P9-AGH-625

Buffalo Bill's Wild West Warriors

SMITHSONIAN NATIONAL MUSEUM OF AMERICAN HISTORY
WASHINGTON, D.C.

An Imprint of HarperCollinsPublishers

Buffalo Bill's Wild West Warriors

A Photographic History by Gertrude Käsebier

Michelle Delaney

HarperCollins books may be purchased for educational, business, or sales promotional use. For information, please write: Special Markets Department, HarperCollins Publishers, 10 East 53rd Street, New York, NY 10022.

FIRST EDITION

BOOK DESIGN BY SHUBHANI SARKAR

Library of Congress Cataloging-in-Publication Data is available upon request.

ISBN: 978-0-06-112977-3
ISBN-10: 0-06-112977-1

07 08 09 10 11 DT/TOP 10 9 8 7 6 5 4 3 2 1

Dedicated to

the late Eugene Ostroff,
longtime Smithsonian curator of photography,

and my parents,
Barbara and the late Michael J. Titanic

Contents

Acknowledgments

TWENTY YEARS AGO, AS A GRADUATE STUDENT IN AMERICAN Studies at the George Washington University, I was first introduced to the vast collections of the Smithsonian Institution's National Museum of American History (NMAH). Following a series of volunteer and internship positions, I was hired for a position in the Division of Photographic History. Even as a novice in the field of photography, I was quick to absorb the outstanding nature of this unique century-old collection incorporating the history of the science, technology, and art of photography from its beginnings in 1839 to the present.

It has always been my expectation to research, publish, and exhibit the Native American portraits of the Museum's Gertrude Käsebier collection. The Smithsonian's holdings represent one of the finest collections of her work. As the leading American portrait photographer of her time, Käsebier's role in the establishment of photography as a fine art in this country cannot be understated. As a founding member of the Photo-Secession in 1902, she worked with photographers Alfred Stieglitz and Edward Steichen to reach broader audiences and inspire photographers across the nation, and in Europe, to the possibilities of pictorialism, or art photography.

The Smithsonian holds more than 100 of Käsebier's original platinum photographs (portraits) of the Sioux Indian performers with Buffalo Bill's Wild West. Previous articles and book research have never yielded a comprehensive discussion or presentation of these images. I hope this book will serve as an important reference tool for those interested in the history of American photography, Native Americans, Buffalo Bill Cody, and the real and mythic Wild West.

My research efforts have benefited greatly from the assistance and guidance of the following curators, librarians, and archivists: Linda Clark and Ann Marie Donoghue, McCracken Research Library, Buffalo Bill Historical Center, Cody, Wyoming; Verna Curtis, Department of Prints and Photographs, Library of Congress, Washington, DC; Mia Fineman, Department of Photographs, Metropolitan Museum of Art, New York, NY; Simon Bieling, Department of Photographs, Museum of Modern Art, New York, NY; Stephen Pinson, Department of Prints and Photographs, New York Public Library, New York, NY; staff of the Manuscript Division,

New York Public Library, New York, NY; Marsha Morton, Pratt Institute, Brooklyn, NY; L. Rebecca Johnson Melvin, Gertrude Käsebier Papers, University of Delaware Library, Newark, DE; and Janet Broske, University Gallery, University of Delaware, Newark, DE.

Fellow staff at the Smithsonian have generously supported my book project and research. They include many of my colleagues at the National Museum of American History and from across the Institution: Shannon Perich, Photographic History Collection; Jim Gardner, Office of Curatorial Affairs; David Allison, Division of Information Technology and Communications; Joan Boudreau and Helena Wright, Graphic Arts Collection; Nancy Brooks, editor, Office of Museum Management Services; Vanessa Broussard, David Haberstich, Craig Orr, Kay Peterson, and Susan Strange, Archives Center; Bonnie Lilienfeld, Fath Ruffins, Rayna Green, and Steve Velasquez, Home and Community Life Collection; Dwight Bowers Blocker and Stacey Kluck, Division of Music, Sports and Entertainment; Ann Shumard and Frank Goodyear, Department of Photographs, National Portrait Gallery, Smithsonian Institution; Eleanor Harvey, Smithsonian American Art Museum; Joanna Cohan Scherer, Handbook of North American Indians, National Museum of Natural History, Smithsonian Institution; Daisy Njoku and Vyrtis Thomas, National Anthropological Archives, National Museum of Natural History, Smithsonian Institution; Chris Cottrill, Mike Hardy, Jim Roan, and Stephanie Thomas of the Smithsonian Libraries; and my extraordinary Smithsonian interns Meg Angelakos, Tim Bauer, Kate Diggle, Samia Elia, Heather Heckler, Katie Morris, and Vanessa Pares. I am also grateful to the many members of the NMAH Collections Committee for their support of the project.

A few scholars have generously mentored me throughout various stages of research: Paula Fleming, retired archivist and specialist in Native American photography at the Smithsonian's National Anthropological Archives; Joy Kasson, author and professor of American studies and English at the University of North Carolina, Chapel Hill; and Barbara L. Michaels, photo historian and author of the only comprehensive Käsebier biography.

Smithsonian photographers John Jones and John Dillaber, and David Sterling of Sterling Prepress all labored diligently, dedicating countless hours to producing the best digital reproductions of the Käsebier photographs for this publication.

HarperCollins editor Donna Sanzone and her colleagues have continually provided enthusiasm and invaluable guidance for this project from their first glance at Käsebier's original prints.

To my family and close friends, I thank you for your patience and encouragement, especially my husband, Paul, and sons, Paulie and Connor, who have helped me to balance work, research, and family fun, including one great trip to the Wild West!

Buffalo Bill's Wild West Warriors

Historical Overviews

1. Gertrude Käsebier in her studio by W. and G. Parrish, St. Louis, MO, circa 1910, reproduced in the *Bulletin of Photography*, June 8, 1910.

Introduction

IN 1898, NEW YORK PHOTOGRAPHER GERTRUDE KÄSEBIER (1852–1934) EMBARKED ON A DEEPLY PERSONAL PROJECT, CREATING A SET OF PRINTS THAT RANK AMONG THE MOST COMPELLING OF HER CELEBRATED BODY OF WORK. KÄSEBIER WAS on the threshold of a career that would establish her as both the leading portraitist of her time and an extraordinary art photographer. Her new undertaking was inspired by viewing the grand parade of Buffalo Bill's Wild West troupe en route to Madison Square Garden for several weeks of performances. Käsebier had spent her childhood on the Great Plains, and retained many vivid, happy memories of living near, and playing with, Native American children. She quickly sent a letter to William "Buffalo Bill" Cody (1846–1917), requesting permission to photograph Sioux Indians traveling with the show. Within a matter of weeks, Käsebier began a unique and special project photographing the Indians—men, women, and children—formally and informally. Friendships developed, and her photography of these Native Americans continued for more than a decade.

Käsebier pursued this priceless opportunity to document the "fast-vanishing life and customs of the Western tribes."[1] Unlike many other photographers working to photograph Native Americans at the turn of the century—especially Edward Curtis—she initiated a studio project aimed at representing Indian performers as individuals in a time of transition. Her reputation as a pictorialist, or art photographer, may have been discussed with Cody, further encouraging the portrait sessions. Within several years, Käsebier was to establish herself as the leading portrait photographer in the United States and one of the few Americans accepted into the prestigious international photographic salons of Europe.

Cody and Käsebier were similar in their abiding respect for Native Americans and their culture. This set them apart dramatically from most Americans who retained a more romantic concept of "vanishing Indians," fostered by government and news sources, which helped to sustain the notion of Indians as wild savages. At different points in their respective lives, each had maintained meaningful relationships with Plains Indians. Although there is no evidence that Cody and Käsebier ever spent time together, there are many commonalities linking their independent interests in Native Americans, their heritage and their potential place in twentieth-century American society. Cody used his influence with United States government officials in Washington, D.C., to secure Indian performers for his Wild West show. Vastly popular with the general public, the "Show" Indians were freed from the

2. "I Am Coming," color lithographic poster for Buffalo Bill's Wild West by Courier Lithographic Co., 1900.

restraints of the government reservations and allowed to travel the United States and Europe. Their performances included reenactments of famous battles, horse races, and tribal dances. Of course, Cody benefited financially from his long-standing relationship with the Dakota Sioux Indians and various other tribes.

Käsebier benefited in other ways. Her project led to the creation of what is arguably the most respected set of photographs produced during her career. The portraits were selectively, and infrequently, exhibited and reproduced in journals of the time. While Käsebier received some of the highest prices in the nation for photographic work, she often gave away the Sioux portraits to those individuals expressing a genuine interest in and appreciation for Native American culture.

It is not clear from Käsebier interviews or family records exactly how many prints were produced from negatives made between 1898 and 1912. The largest and most comprehensive selection of the photographs, more than 100, along with the 14 drawings made when the Sioux visited the studio, was deposited by donation from Käsebier's granddaughter, Mina Turner, to the Smithsonian Institution in 1969. Today, the collection remains a highlight of the National Museum of American History's Photographic History Collection.

Gertrude Käsebier

A PHOTOGRAPHER'S LIFE AND WORK

WHILE GERTRUDE KÄSEBIER RANKS AS ONE OF THE MOST IMPORTANT AMERICAN PHOTOGRAPHERS OF HER TIME, FEW PUBLICATIONS HAVE FOCUSED ON HER LIFE AND THE BREADTH OF HER WORK AND LEGACY. MANY AMERICANS TODAY KNOW little of her extraordinary career as a prominent woman in American photography. She worked for more than twenty years as a commercial portrait photographer of influential Americans and Europeans—statesmen, socialites, industrialists, artists, and authors. As the art historian William Innes Homer observed, "Her contribution to portrait photography revolutionized the medium and influenced countless practitioners in her own time and in later decades."[2]

Married and the mother of three, Käsebier established an independent career, using her professional studio and finished prints to advance the acceptance of photography as a fine art. Gertrude Käsebier achieved much in her private and professional life, while remaining devoted to motherhood and family. Her portraits and photographs are expressive, reflecting an interest in her subjects as individuals. Käsebier biographer Barbara L. Michaels appropriately emphasizes the two basic themes of the photographer's work: independence and solitude.[3] Photography provided Käsebier the means for an independent professional life and artistic achievement.

Käsebier's life was an unlikely journey from a childhood spent in the Gold Rush camps of Colorado to the dynamic world of modern art in early–twentieth-century New York City. Born Gertrude Stanton in Fort Des Moines, Iowa, in 1852, she contracted scarlet fever at the age of three, causing permanent hearing loss in one ear. Her parents, John W. and Muncy Boone Stanton, moved the family to Colorado Territory in 1859, during the Gold Rush. Traveling by covered wagon, the family endured the hardships of nineteenth-century life on the Great Plains—harsh weather extremes, fear of Indian attacks, and separation from earlier homes and friends. John operated a sawmill and, in 1860, was elected mayor of the mining town of Golden in the Colorado Territory.

Despite their remote locale, the Stantons attempted to provide well for their children, Gertrude and Charles, her older brother. Hoping to inspire a career for her daughter in music, Muncy Stanton arranged for the purchase and shipment of a piano for Gertrude. But Gertrude's vivid imagination and general curiosity led her instead toward drawing and sketching. Lacking children her own age to play with in camp, Gertrude was often alone. From oral histories it is known that, occasionally, she was allowed to play with Indian children from local tribes.

And, at Christmastime, her Indian neighbors presented her with beaded gifts, which she cherished much more than the gold nuggets she received from the miners.

In 1864, as the Civil War made settlers' lives even more difficult, the Stanton family moved east to Brooklyn, New York. John gained work as a refiner of sodium carbonate, which he brought with him from the Colorado Territory. Muncy took in boarders for extra income. From 1868 to 1870, Gertrude was sent to live with her grandmother in Bethlehem, Pennsylvania. There she attended and graduated from the Moravian Seminary for Young Ladies. She then rejoined her mother in New York.[4] Gertrude's family life, especially the influences of her mother and her grandmother, had nourished an independent strength in the young woman while simultaneously reinforcing the values of marriage and motherhood.

On May 18, 1874, Gertrude married Edward Käsebier, a shellac importer from Wiesbaden, Germany, and a tenant in the Stantons' house in Brooklyn. The following year their son Frederick William was born. A daughter, Gertrude Elizabeth, arrived in 1878, followed by Hermine Mathilde in 1880.

While both were devoted to their young family, Gertrude and Edward had little else in common. Her recollections about her acceptance of Edward's marriage proposal refer to his "good legs" rather than an overwhelming love.[5] The Käsebiers lived comfortable, if somewhat separate, lives in a succession of homes in Brooklyn and metropolitan New York, often with hired staff to assist Gertrude. Edward did not share his wife's interest in the arts, but he willingly paid for her to attend art school when their children were older. And when Gertrude enrolled in Brooklyn's Pratt Institute to study portrait painting in 1889, Edward agreed to move from their home in New Jersey back to Brooklyn. Gertrude graduated four years later, but remained enrolled for another two years of study at the art school. During that time she also enjoyed summer excursions to the 1893 World's Columbian Exposition in Chicago, and Europe while chaperoning Frank Vincent DuMond's Pratt art classes studying in Paris and Crécy-en-Brie, France, in the summer of 1894.

Gertrude's growing fascination with photography transformed her life as she applied her classical art training to the new medium. Her Pratt instructors attempted to dissuade Käsebier from pursuing her interest in photography—even from taking a camera to Europe—but each successful photograph reinforced her desire to continue. Arranging for her daughters to spend time with their grandmother Käsebier in Germany, she apprenticed in photography with a German chemist. This period of study provided Käsebier a strong technical foundation for her artistic achievement.[6]

When back in New York City, Käsebier began her professional career. She apprenticed for a short time with Brooklyn photographer Samuel Lifshey, and opened her first New York City photography studio in 1897. The additional exposure to the New York art world, camera clubs, and many photography journals published at the time readied her for the professional career.

In her professional and personal work, Käsebier incorporated elements of Japanese art taught to her at Pratt by Arthur Wesley Dow: simplicity, harmony, and flat pattern. Käsebier's decoration of her studio, and the atmosphere she created, suggest the kind of art she wished to make. Art historian Elizabeth Hutchinson's research documenting the studio correctly links the simplicity of the décor to the Arts and Crafts movement in America at the turn of the century. Käsebier's studio featured hardwood floors, plain muslin curtains, and furnishings that were simple, elegant, and not theatrical.[7]

Käsebier's first solo exhibitions of photography were held at the Boston Camera Club and at the Pratt Institute, both in 1897, expanding awareness of her skill in artistic portraiture and painterly printing techniques. Poised on the forefront of an emerging American art photography movement, Käsebier within two years established herself as a ranking professional, and her photographs were included in the article "The Pose in Portraiture," published in *Photo-Miniature*, May 1899. Her portraits of young models were illustrations of the best effort yet made by a photographer to capture likenesses that "preserve simplicity in the portrait, so that the interest concentrates on the personality of the sitter, and all else is subordinated."[8] The author also used the term "human documents" for portraits, a term used at the time, and one that Käsebier herself would adopt when characterizing and titling several of her own portraits.[9] Photographs by Käsebier's contemporaries and close friends, including Frances Benjamin Johnston, of Washington, D.C., and Clarence H. White, of Newark, Ohio, were also included in the article. Such journals and manuals of photography were made widely available to guide new photographers in the best practices in portraiture.

Pictorialism, or art photography, was a growing movement in 1890s America, especially in cities with established photographic communities like New York, Boston, Philadelphia, and Washington, D.C. For more than a decade, photographers in England and Europe had been pursuing new techniques and processes to lift photography to the status of fine art. Soft focus was a predominant characteristic of pictorialism. And other qualities, including texture, "sketchy" effects, and range of colors and tones, were frequently used to obtain the desired painterly look in the photographic prints. Darkroom printing, especially the platinum process with its rich, dark tones of black and gray, or the manipulated brush-stroked textured look of the gum-bichromate process, were preferred by many of the pictorialists.[10]

Even when the handheld Kodak camera

3. ACROSS: *Mother and Child*, sometimes titled *Adoration* or *The Vision*, platinum print by Käsebier, 1897.

4. BELOW: *The Terminal*, photogravure by Alfred Stieglitz, 1893.

was introduced in 1888 by George Eastman, pictorialists remained dedicated to their bulky wooden view cameras on tripods. They resisted Eastman's film camera and company processing of film, continuing to use the older-style cameras and to develop glass plate negatives in their own darkrooms. Fortunately, the pictorialists, mostly serious amateurs, were generally a wealthier group with the resources and time available for the relatively expensive hobby.

Professionals, like Käsebier, and amateur pictorialist photographers formed camera clubs to focus more attention on the topic of photography as fine art. Through the active support of club leader Alfred Stieglitz, and members Edward Steichen and Käsebier, the Camera Club of New York, and later their Photo-Secession group (1902), became dominant forces in American photography. Stieglitz coordinated the work of the Camera Club, organizing exhibitions and publishing journals to further the national debate of photography as art. Stieglitz's exhibition galleries and publications promoted a select group of art photographers and contemporary artists. The small group of New York and American photographers working with Stieglitz included Käsebier, who was also recognized by her peers as a leader who established the standard for artistic portraiture in America.

"The American School" of photography was the subject of many articles written for the English journal *Photograms of the Year* by photographer Joseph T. Keiley, a New York contemporary of Käsebier and Stieglitz. For Keiley and other critics writing at the time, the years 1898 and 1899 were the most important for the beginnings of art photography in America. Gertrude Käsebier's developing career paralleled and influenced this movement, primarily centered along the nation's eastern seaboard. Exhibitions and salons highlighting the work of a small minority of photographers experimenting in pictorialism were critiqued and dissected in the amateur photography journals. The Philadelphia Salon of 1898 was the first photography exhibition to attain the professional standard set in Europe. Käsebier's photography was prominent among the works selected for the showing, second in number of entries only to her friend and New York colleague, Alfred Stieglitz. Her teacher Dow commented:

5. BELOW: Exhibition installation photograph, Käsebier (right) and Frances B. Johnston photographs shown at the 1899 Philadelphia Salon by William Rau. Includes at center of Käsebier display *The Manger*.

> Mrs. Käsebier is answering the question whether the camera can be substituted for the palette. She looks for some special evidence of personality in the sitter, some line, some silhouette, some expression or movement; she searches for character and beauty in the sitter. Then she endeavors to give the best presention [*sic*] by the pose, the lighting and the focusing [*sic*], the developing, the printing—all the processes and manipulation of her art which she knows so well. She is not dependent upon an elaborate outfit, but gets her effects with a common tripod camera, in a plain room, with ordinary light and quiet furnishing.[11]

This description led Joseph Keiley to comment in his review that

> Mrs. Käsebier, who is a professional photographer, has quickly won for herself the position of the first portrait photographer in America. An artist by training and instinct, she has brought to her art that knowledge and feeling essential to the creation of good work, and there is no better sign of the changes in the public taste in such matters than the ever-increasing number of artists who are seriously turning to photography.[12]

The New York Camera Club responded later in 1898, and again in 1899, with exhibitions under the leadership of Alfred Stieglitz, who continued his support of Käsebier's art photography and portraiture. Keiley's review of American photography in 1899 included his praise of Stieglitz:

6. Portrait of sculptor Auguste Rodin, platinum print by Käsebier, 1907.

> . . . by far the most important development of the year, has been accomplished largely through the ceaseless efforts and tireless zeal of one man, and the instrumentality of the most unique photographic publication in the world. With an edition limited to one thousand, *Camera Notes,* the organ of the New York Camera Club, a quarterly magazine, edited by Alfred Stieglitz in the interest of pictorial photography, has made itself known and felt throughout the country; has raised the standard of photographic excellence in both amateur and professional circles far above any previously established; has brought the leaders in touch with students and with each other; has educated the public taste to an understanding of what really good work is; and finally has created an art movement in the photographic world that gives every indication of maturing into a distinctly American school that will reflect all the intellectual vigor of the different sections of the country.[13]

When the 1899 Philadelphia Salon was being organized, Käsebier and Clarence H. White, of Newark, Ohio, were selected by the Pennsylvania Academy of Fine Arts to serve as jurors. The Photographic Society of Philadelphia selected the remaining three jurors: Miss Frances Benjamin Johnston, of Washington, D.C.; F. Holland Day, of Boston; and Henry Troth, of Philadelphia. The group was charged with selecting photographs of a "class of which there is a distinctive evidence of individual artistic feeling and execution."[14]

In all, 954 photographs were submitted. Of these, 772 were rejected. All five judges received ample space for display of their own best work. Käsebier's photograph, *The Manger,* was among the most popular images shown in the salon, and established a sales record of $100 for a pictorial photograph.[15]

Käsebier worked with her sitters like a painter, as she had been trained to do at Pratt. She studied each sitter, taking much care and time to pose them. Normally, her portrait sessions with one individual could last hours. She used older equipment, a large wooden view camera on a stand for portraits, probably a Century camera. Instead of using faster modern mounted automatic shutters, she continued to remove the lens cap and count three to five seconds, usually, for the exposures on glass plate negatives 6½ by 8½ inches and sometimes larger.[16] Käsebier was reluctant to retouch any photograph, but printed as many as a dozen images in the darkroom to achieve what she deemed perfection. The photographer's granddaughter, Elizabeth O'Malley, recalled that "above all else, [Käsebier] has sought to give those she photographed, the best of themselves," in typical motherly fashion.[17]

7. Portrait of painter Robert Henri, platinum print by Käsebier, 1907.

Popular American and European photographic journals of the time ran articles sharing technical advice and aesthetic considerations that read as a homage to Käsebier, as her technique and skill established her as the leading American portraitist of her time. Despite her limited training in photography, even her earliest prints proved elegant and graceful likenesses. The pose of each sitter, the composition and arrangement of space, were seen as vital to the success of each photograph. Käsebier's professional work habits and style reflected her own femininity and nineteenth-century upbringing. She nurtured her sitters in conversation as best she could, to create a comfort level, while intuitively attempting to convey a provocative portrait true to their character and life. However, I believe, she looked repeatedly to find the characteristics so important to her in her own life: independence and personality.

Käsebier's appreciation of European Old Masters influenced her portrait work, but she subordinated poses and accessories, using tone and lighting to avoid self-conscious, rigid portraits. Decisions on the point of view of each image, and the positioning of the camera, were crucial. Journal articles suggested fixing the camera lens level with the sitter's mouth or chin. Käsebier explored the use of all formats: bust portraits, half-length, three-quarter- and full-length; standing, seated, and group images. Her photographs often were used to illustrate journal and magazine articles as the best examples of artistic portraits being made. Fashionable posing styles for men, women, children, and groups were explained, and problems to avoid were described. Käsebier and other portrait photographers of her day were encouraged to develop "the cultivation of instinct," or the "continual observation of what is interesting and what has grace or beauty in nature and art as we see them in everyday life . . . that sympathetic interpretation which compels at once our interest and admiration."[18] Käsebier's striking platinum photographs in strong tones of black or brown, and her painterly textured

8. Portrait of photographer Robert Demachy, gum-bichromate print by Käsebier, circa 1905.

gum-bichromate portrait photographs, and those of her close friends and/or contemporaries Frances Benjamin Johnston, Zaida Ben-Yusuf, Mathilde Weil, and Clarence H. White, continued to be reproduced as photogravure prints illustrating articles in leading photography magazines and journals.

While building and solidifying her professional reputation and support within the photographic community, Käsebier sought an opportunity to bring her lifelong interest in Native American culture to a portrait project of great personal significance. As she watched the 1898 parade of Buffalo Bill's Wild West troupe pass her Fifth Avenue studio toward Madison Square Garden, her focus locked on the Native American performers. Memories of her childhood on the midwestern plains came flooding back, and her affection and respect for their culture inspired her to write a note to William "Buffalo Bill" Cody requesting a studio visit with the Sioux Indians traveling with the arena show: a visit with "an old friend of their tribe" and a portrait sitting. A few weeks passed before she had an answer—Cody had granted her request.[19] Käsebier's friend Adele Miller may have helped to arrange the studio visit through her family's friendship with Buffalo Bill.[20]

On Sunday morning, April 24, 1898, Käsebier prepared with great anticipation to receive her special guests for tea at ten o'clock, and later to make their portraits. She hoped to photograph three or four of the Native Americans. Cody and his managers selected nine Sioux men to send to the studio: Chief Iron Tail, High Heron, Has-No-Horses, Samuel Lone Bear, Joseph Black Fox, Red Horn Bull, Shooting Pieces, Phillip Standing Soldier, and Kills-Close-to-the-Lodge. An eager Käsebier planned to arrive at the studio an hour early for final preparations, but her guests, equally eager, were waiting for her inside when she arrived. The Sioux and their Wild West chaperone were served tea and "hot frankfurters between unbuttered bread," followed by a lengthy three-hour portrait session. Käsebier found her visitors polite and candid but possessing a strong and almost impenetrable reserve when posing for the camera.[21]

The tea and portrait session was reported immediately on the women's page of the *New York Times,* and several years later in the popular journal *Everybody's Magazine,* January 1901. An article, possibly written by Käsebier or a close friend, reproduced her photographs, drawings made for her by the Sioux Indians at her studio, and excerpts of letters exchanged. In "Sioux Chief's Party Call," the *Times* detailed the meeting and friendships made. The resulting portraits were termed a "great success . . . works of art," and as far as the author could discern, appreciated by the sitters.[22] *Everybody's Magazine* described the clothing worn by the men especially for the occasion:

> They wore feathered head-dresses that were marvels; short jackets fairly covered with elaborate designs in solid beadwork; flannel shirts of vivid red, blue, and green; blankets beaded and decorated with patterns of United States flags; moccasins edged with beads or dyed porcupine quills; and furs of otter skin. Brass and silver bands and silver rings . . .[23]

Since the beginnings of photography in the mid–nineteenth century, many American photographers pursued a specialty in photographing Native Americans, documenting the vanishing Indian. Käsebier did not pursue the same path. One photographer, Edward Curtis, tried to fully document Native Americans at the turn of the century. Curtis began a multivolume project in 1906 of photographing and romanticizing Native Americans and their culture, using costumes and props for the Indians so photographed. David F. Barry, Frank Matsura, and Karl Moon were also well known for their portraits of Indians. Photographers Heyn and Matzen of Omaha, Nebraska, photographed some of the same Sioux Indians as Käsebier. Her personal project, on the other hand, resonated from her interest in the group of Sioux traveling with Buffalo Bill's Wild West.

9. Group of Sioux Indians from Buffalo Bill's Wild West photographed by Käsebier at her Fifth Avenue, New York City, studio, platinum print, 1898.

Käsebier's photography emphasizes a small group of "chosen" Indians living a drastically different lifestyle than most of their tribe for six months each year. However, there is no evidence that Käsebier participated in any of the known active Indian reform groups of the period working to improve the lives of Native Americans. Historian Rayna Green reflected on the Smithsonian's Käsebier collection of Indian photographs in a short article in the *History of Photography Journal,* Spring 2000 issue: "Most [Indians] who did not look like Buffalo Bill's show Indians did not get their pictures taken . . . certainly not the impoverished, just reservationized, defeated, hungry, missionary donation-box clothed aboriginals."[24] The Indians traveling with the Wild West wore traditional clothing then forbidden on the reservation.

Käsebier's own fascination with the Sioux Indians can be compared with that of the daily audiences crowding performances of the Wild West, interested in meeting the performers.[25] Many ticket holders visited the Wild West camp prior to performances, meeting with the Indians or other members of the Congress of Rough Riders, and seeing how they lived while traveling with Cody. But Käsebier's status as a professional photographer allowed her to arrange the private meeting with the Indians for her own purposes.

No record is known of Cody receiving any of the portraits from the initial or later sittings. Nor is there any evidence of use of the Käsebier photographs in any of the Buffalo

10. ABOVE: Chiefs Joe Black Fox and Iron Tail photographed by Heyn and Matzen, Omaha, Nebraska, circa 1900.

11. BELOW: Portrait of Chief Iron Tail by unknown maker, gelatin silver print, circa 1900.

12. *The Red Man,* platinum print by Käsebier, circa 1898.

Bill's Wild West program booklets or promotional posters. The images were not made for commercial use, and never were used for that purpose. Only one of the portraits, *The Red Man,* apparently considered the best artistic portrait of the collection, was submitted to exhibitions or salons. A few of the photographs were reproduced in Stieglitz's *Camera Notes* journal. Today, the photographs remain among the most significant made by Käsebier during her distinguished career. The images are simple, thought-provoking, modern portraits of individuals involved in a cultural transition.

Käsebier seated the Indians one by one in her posing chair, and treated the Sioux performers as friends. While on the road with Buffalo Bill's Wild West, they were treated like celebrities. In city after city, news articles chronicled them as the stars of the show, after Cody. Their roles in the program were carefully scripted; they played the enemy to Cody, the military, and the cowboys. Younger members of the group visiting Käsebier, like Samuel Lone Bear and Phillip Standing Soldier, were educated at government-run Indian schools. They spoke in English with Käsebier, and continued to write her letters for years after their first meeting. Four photographs in the Käsebier collection are views of what may be the Plains of South Dakota showing Sioux women in missionary dresses moving their children and belongings with horse travois, using tipi poles as supports (see pages 44–45).[26] These photographs are pictorial in nature, and seemingly in Käsebier's style, but no personal record exists to document her visiting the Indians on the reservation.

Preparing for their visit to Käsebier's photography studio, the Sioux at the Wild West camp met to distribute their finest clothing and accessories to those chosen to be photographed. The photographer admired their efforts, but desired to, in her own words, photograph "a real 'raw' Indian," "the kind I used to see when I was a child," referring to her early years in Colorado and on the Great Plains. She selected one Indian, Chief Iron Tail, to approach for a photograph without regalia. He did not object. The resulting photograph was exactly what Käsebier had envisioned: a relaxed, intimate, quiet, and beautiful portrait of the man, devoid of decoration and finery, presenting himself to her and the camera without barriers.[27]

Several days later, however, when presented with the photograph, Iron Tail immediately tore up the image, stating it was too dark. Käsebier photographed him once again, this time in his full feather headdress, much to his satisfaction (see pages 78–79). Like Iron Tail, others of the Sioux men set aside their feathers and blankets for Käsebier. No other stories like his were recorded during the portrait session. An elder battle hero in his tribe, Iron Tail was probably at the Battle of Little Bighorn with Sitting Bull. Each feather in his headdress, or war bonnet, represented an act of bravery over a lifetime, like medals to a military man. Käsebier kept the original Iron Tail photograph, and used it as the frontispiece of the 1901 *Everybody's Magazine* article. She believed all the portraits were "a revelation of Indian character," showing the strength and individual character of the Native Americans in "new phases for the Sioux."[28] The portraits, pictograph drawings made by the Indian men for Käsebier during visits to the studio, and letters of correspondence are cited in the January 1901 issue of *Everybody's Magazine.*

The drawings and letters to Käsebier include general references to both life on the road with the Wild West and a longing for life at home on the Plains. The drawings made by Iron Tail, Joe Black Fox, Samuel Lone Bear, Phillip Standing Soldier, William H. Frog, and "Paul" are renderings of buffalo, horses, deer, tipis, and Indian figures draped in blankets, on horseback, and performing a war dance. Whether Käsebier requested any subjects for the drawings or how conversation directed the artist's drawing is not known. Several of the Indians were seated very near the sole window of the studio while drawing, yet none of the drawings reflect the New York metropolis outside or the Wild West show directly. One drawing given to Käsebier includes a description of the Battle of Little Bighorn, or Custer's last battle, written in Sioux. Animals, weapons, shields, tipis, and figures line the border of this statement.[29] However, most are similar to other documented collections of Sioux drawings. Many of the drawings show blanketed figures, men and women, participating in courtship traditions; others are drawings of animals—buffalo, deer, horses.[30]

The letters from Samuel Lone Bear, Joe Black Fox, Amos Two Bulls, and David Bull Bear reflect friendship and affection for Käsebier, longing for life at home on the Plains, and reports of illnesses or deaths that occurred while they were traveling with the show. This correspondence encouraged further meetings and photography. Käsebier visited the Wild West show yearly during its performances in the New York City area: at Manhattan's Madison Square Garden, Brooklyn's Ambrose Park, and Coney Island. Käsebier's granddaughter, Mina Turner, was interviewed prior to disseminating the photographer's collections to various museums and universities. She remembered clearly visiting the Indians of Buffalo Bill's Wild West, the Pawnee Bill, and 101 Ranch shows in New York and Brooklyn as a child.

One of the shows Turner attended when four years old was held at Coney Island. The program was interrupted when the Indians spotted "Granny" in the grandstand and shouted their greetings. After the show, Käsebier took her granddaughter to meet with her Indian friends outside the tent. Sammy Lone Bear lifted little Mina onto his horse with him and, to the photographer's delight, rode the little girl around the arena. Turner also recounted taking gifts of mirrors, perfume, and handkerchiefs to the Wild West Indians, returning their generosity. The Sioux Indians who visited with Käsebier at her studio and at their Wild West camp also traveled to her Quincy Street home in Brooklyn, her Oceanside, Long Island, home, and even to a summer residence in Newport, Rhode Island. Every year Käsebier received gifts of "tomahawks, beaded jackets, belts, bags, moccasins, arrow quivers, peace pipes, etc." The visits prompted the concern and disbelief of her neighbors. Nonetheless, Käsebier regularly hosted her friends for tea, cakes, and talk.[31] This ongoing relationship with the Sioux led to another opportunity to produce an equally significant, if smaller, set of portraits of Zitkala-Ša, also known as Gertrude (Simmons) Bonnin.

The nine existing Käsebier portraits of Zitkala-Ša, or "Red Bird" (1876–1938), show the young woman in both Native American and western dress as she lived her life divided between two very different cultural worlds: her mother Yankton Sioux, her father white. Against her mother's wishes, Zitkala-Ša left the Pine Ridge Agency reservation to pursue further education at the Carlisle Indian School in Pennsylvania, Earlham College in Indiana, and later the Boston Conservatory of Music. By the time she and Käsebier met at the photographer's studio, Zitkala-Ša was already an accomplished violinist, performer, composer, lecturer, and author in the world outside the reservation. Zitkala-Ša posed in contrasting outfits worn for her public performances. In some portraits she portrays her Euro-American persona, photographed in a flowing white gown holding her violin or a book in front of Victorian floral wallpaper. But for two of the portraits in profile, she wears an Indian buckskin dress and gazes far in the distance as if looking across the Plains of her homeland. Zitkala-Ša, like the Sioux men of the Wild West, posed comfortably for Käsebier and the camera. Käsebier used dark profiles and silhouettes to suggest quiet, contemplative moments in front of the camera, emphasizing Zitkala-Ša's femininity and potential vulnerability, despite her strong character and many accomplishments. Soon after the portraits were taken, the young woman decided to return to the reservation, dedicating her life to Indian reform, voting rights, and education. She and her husband, Raymond T. Bonnin, eventually moved to Washington, D.C., lobbying against any oppression of Native Americans well into the 1930s.[32]

13. Portrait of Zitkala-Ša (Gertrude Simmons Bonnin) holding violin, platinum print by Käsebier, circa 1898.

14. Portrait of Zitkala-Ša in Native American attire, platinum print by Käsebier, circa 1898.

15. The cast of Buffalo Bill's Wild West in Philadelphia, 1908. Photograph by W. M. Jennings.

Indian Performers and Buffalo Bill's Wild West

MANY BOOKS HAVE BEEN WRITTEN INTERPRETING PHOTOGRAPHS OF NATIVE AMERICANS TAKEN IN THE LATE NINETEENTH AND EARLY TWENTIETH CENTURIES, FROM IMAGES OF INDIVIDUALS, GROUPS, AND TRIBES, TO DEPICTIONS OF HOMELANDS.

Few of these works document the relatively small number of Indians who chose to leave the government-imposed reservation system to participate as performers in the popular Wild West shows of the period. The controversy arising from contracts that William F. ("Buffalo Bill") Cody entered into with the United States government to employ American Indians actually fueled the efforts of the federal Bureau of Indian Affairs and Christian reformers alike to press the government for better treatment of all Indians in the country. Legislative battles over the rights of American Indians continued in Washington, D.C., throughout the existence of Buffalo Bill's Wild West, from 1883 to 1913. But whether or not they were exploited by the Wild West show, many Indians welcomed the opportunity to travel with Cody, thereby freeing themselves for six months each year from the degrading confines of the reservations where they were forbidden to wear tribal dress, hunt, or dance.

Many of the "Show Indians," as they would come to be known, were Sioux Indian men from the Pine Ridge Agency reservation in South Dakota. The Smithsonian's collection of more than 100 portraits by Käsebier includes likenesses of select members of the Sioux who performed with Buffalo Bill's Wild West about 1898. These humanizing photographs are far from the exploitive marketing images and posters created by the Wild West Company to promote their arena show. The Käsebier photographs were made for her own personal project and consumption. She shared them primarily with family and her peers working in the New York modern art scene of the period.

The American West underwent a rapid and sweeping transformation quickly in the last half of the nineteenth century. Railroads and stagecoaches carried settlers west to develop land, pan for gold, and dream of fortunes. "Buffalo Bill" Cody (1846–1917) keenly understood the profound changes taking place, and invested and supported development in his native western lands. He grew up in the plains of Iowa, Nebraska, and Kansas. He lived a pioneer's existence working on wagon trains, panning for gold, riding with the Pony Express as a teenager, and serving in the U.S. Civil War as part of the 7th Kansas Volunteer Cavalry. Cody later worked as an Indian scout with the U.S. Cavalry, and is reputed to have killed thousands of buffalo while working for the Kansas Pacific Railroad.[33] The Indian wars ended with the Battle of Wounded Knee, South Dakota, in 1890.

16. Woodburytype portrait of William F. "Buffalo Bill" Cody by unknown maker, circa 1887.

Cody's name was synonymous with the frontier. His fame as a scout gained him priceless media attention, eventually leading to an acting debut. In *The Border Drama,* a play based on Ned Buntline's novel *The Scouts of the Prairie,* Cody, Texas Jack Omohundro, and Wild Bill Hickok basically portrayed themselves—heroes of the American West. Cody toured for ten years, from 1873 to 1883, acting in plays on Broadway and throughout the United States. He came to fully appreciate the general public's interest in the changing nature of the West, and the importance of the representation of its past, including adapting his own life experiences into a mythology of the West. His acting career—begun in order to finance his own return to ranching—resulted in establishing William F. "Buffalo Bill" Cody as one of the most celebrated Americans of the era.[34] His popularity, coupled with public fascination with the romanticized American West, eventually led Cody to explore the creation of a new kind of theatrical experience—Buffalo Bill's Wild West.

Cody used his friendships and knowledge of Native American culture to build a mass entertainment phenomenon. For much of his adult life, he was a scout for the federal government and sometimes private companies that were expanding throughout the American West. As a scout before and after the Civil War, Cody was responsible for tracking the movements of Indians, observing them, and providing information to prevent attacks as white Euro-Americans pushed farther west across the Great Plains. In expanding commerce and transportation routes, the U.S. government depended on the knowledge and judgment of scouts to protect new settlements. Cody learned Indian customs and warfare tactics and was prominent among scouts working across the United States. He also gained a lifelong respect for Indian ways. And, despite participating in deadly

17. Cover, "Historical Sketches & Programme" for Buffalo Bill's Wild West and Congress of Rough Riders of the World, 1894.

battles against tribes, Cody developed lasting friendships with Native Americans that would influence his own future.[35]

Cody embarked on his most successful business endeavor in 1883, Buffalo Bill's Wild West. He organized his first show, the "Old Glory Blow-Out," in North Platte, Nebraska, on July 4, 1882. This onetime performance led to the formation of traveling arena programs featuring dramatic re-creations of the history and myths of the American West—cowboys, Indians, battles, and buffalo. He partnered with friend and sharpshooter Doc Carver to tour the country with "The Wild West, Rocky Mountain and Prairie Exhibition" in 1883. The *Chicago Evening Post* praised the show as "the truth as it was."[36] Eventually, over its thirty-year run, Buffalo Bill's Wild West entertained millions and presented Cody's version of the lore of the American West. Cody employed American Indian performers and a "Congress of Rough Riders of the World," including a wide array of "exotic" cast members from around the nation and the world to thrill his audiences.

Surviving photographs, early films, programs, news clippings, advertisements, and posters of Buffalo Bill's Wild West show document how Cody and his performers presented both the real and a mythic American West to vast audiences across the United States and Europe between 1883 and 1913. Cody hired American Indians and an array of international cast members—American cowboys, Mexican vaqueros, Russian Cossacks, British military, and Arab performers—to re-create historic and infamous battles, race horses, display marksmanship skills, and generally intrigue visitors with live dramatic performances.

The show's touring schedule was grueling, each spring through fall, with performances twice daily, weather permitting. For their participation, performers received

OFFICIAL ROUTE — Season of 1898.

MARCH.

Date.	Place.	State.	Railroad.	Mls.
29 Tue	Parade N.Y.C'y	N. Y.		
30 Wed	{ Madison Sq're	"		
31 Thu	{ Gar'n, N.Y.C.	"		

APRIL.

Date.	Place.	State.	Railroad.	Mls.
1 Fri	New York City	N. Y.		
2 Sat	"	"		
	SUNDAY.			
4 Mon	New York City	N. Y.		
5 Tue	"	"		
6 Wed	"	"		
7 Thu	"	"		
8 Fri	"	"		
9 Sat	"	"		
	SUNDAY.			
11 Mon	New York City	N. Y.		
12 Tue	"	"		
13 Wed	"	"		
14 Thu	"	"		
15 Fri	"	"		
16 Sat	"	"		
	SUNDAY.			
18 Mon	New York City	N. Y.		
19 Tue	"	"		
20 Wed	"	"		
21 Thu	"	"		
22 Fri	"	"		
23 Sat	"	"		
	SUNDAY.			
25 Mon	Brooklyn	N. Y.	N. Y., N. H. & H.	56
26 Tue	"	"		
27 Wed	"	"		
28 Thu	"	"		
29 Fri	"	"		
30 Sat	"	"		

MAY.

Date.	Place.	State.	Railroad.	Mls.
	SUNDAY.			
2 Mon	Philadelphia	Pa.	Pennsylvania	90
3 Tue	"	"		
4 Wed	"	"		
5 Thu	"	"		
6 Fri	"	"		
7 Sat	"	"		
	SUNDAY.			
9 Mon	Washington	D. C.	Pennsylvania	137
10 Tue	"	"		
11 Wed	Baltimore	Md.	"	43
12 Thu	"	"		
13 Fri	Wilmington	Del.	"	69
14 Sat	Norristown	Pa.	"	43
	SUNDAY.			
16 Mon	Trenton	N. J.	Pennsylvania	52
17 Tue	Bridgeton	"	"	71
18 Wed	Camden	"	"	38
19 Thu	New Brunswick	"	"	58
20 Fri	Newark	"	"	23
21 Sat	Jersey City	"	"	7
	SUNDAY.			
23 Mon	Mount Vernon	N. Y.	N. Y., N. H. & H.	13
24 Tue	Stamford	Conn.	"	20
25 Wed	Meriden	"	"	59
26 Thu	Hartford	"	"	18
27 Fri	Willimantic	"	N. Y. & New England	31
28 Sat	Providence	R. I.	"	58
	SUNDAY.			
30 Mon	Boston	Mass.	Old Colony	44
31 Tue	"	"		

JUNE.

Date.	Place.	State.	Railroad.	Mls.
1 Wed	Boston	Mass.		
2 Thu	"	"		
3 Fri	"	"		
4 Sat	"	"		
	SUNDAY.			
6 Mon	Newburyport	Mass.	Boston & Maine	37
7 Tue	Gloucester	"	"	32
8 Wed	Lynn	"	"	20
9 Thu	Waltham	"	B. & M. and Fitchburg	21
10 Fri	Keene	N. H.	Fitchburg	82
11 Sat	North Adams	Mass.	"	135
	SUNDAY.			
13 Mon	Troy	N. Y.	Fitchburg	48
14 Tue	Albany	"	Delaware & Hudson	6
15 Wed	Kingston	"	West Shore	53
16 Thu	Newburgh	"	"	32
17 Fri	Paterson	N. J.	Erie	46
18 Sat	Morristown	"	D., L. & W.	27
	SUNDAY.			
20 Mon	Danville	Pa.	D., L. & W.	183
21 Tue	Shenandoah	"	Pittsburg & Reading	66
22 Wed	Lebanon	"	"	91
23 Thu	Lancaster	"	"	70
24 Fri	Carlisle	"	"	104
25 Sat	Huntington	"	Cent. Vt. and Pennsyl'a.	125
	SUNDAY.			
27 Mon	Altoona	Pa.	Pennsylvania	39
28 Tue	Johnstown	"	"	38
29 Wed	Indiana	"	"	44
30 Thu	East Liberty	"	"	69

JULY.

Date.	Place.	State.	Railroad.	Mls.
1 Fri	McKeesport	Pa.	Baltimore & Ohio	15
2 Sat	Uniontown	"	"	55
	SUNDAY.			
4 Mon	Wheeling	W. Va.	Baltimore & Ohio	142
5 Tue	Washington	Pa.	"	33
6 Wed	Butler	"	B. & O. and P. & W.	78
7 Thu	New Castle	"	Pittsburgh & Western	46
8 Fri	Oil City	"	W. N. Y. & P. and L. S.	65
9 Sat	Erie	"	Lake Shore	128
	SUNDAY.			
11 Mon	Ashtabula	Ohio.	Lake Shore	41
12 Tue	Sandusky	"	"	119
13 Wed	Monroe	Mich.	"	72
14 Thu	Detroit	"	"	41
15 Fri	Flint	"	Flint & Pere Marquette	74
16 Sat	Saginaw	"	"	33
	SUNDAY.			
18 Mon	Manistee	Mich.	Flint & Pere Marquette	146
19 Tue	Traverse City	"	Manistee & Northeastern	70
20 Wed	Big Rapids	"	Grand Rapids & Ind.	89
21 Thu	Grand Rapids	"	"	56
22 Fri	Kalamazoo	"	"	49
23 Sat	South Bend	Ind.	Lake Shore	71
	SUNDAY.			
25 Mon	Chicago	Ill.	Lake Shore	86
26 Tue	"	"		
27 Wed	"	"		
28 Thu	"	"		
29 Fri	"	"		
30 Sat	"	"		
31 Sun	Milwaukee	Wis.	Chic. & North-Western	85

AUGUST.

Date.	Place.	State.	Railroad.	Mls.
1 Mon	Watertown	Wis.	Chicago & N.-W.	63
2 Tue	Oshkosh	"	"	64
3 Wed	Wausau	"	"	99
4 Thu	Eau Claire	"	"	121
5 Fri	Ashland	"	"	161
6 Sat	Duluth	Minn.	Northern Pacific	76
	SUNDAY.			
8 Mon	Minneapolis	Minn.	St. Paul & Duluth	160
9 Tue	St. Paul	"	"	28
10 Wed	Red Wing	"	Chic., Mil'kee & St. Paul	59

AUGUST — Continued.

Date.	Place.	State.	Railroad.	Mls.
11 Thu	LaCrosse	Wis.	Chic., Mil'kee & St. Paul	86
12 Fri	Dubuque	Iowa.	"	121
13 Sat	Clinton	"	"	60
	SUNDAY.			
15 Mon	Davenport	Iowa.	B., C. R. & N.	77
16 Tue	Kewanee	Ill.	Chic., Bur'ng'n & Q'cy.	89
17 Wed	Burlington	Iowa	"	75
18 Thu	Keokuk	"	St. L., K. & N. W.	43
19 Fri	Jacksonville	Ill.	Wabash	93
20 Sat	Hannibal	Mo.	"	67
	SUNDAY.			
22 Mon	Chillicothe	Mo.	Hannibal & St Joseph	130
23 Tue	St. Joseph	"	"	77
24 Wed	Red Oak	Iowa.	H. St. J. and C., B. & Q.	116
25 Thu	Creston	"	Chic., Bur'ng'n & Qu'cy.	51
26 Fri	Ottumwa	"	"	115
27 Sat	Des Moines	"	Chic., Rock Is. & Pacific.	87
	SUNDAY.			
29 Mon	Atlantic	Iowa.	Chic., Rock Is. & Pacific	82
30 Tue	Omaha	Neb.	C., R. I. & P. and U. P.	62
31 Wed	"	"		

SEPTEMBER.

Date.	Place.	State.	Railroad.	Mls.
1 Thu	Lincoln	Neb.	Burling. & Miss'ri River.	55
2 Fri	Grand Island	"	"	92
3 Sat	North Platte	"	Union Pacific	138
	SUNDAY.			
5 Mon	Cheyenne	Wyo	Union Pacific	225
6 Tue	Denver	Colo	"	107
7 Wed	"	"		
8 Thu	Colorado Sp'gs.	"	Atch., Top. & Santa Fe	74
9 Fri	Pueblo	"	"	43
10 Sat	Trinidad	"	"	144
	SUNDAY.			
12 Mon	Hutchinson	Kan.	Atch., Top. & Santa Fe	418
13 Tue	Wichita	"	"	61
14 Wed	Winfield	"	"	39
15 Thu	Independence	"	"	81
16 Fri	Ottawa	"	"	108
17 Sat	Emporia	"	"	56
	SUNDAY.			
19 Mon	Topeka	Kan.	Atch., Top. & Santa Fe	62
20 Tue	Atchison	"	"	50
21 Wed	Leavenworth	"	"	32
22 Thu	Kansas City	Mo.	"	39
23 Fri	Sedalia	"	Missouri Pacific	95
24 Sat	Nevada	"	"	130
	SUNDAY.			
26 Mon	Joplin	Mo.	Missouri Pacific	64
27 Tue	Aurora	"	St. Louis & San Fran	63
28 Wed	Fayetteville	Ark.	"	84
29 Thu	Ft. Smith	"	"	[illegible]
30 Fri	Russellville	"	Iron Mountain	89

OCTOBER.

Date.	Place.	State.	Railroad.	Mls.
1 Sat	Little Rock	Ark.	Iron Mountain	76
	SUNDAY.			
3 Mon	Newport	Ark.	Iron Mountain	83
4 Tue	Poplar Bluff	Mo.	"	96
5 Wed	Cairo	Ill.	"	74
6 Thu	Carmi	"	C., C., C. & St. L.	103
7 Fri	Vincennes	Ind.	"	57
8 Sat	Evansville	"	E., T. H. & St. L.	52
	SUNDAY.			
10 Mon	New Albany	Ind.	L., E. & St. L.	116
11 Tue	Frankfort	"	Louisville & Nashville	66
12 Wed	Covington	Ky.	"	120
13 Thu	Maysville	"	Chicago & Ohio	40
14 Fri	Huntington	W. Va	"	102
15 Sat	Charleston	"	"	50

"HOME, SWEET HOME."

Date.	Place.	State.	Railroad.	Mls.
	Bridgeport	Conn	{ Chicago & Ohio	369
			{ Pennsylvania	228
			{ N. Y., N. H. & H.	56

OFFICIAL ROUTE — Season of 1899.

Date.	Place.	State.	Railroad.	Mls.
Mar. 29th to Apr. 15th,	New York City.	N. Y.	N. Y., N. H. & H.	56

APRIL.

Date.	Place.	State.	Railroad.	Mls.
	SUNDAY.			
17 Mon	Baltimore	Md.	Pennsylvania	186
18 Tue	"	"		
19 Wed	Washington	D. C.	Pennsylvania	43
20 Thu	"	"		
21 Fri	Richmond	Va.	Penna. and R. F. & P.	116
22 Sat	Staunton	"	C. & O.	136
	SUNDAY.			
24 Mon	Lynchburg	Va.	C. & O.	141
25 Tue	Roanoke	"	N. & W.	53
26 Wed	Bluefield	W. Va.	"	107
27 Thu	Bristol	Tenn.	"	169
28 Fri	Knoxville	"	Southern	135
29 Sat	Chattanooga	"	"	111
	SUNDAY.			

MAY.

Date.	Place.	State.	Railroad.	Mls.
1 Mon	Nashville	Tenn.	N. C. & St. L.	151
2 Tue	Bowling Green.	Ky.	L. & N.	72
3 Wed	Louisville	"	"	114
4 Thu	Madison	Ind.	P. C. & St. L.	110
5 Fri	Indianapolis	"	" "	86
6 Sat	Richmond	"	" "	68
	SUNDAY.			
8 Mon	Cincinnati	Ohio.	P., C., C. & St. L. and [C., H. & D.	74
9 Tue	"	"		
10 Wed	Dayton	"	C., H. & D.	59
11 Thu	Springfield	"	C., C., C. & St. L.	24
12 Fri	Columbus	"	" "	45
13 Sat	Newark	"	P., C., C. & St. L.	33
	SUNDAY.			
15 Mon	Pittsburg	Pa.	P., C., C. & St. L.	165
16 Tue	"	"		
17 Wed	Tyrone	"	Pennsylvania	132
18 Thu	Williamsport	"	"	79
19 Fri	Wilkes-Barre	"	"	103
20 Sat	Towanda	"	Lehigh Valley	78
	SUNDAY.			
22 Mon	Scranton	Pa.	L. V. and C. of N. J.	96
23 Tue	Easton	"	C. of N. J.	119
24 Wed	Allentown	"	"	17
25 Thu	Pottsville	"	P. & R.	71
26 Fri	Reading	"	"	35
27 Sat	Chester	"	"	68
	SUNDAY.			
29 Mon	Philadelphia	Pa.	P. & R.	12
30 Tue	"	"		
31 Wed	"	"		

JUNE.

Date.	Place.	State.	Railroad.	Mls.
1 Thu	Philadelphia	Pa.	P. & R.	
2 Fri	"	"		
3 Sat	"	"		
	SUNDAY.			
5 Mon	Long Branch	N. J.	Pennsylvania	94
6 Tue	Elizabeth	"	"	35
7 Wed	Yonkers	N. Y.	Penna. and N. Y. C.	35
8 Thu	Poughkeepsie	"	N. Y. C.	58
9 Fri	Winsted	Conn.	C. N. E.	80
10 Sat	Hartford	"	"	35
	SUNDAY.			
12 Mon	Boston	Mass.	N. Y., N. H. & H. and [B. & A.	131
13 Tue	"	"		
14 Wed	"	"		
15 Thu	"	"		

18. ACROSS: Performance schedule for Buffalo Bill's Wild West, 1898 Route.

wages, food, transportation, and living accommodations while far away from their homes. Behind the painted backdrops of the show, cast members lived in the Wild West's "village," or encampment, where visitors could stroll, meet performers, and explore the Indian tipi village.

19. Cover, "Historical Sketches & Programme" for Buffalo Bill's Wild West and Congress of Rough Riders of the World, 1900.

Cody worked with his longtime Wild West Company partner and vice president, Nate Salsbury, and general manager Major John M. Burke, to orchestrate the elaborate, complicated logistics for the traveling arena show. Each year the show highlighted Buffalo Bill's own life experiences, those of the American Indians, and demonstrations of expert marksmanship and horsemanship by men and women from throughout the world. Horse races, football, and native dances were popular segments repeated yearly in Buffalo Bill's Wild West, even being referred to as "the greatest show on earth" in a newspaper description.[37] Cody's show was serious competition for the circuses, minstrel shows, and theatrical traveling companies of the time. Cody, like P. T. Barnum, was a consummate entertainer, exciting crowds yearly in American and, occasionally, European cities. Buffalo Bill's Wild West show played at World's Fairs in New Orleans, London, Paris, and Chicago, and was visited by United States presidents and generals and European royalty.

Buffalo Bill's presence as the main draw for audiences was significant, but the hundreds of American Indians he contracted with each season were also immensely popular with audiences. The Show Indians performed the most popular selections on the programs, such as the "Attack on the Deadwood Mail Coach" and the "Battle of Little Bighorn." According to historian Joy Kasson, despite "all its complexity, the audience's encounter with

20. "All Roads Lead to Buffalo Bill's Wild West and Congress of Rough Riders of the World at Ambrose Park." Back cover, "Historical Sketches & Programme" for Buffalo Bill's Wild West and Congress of Rough Riders of the World, 1894.

21. "Show Indians" entering the Wild West arena for performance, from J. S. Johnston's Series of American Stereoscopic Views, unknown location and date.

the American Indian performers continued to be one of the Wild West's defining features."[38]

When Cody launched his Wild West traveling show in 1883, the Indian wars were nearing an end. The victorious U.S. government claimed the land and efforts were made to encourage American Indians to assimilate into existing society and adopt "civilized" ways. As a result of negotiated treaties, the Indians were forced to live according to the reservation system. Few options beyond reservation life or faraway government-run Indian schools existed for American Indians, no matter what tribe.

Ironically, the Show Indians at times performed programs that dramatized the very battles, raids, and massacres in which they had actually participated. The Indians played roles in the show concurrent with the image of Native Americans perpetuated by the U.S. government and news media, in Native American historian L. G. Moses's words, as "an Indian [as] noble savage, a rapacious killer; a reservation idler, the vanishing American, or a war-bonneted equestrian raider of the plains."[39] While actively marketing and exploiting the lives of these Indians, Buffalo Bill firmly believed himself a friend to the

22. Group photograph, Pawnee Indian School, unknown location and date.

Indians, despite the years of Indian scouting for the U.S. military and vicious duels with Indians such as Yellow Hair, whom he reportedly scalped in July 1876.[40] Cody worked within the federal government system, negotiating with agents of the Bureau of Indian Affairs (BIA) and obtaining signed contracts that allowed Indians to leave their reservations and travel with Buffalo Bill's Wild West.

Moses's research also concluded that the "Indians who performed in the Wild West shows beginning in the 1880s had known life before the reservation experience profoundly altered their cultures. They were members of a transitional generation, one that encountered for the first time the full weight of comprehensive government programs to eradicate native life . . . neither the reformers nor the members of the Indian service could compel the Indians to remain at home and lead more 'productive' lives."[41] Each season American Indians selected by Buffalo Bill and his representatives accepted the conditions and terms of their government contracts as a way out of the harsh existence on the newly formed reservations. The Indians agreed to obey the rules and regulations of the Wild West Company. Their contracts specifically included wording requiring that each Indian would return to his or her homeland when the show tour ended.[42]

The National Archives and Record Administration preserves an original contract agreement between Cody and partner Nate Salsbury of the Buffalo Bill Wild West Company and the American Indian "Rocky Bear" of the Pine Ridge Agency reservation, South Dakota. A monthly salary of $75.00 was listed for Rocky Bear's accompanying "the exhibition." The document stated that Cody and Salsbury were responsible for providing "proper food and raiment, all traveling and needful incidental expenses." They were to protect said Indian from "immoral influences and surroundings, provide medical attention and medicine," and therefore were liable for the health, welfare, and comfort of any Indian in their employment.[43]

Rocky Bear's participation with the show included the European tour in 1890, which included appearances in Venice and at the Vatican in Rome for the twelfth anniversary of Pope Leo XIII. A special correspondent to the *New York Herald,* March 4, 1890, reported:

> One of the strangest spectacles ever seen within the venerable walls of the Vatican was the dramatic entry of "Buffalo Bill" and the head of his Indians and cow-boys this morning, when the ecclesiastical and secular military court of the Holy See assembled to witness the twelfth annual thanksgiving of Leo XIII for his coronation. In the midst of the splendid scene, crowded with the Old Roman aristocracy, and surrounded by walls immortalized by Michael Angelo [*sic*] and Rafael, there suddenly appeared a host of savages in war paint, feathers and blankets, carrying tomahawks and knives.
>
> A vast multitude surged in the great square before St. Peter's early in the morning to witness the arrival of the Americans. Before half-past nine o'clock the Ducal Hall, Royal Hall, and Sextine Chapel of the Vatican, were packed with those who had influence enough to obtain admittance. Through the middle of the three audiences, the pathway was bordered by brilliant uniforms of the Swiss Guards, Palatine Guards, Papal gendarmes and private chamberlains. The sunlight fell upon lines of glittering steel, nodding plumes, golden chains, shimmering robes of silk, and all the blazing emblems of pontifical power and glory.
>
> Suddenly, a tall and chivalrous figure appeared at the entrance, and all eyes turned toward him. It was Colonel W. F. Cody, "Buffalo Bill." With a sweep of his great sombrero, he saluted the chamberlains, and then strode between the guards with his partner, Mr. Nate Salsbury, by his side.
>
> "Rocky Bear" led the Sioux Warriors, who brought up the rear. They were painted in every color that Indian imagination could devise. Every man carried something with which to make big medicine in the presence of the great medicine man sent by the Great Spirit.
>
> "Rocky Bear" rolled his eyes and folded his hands on his breast as he stepped on tip-toe

23. "St. Peter's & Vatican, Rome," reproduction from original photograph, in "Historical Sketches & Programme" for Buffalo Bill's Wild West and Congress of Rough Riders of the World, 1894.

24. "Colosseum, Rome," reproduction from original photograph, in "Historical Sketches & Programme" for Buffalo Bill's Wild West and Congress of Rough Riders of the World, 1894.

through the glowing sea of color. His braves furtively eyed the halberds and two-handed swords of the Swiss Guards.

The Indians and cow-boys were ranged in the south corners of the Ducal Hall. Colonel Cody and Mr. Salsbury were escorted into the Sextine Chapel by Chamberlains, where they were greeted by Miss Sherman, the daughter of General Sherman. A princess invited Colonel Cody to a place in the tribune of the Roman nobles.

He stood facing the gorgeous Diplomatic Corps, surrounded by the Prince and Princess Borghesi, the Marquis Serlupi, Princess Bandini, Duchess di Grazioli, Prince and Princess Massimo, Prince and Princess Ruspoli, and all the ancient noble families of the city.

When the Pope appeared in the *sedia gestatoria*, carried above the heads of the Guards, preceded by the Knights of Malta and a procession of cardinals and Archbishops, the cow-boys bowed and so did the Indians. "Rocky Bear" knelt and made the sign of the cross. The Pontiff leaned affectionately toward the rude group and blessed them. He seemed to be touched by the sight.

As the Papal train swept on, the Indians became excited, and a squaw fainted. They had been warned not to utter a sound, and were with difficulty restrained from whooping. The Pope looked at Colonel Cody intently as he passed, and the great scout and Indian fighter bent low as he received the Pontification benediction.

After the Thanksgiving Mass, with its grand choral accompaniment, and now and then the sound of Leo XIII's voice heard ringing through the chapel, the great audience poured out of the Vatican.[44]

Thousands of Europeans were introduced to Native American culture and history through performances of the Wild West and the extensive newspaper coverage of Buffalo Bill's troupe on tours of local areas and in meetings with dignitaries.

Undoubtedly, the most well-known Indian chief to travel with Buffalo Bill's Wild

IRON TAIL
LAST OF THE
GREAT CHIEFS
NOW WITH
BUFFALO BILL
PAWNEE BILL
SHOWS

25. ACROSS: Poster, "Chief Iron Tail, Last of the Great Chiefs," advertising the Buffalo Bill and Pawnee Bill shows, copyrighted 1912, by the U.S. Lithograph Co., Russell Morgan Print, Cincinnati and New York.

West was Chief Sitting Bull of the Hunkpapa Sioux, who spent just one season with the show, in the summer of 1885. Sitting Bull was infamous for his involvement with the massacre of U.S. Cavalry troops at the Battle of Little Bighorn in the summer of 1876. He and his tribe then fled American soil for Canada for approximately four years, during which hardships plagued the group. With little food or resources, Sitting Bull eventually decided to make the trip back to his homelands, and surrendered to United States officials on July 20, 1881. As a prisoner of war, he would, for the rest of his life, be a ward of the American government. Sitting Bull was made to live and farm at the Standing Rock Agency, and report to Indian agent James McLaughlin. His efforts and that of his devoted Sioux could no longer prevent the advances of the U.S. military who sought final control of all the Indians' western homelands. Although forced to remain on the reservation, Sitting Bull had established himself as a notable figure among Native Americans. Cody immediately recognized the possibilities for Sitting Bull's celebrity stature.

Initially, the secretary of the interior was opposed to Sitting Bull joining Cody's tour. But Cody and his general manager, John Burke, relentlessly pursued the contract for Sitting Bull's services, finally arranging for Sitting Bull's appearances in the show's parade and in the arena but not in the dramatic segments. His pay was set at $50 per week, with a bonus of $125. His interpreter, William Halsey, and five men and three women would also be allowed to travel with the show at smaller salaries. Sitting Bull also was granted the right to sell his portrait photographs and autographs during the tour. Once on opposite sides of war, Cody and Sitting Bull performed together for the one season. Huge crowds flocked to the performances. Ticket sales soared and Cody's finances stabilized to ensure the future of Buffalo Bill's Wild West.[45]

Like all Indians with the troupe, Sitting Bull was exposed to the Euro-American lifestyle and culture while sharing tribal culture with audiences. Indians received thunderous applause and ovations for their appearances and participation in each program segment. Viewing the thrilling battles and painted warriors from the safety of their grandstand seats, visitors encountered, most for the first time, the skills and strength of the American Indians.[46]

The 1885 contract, while satisfying both Cody and Sitting Bull, would be the only one ever allowed. Sitting Bull's status concerned the Bureau of Indian Affairs and agent McLaughlin. Sitting Bull was never again allowed to leave Standing Rock. His interest in the Ghost Dance movement of his people and religious missionaries led to his death in December 1890. Sitting Bull was shot by Indian police attempting to arrest him at his home. Just two weeks later, tensions led to the massacre of Sioux families at Wounded Knee, a devastating and virtual end to the Indian wars for their sovereignty over their

26. Iron White Man wearing a Buffalo Bill's Indian Police badge, platinum print by Käsebier, 1898.

lands. Indians remained sequestered, living on reservations or sent to government-run schools for "Americanization." The U.S. government closely guarded its control of land and all Native Americans.

The government would not ban the Indians' participation in Buffalo Bill's Wild West or any later competing shows, but regulated it through the Bureau of Indian Affairs. Moses's research shows that reformers believed the shows/exhibitions were "contrary to the best interests of the Indians . . . Ironically, the approach of Cody's Wild West organization was not unlike that of the reformers: both favored assimilation of the First Americans. Indeed, Buffalo Bill continually emphasized that Indians should adapt to a modern world. So did the Indians themselves."[47] The Show Indians were at times interviewed by government agents or the press. Rocky Bear stated: "If [the show] did not suit me, I would not remain any longer. [The Indians] eat everything; that is the reason I am getting so fat. When I come back to the reservation I am getting poor."[48] While Black Heart stated: "These men [Cody, Burke, and Salsbury] have got us in hand. We were raised on horseback; that is the way we had to work. These men furnished us the same work we were raised to; that is the reason we want to work for these kind of men . . . If Indian wants work at any place and earn money, he wants to do so; white man got privilege to do the same—any kind of work that he wants."[49]

Chiefs were often reluctant to let their people go, but Buffalo Bill and John M. Burke, Wild West manager, proved persuasive in most cases.[50] The federal contract stipulated that the Indians must "obey orders, refrain from all drinking, gambling and fighting." Burke organized Buffalo Bill's Indian Police. The number of Indian "policemen" chosen depended on the number of Indians traveling with the show each season, a usual ratio being one policeman for every dozen Indians. In any given season of the Wild West, Indian performers normally ranged in number from 100 to 200. Indian policemen, elected from within the ranks of Indian performers, were given badges and paid $10 more in wages per month.[51] Chiefs Iron Tail and Short Man were leaders of the Indian Police in 1898.

But the Indian men, women, and children of the Wild West Show lived peacefully, coexisting with the diverse groups living and working in the Wild West village and among the many curious visitors. When not performing for sold-out crowds, the Indians would venture out by automobile or by train, sightseeing on their own at major city attractions.[52] Interpreters translated for them inside and outside the Wild West camp.

Burke, in a newspaper interview, addressed the fact that many of the Indians did not initially understand the nature of arena performances. Would they be massacred? Cody and Salsbury's "realistic" and "historical" approach to show segments led to Indian defeat every time. But crowds of 10,000 or more cheered the arrival and actions of the Show Indians in every performance. Cody, the *New York Times* wrote, "always designed [Buffalo Bill's Wild West] to be a series of pictures," an exhibition. Burke indicated that "most Indian Acts in the Wild West show [were] devised by Indians themselves," especially the dance segments.[53]

Program segments were practiced before the start of each season at the Wild West home base in Bridgeport, Connecticut. The set included scenes with backdrops of sweeping scenes, special electric lighting, and windstorm effects to closely duplicate the rolling landscape of the American West. Cody's frontier spirit and that of the Indians were revived daily during the grand parades, battles, and rescues. All acts were meticulously choreographed to represent an American West that was becoming a distant memory. As L. G. Moses writes:

> Indians survived "Winning the West," both in reality and then as portrayed in the shows. Whether on or off the reservations, they drew strength from their cultures to sustain them. It is a testimony to their remarkable resilience that, given the hostile environment created by the governments [*sic*] and Euroamericans between 1883 and 1917, the time of Buffalo Bill's career in the Wild West, Indians and their cultures endured.[54]

Today, Buffalo Bill Cody's scrapbooks of newspaper clippings from virtually every city visited on the Wild West yearly program provide invaluable references to scholars. Whether in New York, Chicago, or Kansas City, publicists for the show supplied local journalists with updates on the program, and the year's highlights. The 1898 season, corresponding with the making of Käsebier's first portraits, was the first to include the Cuban Rough Riders, wounded freedom fighters on furlough awaiting their return to Cuba to battle the Spanish. Their story and their horsemanship rivaled that of the American Indians in popularity with the audience. Many articles in the 1898 scrapbook reference Buffalo Bill's readiness to join the American forces fighting in the Spanish-American War as a scout for the Army. He boasts in one article for *The World,* April 3, 1898, "How I Could Drive Spaniards from Cuba with 30,000 Indian Braves," acknowledging his respect for Native American skills in warfare.[55]

THE WORLD: SUNDAY, APRIL 3, 1898. 27

BUFFALO BILL WRITES ON "HOW I COULD DRIVE SPANIARDS FROM CUBA WITH 30,000 INDIAN BRAVES."

Buffalo Bill says there are in the country fully 30,000 Indians who can fight and who would be glad to enlist under Uncle Sam's banner for guerilla warfare in Cuba. Lieut. Emyerich and Lieut.-Col. Delgado, Cuban veterans, say that such a body of galloping, fearless troops could take Havana in one dashing charge. The Indian has a taste for war, and he hates the Spanish for bringing the white man to this continent and for their horrible cruelty to the red men.

IN response to your request for a statement regarding the probable conduct and possible usefulness of the American Indian in the event of war, I wish to say first that every Indian would be loyal to the American flag.

There are in the United States to-day fully 30,000 full-blooded Indian warriors and at least 10,000 more youths and aged Indian men who can fight.

With the 30,000 young redmen, mounted on their wiry ponies, acting in conjunction with the insurgents with an adequate amount of artillery, and using the same military tactics that they and their fathers used in fighting the whites in the wild West, I do not think that the Spaniards would last more than sixty days in a land war in Cuba.

Havana is the stronghold of the Spaniards. If Havana were to fall the subjection of the rest of the island, with the help of the gallant insurgents, could be accomplished. The country surrounding Havana is well adapted to the American Indian method of warfare.

From a hurried study of the inland defenses of the city and from questioning the veteran insurgents who have just come from Cuba to take part in my Wild West Show, I am led to believe that, with the aid of the six or seven thousand insurgents from Pinar del Rio and Matanzas provinces, who could be easily moved to the region of Havana on short notice, the city could be taken by these armed forces, at least with a naval attack engaging the guns in the forts at the same time.

The most experienced of the Cuban fighters who are with me, men thoroughly acquainted with the region about Havana, assure me that this could be done. Lieut.-Col. Emyerick, who carries eight ugly wounds, is a veteran of two Cuban wars and has fought from one end of the island to the other, has said that the Indians could do it. He also says that he would guarantee to be able to land Indian or any other kind of American troops on any part of the Cuban coast not fortified by the Spaniards.

Lieut.-Col. Delgado, who fought with Gen. Maceo in his last battle and was twice wounded, and Lieut. Mazurro, who composed the Cuban national hymn and is the head of the Wild West Show's band of insurgents, also say that the Indians, operating in their own peculiar way, would make effective fighters in Cuba, and that 30,000 of them could capture Havana. Others of the wounded veterans have said the same.

These men have been thoroughly impressed by the appearance of the fierce Sioux Indians whom they have met in Madison Square Garden, and have been even more impressed by what they have learned of the history and fighting qualities of the American red men.

Would the Indians fight the Spaniards? They most certainly would. The American Indian has by no means forgotten how to fight. He is a natural-born fighter, and is just as anxious to go to war now as he ever was, and he would rather fight Spaniards than any other people on earth. Why? Because Spain sent the first white man to America. They hate Spain for having done that.

Most people who have had no experience with Indians will consider that a trivial thing for me to say. It is not. American Indians know about Columbus and who sent him here. I took a band of them to Barcelona, Spain, with me several years ago. I showed them the big statue of Columbus there. They gazed at it in silence and disgust for some time, and then I asked them what they thought about it.

"Bad medicine," replied the leading man among them—the medicine man. If they consider a thing good they call it "good medicine," if bad it is "bad medicine." I asked for a further explanation and the medicine man said that they could never forgive Columbus for coming to rob their fathers of their beautiful land nor Spain for sending him. Trouble has been the Indian's lot, he said, ever since.

The American Indian has a natural appetite for war, and he is hungry to fight the nation that is responsible for his being disturbed in his Arcadian simplicity.

There are many great Indian chiefs still living, perhaps fifty chiefs and important sub-chiefs, who would make gallant and effective leaders in an Indian campaign in Cuba. There is American Horse, Sioux Chief, who, since the great Chief Red Cloud is totally blind, would be the great Sioux leader. After him would come He Dog, Little Wound, Hump, Red Horn Bull, all Sioux chiefs, and Big Road, Kicking Bear and Short Bull, of the Ogallalla Sioux.

Red Horn Bull is with my show. He was in the battle of the Little Big Horn River in 1876, known as the Custer massacre, where Gen. Custer and his entire command were slain. Red Horn Bull carries the ugly mark of the last bullet from Custer's revolver. In the thick of the fight he came face to face with the gallant General, who, having lost his sword, drew his revolver and began firing. Red Horn Bull says that he grabbed the revolver, and as he did so the hammer fell and the 41-calibre bullet went through his jaw, carrying away part of the bone and knocking him down. He is very proud of Gen. Custer's bullet-hole.

An Indian with a record like that could be relied on to get the better of a good many Spaniards if he met them face to face. He said just a few days ago that he would like to fight Spain and would be glad to fight under the American flag. That, I believe, is the feeling among all Indians.

Then there is Chief Joseph, of the Nez Perces, one of the greatest Indian generals that this country ever produced and certainly the most humane of all Indian chiefs. He is in the prime of life, and so is his sub-chief, Ollicutt. Geronimo, the vicious chief of the Apaches, is at present a prisoner of war, but he is a great and wicked general and must be considered in any speculation like the present. These are only a few of the chiefs, still living, any one of whom is capable of leading his people to war against the Spaniards and to conduct a telling campaign.

Every one of the 30,000 or more Indian warriors is prepared for war. He could go on a moment's notice. Each owns his own war horse, many having numbers of them, and each is constantly equipped with arms and ammunition. All that would be necessary would be to load them, their horses and equipments on trains and ship them to the sea coast. Nothing would please the Indians more than an order to go to battle. Even their religion teaches them that it is good to fight. The better record an Indian has as a warrior on earth the better his chance of happiness in the hereafter, he is taught.

Ships could be provided for transporting the Indians from the United States sea coast to Cuba and I am assured by insurgents and others that a landing there could be effected even at so favorable a point as the open country about midway between Havana and Matanzas; not more than twenty miles from the capital, in fact.

If, as I have been told, there are bands of insurgents constantly camped within two or three miles of Havana, the Indians could be mobilized in the hills that surround the city. The conditions seem to be peculiarly favorable to Indian warfare. No people on earth can get the "lay" of a new country quicker than the American Indian. He is a natural astronomer and astrologer. He observes landmarks with unerring accuracy and has a wonderful faculty of determining direction. From the crest of some high hill one long sweep of the eyes would be enough to give each leader of the Indians the "lay of the land" and tell how best to employ his forces. The Indian is a great strategist.

If these 30,000 shouting Indian braves on horseback, resplendent in brilliant war paint, the eagle feathers on their war bonnets fluttering in the wind, should sweep down on Havana in a grand charge what a picture it would make! Taken unawares, hundreds of thousands of men could not withstand such an onslaught.

As to the rest of the island, it is just the kind of country in which Indians fight best. A ridge of mountains runs the whole length of the island about midway between the coasts, and the generally hilly nature of the rest of the island makes it adaptable to ambush fighting and sudden charges, the tactics employed most effectively by the Indians.

Of course all this is speculation. It perhaps can never come to pass; but it is interesting to reflect on what has been and what might still be accomplished by that noble but rapidly dying race, the American Indian.

WILLIAM F. CODY (Buffalo Bill).

The newspaper accounts of the 1898 season of Buffalo Bill's Wild West, much as in other years, chronicles attendance statistics and interesting moments along the six-month tour. Numerous reports focus on the Show Indians and their daily lives and activities while on tour. The *New York Journal*, April 17, 1898, one week prior to the Indians' visit to Käsebier's studio, reported their appearance in the annual Fifth Avenue Easter Parade, attracting attention in their colorful coats, feathers, blankets, and moccasins.

The *Baltimore News* of May 12, 1898, ran a commentary titled "How the Indians and Other People of the Show Live," reporting that "Indians consider it a great privilege to travel with the show and make money." The Indian Police force was described as keeping order among the warriors. Offenders, those who broke established rules, were sent back to the reservation, and another Indian sent as a replacement. Four women and two children traveled with the troupe in 1898. The "wigwam encampment" was set up in back of the main

27. ACROSS: "How I Could Drive Spaniards from Cuba with 30,000 Indian Braves," *The World*, April 3, 1898, in 1898 Buffalo Bill Scrapbook.

tents and was easily accessible to visitors. The Indians ate in the large dining tent, were served the same food as other performers and workers but, curiously, no desserts, as was their stated preference. The press, like thousands of spectators to the show, was repeatedly fascinated with the apparent ease with which the Show Indians adapted to a theatrical life, and one so far from the Great Plains.[56]

One of the most intriguing descriptions of Buffalo Bill's Wild West and the Show Indians can be found in an edited journal, "The Idle Record of an Idle Summer," dated 1909, in the Smithsonian's Photographic History Collection. The author, a woman living near Atlantic City, New Jersey, carefully documented, as a Christmas present for a friend, the events occurring in the seaside city in June of 1909. The author's husband served as photographer, thus illustrating the journal. In typical early–twentieth-century fashion, the author describes "Buffalo Bill Coming to Town."

> "Lo! The poor Indian!" is no more of a stoic. We have watched him too under gray cold skies for Buffalo Bill has come and gone and we "assisted" just as we did at the circus:—from the outside. Poor Buffalo Bill! Poor Lo! That tricky calendar said "June," the weather man chuckled and switched on October!
>
> There was no parade but the "braves" marched up the boardwalk to one of the piers clad in war-paint, feathers and skin—little else! The squaws had not been invited to the performance. After they gave one squint at the sky, they seemed glad they were not. The wigwam was cosy and the mess-tent warm. The braves marched boldly accompanied by half the small boys of the neighbourhood [*sic*]. The other half were green with envy. It was Saturday morning, "no chores, no fun!" "Tickets for the show must be earned," said mother. But—oh what joy to walk proudly beside a "real" Indian, to touch him and know that was only skin, that smooth, brown, polished surface streaked with red and yellow paint; to see him toss his feathers and maybe ! oh, bliss! pick up an arrow, a tomahawk, a lariat he had dropped. Wasn't that almost as good as going to the show?
>
> We, two, trotted down to the boardwalk and watched the procession move by. There we sauntered down the quarter-mile to the "camp" and hung over the rail with our neighbors watching "doings" on the sand below.[57]

Pictures depicting the Wild West camp in the sand of Atlantic City show the casual parade of the Show Indians, announcing their arrival with a stroll down the boardwalk, the tipis and camp on wash day, and the exuberant local young boys working outside the tents not for pay, but for tickets.

In conclusion, the diary author writes of the show's departure from her city: "The Indians, wigwams, elephants, cowboys, burros and babies vanished in the night . . ." Buffalo Bill's Wild West, its hundreds of staff, performers and Show Indians, quietly moved on almost daily through their tour schedule, leaving lasting memories with their audiences.[58]

28–30. American Indians parade and set up camp at Atlantic City, New Jersey, June 1909, in the edited journal "The Idle Record of an Idle Summer."

Epilogue

ONE HUNDRED YEARS LATER, GERTRUDE KÄSEBIER'S PORTRAITS, PRESERVED IN THE SMITHSONIAN, REMAIN IMPORTANT VISUAL RECORDS ENCOURAGING FURTHER CONTEMPLATION AND RESEARCH INTO THE LIVES OF THESE SIOUX PERFORMERS and their nation. Käsebier documents a complexity in the portraits of the Sioux performers of the Wild West show, actors playing themselves. This valuable collection of portraits makes Native American specialist Rayna Green wish that "[Käsebier] had followed her Dakota friends into the photographic void of the early twentieth century where individual and collective Native character, devoid of props, was all there was to shoot."[59]

Sitting for their portraits, the Sioux Indian men and Zitkala-Ša befriended Gertrude Käsebier, and allowed her to preserve both their likenesses and spirit for history. "It takes a genius to eliminate the traces of labor from his production," Käsebier once stated. Lecturing for the Department of Photography at the Brooklyn Institute in 1914, she reflected on photography, advising fellow artists in the audience to avoid the ultradramatic and self-exploitation—to cultivate simplicity.[60] Her biographer, Barbara Michaels, concludes: "Käsebier's pictures fascinate in part because they do defy precise explanation. Because she aimed to excite emotions through nuanced, evocative images, her pictures often remain ambiguous, dreamlike, timeless."[61] Gertrude Käsebier's collection of Native American portraits is a poignant testimony to her independent spirit and her modern awareness of the possibilities of fine art photography.

31. Portrait of Gertrude Käsebier by Alvin Langdon Coburn, circa 1902–1903.

Notes

1. "Some Indian Portraits," *Everybody's Magazine* 4 (January 1901): 24.
2. William Innes Homer, *A Pictorial Heritage: The Photographs of Gertrude Käsebier* (Wilmington, DE: University of Delaware and Delaware Art Museum, 1979), 20.
3. Barbara L. Michaels, *Gertrude Käsebier: The Photographer and Her Photographs* (New York: Harry N. Abrams, 1992), 164.
4. Ibid., 13–14; Homer, *Pictorial Heritage*, 9–15; Gertrude Käsebier Papers, University of Delaware Library, Newark, DE.
5. Quoted in Homer, *Pictorial Heritage*, 12.
6. Ibid.; Weston J. Naef, *The Collection of Alfred Stieglitz: Fifty Pioneers of Modern Art* (New York: Metropolitan Museum of Art and Viking Press, 1978), 387–93.
7. Elizabeth Hutchinson, "When the Sioux Party Calls: Käsebier's Indian Portraits and the Gendering of the Artist's Studio," *American Art* 16 (Summer 2002): 48–49.
8. "The Pose in Portraiture," *The Photo-Miniature* 1 (May 1899): 51.
9. Ibid., 45–51.
10. Ibid., 45–82; "The Platinotype Process," *The Photo-Miniature* 1 (October 1899): 319–22.
11. Joseph T. Keiley, "The American School," *Photograms of the Year* (1899): 22.
12. Ibid., 22.
13. Ibid., 13–14.
14. Ibid., 22.
15. Ibid., 18–22.
16. Homer, *Pictorial Heritage*, 15–16, 32.
17. Gertrude Käsebier Papers, University of Delaware Library, Newark, DE.
18. Ibid., 81–82.
19. "Sioux Chief's Party Calls. The Indians Make Daily Visits to the Studio Where They Were Entertained at Tea," *New York Times* (April 24, 1898): 14.
20. Michaels, *Gertrude Käsebier*, 8.
21. "Sioux Chief's Party Calls," 14.
22. Ibid.
23. "Some Indian Portraits," 4.
24. Rayna Green, "Gertrude Käsebier's 'Indian' Photographs," *History of Photography Journal* 24 (Spring 2000): 59.
25. Hutchinson, "When the Sioux Party Calls," 38.
26. Green, "Gertrude Käsebier's 'Indian' Photographs," 59–60.
27. "Some Indian Portraits," 7–12.
28. Ibid.
29. Mina Turner accession records, Gertrude Käsebier Collection, Photographic History Collection, National Museum of American History, Smithsonian Institution, Washington, DC.
30. William K. Powers, "The Art of Courtship among the Oglala," *American Indian Art Magazine* (Spring 1980): 41–47.
31. Gertrude Käsebier Papers, University of Delaware Library, Newark, DE.
32. Arlington National Cemetery, Gertrude Simmons Bonnin biography, http://www.arlingtoncemetery.net/gsbonnin.htm; Famous Native American Women, Gertrude Simmons Bonnin, http://nativeamericanrhymes.com/women/bonnin.htm.
33. *Buffalo Bill Historical Center*, museum catalog (Cody, WY: 1995), 18–21.

34. Ibid.
35. Original Buffalo Bill's Wild West programs, dated 1894 and 1900, Wild West collection, Archives Center, National Museum of American History, Smithsonian Institution, Washington, DC.
36. "How the Wild West Show Was Developed," *New York Times* (April 7, 1901): 26; Buffalo Bill Historical Center, 21.
37. 1898 Buffalo Bill Cody Scrapbook, McCracken Research Library, Buffalo Bill Historical Center, Cody, WY.
38. Joy Kasson, *Buffalo Bill's Wild West: Celebrity, Memory, and Popular History* (New York: Hill and Wang, 2000), 217–19.
39. L. G. Moses, *Wild West Shows and the Images of American Indians 1883–1933* (Albuquerque, NM: University of New Mexico Press, 1996), 4.
40. Buffalo Bill Historical Center, 20, 35.
41. Moses, *Wild West Shows,* 7–8.
42. Curator's files, "Indians with the Wild West," McCracken Research Library, Buffalo Bill Historical Center, Cody, WY.
43. Ibid.
44. Original 1894 Buffalo Bill's Wild West program, Archives Center, National Museum of American History, Smithsonian Institution, Washington, DC.
45. Kasson, *Buffalo Bill's Wild West,* 170–71.
46. Ibid., 174–82.
47. Moses, *Wild West Shows,* 63–64.
48. Ibid., 101.
49. Ibid., 103.
50. Ibid., 26.
51. "Indians in the Wild West Show: Even When Not Performing They Wear Native Dress," *New York Times* (April 21, 1901): 20.
52. "Indians See the Fish," *New York Times* (April 29, 1900): 7; "Redskin Commuters a Civilized Type," *New York Times* (April 15, 1907): 5.
53. "Indians in the Wild West Show," 20.
54. Moses, *Wild West Shows,* 194.
55. 1898 Buffalo Bill Cody Scrapbook, McCracken Research Library, Buffalo Bill Historical Center, Cody, WY.
56. Ibid.
57. Edited diary/journal, "An Idle Record of an Idle Summer," catalog number 77.29, June 1909, Photographic History Collection, National Museum of American History, Smithsonian Institution, Washington, DC.
58. Ibid.
59. Green, "Gertrude Käsebier's 'Indian' Photographs," 60.
60. Gertrude Käsebier lecture given at the Brooklyn Institute, Department of Photography, February 13, 1914, included in the Gertrude Käsebier Papers, University of Delaware Library, Newark, DE.
61. Michaels, *Gertrude Käsebier,* 165.

Illustration Credits

1. Smithsonian Libraries.
2. Department of Prints, National Portrait Gallery, Smithsonian Institution.
3. Photographic History Collection (PHC), National Museum of American History (NMAH), Smithsonian Institution.
4. PHC/NMAH.
5. PHC/NMAH.
6. PHC/NMAH.
7. PHC/NMAH.
8. PHC/NMAH.
9. PHC/NMAH.
10. National Anthropological Archives, National Museum of Natural History, Smithsonian Institution.
11. Department of Photographs, National Portrait Gallery, Smithsonian Institution.
12. Department of Prints and Photographs, Library of Congress.
13. PHC/NMAH.
14. PHC/NMAH.
15. Buffalo Bill Historical Center, Cody, WY.
16. Department of Photographs, National Portrait Gallery, Smithsonian Institution.
17. Warshaw Collection, Archives Center, NMAH.
18. Buffalo Bill Historical Center, Cody, Wyoming.
19. Warshaw Collection, Archives Center, NMAH.
20. Warshaw Collection, Archives Center, NMAH.
21. PHC/NMAH.
22. PHC/NMAH.
23. Warshaw Collection, Archives Center, NMAH.
24. Warshaw Collection, Archives Center, NMAH.
25. Division of Music, Sports and Entertainment, NMAH.
26. Department of Photographs, Museum of Modern Art, NY.
27. Buffalo Bill Historical Center, Cody, WY.

28–30. PHC/NMAH.

31. PHC/NMAH.

Käsebier's Native American Portraits

The Gertrude Käsebier Collection

Photographs of Dakota Sioux Indian performers with Buffalo Bill's Wild West Show, circa 1898

PLATINUM AND GUM PHOTOGRAPHS AND PHOTOGRAVURE PRINTS, MADE FROM ORIGINAL 6½″ × 8½″ GLASS NEGATIVES, AND PICTOGRAPH DRAWINGS MADE BY THE INDIANS AT KÄSEBIER'S STUDIO

While Käsebier primarily photographed her Native American subjects in the studio, there are existing photographs among her personal collection showing the Dakota Sioux Indians in the West, probably an area within their Pine Ridge Reservation, South Dakota. To date, no correspondence has been located regarding a trip for Käsebier to the Great Plains.

The Sioux are shown moving through the barren landscape of the Black Hills, South Dakota, hunting on horseback and transporting their children and tipi homes.

From left to right: Sammy Lone Bear, Phillip Standing Soldier, Joe Black Fox, and Chief Iron Tail drawing for Käsebier while visiting the studio. Each of these men developed lasting friendships with the photographer, presenting her with sketches, corresponding through letters over the years, and visiting with Käsebier when the Wild West show performed annually in New York City.

The natural light provided by the single window in Käsebier's studio accents this group portrait of the Dakota Sioux chiefs and men visiting in April 1898. Käsebier often used lighting effectively in portraits for highlighting her subjects, and created dramatic effects and strong visual lines through her technical skills in developing and printing the images.

ACROSS: Near the window of Käsebier's Fifth Avenue, New York, studio, two young Sioux men wait during the portrait session. Pausing momentarily from drawing, one glances outward, contemplating the vast city and skyscrapers.

ABOVE: Little Finger posed casually in front of a tipi holding a spear with shield and wearing a gun, a bone breastplate, armbands, and feather and fur accessories. Possibly photographed at Buffalo Bill's Wild West camp set up in New York during performances.

ACROSS: Black Horse with woman and another man in front of tipi.

Left and right close-up profile views of Amos Two Bulls. These platinum images are toned in shades of black and brown, respectively, which were expertly applied by

Spotted Tail, his wife, and son standing in front of two tipis. Each tipi is painted with drawings significant to the family or tribe. Spotted Tail stands with a traditional Sioux blanket wrapped at his waist. His wife's dress is adorned with elk teeth and a beaded scarf. The boy, who leans close to his father, warily looking at the photographer, is dressed similarly to Spotted Tail.

Kills First looks directly into the camera for the first of two portraits by Käsebier. In the second, he holds two arrows and turns in profile, allowing for closer inspection of his clothing and the feathers, beads, and medallions of his attire.

Short Man is photographed by Käsebier seated presumably in the middle of the studio, allowing a view of the wall with framed photographs in the background. In full war bonnet, or feather headdress, and bone breastplate, Short Man sits wrapped in a blanket, holding a war club, and wearing a vest, with an Indian Police badge for Buffalo Bill's Wild West, on his left breast. The chiefs and leaders of Buffalo Bill's Indian Police were responsible for overseeing all Native Americans traveling with the show and received slightly more pay than other Indians.

In his photographs, Joe Black Fox seems quite at ease with Käsebier and being in front of a camera. Black Fox almost smiles, grinning for the portraits. This is generally uncharacteristic for Native Americans—in 1898 many still believed in the potential for the lens to steal their soul. Black Fox poses dutifully in his feather headdress and then playfully with cigarette in hand, relaxed, wrapped in a blanket and wearing a patterned silken scarf with pin, earrings, and beaded lizard-shaped accessory in his hair.

Jos Black Fox

Mrs Barstow

Pencil drawing, deer, signed "Joe Black Fox."

Pencil drawing, one figure draped in blanket, signed "Joe Black Fox."

ACROSS: Pencil drawing, "Mrs. Barstone" and "Joe Black Fox," two figures draped in blankets.

The *New York Times* reported yearly on Buffalo Bill's Wild West show's arrival in the city. Several articles referenced the friendships, and in one case elopement, of Indian performers and local white women. Women's social reform groups of the time would have included Indian rights as an important issue and, therefore, were concerned for the well-being and fair treatment of Indians traveling with the Wild West show.

ABOVE: Has No Horses appears complacent in posing for his portraits, potentially patient with the photographer for his front view, and left and right profiles. He agrees, like many of the other Native Americans visiting Käsebier's studio, to pose in full dress with war bonnet, then without, and a third time with a war club. A blanket, or rug, is hung as a backdrop.

ACROSS: Käsebier poses High Heron and Has No Horses (standing) together, similarly dressed and equally displaying strong composure. Has No Horses tightly grips his blanket wrap with one hand and lightly touches his chin with the other, revealing vulnerability. The intricate white beadwork of his vest and blanket are highlights among the otherwise dark portrait.

Chief Lone Bear's family maintained a lasting and meaningful friendship with Käsebier following the initial portrait session, visiting her when possible. His son, Sammy, and daughter, Mary, were also photographed.

Chief Lone Bear's badge reads "Buffalo Bill's Police." The beaded embroidery above the vest badge is a flag pattern similar to the blanket held by Sammy and shown on others photographed within this group.

Samuel Lone Bear developed the closest lasting friendship with Gertrude Käsebier following this initial portrait sitting in 1898. "Sammy" was educated at a government Indian school and wrote letters to Käsebier in English over many years, dated as late as 1912. Käsebier's granddaughter Mina Turner remembered vividly one visit to a Wild West show performance, and having Sammy pull her from the ground for a ride around the arena with him on horseback. "Granny" waved happily from the stands.

Lone Bear poignantly stands alone for the third portrait, in the midst of the Fifth Avenue studio, a table covered in white behind. Embroidered American flags are clearly visible on his blanket border.

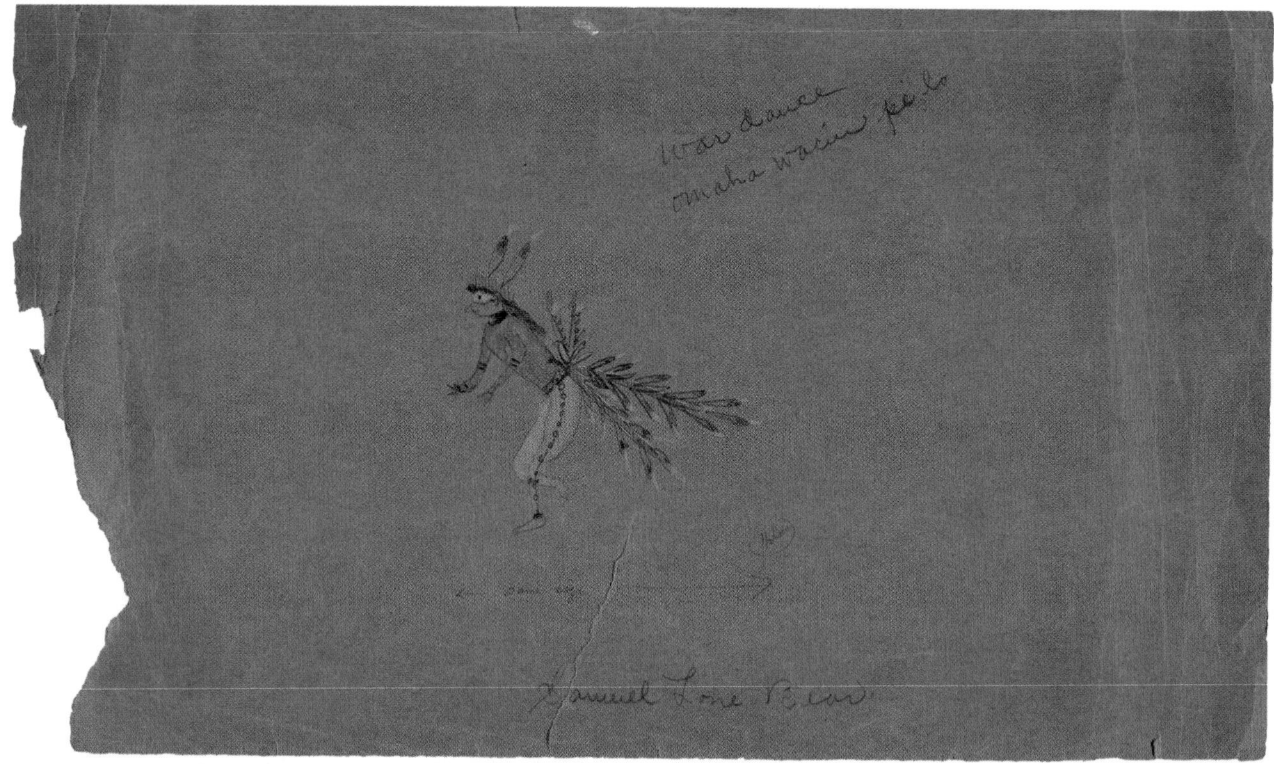

Pencil and crayon drawing of an Indian figure with feathers, dancing, titled "War dance, Omaha waciu pi lo," and signed "Samuel Lone Bear."

ACROSS, TOP: Pencil drawing, "Catch girls," showing four figures and a tipi. Signed by "Sammy Lone Bear Jr.," and dated March 6, 1899.

This pictograph drawing, like many of those made at Käsebier's studio, contains references to a Sioux courtship tradition, "the chase" and the courting blanket.

ACROSS, BOTTOM: Pencil drawing, "Wild buffalo," signed "Sam Lone Bear Junior."

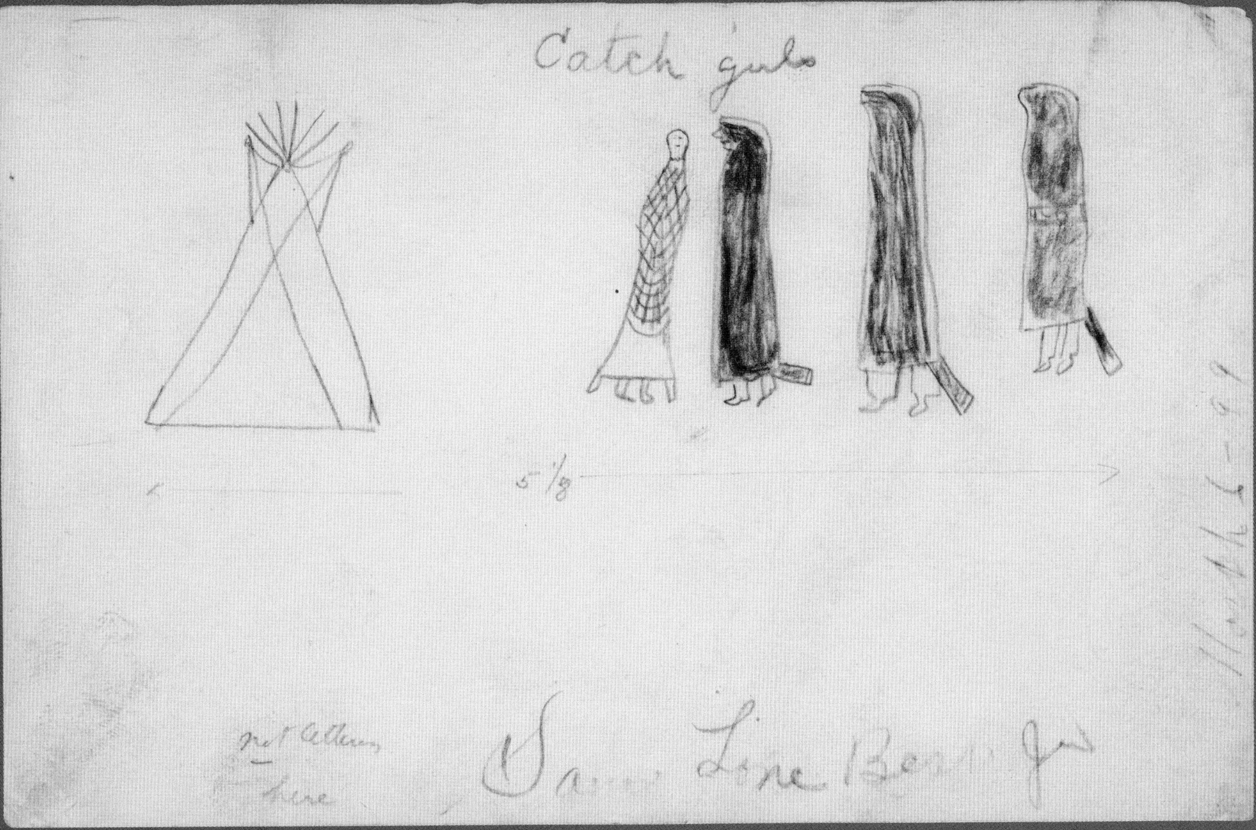

Catch girls

5 1/8

Sam Lone Bear Jr

Sam Lone Bear Junior

3

Wild buffalo

I told the indians I wanted to
photograph a papoose. They said the
squaws had a superstion that it would
kill the child. I told them they ought
to know better, having been to Carlisle
school and around the world with the
show. They brought me Mary Lone
Bear, nine years old.
Six weeks later I visited the show
and went out to the tepees to visit.
The squaws grabbed their kids and
ran looking at me viciously.
I asked the men what was the
matter. They told me Mary Lone
Bear had died.
What killed her?

Mary Lone Bear was one of the few Sioux children Käsebier was allowed to photograph. Her father Chief Lone Bear and brother Samuel "Sammy" Lone Bear were also photographed. Sammy remained friends with the photographer for many years, visiting her and inviting her to performances.

A note that accompanies the photographs in the Smithsonian's collection, written by Käsebier, reads:

> I told the Indians I wanted to photograph a papoose. They said the squaws had a superstition that it would kill the child. I told them they ought to know better having been to Carlisle School and around the world with the show. They brought me Mary Lone Bear, nine years old.
>
> But weeks later I visited the show and went out to the tepees to visit. The squaws grabbed their kids and ran looking at me viciously. I asked what was the matter. They told me Mary Lone Bear had died.
>
> What killed her?

Shooting Pieces seated on a simple curved wooden bench, wrapped in a blanket, and holding a war club.

ACROSS: Clockwise: Black Cat, Big Elk, Shooting Pieces, and Andrew grouped in the corner of the studio. Käsebier may have simply turned her camera stand to seize this casual image while the Sioux waited for others to be photographed.

Flying Horse, shown in a close-up profile view. Käsebier uses natural studio light to reflect strongly on his face, and the light-colored feathers and beads of his vest and hair, while contrasting his dark clothing and the light-colored wall.

Chief Iron Tail was the elder chief in the group of Sioux Indians selected by Buffalo Bill Cody to visit Gertrude Käsebier's photography studio. Iron Tail was a veteran of the Indian Wars, including the Battle of Little Bighorn. Later, he became friendly with Buffalo Bill and traveled with the Wild West troupe for almost twenty years. Iron Tail was one of several Native Americans whose profile inspired the face appearing on the United States buffalo nickel early in the twentieth century.

Surprisingly Chief Iron Tail agreed to remove his feather war bonnet for the portrait sitting with Käsebier, although the headdress and feathers were badges of his place of importance within the tribe. The photographer hoped to achieve "raw" photographs of each Sioux Indian, representing their individuality and personal character. Käsebier was pleased with her results and made a copy of the finished print for the chief. When Iron Tail saw the print, he immediately tore it in half, upset with the image. Later, he sat for Käsebier in full regalia.

Pencil drawing, one figure on horseback and two Indians near a tipi, signed "Iron Tail."

Iron Tail

266

267

Chief Red Horn Bull seated, holding war club. His face appears scarred and deformed from years of battle and hard life on the Plains.

Kills Close to the Lodge, seated, holding war club.

Identified as both Kills Close to the Lodge and Sitting Holy on the photographer's mounts, the original Käsebier negative held by the Library of Congress identifies this Sioux Indian as Luke Big Turnips.

LEFT & ACROSS: Phillip Standing Soldier, shown in one photograph with a pipe to his lips, was one of the youngest of the Wild West Indian performers photographed by Käsebier. Younger Sioux were trained in English and a variety of subjects at government-run Indian schools.

BELOW: Pencil drawing, horse, drawn by "Phillip S. Soldier."

RIGHT: Identified as Whirling Hawk in the 1901 *Everybody's Magazine* article "Some Indian Portraits," this Native American is Charging Thunder according to original Käsebier negatives held in the Library of Congress. The feathers worn in his hair, his fringed shirt, medallions, pins, and wrist cuffs are distinctive in comparison with the other Sioux photographed.

ACROSS: Young Whirling Hawk is seated and photographed against the darkest of the backdrops used by Käsebier. Studio lighting highlights his profile, and details on the bone breastplate, intricate embroidery of the vest, feathers, headdress, and armbands.

ABOVE: “Sioux+Wigwam” is the caption Käsebier used for this photograph of four Sioux men in front of a tipi. This image was probably taken by Käsebier while visiting the Buffalo Bill’s Wild West camp set up in Brooklyn, relatively close to the Käsebier family home.

ACROSS: High Heron mounted on horseback, posed in front of two tipis, possibly at the Buffalo Bill’s Wild West camp in Brooklyn. Four individuals are visible in the background. Ticket holders were able to tour the performers’ camp and living quarters before the show and attend rehearsals.

RIGHT & ACROSS: Whirling Horse photographed in full headdress and draped in blanket.

BELOW: Photograph of Whirling Horse, mounted on sketch paper with drawings of a tipi, buffalo, and Indian on horseback, presumably made by Whirling Horse during the portrait session and given to Käsebier.

Portrait of Flying Hawk.

Käsebier said that it took three years to get the Sioux Indians, who were fearful that if photographed a child would die, to agree to let her photograph their children. Willie Spotted Horse, dressed like his elders in full feather headdress and bone breastplate, is posed resting one arm on a stool, gazing directly into the camera lens.

BELOW: Käsebier's portrait of American Horse and his wife is unusual and significant, when compared with most Native Americans photographed at the time. Käsebier successfully reflects the intimacy expressed through the pose and direct gaze into the camera lens when printing this soft-focused platinum print.

Portraits of Amos Little.

Portraits of White Wolf.

Portrait of Plenty Wounds.

Portrait of William Frog seated on the studio floor, posed with a pipe.

Cow Boy
Cow

Pencil drawing, one figure, inscribed "Cowboy, horse, and cow," and signed "Wm. H. Frog."

Side/back view of Bad Bear. In later oral interviews with family members, Käsebier detailed the difficulty she had getting some of the men to sit for their photographs.

LEFT: Portrait of Takes Enemy, holding a spear or staff.

ACROSS: Portrait of Whirlwind Horse, wearing a full feather headdress and tailored fabric shirt.

ABOVE: Unidentified Sioux male, possibly Bad Bear.

ACROSS: Profile portrait of Iron White Man, who wears two strings of beads, a circular ring on his head, tailored shirt, and vest.

In addition to photographing the group of Sioux performers sent by Buffalo Bill Cody to the studio, Käsebier was able to arrange a portrait session with Zitkala-Ša, "Red Bird," also known as Gertrude Simmons Bonnin (1876–1938), a Yankton Sioux woman of Native American and white mixed ancestry. She was born on the Pine Ridge Reservation in South Dakota, like many of the Sioux traveling with the Wild West show. She was well educated at many schools, including reservation schools, Carlisle Indian School, Earlham College in Indiana, and the Boston Conservatory of Music. Zitkala-Ša became an accomplished author, musician, composer, and dedicated worker for the reform of Indian policies in the United States.

Käsebier photographed Zitkala-Ša in Native American dress and Western clothing, clearly identifying the two worlds in which this woman lived and worked. In many of the images, Zitkala-Ša holds her violin or a book, further identifying her interests. Käsebier experimented with changing backdrops, including a Victorian floral print, and printing using the painterly gum-bichromate process for several of these images, adding increased texture and softer tones to the photographs.

Additional Drawings in the Käsebier Collection

Pencil drawing, "This is a Black Horse with white legs + face, Branded US on."

This is a Black Horse
with white legs + fac
Brandid WS on
WS

This is a spotted Horse
with teepee & D Branded my brand.

Pencil drawing, “This is a spotted Horse with teepee + D Branded my brand.”

This is American Bison

Pencil drawing, "This is American Bison."

Paul

Pencil drawing, "Paul," showing three figures and a tipi.

Pencil drawing and text, the story of the Custer Fight told in Sioux with sketches of figures, animals, tipis, arrow quivers, and shields around the border.

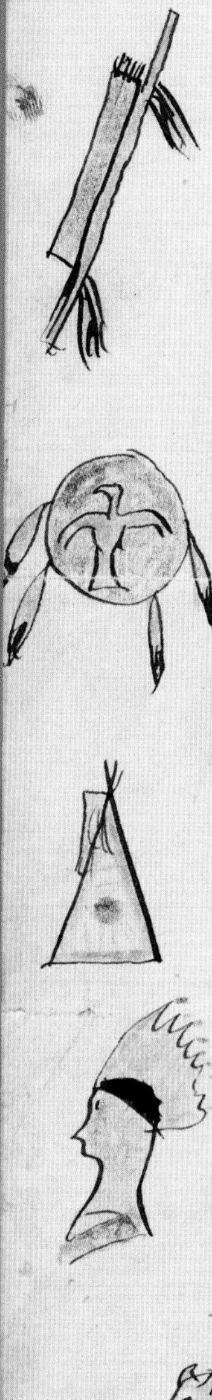

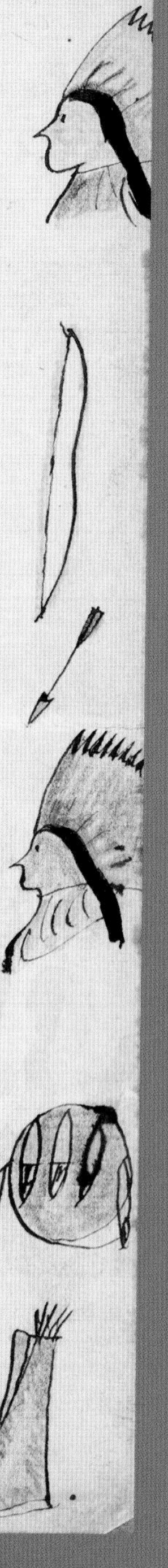

Tatanka ptecela toka gnuya i
nan Wasincu Ob kici zapi
nan akicita kin iyuha wi
ca kte pi nan etan lakota
wikcemnan sam ayamni wi
ca kte pi nan akicita aki
cita kin Opawinge wica
kte pi nan hehanl oke pe
kin han ska kasota pi el
Opa ca he wicasa kin he
isnanla lila wanka tu oya
ca ake tohantu iksa tu wa
cin ehantans Tatanka pte
cela kiginkta lila cin 6
kin nigan hecel cin un
we lo Ho he cetu welo
Wanna henanla ojelo

Tatanka ptecela

COL. W. F. CODY.

BUFFALO BILL'S... WILD WEST

AND

Congress of Rough Riders of the World.

NATE SALSBURY.

OFFICIAL PROGRAMME.

1—**OVERTURE,** "Star Spangled Banner," . . COWBOY BAND, WM. SWEENEY, Leader.

2—**GRAND REVIEW,** introducing the ROUGH RIDERS OF THE WORLD—Indians, Cowboys, Mexicans, Cossacks, Gauchos, Arabs, Scouts, Guides and detachments of fully equipped Regular Soldiers of the Armies of America, England, Germany and Russia, a Color Guard of Cuban Veterans, and a squad of Porto Rican and Filipino Rough Riders.

3—**MISS ANNIE OAKLEY,** Celebrated Shot, who will illustrate her dexterity in the use of firearms.

4—**RACE OF RACES.** Race between a Cowboy, a Cossack, a Mexican, an Arab, a Gaucho, and an Indian, on Spanish-Mexican, Bronco, Russian, Indian and Arabian horses.

5—**U. S. ARTILLERY DRILL,** by veterans from Capt. Thorpe's Battery D, Fifth Regiment, U. S. Artillery.

6—**ILLUSTRATING A PRAIRIE EMIGRANT TRAIN CROSSING THE PLAINS.** It is attacked by marauding Indians, who are in turn repulsed by "Buffalo Bill" and a number of Scouts and Cowboys.

7—**PONY EXPRESS.** A former Pony Post Rider will show how letters and telegrams of the Republic were distributed across our Continent previous to the building of railways and telegraph.

8—**A GROUP OF MEXICANS** from Old Mexico will illustrate the use of the lasso and perform various feats of horsemanship.

9—**THE BATTLE OF SAN JUAN HILL.** Introducing detachments from Roosevelt's Rough Riders, Twenty-fourth Infantry, Ninth and Tenth Cavalry, Grimes' Battery, Garcia's Cuban Scouts, Pack Train, etc., etc.

SCENE 1—BEFORE THE BATTLE. THE BIVOUAC.
(Several hours are supposed to elapse before the opening of the second scene.)

SCENE 2—STORMING OF THE HILL.

V

10—**A GROUP OF RIFFIAN ARAB HORSEMEN** will illustrate their style of horsemanship, together with native sports and pastimes.

11—**JOHNNIE BAKER,** Celebrated Young American Marksman.

12—**COSSACKS,** from the Caucasus of Russia, in feats of horsemanship, native dances, etc.

13—**RELAY RACE,** four teams:

1	2	3	4
Filipino Woman	Mexican	Arab Woman	Cowboy
vs.	vs.	vs.	vs.
Indian Squaw.	Filipino.	American Girl.	Cossack.

14—**COWBOY FUN.** Picking objects from the ground, lassoing wild horses, riding the buckers, etc.

15—**INDIANS** from the Sioux, Arrapahoe, Brulé and Cheyenne tribes will illustrate the Indian mode of fighting, war-dances and games.

16—**MILITARY MUSICAL DRILL** by a detachment of Irish Lancers, a detachment of the Garde-Kurassiers of His Majesty, Kaiser Wilhelm II, and of the Tenth U. S. Cavalry (colored).

17—**VETERANS FROM THE SIXTH U. S. CAVALRY** in military exercises and an exhibition of athletic sports and horsemanship.

Note.—The men will wear the uniforms adopted by the U. S. Army on the frontier. The horses are Western range horses, used in this manner for the first time in history. The Army and National Guard use the "American" horse.

18—**ATTACK ON THE DEADWOOD MAIL-COACH BY INDIANS,** Repulse of the Indians, and rescue of the stage, passengers and mail, by "Buffalo Bill" and his attendant Cowboys.

19—**RACING BY INDIAN BOYS ON BAREBACK HORSES.**

20—**THREE MINUTES WITH THE ROUGH RIDERS OF THE WORLD.**

21—**COL. W. F. CODY** ("Buffalo Bill") in his unique feats of sharpshooting while riding at full speed.

22—**BUFFALO HUNT,** as it was in the Far West of North America, by "Buffalo Bill" and Indians, exhibiting the last of the only known native herd of buffalo.

23—**ATTACK ON SETTLERS' CABIN** and rescue by "Buffalo Bill" and a band of Cowboys, Scouts and Frontiersmen.

24—**SALUTE,** by the entire company.

N. B.—The Management reserves the right to change Programme according to circumstances, occasion or accident.

NOTICE.—In order not to disturb the audience all persons are earnestly requested to remain seated until the end.

Any discourtesy on the part of the Ushers or other employees should be at once reported to the Manager. All articles found will be sent to the Manager's Office.

Several Experienced Detectives are in attendance at every performance for the Protection of our Patrons.

COLONEL CODY uses Winchester Rifles and Winchester Ammunition exclusively in all his exhibitions.

Address all business communications pertaining to the Arenic Department of the Wild West Exhibition to Mr. Johnnie Baker.

Original Buffalo Bill's Wild West program, 1900,
Archives Center, National Museum of American History, Smithsonian Institution.

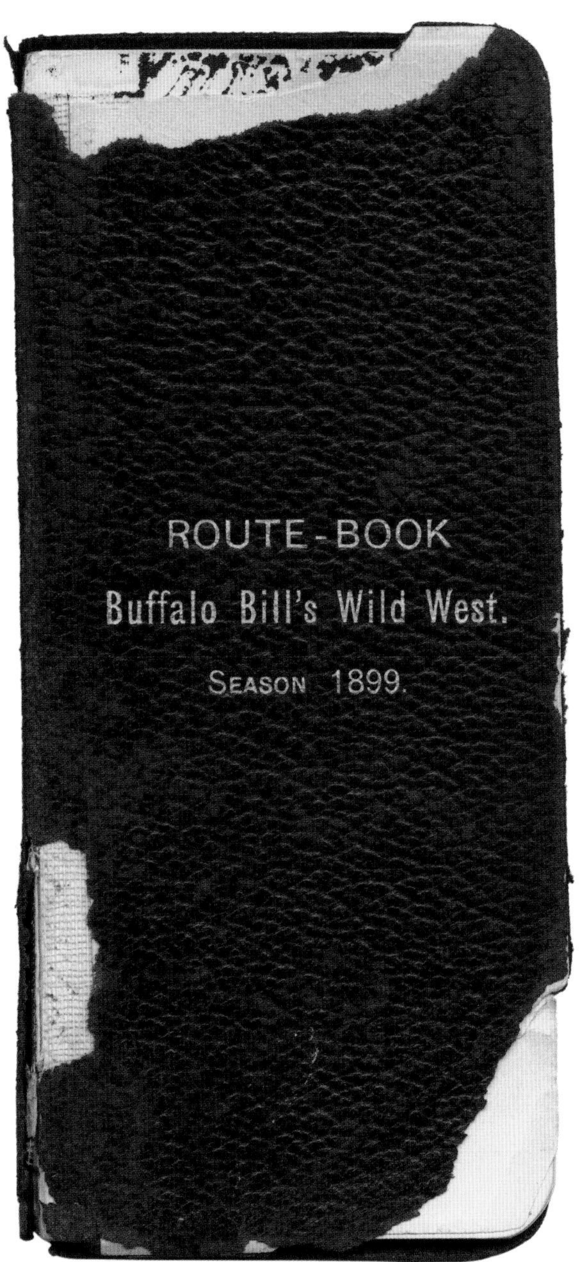
ROUTE-BOOK
Buffalo Bill's Wild West.
SEASON 1899.

HENRY H. R. COE
620 17th Street
Cody, Wyoming
ROUTE-BOOK
Buffalo Bill's Wild West
1899.
CONTAINING ALSO THE OFFICIAL ROUTES
SEASONS OF
1895, 1896, 1897, 1898.
COMPILED BY
GEORGE H. GOOCH.
BUFFALO, N. Y.
THE MATTHEWS-NORTHRUP CO.

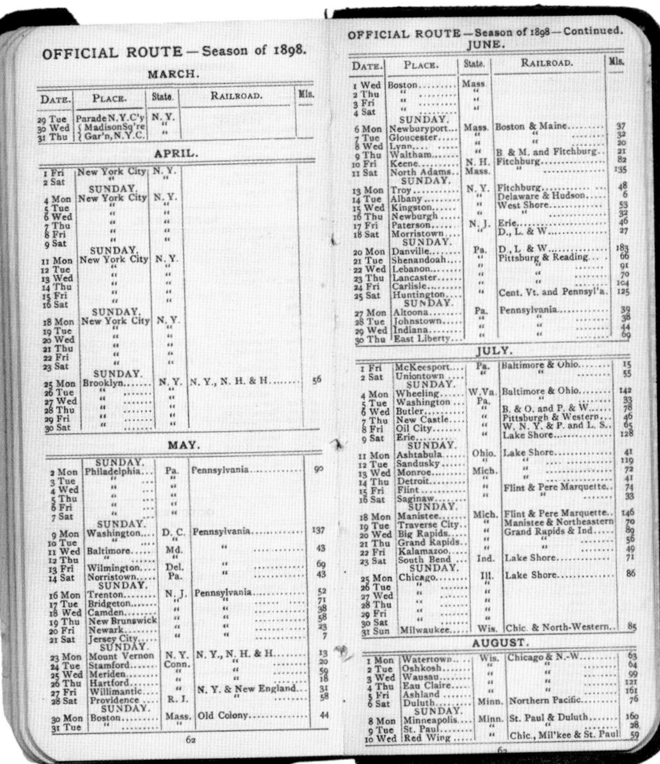

OFFICIAL ROUTE — Season of 1898.

MARCH.

Date.	Place.	State.	Railroad.	Mls.
29 Tue	Parade N. Y. C'y	N. Y.		
30 Wed	Madison Sq're	"		
31 Thu	Gar'n, N. Y. C.	"		

APRIL.

Date.	Place.	State.	Railroad.	Mls.
1 Fri	New York City	N. Y.		
2 Sat	"	"		
	SUNDAY.			
4 Mon	New York City	N. Y.		
5 Tue	"	"		
6 Wed	"	"		
7 Thu	"	"		
8 Fri	"	"		
9 Sat	"	"		
	SUNDAY.			
11 Mon	New York City	N. Y.		
12 Tue	"	"		
13 Wed	"	"		
14 Thu	"	"		
15 Fri	"	"		
16 Sat	"	"		
	SUNDAY.			
18 Mon	New York City	N. Y.		
19 Tue	"	"		
20 Wed	"	"		
21 Thu	"	"		
22 Fri	"	"		
23 Sat	"	"		
	SUNDAY.			
25 Mon	Brooklyn	N. Y.	N. Y., N. H. & H.	56
26 Tue	"	"		
27 Wed	"	"		
28 Thu	"	"		
29 Fri	"	"		
30 Sat	"	"		

MAY.

Date.	Place.	State.	Railroad.	Mls.
	SUNDAY.			
2 Mon	Philadelphia	Pa.	Pennsylvania	90
3 Tue	"	"		
4 Wed	"	"		
5 Thu	"	"		
6 Fri	"	"		
7 Sat	"	"		
	SUNDAY.			
9 Mon	Washington	D. C.	Pennsylvania	137
10 Tue	"	"		
11 Wed	Baltimore	Md.	"	43
12 Thu	"	"		
13 Fri	Wilmington	Del.	"	69
14 Sat	Norristown	Pa.	"	43
	SUNDAY.			
16 Mon	Trenton	N. J.	Pennsylvania	52
17 Tue	Bridgeton	"	"	71
18 Wed	Camden	"	"	38
19 Thu	New Brunswick	"	"	58
20 Fri	Newark	"	"	23
21 Sat	Jersey City	"	"	7
	SUNDAY.			
23 Mon	Mount Vernon	N. Y.	N. Y., N. H. & H.	13
24 Tue	Stamford	Conn.	"	20
25 Wed	Meriden	"	"	59
26 Thu	Hartford	"	"	18
27 Fri	Willimantic	"	N. Y. & New England	31
28 Sat	Providence	R. I.	"	58
	SUNDAY.			
30 Mon	Boston	Mass.	Old Colony	44
31 Tue	"	"		

62

OFFICIAL ROUTE — Season of 1898 — Continued.

JUNE.

Date.	Place.	State.	Railroad.	Mls.
1 Wed	Boston	Mass.		
2 Thu	"	"		
3 Fri	"	"		
4 Sat	"	"		
	SUNDAY.			
6 Mon	Newburyport	Mass.	Boston & Maine	37
7 Tue	Gloucester	"	"	32
8 Wed	Lynn	"	"	20
9 Thu	Waltham	"	B. & M. and Fitchburg	21
10 Fri	Keene	N. H.	Fitchburg	82
11 Sat	North Adams	Mass.	"	135
	SUNDAY.			
13 Mon	Troy	N. Y.	Fitchburg	48
14 Tue	Albany	"	Delaware & Hudson	6
15 Wed	Kingston	"	West Shore	53
16 Thu	Newburgh	"	"	32
17 Fri	Paterson	N. J.	Erie	46
18 Sat	Morristown	"	D., L. & W.	27
	SUNDAY.			
20 Mon	Danville	Pa.	D., L. & W.	183
21 Tue	Shenandoah	"	Pittsburg & Reading	66
22 Wed	Lebanon	"	"	91
23 Thu	Lancaster	"	"	70
24 Fri	Carlisle	"	"	104
25 Sat	Huntington	"	Cent. Vt. and Pennsyl'a.	125
	SUNDAY.			
27 Mon	Altoona	Pa.	Pennsylvania	39
28 Tue	Johnstown	"	"	38
29 Wed	Indiana	"	"	44
30 Thu	East Liberty	"	"	69

JULY.

Date.	Place.	State.	Railroad.	Mls.
1 Fri	McKeesport	Pa.	Baltimore & Ohio	15
2 Sat	Uniontown	"	"	55
	SUNDAY.			
4 Mon	Wheeling	W. Va.	Baltimore & Ohio	142
5 Tue	Washington	Pa.	"	33
6 Wed	Butler	"	B. & O. and P. & W.	78
7 Thu	New Castle	"	Pittsburgh & Western	46
8 Fri	Oil City	"	W. N. Y. & P. and L. S.	65
9 Sat	Erie	"	Lake Shore	128
	SUNDAY.			
11 Mon	Ashtabula	Ohio.	Lake Shore	41
12 Tue	Sandusky	"	"	119
13 Wed	Monroe	Mich.	"	72
14 Thu	Detroit	"	"	41
15 Fri	Flint	"	Flint & Pere Marquette	74
16 Sat	Saginaw	"	"	33
	SUNDAY.			
18 Mon	Manistee	Mich.	Flint & Pere Marquette	146
19 Tue	Traverse City	"	Manistee & Northeastern	70
20 Wed	Big Rapids	"	Grand Rapids & Ind.	89
21 Thu	Grand Rapids	"	"	56
22 Fri	Kalamazoo	"	"	49
23 Sat	South Bend	Ind.	Lake Shore	71
	SUNDAY.			
25 Mon	Chicago	Ill.	Lake Shore	86
26 Tue	"	"		
27 Wed	"	"		
28 Thu	"	"		
29 Fri	"	"		
30 Sat	"	"		
31 Sun	Milwaukee	Wis.	Chic. & North-Western	85

AUGUST.

Date.	Place.	State.	Railroad.	Mls.
1 Mon	Watertown	Wis.	Chicago & N.-W.	63
2 Tue	Oshkosh	"	"	64
3 Wed	Wausau	"	"	99
4 Thu	Eau Claire	"	"	121
5 Fri	Ashland	"	"	161
6 Sat	Duluth	Minn.	Northern Pacific	76
	SUNDAY.			
8 Mon	Minneapolis	Minn.	St. Paul & Duluth	160
9 Tue	St. Paul	"	"	28
10 Wed	Red Wing	"	Chic., Mil'kee & St. Paul	59

63

OFFICIAL ROUTE — Season of 1898 — Continued.

AUGUST — Continued.

Date.	Place.	State.	Railroad.	Mls.
11 Thu	LaCrosse	Wis.	Chic., Mil'kee & St. Paul	86
12 Fri	Dubuque	Iowa.	"	121
13 Sat	Clinton	"	"	60
	SUNDAY.			
15 Mon	Davenport	Iowa.	B., C. R. & N.	77
16 Tue	Kewanee	Ill.	Chic., Bur'ng'n & Q'cy.	89
17 Wed	Burlington	Iowa	"	75
18 Thu	Keokuk	"	St. L., K. & N. W.	43
19 Fri	Jacksonville	Ill.	Wabash	93
20 Sat	Hannibal	Mo.	"	67
	SUNDAY.			
22 Mon	Chillicothe	Mo.	Hannibal & St Joseph	130
23 Tue	St. Joseph	"	"	77
24 Wed	Red Oak	Iowa.	H. St. J. and C. B. & Q.	116
25 Thu	Creston	"	Chic., Bur'ng'n & Qu'cy.	51
26 Fri	Ottumwa	"	"	115
27 Sat	Des Moines	"	Chic., Rock Is. & Pacific	87
	SUNDAY.			
29 Mon	Atlantic	Iowa.	Chic., Rock Is. & Pacific	82
30 Tue	Omaha	Neb.	C., R. I. & P. and U. P.	62
31 Wed	"	"		

SEPTEMBER.

Date.	Place.	State.	Railroad.	Mls.
1 Thu	Lincoln	Neb.	Burlng. & Miss'ri River	55
2 Fri	Grand Island	"	"	92
3 Sat	North Platte	"	Union Pacific	138
	SUNDAY.			
5 Mon	Cheyenne	Wyo	Union Pacific	225
6 Tue	Denver	Colo	"	107
7 Wed	"	"		
8 Thu	Colorado Sp'gs	"	Atch., Top. & Santa Fe	74
9 Fri	Pueblo	"	"	43
10 Sat	Trinidad	"	"	144
	SUNDAY.			
12 Mon	Hutchinson	Kan.	Atch., Top. & Santa Fe	418
13 Tue	Wichita	"	"	61
14 Wed	Winfield	"	"	39
15 Thu	Independence	"	"	81
16 Fri	Ottawa	"	"	108
17 Sat	Emporia	"	"	56
	SUNDAY.			
19 Mon	Topeka	Kan.	Atch., Top. & Santa Fe	62
20 Tue	Atchison	"	"	50
21 Wed	Leavenworth	"	"	32
22 Thu	Kansas City	Mo.	"	39
23 Fri	Sedalia	"	Missouri Pacific	95
24 Sat	Nevada	"	"	130
	SUNDAY.			
26 Mon	Joplin	Mo.	Missouri Pacific	64
27 Tue	Aurora	"	St. Louis & San Fran	63
28 Wed	Fayetteville	Ark.	"	84
29 Thu	Ft. Smith	"	"	62
30 Fri	Russellville	"	Iron Mountain	89

OCTOBER.

Date.	Place.	State.	Railroad.	Mls.
1 Sat	Little Rock	Ark.	Iron Mountain	76
	SUNDAY.			
3 Mon	Newport	Ark.	Iron Mountain	83
4 Tue	Poplar Bluff	Mo.	"	96
5 Wed	Cairo	Ill.	"	74
6 Thu	Carmi	"	C., C., C. & St. L.	103
7 Fri	Vincennes	Ind.	"	57
8 Sat	Evansville	"	E., T. H. & St. L.	52
	SUNDAY.			
10 Mon	New Albany	Ind.	L., E. & St. L.	116
11 Tue	Frankfort	"	Louisville & Nashville	66
12 Wed	Covington	Ky.	"	120
13 Thu	Maysville	"	Chicago & Ohio	40
14 Fri	Huntington	W. Va	"	102
15 Sat	Charleston	"	"	50

"HOME, SWEET HOME."

Date.	Place.	State.	Railroad.	Mls.
	Bridgeport	Conn	Chicago & Ohio Pennsylvania N. Y., N. H. & H.	369 228 56

64

OFFICIAL ROUTE — Season of 1899.

Date.	Place.	State.	Railroad.	Mls.
Mar. 29th to Apr. 15th,	New York City	N. Y.	N. Y., N. H. & H	56

APRIL.

Date.	Place.	State.	Railroad.	Mls.
	SUNDAY.			
17 Mon	Baltimore	Md.	Pennsylvania	186
18 Tue	"	"		
19 Wed	Washington	D. C.	Pennsylvania	43
20 Thu	"	"		
21 Fri	Richmond	Va.	Penna. and R. F. & P.	116
22 Sat	Staunton	"	C. & O.	136
	SUNDAY.			
24 Mon	Lynchburg	Va.	C. & O.	141
25 Tue	Roanoke	"	N. & W.	53
26 Wed	Bluefield	W. Va.	"	107
27 Thu	Bristol	Tenn.	"	169
28 Fri	Knoxville	"	Southern	135
29 Sat	Chattanooga	"	"	111
	SUNDAY.			

MAY.

Date.	Place.	State.	Railroad.	Mls.
1 Mon	Nashville	Tenn.	N. C. & St. L.	151
2 Tue	Bowling Green	Ky.	L. & N.	72
3 Wed	Louisville	"	"	114
4 Thu	Madison	Ind.	P. C. & St. L.	110
5 Fri	Indianapolis	"	" "	86
6 Sat	Richmond	"	" "	68
	SUNDAY.			
8 Mon	Cincinnati	Ohio.	P., C., C. & St. L. and [C., H. & D.	74
9 Tue	"	"		
10 Wed	Dayton	"	C., H. & D.	59
11 Thu	Springfield	"	C., C., C. & St. L.	24
12 Fri	Columbus	"	" "	45
13 Sat	Newark	"	P., C., C. & St. L.	33
	SUNDAY.			
15 Mon	Pittsburg	Pa.	P., C., C. & St. L.	165
16 Tue	"	"		
17 Wed	Tyrone	"	Pennsylvania	132
18 Thu	Williamsport	"	"	79
19 Fri	Wilkes-Barre	"	"	103
20 Sat	Towanda	"	Lehigh Valley	78
	SUNDAY.			
22 Mon	Scranton	Pa.	L. V. and C. of N. J.	96
23 Tue	Easton	"	C. of N. J.	119
24 Wed	Allentown	"	"	17
25 Thu	Pottsville	"	P. & R.	71
26 Fri	Reading	"	"	35
27 Sat	Chester	"	"	68
	SUNDAY.			
29 Mon	Philadelphia	Pa.	P. & R.	12
30 Tue	"	"		
31 Wed	"	"		

JUNE.

Date.	Place.	State.	Railroad.	Mls.
1 Thu	Philadelphia	Pa.	P. & R.	
2 Fri	"	"		
3 Sat	"	"		
	SUNDAY.			
5 Mon	Long Branch	N. J.	Pennsylvania	94
6 Tue	Elizabeth	"	"	35
7 Wed	Yonkers	N. Y.	Penna. and N. Y. C.	35
8 Thu	Poughkeepsie	"	N. Y. C.	58
9 Fri	Winsted	Conn.	C. N. E.	80
10 Sat	Hartford	"	"	35
	SUNDAY.			
12 Mon	Boston	Mass.	N. Y., N. H. & H. and [B. & A.	131
13 Tue	"	"		
14 Wed	"	"		
15 Thu	"	"		

65

Buffalo Bill's Wild West.

COL. W. F. CODY, *President.*
NATE SALSBURY, *Vice-President.*
MAJOR J. M. BURKE, *Gen'l Manager.*

DIRECTORS OF TOUR.
JAS. A. BAILEY, W. W. COLE,
LOUIS E. COOKE, *General Agent.*

BUSINESS MANAGERS.
For Cody & Salsbury, JULE KEEN. For Bailey & Cole, ERNEST COOKE.

SECRETARIES.
For Cody & Salsbury, L. E. DECKER, For Bailey & Cole, JOS. F. QUAID.

TREASURERS.
For Cody & Salsbury, JULE KEEN. For Bailey & Cole, FRED B. HUTCHISON.

DIRECTOR OF ENTERTAINMENT.
JOHN BAKER.

SUPERINTENDENT OF GROUNDS.
HENRY BARNUM.

MANAGERS OF PRIVILEGES.
Messrs. DREW AND CAMPBELL.

2

GENERAL STAFF.
John Baker, ... *Arenic Director.*
John McLaughlin, *Master of Transportation.*
Dan Taylor, ... *Master Mechanic.*
M. B. Bailey, . . *Sup't of Electric Lights.*
Jake Platt, ... *Sup't of Canvas.*
Chas. Evans, . . *Sup't of Baggage Stock.*
W. W. Reedy, . . *Sup't of Bronco Stock.*
C. W. Ramsey, *Sup't of Confectionery Dep't.*
Wm. Sweeney, ... *Leader of Band.*
Wm. McCune, . . . *Officer of the Day.*
Morris Kern, . . *Principal Door Tender.*
J. W. Rogers, ... *Detective.*
J. J. McCarthy, ... *Orator.*
Lou. Decker, ... *Mail Carrier.*
John Noble, ... *Head Car Porter.*
Keen & Langan, ... *Caterers.*
M. Martin, ... *Head Waiter.*
John Stacks, ... *Parade Wardrobe.*
Chas. Wichelhausen, ... *Properties.*
Wm. Smith, ... *Ammunition.*

DEPARTMENT OF PUBLICITY.
Louis E. Cooke, *General Advance Manager.*
M. Coyle, ... *Railway Contractor.*
Edward Arlington, . . *Excursion Agent.*
Major John M. Burke, *General Press Agent.*
Frank J. O'Donnell, *Contracting Press Agent.*
Miss Maymie Jester, . *Special Press Agent.*
Dexter E. Fellows, . . *Special Press Agent.*
S. H. Semon, . *General Contracting Agent.*
E. H. Woods, *Assistant Contracting Agent.*
M. Manton, }
Chas. Curtis, } . . . . *Bill Inspectors.*

ADVERTISING CAR No. 1.
P. S. Mattox, *Manager.*
W. H. Alberts, ... *Boss Bill Poster.*
Tom Lyons, ... *Boss Lithographer.*
Chas. Hayes, ... *Secretary.*
John Lewis, ... *Programmer.*

BILL POSTERS.
Lew Curry, Richard Le Fever,
Oliver Lester, Chas. Welsh,
Geo. Baldwin, Martin Slivers,
Harry Campbell, John Alvather,
Pete Dunn, Sam Sanders,
R. L. Bean, *Car Porter.*

3

LITHOGRAPHERS.
Fred Seyboth, John Gray,
Chas. R. Coleman.

ADVERTISING CAR No. 2.—EXCURSION DEPARTMENT.
Al. Riel, *Manager.*
Geo. Frazier, ... *Boss Bill Poster.*
Kurt Eisfeldt, ... *Lithographer.*
Chas. Venable, ... *Banner Man.*
Al. Boshell, ... *Board Man.*
Victor Cooke, ... *Card Man.*

EXCURSION BILL POSTERS.
Thos. Deansfield, H. Sayers,
Wm. Shea, Chas. Dering,
A. J. Choffin, Wm. Fannon,
Geo. Houghtaling, Geo. Nelson,
Dan Pheney, H. Robinson,
H. Leschinsky, Chas. Loughridge,
Geo. Hurst, *Car Porter.*

OPPOSITION BRIGADE.
Fred Beckman, *Manager.*
Dan Pheney, ... *Boss Bill Poster.*
Kurt Eisfeldt, ... *Lithographer.*
Herman Leschinsky, }
Frank Raymond, } . . . *Bill Posters.*

LAYERS-OUT.
Harry G. Barnum, Thos. Clear.

TICKET SELLERS.
MAIN TICKET WAGON.
Fred B. Hutchison, John Flandreau.

OUTSIDE TICKETS.
John Tippetts, Lou. Decker,
Frank Cloud.

DOWN-TOWN OFFICE.
Harry Gray.

DOWN-TOWN ORATOR.
S. H. Davis.

4

RESERVED-SEAT TICKETS.
Jule Keen *in charge.*
Starr Pixley, Geo. Dittmar,
Sam. T. Bitmead.

MAIN DOOR TENDERS.
J. P. Brogan, Dan. Taylor,
Morris Kern, John McLaughlin.

RESERVED-SEAT TENDERS.
Walter H. Cleary, Arthur Waterman.

USHERS.
Wm. McCune, *Head Usher.*
Dave Jarrett, *Assistant.*
Eddie Walton, *Assistant.*

RESERVED-SEAT USHERS.
Ed. Barry, Wm. Hunter,
M. Quinlan, Ed. Howard,
Geo. Davis, Wm. Hutton,
Ed. Gallagher, Sam. Maitland,
Wm. King.

BLUE SEATS.
Wm. Arnold, Lee Fuller,
Mike Burns, Wm. Murphy,
Larry Eagan, T. McBurney,
Fred Gibson, G. Pratt,
Geo. Smith, J. White.
John Condon, *Director.*
Jos. Collins, *Wardrobe.*

COWBOY BAND.
Wm. Sweeney, *Leader.*
Wm. Sweeney, ... Solo Cornet.
Albert Ziehm, ... Solo Cornet.
Floyd O'Hara, ... Solo Cornet.
Jas. Allen, ... First Cornet.
W. N. Tinkham, ... Second Cornet.
Elmer Parlett, ... *Eb* Cornet.
Harry Nelson, . . . Solo *Bb* Clarionet.
Christian Schetting, . . Solo *Bb* Clarionet.
Frank Genter, ... First Clarionet.
Harvey Benham, . . . Second Clarionet.

5

COWBOY BAND.—Continued.

Frank Carothers, ... E♭ Clarionet.
Chester C. Larned, ... Piccolo.
Ed. Weber, ... First Alto.
John C. Howard, ... Second Alto.
W. H. Dickin, ... Third Alto.
John Galligan, ... First Trombone.
Lon Williams, . . . Second Trombone.
Chas. Baas, ... Third Trombone.
Thos. V. Murphy, . . . First Baritone.
John Schilling, . . . Second Baritone.
W. A. Frank, ... Bass.
M. A. McAdams, ... Bass.
Geo. C. Foehlinger, ... Small Drum.
Geo. W. Turner, ... Bass Drum.

Johnnie Baker, *Expert Marksman.*
Miss Annie Oakley, *Lady Rifle Shot.*
Frank Butler, *Manager for Miss Oakley.*

DRIVER OF STAGE COACH.

John F. Burke.

U. S. CAVALRY.

Jas. G. Warren, *Sergeant.*
Chas. Rieth, *Color Bearer.*

Wm. Baker, Frank Stryker,
J. Wortman, W. J. Taylor,
Dennis Langan, Chas. Humberstone,
Peter Fay, Ed. Gallagher,
Harry Jackson, Jas. Brown,
Granville Corr, Andy Milen,
Frank McCormack.

U. S. ARTILLERY.

Herman Kanstein, *Sergeant.*

PIECE No. 1.	PIECE No. 2.
J. R. Myerly, } *Drivers*	Harry Wilkes, } *Drivers*
Thos. Gibney,	R. I. Clapham,
Chas. Wolff,	Jas. Ryan,
Jack Langan, *Corp.*	Victor Hudson, *Corp.*
L. Wagner, No. 1.	C. Triangel, No. 1.
R. Hegeman, No. 2.	Pony Moore, No. 2.
C. Hobart, No. 3.	A. Miller, No. 3.
Jas. Degnen, No. 4.	Geo. Davis, No. 4.

6

ROOSEVELT'S ROUGH RIDERS.

G. A. Webb, *Sergeant.*
Wm. McGinty, *Color Bearer.*

M. L. Newcomb, J. Kline,
F. Beal, Ed. Loughmiller,
T. Holmes, F. Byrne,
W. Cook, Ben Miller,
Tom Isbell, H. Meagher,
V. D. Miller, J. H. Tait,
Jess Langdon, L. Muxlow.

AMERICAN COWBOYS.

Joe Esquivel, *Chief.*
John Franz, *Assistant.*

Silas Compton, Jesse Nelson,
Bert Schenck, Tom Hunter,
Jim Gabriel, Bob Singletree,
Jas. Jennings, Lem Hunter,
Walter Scott, Carl Sorrensen,
Jack Joyce, A. McCann.

ENGLISH LANCERS.

Thos. Cook, *Sergeant.*
W. House, *Color Bearer.*

Fred Rapley, E. Plummer,
J. Clarke, W. Ridgwell,
Jas. Ryan, W. Barrett,
Wm. Wandland, T. Dennis,
P. Shingler, A. Brown,
T. Pigott, W. Pocock.

GERMAN CUIRASSIERS.

Julius von Natzmer, *Captain.*
Heinrich Sprittule, *Sergeant.*
O. Weinrich, *Color Bearer.*

E. Wittmann, T. Schwark,
C. Shultz, H. Damm,
G. Kaempfer, A. Zippliss,
A. Rother.

7

MEXICANS.

Vicente Orapeza, *Chief.*

Manuel Pena, Pedro Aleman,
Epifania Martinez, Yrineo Munoz,
Luio Alba, Manuel Castillo,
Santiago Munoz, Agapita Alba.

COSSACKS.

David Cadjaia, *Chief.*

Dimetri Mgaloblichvily,
Toma Baramidzi,
Miron Tschonia,
Ivan Baramidzi, Ermile Antadzi,
Loucas Tschartishvily,
Michael Antadzi,
Vladimir Jacutahvily.

ARABS.

Sheik Hadji Tahar, *Chief.*
Hadji Cheriff, *Whirling Dervish.*

Moly Ambark, Oshan,
Ameen Abou Hamed, Masand,
M. Muzie, Nagim Abdullah,
H. Abachi, Nageeb Ballish,
Mohammed Agram, Willie Masand,
Hadji Hamid, Brodie ben Hadji,
Togler ben Hadji.

CUBANS.

Col. Mariano Aymerich, *Chief.*
Lieut. Evaristo M. Alonso.
Lieut. Andres Fontanilla.

Antonio Marti, Manuel Portuondo,
Rafael Rodriguez, Ramon Ferreno,
Benito Carreras.

HAWAIIANS.

David Kipi, K. Natsia,
J. Kulia, W. Hopili,
G. Makalina, Isabella Pary,
Ribaka Natsia.

8

FILIPINOS.

Felix Alcantara, Geronimo Momo,
Isidora Alcantara.

INDIANS.

CHIEFS.

Iron Tail, Growler,
Black Fox, Iron Cloud,
Has No Horse.

BRAVES.

Spotted Weasel, Sam Stabber,
Good Horse, White Belly,
Comes Out Holy, Eagle Fox,
Flying Horse, Pluck Porcupine,
John Kills Brave, Red Calf,
Standing Soldier, Jacob Iron Eagle,
White Bird, Charging Thunder,
Little Bull, Dreamer,
Comes Last, Wounded,
Comes Out Bear, Loud Thunder,
Richard Lip, Frank Meat,
Spotted Horse Fight, Albert Thunder Hawk,
White Bonnet, Ed. Porcupine Knee,
Kills in Loge, Sam Lone Bear,
Comes Killing, Mounted Sheep,
Holy Bear, Whirlwind Horse,
Kills Enemy.

SQUAWS.

Mary Kills Enemy, Jennie Spotted Horse,
White Cow.

PAPOOSE.

Willie White Bird.

INTERPRETER.

David Bull Bear.

WATCHMAN OF INDIAN CAMP.

J. J. Ryan.

9

"BRONCHO" STABLE.

W. W. Reedy *in Charge.*

J. F. Meade, Hugh Harkins, . . . Cowboy String.
Jas. Bass, ... English Lancers.
M. T. McKenzie, . . . Rough Riders.
Naber E. Smith, ... U. S. Cavalry.
Geo. Bare, ... Mexican.
Dan White, . . Hawaiians and Filipinos.
Al Hook, ... Cossack.
Wm. Jones, ... Arab.
Chris Peterson, ... German.
Chas. Judd, Sam. Harkins, ... Artillery.
Marshall Ochoa, W. Dyer, Dewitt Genung, Chas. Kelly, ... Indian.
J. W. Porter, ... Mules.
Russell Churchill, . . . Bucking Horses.
Giess Stine, ... Col. Cody's Stock.
Jas. Murphy, . . Col. Cody's Coachman.
J. R. Ziegler, Driver of "Buffalo" Wagon.
Harry Murphy, . In Charge of Buffaloes.

"WILD WEST" BLACKSMITHS.

Fred Kurz, Joseph Ferren.

WARDROBE AND PROPERTIES.

Chas. Wichelhausen.
Chas. J. Ansert, Wm. Monday,
Jas. Fish, Martin Dillon.

AMMUNITION.

Wm. Smith *in Charge.*
Tom Edwards, Roy Myers,
Jas. Berger.

BAGGAGE STOCK.

Chas. Evans, *Superintendent.*
Wm. McNaul, *Assistant.*

10

EIGHT-HORSE DRIVERS.

DRIVER.	HELPER.
Jas. Thomas,	Henry White,
Perry Camp,	Andy Johnson,
S. W. Elliott,	Chas. Miller,
David Denio,	Chas. Foley.

SIX-HORSE DRIVERS.

Ed. Miller, Jas. Robinson,
Wm. Montgomery, Grant Hulvey,
Chas. Mitchell, Jas. McGovern,
Harry E. Mills.

FOUR-HORSE DRIVERS.

Jas. Afford, Jas. Williams,
Sam Woodman, Wm. Donohue,
John Gallagher, J. F. Tewell,
Geo. Eastman, Rob't Burns.

PULL-UP TEAMS.

John Laird, Chas. Cook,
Thos. Lee.

BUGGY STOCK.

Jack Lewis.

LEAD BARS AND BODY POLES.

Frank Emery.

FEED.

John Puget.

BLACKSMITH AND REPAIR DEPARTMENT.

Dan Taylor, *Master Mechanic.*
Fred Keller, ... Carpenter.
E. J. Collins, ... Harness Maker.
John Norbury, ... Blacksmith.
Alex. Young, ... Blacksmith.

11

RAILROAD DEPARTMENT.

John McLaughlin, *Master of Transportation.*
R. P. Murphy, *Assistant.*
John Rose, ... Car Inspector.
A. H. Miller, . . Watchman 1st Section.
Joe Brown, . . . Watchman 2d Section.
Wm. Remack, ... Chandeliers.
Paul Spearing, Frank Arnett, ... Polers.

TRAINMEN.

Frank Coyle, A. E. Meyer,
L. D. Bottarff, John Bennett,
John Fallon, Jere Murphy.

SPECIAL WATCHMEN.

John Stacks, . . . White Ticket Wagon.
Frank Quinn, ... Private Office.
M. Hogan, ... 2d Section Stock.

CAR PORTERS.

John Noble, *Head Porter.*
Wm. Vogel, Car 51, Pete Wallace, Car 54,
Geo. Long, Car 52, Chas. Carroll, Car 55,
Harry Gears, Car 53, F. C. Hawley, Car 56,
Wm. Reilly, Car 57.

COL. CODY'S PRIVATE CAR No. 50.

Alfred Heimer, *Porter,*
W. L. Brown, *Cook.*

SIDE-SHOW.

Messrs. Drew & Campbell, *Managers.*

PERFORMERS AND CURIOS.

Ashida and Koh, . . . Japanese Magic.
Olga, ... Snake Enchantress.
Wm. Baker, ... Boy Giant.
Chemah and Pearl Robinson, . Midgets.
J. G. Sheidler, ... King of Cards.
Balbroma, ... Fire King.
Victorina, ... Sword-swallower.
Val Vino, ... Juggler.
Millie Owen, ... Long-haired Lady.
Prince Oskazuma, ... Kaffir Warrior.
Ben Casper, W. F. Greiner, . Venetian Glass Blowers.
J. McClellan, Ben Powell, Electrograph and Mind-readers.

12

LECTURER.

Burt Davis.

ORATORS.

P. J. Staunton, Jos. F. Ferris,
Frank Cloud.

DOOR TENDER.

Frank Quinn.

SIDE-SHOW CANVASMEN.

H. E. Tudor, *Superintendent.*
Wm. Powers, J. Martin,
Wm. Allen, Geo. Fuller,
Jno. McLean.
Harry Tudor, ... Inside.

SIDE-SHOW BAND.

L. Sacketts, *Leader.*
F. Rechhia, ... B♭ Clarionet.
F. Donato, ... E♭ Clarionet.
G. Grella, ... Solo B♭ Cornet.
A. Scerni, ... First B♭ Cornet.
E. Renzi, ... B♭ Baritone.
L. D. Paolo, ... B♭ Trombone.
W. Pellazzo, ... E♭ Alto.
D. Zuglielmo, ... Bass Drum.
D. Barbieri, ... Small Drum.

CONFECTIONERY DEP'T.

Chas. L. Ramsey, *Superintendent.*
S. H. Davis, *Assistant.*
C. W. Spadi *in Charge of Supplies.*

BUTCHERS.

C. E. Fearn, C. E. Brooks,
Harry Merrick, Fred Roteman,
Jas. White, Arthur W. Horton,
Joe Burke, Garrett Henry,
A. Watt, Lou C. Cloud.

NEW ENGLAND POP-CORN FACTORY.

M. C. Bowers.

13

CONCERT COMPANY.

"The Ramseys," . . . . Comedy Duo.
Bessie Searles, ... Serio-Comic.
Schafer and Read, . . Musical Comedy.
Cloud and Kershaw, . . Irish Comedians.
"The Brannigans," . . . . Jig Dancers.
Nellie Waters, ... Comedienne.

CONCERT ORCHESTRA.

J. Schilling, ... First Violin.
Ed. Weber, ... Second Violin.
Wm. A. Frank, ... Viola.
M. A. McAdams, ... Bass.
F. Genter, ... Clarionet.
A. Ziehm, ... Cornet.
L. Williams, ... Trombone.

OFFICIAL PROGRAMMES.

J. & H. Mayer, *Publishers.*
Tom Burke *in Charge.*
H. Mayer, *Solicitor.*

AGENTS.

Wm. Conroy, Frank Clear,
Walter Miller, Ed O'Connell.
Geo. Manchester,
Agent for "Buffalo Bill's" History.

ELECTRICAL DEPARTMENT.

M. B. Bailey, *Superintendent.*
D. MacDonald, *Chief Electrician.*
Wm. J. Connor, *Chief Engineer.*

FIREMEN.

Archie Clements, Wm. M. Penn.

ASSISTANTS.

Maurice Doody, Joe McCann,
Geo. H. Gooch, Bernie McBride,
Henry Reever, Larry Murphy.

CALCIUM LIGHTS.

Maurice Doody, Geo. H. Gooch.

14

CHANDELIERS.

Jack Cullen *in Charge.*
Ed. A. Combs, *Assistant.*

CANVAS DEPARTMENT.

Jake Platt, *Superintendent.*
John Eberle, *First Assistant.*
David Jarrett, *Second Assistant.*
Jack Dawson, *Horse Tents.*
Wm. Smithey, *Dressing Room and Backing.*

Jas. McCaffrey, M. Mack,
John Condon, Larry Sullivan,
John White, Wm. Cronin,
R. Callahan, John Murphy,
Sam Maitland, Wm. Hunter,
Herbert Parkes, Mike Jones,
Ed Barry, John Weaver,
Wm. Hutton, Ed Howard,
John Halpin, Pat Burke,
Mike Burns, Lee Fuller,
Andy Wood, Thos. Ryan,
Geo. Davis, M. Quinlan,
Alex. McFrine, Larry Eagan,
Walter King, Wm. Murphy,
Lyman Mayo, Wm. Thomas,
Mike McManus, Jos. Collins,
Wm. Sampson, Geo. Amos,
Chas. Lavesta, Chas. Vanberg,
Geo. Smith, Ernest Yelland,
Wm. Arnold, Edward Bitting,
Chris Cair, Geo. Pratt,
Jos. Trempley, Mike Keating,
Thos. Foley, John Walsh,
Harry Buckner, Jack Bryan,
John D. Fulton, John Morrow,
John Bergeman, Jas. Harrison,
John Tracy, John Rassler,
Harry Peterson, Harry Hoskins,
Unix Robia, John Bauersis,
Geo. Hunt.

FRONT END.

John A. Eberle, *Superintendent.*

SEATS.

Jas. McCaffrey, *in Charge.*
John Condon, *Assistant.*
John White, *Leveler.*

15

JACK SETTERS.

Bob Callahan, Herbert Parkes,
Sam Maitland, Wm. Hutton,
Hugh Gallagher.

TOE-PIN DRIVERS.

John Halpin, Andy Wood,
Ed Barry, Geo. Davis,
Mike Burns, Alex. McFrine.

BLOCKS.

Lyman Mayo.

KIDS.

Walter King.

BACK END.

Dave Jarrett, *Superintendent.*

SEATS.

M. Mack *in Charge.*
Larry Sullivan, *Assistant.*
Wm. Hunter, *Leveler.*
Mike Jones, *Toe Leveler.*

JACK SETTERS.

John Weaver, Pat. Burke,
Ed. Howard, Lee Fuller,
Thos. Ryan.

TOE-PIN DRIVERS.

Larry Eagan, Mike McManus,
Wm. Murphy, Wm. Sampson,
Wm. Thomas, Chas. Lavesta.

BLOCKS.

Geo. Smith.

KIDS.

Wm. Murphy.

16

RESERVED SEATS.

M. Quinlan *in Charge.*

STRINGER SETTERS.

Wm. Arnold, Chris Cair.

JACK SETTERS.

Jos. Trempley, Thos. Foley,
Wm. Murphy, Harry Buckner.

TOE-PIN DRIVERS.

Harry Hoskins, John Rossler,
Ed Daily, Wm. Ryan.

BLOCKS.

Chas. Vanberg.

KIDS.

Jos. Collins.

BIG TOP STAKE AND CHAIN, Nos. 6 and 11.

John Murphy, Wm. Cronin.

HORSE TENTS.

John Dawson, *Superintendent.*

Wm. Ryan, Unix Robia,
John Tracey, Ed Dailey,
Geo. Amos, Harry Peterson,
John Rassler, Harry Buckner,
John Welsh, Thos. Foley,
Jas. Harrison, Thos. Murphy,
Wm. Carey, Harry Hoskins.

STAKE WAGON No. 14.

John Walsh.

17

BACKING AND DRESSING ROOM.

Wm. Smithey, *Superintendent.*

RIGHT CURTAIN.

John Bauereis, Geo. Hunt.

CENTER CURTAIN.

Edward Bitting, John Bergeman,
Ernest Yelland, John Morrow.

LEFT CURTAIN.

Jack Bryan, John D. Fulton.

FRONT-DOOR MEN.

Geo. Pratt, Mike Keating.

SAIL MAKERS.

John Weaver, Geo. Halpin,
John Walsh.

COOK HOUSE.

Messrs. Keen & Langan, *Caterers.*
Chas. W. Petty, *Advance.*
Fred Bowman, *Accountant for Wild West.*
Sam. T. Bitmead,
Accountant for Keen & Langan.

COOKS.

Wm. Myers, *Head Cook.*
Harry Holmes, Henry Hiler,
John Hammond.

BUTCHER.

Chas. Felix.

CAMPFIRE.

Mike Connelly.

WAITERS.

M. Martin, *Head Waiter.*
Wm. Walsh, *Assistant Head Waiter.*

18

TABLE No. 1—STAFF.

Fred. Adams, Eddie Walton,
Thos. Rafferty, Coffee-boy.

TABLE No. 2—COWBOYS AND BAND.

H. Stewart, Jos. McCaffrey,
Joe Gillin, Coffee-boy.

TABLE No. 3—PRIVILEGE.

Jas. Kelly, W. Sproegal.

TABLE No. 4—ARABS, ETC.

J. Coleman, H. Bird,
G. Packett.

TABLE No. 5—AMERICAN SOLDIERS.

C. Hutchison, J. Hobson,
B. Palmer, Coffee-boy.

TABLE No. 6—ENGLISH AND GERMAN SOLDIERS.

N. Nist, Chas. Black,
J. Ruffells, Coffee-boy.

TABLE No. 7—INDIANS.

J. Furlong.

WORKMEN'S TABLES Nos. 8, 9 AND 10.

C. Carson, C. Whitney,
W. Binne, Wm. Ives,
W. Wagstaffe, Wm. Basman.
Jas. Knight, John Kehoe, } Coffee-boys.

DESSERT BOYS.

L. Routledge, Bert Cohn.

DISHWASHERS.

Jesse Jackson, Jos. Jackson.

LAUNDRYMAN.

D. McMillan.

NIGHT WATCHMEN.

Chas. Nicholson, Thos. Devine.

NIGHT-LUNCH STAND.

Tom Austin.

19

68

SUMMARY.

	1895.	1896.	1897.	1898.	1899.
Distance traveled, miles, . . .	8,980	10,787	8,041	10,253	11,111
Railroads used, ...	34	42	41	40	40
Length of season, days, . . .	195	190	189	200	200
Number of stands, ...	131	132	104	133	132
Number of performances, . . .	321	332	320	345	341
Lost performances, ...	3	5	6	12	7

1898 Route Book Summary

Distance Traveled, Miles	10,253
Railroads Used	40
Length of Season, Days	200
Number of Stands	133
Number of Performances	345
Lost Performances	12
Longest run from one stand to next (Trinidad, Colo. to Hutchinson, Kans.)	418 miles
Shortest run from one stand to next	7 miles
States Covered	26
Days No Performances	2
Days Only One Performance	6
Total Lost Performances	10
Transportation	
Baggage Wagons	35
Water Tanks	2
Engines for Electric Light	2
Buggies	4
Prairie Schooners	2
Field Pieces and Caissons	2
Stage Coach	1
Trains	
Flat Cars	16
Stock Cars	15
Sleeping Coaches	8
Traveling with Show	467 people
Stables	
Horses	329
Mules	6
Draught horses	118
Biggest arena, Boston, Mass.	198 × 397 feet
Smallest arena, Uniontown, Pa.	125 × 325 feet
Standard	166 × 347 feet
Most memorable show	Trinidad, Colo., September 10

Tents erected and performance given in heavy snowstorm

SOURCE: 1899 Route Book, McCracken Research Library, Buffalo Bill Historical Center, microfilm.

Selected Bibliography

Collections

Archives Center, National Museum of American History, Smithsonian Institution, Washington, DC.
Department of Photographs, Metropolitan Museum of Art, New York, NY.
Department of Photographs, Museum of Modern Art, New York, NY.
Department of Photographs, National Portrait Gallery, Smithsonian Institution, Washington, DC.
Department of Prints and Photographs, Library of Congress, Washington, DC.
Department of Prints and Photographs, New York Public Library, New York, NY.
Division of Music, Sports and Entertainment, National Museum of American History, Smithsonian Institution.
Gertrude Käsebier Collection, Photographic History Collection, National Museum of American History, Smithsonian Institution, Washington, DC.
Gertrude Käsebier Papers, University of Delaware Library, Newark, DE.
Handbook of North American Indians, National Museum of Natural History, Smithsonian Institution, Washington, DC.
Manuscript Division, New York Public Library, New York, NY.
McCracken Research Library, Buffalo Bill Historical Center, Cody, WY.
National Anthropological Archives, National Museum of Natural History, Smithsonian Institution, Washington, DC.
University Gallery, University of Delaware, Newark, DE.

Periodicals

American Amateur Photographer
British Journal of Photography
Bulletin of Photography
Camera Notes
Camera Work
History of Photography
Photograms of the Year
New York Times
Photo-Era
Photo-Miniature
Photographic Times
Wilson's Photographic Magazine

Exhibition Catalogs

Catalogue of Prints, The Photographic Section, American Institute, National Academy of Design, New York City, September 26–October 8, 1898.
Exhibition of Photographs, Corcoran Gallery of Art, Washington, DC, 1904.
Photographic Salon, The American Institute, New York City, December 4–23, 1899.
The Second Philadelphia Photographic Salon, Pennsylvania Academy of Fine Arts and The Photographic Society of Philadelphia, October 22–November 19, 1899.

Articles by Käsebier

Käsebier, Gertrude. "Studies in Photography." *Photographic Times* 30 (June 1898): 269–72. Reprinted in Peter C. Bunnell, ed., *A Photographic Vision: Pictorial Photography, 1889–1923*. Salt Lake City: Peregrine Smith, 1980.

———. "To Whom It May Concern." *Camera Notes* 3 (January 1900): 121–22.

———. "Attracting Customers to the Studio: A Public for Every Class of Work." *British Journal of Photography*, October 14, 1910, 777.

———. "Praise from Mrs. Käsebier." *Bulletin of Photography*, September 18, 1912, 419–20.

———. "Picture Making: A Talk to the Department of Photography, Brooklyn Institute." *American Photography* 9 (April 1915): 224, 226.

Articles (chronological order)

D. M. N. [Dora M. Norton]. "Art Studies in Photography." *Pratt Institute Monthly* 5 (March 1897): 221–23.

"Sioux Chief's Party Calls. The Indians Make Daily Visits to the Studio Where They Were Entertained at Ten." *New York Times*, April 23, 1899, 20.

"The Indian as a Gentleman. Those of the Wild West Are Most Chivalrously Inclined as Shown at a Reception and 'Show' Party." *New York Times*, April 23, 1899, 20.

Dow, Arthur W. "Mrs. Gertrude Käsebier's Portrait Photographs." *Camera Notes* 3 (July 1899): 22–23.

Hartmann, Sadakichi. "Portrait Painting and Portrait Photography." *Camera Notes* 3 (July 1899): 13–19.

Keiley, Joseph T. "Mrs. Käsebier's Prints." *Camera Notes* 3 (July 1899): 34.

Stieglitz, Alfred. "Our Illustrations." *Camera Notes* 3 (July 1899): 24.

Cram, R. A. "Mrs. Käsebier's Work." *Photo Era* 4 (May 1900): 131–36.

Hartmann, Sadakichi. "Gertrude Käsebier." *Photographic Times* (May 1900): 195–99.

"Some Indian Portraits." *Everybody's Magazine* 4 (January 1901): 2–24.

"Artist Receives Indians. Mrs. Käsebier Invites Children. Friends to Meet a Contingent from Buffalo Bill's Show." *New York Times*, April 14, 1901, 7.

Caffin, Charles H. "Mrs. Käsebier and the Artistic-Commercial Portrait." *Everybody's Magazine* 4 (May 1901): 408–95. Included in *Photography as a Fine Art*. New York: Doubleday, Page & Co., 1901. Reprinted: Hastings-on-Hudson, NY: Morgan & Morgan, 1971, and New York: Amphoto, 1972.

Johnston, Frances Johnston. "The Foremost Women Photographers of America: The Work of Gertrude Käsebier." *Ladies Home Journal* 18 (May 1901): 1.

Caffin, Charles H. "Mrs. Käsebier's Work—An Appreciation." *Camera Work*, no. 1 (January 1903): 17–19.

Editors. "The Pictures in This Number." *Camera Work,* no. 1 (January 1903): 63.
Johnston, Frances Benjamin. "Gertrude Käsebier, Professional Photographer." *Camera Work,* no. 1 (January 1903): 20.
Bayley, R. Child. "Things Photographic in the United States of America: Mrs. Käsebier." *Photography* 15 (January 17, 1903): 63. Reprinted as "A Visit to Mrs. Käsebier's Studio." *Wilson's Photographic Magazine* 40 (February 1903): 73–74, and as "Mrs. Käsebier." *American Amateur Photographer* 15 (February 1903): 78–79.
Keiley, Joseph T. "Gertrude Käsebier." Photography, March 19, 1904, cover, 223–27, 237. Reprinted: *Camera Work,* no. 20 (October 1907): 27–31.
"Gertrude Käsebier at the Photo-Secession." *Photo-Era* 16 (March 1906): 215.
Roberts, Mary Fanton [Giles Edgerton]. "Photography as an Emotional Art: A Study of the Work of Gertrude Käsebier." *Craftsman* 12 (April 1907): 80–93. Reprinted: *Image* 15 (December 1972): 9–12.
Caffin, Charles, H. "Emotional Art. (After reading the *'Craftsman,'* April 1907.)" *Camera Work,* no. 20 (October 1907): 32–34.
Lohmann, Helen. "Gertrude Käsebier—Photographer." *Abel's Photographic Weekly,* February 20, 1909, 130.
Hord, Spencer B. [Chippendale]. "Gertrude Käsebier, Maker of Photographs." *Bulletin of Photography,* June 8, 1910, 363–67.
Ward, H. Snowden. "Gertrude Käsebier and Her Work." *Amateur Photographer and Photographic News,* December 13, 1910, 590–91. Reprinted: *Abel's Photographic Weekly,* December 24, 1910, 267–68.
Todd, F. Dundas. "My Photographic Reminiscences." *Abel's Photographic Weekly,* January 12, 26, 1924, 30–31, 80–81.
"Threescore Years and Sixteen Is Ardent Exponent of Photography." *New York Sun,* January 5, 1929, 21. Reprinted as "Gertrude Käsebier Is Interviewed." *Photo Era* 62 (March 1929): 129–30.
Hervey, Dr. Walter L. "Gertrude Käsebier—Photographer." *Photo Era* 62 (March 1929): 131–32.
"Mrs. G. E. Käsebier Dead at 82." *New York Times,* October 14, 1934, 28.
Holm, Ed. "Gertrude Käsebier's Indian Portraits." *The American West,* July 10, 1973, 38–41.
Doherty, Amy S. "Frances Benjamin Johnston 1865–1952." *History of Photography Journal* 4 (April 1980): 97–111.
Powers, William K. "The Art of Courtship among the Oglala." *American Indian Art Magazine* 5 (Spring 1980): 40–47.
Anderson-Spivy, Alexandra. "Portraits of the Oglala Sioux Who Rode with Buffalo Bill." *Esquire Sportsman,* Autumn 1992, 53–58.
Green, Rayna. "Gertrude Käsebier's 'Indian' Photographs." *History of Photography Journal* 24 (Spring 2000): 58–60.
Hutchinson, Elizabeth. "When the Sioux Party Calls: Käsebier's Indian Portraits and the Gendering of the Artist's Studio." *American Art* 16 (Summer 2002): 40–65.

Books

Berkhofer, Robert F. Jr. *The White Man's Indian.* New York: Vintage Books, 1978.

Buffalo Bill Historical Center (museum catalog). Cody, WY: Buffalo Bill Historical Center, 1995.

Cody, Colonel W. F. *Buffalo Bill's Life Story: An Autobiography.* New York: Dover Publications, 1998 commemorative edition.

Doty, Robert. *Photo-Secession.* Rochester, NY: The George Eastman House, 1960.

Fleming, Paula Richardson. *Native American Photography at the Smithsonian.* Washington, DC: Smithsonian Books, 2003.

Goodyear, Frank III. *Red Cloud: Photographs of a Lakota Chief.* Lincoln, NE: University of Nebraska Press, 2003.

Gover, C. Jane. *The Positive Image: Women Photographers in Turn of the Century America.* Albany, NY: State University of New York Press, 1988.

Green, Jonathan. *Camera Work: A Critical Anthology.* New York: Aperture, 1973.

Greenough, Sarah, et al. *Modern Art and America: Alfred Stieglitz and His New York Galleries.* Boston: National Gallery of Art & Bulfinch Press, 2000.

Homer, William Innes. *A Pictorial Heritage: The Photographs of Gertrude Käsebier.* Wilmington, DE: University of Delaware and Delaware Art Museum, 1979.

———. *Alfred Stieglitz and the American Avant-Garde.* Boston, MA: New York Graphic Society, 1977.

Kasson, Joy. *Buffalo Bill's Wild West: Celebrity, Memory, and Popular History.* New York: Hill and Wang, 2000.

Kort, Pamela, and Max Hollein. *I Like America: Fictions of the Wild West.* Munich, Germany: Prestel, 2006.

McMaster, Gerald, and Clifford E. Trafzer, eds. *Native Universe: Voices of Indian America.* Washington, DC: National Museum of the American Indian and National Geographic, 2004.

Michaels, Barbara L. *Gertrude Käsebier: The Photographer and Her Photographs.* New York: Harry N. Abrams, 1992.

Morton, Marsha. *Pratt and Its Gallery: The Arts and Crafts Years.* New York: Pratt Institute, 1999.

Moses, L. G. *Wild West Shows and the Images of American Indians, 1883–1933.* Albuquerque, NM: University of New Mexico Press, 1996.

Naef, Weston J. *The Collection of Alfred Stieglitz: Fifty Pioneers of Modern Art.* New York: Metropolitan Museum of Art and Viking Press, 1978.

Panzer, Mary. *Philadelphia Naturalistic Photography, 1865–1906.* New Haven, CT: Yale University Art Gallery, 1982.

Peterson, Christian A. *Alfred Stieglitz's Camera Notes.* New York: W. W. Norton & Co. and The Minneapolis Institute of Arts, 1993.

Trachtenberg, Alan. *Shades of Hiawatha: Staging Indians, Making Americans 1880–1930.* New York: Hill and Wang, 2004.

Tucker, Anne. *The Woman's Eye.* New York: Alfred A. Knopf, 1973, 2, 6–7, 13–27.

Whelan, Richard. *Stieglitz on Photography: His Selected Essays and Notes.* New York: Aperture Books, 2000.

Wetmore, Helen Cody, and Zane Grey. *Buffalo Bill: Last of the Great Scouts.* Lincoln, NE: University of Nebraska Press, 2003 commemorative edition.

Web Sites

Archives, Oglala Lakota College, Kyle, South Dakota, http://library.olc.edu/Archives/archindex.htm
Arlington National Cemetery Web Site, http://www.arlingtoncemetery.net/gsbonnin.htm
Famous Native American Women, Native American Rhymes, Rhodes Educational Publications, http://nativeamericanrhymes.com/women/bonnin.htm
Oglala Sioux Tribe of the Pine Ridge Indian Reservation, South Dakota, http://www.lakotamall.com/oglalasiouxtribe/
National Museum of the American Indian, Smithsonian Institution, Washington, DC, http://www.nmai.si.edu/
Voices from the Gaps: Women Artists and Writers of Color, An International Web Site University of Minnesota, Minneapolis, MN, http://voices.cla.umn.edu/vg/Bios/entries/bonnin_gertrude_simmons_zitkalasa.html

Index

Page numbers in *italic* type indicate illustration captions.

Foundations of

AURAL REHABILITATION

Children, Adults, and Their Family Members

Foundations of

AURAL REHABILITATION

Children, Adults, and Their Family Members

Nancy Tye-Murray, PhD

5521 Ruffin Road
San Diego, CA 92123
e-mail: information@pluralpublishing.com
Web site: http://www.pluralpublishing.com

Typeset in 11/13 Adobe Garamond by Achorn International
Printed in the United States of America by McNaughton & Gunn, Inc.

Library of Congress Cataloging-in-Publication Data

Names: Tye-Murray, Nancy, author.
Title: Foundations of aural rehabilitation : children, adults, and their families / Nancy Tye-Murray.
Description: Fifth edition. | San Diego, CA : Plural Publishing, [2020] |
Includes bibliographical references and indexes
Identifiers: LCCN 2018045681 | ISBN 9781635500738 (alk. paper) | ISBN 1635500737 (alk. paper)
Subjects: | MESH: Correction of Hearing Impairment—methods | Family Relations | Persons With Hearing Impairments—psychology | Persons With Hearing Impairments—rehabilitation | Case Reports
Classification: LCC RF297 | NLM WV 276 | DDC 617.8/06—dc23
LC record available at https://lccn.loc.gov/2018045681

CONTENTS

PART 3 AURAL REHABILITATION FOR CHILDREN

PREFACE

What exactly is aural rehabilitation? The answer to this question can conceivably include every aspect of audiology, education, and speech-language pathology for adults and children who have hearing loss and related services for their family members. Under the rubric of aural rehabilitation may fall any of the following topics: identification, quantification, and diagnosis of hearing loss and other hearing-related communication difficulties, assessment of visual-only and audiovisual speech recognition, selection and fitting of listening devices, speechreading and auditory training, patient and family counseling, psychosocial support, follow-up services, communication strategies training, tinnitus treatment, literacy promotion, speech and language therapy, classroom management, parent instruction, sign language instruction, noise protection, workplace accommodations, and school and nursing home in-services. The threads that run through the various services and that unify them into the discipline of aural rehabilitation include an emphasis on understanding and addressing the needs of patients who have hearing loss and their family members and an emphasis on ensuring that patients and their communication partners achieve maximum communication success in their everyday environments. Aural rehabilitation draws from a variety of disciplines. This text cites literature from the fields of cognitive psychology, counseling, medicine, occupational therapy, sociolinguistics, second language learning, and general education, as well as audiology, speech-language pathology, and deaf education.

This book presents an evidence-based approach to the discipline of aural rehabilitation, and reviews the scientific underpinnings that underlie much of what occurs in clinical practice. For some readers, *Foundations of Aural Rehabilitation: Children, Adults, and Their Family Members* may be their only textbook that is entirely devoted to aural rehabilitation, while for others, it may be their first followed by a more advanced class and corresponding textbook. The book can serve as an introduction to aural rehabilitation and as a reference that can be revisited by practicing professionals. It may also serve as a starting point for researchers and scientists. By design, the book is translational and is based on the premise that clinical practice informs scientific research and scientific research informs clinical practice.

The book includes a number of case studies, and general demographic, medical, and pop-cultural trends are considered in parallel with corresponding developments in aural rehabilitation. Sidebars, illustrations, and chapter inserts provide lively additions to the text and include quotations by patients, professionals, and family members, bulleted points, historical notes, and tangential asides.

New Features

The fifth edition has been reorganized so that after Chapter 1, which is an introductory chapter, other chapters are now grouped into three parts. Part 1 concerns the components of an aural rehabilitation plan, Part 2 concerns adults and their family members, and Part 3 concerns children and their parents or guardians. In previous editions, adults and children were considered separately, for each of the services comprised by aural rehabilitation, such as speechreading training and communication strategies training. The presentation has been streamlined, with greater focus on the "take-home message" of current research and its clinical implications. I hope that instructors will find this new organization easier to teach and students will find the materials easier to learn.

This edition includes several new features. For example, much has happened in the last five years in the field of auditory training and Chapter 4 presents a state-of-the-science review of the most current research as well as an overview of what it is like to listen with hearing loss. Chapter 5 concerns audiovisual speech perception, and since this is my area of research expertise, I took special pleasure in updating it, as nothing excites me more than sharing my enthusiasm with students. My goal in writing this chapter (and all the chapters) was to make audiovisual speech perception, as well as all aspects of aural rehabilitation, as interesting and compelling for my readers as it is for me. Chapter 15 presents emerging trends in speech and language therapy, including specific examples of therapy techniques. In this edition, I combined Chapters 2 and 11 from the fourth edition so as to consolidate the presentation about aural rehabilitation plans for adults and to minimize redundancies. Finally, this edition has more illustrations and figures than any of the previous editions—I truly believe that a picture is worth a thousand words.

The fifth edition addresses a global audience whenever possible, without sacrificing the importance of including information that might be uniquely relevant to students who intend to work in the United States. There are many reasons for this broad focus, including the increasing globalization and cross-pollination of speech and hearing services, the mobility of students, and the increased likelihood that they may practice and study in different countries, as well as the advent of telepractice, which means that students may someday provide services via telecommunications to patients living abroad.

Target Audience

The book targets undergraduate students who are in their junior or senior year in a university or postsecondary program and graduate students who are in their first year of graduate training. It can serve as a primary resource for the disciplines of audiology, speech-language pathology, education of children who are deaf and have hearing loss, and speech and hearing science, and as a supplemental source for training programs in special education, medicine, nursing, occupational therapy, psychology, and vocational rehabilitation counseling.

I immensely enjoy hearing from my readers and can be contacted at nmurray@wustl.edu.

Nancy Tye-Murray, Professor
Washington University in St. Louis School of Medicine
St. Louis, MO

To the professors and instructors who teach aural rehabilitation: I salute you.

Foundations of

AURAL REHABILITATION

Children, Adults, and Their Family Members

CHAPTER 1

Introduction

OUTLINE

- The World Health Organization (WHO) and Hearing-Related Disability
- Services Included in the Aural Rehabilitation Plan
- Where Does Aural Rehabilitation Occur?
- Who Provides Aural Rehabilitation?
- Hearing Loss
- Service Needs
- Cost-Effectiveness and Costs
- Evidence-Based Practice
- Case Study: Applying the WHO's International Classification of Functioning, Disability and Health
- Case Study: Evidence-Based Practice Decision Making
- Final Remarks
- Key Chapter Points
- Terms and Concepts to Remember
- Appendix 1–1
- Appendix 1–2
- Appendix 1–3

Hearing loss has been called the "invisible condition," yet its impact may be anything but invisible. People with hearing loss may miss out on casual conversations, on conversations that establish intimacy and friendship, and on conversations that convey important information or promote life goals. Everyday activities that people with normal hearing take for granted, such as talking on the telephone or with a store clerk, may be effortful and frustrating (Figure 1–1). For children, the difficulties may relate not only to hearing spoken messages, but also to interpreting and expressing messages because of their limited language skills. In addition, children may have restricted speech skills, world knowledge, and experience with social conventions, which will further constrain their conversations and other interactions.

© pathdoc | Shutterstock.com

FIGURE 1–1 Hearing loss affects everyday activities. Activities that persons with normal hearing take for granted may become effortful or frustrating for persons who have hearing loss.

Aural rehabilitation is intervention aimed at minimizing and alleviating the communication difficulties associated with hearing loss.

Aural rehabilitation is aimed at restoring or optimizing people's participation in activities that have been limited as a result of hearing loss. It may be aimed at benefiting their communication partners as well. The goals of aural rehabilitation are to:

- Alleviate the difficulties related to hearing loss and
- Minimize its consequences.

Conversational fluency relates to how smoothly conversation unfolds.

A **hearing-related disability** is a loss of function imposed by hearing loss. The term denotes a multidimensional phenomenon, and may include pain, discomfort, physical dysfunction, emotional distress, and the inability to carry out typical activities.

Achieving these goals will enhance conversational fluency and reduce hearing-related disability. **Conversational fluency** refers to how smoothly conversation unfolds and how easily communication partners can exchange information, as well as to any restrictions in topic selection (e.g., Does hearing loss restrict them to talking about only simple topics, such as the weather?). **Hearing-related disability** is a loss of function caused by hearing loss or an inability to perform an activity and is a multidimensional phenomenon. Disability is not an attribute of the individual per se. It arises from a complex collection of conditions, some of which stem from the individual's real-world environment.

Those Whom We Serve

Children who receive aural rehabilitation services are often referred to as *students*, especially in the context of an educational setting. Terminology for adults who receive services is more variable and includes *patients, clients,* and *consumers.* Hernandez

(continues)

Those Whom We Serve *(continued)*

and Amlani (2004) mailed out 1,428 surveys to a random sample of Fellows of the **American Academy of Audiology (AAA)**. Thirty-two percent of the surveys were returned. The results showed that an overwhelming majority (90%) preferred the term *patient*, which is the term that is used in this text.

The **American Academy of Audiology (AAA)** is a professional organization for audiologists that advances the profession of audiology through leadership activities, advocacy, educational programs, public awareness, and research support.

This chapter introduces the subsequent topics in this book. We will first consider a model of hearing-related disability and how it shapes the aural rehabilitation intervention plan. We will then review general issues and terms associated with aural rehabilitation and hearing loss as well as locales where aural rehabilitation might occur, who might provide it, and who might receive it, and then finally, review how you might go about selecting appropriate intervention services.

THE WORLD HEALTH ORGANIZATION (WHO) AND HEARING-RELATED DISABILITY

The **World Health Organization** (WHO) developed the **International Classification of Functioning, Disability and Health** (ICF), a classification system that provides a **biopsychosocial** framework for describing and considering a health condition (WHO, 2001). The ICF couches the consequences of a health-related condition within the context of a patient's environment and circumstances (Figure 1–2). It takes into account the nature and extent of a patient's functioning and how it may be limited in quality or quantity. The focus is not on a patient's hearing loss with the idea of "fixing" it, but rather, on how hearing difficulties affect the patient in everyday life and how hearing-related disability might be alleviated.

The **World Health Organization (WHO)** is an agency within the United Nations system that is responsible for providing leadership on global health issues, for setting health research agendas and health standards and norms, for dispensing evidence-based policy options, and for monitoring and assessing international health standards.

The **International Classification of Functioning, Disability and Health (ICF)** is an internationally recognized classification system for describing consequences of health conditions and for considering the dimensions of health and functioning, and can be applied to all rehabilitation sciences.

A **biopsychosocial** framework implies that biological, psychological (e.g., thoughts, emotions, behaviors), and social factors influence how a health condition may affect human functioning.

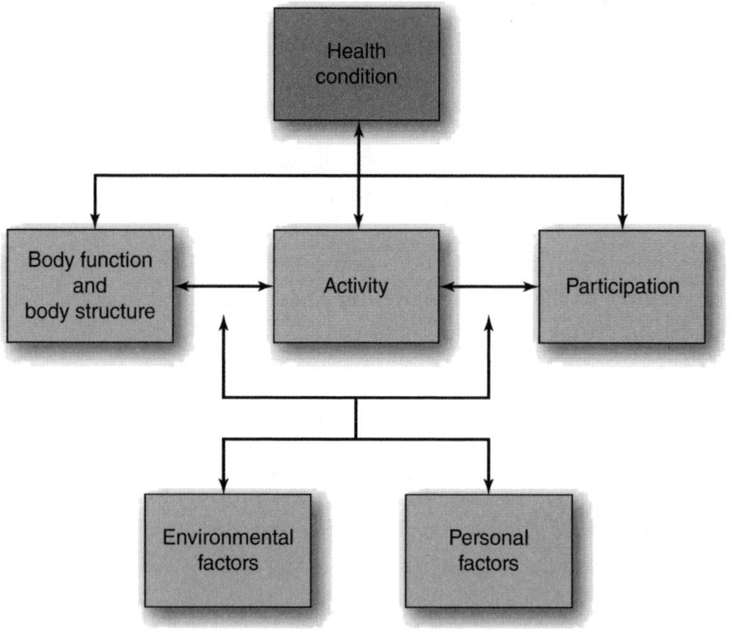

FIGURE 1–2 The International Classification of Functioning, Disability and Health (ICF) that is utilized and promulgated by the World Health Organization (WHO). The ICF provides an international common language and conceptual framework for considering the effects of a health condition on functioning, disability, and health.

A **body structure**, as defined by WHO, is an anatomical part of the body, such as organs (e.g., the cochlea), limbs, and their components.

Body functions are physiological functions of body systems, including psychological functions.

An **activity** is the execution of a task or action by an individual; it is an endeavor that a patient wants or needs to do with hearing (e.g., alerting to sound; recognizing speech).

Participation is involvement in a life situation; it represents the societal perspective of functioning (e.g., participating in a dinner table conversation).

An **activity limitation** is a change at the level of the person brought about by an impairment at the levels of body structure (e.g., loss of hair cells in the cochlea) and function (e.g., loss of an ability to discriminate pitch); for example, a patient may no longer be able to engage easily in casual conversation.

A **participation restriction** is an effect of an activity limitation that results in a change in the broader scope of a patient's life; for example, a patient may avoid social gatherings.

The central row of Figure 1–2 depicts reciprocal relationships between the **body structures** and **body functions** and activity and participation. An **activity** is, quite literally, the execution of a task or action by an individual. A **participation** is an involvement in a life situation. An **activity limitation** is a change at the level of the patient, such as an inability to recognize speech over the telephone, whereas a **participation restriction** is the effect of a change in participation on the broader scope of life, such as a patient's avoidance of social situations for fear of being left out. Activity limitations and participation restrictions are often intertwined. For example, a woman who cannot respond to questions in a crowded room has an activity limitation because she cannot recognize speech in the presence of background noise. She also has participation restrictions because she avoids noisy restaurants and parties as a result (Figure 1–3).

FIGURE 1–3 Activity limitations and participation restrictions. A patient may experience difficulty in recognizing speech in the presence of background noise. This activity limitation may restrict the ability to participate in social gatherings.

Environmental factors are external to a patient, and are composed of the physical, social, and attitudinal environment in which the patient lives and conduct his or her life.

Social factors are the prevailing viewpoints of one's society.

Personal factors pertain to the patient, and encompass an individual's age, lifestyle, race, coping styles, attitudes, self-efficacy, lifestyle, habits, preferences, socioeconomic background, and other health conditions.

The lower row of boxes in Figure 1–2 shows how the ICF takes into account two types of contextual factors, environmental factors and personal factors. **Environmental factors** include the physical, social, and attitudinal influences that a person regularly experiences. For example, **social factors** (also referred to as cultural factors) are the prevailing viewpoints of the people in a person's social milieu. If the prevailing view is that hearing loss is a negative state, as when it is a sign of aging in a youth-oriented society or of inadequacy to perform in the workforce, then the participation restrictions and other consequences may increase. **Personal factors** include gender, age, race, fitness, lifestyle, habits, social background, profession, family, coping styles, past and current experience, personality, values, preferences, knowledge, and any other health conditions. Personal factors also encompass a person's attitude toward the hearing loss. For example hearing loss might be a source of shame or it may seem inconsequential in comparison to other life events, such as diabetes or cancer.

Environmental and personal factors influence the magnitude of hearing-related disability. For example, a computer programmer and a car salesperson may have the same degree of hearing loss, yet their activity limitations and participation restrictions likely differ. The programmer may rarely experience conversational difficulties while working alone at a computer station. Conversely, the car salesperson must converse with customers throughout the workday, and may frequently misunderstand questions and hesitate to use the telephone.

The components of the model shown in Figure 1–2 are interlinked. For example, because a musician played the electric guitar (an *activity*) and performed in loud concert halls on a regular basis (a *participation*), he damaged hair cells in his inner ears (a change in *body structure*) and incurred a bilateral hearing loss (a change in *body function*). Now he can no longer regulate his voice pitch (an *activity limitation*) and no longer sing harmony with his band (a *participation restriction*). He wears earplugs during concerts to prevent further hearing loss (a positive effect on *body structures* and *body function* from an *environmental factor*) and avoids all publicity interviews because he is a proud man and does not want to be humiliated because he cannot understand questions (a negative effect on *participation* by a *personal factor*).

The Perils of Loud Music

"I have unwittingly helped to invent and refine a type of music that makes its principal components deaf. Hearing loss is a terrible thing because it cannot be repaired."

—Peter Townshend, guitarist, vocalist, and songwriter for *The Who*, a rock band of the 1960s and 1970s

(Townshend, 2013)

The ICF may extend to a patient's families and communication partners. The behaviors and attitudes of **frequent communication partners** (the people the patient interacts with most often at home, in the workplace, in school, or during social activities) for the most part may fall under the rubric of *personal factors*, although in practice, they deserve more attention than the model shown in Figure 1–2 implies. Frequent communication partners can exert a significant effect on a patient's activities and participation. For example, a frequent communication partner who mumbles and who resents the patient's hearing loss may exacerbate the consequences of hearing loss, whereas one who speaks clearly and who empathizes may alleviate them.

Frequent communication partners are persons with whom another often converses, such as a family member.

Perceived quality of life "reflects self-assessment of the current life experiences and includes such things as enjoyment, meaning, purpose, usefulness, value, freedom of choice, and independence. . . . It is influenced by function, activity, and participation, but is by no means completely determined by them" (Boothroyd, 2007, p. 64).

A **third-party disability** refers to changes in life functioning that accrue as a result of a family member's health condition.

The patient's hearing loss may impose an adverse effect on a frequent communication partner's **perceived quality of life**. The WHO labels the effects of hearing loss on the frequent communication partner as **third-party disability**. For example, answering interview questions about how their partner's hearing loss affects everyday life, one respondent wrote, "There's that thing of not wanting to go somewhere because there might be too many people around . . . [he] will find an excuse for not wanting to go out. So that affects me then because I might retract from something if somebody suggests we do something." Another wrote, "What I don't like is when I'm watching a television show and [he] would say "Can you turn that up?" And I'd just about bounce out of my chair. I think, you've got to be kidding me! . . . I'm not having a happy time" (Scarinci et al., 2009, pp. 2095–2096). In these two examples, one patient's hearing loss has limited his frequent communication partner's social life and another patient's hearing loss has caused auditory distress.

Participation Restrictions: A Very Famous Case Study

Ludwig van Beethoven (Figure 1–4) began to suffer hearing loss and chronic tinnitus at the age of 26 years, making it difficult for him to hear his music (activity limitation) and play the piano before an audience (participation restriction). At the age of 28 years, he sent this letter to his two brothers, Carl and Johann. Despite his enormous success as a composer, Beethoven still suffered the participation restrictions imposed by significant hearing loss:

> Though born with a fiery, active temperament, even susceptible to the diversions of society, I was soon compelled to isolate myself, to live life alone. If at times I tried to forget all this, oh how harshly was I flung back by the doubly sad experience of my bad hearing. Yet it was impossible for me to say to people, "Speak louder, shout, for I am deaf." Ah, how could I possibly admit an infirmity in the one sense which ought to be more perfect in me than others, a sense which I once possessed in the highest perfection, a perfection such as few in my profession enjoy or ever have enjoyed. Oh I cannot do it; therefore, forgive me when you see me draw back when I would have gladly mingled with you. My misfortune is doubly

(continues)

© Georgios Kollidas | Dreamstime.com

FIGURE 1–4 Ludwig van Beethoven.

Participation Restrictions: A Very Famous Case Study *(continued)*

painful to me because I am bound to be misunderstood; for me there can be no relaxation with my fellow men, no refined conversations, no mutual exchange of ideas. I must live almost alone, like one who has been banished; I can mix with society only as much as true necessity demands. If I approach near to people a hot terror seizes upon me, and I fear being exposed to the danger that my condition might be noticed.

(Beethoven, 1802)

Communication partners of persons who have hearing loss may experience:

- Difficulties in communicating with their partners in background noise
- Difficulties in coping with the high volume of the television set
- Annoyance as to having to respond on behalf of their partners and having to repeat or clarify their utterances during conversations
- Similar levels of frustration and irritation as their partner
- Irritation during one-on-one conversations and group conversations
- A similar degree of reduced social interactions

(Scarinci et al., 2009, p. 2089)

Tinnitus is the perception of sound in the head without an external cause.

Hearing protection is means to prevent or minimize the deleterious effects of loud sound on the auditory system.

SERVICES INCLUDED IN THE AURAL REHABILITATION PLAN

Table 1–1 presents services often included in an aural rehabilitation plan. The plan typically includes diagnosis and quantification of the hearing loss and provision of appropriate listening devices. It may include communication strategies training, counseling related to hearing loss, assertiveness training, psychosocial support, auditory and speechreading training, and counseling and instruction for family members, colleagues, teachers, or caretakers. For adults, it may also include means and strategies to measure and manage **tinnitus** and a **hearing protection** component. For children, the plan may include interventions related to speech, language, and academic achievement.

TABLE 1–1 Components of a Typical Aural Rehabilitation Program

COMPONENT	DESCRIPTION
Diagnosis	Assessment of hearing loss and speech-recognition skills
Provision of appropriate listening device	Provision of hearing aid(s) or participation on a team that results in cochlear implantation and follow-up services
Provision of appropriate hearing assistance technology systems (HATS), inclusive of assistive listening devices (ALDs)	Explanation and dispensing of devices that supplement or replace a hearing aid or that serve to lessen hearing-related communication difficulties and other devices that facilitate the reception and identification of non-speech auditory signals
Tinnitus management	Assessment of tinnitus disability and provision of means to gain relief or control over the sensation of tinnitus
Hearing protection	Assessment of sound levels and provision of hearing protection materials
Auditory training	Structured and unstructured listening instruction and practice
Communication strategies training	Teaching of strategies that enhance communication and minimize communication difficulties (facilitative strategies, repair strategies, environmental management)
Informational/educational counseling	Instruction about normal hearing, hearing loss, listening device technology, speech perception, available services
Personal adjustment counseling	Intervention to enhance the management and acceptance of hearing loss and communication difficulties
Psychosocial support	Addressing the psychological and social impact of hearing loss on the person with hearing loss, family, and friends (may include stress management and relaxation techniques)

(continues)

TABLE 1–1 *(continued)*

COMPONENT	DESCRIPTION
Frequent communication partner training	Communication training for the spouse, partner, family, friends, or coworkers
Speechreading training	Training speech recognition via both auditory and visual channels
Speech-language therapy	For children primarily, therapy that teaches children to produce the sounds and words of their language and that emphasizes developing strategies to monitor one's own speech production and therapy that develops their vocabulary, syntax, and pragmatics
In-service training	Specialized training for other professionals, such as teachers in the public school system or caretakers in senior citizen centers

A survey of 1,625 audiologists in the United States indicated that they provided the following services:

- 86% provided counseling about communication strategies and realistic expectations
- 81% demonstrated and fit hearing assistive technology and hearing aids
- 60% measured patients' unaided and aided speech recognition abilities
- 45% provided services to babies ranging in age from birth to 6 months
- 41% validated their treatment outcomes by administrating self-questionnaires
- 17% provided auditory training
- 12% programmed and fit cochlear implants
- 4% provided speechreading training

(*ASHA Leader*, May 2013, p. 22)

Other Terms Related to Aural Rehabilitation

Sometimes the terms *aural habilitation* or *audiologic rehabilitation* are used instead of *aural rehabilitation*. The term **aural habilitation** might be used when the person receiving the services is a child rather than an adult because in the strict sense, *rehabilitation* means to restore something that was lost. When providing auditory training or speech and language therapy to children who have hearing loss, the goal is not to restore lost function, but rather to develop (i.e., habilitate) skills that were not present beforehand.

The term **audiologic rehabilitation** implies an emphasis on the diagnosis of hearing loss and the provision of listening devices and a lesser emphasis on follow-up support services, such as communication strategies training. Moreover, it implies services provided exclusively by an audiologist as opposed to those provided by other professionals, such as a speech-language pathologist or a classroom teacher.

Aural habilitation is intervention for persons who have not developed listening, speech, and language skills.

Audiologic rehabilitation is a term often used synonymously with aural rehabilitation or aural habilitation; it may entail greater emphasis on the provision and follow-up of listening devices and less emphasis on communication strategies and auditory and speechreading training.

WHERE DOES AURAL REHABILITATION OCCUR?

Aural rehabilitation may occur in a variety of locales. For example, it may be provided in any of the following settings:

- A university speech and hearing clinic
- An audiology private practice
- A hearing aid dealer's private practice
- A hospital speech and hearing clinic
- A community center or nursing home
- A school
- An otolaryngologist's office
- A speech-language pathologist's office
- Consumer organization meetings
- The home, sometimes with the aid of a computer and possibly Web-based communications
- Military veterans' organizations, such as a VA hospital or military or veterans center

A Rose By Any Other Name . . .

Other terms include:

- Hearing rehabilitation
- Hearing therapy
- Listening therapy
- Auditory management
- Listening rehabilitation

(*Hull, 2018*)

WHO PROVIDES AURAL REHABILITATION?

Aural rehabilitation might be provided by an audiologist, a speech-language pathologist, or a teacher for children who are deaf and hard of hearing. An audiologist usually takes the lead role in developing an adult's aural rehabilitation plan and coordinating the services provided by other professionals, whereas a speech-language pathologist often plays the lead role for a child, especially in a school environment. For example, the speech-language pathologist is most likely to provide speech and language therapy and often is the professional who provides auditory and speechreading training. Whereas the audiologist may fit and maintain a child's hearing aids and equip the classroom with appropriate **assistive listening devices (ALDs)** and hearing assistive technology, the speech-language pathologist may be the person who has extended one-on-one contact with a child and the one who knows the child well. For a very young child, a teacher for children who are deaf and hard of hearing often takes the lead, and may interact frequently with the child's parents.

An **assistive listening device (ALD)** is an instrument designed to provide awareness or identification of environmental signals and speech and to improve signal-to-noise ratios.

The **American Speech-Language-Hearing Association (ASHA)** is a professional, scientific, and credentialing organization for audiologists, speech-language pathologists, and speech, language, and hearing scientists in the United States and internationally.

The **American Speech-Language-Hearing Association (ASHA)** convened a working group on audiologic rehabilitation (ASHA, 2002). Its charge was to summarize the knowledge and skill sets that audiologists and speech-language pathologists should have if they are to provide aural rehabilitation. These outlines are presented in Appendix 1–1 (audiologists) and Appendix 1–2 (speech-language pathologists).

In addition to a general knowledge about basic communication processes, audiologists who provide aural rehabilitation are expected to understand the auditory system function and disorders, developmental status, cognition, sensory perception, audiologic assessment procedures, speech and language assessment procedures, evaluation and management of listening devices, effects of hearing impairment on functional communication, case management, interdisciplinary collaboration and public advocacy, and hearing conservation and acoustic environments.

In addition to general knowledge about the basic communication processes, speech-language pathologists are expected to have a broad knowledge of auditory system function and disorders, developmental status, cognition, sensory perception, audiologic assessment procedures, assessment of communication performance, listening devices, effects of hearing loss on psychosocial, educational, and vocational functioning, management, interdisciplinary collaboration and public advocacy, and acoustic environments.

HEARING LOSS

Hearing loss may be categorized along four dimensions: degree, onset, causation, and time course (Figure 1–5). In terms of degree, hearing loss may be characterized as mild, moderate, moderate-to-severe, severe, or profound.

The **pure-tone average (PTA)** is the average of the thresholds at 500, 1000, and 2000 Hz.

Degree of hearing impairment is often defined by the **pure-tone average (PTA)**, the average of the individual's pure-tone frequencies at 500, 1000, and 2000 Hz obtained with headphones. The following descriptors are often used to denote degree:

Normal: The PTA is 25 dB HL or better; for children, 15 dB HL or better.

Mild: The PTA is between 26 (or 15) and 40 dB HL.

Moderate: The PTA is between 41 and 55 dB HL.

Moderate-to-severe: The PTA is between 56 and 70 dB HL.

Severe: The PTA is between 71 and 90 dB HL.

Profound: The PTA is poorer than 90 dB HL.

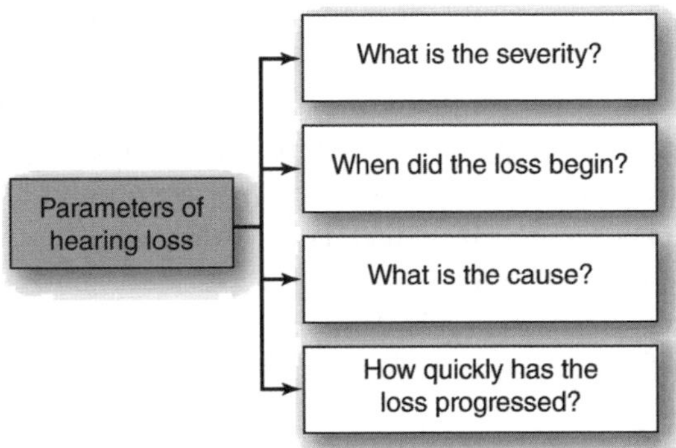

FIGURE 1–5 Parameterization of hearing loss along four dimensions: degree, onset, causation, and time course.

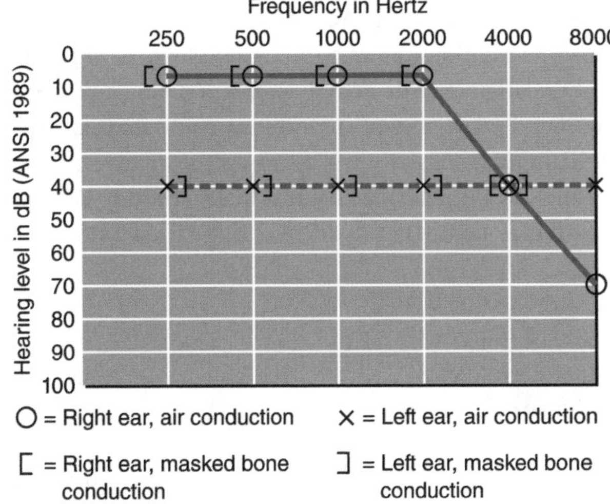

FIGURE 1–6 An audiogram that depicts an asymmetrical hearing loss. The left ear has a "flat" hearing loss; the right ear has a "high-frequency" hearing loss.

Closely related to the degree of hearing loss is its **configuration**. Configuration of hearing loss reflects the extent of hearing loss at each of the audiometric frequencies (**audiograms** indicate hearing sensitivity at the frequencies of 250, 500, 1000, 2000, 4000, and 8000 Hz) and provides an overall picture of hearing sensitivity. For example, a person who has normal hearing for the frequencies 250–2000 Hz and then reduced sensitivity for the frequencies 4000–8000 Hz may be described as having a "high-frequency hearing loss." A person who has equal sensitivity across the audiometric frequencies has a "flat hearing loss" (Figure 1–6). Other descriptors associated with degree of hearing loss include the following:

Configuration refers to the extent of the hearing loss at each frequency and gives an overall description of the hearing loss.

An **audiogram** is a graphic representation of hearing thresholds as a function of stimulus frequency.

- *Bilateral versus unilateral.* Bilateral hearing loss means both ears have reduced sensitivity, whereas unilateral means only one ear is affected.
- *Symmetrical versus* **asymmetrical**. Symmetrical hearing loss means the degree and configuration of hearing loss are the same in each ear, whereas asymmetrical means the two ears differ.
- *Fluctuating versus stable.* Sometimes a person's hearing sensitivity may fluctuate (e.g., if a child has fluid in the ear), whereas at other times sensitivity remains stable.

An **asymmetrical** hearing loss is one in which the degree and/or configuration of loss in one ear differs from that in the other ear.

Hard of hearing means having a hearing loss; usually not used to refer to a profound hearing loss.

Deaf usually means having minimal or no hearing.

A person who has a mild, moderate, or moderate-to-severe hearing loss (i.e., a hearing loss between 26 and 70 dB HL) is often called **hard of hearing**. Sometimes the term *hearing impaired* is used in lieu of the term *hard of hearing*. Many persons dislike it as it connotes that they may be exactly that, impaired, even though they may function effectively in their everyday lives. A person who has a profound hearing loss (and less often, severe) may sometimes be called **deaf**. People who belong to the Deaf community, often people who were born deaf or who grew up with deaf family members, may refer to themselves as *Deaf*. The capital "D" denotes their membership in the Deaf culture. Members of the Deaf culture share a similar sign language, culture, and often, educational experience.

Prelingual refers to a hearing loss acquired before the acquisition of spoken language.

A label of **congenital** implies the hearing loss was present at birth.

A label of **acquired** implies the hearing loss was incurred after birth.

Perilingual refers to a hearing loss acquired during the stage of acquiring spoken language.

Postlingual refers to a hearing loss incurred after the acquisition of spoken language.

In terms of onset, a hearing loss may be described as prelingual, perilingual, or postlingual. A person who has a **prelingual** hearing loss incurred the loss before acquiring language. Although there is no universally agreed cutoff time as to when the prelingual phase ends, generally, a child who incurs a hearing loss before the age of 2 years is said to have a prelingual loss. A **congenital** hearing loss is thought to be present at birth or associated with the birthing process. An **acquired** hearing loss is not present at birth but is incurred later, either as a child or as an adult. A child who lost his or her hearing after acquiring some spoken language but before acquisition was complete is said to have a **perilingual** hearing loss. Finally, a **postlingual** loss is one that occurred after the acquisition of speech and language. Again, there is no agreed-upon age at which the perilingual stage ends and the postlingual stage begins, but it is around the age of 5 years. The postlingual distinction may be further divided into four additional cohorts. These are:

- Prevocational (around the ages 5–17 years)
- Early working age (18–44 years)
- Later working age (45–64 years)
- Retirement age (65 years and older)

Depending on a patient's membership in a cohort, his or her aural rehabilitation needs may vary. For example, someone who is prevocational may benefit from having a special amplification system available in the classroom, and the child's family may benefit from communication strategies training. Another person of later working age may require personal adjustment counseling and even psychosocial support to accept his or her change in abilities. The consequences of *not* receiving aural rehabilitation will also vary because of cohort membership. For example, a toddler who incurs hearing loss and who does not receive an appropriate listening aid will likely experience significant spoken language delay. An older man who incurs hearing loss will maintain normal speech and language, but may withdraw and isolate from family and friends and experience depression.

A **conductive loss** results from an obstruction within the outer or middle ear.

Microtia is a congenitally small external ear.

A congenital closure of the external auditory canal is called **atresia.**

Cerumen is earwax.

Otitis media is an inflammation of the middle ear, often accompanied by the accumulation of fluid in the middle ear cavity.

Sensorineural hearing loss is a type of hearing loss that has a cochlear or retrocochlear origin.

The third dimension used to categorize hearing loss is causation. A hearing loss may be conductive, sensorineural, or a combination of both (a mix), and it may be of central origin. The source of impairment determines the type.

A **conductive loss** stems from an obstruction in either the outer or middle ear that prevents sound from reaching the sensorineural structures in the inner ear. An obstruction might be congenital, such as **microtia** or **atresia**, or it might be acquired, such as **cerumen** accumulation in the ear canal or **otitis media** in the middle ear. Many conductive hearing losses resolve with medical treatment or the passage of time. In instances when a loss in hearing sensitivity remains, effective amplification can minimize listening difficulties. Conductive losses result in speech being attenuated. If the speech can be amplified loud enough, the patient usually can recognize speech quite easily. Conductive losses typically are limited in degree as once the level of the sound rises above about 50 or 60 dB SPL, it is transmitted directly to the inner ear by bone conduction.

A Quick Tour of the Human Ear

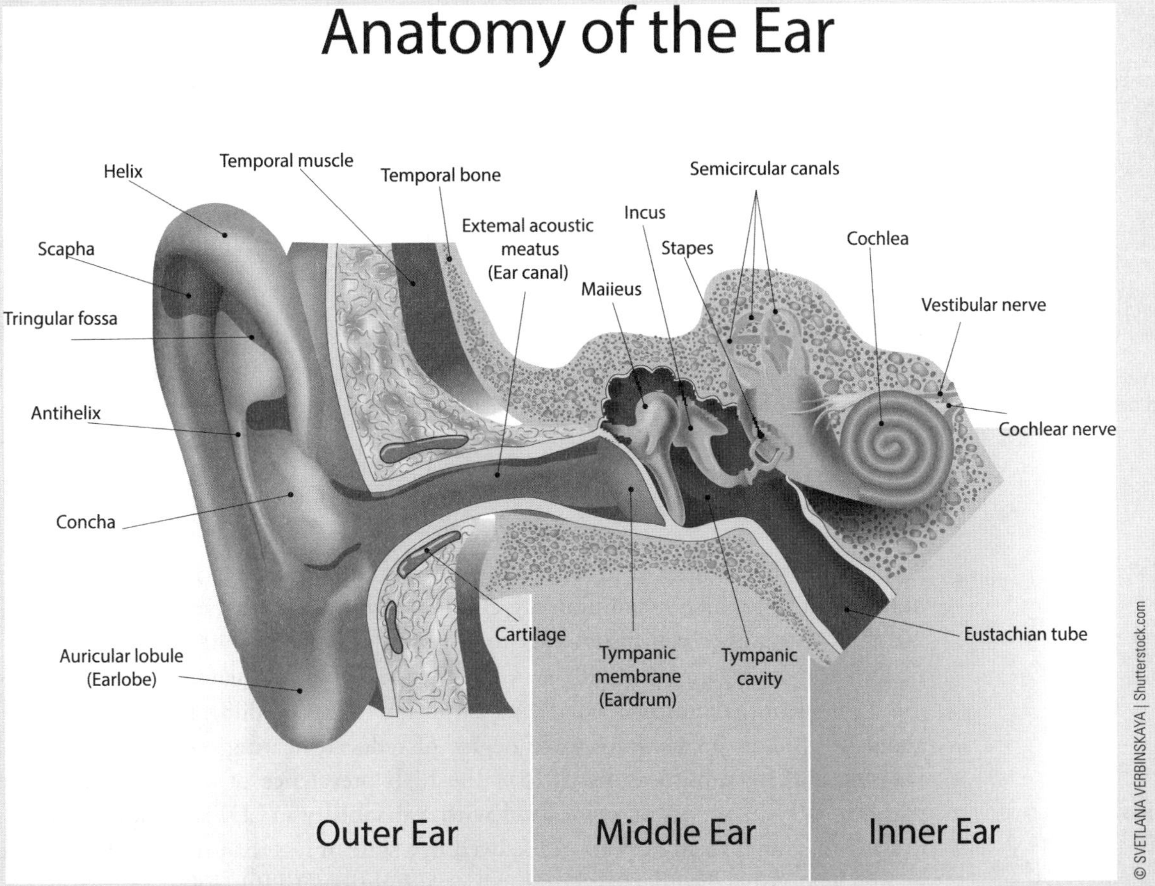

Anatomy of the Ear

Helix
Temporal muscle
Temporal bone
Semicircular canals
Scapha
Extemal acoustic meatus (Ear canal)
Incus
Stapes
Cochlea
Tringular fossa
Maiieus
Vestibular nerve
Antihelix
Cochlear nerve
Concha
Cartilage
Eustachian tube
Auricular lobule (Earlobe)
Tympanic membrane (Eardrum)
Tympanic cavity
Outer Ear
Middle Ear
Inner Ear

FIGURE 1–7 The human ear.

The types of hearing loss are classified by where in the human auditory pathway the impairment occurs (Figure 1–7). The auditory system has the following three anatomical regions plus the auditory nerve and central mechanisms:

- Outer ear, which includes the outside of the ear and the ear canal up to the level of the tympanic membrane (eardrum)
- Middle ear, which includes the cavity behind the tympanic membrane that houses the three tiny bones or ossicles (malleus, incus, stapes) responsible for mechanically conducting sound waves to the inner ear
- Inner ear, the cavity next to the middle ear that houses the cochlea, the snail-like structure that houses the cells responsible for responding to sound and transmitting it to the auditory nerve, and the labyrinth, a structure that is integral to our sense of balance and includes the semicircular canals
- Auditory nerve and central mechanisms, the eighth cranial nerve, which is responsible for conveying sound from the inner ear to the brainstem, and the central mechanisms comprising the brainstem, midbrain, and auditory cortex

Sensorineural hearing loss stems from a disturbance in the inner ear, eighth nerve, brainstem, midbrain, or auditory cortex. Sensorineural losses are typically permanent. Prelingual sensorineural hearing losses might be caused by any number of factors, including genetic makeup, maternal infections, or postnatal infection such as **meningitis** or **encephalitis**. Postlingual sensorineural hearing losses might relate to noise exposure,

Meningitis is a common cause of childhood sensorineural hearing loss caused by bacterial or viral inflammation of the meninges. The meninges are the membranous linings of the brain and spinal cord.

Encephalitis is an inflammation of the brain.

Ototoxic drugs are harmful to the structures of the inner ear and the auditory nerve.

the ingestion of **ototoxic drugs**, or aging. People who have sensorineural hearing loss often experience decreased ability to recognize speech, even if they are using appropriate amplification, because they have reduced or ablated neural capacity for conveying sound to the brain.

A hearing loss that has both a conductive and a sensorineural component is called a **mixed hearing loss.**

Sometimes an individual can have both a conductive and a sensorineural hearing loss. For example, a child who has a congenital sensorineural hearing loss may have **mixed hearing loss** if he or she suffers a bout of otitis media.

A central hearing loss, which is a kind of sensorineural hearing loss, stems from a disorder in function in the central auditory structures. It may be characterized by seemingly normal hearing thresholds coupled with a difficulty in understanding speech, especially in noisy settings, and in localizing sounds.

A **progressive hearing loss** is a hearing loss that increases over time.

A **sudden hearing loss** is a hearing loss that has an acute and rapid onset.

Finally, a hearing loss may be categorized as progressive or sudden. A hearing loss that occurs over the course of several months or years is a **progressive hearing loss.** A loss that occurs abruptly, say as a result of head trauma, is a **sudden hearing loss.**

SERVICE NEEDS

As of 2018, the number of people who suffer from disabling hearing loss worldwide is 466 million, of which 44 million are children (World Health Organization [WHO], 2018). This number will likely swell to almost a billion (i.e., 900 million people) by 2025 (Hear-it Organization, 2012). Globally, the WHO estimates that hearing loss is more prevalent than any other disabling condition (WHO, 2008). In the United States, about 48 million people have some degree of reduced hearing sensitivity (Center for Hearing and Communication, 2018). The high prevalence of hearing loss coincides with the WHO's report of **years lived with a disability (YLD)** statistics. Adult-onset hearing loss ranks third in years of life lived in a state of less than full health, outranked by only depressive disorders and unintentional injuries (WHO, 2006).

Years lived with a disability (YLD) is a term used by the WHO and refers to years of life lived with a disability, taking into account severity.

An **unserved** population refers to a group of patients in need of but not receiving services.

An **underserved** population is a group of patients receiving less than ideal services.

Many individuals who have hearing loss are unserved or underserved. **Unserved** means that they are not served as a result of policy, practice, or environmental barriers. **Underserved** means that they are inadequately served. In developing countries, 97% of people with hearing loss are unserved or underserved (Tucci, Merson, & Wilson, 2009). Developed and affluent countries also suffer from a shortage of services. For example, Margolis and Morgan (2008) estimate that by the year 2050, the United States will experience an annual shortfall of 15 million audiograms. The problem of being underserved is especially acute in rural settings, as only 13% of audiologists in private practice work in rural communities (ASHA, 2015).

Patients are unserved and underserved, in part, because there are too few speech and hearing professionals. For example, the average ratio of audiologists to the general population is 1 to 20,000 in developed countries and as high as 1 to every 6.25 million people in developing countries (Fagan & Jacobs, 2009). Other reasons include (Swanepoel et al., 2010, p. 197):

- Poor professional and public awareness
- Shortage of professional training programs
- A lack of outreach and immediate or extended support services
- Geographical barriers such as distance or remote terrains
- Natural barriers, such as severe weather
- A lack of government support and reimbursement policies for services

Increasingly, people with hearing loss and their families are exerting pressure on lawmakers and policy makers to ensure the availability of age-appropriate aural rehabilitation services (Figure 1–8).

FIGURE 1–8 Demand for aural rehabilitation services across the life span.

Infants and Toddlers

Advances in neonatology and critical-care medicine have led to better survival rates of high-risk babies. Infants who might have died in earlier times now survive, often with medical conditions that include hearing loss. Public policy in the United States provides for early identification of hearing loss and subsequent service provision, under the auspices of Public Law 105-17 (Individuals with Disabilities Education Act Amendments, 1997) (Chapter 12).

School-Age Children and Teenagers

Once children enter school, they face the challenge of learning to read and master academic material. They encounter new independence away from the home. Friends and classmates become increasingly important, and often, learning how to communicate effectively with their peer group becomes a high priority. Services for children and teenagers may include educational planning, accommodation in the classroom, including the use of assistive technology, and support in transitioning from elementary school to secondary school to postsecondary school settings.

Adults

Individuals in the center of the life cycle also may desire aural rehabilitation services. With appropriate support, adults with even significant hearing loss can function effectively in their workplace, community, and home environments. The passage of the Americans with Disabilities Act (ADA, 1990), which is landmark legislation that calls for equal access for all persons with disabilities (Chapter 10), requires that workplaces and public spaces accommodate people with hearing loss.

Older Adults

With the aging of the "baby boom" population, age-related hearing loss affects an increasing percentage of the world's population (Figure 1–9). Older adults often are unwilling to, nor should they be expected to, sit on the sidelines of life because they are unable to communicate with those around them. They have a demand for services that

FIGURE 1–9 Aural rehabilitation and older persons.

will enhance their ability to communicate with their families and friends, to participate in community activities and volunteer work, and to stay in touch with their world via multimedia technology. Some desire to continue in their professional careers and postpone retirement. With increased awareness of preventative medicine routines and a growing sophistication in medical practice, an ever growing number of older persons live longer, and many have few health problems other than hearing loss that restrict their day-to-day functioning.

Family and Frequent Communication Partners

A primary goal of any aural rehabilitation plan is to develop and enhance communication between the person with hearing loss and his or her family and communication partners. Implicitly, this goal suggests that the plan must target not only the individual, but also the people with whom the individual interacts during everyday activities. For an adult patient, the aural rehabilitation might include those people in the home, social/vocational settings, and the workplace. Figure 1–10 shows these communication realms as intersecting, because some communication partners may interact with the individual in both work and social environments. For a child, the plan might target the communication partners in the school system, social and extracurricular activities, and the home.

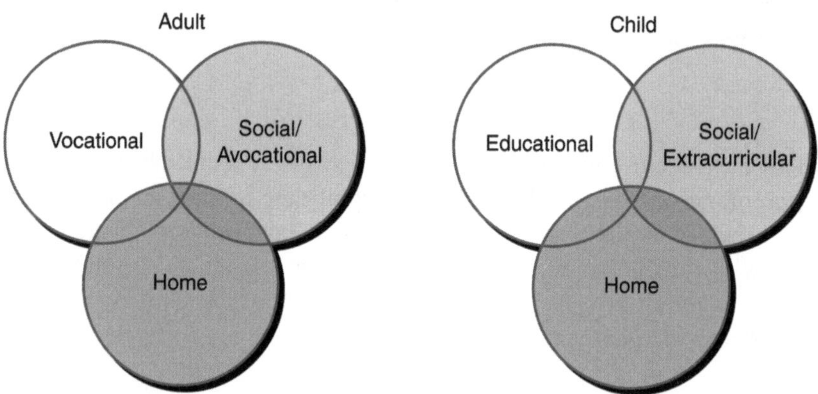

FIGURE 1–10 The aural rehabilitation plan and the individual's communication realms.

Communication partners of persons with hearing loss can learn effective communication techniques. For example, a husband may learn how to speak slowly and clearly so that his partner might better speechread him. A mother might develop techniques for stimulating conversation between herself and her daughter. In addition, communication partners sometimes need additional support from a speech and hearing professional. Parents may need personal adjustment counseling as they reconcile themselves to their baby's hearing loss. A woman may need to adjust to the changed hearing status of her partner who may have just received a cochlear implant.

COST-EFFECTIVENESS AND COSTS

Cost-effectiveness is the relationship between the money spent and the benefits accrued.

Cost-effectiveness relates to the relevance of aural rehabilitation, whereas the costs of providing services relate to the reality of providing services in an environment where health care expenses are spiraling, and services are being cut for economic reasons.

Aural rehabilitation can promote an individuals' quality of life and increase their conversational fluency in the home, workplace, and community. In the case of children, appropriate aural rehabilitation can promote success in school as well. For example, children who receive cochlear implants and then receive follow-up aural rehabilitation, particularly auditory speech stimulation, are more likely to develop language, speech, and literacy skills than those who do not receive follow-up support (e.g., Geers, Nicholas, & Seedy, 2003). Research shows that when counseling and follow-up programs are provided, adult patients are less likely to return their hearing aids to the audiologist than when they are not provided (Northern & Beyer, 1999) and that the benefits of an aural rehabilitation program justify the expense (Abrams, Chisolm, & McArdle, 2002).

A primary obstacle to providing aural rehabilitation relates to the short-term costs of providing services. Aural rehabilitation can be expensive for two reasons: (1) listening device technology is often costly and (2) providing services such as communication strategies training is labor intensive. Often such costs are not covered by insurance companies and must be borne by the individual.

In the United States, coverage policies can be classified as private (e.g., health maintenance organizations [HMOs]), state (e.g., Blue Cross and Blue Shield), federal (e.g., **Medicare**), or a combination of state and federal (e.g., **Medicaid**). Policies vary in the costs they cover. For example, private insurance plans are governed by the terms of the individual policy. Sometimes when insurance plans provide coverage for services following receipt of a listening device, they do so only when a speech-language pathologist rather than an audiologist provides the services. Medicaid permits flexibility to the states in implementing their programs, but typically, hearing aids are covered if they are deemed medically necessary for a patient and the patient qualifies for Medicaid. Some states offer low-cost loans, with hearing aids being one of the common devices purchased with the loan funds (Hager, 2007).

Medicare is a program under the United States Social Security Administration that reimburses hospitals and physicians for medical care they provide to qualified people who are 65 years or older.

Medicaid is a program in the United States authorized by Title XIX of the Social Security Act that is jointly funded by the federal government and state governments, which reimburses hospitals and physicians for providing health care to qualified people who cannot otherwise afford services.

EVIDENCE-BASED PRACTICE

In the following chapters, we will consider the services that may be included in an aural rehabilitation plan and how they might be customized for both adult and pediatric populations. To the extent possible, the focus will be on services that are based on an **evidence-based practice (EBP)** approach.

Evidence-based practice (EBP) is clinical decision making that is based on a review of the scientific evidence of benefits and costs of alternative forms of diagnosis or treatment, on clinical experience, and on patient values.

Many aural rehabilitation services that are routinely provided to patients, and the techniques for providing them, have been well researched and shown to work. Some, however, are supported more by tradition and expert opinion than by scientific evidence. Historically, there has been a paucity of well-controlled experiments for such reasons as the following:

- The heterogeneity of patient populations, which makes generalization of research results problematic and sometimes makes definitions of success patient specific; some therapies work for some patients but not for others.
- The role played by the skill of the clinician in determining outcome; as one clinician-researcher asked, "When we get good outcomes, is it the therapies or the therapists?" (Ratner, 2006, p. 206).
- The lack of agreement among researchers and clinicians about **outcome measures**; for example, a patient with significant bilateral hearing loss may never regain normal function in all situations and decisions will have to be made about how to gauge success.
- The tendency for journals not to publish non-significant results; journals publish what works as opposed to what does not work.
- Ethical concerns about data collection; for example, a researcher might not be able to justify assigning patients who might benefit from an intervention to a

An **outcome measure** indicates the amount or type of benefit experienced by either an individual or a group of individuals to a treatment or series of treatments, and/or indicates a response.

Using a Grand Rounds Format to Promote EBP

A grand rounds format is an educational methodology that has long been used to instruct physicians, residents, and medical students. This format can be adapted for the purpose of teaching faculty and students about EBP in aural rehabilitation. Here are tips for creating a grand rounds program:

- Schedule the grand rounds on a weekly basis, to last for one hour, typically early in the day before classes and clinics begin.
- Invite students and faculty alike to attend.
- Have a student present a case study at the onset of the grand rounds, along with a review of literature that is relevant to the case.
- Invite a faculty member to lead a question-and-comment session after the student presentation.
- Occasionally invite a visiting professor or a local audiologist to serve as a guest speaker.
- Enhance the diversity of cases that are presented via periodic teleconferences with other universities and clinics.

(Hall, 2018, p. 86)

control group for the sake of comparing their outcome to that of those assigned to an **experimental group**.

Nonetheless, in this age of managed care and accountability, increasingly the services included in an aural rehabilitation plan must be supported by empirical evidence. ASHA encourages that whenever possible, services be based on an EBP approach (ASHA, 2004a). EBP entails integrating the best research evidence with clinical expertise and patient values. In such an approach, you will judiciously integrate scientific evidence into your clinical decision making, along with your own clinical expertise and knowledge about the particular preferences, environment, needs, culture, and values of your patient (ASHA, 2004a) (Figure 1–11). Even though it is tempting to rely primarily on past clinical experience and the opinions of colleagues to guide clinical decision making, as many professionals do (Zipoli & Kennedy, 2012), services should not be provided just because "that is what we have always done" and "this is the way we have always done it." Rather, selection of services should also be driven by relevant and valid data obtained from clinically oriented studies.

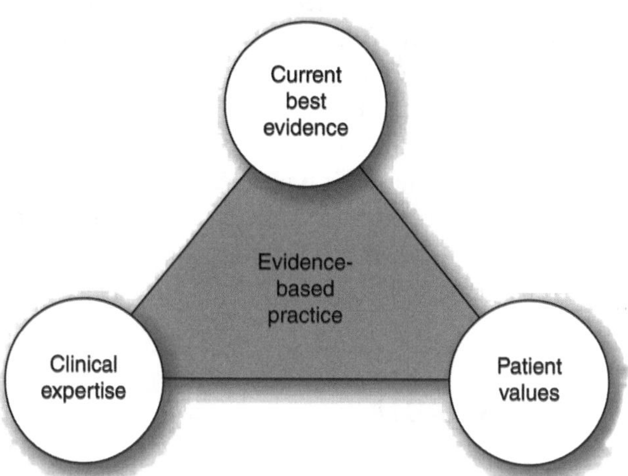

FIGURE 1–11 An evidence-based practice approach, which takes into account quality research evidence, clinical experience, and patient values and needs.

The most compelling evidence for selecting services, sometimes referred to as "Level 1" evidence, results from a meta-analysis of more than one randomized controlled trial. A **randomized controlled trial** entails comparing participants who have been **randomly assigned** to receive a test treatment to participants who receive no such treatment or a different test treatment (Figure 1–12). For example, if you were a clinical researcher, you might opt to compare the efficacy of a particular eight-week-long computer-based auditory training program and determine whether it improves the ability of new hearing aid recipients to recognize speech in the presence of background noise. You might include two groups in your experimental design, one group that receives training and one group that receives no training (the control group). In this example, the eight weeks of computer-based auditory training is the independent variable of the experiment and measures of participants' ability to recognize speech in the presence of noise are the dependent variables. An **independent variable** is the **variable** that is manipulated (e.g., provision of auditory training). The variable that is measured (e.g., speech recognition ability) is the **dependent variable** (Figure 1–13).

A **control group** is composed of research participants who closely resemble members of the experimental group but who do not receive the experimental treatment and thereby serve as a standard against which to detect and measure changes in the experimental group due to the treatment.

An **experimental group** is composed of research participants who receive the treatment under study.

In a **randomized controlled trial,** investigators randomly assign eligible people into treatment and control groups and then compare outcomes. The chance assignment reduces the likelihood that differences stem from pre-existing differences between the two groups.

Because it is unlikely that a single study will provide a definitive answer to a single scientific question, a **meta-analysis** of the existing studies, where results from several studies

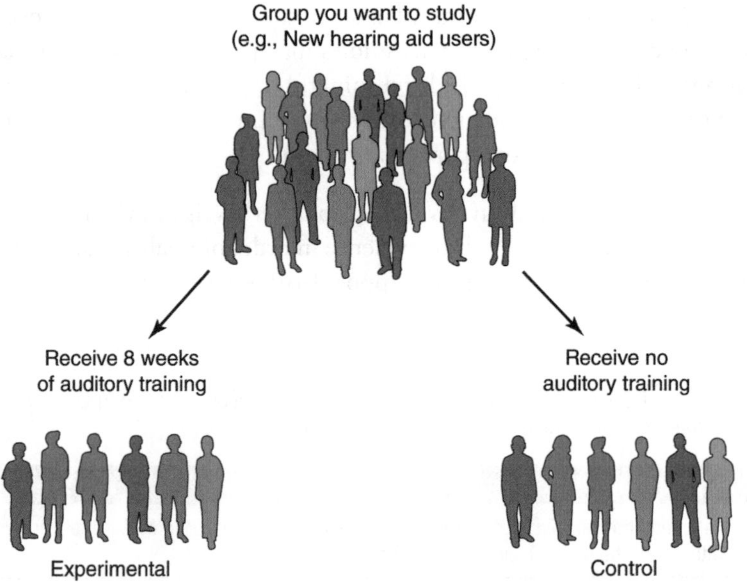

FIGURE 1–12 Random assignment. Each participant in the available population of new hearing aid users has an equal chance of being assigned to a level of the independent variable, which in this example, is either eight weeks of auditory training or 0 weeks of auditory training. The *available population* is called a "convenience sample" because it is a subgroup of a larger population and implies that these are participants who are available and willing to participate in the particular experiment.

Random assignment is a method of placing research participants into the conditions or treatments of an experiment in such a way that every participant has an equal chance of being assigned to any of the conditions or to any level of the independent variable.

The **independent variable** in an experiment is the variable that is manipulated by the experimenter in order to assess its consequences or impact on the dependent variable.

A **variable** is something that can vary and that research can measure.

The **dependent variable** in an experiment is the variable that is affected by the treatment or manipulation of the independent variable and can be measured.

A **meta-analysis** is a study of studies that combines the results of a set of studies on the same topic to reach a general conclusion.

1	2	3	4	5
Select an auditory training program	Make random assignment	Measure speech recognition	Assess and compare	Make conclusions
Independent variable	→ Control group → Experimental group	↘ ↗ Dependent variable	→ Control group's results versus those of the experimental group	→ Do the results support the treatment?

FIGURE 1–13 A randomized controlled experimental design for assessing the benefits of auditory training. The independent variable is eight weeks of auditory training. The dependent variable is participants' ability to recognize speech.

Meta-Analysis: The Gold Standard

Researchers who perform a meta-analysis summarize the results of many studies that have addressed the same topic. For example, in a now classic study, Sweetow and Palmer (2005) surveyed the literature to address the question, *Is there evidence of improvement in communication skills through individual auditory training in an adult hearing-impaired population?* The researchers identified a possible 213 articles in the literature that provide results pertinent to this question. Rather than simply counting up the number of positive and negative findings to derive an answer, they instead identified those studies that had adequate sample sizes, sufficient detail, and good methodological rigor and culled the number of studies to consider down to 6. They then looked at the size of each effect (i.e., whether a large gain in skills occurred, a small gain, or no gain) and concluded that in general, auditory training leads to enhanced skills.

are synthesized, provides the optimum basis for choosing treatment. Especially in an active field of research, where numerous studies may produce inconsistent results (e.g., whether or not auditory training yields meaningful improvement in speech recognition skill), a meta-analysis will provide guidance to the clinician about whether a particular intervention will be effective for a particular patient.

This kind of evidence is not always available, so other levels of evidence might have to suffice. Table 1–2 presents the levels of evidence in order of quality and credibility, from most optimal to least optimal, that can support EBP services.

TABLE 1–2 Levels of Evidence to Support EBP Treatment Interventions, Ranked in Order of Highest/Most Credible (Ia) to Lowest/Least Credible (IV) (Adapted from ASHA, 2004a, p. 2)

LEVEL	DESCRIPTION
Ia	*Systematic meta-analysis of more than one randomized controlled trial.* A meta-analysis is a synthesis of the major findings of a group of studies.
Ib	*Well-designed randomized controlled trials.* In a randomized controlled trial, participants are assigned randomly to either a treatment or a control group. One reason that a researcher may opt not to conduct a randomized trial pertains to the ethical issue of withholding treatment.
IIa	*Well-designed controlled trials without randomization.* These are less reliable than randomized trials because the participant groups might differ in unanticipated or unrecognized ways.
IIb	*Well-designed quasi-experimental studies, e.g., cohort studies.* A cohort study is one in which a group of patients exposed to a particular treatment is followed over time and is compared with an unexposed group. It is not as reliable as a randomized controlled trial because the two groups may differ in ways that are not readily apparent.
III	*Well-designed nonexperimental studies, e.g., correlational and case studies.* A correlation study determines the relationships (correlations) between variables but does not permit causal interpretations. A case study is an uncontrolled study of a single individual or a series of individuals for the purpose of observing the outcome of an intervention. Neither one includes a control group.
IV	*Expert committee report, consensus conference, and expert opinion.* A committee report might define required procedures and practices, based on scientific data and/or expert opinion. Consensus is an agreement among experts about an issue, whereas an expert opinion reflects the scholarly knowledge and clinical experience of recognized leaders in the field.

When engaging in EBP, many clinicians follow a five-step approach (adapted from Affiliate Representatives, 2003, p. 5, Figure 1–14):

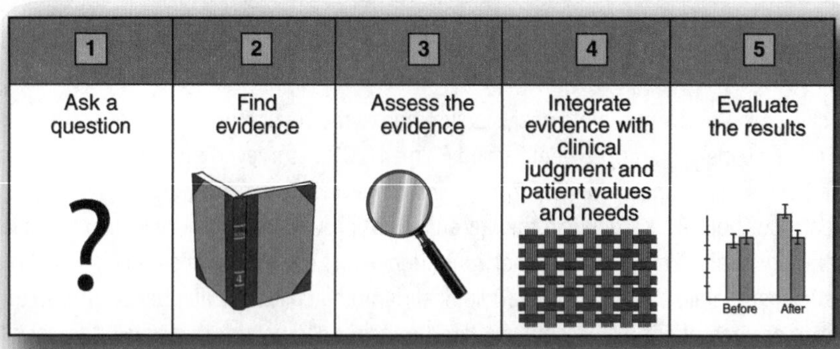

FIGURE 1–14 The five-step approach for engaging in EBP.

1. *Ask a straightforward question.* For example, in developing an aural rehabilitation plan for a business executive who is experiencing communication difficulties, you might pose the question: Does group communication strategies training, as compared with individual training, result in better adjustment to hearing loss? Your purpose is to determine whether you should recommend group communication strategies training for this patient, individualized training, or neither.
2. *Find the best evidence to answer the question.* You might consult a journal or textbook, conduct a database search with an electronic bibliographic database, search the internet, or engage in a citation search, where you determine if an article has been included in a review article bibliography (see Appendix 1–3 at the end of this chapter). You might also contact professional organizations such as ASHA or the AAA or government agencies such as the **National Institutes of Health (NIH)**'s agency, the **National Institute on Deafness and Other Communication Disorders (NIDCD)**, for information.
3. *Critically assess the evidence and decide if the results pertain to your patient.* You might consult with Table 1–2 and determine the level of evidence available for EBP and consider effect size, or the magnitude of benefit provided by a particular intervention, and consider whether this effect is of **clinical significance**. For example, a treatment might be shown to have a significant effect on a test group of patients, but the effect might be inconsequential to everyday communication or might not justify the time and effort entailed in providing the service.
4. *Integrate the evidence with your clinical judgment and the patient values and needs.* In considering the applicability and feasibility of an aural rehabilitation plan, you will talk to the patient and/or to the patient's family about possible options and weigh the potential benefits and disadvantages of each; for instance: Can the patient afford individualized communication strategies training and is there time in your workday to provide it?
5. *Evaluate the performance after having implemented your plan.* For this, you will choose measures to monitor progress and adjust your decisions if the desired outcomes are not being achieved.

The **National Institutes of Health (NIH)** is the medical research agency of the United States and has the mission of acquiring knowledge to help prevent, detect, and treat disease and disability.

The **National Institute on Deafness and Other Communication Disorders (NIDCD)** supports research activity concerning the normal and disordered processes of hearing, speech, language, balance, taste, and smell and about problems experienced by people with communication impairments.

Clinical significance relates to whether an experimental result has practical meaning to either the patient or the clinician.

A **case study** involves an in-depth examination of a patient, either because the patient is considered to be unusual or because the patient might be representative of a larger group, although that possibility can only be considered speculative.

What Exactly Is a Case Study?

A **case study** provides an in-depth description of an individual, sometimes because that individual is unusual and sometimes because that individual might possibly be representative of a population, although whether that is so can only be speculative. For example, a set of identical twins were once studied because one had incurred a profound hearing loss shortly after birth. The researchers were interested in studying the effects of hearing loss on language development, and in this situation, the two children were otherwise very comparable in terms of genetic makeup and home environment (variables that could affect language development), so the situation presented an ideal window of opportunity. In another example, a patient who received a cochlear implant was studied because she improved her speech recognition by listening to books-on-tape according to a predetermined schedule.

Although case studies provide information about an individual and might provide direction for future research, the results cannot be generalized. In the first example, it is not possible to conclude that other children will experience the same degree of language delay that was experienced by the twin because of significant hearing loss. Children vary in their language experiences, educational opportunities, sociability, and all manner of other variables, so the outcomes noted for one child cannot possibly be extrapolated to a population. In the second example, it is not possible to conclude that listening to books-on-tape will improve the speech recognition of new cochlear implant recipients. Patients may respond differently to this treatment, perhaps as a function of their entry level speech recognition abilities, their brand of cochlear implant, or their vocabulary and level of education.

Many professionals who provide aural rehabilitation bemoan the time that they have available to read the literature and cite limited time as a reason for not engaging in EBP. For example, in a survey of 1,000 audiologists and speech-language pathologists, 60 percent of audiologists and 75% of speech language pathologists indicated that they had insufficient time to engage in EBP. Sixty-two percent of the school-based respondents indicated that the cost of continuing education was a barrier to learning about and implementing evidence-based interventions (Schooling & Solomon, 2017).

The good news is that, increasingly, professional journals are providing web-based access to research abstracts, full-text articles, and tutorials. Professional organizations such as ASHA and AAA are packaging best practice evidence into user friendly formats such as position papers, clinical practice guidelines, and evidence maps. For example, ASHA's National Center for Evidence-Based Practice in Communication Disorders (N-CEP) launched a series of evidence maps, each of which is organized around the three lynchpins of EBP: scientific evidence, clinical expertise, and patient values and perspectives (https://www.asha.org/Evidence-Maps/). For a particular topic (e.g., hearing loss–children, hearing loss–adults), the N-CEP searches and then reviews the scientific literature and provides summaries of key findings and recommendations. The maps are organized by clinical topic and can be searched by typing in clinical questions or situations (Schooling & Solomon, 2018).

Selecting the components to include in an aural rehabilitation plan is not always a straightforward or easy proposition, and many variables will factor into the decision making process. These variables will include the needs and desires of the patient, the availability of services within an aural rehabilitation practice and the surrounding community, and the cost-effectiveness of providing a particular intervention or treatment. An EBP approach is a means to ensure that the services that are included in the plan will likely result in the desired and predicted outcomes.

CASE STUDY

Applying the WHO's International Classification of Functioning, Disability and Health

Hickson and Scarinci (2007, pp. 288–289) introduce their readers to Hugh, a 72-year-old man who rarely uses his hearing aids at home, despite pleas from his wife, Lorna, that doing so would enhance their conversational fluency significantly (and thereby reduce activity limitations, see Figure 1–1). Hugh believes that his hearing *isn't all that bad* and that *I hear well enough at home* (psychosocial factor). Thus, Lorna experiences a third-party disability, and in the home environment, experiences a greater communication activity limitation than does Hugh. Hugh rarely attends social gatherings because of his inability to recognize speech in noisy situations, resulting in participation restrictions for both himself and his wife. Lorna misses socializing with the couple's friends, but does not want to attend functions alone and leave Hugh to fend for himself on a Friday night. The couple discussed these ongoing communication activity limitations and participation restrictions with their audiologist, who recommended that they participate in a communication strategies training class. Hugh and Lorna took the class, where they met other couples who were experiencing similar communication activity limitations and participation restrictions. The couple appreciated their classmates' empathy and support, and with input from the audiologist who led the class, developed the following list of communication strategies to reduce both of their communication activity limitations and participation restrictions:

- Lorna will use repair strategies and clear speech to promote conversational fluency.
- Lorna will make sure that Hugh can see her face so he can read her lips as well as hear her voice.
- Lorna will gain Hugh's attention before beginning to speak, so he is aware that she is speaking.
- Hugh will wear his hearing aids more often in the home and when going out to social situations, which should lead to fewer participation restrictions for both Hugh and Lorna.

The happy ending is that Hugh now wears his hearing aid more often and their Friday nights are much more fun.

CASE STUDY

Evidence-Based Practice Decision Making

Cox (2005) describes a 75-year-old woman who lives alone on a fixed income. The woman has a bilateral, moderate, sensorineural hearing loss. She does not socialize often, but does visit her children for lunch every Sunday. She has difficulty in understanding their conversations around the dining table. Her daughter has accompanied her to today's audiology appointment. She is interested in purchasing one of the fancy "digital" hearing aids for her mother. Here are the steps that the audiologist pursues in practicing EBP:

Step 1: Generates the question. "Will an older woman with moderate bilateral presbycusis obtain better speech understanding in noise with digital processing hearing aids than with . . . analog devices . . . ?" (p. 422). Note that the key elements in this question are *the person* (i.e., an older woman with some social contacts), *the problem* (difficulty understanding conversation in social situations), *the proposed treatment* (digital hearing aids), a *comparison treatment* (analog hearing aids), and an *outcome measure* (how well the woman will recognize speech using a hearing aid in the presence of background noise).

Step 2: Finds the best available evidence. The audiologist conducts an Internet search of an online database. She enters into the search field the items: "hearing aid AND digital AND (analog OR analogue)" (p. 423). The database that she uses, PubMed (see Appendix 1–3), allows her to limit her search from 1995 to the present. The search yields 13 English-language articles. A quick reading of the articles' abstracts eliminates 5 as irrelevant to the question posed in Step 1.

Step 3: Evaluates the evidence. Beginning with the most recent article and working backward in time, the audiologist selects a subset of the remaining eight articles for a careful review. She assesses the strengths and weaknesses of the evidence.

Step 4: Makes a recommendation. The audiologist considers the similarities and differences between her patient and the participants included in the research studies that she has just read (their ages, health, gender, education, and so forth) to determine the extent to which the evidence applies to her patient. She synthesizes this information with her own clinical judgment and what she knows about her patient, and decides on an appropriate course of action. She shares her recommendation with the patient and her daughter. A hearing aid is ordered for the patient.

Step 5: Follows up. After the patient is fitted with her new hearing aid, the audiologist schedules a follow-up clinic visit in case the recommendation is not successful and needs to be modified.

FINAL REMARKS

A number of professional journals deal with aural rehabilitation. These journals are listed in Appendix 1–3 at the end of this chapter. They can provide additional and timely information about the topics covered in this text. They are also a source for EBP.

KEY CHAPTER POINTS

- The WHO uses the ICF for considering a health-related disability.
- Hearing loss may limit communication activity and impose participation restrictions on everyday activities.
- The impact of hearing loss on a patient may be mediated by environmental and personal factors—for example, a patient's use of listening aids, his or her physical environment, lifestyle and frequent communication partners, and individual characteristics such as personality.

- Aural rehabilitation for adults may include diagnosis and quantification of hearing loss, provision of appropriate listening devices, training in communication strategies, counseling related to hearing loss, vocational counseling, noise protection, and counseling and instruction for family members. It may or may not include auditory and speechreading training.
- Aural rehabilitation for children may include diagnostics, provision of appropriate amplification, auditory and speechreading training, communication-strategies training, family training, and intervention related to speech, language, and educational development.
- Aural rehabilitation may occur in a variety of locales, including schools, hospitals, university speech and hearing clinics, and audiology private practices.
- Aural rehabilitation may be provided by an audiologist, speech-language pathologist, or educator.
- Hearing loss may be categorized by degree, onset, causation, and time course.
- The aural rehabilitation plan includes the communication realms of the person who has hearing loss.
- Aural rehabilitation is relevant for at least two general reasons: demographics and cost-effectiveness.
- EBP approaches reflect best research evidence, clinical expertise, and patient values.
- Randomized controlled trials typically compare groups of individuals who have been randomly assigned to a treatment or to a control condition.
- When engaging in EBP, clinicians ask a question, find evidence to answer it, assess the evidence, integrate the evidence with their judgment and patient values, and then evaluate performance.

TERMS AND CONCEPTS TO REMEMBER

Conversational fluency
Hearing-related disability
World Health Organization (WHO)
International Classification of Functioning, Disability and Health (ICF)
Activity limitations
Participation restrictions
Environmental factors
Personal factors
Third-party disability
Frequent communication partner
Perceived quality of life
Unserved and underserved
Evidence-based practice (EBP)
Randomized controlled study
Levels of evidence
Evidence-based practice five-step approach
Clinical significance

Appendix 1–1

Basic Areas of Knowledge and Skills

Source: from ASHA, Supplement No. 22, April 16, 2002, pp. 90–92.

Audiologists who provide aural rehabilitation services demonstrate **basic knowledge** in the areas that are the underpinnings of communication sciences and disorders. These include the following:

Basic knowledge is demonstrated by the recall of specifics, universals, methods, and processes, or the recall of a pattern, structure, or setting (Bloom, Hastings, & Madaus, 1971, p. 271).

I. General Knowledge

- **A.** General psychology; human growth and development; psychosocial behavior; cultural and linguistic diversity; biological, physical, and social sciences; mathematics; and qualitative and quantitative research methodologies

II. Basic Communication Processes

- **A.** Anatomic and physiologic bases for the normal development and use of speech, language, and hearing (including anatomy, neurology, and physiology of speech, language, and hearing mechanisms)
- **B.** Physical bases and process of the production and perception of speech and hearing (including acoustics or physics of sound, phonology, physiologic and acoustic phonetics, sensory perceptual processes, and psychoacoustics)
- **C.** Linguistic and psycholinguistic variables related to the normal development and use of speech, language, and hearing (including linguistics [historical, descriptive, sociolinguistic, sign language, second-language usage], psychology of language, psycholinguistics, language and speech acquisition, verbal learning and verbal behavior, and gestural communication)
- **D.** Dynamics of interpersonal skills, communication effectiveness, and group theory

Special Areas of Knowledge and Skills

Audiologists who provide aural rehabilitation have **special knowledge** in the following areas and demonstrate the itemized requisite skills in those areas:

Special knowledge permits application, analysis, synthesis, and evaluation; an individual not only possesses knowledge but can apply and elaborate upon that knowledge (Bloom et al., 1971).

III. Auditory System Function and Disorders

- **A.** Identify, describe, and differentiate among disorders of auditory function (including disorders of the outer, middle, and inner ear; the vestibular system; the auditory nerve and the associated neural and central auditory system pathways and processes)

IV. Developmental Status, Cognition, and Sensory Perception

- **A.** Provide for the administration of assessment measures in the client's preferred mode of communication
- **B.** Verify adequate visual acuity for communication purposes
- **C.** Identify the need and provide for assessment of cognitive skills, sensory perceptual and motor skills, developmental delays, academic achievement, and literacy
- **D.** Determine the need for referral to other medical and nonmedical specialists for appropriate professional services
- **E.** Provide for ongoing assessments of developmental progress

V. Audiologic Assessment Procedures

- **A.** Conduct interview and obtain case history

- **B.** Perform otoscopic examinations and ensure that the external auditory canal is free of obstruction, including cerumen
- **C.** Conduct and interpret behavioral, physiologic, or electro-physiologic evaluations of the peripheral and central auditory systems
- **D.** Conduct and interpret assessments for auditory processing disorders
- **E.** Administer and interpret standardized self-report measures of communication difficulties and of psychosocial and behavioral adjustment to auditory dysfunction
- **F.** Identify the need for referral to medical and nonmedical specialists for appropriate professional services

VI. Speech and Language Assessment Procedures

- **A.** Identify the need for and perform screenings for effects of hearing impairment on speech and language
- **B.** Describe the effects of hearing impairment on the development of semantic, syntactic, pragmatic, and phonologic aspects of communication, in terms of both comprehension and production
- **C.** Provide for appropriate measures of speech and voice production
- **D.** Provide for appropriate measures of language comprehension and production skills and/or alternate communication skills (e.g., signing)
- **E.** Administer and interpret appropriate measures of communication skills in auditory, visual, auditory-visual, and tactile modalities

VII. Evaluation and Management of Devices and Technologies for Individuals with Hearing Impairment (i.e., hearing aids, cochlear implants, middle ear implants, implantable hearing aids, tinnitus maskers, hearing assistive technologies, and other sensory prosthetic devices)

- **A.** Perform and interpret measures of electroacoustic characteristics of devices and technologies
- **B.** Describe, perform, and interpret behavioral/psychophysical measures of performance with these devices and technologies
- **C.** Conduct appropriate fittings with and adjustments of these devices and technologies
- **D.** Monitor fitting of and adjustment to these devices and technologies to ensure comfort, safety, and device performance
- **E.** Perform routine visual, listening, and electroacoustic checks of clients' hearing devices and sensory aids to troubleshoot common causes of malfunction
- **F.** Evaluate and describe the effects of use of devices and technologies on communication and psychosocial functioning
- **G.** Plan and implement a program of orientation to these devices and technologies to ensure realistic expectations; to improve acceptance of, adjustment to, and benefit from these systems; and to enhance communication performance
- **H.** Conduct routine assessments of adjustment to and effective use of amplification devices to ensure optimal communication function
- **I.** Monitor outcomes to ensure professional accountability

VIII. Effects of Hearing Impairment on Functional Communication

- **A.** Identify the individual's situational expressive and receptive communication needs

- **B.** Evaluate the individual's expressive and receptive communication performance
- **C.** Identify environmental factors that affect the individual's situational communication needs and performance
- **D.** Identify the effects of interpersonal relations on communication function

IX. Effects of Hearing Impairment on Psychosocial, Educational, and Occupational Functioning

- **A.** Describe and evaluate the impact of hearing impairment on psychosocial development and psychosocial functioning
- **B.** Describe systems and methods of educational programming (e.g., mainstream, residential) and facilitate selection of appropriate educational options
- **C.** Describe and evaluate the effects of hearing impairment on occupational status and performance (e.g., communication, localization, safety)
- **D.** Identify the effects of hearing problems on marital dyads, family dynamics, and other interpersonal communication functioning
- **E.** Identify the need and provide the psychosocial, educational, family, and occupational/vocational counseling in relation to hearing impairment and subsequent communication difficulties
- **F.** Provide assessment of family members' perception of and reactions to communication difficulties

X. AR Case Management

- **A.** Use effective interpersonal communication in interviewing and interacting with individuals with hearing impairment and their families
- **B.** Describe client-centered, behavioral, cognitive, and integrative theories and methods of counseling and their relevance in AR
- **C.** Provide appropriate individual and group adjustment counseling related to hearing loss for individuals with hearing impairment and their families
- **D.** Provide auditory, visual, and auditory-visual communication training (e.g., speechreading, auditory training, listening skills) to enhance receptive communication
- **E.** Provide training in effective communication strategies to individuals with hearing impairment, family members, and other relevant individuals
- **F.** Provide for appropriate expressive communication training
- **G.** Provide appropriate technological and counseling intervention to facilitate adjustment to tinnitus
- **H.** Provide appropriate intervention for management of vestibular disorders
- **I.** Develop and implement an intervention plan based on the individual's situational/environmental communication needs and performance and related adjustment difficulties
- **J.** Develop and implement a system for measuring and monitoring outcomes and the appropriateness and efficacy of intervention

XI. Interdisciplinary Collaboration and Public Advocacy

- **A.** Collaborate effectively as part of multidisciplinary teams and communicate relevant information to allied professionals and other appropriate individuals
- **B.** Plan and implement in-service and public-information programs for allied professionals and other interested individuals

C. Plan and implement parent-education programs concerning the management of hearing impairment and subsequent communication difficulties

D. Advocate implementation of public law in educational, occupational, and public settings

E. Make appropriate referrals to consumer-based organizations

XII. Hearing Conservation/Acoustic Environments

A. Plan and implement programs for prevention of hearing impairment to promote identification and evaluation of individuals exposed to hazardous noise and periodic monitoring of communication performance and auditory abilities (e.g., speech recognition in noise, localization)

B. Identify need for and provide appropriate hearing protection devices and noise abatement procedures

C. Monitor the effects of environmental influences, amplification, and sources of trauma on residual auditory function

D. Measure and evaluate the environmental acoustic conditions and relate them to effects on communication performance and hearing protection

Appendix 1–2

Source: from ASHA, Supplement No. 22, April 16, 2002, pp. 90–92. Copyright © by the American Speech-Language-Hearing Association. Reprinted with permission.

Basic Areas of Knowledge and Skills

Speech-language pathologists who provide aural rehabilitation services demonstrate knowledge in the basic areas that are the underpinnings of communication sciences and disorders. These include the following:

I. General Knowledge

A. General psychology; human growth and development; psychosocial behavior; cultural and linguistic diversity; biological, physical, and social sciences; mathematics; and qualitative and quantitative research methodologies

II. Basic Communication Processes

A. Anatomic and physiologic bases for the normal development and use of speech, language, and hearing (including anatomy, neurology, and physiology of speech, language, and hearing mechanisms)

B. Physical bases and process of the production and perception of speech and hearing (including acoustics or physics of sound, phonology, physiologic and acoustic phonetics, sensory perceptual processes, and psychoacoustics)

C. Linguistic and psycholinguistic variables related to the normal development and use of speech, language, and hearing (including linguistics [historical, descriptive, sociolinguistic, sign language, second-language usage], psychology of language, psycholinguistics, language and speech acquisition, verbal learning and verbal behavior, and gestural communication)

D. Dynamics of interpersonal skills, communication effectiveness, and group theory

Special Areas of Knowledge and Skills

Speech-language pathologists who provide aural rehabilitation have special knowledge in the following areas and demonstrate the itemized requisite skills in those areas:

III. Auditory System Function and Disorders

- **A.** Identify, describe, and differentiate among disorders of auditory function (including disorders of the outer, middle, and inner ear; the vestibular system; the auditory nerve and the associated neural and central auditory system pathways and processes)

IV. Developmental Status, Cognition, and Sensory Perception

- **A.** Provide for the administration of assessment measures in the client's preferred mode of communication
- **B.** Verify adequate visual acuity for communication purposes
- **C.** Identify the need and provide for assessment of cognitive skills, sensory perceptual and motor skills, developmental delays, academic achievement, and literacy
- **D.** Determine the need for referral to other medical and nonmedical specialists for appropriate professional services
- **E.** Provide for ongoing assessments of developmental progress

V. Audiologic Assessment Procedures

- **A.** Conduct audiologic screening as appropriate for initial identification and/or referral purposes
- **B.** Describe type and degree of hearing loss from audiometric test results (including pure-tone thresholds, immittance testing, and speech audiometry)
- **C.** Refer to and consult with an audiologist for administration and interpretation of differential diagnostic procedures (including behavioral, physiological, and electrophysiological measures)

VI. Assessment of Communication Performance

- **A.** Provide for assessment measures in the client's preferred mode of communication
- **B.** Identify and perform screening examinations for speech, language, hearing, auditory processing disorders, and reading and academic achievement problems
- **C.** Identify and perform diagnostic evaluations for the comprehension and production of speech and language in oral, signed, written, or augmented form
- **D.** Provide diagnostic evaluations of speech perception in auditory, visual, auditory-visual, or tactile modalities
- **E.** Identify the effects of hearing loss on speech perception, communication performance, listening skills, speechreading, communication strategies, and personal adjustment
- **F.** Provide for clients' self-assessment of communication difficulties and adjustment of hearing loss
- **G.** Monitor developmental progress in relation to communication competence

VII. Devices and Technologies for Individuals with Hearing Loss (i.e., hearing aids, cochlear implants, middle ear implants, implantable hearing aids, hearing assistive technologies, and other sensory prosthetic devices)

- **A.** Describe candidacy criteria for amplification or sensory-prosthetic devices (e.g., hearing aids, cochlear implants)
- **B.** Monitor clients' prescribed use of personal and group amplification systems

C. Describe options and applications of sensory aids (e.g., assistive listening devices) and telephone/telecommunication devices

D. Identify the need and refer to an audiologist for evaluation and fitting of personal and group amplification systems and sensory aids

E. Implement a protocol, in consultation with an audiologist, to promote adjustment to amplification

F. Perform routine visual inspection and listening checks of clients' hearing devices and sensory aids to troubleshoot common causes of malfunctioning (e.g., dead or corroded batteries, obstruction or damage to visible parts of the system)

G. Refer on a regularly scheduled basis clients' personal and group amplification systems, other sensory aids, and assistive listening devices for comprehensive evaluations to ensure that instruments conform to audiologists' prescribed settings and manufacturers' specifications

H. Describe the effects of amplification on communication function

I. Describe and monitor the effects of environmental factors on communication function

VIII. Effects of Hearing Loss on Psychosocial, Educational, and Vocational Functioning

A. Describe the effects of hearing loss on psychosocial development

B. Describe the effects of hearing loss on learning and literacy

C. Describe systems and methods of educational programming (e.g., mainstream, residential) and facilitate selection of appropriate educational options

D. Identify the need for and availability of psychological, social, educational, and vocational counseling

E. Identify and appropriately plan for addressing affective issues confronting the person with hearing loss

F. Identify appropriate consumer organizations and parent support groups

IX. Intervention and Case Management

A. Develop and implement a rehabilitative intervention plan based on communication skills and needs of the individual and family or caregivers of the individual

B. Provide for communication and counseling intervention in the client's preferred mode of communication

C. Develop expressive and receptive competencies in the client's preferred mode of communication

D. Provide speech, language, and auditory intervention (including but not limited to voice quality and control, resonance, phonologic and phonetic processes, oral motor skills, articulation, pronunciation, prosody, syntax/morphology, semantics, pragmatics)

E. Facilitate appropriate multimodal forms of communication (e.g., auditory, visual, tactile, speechreading, spoken language, Cued Speech, simultaneous communication, total communication, communication technologies) for the client and family

F. Conduct interviews and interact effectively with individuals and their families

G. Develop and implement a system to measure and monitor outcomes and the efficacy of intervention

X. Interdisciplinary Collaboration and Public Advocacy

- **A.** Collaborate effectively as part of multidisciplinary teams and communicate relevant information to allied professionals and other appropriate individuals
- **B.** Plan and implement in-service and public-information programs for allied professionals and other interested individuals
- **C.** Plan and implement parent-education programs concerning the management of hearing impairment and subsequent communication difficulties
- **D.** Plan and implement interdisciplinary service programs with allied professionals
- **E.** Advocate implementation of public law in educational, occupational, and public settings
- **F.** Refer to consumer-based organizations

XI. Acoustic Environments

- **A.** Provide for appropriate environmental acoustic conditions for effective communication
- **B.** Describe the effects of environmental influences, amplification systems, and sources of trauma on residual auditory function
- **C.** Provide for periodic hearing screening for individuals exposed to hazardous noise

Appendix 1–3

Professional Journals That Might Be Consulted for Evidence-Based Practice

Source: from ASHA, Supplement No. 22, April 16, 2002, pp. 90–92. Copyright © by the American Speech-Language-Hearing Association. Reprinted with permission.

Advance for Audiologists

Advance for Speech-Language Pathologists and Audiologists

American Annals of the Deaf

American Journal of Audiology: A Journal of Clinical Practice

American Journal of Speech-Language Pathology: A Journal of Clinical Practice

ASHA (American Speech-Language Hearing Association)

Asian Pacific Journal of Speech, Language, and Hearing

Audiology and Neurotology

Deafness and Education

Ear and Hearing

Educational Audiology Review

Hearing Journal

Hearing Review

International Journal of Audiology (formerly *Audiology, British Journal of Audiology*, and *Scandinavian Audiology)*

International Tinnitus Journal

Journal of the Academy of Rehabilitative Audiology

Journal of the American Academy of Audiology

Journal of Child Language

Journal of Communication Disorders

Journal of Deaf Studies and Deaf Education
Journal of Educational Audiology
Journal of Speech, Language, and Hearing Research
Language and Speech
Language, Speech, and Hearing Services in the School
Noise and Health
Noise Regulation Report
Perspectives on Aural Rehabilitation and Its Instrumentation
Seminars in Hearing
Seminars in Speech and Language
Speech Communication
Tinnitus Today
Topics in Language Disorders
Trends in Amplification
Volta Review
Volta Voices

Electronic Databases That Might Be Consulted for Evidence-Based Practice

Medline, at http://www.nlm.nih.gov/, spotlights medical and health-related research (see also PubMed, www.pubmed.gov).

PsychINFO, at http://www.apa.org/pubs/databases/psycinfo/index.aspx, spotlights the psychological literature.

Educational Resource Information Center (ERIC), at http://www.eric.ed.gov/, spotlights educational research.

ASHA National Center for EBP in Communication Disorders, at https://www.asha.org/Evidence-Maps/

ComDisDome, at http://search.proquest.com/login?accountid=15159, lists dissertations and monographs that are peer-reviewed.

CINAHL, at http://www.ebscohost.com/academic/cinahl-plus-with-full-text/, lists trade journals.

PART 1

The Components of an Aural Rehabilitation Plan

CHAPTER 2

Assessing Hearing Acuity and Speech Recognition

OUTLINE

- Review of the Audiological Examination and the Audiogram
- Purpose of Speech Recognition Testing
- Patient Variables
- Stimuli Units
- Test Procedures
- Difficulties Associated with Speech Recognition Assessment
- Multicultural Issues
- Case Study: Reasons to Go with a Test-Battery Approach
- Final Remarks
- Key Chapter Points
- Terms and Concepts to Remember
- Key Resources

Speech recognition is the ability to perceive a spoken message and make decisions about its lexical composition using auditory and sometimes visual information.

Speech recognition testing is performed in order to determine how well an individual can recognize speech units.

A key element in promoting conversational fluency and reducing hearing-related disability is to optimize a patient's ability to recognize speech. The reason that conversational fluency is often degraded is that persons with hearing loss cannot recognize the spoken messages of their communication partners. **Speech recognition**, also called speech perception, refers to how well people use auditory and/or visual information to understand spoken messages. **Speech recognition testing** involves assessing how well someone can recognize speech units such as phonemes, words, and sentences. The first phase of most aural rehabilitation plans is to assess a patient's hearing acuity and assess how well the person can recognize speech. Depending upon a patient's hearing status and communication needs, he or she may then go on to receive a listening device such as a hearing aid or a cochlear implant and may engage in communication strategies training, auditory training, or speechreading training, or any combination of the three. To the extent that speech recognition performance can be optimized, there will be a concomitant enhancement of conversational fluency and a reduction of hearing-related disability.

The audiogram provides a general description of the magnitude of a patient's hearing loss. However, the audiogram does not adequately portray the communication difficulties an individual may experience or an individual's aural rehabilitation needs. Speech recognition measurement is an important element in assessing how hearing loss affects someone's life and communication interactions.

In this chapter, we will focus on four considerations underlying the assessment of speech recognition: purpose, patient variables, stimuli units, and test procedures (Figure 2–1). Before considering these topics, we will first review the audiogram and other components of the audiological examination. A later chapter, Chapter 12, will present a more in-depth consideration of testing infants and young children.

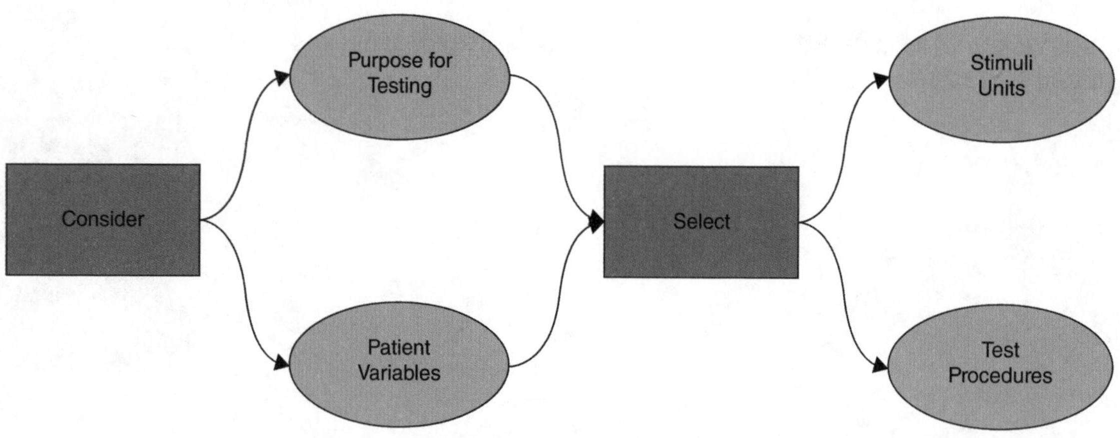

FIGURE 2–1 Four variables to consider when assessing speech recognition.

REVIEW OF THE AUDIOLOGICAL EXAMINATION AND THE AUDIOGRAM

A typical audiological assessment includes an audiogram, a determination of speech recognition threshold, and an assessment of speech recognition. Sometimes the examination might entail a determination of most comfortable loudness and uncomfortable loudness levels for speech as well. It is not unusual that a patient receives an audiogram after failing a hearing screening.

Hearing Screening

Many people experienced their first **hearing screening** in a school setting as children (Figure 2–2), and many adults who work in noisy settings, such as a baggage handler at an airport, routinely receive hearing screenings. The screening may be conducted by an audiologist or another health care professional such as a nurse. It typically occurs in the quietest room available. The purpose of a hearing screening test is to separate individuals into two groups: those who are likely and those who are unlikely to have a hearing loss. A hearing screening entails presenting a limited range of **pure tones** (usually 500–4000 Hz) at only one intensity level (usually 20 decibels hearing level [dB HL]). If an individual fails a hearing screening and is deemed a member of the group that is likely to have a hearing loss, that individual is referred for more in-depth audiological testing.

A **hearing screening** presents a rapid and truncated audiological assessment to a large group of individuals with the goal of identifying those who require additional diagnostic procedures.

A **pure tone** has only one frequency of vibration.

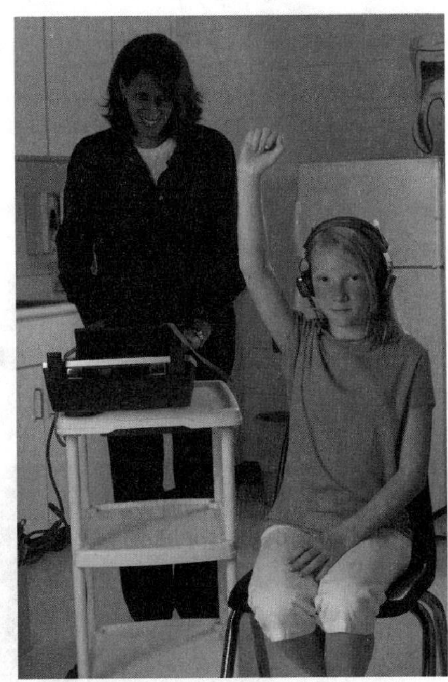

© Brian Eichhorn | Shutterstock.com

FIGURE 2–2 Hearing screenings. Most people undergo their first hearing screening in a school setting as children. Adults who work in a noisy environment, such as a factory or on an airport tarmac, often undergo a hearing screening on an annual basis.

Simple questions that might be asked during a screening procedure:

- Can you hear on the telephone?
- Do people tell you that you set the TV volume too high?
- Do you often ask people to repeat?
- Do you have problems listening in a noisy room?
- Do people seem to mumble?
- Are women and children especially difficult to hear?

Pure-Tone Audiometry

The audiogram provides a quantitative assessment of an individual's ability to detect sounds. An audiologist typically performs the test, with the use of an **audiometer** (Figure 2–3). The audiometer presents tones and the individual indicates when he or she hears them. The goal is to determine the softest sound level at which the tones can be detected, or the threshold of audibility. A **threshold** is the level of sound so faint that it can be detected only 50% of the time. Hearing threshold levels are typically assessed across a range of **octave** frequencies from 250 to 8000 Hz.

An **audiometer** is an instrument for measuring hearing sensitivity for a range of frequencies.

The level at which sound can be detected only 50% of the time is called a **threshold.**

An **octave** is the interval between two frequencies having a 2 to 1 ratio.

Impetus for Inventing the Audiometer

"I can't bear to hear that even my friends should think that I stumbled upon an invention and that there is no more good in me."

—Alexander Graham Bell, whose first invention was the telephone, writing about why he continued to develop and promote new inventions, including the audiometer

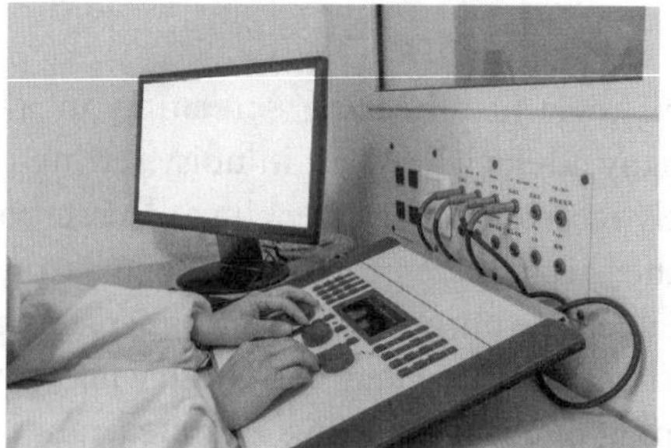

© xiao yu | Shutterstock.com

© Doro Guzenda | Shutterstock.com

FIGURE 2–3 An audiometer and air conduction testing. An audiologist presents tones with an audiometer (upper panel) to a patient who is wearing headphones (lower panel). The patient indicates that he has heard a tone by depressing a response switch.

Mr. Bell's Other Invention

Alexander Graham Bell (Figure 2–4), who was married to a woman with significant hearing loss, invented the first audiometer in 1879. It consisted of a pair of induction coils and a telephone receiver. Calibrated frequencies of calibrated intensity could be generated to measure the hearing abilities of individuals. Bell's audiometer revealed "unsuspected vestiges of hearing in many previously classed as totally deaf. Once recognized, even a slight hearing capacity was useful in developing articulation and speechreading. The device also detected hearing impairment in many public school children whose handicap had been taken for stupidity or inattention. In exhibiting his audiometer to the National Academy of Sciences in 1885, Bell reported that of seven hundred pupils whom he and an assistant had tested with it, more than ten percent had some hearing impairment" (Bruce, 1973, p. 394).

© Georgios Kollidas | Dreamstime.com

FIGURE 2–4 Alexander Graham Bell. The first transmission of voice sounds occurred on June 3, 1875. Alexander Graham Bell spoke to his assistant, Thomas Watson, via a diaphragm made of stretched animal membrane.

The tones may be presented by **air conduction**, either through **insert earphones**, supra-aural earphones, or sound field, or by **bone conduction**, through a bone conduction oscillator placed against the skull, either on each mastoid process or the forehead. Air conduction test results indicate hearing losses that might be either conductive (involving the outer or middle ear) or sensorineural (involving the inner ear, eighth nerve) in nature. Bone conduction test results reflect only the sensorineural component. By comparing the air and bone conduction results, the audiologist can determine whether there is hearing loss stemming from a problem in either the outer or the middle ear. The difference between the two sets of thresholds is termed the **air-bone gap**.

Audiological thresholds are plotted on an audiogram, where the y-axis indicates **sound level** (loudness) and the x-axis indicates **frequency** (pitch). As shown in Figure 2–5, an X on the audiogram represents the left-ear and an O represents the right-ear thresholds when the test signals are presented via air conduction. A less-than sign (<) indicates an unmasked bone conduction threshold for the right ear and a left bracket ([) indicates a masked bone conduction threshold. A greater-than sign (>) indicates an unmasked bone conduction threshold for the left ear and a right bracket (]) indicates a masked bone conduction threshold. The capital letter *A* denotes an aided threshold or how the patient hears when wearing a hearing aid. An *R* subscript below the *A* is used to refer to testing with the right hearing aid worn and an *L* subscript is used to refer to testing with the left hearing aid worn. The capital letter *C* denotes a threshold when the patient is wearing a cochlear implant. In this figure, the patient's audiogram indicates that the threshold for 250 Hz is 10 dB HL in the right ear and 55 dB HL in the left ear. As noted in Chapter 1, the pure-tone average (PTA) is often used to denote degree of hearing loss. Table 2–1 indicates the relationship between degree of hearing loss and speech recognition, as a function of the descriptors *mild, mild-to-moderate, moderate, severe,* and *profound.*

Another class of descriptors often assigned to a patient's audiogram is the configuration of the hearing loss. Four common configurations of hearing loss appear in Figures 2–6, 2–7, 2–8, and 2–9, which illustrate a flat configuration of hearing loss, a high-frequency

Air conduction refers to when sound travels through the air into the external auditory canal and stimulation progresses through the middle ear, inner ear, and to the brain.

An **insert earphone** is an earphone whose receiver is attached to a tube that leads to an expandable cuff. It can be inserted into the external auditory canal.

Bone conduction refers to the transmission of sound through the bones in the body, particularly the skull.

An **air–bone gap** is the difference between air and bone conduction thresholds; a difference may indicate a conductive component in the hearing loss.

Sound level is the intensity of sound expressed in decibels.

Frequency is the number of regularly repeated events in a given unit of time; usually measured in cycles per second and expressed in Hertz (Hz).

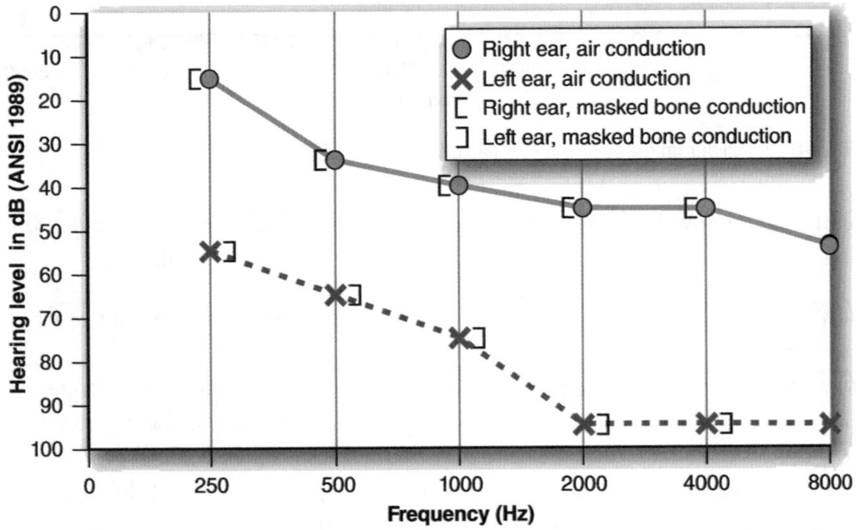

FIGURE 2–5 An audiogram for someone who has a PTA of 40 dB HL in the right ear (a mild hearing loss) and 73 dB HL in the left ear (a severe hearing loss).

TABLE 2–1 How Degree of Hearing Loss Affects Speech Recognition (Flexer, 1999)

HEARING LOSS	EFFECT ON WORD RECOGNITION
Mild (PTA = 26–40 dB HL)	In quiet situations, speech recognition will be fairly unaffected. In the presence of noise, speech recognition may decrease to 50% words correct if the PTA is 40 dB HL. Consonants are most likely to be missed, especially if the hearing loss involves primarily the high frequencies.
Mild-to-Moderate (PTA = 41–55 dB HL)	The patient will understand much of the speech signal if it is presented in a quiet environment face-to-face, and if the topic of conversation is known and the vocabulary is constrained. If a hearing aid is not used, the individual may miss up to 50–75% of a spoken message if the PTA is 40 dB HL and 80–100% if the PTA is 50 dB HL.
Moderate (PTA = 56–70 dB HL)	If the patient does not use a hearing aid, he or she may miss most or all of the message, even if talking face-to-face. He or she will have great difficulty conversing in group situations.
Severe (PTA = 71–90 dB HL)	The patient may not even hear voices, unless speech is loud. Without amplification, the individual probably will not recognize any speech in an audition-only condition. With amplification, he or she may recognize some speech and detect environmental sounds.
Profound (PTA = 90 dB HL or greater)	The patient may perceive sound as vibrations. An individual will rely on vision as the primary sense for speech recognition. He or she may not be able to detect the presence of even loud sound without amplification.

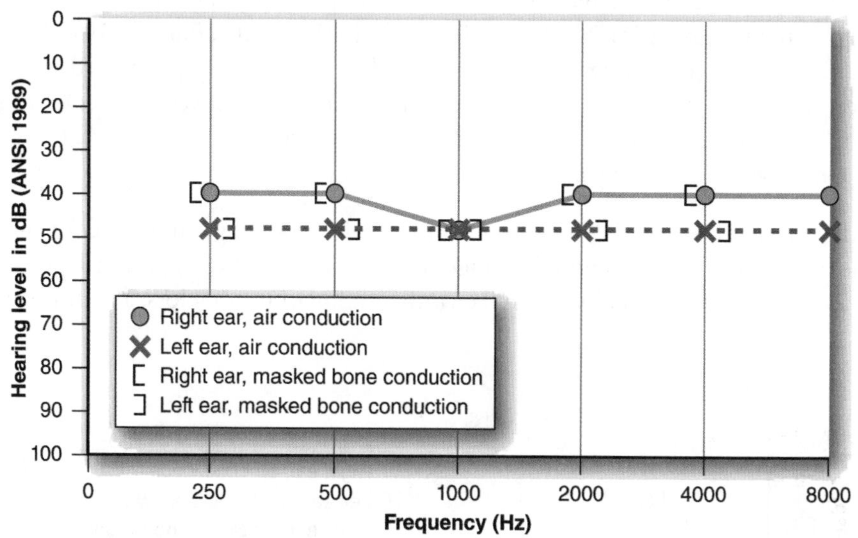

FIGURE 2–6 An audiogram for someone who has a flat configuration of hearing loss.

configuration, a low-frequency configuration, and a saucer-shaped configuration of hearing loss, respectively. These configurations may be defined as follows:

- *Flat*: Thresholds are within a 20-dB range of each other across the span of frequencies tested.
- *High-frequency*: Thresholds are within normal range for the low and mid-frequencies, but decline for the higher frequencies. A high-frequency loss may be described as *precipitous* if the loss at each of the higher frequencies is at least 20 dB greater with each ascending frequency. It may be described as *sloping* if thresholds for the higher frequencies are 20 dB or poorer than for the lower frequencies.
- *Low-frequency*: Thresholds are lowered for the low frequencies but are within normal range for the mid-frequencies and higher frequencies.
- *Saucer-shaped*: The loss is confined to the mid-frequencies.

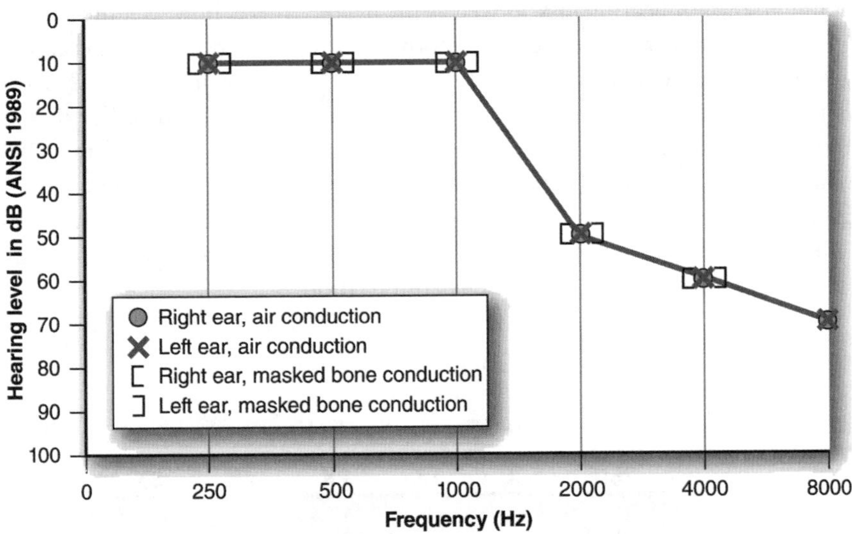

FIGURE 2–7 An audiogram for someone who has a high-frequency configuration of hearing loss.

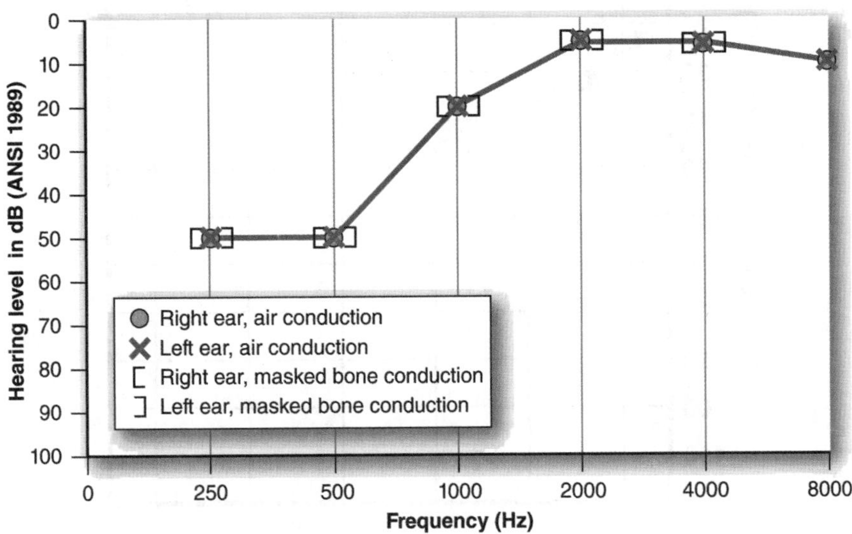

FIGURE 2–8 An audiogram for someone who has a low-frequency configuration of hearing loss.

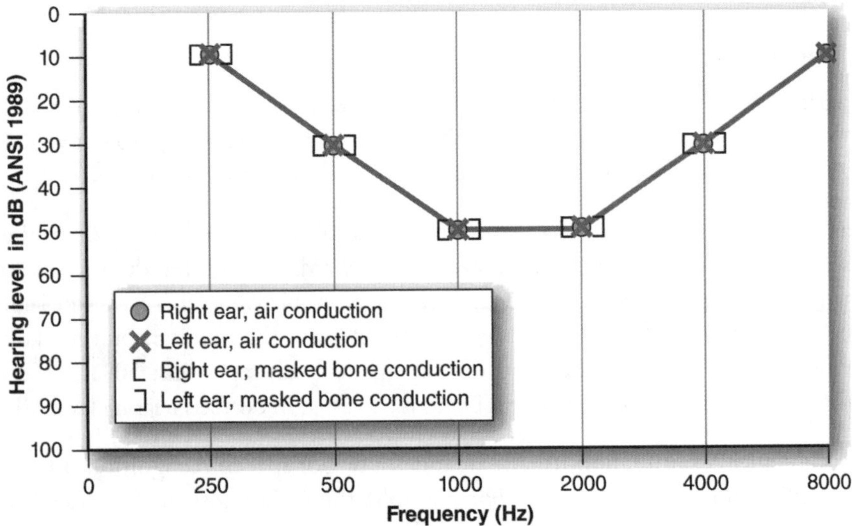

FIGURE 2–9 An audiogram for someone who has a saucer-shaped configuration of hearing loss.

The configuration of hearing loss, as well as the degree, affects how well the patient may recognize speech. Most of the acoustic information that contributes to speech recognition lies within the frequency band of 250 to 6000 Hz, as shown in Figure 2–10, which shows the approximate intensity and frequency of the speech sounds. For this reason, someone who has a low-frequency audiogram configuration (Figure 2–8) may likely receive more speech information and hence recognize more speech than someone who has a high-frequency configuration (Figure 2–7), even if they have similar PTAs. The person with the latter audiogram will likely not hear such high-frequency consonant sounds as [s, ʃ, t, p, k, f] while listening to everyday conversation.

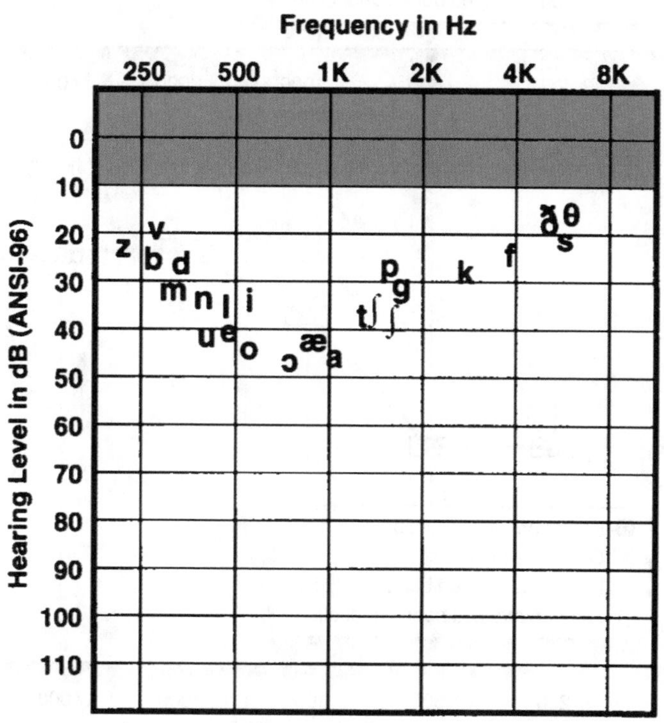

FIGURE 2–10 Generalized phonetic representations of speech sounds occurring at normal conversational levels plotted on an audiogram.

Speech Audiometry

The audiological examination usually includes speech testing in addition to the audiogram. Results will indicate how hearing loss affects a patient's ability to detect and recognize speech and the level of sound necessary for comfortable listening.

Speech reception threshold (SRT) is the lowest presentation level for spondee words at which 50% can be identified correctly.

A **spondee** is a two-syllable word spoken with equal stress on each syllable.

When determining the **speech reception threshold (SRT)**, the audiologist determines the softest level at which a patient can understand simple words. In one procedure, an audiologist might ask the patient to repeat **spondees**. These are bisyllabic words that have equal stress on both words, such as *baseball, ice cream, hotdog,* and *sidewalk.* The words are presented through the audiometer, and the level is varied until the patient can repeat just 50% of the words correctly. This level is recorded as the SRT, and is expressed in decibels hearing level (dB HL).

A **word recognition score (WRS)** refers to the percentage of monosyllabic words presented at a comfortable listening level that can be correctly repeated.

The audiological examination usually includes a test of speech recognition, in addition to the audiogram and SRT testing. For example, the audiologist might present monosyllabic words at a comfortable listening level and expect the patient to repeat each word in order to obtain a **word recognition score (WRS)**. Many audiologists present a list of

50 **phonetically balanced (PB)** words, which is a list that contains all the phonemes of English in approximately the same proportion as occurs in connected discourse. WRS is recorded in terms of percent words repeated verbatim.

A **phonetically balanced (PB)** word list presents a set of words that contain the speech sounds with the same frequency in which they occur in everyday conversations.

Sometimes the audiologist might want to determine the hearing level at which speech is most comfortable to listen to and the level at which it becomes too loud. The **most comfortable loudness level (MCL)** typically is determined by asking the patient to listen to running speech. The initial presentation level may be just above the level of the SRT, and then it is gradually increased. The patient indicates when it is at a comfortable level, when it is too soft, and when it is too loud. The **uncomfortable loudness level (UCL)**, sometimes called the *threshold of discomfort*, is the threshold level at which the speech changes from being comfortably loud to being uncomfortably loud. Sometimes patients will refer to a scale like that shown in Figure 2–11 to indicate MCL and UCL. A **dynamic range** for speech may be computed by subtracting the decibel value of the patient's SRT

Most comfortable loudness level (MCL) is the intensity level at which sound is most comfortable for a listener, usually expressed in dB HL.

The **uncomfortable loudness level (UCL)** is the level at which sound becomes uncomfortably loud for a listener.

A **dynamic range** is the difference in decibels between a person's threshold for just being able to detect speech and the person's threshold for uncomfortable listening.

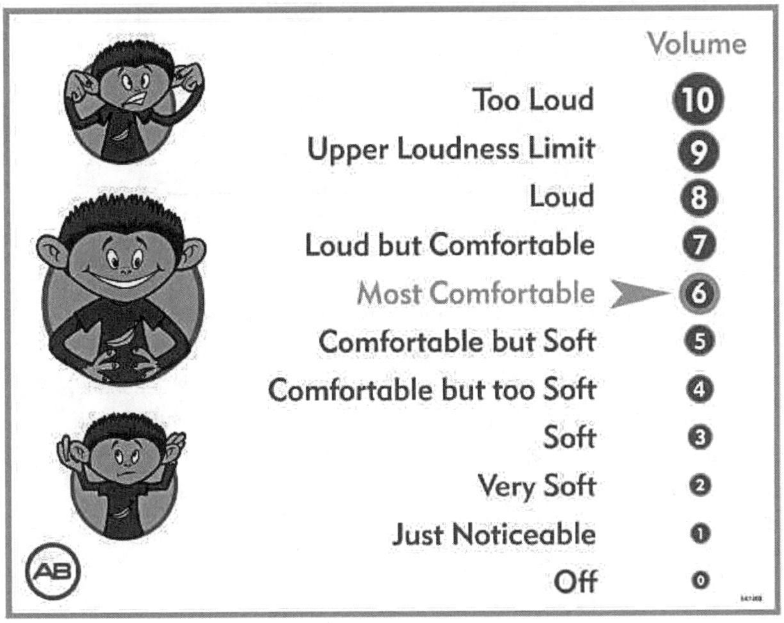

FIGURE 2–11 Measuring most comfortable loudness level (MCL) and uncomfortable loudness level (UCL). A diagram such as this presents a visual representation of MCL and UCL.

Sound Field Testing

Often, tests of speech recognition are presented in sound field as opposed to under headphones. If a patient typically wears a hearing aid, he or she often wears the aid for testing. When recording the results of sound field testing on the audiogram, the audiologist will usually indicate the **loudspeaker azimuth** (Figure 2–12). This is the direction of the **loudspeaker** in relation to the patient, measured in angular degrees in the horizontal place. If the loudspeaker is located directly in front of the patient, then the azimuth is 0 degree. If it is located directly behind the patient, the azimuth is 180 degrees. Sound field measures are typically indicated with the letter *S* on the audiogram. Newby and Popelka (1992) discussed the reasons for sound field testing:

(continues)

Loudspeaker azimuth is the position of the loudspeaker relative to the listener, measured in angular degrees in the horizontal plane.

A **loudspeaker** converts electrical energy into sound.

Sound Field Testing *(continued)*

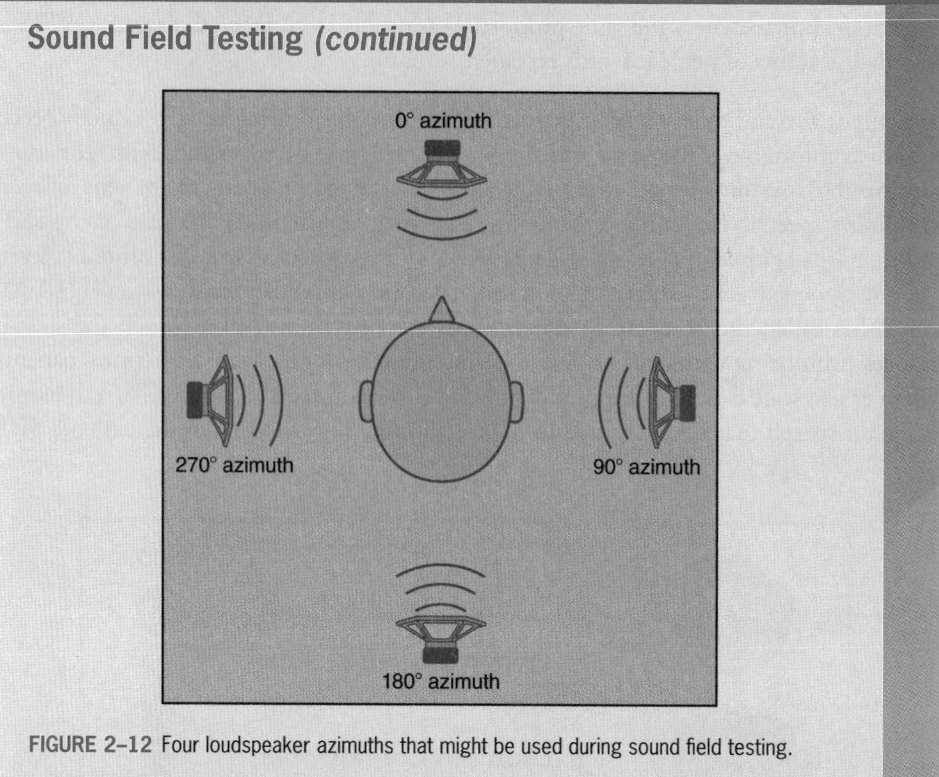

FIGURE 2–12 Four loudspeaker azimuths that might be used during sound field testing.

Sound field testing determines hearing sensitivity or speech recognition ability by presenting signals in a sound field through a loudspeaker.

Testing with a loudspeaker is referred to as **sound field testing** because the sound is not confined, as it is in an earphone, but is circulated in a field about the patient's head. Unless we are talking over the telephone, or for some reason listening through earphones, all our listening throughout the day is of the sound field type. To judge how the patient hears in a typical sound field listening situation is the main reason that we give speech tests through a loudspeaker. (pp. 182–183)

from the decibel value of the patient's UCL. The dynamic range will often influence the selection and programming of an individual's listening device and sometimes the design of the patient's auditory training program.

Test Environment

Dead-air spaces are unventilated air spaces.

Ideally, audiological testing occurs in a sound-isolated chamber so as to obtain the patient's best performance (Figure 2–13). A sound-isolated chamber is acoustically isolated from the rest of the building through the use of mass (e.g., concrete), insulation (e.g., fiberglass), **dead-air spaces**, and doors with tight acoustic seals. Sometimes the ideal test environment is unavailable, especially when conducting on-site assessments in industry or in a school. On these occasions, testing might occur in the quietest room available, using specially designed earphone enclosures or by inserting earphones. A description of the less-than-ideal environment should be included in the audiogram comments section so that the test results might be interpreted accordingly. Sometimes an audiologist opts not to test at 250 Hz, as ambient room noise (such as a refrigerator, see Figure 2–2) may mask presentation of this tone. If background noise is a problem, the audiologist may assume that elevated thresholds that do not exceed 30 dB HL may not be indicative of reduced hearing sensitivity, but rather, of the noisy test conditions.

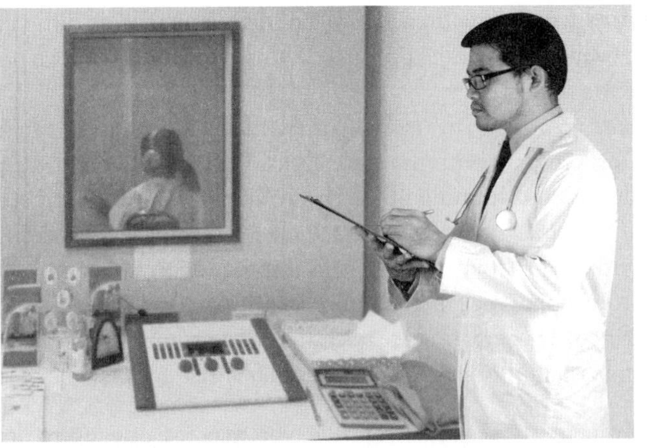

FIGURE 2–13 A patient seated in a sound-isolated chamber for audiological testing.

PURPOSE OF SPEECH RECOGNITION TESTING

When designing an aural rehabilitation plan for a particular patient, you will almost always want more information about the patient's speech recognition skills than that provided by a traditional audiological examination. There are many ways to use the results of an in-depth assessment. These include the following:

- *To determine need for amplification.* If a patient demonstrates reduced speech recognition, then amplification might be considered.
- *To compare performance with a listening aid to performance without an aid and to build patient confidence.* This comparison can be accomplished by measuring speech recognition with and without the device. Sharing the results might motivate a patient to wear a hearing aid and might enhance the individual's confidence for everyday listening tasks.
- *To compare different listening devices.* A patient might be tested with one listening device and then another to determine the device that affords the best performance. This testing is feasible when two or three devices are being compared, but becomes problematic when many devices are under consideration. In recent practice, speech recognition testing has been used less frequently for the purpose of selecting listening devices than in former times.
- *To demonstrate to patients that their ability to recognize speech is diminished.* Especially during counseling, information gained from speech testing can illustrate how speech understanding is impaired relative to persons who have normal hearing.
- *To obtain information that might elucidate environmental listening issues.* By performing speech testing in the presence of background noise, and comparing the results to performance in quiet, an audiologist can gain information that can be used to counsel patients about their particular listening difficulties. For example, background noise may be more problematic for certain people, such as older persons, than for others.
- *To assess performance longitudinally.* There may be instances where a speech and hearing professional may want to monitor speech recognition over time and answer questions such as, "Is the patient's hearing deteriorating because of use of a listening device?" or "Has speech recognition changed as a result of auditory training?" Care must be taken that measurements are not affected by the learning of test materials with repeated administration.

- *To determine need for auditory training.* If a patient experiences difficulty in recognizing speech, even when using appropriate amplification, then the patient may be a candidate for training.
- *To determine placement within a training curriculum.* Not everyone begins an auditory training program with the same tasks. Patients will enter training with different skill levels, and training objectives will need to be selected accordingly.
- *To determine if expected benefit has been achieved.* One goal of providing a listening aid or providing auditory training is to improve speech recognition. A speech and hearing professional may assess whether individuals obtained expected benefit by comparing their performance with that of a group of persons who have a similar hearing loss or who have received similar interventions.

The purpose may dictate the test. For example, you may use one test to determine placement in an auditory training curriculum and another test for assessing benefit from a hearing aid.

PATIENT VARIABLES

In selecting appropriate test materials for assessing word recognition, it is important to consider variables such as cognitive/linguistic level and hearing ability, for these will affect how someone performs on a particular test. A consideration of patient variables will help you choose between test stimuli, response format, testing conditions, and whether to use live or recorded stimuli.

The patient must have the cognitive skills to take the test. For example, it would be inappropriate to expect an elderly patient with dementia to repeat a seven-word sentence. The degree of hearing loss and experience with a listening device will affect test selection. For example, if a patient just received a cochlear implant, it may be inappropriate to administer a monosyllabic word test in an audition-only condition with background noise, because the individual likely will exhibit a "floor" performance.

Communication mode is the means used by a sender to share information with a receiver and may include speech, sign writing, hand gestures, or any other system of shared symbols.

Sometimes there will be a need to consider **communication mode** and other disabilities. For example, if a patient uses sign language, the test instructions should be presented with sign, and provisions for recording the patient's responses must be made (i.e., if the patient signs responses, then someone must interpret them). If a patient has decreased speech intelligibility as well as a hearing loss, and is not a young child, you might ask the patient to write down what he or she hears.

STIMULI UNITS

Once the purpose for testing has been identified and patient variables have been considered, test selection can be made. Test stimuli that are used typically to assess speech recognition are summarized in Table 2–2 and shown in Figure 2–14. Examples of tests that correspond with each type are also listed. Each kind of stimulus presents both advantages and disadvantages.

Phonemes and Phoneme Contrasts

A **phoneme** is the smallest class of speech sounds in a language.

Nonsense syllables are syllables of speech that have no meaning.

Phoneme testing permits phonetic errors to be examined. The items may be designed to assess consonant or vowel recognition. Although often referred to as phoneme testing, technically, these stimuli are **nonsense syllables**.

TABLE 2–2 Examples of Word Recognition Tests That Use Phoneme, Word, and Sentence Stimuli for Children and Adults (these tests typically are administered in an audition-only condition)

TEST	AUTHOR(S)	STIMULUS TYPE	STIMULUS UNITS	RESPONSE FORMAT
Speech Pattern Contrast Test (SPAC)	Boothroyd (1984)	Phoneme (also includes test of suprasegmental contrasts, such as word stress)	Words and phrases	Closed set
Iowa Consonant Confusion Test	Tyler et al. (1986)	Phoneme	Nonsense bisyllables, including *eemee, eesee, eedee, eebee*	Closed set (13-choice)
Iowa Vowel Confusion Test	Tyler et al. (1986)	Phoneme	Monosyllables with an [hVd] format, including *heed, who'd, had, head*	Closed set (9-choice)
Nonsense Syllable Test (NST)	Edgerton and Danhauer (1979)	Phoneme	Nonsense bisyllables	Open set
Consonant-Nucleus-Consonant (CNC) Words	Peterson and Lehiste (1962)	Word	Lists of 50 phonemically balanced words, each containing a consonant, vowel or diphthong, consonant	Open set
Northwestern University Auditory Test No. 6 (NU-6)	Tillman and Carhart (1966)	Word	Monosyllabic words	Open set
Central Institute for the Deaf (CID) Auditory Test W-22	Hirsh et al. (1952)	Word	Phonetically balanced monosyllabic word lists	Open set
Words in Noise (WIN) Test	Wilson, Carnell, and Clehorn (2007)	Word	Monosyllabic words are presented in seven signal-to-noise ratios of multi-talker babble	Open set
Central Institute for the Deaf (CID) Everyday Speech Sentences	Davis and Silverman (1978)	Sentence	Sentences that vary in length and structure	Open set
AzBio Sentences	Spahr et al. (2012)	Sentence	Fifteen sentence lists that have an equivalent level of difficulty	Open set
Revised Speech Perception in Noise (SPIN)	Bilger, Nuetzel, Rabinowitz, and Rzeczkowski (1984)	Sentence	Sentences that have either high context for the last word in the sentence or low context	Open set, presented with a background of speech babble
CUNY Sentences	Boothroyd, Hanin, and Hnath-Chisholm (1985)	Sentence	Unrelated sentences	Open set
Hearing in Noise Test (HINT)	Nilsson, Soli, and Sullivan (1994)	Sentence	Unrelated sentences delivered in groups of 10	Open set, presented with a background of speech-shaped noise (scored by the signal-to-noise ratio at which 50% of the sentences are repeated correctly)
The Connected Speech Test (CST)	Cox, Alexander, and Gilmore (1987)	Sentence	Sets of 10 related sentences pertaining to familiar topics	Open set
The Synthetic Sentence Test (SSI)	Jerger, Speaks, and Trammell (1968); Speaks and Jerger (1965)	Sentence	Synthetic sentences with minimal contextual cues and minimal redundancy	Closed set
Quick Speech in Noise Test (QuickSIN)	Etymotic Research (2001)	Sentence	Sets of six unrelated sentences	Open set, presented with a background of four-talker babble that varies in 5-dB steps, starting at +25 SNR

(continues)

TABLE 2–2 *(continued)*

TEST	AUTHOR(S)	STIMULUS TYPE	STIMULUS UNITS	RESPONSE FORMAT
Speech Sound Pattern Discrimination (SSPDT)	Bochner, Garrison, Palmer, MacKenzie, and Braveman (1997)	Sentence	Sets of three sentences, one standard and two comparison (e.g., *Free books are available* is a standard, *Three books are available* is a comparison)	Closed set, requiring a same or different judgment
Speech in Noise (SIN)	Killion and Vilchur (1993)	Sentence	Sentences	Open set, presented with varying levels of four-talker babble

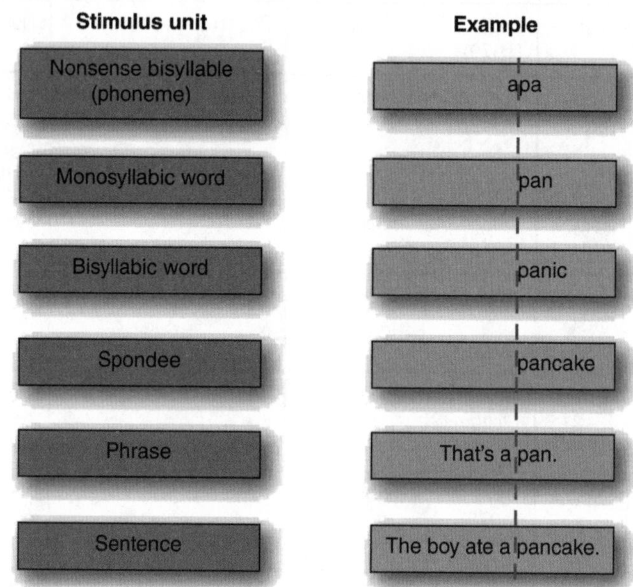

FIGURE 2–14 Stimuli units that might be used for speech recognition testing.

Speech features are categorical properties of phonemes; a phoneme can be described as a bundle of speech features.

An **information transmission analysis** is a statistical procedure that analyzes the transmission of speech features by scoring confusions between test stimuli that are grouped based upon the presence or absence of those features; for example, the phonemes /p/ and /t/ share the feature of being "unvoiced." If a patient confuses *eepee* for *eetee*, the patient will receive credit for having correctly utilized the "voicing" feature but not the "place" feature.

Multidimensional scaling is a statistical procedure whereby data points are represented in a geometric space; for example, two phonemes that sound similar to a patient will be plotted near to each other and two phonemes that sound dissimilar will be plotted far from each other.

Cluster analysis is a statistical approach to information in a database that aims to determine which data points fall into groups or clusters; for example, it is not uncommon for the phonemes /b,d,g/ to cluster together because they often sound similar to people who have significant hearing loss.

Test results indicate the kinds of **speech features** utilized during speech recognition. For example, a patient may not have scored high on a test that presents a closed set of items such as *eemee, eenee, eesee, eebee, eepee*, and *eetee*. However, an analysis of errors may reveal that even though overall performance was poor, the individual consistently utilized the voicing feature. For example, *eepee* may have been heard as *eetee* or *eesee*, both of which contain unvoiced elements, but never as *eebee* or *eenee*, which contain only voiced elements. Thus, in designing auditory training goals, a speech and hearing professional might aim to build on this ability to utilize the voicing feature.

Although a speech and hearing professional can evaluate subjectively an individual's errors and qualitatively assess error confusions, formal statistical and mathematical analyses can be performed on the results. These provide a quantitative indication of the kinds of information an individual utilizes during speech. Such analyses include **information transmission analysis** (Miller & Nicely, 1955), **multidimensional scaling**, and **cluster analysis**.

A feature analysis of consonant phoneme confusion errors indicates which parameters of the speech signal are detected and utilized. Features that typically are considered in this kind of analysis include nasality, voicing, duration, frication, place, and envelope. A commonly used consonant classification system appears in Table 2–3.

TABLE 2–3 An Example of a Classification System for Consonants That May Be Used to Classify Consonant Phonemes for a Feature Analysis (the numbers are arbitrary and serve only to indicate the group to which a sound belongs within a feature)

CONSONANT	VOICING	PLACE	NASALITY	DURATION	FRICATION	ENVELOPE
B	1	0	0	0	0	1
D	1	1	0	0	0	1
G	1	3	0	0	0	1
P	0	0	0	0	0	0
T	0	1	0	0	0	0
K	0	3	0	0	0	0
V	1	0	0	0	1	1
F	0	0	0	0	1	2
Z	1	1	0	1	1	1
S	0	1	0	1	1	2
ò	0	2	0	1	1	2
M	1	0	1	0	0	3
N	1	1	1	0	0	3

For the nasality feature, consonants /m/ and /n/ are classified as nasal consonants. A person who appears to hear the nasality feature is probably responding to the frequencies around and below 300 Hz. Consonants that are aperiodic in nature (/p, t, k, f, s, ʃ /) are grouped together for the voicing feature, whereas the relatively long-duration consonants are grouped together for the duration feature (/z, s, ʃ /). The voicing and duration features probably relate to temporal cues and the voice pitch. Consonants produced with steady turbulence (/v, f, z, s, ʃ /) usually are grouped together for the frication feature. This feature relates to high-frequency turbulence. The place feature, for which consonants are categorized according to whether they are produced in the front, middle, or back of the vocal tract, is cued by spectral or frequency changes over time, particularly in the region of the second vowel formant. Finally, the envelope feature reflects time-intensity variations in the audio signal. To recognize words, persons must detect and utilize at least some of these features in the signal. A feature analysis indicates how well a patient can distinguish these cues from one another.

An advantage of using phoneme stimuli is that performance is relatively independent of a patient's vocabulary level. It is not important that patients be familiar with the test stimuli, and indeed, the stimuli are often *nonsense syllables*, such as *eesee* and *eetee*. The principal disadvantage of using phoneme stimuli is poor face validity. People do not communicate with these kinds of stimuli and it is not straightforward how recognition relates to conversational speech understanding. For example, nonsense syllables do not require individuals to organize streams of information into linguistically meaningful chunks or to process speech information with the same rapidity as ongoing speech.

Advantages of nonsense syllables:

- Performance unaffected by a patient's vocabulary level
- A feature analysis can often be performed

Disadvantages of nonsense syllables:

- Poor face validity

Words

The most commonly used stimuli for assessing speech recognition are monosyllabic words. Many word lists are designed to be phonetically balanced, such as the Northwestern University Auditory Test Number 6 (NU-6) word lists developed by Tillman

An **acoustic lexical neighborhood** comprises a set of words that are acoustically similar and have approximately the same frequency of occurrence.

Frequency of occurrence refers to the frequency with which a word is likely to occur in everyday speech or common usage.

A **dense neighborhood** has many members.

A **sparse lexical neighborhood** has few members.

Advantages of word stimuli:

- Have a somewhat higher face validity than nonsense syllables
- Easy to score
- Permit fine-grained scoring
- Performance is not affected by a patient's ability to use context or knowledge of linguistic structure

Disadvantages of word stimuli:

- May not index everyday listening performance
- May not be appropriate for some patients who have limited vocabulary
- May not be useful for some purposes, such as evaluating the effectiveness of an automatic gain control feature on a hearing aid, because of their short duration

and Carhart (1966). Some word lists for testing purposes have been based on principles of **acoustic lexical neighborhoods** (Luce, 1986; Luce & Pisoni, 1998)—for example, the Lexical Neighborhood Test (LNT) and the Multisyllabic Lexical Neighborhood Test (MLNT) (Kirk, 1998; Kirk, Pisoni, & Osberger, 1995). Words that have a similar **frequency of occurrence** (i.e., how often the words occur during everyday language use) and that share similar acoustic-phonetic characteristics belong to the same neighborhood. A word that belongs to a **dense neighborhood** (many words that are similar, such as *cat, mat, sat, fat, pat, bat,* etc.) is typically more difficult to recognize than a word that belongs to a **sparse lexical neighborhood** (few words that are similar; the words *thumb, tea,* and *lost* each belong to sparse neighborhoods). Most word lists are comprised of monosyllables that have the phonemic structure of consonant-vowel-consonant (e.g., *cat, man*). Word stimuli generally are difficult to recognize, more so than phrases or simple sentences.

One advantage in using real words is that they have somewhat higher face validity than nonsense syllables designed to assess phoneme recognition. People communicate with words in daily conversation. Word tests might be comprised of monosyllabic words, bisyllabic words, and/or spondees. The tests are also easy to score and allow a wide range of skill levels to be assessed. Responses from a word test can be scored by percentage of words repeated verbatim or percentage of phonemes correct (e.g., if the word is *bat,* and an individual responds *pat,* two of the word's three phonemes are scored as correct). The reasons that percentage phoneme scores are sometimes computed are to obtain a fine-grained understanding of an individual's performance and to provide a different vehicle for comparing test results. For example, two people might achieve the following scores on the same test:

Person 1: 30% words correct, 40% phonemes correct

Person 2: 30% words correct, 65% phonemes correct

Even though they both erred an equal number of times in repeating the words, Person 2's errors better approximate the target than do Person 1's error responses. Thus, the second person may have better listening ability than the first person.

As with phonemes, word stimuli may not reflect adequately how an individual performs in everyday listening situations because people typically listen to connected discourse. For example, words are presented rapidly during conversation. A person typically does not pause to think about the identity of each word as it is spoken, as one does when taking a test of isolated word recognition. During normal conversation, we might receive speech at between 140 and 180 words per minute (Miller, Grosjean, & Lomanto, 1984). It is possible for two people to perform similarly on a word test, in which the demands of fast online processing are not great, and yet function differently in everyday conversation. Another problem in using words as test stimuli may arise if the test taker has a language delay because performance on word tests may be influenced by vocabulary. A patient who has a limited vocabulary may perform poorly simply because he or she is unfamiliar with the test words. As an example of a word test, lists from the Lexical Neighborhood Test (Kirk et al., 1995) appear in the Key Resources.

Phrases and Sentences

A speech recognition test may consist of a series of unrelated phrases or sentences. For example, the test may commence with the sentence, *The cook cut the apple,* and then continue with *The boy and girl walked to school,* which is contextually unrelated to the first sentence. Alternatively, the test may present sentences centered on a common theme. For example, before the test begins, the patient may be informed, "The sentences you will hear concern activities to do at the lake." The first sentence may then be *We paddled a canoe*. The second sentence may be *We went for a swim this morning*, and so forth. Performance will be better for topic-related than unrelated sentences.

Sentence stimuli have high face validity because people typically communicate with phrases, sentences, and paragraphs. As such, performance on a sentence test may better reflect how a person performs in the real world than performance on a phoneme or isolated word test. Sentences have the following features, which are characteristic of everyday speech:

- **Prosodic cues**: When people listen to speech, they attend not only to individual sounds, but also to intonation, rate, and duration cues, and these help them identify words and understand meaning. For example, an individual may be presented with a complete sentence, but because of hearing loss, the person may hear only *mmm mm-mm mmm?* Even though the individual receives a gross approximation of the message, there is still enough information to know that a question is being asked and that the question contains four syllables, and possibly, enough information to know that it contains three words.
- **Contextual information**: The words in a sentence provide contextual redundancy. Recognition of some words facilitates recognition of other words. If an individual hears *Mary closed the* ________, it is possible to deduce that the final word is a noun, based on grammatical context, and that the word might be *door*, based on semantic cues.
- **Coarticulation**: When words are spoken in succession as in a sentence, they blend together and vary as a function of what precedes and follows. For example, the schwa sound in the word *the* will sound different if the word *blue* follows than if the word *green* follows. These coarticulation effects provide redundant cues for word recognition.

Prosodic cues are cues provided by intonation, rate, and duration of speech sounds.

Contextual information is linguistic support available for identifying a target word, phrase, or sentence.

Coarticulation is the influence of one phoneme on either a preceding or succeeding phoneme.

Even though sentences have these features of everyday speech, they also pose some disadvantages for assessment. One disadvantage of using sentence-level stimuli is that performance can be influenced by linguistic knowledge and familiarity with the topic. For example, a child with limited grammatical knowledge may not perform as well as a child who has good language skills, even though the two children might have similar perceptual skills. Memory also may affect results. If an audiologist presents a 10-word sentence to a patient with dementia, the patient may forget the beginning of the sentence by the time it ends.

Advantages of sentence stimuli:

- High face validity
- Likely to reflect real-world performance

Disadvantages of sentence stimuli:

- Performance may be influenced by linguistic knowledge
- Performance may be influenced by familiarity with the topic

Sentence tests are usually scored by computing a percentage words correct score, although sometimes they are scored for percentage phonemes correct and sometimes only selected key words are assessed. For a word to be scored as correct, it must be repeated verbatim. If the sentence is *The girls walked to school*, and a patient responds, "The girl walked to school," that sentence is scored as four out of five words correct. The omission of /s/ from *girls* makes it an incorrect repetition. As an example of a sentence test, lists from the CID Everyday Sentence Test (Silverman & Hirsh, 1955) appear in the Key Resources.

Selection of Test Stimuli

There are no cookbook procedures to follow when deciding which test stimuli to use. However, one guiding principle is that the measures chosen should be informative about how a patient performs in natural situations and should be independent of confounding factors such as vocabulary and grammatical knowledge, cognitive abilities, and memory. Often, clinicians opt to use a test-battery approach, using more than one test so that the aggregate presents different kinds of speech units.

TEST PROCEDURES

Once a test has been selected, decisions must be made about the protocol that will be followed for administering the test. Considerations for assessing speech recognition include the test condition, the type of response set, and whether testing occurs with live voice or recordings.

Test Condition

The auditory speech signal may be presented in quiet or in the presence of noise.

Noise may be introduced to increase the difficulty of the listening task or to gain a better understanding of how the person performs in the real world. The noise signal may be talker babble (e.g., six people read text and their speech signals are overlaid to create a single noise source) or **white noise** (which sounds like a radio off-station). Speech noise and cafeteria noise may also be used. **Speech noise** has approximately the same energy at each frequency as does running speech, whereas cafeteria noise is noise that was recorded in a cafeteria and then overdubbed several times. Sometimes the competing noise signal is semantically meaningful, say, a single talker reading a passage. A meaningful competing signal might be used to determine how well an elderly individual can tune out distracting competitors.

White noise is broadband noise that has equal energy at all frequencies.

Speech noise is broadband noise that has been filtered so that it resembles the speech spectrum.

Turn Off the Noise So I Can Read Your Lips

Background noise not only diminishes a person's ability to hear what a conversational partner is saying, but it also diminishes a person's ability to read lips. As will be noted in Chapter 5, people with hearing loss are often heavily dependent upon visual speech information for understanding conversation, so they may receive a "double whammy" if they are forced to engage in conversation in a noisy room, because they may not be able to maximally utilize their residual hearing or their lipreading skills.

Myerson et al. (2016) administered a speech recognition test to older participants in a vision-only condition (i.e., the participants saw but did not hear the test talker speak sentences) with three presentation modes: (1) in quiet, (2) with simultaneous white noise, and (3) with simultaneous talker babble. Performance became progressively worse across the three conditions, with participants being significantly less able to recognize words when babble was present and being also affected by the white noise, but to a lesser extent. In the case of background babble, participants may have instinctively been monitoring it in an attempt to extract auditory speech information that corresponded with the visual signal they were seeing.

When a speech recognition test is performed in the presence of noise, the audiologist records the **signal-to-noise ratio (SNR)**, which indicates the difference between the sound level of the signal and the sound level of the noise. Thus, if the signal is presented at 40 dB HL, and the noise is presented at 30 dB HL, the SNR is +10. An example of a sentence test designed to be presented in noise, the QuickSIN (Etymotic Research, 2001), appears in the Key Resources. The sound level for presenting the speech stimuli is often at a normal or moderately loud conversational level (60–70 decibels sound pressure level [dB SPL]). Alternatively, the level might be set at about 30 to 40 dB above the patient's SRT. When this latter level is chosen, it is said to be 30 to 40 dB **sensation level (SL)**. The intent of using sensation levels is to liken functional listening levels across patients.

Signal-to-noise ratio (SNR) is the level of a signal relative to a background of noise.

Sensation level (SL) is the level of a sound in dB above a person's threshold.

Response Format

Another important issue to consider when testing speech recognition is what kind of response format will be used to elicit responses. Many standardized tests have an **open-set** format. This format means that no response choices and no contextual cues are provided. The materials are not familiar to the patient, and have never been practiced, say during training.

An **open-set** task or test does not provide choices.

Closed-set tests provide a limited set of response choices and are easier than open-set tests. Items and foils are presented as written stimuli, pictures, or objects. The members and the size of the response set can be selected to test features of speech recognition and to vary test difficulty. For example, if a clinician is interested in determining whether a new cochlear implant user utilizes suprasegmental cues, the response choices when the test word *ball* is spoken might be *ball, ice cream*, and *bicycle*, words that vary in duration and stress pattern. On the other hand, if the clinician is testing an experienced cochlear implant user, the response set might be *ball, bill, bowl*, and *bell*, which will require the patient to attend to more fine-grained segmental cues. The task will be more difficult when there are four response choices as opposed to only three.

A **closed set** is a stimulus or response set that contains a fixed number of items known to the patient.

Live-Voice versus Recorded Test Materials

The next issue to consider in regard to selecting speech recognition test materials is whether testing will be performed with **live-voice testing** or with **recorded stimuli**. As the terms imply, test items can be presented by a live talker or they can be presented via a playback system, such as a computer or compact disc (CD) player. The advantages of using live voice are that no playback equipment is required and the talker can adjust the rate of stimulus presentation to meet performance needs. Some older patients are more comfortable with a live-voice test paradigm than a recorded-voice paradigm.

During **live-voice testing**, stimuli in a test of speech recognition are spoken by a talker in real time as opposed to being recorded and played back.

Recorded stimuli are presented via a computer, tape recorder, compact disk (CD) player, MP3 player, or a digital video disk (DVD) player.

Despite these advantages, there are even more disadvantages associated with using live voice rather than recorded speech. Live talkers can introduce variability from one test session to the next and from one test site to another. Talkers have different speaking styles and they may vary in their style from one day to another. For example, test talkers may vary on any of the following variables:

- *Voicing frequency*: Female test talkers usually have high pitches and may be more difficult to understand than male test talkers, who have characteristically low-pitched voices. Most people have better hearing in the lower frequencies than in the mid and high frequencies.
- *Intonation*: Sentences spoken with appropriate and expressive intonation are generally easier to understand than ones spoken with a monotone or inappropriate intonation. Thus, a test talker who uses more voice inflection while speaking the test sentences will be easier to understand than a test talker who uses less inflection.
- *Speech rate*: Rapidly spoken speech is more difficult to recognize than moderately slow speech. One test talker may speak slowly whereas another may speak more quickly.
- *Clarity of articulation*: Clearly articulated speech is easier to recognize than conversational or mumbled speech. Test talkers may vary in their ability to speak clearly.
- *Physical characteristics*: In an audition-plus-vision or vision-only condition, talkers who have pronounced lip and jaw displacement, no facial hair, and expressive facial movements will be relatively easier to speechread or lipread.

It is important that talker characteristics not confound test results. Otherwise, a clinician will not be able to monitor an individual's performance over time or compare his or her performance with that of other people who have been tested in other clinics. In today's world, most audiology clinics and other hearing-related settings rely exclusively on recorded materials to assess speech recognition. Live-voice testing is rare.

Synthesized and Altered Speech

Most recorded test materials present speech spoken by an adult talker, speaking as clearly as possible. However, two other kinds of recorded materials sometimes are used to assess word recognition: synthesized speech and altered speech.

Synthesized speech is created with a computer, not the human vocal tract.

Synthesized speech is created with a computer or other technological apparatus and not by a human vocal tract. Synthesized speech may be used if the tester wants to determine how a patient utilizes a specific cue for speech recognition. For example, a series of acoustic waveform samples may be created so that there is a systematic variation in the voice-onset time for /b/ in the word *bat*. The tester then might determine at what step in the continuum the patient hears the word *bat* versus *pat*.

Altered speech is human speech that is recorded and then altered in some way.

Time-compressed speech is speech that has been accelerated by removing segments of the waveform and then compressing the remaining segments together without changing its frequency composition.

Expanded speech is recorded speech that is altered by duplicating small segments of the signal so that it sounds like a slow speaking rate.

Filtered speech is passed through filter banks for the purpose of removing or amplifying frequency bands in the signal.

Low-pass filtered speech has been passed through filter banks that removed the higher, but not the lower, frequencies.

High-pass filtered speech has been passed through filter banks that removed the lower, but not the higher, frequencies.

Altered speech is human speech that is recorded and then altered in some way, usually by means of computer software. Altered speech may be time-compressed, extended, or filtered. **Time-compressed speech** has been digitized and then processed so that small segments are periodically deleted from the ongoing signal waveform. When it is played back, time-compressed speech sounds like natural speech produced at a fast speaking rate. Conversely, **expanded speech** is created by duplicating small segments of the signal so that the speech sounds as if it were produced with a slow speaking rate. **Filtered speech** is created by passing the speech signal through filter banks. **Low-pass filtered speech** includes the lower but not the higher frequencies whereas **high-pass filtered speech** includes the higher but not the lower frequencies. Altered speech sometimes is used when the tester is interested in how well the patient can recognize speech when the auditory system is challenged.

In sum, synthesized speech and altered speech often are used to examine the effects of specific acoustic cues on speech recognition or to create a difficult speech-listening condition. These stimuli might be used to address the following questions:

- Does an individual utilize the plosive burst cue when distinguishing a /t/ from an /s/?
- Even though a young and an aged person have similar hearing thresholds, is the older person less able to understand time-compressed speech, which is a more taxing listening task?

DIFFICULTIES ASSOCIATED WITH SPEECH RECOGNITION ASSESSMENT

There are several problematic issues that should be considered when attempting to evaluate speech recognition and the effects of training on speech recognition performance. Three of the more significant issues are learning effects, test–retest variability, and clinical significance.

Learning effects occur when performance on a test improves as a function of familiarity with the test procedures or items, not as a result of a change in ability.

Learning Effects

Patients sometimes learn the test items when they are presented more than once, even when several weeks separate the test periods. Thus, because of **learning effects**, performance improves for reasons other than an aural rehabilitation intervention, such as receipt of auditory training. For example, suppose someone was presented with the sentence, *The boy and girl are walking to school* during a speech recognition test and recognized the words, *The boy* _____ _____ _____ *walking* _____ _____. If the patient repeated the test three months later, he or she might recognize all of the words, because he or she remembered the sentence remnant and used that information as contextual cues for identifying the rest of the sentence. Even recognizing the sentence rhythm and syllabic pattern might trigger recall. It may seem implausible that someone can remember dialogue for that length of time, but you simply need to reflect how the words of a song learned in grade school may come back to mind after many years of not hearing it, often after just hearing the first couple of words or the first few notes of the song.

One way in which the learning problem has been addressed is with the use of **equivalent lists**, that is, sets of sentences that are presumed to be equally difficult to recognize. Equivalency is usually established by playing the separate tests to a large group of participants. If, on average, the participants recognize an equal number of words on each list, then the lists are said to be equivalent.

Equivalent lists are typical in the context of speech recognition tests and are collections of items comprised by each list that are presumed to be equally difficult to recognize in the aggregate.

The problem with this tactic is that the lists may be equivalent when some listening devices are used but not others. For example, a group of hearing aid users may perform similarly on two lists of test items, whereas a group of cochlear implant users may not. Similarly, equivalency may vary with the configuration of hearing loss, such that a group of individuals with a sloping mild-to-moderate loss will not perform like a group of individuals who have a flat severe hearing loss. Some researchers have tried to minimize learning effects by constructing tests that have a large number of items, say 100 or more sentences (Tyler, Preece, & Tye-Murray, 1986). With so many test items, patients may be less likely to remember them, even with repeated testing. However, there are few empirical data available to support this assumption. Another tack has been to use a closed-set matrix format (e.g., Gagné, Charest, Monday, & Desbiens, 2006; Tye-Murray, Sommers, & Spehar, 2006). A closed set of words is presented in the context of either a constant sentence frame (e.g., Gagné et al., 2006) or one of four possible frames (e.g., Tye-Murray et al., 2006). The patient receives several practice items before the test is administered. The closed-set nature of the response set ensures list equivalency, and learning effects associated with repeated testing are minimized because the patient is familiarized with the matrix of key words prior to each test session by means of a practice session, and the same sentence need never be presented twice. Table 2–4 presents the response screen for a matrix test. In this example, every possible sentence has the same syntactic structure (i.e., *The ___ and the ___ watched the ___ and the ___*) and contains four key words that may be selected from the response matrix. For example, one test sentence might be *The saint and the wife watched the mice and the mole*, and another might be *The bird and the boys watched the mole and the cop*. If enough sentences are recorded, then the patient need never hear the same sentence twice, no matter how many times he or she takes the test. For example, the matrix shown in Table 2–4 permits 863,040 different sentences. Although this format ensures list equivalency and minimizes learning effects, it allows for the assessment of only a limited number of words and may be too easy for those patients who have very good listening abilities.

TABLE 2–4 Example of a Matrix Test Format

In this example, the matrix includes 32 interchangeable key words for each of the four slots in the sentence frame, where a word can be used only once within a single sentence. During testing, the matrix appears on a computer touch screen and the patient responds by touching four consecutive choices.

The ___ and the ___ watched the ___ and the ___.

Please choose from the following words:

Bear	Cat	Deer	Fawn	Men	Saint	Team	Whale
Bird	Cook	Dog	Fish	Mice	Seal	Toad	Wife
Boys	Cop	Dove	Fox	Mole	Snail	Tribe	Wolf
Bug	Cow	Duck	Frog	Moose	Son	Troop	Worm

Test–Retest Variability

Test–retest variability is a measure of the consistency of performance on a test from one presentation to the next.

Another difficulty related to assessment is that patients vary in their performance from day to day. A patient may achieve a score on one day, then take it on another day and achieve a different score, even though it is the same test. There may be several factors that contribute to **test–retest variability**. For example, on some days a patient may be highly motivated to perform well, whereas on others, the patient may be tired and uninterested. As such, scores may improve or decrease over time, not as a result of training, but as a result of fatigue, interest, and mood. The nature of the test also may contribute to variability. Most tests are inherently variable, such that simply taking the test two times will yield somewhat different results, even if all testing parameters are held constant. If a test presents a closed set of choices, the patient may perform better on one day than another as a function of chance. Finally, test conditions can affect variability. Changes in any of the following variables can shift test scores:

- *Mode of presentation*: For example, changing from live-voice stimuli to recorded stimuli may result in a decline in scores.
- *Location*: For example, changing from a sound-treated booth to a clinic office may also lead to decreased performance.
- *Talker*: For example, someone who is familiar versus unfamiliar, and someone who is male rather than female, will typically be easier to understand.
- *The number of times an item is repeated*: For example, presenting a test item twice, or as often as an individual requests, usually leads to better performance than presenting it only once.

Test–Retest Reliability and Validity

Test–retest reliability is the degree to which a group of test takers will achieve the same scores with repeated administrations of a test.

An issue closely related to variability is **test–retest reliability.** Reliability of a test relates to the extent that test results are repeatable, and the level of reliability is expressed in terms of a standard error of measurement. Mendel and Danhauer (1997) describe reliability as follows:

> Reliability concerns the extent to which measurements are repeatable by the same individual using different measures of the attribute, or by different people using the same measure of the attribute without the interference of error. . . . Reliability can be expressed in terms of the standard error of measurement. If a listener is given the same test many times, the score determined from an average of the test scores would approach some value (that is, the true score) more and more closely. The degree to which a single test score approximates the true score determines the reliability of the test. (pp. 10–11)

Validity is the extent to which a test measures what it is assumed to measure.

In addition to being reliable, a test of speech recognition should also have good **validity**, meaning that the corpus of test items representatively sample the domains and indicators of interest and provide a good estimate of the construct of speech recognition ability. Martin and Clark (2006) present three criteria for assessing the validity of a speech recognition test:

1. How well it measures what it is supposed to measure (a person's difficulties in understanding speech)
2. How favorably a test compares with other, similar measures
3. How the test stands up to alterations of the signal (such as distortion or presentation with noise) that are known to affect other speech tests in specific ways (p. 127)

Clinical Significance

Another difficulty associated with speech recognition assessment relates to clinical significance. It sometimes is difficult to determine whether a small change in performance is clinically significant. For example, an individual might recognize 30% of the words in a sentence test prior to receiving auditory training. Afterward, the person might recognize 36% of the words. In this example, the clinician must determine whether listening has improved in a meaningful way.

A within-subject statistical procedure has been used to compare posttraining performance to pretraining performance to establish whether a change is statistically significant. The number of words repeated verbatim in each sentence of a pretraining test can be compared with the number of key words repeated verbatim in the same sentence following training. A paired *t* statistic can be computed using all sentences in a list. Although statistical significance does not necessarily equate with clinical significance, it does indicate whether a change is robust.

MULTICULTURAL ISSUES

With the U.S. population becoming increasingly diverse, multilingual testing has gained importance as an issue in aural rehabilitation. Indeed, this is true in countries throughout the world, as people are increasingly mobile and willing to relocate.

When considering multilingual testing, it is important to determine whether the patient is **monolingual** (speaks only one language) or bilingual (speaks two languages). A **bilingual** individual is sometimes described as being a native speaker, such as a native Spanish speaker, to imply proficiency comparable to that of a language speaker who originates from the country where the language is spoken. Performance on a speech recognition test may vary from one patient to another, depending on whether that person is monolingual or bilingual, and on other such language variables as language history (e.g., When did the individual begin to learn English? Which language was learned first?) and competency (e.g., the individual's proficiency in a language). Monolingual and bilingual individuals perform differently from each other on speech recognition tests, and Spanish tests of speech recognition yield better performance than English tests for native Spanish bilingual individuals (see Von Hapsburg & Peña, 2002, for a review). Some evidence suggests that Spanish-English bilingual listeners are more adversely affected by background noise than are monolingual English listeners (Von Hapsburg, Champlin, & Shetty, 2004).

Monolingual describes a person who speaks only one language.

Bilingual describes a person who speaks two languages.

There is a demand for speech recognition materials that are appropriate for non–English-speaking patients or patients who use English as a second language. Unfortunately, the demand at present exceeds the supply. The few examples of tests that have been developed for Spanish-speaking patients include the Spanish Bisyllables (Weisleder & Hodgson, 1989), 50-word lists of bisyllabic consonant-vowel-consonant-vowel Spanish words presented in an open-set response format; and the **Synthetic Sentence** Identification (SSI) test (Benitez & Speaks, 1968). One difficulty in assessing nonnative English speakers for clinicians is that they may not understand the language of their patients, and hence, may have difficulty in scoring responses to test materials. At least one test, the Spanish Picture-Identification Test (McCullough, Wilson, Birck, & Anderson, 1995), has been modified to circumvent this problem (McCullough & Wilson, 2001). The test consists of two 50-word lists. The test words (spoken in a carrier phrase context) are common bisyllabic nouns and verbs that can be easily pictured. The items are presented in a four-choice closed set, with the foils (or alternative responses) rhyming with

Synthetic sentences are syntactically correct but meaningless sentences, and usually include a noun, verb, and object.

the target word. The choices are presented in picture form to patients via a computer screen monitor. The advantage of using the picture-based closed-set format is that the clinician administering the test does not need to understand Spanish to test the patient. The word lists appear in the Key Resources as an example of a Spanish-language test.

Bilingualism Defined

"The broadest definition of a bilingual includes anyone who knows two languages (Baker, 1993). Yet, this definition remains too broad to be useful, because the degree to which an individual knows each language depends on many circumstances. Factors such as when the languages were learned, how the languages were learned, what language skills (reading, writing, speaking, listening) were acquired, and how the languages are used on a daily basis affect the state of bilingualism in any individual. Some consider bilinguals only those who are equally fluent in both of their languages, known as *balanced* bilinguals or *ambilinguals*. . . . A functional or holistic view of bilingualism takes into consideration that individuals learn and use each of their languages for different purposes and in different communication contexts. Therefore, a functional view of bilingualism recognizes that a bilingual may become more competent in one language in certain communication contexts and competent in the other language for other contexts. From the functional perspective, then, it becomes important to ask why the languages were acquired, how they were acquired, when they were acquired, and how they are used" (Von Hapsburg & Peña, 2002, p. 203).

CASE STUDY

Reasons to Go with a Test-Battery Approach

Lindsey Mooreland, an audiologist, wanted to compare the listening skills of three of her older male patients. At first, she thought she might administer only a word test, the NU-6. Because she had extra time, she went ahead and administered a consonant test (the Iowa Consonant Test) and a sentence test (the Iowa Sentence Test) too. The results for the three real-life patients appear in Table 2–5.

TABLE 2–5 Percentage Correct Scores for Three Patients on Three Different Tests That Each Present a Different Stimulus Type, Presented in an Audition-Only Condition

TEST AND STIMULUS TYPE	PATIENTS' SCORES IN %		
	Al	Tom	Bob
Iowa Consonant Test (Consonants)	55	61	87
NU-6 (Words)	45	45	30
Iowa Sentence Test (Sentences)	58	38	48

If she had administered only the word test, the three men would have appeared similar in their listening skills. Scores ranged from a low of 30% words correct (Bob) to a high of 45% (Al and Tom).

The test-battery approach reveals a more complex picture, and the conclusions as to which patient has the best listening skills is not as straightforward as it would have been if she had administered only a word test. In terms of consonant recognition, Bob scored the highest of the three (87% consonants correct), whereas Al scored the lowest (55% correct). For sentence recognition, Al scored the highest (58% words correct) and Tom scored the lowest (38%).

Time available for testing and the purpose for assessment will dictate in large part which and how many tests are administered to a patient. However, if a clinician administers only a single test, it is important to be aware that the test result may not provide a complete picture of the construct of speech recognition for a particular patient.

FINAL REMARKS

In this chapter, considered in a general way how to assess patients' ability to recognize speech. We have not focused on particular tests, but rather, on the principles that must be considered when choosing a test for a particular individual. The results of speech recognition testing are invaluable when designing an aural rehabilitation plan.

KEY CHAPTER POINTS

- A typical audiological assessment includes an audiogram, a determination of speech recognition thresholds, and an assessment of speech recognition. The audiogram by itself does not always adequately reflect the magnitude of a patient's communication difficulties.
- The optimal test environment is a sound-treated booth.
- A speech and hearing professional might assess speech recognition abilities for any number of reasons. For example, an audiologist might be interested in evaluating a patient's need for amplification or assessing the patient's performance over time.
- Patient variables, such as the cognitive/linguistic skill of the test taker, will influence selection of test materials. For example, an audiologist would not select a sentence test for evaluating a 3-year-old child.
- Test stimuli may be phonemes, words, phrases, unrelated sentences, or topically related sentences. Each kind of stimulus offers advantages and disadvantages.
- Once test materials have been selected, decisions can be made about test procedures. For example, an audiologist might opt to present the stimuli in an audition-only condition, using recorded voice and background noise.
- Patients may learn the items in a test with repeated testing.
- A test should have good reliability and validity.
- Test–retest variability sometimes is an important issue.
- Some people, especially children, may vary in their performance from day to day.
- Although multicultural testing is ever more commonplace, the need for speech recognition tests in languages other than English outstrips the current supply.
- Bilingual individuals perform better on tests administered in their native language than on tests administered in their second language.

TERMS AND CONCEPTS TO REMEMBER

Audiogram
Degree of hearing loss
Effects of hearing loss on word recognition
Test selection
Speech features
Information transmission analysis
Speechreading enhancement
Closed and open sets
Reliability and validity
Bilingual

KEY RESOURCES

Examples of the Lexical Neighborhood Test

(Kirk et al., 1995)

List 1

Easy words: juice, good, drive, time, hard, gray, foot, orange, count, brown, home, old watch, need, food, dance, live, stand, six, cold, push, stop, girl, hurt, cow.

Hard words: thumb, pie, wet, fight, toe, cut, pink, hi, song, fun, use, mine, ball, kick, tea, book, bone, work, dad, game, lost, cook, gum, cap, meat.

Examples of CID Everyday Sentences

(Silverman & Hirsh, 1955)

List A

1. Walking's my favorite exercise.
2. Here's a nice quiet place to rest.
3. Our janitor sweeps the floors every night.
4. It would be much easier if everyone would help.
5. Good morning.
6. Open your window before you go to bed!
7. Do you think that she should stay out so late?
8. How do you feel about changing the time when we begin work?
9. Here we go.
10. Move out of the way!

Examples of the Quick SIN Test

(Etymotic Research, 2001)

(*Note.* The sentences are presented in increasing levels of noise. The first sentence is presented with a +25 SNR with the noise level increasing in 5-dB increments such that the sixth sentence is presented at a 0 SNR. The test includes 18 lists, consisting of six sentences each.)

A sample list.

1. A white silk jacket goes with any shoes.
2. The child crawled into the dense grass.
3. Footprints showed the path he took up the beach.
4. A vent near the edge brought in fresh air.

5. It is a band of steel three inches wide.
6. The weight of the package was seen on the high scale.

Examples of Words in the Spanish Picture-Identification Task

(McCullough & Wilson, 2001)

LIST 1	LIST 1 (*continued*)
Balón (balloon)	Mono (monkey)
Barba (beard)	Niña (girl)
Barca (boat)	Ojo (eye)
Besa (kiss)	Oso (bear)
Boca (mouth)	Pala (shovel)
Bola (ball)	Papa (potato)
Bota (boot)	Pico (sting)
Caja (box)	Pito (whistle)
Canta (sing)	Prisa (hurry)
Capa (cape)	Queso (cheese)
Cara (face)	Rama (twig)
Carne (meat)	Ratón (rat)
Cárcel (jail)	Reza (pray)
Coger (catch)	Roja (red)
Cono (cone)	Ropa (rope)
Corer (run)	Rota (broken f.)
Foto (photo)	Sala (living room)
Gorro (cap)	Salto (jump)
Hueso (bone)	Santo (Saint m.)
Jota (J)	Talon (heel)
Ladrón (robber)	Tasa (cup)
Llama (knock)	Toca (knock)
Manta (blanket)	Toro (bull)
Masa (dough)	Viña (vine)
Misa (mass)	Voto (vote)

CHAPTER 3

Listening Devices and Related Technology

OUTLINE

Depending upon the results of the audiological assessment, a patient may receive a listening device in order to minimize conversational difficulties and maximize the use of residual hearing for daily functioning. In this chapter, we will review three kinds of listening devices, hearing aids, cochlear implants, and hearing assistive technology systems, with an emphasis on assistive listening devices. It will serve as an introduction for readers who are unacquainted with them and a key-points review for those who are familiar with them.

HEARING AIDS

Prior to the 20th century, there were three ways to help a person with hearing loss hear better: (1) speak loudly, (2) talk right into the person's ear, or (3) provide the person with an ear horn, speaking tube, trumpet, or other similar device (Figure 3–1). The advent of electronic hearing aids revolutionized the methods available to assist patients to hear more, beginning with analog hearing aids toward the beginning of the last century and then with digital hearing aids toward its closing.

Two major trends are evident in modern hearing aid design: miniaturization and enhanced signal processing. Over time, hearing aids have become smaller. Early hearing aids were so large and cumbersome that they were not portable. These tabletop electrical aids were often used only in educational settings where teacher and students might sit around a shared table or in meeting situations (Figure 3–2). The early portable aids were not much of an improvement over the tabletop devices. They were housed in large cases that had to be carried on the body or with the hand and were operated with vacuum tubes. Vacuum tubes were replaced by transistors, which made it possible for hearing aids to be worn on the head. In the last several decades, there have been advances toward miniaturization so that now it is possible to use a hearing aid and have it be essentially invisible. Probably the primary factor spurring this trend toward miniaturization is patients' cosmetic concerns. Along with miniaturization, there has been another trend in hearing aid designs, and that is sophistication in their **signal processing** capabilities (ability to alter the signal in some way, usually according to a processing **algorithm**), all in virtual real time.

Signal processing involves manipulation of various parameters of a signal.

An **algorithm** is a mathematical formula that provides step-by-step rules to perform a specific function or task, such as processing and amplifying an acoustic signal.

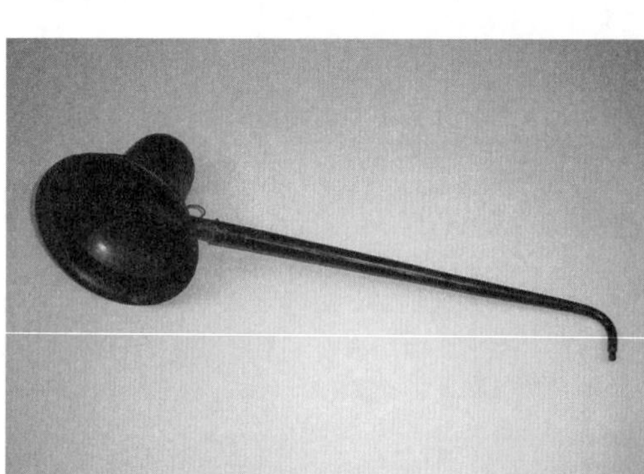

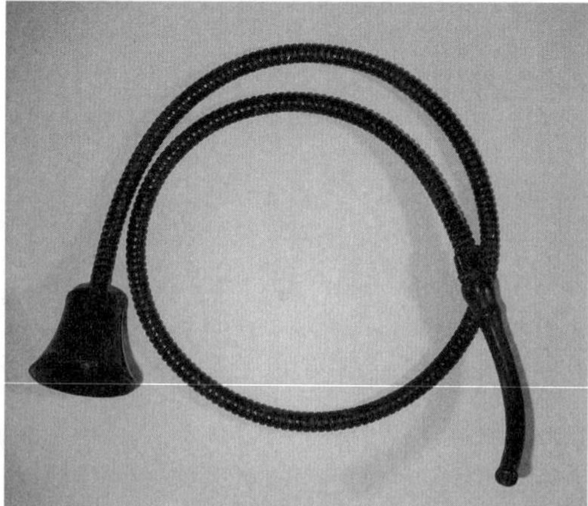

FIGURE 3–1. An ear trumpet and speaking tube. The black metal London hearing trumpet, shown on the left, is about 26 inches long. The rubber "conversation tube," shown on the right, has a vulcanite mouthpiece and earpiece. Both devices exemplify available listening technology in the nineteenth century. Courtesy of Becker Medical Library, Washington University School of Medicine.

FIGURE 3–2. A desktop hearing aid and a group of men using the aid. The device shown on the left was designed to rest on a table. The multiple funnels collected sound from talkers seated around the table, as shown on the right side of the figure. A long elastic tube conveyed the talkers' speech to the ear of the person with hearing loss. This device was manufactured in 1875, and was still in use in 1926. Courtesy of Becker Medical Library, Washington University School of Medicine.

Hearing Aid Components

Figure 3–3 provides a schematic of a digital signal processing (DSP) hearing aid. Digital hearing aids (as opposed to analog hearing aids) first appeared on the market in 1987, and have since come to dominate the market, accounting for about 95% of all hearing aids sold in the United States (Strom, 2007). Digital signal processing means that the acoustic signal is converted into a series of binary numbers and then processed using algorithms.

The **microphone** picks up the acoustic signal from the ambient environment. The microphone component converts the acoustic signal into an electrical signal. The electrical signal then passes to the **amplifier**, where the signal is selectively amplified. For example, only the high frequencies of a signal may be boosted. From the amplifier, the processed electrical signal passes to the **receiver**. The receiver converts the processed electrical signal back into an acoustic signal and passes it on through any tubing and earmold.

A **microphone** is a transducer that converts an audio signal into an electronic signal.

An **amplifier** increases the intensity of sound.

A **receiver** is an instrument that converts electrical energy into acoustic energy, as in a hearing aid. The term also refers to the component of an FM system worn by the listener to receive signals from the FM transmitter.

The hearing aid also carries **batteries**, which provide power for its operation. Batteries come in at least five sizes (denoted by the following codes, from largest capacity or milliamp hours to smallest: 675, 13, 312, 10, and 5). Although battery life is dependent on a number of factors, such as the kind of battery it is, the style of hearing aid in which it is used, and the volume control setting, a zinc battery will last anywhere from a few days to a few weeks. Some hearing aids operate with rechargeable batteries (Friedman, 2017).

A **battery** is a cell that provides electrical power.

Microphones

Microphones are designed to respond to sound, without distorting it or introducing extraneous noise. The microphone is a transducer that converts the audio signal into an electrical signal.

There are two general types of microphones: directional and omnidirectional. **Directional microphones** are designed to respond primarily to sound originating from in

Directional microphones are more sensitive to sound originating from in front of the user than to sound coming from behind the user.

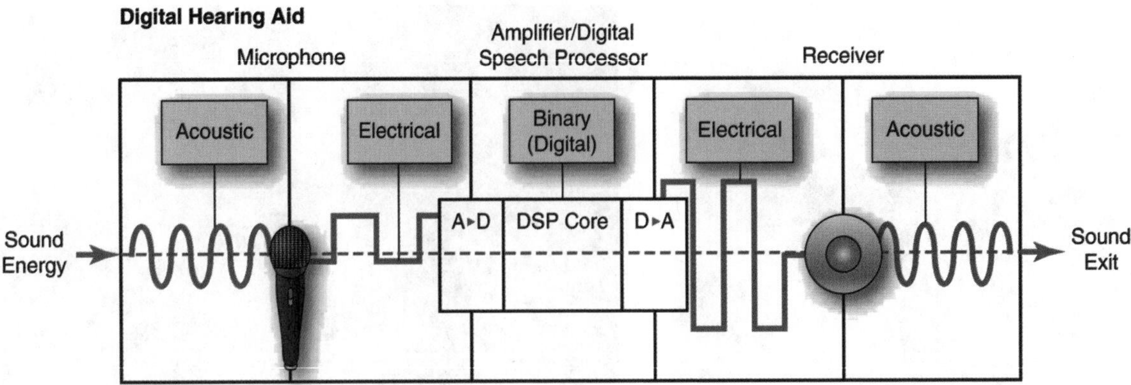

FIGURE 3–3 Schematic of a digital hearing aid. A = analog; D = digital; DSP = digital speech processing.

front of the user, and not from the back. **Omnidirectional microphones** respond to sound originating from all directions. Directional microphones enhance the signal-to-noise ratio for the user. For example, a hearing aid with a directional microphone system will pick up the speech of a talker who stands in front of the user, but not from two individuals who speak about something else in the back of the room. The system has two microphones or microphone ports (a *dual-microphone system*) that when activated results in a boosting of the level of sounds coming from the front and decreases the level of sounds coming from behind. As such, directional microphones are often desirable for listening in noisy situations. Some hearing aids include automatic directional systems, which have a switching algorithm that automatically switches the patient's hearing aid between an omnidirectional microphone mode in quiet situations and a directional mode in noisy situations, according to such factors as signal-to-noise ratio and the level of the sound. Some **automatic directional microphones (ADMs)** even alter their directional response patterns so as to optimize the signal-to-noise ratio in continuously changing environments. Many hearing aids offer a control on the device or a remote control option whereby the user can switch from omnidirectional to directional. Research suggests that patients perform better in noisy environments with directional microphones and ADMs than with omnidirectional microphones (Keidser, 2012).

Omnidirectional microphones are sensitive to sound coming from all directions.

Automatic directional microphones (ADMs) automatically switch between an omnidirectional and directional mode according to environmental conditions.

Amplifiers

An amplifier is also a component in all hearing aids. Amplifiers increase the level of the signal. **Gain** describes the amount of amplification provided by an amplifier and is defined as the difference between the hearing aid's input and output. For example, if an input signal is 30 dB sound pressure level (SPL) and the output is 60 dB SPL, the gain of the hearing aid is 30 dB.

The signal is selectively processed and amplified. In many hearing aids, the signal passes through three stages of the amplification process. In the **preamplifier stage**, the signal received from the microphone is boosted. During the **signal-processing stage**, the signal is manipulated to enhance the quality of the sound for the patient. Some amplifiers include **digital noise reduction (DNR)** schemes designed to amplify speech but not background noise. During the **output stage**, the processed signal is amplified and sent to the hearing aid receiver. Almost all modern hearing aids have a digital processor, where sound is converted from an analog signal into a digital representation. The processing

The **gain** of a hearing aid is the difference in decibels between the input level of an acoustic signal and the output level.

In the **preamplifier stage**, the signal from the microphone is amplified.

In the **signal-processing stage**, the signal is manipulated to enhance or extract component information.

Digital noise reduction (DNR) is processing designed to reduce gain in the low frequencies or specific frequency bands when noise is detected.

In the **output stage**, the process signal is boosted.

is performed on this computer language version. The processed signal is then converted back into an analog signal. The three components involved in this process are as follows:

- *The analog to digital (A/D) converter*, where the signal is changed to a sequence of 1s and 0s.
- *The core*, where it is filtered into channels (frequency bandwidths) and manipulated according to the programmed settings for the patient's particular hearing loss.
- *The digital to analog (D/A) converter*, where the digital signal is converted back to an analog signal that now has the prescribed signal manipulations.

Amplifying algorithms may be classified as one of two types: peak-clipping or compression. These terms refer to their mode of limiting the output of the signal so that it is not so loud as to be uncomfortable to the user nor has the potential to cause a noise-induced hearing loss. The goal of peak-clipping or compression is to limit the **maximum power output** (MPO) of the hearing aid, which is the maximum output level a hearing aid will put out in response to a very loud input signal.

Maximum power output (MPO) is the maximum intensity level that a hearing aid can produce, sometimes called *saturation sound pressure level.*

A **peak-clipping** circuit provides a constant or linear amount of gain (or amplification) across a range of input levels. A one-to-one relationship exists between the input and output, so that the sound is amplified by a consistent amount until it reaches a saturation level. At this **saturation level**, sound coming into the amplifier circuit is so loud that the amplifier begins to "clip" or cut off the peaks of the signal. Although this effectively limits the level of the audio signal, it also introduces distortion; therefore, sound quality decreases. Figure 3–4 presents an example of the relationship between input and output levels of the hearing aid in a peak-clipping system.

Peak-clipping is a method of limiting hearing aid output in which a constant or linear amount of gain is provided across a range of input levels until it reaches a saturation level, at which time the amplifier begins to "clip" off the peaks of the signal.

Saturation level is the point at which an amplifier no longer provides an increase in output compared with input.

Most modern hearing aids employ a nonlinear amplification system. A nonlinear amplifier system functions with a **compression** circuitry. The use of compression has three purposes. One purpose of compression is to limit the maximum output of the hearing aid, so that sound is never so loud as to cause discomfort to the user.

Compression is a nonlinear form of amplifier gain used to determine and limit output gain as a function of input gain.

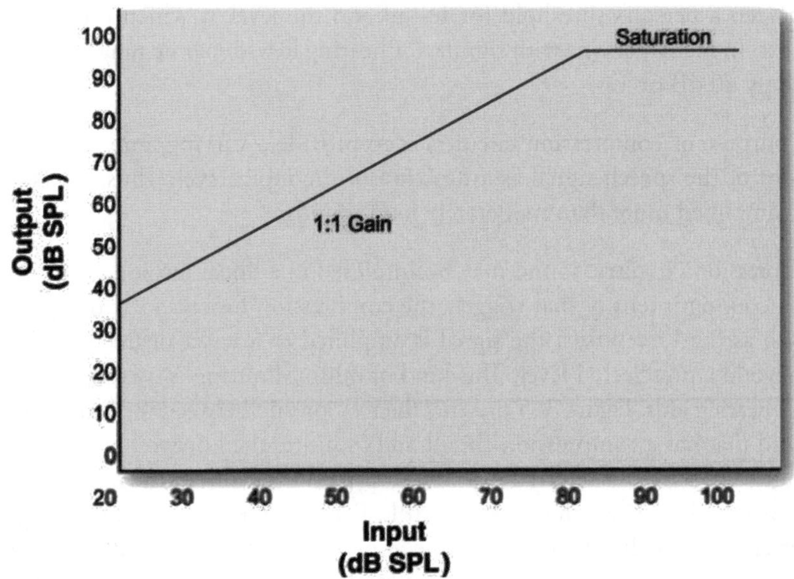

FIGURE 3–4 Input–output loudness function for a hearing aid that uses peak-clipping to limit output.

Over-the-counter hearing aids (OTCs) are hearing aids meant for adults who have mild-to-moderate hearing loss and are available without involvement of a hearing health care professional via stores, mail, or Internet.

Personal sound amplification products (PSAPs) are worn in the ear and amplify sounds, but they do not address other aspects of hearing loss, such as the configuration of the loss or distortion.

Key points about PSAPs:

- Wearable electronic products
- Not intended to compensate for hearing loss
- Amplify sound but otherwise usually do not process the sound in any way to accommodate hearing loss
- Not subject to FDA approval because they are not considered to be medical devices
- Cannot be marketed as a treatment for hearing loss
- Inexpensive compared with hearing aids

(Calderone, 2017; Sydlowski, 2018)

Personal Sound Amplification Products and Over-the-Counter Hearing Aids

In response to calls for better affordability and accessibility of hearing aids, several agencies (e.g., the Federal Trade Commission; the National Academies of Sciences, Engineering, and Medicine) have advocated easy availability of **over-the-counter (OTC) hearing aids**. Some believe that hearing aids are too expensive for many people, especially since the price is often not covered by third-party payers. In addition, many people, especially those in rural areas, do not have ready access to audiologists and other hearing health care professionals. The Food and Drug Administration (FDA) is developing proposed regulations that will allow hearing aids to be sold over the counter without the supervision or involvement of a hearing health care professional. In October, 2018, the FDA approved the first OTC hearing aid developed by Bose Corporation.

Currently, some consumers who cannot afford hearing aids or who do not have ready access to hearing health care buy **personal sound amplification products (PSAPs)**, which are worn in the ear and amplify sound. Typical uses for PSAPs include watching television and engaging in other recreational activities.

The OTC law recently passed by Congress defines an OTC device as follows:

- Uses the same scientific technology as air conduction hearing aids.
- Targeted at adults who have mild-to-moderate hearing loss.
- May be user controlled through the use of tools, tests, or software so as to provide a customized fit.
- May use wireless technology, including tests for self-assessment of hearing loss.
- Available over the counter, without involvement of a licensed person, via in-person transactions, mail, or online.

(Sydlowski, 2018, p. 21).

Qualms about OTCs

"When you use an over-the-counter device, it's going to be an experiential thing; it's going to be an experiment. It either works or doesn't work. . . . [T]here's really no way to predict, without evidence from a hearing test . . . whether that's going to be a successful fit or not."

—David Zapala, PhD, member of the National Academies of Sciences, Engineering, and Medicine

(Special Report, 2017, p. 10)

A second purpose of compression is to provide a range of sounds to the user within the person's dynamic range. As noted in Chapter 2, dynamic range is defined as the difference between a person's threshold for sound and the level at which the sound causes discomfort. In many persons with significant hearing loss, dynamic range is reduced and may be only 40 dB or less.

A third purpose of compression circuitry is to provide a varying amount of gain (amplification) of the speech signal as a function of the input level. Thus, soft sounds are typically amplified more than moderately loud sounds.

Kneepoint is the point on an input–output function where compression is activated.

Compression ratio is the decibel ratio of acoustic input to amplifier output.

Attack time is the time between when a signal begins to the onset of its steady-state amplified value.

In a compression circuitry, sound may be amplified in a linear fashion until it reaches a level of incoming intensity that triggers the compression function. At this point, often referred to as the **kneepoint**, the signal is amplified to a lesser degree, and never amplified beyond a preselected level. This kind of output limiting is used most commonly in today's hearing aids. Figure 3–5 presents the relationship between input and output of a hearing aid that has a compression circuit and indicates the kneepoint. The relation between input and output is referred to as the **compression ratio**, or the ratio of the change in input SPL to the change in the output SPL. For example, if a sound entering into the amplifier changes by 20 dB but leaves the amplifier changed by 10 dB, that compression ratio is 2:1. The length of time it takes for a compression system to react to a loud sound and compress it is referred to as an **attack time**. For example, if it takes 50 ms for a sound of 120 dB SPL to be compressed to a level of 90 dB SPL, then the attack

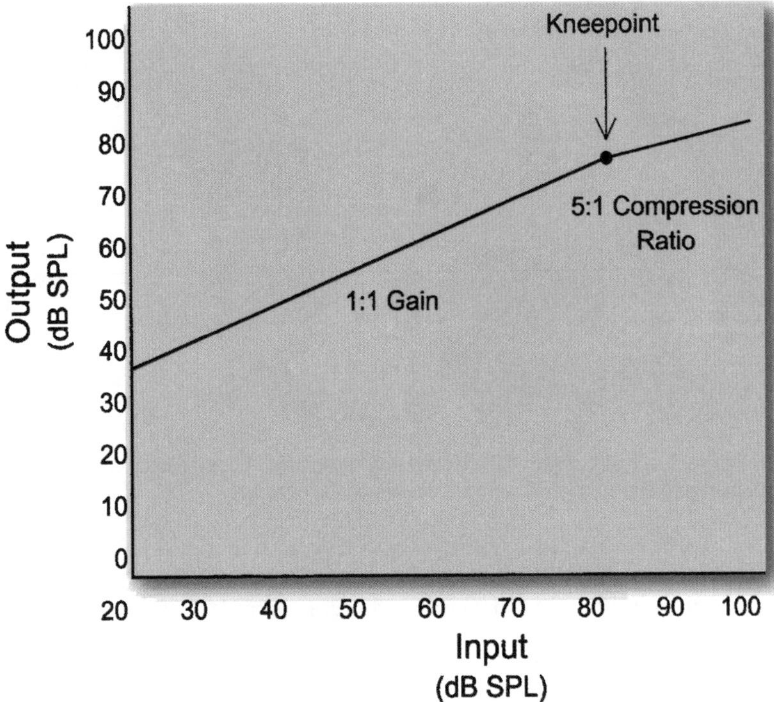

FIGURE 3–5 Input–output loudness function for a hearing aid that uses compression circuitry to limit output.

time is 50 ms. Similarly, the **release time** is the length of time for a compression system to increase its gain after a loud sound has ceased. There are different kinds of compression circuits. For example, the K-AMP circuit provides more gain for high frequencies than low frequencies at low-intensity input levels, but not for high-intensity input levels. **Multiband compression** permits different degrees of compression and output limiting for different frequency bands in the incoming signal, so that the growth of loudness in a signal can be controlled, and the signal can be shaped to maximize speech recognition.

Release time is the time it takes for an amplifier to return to its steady state after a loud sound ends.

Multiband compression is a method of shaping the loudness growth of a signal to maximize speech for the listener using different degrees of compression and output limiting for different frequencies.

Receivers

The processed electrical signal enters the other energy transducer of the hearing aid, the receiver, where it is converted back to acoustic energy. In a sense, the receiver is a mini loudspeaker or a microphone in reverse (i.e., whereas the receiver converts the electrical signal into an acoustic signal, the microphone converts the acoustic signal into an electrical signal).

Earmolds

In addition to a microphone, amplifier, and receiver, some hearing aids require the use of earmolds (whereas the casing actually replaces the **earmold** in many other kinds of hearing aids). Earmolds deliver sound from the receiver to the ear and help hold the hearing aid in place. Figure 3–6 presents two general types of earmolds, the conventional earmold on the left side and the open-fit technology version on the right side.

An **earmold** is a coupler customized to fit into the auricle that channels sound from the earhook of a hearing aid into the auditory canal.

Conventional earmolds typically are custom-made to fit into the ear canal of the user. An earmold attaches to plastic tubing, which leads to the hearing aid receiver. It can be constructed in a variety of configurations to suit the needs of the individual user. For example, some earmolds fill the entire concha of the ear whereas others consist only of

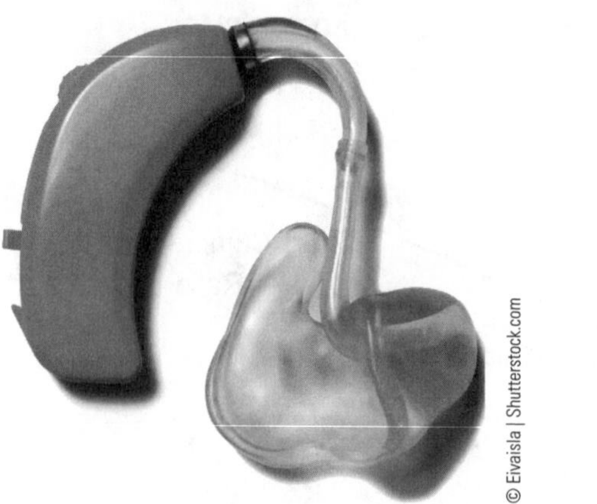

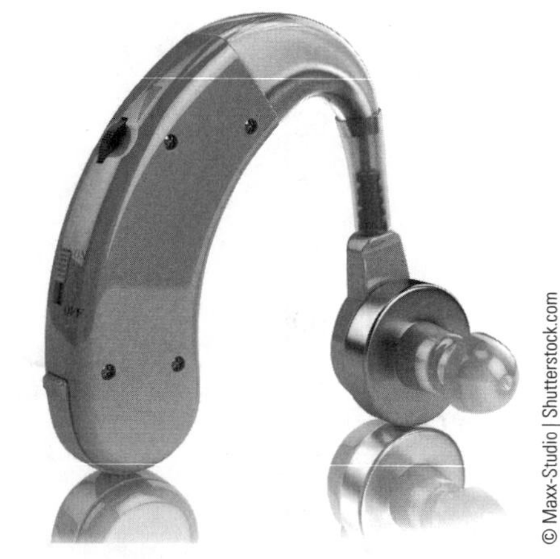

FIGURE 3–6 Two general types of earmold attached to a hearing aid. A conventional earmold is shown on the left side of the figure and an open-fit earmold appears on the right side.

a half-ring that anchors it within the concha. The former style of earmold might be used for a severe or profound hearing loss and the latter for a mild loss.

The open-fit concept is typically not a custom-made coupler but instead consists of a dome-shaped coupler that comes in standard sizes to fit different shapes and sizes of ear canals. Custom-made couplers can be constructed when feedback or retention in the ear canal are at issue. The open-canal fittings are generally used when the patient has a high-frequency hearing loss and normal or near-normal hearing in the frequencies at and below 2000 Hz. By not occluding the ear canal, low-frequency sound can pass through the ear canal unobstructed, allowing natural hearing. High-frequency sound is amplified and passed through the coupler into the ear canal.

Other Features of Hearing Aids

In addition to the components just discussed, some hearing aids include additional features. These include an on–off control, a volume control, a telecoil, and a remote control.

On–Off Control

The **on–off control** is a small switch that moves back and forth to turn the hearing aid off when not in use and on when needed and may be incorporated into the volume wheel.

The **on–off control** may be a small switch that moves back and forth to turn the hearing aid off when not in use and on when the hearing aid is needed. The on–off control also may be incorporated into the volume control wheel. When a hearing aid does not have an on–off switch, the hearing aid is activated by inserting the battery.

Audio Input

Direct audio input (DAI) is a hardwired connection that leads directly from the sound source to the hearing aid or other listening device.

An **audio boot**, also called a *shoe*, is a device that is used with a behind-the-ear hearing aid for coupling to a direct audio input cord.

Many behind-the-ear hearing aids have an audio input that allows an audio signal to be input directly from the signal source. This **direct audio input (DAI)** eliminates distortion from the surrounding environment. For example, a cable may be used to couple the hearing aid directly to a television or radio. The audio input consists of electrical contacts that accommodate a plug or an **audio boot**. It has a separate preamplifier from the microphone.

Telecoil

A **telecoil** is an induction coil that receives electromagnetic signals from a telephone or loop amplification system.

The **telecoil** (sometimes called a *t-coil* or an *audiocoil*) is an inductive coil within a hearing aid (i.e., a coil of wire wrapped around a magnetized metal rod) that enhances telephone communication. The telephone receiver emits electromagnetic signals, which are picked up by the hearing aid telecoil. The hearing aid microphone thus is bypassed. The signal picked up by the telecoil is amplified and transduced to an audio signal, and then delivered to the ear. If the hearing aid has an on–off switch, it may have an **MTO** (**M**icrophone, **T**elephone, and **O**ff) that includes a *T* position for telecoil and an *M* position for microphone, so the user can switch on the telecoil before using the telephone. An MT option on the on–off switch allows for simultaneous use of both the telecoil and microphone. Many hearing aids include a "touchless telecoil," where close proximity of a telephone automatically switches the hearing aid's microphone to the telephone mode. Use of a telecoil minimizes **acoustic feedback** problems and prevents the transmission of ambient room noise. As will be noted later in this chapter, telecoils can be used to pick up signals from ALDs too. Some of the small hearing aid models are sometimes too small to incorporate telecoils.

MTO is an abbreviation that refers to the three settings of a hearing aid on–off switch: **M**icrophone, **T**elephone, and **Off**.

Acoustic feedback occurs when the output from a hearing aid receiver re-enters the microphone, sending the system into oscillation and creating a "squeal."

Volume Control

A **volume control** allows the user to adjust the level of amplification. It usually is a rotating wheel.

The **volume control** on a hearing aid is used to adjust its output and may be manual or automatic.

Remote Control

A **remote control** is a handheld device that can serve two purposes. First, it can be used to program the electroacoustic properties of a hearing aid. Second, a remote control can be used to switch the hearing aid from one channel to another, to adjust the volume, and to turn it off and on.

A **remote control** is a handheld device that permits adjustments in the volume or changes in the program of a programmable hearing aid.

A Menu of Options

Some of the options related to signal processing and hearing aid design from which a patient and audiologist may choose include the following:

- ***Multiple memories***, so that a patient might adjust the hearing aid one way when listening in quiet and another way when listening in noise, to maximize sound quality and speech reception, and even adjust to a music or work environment situation. Hearing aids that provide access to different amplification characteristics sometimes are referred to as ***multiple-memory hearing aids***.
- ***Acoustic feedback cancellation***, so that hearing aids will not "whistle" when sound escapes from the receiver
- ***Multiple channels***, which allow frequency shaping, a signal-processing technique wherein the signal is filtered into frequency bands so that some bands (such as the high-frequency bands or the bands that carry speech information) receive more gain or amplification than other bands (such as the low-frequency bands or bands that contain a high level of noise)
- *Restoration of binaural hearing*, made possible by the possible linkage of signal processing from bilaterally fitted hearing aids, through ***high-frequency directionality*** and ***binaural gain control*** (Keidser, 2012)
- *Data storage*, whereby the hearing aid can collect and store such information as use time, noise in the listening environment, and the level of input signals

Some hearing aids have **multiple memories** that allow the speech signal to be processed in more than one way.

Multiple-memory hearing aids allow the user to select the processing strategy according to the listening environment.

Acoustic feedback cancellation is a feature that avoids the annoying squeal produced by hearing aids when the microphone picks up the amplified sound from the hearing aid and reamplifies it.

A hearing aid that uses **multiple channels** filters the signal into frequency bands so that some bands (usually the high-frequency bands) can receive more gain than others.

High-frequency directionality entails the hearing aid microphone reproducing the effects of the pinna by amplifying high frequencies in a way similar to an ear that is not occluded with a hearing aid earmold, and thereby enhancing posterior/anterior and up/down localization.

Binaural gain control aims to provide interaural difference cues (typically resulting from the head shadow effect) that are like those experienced in unaided ears by means of wireless communication between the two hearing aids.

Hearing Aid Styles

There are at least seven styles of hearing aids: (1) body aids, (2) behind-the-ear (BTE) aids, (3) receiver-in-the-ear (RITE), (4) in-the-ear (ITE) aids, (5) in-the-canal (ITC) aids, (6) completely-in-the-canal (CIC) aids, and (7) implantable hearing aids.

Body Hearing Aids

A **body hearing aid** includes a box worn on the torso and a cord connecting it to an ear-level receiver.

The body-aid casement is about the size of a deck of cards and is worn on the torso. The casement leads to a custom-made earmold by means of a long cord. The body-worn casement houses the microphone, amplifier, and receiver. **Body hearing aids** may provide powerful amplification and are useful for severe and profound hearing losses. They also have large controls, so they can be used by individuals who have reduced manual dexterity. Body aids are durable and can be harnessed to a patient who might have memory difficulties so that the likelihood of the hearing aid being lost or damaged may be reduced.

A **bone conductor** is a vibrator or oscillator used to transmit sound to the bones of the skull by means of vibration.

A **bone-conduction hearing aid** delivers the amplified signal via a bone vibrator placed over the mastoid directly to the cochlea, bypassing the middle ear.

Despite these advantages, body aids are not common today in either the United States or Europe. They are somewhat bulky and highly visible. The placement of the microphone on the chest rather than near the ear also may decrease a patient's ability to localize sound. They sometimes are used with patients who have a pinna that cannot support a BTE hearing aid and with patients who have atresia, microtia, or chronic otitis media. For these latter patients, the body aid may be attached to a **bone conductor**, converting it into a **bone-conduction hearing aid**. In this arrangement, sound is delivered to the inner ear via the bone vibrator worn behind the pinna and over the mastoid bone. The vibrations are transmitted through the bones of the skull directly to the cochlea, bypassing the middle ear altogether. Body aids are comparatively inexpensive and are sometimes promoted in emerging markets because of their lower cost.

Behind-the-Ear Hearing Aids

The style of hearing aid known as **behind-the-ear (BTE)** is worn over the pinna and coupled to the ear by means of an earmold.

An **earhook** connects the case of a BTE to the earmold tubing and hooks atop the ear.

The **behind-the-ear (BTE)** hearing aid components are built into a small shell that fits behind the pinna. Appropriate for mild to profound hearing losses, the **earhook** of the hearing aid case typically connects to an earmold by a small plastic tube. In BTEs with open-ear fittings, there may be only a tubing system or there may be a skeleton mold or a tulip tip to hold the device in place. The BTE is probably the most flexible style of hearing aid because it can be fitted with many available options, such as a powerful telecoil circuit. In addition, an earmold can be constructed to accommodate the user, which may be desirable for several reasons. For example, if a patient suffers from chronic otitis media, then he or she might not be able to use a device that occludes the ear canal, as does an ITE aid. Other advantages of BTEs include the following:

- When used with a soft earmold, a BTE affords greater safety than an ITE hearing aid. This aspect is important especially for an athlete, who may be at high risk for being hit in the ear, say, by a ball in a weekend football game.
- A BTE has the capability of DAI, so it can be hardwired to an assistive listening device.
- BTEs have fewer problems with feedback.
- There are fewer repair problems than with other hearing aid styles.
- BTEs are relatively easy to clean because the earmold can be detached and washed with warm soapy water. This aspect is important for individuals who perspire a lot, have wax buildup, or have chronic otitis media.
- A BTE can be used with a nonoccluding earmold, which may be important if the individual has chronic otitis media or is unable to have an occluded ear canal for other reasons.

A patient who is concerned about cosmetics may reject a BTE, because it is typically visible, unless covered by long hair. However, hearing aid designers are increasingly concerned with developing aesthetically pleasing, even trendy (think leopard spots), hearing devices (Figure 3–8). Instead of being stodgy medical devices, the goal is to make them more desirable, like iPods and Bluetooth technology.

When You Only Have One Good Ear to Work With

Patients who have unilateral hearing loss may be candidates for a **contralateral routing of the signal (CROS)** hearing aid. In its simplest manifestation, a microphone is worn on the "poor ear" and an amplifier and receiver are worn on the "good ear" (Figure 3–7). The poor ear may have severe hearing loss, poor speech discrimination, chronic infection, or malformation. The sound is routed from the poor ear to the good ear, typically wirelessly. A **bilateral contralateral routing of the signal (BICROS)** fitting is appropriate when both ears have hearing loss, but the loss is asymmetrical.

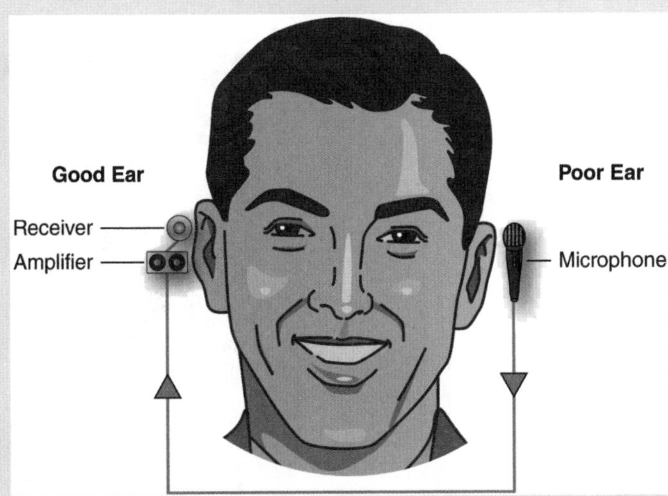

FIGURE 3–7 Schematic for a contralateral routing of the signal (CROS) hearing aid. Sound is routed from a microphone in the poor ear to an amplifier and receiver in the good ear.

A **contralateral routing of signals (CROS)** fitting is designed for unilateral hearing loss and entails placing the microphone on the poor ear side and the amplifier and receiver on the good ear side so that sound can be routed to the good ear.

A **bilateral contralateral routing of signals (BICROS)** fitting is designed for asymmetrical hearing loss and entails a microphone at each ear, with both microphones leading to a single amplifier and receiver in the better ear.

Receiver-in-the-Ear Hearing Aids

Also called a receiver-in-the-canal (RITC) aid or full shell (Figure 3–8), the receiver-in-the-ear (RITE) hearing aid style has a small casing that rests behind the ear. The diminutive casing houses all of its components except the receiver. The receiver resides in a plastic tubing that inserts into the ear canal. RITEs are typically recommended for hearing losses ranging from mild to severe.

In-the-Ear and In-the-Canal Hearing Aids

In-the-ear (ITE) also called half shell and **in-the-canal** (ITC) hearing aids fit completely in the external ear. A primary difference between the two styles is that the ITC fills less of the concha than does the ITE. Figure 3–9 shows two images of an ITC. The

An **in-the-ear (ITE)** hearing aid fits into the concha of the ear.

An **in-the-canal (ITC)** hearing aid fits in the external ear canal, only partially filling the concha.

FIGURE 3–8 A hearing aid designed to allay the cosmetic concerns of patients. This stylish design is available in 13 different colors, including Samoa Blue, Vivid Lilac, and Think Pink. This is an example of a receiver-in-the-ear (RITE) hearing aid, a style that is increasingly popular.

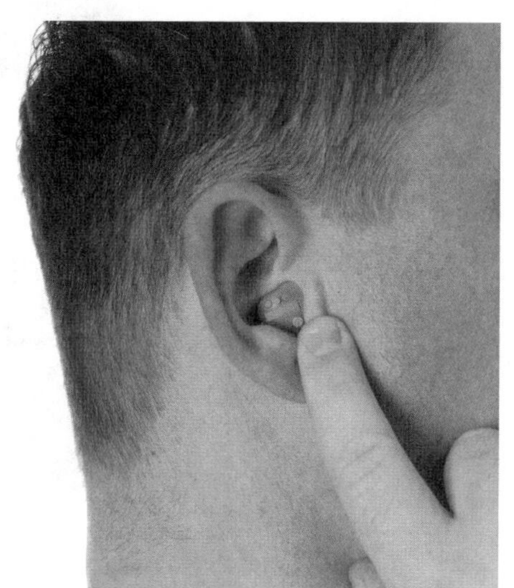

FIGURE 3–9 An in-the-canal hearing aid shown out of the ear (left) and inserted into an ear (right). The ITC, which inserts into the ear canal and fills less of the concha than an ITE, is cosmetically appealing to many patients.

two styles of listening devices must be custom-fitted to the user's ear. The audiologist takes an earmold impression of the ear and then sends the impression to the manufacturer for construction of the aid. The casings of ITEs and ITCs house all of the hearing aid components and no additional tubing or earmold is necessary. ITEs are typically prescribed for patients with mild to severe hearing losses and ITCs are typically prescribed for patients with mild to moderately severe hearing losses. ITCs are generally not recommended for patients with good hearing in the lower frequencies because they magnify an occlusion effect. An **occlusion effect** is the enhancement of low frequencies via **bone conduction** that is caused by the occlusion of the ear canal and may create the sensation of "listening in a barrel."

An **occlusion effect** is the enhancement of low-frequency sounds that occurs via bone conduction and is caused by the occlusion of the ear canal.

Bone conduction delivers sound by means of vibrating the skull.

The ITE hearing aid offers at least a couple of benefits over BTE aids. The position of the microphone enhances the amplification of high-frequency sounds relative to the BTE aid, and the closeness of the receiver to the tympanic membrane means that less gain is required to provide adequate amplification for a particular level of hearing loss. Although at one time ITE aids did not accommodate telecoils, most modern versions include them. Also, earlier versions often did not supply adequate amplification for more severe hearing losses, whereas current versions do. They are not as susceptible to wind noise as are the larger hearing aids. An ITE aid has cosmetic appeal relative to a BTE aid, but does have some disadvantages comparatively. For example, ITEs are highly subjected to cerumen buildup, so a person who produces a lot of cerumen should not be fitted with an ITE style. Some patients report that their own voices sound distorted or too loud, probably because the entire ear canal is blocked and disrupts how one hears him or herself.

Completely-in-the-Canal Hearing Aids

Completely-in-the-canal (CIC) hearing aids are worn completely inside the ear canal and do not occupy the concha. They are inserted and removed from the ear canal by means of a short clear cord attached to the hearing aid casement. CIC aids are so small that options often are not available, such as an on–off switch, a volume control, and a telecoil. Some newer devices that use digital technology have remote controls that permit adjustments in gain and program selection. They offer many advantages. They tend to be easy to insert and remove, often more so than trying to insert an earmold, as with a BTE aid. Some people report a better sound quality with CIC aids than with other styles, which is due in part to the absence of an occlusion effect. The advantages of CIC aids can be summarized as follows:

A **completely-in-the-canal (CIC)** hearing aid fits entirely within the external ear canal.

- Reduction of feedback
- Improved sound localization
- Less electronic gain needed than with other styles, because the volume between the end of the hearing aid and the tympanic membrane (eardrum) is minimal
- Elimination of wind noise
- Enhanced telephone use without the need for additional assistive listening devices
- Virtually invisible to others when inserted into the user's ear canal
- Greater high-frequency gain

Despite the advantages, CIC hearing aids are high-maintenance devices. Cerumen tends to build up, requiring the patient to clean the hearing aid frequently. Because CIC hearing aids are so small, a person with manual dexterity problems may experience difficulty in inserting and removing them. They are also easily lost.

Implantable Hearing Aids

Implantable hearing aids are options for patients who cannot wear an external hearing aid or who choose not to do so.

A middle ear implantable hearing aid converts the sound signal into a micromechanical vibration and transmits it directly to the ossicular chain. The **ossicular chain**, comprised of the malleus, incus, and stapes, spans the middle ear volume, stretching from the tympanic membrane to the oval window of the cochlea (see Figure 1–7).

The **ossicular chain** comprises the three small bones of the middle ear, the malleolus, incus, and stapes, and extends from the tympanic membrane through the tympanic cavity to the round window.

The first middle ear implants had outer and inner components. The outer components include the power supply (battery), the microphone, and electronic components that

Binaural versus Monaural Fitting

Often, an audiologist will recommend that a patient receive two hearing aids instead of one, especially if the hearing loss is moderate or severe. Even though two hearing aids are more expensive than one and may require more effort to maintain, binaural amplification fitting offers many advantages over a monaural fitting, including the following:

- ***Elimination of head shadow***: With one hearing aid, sound coming from the unaided side of the head may be attenuated by as much as 12 to 16 dB, especially high-frequency sounds. Use of two hearing aids allows sound to be received on both sides of the head.
- ***Loudness summation***: When sound is received by both ears, a summing of the two signals results. Thresholds for sound may improve by 3 dB or more compared with monaural thresholds in either ear.
- ***Binaural squelch***: Listening performance will be better in noise when the user wears two hearing aids instead of one. This improvement in signal-to-noise ratio may be 2 or 3 dB.
- ***Localization***: People with normal hearing are sensitive to interaural differences in a sound's intensity and phase and this allows them, in part, to perceive the direction and the location of a sound source and to segregate one sound source from another. A monaural hearing aid fitting disrupts these cues, whereas binaural hearing aids serve to preserve this localization ability.

Attenuation of sound to one ear because of the presence of the head between the ear and the sound source is called the **head shadow** effect.

Loudness summation is a summing of the signals received by each ear, resulting in a 3 dB advantage for binaural over monaural hearing.

Binaural squelch is an improvement in listening in noise when wearing two hearing aids instead of one, resulting in a 2 to-3 dB improvement in signal-to-noise ratio.

Localization is the ability to locate the source of a sound in space due to the normal ear's sensitivity to interaural differences in phase and intensity.

transduce the auditory signal into an electromagnetic signal. The internal components include a receiver, a cable, and a vibrator that deliver the micromechanical vibration to the ossicular chain.

The implantable middle ear device has not been widely used. Most often, it is considered to be appropriate for patients who have moderately severe to severe hearing losses, although some patients who have a mild loss are also candidates (Miller & Fredrickson, 2000). The loss might be sensorineural, conductive, or mixed. The middle ear implant is purported to bypass some of the shortcomings of more traditional hearing aid styles, including problems with feedback, occlusion effects, and buildup of cerumen. The downside includes high cost and the necessity of undergoing anesthesia for a surgical procedure for the implant.

A **bone-anchored hearing aid (BAHA)** is a bone-conduction hearing aid that is anchored in the mastoid and attached percutaneously to an external processor, and is often used for conductive hearing loss in the presence of chronic middle ear disorder or atresia.

Another type of implantable hearing aid is the **bone-anchored hearing aid (BAHA)**. A BAHA is a bone conduction hearing aid that uses a surgically implanted titanium screw to transmit sound through the skull to directly vibrate the cochlea and stimulate the hair cells. The external component is worn behind the ear, coupled to an external abutment via a spring or clip. Patients with conductive or mixed hearing loss, who typically have external ear canal problems such as atresia or eczema, and with middle ear malformations and chronic infection are candidates for these devices.

Selecting a Hearing Aid Style

A consideration of hearing aid styles leads to the question, "How do you determine which style to provide to a particular individual?" There is no pat answer to this question, but the selection of a particular style of hearing aid often is dependent on the degree of hearing loss, the patient's preference, the cost of the device, the person's age and lifestyle, and his or her physical status.

In order of descending willingness-to-pay-for-attributes cited by patients:

- The ability of the hearing aid to perform well in quiet settings
- The hearing aid's capacity to repel moisture and sweat
- Total amount of money spent
- Minimal acoustic feedback
- Long battery life

(Bridges, Lataille, Buttorff, White, & Niparko, 2012)

Degree of Hearing Loss

Going Blue

Bluetooth first appeared in 1994 and used radio frequencies to permit devices to communicate without wires or cables. The Bluetooth device transmits sound directly to the hearing aid so the microphone is bypassed, allowing sound from television, Bluetooth-enabled mobile phones, and music players to be accessed wirelessly and hands-free. Hence, a frequent communication partner's common complaint, "The television is cranked up too loud!" can be eliminated.

The magnitude and configuration of an individual's hearing loss will help to determine the style of hearing aid selected. For example, if an individual has a profound hearing loss, a CIC device is not appropriate because it likely will not provide enough amplification for the person's listening needs or will be susceptible to acoustic feedback because the amplified sound can readily feed back into the microphone and be re-amplified.

User Preference

Probably as important as the magnitude and configuration of the hearing loss in selecting a hearing aid style is the preference of the user. The audiologist will talk with the patient and carefully consider his or her preferences and prejudices concerning hearing aid styles. If user preferences are not considered, the hearing aid may not be used. For example, if an audiologist provided someone with a BTE, and the individual turned out to be too self-conscious to wear it, then the BTE probably was an inappropriate selection on the audiologist's part.

Costs

A closely related issue to preference is cost. CIC and digital hearing aids with many "bells and whistles" constitute the most expensive hearing aids. ITC and CIC instruments are subject to the deleterious effects of perspiration and cerumen since they are inserted into the ear canal and hence can incur costly repair bills. You will want to explore an individual's financial resources to purchase certain hearing aid styles early in the selection process. Those styles the patient deems too expensive can then be eliminated from consideration.

Lifestyle

Lifestyle influences the selection process. For example, a physician or nurse who often uses a stethoscope and does not want to use one with a built-in amplifier, may want a CIC aid because this style can be used with a stethoscope. A patient who uses the telephone for a good part of the working day may opt for a BTE hearing aid that has a powerful telecoil circuitry.

Physical Status

Physical status includes an individual's manual dexterity and the condition of the ear. It is important to assess a patient's gross and fine motor skills and to evaluate how well the individual can move hands, fingers, and arms because both fine and gross motor skills are necessary for putting on and taking off a hearing aid. In addition, fine motor control is necessary for manipulating the controls, changing batteries, and inserting and removing the hearing aid from the ear. If a patient has poor skills, it might be best to consider a BTE aid, a body aid, or an ALD such as a handheld amplifier.

An examination of the ear will indicate whether a patient has chronic ear infections or a deformity in the ear canal. For example, in the case of chronic otitis media, if an ITE aid is prescribed, secretions might damage the device. Hence, this is one reason a BTE aid may be more appropriate. A deformed or nonexistent ear canal also may limit (or preclude) the use of certain styles of hearing aids.

In addition to the health of the ear and physical malformations, the curve of the ear canal may influence a selection. If a patient has a straight ear canal, without a bend, then he or she probably should not receive a CIC aid. The device will not stay in place. Similarly, if the patient has a shallow concha, an ITC aid may be difficult to keep in the ear.

Electroacoustic Properties

In addition to selecting a hearing aid style, certain decisions must be made concerning the electroacoustic properties of the hearing aid. These properties affect how the hearing aid processes the audio signal. These properties include saturation SPL and gain/frequency response:

- ***Output sound pressure level (OSPL)***: Once called the *saturation sound pressure level (SSPL)*, this term refers to the maximum sound pressure level that can be delivered to the ear when the volume control is turned full on and the input signal is 90 dB SPL. This value is determined to ensure that the hearing aid's maximum power does not exceed the user's **loudness discomfort level (LDL)**, also called uncomfortable loudness level (UCL). The LDL is the threshold at which sound becomes so loud that the hearing aid user cannot tolerate it, even for a brief exposure. An **OSPL90** curve is obtained by measuring the hearing aid's output in a hearing aid test chamber called a **hearing aid test box**. The hearing aid is connected to a 2-cc coupler that simulates the human external ear canal volume. An input signal then is presented that sweeps across frequencies, at 90 dB SPL. The output of the hearing aid is measured.
- ***Gain/frequency response***: The difference between the amplitude of the input signal and the amplitude of the output signal across frequencies is referred to as the gain/frequency response of a hearing aid. Typically, a hearing aid for an individual is adjusted to deliver the greatest amount of gain for those frequencies for which the individual has the poorest thresholds.
- ***Total harmonic distortion (THD)***: The amplitude distortions in the form of additional harmonic components of an input sine wave. These unwanted signals, created by the hearing aid, typically are reported for the frequencies of 500, 800, and 1600 Hz.

The **output sound pressure level (OSPL)** is the maximum output generated by a hearing aid receiver, determined when the hearing aid has its gain turned full on and is receiving a 90 dB SPL signal.

Loudness discomfort level (LDL) is the level at which sound is perceived to be uncomfortably loud.

An **OSPL90** is an electroacoustic assessment of a hearing aid's maximum level of output signal, expressed as a frequency response curve to a 90 dB SPL signal, with the hearing aid volume control set to full on; also called *SSPL90*.

A **hearing aid test box** is a chamber that provides an electroacoustic analysis of hearing aids and probe-microphone measurements. It provides an off-the-ear determination of OSPL-90 in which the hearing aid is connected to a 2-cc coupler to simulate the human ear canal; an input signal that sweeps across the frequencies at 90 dB SPL is input, and the aid's output is measured.

Gain/frequency response is the difference between the amplitude of the input signal and the amplitude of the output signal across frequencies.

Determining Gain and Assessing Benefits

In determining how a hearing aid will shape incoming sound to accommodate a patient's degree and configuration of hearing loss, a formula for gain is typically applied, which is a formula used to compute the desired amount of amplification at each frequency. This strategy is referred to as a **prescription procedure**. For example, in one of the earliest prescription procedures, the goal was to restore hearing thresholds to normal. The amount of gain prescribed at each frequency corresponded to the degree of hearing loss. In a more recent prescriptive procedure, high frequencies are amplified more than low frequencies to maximize speech audibility. Some prescriptive formulas determine targets for soft, moderate, and loud sounds. Incorporated in most prescriptive formulas is the patient's LDL, so sound is not presented at an uncomfortably loud level. Most hearing aid manufacturers preprogram a hearing aid according to their preferred prescription formula and the patient's particular hearing loss, but the audiologist can alter the settings using the manufacturer's computer software.

Prescription procedures are strategies for fitting hearing aids by using a formula to calculate the desired gain and frequency response.

Verification

Implicit in the use of prescriptive methods of hearing aid selection is the need to verify that the prescriptive targets have been met and that the fitting is appropriate for the particular patient. **Verification** determines whether the hearing aid is acoustically working as desired on the patient's ear. Verification is typically accomplished with **probe microphone** technology and is considered by the American Speech-Language-Hearing Association (ASHA) and the American Academy of Audiology (AAA) as being the *best practice* (AAA, 2006; ASHA, 1998). A small flexible tube is inserted into the ear canal and positioned near the tympanic membrane. The tube connects to a microphone, which records the decibels of power delivered at the end of the ear canal. First, sound is measured near the tympanic membrane, so the measure is influenced by the natural resonance of the ear canal. Measurements are then repeated, but this time with the hearing aid worn by the patient. These measures are called **real-ear measures**. Although these measures do not indicate how well an individual can hear when wearing the hearing aid, results indicate whether the hearing aid delivers the prescribed gain at each frequency, also called the **target gain**.

Verification means to determine that the hearing aid meets a set of standards, including standards of basic electroacoustics, real-ear electroacoustic performance, and comfortable fit.

A **probe microphone** is a microphone transducer that is inserted in the external ear canal for the purpose of measuring sound near the tympanic membrane.

Real-ear measures entail the use of a probe microphone to measure hearing aid gain and frequency response delivered by a hearing aid at the tympanic membrane.

Target gain is the gain prescribed for each frequency of a hearing aid, against which the actual hearing aid output is compared.

A recent trend has been to include **speech mapping** in the probe-measure repertoire, which ensures that the patient can optimally hear those frequencies comprised by the speech spectrum. In this procedure, the patient wears the hearing aid while he or she is coupled to the programming computer, along with a probe microphone in the ear. Continuous speech is presented at a constant level, typically twice, once at a conversational level and then once at a fairly loud level. The output of the probe microphone displays on the computer screen. This display is evaluated in terms of the patient's audiogram, LDL, targeted gain levels, and a spectral display of conversational speech. In particular, the soft and loud peaks of speech are assessed to ensure that they do not approach an uncomfortable level but are loud enough to be heard.

Speech mapping is a visual display of the impact of amplification on the average speech spectrum.

Validation

In addition to verifying that a hearing aid meets particular targets, **validation** measures are collected to ensure that hearing-related disability has been reduced. Validation may entail collecting speech recognition measures and subjective impressions.

Validation determines the extent to which hearing-related disability has been reduced by an intervention, such as receipt of a hearing aid.

Speech recognition testing indicates the extent to which the patient can recognize more speech with the hearing aid versus without the hearing aid and ostensibly reflects a concomitant decrease in hearing-related disability. Patients are tested with and without their hearing aid, and the amount of improvement in percent words correct is computed. According to Bentler (2009), the most commonly used tests for this purpose are the CID W-22 Test (Hirsh et al., 1952), the NU-6 Test (Tillman & Carhart, 1966), the Speech-in-Noise (SIN) Test (Killion & Vilchur, 1993), the QuickSIN Test (Killion, Niquette, & Gudmundsen, 2004), and the Connected Speech Test (CST) (Cox, Alexander, & Gilmore, 1987). The Hearing in Noise Test (HINT; Nilsson, Soli, & Sullivan, 1994) is also recommended for this purpose (Mendel, 2011).

A second, subjective procedure to validate hearing aid benefit is to administer a questionnaire or an inventory. Patients may complete a checklist about what they can or cannot hear with the hearing aid, and may indicate satisfaction with the device. Cox (2003) identified seven categories of self-report outcome data. Choice of a particular self-assessment scale might be based on which of these seven categories you are interested in assessing:

1. *Benefit*, or the change in hearing-related disability that has resulted from the use of amplification
2. *Satisfaction*, or an overview of the physical, social, psychological, and financial changes that have resulted from the use of amplification
3. *Use time*, which is often related to the severity of the hearing loss and contextual factors, but is an indicant of how helpful and beneficial the hearing aid is for the patient
4. *Residual activity limitations*, or the hearing-related difficulties that the patient continues to experience despite the use of amplification
5. *Residual participation restrictions*, or limitations that prevent an individual from fulfilling a role in life
6. *Impact on others*, usually determined by a frequent communication partner (not many instruments are available for this purpose)
7. *Quality of life*, including improvements in social life and mental health

   Other subjective indices include asking such questions as:

   - Does my speech sound natural?
   - Can you hear me clearly when I count from one to ten?
   - Am I too loud?
   - Does your own voice sound natural?
   - Is it tinny or mechanical sounding?

Table 3–1 summarizes several self-assessment scales that may be used to validate the goodness of a hearing aid. Some of the scales are geared more toward gauging benefit (e.g., Profile of Aided Loudness [PAL]; Mueller & Palmer, 1998), whereas others are geared more to assessing satisfaction with the device (e.g., Satisfaction with Amplification in Daily Life [SADL]; Cox & Alexander, 1999).

Hearing Aids Are Not Always a Be-All End-All Solution

"It's not all about the hearing aid! A good community-based marketing program will educate local communities on the importance of hearing healthcare, including counseling and aural rehabilitation."

—Christine Throm, AuD, a practice owner in Los Gatos, CA

(The Hearing Journal Special Report, 2018, p. 21)

Hearing Aid Orientation

Once the audiologist receives the prescribed hearing aid from the manufacturer, the patient returns to the clinic to be fitted with the device. The audiologist will make sure that the hearing aid fits comfortably into the patient's ear. At this time, benefit also is

TABLE 3–1 Examples of Self-Report Measures That Have Been Developed to Assess a Patient's Perceived Benefit from a Hearing Aid

MEASURE	PURPOSE	REFERENCE
Glasgow Hearing Aid Benefit Profile (GHABP) The prespecified element of the instrument presents four listening situations with six questions about each, and includes six scales to evaluate effectiveness of aural rehabilitation for initial disability, handicap, hearing aid use, satisfaction, and residual disability	To assess individual patient concerns and expectations in a variety of difficult listening situations Example: *In this situation [having a conversation with several people in a group], what proportion of the time do you wear your hearing aid? (5-point scale: 1 = never/not at all; 5 = all the time)*	Gatehouse (1999)
Hearing Aid Needs Assessment (HANA) A questionnaire designed to assess the relationship between perceived communication needs and expectations with realized benefit with a newly fitted hearing aid.	To compare perceived communication needs with actual benefit eventually achieved with hearing aids Example: *You are at home listening to your stereo system.* (Ratings for *how often, how much trouble, and how much help expected*)	Schum (1999)
Hearing Aid Performance Inventory (HAPI) 64 items, based on 12 bipolar features (e.g., visual signal present/absent), assess noisy situations, quiet situations, situations with reduced signal information, and situations with non-speech stimuli	To assess the benefits of amplification in varying listening situations Example: *You are alone at home talking with a friend on the telephone. (5-point scale: 1 = very helpful; 5 = hinders performance)*	Walden, Demorest, and Helper (1984)
Hearing Aid Users Questionnaire 11-item questionnaire that assesses hearing aid use, benefit, and related problems and satisfactions	To detect problems that affect a patient's ability to use hearing aids and receive benefit Example: *How would you describe your satisfaction with your hearing aid? (4-point scale: 1 = very satisfied; 4 = very dissatisfied)*	Dillon, Birtles, and Lovegrove (1999)
Hearing Problem Inventory 50 items about emotional reaction to hearing loss; effect of hearing loss on everyday activities; signal and environmental influences; use of visual cues; use, fit, and care of hearing aid	To assess benefit of using a hearing aid and to identify some of the influences on a patient's perception of his or her problems and hearing aid use Example: *The telephone pickup on my hearing aid is good. (5-point scale: 1 = almost always; 5 = almost never)*	Hutton (1980)
The International Outcome Inventory for Hearing Aids (IOI-HA) 7-item inventory designed to assess the efficacy of hearing aid treatments (see Chapter 10, Key Resources)	To measure 7 dimensions of hearing intervention outcome: daily use, benefit, residual activity limitations, satisfaction, residual participation restrictions, impact on others, and quality of life Example: *Think about how much you used your present hearing aid(s) over the past 2 weeks. On an average day, how many hours did you use the hearing aid(s)?* (Range of hours, from *None to More than 8 hours)*	Cox and Alexander (2002)

(continues)

TABLE 3–1 *(continued)*

MEASURE	PURPOSE	REFERENCE
The Client-Oriented Scale of Improvement (COSI) The patient identifies the most pressing listening needs and then rates in terms of degree of change and final ability as to how the hearing aid has affected these needs (see Chapter 10, Key Resources)	To address directly whether the patient's most important listening difficulties have been alleviated or eliminated; may also be used to guide the general aural rehabilitation plan Example: *Because of the new hearing instrument, I now hear . . . worse, no difference, slightly better, better, much better [for the specific need noted]*	Dillon, James, and Ginis (1997)
Profile of Aided Loudness (PAL) 12 items across categories of soft, average, and loud sounds	To determine whether amplification has restored loudness Example: *You are chewing soft food: Loudness rating (scale from 0 to 7: 0 = do not hear; 7 = uncomfortably loud); Satisfaction rating (scale from 5 to 1: 5 = just right; 1 = not good at all)*	Mueller and Palmer (1998); Palmer, Mueller, and Moriarty (1999)
Profile of Hearing Aid Benefit (PHAB) 66 items in seven subscales designed to assess the following: familiar talkers, ease of communication, reverberation, reduced cues, background noise, aversiveness of sounds, and distortion of sounds	To generate a measure of hearing aid benefit computed from the difference between aided and unaided conditions Example: *(Answered with and without hearing aid) Women's voices sound shrill (7-point scale: A = always; G = never)*	Cox, Gilmore, and Alexander (1991); Cox and Rivera (1992)
Abbreviated Profile of Hearing Aid Benefit (APHAB) Uses a subset of 24 of the 66 items from the PHAB, four scales designed to assess ease of communication, reverberation, noise, and aversiveness	To generate a measure of hearing aid benefit in a clinically feasible amount of time, see example (above)	Cox and Alexander (1995)
Profile of Hearing Aid Performance (PHAP) 66 items designed to measure two aspects of performance with a hearing aid, speech communication in a variety of typical workday situations and reactions to loudness or quality of environmental sounds	To generate a measure of performance rather than benefit Example: *When I am in a quiet restaurant, I can understand conversation (7-point scale: A = always; G = never)*	Cox and Gilmore (1990)
Satisfaction with Amplification in Daily Life (SADL) 15 items in four subscales: positive effects, service and costs, negative features, and personal image	To quantify hearing aid satisfaction Example: *Are you convinced that obtaining your hearing aid was in your best interest? (7-point scale: A = not at all; G = tremendously)*	Cox and Alexander (1999)
The Speech, Spatial, and Qualities of Hearing Scale (SSQ) 14 items about speech hearing, 17 items about spatial hearing, 18 items about other functions; when applied to aided listening, additional items are included	To assess the recognition of speech in a variety of competing contexts, with particular attention to interventions that involve binaural hearing Example: *Do you have the impression of sounds being exactly where you would expect them to be? (10-point scale: 0 = not at all; 10 = perfectly)*	Gatehouse and Noble (2004)

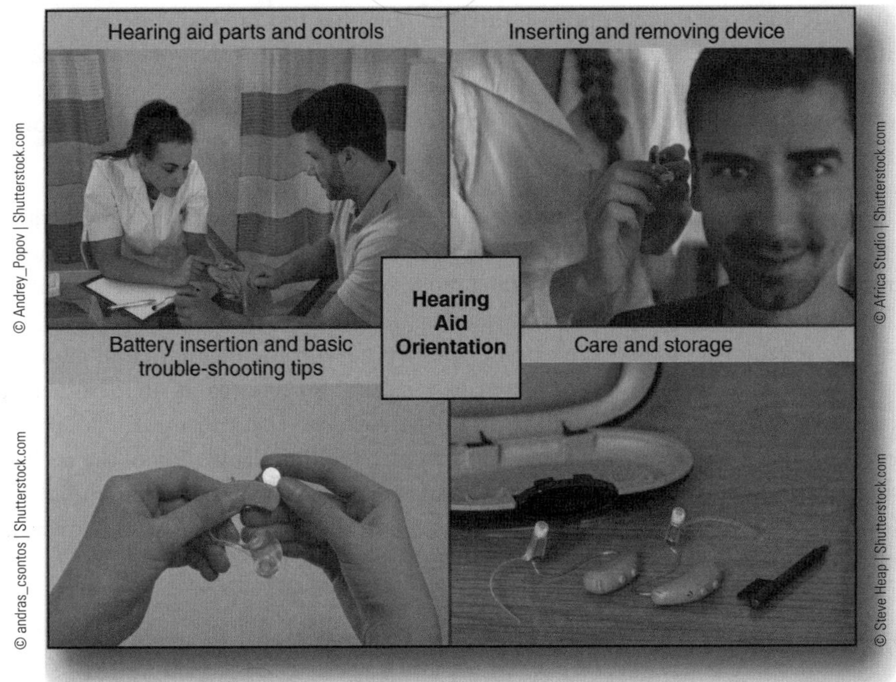

FIGURE 3–10 The hearing aid orientation. Some of the topics covered in the hearing aid orientation include a description of the parts and controls, instruction on insertion, battery information, and issues related to maintenance, warranty, and care.

assessed, and the patient receives a **hearing aid orientation (HAO)**. The HAO includes the following services (Figure 3–10):

- The audiologist describes the function of each part of the hearing aid and ensures that the patient can adjust any controls.
- The patient practices inserting and removing the hearing aid (sometimes with the aid of a mirror) and practices inserting and removing batteries from the hearing aid battery compartment.
- The audiologist reviews basic hearing aid maintenance and ways to clean the device, protect it from moisture, and store it at night, and discusses battery life, storage, disposal, and how to order new batteries.
- The patient practices using the telephone, using the telecoil switch if the hearing aid has one.
- The audiologist reviews realistic expectations and the limitations of amplification, and why the particular hearing aid was selected.
- The patient and audiologist determine an appropriate use pattern for the first few weeks of using the new hearing aid.
- The patient learns how to **troubleshoot** the device for common problems such as weak or no sound (e.g., one possible solution is to check the battery and replace) and feedback (e.g., one possible solution is to clean the wax guard).
- The patient receives printed information about the hearing aid and warranty.
- The patient and audiologist agree on a follow-up time table and talk about how to monitor performance with the hearing aid.

Hearing aid orientation (HAO) is the process of instructing a patient (and a family member) to handle, use, and maintain a new hearing aid.

Troubleshoot refers to a series of steps to follow when the hearing aid will not turn on, if the sound is faint or distorted, or feedback occurs, the objective being to locate and correct the source of malfunction.

Caring for your hearing aid:

- Keep hearing aids away from heat and moisture
- Clean hearing aids as instructed
- Avoid using hairspray or other hair care products while wearing hearing aids
- Turn off when not in use
- Replace dead batteries immediately
- Keep away from children and pets

COCHLEAR IMPLANTS

Not all patients who have hearing loss have the potential to benefit from a hearing aid. For example, someone who has little, if any, residual hearing will probably never recognize the auditory speech signal, no matter how it is processed or how much it is amplified. Another intervention available besides a hearing aid is the cochlear implant. Cochlear implants, virtually unheard of 40 years ago, are now fairly commonplace. About 325,000 people worldwide use a cochlear implant (NIDCD, 2017). A minority of patients use bilateral cochlear implants (one cochlear implant in each cochlea).

Most sensorineural hearing loss results from a dearth or absence of hair cells (the sensory receptors of hearing) in the cochlea and not because of a damaged auditory nerve or central dysfunction. A cochlear implant replaces the hair-cell transducer system by stimulating the auditory nerve directly, bypassing the damaged or missing hair cells. The nerve impulses then progress to the brain, following the route of the neural auditory pathway, as if the cochlea were stimulated in a natural way. Implants are designed to interface with the **tonotopic organization** of the cochlea. The implant divides sound into a series of frequency bands and then delivers each band to that region of the cochlea for which it is best suited. High-frequency bands are delivered to the basilar end of the cochlea, whereas low-frequency bands are delivered to the apical end. The level of stimulation serves to code sound intensity.

Structures within the peripheral and central auditory nervous system are arranged topographically according to tonal frequency; that is, they have a **tonotopic organization**.

A Brief History

Although cochlear implants are a relatively new development, scientists have long been tantalized by the idea of providing sound sensation by means of electrical stimulation. One of the first recorded attempts in history to stimulate the ear electrically occurred in 1790, when Alessandro Graf Volta inserted metal rods into each of his ears. The rods were connected to 30 or 40 of his newly invented electrolytic cells. With one deft move, Volta delivered approximately 50 volts to himself. The results were staggering. He perceived a sensation similar to "a blow to the head," followed by "a sound like the boiling of a viscous liquid" (Luxford & Brackmann, 1985, p. 1). The experiment was not repeated.

The more recent history of cochlear implants hails back to France in the 1950s. The electrophysiologist Andre Djourno developed an electrical auditory prosthesis in the mid-1950s for stimulation of motor nerves. He was able to trigger jumping action in both frogs and rabbits. On February 25, 1957, the otolaryngologist Charles Eyries implanted a human with profound hearing loss with an identical device to stimulate the auditory nerve (Seitz, 2002). The patient reported hearing a sound like "crickets chirping" or "a roulette wheel spinning" (Luxford & Brackmann, 1985). Reports of this early implant work filtered to the medical communities in the United States and Australia. Shortly thereafter, in the 1960s and 1970s, much activity was aimed toward the development of wearable devices. Names often associated with this work are Dr. William House of Los Angeles, California, Dr. Graham Clarke of Melbourne, Australia, and the scientists Ingeborg and Erwin Hochmair, of Vienna, Austria. The following excerpt from an interview with Dr. House captures the excitement of this era:

> The story started shortly after I finished my residency in ENT at the USC Los Angeles County Hospital [in 1956]. Several parents brought their children who were obviously hearing impaired. The trouble is that there was so little that we could do. It gave me a bad feeling [because] all I could do would be to say, go and see if you can get a hearing aid and learn lipreading. . . . Fortunately, about this time a patient brought me a newspaper clipping . . . about a patient in France who had a destroyed cochlea. Two French doctors put a coil of wire where the patient's destroyed cochlea should have been, at the nerve stub, and found that the patient could hear sound. I was very impressed with this . . . and [I felt] this was a breakthrough we should explore. (Zeng, 2012, p. 32)

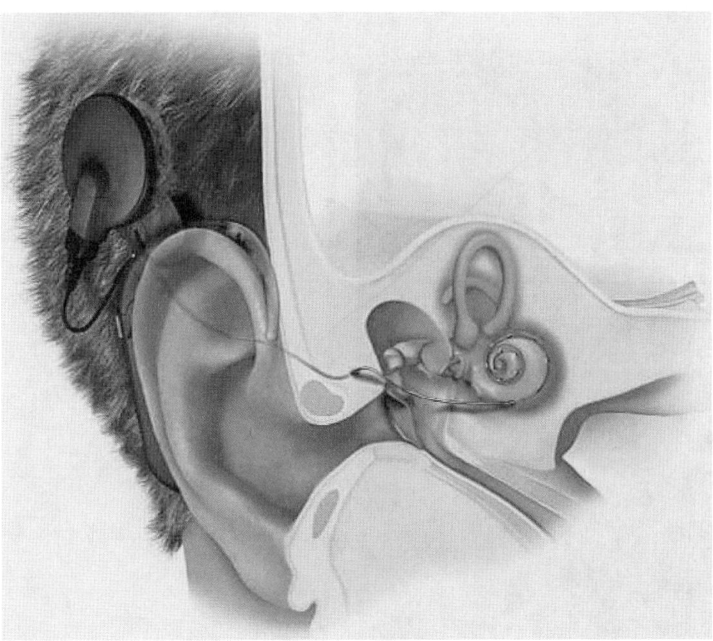

FIGURE 3–11 Schematic of the internal and external components of a typical cochlear implant.

The FDA approved the first multichannel cochlear implant in 1984 for adults. Since the 1990s, miniaturization has occurred, so most users now wear a BTE processor that is about the same size as a BTE hearing aid. Relatively recent advances include a totally implantable device, called a **completely implantable cochlear implant (CICI)**, also referred to as a totally implantable cochlear implant (TICI) (Briggs et al., 2008).

The cochlear implant of the future may be a **completely implantable cochlear implant (CICI)**, which will comprise only internal components.

Overview

Commonly, cochlear implants include internal and external components. The **internal components** are implanted in the skull, in close proximity to the inner ear (Figure 3–11). The internal components typically include an internal receiver, which is placed on the mastoid bone, and an electrode array, which is inserted into the cochlea. These components are not visible after implantation, but are covered by skin and hair. The user may have a small incision scar and a slight convex protrusion behind the pinna.

In cochlear implants, the **internal components** are implanted within the skull.

The **external components** include a microphone, connecting cables, a speech processor, and a transmitter (Figure 3–12). The microphone and transmitter typically are worn behind the ear. Figure 3–12 presents a photograph of a cochlear implant in place on the user's head.

In cochlear implants, the **external components** are worn on the outside of the body.

The microphone of a cochlear implant picks up sound from the environment, converts it to an electrical signal, and then delivers it via connecting cables to the speech processor. The **speech processor**, as the name implies, processes the signal. Each cochlear implant design utilizes a speech-processing strategy, or algorithm, for determining how the signal is processed. The signal is digitized, filtered, and then segmented so that different components of the signal are presented to different electrodes in the electrode array.

A **speech processor** is the component of a cochlear implant where the input signal is modified for presentation to the electrodes in the electrode array.

The processed electrical signal leaves the speech processor and is delivered to the electrode array via a transmitter and an internal receiver. The transmitter often is worn outside of the head and delivers the signal to an internal receiver. The transmitter may

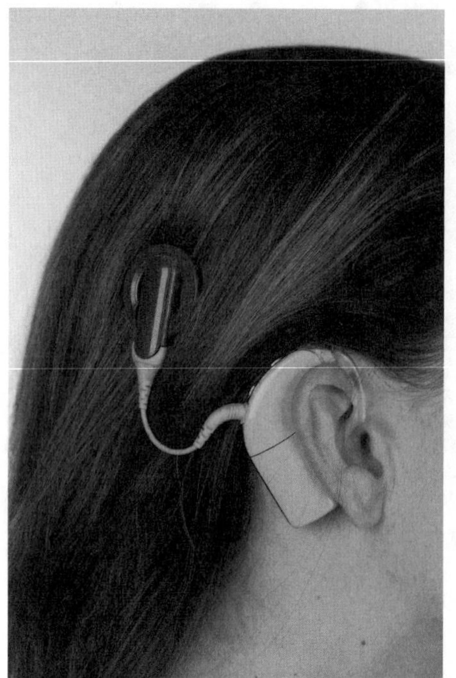

FIGURE 3–12 A cochlear implant as worn by a user. Courtesy of MED-EL.

be held in place by a magnet. The electrical signal typically is transmitted across the skin by either electromagnetic induction or radio frequency transmission. From the internal receiver, the electrical signal passes on to the electrode array.

The **electrode array** is a component of a cochlear implant composed of electrodes separated by insulation; it is inserted into the cochlea and placed in close approximation to the ganglion cells that are responsible for transmitting electrical impulses to those brain regions responsible for processing sound.

The **round window** is a membrane-covered opening between the middle ear space and the scala tympani section of the cochlea in the inner ear.

If a device is **multichannel**, it has more than one channel. The term is often used to describe cochlear implants that present different channels of information to different parts of the cochlea.

Interleaved pulsatile stimulation is a cochlear implant processing strategy in which trains of pulses are delivered across electrodes in the electrode array in a nonsimultaneous fashion.

The **electrode array** is a small wire, inserted into the cochlea, usually through the **round window**. The electrode array carries electrode pairs. The electrode pairs, which are tiny exposed balls or rings on the wire, have positive and negative polarity contacts, between which passes current. The current stimulates the fibers of the auditory nerve.

Most cochlear implants in use in the United States today are **multichannel** devices. This means that the electrode pairs in the electrode array present different information to different regions of the cochlea. In the normal ear, different frequencies of the auditory signal excite different neurons along the cochlea. The goal of a multichannel system is to simulate the normal cochlea and present high-frequency components of the signal to the basal end of the cochlea and low-frequency components of the signal to the apical end.

Although there are some variations in the processing strategies used by different models of cochlear implants, many current cochlear implants utilize an **interleaved pulsatile stimulation** algorithm. In this design, each electrode pair in the electrode array is designated to represent different frequency bands. The audio signal is processed and delivered to the electrode array by spreading pulses, in a nonsimultaneous manner (hence, they are interleaved) across the electrode pairs, from high to low or from low to high frequencies.

The cochlear implant is powered by either a disposable battery or a rechargeable battery. Most cochlear implants can be used in conjunction with an ALD. DAI cables can couple the cochlear implant to CD players, auxiliary microphones, and other portable players. Some devices have an integrated telecoil and some can be plugged into an external telecoil and some are Bluetooth friendly.

In the United States, three manufacturers, Cochlear Corporation, Med-El, and Advanced Bionics, provide most of the devices. Their processing strategies are continually

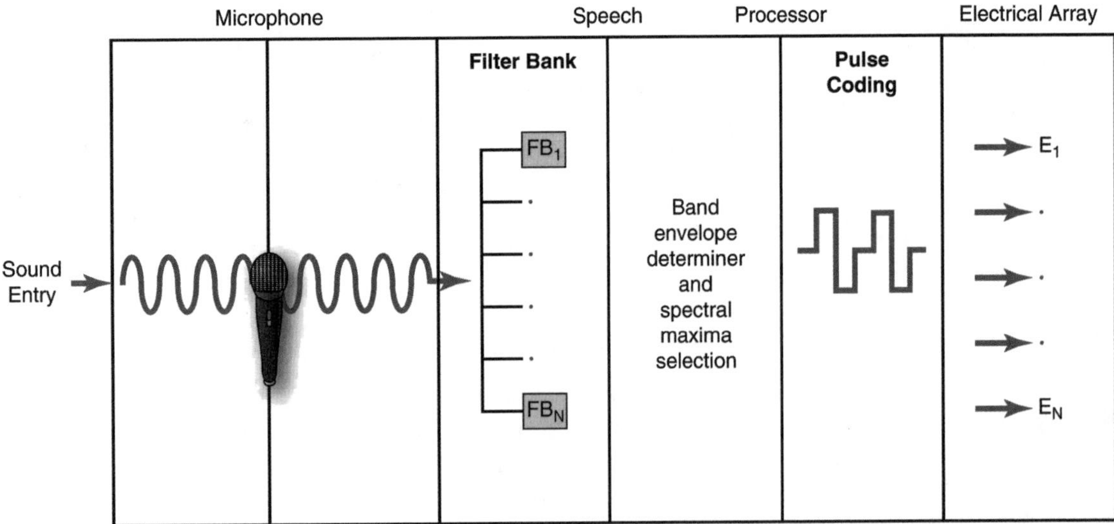

FIGURE 3–13 A simplified schematic of a continuous-interleaved-sampling coding strategy. Sound passes into the microphone and then is filtered and digitally processed before being decoded into pulses and presented to the electrical array inserted into the cochlea. FB = filter bank; E = electrode.

under development. However, for the past 20 years, variants of a continuous interleaved sampling (CIS) coding strategy have dominated the markets, regardless of the manufacturer. A simplified version of a CIS is presented in Figure 3–13. In a CIS scheme, the acoustic signal is picked up by the microphone and then filtered into bands of frequencies with a bank of **band-pass filters**.

A **band-pass filter** is an electronic filter that allows a band of frequencies to pass, while blocking the passage of frequencies below or above the band of specified limits.

A relatively new development in processing strategies is combined **electrical auditory stimulation (EAS)**, which is part of what is sometimes referred to as a **hybrid** cochlear implant. This device has a shorter electrode array than traditional cochlear implants (so does not insert as far into the cochlear capsule) and patients hear sounds through a combination of electrical stimulation and traditional acoustic amplification. The goal is to preserve existing hearing sensitivity, which for many patients who have hearing loss exists to some extent for low and even mid frequencies. The device delivers amplified sound for the lower frequencies and electrical stimulation for the higher frequencies. Studies show that patients with EAS devices achieve good word recognition compared with performance presurgery with only a hearing aid, even in the presence of background noise. They experience relatively good music perception, a benefit that eludes many users of traditional cochlear implants (Gfeller et al., 2012; Muller et al., 2012) and relatively good perception of speech prosody.

Electrical auditory stimulation (EAS) presents combined electrical and acoustic stimulation to the same ear; developed for patients who have profound hearing loss in the high frequencies and significant residual hearing loss in the low frequencies.

Hybrid devices are listening aids that combine a cochlear implant system with hearing aid technology.

Candidacy

The primary candidacy requirements for implantation are the presence of irreversible hearing loss and good general health. Typically, audiometric thresholds must indicate a severe or profound hearing loss, although criteria have relaxed in recent years and Cochlear Corporation and Medicare in particular now specify bilateral moderate-to-profound sensorineural hearing loss. Good general health is desirable, as patients must undergo surgery and anesthesia.

For adults, there is no upper age of implantation. Although most adult cochlear implant recipients have postlingual hearing losses, prelingual hearing loss does not preclude candidacy (see Dowell, 2005; UK Cochlear Implant Study Group, 2004). Until fairly recently, patients with asymmetric hearing loss, where hearing in the better ear is relatively good, were not considered candidates, but some patients have received a cochlear implant in the poor ear, with positive outcomes (Firszt, Holden, Reeder, Cowdrey, & King, 2012).

In a study analyzing the outcomes in 465 adult patients who received a cochlear implant between 1994 and 2006, the following five variables were found to predict successful speech recognition scores, in descending order of importance:

- Postlingual onset of significant hearing loss
- Shorter duration of severe sensorineural hearing loss
- Age (younger recipients achieve better outcome)
- Style of electrode array (a "perimodiolar" style portends a better outcome)
- Better preoperative speech recognition scores in the better aided ear

(Dowell, 2012)

For children, the FDA has approved implantation for infants as young as 12 months, although if they are under the age of 24 months, they should have at least a 3-month trial of wearing hearing aids bilaterally. Exceptions to this trial period occur, say, when a child has had meningitis, and there is danger of imminent ossification of the cochlea. Children who receive limited or no benefit from using hearing aids are candidates. In infants and toddlers, this means that they do not develop simple auditory skills such as responding to their name or startling to loud sound over a 3- to 6-month period. For older children, this means that they recognize less than 30% of words in an open-set test format.

Binaural Cochlear Implants

A minority of patients have received bilateral implant surgery and wear a cochlear implant in each ear. There is some evidence that use of two cochlear implants affords a modest increase in speech recognition compared with using only one device, especially when listening in the presence of background noise. Use of two cochlear implants may also enhance sound localization because the use of two devices reinstates the interaural amplitude and timing cues that underlie the ability to lateralize sounds in a horizontal plane (Ching & Incerti, 2012).

Many other cochlear implant users continue to use a hearing aid in the unimplanted ear. When a patient wears binaural hearing aids and then receives a cochlear implant in one ear, the patient typically will experiment with using both the cochlear implant and the hearing aid. In some cases, a patient will find that simultaneously listening to both the electrical and the amplified signals is confusing and will opt to use only the cochlear implant. In other cases, the patient will find that the simultaneous signals enhance his or her ability to listen in noise and to localize sound, so will opt to use both devices. A patient who uses a cochlear implant in one ear and a hearing aid in the other is said to have **bimodal stimulation**.

Bimodal stimulation refers to the use of a cochlear implant in one ear and a hearing aid in the other.

Process

Acquiring a cochlear implant is a multistage process. It often begins with a comprehensive audiological evaluation and, if the patient has never used appropriate amplification, a trial period with amplification. Once a patient has been deemed a candidate, he or she undergoes surgery, at which time the internal components are implanted under the skin behind the pinna. Four to six weeks later, the patient returns and the external components of the device are fitted. The audiologist adjusts the stimulus parameters of the speech processor to optimize speech recognition in a process called **mapping**. Ideally, the patient then engages in a comprehensive aural rehabilitation program to develop new listening skills and maintains contact with the cochlear implant center through regularly scheduled follow-up visits.

Mapping is a term used to describe the process of programming the speech processor of a cochlear implant.

How to Establish a Map

Most cochlear implants are established by programming the following parameters:

- *Dynamic range.* In adjusting the speech processor, each electrode in the electrode array is programmed according to the threshold of stimulation and maximum acceptable loudness level. The difference between these two current levels defines a dynamic range. An **electrical threshold (T-level)** is the amount of current that must be passed through an electrode so the patient is just aware

(continues)

The **electrical threshold (T-level)** is the amount of current that must be passed through an electrode so that the patient is just aware of a sound sensation.

How to Establish a Map *(continued)*

of a sound sensation. **Maximum comfort level (C-level or M-level)** is the maximum current level that can be introduced before the individual experiences discomfort. The thresholds and maximum comfort levels will vary among electrodes and between patients as a function of neuronal survival in the auditory nerve.

- *Loudness balancing.* Through **loudness balancing**, the speech processor is programmed so stimulation across electrodes preserves the loudness contour of the speech signal. Patients must judge the relative loudness of signals presented to different electrodes in the cochlear implant electrode array. If the electrodes are not balanced, the patient might experience occasional popping sounds and may not hear some speech information.
- *Pitch and pitch ranking.* Electrodes situated near the basal end of the cochlear are programmed to represent the high-frequency range and those near the apical end represent the low-frequency range. This representation matches the tonotopic organization of the cochlear. **Pitch ranking** determines the ability to discriminate pitch from the basal to the apical electrodes. During pitch ranking, two electrodes are stimulated, one right after the other. The patient's task is to indicate which stimulus pulse has a higher or lower pitch.

The **maximum comfort level (C-level or M-level)** is the maximum intensity level that can be listened to comfortably for a prolonged duration of time, sometimes referred to as *MCL*.

Loudness balancing is programming the speech processor so that stimulation follows the loudness contour of the incoming speech signal.

Pitch ranking determines the ability to discriminate pitch from stimulation of the basal to apical electrodes.

HEARING ASSISTIVE TECHNOLOGY SYSTEMS (HATS) AND ASSISTIVE LISTENING DEVICES (ALDS)

In addition to, or in lieu of, hearing aids or cochlear implants, patients may also receive an assistive listening device (ALD) or **hearing assistive technology systems** (HATS). HATS are listening, alerting, and/or signaling devices that facilitate a patient's communication with the environment or enhance the patient's personal safety through the use of auditory, visual, or tactile modalities. Sometimes used synonymously with the term "ALD," HATS may not always entail "listening" per se, as the term "ALD" would imply, but may also include such devices as a flashing doorbell or a vibrating alarm clock.

Hearing assistive technology systems (HATS) are listening, alerting, and/or signaling devices that facilitate patients' communication with the environment or enhance their personal safety through the use of auditory, visual, or tactile modalities; encompass assistive listening devices and other assistive devices.

Hearing aids and cochlear implants are listening devices that may be worn during almost all waking hours and in almost all communication settings. By contrast, HATS usually are used in specific situations, such as when listening in a public hall or conversing in a restaurant when a hearing aid or cochlear implant either are inadequate to permit good communication or are not desirable to the patient.

HATS facilitate four communication needs (ASHA, 2009):

- Face-to-face communication that may occur in such places as the home, a restaurant, a business meeting, a place of worship, concert, lecture, automobile, courtroom, or classroom
- Broadcast and other electronic media, including radio, television, and movie theater
- Telephone conversation, as on the telephone or intercom
- Sensitivity to alerting signals and environmental stimuli, including such sounds as the doorbell, smoke detector, telephone ring, appliance timer, baby's cry, child's voice, alarm clock, and door knock

The primary objectives for providing an individual with a listening device or a HATS may include the following:

- To make speech audible, without introducing distortion or discomfort
- To restore a range of loudness experience
- To augment communication through nonauditory means
- To enhance personal safety or environmental awareness

TABLE 3–2 Situations in Which the Use of an Assistive Device Might Be Appropriate

HOME	COMMUNITY	WORKPLACE	TRAVEL AND RECREATION	SCHOOL
One-on-one conversation	Medical treatment (visiting a physician, dentist, hospital)	Office conversation	One-on-one conversation (e.g., in the car)	Communication with the teacher or professor
Group conversation	Volunteer activities	Lectures	Television reception	Communication with classmates
Television reception	Religious services	Telephone communication	Public spaces	
Radio reception	Post office and other community service centers	Conferences and group meetings	Restaurants	
Reception of environmental signals such as the doorbell		One-on-one meetings	Hotel rooms	

In selecting devices for a particular patient, you will want to consider the patient's communication demands in the home, work, community, recreational, or school environments. Table 3–2 presents a list of situations in each of these settings in which use of an ALD or HAT may be appropriate.

HATS are especially useful when the audio signal is presented at a distance or when the listening conditions are less than ideal. Conditions that might compromise a listening environment, and where a HATS may be especially helpful, include the following:

- ***Ambient noise***: Noise that is present in a room when it is unoccupied. This noise may emanate from open windows, air-handling systems, computers, fluorescent lighting systems, or piped-in music.
- ***Reverberation***: Echoes caused by sound rebounding off surfaces such as walls, floors, and ceilings. Rooms that have high ceilings, hardwood floors, and plaster walls tend to be highly reverberant, whereas those that have carpet and heavy draperies tend to have less reverberation.
- ***Background noise***: Undesirable noise that masks the auditory signal of interest. For example, in a lecture hall, the speaker's voice may be the target signal, and the rustling of programs, coughing, and the shuffling of feet might be undesirable background noise.

In principle, ALDs work by collecting sound from the sound source (e.g., the talker's mouth) and delivering it to the user's ear. In this way, the audio signal is presented at an audible level, with a favorable signal-to-noise ratio, with minimal ambient noise, without the effects of reverberation, and with little background noise. ALDs can be categorized as one of two kinds: wireless and hardwired.

Wireless Systems

As the name implies, a wireless system does not use wire between the microphone and the unit that delivers the signal to the user's ear. Sound is transmitted from the sound source to the individual by means of radio waves or infrared signals. These kinds of systems may be used when the individual is far from the sound source—for example, in a religious service, when attending a theater play, or when several people must attend to a talker, as adult learners do when listening to a lecturer. A wireless system picks up the audio signal, either through a microphone placed near the sound source or by means of a direct electrical plug-in. The sound is then converted into an electrical signal by a transmitter and delivered through the air to a receiver worn by the user, often by means of radio waves or infrared (invisible light). The signal may be delivered to the ear either via earphones or through the individual's hearing aid. Wireless systems can be further classified as frequency modulation (FM), infrared, induction loop, or simple amplification.

FM Systems

Frequency modulation (FM) systems utilize radio waves to transmit sound from the source to the user. The Federal Communications Commission (FCC), which regulates FM systems, has allocated a range of bandwidths for exclusive use by persons with hearing loss. FM systems may be described as either personal systems or sound-field systems. When using a **personal FM system (trainer)**, the main talker (e.g., a classroom teacher) wears a microphone usually on a cord around the neck or clipped onto the shirt. The speech signal is conveyed into a transmitter, where it is frequency modulated on radio frequency carrier waves and transmitted through the room to the person with hearing loss, who wears a receiver. The receiver may connect to the person's hearing aid by a direct auditory interface and an audio boot connection, or the person may wear an **FM boot** at the bottom of the hearing aid. Some FM systems utilize a **neckloop** that transmits sound to the hearing aid via the hearing aid's telecoil. Ear-level FM receiver units and hearing aids with built-in FM receivers are also available. If there is more than one patient who has hearing loss in a group gathering, then each patient wears a receiver and may receive the talker's signal.

Frequency modulation (FM) is the process of creating a complex signal by means of sinusoidally varying a carrier wave frequency.

A **personal FM system (trainer)** is a listening device in which the speaker wears a wireless microphone and the speech is frequency modulated on radio waves transmitted through the room to the listener who wears a receiver.

An **FM boot** is a boot-like device that houses an FM receiver. It attaches to the base of a behind-the-ear hearing aid.

A **neckloop** is a transducer worn around the neck, often as part of an FM assistive device system. It consists of a cord from a receiver and transmits signals via magnetic induction to the telecoil of the user's hearing aid.

A **sound-field FM system** is a listening system, similar to a personal FM system, in which sound from a microphone is transmitted to loudspeakers that are positioned throughout the room.

A sound-field FM system operates similarly to a personal FM system. A **sound-field FM system** differs from the personal system because the sound is transmitted to loudspeakers that are positioned throughout the room, usually two in the back of the room and one near the front. There, the signal is converted to an audio signal and played into the environment, as with a standard public address system. A patient's personal hearing aid microphone picks up the signal. Whereas a personal FM system offers better signal-to-noise ratios, the sound-field system is advantageous because it can be beneficial for an entire room, even for those present who do not have a hearing loss. For example, even children with normal hearing might benefit from the amplification of the teacher's voice. FM sound-field systems also do not require a patient to wear a special FM receiver. Hence, the patient wears less hardware.

Situations and settings in which FM systems may be used include group lectures, religious services, theaters, classrooms, and one-on-one communication. Large-area listening environments, such as churches, synagogues, and theaters, sometimes incorporate an FM transmitter into their public or large-area broadcasting systems. Listeners then may check out a receiver unit for a particular event or presentation. In one-on-one communication, the person with hearing loss might connect his or her hearing aid to an FM receiver and hold a small FM transmitter toward the talker. The talker then speaks into a small handheld or table-mounted FM transmitter microphone.

Infrared Systems

Infrared systems operate similarly to FM units, but use infrared signals to transmit sound. A transmitter/emitter sends the signal encoded in infrared light waves to a wireless receiver, which contains a photo detector diode. A photo detector diode picks up

An **infrared system** is an assistive listening device that broadcasts from the sound source to a receiver/amplifier by means of infrared light waves.

the infrared signal and converts it back to the audio signal. A patient either may wear an infrared receiver that inputs directly into the ears or may receive the signal through a neckloop, DAI, or headphones. Common situations in which infrared systems are used include television watching and movie theaters. Infrared systems are not appropriate for outdoors, as sunlight interferes with transmission. The infrared signals also cannot travel through walls. A "line of sight" is required for the signal to be received.

Induction Loop Systems

An **induction loop system** works by running a wire around the circumference of a room or table that conducts electrical energy from an amplifier and thus creates a magnetic field, which induces the telecoil in a hearing aid to provide amplified sound to the user.

The third kind of wireless system is the induction loop system. For an **induction loop system** to operate, a loop of wire must be placed around the circumference of a room. Sound is picked up by means of a microphone or a direct input (e.g., a television direct connection). Sound is converted into electrical signals and fed through the loop. Electromagnetic energy is broadcast throughout the room and can be picked up by a hearing aid (and some cochlear implants) when the telecoil circuit is activated. The listener must sit either inside of the loop of wire or beside it. Some religious settings, convention halls, train, bus, and airplane terminals, and theaters have permanent loop systems in place. There are portable induction loop systems so that any room can be optimized for communication. A variation of the large-area loop system is an induction loop wire system that can be worn around the neck. Induction systems are becoming increasingly popular, in large part because they are convenient for the user, who need only wear a hearing aid with a telecoil. Especially throughout the United Kingdom, Scandinavia, and elsewhere in Europe, it is not unusual to find induction loop systems in banks, post offices, senior citizen centers, government buildings, and tourist information centers.

A **closed caption (CC) decoder** in a television set or electronic appliance extracts previously encoded closed caption data from a received video signal and displays it on a screen.

Watching the Tube and Other Pleasures

At one time, persons with significant hearing loss either had to forgo watching television and movies altogether or had to struggle to understand the dialogue and other important auditory signals. Thanks to closed captioning, this is no longer true for individuals who can read.

Since 1993, the Americans with Disabilities Act (ADA) has stipulated that all television sets sold in the United States with screens of 13 inches or larger must contain a **closed caption (CC) decoder**. A CC decoder projects dialogue orthographically on the screen and in relative synchrony with the spoken messages as well as a description of relevant sounds, such as a telephone ringing or an alarm. Often, the coding can be activated by means of the television set's remote control.

Some movie theaters also offer closed captioning, using either an open or closed system. In open captioning, subtitles are projected onto the screen, just as in foreign films, and can be seen by the entire audience. In closed captioning (sometimes called rear-window captioning), the captions are available only to individuals who attach a clear acrylic reflector panel to their seats. A rear-window captioner, which displays reversed captions via a light-emitting display (LED) system, is mounted at the back of the theater. It projects the captions onto the reflectors. The result is that the viewer sees captions superimposed on or beneath the movie screen.

Web-based video also permits closed captioning for video. Web-based captioning can be accessed with such technologies as QuickTime (http://www.apple.com/quicktime/), RealOne Player (http://www.real.com/), and Media Player (http://www.microsoft.com/downloads).

Simple Amplification

Simple amplification systems merely amplify the audio signal so that it may be more audible to the person with hearing loss. The most common implementation of simple amplification systems is in telephones. **Telephone amplifiers** either replace the telephone handset or clip onto existing handsets. Replacement handsets have built-in amplifiers, so that the signal is amplified before it is delivered to the user's ear. Often, telephones with amplifiers have volume controls; therefore, they may also be used by persons who have normal hearing who might wish to turn down the volume after the person with hearing loss uses the device. Many units include options for amplifying the ring and the dial tone.

Simple amplification systems amplify the audio signal so that it is more audible to a person with hearing loss.

Telephone amplifiers amplify sound from a telephone receiver.

Hardwired Systems

The other kind of ALD can be described as hardwired. **Hardwired assistive listening devices** connect the sound source to the listener by actual wire. A microphone may pick up the audio signal and deliver it to the patient's hearing aid by means of a DAI, or there may be a DAI jack that plugs into a piece of equipment, such as a television. The audio signal is converted into an electrical signal. It travels through the connecting wire, terminating at the user's hearing aid, headphones, or a neckloop. This system provides a favorable signal-to-noise ratio to the user and, usually, an adjustable amount of signal amplification. These kinds of systems are used most often for listening to television, radio, or music. However, such systems require the user to be tethered to the sound source, a feature most patients do not want.

Hardwired assistive listening devices are directly connected by wires.

Other Kinds of Hearing Assistive Technology Systems

Some assistive technology facilitates reception of information that is not speech, and auditory information by means other than amplification, such as by vibrotactile stimulation or visual display. One example is an alarm clock that simultaneously beeps, flashes a lamp, and shakes the bed (not to be used after a rowdy New Year's Eve party). Other examples include:

- A doorbell signal coupled to a lamp, which flashes when the doorbell is rung
- A smoke detector, where light flashes signal the presence of smoke
- A baby cry alert system, where a parent can be signaled if a baby begins to cry in another room
- A telephone ring signaler that causes a lamp to flash

I Need to Make a Call

Although many persons with significant hearing loss often rely on the internet or text messaging for communication at a distance, most persons still have a need to use a telephone. In addition to using a telephone amplifier, these individuals have at least four other options available for using the telephone. These options are:

- *Audiovisual cell phone displays*: Many cellular telephones permit visual displays, so the caller can opt to both see and hear the person on the other end of the phone call, and thereby can engage in speechreading.
- *Captioned telephones*: Working much like a closed caption television set, this special telephone has a built-in-screen. When the user receives a telephone call, the

(continues)

I Need to Make a Call *(continued)*

screen displays word-for-word captions while the user simultaneously hears the caller's voice. The transcription, performed by a remote operator with the help of speech-to-text software, occurs almost in real time.

- *Text telephones (TTs)*: A telephone terminal comprised of a telephone, a keyboard, and a message display screen. The telephone handset fits into the terminal cradle. Both parties must have a terminal set. They communicate by typing their messages to one another. The messages are displayed on the message display screen. TTs are sometimes referred to as telecommunication devices for the Deaf (TDDs). Modern systems include features such as automatic dialing, storage of frequently used words and phrases, and personal directories.
- ***Relay systems***: A trained operator serves as an intermediary in a telephone conversation. The person with hearing loss communicates with the operator via a TT (and possibly voice), whereas the person with normal hearing communicates with the operator via voice. To place a call, the initiator contacts a relay operator, who in turn contacts the recipient of the call.

A **relay system** is used by persons with significant hearing loss for telephone access; an individual contacts a relay operator who serves to transmit messages between the caller and the person called by means of teletype or voice.

COMPUTER-BASED TECHNOLOGY

Patients, and in particular members of the Deaf community, have quickly learned to exploit modern technology such as cell phone texting and instant message systems to overcome many of the communication barriers posed by hearing loss. Users can text important points to a target audience with perfect intelligibility, even in the noisiest of settings. The technology is unfettered by proximity so users can converse with communication partners no matter where they might be, whether right next to them or halfway around the world. Users can even multitask multiple conversations at a time. They also can efficiently and easily communicate with their peers with normal hearing, even if their peers do not know sign language and the user with hearing loss does not have intelligible speech. Web-based systems such as Twitter and Facebook have also expanded opportunities for easy communication.

Users can conduct face-to-face conversations and exploit speechreading or sign language conversations using the audio-video capabilities of a cell phone or computer. For a conversation conducted in sign language, the user might hold a cell phone in one hand and sign a kind of pigeon sign with the other hand. Communicating in sign language typically requires the use of both hands, but a one-handed version is evolving, much like shorthand word and phrase spellings emerged for text messaging. One blogger captured the dramatic change in lifestyle wrought by technology (K's Blog, 2011):

> Quietly over the last decade, phones that make text messaging easy have changed life profoundly for millions of Deaf people. Gone are the days of a Deaf person driving to someone's house just to see if they are home. Wives text their Deaf husbands in the basement, just as a hearing wife might yell down the stairs. Deaf teens blend in with the mall crowd since they're constantly texting, like everyone else in high school. For the first time, a generation of Deaf people can communicate with the world on its terms, using cell phones, BlackBerrys, or iPhones.

Just Another Customer Using His iPhone and Sipping a Cup of Joe

"I put the iPhone on the table. I point it at whoever's talking, and I can have conversations with them. Soon we forget the iPhone is sitting there."

Richard Einhorn, a patient with hearing loss who uses his iPhone and an app to achieve a favorable signal-to-noise ratio to converse with his friends

(Eisenberg, 2012, p. BU3).

A new wave of technological innovations entails the use of speech-to-text software, where a listener with hearing loss can follow a real-time orthographic transcription of a talker's spoken message using a small display monitor and a microphone or a pair of eyeglasses. Already telephone systems are available that exploit speech-to-text software.

CASE STUDY

Audio Technology

Richard Einhorn is a music composer who incurred sudden hearing loss in 2010. As the *New York Times* reports (Eisenberg, 2012), Mr. Einhorn is a man adept at using modern audio technology. Although "it takes time and practice to learn where they work well, and to switch from one device to another" (p. BU3), he now routinely implements the following solutions:

- *Quiet settings*: He relies on his state-of-the-art digital hearing aid.
- *With friends in a bustling coffee café*: Mr. Einhorn removes his hearing aid and snaps a directional microphone called a Blue Mikey onto his iPhone and inserts a pair of earbuds (Etymotic hf5) into his ears. The iPhone has an app (*sound AMP R*) that amplifies and processes the sound. The system affords a good signal-to-noise ratio and attracts little attention—just one of many iPhones lying on customers' tables.
- *Cell phone calls*: When Mr. Einhorn wants to make a cell phone call, he uses his hearing aid and a companion device he wears around his neck. Sound is transmitted from his iPhone to his Bluetooth digital hearing aid via the neck-worn device.
- *Television viewing*: Mr. Einhorn switches his MTO switch to the "T" position. His viewing room is looped with a system called Contacta, and it connects to the audio output of his television set. If he sits on the couch within the periphery of the loop, with the telecoil of his hearing aid turned on, the broadcast is "crystal clear."
- *Pharmacies and medical offices*: Although this one is not yet in "routine use," Mr. Einhorn looks forward to the near future, when Encom Systems perfects its "small mat" with a built-in hearing loop. The loop will be connected to a microphone. When standing on this mat, he will be able to conduct relatively quiet and clear conversations with the pharmaceutical or medical staff.

CASE STUDY

Listen to the Music

Newsweek magazine (Stone, 2002) featured an article about cochlear implants and included a case study about a woman who longed to listen to music, opera in particular. The case study presented here is much like this woman's story. Added here are references to the literature that support the statements about music perception and music training.

Sally Anderson, a former music teacher from Des Moines, Iowa, went to the opera with her husband, David, and imagined the lyrics and the music. If they went to parties, David would serve as translator and repeat everything that was said in a group conversation. Similarly, on a trip to England, he repeated the tour guides' commentaries during museum and cathedral visits.

Like her aunt, Sally began to lose her hearing in her late 20s and lost much more of it after her second pregnancy. For the next 15 years, Sally graduated to a series of increasingly powerful hearing aids. The realization of deafness occurred when she was sitting next to the telephone one evening while reading the newspaper. "Answer the phone," her teenage daughter said, poking her in the shoulder. Sally had not heard it ringing.

A year ago, her husband convinced her to contact a cochlear implant center after he read an article about cochlear implants in the newspaper. An audiological examination revealed a bilateral profound hearing loss. After a comprehensive medical examination to ensure good health and no cochlear anomalies, Sally signed up for surgery. "It was an opportunity I couldn't pass up. They said I was a prime candidate. I'd had hearing until adulthood, I hadn't been totally deaf for a very long time, and I was

(continues)

CASE STUDY (*continued*)

Listen to the Music

highly motivated to hear." She told her audiologist that she could not wait to hear the birds sing or the radio play. The price was off-putting—$50,000 for the surgery alone, and that fee did not include follow-up aural rehabilitation—but the clinical coordinator at the implant center helped Sally determine that her insurance company would provide coverage.

Immediately upon hookup of the instrument, Sally recognized the sound of chairs scraping against the floor, a door banging, and a telephone ringing. The audiologist administered a sentence test in an audition-only condition, and she recognized about 20% of the words. During her first six months of use, her score on the sentence test rose to almost 60% words correct. Her audiologist encouraged her to continue wearing the hearing aid she had long used in her unimplanted ear, as some researchers have shown that a hearing aid provides additional benefit, especially when listening in noisy backgrounds (e.g., Ching, Incerti, & Hill, 2004). Sally eventually discontinued wearing the hearing aid, saying that the little sound she received from it just made listening with the cochlear implant "more confusing" (see also Mak, Grayden, Dowell, & Lawrence, 2006). Over the course of a year she became a telephone user, and was even able to hear the dial tone. She occasionally used an FM system.

Her disappointment with the device pertained to music. It just did not sound like she remembered it. During the second week of implant use, she talked her husband into taking her to a symphony concert. The experience was so disturbing she had to turn her device off midway through the concert.

Sally enrolled in a music-based aural rehabilitation program (e.g., Gfeller, Mehr, & Witt, 2001). A music therapist with experience working with cochlear implant users started Sally on a simple program where she listened to recorded tunes of familiar songs, such as "Twinkle, Twinkle Little Star" and "Happy Birthday to You." The renditions of the songs consisted of simple orchestrations and a male solo singer. Sally easily identified the melodies, and this success motivated her to continue with the training. During the past few months, she has graduated from familiar songs (her favorites are Beatles' tunes from the 1960s), to country and western music (which, for many implant users, is pleasurable because of its rhythmicity and repetitiveness), to familiar symphonic pieces.

Last week, David Anderson took his wife to a presentation of the play *South Pacific*. Following the advice of her aural rehabilitation music therapist, Sally took a score of the music with her. The couple sat in the balcony, where Sally could discreetly set up the music sheets and follow along. This time, she left the auditorium with tears of joy in her eyes. Sally said she recognized some of the tunes and every lyric.

FINAL REMARKS

Listening and communication technology is rapidly evolving. One of the main trends is waterproofing. At least one cochlear implant manufacturer has developed a waterproof processor that can be worn while swimming and bathing and another has a water-resistant device that can be worn in water for a short period of time. Waterproof hearing aids permit children (and adults) to wear their devices during all waking hours, without having to miss out while swimming, bathing, or participating in other water sports.

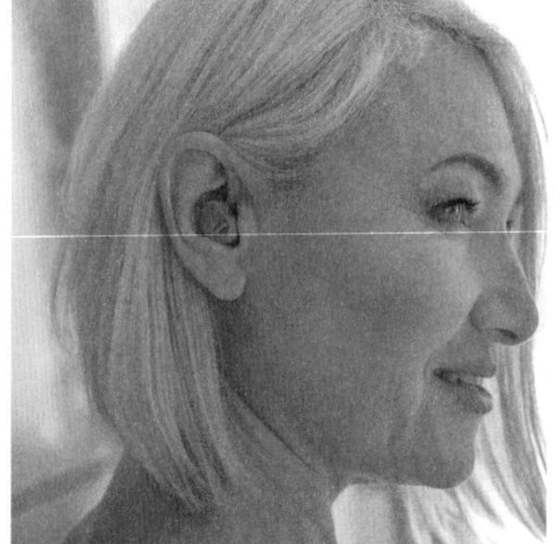

KEY CHAPTER POINTS

- The objectives for providing a patient with a listening device are to make speech audible, without introducing distortion or discomfort, and to restore a range of loudness experience.
- Hearing aids, cochlear implants, and assistive listening devices are the primary listening devices available to persons who have hearing loss.
- Two major trends in modern hearing aid design are miniaturization and enhanced signal processing.

- Hearing aids have three fundamental components: a microphone, an amplifier, and a receiver. They also have a power source. Microphones may be directional or omnidirectional. Amplifiers may use peak-clipping for output limiting or compression.
- There are seven general styles of hearing aids. Selection of style is dependent on the degree of hearing loss, user preference, costs, patient lifestyle, and the patient's physical status.
- Hearing aid benefit may be assessed with behavioral measures, probe microphone technology, and self-assessment scales.
- Cochlear implants provide sound sensation by means of directly stimulating the auditory nerve. Candidacy requirements for implantation include the presence of irreversible sensorineural hearing loss and good general health.
- Most cochlear implants in use are multichannel devices and many of them utilize an interleaved pulsatile stimulation algorithm.
- Assistive listening devices are used to address communication needs related to face-to-face communication, broadcast and other electronic media, and telephone use. General categories of devices are wireless and hardwired.
- Hearing assistive technology includes ALDs as well as devices that facilitate the reception of auditory information that is not speech and that provide auditory information by means other than amplification.

TERMS AND CONCEPTS TO REMEMBER

Miniaturization
Signal processing
Hearing aid components
Omnidirectional microphone
Gain
Telecoil
Hearing aid styles
Binaural fitting
Prescription procedures
Validation
Tonotopic organization
Cochlear implant components
Cochlear implant candidacy
Compromised listening environments
Wireless systems
FM sound-field system
Induction loop
Computer-based technology

CHAPTER 4

Auditory-Only Speech Perception and Auditory Training

OUTLINE

Only 40–60% of hearing aid owners are sufficiently satisfied with the benefits of hearing aids to use them on a regular basis (Kochkin, 2005a). The profile for the entire population of adults is similarly bleak. Only 24% of the 31.5 million persons in the United States who have hearing loss currently own hearing instruments (Kochkin, 2005b). Taken together, these statistics indicate that a large segment of at least our adult population experiences communication difficulties in everyday conversations because of untreated hearing loss.

One of the principal reasons for the high dissatisfaction rate with amplification, as well as with cochlear implants, is that the listening devices do not overcome the most common complaint voiced by patients, namely, that they can detect spoken language but cannot understand it, especially in the presence of competing sounds. Although recent advances in digital signal processing have improved how well listening aids restore audibility, listening in noise remains highly problematic for most patients (Figure 4–1).

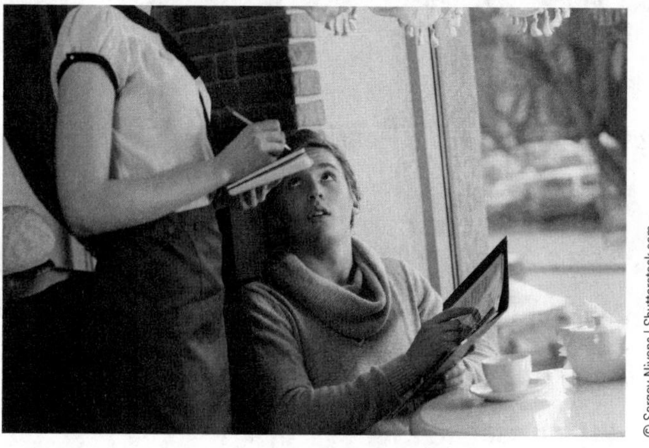

FIGURE 4–1 Listening in noisy environments. Many patients seek auditory training because they are challenged by noisy listening environments such as restaurants. Many auditory training programs present training items in the presence of noise so that patients can practice listening in noise and so that they can develop their confidence to handle noisy environments.

In this chapter, we will consider how hearing loss affects speech recognition and then consider auditory training first for speech recognition and then for music listening, including the types of auditory training and evidence for training efficacy.

LISTENING TO SPEECH WITH A HEARING LOSS

A **spectrogram** is a three-dimensional graph of speech that displays frequency on the ordinate (*y*-axis), time on the abscissa (*x*-axis), and amplitude by the density of the tracing.

The most obvious effect of sensorineural hearing loss on speech listening is a decreased sensitivity to the signal, especially for the frequencies of speech that have characteristically low amplitude. Figure 4–2 presents two versions of a **spectrogram** for the sentence *Beth washed the cat*, where frequency is plotted on the y-axis and time is on the *x*-axis. The left signal presents the signal as a person with normal hearing would hear it and the right side presents the signal as a person with a flat moderate-to-severe sensorineural hearing loss would hear it. Note that on the left side, energy is present throughout the range of frequencies found for speech, roughly those frequencies up to 8000 Hz. In contrast, the right side spectrogram shows attenuated energy, and energy only in the lower and some of the middle frequencies. Hearing loss acts as a filter and attenuates or eliminates those sounds that are not of relatively high amplitude. As a result,

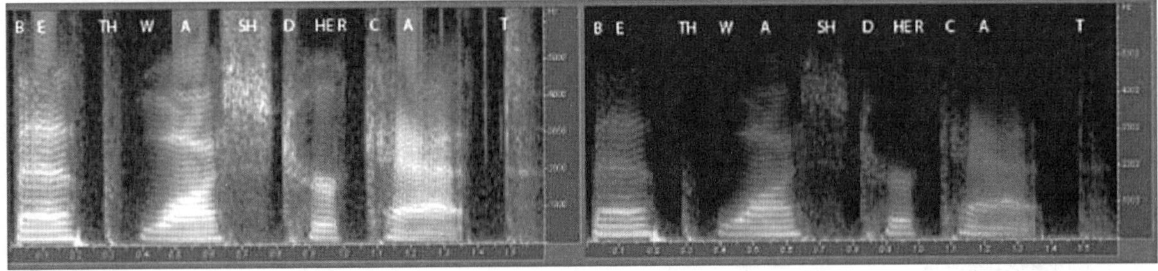

FIGURE 4–2 Spectrograms of the sentence *Beth washed the cat*. The left side of the figure shows the unfiltered version and the right side shows a version that has been filtered to simulate a severe hearing loss. The *y*-axis corresponds to frequency and the *x*-axis corresponds to time.

some sounds are no longer present and some sounds are acoustically more like one another. For instance, on the left side, the [ʃ] in *washed* has high energy in the high frequencies for a relatively long duration compared with the [k] in *cat*. However, on the right side, these two sounds look similar and are not distinguished from one another by high-frequency information. Many patients with sensorineural hearing loss have a sloping loss, so the attenuation and elimination of mid- and high-frequency speech information becomes exacerbated.

The presence of background noise can further reduce the audibility of the speech signal and the clarity of speech sounds. Even if they can hear speech in quiet like persons with normal hearing, most persons with sensorineural hearing loss will have comparatively greater difficulty recognizing speech in the presence of background noise, particularly if they have more significant hearing loss.

Many people with sensorineural hearing loss have impaired frequency selectivity and impaired temporal resolution. For instance, if they are presented with two different tone pulses, one after another, they require a greater difference in frequency between the two pulses in order to perceive that they are "different pitches" than do persons with normal hearing. This is a hallmark of impaired **frequency selectivity**. If they are asked whether a pulse has an interval of silence embedded in its center (i.e., tone pip-silent interval-tone pip), they require a longer temporal "gap" of silence before they say "yes." This is a hallmark of impaired **temporal resolution**. Since the speech signal comprises a wide range of frequencies and changes rapidly over time, impaired frequency selectivity and impaired temporal resolution negatively affect speech recognition, even when the signal is loud enough to hear. For instance, the two spectrally similar words *me* and *knee* may be clearly audible to a patient with hearing loss, but because the patient has impaired frequency selectivity and is unable to make fine frequency discriminations, the two words may sound alike.

Listening with a hearing loss has more subtle effects on speech recognition besides inaudibility, impaired recognition in noisy situations, and frequency and temporal distortion. A person with hearing loss often expends more **perceptual effort** in attending to the speech signal. Because more effort is required to identify spoken words, fewer cognitive resources may be available to process what is being heard and to encode the speech content into memory (McCoy et al., 2005). For instance, patients may have poorer recall for spoken strings of numbers. They may be able to repeat back sentences presented one at a time, but after three sentences, they will be unable to remember some of the content from the first sentence. Fewer cognitive resources are available to process information as it comes into **working memory** and to place the information into **long-term memory**.

Hearing loss is more than just hearing loss.

"You can treat hearing loss with a device such as a hearing aid or cochlear implant, and it will make sounds more audible. But that doesn't compensate for changes that occur with aging beyond the ear. Some problems aren't simply not being able to hear, but not being able to process it well either."

—Samira Anderson, PhD, University of Maryland, 2017 *(http://hearinghealthmatters.org/hearingnewswatch/2017/university-maryland-hearing-loss-brain-function-research-grant/)*

Frequency selectivity is the auditory system's ability to respond differentially to different frequencies and bands of frequencies.

Temporal resolution is the auditory system's ability to perceive or discriminate sound segments occurring closely in time as separate events.

Perceptual effort is the effort that a person expends to recognize speech, sometimes at the cost of using processing resources that might otherwise be allocated toward encoding speech into memory.

Working memory is the cognitive system used to temporarily store information that is required to perform complex cognitive tasks such as reasoning, comprehension, and learning, and is thought to have limited capacity.

Long-term memory is the cognitive system used to maintain information for extended periods of time, even a lifetime, and is thought to have unlimited capacity.

Why some people with hearing loss feel like a tuckered-out cat at the end of the day

According to Pichora-Fuller et al. (2016), listeners with hearing loss "expend more mental effort to direct attention to and concentrate on . . . comprehending, remembering, and responding to [speech]. . . ." And as a result, "they may experience fatigue and/or decide to quit the task at hand to avoid becoming fatigued." To counteract hearing-related cognitive fatigue:

- Patients should "chill out" with quiet time every day at about the same time of day, limiting verbal input, even reading, for about 20 minutes.
- If warranted, use appropriately fitted hearing aids, ideally with noise reduction circuitry.
- Engage in auditory training (e.g., Sommers et al., 2015).

Noise-Induced Hearing Loss

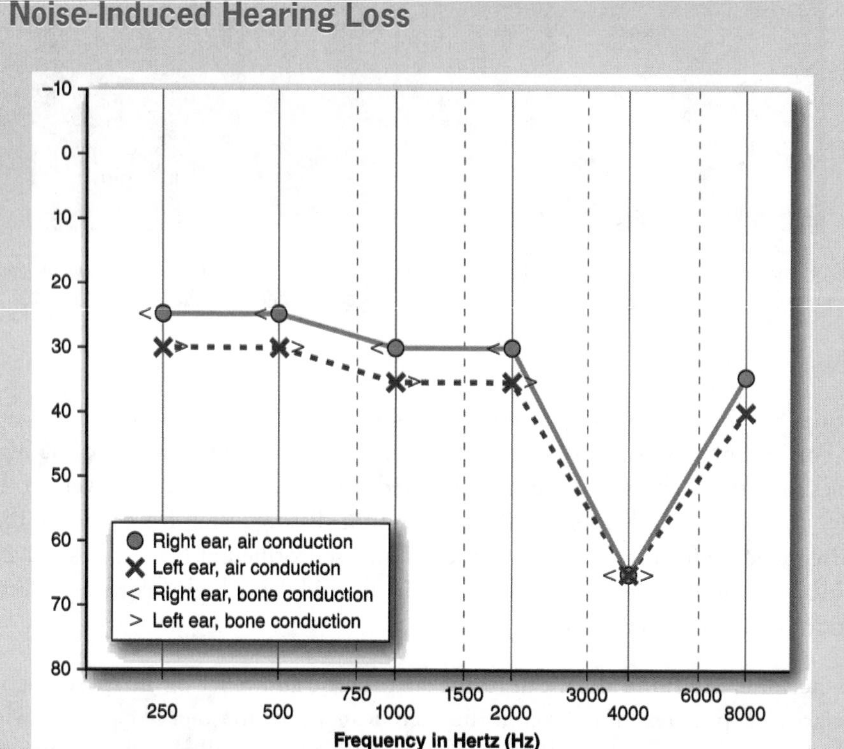

FIGURE 4–3 An audiogram characteristic of a noise-induced hearing loss. Hearing sensitivity is decreased at 4000 Hz, relative to thresholds for other frequencies.

One of the most common causes of adventitious hearing loss is exposure to loud sound. A transient but powerful noise can lead to hearing loss, as in the impulse noise generated by a munitions explosion, as can prolonged exposure to excessive noise levels, as in the unrelenting noise generated in an automobile assembly line. Noise can lead to damaged hair cells and damage to the auditory nerve, which in turn results in hearing loss and, very often, tinnitus. Figure 4–3 shows a characteristic **noise notch** audiogram, so called because hearing loss initially occurs in the frequencies between 3000 and 5000 or 6000 Hz. Individuals who are regularly exposed to loud sound should be encouraged to wear protection such as earplugs and earmuffs. An estimated 15% of the US population between the ages of 20 and 69 years have noise-induced hearing loss (about 26 million Americans), so many patients who seek auditory training may well have a noise notch.

A **noise notch** refers to the characteristic dip in hearing sensitivity at around 4000 Hz that is associated with an audiogram for a patient who has noised-induced hearing loss.

GOALS OF AUDITORY TRAINING

The primary goal of auditory training is to develop patients' ability to recognize speech using the auditory signal and to interpret auditory experiences. Both patients who use hearing aids and who use cochlear implants stand to benefit from auditory training.

Hearing aid users may learn to use their residual hearing to their maximum capability. For example, if someone has just received a hearing aid for the first time, auditory training "recalibrates" that person's brain for listening. Changes in brain structures have most likely occurred gradually over time because of decreasing and deteriorating auditory stimulation. When the person suddenly receives an amplified, spectrally shaped speech signal, the brain needs to undergo reorganization. Auditory training can accelerate and complement this process and promote sensory neuroplasticity (e.g., Kraus & White-Schwoch, 2015).

Auditory training can help cochlear implant users learn to interpret the electrical signal. For example, if someone has had significant hearing loss for a long time, memories of auditory speech may have faded and even disappeared. Auditory training will revive memories of speech and help new users map what they remember words as sounding like onto their new percepts, which might quite sound different because of how an implant electrically stimulates the auditory nerve. Auditory training is especially essential for children who receive cochlear implants, particularly for children who have prelingual hearing loss because they must learn to recognize speech starting from "square one."

Although auditory training typically concerns speech recognition, another goal of auditory training, particularly for patients who use cochlear implants, may be to enhance music perception. Many cochlear implant users who have adventitious hearing loss are disappointed that music sounds so different from how they remember it as sounding.

HISTORICAL NOTES

Systematic auditory training dates back to as early as 1805, when Jean Marc Gaspard Itard worked with students enrolled in the Paris School for Deaf-mutes. He noted that if he blindfolded students and asked them to raise a hand when they heard a bell chime, they did so with great uncertainty at first but grew more confident with practice. His realization that listening practice could enhance sound awareness was like "a ray of light illuminating the path which must be followed to bring life to a sense paralysed [*sic*] at birth" (Wedenberg, 1951, p. 15). Itard went on to develop one of the first formal auditory training curricula. In early exercises, he asked students to respond when he struck his oversized bell. If students performed well, he would wind his handkerchief around his stick so as to decrease the sound intensity. In later auditory training exercises, he used a flute to develop students' abilities to discriminate two notes, and eventually, and in the best case scenario taught students to identify vowel sounds and to comprehend sentences.

This progression of listening skill training exercises—starting with sound awareness, moving on to sound discrimination, then to sound (and word) identification, and culminating in sentence (and discourse) comprehension—came to dominate the structure of subsequent auditory training curricula, and still does so for children. This hierarchy of listening skill development will be considered in-depth in Chapter 13, when we review principles of auditory training for infants and toddlers.

Toward the end of the nineteenth century, two European gentlemen played a lead role in promoting formal auditory training for adults with adventitious hearing loss. Victor Urbantschitsch of Austria, an otologist, advocated an analytic style of auditory training, whereas Friederich Bezold of Germany, also an otologist, advocated a synthetic style of auditory training. In **analytic training**, students focus their attention on fine-grained acoustic differences between the elements composing spoken communication, with the notion that a student must perceive each of the basic parts of speech before the whole can be identified. In a typical exercise, a student might have been asked to discriminate the word *pop* from the word *top*. In order to do so, the student would need to attend to the initial sounds of both words. In **synthetic training**, students learn to understand the meaning of an utterance, even if they do not understand every word, with the notion

Analytic training emphasizes the recognition of individual speech sounds or syllables.

Synthetic training emphasizes the understanding of meaning and not necessarily the identification and comprehension of every word spoken in an utterance.

that perception of the whole is paramount. In a typical exercise, a student might have listened to a clinician read a paragraph and then answered questions about the paragraph content. At the time, these two seemingly disparate approaches engendered lively debate among physicians and educators who worked with patients who had hearing loss. As will be reviewed in Chapter 5, early speechreading programs also advocated either analytic or synthetic training, and in time, many speechreading curricula came to include a combination of both.

Three developments spurred the popularity of auditory training in the 20th century. First, the advent of wearable hearing aids meant that patients could maximize their residual hearing and had greater potential to benefit from auditory training. Whereas speechreading training had held center stage previously, auditory training became an increasingly commonplace aural rehabilitation intervention. Second, mid-century, many World War II veterans returned to their homes with **noise-induced hearing loss**, victims of the gun, cannon, and bomb blasts of modern warfare. Veterans' organizations and hospitals provided auditory training routinely to former soldiers. Raymond Carhart of Northwestern University led many of these efforts. He developed a curriculum that followed the hierarchy of listening skills set by Itard (i.e., detection, discrimination, identification, and comprehension), and was probably one of the first teachers to provide training items in the presence of competing noise. The third development, toward the end of the last century, was the emergence of cochlear implant technology. In the amount of time it took to activate a cochlear implant, a patient went from having no hearing to having hearing potential. Auditory training could maximize this potential by accelerating the learning curve and by raising the level to which listening performance eventually plateaued.

Noise-induced hearing loss is a permanent sensorineural hearing loss caused by exposure to excessive sound levels.

CANDIDACY FOR AUDITORY TRAINING

Adult patients who receive auditory training often are those who have experienced a recent change in hearing status. For example, someone who has just received a cochlear implant may receive auditory training to accelerate the learning process that often occurs during the first months following implantation. Patients who have incurred hearing loss following trauma or the ingestion of ototoxic drugs may receive training to adjust to their radically altered listening state. Patients who are using a hearing aid for the first time, or who have received a new model of hearing aid, may also receive auditory training, as their hearing status has also changed. Research shows that new hearing users realize greater benefits from training compared with experienced hearing aid users (Olsen, 2010; Olson, Preminger, & Shinn, 2013), although experienced hearing aid users too have shown benefits from training (e.g., Stecker et al., 2006; Tye-Murray et al., 2017). Many audiologists will "bundle" complimentary auditory training sessions into the price of the hearing aid.

Patients who are veteran hearing aid users may also enroll in auditory training, even though they have not experienced a recent change in hearing status. Typically, these patients are dissatisfied with their aided listening performance. They may benefit from receiving auditory training in the presence of background noise, as listening in noisy settings tends to be their most common concern.

Almost all children with meaningful hearing loss can benefit from auditory training. Although much that will be considered in this chapter applies to both adults and school-age children, as noted earlier, auditory training specifically for infants and toddlers will be addressed in Chapter 13.

BRAIN PLASTICITY AND AUDITORY TRAINING

Brain **plasticity** is the brain's ability to change as a result of experience, behavior, environment, or changes resulting from sensory deprivation or stimulation. Throughout the lifespan, the brain is capable of changing its existing neural pathways. Willott (1996) suggests three reasons why brain plasticity is relevant to aural rehabilitation:

- *Acquired hearing loss may cause functional changes in the central auditory system, changes that can affect speech perception.* For instance, Dietrich, Nieschalk, Stoll, Rajan, and Pantev (2001) reported that their participants who suffered a sudden high-frequency hearing loss had a different tonotopic map of the primary auditory cortex than their participants who had normal hearing. Specifically, in the participants with hearing loss, regions in the brain formerly responsive to high frequencies were now responding to the highest frequency that still had a normal threshold.
- *Receipt of a hearing aid or cochlear implant may lead to secondary brain plasticity, and lead to secondary changes in speech perception.* For example, Tye-Murray, Tyler, Woodworth, and Gantz (1992) tested patients' word recognition ability after they had received 1 month of experience with their cochlear implant and then after they had received 9 months. On average, scores rose by almost 10 percentage points, suggesting that patients had learned to perceive the electrical signal as a function of exposure. Some patients showed improvement after even 18 months of experience.
- *Neuronal changes may occur in the central auditory system as a result of auditory training.* For example, Tremblay, Kraus, Carrell, and McGee (1997) showed that auditory training led participants to better identify differences between synthetic versions of the syllable /da/.

Road Maps on the Brain

"A useful analogy for brain plasticity is to think of the brain as a road map covered in roads and roundabouts (or highways and intersections). If you compare your old road map with a more recent one you are likely to see some changes: New highways and intersections may have appeared and some previous ones may have been modified or even disappeared. So, just like road maps, the brain is dynamic, and it is changed by the environment in which it functions. This happens in the auditory and other parts of the brain."

—Kevin Munro, Associate Professor of Audiology at the University of Manchester and researcher interested in brain plasticity

(Mueller, 2010)

Plasticity is a term used to refer to the physiological changes in the central nervous system that occur as a result of sensory experiences.

Answers to Three Questions That People with Hearing Loss Might Ask

1. "How does hearing loss change my brain?"
   - Answer: When you begin to lose your hearing, those pathways in your brain that used to be designated for understanding speech begin to reorganize and rewire themselves. As a result, you may have lost some of the mental tools that are necessary to process and comprehend speech.
2. "If I begin to use hearing aids, will my brain automatically regain those mental skills that I lost because of hearing loss?"
   - Answer: Possibly, but if this does happen, regaining them will take time and you may never become the listener that you were before you acquired hearing loss. However, help is available. Auditory training can trigger and accelerate your brain's rebuilding process.
3. "But aren't hearing and listening the same thing?" (Figure 4–4)
   - Surprisingly, they are not. Hearing allows you to receive acoustic information (speech), while listening requires your brain to attend to and interpret speech. Once a speech signal enters your ear, your brain must rapidly process each word and hold that string of words in memory long enough to comprehend and make sense of its meaning. Not only must your brain distinguish each word from all other possible words, but it must invoke mental skills such as auditory memory, auditory attention, and auditory processing speed in order for you to engage successfully in conversation. Auditory training can help you develop more effective listening skills.

(continues)

(continued)

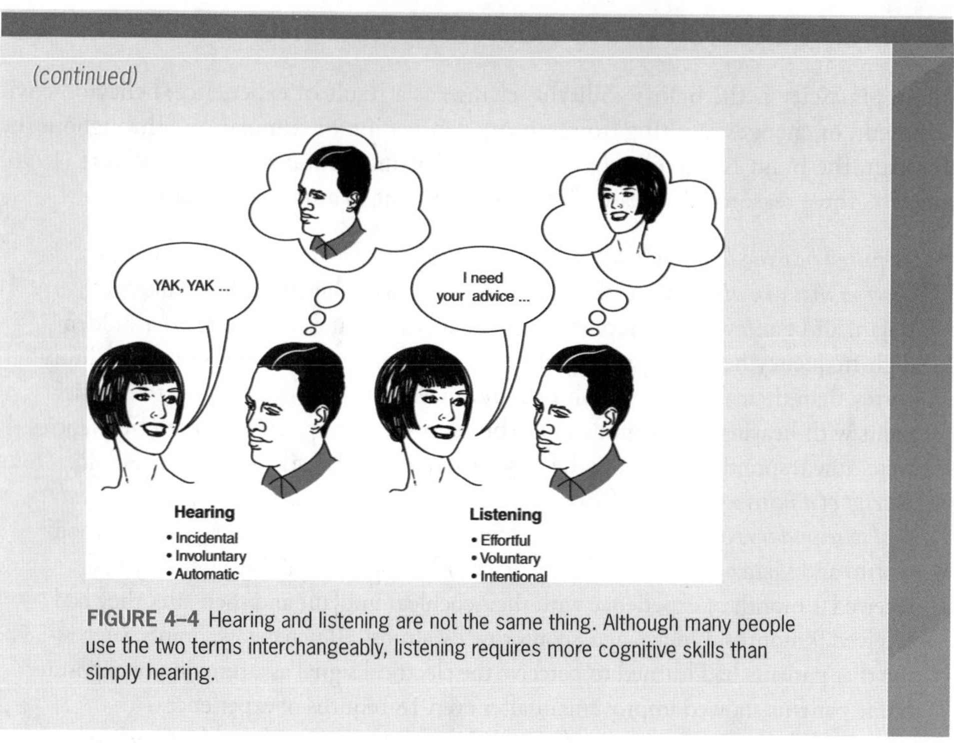

FIGURE 4–4 Hearing and listening are not the same thing. Although many people use the two terms interchangeably, listening requires more cognitive skills than simply hearing.

THEORETICAL UNDERPINNINGS FOR AUDITORY TRAINING

Transfer-Appropriate Processing theory implies that the benefits of auditory training will be tied to what is transfer appropriate: the greater the overlap between what is trained and what the desired outcomes are, the greater will be the training benefits.

Meaning-based orientation refers to using tasks in auditory training that require a student to engage in meaning-related processing and to activate the semantic regions of the brain.

Affective filter hypothesis is a hypothesis that acknowledges that affective factors can impede perceptual and linguistic learning.

Three theoretical underpinnings for auditory training have emerged in recent years, guided by the influence of principles of second language learning (Krashen, 1985, 1994). They are **Transfer-Appropriate Processing (TAP)**, a **meaning-based orientation**, and the **affective filter hypothesis** (Barcroft, 2007, 2015).

Transfer-Appropriate Processing (TAP) Theory

TAP theory posits that human learning depends upon the degree of compatibility between the training tasks and measures of desired outcome. One of the most robust findings from research on auditory training concerns the relationship between talkers and tasks used during training and assessment. A number of studies (e.g., Barcroft et al., 2011; Burk & Humes, 2007), including meta-analyses of studies (Bronus & Pryce, 2011; Sweetow & Palmer, 2005) indicate that benefits are tied to what is transfer appropriate: auditory training is most effective when using the same talker during both training and assessment and when using the same tasks during both training and assessment. Additionally, when different tasks or talkers are used in training compared with assessment, the greater the overlap between the talkers (e.g., one of six talkers overlapping as opposed to zero of six talkers) and task type, the greater the benefit.

For example, Barcroft et al. (2016) had two groups of patients complete 12 hours of meaning-oriented auditory training, where one group trained with the speech of a single talker (one of six available talkers) and a second group training with the speech of all six talkers intermixed. A control group completed 12 hours of American Sign Language training. The researchers used tests with each of the single talkers to assess benefit. The results showed that the participants in the auditory training groups improved on the tests, whereas those in the control group did not. Moreover, and importantly for TAP theory, gains were highest for the talker with whom they trained.

The bottom line is this: Effective training tasks focus on what the patient wants to learn. If the patient wants to understand his or her spouse better (Figure 4–5), use speech stimuli

FIGURE 4–5 Transfer-Appropriate Processing theory. If a patient wants to better recognize the speech of her spouse, then she should train with that person's voice. Here, a spouse is recording training items that are then automatically inserted into the computerized auditory training games in the clEAR auditory brain training program. A study showed that even when couples have been married an average of 14 years, auditory training can help the person with hearing loss better discriminate the speech of the spouse in the presence of background noise and reduce listening challenges (Tye-Murray et al., 2016).

produced by the spouse as training stimuli (Tye-Murray et al., 2016). If the patient wants to understand everyday conversation spoken by various communication partners, use the words that have a **high frequency of usage** as training stimuli so the patient can quickly and easily recognize those words most likely to be spoken on a regular basis (e.g., Burk et al., 2006).

High frequency of usage applies to words that occur frequently in everyday conversation.

Meaning-Based Orientation

When a training task is meaning oriented, the patient must semantically process the speech signal, which entails activating regions of the brain that process semantic content. By contrast, when a training task is form oriented, no semantic processing occurs, so activation of the semantic regions of the brain may be unnecessary. Table 4–1 presents examples of meaning-oriented versus form-oriented auditory training tasks. In the form-oriented examples, a patient can complete the task without paying attention to the meaning of the word, sentence, or discourse passage. Conversely, in the meaning-oriented examples, just like in real-world communication, the patient must attend to meaning at all levels of linguistic complexity. Sound discrimination and word recognition takes places as a natural by-product of language communication, and form is never divorced from meaning.

TABLE 4–1 Examples of Form-Oriented Versus Meaning-Oriented Auditory Training Tasks at the Level of Phonetic/Phonemic, Word, Sentence, and Discourse Linguistic Categories

LEVEL	FORM-ORIENTED	MEANING-ORIENTED
Phonetic/ Phonemic	Stimulus: *Ba-Ma* Task: Answer the question, *Are these syllables the same or different?*	Stimulus: *bat-cat* Task: Point to one of four sets of picture pairs that illustrate these two words and in this order. (The patient is shown the following sets of pictures: a bat and a bat; a cat and a cat; a bat and a cat; a cat and a bat)
Word	Stimulus: *cat-caterpillar* Task: Answer the question, *Which word is longer?*	Stimulus: *cat* Task: Point to one of four pictures that illustrates this word. (The patient is shown the following four pictures: a cat; a rat; a cab; a hat)
Sentence	Stimulus: *The chef made an apple pie.* Task: Listen to this sentence and then repeat it verbatim.	Stimulus: *The chef made an apple pie.* Task: Answer the question, *What kind of pie did the chef make?*
Discourse	Stimulus: A read passage Task: As you hear this passage, follow along in the text with your finger.	Stimulus: A read passage Task: Listen to this passage, then answer questions about the content of the passage.

The Affective Filter Hypothesis

"If the [student] is anxious, has low self-esteem, doesn't consider him/herself to be a potential member of the group that speaks the language, s/he may understand the input, but it will not reach the language acquisition device—a block, the Affective Filter, will keep the Input out." (*Krashen, 1994, p. 46*)

The affective filter hypothesis recognizes that emotional factors can block input into a second language learner's language acquisition process. If a person feels like a hopeless, hapless outsider, the person may raise an affective filter that effectively blocks input that would allow him or her to progress in acquiring a new language. Similarly, if a person with hearing loss experiences high anxiety during everyday listening, continuous failure in recognizing speech, and low self-esteem, listening skills are unlikely to improve. Auditory training can be tailored to reduce a patient's anxiety and to enhance a sense of community with other people who have hearing loss. For example, some computer-based training programs adaptively vary background noise during training so that patients always experience an 80% success rate, Some programs use the internet to connect patients through shared training goals and community message boards (Tye-Murray, 2016a; 2017; e.g., http//:www.clearworks4ears.com).

AUDITORY TRAINING TO IMPROVE SPEECH RECOGNITION

Patients should be fitted with an appropriate listening device before starting an auditory training program. By ensuring that patients have the best listening system possible, you will increase the raw material they have to work with and enhance their potential to benefit from training.

Implementing a Training Program

If you are providing formal auditory training using live voice, you probably will not encourage students to watch your mouth movements as you speak. In fact, you may obscure your mouth, either by covering it or by sitting out of view (Figure 4–6).

© Photographee.eu | Shutterstock.com

FIGURE 4–6 Providing auditory training with live voice. The clinician either sits out of view of the student or uses a mesh screen to hide her mouth movements.

Increasingly, auditory training is computerized, and the student sits before a computer screen, or uses a small portable laptop computer or an inexpensive mobile digital device such as an iPad. The student performs exercises with digitized speech samples, often in a game-like format, without seeing a concomitant visual speech signal. In these scenarios, your role may be to introduce the student to training, and to monitor the student's progress, either in person or by means of the internet, computer record, or telephone.

There is flexibility in how often you schedule training sessions. For example, Humes et al. (2014) showed that 15 hours of auditory training dispensed twice a week was as effective as the same amount dispensed three times a week.

Game-like Auditory Training

FIGURE 4–7 Gamified auditory training. In order for the brain to learn new perceptual skills, it must be aroused by and engaged in the learning process.

Training activities have become much more game-like, more similar to the kinds of games that keep children and adults alike playing on the Internet for hours (Figure 4–7). This is because in order for the brain to learn new perceptual skills, it must be aroused by and engaged in the learning process. The rationale for gamifying auditory training is as follows:

- Playing video games is pleasurable.
- Pleasant activities cause the brain to increase production of dopamine, which is a neurotransmitter that acts as a "messenger" between brain cells.
- Research has shown that playing video games increases production of dopamine.
- Increased dopamine levels enhance neural plasticity.
- Enhanced neural plasticity allows for greater perceptual learning.
- Hence, individuals with hearing loss have better potential for learning to use their residual hearing when playing auditory training games than when engaging in rote auditory training tasks.

There are several advantages to using computerized instruction. These include the following:

- Many different talkers can speak training items, which may lead to training benefits generalizing to the real world, where many different talkers are encountered.
- Many training items can be presented in a relatively short period of time; concentrated training may lead to faster learning and maintains a student's interest.
- Training is interactive, which means that a student's response to one training item determines what will happen next; response contingency may lead to enhanced learning.
- A record can be maintained of correct and incorrect responses, which affords a means for the clinician to monitor progress.

- Training difficulty can vary adaptively, based on a student's performance.
- Instruction is self-paced; students can proceed through an exercise as slowly or as quickly as they choose.
- Training can occur in the student's home and at the student's convenience.
- Training can be self-guided, meaning that a student can choose which activities and exercises to complete.
- Costs may be less than labor-intensive clinician-based training.

Some research about computer-based training in the home environment has shown poor patient compliance (Saunders et al., 2018). For example, Sweetow and Sabes (2010) lamented that from over 3,000 patients enrolled in the Listening and Communication Enhancement (LACE) computer-based program, a program that patients complete on a personal computer in their homes, less than 30% of the patients completed the program. By contrast, when more than 90 patients completed computer-based training in a clinic setting and had clinician contact—the clinician greeted the patient and then returned following the training session to answer questions and provide support—compliance was 100% (Tye-Murray, Barcroft, & Sommers, 2011).

Modern programs take advantage of the internet as a means for a clinician to provide ongoing coaching and feedback to patients on a weekly basis. For example, clEAR (customized learning: Exercises for Aural Rehabilitation; Tye-Murray, 2016a, 2016b) presents patients with a weekly lesson plan, telling them which training games to play that week and, importantly, why they are playing the particular games. The program has lesson plans that are uniquely tailored to the patient's particular listening needs, consonant with TAP theory. For example, clEAR has a lesson plan for the patient with a new hearing aid, for the patient who wants to understand speech better in the presence of background, and for the patient who wants to train with the speech of a spouse or other important communication partner. The clinician has access to the patient's feedback charts (Figure 4–8), so can not only send a lesson plan each week, but provide specific feedback based upon the patient's charts.

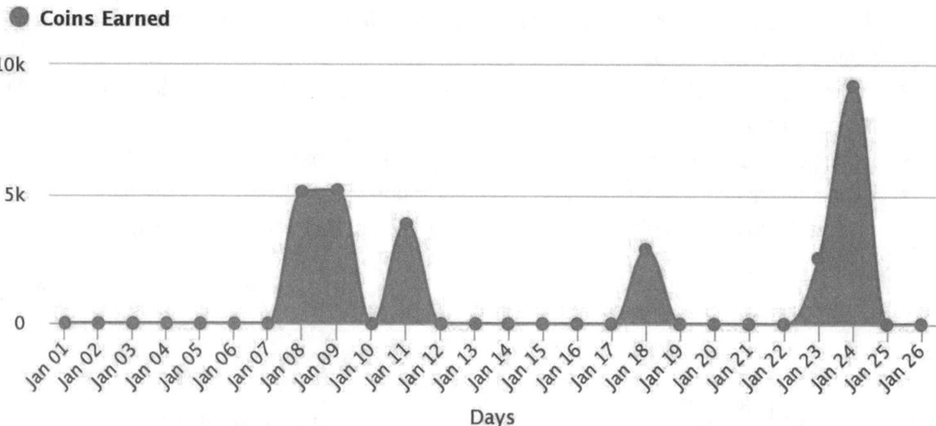

FIGURE 4–8 Feedback charts about performance. When auditory training is administered via the Internet, the clinician can monitor a patient's progress with feedback charts like this one, which shows the number of coins earned during the preceding three weeks. In the clEAR program, users earn coins for each correct response.

Training Programs

Although no two auditory training programs are alike, current programs typically present at least one of four general types of training in the course of a single training session, and many of the programs present two or more of the types. These types of training are: phoneme-based, word-based, sentence-based, and cognitive skill-based.

Phoneme-Based Training

Phoneme-based training may present nonsense syllables in vowel-consonant-vowel context, such as *aba* and *ata*, and/or in consonant-vowel and vowel-consonant context, such as *ba* and *ab*, or may present real words in a static context, such as vowels in an *h–d* context. One rationale for phoneme-based training is that learning to discriminate phonemes in nonsense syllables is akin to acquiring the "building blocks" of language, and this learning will generalize to recognizing larger speech units such as words and sentences (e.g., Moore, Rosenberg, & Coleman, 2005). Phoneme-based training hones **bottom-up processing**, which is the ability to recognize the constituents of syllables: their onsets, nuclei, and coda (offsets). A patient may hear two syllables (e.g., *ba-da*) and be asked to determine whether the two are the *same* or *different*.

Bottom-up processing refers to the processing of sound that is influenced only from input from the auditory periphery, with minimal cognitive processing in terms of expectations or prior knowledge.

The use of nonsense syllables violates the meaning-based orientation considered earlier. For this reason, phoneme-based training may be modified in a way that requires a patient to both attend to meaning as well as engage in phoneme discrimination. Figure 4–9 presents a training screen for a four-choice discrimination task. The patient may hear the words *net* and *nest.* Instead of simply indicating that the two words are the *same*, the student must understand the two words and then select the corresponding illustration from a closed set of four choices.

FIGURE 4–9 Response screen from a computerized auditory training activity. Although this is a simple phoneme-level discrimination task, students must attend to both meaning and form to respond correctly.

Word-Based Training

Word-based training emphasizes meaningful speech units, as opposed to the "building block" or sublexical approach of phoneme-based training. In a typical training protocol, a student might identify which of a member of possible word choices occurred. For example, Humes, Burk, Strauser, and Kinney (2009) taught students to recognize the 600 most frequently used words of the English language, as these words represent about 80–90% of the words used in the course of everyday conversation. A sample of these commonly used words, which during training were presented in closed-set groups, includes the following: *am, always, answer, change, control, day, even, life, remember, sun, third, together, understand, wind, and yes.* A student might hear a word during training and then indicate which word was spoken from a closed set of choices.

Sentence-Based Training

Sentence-based training presents sentences as training stimuli. For instance, in the Computer-Assisted Speech Perception Sentence training program (CasperSent) (Boothroyd, 2008), each sentence in a training exercise pertains to one of 12 topics, such as *food* or *work*. Example sentences are *Make sure that you don't overcook the shrimp* and *Take the job only if you feel the work will be more challenging*. The student listens to a sentence and then self-scores the sentence by clicking on the words heard correctly once the orthographic version of the sentence appears on the computer screen. In the event of errors, the sentence replays before the program moves on to the next sentence.

Sentence-based training requires students to use both bottom-up processing and top-down processing skills, which is what they must do during everyday speech recognition. **Top-down processing**, as it pertains to speech recognition, entails the listener using social and linguistic knowledge as well as expectations based on contextual evidence to identify sentences, in balance with the sensory evidence and bottom-up processing.

Top-down processing refers to the processing of a speech signal that is influenced by expectations and prior knowledge, and the way that advanced cognition affects perception of sensory inputs.

Cognitive Skill–Based Training

Cognition refers to those mental processes involved in obtaining knowledge, in comprehending, and in thinking, including such mental acts as remembering, judging, and problem solving.

Cognition includes those mental processes that are used for perceiving, remembering, and thinking. This relatively new type of auditory training has been motivated by research showing interactions exist between the effects of peripheral hearing loss and cognitive functions such as working memory and selective attention (e.g., Pichora-Fuller & Levitt, 2012; Pichora-Fuller & Souza, 2003; Wingfield & Tun, 2001).

Working memory is a temporary storage mechanism that allows incoming information to be actively manipulated (Baddeley, 1992). A larger working memory allows one to better comprehend connected discourse (Caplan & Waters, 1999). The Target Word exercise of the LACE program is an example of a training activity designed to develop auditory working memory (Sweetow & Sabes, 2006). In early training, a target word is visually presented before a sentence is played in quiet. After listening to the sentence, the student must indicate on a multiple-choice response screen what word occurred just prior to the target word in the sentence. In later training, the target word is presented after the patient hears three sentences, and the patient must remember back to the first sentence and recall the word that occurred before the target word.

Selective attention is a selective narrowing of mental focus and receptivity.

Selective attention is the ability to disregard or attenuate a competing signal while attending to and processing a target signal. Selective attention is often impaired in persons with hearing loss because their auditory systems do not fully encode frequency, duration, and intensity cues. This in turn may hinder auditory object formation. For instance, if patients with hearing loss attempt to recognize one sentence while another sentence is spoken simultaneously, they may not filter out the competing sentence and hence not discern which words belong to which sentence or decipher the sounds from one word from those of a simultaneously spoken word (Shinn-Cunningham & Best, 2008). In order to train selective listening attention, the Competing Speaker exercise of LACE requires students to focus on either a man's, a woman's, or a child's voice while ignoring a competing voice in the background. For instance, a woman's voice speaks a sentence while a man's voice speaks a competing sentence. An orthographic transcription of the woman's sentence then appears on the computer screen and students must indicate whether they recognized every word in the sentence.

Most recently, a group of investigators have developed a procedure they call audiomotor perceptual training to enhance speech recognition in the presence of background noise (Whitten et al., 2017). In this video game–like task, students build a puzzle by using their finger to trace the perimeter of hidden puzzle pieces on the monitor screen. Changing tones guide them, and background noise grows in intensity, making the tones more difficult to hear. Just like playing an action video game, training with a sensorimotor task may lead to perceptual learning.

AUDITORY TRAINING TO IMPROVE MUSIC PERCEPTION

Many cochlear implant users yearn to enjoy music, and after spoken language, they cite it as being an important auditory stimulus in their lives. Unfortunately, many cochlear implant recipients are disappointed. They might be able to hear the rhythm of music, and this may allow them to clap or dance to the rhythm of the beat, but they typically cannot perceive or appraise pitch, timbre (tone quality), or melody very well (Gfeller et al., 2008; Macherey & Delpierre, 2013).

The cochlear implant cannot replace or simulate the exquisite architecture of an intact cochlea. A normal cochlea encodes pitch by place of stimulation, where the apical end corresponds to low pitches and the basal end corresponds to high pitches, and by the rate at which the fibers of the auditory nerve fire, where a faster firing rate corresponds to a higher pitch. Whereas the normal cochlea has 3,500 inner hair cells to convey frequency information, the implanted electrode array has only 8 to 24 electrodes to specify frequency. Moreover, the electrode array may not provide stimulation along the entire length of the basilar membrane. The firing rates of the electrodes either are set or do not effectively transmit fine timing changes. The technological constraints that limit place-pitch and rate-pitch in turn impair melody perception. Melody perception is built upon a person's ability to perceive changes in pitch, to perceive the interval distance between two consecutive notes, and to perceive the overall contour of a series of notes. Since pitch perception is poor, many cochlear implant users cannot recognize such simple and well-known melodies as "London Bridge" and "Twinkle, Twinkle Little Star" (Gfeller et al., 2002).

Tips for cochlear implant users about how to listen to music:

- Choose a quiet listening environment
- Choose music selections carefully
- Be strategic and realistic about listening
- Make the sound as good as possible
- Use visual input to help out your ears and brain
- Broaden your music listening goals

(Gfeller, 2009)

Listen to the music? No thank you.

"The perception of music, even among the upper echelons of implant performers, may be very limited, and can be an extremely disappointing part of the implant experience. It has been said that current technology in cochlear implantation may not provide the spectral resolution and fine structures necessary for music perception, as high scores in speech understanding in quiet are not predictive of music enjoyment and perception."

(Smith, Bartel, Joglekar, & Chen, 2017)

Training Approaches

There are at least two approaches for training music perception: the musical feature approach and the whole song approach. The musical feature approach trains students to perceive the structural features of music, such as **rhythm**, **pitch**, **melody**, and **timbre**. Because music is a complex combination of features, a starting point in learning to perceive and organize these features is to learn to perceive and appraise them one by one. These skills may then generalize to more realistic music listening, and the experience may become more pleasurable. The whole song approach provides a more holistic experience, and teaches students to enjoy songs and to recognize musical styles. The student focuses on the overall musical experience. These approaches are not mutually exclusive, and both kinds of approach activities may be included within a single music auditory training lesson.

Rhythm refers to a pattern of sounds and silences that is repeated.

Pitch is a perceptual phenomenon that allows the ordering of sounds along a frequency scale, and is a psychological impression of frequency.

A **melody** is a sequence of musical tones that are perceived as a single entity.

Timbre is the quality of a musical note that distinguishes different sound sources, such as wind instruments (e.g., a flute) and string instruments (e.g., violin).

Musical Feature Approach

A typical exercise in the musical feature approach might be to train the recognition of musical instruments, a skill that requires timbre perception. For instance, students might be presented the same simple melody over and over, each time produced with one of 12 different instruments (bells, harp, guitar, drums, piano, flute, saxophone, clarinet, violin, cello, trombone, and trumpet). The student's task is to identify which instrument played a given sample (Driscoll, 2012; Driscoll, Oleson, Jiang, & Gfeller, 2009). Alternatively, students might identify simple melodic contours and indicate whether a five-tone melody has a rising or falling pitch contour (Galvin, Fu, & Nogaki, 2007).

Whole Song Approach

The whole song approach provides positive and ultimately pleasurable music listening experiences, and is epitomized by some of the activities developed for Med-El and for cochlear implant users seen at the Hearing Rehabilitation Foundation (Plant, 2009). In this particular training program, students cycle through the following activities: (1) listening to familiar melodies such as "Yankee Doodle" and "This Land Is Your Land"; (2) listening to songs with simple musical styles; these are songs that have "easy-to-access" lyrics and minimal instrumental accompaniment (e.g., songs by John Denver and James Taylor); (3) playing music videos so they can watch the performer's mouth form the words to the lyrics and see the performer's body sway to the rhythm; (4) experiencing a live performance, as when a clinician plays the guitar and encourages the patient to sing along; and (5) listening to music composed for cochlear implant users, music that is characterized by low frequency timbres, many instrumental solos, and avoidance of complex harmonies.

BENEFITS OF AUDITORY TRAINING

Efficacy of auditory training is difficult to assess. When hearing and speech professionals say "auditory training" or when they see the term in a research article, they often believe that the term always refers to a similar training experience. The problem with this kind of assumption is that different training curricula may lead to different results. For example, Sweetow and Palmer (2005) surveyed the literature to answer the following question: "Is there evidence of improvement in communication skills through individual auditory training in an adult hearing-impaired population?" (p. 494). Not surprisingly, the answer was equivocal. For the six research studies that met the authors' criteria of methodological rigor, four reported that auditory training enhanced listening performance, one did not, and one reported mixed results. All six studies had a different instantiation of auditory training. Similarly, Henshaw and Ferguson (2013) performed a meta-analysis of the benefits of computerized auditory training. Based on the authors' examination of 13 research studies that met their inclusion criteria of good experimental design, they concluded that overall, results were not always consistent or robust but it appeared that training results in modest gains in speech recognition. Saunders et al. (2016) reported no benefits of LACE auditory training for a group of veterans as opposed to a placebo auditory training with books-on-tapes for another group, whereas Barcroft et al. (2016) and Tye-Murray et al. (2017) reported significant gains for a group of older adults using clEAR.

Because there are many different philosophies about how to structure auditory training, its effectiveness should be considered within the context of what constitutes the training experience. Many programs vary in length, from one day (e.g., Bode & Oyer, 1970) to six weeks or longer (Tye-Murray et al., 2012), and evaluation of the effectiveness of training is likely confounded by duration of training. Some programs present training that is rote and repetitive (e.g., LACE) and some programs emphasize engaging the student in the learning process by gamifying training (e.g., clEAR).

With that caveat, overall, several studies have suggested that auditory training is effective in improving speech discrimination and recognition in adults (e.g., Barcroft et al., 2011; Burk & Humes, 2007b; Burk, Humes, Amos, & Strauser, 2006; Casserly & Barney, 2017; Fu & Galvin, 2007; Gil & Lorio, 2010; Olson et al., 2013; Stecker et al., 2006; Sweetow & Sabes, 2007; Tobey et al., 2005; Tye-Murray et al., 2017; Woods & Yund, 2007), whereas at least two have not (Stacy et al., 2010; Saunders et al., 2016). At least two have suggested that auditory training is effective for school-age children (Hnath-Chisolm, 1997; Sullivan, Thibodeau, & Assmann, 2013).

Some studies have used indices other than speech tests to assess benefits. In one study, 93 adult research participants on average indicated that they were now more confident in talking with both familiar and unfamiliar talkers following auditory training (Tye-Murray et al., 2012). Another study compared the hearing aid return rates of 173 research participants who had just received a new hearing aid and who had participated in auditory training versus the return rates of 452 participants in a control group. Thirteen percent of the participants in the control group returned their hearing aids for credit, whereas only 4% of the participants who received auditory training did so (Martin, 2007). Finally, Sommers et al. (2015) showed that 83 experienced adult hearing aid users required significantly less perceptual effort to attend to speech following 12 sessions of clEAR auditory training.

There are mixed data about the benefit of music training. For instance, Galvin et al. (2007) provided musical feature training exercises to six research participants and found that melodic contour identification improved with training, and Driscoll (2012) showed that a five-week training program comprising a total of three training sessions improved the ability of 71 adults with cochlear implants, on average, to recognize excerpts recorded with eight different musical instruments. Smith et al. (2017) found that those individuals with a "high" musical background (e.g., able to read sheet music, several years playing an instrument) received relatively little benefit from a home-based computerized program, whereas those with a "low" musical background did demonstrate improved music perception skills. Gfeller and her colleagues reported only modest effects of training, however (Gfeller, Witt, Stordahl, Mehr, & Woodworth, 2000). Twelve cochlear implant users enrolled in a three-month home training program (48 lessons) and 12 cochlear implant users served as control participants and completed no formal music training. Training included both musical feature and whole song training, with the following activities: pitch sequence perception, song recognition, timbre recognition and appraisal, and appraisal of different musical styles. The training group showed no change in their ability to recognize or appreciate simple songs such as "Happy Birthday" relative to the control group, but did show change with complex music such as Beethoven's Fifth Symphony. Looi, King, and Kelly-Campbell (2012) found that although music auditory training did not change their ability to identify timbre or rate-pitch, on average, 18 adult cochlear implant users gained greater music enjoyment following training, suggesting that music enjoyment can change, independently of perceptual accuracy.

CASE STUDY

Learning to Hear Again

Good Housekeeping tells the story of 32-year-old Kelly Gilkey, a woman with a severe prelingual hearing loss (Allen, 2012). Kelly received a cochlear implant and one year later, as she approached the year's end, "she enjoy[s] sounds she has never heard before, like the peal of church bells [and is] . . . able to hear her boys [ages 2 and 3 years] in the living room or even upstairs, playing with their new toys" (p. 59).

Like many successful adult cochlear implant users who have prelingual hearing loss, Kelly had some residual hearing up until her second pregnancy and wore hearing aids starting from early childhood. She never relied on sign language for communication, and went through school using her speech and hearing. This past year has been a "journey of daily discovery."

The day of her device activation brought surprises, both pleasant and unpleasant. At first, "It was horrible!" Kelly relates. "I heard a lot of background noise—air conditioning, people moving about. . . . When the audiologist and my mom started talking, they sounded like Minnie Mouse on helium." Her husband's deep voice sounded "much better," and hearing it was "pretty incredible" (p. 62).

(continues)

CASE STUDY

Learning to Hear Again (*continued*)

"Like others who receive cochlear implants, Kelly had to learn how to identify sounds—as dizzying as a crash course in a new language. 'It's like you're rebuilding your auditory database,' she says. Questions would run through her head continually: *What's that sound? OK, that's the refrigerator, I can ignore that. What's that sound? It's my dog snoring. OK, I can ignore that.* Sometimes just to give her brain a rest, she would take off her sound processor, grateful for the relative quiet" (p. 62).

It took about a week for voices not to sound like cartoon characters, but for several months they sounded robotic. Now they sound normal. She was surprised that things she had not realized made sound indeed did make sound—like a clock ticking or her fingers tapping on a computer keyboard.

Kelly engaged in formal auditory training with her audiologist. After a while, she could discriminate an /s/ sound from an /ʃ/ sound and a /ʒ/, high-frequency sounds that she had not been able to hear with her hearing aid. At home, she honed her listening skills by listening to audio books on tape. Her favorite was reading along with the *Harry Potter* series (she could hear the British accent!).

She is currently "training her brain" to hear the sounds of music, and recently went to hear a symphony with her husband. For the first several months of device use, she hesitated to listen to music, afraid she would be disappointed with how it sounded. She was "shocked at how I was able to distinguish the instruments" (p. 65).

Kelly's story illustrates the importance of incidental learning of sounds and speech, the value of auditory training, and how patients sometimes develop home-based listening practice activities. It also shows that music appreciation comes slowly, often after ample experience with a cochlear implant.

FINAL REMARKS

The importance of the audiologist's or other hearing health care provider's ongoing involvement during training cannot be overemphasized. If you tell a patient to "go home and train with these computerized auditory training programs," the outcome will likely not be very good. On the other hand, the outcome might be positive if there is a hearing health care provider involved in every step of the way—a professional who provides a structured training curriculum, who provides ongoing feedback about progress and compliance, and who makes the patient feel as if someone cares that he or she is engaging in training. Tye-Murray et al. (2012) asked a group of about 100 patients what they liked best about their auditory training experience, which entailed weekly contact with an audiologist, and one of the most common answers was "regular contact with my audiologist." The other most common answer was "feeling empowered to manage my hearing loss."

KEY CHAPTER POINTS

- Adults with new listening devices or a change in hearing status and children with meaningful hearing loss are most likely to receive auditory training.
- Hearing loss makes some sounds inaudible, may impair frequency selectivity and temporal resolution, and may result in increased perceptual effort during listening.
- Because brain plasticity extends well into adulthood, many adult patients have the potential to benefit from auditory training.

- The theoretical substrate underlying more recent auditory training programs comes from second language learning and includes Transfer-Appropriate Processing (TAP) theory, meaning-based orientation, and affective filter hypothesis.
- Many of today's auditory training programs are computer based.
- Many auditory training programs present one or more of these types of training: phoneme-based, word-based, sentence-based, and cognitive skill–based.
- Many cochlear implant users are disappointed with the way music sounds and some seek music training, which may be based on music features such as timbre or on whole song recognition.
- Several published reports suggest that auditory training is beneficial. In addition, brain activity appears to change as a result of auditory learning.

TERMS AND CONCEPTS TO REMEMBER

Noise-induced hearing loss
Frequency selectivity
Temporal resolution
Perceptual effort
Working memory
Brain plasticity
Selective attention
Gamification
Transfer-Appropriate Processing theory (TAP)
Meaning-based orientation
Affective filter hypothesis

CHAPTER 5

Audiovisual Speech Perception and Speechreading Training

OUTLINE

- Speechreading for Communication
- Characteristics of a Good Lipreader
- What Happens When Someone Lipreads?
- The Difficulty of the Lipreading Task
- What Happens When Someone Speechreads?
- Importance of Residual Hearing
- Factors That Affect the Speechreading Process
- Assessing Vision-Only and Audiovisual Speech Recognition
- Traditional Methods of Speechreading Training
- Speechreading Training Today
- Benefits of Speechreading Training
- Oral Interpreters
- Case Study: An Exceptional Lipreader
- Final Remarks
- Key Chapter Points
- Terms and Concepts to Remember

Lipreading is the process of recognizing speech using only the visual speech signal and other visual cues, such as facial expression.

Speechreading is speech recognition using both auditory and visual cues.

The terms *lipreading* and *speechreading* sometimes are used interchangeably, but for the sake of clarity in this chapter, they will be used to refer to two different processes. When **lipreading**, a person relies only on the visual signal provided by the talker's face for recognizing speech. When **speechreading**, the person attends to both the talker's auditory and visual signals, as well as the talker's facial expressions and gestures, and any other available cues.

In this chapter, we will consider the lipreading and speechreading processes and how visual speech information enhances the intelligibility of degraded auditory information and then consider means that have traditionally been used to enhance speechreading performance as well as current practices, and finally, consider efficacy of instruction.

SPEECHREADING FOR COMMUNICATION

Functional magnetic resonance imaging (fMRI) is an imaging technology used to study the activity of the brain; the computerized images show which brain structures are active during a particular mental activity.

The **auditory cortex** is the region of the brain that is responsible for processing auditory information and is located in the temporal lobe of the cerebral hemisphere, just forward of the occipital lobe.

People with normal hearing routinely rely on speechreading. Consider these examples: When we are at a noisy restaurant, we understand more if we watch the talker's face while we listen (Figure 5–1). We may feel unsettled when we view dubbed foreign films because the words we hear do not match those we see. A raised eyebrow imparts additional meaning to the question "You're not working today?" A number of experimental paradigms have been developed that demonstrate that even if an individual has normal hearing, that person relies on visual speech information to recognize and comprehend a message. If someone reads aloud Kant's *Critique of Pure Reason*, which is difficult-to-grasp philosophy, the audience will better understand the content if the members see and hear the reader than if they only hear the person's voice (Arnold & Hill, 2001; Reisberg, McLean, & Goldfield, 1987). If a talker "shadows" someone who is reading a passage, that is, attempts to repeat each word the reader speaks as quickly as possible, the individual will do so at a faster rate if he or she sees and hears the reader than by listening alone (Reisberg et al., 1987). Studies employing **functional magnetic resonance imaging (fMRI)**, a noninvasive means of mapping brain activity, have shown that when someone tries to recognize speech using the visual signal only, the **auditory cortex** becomes activated (Venezia et al., 2017; Wilson, Alsius, Paré, & Munhall, 2016). Even infants engage in speechreading. If a 5-month-old baby hears someone phonate "eeeeeee" and simultaneously views a side-by-side projection of the same talker, on one side saying "eeeeeee" and on the other side saying "aaahhhh," the baby most likely will fixate on the visual signal that corresponds to the acoustic signal (Kuhl & Meltzoff,

FIGURE 5–1 The visual speech signal can enhance speech recognition, particularly in the presence of hearing loss and/or background noise.

1982). Babies can visually recognize when a familiar word is mispronounced, as when the word *bottle* is spoken as *dottle* (Weatherhead & White, 2017).

A person with hearing loss will depend more on the visual signal for speech recognition than will people who have normal hearing. The greater the hearing loss, the more a person will rely on visual information for communication.

CHARACTERISTICS OF A GOOD LIPREADER

People vary widely in their lipreading performance. Some individuals can score 80% words correct or better in a vision-only test condition, as measured by verbatim repetition of test words, whereas others score 5% or worse on the same stimuli (Sommers, Tye-Murray, & Spehar, 2005). Although many researchers have asked the question *Why do some people lipread better than others?*, we still do not have a clear answer. However, we can divide our existing knowledge into three categories: Variables that do not have predictive power, variables that do, and variables that may or may not. Most likely a combination of variables is predictive, and that combination may differ across groups of people.

Variables That Appear Not to Have Predictive Power

Performance cannot be predicted by an individual's intelligence, educational achievement, presence and duration of acquired hearing loss, gender, or gaze behavior (Hygge, Rönnberg, Larsby, & Arlinger, 1992; Rönnberg, 1995; Tye-Murray, Sommers, & Spehar, 2007a, 2007b). For example, adults with acquired hearing loss, and hence they are practiced in lipreading, lipread no better than adults with normal hearing (Tye-Murray et al., 2008). Women and men perform equally well on tests of vision-only consonant recognition, word recognition, and sentence recognition (Tye-Murray et al., 2007b). **Gaze behavior**, which refers to how the eyes scan the face of the talker, does not predict (Wilson, Alslius, Paré, & Munhall, 2016). For example, people who fixate longer on the mouth are not better lipreaders than people who fixate longer on the eyes.

Gaze behavior, in reference to lipreading or speechreading, refers to how the eyes shift their focus around the talker's face as the talker speaks.

Variables That Appear to Have Predictive Power

At least three variables appear to have predictive power, the first being cognitive skills. In one of the most comprehensive studies on the topic, Feld and Sommers (2009) administered a matrix-type lipreading test to 43 young adults and 38 older adults along with a battery of tests measuring verbal working memory, spatial working memory, processing speed, and perceptual ability. As with verbal working memory (the type of working memory considered in the previous chapter), **spatial working memory** is measured with a span task, but instead of asking research participants to remember strings of digits, participants must recall varying length of strings of nonverbal items, such as the position of red lines drawn within a box. The researchers found that spatial working memory and **processing speed** predicted lipreading scores for both young and old participants (together accounting for 46% of the variance). Processing speed refers to how quickly someone can perform a cognitive task and is often measured with reaction time tasks, such as how quickly a person can determine whether or not the words *thyme* and *lime* rhyme. Intuitively, these findings make sense, as lipreading entails processing visual information and doing so rapidly because speech unfolds very quickly.

Spatial working memory is responsible for temporarily storing visual information and permits active utilization and updating of visual information from the environment and about one's spatial position.

Processing speed is the rate at which information is conducted and manipulated throughout the nervous system.

A second variable that predicts lipreading performance is age. Young adults lipread better than older adults, suggesting that aging adversely affects lipreading ability (e.g., Stevenson et al., 2015; Taitelbaum-Swead & Fostick, 2016; Tye-Murray et al., 2016).

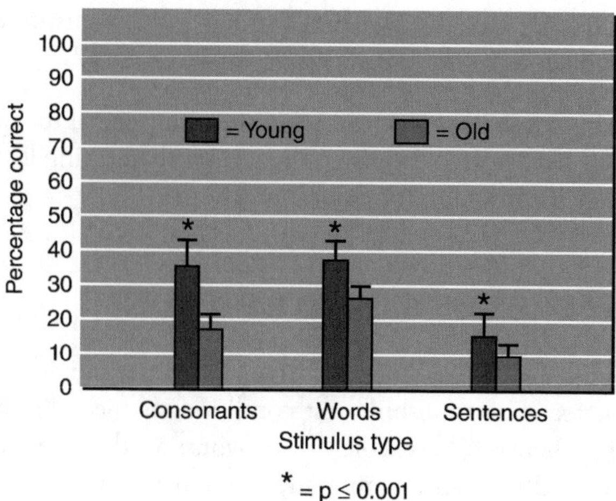

FIGURE 5–2 Percentage correct scores for a group of 45 young lipreaders (ages 18–24 years) and a group of 45 older lipreaders (ages 65 years and older). The asterisks indicate a significant difference in performance between the two groups.

Figure 5–2 shows the difference between how well young and old adults lipread consonants, words, and sentences. The research participants had normal hearing and no visual impairment. As the figure suggests, the younger adults lipread all three types of speech stimuli better than the older adults.

Third, even though individuals who have acquired hearing loss do not appear to develop superior lipreading skills to those individuals who have normal hearing, individuals who have congenital hearing loss lipread better than individuals who are born with normal hearing. For example, cochlear implant users with congenital deafness who receive their cochlear implant later in life appear to be better lipreaders than those who receive an implant earlier, presumably because they have been reliant on the visual speech signal for a greater length of time (Pimperton et al., 2017). Children with hearing loss lipread words and sentences with greater accuracy than do children with normal hearing (Tye-Murray et al., 2015).

Variables That May (or May Not) Have Predictive Power

Some speech and hearing professionals have cited more nebulous characteristics that may relate to lipreading performance, including individuals' ability to capitalize on contextual cues, their willingness to guess, their mental agility, and their willingness to revise interpretations of a partially recognized message. Linguistic and world knowledge can constrain proficiency. Someone who has a limited vocabulary and limited knowledge of grammar will likely experience lipreading difficulties.

WHAT HAPPENS WHEN SOMEONE LIPREADS?

Visual fixation occurs when the eyes fixate gaze on a single location.

A **saccade** is a rapid and intermittent eye movement such that the eyes fixate on one point and then another point in the visual field.

A talker's face presents salient cues for recognizing the sounds of speech and the prosodic patterns of sentences. For example, when a talker speaks the sound /m/, the lips press together. When the talker makes the /u/ sound, the lips pucker slightly. The eyebrows rise when a talker incredulously asks a question (e.g., *You did what?*). When someone lipreads, the person's eyes scan the talker's face, seeking both phonetic and prosodic cues as to what is being said. Eyes may stabilize, for a **visual fixation**, or rotate in quick, high-velocity shifts, for a **saccade**. When processing a visual scene, viewers will interweave a series of visual fixations with saccades.

Researchers have studied eye movement behavior during lipreading using equipment that tracks the center of the pupil. One study found that lipreaders monitor different regions of the face, according to the kind of information they seek (Lansing & McConkie, 1999). Research participants were asked to discriminate either phonetic contrasts (e.g., *Ron ran* vs. *We won*) or questions and statements (e.g., *Ron ran?* vs. *Ron ran*). In general, participants tended to direct their eye gaze toward the talker's eyes, nose, and mouth, with occasional shifts to the regions of the forehead, cheeks, and chin. When seeking prosodic information about questions versus statements, they focused more on the upper face (most likely monitoring events such as forehead wrinkling, eyebrow raising, and eye widening), and when making phonetic judgments, they focused more on the lower face, monitoring lip and jaw movement. Eye gaze tended to shift to the talker's eyes at the end of an utterance, regardless of what the subjects' lipreading task happened to be. Another study, assessing sentence recognition, showed that under optimal listening and viewing conditions, research participants used saccades and fixated on various points on the talker's face. For example, during the course of speechreading a single sentence, one participant fixated on the talker's left eye, then had a saccade to the talker's nose, then to the inner corner of the right eye, and ended by fixating on the tip of the talker's nose. When test conditions became unfavorable, because of loud background noise or a competing visual speech signal, participants fixated on points on or near the talker's mouth and used a "saccades-toward-mouth" gaze strategy (Yi, Wong, & Eizenman, 2013).

THE DIFFICULTY OF THE LIPREADING TASK

When lipreading, most people recognize less than 20% of the words they see. (Look back at Figure 5–2 and examine the percentage correct scores for words in a sentence context.) Why is lipreading so difficult? The answer to this question relates to the five variables listed in Table 5–1, which are: (1) the visibility of sounds, (2) the rapidity of speech, (3) coarticulation and stress effects, (4) visemes and homophenes, and (5) talker effects.

TABLE 5–1 Factors That Influence the Difficulty of the Lipreading Task

FACTOR	EFFECT
Visibility of sounds	Many sounds are not associated with visible mouth movement.
Rapidity of speech	Often sounds occur in sequence faster than the eye can resolve them.
Coarticulation and stress effects	The appearance of words vary as a function of how they are spoken.
Visemes and homophenes	Many sounds and words appear alike on the face.
Talker effects	Talkers speak sounds and words with different mouth movements.

Visibility of Sounds

Many sounds entail minimal visible mouth movement. Woodward and Barber (1960) estimated that 60% of speech sounds are not visible on the mouth or cannot be seen readily.

Words that are more visible on the face tend to begin with consonants that are made with bilabial closure (/p, b, m, w/), the upper teeth pressing the lower lip (/f, v/), or the tongue tip contacting the upper teeth (/θ, ð/). Consonants with limited visibility include sounds that are produced within the mouth, such as /k, g, t, n/. Some features of phonemes are simply not visible at all. For example, there is no visible evidence indicating that a

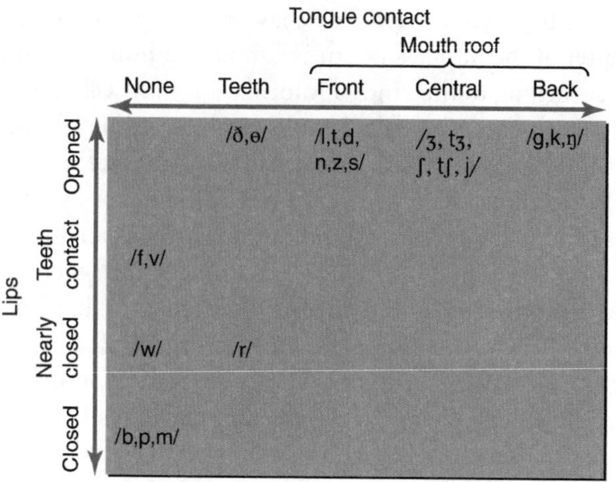

FIGURE 5–3 Consonant production as a function of tongue and lip activity.

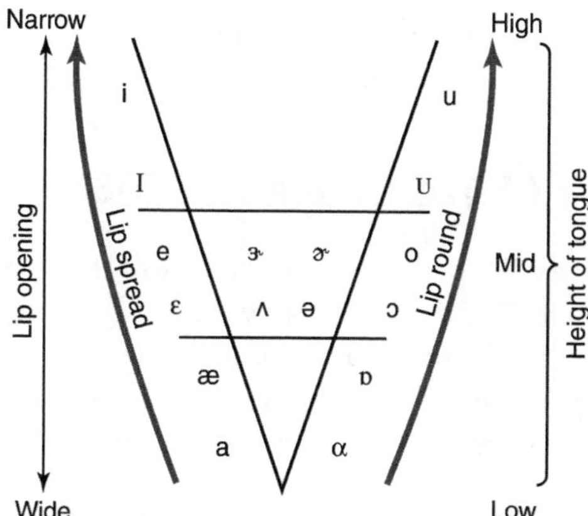

FIGURE 5–4 Vowel production as a function of lip opening, lip spreading, and tongue height. *Modeled after Berger (1972, p. 78).*

phoneme is either voiced (e.g., /b, d, g/) or unvoiced (e.g., /p, t, k/). Figure 5–3 presents the consonants (excluding /h/) according to the activity of the lips and tongue. Those consonants that have lips closing during production tend to be more distinctive than those that do not; the consonants that are produced with tongue activity toward the front of the mouth tend to be more distinctive than those produced at the back of the mouth.

Vowels are not particularly visibly distinctive. They may or may not be distinguished by lip spreading (e.g., *beak* vs. *book*, where /i/ involves more lip spreading than /U/), tongue and jaw height (e.g., *bit* vs. *bought*, where /I/ is associated with greater tongue and jaw height than /a/), and lip rounding (*boot* vs. *bet*, where /u/ is associated with more lip rounding than /¾/) (Figure 5–4). Fortunately, even though many vowels do not entail distinctive mouth movements, they tend to be acoustically salient to individuals who have hearing loss because they are relatively intense, change slowly over time in their frequency composition, and are relatively long in duration.

Rapidity of Speech

When speaking conversationally, a talker may speak anywhere from 150 to 250 words per minute, or roughly 4 to 7 syllables per second, excluding time spent pausing. Whereas a typical talker may produce an average of 15 phonemes per second, the human eye may be capable of registering only about 9 or 10 discrete mouth movements in this time interval. Thus, the lipreader (speechreader) has little time to ponder the identity of a particular word and even may not realize the occurrence of every word. The individual may have difficulty determining when one word ends and the next word begins, as word boundaries may not be clearly demarcated visually.

Coarticulation and Stress Effects

Coarticulation and stress effects may result in the same sound looking different depending on its phonetic and linguistic context. For example, the sound /b/ looks different in the word *boot* versus *beet*. The lips begin to round in anticipation of the following /u/ in the first case; the lips begin to spread in anticipation of the following /i/ in the second case. If an alveolar consonant follows a rounded vowel such as /u/ in the word *hoot*, the lip rounding may hide the tongue and the teeth.

Coarticulation refers to the overlapping of articulatory and acoustic patterns resulting from the articulators anticipating production of a speech sound or feature.

Stress can also affect the appearance of a word. The word *you* looks different in the following question, depending on the talker's stress pattern:

What did ya do yesterday?

What did YOU do yesterday?

Visemes and Homophenes

The fact that sounds belong to viseme groups and many words are homophenous increases lipreading and speechreading difficulty. **Visemes** are groups of speech sounds that look alike on the face. The sounds /b, m, p/ are visemes. When these sounds are spoken without voice, as in *bat, mat,* and *pat,* they are indistinguishable on the mouth. There is some disagreement among researchers as to which sounds constitute a viseme, although all agree that there are fewer visemes than phonemes. Two listings of consonants grouped as visemes as compiled by two different sources appear in Table 5–2.

Visemes are groups of speech sounds that appear identical on the lips (e.g., /p, m, b/).

TABLE 5–2 Consonants Grouped as Sets of Visemes. Sets Are Presented from Two Different Research Groups

ERBER (1974)	LESNER ET AL. (1987)
/p, b, m/	/p, b, m/
/f, v/	/f, v/
/u, ð /	/u, ð /
/ʃ ʒ/	/ʃ, ʒ, dʒ, tʃ/
/w, r/	/w, r/
/l/	/l/
/n, d, t, s, z/	/t, d, s, z, n, k, g, j/
/k, g/	
/h/	

Sources: Adapted from Lesner, K., Sandridge, S., & Kricos, P. (1987). Training influences on visual consonant and sentence recognition. *Ear and Hearing, 8,* 283–287; Erber, N. P. (1974). Visual perception of speech by deaf children: Recent developments and continuing needs. *Journal of Speech and Hearing Disorders, 39,* 178–185.

Homophenes are words that look identical on the mouth.

Homophenes are words that look the same on the mouth. It is not always intuitively clear which words are homophenous and which words are not. For example, as different as the words *grade* and *yes* sound, they are nonetheless homophenous. When only the visual signal of the talker is presented, an individual will likely not discriminate one word from the other. On the other hand, even though the words *boon* and *doom* sound similar, and might be confused with one another if the listening environment is noisy, an individual will have no problem in distinguishing them as different words if the talker's face is visible. Table 5–3 presents a list of other homophenous word pairs.

Somewhere between 47% and 56% of words in the English language are homophenous (Auer & Bernstein, 1997). Grammatical sentence cues and other linguistic and situational cues can decrease the confusion about word identity, and some talkers will better distinguish words on the basis of the visual signal than will other talkers. Nonetheless, the existence of homophenous words may thwart lipreading. Often, the word choices that a lipreader must consider are numerous, as illustrated in the example *Pat sat on a log*. Table 5–4 is a matrix of possible confusions that could be made for each word. You might come away with any number of meanings after lipreading this simple sentence, including:

1. Matt tracked its dog.
2. Bess stacked hot dogs.
3. Brad tanned on a dock.
4. Paul set his lock.

TABLE 5–3 Examples of Homophenous Word Pairs

HOMOPHENOUS WORD PAIRS (WORDS THAT LOOK ALIKE ON THE FACE)	
Rise	Rice
Perch	Merge
Marry	Bury
Mat	Man
Bind	Mite
Aunt	Hand
Van	Fat
Pass	Ban
Down	Stout

TABLE 5–4 Matrix of Homophenous Words That Correspond with the Words in the Target Sentence

PAT	SAT	ON	A	LOG
Matt	set	in		dog(s)
Brad	tanned	hot		sock
Bess	stacked	his		dock
Paul	tracked	its		lock

Talker Effects

Talker effects may confound lipreading efforts because the same sound may look different when spoken by two different people. For example, two talkers may differ in the degree of mouth opening used for speaking the vowels in the sentence *That is Pat's*. A person who has a pronounced accent may appear different when talking than a person who has the same regional accent as the lipreader. For example, a native of Minnesota may not recognize visually the word *rice* when it is spoken by a Texan.

WHAT HAPPENS WHEN SOMEONE SPEECHREADS?

When people speechread, they integrate what they hear with what they see. For example, if you were to hear a burst of air followed by an audible low-pitched sound and simultaneously see the lips press together and then release, you would most likely experience the percept of a /b/ sound. Your brain would have combined the sounds that you heard with the facial movements that you saw.

How does **audiovisual integration** happen? We don't know, although many research teams have devoted a good deal of effort trying to sort out this issue. One widely explored puzzle is, at what point do we integrate auditory and visual information? Do we process the two signals independently and then combine them, or do we process them interactively? For example, it may be that visual and auditory information are mapped onto some kind of "phonetic prototype" at the same time, or it may be that vision biases phonetic decisions about the auditory signal before a decision is made about what is being heard.

Audiovisual integration occurs when information from the auditory and the visual signal combine to form a unified percept.

What we do know unequivocally is that what we hear influences what we see, and what we see influences what we hear. Sometimes, the whole is difficult to predict from the parts. One of the most influential experimental paradigms that illustrates this is the "McGurk effect," so called because it was discovered in an experiment reported by McGurk and MacDonald (1976). McGurk and MacDonald presented discrepant auditory and visual speech stimuli to a group of research participants who had normal hearing. The stimuli were consonant–vowel monosyllables. For example, a participant may have heard the syllable *ba* while simultaneously seeing someone speak *da*. For some combinations of consonants, participants perceived a third consonant that differed from the two syllables. When they heard *ba* and saw *ga*, they typically perceived the syllable *da*. These results suggest that, when we recognize speech, we integrate auditory and visual speech information so we perceive a unified percept, and that this integration is obligatory (i.e., we cannot help but do it).

The **ventriloquism illusion** occurs when a ventriloquist induces the perception of speech as coming from a puppet's mouth by moving the puppet in synchrony with the sound.

For a Dummie, He Talks Pretty Well

A talented ventriloquist will have you believing that the little puppet sitting on his lap is alive and spewing wisecracks (Figure 5-5). Speech seems to emanate from the puppet's mouth—its lips move while those of the ventriloquist tremble, but only just. Some investigators suggest the **ventriloquism illusion** demonstrates the brain's propensity for treating information received from two different sensory modalities as if it originated from a common source or articulatory event, so to perceive a synchronized and integrated percept. Interestingly, if you close your eyes while watching a

(continues)

FIGURE 5-5 The ventriloquist effect.

For a Dummie, He Talks Pretty Well *(continued)*

ventriloquist's performance, you may hear that many consonants sound distorted because of the ventriloquist's closed mouth. Open your eyes, and the visible opening and closing of the puppet's mouth will make the consonants sound more normal. This phenomenon is known as **crossmodal enhancement**, and refers to those situations where the presentation of a stimulus in one sensory modality affects our ability to respond to a stimulus presented in another modality (Spence, Senkowski, & Röder, 2009).

Crossmodal enhancement occurs when the response to a stimulus presented through one modality (e.g., hearing) is augmented or modulated by another stimulus presented through a different modality (e.g., sight).

A number of investigators have proposed that audiovisual integration occurs at a distinct stage of the speech recognition process (e.g., Grant, Walden, & Seitz, 1998; Massaro, 1998; Ouni, Cohen, Ishak, & Massaro, 2007). For example, Figure 5–6 illustrates three stages, including an initial stage of perceiving the auditory and visual signals, a second stage where integration occurs, and a third stage where discrete phonetic and lexical decisions are reached. The possible existence of a distinct stage of integration has motivated some investigators to evaluate whether an integration ability is a quantifiable skill and whether it might be amenable to intervention. For example, if someone has poor integration, then perhaps aural rehabilitation and speechreading training might be directed toward enhancing this skill.

Doubt has arisen as to whether a distinct stage, as shown in Figure 5–6, is the most accurate way to conceptualize how individuals combine the auditory and visual speech signals. In particular, age has been shown to impact negatively upon one's ability to lipread but it has either minimal or modest impact upon one's ability to integrate (Cienkowski & Carney, 2002; Spehar, Tye-Murray, & Sommers, 2008; Tye-Murray, Spehar, Myerson, Hale, & Sommers, 2016), and older individuals with age-appropriate hearing loss have integration abilities similar to those of older individuals who have normal hearing (Tye-Murray et al., 2007a). Perhaps there are minimal or modest differences between older and younger persons' abilities to integrate because there is no distinct stage of integration. An alternative view of audiovisual speech recognition appears in Figure 5–7.

This Is How I Do It

"I can hear you and I can watch your mouth move, and then I put together the sounds and the visual image, and I can understand the words as I integrate the two signals."

—Marlee Matlin, Academy Award–winning actress and person with significant hearing loss

(Brainy Quote, 2013)

The model of audiovisual speech recognition presented in Figure 5–7 is based on the Neighborhood Activation Model (NAM; Luce & Pisoni, 1998). In this model, presentation of a spoken word activates a set of lexical candidates, or a lexical neighborhood, the members of which "compete" as a match for the incoming stimulus. As noted in Chapter 3, an acoustic lexical neighborhood of words comprises words that sound alike with the exception of a single phoneme (e.g., *kit, can, cab*, and *scat* are all neighbors of the auditory word *cat*). In an auditory-only condition, members of the neighborhood are activated with the onset of the spoken word and candidates are eliminated as the word unfolds until only one word remains. So-called top-down information affects

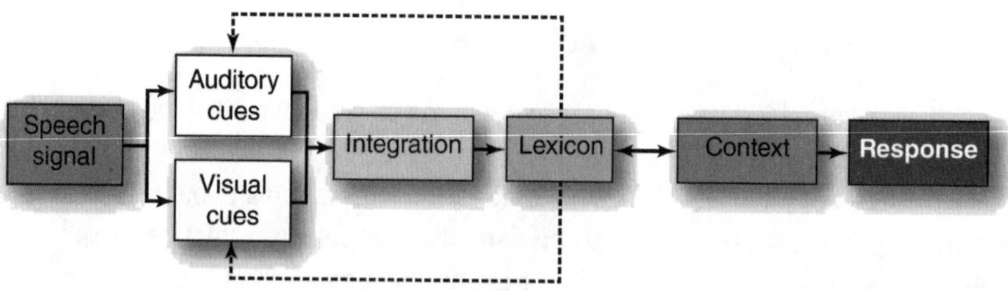

FIGURE 5–6 A model of audiovisual speech recognition, similar to that proposed by Grant et al. (1998). The model includes distinct stages for perceiving the auditory and visual speech cues, for integrating the two kinds of cues, and for accessing the mental lexicon. The dotted lines indicate that the words in the lexicon, in some instances, might affect the perception of auditory and visual cues.

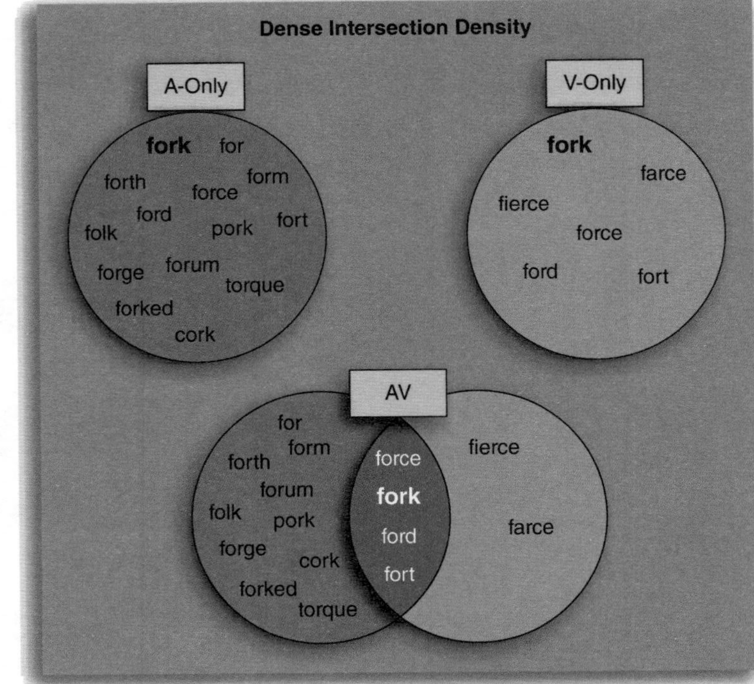

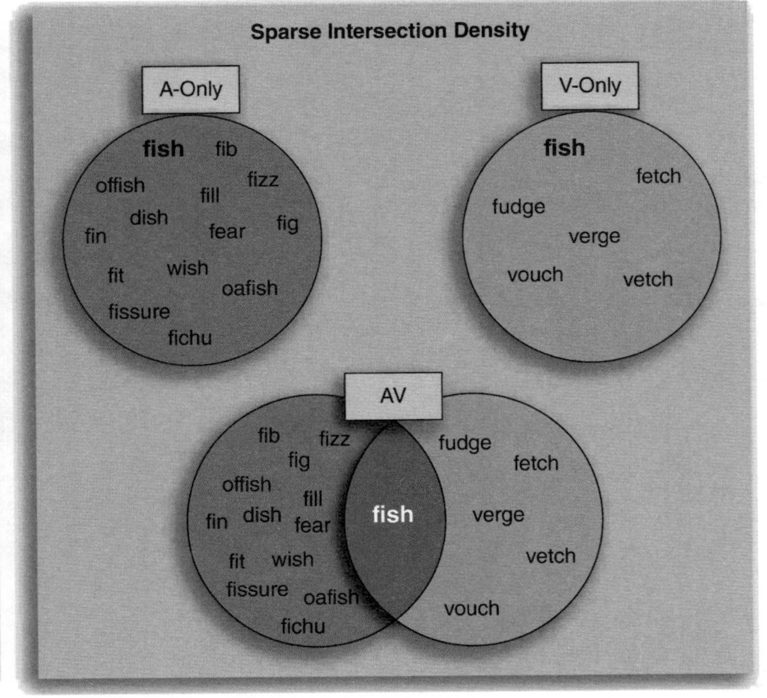

FIGURE 5–7 An alternate model of audiovisual speech recognition. The left half of the figure illustrates the auditory and visual lexical neighborhoods for the word *fork*, whereas the right side of the figure illustrates the auditory and visual lexical neighborhoods for the word *fish*. The upper half of the figure indicates that both words have similar densities for their auditory and visual neighborhoods. However, the lower half of the figure illustrates that the two words have different intersection densities. In less than ideal viewing and listening conditions, a patient would likely recognize the word *fish* more readily than the word *fork*. *Adapted from Tye-Murray et al. (2008, p. 236).*

Words with a **low frequency of usage** are words that occur infrequently in everyday conversation.

Visual lexical neighborhoods are groups of words that look alike on the face and have approximately the same frequency of occurrence.

recognition. For example, a word with a high frequency of usage will receive more activation than a word with a **low frequency of usage**.

Evidence suggests that words belong not only to auditory lexical neighborhoods, but also to **visual lexical neighborhoods** (Feld & Sommers, 2011; Tye-Murray, Sommers, & Spehar, 2008). For example, a word like *elephant* has few words that resemble it visually and so it is much more likely to be recognized by a lipreader than a word such as *cheese*, which has many words that resemble it visually.

Figure 5–7 shows how the NAM might apply to audiovisual integration. The left side of the figure shows a lexical neighborhood schematic for the word *fork*. The first sphere in the top half of the diagram represents the auditory lexical neighborhood, whereas the second sphere represents the visual lexical neighborhood. The bottom half of the figure demonstrates what happens when someone speechreads. The candidate choices are fewer than for either the auditory-only or visual-only conditions but ambiguity still exists. If the individual has a hearing loss, the individual might well misperceive the word. The right side of the figure shows a lexical neighborhood schematic for the word *fish*. Again, the first sphere represents the auditory lexical neighborhood, whereas the second sphere represents the visual lexical neighborhood. The bottom half of the figure demonstrates what happens when the word is presented audiovisually. Only one choice is available at the intersection. As such, the word *fish* is much more likely to be recognized than the word *fork* by someone who has hearing loss. Tye-Murray et al. (2008; also Feld & Sommers, 2011) showed that words having few items in the overlapping regions of their intersections are more likely to be recognized correctly than words having many items in an auditory-plus-vision condition. This finding suggests that during speechreading, there occurs a simultaneous activation of acoustic and visual lexical neighborhoods, leading to a winnowing of members in the intersection of the auditory and visual neighborhoods as the speech signal unfolds.

Audiovisual Speech

"Multisensory speech is the *primary* mode of speech perception and it is not a capacity that is 'piggybacked' onto auditory speech perception. Human speech is bimodal, dynamic, and forms a large proportion of the sensory signals encountered by humans in social contexts."

—Researchers at Princeton University *(Chandrasekaran et al., 2009, p. 1)*

Audiovisual speech recognition is not quite as simple as depicted in either Figure 5–6 or Figure 5–7 because both residual hearing and a number of other factors can influence the process.

If Hula Hoops Could Talk

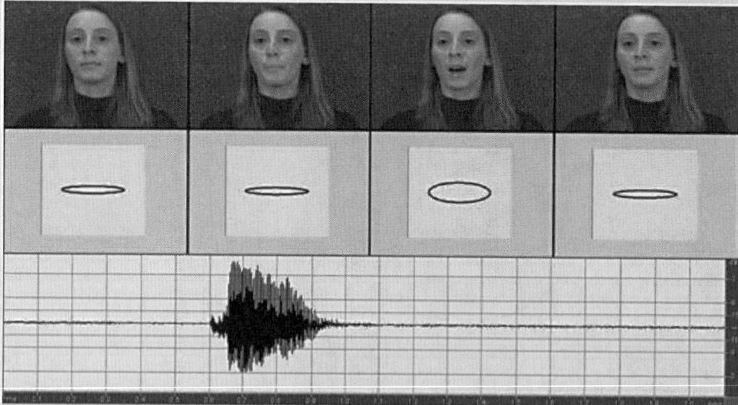

FIGURE 5–8 Crossmodal enhancement. An undulating Lissajous figure can enhance speech perception.

Crossmodal enhancement is sometimes assessed with a single syllable speech detection paradigm. In this paradigm, a participant listens for a single spoken syllable such as /ba/, presented with a background of speech-shaped noise. Sometimes the syllable is presented in the noise and sometimes it is not presented. The level of the signal is adaptively varied to establish the

(continues)

If Hula Hoops Could Talk *(continued)*

signal-to-noise ratio at which the syllable can be detected with 50% accuracy (the threshold of detection). When the talker's face is presented simultaneously with the acoustic signal of the syllable, the threshold is achieved with a poorer signal-to-noise ratio than when it is presented in an audition-only condition.

Even a signal that parodies the moving lips can affect performance in young adults. When the /ba/ syllable is coupled with an animated Lissajous figure (i.e., an undulating horizontal oval, Figure 5–8), participants can tolerate a poorer signal-to-noise ratio than when it is presented in an auditory-only condition, although the Lissajous figure does not provide as much benefit as does the video clip of the talker's face (Tye-Murray, Spehar, Myerson, et al., 2011).

IMPORTANCE OF RESIDUAL HEARING

Rosen, Fourcin, and Moore (1981) asked a test talker to produce a series of nonsense syllables with varying medial consonants, such as /apa/, /ama/, /ada/, and /asa/. A laryngograph was placed on his throat, which reflected vocal fold vibration, and the output was used to develop an auditory signal that reflected the changes over time in the talker's **fundamental frequency** (voice pitch). The speech signal sounded as if someone were speaking with his or her hand clamped over the mouth. When the research participants (who had normal hearing) saw but did not hear the talker, they identified 44% of the consonants correctly. When they saw the talker speak and heard the concomitant changes in fundamental frequency, their performance improved to and impressive 72% consonants correct.

Fundamental frequency is the lowest frequency (first harmonic) of a complex waveform.

Even Babies Use Visual Speech

© kryzhov | Shutterstock.com

FIGURE 5–9 Infants and speechreading. Infants attend to the visual speech signal as they learn their native language.

Have you ever held an infant and noticed how the baby gazes intently at your mouth while you speak (Figure 5–9)? One study suggests that one reason babies attend to faces is that visual speech may play a critical role in helping them to narrow down their perceptual sensitivities to match the phonetic and linguistic distinctions of their native language. In a study performed in British Columbia, researchers presented videotaped sentences to babies in a vision-only condition (Weikum et al., 2007). The sentences

(continues)

Even Babies Use Visual Speech *(continued)*

were spoken in English (or French) until the baby became bored or looked away. That was followed by the same talker speaking the same sentences but in the other language in order to determine whether the change in languages caught the infant's attention. The results showed that babies who were being raised in a monolingual household were sensitive to the change in language at the ages of 4 and 6 months, but were no longer so at the age of 8 months. Conversely, babies who were being raised in a bilingual household remained sensitive to the change even at 8 months. The authors concluded that bilingual infants "advantageously maintain the discrimination abilities needed for separating and learning multiple languages" (p. 1159).

These results help to explain why people with even profound hearing losses are dependent upon their hearing aids for successful communication. Even though they receive minimal auditory information, their ability to speechread is enhanced by the amplified signal. In listening to connected speech, such as sentences, residual hearing can help to extract suprasegmental patterns, which can convey information about syllabic structure and word boundaries as well as information about syntax (e.g., a question vs. a statement) and semantics (e.g., a word spoken with emphasis may have a different meaning than the same word spoken without emphasis). The degraded auditory signal may provide segmental information as well, such as whether a sound is voiced or unvoiced.

FACTORS THAT AFFECT THE SPEECHREADING PROCESS

How well someone speechreads in a particular situation is influenced by at least four factors. As Table 5–5 indicates, these factors are: (1) the talker, (2) the message, (3) the speechreading environment and communication situation, and (4) the speechreader.

TABLE 5–5 Factors That Influence the Speechreading Task

TALKER	MESSAGE	ENVIRONMENT	SPEECHREADER
Facial expressions	Length	Viewing angle	Lipreading skill
Diction	Syntactic complexity	Distance	Residual hearing
Body language	Frequency of word usage	Background noise	Use of appropriate amplification
Speech rate	Shared homophenes	Room acoustics	Stress profile
Familiarity to the speechreader	Context	Distractions	Attentiveness
Accent			Fatigue
Facial characteristics			Motivation to understand
Speech prosody (intonation, stress, and rhythm)			Language skills
Objects in or over the mouth			Uncorrected vision impairment

The Talker

The talker can increase or decrease the difficulty of the speechreading task (Table 5–6). For example, many audiologists and speech-language pathologists have learned to speak with clearly articulated speech and ample, albeit not exaggerated, mouth movements. Patients sometimes complain to their clinician, "I can speechread you just fine. It's when I get out in the real world, talking to people that I don't know, and who don't move their lips, that I get into trouble with my speech understanding." The talker's speaking style and use of body language, the familiarity of the talker to the speechreader, and even the talker's gender may all affect speechreading performance.

TABLE 5–6 Speaking Behaviors That Impede the Speechreading Task

I have a difficult time speechreading when the talker:

- Mumbles
- Doesn't look at me when talking
- Chews gum
- Has an unusual accent
- Has a speech impediment
- Smiles too much
- Moves around while talking
- Uses no facial expressions
- Shouts
- Has a high-pitched voice
- Talks too fast
- Uses long, complicated sentences and obscure vocabulary words
- Has a beard and/or mustache
- Wears dark glasses

Note. This list was generated during a group discussion with adults who have hearing loss.

People who speak with clear speech include:

- An elementary school teacher
- A newscaster
- An airport employee who announces airline arrivals and departures
- A public radio broadcaster
- A politician
- British royalty

The following behaviors make a talker difficult to speechread:

- Shouting
- Mumbling
- Turning away
- Speaking rapidly
- Covering the mouth with a hand
- Smiling simultaneously while talking

People who speak with clear speech are easier to hear and speechread than people who do not. **Clear speech** is characterized by a somewhat slowed speaking rate and good (although not exaggerated) enunciation. Some sounds might be slightly longer than normal and more fully differentiated. Key words are emphasized and pauses are inserted at clause boundaries. Overall, the duration of utterances is longer. An utterance that is spoken with clear speech is more likely to be recognized in an auditory-only (Uchanski et al., 1996), vision-only (Gagné & Boutin, 1997), and in an audition-plus-vision condition (Helfer, 1997) than when it is spoken conversationally. For example, on a sentence

Clear speech is a way of speaking to enhance one's intelligibility; it entails speaking with a slowed rate and good but not exaggerated enunciation of words.

recognition test, a group of research participants recognized significantly more of the words when the sentences were spoken with clear speech in an audition-plus-vision condition than when they were spoken conversationally. The biggest effect occurred for words in the middle of sentences, suggesting that clear speech helps to demarcate word boundaries (Helfer, 1997). The following represents examples of conversational speech and the more intelligible clear-speech counterpart:

D'yeet yet? for *Did you eat yet?*

Go-in fishin' 'morrow af'ernoon for *I'm going fishing tomorrow afternoon.*

D'yever see 'em? for *Did you ever see them?*

Gestures and facial expressions are other talker features that influence speechreading performance. For example, a talker who speaks a happy script with a happy facial expression will be more intelligible than one who speaks it with a sad facial expression. Similarly, a talker who speaks a somber script with a sad facial expression will be more intelligible than one who speaks it with a happy facial expression (Rönnberg, 1996). Facial expression can also serve to convey prosodic cues, such as a question versus a statement intonation (Srinivasan & Massaro, 2003).

How Something Is Said Will Affect How Someone Lipreads It

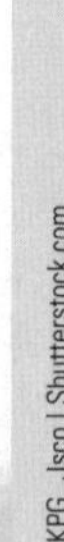

FIGURE 5–10 Body movements and facial expression can affect performance.

Try this experiment. Say to a friend, without using your voice, "Oh my aching back." As you speak, use minimal facial expression and body movements (Figure 5–10). Ask your friend to guess what you have said. Chances are, the guess will be incorrect. Now mouth the phrase again, but this time, assume a pained expression and rub your back with your hand. The odds are high that the friend will quickly recognize your utterance this second time around. This experiment reveals an important principle in speechreading: *Context cues can dramatically affect an individual's ability to speechread.*

People who have hearing loss will have an easier time recognizing the speech of someone who is familiar, such as a family member, than someone who is unfamiliar, because they are accustomed to the talker's mouth movements and speech patterns (e.g., Lee & Harrison, 2017). Someone with an unfamiliar accent, such as someone from a different country, will be harder to speechread than someone from the same country.

The gender of the talker may influence performance because the higher fundamental frequency of the female voice is harder for most persons with hearing loss to hear than the lower fundamental frequencies associated with male voices. The average fundamental frequency of males is about 117 Hz, whereas the average fundamental frequency for females is 217 Hz (Fitch & Holbrook, 1970). For this reason the female voice may not enhance the visual speech signal to the same extent that the male voice does during speechreading. Conversely, for male talkers, the presence of facial hair, as with a moustache or beard, can impede speechreading by obscuring lip and jaw movement.

The Message

The message's structure, frequency of use of the component words, the number of similar-looking words, and the supporting context all affect speechreading performance. For example, if a talker were to say, "That elephant is big," a person with hearing loss would likely recognize what was said, especially if the talker were standing in a zoo next to an elephant cage when he or she said it. The word *elephant* is highly visible on the face and has few words that look similar to it. The sentence is short and syntactically simple, and the adjective *big* begins with the highly visible phoneme /b/. The setting of the zoo provides situational clues for understanding the sentence.

On the other hand, if out of the blue someone were to say, "The hen sat on the cardigan," most people with hearing loss would not understand the sentence. The component words do not entail many highly visible mouth movements and there is no supporting context. Moreover the word *cardigan* is uncommon. A word with a higher frequency of usage and greater visibility, such as *sweater*, would be easier to speechread. Words that have fewer response possibilities are also easier to recognize. For example, the word *bat* may be difficult to recognize, even though it begins with a highly visible mouth movement, because it has many visual lexical neighbors (e.g., *bad, bet, mat, met, pat*) and acoustic (e.g., *cap, cat, scat, bad*).

As an example of how even contrived situational cues can facilitate speechreading. people will recognize significantly more words in a sentence like *She put the potatoes on the pot* if they see the picture shown in Figure 5–11 right beforehand (Spehar et al., 2016).

Topical Cues Can Help

Simply knowing the topic of conversation can enhance a speechreader's performance. For example, if you ask a patient to read the word *homes* before asking the patient to speechread the sentence *She just moved into a three-bedroom apartment*, the patient will speechread more words correctly than if no topical word is presented beforehand (Hanin, 1988). The sentence *I cut my finger with a knife* will be easier to speechread if it is preceded by a related sentence such as *I was careless with a sharp blade* than if it is preceded by an unrelated sentence such as *You need special watering tools* (Gagné, Tugby, & Michaud, 1991).

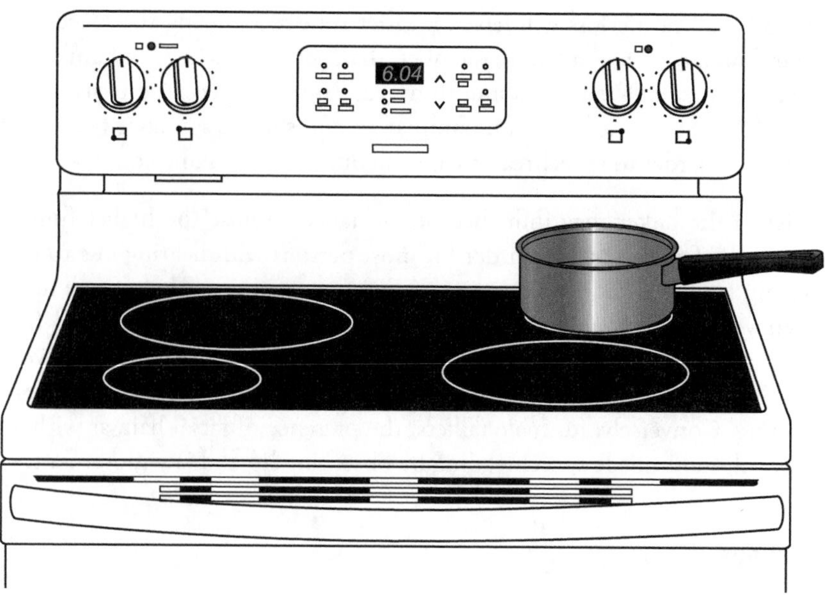

FIGURE 5–11 Situational or pictorial cues can facilitate lipreading and speechreading. For example, a person is more likely to lipread the sentence *She put the potatoes in the pot* if he or she sees this picture beforehand than if the sentence were to be spoken in isolation.

The Speechreading Environment and Communication Situation

Envrionmental factors such as the viewing angle, the distance from the talker, room conditions, and the presence or absence of background noise may all affect how well patients speechread in any given environment or communication situation (Figure 5–12). Patients often avoid social situations because they cannot hear in certain environments. "I hate parties," a patient may complain. "The lighting is always dim and the music is too loud." Another may say, "I bought a round dining table. With our old rectangular one, I could never read anyone's lips."

FIGURE 5–12 Viewing angle. Speechreading someone in profile is more difficult than speechreading someone who is directly facing you.

FIGURE 5–13 Illumination. Poorly lit talkers are difficult to speechread, especially when the available light casts shadows on the face.

The best angle for speechreading appears to be a frontal viewing angle (0 degrees azimuth) and an intermediate angle (30–45 degrees) appears to be better than a lateral angle (90 degrees) (e.g., Erber, 1974; although see Bauman & Hambrecht, 1995). If a conversation is occurring in a group setting, as in a conference held around a rectangular table, the participants often may not have an advantageous viewing angle of a talker, particularly if talkers turn their heads toward various participants as they speak. A participant in the conversation may also miss the beginnings of many utterances, as one person and then another speaks, because the participant must locate the talker first. Moreover, the participant will nearly always miss the onset of visible facial motion, because it typically precedes the onset of sound by anywhere from 100 to 300 ms (Chandrasekaran et al., 2009).

Distance from the talker may affect performance, particularly if the speechreader is too far away to view the talker's mouth movements. A patient who is speechreading from the back row of a convention center conference hall will not recognize as much of the presenter's spoken message as one who sits in the front row and has **favorable seating**. For example, Gagné, Charest, Monday, and Desbiens (2006) reported that a group of 16 young adults scored about 16% words correct better when they were separated from the recorded talker by a distance of 1.8 meters than when they were separated by a distance of 7.3 meters.

Favorable seating for speechreading includes being close enough to see the talker's lip movements and being able to see the talker full-face rather than in profile.

Lighting is important (Figure 5–13). For example, when Tye-Murray et al. (2010) degraded the visual speech signal by reducing contrast sensitivity to a point where research participants could just barely tell that the mouth was opening and closing, as might happen when speechreading in early evening, the participants still received benefit. They scored about 65% words correct in an auditory-plus-degraded vision condition compared with just under 40% words correct in an auditory-only condition on a matrix sentence test. However, they received even more benefit when the visual signal had good clarity, as would occur when speechreading a talker at close range at high noon, scoring 80% words correct.

Talking with an Avatar

Work is underway in many laboratories to create synthetic talkers or avatars, to provide realistic facial movements that are synchronized with a simulated acoustic speech signal (Figure 5–14). For example, the Talking Head "MASSY" (Modular Audiovisual Speech Synthesizer) has been used to assess the speech reception abilities of persons with normal hearing and experienceed cochlear implant users (Schreitmüller

(continues)

Talking with an Avatar *(continued)*

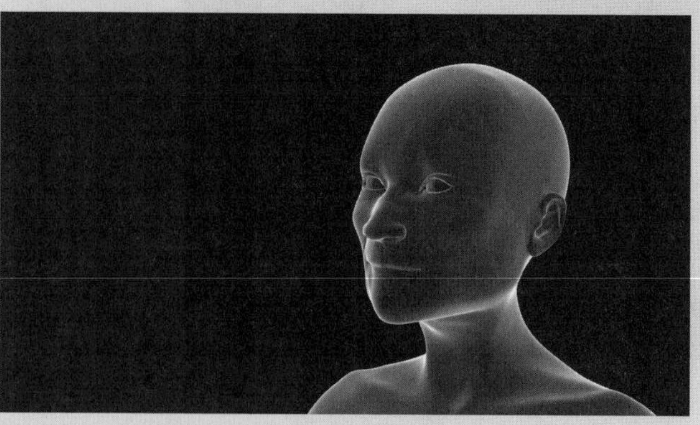

FIGURE 5–14 Avatars are occasionally used for assessment or training.

et al., 2017). The three-dimensional head floats on the computer screen. When he talks, his lips move and pucker, his eyebrows raise, and his chin and facial features vary, depending on what he is saying.

There are several possible uses for animated synthetic speech such as MASSY in addition to testing lipreading and speechreading abilities. The system might provide speechreading practice using a computer or be used as a tool to study the basic process of audiovisual speech perception and audiovisual integration. For example, it is possible to make Baldy's lips appear to say one thing and the accompanying sound to say another (as when performing a McGurk effect experiment).

Speechreading enhancement Speechreading enhancement is computed by comparing a patient's speech recognition score in a vision-only condition with the score obtained in an audition-plus-vision condition.

Just as with listening performance, the presence of background noise can impair someone's speechreading performance. Table 5–7 lists common sources of room noise that can interfere with the speechreading task. A noisy environment can mask speech and decrease the **speechreading enhancement** effect afforded by residual hearing, as well as distract the speechreader from the speech recognition task.

Other environmental factors that affect performance include excessive room reverberation, the availability of assistive devices, and interfering objects such as a support beam extending from a room's floor to ceiling. The presence of visible movement, such as movement by others in the room or activity seen from a window, also can be distracting.

The Speechreader

Speechreading performance relates to lipreading skill, as well as to an individual's hearing acuity. Generally, the better the lipreading skill and the greater the amount of residual hearing, the better the speechreading performance (e.g., Sommers et al., 2005). However, the nature of the hearing loss also affects performance. For example, persons who have hearing loss in the high frequencies but not in the low frequencies typically will benefit more from the addition of visual cues to the auditory speech signal than persons who have hearing loss in the low frequencies. This is because lip and jaw movements are more correlated with high-frequency speech information than with low-frequency

TABLE 5–7 Examples of Noise Sources Common to Various Communication Settings

HOME	RESTAURANTS	WORKPLACE	CLASSROOM
Kitchen sink/running water	Dishes/silverware	Computers	Students talking
Washer/dryer	Music	Printers	Paper rustling
Air conditioner	Guests talking	Machinery	Shoes scuffling
Furnace			Chairs moving
Vacuum cleaner			Projectors
Television			Fans, ventilator, furnace, air conditioner
Radio			Hall noise
Family members talking			
Open window/door (lawn mower, leaf blower, traffic)			
Refrigerator			

information. Seeing the talking face provides complementary information to what a person with high-frequency hearing loss will hear but redundant information to what a person with a low-frequency hearing loss will hear (see Grant, Bernstein, & Summers, 2013, for a review).

Speechreading performance also is influenced by patients' use of appropriate amplification and use of eyeglasses when needed. Not surprisingly, poor visual acuity, such as that stemming from cataracts, will also hinder performance.

An individual's level of stress, fatigue, and attentiveness can affect performance. For example, if the speechreader is engaged in a job interview, anxiety may impair his or her speechreading performance. A business person, fatigued from a long day of concentrating on coworkers' auditory and visual signals, may not speechread family members very well at home.

Speechreading Can Be Exhausting

"I find lipreading very stressful and frustrating because I am often confused. For example, if you look at a person's lips saying *dog* and *saw*, they look the same. With my hearing aid alone, I do not hear "s" or "d" sounds. So usually I have to use my common sense. For example, if someone said, "The dog is running across the street," then I know it was not the saw who ran across the street—it was the dog. Most hearing people do not understand that people in my position have to think incredibly fast in order to keep up with conversations. . . . Lip reading is a grueling and exhausting mental exercise and lip readers are constantly thinking and trying to discern what is actually being said. I get real mad at those who think that I am stupid simply because I cannot hear. The truth is I get exhausted after a while and simply cannot keep up. At that point, I begin to guess at what is being said and eventually give up and choose to be quiet."

—Heather Whitestone, Miss America 1994

(Whitestone, 2007)

ASSESSING VISION-ONLY AND AUDIOVISUAL SPEECH RECOGNITION

Before patients begin formal speechreading classes, they typically take speech recognition tests in both a vision-only and audition-plus-vision condition. Testing is repeated following training. The purpose is to determine how well they can recognize speech in an audition-plus-vision condition, which is how we communicate typically in face-to-face conversations, and to determine their speechreading enhancement, which indicates how effectively they are using residual hearing to augment the visual speech signal.

Speechreading testing may also be performed for counseling purposes. For example, if a patient is reluctant to wear a hearing aid, the results from testing can provide objective evidence of the benefits of amplification for everyday communication.

Why Test Lipreading Abilities?

"Knowing whether a patient is a good or a poor lipreader provides an excellent counseling tool. I tell patients who are good lipreaders to capitalize on their talents and attend to the faces of their communication partners, and those who are poor lipreaders to consider enrolling in an auditory training program."

—An AuD student who had just completed a Capstone project that required him to administer lipreading tests to patients with hearing loss

Vision-Only

In a recorded test of speech recognition that is administered in a vision-only condition, the visual signal typically is comprise of the talker's head and shoulders, with the talker facing the patient head-on. The talker should be well lit, so his or her face is fully visible and not in shadows. The talker usually speaks before a plain, non-distracting background. As with auditory-only testing (Chapter 2), test stimuli might include phoneme contrasts, words, or sentences.

Audition-Plus-Vision

Both the vision-only and audition-plus-vision conditions are included when accessing speechreading enhancement or determining goals for speechreading training. Speechreading enhancement (sometimes referred to as *auditory enhancement*) is computed by comparing speech recognition scores in a vision-only condition to scores obtained in an audition-plus-vision condition. It indicates how much better a patient can recognize speech when listening and watching the talker compared with watching alone. Two different computations may yield a speechreading enhancement score. First, a simple difference score may be computed by subtracting the percentage correct score obtained in a vision-only condition (V) from the percentage correct score obtained in an audition-plus-vision condition (AV): AV% correct – V% correct. The greater the difference between the two scores, the greater the amount of enhancement provided by the auditory signal.

A Brief History of Vision-Only Speech Testing

Visual tests have a history extending almost as far back as the film industry. The first test of vision-only speech recognition was filmed by the lipreading teacher Edward Nitchie in 1913. It included three proverbs: *Love makes the world go around, Spare the rod and spoil the child, and Fine feathers make fine birds.* The test had obvious shortcomings. The proverbs were well known to that era's generation, so after recognizing a few words of one, a patient was likely to guess the rest. In addition, performance with just three items probably could not adequately reflect general word recognition ability. Nonetheless, this test represented a beginning. In the 1940s, Utley (1946) developed a test for adults called How Well Can You Read Lips? Well into the early 1980s, it remained a widely used test of vision-only and audition-plus-vision word recognition. It included a word test, a sentence test, and a story test.

The advent of cochlear implants in the 1980s coincided with the development of several new tests (e.g., Boothroyd, Hanin, & Hnath-Chisholm, 1985; MacLeod & Summerfield, 1987; Tyler, Preece, & Tye-Murray, 1986; Walden, Erdman, Montgomery, Schwartz, & Prosek, 1981), whereas advances in computer technology led to more widespread usage. Initially, researchers and clinicians viewed cochlear implants as an aid for lipreading as much as a hearing device per se, so tests were needed to assess how well the electrical speech signal augmented vision-only speech recognition. New computer technologies permitted visual files to be stored digitally and eliminated the need for elaborate test setups comprised of screens and projectors. Computer technology also allowed for faster testing as test items no longer had to be spaced on the recorded film to accommodate slow respondents. Computer-controlled testing allows

A Brief History of Vision-Only Speech Testing *(continued)*

test item presentation to be paced according to patient performance and allows for on-line scoring. Tests for adults include the Iowa Phoneme and Sentence Test (Tyler et al., 1986) and the City University of New York (CUNY) Sentences (Boothroyd et al., 1985). Tests for children include the Children's Audiovisual Enhancement Test (CAVET; Tye-Murray & Geers, 2001) and the Children's Build-A-Sentence Test (Tye-Murray et al., 2015).

TABLE 5–8 Two Formulas to Compute Speechreading Enhancement Two different formulas may be used to compute speechreading enhancement. In this example, Sam J. achieved an enhancement score of 25% when it was computed with the difference score formula and an enhancement score of 50% when it was computed with the normalized difference formula. Max H. achieved an enhancement score of 45% when it was computed with the difference score formula and an enhancement score of 50% when it was computed with the normalized difference formula.

PATIENT	V-ONLY SCORE	AV SCORE	DIFFERENCE SCORE: (AV – V)	NORMALIZED DIFFERENCE SCORE: (AV – V) ÷ (100 – V)
Sam J.	50% correct	75% correct	75 – 50 = 25	(75 – 50) ÷ (100 – 50) = 50
Max H.	10% correct	55% correct	55 – 10 = 45	(55 – 10) ÷ (100 – 10) = 50

Second, a normalized ratio score may be computed. This computation is done by first figuring out how much room for improvement there is in a vision-only condition, then referencing the amount of improvement gained with the addition of the auditory signal to that amount available. The formula for computation is: AV% correct—V% correct/100% – V% correct. Table 5–8 presents an example of the two computation methods. In this table, Patient Sam H. recognized 50% of the words correct when a test was presented in a vision-only condition and 75% words correct when the auditory signal was added. Patient Max J. recognized 10% and 55% of the words in the two conditions, respectively. Note that whereas Max J. appears to have achieved greater speechreading enhancement than Sam H. when the simple difference score is used, they appear to have equal gains with the addition of the auditory signal when the normalized difference score is employed.

TRADITIONAL METHODS OF SPEECHREADING TRAINING

At the beginning of the 20th century, speechreading training was a principal component of most aural rehabilitation programs, in large part because there were few alternative means for alleviating communication problems experienced by persons with hearing loss. Professionals simply did not have the technology to reduce hearing difficulties. In those times, persons would attend speechreading classes and perform drill activities at home. Four speechreading training methods were popular in the United States (Berger, 1972). These methods were advocated originally by Bruhn, the Nitchies, the Kinzes, and Bunger.

In 1902, Martha Emma Bruhn introduced the Mueller–Walle method to North America, a primarily analytic speechreading training method that originated in Germany. As noted in the last chapter, analytic training emphasizes the recognition of individual speech sounds. Bruhn published three textbooks, the last of which was the *Mueller-Walle*

Features of the Mueller–Walle method:

- Speech sounds categorized according to their visible characteristics
- Lessons based on a sound movement or group of movements
- Rapid, rhythmic syllable drills
- Simple sentences

Method of Lip Reading for the Hard of Hearing (Bruhn, 1947). The hallmark feature of this program was an emphasis on rapid syllable drill, such as *she-ma-flea* and *she-may-free* and rapid phrase recognition, such as *We saw the zoo, We saw the moo*, and *She saw the zoo*. Students also practiced recognizing homophenous words, using sentence context cues to distinguish between possible meanings, such as *ROB won the game* versus *The children like to ROMP in the garden.*

Examples of Analytic Training Objectives

Most speechreading training programs that emphasize analytic training follow a specific hierarchy of training objectives and are designed to contrast three features of articulation. Place (i.e., where in the mouth the primary constriction for the sound occurs, as in /b/ versus /d/), voicing (whether the sound is produced with or without voicing, as in /p/ versus /b/), and manner (how the sound is produced, as in /m/, a nasal, versus /b/, a plosive). The feature of place tends to be most visible on the face, whereas the feature of voicing provides virtually no visual cues, so early objectives might stress use of visual place cues while later objectives might stress use of voice cues. Here is a sample hierarchy of consonant analytic speechreading training objectives, edited out from a more extensive list. Note how the speechreading task progresses in difficulty, from requiring students to distinguish from two words, four words, and then six words, and finally culminates in open-set word recognition.

The student will:

1. Discriminate consonant pairs that differ in place of production and voice; for example, *tag* from *bag*.
2. Discriminate consonant pairs that share similar place of production but differ in manner and voice; for example, *pan* from *man*.
3. Will discriminate consonants that differ in place of production, using a four-item and then a six-item response set; for example, *tag* from the response set of *tag, bag, back*, and *gas*.
4. Will discriminate consonants from a four-item and then a six-item response set of voice or voiceless consonants; for example, *pop* from the response set of *pop, cop, cap*, and *top*.
5. Will identify words from an open set of familiar vocabulary.

Edward B. Nitchie, who published his first book, *Lip-reading Principles and Practices*, in 1912, rarely employed syllable drill. Instead, he promoted synthetic training, and emphasized the importance of psychological processes of speechreading. As noted in the last chapter, synthetic training emphasizes the understanding of meaning and does not require every word spoken to be recognized correctly. Practice usually centered on sentence and story materials and the identification of homophenous words through contextual cues. Students sometimes practiced speechreading themselves by talking before a mirror. He emphasized that students focus on speech movements as opposed to static articulatory postures, and emphasized the importance of understanding the gist of a message as opposed to every word. Typically training was conducted without voice. Nitchie's text was updated by his wife, Elizabeth, and it was one of the most widely read texts on the subject in the 20th century (Nitchie, 1930).

Examples of Synthetic Training Objectives

Speechreading training programs that emphasize synthetic training incorporate a logic in which training objectives progress from simple tasks, such as discriminating words from phrases, to very challenging tasks, such as recognizing a series of unrelated sentences. Here is a sample hierarchy of synthetic speechreading training objectives, edited out from a more extensive list.

The student will:

1. Discriminate multiword utterances from single-word utterances, using a closed response set; for example, *How are you today?* from *Hi!* Later, the student can be asked to discriminate long words from short words; for example, *Halloween* from *cat.*
2. Discriminate between words having the same number of syllables; for example, *That's my cat* from *That's my dog.*
3. Will identify picture illustrations from a closed set, after hearing a one-sentence description.
4. Will answer simple questions that are related in content; for example, *Where are you going next summer? How will you get there?*

Features of the Nitchie method:

- Mirror practice
- A synthetic approach
- Speech movements as opposed to static postures
- Importance of grasping message gist
- Use of stories, humorous anecdotes, and sentences to effect "mind training"

Synthetic Speechreading Practice with Ed

To the reader/patient: "Have your assistant read the story (e.g., about Benjamin Franklin) to you, without voice, without interruption, [lipread] not for every word but for the thought of each sentence. . . . Have your assistant tell the story to you in different words. . . . Should you fail to understand a certain word, don't stop your assistant in the middle of the sentence, wait until the sentence is finished, while you try to follow along as much as you can [and then ask for clarification]."

—Edward G. Nitchie (1930)

Cora Kinze studied with both Bruhn and Nitchie before establishing her own school for speechreading training with her sister Rose in 1917. Not surprisingly, the sisters developed an eclectic method, combining the analytic syllable drill of Bruhn with the more synthetic exercises of Nitchie.

The Jena method was developed by Karl Brauckmann, who lived in the city of Jena, Germany, and published two brief textbooks in 1925. The Jena method was introduced into the United States by Anna Bunger in 1927 (Bunger, 1944). A hallmark of Brauckmann's approach was its emphasis on **mimetic** and **kinesthetic** forms and sensations, and the recognition that our ability to produce speech relates to our ability to perceive it. In this method, students focus on the mouth movements of the instructor, while simultaneously speaking the training materials. Training materials include repeated syllables and then words derived from the syllables.

Features of the Jena method:

- Sounds described according to whether movement involves lips, tongue, or tongue–soft palate
- Syllable drill
- Student speaks in unison with the clinician
- Student concentrates on his or her kinesthetic and tactile sensations

Mimetic means imitating or copying movements.

Kinesthetic relates to the perception of movement, position, and tension of body parts.

Read My Lips: It's Easier When They're Your Own

Even though you likely do not practice lipreading yourself in a mirror, you probably can lipread yourself better than you can lipread most other people (Figure 5–15). In a study that explored the link between speech production and speech perception, research participants recorded nonsense sentences constructed from a matrix sentence test (e.g., *The duck watched the boy* and *The snail watched the goose*). A few weeks later, they returned to our laboratory and lipread sentences recorded both by themselves and by nine other participants. Participants consistently scored higher when lipreading themselves than when lipreading the nine other talkers. The findings suggest that seeing someone talk activates mental processes that link seen words

(continues)

Read My Lips: It's Easier When They're Your Own (continued)

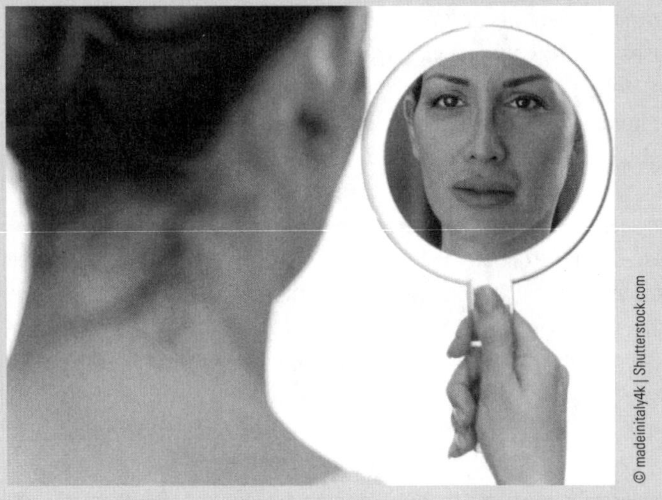

© madeinitaly4k | Shutterstock.com

FIGURE 5–15 Reading lips: It's easier when they're your own.

with actual words in your mental lexicon, and this activation is particularly potent when you see yourself speak. A strong link may exist between how we perform actions and how we perceive actions, and we may activate the same mental representations when we speak and when we listen, lipread, or speechread. The findings have implications for how we might learn new actions, and in particular, for how we might learn to recognize and produce speech (Tye-Murray, Spehar, Myerson, Hale, & Sommers, 2013). The self-advantage also happens for audiovisual speech perception (Tye-Murray, Spehar, Myerson, Hale, & Sommers, 2015, but see Treille, Vilain, Kandel, & Sato, 2017).

SPEECHREADING TRAINING TODAY

Content for a speechreading training program that is interwoven with communication strategies training:

- Assessment of speechreading skills
- Overview of speechreading, with a consideration of the process
- Opportunity to reflect on habits and skills
- Tips and rules to follow (e.g., *Keep a positive attitude*)
- Identification of difficult communication situations and formulation of solutions
- Formal speechreading lessons may (or may not) commence

With the advent of hearing aids, cochlear implants, and assistive listening devices, individuals are better able to use their residual hearing. Concomitantly, the popularity of speechreading training has waned, so that now it rarely is found as the sole element of an aural rehabilitation program. Nonetheless, some of the fundamental principles underlying the seminal training programs are evident in modern training curricula. In a single lesson, students might receive analytic training, where their attention is focused on sound and word identification (as in the Mueller–Walle method), as well as synthetic training, where their attention is focused on recognizing the gist of a sentence (following Nitchie).

The first class (and sometimes the only class) of a modern speechreading training program often is informational in nature and includes a consideration of the speechreading process. A handout like the one reprinted in Table 5–9 might be used to guide discussion amongst patients. This handout reviews factors that affect the speechreading process and the importance of using speechreading cues maximally.

In addition to considering the principles outlined in Table 5–9, class participants also might reflect on their speechreading habits and listening difficulties. They often review rules to follow when speechreading, such as those listed in Table 5–10. For example, although *Watch*

TABLE 5–9 A Handout That Might Be Distributed to Students to Stimulate Discussion About the Speechreading Process

Speechreading is a process of attending to auditory and visual information to recognize a spoken message. Speechreading is not just watching others' lips to identify the words they are saying. It also consists of making the most of your hearing, and using your mind to collect all the information available to make a "best guess." Speechreading includes the following:

1. Lipreading: Watch the mouth movements of the talker, including the lips, jaw, and tongue tip. It is impossible to identify every word, but you can identify some words and sounds that will help you ascertain what is being said.
2. Facial expression: It is possible to identify people's moods or how they feel by the expression on their faces. You can also glean subtle nuances of meaning in their messages by attending to facial expressions.
3. Gesture, posture, and movement: What people are doing, how they are sitting, and the gestures they make give clues to what they are thinking about and what they might say.
4. Situational cues: You can anticipate what a person is going to talk about by the situation or place they are in and the relationships of the people present.
5. Knowing the topic: It is easier to follow conversation when you know what the talker is talking about. The easiest way to find out is to ask someone else who is listening. You might say, "What are we discussing?"
6. Knowledge of language: You might be able to make educated guesses about a particular word missed on the basis of sentence structure.
7. Keeping informed: Knowing what news items or subjects are of current interest to people may help you to anticipate what will be talked about. Read newspapers and magazines and watch the news on television.
8. Emotional factors: Keep motivated and develop self-confidence even though there will be times that you make errors.
9. Use your hearing: Although you have a hearing loss, you may be able to hear sounds and words that help you to identify the message or idea.
10. Until now, you have been taking advantage of these clues to some extent. One goal of this class is to make you more conscious of them so you use them maximally. Using these clues, much of the message can be predicted. Some parts of the message are less predictable (e.g., hearing a new name), making them more difficult. Therefore, you must use two kinds of information: (a) the part of the message you did understand and (b) any additional knowledge that can help you to fill in the gaps in order to figure out the whole message.

Source: Adapted from "Speechreading instruction for adults: Issues and practices," by R. Cherry & A. Rubinstein, 1988, p. 302. *Volta Review*, 289–306.

If you have a hearing loss and like to eat out at restaurants....

- Sit in a place where you cannot see a television monitor because the visual distraction will decrease your ability to speechread and to pay attention to conversation that is occurring at your table.
- If you have a "better ear"(one which has more hearing than the other), select seating or positioning that will allow you to have the talker on your better side.
- Choose a padded booth because the padding will provide a buffer to other noise in the restaurant.
- Sit with your back to the rest of the room, especially if your hearing aids have directional microphones so that your hearing aids will not amplify noise that is coming from behind.

TABLE 5–10 Rules to Follow When Speechreading (a handout like this might be discussed during a group class)

1. **Watch the face.**

   This seems obvious, but you can be distracted by other events in the room or by a handheld device. If you feel a little self-conscious and think that your conversational partner wonders why you never look away (e.g., *Do I have jam on my cheek?*), explain your speechreading strategy in a concise way (e.g., *It helps me to look at your face because I rely on reading lips to understand words*). By saying this, you also provide implicit and subtle instruction: You are saying without actually saying, *Make sure I can see you when you speak.*
2. **If your conversational partner is engaging in a behavior that makes it difficult to speechread, say something!**

   For example, if your conversational partner is talking with a hand over the mouth (it is amazing how often people talk this way, as anyone with hearing loss well knows), let the person know that this behavior diminishes your ability to speechread. When people say something in a conversation, they want their listener to understand, so it is unlikely that anyone will take offense.
3. **Make ambient lighting work for you and not against you.**

   For example, if you are sitting at an outdoor coffee shop, choose a chair at the table where you are not looking into the morning sun. Direct sunlight in your eyes will compromise your speechreading performance. Moreover, the sunlight streaming around your partner's head will cast shadows on the person's face and further hamper your speechreading. At restaurants, sit by a window in the day and near a light source in the evening.

(continues)

TABLE 5–10 *(continued)*

4. **Minimize background noise.**
   Roll up the car windows, move to a quiet room, turn off the kitchen faucet, mute the television, quiet the kids, stop the music . . . silence is golden (at least in the background) when trying to speechread.
5. **Location, location, location . . .**
   And we are talking real estate—sort of. Try to ensure that you have favorable seating so you can easily see the talker's face, ideally from a frontal view. If you are at a lecture, opt for a front row seat. If you take a walk with a friend, choose a trail where you can walk side-by-side and look at each other while walking and talking. If you are at a casual restaurant or sports bar, do not sit where you can see a television monitor as the flickering image may be distracting.
6. **Chill.**
   Speechreading can be tiring and stressful. Unfortunately, the perceptual effort, the anxiety, and the self-doubt that can accompany "not getting every word" can be self-defeating. Hang in there, focus on what your conversational partner is saying, and turn off the internal dialogue, (e.g., *Oh no! I'm not getting any of this! Is she going to think I'm stupid?*), and as best you can, relax and go with the flow. By so doing, you will understand a lot more. Chill.

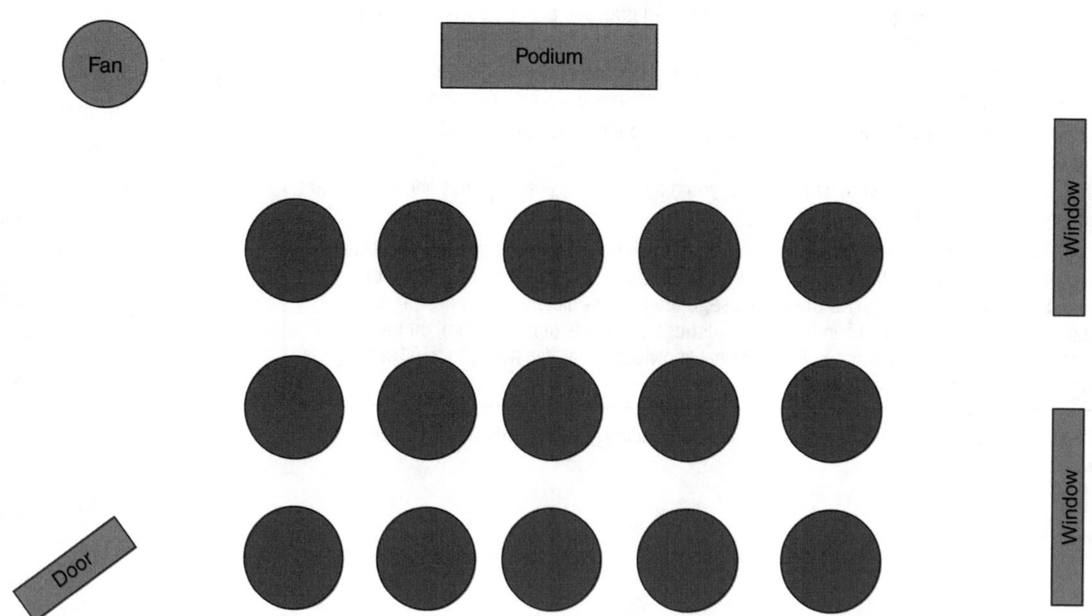

FIGURE 5–16 A chart for discussing listening environments and ways to minimize speechreading difficulties. Students might be asked to identify where they might sit to optimize speechreading performance.

the talker's lips, the first rule presented in Table 5–10, seems like an obvious recommendation, some people become distracted by watching the talker's hand gestures or they have a habit of listening with lowered eye gaze instead of concentrating on the talker's mouth movements. As a result, their speechreading performance is not as good as it could be.

During an introduction to speechreading, class students might review charts like the one presented in Figure 5–16 to identify difficult listening situations and to formulate solutions for rectifying the difficulties. They might be asked to identify which seats present the most favorable circumstances for lipreading and speechreading, and which seats present the least favorable. This kind of activity sensitizes students to the concept of favorable speechreading conditions.

Following this kind of introduction, students may or may not receive formal speechreading training. In today's world, rarely if ever do participants in an aural rehabilitation class practice lipreading (vision-only speech recognition). Rather, they practice recognizing speech using both auditory and visual signals. As with auditory training, many programs are computer-based, and training may occur in the presence of recorded background noise, either to make the training task more difficult or to mimic real-world communication settings.

Two examples of formal speechreading programs, both computerized, are *Read My Quips* (SenseSynergy, www.sensesynergy.com) and *Seeing and Hearing Speech* (Sensimetrics Corp., http:/www.sens.com). *Read My Quips* trains sentence comprehension in the presence of contextual cues. During an exercise, a woman appears on the computer screen and speaks a witty sentence or aphorism (hence, the name *Quips*). Afterwards, a crossword game displays on the computer screen. Each box in the game corresponds to a word of the sentence rather than to a letter. Examples of sentences are *We would all like to vote for the best man but he is never a candidate* and *A sweater is a garment worn by a child when his mother is feeling cold.* In these two examples, the bolded part of the sentence is provided to the student (thus supplying contextual cues), and the student's task is to type the remaining words into the crossword puzzle after speechreading the talker. Items are presented in noise.

In the *Seeing and Hearing Speech* program, a variety of talkers speak sounds and sentences. Training is divided into the categories of *phonemes* (which in turn is subdivided into *vowels* and *consonants*), *stress-intonation-length*, and *everyday conversation*. Vowel activities are sorted into such groups as *rounded-lip vowels, spread-lip vowels*, and *relaxed-lip vowels,* and vowels are contrasted in words that are spoken in isolation, phrases, and sentences. In a stress-intonation-length activity, the student has the option of comparing the same sentence that is spoken with different stress patterns, e.g., *JOHN loves Mary, John LOVES Mary*, and *John loves MARY*, and at different film rates. Everyday activities include training for greetings, sentences about the weather, and simple questions.

How to practice speechreading:

- Work with a partner
- Talk about real-life things
- Practice viewing the speaker from various angles and distances
- Know the subject at hand
- Speechread for overall content rather than individual words
- If you cannot fill in the missing pieces, ask the speaker to reword the entire sentence [rather than] single words
- If you are unable to understand, do not [automatically] interrupt . . . because you may be able to comprehend the meaning once the sentence is complete
- After you have gained a level of competency, practice with background noise

(Alexander Graham Bell Association for the Deaf and Hard of Hearing, 1988, p. 1)

BENEFITS OF SPEECHREADING TRAINING

Many researchers have considered whether lipreading and speechreading skills can be developed through training and practice. Just as with auditory training, investigations aimed at assessing efficacy are difficult to design because the outcome can be influenced by a number of variables, including the heterogeneity of the research participants (including such factors as age, degree of hearing loss, level of motivation to participate in training), variations in training stimuli and methods, variations in the duration of intervention, and the talent of the instructor. For example, a participant who has engaged in six weeks of speechreading training may be more motivated to perform well on a posttraining test of audiovisual speech recognition than a control participant who has received no training.

A relatively large number of investigators report that training improves performance (e.g., Bernstein et al., 2001; Sims, Dorn, Clark, Bryant, & Mumford, 2002; Walden, Prosek, Montgomery, Scherr, & Jones, 1977; Walden et al., 1981), whereas others report that speechreading training provides little or only marginal benefit (e.g., Lesner et al., 1987; Rishiq, Rao, Koerner, & Abrams, 2016). When improvements do occur, they are often, although not always, modest. For example, some investigators have demonstrated that adults with hearing impairment show only small improvement following training, typically improving by 10–15% in their ability to recognize speech stimuli (e.g., Alcantara, Cowan, Blamey, & Clark, 1990; Gagné, Dinon, & Parsons, 1991; Walden et al., 1981). It appears that tutored self-instruction that occurs in the home with videotaped stimuli can be effective in teaching skills (Lonka, 1995; but see Rishiq et al., 2016), which may bode well for the feasibility of computerized instruction.

Often, results are inconclusive or present contradictory findings. Some people may not show improvement in their performance on a test of audiovisual speech recognition. However, if asked whether they believe they benefited from speechreading training, they may provide an ardent testimonial in support of training or will report benefit via a questionnaire (e.g., Binnie, 1977). Some individuals may become better test takers, so their speechreading skills only appear to improve, rather than actually improving.

An **oral interpreter** sits in clear view of a person who has hearing loss and silently repeats a talker's message as it is spoken.

Oral transliteration is the act of lagging a talker by a few words, mouthing or speaking the words with a normal speaking rate and good enunciation. Although oral transliteration usually does not entail the use of sign language, natural body language, expressions, and gestures are typically presented that support the content of the words.

ORAL INTERPRETERS

The final topic to be considered in this chapter concerning audiovisual speech perception is the oral interpreter. Because many persons who have hearing loss rely on the visual speech signal, situations may arise when an oral interpreter is helpful or even essential. You may be asked on occasion to help locate an oral interpreter. An **oral interpreter** (also called an oral transliterator) is someone who sits in clear view of the individual with hearing loss and silently (or softly) repeats a talker's message as it is spoken, often lagging behind by only one or two words. Through this process of **oral transliteration**, an oral interpreter attempts to convey a talker's mood and intent. National certification is available through the Registry of Interpreters for the Deaf (RID), and includes the Certificate of Transliterating (CT) and the Oral Interpreter Certificate (OIC). Certified interpreters must adhere to a Code of Ethics (1984), which dictates their professional code of behavior. This code includes the following guidelines:

- They cannot share with other individuals information they learn during an interpreting assignment.
- They cannot change the meaning of a message as they interpret it for the person who has hearing loss.
- They cannot add their opinions or personal commentary to a message.

Situations where an oral interpreter might be required:

- A classroom
- A convention hall
- A conference room
- A conversation where one of the talkers is not present, as in a conference call
- A conversation with someone whose speech is difficult to speechread, as with someone who has an unfamiliar accent

CASE STUDY

An Exceptional Lipreader

A few studies have focused on exceptionally good lipreaders (e.g., Andersson & Lidestam, 2005; Lyxell, 1994; Rönnberg et al., 1999) in an effort to understand what makes some people particularly facile at deciphering the visual speech signal. For example, Lyxell (1994) studied a 56-year-old woman, SJ, who lost her hearing at the age of 16, following a bout with meningitis. On a sentence test administered in a vision-only condition, SJ scored 57% words correct. By comparison, the average performance of a control group of 119 research participants in a control group (49 who had hearing loss and 70 who had normal hearing) was 24% words correct. They identified roughly half as many words as SJ. Interestingly, her ability to discriminate words, which means her ability to indicate whether two words spoken in a pair are the same or different, was no better than the average control subject. Thus, even though she is skilled at lipreading sentences, this skill does not transfer to word discrimination.

SJ has developed a specific strategy for lipreading. She reported that when she lipreads, she tries to repeat each spoken word as soon as she can after it is spoken. When possible, she tries to summarize the words into meaningful units, for example, during pauses in the talker's speech. She purposefully fills in missing pieces of information and updates misperceived words.

(continued)

CASE STUDY *(continued)*

An Exceptional Lipreader

A cognitive test battery revealed that SJ has a better than average ability to comprehend read sentences and to recall the last words of a series of sentences presented in text format. This performance suggests that she has a good short-term working memory for complex tasks. For more simple tasks, such as repeating back strings of digits presented sequentially on a computer screen, her performance was unremarkable. She was also found to have an excellent ability to fill in missing words in printed sentences, although she did not exhibit extraordinary skill in filling in letters in words.

The results from the cognitive tests mesh well with her reported strategy for lipreading. She has a large working memory that allows her to buffer information as she lipreads. She can use this stored information to catch up on what she missed and to correct what later turns out to be a misperception.

FINAL REMARKS

Few adults or children receive a great deal of speechreading training, and rarely is it provided in the absence of other aural rehabilitation services. When it is provided, the emphasis is usually placed on effective strategies to minimize the difficulty of the speechreading task, such as ways to manage the environment or ways to encourage appropriate speaking behaviors on the part of their communication partners. A topic that currently is receiving much attention in the research literature pertains to audiovisual integration; that is, how we combine the auditory and visual speech signals. The answer to this question may have important implications for the design of more effective speechreading training protocols.

KEY CHAPTER POINTS

- Even persons with normal hearing rely on the visual speech signal to some degree.
- Some people are better lipreaders than others. Performance cannot be predicted by such factors as intelligence or practice with the lipreading task, but may be related to age and cognitive factors such as spatial working memory and processing speed.
- When people lipread, their eyes both fixate and perform quick shifts. They often focus on the talker's eyes, nose, and mouth.
- Lipreading is difficult. Some of the factors that may compound the lipreading task include the partial visibility or nonvisibility of many speech sounds on the face, the rapidity of speech, coarticulation, the visual similarity of many sound groups, and talker variables.
- Some models of audiovisual integration suggest that the ability to integrate is distinct from the abilities to recognize speech auditorily or to recognize speech visually. An alternative model, based on the concept of lexical neighborhoods, posits that a distinct stage of integration may not be a part of the speech recognition process.
- A little residual hearing can increase markedly a patient's ability to recognize speech when looking and listening simultaneously.
- The talker, message, environment, and state of the person affect how well the individual will recognize a spoken message. For example, a talker who mumbles will be difficult to understand.
- A talker's use of clear speech can effect a dramatic improvement in a patient's ability to lipread and speechread.

- Speechreading training was popular in the first half of the 20th century. The advent of more sophisticated listening devices and questions about the benefits of training have led to a reduced emphasis on speechreading training in most aural rehabilitation programs.
- A relatively large number of investigators have attempted to evaluate the efficacy of speechreading training, using a variety of training methods and tests and focusing on a number of different participant groups.
- Extraneous variables, such as patient motivation, complicate assessments of speechreading training efficacy.
- Speechreading training appears to provide modest benefits.

TERMS AND CONCEPTS TO REMEMBER

Speechreading
Lipreading
Functional magnetic resonance imaging (fMRI)
Auditory cortex
Spatial working memory
Processing speed
Visual fixation
Saccade
Audiovisual integration
Ventriloquism illusion
Crossmodal enhancement
High frequency of usage
Low frequency of usage
Visual lexical neighborhoods
Fundamental frequency
Favorable seating
Luminance
Speechreading enhancement
Mimetic
Variability in individual skill levels
Sound visibility
Coarticulation and stress effects
Visemes
Homophenes
Models of audiovisual integration
Neighborhood Activation Model (NAM)
Variables affecting performance
Clear speech
Frequency of usage
Twentieth-century methods
Kinesthetic
Class handouts
Computerized instruction
Oral interpreter
Oral transliteration

CHAPTER 6

Communication Strategies and Conversational Styles

OUTLINE

- Conversation
- Facilitative Communication Strategies
- Repair Strategies
- Stages of Communication Breakdown
- Research Related to Repair Strategy Usage and Communication Breakdowns
- Conversational Styles and Behaviors
- Case Study: A Couple Conversing
- Final Remarks
- Key Chapter Points
- Terms and Concepts to Remember

Successful everyday communication for individuals with hearing loss is influenced by many variables, including the effectiveness of their listening device, their speechreading skills, and their amount of residual hearing. In addition, success in communication is affected greatly by how well people use communication strategies. A **communication strategy** is a course of action taken to facilitate a conversational interaction or to rectify a problem that arises during conversation. During **communication strategies training**, patients receive instruction about how to manage their conversational interactions effectively. Many speech and hearing professionals recognize that communication strategies training is a powerful way to enhance patients' abilities to manage everyday listening problems.

A **communication strategy** is a course of action taken to enhance communication.

Communication strategies training is instruction provided to persons with hearing loss or to communication partners to maximize their communication potential and to minimize the occurrence of communication breakdowns.

In this chapter, the foundation will be laid for the next chapters about conversational fluency and hearing-related disability assessment and conversation strategies training. First we will consider general issues related to conversation and then focus on communication strategies and conversational styles. The included conversations actually occurred. Some have been edited for brevity or clarity.

CONVERSATION

Much of the fabric of human relationships is woven by our conversations—by what we say, how we say it, and how we listen. We engage in conversation for several reasons (Figure 6–1):

- To share ideas
- To create meaning
- To relate experiences
- To tell stories
- To express needs
- To effect a result
- To instruct
- To influence
- To establish intimacy
- To build understanding

Story Time

"In everyday talk, storytelling is ubiquitous: 'You'll never believe what happened today.' 'I'll never forget the time when . . .' 'Did you hear the one about . . .?' When in doubt—or at loose ends or in the need of attention—we narrate."

—O. Scott, film critic for the *New York Times*

(Scott, 2007, p. 11)

The way people talk with others is guided by their knowledge of implicit rules of conversation (**conversational rules**). A metaphysical reflection about the way we converse might indicate that most of us typically adhere to culturally established conventions. For example, when two or more people begin a conversation, they each:

Conversational rules are implicit rules that guide the conduct of participants in a conversation.

- *Tacitly agree to share one another's interests.* They commit their mental resources to attending to their communication partner's messages and respond to the messages in a way that furthers the discussion.
- *Ensure that no single person does all of the talking.* Most people do not dominate the conversation with their own talking and they do not expect their communication partners to bear the onus of continuing the conversation alone. They share speaking turns. A communication partner should not leave a conversation thinking, "I didn't get a word in because that person wouldn't stop talking," or thinking, "Jess sat like a piece of furniture, not saying a word, as if he didn't care."
- *Participate in choosing what to talk about and participate in developing the topic.* Typically, there is not a "chief" who leads the conversation and who alone decides what is talked about and how that subject is developed. Rather, all participants play a role, at some point or another, in deciding what is talked about and in shaping the direction in which the discussion progresses.

FIGURE 6–1 Reasons to engage in conversation: to share, to instruct, or to inform. Conversations are the fabric of human relationships.

- *Take turns in an organized fashion.* Conversation often unfolds in either a turn-taking or an overlapping style. In a turn-taking interaction, one person finishes speaking before the next person begins and interruptions are infrequent. In an overlapping interaction, it is acceptable for two or more communication partners to speak simultaneously or for one partner to start speaking before another finishes. This latter style might predominate in conversations that are more intimate, spontaneous, and energetic.
- *Try to be relevant to the topic of conversation (topic coherence).* If a conversation is centered on automobiles and someone abruptly begins to talk about a recipe for cornbread, that individual has violated an implicit rule of conversation by not being relevant to the discussion. A sequential ordering principle is in play throughout most conversations. An utterance is usually made in response or in relation to someone's preceding utterance. Even when topics change, the change is typically accomplished in an orderly way. A communication partner may remark, "Which reminds me . . ." or in some such way explicitly or implicitly explain why he or she is not adhering to a *relatedness expectation.*
- *Provide enough information to convey a message without being verbose.* In a conversation, people expect their communication partners to deliver their messages in a fairly succinct way and in a manner that maintains their interest in listening.

Four maxims of conversation (these for the talker):

- Maxim of Quantity: Avoid wordiness
- Maxim of Quality: Be truthful
- Maxim of Relation: Be relevant
- Maxim of Manner: Be perspicuous (orderly, clear in statement, not obscure or ambiguous)

—Paul Grice, English language philosopher
(Grice, 1975)

If one participant in a conversation has a hearing loss, some of the rules of conversation may have to be modified or adapted. For example, interruptions may occur more frequently because the individual must frequently ask for clarification. Other participants may have to exert a greater effort to ensure that the person has an opportunity to contribute to a topic's development. If he or she did not understand or misunderstood something that has been said, the person with hearing loss may sometimes contribute remarks that are not relevant to the ongoing discussion. The individual may also have to use communication strategies, ideally in a way that does not violate the more universally established rules of conversation.

The quality of conversations experienced by persons with significant hearing loss often differs from that experienced by persons who have normal hearing. They may not hear the rhythms created by the ups and downs of a talker's prosody and the alternation of speech and small pauses, those musical elements of spoken language that sweep a listener along during the telling of a narrative or story. Emotional nuances and subtle meaning, say affection or sarcasm, might be lost if the listener cannot register the talker's tone of voice or lexical emphasis. Consider the utterance spoken with a high pitch, "You're NOT going to give me a birthday present AGAIN?" and the same utterance spoken with a low volume, "You're not going to give me a birthday present again." The first version is **keyed** as an introduction to an argument, while the second is keyed as a gentle remonstration.

Keying occurs when a talker's tone of voice, cadence, lexical emphasis, prosody, and other speaking characteristics imbue an emotional stance to an utterance.

With a Wave of the Hand

© wavebreakmedia | Shutterstock.com

FIGURE 6–2 Talking with your hands. In this picture, the woman is using a *beat* gesture to emphasize her words and the man is using a *metaphoric* gesture to indicate his assessment of the woman's message.

Most people supplement their words with complex hand gestures (Figure 6–2). They might spread their palms wide apart when they say the word *big* or shake their finger for emphasis. These gestures can be quite helpful to persons with hearing loss as they try to understand spoken messages. Hand gestures fall into at least six categories (e.g., Cassell, 2001):

- **Emblematic:** Culturally specified gestures; e.g., the "V" gesture might symbolize *victory* to some citizens living in the United Kingdom but *peace* to some citizens living in the United States.

With a Wave of the Hand *(continued)*

- **Iconic:** Gestures that depict an item, action, or feature of something being described; e.g., a talker might slide a hand through the air as he describes a slide into home base that happened at a baseball game.
- **Metaphoric:** Gestures that depict a metaphor; e.g., a talker might make a corkscrew whirling motion with an index finger at her temple while simultaneously saying the word *crazy.*
- **Deictic:** Gestures that locate items, places, or people in space; e.g., a talker might hold out his left palm when referring to people living in the western suburbs of a city and his right palm when referring to persons living in the eastern suburbs.
- **Beat:** Gestures that provide emphasis and serve an evaluative or orienting function; e.g., a talker might flick her wrist as she stresses the unimportance of completing a particular task.
- **Regulatory:** Gestures that help guide the flow of conversation; e.g., a talker may let her hands fall as he nears the end of a speaking turn.

From a broad-brush perspective, the content of a conversation might be limited or its fluency stunted when one of the participants has a hearing loss. Conversations involving someone who has a hearing loss may have any of the following characteristics:

- *Disrupted taking of turns.* When someone comes to an end of a speaking turn, the person often begins to speak slower and his or her intonation contour begins to fall. The person with hearing loss may not hear these signals, and thus, inappropriate silences may occur because he or she does not initiate a conversational turn on cue. In addition, if the person has not understood the message, he or she may be unable to formulate a response or be slow in doing so, and so again, silence ensues. Inappropriately long pauses may cause the communication partner to conclude, " 'You're withholding,' 'You're hostile,' 'You never tell me what's on your mind,' or even 'You have nothing on your mind!' " (Tannen, 2000, p. 393).
- *Modified speaking and listening styles.* Communication partners may speak slowly with precise articulation in order to facilitate speech recognition for the person with hearing loss. They may rely more on nonverbal behaviors to convey their messages, such as more frequent and elaborate hand gestures and exaggerated facial expressions. The listener with hearing loss may utilize unusual eye gaze patterns. For example, the person might stare at the talker's mouth and make infrequent eye contact.
- *Modified conversational style.* Communication partners might refrain from an overlapping style of turn taking because the person with hearing loss is unable to speechread two or more people simultaneously (if more than two people are in the conversation) or the person might miss the beginning of their remarks if they overlap.
- *Less rich imagery.* The communication partner might omit the details that make a story colorful; for example, a talker might describe a motor vehicle as "a junk heap on wheels" to a listener who has normal hearing but as "a car" to the listener who has difficulty in recognizing any but the most common of words. The two descriptions certainly evince different mental images.
- *Inappropriate topic shifts.* The person with hearing loss may not recognize previous remarks and may inadvertently (and inappropriately) change the subject.

- *Superficial content.* Because speech recognition is difficult for the individual who has hearing loss, the participants in a conversation may avoid certain topics for discussion and avoid topics that might evoke unusual vocabulary or complex syntax. A spouse might decide that it is not "worth the effort" to describe the intricacies of a business meeting in response to her husband's question, "How was your day?" Instead, she might simply say, "Fine," and leave it at that.
- *Frequent clarification.* Misunderstandings are commonplace in conversations, even when all participants have normal hearing. When someone has a hearing loss, misunderstandings may become more frequent. Both the person with hearing loss and the communication partner may need to engage in clarification more often, and diversions from the topic of conversation may occur regularly.
- *Violation of implicit social rules.* The person with hearing loss may talk too loudly because the person does not have enough hearing to regulate voice level or to modulate it according to room conditions (e.g., quiet or noisy). The person may appear as "not paying attention" or as "not caring about what is said."
- *Disrupted grounding.* When people engage in conversation, they often employ a **grounding** process, wherein they incorporate a bit of information into the conversation as "common ground" and then this information is presupposed throughout the remaining interaction. A person with hearing loss might miss out on important information early on in a conversation or inadvertently indicate that he or she has understood shared information because of bluffing behavior. The person may then misunderstand later remarks. In a related sense, if the person has a prelingual or perilingual hearing loss, he or she might lack general world knowledge that most people acquire through incidental listening (e.g., names of songs by popular musicians). This person may have an even greater danger of not sharing "common ground." A communication partner might come to realize that grounding must be more deliberate and may have to state assumed information explicitly or state common ground information more than once.

Grounding is a conversational occurrence in which communication partners establish a body of information as shared common ground for an ongoing conversational interchange. It usually entails the presentation of information by one communication partner and the confirmation of mutual understanding by another.

Older Persons and Persons with Hearing Loss: Commonalities in Conversation

Takeoka and Shimojima (2002, p. 189) suggest that conversations with older persons are often slow-paced and filled with repetitions, with the unwanted outcome of being "boring." Communication problems may arise not only because of the presence of hearing loss, but also because of older persons' alleged slowness to understand or stubbornness to accept new ideas. The researchers note that younger people, when conversing with older persons, sometimes adopt a "patronizing speech style." The patronizing style may include:

- Talking only about restricted topics
- Using directive speech
- Using childlike expressions
- Speaking very slowly
- Exaggerating their nonverbal signals
- Paraphrasing frequently
- Decreasing their grammatical complexity
- Talking about fewer topics

Compare this list with the list just reviewed about how conversations involving a person with hearing loss might differ from the norm. Note the similarities. You may find that some of your younger adult patients are frustrated by how some people react to them during conversation.

FACILITATIVE COMMUNICATION STRATEGIES

In Chapter 5, it was noted that four factors influence the speechreading task: the talker, the message, the environment, and the listener. In a communication strategies training program, patients learn to use facilitative strategies. **Facilitative strategies** are used to influence these four factors. Table 6–1 summarizes types of facilitative communication strategies, each designed to influence each of these four factors. Figure 6–3 summarizes the process that persons might engage in when they experience difficulty in recognizing speech during conversation. The individual identifies the source of difficulty, implements a facilitative strategy, and determines whether the difficulty is resolved. If it is, then the conversation can continue. If it is not, the person might implement another strategy.

Facilitative strategies include instructing the talker and structuring the listening environment, to enhance the listener's performance.

Facilitative strategies for the workplace include:

- Avoid noisy environments such as the coffee room at rush hour.
- Schedule private (face-to-face) meetings rather than group meetings.
- Preboard when airplane travel is part of the job.
- Use email and text messaging rather than the telephone.
- Choose favorable seating in a conference room.
- Disclose about hearing loss and ask others to adapt work processes, such as taking notes during meetings.

(Shaw, Tetlaff, Jennings, & Southall, 2013, p. 198)

Strategies That Influence the Talker

Persons with hearing loss use **instructional strategies** to influence communication partners' speaking behaviors. A person asks the talker to change the delivery of the message, as in these examples:

- "When you cover your mouth with your hand, I have a hard time speechreading you."
- "Could you face me, please?"
- "Please slow down your talking. I understand more that way."

To use instructional strategies, people must identify behaviors that impede their speech recognition efforts. Then they may instruct the communication partner about how to change the behavior.

When implementing an **instructional strategy**, the listener asks the talker to change the delivery of the message.

Strategies That Influence the Message

Message-tailoring strategies influence the way someone constructs a message. A person might ask, "Did you go swimming or biking last night?" This question sets the stage for one of two responses, *swimming* or *biking*. Alternatively the individual may not use a message-tailoring strategy, and instead ask, "What did you do last night?" which opens the floodgate for a multitude of answers and a greater likelihood of communication breakdown.

Message-tailoring strategy is a way of phrasing one's remarks to constrain the response of a communication partner.

TABLE 6–1 Facilitative and Repair Strategies

Facilitative strategies may be used to influence:

- **Speech recognition skills**

  Adaptive strategies: The patient implements relaxation techniques.

  Anticipatory strategies: The patient prepares for conversational interactions in advance by anticipating conversational content and potential listening difficulties.

- **Communication environment**

  Constructive strategies: The patient structures the environment to optimize communication by minimizing background noise and ensuring a favorable view of the talker.

- **Communication partner**

  Instructional strategies: The patient influences the communication partner's speaking behaviors by asking the partner to speak clearly, facing forward.

- **Message**

  Message-tailoring strategies: The patient encourages communication partners to use short sentences and employs closed-ended questions.

  Acknowledgment gesture: The patient provides feedback to the communication partner by a nod or shake of the head.

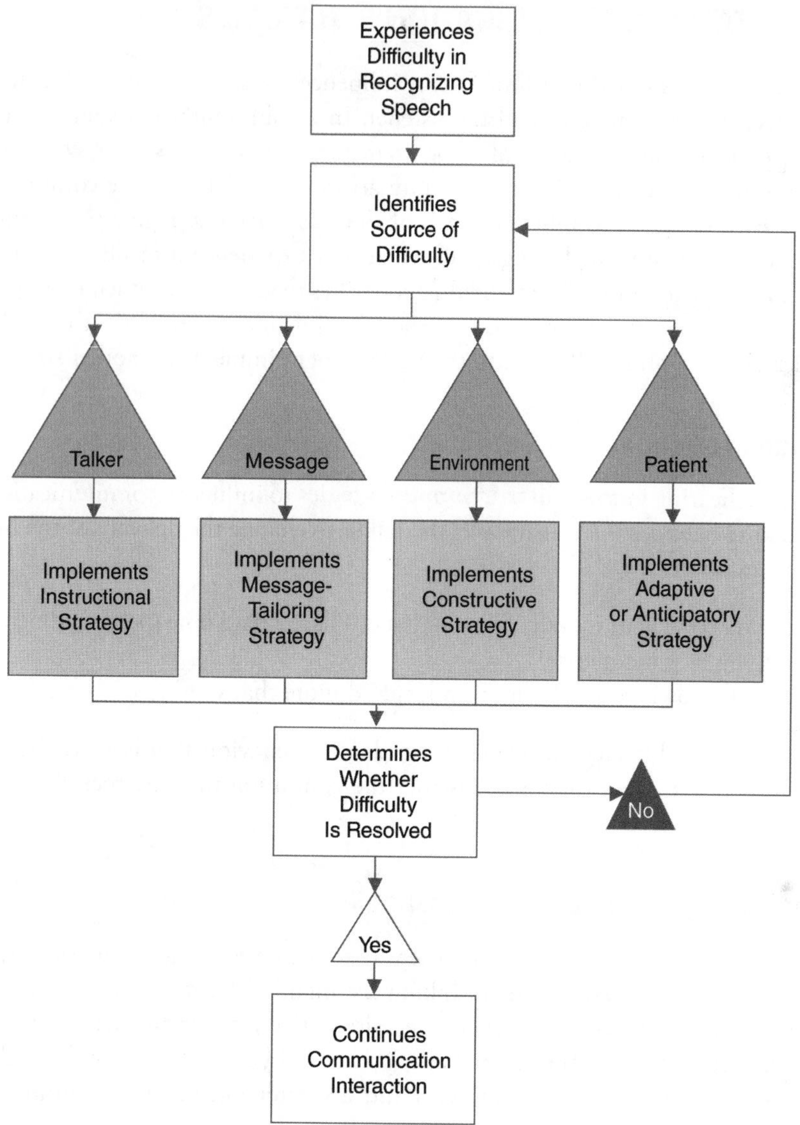

FIGURE 6–3 Process someone may follow when encountering a communication difficulty.

Metacommunication is communication about communication.

Using a message-tailoring strategy requires a kind of **metacommunication** skill. That is, not only must people be able to think about what they want to say, but also they have to consider in their own minds how best to say something in order to effect the desired result.

An **acknowledgment gesture** may consist of a head nod or a head shake. It is often made in response to a remark from a frequent communication partner, who is familiar with the signaling system.

Another way to tailor a communication partner's messages is by means of an **acknowledgment gesture**. Some patients, especially when talking to frequent communication partners, learn to nod their heads when they feel that they have understood a remark and either shake their head or quit nodding when they do not. Their partner might then respond by clarifying the remark without the need to relinquish a speaking turn. The danger of using acknowledgment gestures is that they can sometimes lead to bluffing behaviors, a kind of maladaptive communication act.

Strategies That Influence the Environment

A **constructive strategy** is a tactic designed to optimize the listening environment for communication.

Someone uses a **constructive strategy** to enhance the communication environment. The success of constructive strategies hinges on the ability of the person to analyze the

TABLE 6–2 Examples of Constructive Strategies That Can Be Used to Optimize the Listening and Speechreading Task

- If possible, ensure that the talker is well lit and within easy view. Do what you can to ensure favorable lighting, such as moving away from a window that has sunlight glare. Arrive early to public events so you can get favorable seating, near the talker and with a head-on view of the talker's face.
- When you are riding in the car and talking with your passenger, turn off the radio, roll up the windows, and don't turn the fan up to full blast. If applicable, fix that broken muffler or thumping fan belt!
- If background noise is present, either reduce the noise or move to a quieter setting. Turn down the television set or turn it off; close a door to eliminate unwanted noise; choose a quiet restaurant rather than a noisy one and try to dine during the "off hours" of the restaurant's business.
- During conversation, position yourself in such a way where you will not be distracted by the content on a computer screen or television set. Put down your smartphone or tablet so you can focus on speechreading your conversational partner.
- Going for a walk with a friend? Avoid sidewalks alongside busy streets, choose a trail in a quiet park or woods, and find a trail wide enough so that you can walk side-by-side and turn towards each other as you speak.

Note: This list might be reviewed with the person who has hearing loss, as well as with the person's frequent communication partners.

communication environment and to identify those elements that can be modified or exploited to optimize communication. Table 6–2 presents a sample list of constructive strategies that people with hearing loss may use to optimize communication.

Strategies That Influence the Reception of a Message

Adaptive strategies serve to counteract maladaptive behaviors and include relaxation techniques and other means of dealing with emotions and negative behaviors that stem from hearing loss. For example, some people with hearing loss feel anxious during a conversation with someone who is unfamiliar to them and they worry about what they might miss or what their communication partners think of them. In these instances, they might have to take a deep breath, consciously relax, purposefully redirect their thoughts toward the present conversation, and attend to the talker's lip movements. This adaptive behavior not only can decrease anxiety, but also can enhance message recognition.

Adaptive strategies are methods of counteracting maladaptive behaviors that stem from hearing loss.

Maladaptive Strategies

Sometimes people who have hearing loss implement **maladaptive strategies** to cope with their communication difficulties. These strategies include:

- Bluffing and pretending to understand
- Social withdrawal to avoid communication difficulties
- Dominating conversations so as to be aware of what is being talked
- Succumbing to feelings of anger, hostility, or self-pity

People who characteristically use these kinds of maladaptive strategies have a high incidence of depression (Williams, Falkum, & Martinsen, 2015). Some individuals become unduly anxious and tense, either as they anticipate an upcoming communication interaction (such as a meeting with their boss) or during the interaction itself, as problems in understanding begin to arise. It is well within the purview of a communication-strategies training program to encourage alternative behaviors in lieu of maladaptive strategies.

A **maladaptive strategy** is an inappropriate behavioral mechanism for coping with the difficulties caused by hearing loss in a conversation; they sometimes yield short-term benefit but incur long-term costs.

Anticipatory strategies are methods of preparing for a communication interaction.

An individual uses an **anticipatory strategy** to prepare for a communication interaction. These strategies include anticipating potential vocabulary and conversational content. For example, before a job interview, a person with hearing loss might study related information about the company, such as employee handbooks or news clippings. The individual might buy books about recruitment procedures and learn what kinds of questions are standard during interviews. Should the interviewer mention names of key employees, the person may thus recognize the names because they are already familiar. When the interviewer asks routine questions, they also may be easier to recognize because the person has the appropriate framework in which to listen. More global preparatory work may include considering what vocabulary is likely to occur (e.g., *popcorn* at a movie theater concession stand) and then practice speechreading that vocabulary with a partner. Someone can anticipate spoken remarks by attending to situational cues (e.g., talking with a ticket seller at a movie theater). Predictions can be made on the basis of "knowledge of a partner's typical conversational style (e.g., use of colloquialisms or gestures); common conversational sequences (e.g., as in greeting rituals); and expected responses to utterances of particular types (e.g., to choice questions)" (Erber, 1996, p. 42). An anticipatory strategy may also include anticipating a difficult environment or situation (e.g., there will be a lot of noise at the restaurant) and planning means to minimize problems (e.g., ask for a padded booth near the back of the room).

Ready? Set? Go!

People with hearing loss can implement anticipatory strategies prior to a communication interaction and enhance their probability of recognizing spoken messages. Examples of anticipatory strategies that might be reviewed with a patient are listed below:

- Obtain a synopsis of a play before going to see it. Knowing the plot may help you follow the dialogue that occurs between the play's characters.
- Learn the names of key players and products before you go on a job interview. These words will then likely be more recognizable on the talker's face. Also know how job interviews are structured, from beginning, to middle, to end. This information will help you anticipate what may be said during each segment.
- Keep abreast of current events and movies. If these topics arise during group conversations, you will be better able to fill in the blanks when you miss words here and there.
- Read the textbook before a subject is covered in class (good advice for any student). Knowing the subject matter in advance will help you to follow it in class.

Aside from enhancing actual speech recognition, there may be psychological advantages to using anticipatory strategies. A person with hearing loss might feel more comfortable during an interaction if the person has practiced speechreading the vocabulary that might occur and if the person has obtained some background information. Moreover, simply having a definitive course of action may make individuals feel more in charge of their communication interactions.

There are mixed findings about the effectiveness of anticipatory strategies. One study showed that anticipatory strategies are not effective in enhancing speech recognition when a person is about to enter into a familiar communication situation, as when preparing for an appointment with a physician or a visit to a bank or a gas station (Tye-

Murray, 1992b). However, when the situation is unfamiliar, use of anticipatory strategies appears to be effective in preparing individuals to recognize speech (Rubinstein, Cherry, Hecht, & Idler, 2000). For example, if people learn the plot of a theretofore unfamiliar story, they will later recognize sentences about the story better than if they had not reviewed it.

What They Would and Wouldn't Do

In a study that involved 99 persons with mild hearing loss and 86 persons with severe hearing loss (Hallam & Corney, 2014), a survey revealed what they most likely would and wouldn't do during a conversation to promote conversational fluency. Both groups provided similar responses:

What they would do:

- Make sure they could see the talker's face.
- Pay attention to facial expressions and body language.
- Move closer to the talker.

What they wouldn't do:

- Deliberately ignore the communication partner until he or she implemented more effective speaking behaviors.
- Write down their messages.
- Either ask for the topic of conversation or ask the talker to speak louder.

Asking for the topic of conversation is one of the specific repair strategies suggested in Table 6–3, and it has shown to be an effective one for repairing communication breakdowns (e.g., Tye-Murray et al., 1990). An implication of this finding is that a communication strategies program, the topic of the next chapter, might include instruction about how to implement this strategy in a way that is comfortable and easy to do.

REPAIR STRATEGIES

Communication strategies training also may teach patients to use **repair strategies** to repair **communication breakdowns**. After signaling the occurrence of a communication breakdown, people can request information by using one of many possible **receptive repair strategies** (Table 6–3). The word *receptive* indicates that the repair strategy is used to rectify a communication breakdown when the recipient of a message (in this case, a person with hearing loss) does not recognize the sender's (talker's) message. Examples include: "Could you say that again?" (the *repeat repair strategy*), "Who is going to give you a ride?" (the *answer a question repair strategy*), and "I missed that completely; what are you talking about?" (the *key word repair strategy*). The other type of repair strategy is an **expressive repair strategy**, which is used to rectify a communication breakdown that occurs because the person with hearing loss (the sender) produces an unintelligible utterance and the communication partner (the receiver) does not recognize it. Children with hearing loss and adults with prelingual hearing loss and poor speech intelligibility may often need to use expressive repair strategies in the course of spoken language conversation. Adults with adventitious hearing loss will likely not use them any more often than any adult with normal hearing because usually their speech remains intelligible, although certain high-frequency consonant sounds (e.g., /s, t/) may begin to sound distorted after long-standing hearing loss (Cowie & Douglas-Cowie, 1992).

Repair strategies are tactics implemented by a participant in a conversation to rectify a breakdown in communication.

A **communication breakdown** occurs when one communication partner does not recognize another's message.

A **receptive repair strategy** is a tactic used by an individual when he or she has not understood a message.

Expressive repair strategies are used when the sender produces an unintelligible utterance and the communication partner cannot understand it.

Metacommentary: Talk About Talking

"You're going into quiet mode and I'm not even picking you up" (p. 134).

"Sorry, you're dropping your voice, I'm not hearing you" (p. 136).

A bilateral cochlear implant user in conversation with his wife, using repair strategies that can best be described as **metacommentaries**.

(Lind et al., 2010)

A **metacommentary** is a comment about the talk or conversation.

TABLE 6–3 Repair Strategies That Can Be Used to Repair Communication Breakdowns

Specific repair strategies request the communication partner to:

- Repeat the entire message: *Can you say that again, please?*
- Repeat part of the message: *Jan and Karl are going to what?*
- Confirm the message: *You said, Sheila is bringing the coffee pot, right?*
- Choose between two candidates: *Did you say "floor" or "flower"?*
- Simplify the message: *I didn't hear you properly. Can you try that again with fewer words?*
- Indicate the topic of conversation: *I'm not sure I'm following you. You're talking about . . . ?*
- Answer a question: *What will Janice be doing this afternoon?*
- Elaborate the message: *Tell me more.* (Or ask a question that will elicit more information and possibly lead to understanding.)
- Write
- Fingerspell (if both parties know the manual alphabet) or spell the word aloud.

Nonspecific repair strategies ask:

- *What?*
- *Huh?*
- *Pardon?*

Depending upon how well patients know their communication partners, they might feel comfortable in asking them to write, to use gestures and hand signals, or to spell important topic words. Selection of a particular repair strategy may hinge on a variety of factors, including:

- How useful a particular strategy has been in the past
- How much of the message was understood
- The cause of the communication breakdown
- An assessment of how well a communication partner might follow the instructions
- Whether the communication partner is familiar or unfamiliar

STAGES OF COMMUNICATION BREAKDOWN

Figure 6–4 suggests at least three stages are involved in repairing a communication breakdown. First, the breakdown must be detected, then one of the communication partners chooses a course of action, and then the action is implemented. When communication breakdowns occur, persons with hearing loss might detect immediately that they did not recognize the message. In such cases, an individual might alert the partner and seek repair. "Hold on," the person might say, "I missed that." It sometimes happens that an individual does not realize a breakdown has occurred until much later in the conversation, as in the following example:

Professor: (who has a hearing loss): What was your last assignment?

Film student: I did a 10-minute educational film on Arctic moss.

Professor: (thinking the film student said Arctic *moths*): Oh, you must have had to do that over the summer then.

Film student: Believe it or not, some species live embedded in ice crystals, so we did some shots in early November.

Professor: What do they do, live in caverns?

Film student: Huh?

Professor: (beginning to wonder whether he has missed something): Live in caverns?

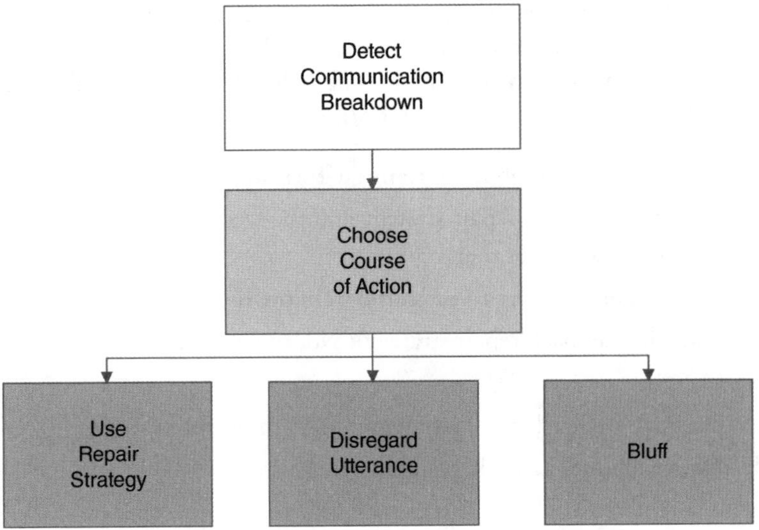

FIGURE 6–4 Stages associated with communication repair.

Film student: (who has hearing loss): Well, I guess there's some moss in caverns up there, but I've never seen any caves.

Professor: *Moss?* [blushing] Oh, I thought we were talking about *moths!*

As the professor sensed an incongruence between the film student's and his own remarks, he gradually realized that he misunderstood an utterance earlier on in the conversation. This is a prime example of not realizing that a breakdown has occurred at its onset.

Often the communication partner is the first to recognize that a communication breakdown has occurred, as in this example:

Classmate: So the midterm exam is next Friday?

James: I'm going to be working on my report on Friday.

Classmate: No, I'm *asking* you if the exam is on Friday.

In this example, the classmate intended her statement to be a yes–no question. Although it is unclear whether James understood the remark and misconstrued its intention or whether he simply did not understand it, the classmate recognized that a communication breakdown occurred and initiated a repair.

Once a misunderstanding becomes apparent, an individual might alert the communication partner and provide instruction about how to repair it. For example, he or she may ask about the topic of conversation (e.g., "What are you talking about?"). This is actually a form of metacommunication between two people because it entails discussion of a communication act.

Usually, breakdowns are repaired with the use of one or two repair strategies, as in this interchange when a request for a partial repetition is made:

Coworker: I'll get a copy of the fax to you tomorrow.

Person with hearing loss: A copy of what tomorrow?

Coworker: The fax. The fax sent by Mr. Roberts.

There are occasions when several exchanges are required. In the worst of circumstances, these interchanges can be awkward for all parties involved in the conversation, as in the following example in which a husband and wife (who recently received a cochlear implant) talked while seated in a speech and hearing test room:

Husband: Laura is going to catch the train on Tuesday.

Wife: (uses a nonspecific repair strategy and the feedback repair strategy): What? I didn't catch any of that.

Husband: I said, Laura is going to catch the train on Tuesday.

Wife: (uses the feedback repair strategy): No, none of it.

Husband: Laura . . .

Wife: (uses the feedback repair strategy): Something about more?

Husband: No, watch me. Laura is going to get the train.

Wife: (uses the feedback repair strategy): Oh, yeah. I got "train."

Husband: Yes, a train. Laura is . . .

Wife: (uses the spelling repair strategy, shaking her head): Nope, nope, none of it. Spell it.

Husband: (spelling): L-A-U-R-A.

Wife: (uses the feedback repair strategy): Oh Laura! What about Laura and the train?

An **extended repair** occurs when many repair strategies are needed to mend a communication breakdown.

At this point, several repair strategies have been implemented and the message is still not conveyed. This is an example of an **extended repair**. It would be easy for both participants in the conversation to abandon repair and say, "Never mind, it's not that important." Indeed, in situations such as this, that is often exactly what happens.

Sometimes when someone uses a repair strategy, the topic of conversation shifts, as indicated in Figure 6–5. Ideally, people use repair strategies in such a way that they do not cause the conversation to stagnate or veer off into a different direction. For example, a student with a hearing loss, Janet, did not use a repair strategy effectively in the following exchange:

Cynthia: I got my grades in the mail last Saturday.

Janet: Grapes? Why are you getting grapes in the mail?

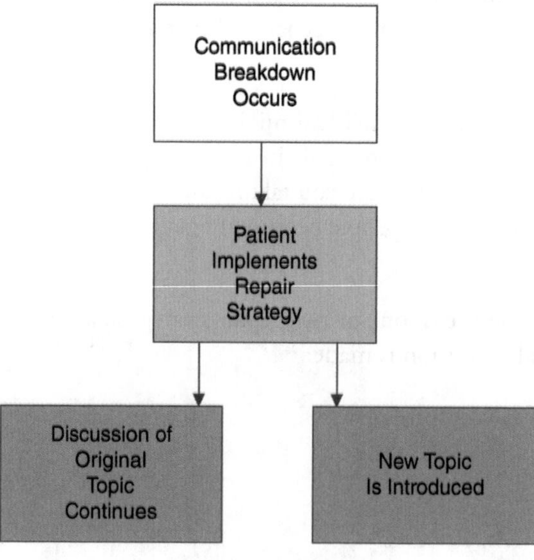

FIGURE 6–5 Possible effects of using a repair strategy.

Cynthia: No, I said *grades*, not *grapes*.

Janet: Oh, I know you make wine, so I thought you had joined some kind of mail-order program. By the way, when am I going to get my bottle?

The problem with this interchange is that the topic of conversation changed inappropriately (from grades to a promised bottle of wine) as a result of the repair strategy used. A seemingly more cooperative and congenial way to repair this communication breakdown is as follows:

Cynthia: I got my grades in the mail last Saturday.

Janet: Grapes?

Cynthia: No, I said *grades*.

Janet: Oh, you got your grades in the mail. How did you do?

In this latter version, Janet asked for confirmation and then steered the conversation back on track.

Sometimes patients bluff and pretend to understand following a communication breakdown, nodding and smiling in agreement with what they do not know. The consequences of **bluffing** can be negative. The person may appear insensitive, uninterested, dull, or inattentive. He or she may begin to feel powerless to manage communication difficulties. When bluffing is used excessively, conversation may leave the person feeling like a failure or angry at himself or herself.

Bluffing is pretending to understand an utterance and behaving in a way that suggests that understanding occurred, even if little or none of the message was recognized.

Bluffing

The following conversation, which occurred between two women who had just met, presents an instance in which bluffing led to the appearance of insensitivity. Woman 2 has just said that she is about to take a trip. Woman 1 has a hearing loss:

Woman 1: Where are you going?

Woman 2: To Portland to see my daughter. She is having a baby.

Woman 1: (nodding; she understood the word *baby*, but not much else): I see.

Woman 2: She has been bedridden for several weeks because she has diabetes and high blood pressure, and now the doctor says they are going to have to induce or the baby you know might be in trouble if it goes much longer than it's been going, even though it will be four weeks premature which we are pretty worried about especially since it's her first.

Woman 1: (lost by the length and convoluted syntax of her partner's utterance, and still not understanding much): Oh, how nice.

Woman 2: No, not really, this is pretty serious.

It's Sometimes Just Smoke and Mirrors

"The single biggest problem in communication is the illusion that it has taken place."

—George Bernard Shaw, Irish playwright, critic, and political activist

(lived 1856–1950)

Inadvertently, Woman 1 has created an unfavorable impression because she bluffed and pretended to understand instead of repairing the communication breakdown.

One reason that someone may bluff is because use of a repair strategy may require a person to acknowledge a hearing loss. For example, an individual might say, "Can you say that again, please?" and the communication partner might respond, "What's the matter?" For some people, it is difficult to acknowledge "I have a hearing loss, and I can't always catch all that is said to me."

Many persons are reluctant to admit a hearing loss, in part because of personal vanity and perceived **social stigma** or self-stigma. Unfortunately, many people have stereotypical

Social stigma is having a condition that is devalued because it deviates from a societal norm and results in a negative status being placed upon a person or group of persons.

views of persons with hearing loss. Some see them as difficult to communicate with or as deserving pity. For many people, revealing a hearing loss to someone who does not know them is a daunting challenge and, hence, they may be reluctant to use repair strategies. Hallberg (1996) suggests that the driving force for all coping strategies, including bluffing and pretending to understand, lies in an individual's efforts to maintain a positive and "I am normal" self-image and to avoid being considered as deviant or deficient by others. Acknowledging a hearing loss, and putting a spotlight on the loss by signaling communication breakdowns and using repair strategies, may result in a spoiled self-identity. These behaviors may also lead others to view the person with hearing loss as an undesirable social deviation from a normal state, a situation that most people would like to avoid. In addition, Hallberg suggests that the reluctance to admit a hearing loss might stem from self-deception or a distortion of reality. There may be a discrepancy between a person's desired self-image and actual circumstances, and the self-deception protects the self-image and helps the individual maintain a positive or normal self-image in the face of hearing loss.

Some people do not blatantly pretend to understand, but rather, when they do not understand a remark, they change the topic of conversation, as in the following exchange, where Frank is a man with hearing loss and Liz is a woman he is meeting for the first time (Tye-Murray, Mauzé, & Schroy, 2010, p. 159). In the course of their 10-minute conversation, Frank shifted the topic eight times. He initiated his topic shifts with such affirmations as, "Right, right!" or, "Yeah, I know," apparently to hide his incomprehension and yet advance the conversation nonetheless. This strategy eventually backfired on him. At the beginning of the conversation, Liz believes they have discovered a mutual acquaintance:

Liz: My mother-in-law is Sally Pitts.

Frank: Is who?

Liz: Sally Pitts.

Frank: Oh right! Yeah! Well, I haven't been back to Illinois since I got my cochlear implant (he then continues talking about his cochlear implant).

Several minutes later, his ruse is revealed, albeit only after more valiant bluffing. Notice below that he uses the *elaborate repair strategy* when he asks Liz about when her mother-in-law had worked at the pharmacy and the *spell repair strategy* when he tries to clarify her last name:

Liz: So, have you ever met my mother-in-law?

Frank: What'd you say her name was?

Liz: Sally Pitts. She kept the books at [your brother's] pharmacy.

Frank: Yeah . . . you know, I don't think I have . . .

Liz: Really?

Frank: Is it *Fix*? *F-I-X?*

Liz: No, *Pitts. P* as in *pumpkin.*

Frank: Yeah. No, no, I got it that time, but no . . . I, uh, when'd she work there?

Liz: Years and years, and just recently quit.

Frank: Oh! (slaps hand to forehead) Yeah! Right! Sorry, Sally Pitts! . . . I knew her! I knew her real well.

Two more maxims of conversation (these for the listener):

- Maxim of Receive Readily: Pay attention and do not let your mind wander or let yourself be distracted from listening.
- Maxim of Recognize Genuinely: Care enough about what your communication partner is saying that you will make the necessary effort to ensure understanding.

(Tye-Murray et al., 2010)

Shifting the topic of conversation in order to mask a communication breakdown can yield negative effects. The video of this conversation was shown to a panel of judges who were asked if they would choose to have a conversation with Frank. One judge who said *no* wrote on his evaluation sheet, "I'd rather repeat myself multiple times than have someone pretend to understand me."

And indeed, a possible outcome of excessive bluffing is that the patient violates one of two maxims governing the conduct of listeners during casual conversations, that being to *recognize genuinely*. The second maxim is *receive readily*.

Two Maxims of Conversation for Listeners

The first maxim is to *recognize genuinely*. When we engage in conversation, we believe that our communication partners are behaving in good faith and when they indicate comprehension, they genuinely perceive our message. A second maxim governing the conduct of listeners is to *receive readily*. Our communication partners should not have to expend undue effort to express their messages. They expect us to pay attention and not be distracted, say, by other conversations co-occurring in the room. Unfortunately, for communication partners with hearing loss, these two maxims often present an either/or situation. If they receive readily, and hence bluff and pretend to understand, they may not recognize genuinely; if they recognize genuinely, and ask their communication partners to clarify their messages (sometimes, again and again and again), they may not receive readily.

Receive Readily

This second maxim for listening underlies another reason why people may bluff. Most people in a conversation desire to be cooperative and agreeable. Some people are unwilling to use repair strategies and bluff because they feel guilty and embarrassed about introducing difficulties into a conversation—they feel that they must *receive readily*. Typically, when we converse, we engage in a cooperative enterprise as we try to ensure that a conversation is as pleasant and rewarding an experience for our communication partner(s) as it is for ourselves. If someone frequently halts the conversation for clarification, it may become less pleasant and less rewarding (Figure 6–6), as in the following exchange:

Patrick: I am going on spring break next week.
Richard: Huh?
Patrick: I said *spring break*.
Richard: Oh.
Patrick: We are driving to Florida in Jason's parents' car.

FIGURE 6–6 Spirit of cooperation during conversation. When we engage in a conversation, we usually try to be cooperative and help make the conversation a pleasurable or meaningful experience for all participants.

Richard: Huh?

Patrick: We are driving to Florida in Jason's parents' car.

Richard: Oh.

Mary: I wish I were going somewhere.

Richard: Huh?

Mary: I wish I were going somewhere.

Richard: Yeah, me too.

As the interchange unfolds, the spontaneity of the conversation becomes stifled by the continual requests for clarification. Maintaining continued conversation will prove laborious and effortful for all involved. It is for such reasons that many persons with hearing loss opt to bluff, particularly when talking to people they do not know well.

While bluffing is generally not a good idea, some patients believe that bluffing is sometimes acceptable, as when they are in a group situation or when they are tired of paying attention. Patients may decide to bluff because they think that if they wait a moment, the meaning of an utterance will register with them or subsequent remarks will clarify what was missed. The challenge, of course, is to know when bluffing is appropriate and when it is not.

RESEARCH RELATED TO REPAIR STRATEGY USAGE AND COMMUNICATION BREAKDOWNS

Although communication breakdowns may occur in any conversation for any variety of reasons, certain conditions increase the likelihood of their occurrence. As noted earlier, environmental conditions, message content, and speaking behaviors all influence how well a person with hearing loss recognizes a spoken message. A study by Caissie (2001) suggests that the dynamic nature of the conversation also affects when communication breakdowns are most likely to occur. For example, if two people are engaged in a conversation and they limit themselves to talking about a single topic, they are less likely to experience communication breakdowns than if they jump from one topic to the next. As the two individuals exchange remarks on their chosen topic, there is more contextual information available to resolve potential misunderstandings.

Topic Shading

Abruptly shifting from one topic to another is more likely to cause communication difficulties than discussing only one topic. Interestingly, even more disruptive than topic changing is topic shading. **Topic shading** happens when a new topic is introduced but is a direct offshoot of something that was just being discussed, as in the following example:

Topic shading occurs when a new emphasis is derived from an ongoing topic of conversation such that the topic remains the same but the relevant details shift.

Janice: (who has hearing loss): I'm going to Chicago tomorrow.

Robert: Are you driving or flying?

Janice: Flying.

Robert: I've got to get my tickets for my New York trip.

Janice: Huh?

In this example, the two participants are still talking about traveling when the topic shifts, but instead of talking about Janice's trip they are now talking about Robert's need to purchase airline tickets. It may be that when an entirely new topic is introduced, the person with hearing loss can contribute a relevant comment, even if she or he has not understood every word. For example, if instead of mentioning his airline tickets, Robert had said, "What are you doing tonight?" Janice might have caught the general gist of his message and might have responded with an appropriate response (e.g., "Not much"). When topics shift subtly, individuals may request clarification to ensure they are following the direction the conversation is veering toward.

Frequency of Bluffing

In a classic study, Hétu, Lalande, and Getty (1987) studied workers with occupational hearing loss. They found that 67% of the respondents when at a family gathering, a party, or a social meeting were likely to *pretend to be understanding while keeping silent*; that is, they engaged in bluffing.

Use of Nonspecific Repair Strategies

Research suggests that most individuals are more likely to ask their communication partners to repeat a message following a communication breakdown than to simplify it, restructure it, or elaborate it (Caissie & Gibson, 1997; Tye-Murray, Knutson, & Lemke, 1993; Tye-Murray et al., 1990; Tye-Murray & Witt, 1996). Moreover, their most common repair tactic is to say, "What?," "Huh?," or "Pardon?" This kind of repair strategy (i.e., what-huh-pardon) is called a **nonspecific** as opposed to a **specific repair strategy**. When using a specific repair strategy, the person with hearing loss often provides explicit instruction to the communication partner about how to repair the breakdown.

A nonspecific repair strategy is a communication strategy that simply indicates a lack of understanding without providing instruction or other feedback to the communication partner.

A specific repair strategy is a communication strategy that provides explicit instructions to the communication partner about how to repair a communication breakdown.

You Say, I Say

When persons with hearing loss implement a repair strategy, they invite a response from their communication partners, thereby establishing a linked speaking turn. Linked speaking turns are called **adjacency pairs**. Examples of adjacency pairs include question–answer (e.g., "Who asked?"— "Bob asked."), greeting–reciprocation (e.g., "Hey there."— "Hi."), and summons–acknowledgment combinations (e.g., "Can you come over here?"— "Sure."). Particular repair strategy–response adjacency pairs often emerge when a person with hearing loss interacts with a person who has normal hearing. These include (Tye-Murray & Witt, 1996):

- *Nonspecific repair strategy—message repetition response.* When an individual with hearing loss implements a nonspecific repair strategy following a communication breakdown, the communication partner typically repeats the original message.
- *Request for information repair strategy—provide information response.* When an individual requests specific information, the communication partner typically provides it.
- *Confirmation repair strategy—feedback response.* When an individual restates the message content, the communication partner usually either confirms or corrects the statement.

Adjacency pairs are linked speaking turns.

Consequences of Using Repair Strategies

When a person uses a repair strategy, how is a communication partner likely to respond? One of the most noteworthy findings pertains to the use of the repeat repair strategy and nonspecific repair strategies. When these are used following a communication breakdown, the communication partners typically repeat the original message verbatim (Caissie & Gibson, 1997; Lind et al., 2010; Tye-Murray, Witt, Schum, & Sobaski, 1995). Thus, if someone says "Huh?" there is a high probability that the communication partner will repeat exactly what he or she has just said.

Additional research suggests that someone is more likely to understand a message following a communication breakdown if the communication partner restructures it rather than simply repeats it (Gagné & Wyllie, 1989), especially if the talker already has repeated the message one time and the person with hearing loss still has not recognized it. For example, someone says, "I bought a new car" and a person responds, "Huh?" Then the first communication partner repeats, "I bought a new car." A third verbatim repetition may be less helpful to a person with hearing loss than if the communication partner had rephrased the message as "I bought a Buick." New words, especially the more visible word *Buick* as opposed to *car*, may be easier for the patient to recognize audiovisually. Caissie and Gibson (1997) found that the most effective repair of communication breakdowns occurred when communication partners either paraphrased or confirmed the message. Repeating the message one time was almost equally effective. And indeed, when people repeat a message, they tend to increase loudness, pitch, and duration, so their communication partners with hearing loss are more likely to hear what they say (Lind et al., 2010). The least effective strategy appeared to be elaboration.

There may be an additional drawback to using nonspecific repair strategies. When persons often say "What?" or "Huh?" during a conversation to rectify communication breakdowns, their communication partners are more likely to perceive them unfavorably and to enjoy the interaction less (Gagné, Stelmacovich, & Yovetich, 1991; Tye-Murray et al., 1995). In the experimental paradigm that was used in these experiments, audiovisual recordings were made of spontaneous conversations between two people, one of whom had a real or simulated hearing loss. The recordings were then shown to a team of judges who were asked to rate each person with hearing loss on a personality 6-point rating scale (e.g., *this person is competent-incompetent*). The judges also rated them on a scale of emotional responses, using a second 6-point rating scale (e.g., *this person makes me feel composed-irritated*). When individuals used nonspecific instead of specific repair strategies, they were rated more unfavorably and they elicited more unfavorable reactions from the judges, perhaps because such use placed the onus of repair on the communication partner.

Despite the drawbacks, there are positive outcomes of using nonspecific repair strategies in some contexts, and they are not necessarily to be avoided on all occasions. First, communication breakdowns that occur during spontaneous conversation between adults in which one partner has a hearing loss often are resolved after the use of a single repair strategy, even if it is a nonspecific strategy (Lind, Hickson, & Erber, 2006; Tye-Murray et al., 1995), suggesting that nonspecific repair strategies can be effective.

Second, a nonspecific repair strategy is minimally disruptive to the flow of ongoing conversation. When an individual asks, "Huh?" he or she assumes the speaking floor briefly, and the communication partner can easily continue a speaking turn. However, when someone uses other repair strategies such as, "I missed that, can you tell me what you are talking about?" and uses them frequently, a conversation can become stilted and less fluent. By using a nonspecific repair strategy, the individual takes a phantom speaking turn and may appear more cooperative in the conversational interchange. Third, the use of nonspecific repair strategies might facilitate the grounding process, wherein one partner presents a bit of information and the other partner provides an acknowledgment (in such instances, the nonspecific repair strategy assumes the same purpose as an acknowledgment gesture). The nonspecific repair strategy might serve to acknowledge that information was not conveyed successfully and thereby establish a lack of common ground.

Finally, a nonspecific repair strategy might indicate the location of a problem. Lind et al. (2006) examined the frequency and effectiveness of repair strategies that occurred during an approximately 20-minute conversation between a cochlear implant user and his wife and found that nonspecific repairs were effective in pinpointing the location of difficulty. The husband sometimes said "Huh?" in the middle of his wife's utterance. Even though he did not identify the source of the breakdown, indicating the time of occurrence led to successful repair. Lind (2009a) suggests that such frequent interjections of repair might be most appropriately used when talking with a frequent communication partner such as a family member, as they might create a social tension while talking with an unfamiliar communication partner.

Disclosing a Hearing Loss

It is impossible to make a blanket statement about whether people tend to disclose their hearing loss, and if so, what the consequences are of doing so, as this scenario will vary as a function of the communication partners involved and the circumstances of the interaction. Even so, studies about disclosure and its consequences illustrate what could happen.

I'll Never Tell

The following summary was included in a report about the communication problems experienced by inpatients at a hospital. This section dealt with reluctance to admit a hearing loss:

> Patients who conceal their hearing loss do so for a variety of reasons, but the most common one is self-consciousness. Some go to great lengths to conceal their disability. Some are very skillful at this concealment, not appreciating how dysfunctional it is. Female patients often adopt hairstyles that cover their hearing aids. One patient admitted that she disliked wearing a hearing aid, because her hair was no longer thick enough to cover it. Many hearing-impaired people pretend to understand what is being said, rather than admit to their difficulties. This can be very misleading and create many problems. One patient said: "My reticence to make my hearing loss known made me the victim of my own vanity." A patient who finally decided to admit to his problem was agreeably surprised that both the doctors and nurses were helpful and understanding. In some cases, patients' deceptions were unexpectedly exposed.
>
> (Hines, 2000, p. 35)

The Acknowledgment Tactic

"At the very beginning of the meeting, I explain to people what it's about. I'm hard of hearing. I've got a cochlear implant. Situations like this are difficult for me, so we've got a captionist. The captionist is confidential, she's bound by confidentialities, and all the information that is there is destroyed after the meeting."

—Federal government employee who routinely uses acknowledgment tactics and relies on closed captioning during meetings

(Jennings, Southall, & Gagné, 2013, p. 176)

The Tendency to Disclose

Hétu and his colleagues conducted a focus study to explore whether and why factory workers who have hearing loss disclose it (Hétu et al., 1990). They found that the workers tended not to disclose their hearing loss. However, for some, their coworkers and some relatives only learned of the participants' hearing loss after they were the subject of a local newspaper story. Afterward, the participants were strongly stigmatized and

Willingness/Unwillingness to Disclose a Hearing Loss

"When you involve someone else in it, you've enlisted their help, their participation, and to some degree, their sympathy. I learned a long time ago that people don't like perfect people. If you can represent yourself as having somewhat of a deficit, whatever it may be, that someone will likely pull for you a little bit more. They'll understand that you're fighting a problem and that you're trying to deal with it. I tell them right up front."

—A teaching associate

"When I give presentations . . . I will say, 'Look guys, I don't hear well in this kind of environment. If I'm walking up close to you, getting in your space, it's all right."

—A director of stewardship

"I'm on the phone and I have to ask them two or three times their address. I ask them to spell it because when you spell it I can usually make out the initials. I don't tell them the truth. Sometimes I just say, 'I don't have a really good connection on this phone, could you speak up a little louder?'"

—A salesperson

"Those people [in a meeting] don't know I have a hearing loss, nor do I have the time to tell them. And there is an agenda, and the boss or the department head just goes *bop, bop, bop*, and if it's important, they are going to either email me or give me the minutes. So I just sit there and wait till the time is over with."

—A business executive

(Tye-Murray et al., 2009)

became the target of demeaning jokes and comments from coworkers and family alike, some of who did not believe their disability was serious ("You can't be very deaf, you talk on the phone") and some of who dismissed them ("He's as deaf as a post, can't hear a thing anymore"). The researchers categorized the participants' reluctance to acknowledge their hearing-related difficulties as *denial* (e.g., "The talker was mumbling"; "I am not a deaf person"), *minimization of the problem* (e.g., "It's more of a problem for my wife than for me"), *reluctance to talk about the problem* ("We're not going to talk about it"), and *attempt at normalization* (e.g., "Anyone who works in a noisy factory gets a hearing loss"). The researchers concluded that reluctance to disclose a hearing loss is an adaptive process that stems from fear of stigmatization.

Times may have changed since Hétu and his colleagues (1990) performed their study or there might exist a difference between office workers' willingness to disclose as opposed to factory workers' willingness. Tye-Murray et al. (2009) conducted a focus group study with 48 office workers and found that 70% of them divulged their hearing loss to at least one person in the office, usually someone who was a close coworker or a supervisor (Tye-Murray et al., 2009). Other participants indicated that they routinely referenced their hearing loss, especially if doing so would enhance their job performance or would prevent people from attributing their communication difficulties to a condition other than hearing loss. For example, various participants suggested that if they did not inform people about their hearing loss, then people may think that they were "slow," "not paying attention," "an idiot," "sleeping at the table," "goofy," or "not very with it." People might also attribute their communication difficulties to Alzheimer's disease or some other memory problem. One of the participants, an attorney, said that people who were unaware of his hearing loss "think [I'm] aloof and [I am] bored and that [I] don't want to have anything to do with them."

Similar to this study, Stevens et al. (2018) also reported a high disclosure rate. In their survey of 1581 patients with hearing loss, 93% of respondents sometimes or often let their health care providers during medical appointments know about their hearing loss. Seventy percent reported that the office "sometimes" or "often" made arrangements to improve communication, which underscores the value of disclosure.

Southall, Jennings, and Gagné (2011) identified several factors that influence someone's reluctance to disclose a hearing loss and provided example comments gleaned from interviews with 12 participants (pp. 703–705):

- *Perceived importance of the situation*: e.g., "[I don't say I have a hearing loss during a job interview]. Self-preservation kind of kicks in. I want this job. I need this job. And I want that salary." —Government worker
- *Perceived sense of control*: e.g., "[I don't say I have a hearing loss]. No. Don't interrupt the conversation with things that don't matter. . . . I guess it comes back to commanding the situation." —Engineering consultant
- *Community affiliation*: e.g., "[I don't ask for accommodations.] You do want to be treated normally. You don't want to be treated differently." —Buyer
- *Burden of communication*: e.g., "If there's someone that doesn't know about it, and it's come to a point where it's probably more than the average person asking, 'What? Can you repeat that?' then I disclose [my hearing loss]. Otherwise, if I think it's within the realm of the average person that asks something to be repeated, then I won't. I won't say anything." —Engineer

Consequences of Disclosure

As just noted, Hétu et al. (1990) found that disclosing a hearing loss can lead to negative consequences (e.g., derogatory comments from coworkers) while Tye-Murray et al.

(2009) reported positive consequences (e.g., communication breakdowns are attributed to the hearing loss and not cognitive conditions such as Alzheimer's). Stevens et al. (2018) also noted positive consequences (e.g., accommodations during medical appointments). So again, just as a person's willingness to disclose a hearing loss is affected by the communication partner and the communication situation, so too are the resultant consequences of doing so. With that said, research has shown subtle consequences of disclosure that can occur.

Reasons why workers choose to disclose or conceal a hearing loss include:

- Importance of the situation
- A worker's perceived sense of control and the balance of power between the worker and the communication partner
- Community affiliation and what is considered to be "normal" in the workplace
- Burden of communication, and perception that hearing loss impedes the natural flow of conversation
- Coexisting issues, such as visibility of hearing aids

(Southall, Jennings, & Gagné, 2011)

Blood and Blood (1999) found a *subtle positive consequence*. They videotaped two young Deaf adults, each participating in rehearsed interviews about school, hobbies, and interests. Both wore a visible behind-the-ear hearing aid. In one interview, the men acknowledged a hearing loss to their unfamiliar communication partner, explaining that they had worn hearing aids since infancy, had received speech-language therapy, and had advocated for persons with hearing loss. In a second interview, they did not disclose their hearing loss. The videotapes were shown to groups of university students who rated the men on 14 bipolar adjective scales, such as *likable–not likable, trustworthy–untrustworthy,* and *sociable–unsociable.* The judges also answered such questions as *Explain how you think the speaker would interact with strangers* and *How do you feel this speaker would act around you?* In the videotapes where the young men talked about their hearing loss, they were rated as more sincere, likable, decisive, reliable, sociable, friendly, employable, and emotionally adjusted compared with when they did not mention their hearing loss. They elicited such comments as, "He was confident and self-assured" and "very honest," as opposed to comments such as "I don't think I could work with him" and "he's not very bright" when they did not disclose their loss. Based on these findings, the researchers suggested that patients might be encouraged to practice using an **acknowledgment tactic** in the aural rehabilitation setting, and then use it to reduce or eliminate such feelings as embarrassment and other difficulties that may occur in social interactions. By talking about their hearing loss, they may also educate unfamiliar communication partners (who may feel ill at ease because they know little about hearing loss), and they may also elicit a more favorable response from them.

People with hearing loss use an **acknowledgment tactic** to disclose their hearing loss and acknowledge a disability when talking to an unfamiliar communication partner for the first time.

Tye-Murray and Witt (1996) uncovered a *subtle negative consequence* of disclosing a hearing loss. In their investigation, a participant who was a cochlear implant recipient was seated at a table with someone who had normal hearing whom the participant did not know (an "unfamiliar communication partner"). The unfamiliar communication partner was told that he or she was participating in a study about conversation but was not told that the participant had hearing loss. Each dyad conversed for 10 minutes with no one else present in the room. The conversations were videotaped and later analyzed. Analyses showed that only 44% of the patients revealed their hearing losses (again, demonstrating that disclosure is influenced by the communication partner and the communication circumstances), even though most experienced many communication breakdowns during the course of the 10-minute conversation. What is perhaps most interesting is what happened when a patient did reveal a loss. Once the patient did so, the conversation began to center around the topic of hearing loss and difficulties associated with hearing loss, rather than other shared topics of interest. This change may be yet another reason why people are reluctant to reveal a hearing loss—they do not want their hearing loss to become the focus of discussion.

CONVERSATIONAL STYLES AND BEHAVIORS

Many communication strategies training curricula include materials that are aimed at developing desirable conversational styles and conversational behaviors. Although there are no right and wrong ways per se of engaging in conversation, and what is appropriate will vary with the situation, some conversational styles and behaviors are nonetheless more effective when communication is hampered by the presence of hearing loss than are other styles and behaviors.

Conversational Styles

Conversational style refers to the set of behaviors and methods that a person implements to relay and receive information during communication activities. Adults who have significant hearing impairment, and even children and teenagers, may exhibit at least four kinds of conversational styles: (a) passive, (b) aggressive, (c) passive-aggressive, and (d) assertive.

A **passive conversational style** is one in which a person plays a lesser role than the communication partner in advancing a conversation and is characterized by not taking conversational turns and by bluffing and pretending to understand.

A person with a **passive conversational style** is someone who wants to appear cooperative at all costs and avoid misunderstandings and conflict. This style entails little risk and is very safe in the short term, but it can be counterproductive in the long term. Someone who engages in a passive conversational style often does the following:

- Withdraws from conversation
- Frequently bluffs and pretends to recognize utterances
- Speaks with a quiet tone, uses little eye contact, and may affect a facial expression that is sheepish or poker-faced in response to a message
- Avoids social interactions and group gatherings in order to avoid communication difficulties

Someone who sits at the bridge table, smiling and quietly nodding, is probably someone who can be characterized as having a passive conversational style. The person gains little by being in the game. The individual may begin to feel frustration, victimization, resentment, and helplessness. After having been passive for too long, the person might display a burst of anger. This person may have a difficult time recognizing his or her own communication needs and knowing how to get them met more effectively.

A person with an **aggressive conversational style** may blame others for misunderstandings.

Persons with an **aggressive conversational style** represent the opposite extreme of persons with a passive conversational style. They may protect their rights at the expense of others and feel a need to come out "on top" of a conversation at all costs. They may exhibit some of the following characteristics during conversation:

- Hostility, regardless of the message, belligerence, and a bad attitude
- Shouting or "soapbox" speech
- Excessive or expansive body gestures
- An intimidating demeanor, such as directing an intense stare at the talker, leaning in to the talker, or standing stiffly erect

The person may purposely or inadvertently embarrass, hurt, or anger his or her communication partners and blame others for communication difficulties. "Quit mumbling, and try to help me out!" someone may demand, or, "You never told me that!" The first utterance is a tacit insult (i.e., it implies, "You could help me out but you have chosen not to"), whereas the second is an accusation ("It's not that I didn't hear you, it's that you never told me in the first place!"). These kinds of utterances have the potential to alienate communication partners and may result in the person with hearing loss being ineffective and even avoided.

A **passive-aggressive conversational style** is one in which aggression is expressed in indirect ways.

Some individuals with hearing loss adopt a **passive-aggressive conversational style**, which incorporates elements of both a passive and an aggressive style. They may forfeit their right to understand a message initially and then manipulate the conversation or take vengeance later. The goal is to avoid communication breakdowns and communication difficulties and then make the communication partner sorry that they occurred or that they were not rectified. The person might say, "I can't understand what you're saying but I realize that it's probably not important." Sometimes the person might act passively to a person's face and then aggressively later. "Yes, yes," an older man might say to a doctor. He then may complain bitterly to his adult daughter later that the doctor was insensitive to his hearing loss and that he will not be returning for follow-up visits. The person with a passive-aggressive communication style may:

- Use sarcasm
- Behave passively to someone's face and then aggressively when the person is gone
- Exhibit sullenness, stubbornness, or procrastination

During communication strategies training, patients often are encouraged to minimize their use of passive, aggressive, and passive-aggressive conversational styles and instead implement an assertive style. The goals of the assertive conversationalist are to communicate effectively and to find solutions that minimize or prevent communication breakdowns. Persons who adopt an **assertive conversational style** usually follow these guidelines during conversation. They:

A person who adopts an **assertive conversational style** takes responsibility for managing communication difficulties in a way that is considerate of communication partners.

- Respect the rights of their communication partners, while honestly and openly expressing their own needs and emotions
- Take responsibility for managing communication difficulties, but do so in a way that is considerate of their communication partners
- Use eye contact when speaking with a person and have facial expressions appropriate to the message
- Use body language that conveys receptiveness and openness
- Acknowledge their communication partner's efforts to promote good communication when appropriate

"Let's get a seat away from the stereo speaker," an assertive person may suggest, "and then you won't have to repeat everything you say." This remark is courteous and provides direct explanation of how to remedy a communication problem.

These four types of conversational styles (passive, aggressive, passive-aggressive, and assertive) may be reviewed in a communication strategies training program. One goal is to make patients aware of their communication styles so that they can learn to communicate more effectively and can recognize ineffective communication behaviors in others. Through practice and hard work, they can develop assertive ways of rectifying their communication problems. They can also learn how to respond effectively to their communication partners when they implement passive or aggressive behaviors.

Sometimes, especially when a psychologist participates in implementing the plan, the aural rehabilitation plan includes **psychosocial therapy**. One of the primary goals of this type of intervention is to encourage assertive behaviors. Participants explore the psychological and social ramifications of hearing loss and some of the underlying reasons why they may not engage in assertive behaviors. For example, some people who behave passively may do so because they feel they burden other people when they ask for assistance. These underlying assumptions are challenged during psychosocial therapy.

Psychosocial therapy is a therapy approach that challenges a patient's erroneous assumptions and helps the person to develop a positive self-image.

Communication Behaviors

Figure 6–7 presents three constellations of behaviors that complement the model of conversational styles just reviewed. The model consists of three circles that are labeled interactive, noninteractive, and dominating.

FIGURE 6–7 Constellations of behaviors that characterize some persons with hearing loss.

Interactive behavior is the use of cooperative conversational tactics, consistent with an assertive conversational style.

Persons who fall within the **interactive behavior** circle use cooperative conversational tactics, which are consistent with an assertive conversational style. These individuals share responsibility with their communication partners for advancing a topic of conversation and selecting topics of conversation. They do not dominate discussion, they show interest in what their communication partners say, and attempt to respond appropriately to their remarks.

Noninteractive behavior is characteristic of a passive behavioral style and is one in which the individual does little to advance the course of the conversation.

Persons who fit the **noninteractive behavior** constellation often can be characterized as having a passive conversational style. They may bluff following a communication breakdown. They may not contribute much to the development of a conversation topic, and they may not participate in selecting a topic to talk about. They also may not respond to turn-taking signals. For example, a communication partner may say, "So . . . you know . . . hmmm," hoping that the person with hearing loss will contribute a remark. The following interchange illustrates a noninteractive conversational style (exhibited by Rose, who has a hearing loss):

Marie: I saw a great movie last night.

Rose: Oh.

Marie: It was on the old-movies channel on cable.

Rose: Hmmm.

Marie: It had Fred Astaire and Ginger Rogers, lots of dancing and, you know, that kind of old-movie stuff . . .

(Rose nods)

Marie: I just love that . . .

(Rose nods)

Marie: I guess it takes me back to when I was going to the movies as a kid.

In this interchange, Rose does not express interest in Marie's remarks and does not share in advancing the topic. Marie begins to talk more in order to fill in the silences.

A noninteractive conversational style often yields unfavorable consequences. In a series of interviews with adults who have hearing loss, Cowie and Douglas-Cowie (1992) were told by one participant, "There are many occasions when I would like to ask questions, but in case I don't hear the answer I just don't do it. I think that probably gives the impression that I'm not interested, which isn't the case, it's just to save embarrassment" (p. 269). An individual's withdrawal can elicit negative reactions from communication partners and create an internal source of stress for oneself.

There is some evidence that two characteristically passive behaviors, avoidance and pretending to understand, are commonly used by persons who have hearing loss. Stephens et al. (1999) provided a questionnaire to 100 consecutive patients attending an audiological rehabilitation clinic in Cardiff, Wales. The patients were asked how often they exhibited certain behaviors in 11 different communication interactions. The most commonly cited behavior (in addition to asking people to repeat a misunderstood message) was *avoidance*, defined as "deliberately avoiding conversations with other people in certain circumstances to avoid the embarrassment of having to ask them to repeat what they say." Another commonly cited behavior was *pretend*, defined as "pretending they are hearing even when they don't, to avoid asking people to repeat themselves."

The final constellation in Figure 6–7 denotes a constellation of **dominating conversational behaviors**, which are characteristic of an aggressive conversational style. Persons who fall into this circle may take extended speaking turns, interrupt, and use abrupt topic changes. They may try to dominate the conversation, in order to always be aware of what is being talked about. Sometimes they will avoid asking questions so that they do not have to give up the speaking floor to hear the answers. Here is an excerpt from one conversation in which Deidre, an older woman with hearing loss, was conversing with her friend's daughter, Carrie:

Dominating conversational behaviors are characteristic of an aggressive conversational style and may include interrupting, taking long speaking turns, and dominating the topic of conversation.

Deidre: Sharon says you are going on vacation.

Carrie: Yes, I am flying with my brother to . . .

Deidre: (interrupting) Oh, I went on a plane once, to see my brother in South Carolina. He has a house down there, one he built himself on a lake.

With one remark, the two are suddenly talking about Deidre's plane trip and her brother rather than Carrie's upcoming travels.

As is the case with a passive conversational style, a dominating conversational style also may have undesired effects. One participant in the interviews conducted by Cowie and Douglas-Cowie (1992) reported, "I have to dominate the meeting, I make myself the artificial center of attention so that people will just speak to me . . . Instead of speaking to the chairman they would be speaking to me" (p. 269). One can surmise that colleagues (or at least the chairman) might react unfavorably to such a dominating conversational style.

In the model illustrated in Figure 6–7, the three circles overlap for two reasons. First, an individual usually demonstrates behaviors that are characteristic of more than one constellation. An individual's use of conversational behaviors may vary during a conversation, as the person becomes more comfortable or the dynamics of the interchange are established. Behavior may vary as a function of the familiarity of the communication partner too, as well as the circumstances in which the conversation is occurring. For example, someone who typically exhibits dominating communication behaviors may exhibit interactive behaviors when trying to talk his or her way out of a speeding ticket with a policeman. The second reason for the overlap is that some people, such as those who have a passive-aggressive conversational style, might demonstrate communication behaviors that appear on a superficial level to be interactive but at a deeper level are actually noninteractive or dominating.

CASE STUDY

A Couple Conversing

In the case study reported by Lind et al. (2006), a 55-year-old cochlear implant user spoke with his wife of 33 years for 23 minutes in an unstructured conversation. They sat in a quiet, well-lit room and spoke face-to-face about any topic they chose to discuss. Despite the optimal communication conditions and their familiarity with one another, they experienced 47 communication breakdowns. The repair activity or repair sequences occupied all or part of 67.7% of their conversational turns. They initiated their repair sequences with specific repair strategies roughly 60% of the time. Below are excerpts from three of the repair sequences (punctuation added). For each one, consider the kind of repair strategies used and the type of conversational style exhibited by the husband. Were the strategies specific or nonspecific? Was the conversational style more characteristic of an aggressive, passive-aggressive, assertive, or passive style? Were all of his remarks consistent with the same style? What style of turn taking predominated?

Excerpt 1 (p. 38):

Wife: Doesn't sound very profitable. I s'pose they make profit on the coffee.

Husband: Don't mumble, what?

Wife: I said I guess they make a profit on the coffee even if they don't sell the book.

Husband: Even if they don't sell the book, yeah.

Excerpt 2 (p. 43):

Wife: We always used to camp in the winter so camping in the winter in Victoria is, is not different?

Husband: Sorry I'm not following.

Wife: I mean if you're going to end up south sooner that's no different to short holidays we used to have, we always used to go away in the winter *time*. . . .

Husband: (overlapping with *time*): Yeah.

Excerpt 3 (p. 44):

Wife: Yeah but these are the phone calls that I have to *make* . . .

Husband: (overlapping with *make*): See you keep dropping, I'm losing you.

Wife: These are the phone calls that I have to make so you know (etc.)

Husband: (overlapping with final word in wife's utterance): Yes.

FINAL REMARKS

Although many of the strategies considered in this chapter seem like common sense, it is surprising that many people either have not explicitly thought about them or do not use them effectively. Moreover, many people are not aware that they may be using a conversational style or conversational behaviors that alienate(s) their communication partners. Although these behaviors may have been adopted as a means of coping with hearing-related difficulties, they may create problems in and of themselves.

KEY CHAPTER POINTS

- Face-to-face conversation usually proceeds in an orderly fashion, with communication partners adhering to implicit rules of conversation.
- Grounding occurs when one communication partner presents information and another partner acknowledges understanding. This information is then presupposed throughout the remaining conversation.
- The accepted rules of conversation often must bend when one of the communication partners has a hearing loss. The overall quality of conversation also may be diminished. For example, there may only be superficial content, and grounding may be disrupted.
- There are two classes of communication strategies, facilitative and repair. Within each of these classes are several kinds of strategies that individuals with hearing loss can use to facilitate conversational interchanges.
- There are at least three stages involved in repairing a communication breakdown: detection, selection of a course of action, and implementation.
- Persons who have hearing loss often bluff and pretend to understand. They may do this because they are reluctant to admit a hearing loss or because they do not want to appear uncooperative.
- Much research has centered on the use of repair strategies. One conclusion that emerges is that the most commonly used repair strategy is the repeat strategy.
- There are both advantages and disadvantages in using nonspecific repair strategies.
- Patients may bluff for many reasons, including to avoid embarrassment about having a hearing loss and to be cooperative and agreeable.
- Whether someone discloses a hearing loss varies as a function of the communication situation, but there may be positive or negative consequences associated with disclosure.
- People with hearing loss may have to violate one of two maxims for listeners who engage in casual conversation: Receive readily, recognize genuinely.
- Persons may be assertive, passive, aggressive, or passive-aggressive in their conversational styles.
- Constellations of communication behaviors might be described as interactive, noninteractive, dominating, or some combination of the three.

TERMS AND CONCEPTS TO REMEMBER

Communication strategy
Communication strategies training

Conversational rules
Keyed
Grounding
Facilitative strategies
Instructional strategies
Message-tailoring strategies
Metacommunication
Acknowledgment gesture
Constructive strategy
Adaptive strategies
Maladaptive strategies
Anticipatory strategy
Repair strategies
Communication breakdowns
Receptive repair strategies
Expressive repair strategy
Metacommentaries
Extended repair
Bluffing
Social stigma
Topic shading
Nonspecific
Specific repair strategy
Acknowledgment tactic
Adjacency pairs
Passive conversational style
Aggressive conversational style
Passive-aggressive conversational style
Assertive conversational style
Psychosocial therapy
Interactive behavior
Noninteractive behavior
Dominating conversational behaviors

CHAPTER 7

Assessment of Conversational Fluency and Communication Difficulties

OUTLINE

Typically, a communication strategies training program begins and ends with an assessment of individuals' conversational fluency and hearing-related disability. The goals of the initial assessment might be to:

- Determine the communication demands placed upon individuals in their everyday life.
- Evaluate the impact of hearing loss on daily activities.
- Identify the settings in which communication problems are likely to arise.
- Document the kinds of social activities in which a person is likely to engage.
- Assess how effectively people use communication strategies in a variety of settings.
- Chronicle employment responsibilities.

The goals of assessment will guide the selection of which measures are administered. For example, if the goal of assessment is to identify communication problems that are especially troublesome, the patient might complete a questionnaire. On the other hand, if the goal is to document conversational fluency, a clinician might determine how well information can be exchanged between two communication partners while maintaining a give-and-take dialogue. Assessment techniques for this purpose may include structured communication interactions or informal conversations.

The final assessment indicates whether a patient's actual or perceived conversational fluency has improved and communication difficulties have diminished as a result of an intervention. Some of the original measures might be repeated to determine whether performance has changed. One-time-only measures also might be administered, such as a questionnaire, in which patients can critique the success of an aural rehabilitation plan.

Because a patient's significant other often participates in a communication strategies program, he or she may also be assessed. The assessment might be aimed at determining the significant other's perception of a patient's conversational fluency or communication difficulties or it might assess how the patient's hearing loss impacts upon the significant other.

In this chapter, we will consider those assessment instruments that pertain to hearing-related communication difficulties in everyday situations and to conversational fluency.

CONVERSATIONAL FLUENCY

The following factors help to define conversational fluency (Erber, 1996, pp. 204–205; Erber, 1998):

- *Time spent in repairing communication breakdowns.* If during the course of a conversation, numerous communication breakdowns occur and they require many interchanges between the person with hearing loss and the communication partner before they are resolved, then conversational fluency is low. On the other hand, if need for clarification is minimal, conversational fluency is high. When analyzing communication breakdowns, consider (a) the proportion of time spent in communication breakdowns, (b) the total number of breakdowns, and (c) the average duration of a breakdown.
- *Exchange of information and ideas.* If the participants in a conversation successfully and easily share information and ideas, and the conversation seems to them to be spontaneous and not stilted, then conversational fluency is high.

- *Sharing of speaking time.* When conversation is smooth-flowing, participants have ample opportunity to speak and no one person dominates with protracted speaking times. Prolonged silences or frequent interruptions are not characteristic of fluent conversations.
- *Time spent in silence.* If the participants sit in awkward silence for an inordinate amount of time, then conversational fluency is poor.

Sociolinguists often index the sharing of speaking time with a measure called **mean length turn ratio (MLT ratio)**. To determine this ratio, **mean length of speaking turn (MLT)** is first computed for each participant in a conversation by determining the average number of words each person speaks (or average duration in seconds of a conversational turn) for some set number of conversational turns (often 50 turns). A **conversational turn** begins when one communication partner starts to speak. The turn ends when the person stops talking and someone else responds to the remark. The MLT ratio is computed by taking a ratio between the MLTs of the two communication partners. Table 7–1 illustrates how MLT and MLT ratio are determined.

Sociolinguists are scientists who belong to a branch of linguistics that studies the effects of social and cultural differences within a community on its use of language and conversational patterns.

Mean length turn ratio (MLT ratio) is the ratio of the mean length of speaking turns spoken by two communication partners during the course of a conversation.

Mean length (speaking) turn (MLT) is computed by determining the average number of words spoken during a set number of conversational turns, or the average duration of conversational turns in seconds.

Conversational turn is the period during which a participant delivers a contribution to the conversation.

The dialogues in Table 7–1 also illustrate two different levels of conversational fluency. In the first example, conversational fluency is high. The two communication partners exchange information with ease and they share responsibility in advancing the topic of discussion. They talk about a fairly uncommon conversational topic, period furniture, which entails using unusual vocabulary such as *French regency* and *deco*. The MLT ratio for this conversation is approximately equal, which is often characteristic of fluent interchanges.

The second conversational excerpt in Table 7–1 presents a sample of low conversational fluency. The topic of discussion quickly becomes superficial, as communication breakdowns occur. In this conversation, Martha bears the onus for advancing the conversation. She must fill in the awkward silences and develop the topic. Conversational fluency of this type is not uncommon when one of the communication partners has a significant hearing loss.

TABLE 7–1 Dialogues That Illustrate Two Levels of Conversational Fluency

EXAMPLE 1—A SAMPLE WITH HIGH CONVERSATIONAL FLUENCY	
Joan: Has your new furniture arrived yet?	
Ann: Yes, and I'm thrilled with it.	
Joan: You said that it was going to be French regency.	
Ann: No, I didn't go with that. My husband wanted a deco look.	
Analysis:	Joan's mean length turn (MLT) = 8.0 words (16 words divided by 2 utterances)
	Ann's MLT = 9.0 words (18 words divided by 2 utterances)
	MLT ratio: 0.9, where 1.0 = equal length speaking turns
EXAMPLE 2—A SAMPLE WITH LOW CONVERSATIONAL FLUENCY	
Martha: Has your new furniture arrived yet?	
Tom: Huh?	
Martha: Your furniture?	
(**Tom** looks around, shakes head)	
Martha: How are you doing? How is your wife? . . . Mary?	
Tom: Fine.	
Analysis:	Martha's MLT = 5.6 words (17 words divided by 3 utterances)
	Tom's MLT = 0.7 (2 words divided by 3 utterances)
	MLT ratio: 6.2, where 1.0 = equal length speaking turns

Why traditional audiological tests might not reflect conversational fluency:

- Most require patients to repeat exactly what they heard; engagement in a conversation usually does not require that.
- Most assess recognition of unrelated words and sentences; conversation comprises utterances related by linguistic and situational context.
- Most do not allow for the use of repair and facilitative strategies; in conversation, a patient may ask communication partners to modify an utterance or modify their speaking behavior.
- Most do not entail assessing speechreading ability, even though most conversations occur face-to-face.

GENERAL CONSIDERATIONS FOR EVALUATING CONVERSATIONAL FLUENCY AND HEARING-RELATED DISABILITY

Conversational fluency and the communication difficulties that are associated with hearing-related disability can be challenging to assess for a number of reasons. First, conversational fluency and success in managing communication difficulties vary as a function of the conversational setting and situation and as a function of the communication partner. For example, conversational fluency may be high when a patient talks with a seasoned speech and hearing professional but low when the patient converses with an unfamiliar store clerk. The speech and hearing professional is likely to be accustomed to talking to persons with hearing loss and probably speaks slowly and clearly and checks for comprehension. The store clerk may not know how to facilitate speech recognition for the person with hearing loss, may turn away when talking (and hence limit the person's ability to speechread), and may speak quickly. A measure of conversational fluency taken from the same patient probably would be high for the first communication partner but low for the second.

A second reason that assessment of conversational fluency may be problematic is because measures vary with the topic of discussion. Conversational fluency may be high for a superficial topic such as the weather, but low for a topic centering on local politics. Thus, depending on what was discussed, conversational fluency with a particular patient might be rated as either high or low.

A third reason is because communication difficulties do not always arise during a conversation. A patient may experience numerous difficulties while conversing in the workplace, but none while talking to a family member in a speech and hearing clinic test room. If communication breakdowns do not occur during the course of an audiological assessment, an audiologist may not gauge how well an individual manages communication difficulties.

A **construct** is an abstract or general idea that is inferred or derived from a constellation of measures or from a group of specific instances.

Finally, no one measure can capture adequately the **construct** of conversational fluency or hearing-related disability because both are defined by several dimensions. That is, both are abstractions that reflect a multitude of factors (e.g., the occurrence of breakdowns and pauses, the fluidity of conversation, MLT ratio, amount of time spent in silence, and the

TABLE 7–2 Some General Procedures for Measuring Conversational Fluency and Communication Needs: One Advantage and Disadvantage of Each

PROCEDURE	ADVANTAGE	DISADVANTAGE
Interview	Yields patient-specific information	Difficult to quantify information
Questionnaire	Quick and easy to administer	May miss patient-specific information
Daily log	Provides quantitative information about an extended time period	Can be a reactive procedure
Group discussion	Stimulates patients to introspection and reflection	Some patients may be reluctant to participate
Structured communication interaction	Has good face validity because assessment is based on actual conversational interactions	Can be time-consuming to score
Unstructured communication interactions	Good ecological validity because it best mimics real-world interaction	Results may vary as a function of the communication partner

superficiality of discussion). A number of measures typically must be performed and the results aggregated and then interpreted. Measures an procedures are listed in Table 7–2, along with some of their advantages and disadvantages.

INTERVIEWS

The most straightforward assessment procedure is the **interview**. Patients talk about their conversational problems and consider possible reasons as to why communication breakdowns happen. They comment on their subjective impressions of conversational fluency in a variety of settings (e.g., the workplace, the home). "Are you able to use the telephone?" the interviewer might ask, or might ask a more open-ended question, such as, "Tell me about your listening difficulties." Patients' answers will indicate their particular concerns and their perceptions of their situation and problems. Simply by interacting with the patient, the interviewer will acquire a sense of how well the patient can converse informally.

Interviews are a basic assessment procedure used to elicit specific information about an individual's hearing-related communication difficulties.

Interviews are effective because they elicit information that is specific to a patient. For example, one patient may report experiencing difficulty communicating during office conferences, whereas another may report experiencing problems while watching television. An open-ended discussion about the workplace may trigger a patient to reflect about particular instances in which communication was difficult in his or her recent past and may provide direction for the aural rehabilitation plan.

The disadvantage of interviews is that remarks cannot be quantified. This is problematic when changes in communication behaviors that result from intervention must be documented. Documentation is essential when a speech and hearing professional seeks reimbursement for providing services to patients from third-party health care providers.

Conducting the Interview

Often, interviews are semi-structured and unfold in a conversational format (Figure 7–1). Broad topics are covered, such as communication difficulties that occur in the home, social settings, school, or the workplace. Discussion progresses from one topic to the next in a logical sequence with transitional statements bridging one topic to the next. At the end of each topic, the clinician summarizes to confirm understanding before progressing to the next topic and to seek any clarification. When interviewing a patient, it is important to engage in **generous listening**, which is listening in a way that lets patients know they are being heard, without being judged, and provides positive attention, regard, and acknowledgment.

Generous listening is listening in a way that lets patients know they are being heard, without being judged, and provides positive attention, regard, and acknowledgment.

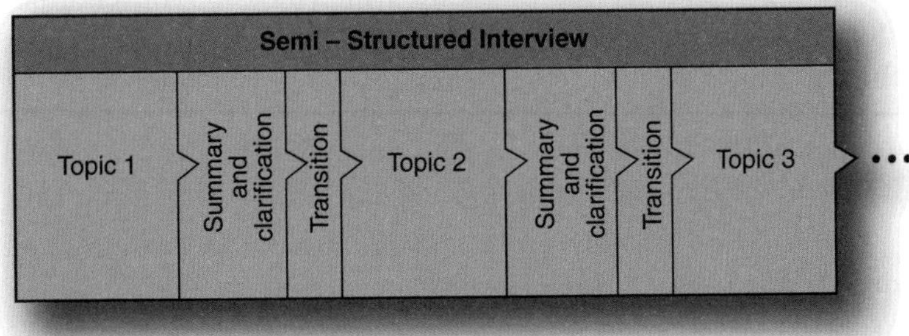

FIGURE 7–1 Semi-structured interviews. Even though the interview may seem like a conversation between clinician and patient, it typically follows a logical, structured format.

Generous Listening

Here are specific tips to keep in mind as when interviewing a patient for the first time (Gitles, 1999):

- Do not get overly involved writing information and do not turn away from the patient. Continue to look at the person, and, most important, listen as if your life depended on it. Listen as if you have never heard any of this before, because you have not, not from this person.
- If the patient pauses, stifle the impulse to ask the next question, interpret what the person is saying, or change the subject. Instead say something like, "Is there anything else?" or "What else can you tell me about that?" or "Tell me more about that."
- Use *how, what,* and *when* questions and avoid *why* questions. People will reveal more to you if they do not feel the need to justify their actions or defend their behavior.
- Encourage patients to talk until they have no more pertinent information to tell you.
- When people answer questions, the more you listen, the greater the depth of the information they will reveal. That is where connectedness and relatedness occur. The more patients reveal, the more they feel it is safe to talk to you, the more they get to weave and listen to their own story about their hearing (which they may have never told a soul), and the greater realization they have of the extent of their problem. As a result, the less reluctant they are about receiving help and the more they begin to let you help them.
- Listen to patients without judgment, evaluation, or opinions. Listen for the emotion and feelings in their expression and be aware of what is *not* being said. Acknowledge patients for having the courage to come in for help and let them know you will support them in whatever way you can.
- The more that you, as a professional, reveal your passion and commitment to helping people—perhaps through a personal story about someone you have helped—the greater the intimacy and relatedness with your patient (pp. 54–56).

Excerpts from two sample interviews demonstrate how an interview may be unsuccessful or successful. In the first interview, the clinician, Dr. Susan Clark, asks a preponderance of yes–no questions. It is almost as if she knows the answer before the patient, Mr. Brown, even responds. A following question is not influenced by the patient's response to a previous question. By the end of the interview, the clinician has gained little information about the patient's communication difficulties or conversational fluency, and the patient probably feels like he has been cycled through a pat list of questions that the clinician fires away at everyone who comes in for a hearing test.

Dr. Clark: (leads Mr. Brown to the testing suite. When he is seated in the testing chair, the clinician begins the interview): So, you think you have a hearing loss?

Mr. Brown: My wife seems to think I do.

Dr. Clark: (makes a tick mark with her pen on the yellow notepad she is holding): You have trouble hearing at home?

Mr. Brown: I do okay.

Dr. Clark (makes a tick mark): What about work?

Mr. Brown: Yeah, that's okay too.

Dr. Clark (makes a tick mark): You can use the telephone?

Mr. Brown: Yeah.

Dr. Clark (makes a tick mark, tucks the pad of paper under her arm): Fine. Let's test your hearing and see what we find.

In contrast, in the excerpt from the second interview, which appears next, the clinician engages in "generous listening." She asks open-ended questions and encourages the patient to elaborate on his responses. Because there is a genuine dialogue occurring, the clinician has a first-person opportunity to observe the patient experience a communication breakdown, giving her some insight into how the patient, Mr. Andrews, handles breakdowns and the ease with which they can be repaired.

Dr. Clark (greets the patient in the waiting room and asks him to follow her to her office for a conversation): Good morning, Mr. Andrews. What brings you here today?

Mr. Andrews: My wife says I have a hearing loss.

(Dr. Clark nods, continues to look Mr. Andrews in the eye.)

Mr. Andrews: I think she mumbles a lot. But then again, I guess I'm cranking up the volume of the TV too high. That probably means something.

Dr. Clark: What happens when she tries to talk to you from another room?

Mr. Andrews: Huh?

Dr. Clark: Say you are in the living room. Your wife is talking to you from the hallway. What happens?

Mr. Andrews: I can't hear her! Same as when she's talking in the kitchen with the water running. I can't hear her.

Dr. Clark: Tell me more about listening at home.

Mr. Andrews describes his difficulties with hearing the doorbell and listening on the telephone. They then discuss the challenges he encounters when listening in the workplace.

Simply by listening, and treating the person as a unique individual and not as Mr. or Mrs. Joe/Jane Patient, Dr. Clark learned much about her patient's communication difficulties. Moreover, she established a bond of human contact that let Mr. Andrews know that she genuinely cared about his hearing health and communication needs.

Sample questions from the *Hearing Handicap Inventory for the Elderly (HHIE)* (Ventry & Weinstein, 1982), where questions are categorized as either *emotional consequences (e) or social and situational effects* (s) and are given points according to answers that are *Yes* (4), *Sometimes* (2), and *No* (0):

- (e) Does a hearing problem cause you to feel embarrassed when meeting new people?
- (e) Does a hearing problem cause you to feel "stupid" or "dumb"?
- (e) Does a hearing problem cause you to want to be by yourself?
- (s) Does a hearing problem cause you to use the phone less often than you would like?
- (s) Does a hearing problem cause you to avoid groups of people?
- (s) Does a hearing problem cause you to go shopping less often than you would like?

QUESTIONNAIRES

Another assessment instrument that is used to assess conversational fluency and hearing-related disability is the questionnaire. Questionnaires might query respondents about how often communication breakdowns occur and whether they typically attempt to repair communication breakdowns and how. Questionnaires are a means of gathering general information easily and quickly (Figure 7–2).

One drawback in using questionnaires is that it is possible to miss important information about communication difficulties that are specific to a patient simply because such information is not covered by items in the questionnaire. A true–false statement such as *I always verify what I understood during a meeting with a coworker afterward* is irrelevant to the respondent who does not work or does not attend meetings. Moreover, responses

FIGURE 7–2 Questionnaires. Questionnaires are an effective means of obtaining information about communication difficulties and conversation in an easy and fast way. Questionnaires are available for both patients and communication partners.

Hearing loss–specific quality of life (HLQoL) refers to the activity limitations and participation restrictions imposed by hearing loss, and its impact on psychosocial functioning.

Sample questions from the *Self-Assessment of Communication (SAC)* (Schow & Nerbonne, 1982), where questions are categorized as either *Disability (activity limitation, AL)* or *Handicap (participation limitation, PL)*, and are given points according to answers that are *almost never, occasionally, about half of the time,* and *frequently*:

- (AL) Do you experience communication difficulties in situations when speaking with one person (at home, at work, in a social situation, with a waitress, a store clerk, a spouse, a boss, etc.)?
- (AL) Do you experience communication difficulties in situations when conversing with a small group or several persons (with friends or family, coworkers, in meetings or casual conversations, over dinner or while playing cards, etc.)?
- (PL) Do you feel that any difficulty with your hearing limits or hampers your personal or social life?
- (PL) Do others leave you out of conversations or become annoyed because of your hearing loss?

It Is the Quality That Matters

Some questionnaires are designed to assess a patient's **hearing loss–specific quality of life (HLQoL**; Abrams, Chisholm, & McArdle, 2005). HLQoL captures the physical, emotional, and social consequences imposed by hearing loss and assesses the activity limitations and participation restrictions experienced by the patient. For example, the Hearing Handicap Inventory for the Elderly (HHIE; Ventry & Weinstein, 1982) includes two subscales, *social function* and *emotional function,* designed to identify activity limitations and participation restrictions and to measure an individual's emotional response and attitude toward having a hearing loss.

to questionnaires may not reflect the importance of each communication difficulty or communication situation to the patient. An inability to talk on the telephone may be disruptive to the lifestyle of one person but only a minor annoyance to another.

A number of self-assessment questionnaires are available. Members of the Academy of Rehabilitative Audiology consider at least four instruments to be valid and useful: the Hearing Handicap Inventory for the Elderly (HHIE), the Self-Assessment of Communication (SAC), the Hearing Handicap Inventory for Adults (HHIA), and the Communication Profile for the Hearing Impaired (CPHI) (Dancer & Gener, 1999).

The popularity of these instruments relates in part to the fact that subjective impressions of communication difficulties often do not correspond to patients' audiograms. An audiogram may indicate that a person has a significant hearing loss. However, the patient, when completing a questionnaire, may describe the loss as a minor nuisance, but not overly problematic. In considering the discrepancy that sometimes exists between audiological and questionnaire information, Erdman (1994, p. 69) notes:

> Self-reports simply constitute different measures; the method of measurement differs as does the content of the measurement. Audiometric tests assess maximum potential or best performance of the central or peripheral hearing mechanism. Self-report instruments, on the other hand, assess typical performance in behavioral utilization of hearing ability.

Questionnaires may yield either quantitative or qualitative information, depending upon the design of the questionnaire items. **Open-ended questions** typically elicit qualitative data. Examples of open-set items include the following:

Open-ended questions are questions that do not confine responses to a closed set of options as might a *yes–no* question.

- *Describe the situations wherein you typically have problems communicating.*
- *What do you usually do when you do not understand someone?*

Closed-ended questions may be used to gather quantitative or categorical information. An example of a quantitative questionnaire item appears next. On this item, the respondent's task is to write a number between 1 and 10 on each response blank, where 1 means *never* and 10 means *always*:

Closed-ended questions are used to gather quantitative or categorical information.

> *I am at a department store. The clerk asks me a question, but I do not understand her. I am most likely to:*
>
> ______ *ask the clerk to repeat the question*
>
> ______ *ask the clerk to say the question in a different way*
>
> ______ *shake my head to indicate that I missed what the clerk said*
>
> ______ *say and do nothing*

Both kinds of questionnaire items offer advantages and disadvantages. Open-ended items are less restrictive and might yield information from a patient that could not have been anticipated. However, sometimes answers to open-ended items are rambling or off-topic, and they may be difficult to quantify, which may be important if you plan to compare pre- and postintervention performance. Closed-ended items allow for a quantitative analysis of responses. However, important information may be missed if the questionnaire does not include items that tap information relevant to a patient's communication difficulties.

DAILY LOGS

Daily logs are self-reports of behavior used by respondents for self-monitoring.

In completing a **daily log**, respondents perform a self-monitoring procedure regarding behaviors of interest and provide self-reports. For example, they may log how many times a day they experience communication difficulties and in which communication settings (e.g., the home, the workplace). In completing logs, patients may answer a series of questions about their communication difficulties or behaviors every day for a set number of days. Example items from a daily log appear in Table 7–3.

When patients complete a log for several consecutive days, their responses may provide a general index of their daily use of communication strategies, their conversational fluency, and their communication difficulties. Responses also may provide information about their aural rehabilitation needs. For example, if someone reports that he or she never spoke on the telephone during six consecutive days, it might be inferred that this person may be unable to use the telephone successfully and therefore avoids telephone conversations. The aural rehabilitation plan may thus be designed to provide telephone training and a telephone receiver amplifier. Individuals can perform a daily-log activity before and after participating in a communication strategies training program, and trends in responses can be compared before and after training. For example, if after completing a communication strategies training program and after receiving a telephone receiver amplifier, the person reports using the telephone an average of two times every day (compared with never), then it might be concluded that intervention provided benefit.

TABLE 7–3 Example Items from a Daily Log Designed to Monitor Someone's Communication Behaviors

1. **Think about your communication interactions today. For the following situations, circle the term (never, a few times, many times) that best describes how much time you spent talking today (beyond a greeting). Circle one response for each condition:**

In a quiet place	never	a few times	many times
In a noisy place	never	a few times	many times
On the telephone	never	a few times	many times
From another room	never	a few times	many times
In a group of people	never	a few times	many times

2. **For the following two situations, write down a number between 0 and 100 (0 = nothing and 100 = everything) that indicates how much of what was said to you today you believe you understood.**

   _____ while watching the talker and listening

   _____ while listening only

3. **Did you ever indicate that you did not understand a spoken message today? (yes or no)**

   _____

4. **What did you do when you did not understand a message? Check all that apply.**

   _____ I asked the talker to repeat the message.

   _____ I said "Huh" or "Pardon."

   _____ I asked the talker to rephrase the message.

   _____ I asked the talker to indicate what he or she was talking about.

   _____ I decided the message was not important enough to keep trying.

   _____ I asked the talker to spell or write the message.

   _____ Other (describe) ______________________________

5. **Consider the conversations that you had with relatives today. Check all of the statements below that apply.**

   _____ I felt anxious when I tried to talk with my relative today.

   _____ I was able to understand my relative's spoken messages.

   _____ I felt satisfied with the success of our communication interactions.

   _____ I avoided talking about unimportant topics.

Guidelines for Constructing a Daily Log

Although there are a few examples of daily logs for aural rehabilitation applications available in the literature (e.g., Palmer, Bentler, & Mueller, 2006), a speech and hearing professional may have to design them and tailor them to track the pertinent activities and behaviors of each patient. Five guidelines to consider when developing a daily log are:

1. Include detailed instructions at the beginning of the daily log and at the start of each section that initiates a new format. Make the instructions clear and concise.
2. Use active sentences rather than passive sentences when writing daily-log items.
3. Log items should have a minimum of prepositional phrases.
4. Avoid professional jargon or terms used often within the speech and hearing communication field but not by the general public.
5. Limit the number of items in a daily log to a maximum of seven. Otherwise, it may be too taxing for a patient to complete or too much of an imposition in the daily routine.

Self-monitoring can be a **reactive** procedure because it may influence a person's communication behaviors and how he or she uses communication strategies. For example, researchers have shown that when individuals complete self-monitoring diaries, they often improve their academic performance, reduce their consumption of alcohol, or decrease the number of cigarettes smoked (e.g., Johnson & Wilhite, 1971; McFall, 1970). Similarly, by monitoring use of communication strategies, patients may actually improve their use of them. As such, the use of daily logs can be used as a training procedure as well as an assessment procedure. However, for this very reason, it can be problematic when someone is trying to assess the effects of an intervention program.

Reactive is acting in response to a stimulus or an experience rather than initiating or controlling it; procedure, such as self-monitoring, that may influence how a person uses communication behaviors and strategies.

GROUP DISCUSSION

In a **group discussion** (Figure 7–3), usually convened on the first meeting of a communication strategies training program, members of the class construct a list of their communication problems and the topics they would like included in the syllabus. The remainder of the program then focuses on these issues. This procedure can be used any time that instruction occurs in a group setting as opposed to one-on-one. Table 7–4 lists some concerns that have emerged during this kind of group session.

Group discussion provides a forum for class members to discuss communication issues.

FIGURE 7–3 Group discussion. Participants may sit in a semicircle to enhance their ability to speechread each other.

TABLE 7–4 Common Concerns That Might Be Identified During a Group Discussion

- Difficulty talking on the telephone
- Impatience on the part of a spouse
- Inability to manage communication breakdowns effectively
- Avoidance by old friends
- People talk to my spouse instead of me
- Feelings of isolation and loneliness
- Feelings of incompetence and anger
- Difficulty conversing in noisy settings
- Difficulty in communicating with my coworkers
- Anxiety about not being able to hear warning signals
- Frustration that family does not understand my hearing loss
- Frustration that most people do not know what it is like to have a hearing loss
- Feelings of being "left out"

Source: Adapted from Trychin, S. (1994). Helping people cope with hearing loss. In J. G. Clark & F. N. Martin (Eds.), (pp. 247–277). Englewood Cliffs, NJ: Simon & Schuster.

Tips on Conducting a Group Discussion

The success (or failure) of a group discussion often hinges on the skill of the speech and hearing professional who conducts the session. Procedures that might be followed when conducting a group discussion include the following:

- Establish the ground rules at the very beginning. Ground rules might include *Avoid interruptions* and *Raise your hand before you speak so everyone will be looking at you when you start talking.*
- Encourage everyone to participate in the discussion, perhaps by asking group members to take turns one at a time around the table.
- Record remarks on a whiteboard, on an overhead projector slide, or on an oversize hanging notebook, even if they seem off-topic or minor.
- Make sure that no one is made to feel embarrassed or foolish for making a contribution.
- Ask some questions that guide the discussion and engage the students in the discussion. For example, you might say, "Mrs. Smith, you work in a pharmacy. What kinds of listening difficulties do you experience when you are behind the counter?"
- Come to the class prepared to draw specific material from the participants.

Structured communication interactions are simulated conversations used to reflect a patient's communication difficulties.

TOPICON is an example of a structured communication interaction activity. The clinician and patient are independently provided with conversational topics. One of them selects a topic and initiates a conversation about it. The two then conduct a brief conversation on the chosen topic, during which the clinician monitors and evaluates the events. The clinician might evaluate "naturalness" and "topic maintenance" and might maintain a count of communication breakdowns.

Example topics for *Topicon*:

Babies
Types of cheese
Going shopping
Tennis
Books
Today's news
Car repair

(Erber, 1996, p. 92)

STRUCTURED COMMUNICATION INTERACTIONS

Structured communication interactions also can be used during both assessment and training. **Structured communication interactions** are simulated conversations that reflect some of the difficulties that actually occur in a patient's typical day. ***TOPICON*** (Erber, 1988) is an example of a structured communication interaction activity that may be used for both assessment and training purposes. In this procedure, the patient carries on a conversation with the clinician. The clinician monitors and evaluates conversational difficulties that occur. Afterward, the clinician and student discuss the fluency of the interaction. They talk about the problems that arose and alternative ways of handling them. They consider who spoke more during the interaction and why. They discuss the direction of information flow and they identify which communication strategies were applied and whether or not they were effective. Conversation fluency can be evaluated with a consideration of the following: (a) number of prolonged pauses, (b) number of restarts, (c) number of topic shifts, (d) interruptions of turn-taking, (e) level of abstraction and superficiality, (f) presence of self-consciousness, and (g) the degree of understanding (Erber, 1988, p. 79).

Another kind of structured communication interaction activity is called **referential communication** and concerns the transmission of information between two communication partners. For example, both patient and clinician might sit before an array of photographs. The clinician describes one of the photographs. The patient's task is to identify the intended referent. When the patient does not understand one of the clinician's descriptions, he or she is expected to use repair strategies.

During a **referential communication** interaction, one communication partner is expected to convey information to another partner by means of an interactive exchange.

UNSTRUCTURED COMMUNICATION INTERACTIONS

As the name implies, an unstructured communication interaction is a fairly spontaneous interaction that has few external constraints. Typically, it is a free-flowing conversation

Question–Answer Sessions (Quest?AR)

Quest?AR is a structured communication procedure that can be used to assess communication difficulties. In the procedure, the clinician asks a series of scripted questions, and the patient responds. Occasionally, listening difficulties are added to induce communication breakdowns. Performance is then evaluated in terms of the frequency of communication breakdowns, and the patient's facility in repairing them. An example of the procedure is presented next (quoted from Erber & Lind, 1994, p. 280).

	Difficulty Added	Difficulty Identified
1. Why did you go there?	______	______
2. When did you go?	______	______
3. How many people went with you?	______	______
4. Who were they (relations/names)?	______	______
5. What did you take with you?	______	______
6. Where is (the place where you went)?	______	______
7. How did you get there?	______	______
8. What did you see on the way?	______	______
9. What time did you get there?	______	______

Quest?AR is a structured communication procedure that can be used to assess communication difficulties.

between a patient and a communication partner that is most often scored after the fact, although sometimes it is evaluated as it unfolds. In order to ensure that communication breakdowns occur, a clinician might decide to use an **elicitation technique**. To observe a patient's use of a receptive repair strategy, a clinician might purposely mumble an utterance and see what happens next. The advantage of using elicitation is that a clinician can ensure that a communication breakdown occurs; the disadvantage is that the breakdown is not genuine. A patient might think that the clinician is "teasing" or might grow impatient, especially if communication breakdowns are induced several times during the conversation. Thus, the results may have reduced ecological validity.

To ensure that communication breakdowns occur during an unstructured interaction, the clinician might use an **elicitation technique** and purposely induce a communication breakdown.

Unstructured conversations can be assessed informally or more formally. At least two ways have been developed to evaluate unstructured communication interactions: transcription analysis and ratings. Both ways typically entail obtaining an audio-videotape recording of the patient engaged in conversation with a communication partner (although sometimes for the rating procedure, or *Dyalog*, the analysis is scored on the spot). The partner might be a frequent communication partner, such as a spouse, an offspring, or a parent, or an unfamiliar communication partner, such as a clinician or a naive communication partner. This latter kind of partner is someone who is unfamiliar to the patient and is also naive about hearing loss. The use of different types of communication partners may indicate how conversational dynamics vary as a function of the familiarity of the partner.

The conversation sample is typically recorded in a quiet room or a room with background noise (e.g., music playing on a radio to induce communication breakdowns). The camera is mounted on a tripod and turned on, and then the camera operator leaves the room so the patient and communication partner can begin to converse. The conversation might be stimulated with the use of "conversation cards" that list topics to talk about. For example, topics might consist of the following:

- What did you do last weekend?
- Where are you going this summer?
- What is your favorite restaurant?
- Do you have any hobbies?
- Tell me about your family.

Transcription Analysis

During **transcription analysis**, conversation is transcribed word for word and then analyzed.

In the **transcription analysis** method of evaluation, the conversation is transcribed word for word and then analyzed. There are at least two approaches for performing a transcription analysis. One is more typically used by social psychologists and the other is more typically used by sociolinguists. Both have been used by researchers and clinicians who are interested in aural rehabilitation.

Social psychologists who study conversations often implement counting and statistical techniques that involve coding certain speech events into predefined categories. For example, they might count the number of communication breakdowns that occurred during the conversation, the number of turn exchanges required to resolve the breakdowns, the number of interruptions, the number of fillers, and the number of different topics discussed. A clinician who is interested in how communication strategies training affected the conversational fluency between a patient and the significant communication partner might quantitatively compare such numbers derived from conversational interactions that were collected before and after training.

Dyalog is a computer-based technique that analyzes conversations, and may include measuring the length of speaking turns and silences by means of pressing a keyboard.

A computer-based technique, which was first developed by Erber (called **Dyalog**, 1998) and requires a computer program, permits relatively fast analyses of unstructured communication interactions and is a variation of the social psychology approach. The clinician watches the conversation from one to three times, depending on how much information is desired. In the three-times version, the clinician first watches it for the purpose of recording talk time for the patient. Every time the patient begins talking, the clinician presses the space bar of the computer keyboard. When the patient stops talking, the clinician releases the space bar. In the second viewing, the clinician records the intervals in which the communication partner talked. Finally, for the third viewing (and the first viewing if only watching one time), the clinician, who by now is well familiarized with the interaction, presses the space bar at the onset of a communication breakdown and releases it at the offset of the breakdown. The following information is then computed: mean length turn in seconds for the patient, mean length turn for the communication partner, MLT ratio, time spent in silence, time spent in communication breakdown, and average length of communication breakdown. Heydebrand et al. (2005) used Dyalog to evaluate the effects of psychosocial support on the occurrence of communication breakdowns between cochlear implant users and their frequent communication partners.

Sociolinguists are typically concerned with how conversational partners collaborate to conduct meaningful conversation, how they manage turn-taking, and how they repair breakdowns in communication. In their approach to transcription analysis, they attempt to describe how communication partners understand and respond to one another and how communication partners "display in their sequentially 'next' turns an understanding of what the 'prior' turn was about" (Hutchby & Wooffitt, 2008, p. 13). For example, the question "What?" can serve at least two functions in the following exchange. It can indicate noncomprehension:

Husband: I bought a fishing rod at the outlet store.
Wife: What?

Husband: I bought a fishing rod at the outlet store.

Alternatively, the question can represent a protest, as in this exchange:

Husband: I paid five hundred dollars for tickets to the baseball game.

Wife: What?

Husband: Hey, our team will probably never go to the World Series again.

The husband's response to his wife's question reveals the wife's intent, which was different in the two exchanges despite being the same response. In the first example, it was a nonspecific repair strategy and in the second, it was a remonstration. This kind of analysis focuses on the organization of turn-taking, and includes the number and length of conversational turns for each conversational partner and the units that correspond to linguistic or pragmatic categories (Beattie, 1983). Researchers have performed this kind of analysis to gauge the effects of repair strategies on communication partners (e.g., Lind, Hickson, & Erber, 2006). A clinician might use this kind of analysis to determine whether assertiveness training affected the ways in which a patient interacts with a frequent communication partner.

Ratings

A second way to analyze an unstructured communication interaction is to obtain ratings from trained students or clinicians. The observer watches the sample and then assigns a number from 1 (poor) to 4 (good) to indicate how smoothly the conversation flows without the need for clarification (Erber, 1996). This kind of rating gives a gross assessment of overall fluency and has proven to be a reliable measure both within and between raters.

THE SIGNIFICANT OTHER

Significant others experience numerous difficulties because of a patient's hearing loss, including having to repeat themselves during conversations, having to cope with the high volume of the television set, and having to respond or interpret on behalf of their partner. They often experience a restricted social life because of their partner's hearing loss and they may experience more negative emotions and experience them more often, including stress, irritation, and anxiety (e.g., Brooks, Hallam, & Mellor, 2001; Hétu, Jones, & Getty, 1993; Hétu et al., 1988; Stephens, France, & Lormore, 1995). As noted in Chapter 1, the World Health Organization's International Classification of Functioning describes the effect of hearing loss on the patient's partner or spouse as a third-party disability: Even though the frequent communication partner does not have a hearing loss, the person can experience activity limitations and participation restrictions because of the patient's hearing loss.

Questionnaires are available to measure third-party disability and third-party HLQoL for spouses and partners of patients with hearing loss (Preminger & Meeks, 2012; Scarinci et al., 2009a). Examples of items that might probe participation restrictions include the following (Preminger & Meeks, 2012, p. 819, called *social impact* factors in the questionnaire):

- *Do you feel that your SO's [significant other] hearing loss hampers your social life?*
- *Do you and your SO avoid going to restaurants because of your SO's hearing loss?*

Sample items that probe activity limitations include the following (called *relationship and emotions* factors in the questionnaire):

- *Do you feel that your SO's hearing loss has a negative effect on the intimate communication between the two of you?*
- *Because of your SO's hearing loss, do you talk less often than you used to?*

Sample items that probe emotions tied to the partner's hearing loss include the following (called *relationship and emotions* factor in the questionnaire):

- *Do you get irritated when you try to talk with your SO but she/he cannot understand you?*
- *Does your SO's hearing loss make you feel frustrated?*

You May Be the One with the Hearing Loss but It Is My Problem Too

Hearing loss affects the psychosocial status and quality of life of not only the patient, but also the patient's spouse or partner. Increasingly, when communication difficulties are assessed, the spouse or partner is included in the assessment. Questionnaires or interviews may reveal any of the following effects, emotions, or reactions experienced by the spouse as a result of the patient's hearing loss (see Preminger & Meeks, 2012, p. 809, for a review):

- Increased anxiety and stress
- Exertion of more effort to converse, including having to talk louder and more slowly, having to repeat themselves and help repair communication breakdowns, and having to obtain the patient's attention before beginning to speak
- Changes in social activities, including avoidance of restaurants, social gatherings, and parties because the patient is uncomfortable in such settings
- Resentment because they have to serve as an interpreter (e.g., at a physician's visit)
- Feelings of irritation, because the television may be too loud or they have to answer the telephone more often
- Feelings of sadness, because conversation is so difficult and happens less often
- Feelings of social isolation, frustration, anger, resentment, and guilt

CASE STUDY

He Says, She Says

When one member of a couple has hearing loss and the other one does not, they may have very different opinions as to how the loss affects both of their lives. Preminger and Meeks (2012) describe a couple who has been married for 10 years. They asked the couple to complete questionnaires about the wife's hearing-related difficulties and about the effects of hearing loss on the husband. The 64-year-old wife has a moderate bilateral sensorineural hearing loss and her 65-year-old husband has normal hearing. The questionnaire responses revealed very different viewpoints. The wife believes her quality of life is greatly impacted by hearing loss, whereas her husband believes she experiences only mild disability. However, because of his wife's hearing loss, the husband feels that he suffers mightily, reporting significant disability stemming directly from her hearing loss.

The investigators suggest, "These high levels of reported disability and incongruence may be a result of the poor communication in the marriage or may be a contributing cause to the poor communication in the marriage. It is likely that this couple would benefit from a comprehensive audiological rehabilitation program" (p. 821).

FINAL REMARKS

It is not uncommon for clinicians to use a **test battery approach** and employ more than one type of assessment procedure. This approach can provide a more well-rounded portrait of communication difficulties than the use of a single measure. However, a clinician needs to be careful not to overwhelm patients with assessment procedures. For example, if they spend their entire first class of communication strategies training on assessment and do not perceive they have benefited by attending, they are not likely to show up for a second class.

A **test battery approach** employs more than one type of assessment procedure.

KEY CHAPTER POINTS

- Most communication strategies training programs begin and end with an assessment of conversational fluency and hearing-related disability.
- Conversational fluency relates to how smoothly conversation unfolds.
- Hearing-related disability relates to the communication difficulties that arise in daily living activities and includes the psychosocial disadvantages related to the hearing loss.
- Conversational fluency and hearing-related disability are difficult to assess for many reasons. For example, conversational fluency may vary as a function of the communication partner (Is the person familiar? Is the person experienced with talking to people who have hearing loss?) and of the topic of conversation.
- A variety of assessment procedures are available. These procedures include interviews and questionnaires. Each offers both advantages and disadvantages. Often, clinicians opt to use a test battery approach.
- A patient's significant other may complete assessment procedures.

TERMS AND CONCEPTS TO REMEMBER

Sociolinguist
Conversational turn
Mean length of speaking turn (MLT)
Mean length turn ratio (MLT ratio)
Construct
Interview
Generous listening
Hearing loss specific quality of life (HLQoL)
Open-ended questions
Closed-ended questions
Daily log
Reactive
Structured communication
Interactions
Referential communication
Elicitation technique
Transcription analysis
Test battery approach

CHAPTER 8

Communication Strategies Training

OUTLINE

- Self-Efficacy
- Issues to Consider When Developing a Training Program
- Getting Started
- Model for Training
- Program Evaluation
- Short-Term Training
- Communication Strategies Training for Frequent Communication Partners
- Benefits of Training
- Case Study: Patients with an Increased Sense of Self-Efficacy
- Final Remarks
- Key Chapter Points
- Terms and Concepts to Remember
- Key Resources

There are many ways to provide training in the use of communication strategies, ranging from simply making printed materials available in the clinic waiting room to presenting a weekly program that may extend several weeks or even months. Training activities may include paper-and-pencil tasks, role-playing, group discussions, and workbook exercises. When possible, the training program is designed to meet the participants' expectations, age, socioeconomic background, lifestyle, and particular communication problems. Often, communication strategies training is one component of a more comprehensive aural rehabilitation program. For example, a group program for new hearing aid users might consist of four distinct sessions, where the first session is about how to handle and care for a new hearing aid, the second session is about communication strategies, and the third and fourth sessions are about psychosocial support and assertiveness.

In this chapter, we will walk through the process of developing a communication strategies program and consider how to assess its effectiveness. Then we will review research related to the effectiveness of communication strategies training.

In the next chapter, we will consider psychosocial support and assertiveness training. Sometimes, communication-strategies training is blended together with group psychological support and assertiveness training, using a hybrid of the model we will consider in this chapter and the problem-solving framework that we will consider in the next chapter (see Figure 9–13).

The content of a communication strategies training program or session typically concerns problems specifically related to hearing loss and how these problems can be minimized. Content may include training for the two types of communication strategies, facilitative and repair (Chapter 6). Participants typically learn about assertive versus nonassertive behaviors too, and work on developing their skills to deal assertively with communication difficulties (Chapter 9).

Vocational Rehabilitation Programs

In addition to including communication strategies training, a vocational program may also address the issues of hearing aids and other assistive technology, workplace accommodations and environmental management, stress management, training for coworkers and supervisors, and empowerment and supervisor support (see Gussenhoven et al., 2013, for a review). As an example, the program described by Kramer (2008) includes a workplace visit to measure noise levels and to identify listening challenges, provision of hearing aids and assistive devices, and specific recommendations for the workplace environment, including furniture placement, and elimination of noisy machines. Suggestions for how to modify the daily routine, such as elimination of nonessential job functions and inclusion of rest breaks, may also be offered. The program also includes instruction about how best to use communication strategies.

SELF-EFFICACY

Self-efficacy is confidence that a person has for performing a particular task; belief in one's ability to do something.

One goal of a communication strategies training program may be to enhance patients' sense of self-efficacy. **Self-efficacy** is someone's belief that he or she can succeed in performing a task, independent of external odds. It is domain specific. A person may believe that he or she can swim 100 meters in an Olympic-size swimming pool but not in the open ocean. Self-efficacy may or may not be grounded in a sense of self-worth or in reality. Someone who believes that he or she is a great swimmer might actually sink like a stone in a shallow pool. People with a high degree of self-efficacy believe that they have the ability to problem-solve, participate in challenging activities, adapt to changing situations, plan and execute goals, and in general engage in **coping** behaviors.

In aural rehabilitation, self-efficacy refers to patients' beliefs about their abilities to manage difficult communication situations and their beliefs that they can plan and execute a course of action that will improve their communicative interactions in a given environment. Sense of self-efficacy can influence a patient's willingness to engage in activities and conversations. It can influence the efforts patients will invest into completing an activity and the time that they will devote to an activity or challenging communication situation. The higher the sense of self-efficacy, the more determined and perseverant will be a person in the face of obstacles or challenges:

> As hearing care professionals, we often spend a lot of time providing information about hearing loss or hearing aids, how they work, and how to troubleshoot; we don't typically spend much time determining how confident the patient feels about executing our recommendations. This is where we should be focusing our interventions: knowing how confident the patient is to carry out the required new behavior is actually more important than knowing if the patient is motivated.
>
> (Gregory, 2011a, p. 29)

To increase self-efficacy with verbal persuasion:

- Use didactic training to explain.
- Provide realistic feedback focused on patient capabilities or effort.
- Encourage the involvement of a significant other.
- Make accurate and convincing comments about the ease of learning the skills.

(Quoted in part from Smith & West, 2006, p. 52)

Coping refers to a patient's mental and behavioral efforts to manage difficult or demanding situations, even when a situation is perceived as taxing or beyond the person's resources.

Ways to Bolster Self-Efficacy

A clinician can explicitly provide at least four types of experiences during a patient's aural rehabilitation journey to bolster self-efficacy (Bandura, 1994):

Participation in a communication strategies training program may bolster patients' self-efficacy as well as provide patients with concrete means to alleviate communication difficulties.

1. *Mastery experience*: Direct experience in a successful communication interaction is perhaps the most powerful source of self-efficacy. If a patient practices using a repair strategy many times in a safe and comfortable setting and often experiences success when doing so, the patient will likely acquire a sense of mastery and high self-efficacy for this task.
2. *Vicarious experience*: Direct observation of others succeeding can bolster the patient's belief that he or she too can succeed. If a patient watches two other patients resolve a difficult communication situation effectively, the patient might end up thinking, "Hey, I can do that too."
3. *Verbal persuasion*: You might tell or logically explain to your patient that communication difficulties can be managed and that a patient has the tools necessary to manage them. A frequent communication partner can also participate in verbal persuasion. For example, A man with hearing loss will likely have greater self-efficacy if his spouse expresses confidence in his ability to communicate successfully at a noisy party than a man whose spouse frets that his inability to follow conversation might lead to embarrassment.
4. *Emotional arousal*: If a patient breaks out into a cold sweat at the very thought of attending a social event, then that patient probably judges his or her self-efficacy to be low. Activities that lower a person's arousal, such as relaxation or breathing activities, might enhance perceived self-efficacy.

Assessing Self-Efficacy

Questionnaires have been developed to assess patients' self-efficacy for hearing-related issues (e.g., Jennings, 2005; Smith & Fagelson, 2011; Smith, Pichora-Fuller, Watts, & La More, 2011; West & Smith, 2007) and at least one, the Self-Efficacy for Situational Communication Management Questionnaire (SESMQ) (Jennings, 2005), was designed specifically to assess the success of a group aural rehabilitation program for increasing students' sense of self-efficacy in everyday communication situations (Jennings, Cheesman, & Laplante-Lévesque, 2014).

These questionnaires differ from the self-assessment questionnaires considered in the last chapter because they assess patients' beliefs or confidence in their current abilities to succeed in a communication activity rather than their perception of the presence or magnitude of hearing-related communication difficulties. These questionnaires may be useful in identifying those situations where patients need assistance and for assessing how an aural rehabilitation intervention may have affected self-efficacy. Self-efficacy questionnaires typically share common features (Bandura, 2001):

- They have *I can* items rather than *I will* items, so to express current capabilities rather than future expectations.
- The questionnaire items target one behavior at a time because self-efficacy can vary for different behaviors simultaneously.
- They include items that assess varying levels of difficulty, as self-efficacy can vary depending on the level of challenge.

These features are demonstrated in the Listening Self-Efficacy Questionnaire (LSEQ). On a scale ranging from 0% to 100%, where 0% corresponds to *I cannot do this at all* and 100% corresponds to *I am certain I can do this,* respondents complete *I can* items such as the following, which query about listening situations that present an increasingly challenging level of difficulty (Smith et al., 2011, p. 422):

- I can understand conversation spoken by a person I know well, such as a close friend or family member.
- I can understand one-on-one conversation while at a medical appointment.
- I can understand one-on-one conversation with continuous background noise, such as a fan.
- I can understand one-on-one conversation when a person is speaking from another part of the house.
- I can understand one-on-one conversation when several conversations are going on at the same time.

The SESMQ asks respondents to indicate on a 10-point scale how well they can hear in a particular situation, such as when talking on the bus to a stranger who covers his or her mouth with one hand. Respondents then rate how confident they are in managing the situation on a second 10-point scale. A range of situations is polled, including talking with a friend or family in a quiet room or at a noisy wedding reception and attending a public lecture with no front-row seating.

Sensitivity to People's Self-Perceptions

"[Speech and hearing professionals] may find it particularly helpful when working with hard-of-hearing adults and their families to remember that how people perceive communication problems (i.e., their meaning or significance to the people involved) is a very important factor to consider. For example, some hard-of-hearing people believe that, due to their hearing loss, they are a burden on other people, and this belief leads them to withdraw from social contact and also probably leads to depression. As another example, many people believe that hearing aids correct hearing problems to the same degree that glasses correct visual problems. It is difficult for people holding this belief to understand why a person wearing hearing aids does not understand what is being said, and it does not occur to them to think about doing anything else to remedy the situation. So, included in the [communication strategies training] programs I conduct are some ways to help people separate fact from fiction pertaining to hearing loss, and methods for helping hearing-impaired people develop a more realistic appraisal of themselves and their hearing problem" (Trychin, 1994, p. 248).

ISSUES TO CONSIDER WHEN DEVELOPING A TRAINING PROGRAM

In addition to developing the course curriculum and content, additional issues must be considered, including the optimal program length and format (Figure 8–1). Some people will have minimal time to devote to a communication strategies training program and 1 hour may be all that is available. Standard programs that include communication strategies in addition to other aurel rehabilitation topics (e.g., introduction to a new hearing aid, assertiveness training) usually require 12 to 40 hours, and are presented in one of two formats. The course may provide intensive instruction during a weekend-long period, meeting 4 to 7 hours per day, or may be spread over a 6- to 15-week period, with each session lasting a couple of hours each week. Change takes time, so multiple sessions held over a period of time probably leads to the most long-lasting changes. Moreover,

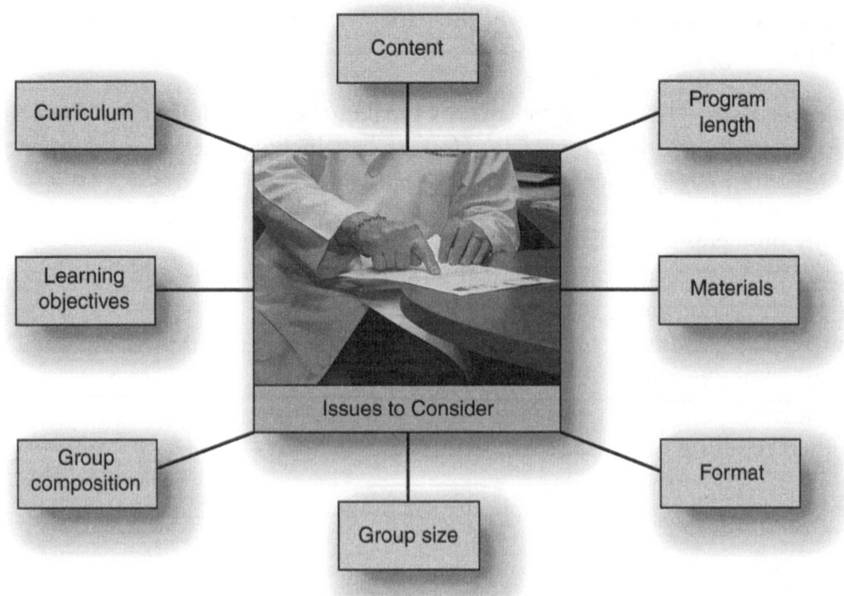

FIGURE 8–1 Issues to consider when designing a group aural rehabilitation program.

The Ida Institute website offers resources for clinicians to help them develop and conduct a group aural rehabilitation program. The following website addresses provide specific topic content (you may have to create an account first in order to access these pages, which can be done at no charge):

- To view videotapes of actual aural rehabilitation group sessions, visit: https://idainstitute.com/tools/group/resources/preparation_and_planning/group_ar_session_intro/
- To learn about value and reimbursement, visit: https://idainstitute.com/tools/group/resources/preparation_and_planning/value_and_reimbursement/
- To learn about group composition, visit: https://idainstitute.com/tools/group/resources/preparation_and_planning/group_composition/
- To learn about program evaluation, visit: https://idainstitute.com/tools/group/resources/preparation_and_planning/program_evaluation/
- To learn about facilitation and methods, visit: https://idainstitute.com/tools/group/resources/facilitation_and_methods/
- To learn about topics and activities, visit: https://idainstitute.com/tools/group/resources/topics_and_activities/
- To learn about group aural rehabilitation classes for parents and teenagers, visit: https://idainstitute.com/tools/group/resources/special_audiences/

participants will have an opportunity to mull over issues arising in one class and return to them in the next, be it a possible strategy for dealing with a communication problem or an emotion about hearing loss that has been heretofore repressed or ignored.

Communication strategies training may be provided during a one-on-one class, a couples session, or in a group. Group sessions are particularly effective because people interact with other people who have hearing loss, as well as interact with their family members. Defenses and recriminations between a patient and a family member may subside when they recognize that other families share common experiences and when they share solutions with people who are in similar situations.

An optimum group size is about 8 to 10 participants, enough people so there is variety in terms of experiences and suggestions but not so many that all participants do not receive time in the "spotlight." Although not always feasible, the group might be tailored so the participants have commonalities in terms of their age and stage of life and their listening device experience and degree of hearing loss.

GETTING STARTED

Before the first session, the clinician usually develops a curriculum and collects materials that will be used during the program. Sample curricula include those presented in *Speechreading: A Way to Improve Understanding* (Kaplan, Bally, & Garretson, 1985), *Learning to Hear Again with a Cochlear Implant* (Wayner & Abrahamson, 1998), *Learning to Hear Again* (Wayner & Abrahamson, 1996), and *Active Communication Education (ACE): A Program for Older Persons with Hearing Impairment* (Hickson, Worrall, & Scarinci, 2006a; Hickson, Worrall, & Scarinci, 2007). The **Ida Institute** offers a curriculum and an array of tools that can be used in a group aural rehabilitation program (https://idainstitute.com/tools/group/) and provides a video of a sample group session called *Proceedings of a Typical Group AR Session* (http://idainstitute.com/toolbox/university_course/videos_and_hanouts/unit_iii/.

Although a curriculum provides a loose blueprint of what will happen in the class, it should be flexible enough to meet the needs of the class participants. A cardinal rule for a communication strategies training program, or any aural rehabilitation plan, is that it should cater to the specific concerns of the patient(s), experienced at the point of time that he or she engages in the program.

Learning **objectives** will guide the content of a program. For example, one communication-strategies program, entitled *Living with Hearing Loss*, includes the following course objectives (Trychin, 2012a). Participants will be able to:

- Identify problems experienced by people who have hearing loss.
- Identify problems experienced by their family members, friends, and coworkers.
- Identify the major causes of communication problems.
- Identify the psychosocial and mental health risks associated with hearing loss.
- List guidelines for effective communication.
- Suggest effective strategies and tactics for preventing communication problems and their resulting psychosocial consequences.

Materials that might be needed to conduct the program may include:

- Name tags
- Handouts and diagrams
- Whiteboard and whiteboard markers
- Videotapes and PowerPoint presentations

The Ida Institute lists several suggestions about how to publicize a group aural rehabilitation program (https://idainstitute.com/tools/group/get_started/):

- Give brochures to your patients.
- Post an announcement on social media, such as Craigslist.
- Submit an announcement to a local newspaper's "community events" section.
- Participate in a community health care fair.
- Speak at elderly centers, libraries, and other community centers.

The **Ida Institute** is a non-profit organization that sponsors a website (https://idainstitute.com), which provides free tools and resources designed to promote person-centered hearing health care worldwide.

A learning **objective** is a result, ideally one that is measurable, which is expected within a particular time period or after a lesson or training program.

TABLE 8–1 Attributes of an Optimal Class Spirit

1. Every class member accepts every other class member with an appreciation of the individual's strengths and a tolerance of the individual's quirks and weaknesses.
2. There is a familiarity of approach among the members of the class, with an awareness of each person's hearing difficulties and backgrounds.
3. Contributions from each class member are encouraged and recognized.
4. Class members can communicate easily with one another, possibly with the use of assistive listening devices.
5. There is acceptance of and conformity to a code of behavior (e.g., "only one person may speak at a time"), usually involving courtesy, mutual respect, and empathy.
6. There is an ability to recognize and use wisely the experiences of individual class members to educate other participants in the class.
7. There is a clear definition of the class agenda and format so each individual knows what to expect.
8. Discussion remains focused, and comments are not made to distract the class.
9. Class members are encouraged to be specific and to use examples.

Source: Adapted from Houle, C. O. (1997). *Governing boards.* San Francisco, CA: Jossey-Bass.

- Planned communication scenarios for role-playing
- FM or infrared system, overhead projector, and PowerPoint
- Workbooks and homework materials

Ideally, the classroom or therapy room will be equipped with a round table, so participants can sit in close proximity and clearly see each other's faces.

When working with groups, it is important to develop a group spirit and esprit de corps and to establish a secure and safe environment so that participants feel comfortable in sharing their feelings and their solutions with one another. The Key Resources presents a class handout for establishing ground rules. Table 8–1 presents attributes of a class group where participants receive optimal benefit from participation

The first session usually begins with an "icebreaker" activity so that everyone feels comfortable in sharing and talking with one another. The group leader might ask a set of simple questions that establish common ground, such as *What do you like to do in your spare time?* and *How long have you lived in [name of your city] and what brought you here?*

After introductions, a common way to begin a communication strategies training program is to ask participants to identify those situations or predicaments in which they most frequently experience communication difficulties. In a group setting, this may be done by going around the table person by person, asking each one to talk about why he or she is attending the class, and when and where and with who each experiences communication difficulties. For example, one person may feel that group meetings at work pose the greatest challenge. Another person may remark that listening to her granddaughter on the telephone is frustrating. These specific examples can be the focus of problem-solving exercises. Participants can brainstorm about how to facilitate communication within specific environments that are problematic for them and how to facilitate communication with specific people whom they interact with on a regular basis.

MODEL FOR TRAINING

The model presented in Figure 8–2 provides a framework for conceptualizing the stages of communication strategies training. The first stage entails formal instruction, the second stage centers around guided learning, and the third stage involves real-world practice. The program may progress through the three stages sequentially or may loop back to a previous stage to reinforce a concept or an idea.

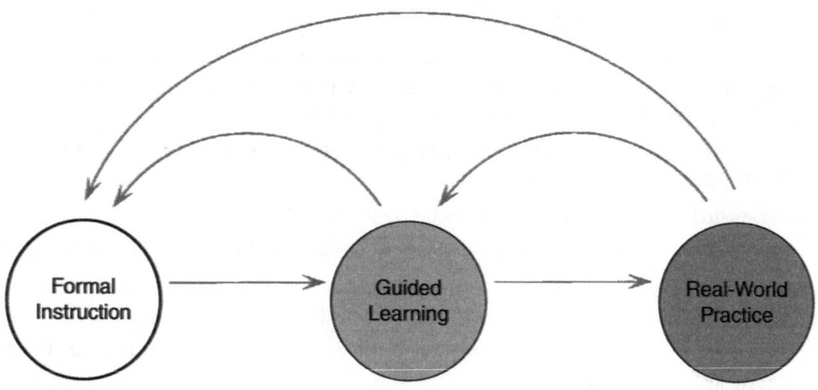

FIGURE 8–2 A framework for conceptualizing the stages of communication strategies training. *Source*: Adapted From Witt, S. (1997). *Effectiveness of an intensive aural rehabilitation program for adult cochlear implant users: A demonstration project*. Unpublished master's thesis, University Of Iowa, Iowa City.

Formal Instruction

Example of a Formal Instruction Training Activity

When sections on passive, aggressive, and assertive conversational behaviors are included in the content of a communication strategies training program, participants reflect on their own styles of handling communication difficulties and consider alternative, perhaps more effective, styles. Following is a paper-and-pencil exercise from Kaplan et al. (1985) that asks respondents to identify communication styles exhibited in each situation. Answers and discussion are provided afterward.

A. "Penny entered the office of her boss, the dean. She noticed it was dark and probably it would be hard to speechread. She pushed past the dean's desk (he was sitting at it!) and opened the blinds. Then she sat down and said, 'Let's get this meeting over with.'"

B. "Wilma replaced the battery in her hearing aid and entered the classroom for the course she signed up for, Feminism in the Deaf Community. She immediately noticed that the room was arranged with desk-chairs in a circle. She was relieved to think that this would facilitate speechreading. However, when the rapid-fire discussions began, she had difficulty identifying which of the 22 participants was speaking. Although she was really interested in the topic, she dropped the course the next week."

C. "Harry stopped at his instructor's office after the first day of his geometry class. He was feeling really frustrated because he was unable to understand the questions being asked of the instructor by class members in front of him; he couldn't see their lips. The instructor suggested he move to the front row and look back at the questioners. The next day he was back again. 'I still have a problem,' he admitted. 'I can't identify the speaker quickly enough to speechread. Could we ask the questioners to identify themselves by holding up their hands a little bit longer?' Harry was able to follow class discussions after that."

Answers

A. Aggressive. Penny's behavior was both rude and demanding.

B. Passive. Wilma didn't try to solve her problem; she gave up on it.

C. Assertive. Harry recognized his problem and worked it out with his instructor (pp. 37–38).

During **formal instruction**, the group leader might ask people to talk about ways they manage their communication difficulties, perhaps in the context of the communication difficulties that the group has just identified. For example, someone in a group might say, "I have difficulty understanding speech in a noisy restaurant. Since I have to eat out a lot as part of my job, this is a big problem." This remark serves as a springboard for a discussion about facilitative strategies. Participants can suggest strategies they have found to be helpful in this specific situation. Their suggestions can lead to a consideration of constructive and instructional strategies. For each solution generated, the group might analyze and evaluate its potential benefits, drawbacks, feasibility, and acceptability. The group leader may also share specific suggestions that were not generated by group members.

Formal instruction provides individuals with explicit information about various types of communication strategies and appropriate listening and speaking behaviors; the first stage in a communication strategies training program.

Writing participants' ideas and responses on a whiteboard or hanging tablet can serve to stimulate contributions to an ongoing discussion (Figure 8–3). Formal instruction usually is most effective when the group leader engages everyone in a dialogue as opposed to making a formal presentation. A long-winded lecture and advice giving will alienate (and anesthetize) participants.

Formal instruction can be used to convey "bullet points" that can then be expanded during group discussion and guided learning. For example, the program by Kaplan et al. (1985) includes three principles for implementing a repair strategy or facilitative strategy to rectify a communication breakdown:

- *Courtesy*: Use courteous language rather than demanding or angry language. (*Could you please . . . ?*)
- *Explanation*: Admit the problem and explain why a situation is difficult. (*I have a hearing loss, and I missed that last word you said.*)
- *Direction*: Do not expect the communication partner to know how to repair a communication breakdown. (*Can you face me when you speak? I understand more when I can watch your lips.*)

FIGURE 8–3 Facilitating group discussions. Whiteboards or hanging tablet can be used to write down ideas and to stimulate discussion during formal instruction.

During a formal consideration of anticipatory strategies, the group leader might ask participants to identify an upcoming event that will pose communication problems (e.g., a holiday office party). Then, using the whiteboard, the group leader will have the group first list what kind of communication difficulties might occur (e.g., loud music will be playing) and then generate anywhere from 5 to 10 solutions for overcoming each difficulty (e.g., find a quiet spot to talk, try to talk one-on-one with other guests and not in a group).

This Isn't Group Therapy

It is important to keep the focus on communication strategies and problem solving during a communication strategies program. As Trychin (1994) notes, "Although the content discussed during class sessions is highly personal and often elicits strong emotional responses, we make every effort to keep an educational focus and to avoid becoming a therapy group and to avoid lapsing into a mutual-sympathy group" (p. 249). His techniques to accomplish this include the following:

- *At the onset of the program, clearly state and write down the goals and objectives*: Impress upon participants that the program will afford them an opportunity to learn and practice effective communication strategies and behaviors, and that they will receive feedback about how well they are using them.
- *Focus on problem-solving and concrete alternative strategies for dealing with communication problems*: Before the discussion devolves into hand-wringing, bring it back on track by saying, "What can be done about it?" or, "Here's what I've tried that works."
- *Keep the focus on communication problems that are hearing-related and maintain an educational orientation*: "It is not always easy to distinguish between those problems that are due to hearing loss, those that are exacerbated by hearing loss, and those that are unrelated to hearing loss. But discussing this distinction can help keep people from blaming all their problems on hearing loss" (p. 249).

Guided Learning

In **guided learning**, the second stage in a communication strategies training program, students use conversational strategies in a structured setting.

The purpose of **guided learning** is to encourage participants to use conversational strategies in a structured setting. Activities for guided learning include modeling, role-playing, analysis of videotaped scenarios, attention, and continuous discourse tracking. Any number or combination of these activities can be included.

Modeling

Modeling is the act of representing or demonstrating a behavior.

Modeling is a technique that entails learning by observing. Although traditionally used with children, it can be used with adults as well. After a formal consideration of effective listening behaviors or communication strategies, a clinician might demonstrate them through modeling. When modeling, the clinician explicitly points out what is appropriate and inappropriate about the modeled behaviors and does not assume students will automatically recognize this independently. During modeling, the group leader might ask someone in the group to help demonstrate the use of a repair strategy. The leader might pretend to misunderstand a remark spoken by the participant and then turn to the group and say, "I didn't understand what she said, did you? I'm going to ask her to tell me what she is talking about." (*The leader is asking for a key word repair strategy.*)

When observing a model, students might pick up on two kinds of information, (a) information about behaviors or strategies and (b) information about what happens to someone as a result of using these behaviors and strategies; that is, they may experience **vicarious consequences**. By watching vicarious consequences, students might become less fearful about implementing communication strategies because they realize that they can use them without incurring negative reactions from others.

When students observe the consequences of a model's behaviors, they experience **vicarious consequences**.

Role-Playing

A hypothetical conversational interaction is staged during **role-playing**. Participants practice using communication strategies and other assertive listening behaviors. If possible, the situation parallels one that is relevant to the participants' everyday experiences. Role-playing can heighten patients' sense of self-efficacy in that it provides them with opportunity to experience success in managing communication difficulties.

In **role-playing**, individuals participate in hypothetical real-world situations and interactions.

In a role-playing scenario, the group leader might suggest that he or she and a patient are at a fast-food restaurant. The patient is charged with ordering dinner for the family and the clinician might play the role of cashier. The leader might occasionally speak with inappropriate speaking behaviors, such as mumbling or speaking in profile. The patient must respond to the questions and, when necessary, use facilitative and repair strategies to promote communication. At the end of a role-playing interaction, the group reviews the interaction, talking about what happened, what worked and what did not work, and what communication strategies were implemented.

Here are additional examples of *wrong way/right way* role-playing opportunities from the Ida Institute (see also Trychin, 2003):

Example 1

1. A participant role-plays a wrong way to tell a communication partner about hearing loss.
2. The participants in the group identify and discuss what was wrong.
3. Another participant role-plays the right way to inform a communication partner.
4. The group identifies and discusses why this alternative way is better.

Example 2

1. A participant role-plays the role of a spouse and intervenes when it is obvious that the person with hearing loss is not following the conversation.
2. The participants in the group identify and discuss what was wrong.
3. Another participant role-plays the right way to inform a communication partner.
4. The group identifies and discusses why this alternative way is better.

Example of a Guided Learning Training Activity

Based on the work of Samuel Trychin (1988, 2003, 2012b), the Ida Institute developed a *wrong way/right way* role-playing activity (https://idainstitute.com/tools/university_course/):

"1. Provide a script and have group members act out an interaction where someone is doing something inappropriate or unhelpful.
2. Have the other participants identify what is 'wrong' and discuss why it is 'wrong.'
3. Other participants act out the scene in the 'right way.'
4. Have participants bring up scenarios from their experience that have been a problem.
5. Have group members act out ways of preventing or reducing the problem."

For example, in the wrong way scenario, a participant may bluff and pretend to understand at a party. The participant ends up giving an off-topic remark as a result. After this role-play, the group discusses what went wrong with the bluffing tactic and considers how the participant might have used specific repair strategies. Other class participants then re-enact the party, using the suggested repair strategies.

Role-playing may involve direct instruction, **prompting**, **shaping**, reinforcement, modeling, and feedback. The following interchange between a clinician and patient illustrates each of these components of role-playing, even though the patient is not told explicitly that he will be engaging in "role-playing" per se because some adults balk at the idea of role-playing. Such an interaction might occur in a group setting or in a one-on-one situation:

Prompting serves to inspire a behavior or an utterance; a technique designed to assist an individual in formulating or remembering a remark.

Shaping serves to reinforce those conversational turns that increasingly approximate sought-after behaviors.

Clinician: Suppose you're at a group meeting at work. You miss something the boss says and you think it's probably important. What might you say?

Bennet: I don't know. I haven't ever told him about my hearing loss before, we just don't talk about it, although he probably knows I miss hearing things.

Clinician: Pretend that I'm your boss and there are two more people at the table here. I've just asked you a question but you didn't understand what I said. What might you say to me?

Bennet: I'm not very good at this.

Clinician: This is just practice, go ahead, give it a try. [*prompting*]

Bennet: (grins mischievously): I'd say, I think that's a good idea. [*role-playing*]

Clinician: You're agreeing with me even though you aren't sure what I said. You might be sorry about that if I said something you don't agree with. [*feedback*] Let's see if we can try using one of the repair strategies that we talked about earlier. [*shaping*] There's no need to bluff. [*direct instruction*] See if you can try something like this: "I was looking at my handout here and missed the last part of what you asked. Can you say that part again?" [*modeling*]

Bennet: That sounds okay.

Clinician: Can you try saying something like this?

Bennet: Okay, let's see . . . I didn't get the first part . . .

Clinician: So what would you say?

Bennet: I missed all of that. Could you please repeat that? [*role-playing*]

Clinician: Much better. [*reinforcement*] That was a direct request for what you need. [*feedback*]

In this example, Bennet both has received instruction about how to handle a difficult communication interaction and has practiced implementing the suggestions. Chances are that when the opportunity arises to signal a communication breakdown in a real-world setting, he will be less anxious and less fearful than he would have been otherwise and have a greater sense of self-efficacy. As this example illustrates, role-playing allows a patient to practice feared behaviors without incurring negative consequences.

Attention

The group leader can reinforce formal instruction by focusing group members' attention on both identifying and rectifying environmental problems and on reinforcing appropriate talker behaviors. For example, a man with hearing loss and his wife with normal hearing might be participants in the class. Before speaking, the wife might flicker her fingers and ensure that her husband has turned toward her and is watching her mouth. The leader might observe to the group, "That was an effective strategy in helping him to speechread. She got his attention first, before speaking, so he could watch her lips."

With respect to communication strategies training and assertiveness training, **videotaped scenarios** are recorded vignettes that provide examples of communication interactions that can be used to stimulate discussion about communication strategies and assertive behaviors.

Analysis of Videotapes and Computer-Based Interactions

Videotaped scenarios help patients identify and talk about their communication problems by providing concrete examples. Individuals view videotaped scenarios that contrast inappropriate with appropriate use of communication strategies. For example, one scenario might show a couple in the living room. One person has a hearing loss and the other one does not. The person with normal hearing talks behind a newspaper to the other one. The person with hearing loss accuses the talker of mumbling and leaves the room in anger. The videotape is stopped at this point so that the class can discuss how the person might have effectively implemented an instructional strategy in this context. After the discussion, the class views a second videotape scenario, where the person with hearing loss demonstrates how to use an instructional facilitative strategy appropriately.

Barrier Games

Barrier games, wherein a sender has to transmit key information to a receiver, can provide guided learning experiences (e.g., Lind, 2009b). In a typical barrier game, the sender and receiver sit across from one another at a table, with a barrier such as a short screen or tented notebook positioned on the table top so that neither one can see the other's prop. In a road map barrier game, the sender instructs the receiver to follow a route on the map (Figure 8–4). The receiver must follow the instructions with 100% accuracy. The receiver, who is typically the person with hearing loss, may ask for information and clarification whenever necessary, giving the sender, often the patient's partner or spouse, an opportunity to practice rephrasing, clarifying, and otherwise creatively repair communication breakdowns. Other barrier game tasks may include producing a drawing or geometric shape or moving game pieces around a game board.

FIGURE 8–4 Guided learning. Barrier games provide a guided learning experience, where a sender may have to convey map instructions and the receiver must track the course.

Real-World Practice

Example of a Real-World Training Activity

Topic = Listening for Directions

Instructions: Ask a partner to hide an object somewhere in your house. Then ask your partner for directions for finding it. Only listen as the directions are told to you, and ask for clarification if necessary. After finding the object, answer the following questions:

1. Did you understand the directions?
2. Did you ask for clarification about any part of the directions? If yes, what did you say? How did your partner respond?
3. Did you have any problems in finding the object? If yes, did you ask for more information from your partner? What did you say?

In **real-world practice**, students practice a new skill or behavior in an everyday environment.

The final stage of the training model shown in Figure 8–2 is real-world practice. **Real-world practice** includes activities that students have performed successfully in the classroom as well as some activities that require them to communicate in a setting that is highly motivating, such as the office or a social gathering. Class participants can report back about their successes and problems, and they can share ideas of how to handle problems in the future. Instructions for the activity can be provided to the students in written form, in language that is simple and easily understood. The students might have a means to record their experiences and to share them later with their instructor and other members of their communication strategies training group.

A participant might maintain a calendar like that shown in Table 8–2. The days of the week are listed in the leftmost column, and the patient's frequent communication partners are listed in the row across the top. The participant's task is to indicate when he or she repaired a breakdown in communication by asking the communication partner for a repair. After one week, the group leader or the group as a whole can review the calendar with the participant.

TABLE 8–2 A Calendar for Recording a Real-World Practice Activity

When Did You Repair a Communication Breakdown?

	WIFE	SON	SISTER	COWORKER
Monday	At dinner			Eating lunch in cafeteria
Tuesday		Watching TV		Weekly meeting
Wednesday		Watching TV		On telephone
Thursday	On the drive home from shopping			
Friday			In the car	
Saturday				
Sunday				

An Example of the Communication Strategies Training Model in Practice: Acknowledgment Tactics

Sam Trychin, PhD, a psychologist and someone who himself has hearing loss, has conducted workshops all over the United States and is the author of several books about communication strategies and assertive listening behaviors. Trychin encourages his students to inform unfamiliar communication partners of their hearing loss during their initial conversation. His process for teaching acknowledgment tactics implicitly incorporates the three stages of communication strategies training that we have reviewed here, as well as illustrates how a group leader might go about developing a patient's sense of self-efficacy (Gregory, 2011a).

Formal Instruction and Verbal Persuasion

Trychin begins by providing participants with examples of different ways to tell people about their hearing loss. That is, he provides *formal instruction* about how one might disclose a hearing problem. He also uses verbal persuasion, one of the techniques for developing self-efficacy, wherein he logically explains that conversations will flow more smoothly if the communication partner knows about a patient's hearing loss, and that patients will feel empowered (and less helpless) after they disclose it.

Guided Learning and Vicarious Experience

Next, Trychin encourages participants to practice acknowledgment tactics in a way that makes them feel comfortable. This *guided learning* experience occurs in the safety of the hearing care office or in the context of a workshop conducted with other students who have hearing loss. The guided learning may include modeling, role-playing (including prompting and shaping), and analysis of videotapes (e.g., Trychin, 2003). For example, a role-play might entail a participant introducing the topic of hearing loss to an unfamiliar communication partner, who is played by another student in the class. The participant practices what to say and how to say it, and learns about what reactions to expect and how to respond to them. Trychin provides feedback when a participant performs the task well and offers constructive criticism when the individual discloses the hearing loss in a manner that might turn people off, say, by sounding as if he or she is seeking pity or by coming across as demanding or angry. Students can identify with the successes of others as they watch their classmates role-play and begin to develop the self-confidence that they can do the same. This vicarious experience is another way to develop self-efficacy.

Vicarious Experience and Role-Playing

"When a person sees another individual accomplish a task, the vicarious experience can have a positive impact on self-efficacy. By observing others like themselves perform tasks, patients make judgments about their own capabilities. Seeing people similar to oneself succeed raises an individual's beliefs that he/she can master comparable activities required to succeed. Observing this effective communication behavior [also] provides the observer with information about what to say, how to say it, and that it is socially acceptable."

—Melanie Gregory, senior audiologist at the Ida Institute, Naerum, Denmark

(Gregory, 2011a, p. 32)

Real-World Practice and Mastery Experience

Finally, Trychin asks his students to practice the new behaviors out in the real world, or to engage in *real-world practice* so that "this essential behavior [of disclosing hearing loss] will be incorporated into a patient's repertoire when he/she has succeeded in performing it in the outside world" (Gregory, 2011a, p. 29). These mastery experiences further promote self-efficacy, and patients will begin to believe that they have the skills to implement the acknowledgment tactics they learned during communication strategies training into their daily lives. In keeping with the third stage of the model presented in Figure 8–2, participants are encouraged to keep a "hearing diary," in which they record and chart positive experiences, remaining challenges, and realistic goals. The hearing diary affords a type of self-monitoring, and makes patients cognizant of their successes, which in turn exerts a powerful influence on their sense of self-efficacy. With the hearing diary, it is also possible to set explicit and shared goals to be accomplished between one class and the next and for class participants to have a tangible means to report back progress to fellow students.

PROGRAM EVALUATION

The reasons for evaluating the program are two-fold: (1) To make sure that the curriculum is meeting the needs of the participants and (2) to make improvements in how the program is conducted. A cardinal rule in evaluation is to keep it simple and quick, so neither the participants nor the group leader are bogged down with long forms and analyses.

At the end of the program (or even after each session), you might ask participants to answer simple questions, such as *What did you like about the program and what might be improved?* and *How has your participation in the program altered what you do in your everyday life?* You might also ask them to remember the communication difficulties that they had cited as being problematic at the beginning of the program and then have them comment about how these difficulties have changed as a result of their participation. One tool that can be useful is the Patient Expectation Worksheet (PEW; Palmer & Mormer, 1999), which is administered at the onset of the program and then revisited at the end. Participants list their goals at the onset and consider their success in achieving these goals at the end (Roman, 2018).

One Size Does Not Fit All

"The largest hurdle in group aural rehabilitation is developing effective goals that address the needs of the groups. Harder still is developing activities that appropriately move the entire group towards these goals."

—Aaron M. Roman, AuD, Assistant Professor at West Chester, Pennsylvania

(Roman, 2018, p. 13)

Formal questionnaires such as the International Outcomes Inventory: Alternative Interventions (IOI-AI) (Noble, 2002) can be administered at the end of the program. The IOI-AI comprises seven questions that utilize a 5-point rating scale. Example items are *Think about how much you used the strategies you learnt in the group program over the past 2 weeks. On an average day, how many hours did you use them?* And, *Think about the situation where you most wanted to hear better, before doing the group program. Over the past 2 weeks, how much have the strategies helped in that situation?*

Learning to Disclose a Hearing Loss

Some people are uncomfortable about revealing their hearing loss to others, often for fear of being stigmatized. If disclosing, they might joke about their loss or minimize its consequences. If concealing, they may pretend to understand or isolate themselves. The benefits of disclosing include the following (West, Low, & Stankovic, 2015, p. 195):

- Greater self-esteem
- Better peer relationships
- Lower anxiety levels
- Reasonable benefits and services (e.g., modified work conditions, telecommunications services)
- Support from others who have hearing loss
- Higher quality of life

Whether and how to disclose a hearing loss will of course depend upon the context and the people involved in the conversation, but it is well within the purview of a communication strategies program to provide training in how to disclose, including phrases that can be used. A study of 337 people with hearing loss revealed three ways that people might disclose it (West et al., p. 198):

- Multipurpose disclosure, where they both disclose a hearing loss and provide guidance to the talker to facilitate communication (e.g., "I don't hear as well out of my right ear. Please walk on my left side")

Learning to Disclose a Hearing Loss *(continued)*

- Basic disclosure, where they disclose their hearing loss in simple terms (e.g., "I am hard of hearing")
- Nondisclosure, where they do not explicitly mention hearing loss but they indicate a problem in communication exists (e.g., "Please speak up")

SHORT-TERM TRAINING

For many reasons, an extended program may not be feasible. A patient may not have time to commit to a longer program or the clinic may not have the personnel available to conduct training. In these situations, short-term approaches are available for providing brief communication strategies training. One approach is to provide materials and self-directed instruction. Another approach is to provide a short tutorial.

Materials Approach

The *materials approach* for providing communication strategies training during a brief time interval includes providing printed and recorded materials to the patient and frequent communication partner about communication strategies. This might be accomplished by means of a clinic library, an audio-videotape station, and printed pamphlets.

The library can be established in a small room adjacent to the clinic waiting room or in the waiting area itself. It might include periodicals and books about hearing loss, communication strategies, speech and auditory training activities, and assistive devices. The materials can be read in the waiting room before or after an appointment, or even checked out and returned by mail. A video monitor also might be placed in the library or waiting room. Individuals can view commercially available videos about hearing loss and communication strategies.

Short Tutorial

Another way to provide a brief communication strategies training program is by means of a short tutorial. WATCH is an acronym that Montgomery (1994) coined to describe his short-tutorial communication strategies training program. This program requires about one hour to administer. The acronym represents the following concepts:

WATCH is an acronym for an example of a short-tutorial program of communication-strategies training.

W Watch the talker's mouth, not his eyes.

A Ask specific questions.

T Talk about your hearing loss.

C Change the situation.

H Acquire health care knowledge.

The clinician discusses with the patient each of these concepts in this order.

During the "W" component, the clinician encourages the patient to focus on the talker's mouth for speechreading, as opposed to hand gestures or other items in the communication setting.

During the "A" component, the patient is encouraged to use specific rather than nonspecific repair strategies.

During the "T" component of the program, the clinician discusses the importance of revealing a hearing loss to one's communication partners. A patient can then manage the communication interaction more effectively and implement instructional strategies.

The clinician asks the patient to identify situations in which communication is problematic during the "C" component. Together, they consider possible ways to overcome these problems.

Finally, the clinician provides information about health care and hearing loss resources during the "H" component of the program.

A short program such as WATCH may not always result in a momentous change in how a patient uses communication strategies. However, much of the program's value lies in the fact that simple ideas have been reviewed. The patient might reflect on these ideas and develop them or even become motivated to enroll in a more extended communication-strategies training program.

COMMUNICATION STRATEGIES TRAINING FOR FREQUENT COMMUNICATION PARTNERS

SPEECH

The acronym SPEECH presents a short tutorial about communication strategies for frequent communication partners (Schow, 2001, p. 20):

- **S**potlight your face and keep it visible. Keep your hands away from your mouth so that the hearing-impaired person can get all the visual cues possible. Be sure to face the speaker when you are talking and be at a good distance (5–10 feet). Avoid chewing gum, smoking cigarettes, and other facial distractions when possible. And be sure not to talk from another room and expect to be heard.
- **P**ause slightly between the content portions of sentences. Slow exaggerated speech is as difficult to understand as fast speech. However, speech at a moderate pace with slight pauses between phrases and sentences can allow the hearing-impaired person to process the information in chunks.
- **E**mpathize and be patient with the hearing-impaired person. Try plugging both ears and listen for a short while to something soft that you want to hear in an environment that is distracting and noisy. This may help you appreciate the challenge of having a hearing loss and it should help you be patient if the responses seem slow. Rephrase if necessary to clarify a point and remember, patience and empathy!
- **E**ase their listening. Get the listener's attention before you speak and make sure you are being helpful in the way you speak. Ask how you can facilitate communication. The listener may want you to speak more loudly or more softly, more slowly or faster, or announce the subject of discussion, or signal when the topic of conversation shifts. Be compliant and helpful and encourage the listener to give you feedback so you can make it as easy as possible for him or her.

SPEECH *(continued)*

- **C**ontrol the circumstances and the listening conditions in the environment. Maximize communication by getting closer to the person. If you can be 5 to 10 feet away, that is ideal. Also, move away from background noise and maintain good lighting. Avoid dark restaurants or windows behind you that blind someone watching you.
- **H**ave a plan. When anticipating difficult listening situations, set strategies for communication in advance and implement them as necessary. This might mean that at a restaurant you communicate with the wait staff instead of having your family member or friend who has hearing loss do so.

People with whom a person with hearing loss converses frequently also may benefit from receiving communication strategies training. A frequent communication partner may be a spouse, a son or daughter, a close friend, or a health care provider. The goals of communication strategies training for frequent communication partners are to foster empathy for the difficulty of the speechreading task, encourage the use of appropriate speaking behaviors, learn how to tailor messages so they are easy to recognize, and learn how to repair communication breakdowns effectively. Table 8–3 summarizes topics that may be reviewed.

The Ida Institute website offers resources for clinicians to help them develop a program for frequent communication partners. The following website addresses provide specific topic content:

- To learn more about third-party disability, visit: https://idainstitute.com/tools/communication_partners/
- To view videotapes of actual sessions with frequent communication partners, visit: https://idainstitute.com/tools/communication_partners/the_tools_in_action/
- To listen to lectures about frequent communication partners and to gain more insight into their predicament, visit: https://idainstitute.com/tools/communication_partners/resources/
- To access "tools" that can be used during a program, visit: https://idainstitute.com/tools/communication_partners/get_started/

TABLE 8–3 Content That May Be Included in a Communication Strategies Training Program for Frequent Communication Partners

Appropriate Speaking Behaviors

Frequent communication partners may be encouraged to:

- Speak clearly and slowly.
- Speak with their faces toward the individual with hearing loss.
- Avoid putting objects in or near their mouths while speaking.
- Stand away from windows or bright light sources when talking to someone who has a hearing loss.

Empathy

Frequent communication partners may be asked to consider:

- The difficulty of the speech recognition task when one must rely on a degraded audio signal, perhaps with the use of filtered speech samples.
- The difficulty of the lipreading task, perhaps with the use of silent video clips of people talking or a lipreading test such as the Iowa Sentence Test (Tyler, Preece, & Tye-Murray, 1986).
- How stress and anxiety levels may rise when someone has a hearing loss, and how persons with hearing loss often may experience fatigue and desire social withdrawal.

Organized Messages

Frequent communication partners may be asked to:

- Avoid verbosity and to use concise and syntactically simple sentences. For example, they might say "Let's go to a movie" rather than "I haven't really thought much about it, but I know we aren't doing much on Saturday, so maybe let's go to a movie."
- Avoid ambiguity by using precise terminology. For example, they might say "The sweater is Sarah's" rather than "It's hers."

Comprehension

Frequent communication partners may be encouraged to:

- Ask their partner often if he or she comprehended a message.
- Ask for verification and listen to the person with hearing loss repeat or paraphrase what they have just said.
- Provide feedback about whether the individual correctly recognized the message.

(continues)

TABLE 8–3 *(continued)*

Repair of Communication Breakdowns

Frequent communication partners may receive coaching about how to use repair strategies optimally. Following a communication breakdown, they might:

- Repeat their messages.
- Rephrase their messages and say them in a different way. For example, the sentence "I left" might be rephrased as "I went home."
- Repeat a key word to indicate the topic of conversation. For example, if the sentence "Tom fell down" was not recognized, the communication partner might repair the communication breakdown by saying "Tom. Tom fell down."
- Simplify the message by using fewer words or by using more commonplace words. For example, the sentence "Jane bought a brown bowler hat" might be simplified to "Jane bought a hat."
- Elaborate, by providing more information and repeating important key words. For instance, if the sentence "I cut the paper" was misunderstood, the frequent communication partner might say "I have some scissors. I cut the paper with the scissors."
- Build from the known by presenting information that can easily be recognized to establish a context. For instance, the original sentence might have been "Please put the wallet in my purse." In repairing a communication breakdown, the communication partner might say "Please put the wallet [and then point to the wallet] in my purse" (with a gesture toward a purse).

Communication strategies training for frequent communication partners often is provided at the same time that the patient receives training, frequently within the same class. The Key Resources section presents the content of an aural rehabilitation program that includes both the patient and the significant other, in an instance when they had separate but complimentary classes.

In addition to receiving communication strategies training, spouses and partners also may receive support and counseling from the speech and hearing professional about adjusting to the changes in life quality that occur because of their relatives' or friends' hearing losses. Communication strategies training, along with counseling, may accelerate their adjustment process and reduce third-party disability.

Spouses or partners of persons who have hearing loss or frequent communication partners can learn how to speak with clear speech. In one study, one spouse received instruction about clear speech, which included a description of clear speech (including a discussion of speech rate, precise articulation, pausing, and key word emphasis) (Caissie et al., 2005). He also listened to demonstrations. He then was provided with an opportunity to practice speaking with clear speech and was given feedback about his performance. He was encouraged to practice clear speech for one week with his wife, who has hearing loss, and he received an information booklet describing the procedures. A second spouse who participated in the study was merely told to "speak clearly." Recordings of the two men's speech were presented to a group of 15 research participants who had normal hearing and 15 research participants who had hearing loss. The results showed that the utterances spoken by the talker who had received training were significantly more intelligible than those by the talker who had received no training and this was especially true for the participants who had hearing loss. These results, although from a case study (see Chapter 1 for a review about the limitations of case study findings), suggest that the aural rehabilitation plan might routinely include clear speech training for frequent communication partners.

There are various ways to instruct communication partners in how to speak with clear speech. You might demonstrate clear speech by first speaking sentences with conversational speech and then with clear speech or you might ask a communication partner to imitate your clear speech productions. Instructions about how to produce clear speech vary and might include *speak clearly, speak to someone with a hearing loss or someone who speaks a different language*, and *hyperarticulate.*

BENEFITS OF TRAINING

Only a few experimental investigations have focused on the benefits of communication strategies training and the conclusions are sometimes difficult to interpret (e.g., Aazh & Moore, 2017). The reason for this is probably because communication strategies training is often packaged together with a hearing aid orientation program or a counseling and psychosocial adjustment class. Rarely does the entire content of an aural rehabilitation program consist of communication strategies training. It is also difficult to gauge changes in communication strategy usage (Chapter 7). Many studies have reported a reduction in perceived hearing-related disability following an aural rehabilitation program based on counseling and communication strategies (e.g., Benyon, Thornton, & Poole, 1997; Chisolm, Abrams, & McArdle, 2004; Habanec & Kelly-Campbell, 2015; Heydebrand, Mauzé, Tye-Murray, Binzer, & Skinner, 2005; Hickson, Worrall, & Scarinci, 2006b; Kramer, Allessie, Dondorp, Zekveld, & Kapteyn, 2005; Preminger, 2003; Preminger & Yoo, 2010; Preminger & Ziegler, 2008; Primeau, 1997). A few have not (e.g., Kricos, Holmes, & Doyle, 1992) and some have reported mixed results (e.g., Brewer, 2001). Brewer suggests that one reason for this variability in findings may relate, in part, to the use of standardized or non-patient-specific measures of handicap and disability rather than some index of how patients perceive their individual communication challenges.

Hawkins (2005) reviewed 12 peer-reviewed studies that assessed the benefits of group aural rehabilitation. His mega-analysis indicated that group programs yield short-term psychosocial benefits, including reduced self-perceived hearing-related difficulties, improved self-perceived quality of life, and improved use of communication strategies.

Research that suggests benefit generally can be categorized as showing (a) good patient participation or compliance, (b) change in communication strategies usage, or (c) change in perceived hearing-related disability.

Good Patient Participation or Compliance

Abrahamson (1991) reported that 89% of the patients who began a six-week communication strategies training program completed it. Attendance rates at the classes averaged 85%. Their willingness to stay with the program suggests that participants benefited from it.

Group aural rehabilitation programs increase compliance with hearing aid use. Northern and Beyer (1999) reviewed records from over seven thousand patients who had just received a new hearing aid. Almost half of the patients had opted to complete a three-session aural rehabilitation program, while the remaining patients had not. The program included designated segments entitled, *How To Overcome and Accept Hearing Loss, Tips for Communicating Effectively, Learning to Listen, Cues to Help Speech Understanding,* and *Controlling the Listening Environment.* Only 3% of the patients who completed the aural rehabilitation classes returned their hearing aids for refunds, compared with 9% of the patients who did not take the classes.

Change in Communication Strategies Usage

Chisolm et al. (2004) also found improvement, on average, in the use of communication strategies (i.e., anticipatory, repair, and constructive) by 53 veterans who had received new hearing aids and who had participated in a four-week aural rehabilitation program. Measures were obtained six months following the program's end. The 53 participants in the control group showed no such improvement.

One investigation showed that patients changed how they used repair strategies after participating in a communication strategies training program that concentrated on repair-strategy use (Tye-Murray, 1991b). Following training, subjects began to use the repair strategies, which they found were especially helpful during their training sessions. For example, if during the course of training an individual found that asking for the topic of conversation helped him or her to understand an unrecognized message, then the individual was more likely to begin using that strategy.

Change in Perceived Hearing-Related Disability

Benyon et al. (1997) measured "handicap," which relates to hearing-related disability. The researchers showed that 21 first-time hearing aid users who participated in a 4-week program in aural rehabilitation had a larger reduction in perceived handicap compared with 26 first-time hearing aid users who did not participate. Habanec and Kelly-Campbell (2015) showed that group aural rehabilitation diminished communication problems for non–hearing aid users in both the home and the workplace, and benefits were maintained 12 weeks following the program's end.

Importance of Including the Frequent Communication Partner

Preminger (2003) demonstrated the importance of involving patients' frequent communication partners. Thirteen patients attended six 90-minute classes consisting of informational sessions, communication strategies training, and speech perception training. The patients who participated with the frequent communication partners received significantly more benefit in terms of reducing hearing loss–related participation restrictions and activity limitations (as measured with the Hearing Handicap Index and the Hearing Handicap Index–Significant Others). She expanded these findings in a follow-up program involving 18 couples among whom only the patient participated in classes and 18 couples among whom both the patient and the spouse participated in classes (Preminger, 2011). Classes for the patient included communication strategies training and structured psychosocial exercises (which we will consider in the next chapter). Classes for the spouses included communication strategies training, clear speech training, and structured psychosocial exercise aimed at resolving the problems one encounters when one lives with a person who has hearing loss. The patients whose spouses participated in classes realized a greater change than those patients whose spouses did not participate in hearing loss–related quality of life and a greater change in negative affect posttraining compared with pretraining. In a later study, Preminger showed that following a program that included both patient and spouse, couples were in greater agreement about the problems associated with hearing loss than they were before the program (Preminger, 2011).

CASE STUDY

Patients with an Increased Sense of Self-Efficacy

Backenroth and Ahlner (2000) compiled a set of case studies from a group of 30 individuals with moderate to severe hearing loss who had participated in a group aural rehabilitation program. The program included counseling and communication strategies training. In general, consequences stemming from their hearing losses included limited participation in recreational activities, avoidance of social interactions, and recurrent irritations within the family. Following the aural rehabilitation program, a majority reported a "more relaxed relationship with their hearing-impairment" and a sense of having "learned to live with it" (p. 228). Several expressed an increased sense of self-efficacy. The investigators noted a problem that is not atypical. It is often difficult to

CASE STUDY *(continued)*

Patients with an Increased Sense of Self-Efficacy

convince adults with hearing loss to sign up for communication strategies training because they do not appreciate its value. Yet, once they enroll, they realize the benefits.

Case Study 1 was a 54-year-old woman who worked as a counselor. She reported that her hearing loss was linked to communication difficulties at work, at home, and at social functions. When asked of her expectations of the aural rehabilitation program, she responded, "I didn't have any high expectations of the audiological rehabilitation and I was hard to convince. I didn't think I needed any rehabilitation. . . . The audiologist convinced me to participate" (p. 228). After the program, she noted that she had received practical information about how to inform others about her hearing loss. "I now inform colleagues at my workplace. . . . The main outcomes of the rehabilitation [are] (a) I have become aware of the hearing impairment and allow myself to be fooled less; (b) I now feel more comfortable when using [a] hearing aid; (c) I dare to talk about my hearing impairment and demand more of others; (d) I have gained insight into the reasons for my tiredness; and (e) I generally [feel] supported by people who understand" (p. 229).

Case Study 2, a self-employed 42-year-old male, also expressed reluctance. "I didn't have any high expectations. I was rather skeptical about taking part in a 3-week rehabilitation program, as I run my own business." Although he acknowledged that hearing loss affected his family and social life, he claimed: "My hearing loss has not affected my work situation." He then went on to add, "I work fewer hours now" (p. 231), suggesting that he had indeed made accommodations because of hearing loss. He expressed satisfaction with the outcome of aural rehabilitation: "I gained further insight into my hearing impairment. I think differently. I understand my situation better, for example that I have difficulty in following group conversations. Before I thought I was the only one. I gained better self-confidence" (p. 232).

Finally, Case Study 3, a 50-year-old male, credited his spouse for his participation: "I didn't have any great expectations. I was persuaded to participate—my wife 'dragged' me there!" (p. 233). His hearing loss, like the other two case studies, affected his everyday life. "My interactions in groups are influenced," he told the interviewer. "I don't participate at big dinner parties or work lunches. I do not enjoy a good social life, as I cannot hear." Following his participation, his sense of self-efficacy had grown. He told the interviewer, "I have increased self-confidence. I have the confidence to remind others about my hearing loss and ask them to make allowances" (p. 234).

FINAL REMARKS

People will vary in the willingness to participate and in the extent to which they benefit. Some individuals are incapable of changing their communication behaviors. Some do not have the metacommunication skills to examine their conversational styles and may not be able to monitor how they interact with their communication partners, regardless of the quality or amount of instruction. For example, an elderly woman might not use communication strategies and might deal with communication problems with excessive aggression, but these behaviors are a part of her personality and likely will not change with aural rehabilitation intervention. In these instances, it is critical that individuals who interact frequently with patients receive instruction as well.

KEY CHAPTER POINTS

- A communication strategies training program should be tailored to accommodate a patient's expectations, age, socioeconomic background, lifestyle, and particular communication problems.
- One goal of communication strategies training is to enhance a patient's sense of self-efficacy.

- The content of a communication strategies training program centers around problems specifically related to hearing loss and how these problems can be minimized. Training may be provided for facilitative and repair communication strategies. Patients may also consider assertive versus nonassertive listening behaviors.
- One model for a training program includes three stages: formal instruction, guided learning, and real-world practice. A variety of exercises and activities can be used for each stage.
- Modeling, which entails learning through observing, allows patients to acquire information about effective communication behaviors and strategies and about what happens to someone as a result of using these behaviors and strategies.
- Role-playing may involve direct instruction, prompting, shaping, reinforcement, modeling, and feedback.
- A communication strategies training program for frequent communication partners often includes instruction for clear speech.

TERMS AND CONCEPTS TO REMEMBER

Self-efficacy
Coping
Ida Institute
Objectives
Formal instruction
Class format
Dialogue versus lecture
Guided learning
Modeling
Vicarious consequences
Role-playing
Prompting
Shaping
Videotaped scenarios
Real-world practice
Record of experiences
WATCH
Appropriate speaking behaviors

KEY RESOURCES

Ground Rules for a Group Aural Rehabilitation Program

1. Only one person speaks at a time.
2. Let us know when you are finished speaking by nodding your head.
3. If we are using a group assistive listening device, wait until you have the microphone before beginning to speak.
4. You have a right to pass on a question.

5. Everything said in this room is confidential.
6. There are no "right" or "wrong" answers or remarks. All comments are welcome and respected.
7. Say what you have to say but be sure that everyone has a chance to talk (speak for yourself and let others do likewise).
8. Be specific and use examples.
9. Indicate when you do not hear or understand something that is said—no bluffing or pretending to understand allowed.
10. Be kind and respectful of each other.
11. Stay on topic and focus on the question or issue under discussion (jumping from topic to topic can lead to communication breakdowns).

Content for a Communication Strategies Training/Psychosocial Program for Patients and Their Signficant Others (each class included an informational lecture, plus the topics listed below; adapted from Preminger, 2011, p. 5)

CLASS	CONTENT FOR PATIENT	CONTENT FOR SIGNIFICANT OTHER
1	*Psychosocial exercise: What is the worst thing about having a hearing loss? *Communication strategies training *Importance of speechreading	*Psychosocial exercise: What is the worst thing about living with someone who has a hearing loss? *Talking clearly for people who have hearing loss *Using repair strategies
2	*Psychosocial exercise: You know I cannot hear you when the water is running! *Communication strategies training *Concentration exercise	*Psychosocial exercise: Your partner cannot hear you when the water is running? *What is it like to have a hearing loss? *How to interpret discretely
3	*Psychosocial exercise: recognizing stress *Asking people to speak clearly *Communication strategies training	Psychosocial exercise: in their own words—letters from people with hearing loss *Talking clearly for the people with hearing loss *Using repair strategies
4	*Psychosocial exercise: The wedding crashers *Communication strategies training—dealing with speaker-based problems	* Psychosocial exercise: The wedding crashers *Communication strategies training *What it is like to have a hearing loss

CHAPTER 9

Counseling, Psychosocial Support, and Assertiveness Training

OUTLINE

- Who Provides Counseling, Psychosocial Support, and Assertiveness Training?
- The Patient's Story and Narrative Therapy
- Counseling
- Psychosocial Support
- Assertiveness Training
- Related Research
- Case Study: Solving Challenging Situations
- Final Remarks
- Key Chapter Points
- Terms and Concepts to Remember
- Key Resources

Hearing-related **counseling** is a professional service designed to help patients better understand and solve their hearing-related problems.

Hearing-related **psychosocial support** is the means by which speech and hearing professionals help patients achieve long-term self-sufficiency in managing the psychological and social challenges that result from hearing loss.

Hearing-related **assertiveness training** is aimed at teaching patients to express themselves assertively in their interpersonal communication interactions and to state both negative and positive feelings directly.

An individual's awareness of one's biological or physical self and personality contributes to a person's **self-image**, as does the individual's sense of identity and self-worth.

One goal of an aural rehabilitation plan may be to help persons with hearing loss and their communication partners realize the effect of hearing loss on their lives and to develop the skill sets and self-acceptance to carry on conversations with each other, using communication strategies effectively. Another goal may be to help them understand the often permanent nature of the hearing loss and to accept the idea of using appropriate listening devices. Hearing-related **counseling**, **psychosocial support**, and **assertiveness training** are means to achieve these goals.

In this chapter, we will consider these three interventions as if they were distinct, however, there is a fine line between hearing-related counseling, psychosocial support, and assertiveness training, and often the boundary between where one begins and the next ends blurs into a continuum. Whereas counseling may center only on issues directly related to hearing loss, psychosocial support may dig deeper and delve into the realms of a person's **self-image** and intrapersonal communication patterns. Assertiveness training may focus on conversational behaviors and effective means for interacting with other people. In this chapter, we will consider each one of these components, beginning with a consideration of who provides the services and then the patient-centered context in which they are provided. Next we will consider how to provide counseling, psychosocial support, and assertiveness training, and then develop a sense of when referral to, or collaboration with, other professionals may be appropriate.

WHO PROVIDES COUNSELING, PSYCHOSOCIAL SUPPORT, AND ASSERTIVENESS TRAINING?

Speech and hearing professionals often provide counseling to patients and their frequent communication partners. This professional might be an audiologist, speech-language pathologist, or a teacher of students who are have hearing loss. Sometimes the patient may receive counseling from another health care professional, such as a physician, nurse, psychologist, school counselor, or occupational therapist. Counseling might be provided in the context of an audiological examination or during the development of an individualized aural rehabilitation plan, or it may be provided during times specifically designated for this purpose, such as when a group of adults enroll in a communication strategies training class.

Responding to the Patient

"If a patient requests information, the response [of the audiologist or speech and hearing professional] should provide information, and if the patient expresses an emotion, the response should let the patient know that the emotion was acknowledged and respected."

(English, Mendel, Rojeski, & Hornak, 1999, p. 35)

The speech and hearing professional may also participate in providing psychosocial support. When this happens, the professional may team up with a certified psychosocial therapist or a clinical psychologist. Advantages of a team approach are that patients benefit from receiving the expertise of two types of professionals, and the two can model and role-play desirable behaviors. In cases where the participants have profound losses, and assistive listening devices cannot be used, one professional can write notes on a whiteboard while the other professional leads the discussion. Disadvantages relate to the cost of labor and the logistics of arranging for two professionals to be at the same place at the same time.

THE PATIENT'S STORY AND NARRATIVE THERAPY

Because the subjective experience of hearing loss cannot be predicted from the objective data of audiometric thresholds and word recognition scores, you and your patient must reach a mutual understanding of how hearing loss affects the patient's life activities and participations. The two of you, and often the three of you when a frequent communication partner may be involved, can form a therapeutic alliance, where you may listen to your patient's narrative (and the partner's narrative) in a way that is person centered, empathetic, interactive, and facilitative. By creating a clinician–patient partnership,

The Person Is Not the Problem, the Problem Is the Problem

Harvey (2012) explains that a narrative therapy approach is "based on the notion that people assign meaning to their lives by organizing key events into stories from which they limit or expand their repertoire of certain behaviors. In particular, individuals with hearing loss often are besieged by problem-saturated narratives from which they learn that seeking assistance will prove futile: e.g., 'People tell me I need help, but I know it won't work.' A narrative approach counters self-fulfilling belief by helping patients discover hopeful, preferred, and previously unrecognized possibilities—to re-author their stores and their lives, instead of feeling helpless and inadequate in an office while they politely nod their head and plan their escape" (p. 52). A speech and hearing professional might convey understanding and elicit stories and alternative stories with questions like the following (p. 55):

- "In about a minute or two, can you at least give me a snapshot of how you're feeling?
- Can you tell me a short story that would illustrate what you expect to happen between you and your husband (wife), with and without hearing aids?
- Would you tell me a personal story about when, where, and with whom you're most and least bothered by hearing loss?
- How did you arrive at the feeling that you don't care what other people think about your hearing aids? How did you arrive at this different way of perceiving this situation, [of] putting your needs first?"

you will foster engagement and self-efficacy on the part of the patient and thereby promote the patient's willingness to engage in therapeutic activities (Erdman, 2011; Figure 9–1).

Techniques for forging an alliance come from **narrative therapy** (White & Epston, 1990). A narrative therapy approach rests on the premise that patients assign meaning to their lives by organizing their experiences into personal stories. Sometimes the patient narrative will be elicited in the context of an initial interview, using some of the techniques that were reviewed in Chapter 7. Sometimes, the narrative will be elicited as part of a counseling or psychosocial support intervention.

Narrative therapy focuses on the narrative during clinician–patient encounters, and holds that our identities are shaped by the stories we derive from our life experiences. A primary goal is to externalize problems so that patients can consider their relationship with their problem, such as hearing loss, and draw upon their personal strengths and positive experiences to engage in constructive problem solving and, if advantageous, to enact an alteration of self-identity.

In narrative therapy, a clinician questions the patient and collaborates with the patient to develop a narrative about how hearing loss affects the patient's life and to develop possible alternative narratives. For example, one patient who enrolled in clEAR's auditory brain training program explained that she was "in a dark place" because she believed her hearing loss had come to define who she was and negated her considerable accomplishments, including having practiced as a lawyer and having competed as a world class equestrian. Her clinician took the time to listen to her narrative and worked with her to recast her predicament.

Once patients view themselves as separate from their hearing loss, an opportunity for change arises. Patients might take ownership of both the problem and the possible solutions. The change may take the form of acknowledging that a hearing loss exists, acceptance of a hearing aid, or willingness to attend a communication strategies training program.

Techniques used in narrative therapy include focusing on the narrative (*eliciting the story*), discussing the problem as being separate from the patient (*externalization*), exploring the influence of the hearing loss on the patient and frequent communication

Nonverbal behaviors that promote effective communication:

- Maintain good eye contact at eye level.
- Avoid writing down things during the patient narrative or typing remarks into a computer.
- Lean toward the patient and use facial expressions that show interest.
- Engage in purposeful and appropriate head nodding.

(Johnson, Jilla, & Danhauer, 2018)

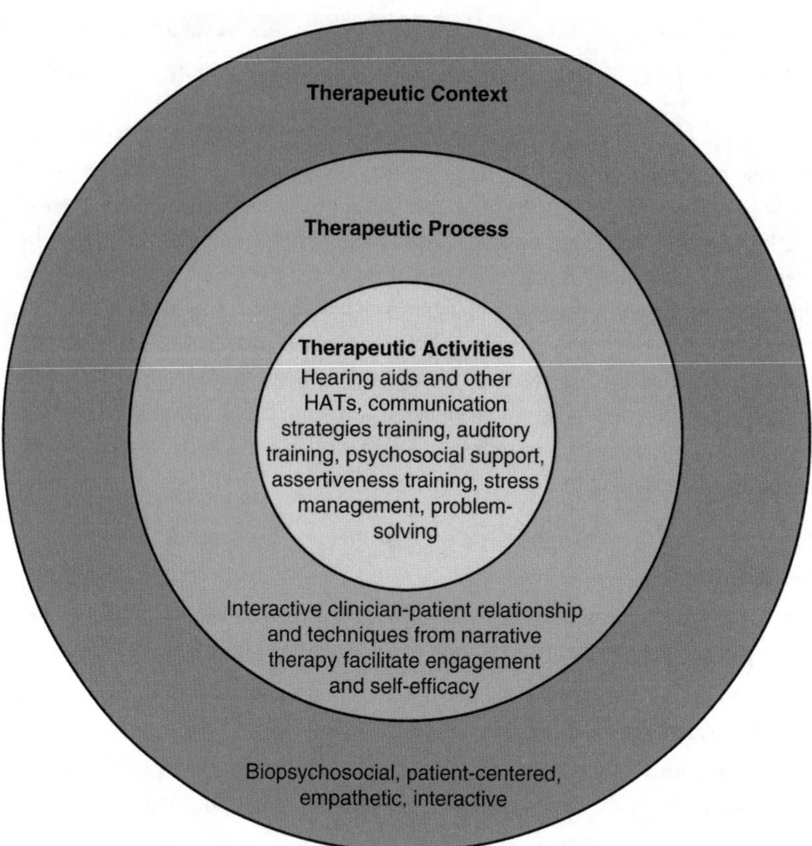

FIGURE 9–1 A narrative therapy approach. The context is patient entered, and the patient is encouraged to provide a narrative about issues related to hearing loss (adapted from Erdman, 2011).

partners (*relative influence questioning*), attaching new meaning to an experience or behavior (*recasting*), and identifying times when there was an exception (*identification of unique experiences or outcomes*) (Etchison & Kleist, 2000). Sometimes the clinician will engage in **clarification** to ensure that there is an accurate and mutual understanding. The clinician might also provide **validation**, letting patients feel what they feel while conveying the message that their feelings make sense, and provide **reassurance**, instilling or restoring confidence that they are capable of handling a hearing-related problem.

Clarification is a counseling technique whereby clinicians abstract the essence of a patient's remarks and summarize them back to their patient.

Validation is a way to corroborate or confirm an experience or feeling. It lets patients know that you understand their feelings and what they are expressing to you, and that their feelings make sense.

Reassurance entails instilling or restoring confidence.

The following interchange between an audiologist and a new patient illustrates some of these and other techniques used in narrative therapy. Notice how the audiologist does not simply ask informational questions, but rather, asks questions that will elicit the patient's story and that will help separate the patient's identity from the problem of hearing loss (adapted from DiLollo et al., 2006, p. 58; Harvey, 2012, p. 55).

Audiologist: In the limited time we have together, please tell me about when you or your brother first noticed that you had a hearing loss. [*eliciting the story*]

Ms. Lin: I think I ignored it at first, just figuring it was people mumbling. Then I noticed that I had to watch people's faces more in order to understand them, and at church, well, I quit going for a while but now, sometimes I just go to the early service, which is small and they don't play the organ.

Audiologist: Thank you for sharing that, Ms. Lin. It seems that there have been times when you have been able to challenge the problems associated with your hearing loss by coming up with strategies that have helped you communicate more effectively. [*recasting*] I'd like you to tell me some more about those times—how you came up with those strategies and what resources you need to make them work. [*identification of unique experiences or outcomes*]

Ms. Lin: I began to realize the importance of watching people's faces, especially when I'm with my book club and many women are talking. I asked my friends not to interrupt each other so often, as they tend to do, so I can focus on one person's face talking at a time.

Audiologist: Can you briefly tell me how your hearing loss is affecting your family? [*relative influence questioning*]

Ms. Lin: I live with my brother. He owns a boutique printing press. He knows we can't talk if we're in the main factory area because I won't hear a word he says. I also have to remind him to look at me when he talks, even when we're in his quiet office.

Audiologist: You've been extremely resourceful in the way you've been able to challenge the impact that hearing loss has on your life. [*externalization*] I'm hopeful we can work together to find more resources that will allow you to overcome the challenges presented by hearing loss. [*encouraging the patient to take ownership*]

Ms. Lin: I've never thought of it that way, but you could be right. I usually do seem to find a way around problems.

In this relatively brief conversation, the audiologist has learned about Ms. Lin's degree of hearing handicap and a little about how hearing loss affects her life and family. Importantly, after telling her personal narrative, Ms. Lin likely feels that the audiologist is genuinely concerned about her predicament and respects her initiative and resourcefulness. Instead of sitting in the audiologist's office dreading a verdict of *You are defective*, Ms. Lin thinks that even though she most likely has a hearing loss, she is quite capable of being proactive to minimize its consequences.

Oh No!

"When my audiologist told me about my hearing loss, it brought back my terror of when doctors thought I had cancer!"

—A patient with newly diagnosed hearing loss

(Harvey, 2018, p. 12)

COUNSELING

Intimately intertwined with eliciting and validating a patient's narrative is the art of targeting counseling needs and then providing them in the form of informational counseling and personal adjustment counseling. Counseling often provides patients with the following benefits:

- Enhanced understanding of hearing loss and its effects on communication
- Better self-disclosure and self-acceptance
- Greater knowledge about how to manage communication difficulties
- Reduced stress and discouragement
- Increased satisfaction with aural rehabilitation services
- Increased motivation to minimize listening problems
- Stronger adherence/compliance with the aural rehabilitation plan, including use of amplification

A Dialogue

"The consultation needs to be a dialogue in which the clinician listens to the patient as well as the other way around. If the patient's ideas are evaded or inhibited, the patient is less likely to remember important information. Even the clinician's anxiety affects recall. Patients remember less when the information is provided by an overtly anxious clinician. Information presented in a manner that emphasizes its importance is more likely to be remembered than information presented in a matter-of-fact manner."

—Robert H. Margolis, Professor and Director of Audiology, University of Minnesota Medical School

(Margolis, 2004b, p. 12)

Informational Counseling

After a hearing test, an audiologist typically explains the nature and degree of hearing loss to the patient, usually in conjunction with a review of the person's audiogram. The audiologist then reviews the relevant steps in the aural rehabilitation plan. This review may include a discussion of the benefits and limitations provided by a hearing aid and

During **informational counseling**, information is imparted to the patient about the hearing loss and hearing disability and the recommended steps for management.

possibly a hands-on demonstration. In this type of interaction, the audiologist provides **informational counseling** (Figure 9–2). The professional instructs, guides, and gives expert information in the format of a give-and-take dialogue. Information provided during this type of counseling may concern the hearing loss itself, listening device technology, community and government services available to persons with hearing loss, and the availability of aural rehabilitation classes, such as auditory brain or communication strategies training.

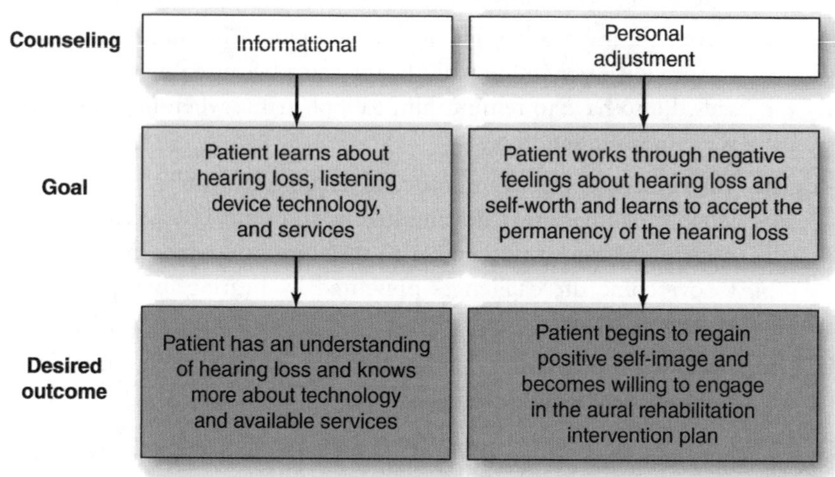

FIGURE 9–2 Two kinds of counseling provided in the aural rehabilitation setting.

More than Just a Number

"I don't expect to have an intimate relationship with my audiologist, but there's a certain feeling that flows between two people when one of them is the care-er, and the other one is being cared for. It doesn't have to be intimate, but you've got to be more than just a number or the next patient."

—A 69-year-old patient

(Armero & Thomas, 2018, p. 19)

An effective clinician understands what the patient is interested in learning about and the level of understanding that the patient is capable of achieving and will present information in a way that the patient understands what is said and remembers the important points. Sensitivity to the patients is critical as patients forget as much as 40% to 80% of information immediately after hearing it in a medical setting. Of this percentage, they may remember about half of it incorrectly (Kessels, 2003).

The method of **explicit categorization**, a way to ensure retention, is an informational counseling technique wherein the clinician enumerates the topics that will be covered and then announces each one before talking about it.

Ways to promote understanding include speaking with easy-to-understand language and supplementing the verbal presentation with graphic materials such as pictures and drawings. Presenting the most important information first and using the method of **explicit categorization** (e.g., "Now that we have talked about your test results, let's talk about the next steps."). The logical and structured format that we reviewed for interviewing techniques in Chapter 7 (see Figure 7–1) also applies for conducting informational counseling. Strategies for ensuring understanding and retention include the following (Margolis, 2004a, p. 15):

- Advice should be given as concrete instructions. "Use ear plugs when you use your power tools," rather than "Keep your noise exposure to a minimum."
- Use easy-to-understand language.
- Present the most important information first to capitalize on the primacy effect.
- Stress the importance of recommendations or other information that you want the patient to remember.
- Use the method of explicit categorization. Tell the patient, "We are going to go over *recommendations*, then we will talk about your specific hearing problem *(diagnosis)*, then we will go over *test results*, then we will talk about how your hearing may change in the future *(prognosis)*." Ask the patient for questions before moving on to the next category.

- Repeat the most important information.
- Don't present too much information.
- Specifically address the patient's reason for seeking a hearing evaluation [or other service].
- Supplement verbal information with written, graphical, and pictorial materials that the patient can take home.

Personal Adjustment Counseling

During **personal adjustment counseling** (Figure 9–2), the focus is on the permanence of the hearing loss and the healthy incorporation of hearing loss into a patient's self-image. The acceptance of hearing loss allows patients to accept the realities of their disability and to adjust their values and priorities while still continuing to lead fulfilled and productive lives. An audiologist might introduce the possibility of using a listening device and listen as a patient expresses a reaction. A speech-language pathologist who is working with a young Deaf adult might explore some of the complicated issues that prevent the person from engaging in social activities with peers or from using an FM assistive listening device in the college classroom.

Personal adjustment counseling focuses on the permanency of the hearing loss and on psychological, social, and emotional acceptance.

Although there are probably as many different approaches to personal adjustment counseling as there are professional counselors, the various approaches can be broadly sorted into three general categories: approaches aimed at modifying thought process *(cognitive)*, approaches aimed at modifying behavior *(behavioral)*, and approaches aimed at modifying emotions *(affective)*. In practice, most counseling entails a combination of all three of these approaches and incorporates many of the techniques that are used in narrative therapy.

Cognitive Approach

A cognitive approach to counseling (e.g., Beck & Emery, 1985; Ellis & Grieger, 1977) relies on intellectual means for addressing problems related to hearing loss. In this approach, faulty thought processes are assumed to underlie inappropriate emotional responses to hearing loss and to underlie erroneous assumptions and self-image difficulties. The speech and hearing professional implements logic to direct and redirect individuals' thoughts, belief systems, perceptions, values, ideas, and opinions. This educational experience is designed to increase self-worth and decrease inferiority feelings and discouragement. For example, a woman with hearing loss may believe she can no longer serve on a corporate board because her hearing loss prevents her from understanding everything that is said during meetings. The clinician might counter this by asking her to consider her experience and expertise, which brought her to serve on the board in the first place, and then by asking her to consider some of the ways she might

Some of the issues that might be addressed during personal adjustment counseling:

- How do I prevent friends and coworkers from avoiding me?
- How do I increase my self-esteem?
- How do I gain confidence to behave more assertively?
- How do I deal with feeling isolated?
- How do I deal with the anger I feel because I experience so many communication breakdowns?
- How do I decrease my dependence on others?

1. **Choose a person at work, a friend or neighbor, or someone in your extended family and tell the person that you have just received a new hearing aid.**
2. **Explain to this person the benefits and limitations you perceive your hearing aid will afford you.**
3. **You might use the results of the speech tests that we collected during your appointment today to explain how well you now understand speech.**

FIGURE 9–3 A counseling homework assignment.

enhance the communication setting during meetings. Sometimes the clinician is passive in a process like this, and at other times, the clinician might direct a counseling session using didactic questioning that may be both accepting and confrontational at the same time. The goal is to eliminate cognitive distortions and arbitrary assumptions and to replace them with positive thoughts and positive perspectives. Techniques that are used in cognitive approaches include questioning, interpreting, goal setting, creation of contracts, and homework assignments. An example of a homework assignment appears in Figure 9–3, and an example of a contract appears in Figure 9–4.

Personal Contract

Name:______________________________

Clinician:______________________________

Before I return to my next appointment, I will:

- **Explain to people that I have a hearing loss**
- **Use repair strategies when I do not understand a spoken message**
- **Not scold myself when I do not recognize a message**
- **Remind my spouse to use optimal speaking behaviors so that I may understand him or her, using language that is assertive but not aggressive**

Signed:______________________________

Date:______________________________

FIGURE 9–4 Example of a contract that might be issued during a counseling session.

Rational Emotive Behavior Therapy (REBT) is a solution-oriented counseling (or therapy) approach that focuses on resolving specific problems using cognitive, behavioral, and affective elements; key to the approach is the idea that emotions result from beliefs rather than events or circumstances.

The **Rational Emotive Behavior Therapy (REBT)** approach, developed by the psychotherapist Albert Ellis, exemplifies a predominantly cognitive approach to counseling. Ellis (2001; Ellis & MacLaren, 1998) describes an A-B-C framework of emotional functioning (Figure 9–5). The A stands for an *activating event* or an *adversity* that a patient confronts. In the context of aural rehabilitation, an example of an activating event might be a young bachelor receiving a diagnosis of hearing loss and a recommendation for a hearing aid from his audiologist. The B stands for the evaluation of the event, which might be *behavioral-affective-cognitive.* For example, the man might conclude, "Only old folks have hearing loss and wear hearing aids." The C is the *consequence* of the patient's evaluation. In this case, the man may decide that he will never wear a hearing aid because he does not want to be perceived as old by his peers.

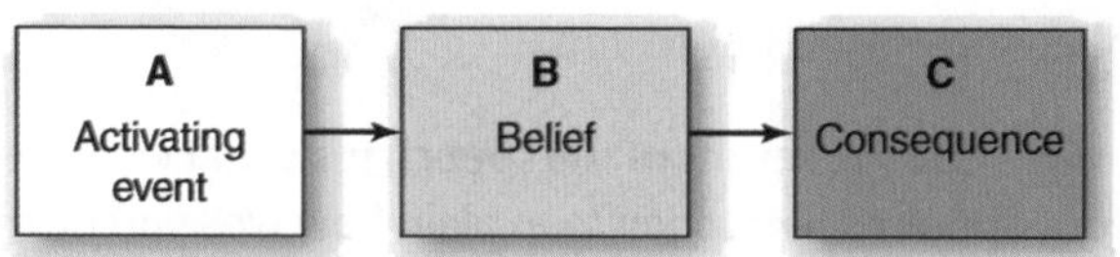

FIGURE 9–5 The A-B-C framework of emotional functioning. A = Audiologist recommends a hearing aid; B = Patient believes potential girlfriends will think that he is too old if he wears a hearing aid; C = Patient declines to participate in a hearing aid evaluation.

The key to counseling is to help the patient realize that his evaluation of the event, and not the activating event itself, is the cause of the undesirable consequence. By obtaining a more rational view of hearing loss and of other people (e.g., young adults do not necessarily equate hearing aids with aging, especially given the ubiquity of ear-level technology), patients are more likely to react to adversity in a more self-serving and adaptive manner. Some clinicians include a D and E component when applying Ellis' model. D stands for *dispute* and E stands for *effective action or philosophy.* In the present example, the audiologist would implement the D component by helping the young man dispute his evaluation of hearing loss and hearing aids; that is, the B of this particular A-B-C-D-E sequence. This might be accomplished by asking the young man to provide evidence for his belief or by asking him to consider what would happen if he abandoned this belief. The result of abandoning or replacing the irrational belief with a rational one results in an effective course of action (the E component); in this case, the use of an appropriate hearing aid. Figure 9–6 presents the stages in the A-B-C-D-E process.

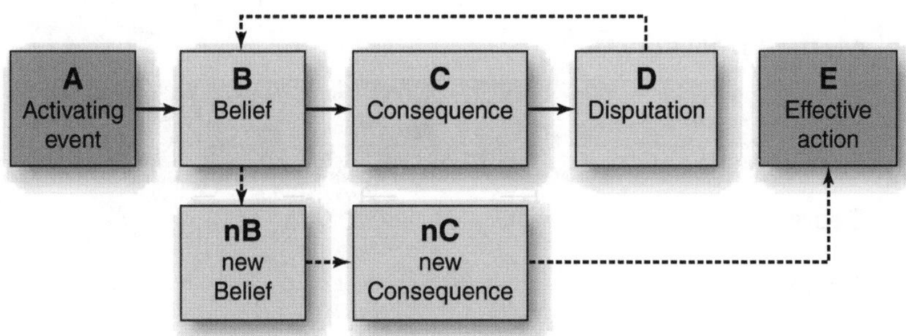

FIGURE 9–6 An example of a cognitive approach to counseling. A = Audiologist recommends a hearing aid; B = Patient believes potential friends will think that he is too old if he wears a hearing aid; C = Patient declines to participate in a hearing aid evaluation; D = Audiologist disputes belief (B) by naming several prominent musicians who wear hearing aids; nB = Patient revises his original belief, that is, develops a new belief; nC = Patient agrees to a hearing aid evaluation, that is, has a new consequence; E = Patient wears hearing aid in everyday situations and becomes a more effective communicator.

Behavioral Approach

Skinnerian learning theory (Skinner, 1953, 1971) forms the basis for many behavioral approaches to counseling. A fundamental tenet is that maladaptive behavior is learned, and as such, it is possible to "unlearn" it. This approach often focuses on observable and measurable behavior foremost, with the idea that changes in cognitive and emotional adjustment will follow behavioral changes. For example, a businessman might hyperventilate before major meetings because he fears he may not understand the other participants' remarks. The clinician may implement a **desensitization** process, which is a strategy to help someone reduce excessive anxiety or fear that occurs in specific situations. The clinician might first ask him to identify those physical symptoms he experiences in response to stress (Figure 9–7), and then introduce him to relaxation techniques, such as that described in Figure 9–8. Behavioral techniques such as these work directly on the physical response to stress and the patient's sense of control.

Desensitization is a way to reduce a patient's negative reactions in specific situations by means of repeatedly exposing the person to them in mild form, either in reality, in role-playing, or in imagination.

Affective Approach

An affective approach (e.g., Rogers, 1980) centers on feelings and on fostering emotional adjustment to hearing loss. The clinician creates an empathetic, accepting environment in which patients can evaluate self-concepts and their reactions to hearing loss. The goal is phenomenological: patients change how they view themselves and their place in the world, even though their circumstance may remain the same. By receiving

Right before a major meeting, I worry that I will not understand what is said at the conference table. I experience the following physical symptoms of stress:
My head pounds.
My palms sweat.
My heart beat races.
My stomach churns.
I feel short of breath.
My neck aches.
I feel dizzy as I walk toward the conference room.
My mouth goes dry.
After the meeting, I think about my performance. Once I get home, I feel the following emotions:
Depression
Anxiety
A sense of being on edge
Anger

FIGURE 9–7 A behavioral approach to counseling. A businessman who has hearing loss is asked to identify his stress reactions to business meetings.

- **Focus on a point one inch below the navel, in the middle of your body**
- **Breath deeply**
- **Expand lower abdomen as you breathe in**
- **Flatten abdomen as you breathe out**
- **Perform this exercise for 10–20 minutes**

FIGURE 9–8 Relaxation techniques to reduce stress responses. These techniques may be reviewed in a behavioral counseling approach (adapted from Hogan, 2001).

What the patient might really be saying when asking whether a hearing loss is permanent:

"This is worse than I thought, I was hoping it was nothing serious."

"I'm worried about the future, how am I going to manage this with so much else going on in my life?"

"I know it sounds silly, but this makes me feel old."

(Clark & English, 2004, p. 76)

unconditional positive regard from their clinician, patients develop a sense of being accepted because the person is who he or she is. Central tenets of Rogers' affective approach are congruence with self, unconditional positive regard, and empathetic understanding. Although these tenets are hallmarks of an affective approach, they should be a part of any counseling interaction between a speech and hearing professional and a patient (or patient's family member).

Congruence with self means that clinicians act as themselves and do not assume an imposing facade of professionalism. They relate to patients honestly and sincerely. Instead of saying to a first-time patient: "Your audiogram indicates a mild-to-moderate sensorineural hearing loss bilaterally with a conductive component," a pronouncement replete with professional jargon, an audiologist might instead say, "I know you are worried about your hearing. My tests seem to agree with your impression that you are not hearing as well as you used to hear. I'd like to answer your questions." With the former statement, the audiologist might inadvertently increase the patient's anxiety. With the latter approach, the audiologist has validated the patient's own opinions and allowed the patient to share the lead in discussing the test results. The audiologist has set the stage for the patient to take responsibility and participate in the aural rehabilitation plan.

Congruence with self is the first tenet of person-centered counseling, in which clinicians act as themselves in interactions with patients and do not assume a facade of professionalism.

A second tenet is **unconditional positive regard**. The clinician assumes that patients know best and that they have the inner resources to overcome their communication difficulties. Hallmarks of unconditional positive regard include the following clinician behaviors:

- Accepts patients as human beings of stature
- Respects them regardless of their employment or social status
- Brings appropriately placed empathy, sincerity, and caring to the interaction
- Engenders a nonthreatening context for patients to express their concerns about their hearing losses, their painful or defensive feelings about their communication difficulties, and their apprehensions about using a listening device

In **unconditional positive regard**, the second tenet of person-centered counseling, clinicians assume that patients know best as well as assume that they have the inner resources to overcome their conversational difficulties.

Rogers' third tenet is **empathetic understanding**. The professional establishes the patient's viewpoints, often through techniques of **reflection** and clarification, and tries to appreciate the patient's situation from the patient's point of view. For example, a person might cite the soft presentation level as a reason for poor performance on a word recognition test. In this instance, the audiologist would probably not say, "I presented the words at a normal conversational level, Mr. Smith. There is no doubt you have a word recognition problem." Instead, **empathizing** with the patient's feelings, the audiologist might respond, "I know the words were not very loud for you. Are there occasions during your typical day when speech seems too soft to hear?" With this remark, the patient's impressions are acknowledged, and the test results are related to situations that are relevant.

Empathetic understanding is the third tenet of person-centered counseling. The clinician listens to the patient's concerns and feelings about the hearing problem, reflects them back to the patient, and helps the patient identify solutions.

Reflection is a counseling technique whereby clinicians paraphrase or summarize what their patient has just said. By this means, clinicians demonstrate that they are listening carefully and accurately, and provide their patients with an opportunity to examine their own views or feelings by hearing them expressed by another person.

Empathizing entails placing yourself in the patient's situation while still remaining objective.

Targeting Counseling

Counseling needs to target the patient's particular concerns. For example, one patient, Candice Brown, commented to her audiologist, "I worry that I can't be there for my 17-year-old daughter the way I want to be. It's too much of an effort for her to talk to me, she says. Lately, she just tunes me out." She noted that she felt a low-grade anxiety throughout many of her waking hours. In this case, the aural rehabilitation plan might include the following counseling tactics:

- *Provide informational counseling by talking to Candice about a group communication strategies training program.* An audiologist might give her a program's brochure and answer her questions about program content. The audiologist might also provide an overview of some of the communication strategies that are typically included in such a program.
- *Provide personal adjustment counseling and help Candice understand that communication between a teenage daughter and her parent is universally problematic and not just an issue for a mother who has hearing loss.* During this process, a speech and hearing professional might follow the steps in the A-B-C-D-E model depicted in Figure 9–6, beginning by identifying an activating event, such as the

daughter's reluctance to talk about school (A), then Candice's beliefs about the event, that is, that she is "not there" for her daughter (B), and third, the consequences of these beliefs, which for Candice is increased anxiety (C). The speech and hearing professional might question Candice's beliefs (D) with the goal of stimulating more effective action on Candice's part (E).

- *Continue personal adjustment counseling.* Once Candice has enrolled in the communication strategies training program, the daughter might be encouraged to attend, so both will have an opportunity to share their frustrations, feelings and ideas for solutions. Desensitization might be provided by allowing them to role-play solutions for difficult communication situations, such as talking on the telephone.

Asking Patients to Respond to an Attitudinal Continuum

"Mr. Jones, I want you to put an X along this line that best describes your feelings about [using a hearing aid]. I'm only going to give you a few seconds so that you don't think about this because there is absolutely no need to justify your feelings."

—A clinician who is helping a patient assess his feelings about using a hearing aid

(Shelton & Faucette, 1999, p. 38)

Interweaving Counseling Approaches: A Clinical Example

An eclectic program that interweaves the three types of counseling is presented by Shelton and Faucette (1999). Designed to encourage patients to use amplification, it is also based on tools made available by the Ida Institute.

Personal Adjustment Counseling with an Affective Approach

Patients begin by exploring their feelings and attitudes about using amplification, both the negative and the positive, and about their sense of self-efficacy. The clinician may administer one or two simple paper-and-pencil tools to stimulate discussion.

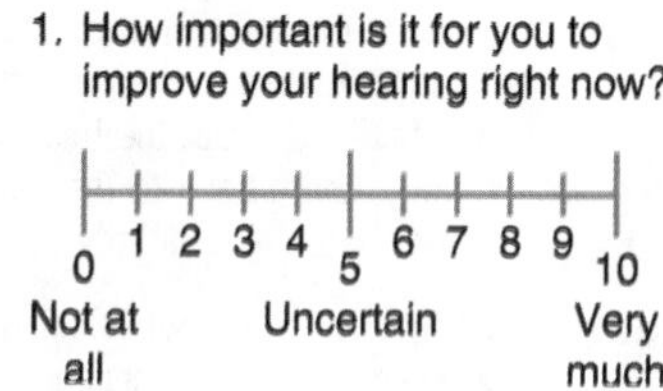

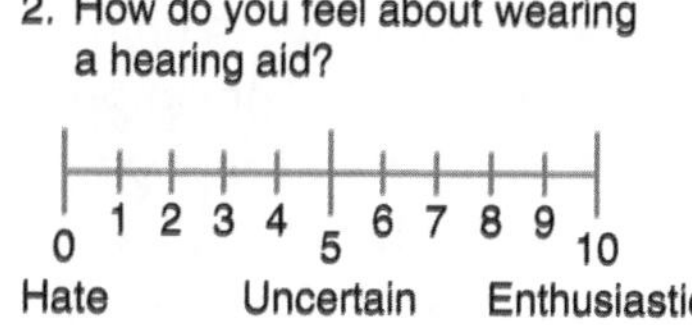

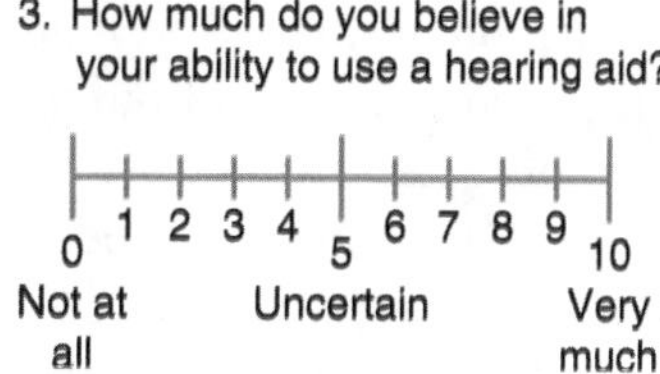

FIGURE 9–9 Three attitudinal continuums that can be used to help a clinician and patient evaluate the patient's desire for change and sense of self-efficacy (adapted from Clark et al., 2012; Shelton & Faucette, 1999).

The first tool presents three attitudinal continuums, which are "thermometers" that allow patients to gauge attitudes and feelings about their current situation and about using a hearing aid. For the first attitudinal continuum, patients indicate on a scale from 0 to 10 how important it is for them to improve their hearing (Figure 9–9). The patient's response serves to pinpoint other issues that may impede or promote hearing aid use, as well as provides information about the patient's goals for aural rehabilitation (Clark, Maatman, & Gailey, 2012). For example, this interchange may occur:

Clinician: You've marked a 4 on this line. Mr. Amos, why did you not mark a 0?
Mr. Amos: I probably need to be hearing better at work, so that's important.
Clinician: And why did you give yourself a 4 instead of an 8?
Mr. Amos: I do okay at home, so my hearing isn't a problem there.

The direct questioning encourages the patient to reflect on his lifestyle needs and to articulate his feelings and opinions.

The next attitude continuum shown in Figure 9–9 explicitly queries about feelings, asking the patient *How do you feel about wearing hearing aids?* Here, the focus narrows and the patient quantifies feelings in a tangible way. The clinician engages in empathetic listening and helps the patient articulate feelings using the counseling techniques of reflection and clarification:

Clinician: You've marked a 6 on the scale.

Mr. Amos: Yeah, I'm doing fine with my hearing at home but work, well, let's just say, not so good.

Clinician: So, listening at work is giving you difficulties . . . [*reflection*]

Mr. Amos: Listening to clients. I work as a carpet salesman and I need to hear my clients. So I marked a 6.

Clinician: So, you feel a hearing aid might be helpful? [*clarification*]

Mr. Amos: Oh yes, I'd be willing to try.

If the patient marks a high number, then there may be no need for further discussion.

The third attitude continuum in Figure 9–9 probes the patient's sense of self-efficacy. Again, if the patient marks a high number, then further discussion may be unnecessary. If the patient marks a low number, the clinician might ask, "Why do feel you won't be successful?" or the clinician might **reframe** the response toward an optimistic bent and ask, "Why did you mark a 3 rather than a 1?"

The second tool asks patients to identify their feelings (Table 9–1). The list includes negative, neutral, and positive emotional descriptors. The patient has 60 seconds to circle five words that best express his or her feelings about using a hearing aid. The brief time

Asking Patients to Respond to a List of Emotional Descriptors

"Okay, Mr. Jones, I want you to do something else for me. Here is a list of words, some having positive connotations, some having negative connotations. I want you to take 60 seconds and circle the five words that you associate with [using a hearing aid]."

—A clinician who is helping a patient take inventory of his feelings about becoming a new hearing aid user

(Shelton & Faucette, 1999, p. 38)

Reframing is a counseling technique that provides the patient with an alternative frame of reference from which to view a problem.

TABLE 9–1 Emotional Labels. Patients are asked to identify five feelings, with no request to give concomitant reasons: "Feelings are caused by perception, not logic. Feelings may change as additional thinking creates change in perception. When you identify your feelings, you should honor them. This acceptance of 'what is right now' mollifies the feelings, thus eliminating its insistence to get your attention" (Adapted from Shelton & Faucette, 1999, p. 40).

Angry	Enthused	Nervous
Anxious	Fearful	Obligated
Assured	Fired up	Panicky
Bewildered	Frightened	Peaceful
Bitter	Guilty	Powerful
Cheated	Hassled	Pressured
Comfortable	Hopeful	Relieved
Competent	Hopeless	Responsible
Confident	Impatient	Satisfied
Confused	Insecure	Secure
Curious	Inspired	Serene
Delighted	Interested	Skeptical
Depressed	Irritated	Strengthened
Disappointed	Jittery	Tense
Discouraged	Lonely	Unsure
Drained	Lost	Useless
Empowered	Misunderstood	Withdrawn
Energetic	Motivated	Worried

precludes the patient from engaging in rational thinking, and limits the patient in trying to justify or judge choices or to dissemble uncomfortable feelings. Identifying emotions by name makes them manageable and provides an opportunity for the clinician to validate and **normalize** them (e.g., "Many patients circle the word *anxious*") and to explore them more fully (e.g., "Let's talk about this word *anxious*. Under what circumstances

Normalizing is a counseling technique that helps patients realize that their feelings are *normal* and helps to decrease any negative emotions, such as shame or embarrassment, that they may have about hearing loss.

Hearing Meetups

© Pipa100 | Dreamstime.com

FIGURE 9–10 Creating opportunities for psychosocial support by means of regular face-to-face gatherings.

One way to create a support network for patients is to encourage them to form a meetup group, which is a local community of individuals who share the common interest of hearing loss and audiology-related topics (e.g., https://www.meetup.com/). For example, Davis Audiology in Greenville, SC conducts meetups that are facilitated by a **Hearing Wellness Advocate (HWA)**, who typically is a patient who has a 'can-do' attitude and is willing to share his or her patient hearing health care journey with others (Davis, 2017). A staff audiologist also attends the meetup to answer clinical and technical questions. Meetups are a "win-win" situation in that patients receive psychosocial support from their peers and the speech and hearing professional differentiates him/herself from other hearing health care providers. Here are Davis' tips for running a hearing meetup:

- Recruit an HWA who is enthusiastic about leading the group.
- Publicize the meetup with a flyer that lists the topics for the next several months. Flyers can be circulated to local entities such as religious and community centers and through email. Facebook and Instagram can also be effective.
- At the meeting, provide nametags so participants can address each other by first names.
- Start the meeting with the HWA recapping his or her hearing journey, which will help newcomers feel welcomed.
- The meeting should explicitly feature one or two topics, such as *Understanding Your Audiogram, Tinnitus and Treatment Strategies*, or *Self-Advocacy*. If possible, include multimedia slides and videos to stimulate discussion.
- Occasionally, invite a guest speaker, such as a local physician, who might discuss related comorbidities, such as diabetes or cardiovascular health.
- Serve refreshments! (Figure 9–10)

might you be anxious to use a hearing aid?"). Once negative feelings are brought out into the open, they have diminished potential to sabotage constructive action. Talking next about positive feelings, such as relief, self-empowerment, hope, and excitement, may recast the patient's perspective, shifting the balance of power so that the positive feelings assume greater importance than the negative. The clinician acknowledges the patient's feelings, never judging or denying their existence.

Personal Adjustment Counseling with a Cognitive Approach

The next step may be to ask the patient to identify the pros and cons of using a hearing aid. Figure 9–11 presents a cost–benefit analysis form (CBAF), which is modeled after the CBAF used in REBT cognitive therapy to promote changes in behavior and to move

Benfits of Not Taking Action	Costs of Not Taking Action
• My wife and I don't go out much anyway, so there's no need for them. *Have you considered that maybe you don't go out because you will experience listening difficulties?* *Do you think your wife misses being more socially active?* • I won't have to take care of them; hearing aids are a lot of work! *What kind of work do you think hearing aids require?* *Why do you think you can't handle this work?* *What other kinds of technology do you use?*	• My wife will be angry that I won't try hearing aids. *Why do you think she wants you to try using them?* • I'll feel useless and sad because I can't talk to people. *In what situations do you feel this way?*
Costs of Taking Action	**Benefits of Taking Action**
• My co-workers may tease me when they see the hearing aids. *How do you react when you see a friend or co-worker who is wearing a hearing aid?* *Where is the evidence that they will tease you?* • My clients may think I'm too old to work with them. *Do you think using a hearing aid will help you hear your clients better?* • They will hurt my ears. *In what ways will they hurt your ears?*	• I will hear what people say at family gatherings. • People won't think I'm going senile because I give off-topic answers to their questions. • I won't feel so helpless about my hearing problems. • I'll be able to go to the symphony and enjoy the music. • My family won't complain that I turn the television up too loud, and my wife will watch shows with me. *Encourage the patient to identify benefits, possibly using such prompts as, "If you can participate in telephone conference calls then..."* *Possibly note benefits that were not listed; e.g., "Some people say they have an easier time on the telephone...."*

FIGURE 9–11 A cost–benefit analysis form. The patient indicates the benefits and costs of taking action versus not taking action. Possible clinician responses are presented in italics.

patients toward action (Dryden & Branch, 2008). It is also offered as a motivational tool by the Ida Institute.

This tool promotes rationality. Patients list the potential costs and benefits of taking no action and the potential costs and benefits of taking action. They work through the box from left to right and top to bottom. Responses in the four quadrants both present a logical structure for decision making and may help patients organize and analyze their thoughts, feelings, and opinions. Typically, the potential benefits of making changes exceed the benefits of maintaining the status quo, and the costs of change are less than the costs of inaction. Indeed, if a review of the CBFA shows that the patient perceives using a hearing aid as more desirable than staying with the status quo, then little time need be spent reviewing the form. However, if the patient appears ambivalent about change, the clinician might review the form and ask empirical questions or use realistic disputation, as exemplified in Figure 9–11. The goal is to discover and deal with the so-called advantages of taking no action versus the perceived disadvantages of taking action. In the case where disadvantages far outweigh advantages, discussion about obtaining a hearing aid might be delayed until a future date.

As the clinician and patient review the CBAF, a natural shift occurs, from personal adjustment counseling to informational counseling. The clinician corrects any misconceptions and affirms accurate perceptions by providing information. For example, the clinician may affirm that the patient will be able to watch television with a lower sound level and will likely enjoy symphonic music more. Correcting misconceptions must be done with respect and sensitivity. For example, instead of challenging the patient's assertion that a hearing aid will cause discomfort, the clinician might encourage the patient to expand on his concern and then present information to address it:

Clinician: Why do you think a hearing aid is going to hurt your ear?

Mr. Amos: I think it's going to bother me to have something in my ear all the time.

Clinician: I can understand why you think that it may be hard to get used to having something in your ear. We will customize the ear mold (shows patient an ear mold) to fit comfortably into your ear. If for any reason it doesn't feel right, I'll make adjustments until you feel no discomfort or irritation.

The patient's list of potential benefits might also help identify patient-specific goals for aural rehabilitation, and the clinician might discuss additional ways the aural rehabilitation plan might address them. Then, the clinician may begin to talk about various hearing aid options and about the next steps for obtaining a hearing aid.

The three distinguishing features of the example program just described are as follows (Shelton & Faucette, 1999, p. 52):

- The weight of the responsibility for decisions shifts from the [clinician] to the patient.
- The focus changes from [clinician]-driven discussion to patient-centered exploration.
- The [clinician] moves from one who controlled the outcome to one who facilitates it.

Components that, taken together, determine psychosocial reaction to hearing loss:

- *Emotional:* May include shame, guilt, anxiety, anger, frustration, embarrassment, depression.
- *Cognitive:* May include inattentiveness, reduced concentration, low self-esteem, low self-confidence, increased effort required for listening comprehension.
- *Interpersonal:* May include bluffing, social withdrawal, dominating conversations, a loss of intimacy.
- *Behavioral:* May include a limitation of activities or social isolation.
- *Physical:* May include fatigue, muscle tension, headaches, stomach problems, sleep problems.

(Preminger, 2007, p. 114)

PSYCHOSOCIAL SUPPORT

Counseling may be expanded to include psychosocial support. Psychosocial support is particularly valuable when patients' emotional responses to hearing loss are negative and when they have experienced communication failure and other people's disapproving attitudes. The goal of the support is to facilitate emotional adjustment in the context of the aural rehabilitation plan. The outcome is increased self-acceptance, increased self-confidence, and more effective use of communication strategies.

Psychosocial Consequences for Persons with Hearing Loss

Losing one's hearing can be devastating, particularly if the loss is severe enough to result in isolation from society (Figure 9–12). The loss, and concomitant changes in how a patient relates to family, friends, and coworkers, can decrease one's self-confidence and foster a negative self-image, which may be reinforced by others' reactions, including their stigmatization. Because acquired hearing loss may restrict one's activities and create unsatisfactory interactions, depression may follow. For example, Knutson and Lansing (1990) showed that adults with profound hearing loss were likely to be depressed, introverted, and lonely and experience social anxiety, particularly if they had inadequate communication strategies. Hétu and Getty (1991) found a prevalence of a negative self-image among individuals with hearing loss.

FIGURE 9–12 Psychosocial consequences of hearing loss. Hearing loss may cause loneliness and social isolation.

Who Am I?

"I confess to being quite stressed with resultant higher cortisol levels, and often, I am not the most pleasant company. I remove my hearing aids just for a break. I believe it was almost easier when I did not 'own' my hearing loss and didn't even wear my hearing aids, nodding to get along in conversation and guessing what was said. Now hearing loss has become the singular characteristic that defines me when I achieved so much in so many fields. So sad."

—A high-powered lawyer who is also a competing equestrian, conservatory-trained musician, artist, and mother of three

Even when the hearing loss is not severe or profound, it can inflict negative psychosocial consequences. A study about working adults with mild-to-moderate hearing loss (mean age of 46 years), and working adults with normal hearing showed that the participants with hearing loss were more prone to depression, anxiety, hostility, and interpersonal sensitivity (Monzani et al., 2008).

Hearing loss also may create **hearing-related stress**, which is an individual's response to either an acute or chronic strain. Stress in turn may create feelings of frustration, anger, and even despair. Adults with hearing loss may experience a three-pronged stress: (a) having to understand speech with impaired hearing, (b) having to adjust to a new self-concept, that of a person with hearing loss, and (c) having to adjust to society's reactions to self-as-hearing-impaired.

Hearing-related stress includes the stress of adjusting to a new self-concept, the stress of living with an impaired sensory system, and the stress of living with the reactions of society to people who have a disability and who experience communication difficulties.

Individuals who suffer a hearing loss, whether it is sudden or gradual, often develop a sense that they have gone from being "able-bodied" to being "abnormal." They no longer are able to communicate as easily as they once did and they may no longer be able to perform their professions and daily responsibilities as effectively because of the hearing loss. Their social and emotional interactions may be less rewarding than before and they may have a lost or diminished sense of independence and self-sufficiency. One woman, when asked how she was different now that she had a hearing loss, responded, "I feel like the world dumped on me." A man, when asked the same question, responded, "I feel like I'm a piece of driftwood drifting away." Hearing loss may lead to feelings of insecurity because patients no longer trust their ears. They may begin to wonder whether they are responding appropriately in any given situation.

Children who are born with hearing loss, or who acquire hearing loss early, may also experience isolation and a negative self-image, especially as they begin to realize they are in some ways different from others in their social and school environments. A child may develop a self-image of being less capable than others. Children's self-esteem may suffer as they experience difficulties in socializing with their peers who have normal hearing or difficulties in learning academic material.

Because hearing loss has a deleterious impact on interactions with others, consequences may include being ostracized by peers, loss of job opportunities, changes or limitations in everyday roles (e.g., as a spouse, a parent, a friend), and increased levels of stress, anxiety, and fatigue (Getty & Hétu, 1991; Hétu & Getty, 1991; Hogan, 2001). A psychosocial feedback loop may develop, where the impaired social, vocational, or academic function related to the hearing loss stimulates a negative self-image (e.g., "I'm inadequate"). A person's coping responses may in turn deteriorate or not develop and the person may experience limited confidence and feelings of helplessness and unworthiness (Heydebrand et al., 2005; Hogan, 2001).

Psychosocial Consequences for Frequent Communication Partners

Communication, which is the centerpiece of intimacy, invariably suffers when a member of a marriage or partnership has hearing loss. The third-party disability experienced by a patient's frequent communication partners may entail activity limitations and participation restrictions in the domains of everyday communication, domestic life, interpersonal relationships, and participation in social, community, and civic events (Scarinci, Worrall, & Hickson, 2009b, 2012). Spouses and partners in particular may experience third-party hearing disability in any or all of the following domains:

- *Emotions*: For example, they may experience feelings of frustration over communication difficulties, impatience (e.g., "Forget it, it's not worth repeating"), anger (e.g., "What am I supposed to do about your problem?"), guilt, a sense of incompetence for not knowing how to minimize the listening problems for the patient, pity, anxiety, empathy, embarrassment, and sadness for the loss of easy communication, on both the patient's and their own behalf.
- *Accommodations*: For example, they may have to repeat themselves and repair and prevent communication breakdowns, they may sometimes have to serve as an intermediary during conversation (as having to answer questions on patient's behalf), they may have to tolerate the loud volume of the television and raise their voice level when speaking, they may have to make phone calls on the patient's behalf, and they may have to explain the patient's hearing problems to others.
- *Social and civic life*: For example, the partner or spouse may no longer be able to go to noisy environments, may engage in activities alone instead of as a couple, may attend fewer social events, may no longer go to the cinema or theater or

musical events as often as they would like, and may participate in fewer extended family gatherings.

- *Intimacy*: For example, the couple may engage in less spontaneous conversation, joking, and "small talk"; they may feel less satisfied with their marital relationship, arguments triggered by the hearing loss (e.g., the patient accuses the partner of mumbling or not talking face-to-face) may occur, and there might be a shifting of roles in the relationship which leads to discomfort on the part of both the patient and the partner.

Eyewitness Accounts

We once posed the following question to a group of people who had spouses with significant hearing losses: "What are some of the most difficult aspects of living with a family member who has hearing loss?" Here are some of the responses:

Rhonda: I'll list some of them: (1) anger—communication is often difficult that he's "not the same"; (2) concession—everyone has to change what it is he or she is doing, or the way they do them [e.g., talking, listening to the TV]; and (3) frustration—things have to be done his way to accommodate his hearing loss. It is just simply a whole new way of life. He has to deal with the fact that he is hearing impaired and being his family and loving him as we do, we deal (well or not) with all of the changes too.

Gerald: I cannot communicate with her by phone when she is alone. I once called a next-door neighbor to tell her of a tornado warning—she is so damn independent she was upset about my doing that.

Mike: Communication with a family member [who has hearing loss] requires patience and determination. I'm sure the frustration is equally disturbing to my wife. Tempers sometimes flare as one or both attempt communication and fail. Oftentimes communication is abandoned by one or both parties, leaving both equally frustrated.

Janelle: We have a captioning device on the TV and the kids sometimes get mad when he wants to see the news captioned and they may go to another TV—poor kids, hah!

Anna: I have to move and make sure he can see my face when I speak to him. And we less and less enjoy "small talk" together. Hearing aids have helped but we have finally reached the point where we cannot talk to each other without extra effort.

Kristen: Trying to do business and explain to him what's going on. Especially if someone else is around, he gets real rude and frustrated at me because he can't hear or understand.

Spouses

"Spouses play [an important role] in initiating aural rehabilitation . . . and may become so frustrated with their partners' hearing loss that they are often the primary reason why the person [with hearing loss] presents for audiological services."

—Nerina Donaldson and colleagues, researchers at the University of Queensland in Australia

(Donaldson, Worrall, & Hickson, 2004, p. 30)

Psychosocial Support Intervention Paradigm

For many persons with hearing loss, the stress that results from their communication difficulties and their perceived inabilities is debilitating. One reason they may seek psychosocial support is to understand who they are and what has happened to them, and to get their lives moving forward. Raymond Hétu and Louis Getty at the University of Montreal performed some of the seminal work on developing a psychosocial support paradigm for adults who have hearing loss (Getty & Hétu, 1991; Hétu & Getty,

1991). Their approach (sometimes referred to as *the Montreal Method*) was based on two principles:

1. Knowing that hearing disabilities affect not only the victims themselves, but also anyone with whom they interact, rehabilitative help must consider several levels of coordinated interventions in order to reach the target individuals, families, social networks, and institutions.
2. In order to facilitate the interaction between victims of [hearing loss] and others, a change in attitudes and behavior is required (Hétu & Getty, 1991, p. 306).

Their objectives were threefold:

1. To offer a psychosocial support to help affected [patients] and their [frequent communication partners] to better deal with the effects of hearing loss.
2. To allow the [patients] and their [frequent communication partners] to understand the nature and the consequences of the hearing problem.
3. To develop new skills that will help in coping with the effects of hearing loss (Getty & Hétu, 1991, p. 318).

Psychosocial support helps patients recognize:

- The impact of hearing loss on their lives and self-image
- How they may have internalized negative perceptions about hearing loss
- How these negative perceptions limit their living a full and satisfying life
- How new attitudes about themselves and others may allow them to live life in a new and proud fashion, where pride can be defined as made up of "self-confidence, ability, self-esteem, security, a sense of the future, and a sense of where I fit in the world" (Hogan, 2001, p. 18)

As noted in Chapter 8, psychosocial support is sometimes incorporated into a group aural rehabilitation program and is usually provided in small groups of three to eight persons. Often, the participants' frequent communication partners are encouraged to attend the sessions because they play a profound role in shaping the participants' self-image and self-confidence and may also have their own psychosocial issues to address. The support may be provided in intensive sessions over two or three days for eight hours a day, or might be provided in shorter sessions over the course of several weeks. A sample curriculum for a two-day program is presented in the Key Resources. This curriculum was adapted from Hogan (2001), which in turn drew heavily from Getty and Hétu (1991).

Social identity is one's sense of belonging to a particular social group, and comprises a part of a person's self-concept.

Subtle advantages of a group program is that group participation may help patients to accept their hearing loss, to decrease their self-stigmatization, and to abandon any belief that they are defective or that they are confronting insurmountable challenges. Participants may develop a shared **social identity** with fellow group members, giving them a sense of belonging, of being valued and supported, and of being understood, and helping them to realize that it is safe to transition to a new social identity without fear of losing important relationships and without being discredited as a person.

Problem-Solving Framework

The framework for psychosocial support is a problem-solving model (Figure 9–13). Through a series of activities or exercises, participants learn to identify the kinds of problems they are experiencing, understand the nature and effect of these problems, and then generate effective solutions for resolving them.

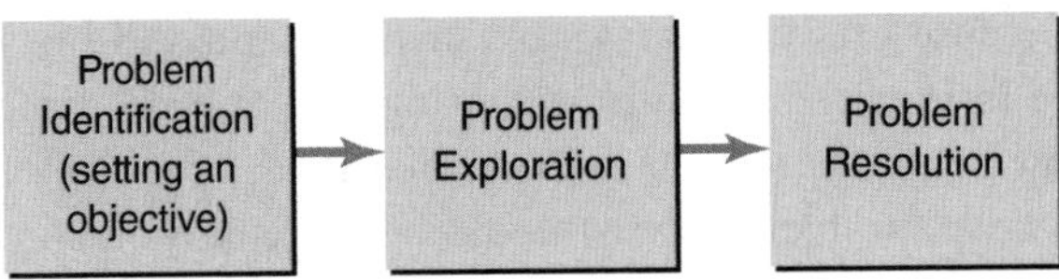

FIGURE 9–13. A problem-solving framework for psychosocial support.

Groups are an ideal venue for:

- "Identifying the problems and concerns of [patients] and their communication partners.
- Providing alternative solutions to the reported hearing loss–related problems.
- Providing opportunity for people to practice new communication skills in a safe, nonthreatening environment.
- Providing feedback about their newly acquired efforts.
- Providing opportunity to practice emotion-regulation procedures."

(Trychin, 2012b, p. 94)

Problem Identification

During problem identification, the participants turn the spotlight on the issues. Problem identification can begin by asking the participants in a psychosocial support group, "What's the worst thing about living with a hearing loss?" Both the person with hearing loss and the person's frequent communication partner respond to this question. Answers can be written on a whiteboard or a hanging easel. Figure 9–14 presents an array of responses that might be elicited during this activity. As this figure demonstrates, the worst thing might range from specific situations that might be easy to address, such as an inability to hear the doorbell, to more general and more difficult-to-address responses, such as depression, stress, anger, and feelings of stupidity. This exercise can be emotionally wrenching for some because it may be painful for participants to verbalize their difficulties to others or to consider how their lives have been affected by the presence of hearing loss. In some cases, the group leader may realize that the psychosocial issues of a particular individual may require referral for more in-depth **psychotherapy**.

Psychotherapy is a treatment for an emotional or behavioral problem in which a mental health expert (e.g., psychiatrist, psychologist, counselor) discusses feelings and problems with a patient, with the goals being the relief of symptoms, changes in behavior leading to improved social, emotional, and vocational functioning, and personality growth.

Joe:	I can't hear the doorbell. People come and ring the doorbell and they think we're not home or I'm rude.
Darren:	Having to ask a couple of times what is being said. I get exasperated and frustrated.
Katie:	Missing out and feeling isolated. I miss the social aspect of being in a group of hearing friends and understanding what they're saying. I also miss not being able to go to movies, and having to wait for the videos to come out. Feeling left out. How many times have I stayed at home because I didn't want to be bored?
Gaylyn:	People treat you like you're two years old or stupid. It makes me feel very, very mad.
Mary:	I've kept it in for so long I can't get the words out. I get angry, depressed, and tongue tied.
Joan:	Stress with my partner.
John:	I tend to shut myself in. If we were having a class reunion tomorrow I wouldn't go because I would have to explain to fifty people about my hearing loss. It makes me uncomfortable.
Jerry:	I miss music.
Archie:	Having to ask for help.

FIGURE 9–14. Responses generated during an identification activity to the question, What is the worst thing about living with hearing loss? Respondents are adult cochlear implant users.

Often, the problem identification segment of the program includes establishment of objectives, which helps make a problem manageable. For example, one woman identified her problem as, "Because I have a hearing loss, my husband and I never talk anymore." To tackle this issue in every conversational setting and at every time of day might be overwhelming. However, if the woman were to identify the problem, and then establish a well-defined objective, problem-solving could be targeted in a concrete manner. For example, in this case, the woman was asked to identify those times when conversation was most important to her. She responded, "Before I begin to fix dinner, after I get home from work." The objective for this woman and her husband then became, "I would like to converse effectively with my husband for 30 minutes every night before I begin to fix dinner." Solutions were then generated to meet this objective (problem exploration, described next) and included *sit together in a quiet place before dinner, turn off the television for 30 minutes*, and *refuse to take phone calls during this time.*

The difficulties identified during this stage will help guide the remainder of the program. For example, if stress seems to be a common theme in the responses, then the participants can discuss ways of managing stress and practicing relaxation techniques. If managing communication breakdowns seems to be the prevailing theme, then the group can focus on using repair strategies effectively.

Move the Flowers?

In an exploration scenario, the group leader set up the following situation:

I'm your wife/husband's cousin. I am having a pretty big dinner party. I want you to meet some of the other people at my party, so I am not going to sit you next to your partner. The flowers are in the center of the table. Would you ask me to move the flowers?

Here is the dialogue that ensued:

Jim: I would explain the situation. I might say, "It would help me to read lips and participate in conversation if you move the flowers."

Group Leader: Is that explaining part hard to do?

Jim: Yes. Admitting a problem is hard to do.

Min: It's hard. It's not fair that we always have to come up with a solution or that we have to explain things.

Mary: When you're a guest in someone's home, you hate to impose on them. After all, it's their house so why should you be telling them what to do?

Notice that during this exercise, some of the emotional underpinnings that prevent people from using facilitative strategies are revealed. Jim is embarrassed to tell people that he has a hearing loss. Min resents that the onus of managing the communication environment always falls on the person who has hearing loss. Mary feels she does not have the right to impose on others.

Problem Exploration

Once problems are identified, they can be explored in more depth. For example, asking a person to turn off the background music requires self-confidence and a healthy self-image (e.g., "I have the right to communicate as effectively as I am able at this gathering"), trust in the communication partner (e.g., the partner could become annoyed or develop a negative perception of the person with hearing loss as a result of the request), and a willingness to be rejected (e.g., the partner could refuse). Often, during periods of exploration, participants in a group will realize that they do not manage their communication problems effectively because they do not want to draw attention to their hearing loss, they are fearful of others' reactions, or they want to take the easiest course of action.

Two means of engaging in problem exploration are through creating scenarios and compiling self-profiles. In creating a scenario, the group leader might describe a hypothetical situation:

> I'm inviting you to my party. There will be lots of people out there. We are going to cook hamburgers and hotdogs out on the grill. The party will be at night, so I'll have a few lanterns burning. And oh yes, I'm going to have some great music. My brother is lending me his boom box. What would keep you from joining us?

The responses to this kind of scenario might range from "I won't be able to speechread anyone" and "The music will be too loud to hear anything" to "No one will talk to me because I'm deaf" and "Parties are boring, I just stand off by myself."

As they speak about their reasons for avoiding social situations, the group members can explore why they might behave in the ways they predict (e.g., "I don't want to burden people"; "It's not fair to my wife to have to interpret everything for me") and what their options are for dealing with difficulties.

In compiling a self-profile, the participants are asked to describe themselves to each other. This might entail pairing off and taking turns talking to one another, drawing a picture of themselves, or creating a collage using pictures torn from magazines. For example, in one session, participants were divided into groups of three and asked to construct a collage using pictures cut out from a stack of old magazines. One group included a picture of a woman falling out of her high heel shoes and another picture of a woman with her back to the camera, holding a telephone receiver to her ear. When describing their collage to the others, the group members noted that the woman falling out of her shoes conveyed their sense of feeling off balance in a hearing world. The woman with her back to the camera conveyed their feelings of being ignored and excluded in everyday events.

Problem Resolution

Problem resolution is the third stage of the process. Some of the techniques described in Chapter 8 can be employed during this stage, particularly if managing communication problems and difficult listening situations has been cited during problem identification and exploration. In developing ways to resolve problems, individuals may engage in self-examination and ask themselves such questions as: *What are my rights as a person with hearing loss? What are the consequences of not managing my problems effectively? How will I feel if I successfully overcome this difficulty?*

Gagné and Jennings (2000, p. 569) present a step-by-step process for problem-solving. First, they suggest that the group or an individual sets an objective and defines a desired outcome. For example, an objective might be, Mr. Smith will use repair strategies during his weekly card game. As a result of his participation in this class, he'll be able to understand messages intended for him after using one or two repair strategies. Step 2 in this problem-solving process is to identify possible solutions. For each of the solutions, the implications of using it (e.g., its feasibility, acceptability, potential advantages, and disadvantages) are considered. The third step in problem solving is to select a solution and to try it out. Finally, the benefits of applying the selected solution are considered, as well as the factors that facilitate or hinder its implementation.

Example of the Problem Identification-Exploration-Resolution Framework

In an actual session, Maria, the wife of a man with hearing loss, said that the most difficult aspect of living with someone who has hearing loss was as follows: "I'm working in the kitchen and Ben is in the living room reading. It takes a very, very, very long time for him to respond to me. He hears talking but he doesn't respond."

After identifying this problem, the participants in the group explored it. They asked the couple about other times when this kind of communication difficulty occurred. They discussed who has control of the situation and who has responsibility. The group leader asked whether the situation could be changed. What core beliefs may get in the way of thinking about the possibility of change? During this discussion, Maria noted ruefully, "If you say something he wants to hear, he'll respond."

This remark prompted another member of the group to observe, "You can't jump to conclusions. I just make sure my mother hears what I say and then I wait for a response."

Later in this discussion, some of the emotional undercurrents of the couple's communication problem emerged:

Maria: I enjoy talking and he doesn't. Finally, I have to just cut it off. There is no point aggravating myself. He doesn't talk anymore, but when I want an answer, I get it.

Ben: This is kind of frustrating or aggravating. Hearing loss is a frustrating situation because now you cannot achieve what you would like regularly. I would love to communicate with her. I would like to talk on the phone, listen to music, and not just noise. A hearing problem is very frustrating.

During the resolution phase of this issue, the group leader asked the participants to generate a list of possible solutions. Here is what they came up with:

- Maria, go over to Ben and wave.
- Maria, yell.
- Maria, throw something at Ben to get his attention.
- Maria, repeat.
- Maria, tap him.
- Ben, read the paper in the kitchen.
- Ben, help prepare dinner.
- The couple should sit together in a quiet, well-lit room for 20 minutes every night before Maria starts to prepare dinner. Communicate then, when conditions are optimal.

The group leader suggested that the couple pick one, try it, and then review its effectiveness.

Offering a Helping Hand

The **Hearing Loss Association of America (HLAA)** is a self-help organization for people with hearing loss and provides information, education, support and advocacy, and for many people, psychosocial support to deal with the stigma and isolation associated with hearing loss. With over 200 local chapters nationwide, people with hearing loss meet with other people who have hearing loss for emotional support, information, and friendship. The organization's guiding premise is that "people with hearing loss can help themselves and one another to participate fully and successfully in society" and that participation in the organization can promote self-confidence and empower them to improve their lives. In addition to attending meetings at their local chapter, members can interact with one another and acquire information about the latest hearing technology through the organization's webinars, message boards, chat rooms, internet courses, a magazine, and annual conventions. The organization offers membership to both citizens and noncitizens of the United States (http://www.hearingloss.org).

The **Hearing Loss Association of America (HLAA)** is a self-help organization for people with hearing loss, and provides information, education, and support and advocacy.

ASSERTIVENESS TRAINING

Although some people who have hearing loss are comfortable with using communication strategies in a secure clinical setting, or even in home situations with familiar communication partners, many often have difficulty using them in other environments. These persons might benefit from assertiveness training. The goal of assertiveness training is to increase the cooperativeness between the person with hearing loss and his or her communication partners while still maintaining equality among the participants who engage in a conversation. Patients develop neutral, nonaggressive behaviors that allow them to maintain their self-esteem without encroaching on the rights of others and that allow them to engage in satisfying conversational interactions. Key elements of assertiveness training often incorporates the constructive and instructional facilitative strategies and acknowledgment gestures that we considered in Chapter 6 and entail learning:

- Ways to indicate a hearing loss (e.g., "I have a hearing loss. I may not understand everything you say to me")
- Means to request a change in the communication environment (e.g., "The light in here is dim. I'm having difficulty reading your lips. May we walk over to another room?")
- Ways to suggest how the communication partner can facilitate the patient's understanding of spoken messages (e.g., "It helps me to understand you if I can clearly see your face")
- Means to provide positive feedback to communication partners to reinforce desirable behaviors (e.g., "I appreciate your coming into the room to talk to me. Thank you")

Issues that might be addressed with assertiveness training:

- How do I tell others what to do so that I can better understand their speech?
- How do I improve my communication partner's speaking habits?
- How do I keep someone from speaking too loudly just because I have a hearing loss?
- How do I enlist my communication partner's help in structuring the listening environment so I can effectively communicate?

Assertiveness training teaches patients and their frequent communication partners ways to manage communication situations. For example a patient may disclose to a waitress that he or she has a hearing loss and ask for a printed list of the daily specials instead of a verbal recitation. If communication difficulties still arise, despite the patient's best efforts to avoid or divert them (e.g., the waitress does not have a printed list; the background music in the restaurant cannot be turned down), the patient can still feel good that he or she took affirmative action to manage the situation. Assertiveness training might also

Words and phrases to use when being assertive:

- Please
- Thank you
- It would help me if . . .
- I need to [see your face; move to a quiet room; turn down the radio]
- Will you . . . ?
- Can you . . . ?

Words and phrases to avoid:

- Won't
- Can't
- Don't
- Never
- You must . . .
- You always [mumble, turn away, talk too fast]

teach patients ways to manage their level of emotional arousal. They can cultivate such positive behavioral traits as being calm, friendly, reasonable, good-humored, and understanding. They can learn methods that will help them decrease physiological arousal and increase their cognitive clarity, methods such as yoga, meditation, progressive relaxation, and deep breathing exercises (Trychin, 2012b, p. 94).

During assertiveness training, emphasis is placed on choice of language and on the consequences of behaviors. For example, patients may compare the consequences of using language such as, "You never speak clearly when I try to talk to you on the telephone even though you know I have a hearing loss!" with those resulting from a statement such as, "It helps me to understand what you are saying when you speak at a slow but not too slow speaking rate." Whereas the former statement is accusatory and puts the communication partner on the defensive, the latter is a neutral statement that provides explicit guidance about how the communication partner can foster understanding.

Assertive behaviors are typically situation specific. That is, assertive behaviors are not always desirable or adaptive. For example, it may inappropriate for a man with hearing loss to remind his supervisor to speak clearly during a conference presentation. Part of the training should include a consideration of the consequences of using assertive behaviors in various situations.

RELATED RESEARCH

Realizations Following Participation in an Aural Rehabilitation Group

"You have to be assertive. If you aren't assertive, you withdraw into yourself. I didn't realize that until we learned that here. We can't let our hearing loss lead us around. We have to grab it and say this is what I can or can't do."

—An accountant who was forced into early retirement because of his progressive bilateral severe-to-profound hearing loss, who as a result of participating in an assertiveness training program experienced a change in his sense of identity that helped him "reestablish his self-esteem and gave [him] the confidence to self-advocate for his needs"

(Jennings & Shaw, 2008, p. 292)

Research suggests that these interventions are effective and that people want these services. For example, patients who do not receive counseling are less likely to use their hearing aids than patients who receive counseling. Counseling reduces the amount of hearing-related difficulties perceived by persons who have hearing loss (Brooks, 1979; Taylor & Jurma, 1999), increases their knowledge about hearing-related issues (Backenroth & Ahlner, 2000; Borg, Danermark, & Borg, 2002; Elkayam & English, 2003), and enhances their abilities to use coping strategies (Backenroth & Ahlner, 2000). After a psychosocial-based communication training program, workers with noise-induced hearing loss were more confident in dealing with their hearing difficulties (Getty & Hétu, 1991), and persons with occupational hearing loss realized at least short-term gains (Hallberg, 1996). Adult cochlear implant users spent significantly less time in communication breakdowns during conversations with an unfamiliar communication partner following their participation in an intensive two-day psychosocial workshop (Heydebrand et al., 2005). They also reported fewer maladaptive behaviors, such as withdrawing, as measured by the Communication Profile for the Hearing Impaired. A group of 46 adults participated in a six-session aural rehabilitation program that included both instruction in the use of hearing assistive technology and communication strategies. The participants made gains in their identified goals following their participation, gains that were still present six months later (Jennings, 2009).

CASE STUDY

Solving Challenging Situations

In assessing the effects of an intensive two-day psychosocial workshop for cochlear implant users and their spouses, we developed a before-and-after measure. The "before" question asked them to describe a common situation where it was difficult

(continues)

CASE STUDY *(continued)*

Solving Challenging Situations

for them to manage hearing another person. Then in a series of "after" questionnaires, we asked them to revisit their "before" answer (we provided them with a photocopied version of their remarks) and determine whether they were managing the situation differently. Here are the responses of Diane, a 39-year-old woman who had used a cochlear implant for two years.

Baseline Challenging Situation

[Diane wrote] "Conversations in groups of three or more in a dark or noisy environment are most difficult, especially if my friends are talking about something exciting. By the time I figure out who is talking, I've missed half of what was said, and then another person starts talking and I have to locate them."

Three-Month Challenging Situation

"I am more assertive in asking friends to repeat what I've missed using appropriate strategies. Sometimes if the conversation is going too fast, I will raise my hand, ask for a time-out, explain to everyone that I can understand them better if they speak slower or one at a time or if they raise their hand before talking—depends on if we are in a meeting or a social gathering. Occasionally, I may quietly ask someone next to me a small part of what I missed . . . rephrasing what I heard and having them fill me in to catch up on the conversation."

Six-Month Challenging Situation

"Really no change from three months ago, although I guess I'm feeling a little more confident these days. I continue to stop and ask friends to repeat or fill me in on conversation. If I get a key word, I may paraphrase it silently to someone next to me in order to catch up. I am doing well and have made significant progress."

Twelve-Month Challenging Situation

"Managing well. I usually ask the group to speak one at a time and at a slower pace. Sometimes they forget and the topic is 'heated' or very fast paced and I will stand up and make a big 'T' and say, 'Time out please. I'm having a hard time keeping up with the conversation, can we slow it down so I can hear and understand what is going on?' I sometimes have to do this two or three times but I've noticed over time that another member of the group will take the time to slow things down and remind others. It just takes repetition and I've gotten *much* better."

FINAL REMARKS

Hearing aids and other listening devices do not always address the problems that patients with hearing loss experience. They may continue to struggle with the changes hearing loss has wrought in their world. When persons experience a catastrophe in their lives, it is not unusual for the educational and health care systems of many countries to provide emotional and psychological support. Certainly, hearing loss should be afforded the same status as other negative life events.

KEY CHAPTER POINTS

- A patient-centered approach entails learning the patient's story and possibly using techniques from narrative therapy.
- Counseling provides many benefits to patients and their families, including better self-acceptance and reduced stress and discouragement. A clinician might provide informational counseling and personal adjustment counseling.

- During informational counseling, the clinician strives to ensure understanding and retention using such techniques as explicit categorization and repetition of important information.
- Personal adjustment counseling approaches are often categorized as cognitive, behavioral, or emotional, or a combination of any of these three.
- Rational Emotive Behavior Therapy (REBT) is a cognitive approach to counseling and, in the aural rehabilitation setting, entails questioning erroneous beliefs about hearing-related issues.
- Desensitization is a technique used in a behavioral counseling approach that aims for a patient to "unlearn" a learned behavior.
- Three tenets of Rogers' affective approach to counseling are congruence of self, unconditional positive regard, and empathetic understanding.
- Useful counseling tools include attitudinal continuums and a cost–benefit analysis form.
- Individuals who suffer a hearing loss, whether it is sudden or gradual, often develop a sense that they have gone from being able-bodied to being abnormal. Some of these individuals might benefit from psychosocial support.
- Psychosocial support aims to facilitate emotional, psychological, and social adjustment to hearing loss. The outcome is increased self-confidence, increased self-acceptance, and more effective use of communication strategies.
- In a problem-solving approach, patients learn to identify the kinds of problems they are experiencing, understand the nature and effect of these problems, and generate effective solutions for resolving them.
- During assertiveness training, individuals learn to increase cooperativeness with their communication partners and to develop neutral nonaggressive behaviors that allow them to maintain their self-esteem without encroaching on the rights of others.
- During assertiveness training, emphasis is placed on choice of language and on the consequences of behaviors.
- Sometimes losing one's hearing constitutes a catastrophic life experience. Individuals require and deserve adequate emotional and psychological support.

TERMS AND CONCEPTS TO REMEMBER

Counseling
Psychosocial support
Assertiveness training
Self-image
Narrative therapy
Clarification
Validation
Reassurance
Informational counseling
Personal adjustment counseling
Explicit categorization
Rational Emotive Behavior Therapy (REBT)
Desensitization
Affective approach

Congruence with self
Unconditional positive regard
Empathetic understanding
Reflection
Empathizing
Reframing
Normalizing
Questionnaires
Hearing-related stress
Social identity
Psychotherapy
Hearing Loss Association of America (HLAA)
Cognitive approach
A-B-C-D-E
Behavioral approach
Problem identification-exploration-resolution
Situation-specific behaviors

KEY RESOURCES

The curriculum for the St. Louis Psychosocial Hearing Rehabilitation Workshop. Persons who use cochlear implants and their frequent communication partners attended this two-day workshop.

Day 1

9:30–9:45 Introduction

Fitting of group FM assistive devices

Outline of group

- About communication strategies (and why it may be hard to use them)
- Problem identification
- Problem exploration
- Problem resolution

Ask group to generate rules of group communication:

- Right to pass on responding to a question
- Mutual respect
- One at a time
- Confidentiality
- "I" statements
- Speak as you want others to speak to you—"clear speech"
- When you finish speaking, signal

Goals

What do you expect from the group? What do you hope to gain by the end of this workshop? [Have participants write down individual goals.]

9:45–10:30 Ice breaker: Spondee exercise: Select one of the spondee cards (e.g., "base" or "ball") and introduce yourself to the person who has the other half of your word.

Take time to talk about when you developed a hearing loss and how it has affected your everyday routine.

10:30–10:40 Break

10:40–11:30 What's the worst thing about living with a hearing loss? For example: What do you miss? If you could change something, what would you change? What frustrates you or upsets you the most?

This group workshop is designed to:

- Help you better understand the problems you face.
- Identify strategies for dealing with these difficulties.

11:30–12:00 Susan's dinner party (schematic of the living room where the party is being held is included in your materials folder)

- Would you come to Susan's party? Why or why not?
- Will you have a good time? Why or why not?
- What might your partner do?
- If you don't do anything, why?
- What does it feel like?
- If you don't come, what would you say to Susan?

Introduction to choices, what is hard/easy about this?

Choices on a continuum, from doing nothing and being passive to being aggressive; brainstorm choices as a group.

General discussion

[Problem identification and exploration]

Which situations do you (or would your partner) find difficult?

What would you do in each situation? What might your partner do? If you don't do anything, why? If your partner would do nothing, why?

[Problem resolution]

Strategies (categories)

- Eliminate the problem.
- Assert your needs.
- Negotiate a better environment.
- Situate yourself away from the noise.
- Put up with it.
- Stay home.

12:00–1:00 Lunch

1:00–2:00 How do you identify yourself? Are you deaf, hard of hearing, impaired, disabled?

- How do you think of yourself?
- Are you happy with how you explain your problem to others?
- Are you comfortable with it?

- Do you see yourself in the hearing world or the Deaf world?
- How do others see you?

Break into groups of four and build a collage, using pictures from magazines, to show the world who you are.

2:00–2:10 Break

2:10–3:00 Exploration of passive, assertive, and aggressive communication behaviors

Marian's social gathering

Identify strategies as passive, assertive, or aggressive

3:00–3:30 The effects of deafness on the body—stress, what is the connection?

- How do you know if you are stressed? (brainstorm)
- What can we do about it? (brainstorm)

Relaxation exercise

3:30–4:00 Wrap up, anticipate possible emotional reactions to what we have done today.

Day 2

9:30–10:00 Review of previous day

How was yesterday's experience for you?

10:00–10:30 Changing roles—participants meet with one clinician, frequent communication partners meet with the other clinician.

- How has your role changed since the onset of the hearing loss? Since the receipt of a cochlear implant?
- How do you feel about your role?
- What style of communication do you use? Why?
- Can you help your frequent communication partner become more assertive? How?

10:30–10:45 Break

10:45–12:00 Explore role changes together

- Being helpful versus taking over.
- What it is like to be a "partner"/dependent.
- Finding the balance.

Partner issues

- Being helpful versus taking over.
- "Rescuing" and dependency.
- What it's like to be a "partner"?
- What has changed since the hearing loss?
- Finding the balance.

12:00–1:00 Lunch

1:00–2:00 How to be assertive

- Role-play difficult situations; discuss communication style and use of communication strategies within the context of each role-playing scenario. For example, at the bank or in the physician's office, are behaviors assertive, aggressive, or passive? Are they effective?

2:00–2:10 Break

2:10–2:45 Individual goals and contracts

Set realistic goals (examples).

What do you want to change?

What are you in control of?

Focus on step-by-step progress.

Keep a journal?

2:45–3:00 Relaxation exercises

3:00–3:45 Evaluation/debriefing

- What was the most important thing you learned during this workshop?
- What was the least useful?
- Will what you have learned help you in your everyday life?
- Has your partner's presence changed anything in how the workshop went for you? What made you decide to come?

PART 2

Aural Rehabilitation for Adults

CHAPTER 10

Adults

OUTLINE

The aural rehabilitation process usually requires the orchestration of a number of interventions, and these services can be integrated in ways to achieve maximum benefit for patients and their frequent communication partners. Services are often affected by a number of variables, including the country or state where delivery occurs and the way that health care is funded, structured, and delivered. For example, in the United States, aural rehabilitation services are largely privately paid, whereas in Scandinavia, services are more likely to be government funded (Gatehouse, 2003). Some U.S. insurance plans provide partial or full coverage for, say, auditory training, whereas others provide no coverage.

In the preceding chapters, we have considered various elements of a possible aural rehabilitation plan, including assessment, listening devices, auditory and speechreading training, communication strategies training, counseling, and group interactions. In this chapter, we first consider adults who have hearing loss and then consider a general strategy for designing an aural rehabilitation plan that incorporates any or all of these aural rehabilitation elements, and one that may also incorporate tinnitus management. The chapter mainly concerns patients who are between the ages of 17 and 60 years. Many individuals in this age bracket participate in family, community, and work situations, and many lead active social lives. A major goal of an aural rehabilitation plan will be to promote conversational fluency with family members, friends, and coworkers. Although much of what is reviewed will apply to the entire adult population, Chapter 10 is devoted specifically to older adults, those over the age of 60 years.

PREVALENCE OF HEARING LOSS AMONG ADULTS

Common stereotypes suggest that adult-onset hearing loss occurs primarily in older persons. However, individuals in their 40s and 50s increasingly experience hearing loss, in large part because of the world becoming an increasingly noisy place and because of increased use of earbuds and headphones. For example, a longitudinal, population-based study of adults in Beaver Dam, Wisconsin, found that the **prevalence** of hearing loss was 3% for adults between the ages of 21 and 34 years, 6% for those between 35 and 44, and 11% for those between 45 and 54. The prevalence jumped to 22% for those between the ages of 55 and 64 (Nash et al., 2011). Most adults lose their hearing gradually over time. The largest segment of adults who have hearing loss has mild or moderate sensorineural hearing loss. Typically, thresholds for the mid and high frequencies are poorer than those for the lower frequencies, regardless of the patient's age (Agrawal et al., 2008).

Prevalence is the percentage of a population that experiences a particular health problem at a point in time.

Factors that increase the risk of adult-onset hearing loss:

- Exposure to occupational, leisure-time, and firearm noise
- Smoking
- Cardiovascular health condition

(Agrawal et al., 2008)

WHO IS THIS PERSON?

In addressing the question *Who is my patient?*, a patient's stage of life, life factors, socioeconomic status, race ethnicity, psychosocial well-being, and home, social, and vocational hearing-related communication difficulties, gender, and other hearing-related conditions such as tinnitus must be considered (Figure 10–1).

Stage of Life

Lee Lieu and his 20-year-old son Kevin survived a devastating car accident on a snowy road. Both received head trauma and, as a result, incurred irreversible bilateral hearing losses (Figure 10–2).

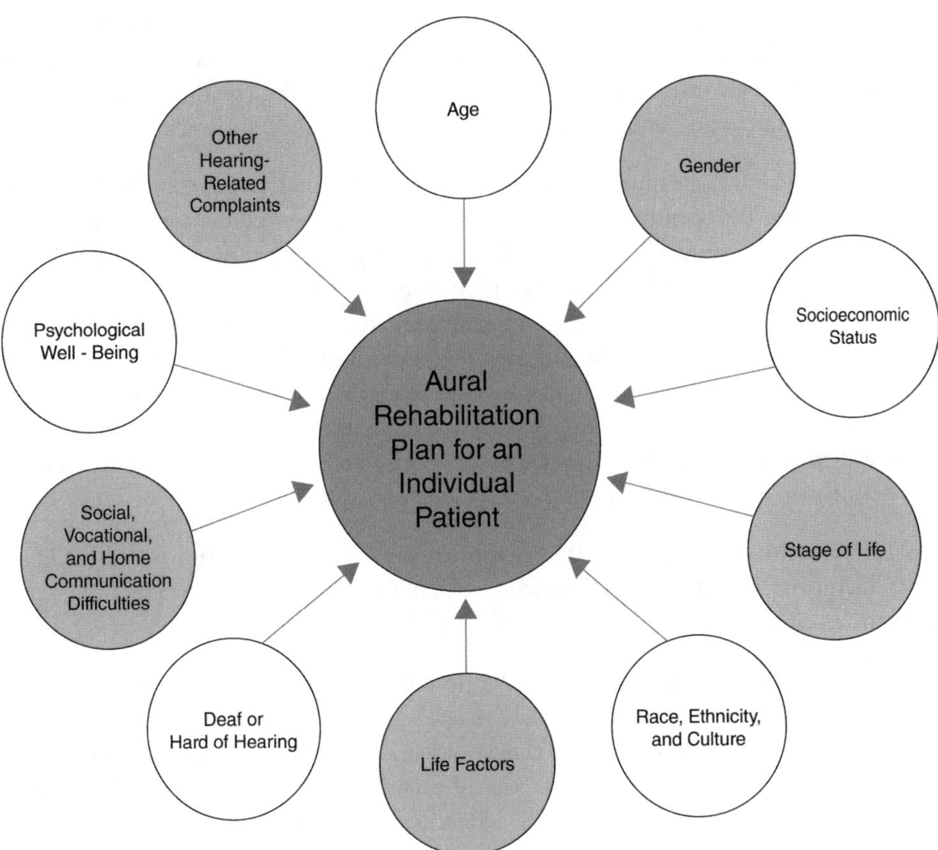

FIGURE 10–1 Variables that influence the design of a patient's aural rehabilitation plan.

FIGURE 10–2 Patient's stage of life. An aural rehabilitation plan may vary as a function of a patient's stage of life.

For both Lieus, life with hearing loss will never be like it was before the accident. However, the impact differs somewhat because the two men are in different stages of life. Lee Lieu owns a small advertising firm, which he started after college graduation. After many years of long hours and hard work, the firm is well established and successful.

Lee believes life has dealt him a blow just when he was experiencing decreased responsibilities and more freedom to pursue leisure activities. He now contemplates early retirement but has misgivings because he had hoped to have a larger savings account before retiring. Lee no longer socializes at executive meetings and he plays less tennis because conversations with colleagues and friends are effortful and exhausting, and if truth be told, demeaning. He either bluffs and pretends to understand or says, "Huh?" again and again and again. He suddenly feels old, and sad thoughts dominate his internal dialogue: He will never hear his grandchildren's voices; his clients don't believe he's competent to spearhead their accounts; his wife misses their once active social life; his friends avoid him because he dampens the spontaneity of conversation.

Lee's son is a junior in college with a major in public relations. Prior to the accident, Kevin Lieu participated in several extracurricular activities and dreamed of creating a public relations empire.

The hearing loss has left Kevin deflated. Because public relations entails communication, he wonders whether he should complete his college program. He feels embarrassed by the use of a professional note taker in class, but fears that asking classmates to share notes might elicit pity, and pity, in his view, would be unbearable. Kevin spends hours alone in the gym lifting weights, bedeviled by concerns for his future.

Life stages are age ranges in which a hearing loss may have different impacts.

Table 10–1 summarizes **life stages** and indicates how hearing loss may have an impact. Adults who have hearing loss often experience similar emotions such as frustration and they experience common difficulties such as communication breakdowns. However, as the example of the Lieu family illustrates, the impact of hearing loss relates to an individual's *stage of life*, that is, whether the individual is in young adulthood, in the 30s, 40s, 50s, or in the later years. Physically, cognitively, and socially, individuals at age 55

Losing That Competitive Edge

"I've been passed over for promotions. I've been denied a lot of things because of my hearing loss."

—A director of horticulture

"Some employers have questioned how well I could hear on the phone. I left an organization because I could not handle the phone work, even after making some attempts to increase the volume."

—A librarian who is a media specialist

(Tye-Murray, Spry, & Mauzé, 2009, p. 478)

TABLE 10–1 Life Stages and the Impact of Hearing Loss*

STAGE	EVENTS ASSOCIATED WITH STAGE	IMPACT OF HEARING LOSS
Young adulthood	Develop intimate relationships with others Accept financial responsibility for self Develop a vision of one's future life and begin to pursue dreams	Begin to reassess dreams Experience self-doubt about finding life partner
The thirties	Reassess life decisions (e.g., Is this the right job?) Career consolidation Modify life structures or reverse decisions that now seem inappropriate Invest self in job, family, and friends	Energy is not invested in reassessment Hesitation about change arises
Middle adulthood	Begin to consider own mortality Note clear signs of physical aging in self May feel that this is last chance to make life changes	Upward mobility may cease Uncertainty about goals and ability to achieve them may increase

(continues)

TABLE 10–1 *(continued)*

STAGE	EVENTS ASSOCIATED WITH STAGE	IMPACT OF HEARING LOSS
The fifties	Children may have left home Career may be well established Time is available to pursue leisure activities	May consider early retirement Fears of aging intensify Withdrawal from leisure activities may occur
Late adulthood	Deterioration occurs in health, physical attractiveness, and strength Friends and family are lost through death or relocation as a result of retirement One begins to review one's life and reflect on its meaning	Other problems related to aging are intensified (e.g., loneliness) Overall sense of loss is exacerbated

*See Van Hecke, 1994.

differ from their 25-year-old selves. Depending on their life stage, patients will confront different issues.

Life Factors

Closely related to stages of life are life factors. By adulthood, most people have established relationships with others, embarked on a vocation, and developed a personality and a personal view of the world. **Life factors** are in place. These factors may be socially and culturally determined, controlled by the individual, fixed, determined by the environment, or influenced by other qualities of the individual and his or her life situation. A patient with a heart problem and an extended family may be less concerned about a mild or moderate hearing loss than someone who has been taking antidepressants and recently lost a job.

Life factors are conditions that help define one's life, such as relationships, family, and vocation.

A **family lifecycle** represents the milestones and emotional and intellectual stages a person passes through as a member of a family, often described in terms of age, marital (partner) status, and ages and the presence/absence of children.

All in the Family

The effects of hearing loss within a family will vary, depending upon where the family is in the **family lifecycle** (Figure 10–3) and the dynamics of family circumstances.

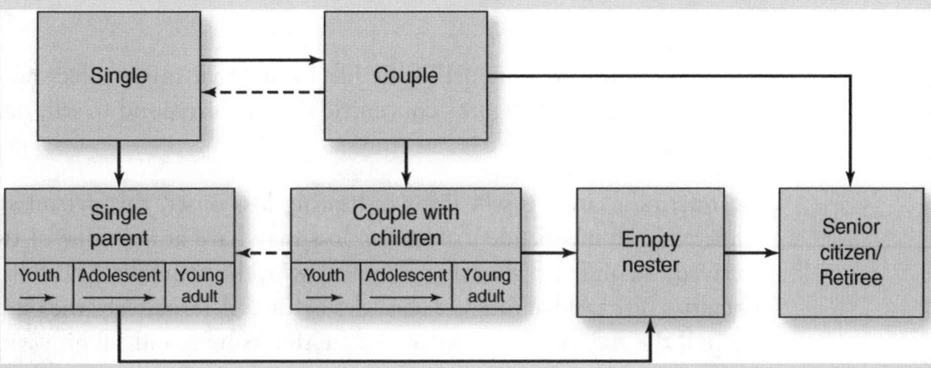

FIGURE 10–3 The family lifecycle. The family lifecycle will exert different effects depending upon where the patient is within that cycle. The patient may be single or a member of a couple, may have children and the children may vary in age from very young to adulthood or may be an empty nester, and may or may not have entered into retirement.

(continues)

All in the Family *(continued)*

You might consider the answers to the following questions:

- Is the patient married or single?
- Are the patient's offspring children, adolescents, or young adults?
- Is the patient an empty nester? A retiree?
- How does the family adapt to the shifting of generational roles?
- What kinds of illnesses and hardships have the family weathered in the past?
- What kinds of resources has the family accumulated?
- What other stresses exist, such as divorce, economic uncertainty, single parenthood, or unemployment?

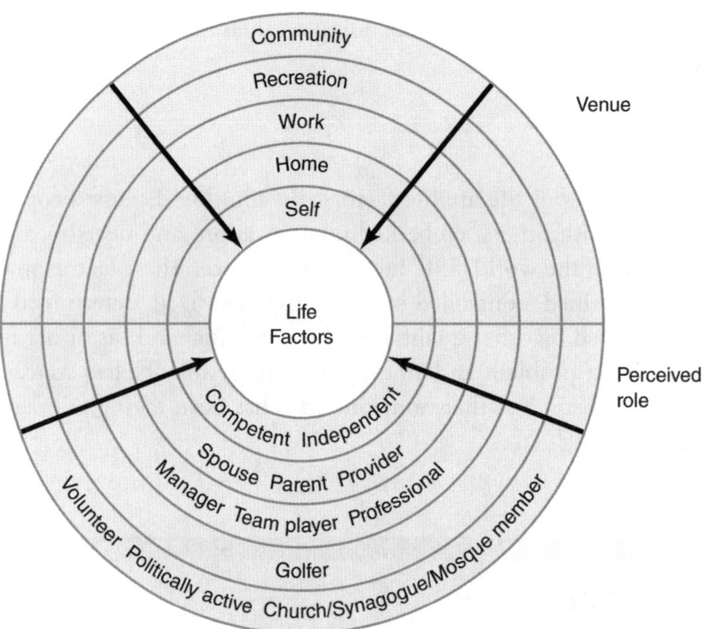

FIGURE 10–4 Life factors. Life factors influence how a patient will react to the onset of hearing loss and will affect the content of an aural rehabilitation intervention plan.

Figure 10–4 presents a model of the life factors that might affect how a male patient views hearing loss. The figure's concentric circles correspond to self, home, work, recreation, and community.

The innermost circle is self. Prior to hearing loss onset, this person viewed himself as competent and independent. Hearing loss may have at least one of two effects on his perceived role and self. He may come away with the belief that "I can handle my hearing difficulties. I've tackled tougher obstacles before." Alternatively, the onset of hearing loss may pull the rug out from under who he thinks he is and fill him with a sense of loss of self.

The next ring represents home and family. We all belong to a family in some way—parents, stepparents, partners, siblings, offspring—and our kinships and relationships bind us to one another and make us feel useful, connected, loved, and needed (Figure 10–5).

FIGURE 10–5 Family as a life factor. Prior to incurring a hearing loss, the patient was a member of a family.

Hearing loss can strain these bindings and cause a patient to feel alone and even rudderless. In turn, the hearing loss may destabilize the family. For example, the patient may fill the role of principal wage earner and believe that hearing loss undermines his or her ability to fulfill this role.

A Family Affair

"When my husband and I join my sons and [wives] at a restaurant, they choose the most advantageous seat for me and speak directly to me. However, sometimes the crosstalk and clatter is still overpowering and I feel like my seat is backing slowly away from the table until I'm just a viewer, not a participant. It's then that I refuse to let my mood sag, but instead sit smiling, giving thanks that they're all there, healthy and I can watch the fun. Inevitably I'm once again included . . . [but] it's a lot of work."

—An empty nester

At work, the hearing loss may hinder interactions with colleagues, especially if he or she is the first person in his company to present significant hearing loss. Some workers believe they have lost that "competitive edge" and have been denied promotions because of hearing loss, and some report having to be overly prepared and having to work twice as hard as their counterparts with normal hearing. For these patients, the overriding issue in developing an aural rehabilitation plan might be *How can we maximize the patient's communication effectiveness and conversational fluency in his or her workplace?*

On the golf course, the person depicted in Figure 10–4 may become the object of subtle teasing from his golf partners, and in the community, he might encounter ignorance and prejudice about disabilities. Such reactions from the community, recreational venues, and even the workplace may cause the patient to feel uncertain and isolated. The constricting arrows in Figure 10–4 reflect a common tendency for patients to withdraw from formerly enjoyable activities and companions.

The influence of community is further detailed in Figure 10–6. Here, the person with hearing loss is represented as a jigsaw puzzle who might be rearranged according to the surrounding community norms, services, and mores. The person will live in a world that has definite notions about who is an ideal citizen and to what extent a disability removes a person from achieving this ideal. The patient may live in a community that views hearing loss as a tragedy, a social problem, or a medical problem. The community, and its prevailing viewpoints, will determine what support services and technologies are available and what expectations are placed on the patient about how he or she should lead life, and help answer such questions as: *What kind of help do I need and where will I get it? How am I to live my life as a person with hearing loss? What kind of financial and technical support might I expect?* and *How am I to contribute to the world around me and live my life?*

Socioeconomic Status

A person's socioeconomic status is based upon a consideration of income, occupation, educational level, and dwelling type. The following examples illustrate ways **socioeconomic status** may affect a patient's aural rehabilitation plan:

Socioeconomic status is a person's position within a hierarchical social structure and is determined by such variables as occupation, wealth, education, income, and place of residence.

An **interpreter** is a person who is specially trained to translate oral or signed communication from one language to another.

A **translator** is a person who is specially trained to translate written text from one language to another.

Culture is a conglomeration of the thoughts, communications, actions, customs, beliefs, values, learned behaviors, and institutions of racial, ethnic, religious, or social groups.

Clock-time orientations are driven by the clock and are characterized by an adherence to time as a factor in determining the length of an interaction or the time-course of an intervention.

TRIBUTE stands for:

- **T**reat each patient as having unique personal and hearing needs.
- **R**espect cultural differences through both your verbal and nonverbal behaviors.
- **I**dentify the personality and learning preferences of each patient.
- **B**egin by learning some basic information on cultural difference through formal learning in courses and worships. Supplement this information with your own informal learning experiences in the workplace and in the community.
- **U**se language and cultural [**interpreters** and **translators**] to keep intended messages clear between you and the patient.
- **T**ell your patients about their hearing loss and hearing needs in plain language, avoiding audiologic jargon.
- **E**xplain that adjusting to hearing loss is a family event, and includes family members whenever possible in the rehabilitation process.

(Dancer, 2006, p. 26)

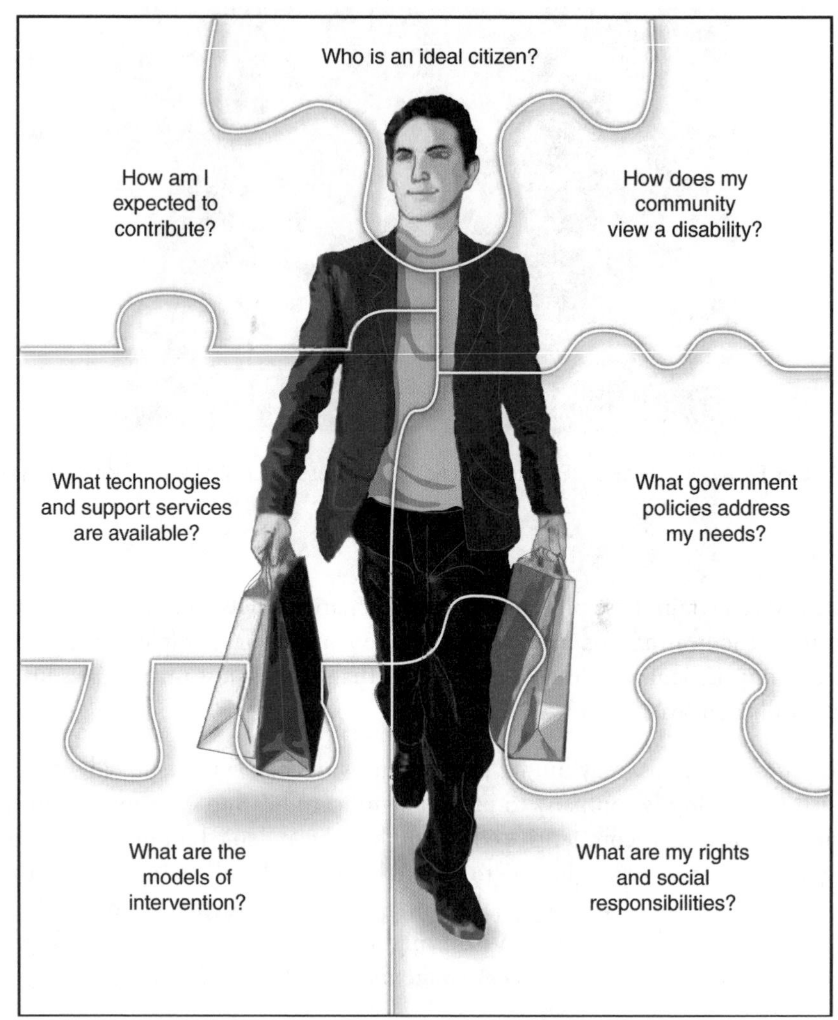

FIGURE 10–6 The community. The community will affect how well a patient functions with hearing loss.

- Financial status may determine whether an individual buys one or two hearing aids and will influence the quality of available health care; for example, patients who live in poorer, less sought after neighborhoods may have health care services that do not match the quality, availability, and affordability of those available in more affluent neighborhoods.
- Educational history may determine how much background knowledge someone has about the anatomy of the ear and its possible disorders and may dictate how a problem is discussed; for example, you will likely use different language when talking to an ophthalmologist than a graphic designer. It also may influence one's willingness to seek amplification or a cochlear implant (e.g., Hjaldahl, Widén, & Carlsson, 2017).
- Employment status may determine whether a patient can access hearing health care services; for example, some patients will hold jobs that do not offer health care benefits or they may be unemployed, so they will have only limited access.

Race, Ethnicity, and Culture

Racial, ethnic, and cultural and linguistic groups often have distinctive customs, beliefs, and service preferences that should be considered when customizing an aural rehabilitation program. For example, some **cultures** value expressing emotions, whereas others do not. Some cultures have concepts of **clock-time**, whereas others have concepts of

event-time. Some cultures incorporate an individualistic perspective—*I speak my mind and I view myself as an "I"*—whereas other cultures follow a collectivist perspective—*I hate to say 'no' for fear of being rude and I view myself as part of an extended family or a "we" group*. Some cultures may hold health care professionals in high esteem, whereas others may not. Some adhere to alternative healing systems such as acupuncture, Ayurvedic medicine, and religious/spiritual ceremonies. Some adults of a minority group may have experienced economic hardship and inadequate medical care growing up and may be inexperienced with interacting with health care professionals or distrustful of them.

Event-time orientations are process driven and are pursued to their natural conclusions no matter how long that might take.

Deaf or Hard of Hearing?

© Monika Wisniewska | Shutterstock.com

FIGURE 10–7 The Deaf culture. Members of the Deaf culture have a shared language. Here, a young woman uses her smartphone's camera to talk with a friend who is also a member of the Deaf culture.

Membership in the **Deaf culture** will affect the aural rehabilitation plan (Figure 10–7). Adult members of the Deaf culture typically lost their hearing early in life and rely on sign language for face-to-face communication and many believe they are culturally and linguistically distinct from hearing society. Membership in the Deaf culture is not determined by one's degree of hearing loss, but rather, by one's identification with Deaf people. For example, two individuals may have identical severe bilateral hearing losses. One of them may use powerful hearing aids and feel a part of the **Hearing culture**, whereas the other may reject listening aids and socialize primarily with Deaf people. One service that might be included in their aural rehabilitation plan might be the arrangement for a **sign interpreter**, who is a professional who does not participate in a dialogue but simply conveys messages from one communication partner to the next by translating spoken language into sign language and vice versa, as in one-on-one conversations, meetings, and lectures.

The **Deaf culture** is a subculture in society that shares a common language (e.g., American Sign Language, British Sign Language), beliefs, customs, arts, history, and folklore; primarily comprising individuals who have prelingual deafness.

The **Hearing culture** is the mainstream culture in the United States and includes spoken language communication.

A **sign interpreter** is a professional who translates the spoken signal into a form of signed English or American Sign Language, or vice versa.

The Deaf culture has the four hallmarks of any culture:

- A shared language, which in the United States is American Sign Language, a visual gesture language (Figure 10–7) that will be described in Chapter 12.
- Behavioral norms, which include ways for getting someone's attention (e.g., hand waving, tapping the person's shoulder) and leave-taking, among others.
- Values, which include Deaf politics, Deaf clubs, and everyday amenities such as visual/vibrating alerting systems and captioning.
- Traditions, which tend to center on face-to-face gatherings of people who are Deaf, which include Deaf alumni events, senior citizen gatherings, and religious services, and other such gatherings that are often replete with folklore, arts, songs, poetry, and joke-telling.

The American Speech-Language-Hearing Association (ASHA, 2011) identified three key culturally related points to consider when delivering speech and hearing services. First, everyone has a culture, a unique set of values and perspectives that have been shaped by the communities and people with whom they have lived and shared experiences. Second, a patient's culture is dynamic, not static, as are his or her cultural norms. People from one culture often acculturate into another, adopting new values and behaviors.

Third, culture is expressed through both explicit and implicit variables. We see explicit variables—a patient's T-shirt logo, a distinctive hat, a choice of food. Implicit variables manifest through behaviors, attitudes and consequences—a person's child-rearing practices, educational values, superstitions, and attitudes. Culture is a dynamic quality, inherent in each of us, continually changing, and expressed both overtly and covertly.

Cultural and linguistic competence is a set of congruent behaviors, attitudes, and policies that come together in a system, in an agency, or among professionals that enables effective work in cross-cultural situations.

In order to improve the quality of aural rehabilitation, many speech and hearing professionals find it valuable to acquire **cultural and linguistic competence**, and to learn more about the patients they serve, by developing relationships with people who act as cultural informants, by attending cultural events in their communities, and by learning how a patient's linguistic and cultural background might influence the clinical decision-making process.

Psychosocial Well-Being

A person with **psychosocial well-being** has a positive self-image and feels like an integral and important part of social relationships.

Stigmatization is a process whereby one's self identity is spoiled by the reactions of others, usually because the person deviates in some way from prevailing social and cultural norms, and is usually described in terms of stereotypes, prejudices, and discrimination.

Self-stigma occurs when a patient is aware of stereotypes (e.g., *Persons with hearing loss are old and decrepit*), agrees with the stereotypes (e.g., *That's right, persons with hearing loss are old and decrepit*), and applies the stereotypes to him or herself (e.g., *I have hearing loss therefore I'm old and decrepit*).

Patients often experience diminished **psychosocial well-being**. Psychosocial well-being relates to a person's positive self-image and sense of being an important and integral part of social relationships. Because hearing loss directly affects their interactions with others, many patients have a psychological experience that closely relates to its social consequences. Colleagues, acquaintances, and even family may begin to ostracize them, which may further diminish psychosocial well-being. **Stigmatization** may occur, which is a societal belief that someone possesses an undesirable attribute (i.e., hearing loss) and/or an undesirable characteristic (i.e., the person is difficult to talk with).

Some patients fall prey to **self-stigma**. Patients who self-stigmatize either consciously or unconsciously adopt the same prejudicial views about hearing loss held by members in their communities and apply those views to themselves. Self-stigma can amplify any feelings of stress, shame, low self-esteem, and degraded self-image and can lead patients to engage in maladaptive behaviors (Southall, Gagné, & Jennings, 2010). For example, self-stigma can lead patients to doubt their abilities and to bypass opportunities. One patient ruefully noted, "I turned down a promotion to be regional sales director because I knew I couldn't handle the volume of phone calls."

Home, Social, and Vocational Hearing-Related Communication Difficulties

How patients spend their time each day will inform their aural rehabilitation plan. For example, a man who spends his free time playing computer games will warrant a different course of action than a man who spends his free time socializing with friends.

Home, Social, and Job Problems

A survey conducted by Prince Market Research (2004) focused on hearing-related difficulties experienced by adults between the ages of 41 and 60 years. The organization conducted interviews with 458 individuals across the United States. The responses obtained are representative of the kinds of problems that patients might report experiencing. Difficulties affecting home and social life were as follows (p. 9):

- Two-thirds of those interviewed reported some difficulty in hearing the television.
- Three-quarters said that they often found themselves in situations where people were not speaking loudly or clearly enough or where the television was not loud or clear enough.

(continues)

Home, Social, and Job Problems *(continued)*

- When asked which areas were most affected by their hearing loss, they responded that they were most likely to avoid watching television with others in the room and most likely to avoid social gatherings.

The issues most commonly cited as affecting their workplace and their jobs were as follows (p. 10):

- One-fourth of those interviewed reported that hearing loss affected their work, including 67% of respondents who had severe hearing loss and 42% of respondents with a moderate hearing loss.
- Among those who said that their hearing loss affected work either "somewhat" or "quite a bit," phone calls (64%) and conversations with coworkers (61%) were reported as being the two areas most impacted by hearing loss.
- Despite the problems that hearing loss created in their workplace, fewer than 5% had asked their employer for help regarding their hearing loss.
- One-fourth of the sample pool said that their hearing loss had decreased their earning potential.

Figure 10–8 presents a model by which to conceptualize how hearing loss affects a patient's daily life. The two-ringed model represents how much relative time a patient spends in home, social, and vocational settings, and allows the patient to identify with whom most communication occurs and the kinds of activities and sounds encountered. In the model template (Key Resources), which actually can be used as a clinic tool, the inner ring depicts time spent in the home, social, and vocational settings, whereas the outer ring depicts the specific communication partners, activities, and environmental sounds encountered in each of the three types of settings. In the versions shown in Figure 10–8, an audiologist asked three patients the following questions:

- Question Set 1: *How big a "slice" of your day is spent at home? At work? At leisure?*
- Question Set 2: *For each slice, with whom do you talk? How do you spend your time?* and *What sounds would you like to hear?*

The complete results for one patient and partial results for the other two patients hold very different implications for an aural rehabilitation plan. Mr. Denby, the patient depicted in the top model of the figure, spends equal time in his home, vocational, and social settings. Mr. Denby indicated that at home his significant communication partners are his wife and 15-year-old son. He watches television and spends time on the internet. Important environmental sounds he hopes to hear are the alarm clock ring and the doorbell. In his pharmaceutical sales job, Mr. Denby identified his significant communication partners as being his boss and clients. He cited important activities as visiting his clients and procuring sales via telephone contact. He identified the paging system used throughout airports and traffic warning signals such as ambulance sirens as important environmental sounds. Socially, Mr. Denby spends time with his golf buddies at the golf course and at parties, and he enjoys listening to dance music.

The daily life listening needs presented by Mr. Denby's double-ring model suggests a very different aural rehabilitation plan from that which would be developed based on the models drawn by Ms. Crawford, whose time expenditures are depicted in the middle

Gender matters. If you are a woman with hearing loss:

- You are twice as likely as a man to disclose your hearing loss (West & Konstantina, 2015).
- You are better at offering suggestions to your conversational partners about how to enhance conversations (e.g., "My left ear has hearing loss, would you mind sitting on my right side?") (West & Konstantina, 2015).
- You are more comfortable with sustained eye contact, so you probably gain more benefit from the visual speech signal and from speechreading.
- You are more likely to use hearing aids and to use them for longer periods at a time (Staehelin et al., 2011).

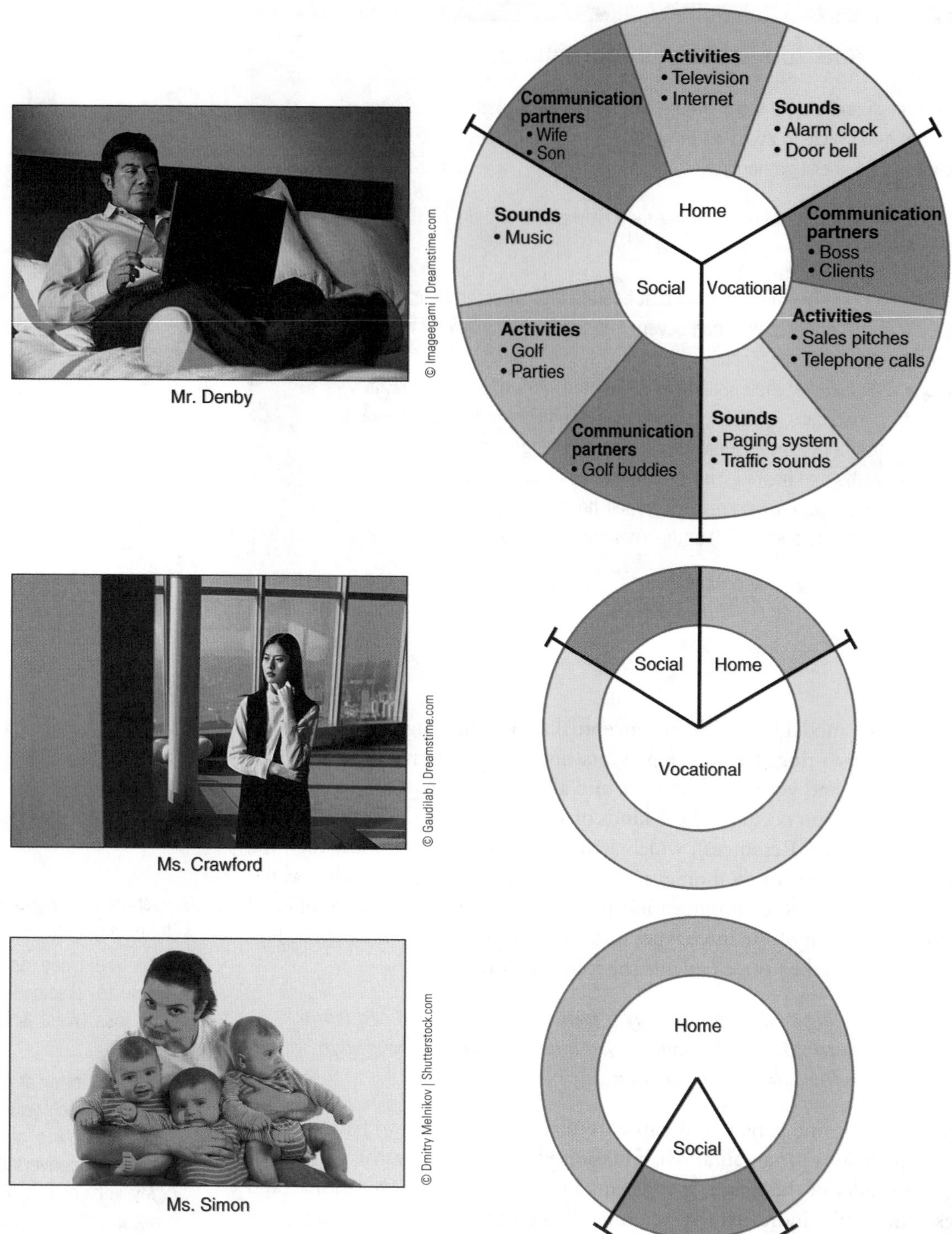

FIGURE 10–8 How hearing loss affects a patient's daily life. The inner ring of the model represents how much relative time a patient spends in home, social, and vocational settings, and the outer ring represents with whom the patient communicates and the types of activities and sounds encountered.

model, or Ms. Simon, whose time expenditures are depicted in the bottom model. Ms. Crawford is a junior-level investment banker, and spends between 12 and 18 hours a day in her office working on her computer. She lives alone and has little time for a social life. Ms. Simon is a stay-at-home mom with baby triplets. She has no vocational listening needs, but has many home-related ones.

Tinnitus

Some patients will experience other impairments related to their hearing loss, the most common being tinnitus. For these patients, the aural rehabilitation plan will also include tinnitus assessment and treatment.

Vertigo

Vertigo is another condition that may accompany hearing loss, more so in older patients than in younger patients. **Vertigo** is a type of dizziness in which a patient inappropriately experiences a sensation of motion, such as a spinning sensation while sitting still or a tilting and swaying sensation while standing upright. The patient may also experience nausea, vomiting, **nystagmus**, falling, faintness, and unsteadiness. The symptom typically arises from a disorder of the **vestibular system** and may occur in the presence of normal hearing. When it co-occurs with hearing loss, the dual symptoms may be indicative of Ménière's disease, acoustic neuroma, viral infection, head trauma, a fistula in the inner ear, and familial progressive vestibular-cochlear dysfunction, among other conditions. An audiologist is often involved in diagnosing the condition and determining whether it relates to a hearing problem. For example, among other diagnostic tests, the audiologist may perform audiological testing, electronystagmogram and videonystagmogram (ENG and VNG) tests, where eye movements are monitored, a Fakuda test, where the patient walks with eyes closed, auditory brainstem response testing (described in Chapter 12), and rotator chair testing, where the patient is spun around while seated. Depending upon the source of the condition, an audiologist may also be involved in the patient's vestibular rehabilitation and provide a type of physical therapy called vestibular rehabilitation therapy, which is a nonmedical treatment in which patients learn different body head positions to relieve vertigo and learn to habituate to triggering stimuli. Vertigo typically requires a team approach for treatment, and in addition to an audiologist, the team may include an **otolaryngologist**, a neurologist, a neuro-otologist, an internist, and/or a physical therapist.

Vertigo is dizziness, often experienced as a sensation of spinning or whirling.

Nystagmus is a pattern of eye movement characterized by a slow lateral drift in one direction followed by a saccade or fast movement in the opposite direction.

The **vestibular system** includes the semicircular canals, the vestibule (otolith and saccule), and the vestibular nerve, and functions to maintain equilibrium and balance, in conjunction with the ocular and proprioceptive systems.

An **otolaryngologist**, also known as an Ear, Nose, and Throat physician, specializes in the diagnosis and treatment of medical conditions of the ear, nose, and throat, including diseases of the related structures of the head and neck.

Most tinnitus is subjective, meaning that it is a phantom sound sensation. A person might perceive sound in the right ear, left ear, both ears, or inside or outside of the head. Common descriptors of tinnitus include:

- Leaves rustling
- The ocean roaring
- Crickets chirping
- A radio playing off-station
- A siren blasting
- A telephone ringing
- A single pure tone, either low-pitched or high-pitched

The word tinnitus derives from the Latin word *tinnire*, which means to ring or tinkle. In a survey of over 3,000 respondents, Kochkin, Tyler, and Born (2011) reported that tinnitus often accompanies adult hearing loss, with about 55% of respondents who reported tinnitus also reporting hearing loss. Tinnitus was found most prevalent among people over the age of 55 years and the typical sufferer experiences it for almost half of each day, with two in five people experiencing it more than 80% of each day.

As Table 10–2 indicates, etiologies of tinnitus are varied. The data reported in this table were collected from 2,369 patients at the Oregon Tinnitus Clinic. Forty percent reported that they could not identify a cause. Of the remainder, etiologies reflected four general categories: (a) noise-related, (b) head and neck trauma, (c) head and neck illness, and (d) other medical conditions, illness, drugs, stress (such as bereavement and loss of employment), and surgery.

TABLE 10–2 Conditions That Have Been Associated with Tinnitus, as Reported from 2,369 Patients from the Oregon Tinnitus Clinic*

CATEGORY OF ASSOCIATED CONDITION	CAUSE	% (AS SINGLE CAUSE)	TOTAL % AS SINGLE CAUSE	TOTAL % AS ONE OF MULTIPLE CAUSES
Noise related			18	22
	Long-duration noise	10		
	Explosion	5		
	Brief intense noise	3		
Head and neck trauma			8	17
	Head injury	4		
	Whiplash/cervical trauma	3		
	Concussion	<1		
	Skull fracture	<1		
Head and neck illness			8	10
	Ear infection, inflammation	3		
	Cold, sinus infection	3		
	Other ear problems	2		
	Sudden hearing loss	<1		
	Allergies, hay fever	<1		
Other medical conditions				
	Other illnesses	2		
	Drugs, medication	2		
	Stress	<1		
	Surgery	<1		
	Possible temporomandibular syndrome	<1		

*Adapted from Henry, Dennis, & Schechter, 2005, p. 1210.

Ménière's disease is an inner ear disorder that is related to idiopathic endolymphatic hydrops and may cause vertigo, hearing loss, tinnitus, and the sensation of fullness in the ear.

An **acoustic neuroma** is a tumor of the auditory or eighth nerve, usually benign, that may cause gradual hearing loss, tinnitus, and dizziness.

Some illnesses associated with tinnitus are **Ménière's disease**, **acoustic neuroma**, and head and neck injuries, such as whiplash. Some tinnitus-inducing agents include aspirin, salicylates, quinine, aminoglycoside antibiotics, and cisplatin. These kinds of drugs may cause either transient or chronic tinnitus.

Diet may exacerbate tinnitus. For example, salt has been found to aggravate tinnitus, especially in patients who have high blood pressure, because it restricts blood vessels, raises blood pressure, and impedes blood circulation (Keate, 2006).

Some patients find tinnitus a minor annoyance, bothersome only in quiet situations, as when trying to sleep. A significant number, however, experience tinnitus as debilitating, the cause of frustration, depression, hopelessness, and even thoughts of suicide. Tinnitus can impair concentration, create listening difficulties because it may mask the speech signal, and disrupt sleep. It can also lead to a reduced quality of life (Nondahl et al., 2007).

Tinnitus Can Be Debilitating

In some people, there is an association between tinnitus and psychopathological characteristics such as depression, anxiety, hysteria, and hypochondria. Though it is not possible to establish a clear cause and effect between tinnitus and such disorders, it appears that tinnitus can impose severe consequences on patients' ability to function in everyday life.

(continues)

Tinnitus Can Be Debilitating *(continued)*

Actor William Shatner, star (Captain Kirk) of the *Star Trek* television series and movies (Figure 10–9), has experienced tinnitus for much of his adult life. As the following excerpt demonstrates, he experienced desperate moments with his tinnitus (Shatner, 1997):

> Over the years I tried herbal remedies. I tried eardrops. I bought masking devices to avoid the silence, and tapes and records of soothing sounds—Japanese music, running water. And inside my house is a little waterfall. The sound of the water is very soothing.
>
> Getting through the nights—that was always the worst. Sometimes I paced the halls. I often turned to writing and exercise, and fatigued myself to sleep. I'd have the television on all night. It affected my marriage; if one person needs noise and the other person is sensitive to it, it can lead to separation. . . . I could not sleep without sound. In my darkest moments I thought to myself, "Will it be this way for the rest of my life, the way I am tormented by it now?" I began to think, "What are the ways to take my life? How does one kill oneself?" I went so far as to start making plans. (pp. 154–155)

Mr. Shatner's essay ended on a somber note. He related, "Recently I made a call to somebody in California, and when I called, his wife answered and said he was dead. He had committed suicide because of tinnitus" (p. 155).

FIGURE 10–9 Even the rich and famous suffer. William Shatner, depicted here in his trademark Star Trek outfit, suffers from tinnitus, probably as a result of having been exposed to loud engine noise.

Because tinnitus is often symptomatic of medical conditions other than hearing loss, a patient should see an otolaryngologist to rule out medical or surgically treatable ear pathology before entering into a tinnitus management program. A visit to an otolaryngologist is especially important if the tinnitus is unilateral, as that may be symptomatic of an acoustic neuroma. In addition to an audiologist and otolaryngologist, other members of a tinnitus management team might include a psychologist, psychiatrist, neurologist, pharmacologist, nutritionist, temporomandibular joint specialist, and biofeedback specialist.

Longing For a Good Night's Sleep

"Once upon a time I mourned my hearing loss and worried about what others would think. Reality caused priorities to change. What I wouldn't give for straight hearing loss without tinnitus. Time will tell if this new midnight tinnitus and resulting insomnia will upend my life or merely severely hamper it."

—A woman who began to experience a high-pitched pulsing tinnitus in addition to a white noise tinnitus

WHERE IS THE PATIENT IN THE JOURNEY?

The question of *Who is this person?* is often accompanied by the question, Where is the person in the patient journey? The term **patient journey** refers to the experiences and processes a patient passes through in the course of experiencing hearing loss and in participating in an aural rehabilitation plan. Most patient journeys begin long before a patient consults a speech and hearing professional and continues long after receipt of a hearing aid or an auditory training class. There are six distinct phases of the patient journey: (1) pre-awareness, (2) awareness, (3) movement, (4) diagnosis, (5) rehabilitation, and (6) resolution (Gregory, 2012) (Figure 10–10).

The **patient journey**, sometimes referred to as the hearing health care journey, is the sequence of experiences and phases a patient passes through during a treatment regimen.

Pre-awareness

With few exceptions, as in the case of adults who have a family history of hearing loss, few individuals ever anticipate they will suffer from hearing loss, especially while still younger than 61 years of age. Thus, when hearing loss begins, it usually takes a person by surprise. In the pre-awareness stage, family and friends may begin to notice that the patient is missing out on conversation, talking too loudly, or ratcheting up the television

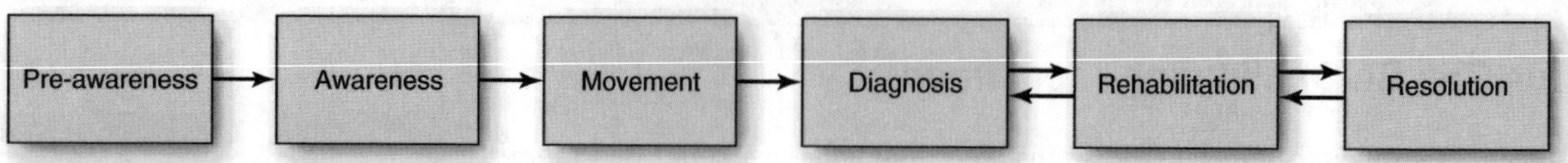

FIGURE 10–10 The six phases in the patient journey. Most patients pass through a series of stages in the course of experiencing a hearing loss (adapted from Manchaiah, Stephens, & Meredith, 2011).

volume. The patient may occasionally feel bewildered or frustrated when trying to converse in noisy settings.

Awareness

Awareness often happens gradually, and if asked when the loss began, a patient may not know. As Hétu (1996, p. 17) noted:

> It takes a rather striking invalidation of one's perceptual experience to start suspecting that one's sense organs no longer work properly. When hearing loss is progressive and symmetrical, there is no internal reference by which to measure the decrease in one's hearing capabilities. Furthermore, a comparison with others' hearing capabilities is very limited.

The advance from pre-awareness to awareness might last anywhere from a few days to many years. Situations that often alert people to a problem include having to ask people to repeat their messages, not hearing a doorbell or someone calling their name, and missing out on conversations that occur in the home. One man, reflecting on this phase, noted ruefully, "For about 2 years, I was snapping at my wife for talking too soft. Then I began to think that other people were mumbling too. It wasn't until my little grandson accused me of not paying attention that I thought to myself, maybe it's my hearing."

Other, less frequently cited indicants include complaining about bad telephone connections and not knowing where sounds are coming from. Family members and others may remark about a patient's coping behaviors and rationalizations. During this phase, a patient may self-test by twisting the radio volume up and down or by listening to speech over a telephone with the receiver held at varying distances from the ear.

Movement

During the movement phase, patients may consult with their family physician, talk to family and friends, search the web, and read articles about hearing, hearing loss, and hearing aids. They may move toward a "tipping point," and decide to consult a hearing health care professional.

Psycological costs, are nonmonetary costs that relate to a person's psychological well-being.

The movement phase may extract **psychological costs**, or nonmonetary, emotional outlays, such as the following:

- Acceptance within themselves that they have a hearing problem
- Anxiety that they may be getting old
- Awkwardness for having to ask for time away from work and having to explain the reason for the request
- Worry that the hearing aid may cost too much or that the audiologist will take advantage of them
- Fear that nothing can be done to alleviate the communication difficulties
- Embarrassment for entering a hearing clinic

Diagnosis

During the diagnostics phase, an audiologist identifies and quantifies the hearing loss. At this point, an individual might expect an audiologist or otolaryngologist to provide a rapid solution, and he or she may expect a treatment and complete cure. After her audiologist diagnosed a moderate bilateral sensorineural hearing loss, one patient responded, "My son had a hearing loss when he was 2 years old and the ear doctor gave him tubes. Now he's fine. You think surgery can help me?"

On realizing that hearing loss is here to stay, many people succumb to anxiety. They worry about possible outcomes, such as decreased professional options, loss of independence, rejection by friends or family members, and altered social status. What has occurred in the awareness and movement phase may mediate a patient's level of anxiety. For example, if someone has long suspected a hearing loss, then diagnosis may be less traumatic.

The Americans with Disabilities Act

As adults adjust to their hearing loss, they may take advantage of some of the provisions included in the 1990 **Americans with Disabilities Act (ADA)**. This key legislation forbids discrimination against persons with disabilities and requires that "reasonable accommodation" be made in public access, including employment and transportation. The law applies to programs and services of federal, state, and local government agencies and applies to goods, services, facilities, advantages, privileges, and accommodations. Table 10–3 presents key features of the ADA.

The **Americans with Disabilities Act (ADA)** is a civil rights law that prohibits discrimination on the basis of disability in employment and in services and activities of federal, state, and local government agencies, as well as in goods, services, facilities, advantages, privileges, and accommodations of public places.

TABLE 10–3 Key Features of the Americans with Disabilities Act as It Pertains to Individuals with Hearing Loss

TITLE	KEY FEATURES
I	Ensures that people with hearing loss have the same opportunities to employment as people without hearing loss and that employers (with 15 employees or more) provide reasonable accommodations to allow them to perform their job. The law does not ensure jobs, but rather, prohibits discrimination for people who are qualified to perform the "essential" functions for a specific job.
II	Requires that state and local government agencies, including transportation programs, make their programs accessible to people with hearing loss. Effective communication must be ensured with auxiliary aids such as assistive listening systems, qualified interpreters, text displays, captioning, provision of TTYs (teletypewriters) and amplified telephones, and transcriptions of audio programs.
III	Requires public places (operated by private entities) including businesses, professional offices, and nonprofit organizations to provide communications access. These entities include hotels, restaurants, movie theaters, stadiums, concert halls, retail stores, transportation terminals, museums, senior centers, and swimming pools. Required accommodations include all of the aids listed above under Title II as well as television decoders and visual alerting devices (in hotel rooms).
IV	Requires that all telephone companies provide relay services throughout the United States on a 24-hours-per-day/7-days-per-week basis free of charge.

Rehabilitation

The rehabilitation phase often is not discrete, as some movement to and from the adjacent phases might occur, which is the reason for the return arrows in Figure 10–10. For example, one patient was so delighted with his new hearing aid that he returned to his audiologist to receive a hearing aid evaluation for his other ear. Another patient who was not yet ready for hearing aids subscribed to an online auditory training program. Her training experience made her realize the extent of her listening difficulties. She went to an audiologist, who diagnosed her with a moderate sensorineural hearing loss and fitted her with bilateral hearing aids. The woman then re-subscribed to the online auditory program so that she could learn to listen with the new aids.

A **patient-centered orientation** focuses on providing care that is respectful of and responsive to a patient's preferences, needs, and values and that ensures that the patient's values guide all clinical decisions.

A **biomedical orientation** focuses on the organs and mechanisms of hearing rather than the person.

A **sales orientation** to aural rehabilitation emphasizes persuading the patient to pursue and procure services, interventions, and listening devices.

Resolution

This phase, sometimes referred to as *postclinical* or *adjustment*, is the time when patients adjust to the ramifications of hearing loss and either accept any remaining hearing-related issues or move back to the rehabilitation phase of the model. Resolution is by no means a static state—many patients may feel that they have resolved their difficulties only to later decide others still exist. Some may early on give up or feel hopeless, but later attempt to tackle their problems anew.

According to the Pickwick Institute, patient-centered care includes the following:

- Effective treatment
- Patient involvement in decisions
- Respect for patients' preferences
- Clear and comprehensive information
- Empathy and emotional support
- Involvement of family and significant communication partners
- Continuity of care

(Balik, Conway, Zipperer, & Watson, 2011)

A PATIENT-CENTERED APPROACH

The **patient-centered orientation** focuses on providing care that respects and responds to a patient's preferances and needs and ensures that clinical decisions are guided by the patient's values.

This simple idea anchors a service practice. Patients are treated with dignity and respect, in a way that builds upon their strengths and promotes their control and independence. Aural rehabilitation entails more than arriving at a correct diagnosis of hearing loss and fitting appropriate listening aids. In a patient-centered program, patients may articulate their concerns, discuss their specific communication difficulties and their expectations, and in conjunction with their hearing health care professional, work to devise solutions to their hearing-related difficulties.

This patient-centered approach is in contrast to a biomedical orientation and a sales orientation. A **biomedical orientation** reduces hearing loss to the biological dimension of disease and illness and focuses on the organs and mechanisms of hearing rather than the person. Hearing-related issues are explained in terms of abnormal structure and function of the hearing organ. A **sales orientation** is based on persuasion: Patients need certain aural rehabilitation services or listening devices and your practice is better than the competition at providing them.

The Expert(s) in the Room

"One of the most important characteristics of the patient-centered approach is that the interaction between the clinician and the patient is perceived as a 'meeting of the experts.' In this case, the audiologist is the expert in the field of audiology and the patient is the expert in his or her own experience of hearing loss."

(Gregory, 2012)

The patient-centered philosophic orientation does not mean that you must begin with a blank slate with every new patient. Rather, certain aural rehabilitation offerings may be more appropriate for some patients than for others and available services can be adjusted to meet a patient need. A patient who has minimal residual hearing may not receive auditory training, but instead, communication strategies training. A patient with a mild hearing loss may receive only a hearing aid and counseling.

THE AURAL REHABILITATION PLAN

Despite the diversity of settings and delivery service models, it is possible (as shown in Figure 10–11) to categorize the components of a patient-centered aural rehabilitation

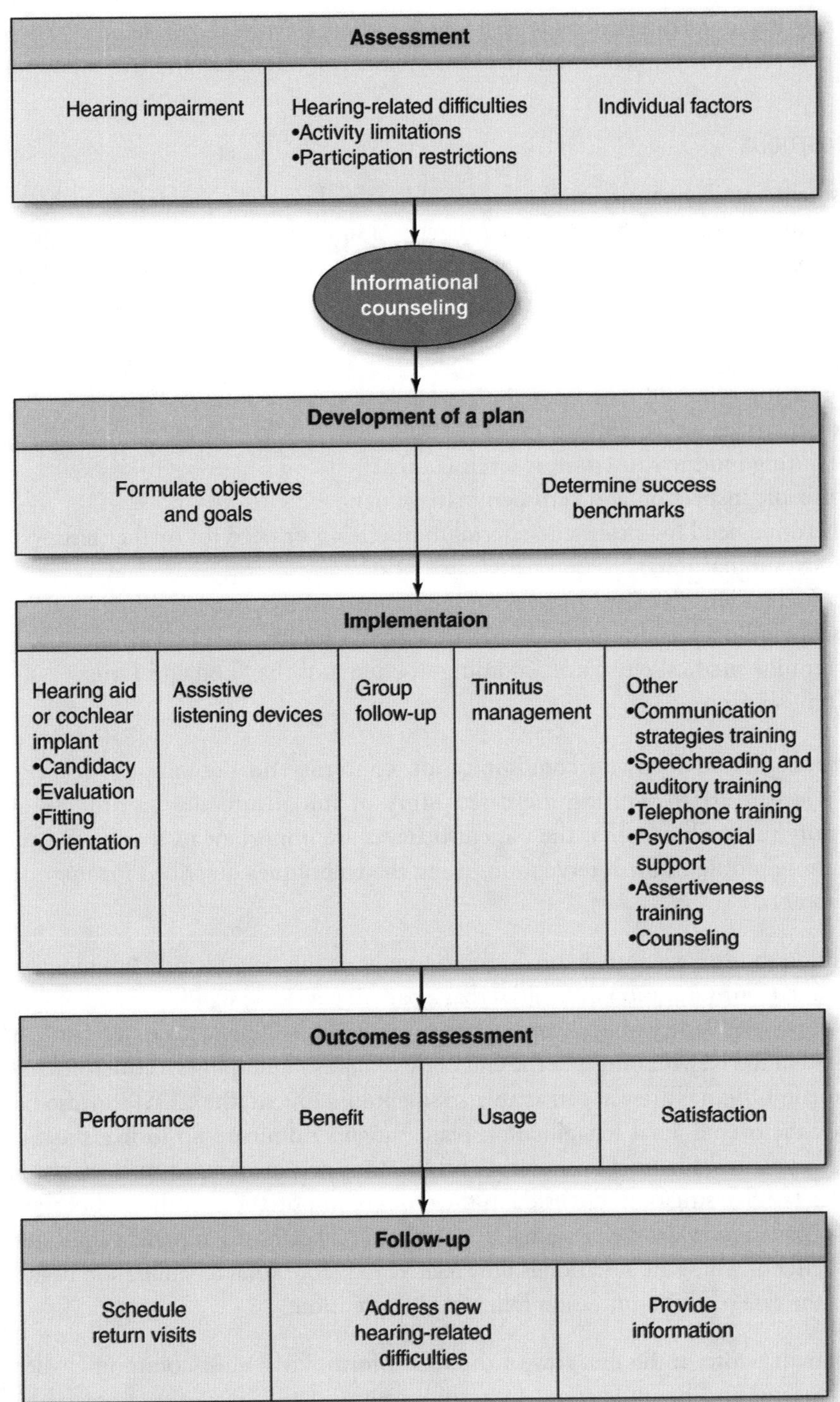

FIGURE 10–11 Stages in the design of an aural rehabilitation plan.

Questions asked during a case history:

- In a biomedical orientation: When did you first notice you might have hearing loss? Is there anything that makes the ringing sound in your ears better or worse?
- In a sales orientation: How did you hear about our clinic? Have you ever considered using a hearing aid?
- In a patient-centered orientation: What are you most concerned about? How do you think your hearing problem is disrupting your life?

plan into six general categories: (1) assessment, (2) informational counseling, (3) development of a plan, (4) implementation, (5) assessment of outcome, and (6) follow-up.

Assessment

Assessment entails quantifying the degree of hearing loss and a patient's speech recognition abilities, following the procedures described in Chapter 2. The American Academy of Audiology (2006, p. 33) recommends that an audiological assessment include the following:

- Comprehensive case history
- Identifying type and magnitude of hearing loss via pure-tone and speech audiometry as well as **immittance**
- Measuring loudness discomfort levels (LDLs)
- Otoscopic inspection and cerumen management
- Determine need for treatment/referral to physician or need for further tests (e.g., vestibular tests)
- Counsel patient, family, caregiver on the results and recommendations
- Assess candidacy and motivation toward amplification
- Determine medical clearance according to criteria of the Food and Drug Administration

Immittance is a term that refers to the energy flow through the middle ear, and includes admittance, compliance, conductance, impedance, reactance, resistance, and susceptance.

Assessment should focus on communication concerns and not simply "hearing concerns" (Jessen, 2018). During the case history or initial interview, a primary goal is to identify the problems that the patient believes are important to resolve and then to target those problems for intervention, using the techniques described for interviewing in Chapter 6.

In addition to interviews, structured-inquiry methods can help identify listening circumstances and communication difficulties that a patient considers significant and of high priority. The Client Oriented Scale of Improvement (COSI; Dillon, James, & Ginis, 1997; presented in the Key Resources at the end of this chapter) exemplifies a structured-inquiry instrument. Originally developed as an assessment instrument, the COSI can also be used to guide the overall aural rehabilitation plan. Patients nominate up to five situations in which they would like to communicate better. They are encouraged to be as specific as possible. The five situations are listed in the order of importance. At the end of the intervention, patients review their original descriptions. For each one, a patient indicates how much better or worse the situation is now relative to before aural rehabilitation began, and what is the ease of communication following intervention.

One patient wrote in the first row of the COSI form, "My most common challenge is to understand and be understood in a noisy room." The clinician encouraged him to be more specific, so the patient added, "I want to hear at clubs, because I enjoy going to clubs. Especially I like going to Maxwell's on Friday nights after work." Specificity pinpoints the intervention and better permits the assessment of outcome. On the second row, the patient wrote, "I have trouble hearing people over the telephone, especially when I'm at work and there are people talking all around me." By completing this form, the patient established specific situations to address. He also indicated the order of importance of his communication needs. After intervention, and after an appropriate adjustment period (of about three months), the patient revisited his original responses. The use of two ratings, that of *improvement* and that of *final ability*, indicated the effectiveness of the aural rehabilitation intervention and potential areas for continued attention. Important to note, the patient developed a sense of having received an individualized intervention program.

Many audiologists opt to provide a written outline to patients that describes what will happen to them, starting from the initial visit through the end of the aural rehabilitation plan. The outline can be basic, as the postcard shows in Figure 10–12, which includes the three components of diagnosis, hearing aid fitting, and listening therapy (a layperson's term for **auditory brain training**). Alternatively, it might be quite detailed. For example, Jessen (2018) provides this template as a written guide for a patient's first visit to a private practice office:

- Complete intake forms
- Determine your top three communication/hearing goals
- Diagnose your degree of hearing loss and ability to recognize words
- Receive educational materials on communication strategies and consumer resources
- Consider treatment options

Auditory brain training is speech perception training that has a heavy emphasis on training those cognitive auditory skills that are necessary to recognize speech (e.g., auditory attention, auditory working memory, auditory processing speed) as well as classic emphasis on analytic and synthetic speech recognition.

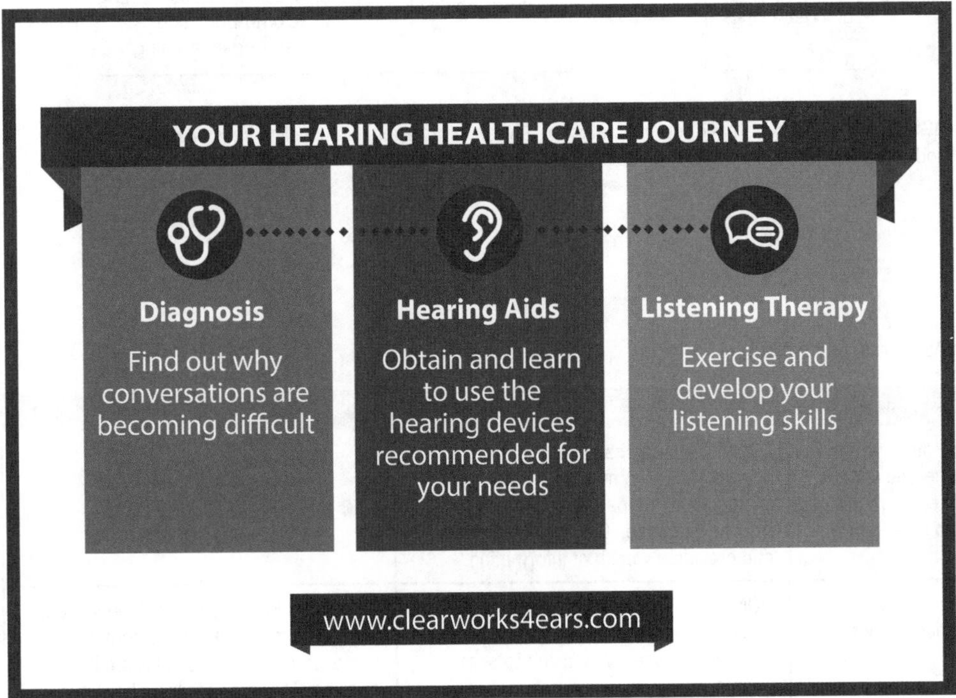

FIGURE 10–12 A postcard sized handout that describes the hearing health care journey (photograph courtesy of clEAR [customized learning: Exercises for Aural Rehabilitation] Auditory Brain Training, used with permission).

Invite a Family Member to the Appointment

Hickson and Singh (2018) note that most patients want a family member included in their audiology appointments. Here are some tips:

What to say when scheduling?

- "There is a lot to discuss and it helps to include family or a friend in the process."
- "Our experience is that it is very helpful if you can bring a family member to your appointment. Who might it be?"

Why invite a family member?

- Better understanding of the patient's hearing-related communication difficulties and how these difficulties affect both the patient and the family.
- Better outcomes, including a greater likelihood that the patient will use amplification.
- You come across as more of a hearing health care professional and less of a salesperson.
- Value is added by a "second set of ears" to remember what was discussed.

How to conduct the appointment?

- Set up the clinic room to accommodate both the patient and the family member.
- Welcome both to the appointment by name.
- Reiterate the reason why both were invited.

(Tips gathered from a workshop conducted by Nerina Scarinci and Louise Hickson, 2018)

Informational Counseling

Although counseling is ongoing, usually a block of time is set aside for informational counseling, typically after (but sometimes before) the assessment and then again, before and after a listening device is fitted, using the techniques described in Chapter 9. The topics covered in the initial counseling session include a summary of the assessment and then progresses to what the next steps might be. Figure 10–13 presents a schematic representation of how an informational counseling session might progress, from a discussion of a patient's hearing-related difficulties to possible management solutions.

Table 10–4 presents a list of suggested *Dos and Don'ts* to follow when talking to patients and their family members about the audiogram and the initial audiological assessment.

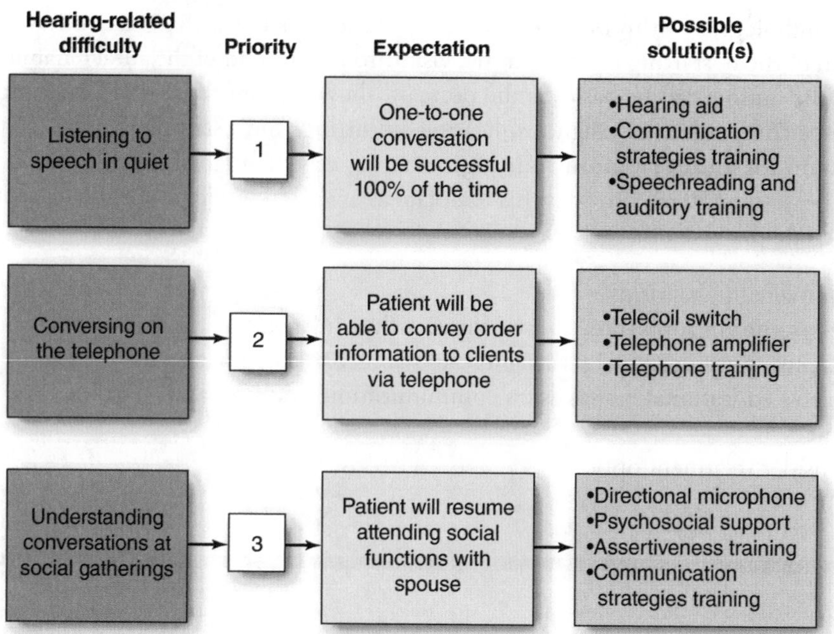

FIGURE 10–13 A schematic representation of how an informational counseling session might progress. Modeled after Gatehouse (2003, p. 2S79).

TABLE 10–4 *Dos and Don'ts* for Describing an Audiogram to a Patient

	DO	DON'T	EXAMPLE
Describing the audiogram	DO: Include the significant other or family member in the session if he/she is at the appointment. Two sets of ears are better than one when it comes to listening to the results.	DON'T: Exclude the people at the appointment who may be in the waiting room unless the patient requests that they be excluded. The family members can provide a wealth of information.	
	DO: Keep it simple. Try and relate everything to what the patient knows.	DON'T: Use jargon. Even words audiologists use daily like *frequency* and *decibel* may seem confusing to some people.	"You heard lots of different beeps. Some were low pitched like a fog horn and some were higher pitched like a bird chirping. This graph tells us how loud we need to turn things up for you to just barely hear these sounds that are important for speech."
	DO: Write information down so the patient can remember what you said later.	DON'T: Assume the patient understands everything you tell him/her. It is a lot of information to take in, especially for a new patient. Often people are coming in for an audiological evaluation because family members think there is a problem and you are the first person to confirm that fact.	Make a copy of the audiogram and make notes on it or let the patient or family member take notes on it as you talk so they have something to take with them.
	DO: Describe what type of hearing loss (sensorineural, conductive, or mixed) the patient has. Focus on what this type of loss means for him/her more than the label.	DON'T: When describing the type of hearing loss, do not get too detailed and confuse matters.	"When you heard the beeps through the headband we put behind your ear, we found the hearing loss is in the nerve so it is what we call a sensorineural hearing loss. This means that we cannot 'fix' the hearing loss with surgery or medication."

(continues)

TABLE 10–4 *(continued)*

	DO	DON'T	EXAMPLE
	DO: Relate the hearing loss back to the problems they reported during the case history.	DON'T: Explain the hearing loss and audiogram without any referent that patients can understand. Telling a patient that he/she has a 50 dB HL loss at 4000 Hz means little. It is more useful to provide examples of speech sounds or noises that the patient may be missing. A *familiar sounds* audiogram or an audiogram with the speech sounds on it can be very helpful.	"You told me that you have trouble hearing the microwave beep when you aren't standing right next to it. Because your hearing loss is in the high pitches, that is one of the sounds you are missing. The further away you stand, the less likely you are to hear it."
Describing word recognition	DO: Be careful when describing word recognition scores. Some patients think if this score is good, they do not have a problem, even if test stimuli were presented at a very loud level.	DON'T: Focus too much on the percent correct score of the word recognition test. Often people walk away thinking that this is their percent hearing or hearing loss. Many times people come into an office and say, "My last test showed a 20% loss," when what really happened is they scored 80% words correct on a word recognition test. Degree of hearing loss and percent words correct are NOT synonymous.	"When I turned up those words you heard loud enough so you could hear them, you understood most of them. This means that if we amplify speech for you—make it very loud—you may understand quite well in quiet. However, we had to turn the words up louder than normal conversational levels for you to recognize words this well."
Psychological reactions	DO: Pay attention to how patients are reacting to the description of their hearing loss. Are they confused? Do they understand what you are saying? Are they getting upset? You are often the first one breaking the news or telling them how significant the problem may be. Be sensitive to that when talking to patients.	DON'T: Assume that if they have no questions now, they won't have any questions when they get home. Sometimes they need to process the information before knowing what they want to ask. Make sure to give them a way to contact you if questions come up later.	
Planning the next steps	DO: Give the patient and his/her family ALL the options available, including doing nothing. Hearing aids aren't always the right answer or even the best solution. Be sure you have taken a thorough enough case history to really understand what the patient's goals are when the test is finished and you have reviewed the results.	DON'T: Tell patients what to do. It is their decision whether to follow your recommendations or not. You need to give them a list of options and *pros and cons* for these options, but the ultimate decision is the patients'.	"You told me when we started today that you really want to be able to hear your grandchildren on the telephone. One thing that could help you do that is an amplified telephone. Another option may be hearing aids. Here are some pros and cons to each . . ."

Information is presented from the patient's perspective, with minimal jargon, and in the context of what the clinician has learned about the patient and the patient's listening concerns during the case history.

Development of a Plan

In Chapter 1, the three elements of evidence-based practice (EBP) were reviewed: research evidence, the clinician's experience, and the patient's goals and preferences. At least two processes are involved in implementing EBP, namely, joint goal setting and shared decision making, and they draw upon these three elements.

In **joint goal setting**, the clinician and patient (and the patient's frequent communication partner) forge a partnership as they discuss and identify meaningful goals and desired outcomes. Defining a goal is the first step toward identifying strategies to solve a hearing-related difficulty and provides a standard by which the effectiveness of an intervention may be assessed. For example, if a patient has difficulty listening during

Joint goal setting entails the patient and clinician creating a partnership to identify meaningful goals and desired outcomes for the aural rehabilitation intervention plan.

Decision Making and Patient Preference

"I've decided what I wanted was the hearing aids. I thought a lot about it, but THAT'S the option for me."

"I already had in my mind, I don't really want a hearing aid, and if I can do anything else to avoid that, I will."

—Two women expressing their preference about hearing aids during a joint decision-making process

(Laplante-Lévesque et al., 2010a, p. 33)

"I prefer to do the group, because I have found when you're doing something in a group, you tend to pick up tricks from people that are participating."

"I get irritated by them. This is a fault of mine, it's the way I am. Somebody in the group begins to talk and I think it's rubbish."

—Two men expressing their preference about participating in a group communication strategies training program during a joint decision-making process

(Laplante-Lévesque, Hickson, & Worrall, 2010b, p. 504)

professional meetings that are conducted at a rectangular table, an FM system might be considered. The plan will also entail establishing success benchmarks and means for assessing them.

Caveat for Goal Setting

Sometimes a clinician must listen for the hidden message when patients talk about their goals, and may have to help the patient clarify true goals. For example, an older patient once stated that his number one priority was to enhance his television-viewing experience. Mr. Lim was spending the majority of his day watching hourly news broadcast shows, and his wife complained that the loud volume of the television set annoyed her. Upon careful questioning and judicious commenting while eliciting the patient narrative, our audiologist discovered that Mr. Lim was viewing an inordinate amount of television because he could not converse easily due to hearing loss. He grumbled that his wife mumbled, his grandchildren avoided him, and his adult children talked to one another as if he were not in the room. The audiologist gleaned that Mr. Lim's means of staying connected to the world was by means of watching news broadcasts rather than by interacting with his family and friends. Hearing loss was affecting his emotional well-being and self-concept and restricting his ability to fulfill the roles of husband, father, grandfather, and friend. Mr. Lim was seemingly unaware that he was withdrawing from daily life, and did not associate his feelings of despondency and low-grade anxiety to the loss of casual conversation. At face value, the solution to Mr. Lim's and his wife's stated goal might have been to provide them with a television-related assistive listening device. However, because the audiologist took the time to hear Mr. Lim's personal narrative, and drew him out with open-ended questioning, other goals were identified, goals targeted toward enhancing conversation fluency between the patient and his family members. Ultimately, the desired goal became that Mr. Lim would spend more quality time interacting with his family members and less time watching the television news.

Shared decision making entails the patient and clinician jointly considering the options to achieve a goal and then making a selection after reviewing related information and taking time for discussion and deliberation.

Shared decision making, as the name implies, means that neither the clinician nor the patient alone decides how the patient's goals are to be addressed. Once they have an appreciation of the nature and extent of the problem, they make joint decisions about which course to pursue. The process entails a review and discussion of the options that might feasibly meet the patient's goals, and then decision making about how to proceed. The process takes into account how a patient makes decisions (e.g., Is this someone who decides quickly or someone who ruminates?) and the patient's personal preferences (e.g., Is this a patient who will reject wearing a visible hearing aid?). The clinician shares expert opinion and experience. For shared decision making to work, the clinician must know the patient's experiences and preferences and the patient must trust the clinician's expertise, motivation, and intentions (Laplante-Lévesque, Hickson, & Worrall, 2010a).

Figure 10–14 presents an example of shared decision making. This patient may desire to participate in social conversations but cannot understand speech in noisy environments, and lacks confidence to use communication strategies. The patient's disclosure of his problems during the interview, perhaps with input from his spouse or frequent communication partner, coupled with the clinician's audiometric results showing poor speech recognition in noise, establishes a joint appreciation of his problem. The patient and

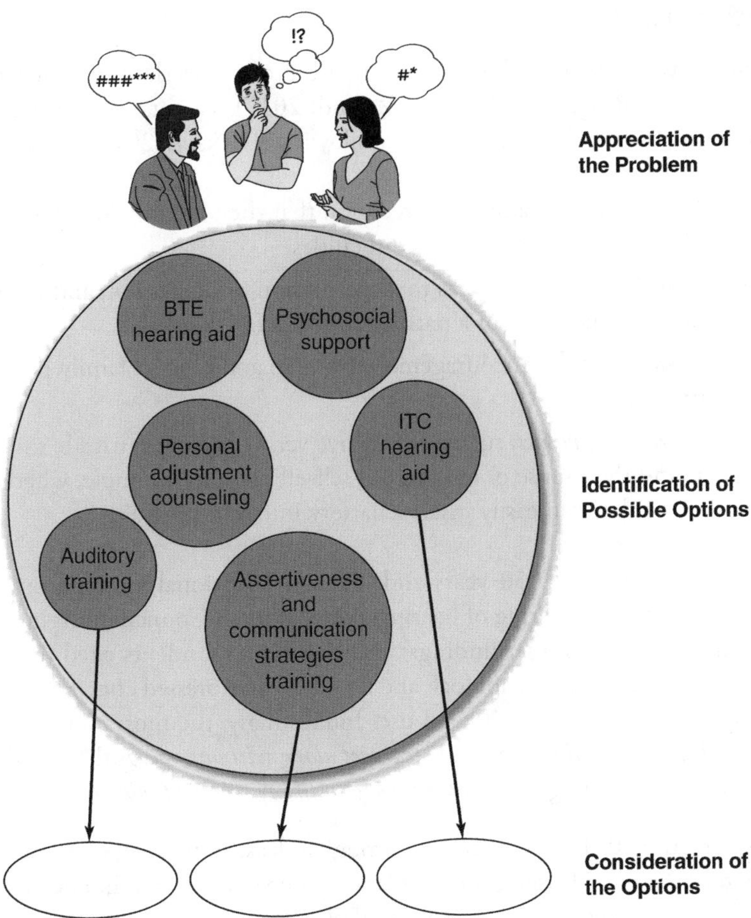

FIGURE 10–14 Shared decision making. Before reaching a decision, both patient and clinician arrive at a shared understanding of the problem, identify possible options drawing heavily on the clinician's expertise, and then consider the options. A patient's significant communication partner may participate in the process.

clinician may decide that one goal is for the patient to be able to participate in conversations involving just three or four people. Possible solutions include use of a hearing aid and receipt of auditory training. The clinician provides information and expert opinion about each option. They then discuss the options and reach a mutual decision as to how to proceed.

Implementation

Implementation of the plan may entail provision of a hearing aid, cochlear implant (see Chapters 11 and 13), or assistive listening devices and hearing assistive listening devices (Chapter 11) and tinnitus management.

Hearing Aids

When determining whether to recommend a hearing aid(s) as part of the aural rehabilitation plan, an audiologist will first determine whether a patient is an appropriate candidate. If the patient meets the audiological criteria and is motivated to use a hearing aid, the audiologist will perform a hearing aid evaluation and provide a hearing aid fitting and orientation. Establishing an appropriate use pattern will be a prominent goal in the aural rehabilitation plan.

Family Influence

"The key reason that new users and potential new users buy hearing aids is the recognition that they have a problem; often motivation comes from the influence of family and friends."

—Sergei Kochkin, Executive Director of the Better Hearing Institute in Alexandria, Virginia

(Kochkin, 2007, p. 48)

Candidacy and Motivation

Motivation to use a hearing aid is an important but often overlooked issue when determining candidacy (Ridgeway, Hickson, & Lind, 2017). Factors that commonly influence persons to obtain a device include the following (Hickson, 2012; Kochkin, 2005a):

- *Subjective factors*, such as patients' perception that their hearing loss is getting worse and their self-reported hearing difficulties
- *Input from family members*, such as their persuasion or dissuasion, and their positive or negative opinions about a patient's use of a hearing aid
- *Professional input*, such as encouragement from an audiologist, family physician, or an otolaryngologist
- *Patients' attitudes and values*, such as a positive versus negative attitude toward hearing aids and their sense of hearing aid self-efficacy; for example, whether or not they believe they can easily insert a battery into a hearing aid

In a survey of 2,300 adults 50 years and older, the National Council on the Aging identified barriers to the wearing of hearing aids (National Council on Aging, 1999; see also Kochkin, 2007, for similar findings). Half of the respondents cited the expense of purchasing a hearing aid as a roadblock and about 20% expressed concerns about vanity and the stigma attached to hearing aid use. Interestingly, the most common responses were *My hearing is not bad enough* and *I can get along without one*. A third of the respondents reported that *[hearing aids] will not help with my specific problem.*

As shown in Figure 10–15, patients pass through at least four stages en route to becoming successful hearing aid users: contemplation, preparation, action, and maintenance (e.g., Laplante-Lévesque, Hickson, & Worrall, 2012).

In the *Contemplation stage*, some patients may be ambivalent to try amplification, while others may be eager. The clinician's role is to inform and educate patients about the magnitude and irreversibility of their hearing loss, about available options for managing hearing-related difficulties, and about the value and limitations of using hearing aids.

In the *Preparation stage,* a patient and clinician will consider how a hearing aid might help the patient achieve the goals they have jointly identified during the goal-setting phase. For example, if a woman who is a teacher has the goal *to hear her students' voices when she is writing on a whiteboard*, they might talk about how a hearing aid with an omnidirectional microphone will enhance listening performance when the teacher turns her back to her class. They may also consider alternative solutions, as a hearing aid may not be the only option for achieving the teacher's goal, and thus, appropriate assistive listening systems might be considered. The teacher might reflect on her personal attitudes, such as whether she holds negative opinions about hearing aid users and if so, the basis for her opinions. She might complete attitudinal line scales, like those considered in Chapter 8, to self-assess her sense of self-efficacy and her motivation for change. She and her clinician might consider the costs and benefits of obtaining and using a hearing aid, either informally through balanced dialogue, or formally, by means of the teacher completing a cost-benefit analysis form (CBAF) (Chapter 9).

In the third stage, *Action*, a clinician and patient talk about the steps involved in obtaining a hearing aid and consider appropriate hearing aid styles. The patient then undergoes a hearing aid evaluation and fitting. A patient may experience a kaleidoscope of emotions during this stage, ranging from excitement, anticipation, and pride for taking constructive action to anxiety, hesitancy, and self-doubt about using technology. A clinician

Patient Stage	Professional's Role	Patient Outcome
Contemplation	Inform and educate	1. Understands the chronic nature of the hearing loss 2. Understands what a hearing aid can and cannot do
Preparation	Address and help develop constructive values and attitudes	3. Revises certain values and attitudes, such as self-stigmatizing beliefs and doubts about self-efficacy 4. Perceives that benefits accrued from using a hearing aid exceed monetary and non-monetary costs 5. Consider how use of a hearing aid will achieve goals formulated in the aural rehabilitation plan
Action	Provide services for hearing aid fitting	6. Learns about appropriate hearing aid styles 7. Understands the steps for acquiring a hearing aid 8. Receives a hearing aid
Maintenance	Support and encourage	9. Completes trial period with a hearing aid 10. Continues appropriate use

FIGURE 10–15 The stages of motivation. Patients may pass through distinct stages in terms of motivation to use a hearing aid.

can help maintain motivation by explaining every step of the process and by providing support, encouragement, and appreciation.

In the fourth stage, *Maintenance*, the patient develops a use pattern and learns to maintain the hearing aid in good working order. Initially a patient may feel overwhelmed or unsettled by the amplified auditory signal and will appreciate the clinician's encouragement and support to continue using the hearing aid. As time passes and the patient begins to experience the benefits of amplification firsthand, motivation will become internalized and self-generated.

When a patient first uses a hearing aid, the patient may feel:

- Self-conscious
- Uncomfortable
- Not his or her "usual" self

Such reactions are:

- Normal
- Part of the "learning curve"
- Transient

(Clark & English, 2004, p. 127)

Establishing a Use Pattern

There are at least three identifiable **hearing aid use patterns** to describe the ways in which adults use hearing aids (Figure 10–16). Those who eventually become full-time users often increase the number of hours per day they use the new hearing aid, so that after several days or weeks, they use it during almost all waking hours. Commonly, patients who reject their hearing aids either return them to their audiologist or tuck them away in a drawer, trying them for only a brief trial period of a few days or weeks. Finally, some individuals never achieve full-time use but do not reject the hearing aid(s). They may experiment with wearing the hearing aid in a variety of situations initially, and then decide they need it only for specific settings. An intermittent use pattern is best established on the basis of experience, so the patient actually tries the device in a variety

Hearing aid use pattern refers to the times, situations, and locations in which a hearing aid user wears the hearing aids.

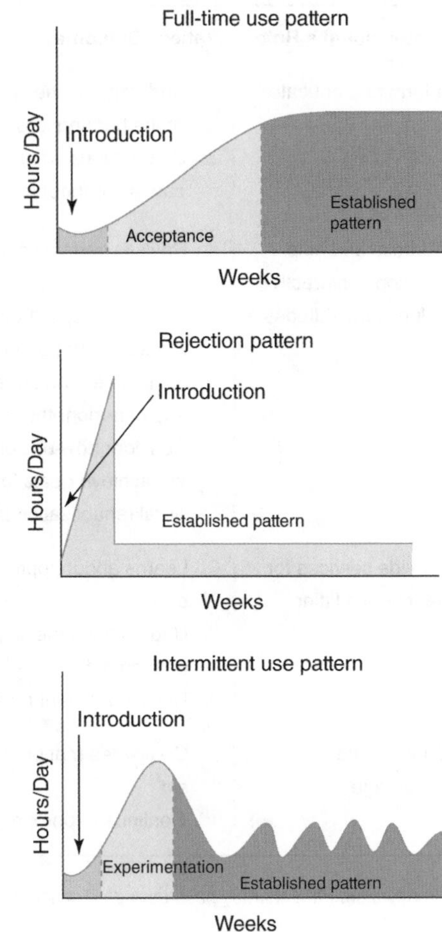

FIGURE 10–16 Patterns of use found in first-time hearing aid users.

of situations before deciding when it is and is not helpful, rather than on assumptions made by either the patient or the audiologist.

Reasons that some individuals choose not to wear their devices include (McCormack & Fortnum, 2013):

- The hearing aid is uncomfortable to wear.
- The hearing aid is difficult to handle.
- The patient is overwhelmed by having to listen in the presence of background noise.
- The patient had unrealistic expectations about what a hearing aid can and cannot do, and is receiving less than expected benefit.
- Speech sounds "tinny" or loud.
- In some instances, patients may have wanted one kind of hearing aid (such as an in-the-ear [ITE] style) but the audiologist prescribed another, one that may have been more appropriate for the hearing loss configuration (such as a behind-the-ear [BTE] style), but ultimately, a wrong choice because the patient now rejects it.

Follow-Up

After the hearing aid orientation, patients typically return about three or more times during the first year, especially if they are first-time hearing aid users. The types of services they might receive include adjustments in the programming of the hearing aid (e.g., increasing the gain), adjustments in the device itself (e.g., shortening the tube length), routine service (e.g., clearing of a clogged tube), and counseling (e.g., training to use the telephone) (Tecca, 2018, p. 21).

Some new hearing-aid users will engage in auditory training to accelerate their adjustment to amplified sound and to enhance their abilities to utilize their residual hearing. It is often a good idea to allow at least a short amount of time between the hearing aid fitting and the onset of auditory training. During this time, a patient can become comfortable with handling the aids (e.g., placing the earmolds in the ear, inserting batteries). After a week or two, when the patient returns for a follow-up visit, the patient can begin auditory training. The patient might receive a handout like that shown in Figure 10–17 at the time of the hearing aid fitting and then be given a more detailed "how-to" sheet at the time that auditory training begins.

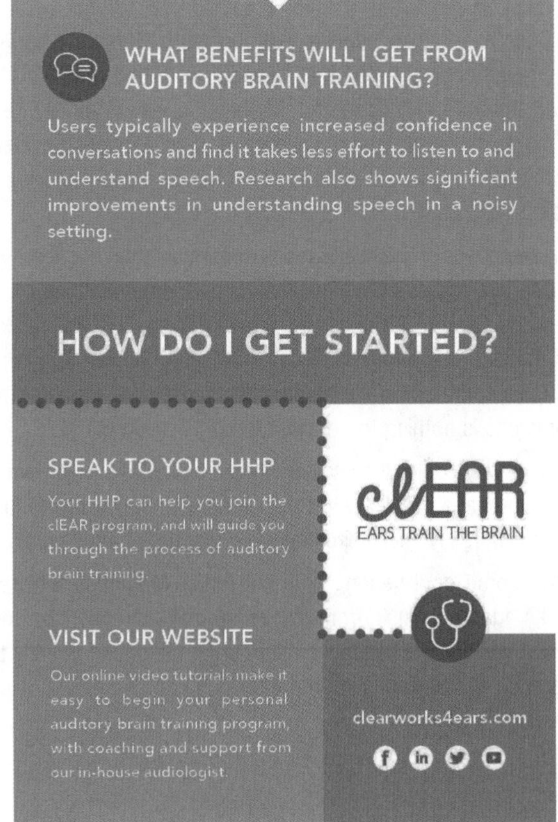

FIGURE 10–17 Auditory training for new hearing aid users. A handout like this might be provided to new hearing aid users before they begin to receive auditory brain training (photograph courtesy of clEAR [customized learning: Exercises for Aural Rehabilitation] Auditory Brain Training, used with permission).

"GLASSES ARE COOL, WHY AREN'T HEARING AIDS?"

FIGURE 10–18 Just like wearing glasses, using a hearing aid can be cool.

Jennifer F. Boylan posed this question in the above caption in an opinion piece that appeared in the *New York Times* (2017) (Figure 10–18). In a nutshell, she suggested that people with hearing loss who could benefit from using hearing aids often opt not to use them because they perceive a social stigma associated with doing so. Readers' responses to her question were highly variable, but over all, there were many who wanted to share how hearing aids had changed their lives. Here are some highlights from the responses, suggesting that hearing aids indeed can be cool:

"I'm 53 and have been rocking my hearing aids for nearly 3 years. I had my hearing checked after my daughter suggested that I needed to (I had promised her I would not behave like her stubborn grandparents). My hearing loss is moderate, and wow, the world sounds so much better when I have my ears in. Besides not having to ask people to repeat themselves, music sounds phenomenal again—and apparently my dryer has a squeak." —Barbara

"For too long many members of the hearing loss community and the hearing public believe that people with hearing loss have intellectual problems. Nothing can be further from the truth. Pres. Bill Clinton, Tom Brokaw, Steve Colbert, NYC Police Commissioner Ray Kelly, Pres. Ronald Reagan and now Jennifer Finney Boylan to name just a few famous people all have come out of the hearing loss closet and it's about time. Listen up America, hearing loss is nothing to be ashamed of." —Howard

"Having hearing aids is way cooler than saying 'What?' over and over or lamely nodding in agreement when you have no idea what the person you're talking to just said. It's also cooler than avoiding noisy social situations like restaurants and parties." —Bruce

"There are definitely some cool hearing aids out there. My latest set are Bluetooth enabled, and with an adapter, music from my phone plays directly into my ears. The same technology connects with a handheld mic to bring the sound directly to the hearing aids. The difference is staggering. Comprehension can rise to 100% even if your hearing loss is severe." —William

New hearing aid users will sometimes participate in a group follow-up orientation program. Information about the care and use of the device that was presented during the hearing aid orientation may be reiterated. Participants may receive supervised practice in handling the device and in using the telephone. Other class topics might include communication strategies, listening, and speechreading. Appendix 10–1 presents an example of a course syllabus for a three-session adult aural rehabilitation group class that has been used by the HEARx network hearing centers (Beyer & Northern, 2000). Each session lasts between 60 and 90 minutes and spouses and family members of the patients are encouraged to attend. If a practice does not offer group classes, then patients might be encouraged to join a local chapter of a self-help group, such as Hearing Loss Association of America (HLAA).

Finally, some patients might want to consider acquiring an assistive listening device in addition to hearing aids, such as a door knock signaler.

Outcomes Assessment

Common outcome measures include direct measurement of performance, interviews, observation of performance, self-report scales and questionnaires, and daily logs. A major goal of assessment is to determine the extent to which activity limitations and participation restrictions have resolved and to determine whether additional concerns remain.

The Gothenburg Profile (Ringdahl, Eriksson-Mangold, & Andersson, 1998), although originally designed to be used during the initial contact with a patient, can also be used as an outcomes assessment instrument. Sample questions include: *Are there occasions when you cannot follow a conversation when you are in your home and speak to one person?; Are there occasions when you cannot hear a speaker at a meeting, even if you are well-positioned?; Are there occasions when you hesitate to meet new people because of your hearing difficulties?;* and *Are there occasions when you avoid social gatherings, because it is hard to follow a conversation?* In responding, patients use a 10-point scale, ranging from *never* to *always.*

Benefit is the improvement gained in an aided compared with an unaided listening condition, and is typically a difference measure. *Benefit* might be assessed through speech recognition tests that are administered in an unaided and then an aided condition, or through self-report measures such as the COSI (see Key Resources; also Chapter 2). If the patient has completed the COSI once, then giving it again can determine whether the patient's goals and expectations were met and indicate whether aural rehabilitation should be modified or extended. Several questionnaires ask respondents to consider aided and unaided conditions, such as the Abbreviated Profile of Hearing Aid Benefit (APHAB; Cox & Alexander, 1995).

A patient is unlikely to benefit from, say, a hearing aid unless the patient uses the device. For example, how long does a patient wear a hearing aid during an ordinary day and in what situations? Although listening device usage is typically assessed, the domain of *usage* can be extended to include the use of communication strategies as well. For example, the daily logs considered in Chapter 7 might be appropriate for tracking one's communication behaviors before and after a communication strategies training course.

Satisfaction can be included in an outcomes assessment, and reflects a patient's contentment with his or her current situation. Satisfaction is positively correlated with benefit (e.g., Brooks & Hallam, 1998; Dillon et al., 1997) but may also be influenced by the patient's expectations (Cox & Alexander, 2000).

An international group of 15 experts who participated in the Eriksholm Workshop held in Copenhagen, Denmark, generated a brief self-report instrument that they believed to be universally applicable, one that allows comparisons across social, cultural, and health care delivery systems (Cox & Alexander, 2000). The International Outcome Inventory for Hearing Aids (IOI-HA) includes seven items, which together query the patient about performance, benefit, usage, and satisfaction. An adaptation of the IOI-HA is included in the Key Resources.

Follow-Up

Aural rehabilitation is a process. If new problems arise or the intervention proves unsuccessful, the aural rehabilitation plan should be adaptable. Patients and their predicaments often change, so the aural rehabilitation plan may require fine-tuning and adjusting as it unfolds. A **predicament** is the sum of the relevant variables affecting the patient, including the hearing loss, situation, attitudes, aptitudes, lifestyles, and communication behaviors. For example, one patient originally sought aural rehabilitation because she could not understand speech in quiet situations. Her audiologist fitted her with a hearing aid that was equipped with a telecoil. She is delighted with how well she recognizes speech, and now finds she wants to use the telephone, something she has avoided using for three years. The patient wants telephone training and telephone-related conversational strategies incorporated into her aural rehabilitation plan. As with the woman considered earlier, who subscribed to an online auditory training program twice, this situation typifies how an aural rehabilitation plan must be adapted to the changing needs of the patient.

Predicament is the "sum of all pertinent aspects of client state and situation, including disorders, impairments, disabilities, handicaps, environments, demands, resources, attitudes, behaviors, and so on" (Hyde & Riko, 1994, p. 351).

During an annual visit, an audiologist can:

- Monitor hearing.
- Make hearing aid adjustments if hearing has changed.
- Examine ear canal for cerumen buildup.
- Review other sources of help (e.g., communication strategies training).
- Clean hearing aids.
- Ensure hearing aids are in good working order.
- Review hearing aid warranty coverage.
- Provide information about new developments (e.g., in federal law).

(Hampton, 2005, p. 79)

Figure 10–19 illustrates the patient's situation. Before aural rehabilitation, she desired to converse more effectively in quiet. The targeted goal was met and now she has a new goal, that being to use the telephone and to solve her telephone-related communication problems.

In performing routine follow-ups, the clinician might provide written materials via mail, and occasionally write short letters inquiring about the patient's satisfaction and progress with amplification. Communication through email can be effective, as well as the use of internet chat rooms centered on hearing loss and aural rehabilitation. Typically, patients return to their audiologists on an annual basis for a hearing test and a hearing aid (or cochlear implant) check. During these visits, the audiologist can assess whether hearing has worsened and whether the hearing aid functions properly, and might encourage appropriate candidates to join a self-help organization (e.g., for tinnitus or advocacy).

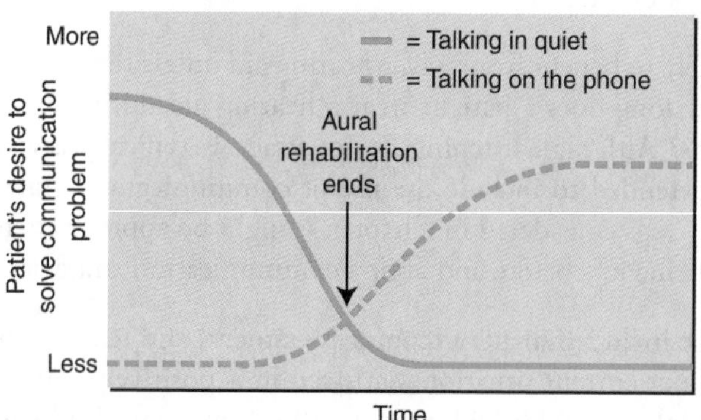

FIGURE 10–19 Flexibility and adaptation. The aural rehabilitation plan may require fine-tuning as patients' predicaments change.

Tinnitus Intervention

Sometimes the aural rehabilitation plan includes the management of tinnitus, which may entail both the assessment of the condition and an intervention. In general, however, few patients pursue treatment. For example, in a large-scale survey assessing nine tinnitus treatment methods, only 7% of respondents reported trying one of the methods (Kochkin et al., 2011).

A tinnitus intake interview may be the first audiological step in addressing a patient's tinnitus concerns. During this interview, an audiologist might ask such questions as: What does your most bothersome tinnitus sound like? Is your tinnitus louder on one side of your head than the other? Would you please describe the onset of your tinnitus? and, How long have you had your tinnitus? (Henry, Zaugg, & Schechter, 2005, p. 26).

The patient might complete a questionnaire. Because tinnitus cannot be measured objectively, it often is difficult to quantify its degree or to understand the magnitude of disability it imparts. Some existing questionnaires include open-ended questions (Tyler & Baker, 1983). Others include quantifiable items, such as those listed below (e.g., Stouffer & Tyler, 1990), presented here with example kinds of questions:

- *Location*: Is it in the left ear, right ear, or both ears?
- *Pitch*: On a continuum corresponding to pitch, is it high pitched or low pitched?
- *Constancy*: Is the tinnitus always present? Is it intermittent? Do you tend to notice it at a particular time of day?
- *Composition*: Do you hear one sound or more than one sound?
- *Fluctuation*: Does the tinnitus change from one sound to another? Does it change in pitch?
- *Loudness*: On a continuum corresponding to loudness, is it loud or soft?
- *Conditions that exacerbate the tinnitus*: What conditions exacerbate the tinnitus (e.g., drinking coffee, smoking)?
- *Annoyance*: On a continuum corresponding to annoyance, can the tinnitus be described as not at all annoying, extremely annoying, or somewhere in between?
- *Effects on concentration and sleep*: Does it have a slight effect? Extreme effect?
- *Depression*: Does it cause minimal depression? Extreme depression?

The patient may also undergo some of the following audiological and medical procedures prior to entering a tinnitus management regime:

- Comprehensive audiological testing, including site-of-lesion testing (e.g., **tone-decay testing**)
- Otoscopic examination, because cerumen can be a cause of tinnitus
- Impedance audiometry, to help establish the functional condition of the patient's middle ear, tympanic membrane, and Eustachian tube and to rule out blockage as a source of tinnitus
- Auditory brainstem response testing (ABR), which records the central auditory system's response to sound, to help distinguish between a cochlear and retrocochlear lesion (retrocochlear means the lesion lies between the cochlea and the brain)
- Vestibular and balance tests, such as eletronystagmography (ENG), where eyeball movement is recorded in response to balance tests such as tracking, optokinetics, and positional testing, and rotary chair and pursuit tracking tests, to determine whether the vestibular system is involved in the patient's condition
- Head magnetic resonance imaging (MRI), to determine whether a tumor is present in the internal auditory canal
- Vascular studies, such as angiography, to explore the possibility of a cardiovascular cause

A **tone-decay test** is a test of auditory adaptation during which a continuous tone is presented at about threshold and any change in perception is monitored over a set time interval; an abnormal adaptation may indicate a retrocochlear site of lesion.

Looking for Relief

"I would use just about any means available to stifle him [tinnitus], to eradicate him from my life, or just to reduce his overwhelming influence on what I have of a life. . . . Others like me want to say to the clinicians and researchers on the leading edge of audiology research: Give us new weapons in our struggle for liberation. We will try just about anything."

—George R. Brown, MD, Chief of Psychiatry, Veterans Administration Medical Center, Mountain Home, TN, and tinnitus sufferer

(Brown, 2004, p. 53)

The **American Tinnitus Association (ATA)** is an organization that supports self-help groups for tinnitus sufferers and funds research about tinnitus.

An audiologist might administer a tinnitus assessment battery. Using psychoacoustical measurement procedures, the battery typically consists of pitch and loudness matching tasks, perceptual location, minimum masking level, and postmasking effects. For example, when determining the minimum masking level, the audiologist might present white noise to the patient through headphones, gradually increasing the level of the signal. The patient's task is to indicate when the noise is just loud enough to mask the percept of tinnitus.

No known cure for tinnitus exists. However, a variety of options provide relief or some control over the sensation of tinnitus. Table 10–5 lists Apps that can be downloaded, which provide sounds and soundscapes that can be used to mask tinnitus. Table 10–6 summarizes some of the more common treatments, which include masking the tinnitus with an auditory signal, signal enhancement, relaxation therapy and mindfulness meditation, biofeedback, counseling, and, in fairly extreme cases, pharmacological interventions that might include sleep aids and medications to reduce anxiety or depression.

Some tinnitus sufferers enroll in a self-help group. The **American Tinnitus Association (ATA)** is the umbrella organization for many such groups. The ATA provides patients with information about tinnitus and current techniques for managing it. The organization sponsors self-help groups, workshops, regional meetings, and seminars, allowing patients to interact with each other and with professionals.

What Every Tinnitus Sufferer Needs to Know

- Tinnitus is not unique to that one patient.
- Tinnitus is not a sign of insanity or grave illness.
- Tinnitus probably is not a sign of impending deafness.
- There is no evidence to suggest the tinnitus will get worse.
- Tinnitus does not have to result in a lack of control.
- Patients who can sleep can best manage their tinnitus.
- Tinnitus is real, and not imagined.
- Tinnitus may be permanent.
- Reaction to the tinnitus is the source of the problem.
- Reaction to the symptom is manageable and subject to modification.
- If significance and threat is removed, habituation or "gating" of attention can be achieved.
- Stay off the internet!

(Sweetow, 2006)

TABLE 10–5 Sound Generator Apps for Masking Tinnitus

NAME OF APP	DESCRIPTION OF SOUNDS PRESENTED	PRICE
White Noise	White noise and a wide selection of environmental and nature sounds, including beach waves crashing, light rain falling, a gentle waterfall, and a cat purring	Free and paid versions available
Sleepmaker Rain	It's all about rain, and choices include constant rainfall, rainfall in the forest, rainfall with distant thunder, rain falling on concrete, rain tapping against windows, rain splattering against a tent	Free and paid versions available
ReSound Relief	Premade soundscapes, such as *Peaceful Morning, At the Beach*, and *Underwater*, and the option of creating customized soundscapes with music clips and nature sounds, such as birds, bubbles, brooks, and whales	Free
Ambient Mixer	Soundscapes where the level of the sound elements can be modulated; for example, the level of the crackling fire in the soundscape called *[Hogwart's] Gryffindor Common Room*; the level of flute music in *Neverland*; the level of Dean's snoring in *Sleeping Next to Dean*	Free and paid versions available

TABLE 10–6 Summary of a Variety of Methods Available for Managing and Controlling Tinnitus

METHOD OF TINNITUS TREATMENT	DESCRIPTION
Relaxation training and exercise	The patient is taught to decrease muscular tension through a series of exercises, sequentially tensing and relaxing targeted muscle groups. Discussion focuses on tinnitus as a source of stress, and the use of relaxation both at home and in real-life situations to relieve stress and associated tinnitus. Relaxation training often focuses on reducing muscle tension in the jaw and neck and reducing teeth grinding, which in turn may lead to decreased tinnitus perception.
Biofeedback	This method is a form of relaxation training in which changes in a person's muscle tension or skin temperature are reinforced with a simple signal, such as a tone that changes in pitch or loudness. This signal helps the patient control arousal level.
Cognitive therapy and counseling	Patients learn to control where their attention is directed or change the content of their thoughts. For example, they learn to replace maladaptive thoughts with constructive thoughts and learn to direct their attention away from the tinnitus. Rational, realistic, and logical perspectives replace irrational, unrealistic, and illogical ones. For instance, a patient who bemoans, "I can't deal with this buzzing noise," might be asked to identify times when he or she has dealt with a difficult situation and proved quite capable in doing so. Patients may also learn stress-management techniques.
Mindfulness-based therapy	Mindfulness therapy stems from mindfulness-based meditation, and exploits the principle of keeping sensation, emotions, and thoughts in present awareness without judgment. The patient trains the mind to be *with* the tinnitus, and not actively ignore it, and to accept any related emotions and reactions as they are. Over time, the sensations and feelings become less threatening and impart a reduced impact on the patient's life (Gans, 2010).
Masking devices, either free standing or patient-worn	The patient wears a masking device (behind the ear) that delivers a sound to the ear that masks the tinnitus, or the patient sets a radio or MP3 player to make continual sound. Possible acoustic stimuli include white noise and ocean waves. The masking sound may be easier to tune out because it is a constant sound, and it also gives the patient a sense of control over the condition because the patient determines whether to hear the masking sound or the tinnitus.
Sound enrichment	Somewhat different from masking, sound enrichment is designed to soothe the limbic system while simultaneously stimulating the auditory neural pathways so that the perceived tinnitus interacts with other sounds that can be ignored. In one approach, sound is filtered in accordance with the patient's hearing loss. An ear-worn device presents fractal tones (which sound like wind chimes), a music-like stimulus that has no sudden changes in tonality, intensity, or tempo (Sweetow & Jeppesen, 2012). Fractal tones may promote relaxation and reduce annoyance induced by tinnitus.
Tinnitus retraining therapy (TRT)	TRT involves a combination of counseling and sound therapy. During counseling, three main points are considered: (a) tinnitus is a form of compensation by the auditory system due to damage or dysfunction within the auditory pathways; (b) tinnitus becomes a problem because of emotional and autonomic responses; and (c) the brain can learn to attenuate these abnormal activations (Jastreboff, 2000). During sound training, patients receive constant broadband low-intensity noise, allowing the patient to still hear tinnitus. The noise generators facilitate habituation and reverse the distress experienced as a result of tinnitus.
Amplification	The hearing aid amplifies ambient noise, which in turn may mask the tinnitus, as well as reduce the contrast between tinnitus and silence. Moreover, since listening may be less effortful, the hearing aid may lead to a reduction in stress and stress-induced tinnitus (Kochkin & Tyler, 2008).

CASE STUDY

One Size Doesn't Fit All

Aural rehabilitation is not a profession of "one size fits all." Patients will vary greatly in the services and support they need before and after they receive a listening device. In this section, three people with differing needs are described.

Doug Kammer has just lost his job as a middle manager because his company merged with another. He is preoccupied with anxieties over his future: Will he get a new job? Does he no longer have the youthful look that employers are looking for? Will his savings tide him over during the interim period of unemployment? He knows at some level that he has a hearing loss and that if he is to be an effective member of a work team, he must be able to communicate effectively. Even so, accepting his hearing loss, taking ownership of his hearing problems, and pursuing a comprehensive aural rehabilitation plan are foreign ideas at this point in his personal turmoil.

(continues)

CASE STUDY (continued)

One Size Doesn't Fit All

Every morning, Mary Saunders starts her day with a flurry of activity—getting children ready for school, making lunches, driving carpool, and cleaning breakfast dishes. All this happens before she heads off to work as an office manager for a small law firm. Life as a single mother of two girls and sole breadwinner seems to be whizzing by her at 100 miles per hour. Some days, she feels like the day has turned into night, without ever providing her with a moment to herself. Lately, she has seemed detached from her surroundings. Her children accuse her of not listening and her coworkers tease her for being absentminded. Is she just overstressed or is something else going on? A few days ago, she realized that she could not hear the high-pitched beeping tone of the office fax machine.

Carl King lost his wife last year. Since then, the new retiree has been struggling to get on with his life. His grown children come by his house several times a week, concerned about his psychological well-being and determined not to let him isolate himself inside his house. His daughter has talked him into going for a hearing test. She thinks one reason her father is withdrawing into himself is that he cannot hear in groups, and he cannot follow family conversations at the dinner table. Carl figures he will go to the hearing clinic to appease his daughter, but that is all he will do. Why get a hearing aid, he asks himself, when he lives alone with no one to talk to?

All these people could benefit from using a hearing aid and from receiving aural rehabilitation services before and after receiving one. Doug, Mary, and Carl live different lives, experience different demands, and harbor different hopes and expectations. Their aural rehabilitation plans must accommodate their differences. Doug needs to come to grips with the presence of his hearing loss and what having a hearing loss means in terms of his self-image. He might develop strategies for managing his hearing loss, both during his search for a new job and then in adjusting and accommodating to a new work setting. Mary might educate her children and coworkers about her communication difficulties and find time in her busy schedule to receive adequate hearing health care. Carl will have to develop the motivation to participate in everyday conversations, which may require him to expand his social network and to take a greater interest in the comings and goings of his children and grandchildren. These people will require many of the same aural rehabilitation services, but these services must be adjusted to accommodate who they are and where they are in terms of adjustment to hearing loss.

FINAL REMARKS

Aural rehabilitation begins with a solid understanding of the patient. In this chapter, we have considered how adults with hearing loss differ in their cultural orientation, their demographics, their reactions to hearing loss, their communication needs and problems, and many other factors. We also have considered the six phases of adjustment to hearing loss.

KEY CHAPTER POINTS

- Most adults lose their hearing gradually over time. Typically, the loss is greatest in the high frequencies and least in the low frequencies.
- Life-factor influences pertain to self, home, work, recreation, and community. For example, the norms, services, and mores that are present in the surrounding community will help the patient answer such questions as "What kind of help do I need and where will I get it?" and "How am I to contribute to the world around me and live my life?"
- Members of varying cultural, ethnic, and racial backgrounds may respond differentially to incurring hearing loss, to interacting with health care professionals, and to an aural rehabilitation plan. It is incumbent upon speech and health professionals to respect a patient's traditions, customs, values, and beliefs related to the aural rehabilitation plan.

- Adults who are have hearing loss may have more psychosocial and vocational difficulties than adults who have normal hearing. They may suffer from feelings of loneliness, self-stigmatization, and decreased self-esteem.
- In developing a patient-centered aural rehabilitation plan, you will determine how hearing loss affects the patient's daily life and consider how much relative time is spent in the home, social engagements, and vocational settings; the patient's communication partners; and what activities and sounds are important to the patient.
- Tinnitus and vertigo are two conditions that sometimes accompany hearing loss in adults.
- The patient journey has six stages: pre-awareness, awareness, movement, diagnosis, rehabilitation, and resolution.
- There are six stages involved in developing an aural rehabilitation plan: assessment, informational counseling, development of a plan, implementation, outcomes assessment, and follow-up. At each stage, the focus will be on customizing the plan for the patient.
- In developing a patient-centered strategy and in implementing an aural rehabilitation plan, a clinician will develop a partnership with his or her patient and develop a problem-solving strategy using joint goal setting and shared decision making. The objectives will be influenced by a patient's priorities and expectations.
- Motivating a patient to use a hearing aid may entail an education process, an examination of the patient's value system and attitudes, and establishment of a hearing aid use pattern.
- A significant number of adults who receive hearing aids do not use them. There are several reasons for nonuse. For example, some people find the sound unacceptable, and others are disappointed that their hearing aids do not provide greater benefit.
- A patient who suffers from tinnitus may undergo a variety of medical and audiological tests.
- Aural rehabilitation is a process and patients' predicaments change over time, so the aural rehabilitation plan must be fine-tuned and adjusted as it unfolds.

TERMS AND CONCEPTS TO REMEMBER

Prevalence
Life factors and life stages
Culture
Cultural and linguistic competency
Stigmatization
Tinnitus
Vertigo
Deaf culture
Americans with Disabilities Act (ADA)
Patient-centered orientation
Patient journey
Formulating objectives
Joint goal setting
Shared decision making
Use patterns
Orientation session

Outcome measure
Performance
Benefit
Usage
Satisfaction
Hearing aid use pattern
Third-party disability

KEY RESOURCES

The NAL Client Oriented Scale of Improvement (COSI)

Used with permission from National Acoustic Laboratories (NAL).

COSI

The NAL Client Oriented Scale of Improvement

Name: ____________________

Audiologist: ____________________

Date: 1. Needs established ____________________

2. Outcome assessed ____________________

Degree of Change

"Because of the new hearing instrument, I now hear..."

Final Ability (with hearing instrument)

"I can hear satisfactorily..."

SPECIFIC NEEDS	Indicate Order of Significance	Worse	No Difference	Slightly Better	Better	Much Better	Hardly Ever 10%	Occasionally 25%	Half the Time 50%	Most of Time 75%	Almost Always 95%
	☐										
	☐										
	☐										
	☐										
	☐										

Tool for Assessing How a Patient Spends a Typical Day

A two-ringed model that can be used as a clinical tool to gain information from patients about how much relative time they spend in home, social, and vocational settings, and to identify with whom and how most communication and listening occurs. You might show the patient this template and ask that he or she answer the two questions listed on the form. In reviewing the model, you will want to ask additional questions, such as *How has hearing loss affected your interactions with your family? Your workmates? Your friends?* and *Has hearing loss caused a change in your lifestyle or the quality of your lifestyle? In what ways?* The patient's answers can then help guide the aural rehabilitation plan. If time is at issue, then the patient might complete the template before an appointment or in the clinic waiting room, and have opportunity to look at sample models, like those presented in Figure 10–21.

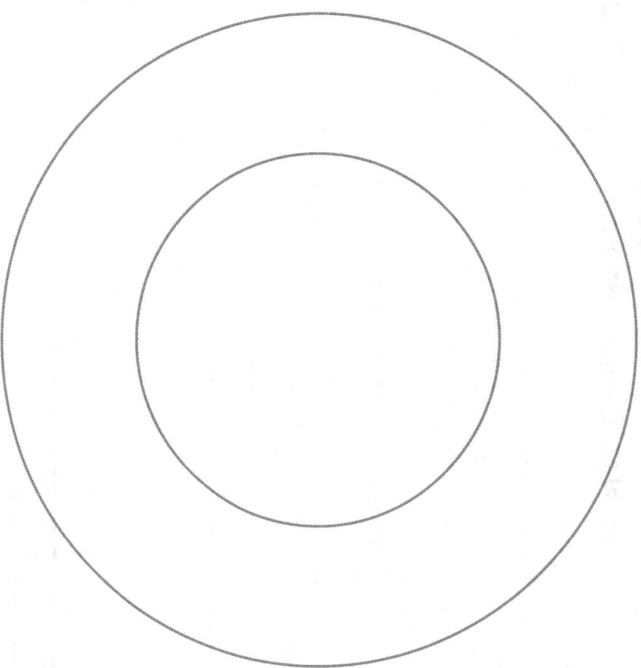

Question 1: How big a "slice" of your day is spent at home? At work? At leisure?

Question 2: For each slice, who do you talk to? How do you spend your time? What sounds would you like to hear?

The International Outcome Inventory for Hearing Aids (IOI-HA)

(adapted from Cox et al., 2000, p. 114S).

1. Think about how much you used your present hearing aid(s) over the past 2 weeks. On an average day, how many hours did you use the hearing aid(s)?

   ☐ none ☐ less than 1 hour a day
   ☐ 1 to 4 hours a day ☐ 4 to 8 hours a day
   ☐ more than 8 hours a day

2. Think about the situation where you most wanted to hear better, before you got your present hearing aid(s). Over the past 2 weeks, how much has the hearing aid helped in that situation?

   ☐ helped not at all ☐ helped slightly
   ☐ helped moderately ☐ helped quite a lot
   ☐ helped very much

3. Think again about the situation where you most wanted to hear better. When you use your present hearing aid(s), how much difficulty do you STILL have in that situation?

   ☐ very much difficulty ☐ quite a lot of difficulty
   ☐ moderate difficulty ☐ slight difficulty
   ☐ no difficulty

4. Considering everything, do you think your present hearing aid(s) is worth the trouble?

   ☐ not at all worth it ☐ slightly worth it
   ☐ moderately worth it ☐ quite a lot worth it
   ☐ very much worth it

5. Over the past 2 weeks, with your present hearing aid(s), how much have your hearing difficulties affected the things you can do?

   ☐ affected very much ☐ affected quite a lot
   ☐ affected moderately ☐ affected slightly
   ☐ affected not at all

6. Over the past 2 weeks, with your present hearing aid(s), how much do you think other people were bothered by your hearing difficulties?

   ☐ bothered very much ☐ bothered quite a lot
   ☐ bothered moderately ☐ bothered slightly
   ☐ bothered not at all

7. Considering everything, how much has your present hearing aid(s) changed your enjoyment of life?

   ☐ worse ☐ no change
   ☐ slightly better ☐ quite a lot better
   ☐ very much better

Appendix 10–1

Topics covered in a three-class group follow-up program for new hearing aid users (adapted from Beyer & Northern, 2000; Northern & Beyer, 1991).

Class 1: Getting to Know Your Hearing Aids (pp. 260–261)

Objectives

1. To demonstrate an understanding of hearing loss and the goals of amplification.
2. To identify realistic expectations of using hearing aids.
3. To identify the limitations of using hearing aids.
4. To understand the importance of binaural amplification.
5. To initiate a comfortable and satisfying hearing aid orientation period.
6. To demonstrate an ability to insert the hearing aids, change batteries, clean the hearing aid, and utilize the telephone effectively.

Class 2: Overcoming Hearing Loss (pp. 261–262)

Objectives

1. To identify the psychological ramifications of hearing loss.
2. To promote the importance of accepting hearing loss as a (usually) permanent yet treatable condition.
3. To introduce positive and assertive coping behaviors that can assist the listener in overcoming communication hardships.
4. To provide tips and strategies for family members of the hearing aid user that will assist in overcoming communication hardships.
5. To identify listening strategies that can improve communication situations.

Class 3: Total Communication (p. 263)

Objectives

1. To identify conditions within a listening environment that can impact communication ability either positively or negatively.
2. To utilize positive and assertive listening strategies to overcome communication barriers.
3. To identify and utilize visual cues that will assist in communication settings.
4. To promote awareness of assistive listening devices and their applications.
5. To provide additional resources on hearing loss and hearing aids.

CHAPTER 11

Older Adults

OUTLINE

- Overview of the Population
- An Aural Rehabilitation Blueprint
- Activity Limitations and Participation Restrictions
- Audiological Status and Otologic Health
- Life-Situation Factors
- Health Variables
- The Effects of Untreated Hearing Loss
- Aural Rehabilitation Intervention
- The Frequent Communication Partner's Journey
- Aural Rehabilitation in the Institutional Setting
- Case Study: Staying Active
- Final Remarks
- Key Chapter Points
- Terms and Concepts to Remember
- Key Resources

This chapter concerns older adults, individuals who are 61 years of age and older. However, this age is an arbitrary benchmark, and people, agencies, and other concerns vary in how they define the term *older.* Theaters, shops, and national parks often confer the status of "senior citizen" to anyone over the age of 55 years. On the other hand, Congress has extended the mandatory age for retirement from 65 to 70 years. One reason for these ambiguous definitions relates to the heterogeneity of the population. One 65-year-old woman may be vibrant and healthy and be a "youthful old," whereas another woman who is 61 years old may be sedentary and afflicted with illness.

In this chapter, we will consider age-related conditions and the unique challenges that they present in formulating and implementing an aural rehabilitation plan.

OVERVIEW OF THE POPULATION

The elderly represent the fastest-growing segment in American society. About 50 million people in the United States are over the age of 65 years, which is about 15% of the population (U.S. Bureau of the Census, 2017). Sixty-nine million are over the age of 60 and 14.6 million are over the age of 85 (Administration for Community Living, 2017). By 2025, the number of adults in America over the age of 65 will have ballooned to almost 72 million, or about 20% of Americans (SeniorCare, 2018) (Figure 11–1).

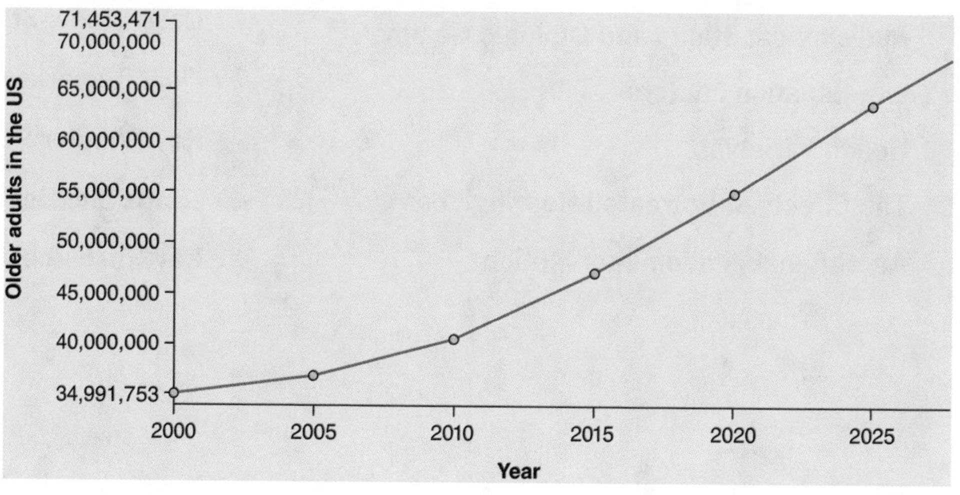

FIGURE 11–1 A growing population. By 2025, over 70 million older adults will be living in the United States (U.S. Census).

The Graying of America

"The aging of baby boomers means that within just a couple decades, older people are projected to outnumber children for the first time in U.S. history. By 2035, there will be 78.0 million people 65 years and older compared to 76.4 million under the age of 18."

—Jonathan Vespa, a demographer with the US Census Bureau

(Vespa, 2018)

As a group, older individuals are healthier than earlier generations. In 1982, 25% of individuals over the age of 65 years had a chronic disability. In 1999, this proportion had dropped to less than 20% (Lyman, 2006). In addition to being healthier, today's older generation is more prosperous and better educated. In 1968, 25% of persons over the age of 65 years lived in poverty (AARP Public Policy Institute, 2010), whereas in 2016, only 9% lived below the poverty line. The over-50 crowd has $2.4 trillion in annual income in the United States, or 42% of all income (after taxes) (Immersion Active, 2017). In 1970, 28% of older persons had a high school diploma, whereas in 2017, 86% held a diploma (Administration for Community Living, 2018).

The implication of these statistics for aural rehabilitation is that older patients will comprise the caseloads of many speech and hearing professionals. These patients are relatively healthy and educated and have financial resources. Many will expect that hearing loss will not prevent them from living active and productive lives. For example, approximately 36% of the younger segment of this group expect to be working beyond the age of 70 (Live Well, 2017).

It's a small world after all . . .

"If all seniors held hands, they would wrap around the world twice."

(SeniorCare.com, 2018)

The older population comprises at least two groups, the more traditional seniors and the baby boomers. The traditional senior and the baby boomer may share many of the same listening difficulties, but may warrant different design and implementation of an aural rehabilitation plan because they differ in both their values and purchasing habits.

Traditional Seniors

Traditional seniors, sometimes known as the "Just Good Enough" generation, may have experienced the deprivations of World War II. They tend to save their money, and many dislike carrying debt. They value trust, service, and quality. Some are resistant to technology, are price oriented, and have a tendency to follow medical advice. Since traditional seniors are now in their eighties and nineties, they are likely to have other age-related health conditions besides hearing loss.

Baby Boomers

The estimated 78 million **baby boomers** include the generation born after World War II, between the years 1946 and 1965 (He, Sengupta, Velkoff, & DeBarros, 2005).

Baby boomers are the generation born between the years 1946 and 1965.

Many baby boomers value active, youthful lifestyles. Convenience and cosmetics may supersede price when they consider whether to use a hearing aid and whether to seek other aural rehabilitation services. Many are technologically savvy and many want to control their health care decisions.

Try it, they like it!

Baby boomers are tech savvy (Figure 11–2):

- 82% belong to at least one social media site, with Facebook being the most popular and Twitter and Instagram much less so.
- 13% use LinkedIn, about the same rate as adults who are between the ages of 18 and 29 years of age.
- They are 19% more likely to share content with others than is any other age demographic.
- They tend to take action based on what they learn from social media, often seeking more information.
- They spend more time online than millennials and outspend them online by 2:1.
- They own 40% of Apple products.

(Immersion Active, 2017; Liquid Lock Media, 2017)

FIGURE 11–2 Baby boomers tend not to be afraid of new technology.

AN AURAL REHABILITATION BLUEPRINT

Figure 11–3 presents a "blueprint" for providing aural rehabilitation to older patients. The model comprises an evaluation stage and an intervention stage. Provision for reevaluation is included, in recognition that as patients continue to age, their circumstances may alter and new interventions become necessary.

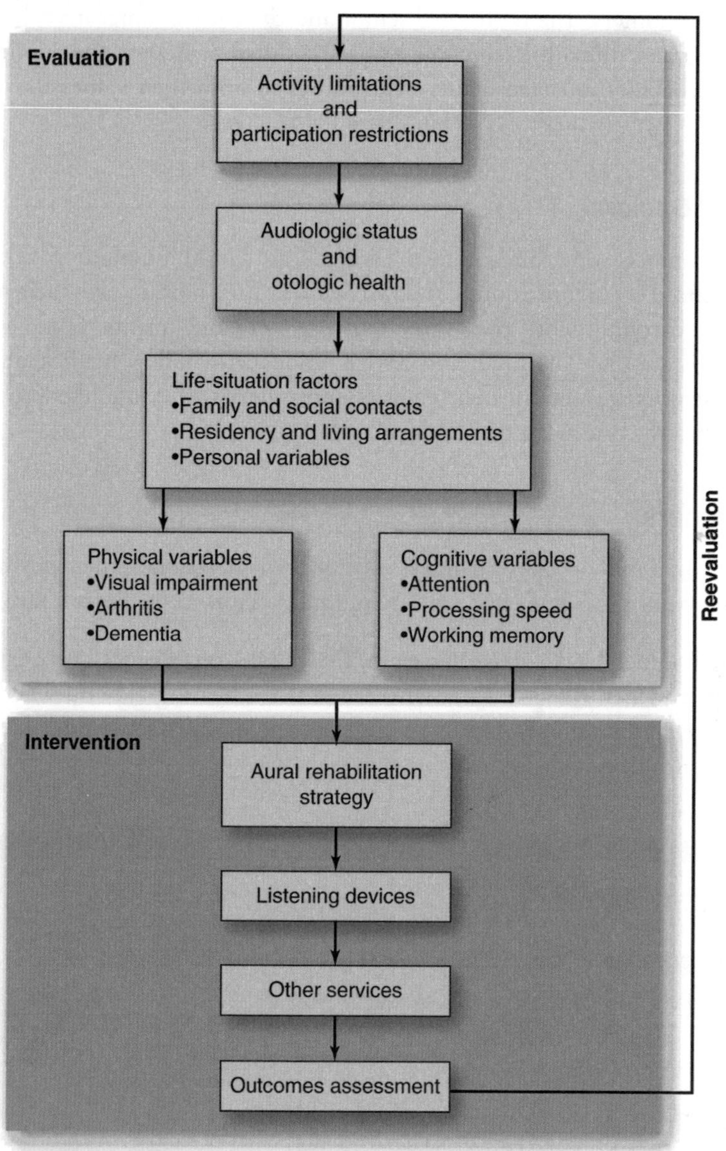

FIGURE 11–3 A model for providing aural rehabilitation services to older patients.

ACTIVITY LIMITATIONS AND PARTICIPATION RESTRICTIONS

One of the first stages of evaluation is to determine a patient's activity limitations and participation restrictions. This evaluation will include collecting a case history. As with younger adults, patients may be asked such questions as "Why are you here?" and "Tell me about . . .":

- The problems you have because of hearing loss.
- How listening difficulties affect your everyday life.
- The activities you would like to do that you have stopped doing.
- The activities that you find more difficult to do now than in the past.
- Any new activities that you would like to try.

The case history also may include a conversation with a family member or caregiver, during which time you might ask about the patient's memory, emotional state, and motivation to participate in an aural rehabilitation program and the feasibility of doing so. Conversational fluency might be assessed informally. You might note the frequency of communication breakdowns and the ways in which the patient attempts to repair them. You might also gather medical data about the following topics:

- Strokes, memory loss, vision problems, dizziness, and medications taken, because they may have an effect on the patient's ability to participate in testing and subsequent aural rehabilitation
- Arthritis and muscle weakness, because these conditions may interact with a patient's ability to handle a listening device
- Ambulation, behavioral changes, and other pertinent conditions, because they may affect the kinds of communication activities in which the patient may engage
- Dementia and Alzheimer's disease, because patients may require assistance from caregivers or family members to use hearing aids, and adjustments may have to be made in the audiological assessment

AUDIOLOGICAL STATUS AND OTOLOGIC HEALTH

An older patient will undergo audiological testing, like that described for adults in Chapters 2 and 10. Sometimes the evaluation will also include measures of auditory processing, such as duration discrimination, **temporal-order discrimination**, and **dichotic-syllable identification**.

Temporal-order discrimination requires a patient to attend to the order in which auditory stimuli are presented. For example, the patient may hear a series of three two-element (or four-element) tone bursts, with either burst having a different frequency. Two elements of the three-element series will be identical, whereas one will have a reversed (or different) order of the bursts. The patient's task is to indicate which one is "different."

A **dichotic-syllable identification** task entails presenting two consonant-vowel syllables to a patient, one to each ear. The patient must identify the two syllables, sometimes from a closed set of alternatives.

Other areas of evaluation may include otologic health, such as presence of impacted cerumen and measures of middle ear pressure and tinnitus.

Tinnitus and Older Adults

Incidence of tinnitus: Between 25% and 30%

Affect on quality of life: Negative impact

(Nondahl et al., 2007)

Audiological Testing

Traditional audiological testing procedures may need to be adapted. An audiologist will likely take more time to instruct older patients and may double-check to ensure that patients understand the instructions. Sometimes re-instruction is necessary, especially if the patient has dementia. Other accommodations for age may include the following:

- During air or bone conduction testing, tone stimuli may need to be presented for a longer duration of time than for younger patients. Some older patients cannot grasp the concept of listening for a soft, brief tone.
- Stimuli for speech recognition testing may need to be presented with a live voice rather than with a recorded voice, and even outside of the test booth so that the patient and clinician sit face-to-face. Some older patients dislike listening to a disembodied, impersonal voice.
- Patients may need rest periods, or testing might be spread over more than one day, as some patients may suffer from fatigue.

- Cerumen removal may be necessary before testing. Older adults have a greater likelihood of impacted cerumen and collapsed ear canals than younger adults, either of which might result in artificial air–bone gaps during audiological testing.
- The use of insert earphones may be required to ensure that a correct audiogram is obtained because of age-related softening of the cartilaginous tissue of the ear canal.
- An audiology assistant or a family member may need to stay with the patient in the test booth.

Presbycusis

Presbycusis is a generic term used to refer to age-related hearing loss.

The **spiral ganglion** comprises the nuclei of the nerve fibers that connect to the hair cells and meet in the central core (which is called the modiolus) of the cochlea.

The **cochlear nucleus** is a cluster of cell bodies in the brainstem where the nerve fibers leading from the cochlea enter and synapse.

Presbycusis is the global term used to refer to hearing loss associated with the aging process. It does not refer to a single pathology but is typically diagnosed when an older person presents a high-frequency hearing loss. Physiologically, two major causes of age-related hearing loss are: (a) neural, meaning a loss of sensory cells and supporting cells, nerve fibers, and neural tissue, and (b) metabolic or strial, meaning a change in the blood supply to the cochlea. Neurologically, hair cells may die and/or the cell bodies of the auditory nerve that comprises the **spiral ganglion** may degenerate. Metabolically, the membranes of the cochlear tissues may begin to thicken, causing occlusion of the capillaries and a loss of blood supply. In addition to neural and metabolic causes, some evidence suggests that the central auditory system may undergo age-related histopathology. For example, the volume of the **cochlear nucleus** may shrink as the myelin surrounding the neural axons begins to thin. A lifetime of noise exposure in both recreational and occupational settings, disease, and exposure to ototoxic agents can be contributing factors. To date, no medical treatments exist to reverse age-related hearing loss other than cochlear implants.

Peripheral presbycusis is fairly common among older adults, but some adults acquire a different kind of of age-related hearing loss called central presbycusis. Here are some basic facts about central presbycusis:

- Who and when: 12% of people over the age of 74 years
- What: Hearing loss characterized by normal thresholds (<40 dB HL) and reduced speech discrimination, especially in the presence of background noise
- Why: Weakening of the brainstem and temporal cortex and/or global vascular degeneration
- Implications: Older adults with central presbycusis are twice as likely as adults with normal hearing or adults with peripheral presbycusis (i.e., hearing loss associated with the cochlea or auditory nerve malfunction) to have mild cognitive impairment (MCI)
- Use of hearing to treat hearing loss could greatly delay or prevent the onset of cognitive neurodegeneration.

(Sardone, 2018)

Figure 11–4 presents median thresholds for females and males for each half-decade of life between the ages of 60 and 84 years (Mills, Schmiedt, & Dubno, 2006). Hearing loss increases with age and men experience a greater decline than do women. By the eighth decade, the display presents a falling slope, with the greatest loss occurring in the high frequencies. The decline in hearing thresholds accelerates over time, with the rate becoming more pronounced after individuals enter into their 70s.

A decline in speech recognition typically accompanies presbycusis. Beyond the age of 60 years, monosyllabic word recognition scores decline by 13% per decade in men and 6% per decade in women (Cheesman, 1997). Speech recognition difficulties are exacerbated when an older person attempts to listen in a noisy environment, more so than is the case for younger listeners. Discourse comprehension overall declines. For example, after listening to a spoken passage in the form of a lecture, narrative, or interview, adults over the age of 65 years will answer fewer comprehension questions correctly than will listeners between the ages of 20 and 64 years (Sommers et al., 2011).

Auditory Processing

In addition to or in conjunction with sensorineural hearing loss and decreased word recognition, some older individuals experience decreased auditory processing abilities. Some older persons cannot discriminate two sounds that differ in pitch, intensity, or duration as well as young persons, and this may reflect decreased auditory processing ability. These changes are indexed by performance on psychophysical tests and on tests of altered speech or demanding listening tasks. Two test batteries of auditory processing that are sometimes used with older adults are the Test of Basic Auditory Capabilities (TBAC; Chirstopherson & Humes, 1992) and the Tonal and Speech Materials for

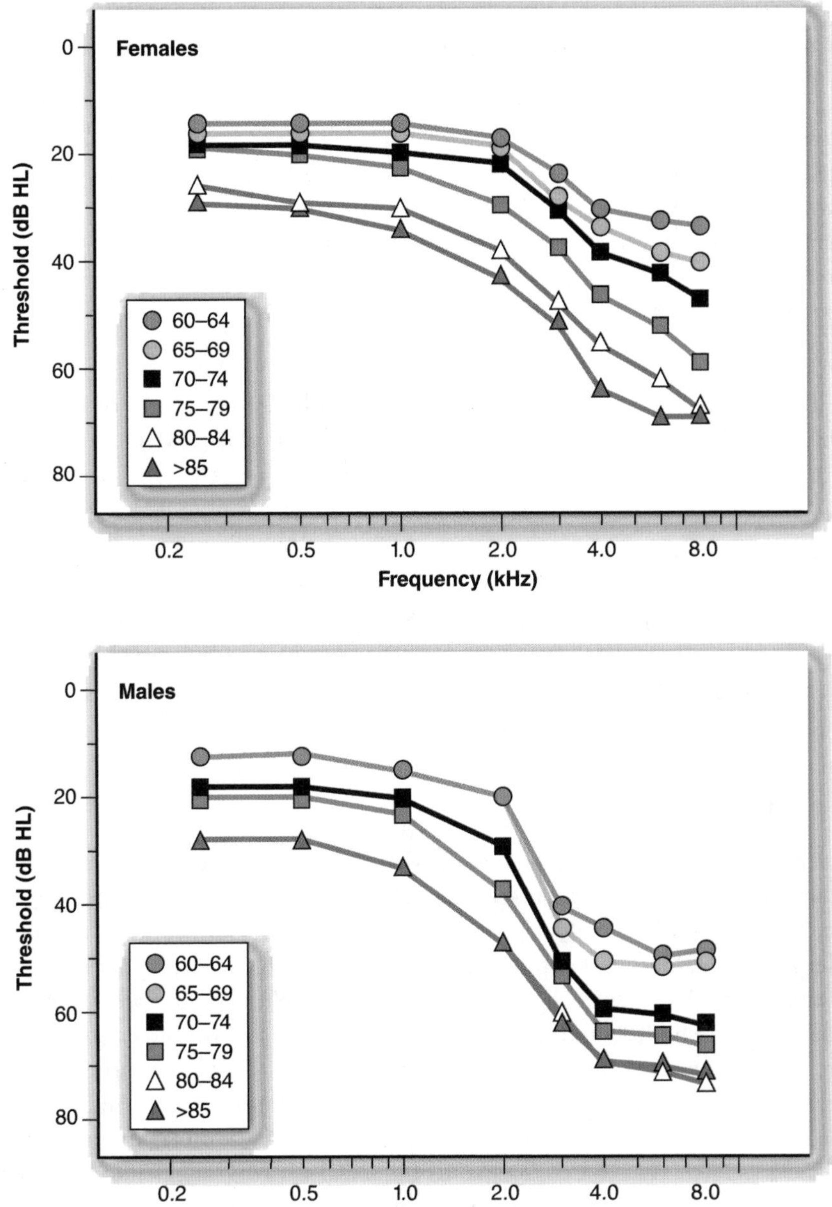

FIGURE 11–4 Average audiograms for groups of females (*n* = 1,358) and males (*n* = 935) at half-decade intervals between the ages of 60 and 84 years. Modeled after Mills et al. (2006, p. 16)

Auditory Perceptual Assessment (Humes, Coughlin, & Talley, 1996; Noffsinger, Wilson, & Musiek, 1994). The tasks in the TBAC require a patient to listen to a "standard" stimulus and then select which of the two subsequent stimuli differ from the standard. An example of a task from the latter test battery is one that requires patients to recognize NU-6 monosyllabic words that have been time-compressed by 45%.

Much research has been conducted to determine the extent to which speech recognition difficulties result from peripheral cochlear pathology (e.g., loss of hair cells in the cochlea) and the extent to which they result from age-related changes in the central nervous system (see Humes, 2005, and Kricos, 2006, for reviews). This is a complex issue, and no consensus exists.

What we do know is that the aging brain demonstrates a number of changes, which may have an impact on speech recognition performance. These changes include the following:

- A loss of neurons
- A reduction in the number of synaptic connections between neurons
- Changes in the excitatory and inhibitory neurotransmitter systems
- Changes in neural transmission along the auditory pathway
- Possibly, changes in cognitive processing of the acoustic signal (e.g., information processing, labeling, retrieval, storage)
- A decrement in long-term and short-term memory

Quite likely, many of these changes in the brain contribute to the declines seen in speech recognition and discourse comprehension experienced by many older adults.

LIFE-SITUATION FACTORS

The next stage in the model presented in Figure 11–3 is the evaluation of life-situation factors. These factors include family and social contacts, residency and living arrangements, and personal factors such as emotional health, mental health, temperament, sense of self-sufficiency and independence, and self-concept.

Family and Social Contacts

The number of people a patient interacts with and the frequency of interaction influence the person's morbidity, mortality, and physical functioning (Strawbridge, Cohen, Shema, & Kaplan, 1996). Older people who have five or more contacts are less likely to suffer from loneliness and depression and more likely to have a higher quality of life than persons who have fewer social contacts. For example, a person who lives within a 30-mile radius of children and grandchildren and works as a volunteer at the local zoo is more likely to have good mental health and be more interested in participating in an aural rehabilitation program than someone who has no family nearby and few interests outside of the home (Figure 11–5). Married people have lower mortality rates (He et al., 2005) and it is likely that marriage expands the social network of extended family members and friends who can provide social contact and support.

FIGURE 11–5 Proximity to family members. Persons who live near family members often are motivated to improve their communication effectiveness.

Social contacts allow an individual to feel more a part of life, more involved in the community, and provide motivation to address a hearing loss. Individuals who do not have communication partners available often do not seek aural rehabilitation services (Figure 11–6).

Just as social relationships influence the impact of hearing loss, hearing loss can affect social relationships. Hearing loss may trigger a negative feedback loop, as illustrated in Figure 11–7. Older persons may withdraw from social interactions because conversation becomes too effortful. In turn, family and friends may perceive them as unsociable, preoccupied with health matters, forgetful, or paranoid (Figure 11–8). These perceptions may lead to an older individual mistakenly being labeled as demented, confused, hostile, or senile. A son may find that his father frequently responds inappropriately to questions and suspect that he is experiencing cognitive decline. In actuality, his father has hearing loss and poor speech recognition. As an older person withdraws, and appears to be less cooperative or less effective as a conversational partner, family and friends may drift away and decrease contact. The older person may increasingly experience anger,

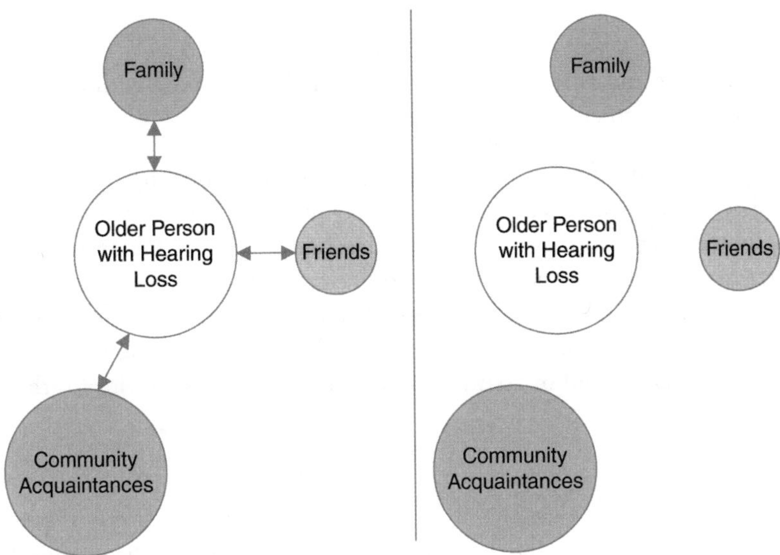

FIGURE 11–6 Social contacts. The number of social contacts and the frequency of contact can affect an older person's desire for aural rehabilitation.

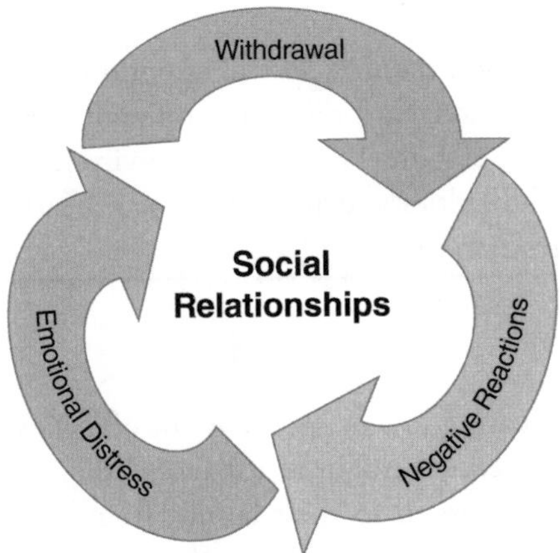

FIGURE 11–7 A negative feedback loop triggered by hearing loss.

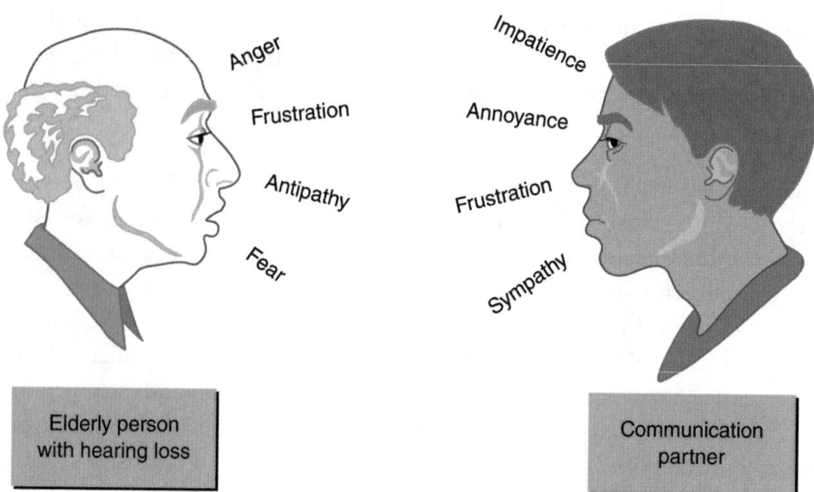

FIGURE 11–8 Miscommunications between an older person and a frequent communication partner. Miscommunications as a result of hearing loss sometimes result in an older person withdrawing from social interactions.

Emotional Reactions

- "Angry, sad, upset, anxious, frustrated . . . all of the above, really."
- "You get anxious about going to new places. I already have trouble seeing, and with the hearing on top of that . . . you start to worry about whether or not you'll be able to cope."
- "I get frustrated with my daughter-in-law for trailing off at the end of sentences, I get frustrated when my wife's rummaging in the cutlery drawer and trying to talk to me when she should know better."

—Comments made by older adults who have hearing loss

(Convery, Meyer, Keidser, & Hickson, 2018, pp. 316–318)

An **assistive living facility** is a living arrangement where patients with special needs, especially older patients, reside and receive help with everyday tasks such as bathing, dressing, and taking medication.

A **nursing home** is a residential, institutionalized facility that has three or more beds and provides nursing care; patients usually require constant nursing care and may require physical, occupational, and other rehabilitative therapies.

frustration, apathy, and anxiety. This situation may lead to more withdrawal and more negative reactions from communication partners.

Counseling family and friends about the ramifications of hearing loss in general and characteristics of the patient's particular loss may prevent the occurrence of the negative feedback loop depicted in Figure 11–7. Family, friends, and caretakers can learn how to counteract an older person's tendency to withdraw and avoid conversational interactions and encourage the individual to obtain aural rehabilitation services. In addition, they can learn how to use communication strategies effectively or learn how to help the older person handle a hearing aid or assistive device, or to handle the device for the person if necessary.

Residency and Living Arrangements

Although most older people live in private residences, some live in nursing homes or **assistive living facilities**. A **nursing home** is commonly defined as an institutionalized facility that has three or more beds and that provides nursing care. The majority of nursing home residents have hearing loss, and half of these have severe loss (Voeks, Gallagher, Langer, & Drinka, 1990).

The residential-care population requires special attention, as patients are likely to have a multitude of health conditions and their environments are likely to be noisier than private home environments (Figure 11–9). Noisy environments can magnify hearing-related communication difficulties and may exacerbate hearing-related activity limitations and participation restrictions.

Personal Variables

Some older people with hearing loss occasionally (or often) experience isolation, anger, insecurity, and loneliness. Patients might feel shame, either from a sense of inadequacy or from a sense of being a burden to their family, friends, and coworkers. Some feel embarrassment because their ears are not "what they used to be." They may hesitate to ask their communication partners to repair communication breakdowns because they

© oneinchpunch | Shutterstock.com

FIGURE 11–9 A patient's residency and the impact on an aural rehabilitation plan. A person in a health care facility or nursing home may have a particular need for assistive devices. In addition, health care workers may need special instruction.

want to "save face" and "save pride." These kinds of emotions and mindsets may lead to lifestyle changes and a diminished quality of life.

Not only will the emotional state of an individual be influenced by the onset of hearing loss, but, in turn, how the individual reacts to hearing loss will be influenced by the individual's psycho-emotional profile. A patient's emotional state is affected by mental health, temperament, sense of self-sufficiency and independence, and self-concept.

The Insidious Effects of a Noisy Home

Environmental noise can have negative and unsettling impacts, especially upon those who may be frail and living in an institutional facility. For example, noise has been associated with sleep interference, hypoxemia, behavioral changes, high anxiety, and increased blood pressure. Unfortunately, nursing homes may have the following characteristics:

- Sound levels that are higher than those recommended for hospital settings
- Noisy dining rooms, especially at dinnertime, thanks to staff talking, the transporting of patients to and from the dining room, and ongoing food preparation and serving activities
- Poor environmental acoustics, such as hard floor tiles and open communal spaces

(Joose, 2011)

One screening tool for depression often used with older patients is the Geriatric Depression Scale (Sheikh & Yesavage, 1986). The scale has 15 yes–no questions, including questions such as:

- Are you basically satisfied with your life?
- Do you feel that your life is empty?
- Do you often feel helpless?
- Do you prefer to stay at home, rather than going out and doing new things?

Positive responses to five or more questions may be reason for referral to a mental health expert.

Mental Health

A person is said to have a **mental health problem** if he or she has psychopathology or clusters of other acute or chronic symptoms. As with any age group, older individuals vary widely in their mental health. However, it is not uncommon for an older person to suffer from depression. Gellis and McCracken (2009) reported that up to 13% of older community-dwelling adults and up to 45% of those who live in nursing homes and

A **mental health problem** is defined as psychopathology or clusters of other acute or chronic symptoms; a psychological or physiological pattern that is not expected as a part of normal functioning, behavior, or culture.

residential care experience depressive symptoms. The following situations may trigger depression:

- Loss of or separation from friends and loved ones
- Change of residence
- Decreased ability to perform physical activities
- Retirement
- Empty-nest syndrome
- A decline in general health

Somatization is a process in which a mental or emotional experience or event is converted into bodily symptoms.

A hearing loss can magnify feelings of hopelessness, loneliness, and helplessness, and depression may decrease desire to seek hearing health care. Indeed, age-related hearing loss is associated with elevated levels of distress, depression, **somatization**, anxiety, and loneliness (Contrera et al., 2017; Nachtegaal et al., 2009; Shiovitz-Ezra & Ayalon, 2010).

Temperament

Temperament refers to stable personality traits.

Some people are, by temperament, more or less able to cope with hearing loss. **Temperament** refers to stable personality traits which sometimes are described in terms of "The Big Five": (1) extroversion, (2) openness to experience, (3) agreeableness, (4) neuroticism, and (5) conscientiousness (Figure 11–10). Temperament often relates to the impact of hearing loss (e.g., Berg & Johansson, 2013). For example, a person might routinely be frustrated by minor irritations, such as getting stuck in traffic, breaking a pencil lead, or forgetting to set an alarm clock. This person may be more affected by hearing loss than someone who has an easygoing temperament. Someone who has a tendency to be introverted may become increasingly isolated and less willing to interact with others as hearing loss progresses. Conversely, someone who is extroverted might readily use repair strategies to repair communication breakdowns and may eagerly use hearing aids.

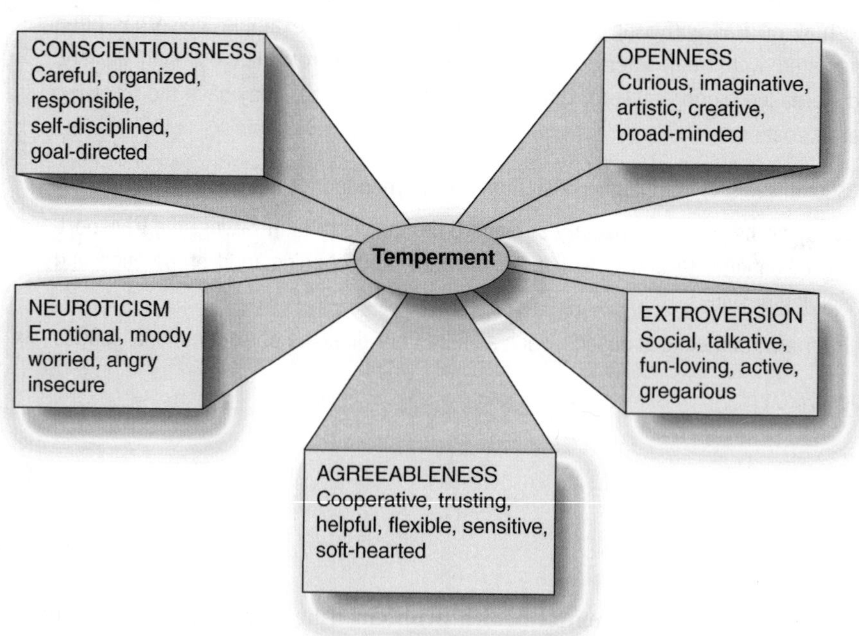

FIGURE 11–10 "The Big Five" personality traits comprised by temperament. Patients' temperament will influence both their reaction to hearing loss and their willingness to engage in aural rehabilitation.

Sense of Self-Sufficiency and Independence

Self-sufficiency and independence relate to whether a person can conduct day-to-day activities without undue reliance on others. Some older people feel increasingly dependent on others for daily activities because they can no longer drive, do their own shopping, and or navigate medical appointments independently. Hearing loss can be yet another signal of increased dependence because a patient may have to rely on others to manage communication difficulties. One man complained, "My wife has to make all my telephone calls for me and I hate it. It makes me feel like I'm 3 instead of 83!"

Self-sufficiency and independence relate to whether a person can conduct day-to-day activities without undue reliance on others.

Self-Concept

Self-concept relates to how people view themselves; for example, does someone think of him/herself as having a hearing impairment? Does the person think that he or she is capable of coping with a disability? Often one's self-concept does not match other peoples' perceptions or an audiological report. One patient commented to her audiologist, "I don't feel old, and I certainly don't think of myself as a senior citizen. But the way people treat me reminds me I'm not young anymore. Someone will take my arm to help me up the stairs, or I go to buy a movie ticket and they give me the senior citizen rate without even asking me if I'm eligible. It's weird." This woman was dismayed when her audiologist proceeded to describe the results of her hearing test, which indicated bilateral moderate hearing loss.

Patients' self-concepts interact with their hearing loss. One patient may experience difficulty in accepting aging altogether and may refuse to wear a hearing aid. Conversely, another may accept hearing loss and readily engage in aural rehabilitation.

HEALTH VARIABLES

Other health care professionals, such as a physician, will be primarily responsible for assessing a patient's general status. Some of the possible conditions that they might identify may affect the aural rehabilitation plan and both the evaluation and intervention stages. Occasionally, a speech and hearing professional might administer a screening instrument, say for dementia, and the results might indicate that a patient be referred to another specialist for further testing.

Printed materials such as education materials, questionnaires, case histories, and contracts should adhere to the following guidelines:

- Font size of 14 or larger
- Ample spacing between the letters and words
- Good contrast, with black print on a white background
- Non-glossy paper
- Crisp visual images, accompanied by large-font figure captions

(Busacco, 2011)

Several physical changes occur as people age. Their skin wrinkles, age spots appear, hair may turn gray, joints stiffen, muscles weaken, and manual dexterity decreases. The rate at which these changes occur varies among individuals, and some people are physically fit well into their 80s and even 90s. Physical fitness interacts with hearing loss to the extent that it may determine the kinds of communication interactions in which a patient engages (e.g., Does the person attend parties? Still work?) and the kinds of listening devices that can be used (e.g., Is manual dexterity a problem if the patient desires an in-the-canal hearing aid?).

In addition to changes in physical fitness, many older persons experience chronic ailments, such as hypertension and cardiac disease. Three common health conditions are especially relevant when considering the impact of hearing loss: (1) visual impairment, (2) arthritis, and (3) dementia.

Visual Impairment

The eyes undergo a number of physical changes with aging. The lens of the eye grows increasingly opaque, becoming more yellow, less elastic, and denser. The pupils shrink and admit less light. The muscles that control the eyes weaken and the number of optic nerve cells declines.

The **visual field** is the entire expanse of space visible to the immobile eye at any point in time.

Contrast sensitivity is the ability to detect differences in luminance.

Color sensitivity is the ability to detect colors of different wavelengths.

As a result of these physical changes, visual acuity declines and the **visual field** constricts, so that a patient cannot detect and use information from the periphery as well. **Contrast sensitivity** and **color sensitivity** (e.g., brown/black, blue/yellow) also decreases. There is poorer accommodation, so that the eyes are less able to shift focus from objects that are near to objects that are far, and delayed adaptation, so that the eyes take longer to adjust to changes in room lighting. Since less light passes through the lens, paradoxically, older persons may require more illumination than younger persons for tasks such as reading, yet they may be more sensitive to glare.

The prevalence of **blindness** in both eyes:

- About 1% for individuals 74 years old
- About 3% for individuals 85 years and older

(Desai, Pratt, Lentzner, & Robinson, 2001)

Visual impairment is defined as a vision loss that cannot be corrected through the use of eyeglasses or contact lenses alone. Anywhere between less than 5% and about 30% of individuals over the age of 70 years have impaired vision, and that the prevalence of visual impairment increases as a function of age (e.g., Bergman & Rosenhall, 2001). Even slight or moderate vision impairment can create problems in everyday situations, interfering with the ability to read, to drive, or to watch television, and can restrict a patient's ability to live independently.

Visual impairment is a vision loss that cannot be compensated for through corrective lenses.

Many older people who have severe visual impairments also have significant hearing loss. It is a sad twist of fate that, in the face of hearing loss, when someone could utilize the visual signal probably more so than at any other time in life for the purpose of speech recognition, this sense also begins to decline. Visual difficulties may relate to **cataracts**, **glaucoma**, **diabetic retinopathy**, or **macular degeneration**, as well as other conditions.

A **cataract** is a progressive retinal disorder that includes a clouding of the lens, causes blurred vision, and impairs contrast sensitivity. Lens-replacement surgery is available as a treatment.

Glaucoma is caused by high fluid pressure within the eye that may damage the optic nerve and result in reduced vision, especially in the peripheral visual field. Medication can often control the condition.

Diabetic retinopathy results from long-standing diabetes, causing blurred and distorted vision in the central visual field or patchy vision, and sometimes a detached retina. Management of the diabetic condition and laser surgery can limit damage to the eye.

Macular degeneration is a deterioration of sensory cells in the central region of the retina that may result in a progressive loss of both reading vision and distance vision.

Two of the more commonly used screening tests for reduced vision are the Snellen Eye Chart and the Pelli–Robson Contrast Sensitivity Chart (Pelli, Robson, & Wilkins, 1998). The Snellen Eye Chart presents alphabetic letters of diminishing height. Patients read the chart while sitting or standing at a distance of 20 feet. Acuity is expressed as a fraction, with the distance at which the patient is standing being the numerator, and the normal maximum legible viewing distance as the denominator. If at 20 feet a patient can read the letters on the row marked "60," the patient has a visual acuity of 20/60 or better. The Pelli–Robson Chart requires patients to read large letters of a fixed size that vary in contrast. Figure 11–11 presents a sampling of letters from this kind of chart.

In addition to performance-based screening tests, vision screening questionnaires are available, including the Functional Vision Screening Questionnaire for Older People (Horowitz, Teresi, & Cassels, 1991) and the National Eye Institute (NEI) Visual Functioning Questionnaire–25 (NEI, 2000). The Functional Vision Screening Questionnaire consists of 15 yes–no questions, including:

- *Do you ever feel that problems with your vision make it difficult for you to do the things you would like to do?*
- *When crossing the street, do cars seem to appear very suddenly?*

A score of 9 or more suggests need for referral to an optometrist or ophthalmologist. The NEI questionnaire, which has an interviewer-administered format, has 25 items that have a graded scale of response options. For example, to the question *Because of your eyesight, how much difficulty do you have finding something on a crowded shelf?* the responses range from *No difficulty at all* to *Stopped doing this because of your eyesight.*

Visual impairment has the following implications for the impact of hearing loss and the design of an aural rehabilitation plan:

- *Audiological testing*: The test booth lighting may have to be adapted to ensure that it is neither darker nor brighter inside than the outside room, and the booth entry and any steps may need to be marked with bright contrasting tape. Furniture inside the booth should be of high contrast, and glare should be minimized with evenly distributed incandescent light.
- *Speechreading*: Degraded visual acuity and decreased contrast sensitivity may mean that an individual will not be able to utilize the visual speech signal maximally, so likely will experience more difficulty in day-to-day speech communication than a person who has similar hearing loss but normal vision (Figure 11–12).
- *Speech perception training*: Speech perception training might be aimed at helping the patient be alert to auditory stimuli and to utilize residual hearing to the fullest extent possible, such as in auditory brain training (Tye-Murray, 2018).
- *Communication strategies training*: The program may include instruction about ways to enhance the visual communication environment, such as a repair strategy of *Come closer.*
- *Communication environment:* A patient who is less visually able will need optimal lighting in his or her communication environment to maximize what clues are available for speechreading. Sometimes, the environment cannot be lit optimally because bright lights cause the patient ocular discomfort. Warm (incandescent) lighting is preferable to harsh or "cold" fluorescent lighting.
- *Hearing aids and assistive devices:* A patient may be unable to manipulate the controls of a hearing aid, see battery polarity, recognize that cerumen has accumulated in the earmold, or change the battery. These considerations may influence recommendations about hearing aid styles and assistive devices. If a hearing aid is recommended, it is important to spend time with the patient so that he or she learns to feel the parts of the hearing aid and learns to adjust it by touch.

FIGURE 11–11 An example of a column of letters that appears on a contrast sensitivity chart.

Arthritis

Arthritis encompasses more than 100 diseases and conditions and entails a painful inflammation of the joints, surrounding tissues, and other connective tissues (Figure 11–13).

Arthritis is inflammation of a joint, often accompanied by pain, swelling, stiffness, and redness of the skin.

Age-related changes in manual dexterity include:

- Joint swelling
- Joint pain
- Decreased sensitivity
- Limitations in range of wrist movement
- (Reduced) fine-motor control
- Less steady movements
- Poorer two-handed coordination

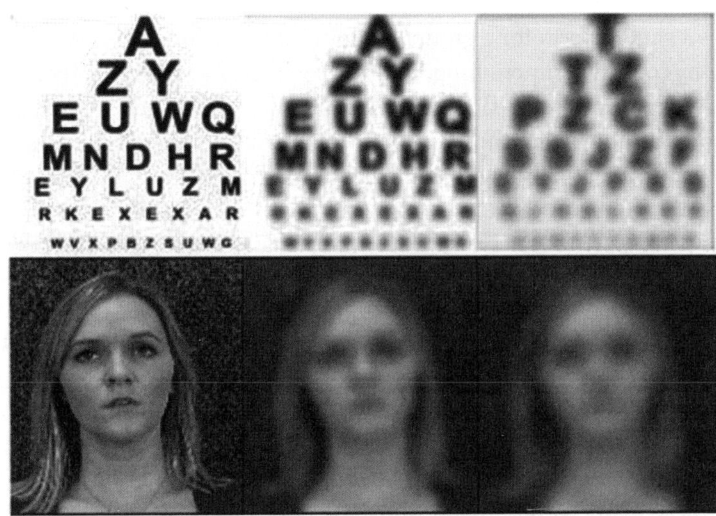

FIGURE 11–12 Blurred vision and lipreading. On a closed-set matrix sentence test, adults who were 66 years old and older dropped from recognizing 55% of the words correctly in a vision-only condition when the visual signal was clear to recognizing less than 10% of the words when the signal was severely blurred through Gaussian blurring (Tye-Murray et al., 2016). A Snellen Eye Chart is included for comparison.

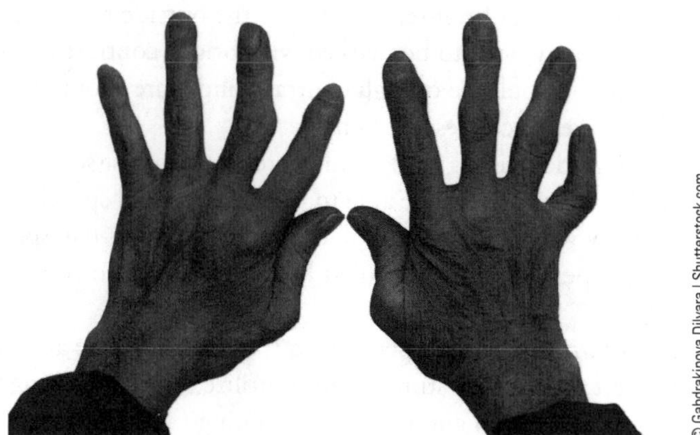

FIGURE 11–13 Arthritis and its effect on the aural rehabilitation plan. Arthritis can cause swelling and pain in the hands, hampering manual dexterity and ability to handle a hearing aid.

Arthritis decreases an individual's ability to perform fine motor activities. About 12% of persons between the ages of 65 and 74 years have activity limitations stemming from arthritis, and about 19% of individuals 75 years and older (National Center for Health Statistics, 2002). Arthritis may decrease a patient's ability to use listening devices. For example, arthritis may pose the following difficulties for tasks related to using a hearing aid:

- Putting the hearing aid on and taking it off
- Opening the battery compartment and inserting batteries
- Removing ear wax and performing other cleaning tasks
- Operating the controls

Recommendations for listening devices will hinge upon a patient's ability to handle them. In some cases, it might be more appropriate to recommend an assistive device that has large controls and is easy to manipulate than to recommend a hearing aid.

Dementia

Dementia refers to a number of diseases that affect reasoning and intellectual faculties; symptoms may include memory loss, deterioration of thought processes, and orientation disorders.

Dementia is a generic term for a group of about 70 to 80 conditions that cause irreversible decline in cognitive functioning, and may relate to a variety of biological mechanisms that damage brain cells. The symptoms of dementia include gradual memory loss, disorientation, decline in the ability to perform everyday tasks, decline in the ability to process and interpret visual images, and loss of language skills.

Alzheimer's disease (AD) is a form of dementia that causes irreversible loss of brain cells.

Alzheimer's disease (AD) is a form of dementia. It is progressive, degenerative, and irreversible. With AD, first memory, then reasoning, and finally language skills deteriorate. The time course between onset and death from AD is usually about 4 to 6 years, but may range from 3 to 20 years. An afflicted patient may become emotionally flat, confused, then incontinent, and eventually, mentally absent. In the final stages, patients cannot recognize loved ones, and they become bed bound. An estimated 5 million Americans suffer from AD. The prevalence could swell to 7.7 million by 2030. Normal aging does not necessarily cause AD, but the prevalence does increase with age. One out of eight people over the age of 65 years has AD, whereas nearly one in two over the age of 85 years has it. It is the seventh leading cause of death for people in the United States (Alzheimer's Association, 2007).

Screening instruments for dementia include the Mini-Mental State (Folstein, Folstein, & McHugh, 1975), the Modified Telephone Interview for Cognitive Status (TICS-M;

Welsh, Breitner, & Magruder-Habib, 1993), the Clock Test (Tuokko, Hadjistavropoulos, Miller, & Beattie, 1992), and the Saint Louis University Mental Status Examination (SLUMS; Banks & Morley, 2003). Sample items from the Mini-Mental State include:

- What is the year? Season? Date? Day?
- Spell the word *world* backward.

The TICS-M can be administered over the telephone in about 5 to 10 minutes. The instrument assesses orientation (e.g., the patient's name, telephone number, the date), attention (e.g., counting backward, counting by serial sevens), and language (phrase repetition, following simple commands, naming). The TICS-M also emphasizes new learning and memory by asking patients for immediate recall of a 10-item list and then delayed recall of the list 5 minutes later. The Clock Test includes three subtests: Clock Drawing, Clock Setting, and Clock Reading. Sample items of the SLUMS include questions about the week and year, as well as a simple math problem and a simple memory task. Other items in the SLUMS ask the patient to identify a triangle from three figure drawings and to name as many animals as possible in a 1-minute time interval.

Frank and Helen, a Happy Story with a Sad Ending

"A man is sitting next to her. She knows his name is Frank, but that is all she knows. She doesn't remember that when they met, she was head cheerleader and he was considered the best-looking guy in town. She doesn't remember that they've been married nearly 63 years and have raised two daughters. . . . She doesn't know that her daughters and Frank, 85, try to watch her constantly because they're terrified she will wander off. She doesn't even know her own name. It is Helen Erskine. She is 81 years old and she has Alzheimer's disease."

(Kantrowitz & Springen, 2007, p. 55)

W.h.e.n s.p.e.a.k.i.n.g t.o o.l.d.e.r p.a.t.i.e.n.t.s*, f.o.l.l.o.w t.h.e.s.e t.i.p.s**:

- Pause* after major syntactic clause boundaries (about 1,300 msec).
- Pause even longer at the end of sentences (about 1,500 msec).
- Speak slowly.
- Avoid sentences with complex syntax, such as those with subject-relative clauses (e.g., *Women that assist men are helpful*) and object-relative clauses (e.g., *Men that women assist are helpful*).

(Piquado, Benichov, Brownell, & Wingfield, 2012)

THE EFFECTS OF UNTREATED HEARING LOSS

Untreated age-related hearing loss may reduce quality of life and increase the chances of both cognitive and physical decline.

Quality of Life

In one of the first studies to investigate the effects of untreated hearing loss in older persons, the National Council on Aging (1999) asked the question "What happens to the quality of life if hearing loss goes untreated in an elderly person?" To answer it, they surveyed 2,304 seniors who have hearing loss. The survey centered only on the use of hearing aids. The findings illuminate what might happen if an older person fails to receive adequate aural rehabilitation intervention. A summary of the survey responses appears in Table 11–1 and Table 11–2.

As Table 11–1 reveals, respondents who do not use hearing aids were more likely to report feeling sad or depressed for a period of two weeks or more during the previous year than respondents who used hearing aids, and they were more likely to report feeling worried, tense, or anxious for a month or more during the past year. They were also more likely to experience paranoia. In fact, nonusers were almost twice as likely to report that "people

TABLE 11–1 Responses to a Nationwide Survey Indicating the Emotional Status of Older Persons Who Have Hearing Loss*

EMOTION	MILDER HEARING LOSS, USES HEARING AID	MILDER HEARING LOSS, DOES NOT USE HEARING AID	MORE SEVERE HEARING LOSS, USES HEARING AID	MORE SEVERE HEARING LOSS, DOES NOT USE HEARING AID
Sadness/depression	14	23	22	30
Worry/tension/anxiety	7	12	12	17
Paranoia	13	24	14	36
Insecure/irritable, fearful/tense	8	10	11	17

*Those who responded affirmatively to the item pertaining to sadness and/or depression had felt either emotion for two or more weeks during the previous year. Those who responded affirmatively to the item pertaining to worry, tension, and anxiety had felt these states for a month or more during the past year. All numbers represent percentages of persons with the indicated hearing loss who use hearing aids.
Source: Adapted from *The Consequences of Untreated Hearing Loss in Older Persons, by the National Council on Aging*, 1999, Washington, DC.

TABLE 11–2 Responses to a Nationwide Survey Indicating the Emotional Status of Older Persons Who Have Hearing Loss (all numbers reflect percentages of hearing loss)

ACTIVITY	MILDER HEARING LOSS, USES HEARING AID	MILDER HEARING LOSS, DOES NOT USE HEARING AID	MORE SEVERE HEARING LOSS, USES HEARING AID	MORE SEVERE HEARING LOSS, DOES NOT USE HEARING AID
Participates regularly in social activities	47	37	42	32
Participates in senior center activities	24	15	21	16

Source: Adapted from *The Consequences of Untreated Hearing Loss in Older Persons, by the National Council on Aging*, 1999, Washington, DC.

get angry with me for no reason." Nonusers were also more likely to describe themselves as feeling insecure, irritable, fearful, or tense. Nonusers were more likely to avoid social activities, such as interacting with neighbors and participating in structured events, and less likely to engage in activities sponsored by senior centers. The percentage of respondents reporting negative emotions increased with the severity of the hearing loss.

In addition to including responses from older persons, the survey included responses from family members. Overall, both hearing aid users and family members reported that following receipt of a hearing aid, improvements occurred in the patient's confidence, independence, relationships with family, and overall outlook on life. Interestingly, the families on average perceived greater improvements than even the users, suggesting that the patients' new ability to hear enhanced the family dynamics of communication.

Cognitive Decline

Untreated hearing loss has been linked with accelerated cognitive decline in older adults. For example, Lin and his colleagues (2013) studied 1,984 adults with a mean age of 77 years for up to 6 years, performing both pure-tone audiological testing and cognitive testing on a regular basis. They found that hearing loss was independently associated with faster cognitive decline and with increased risk for cognitive impairment. They also found, as have other researchers, that using hearing aids may slow the rate of cognitive decline (Amieva, Ouvard, Giuloli, Meillon, Rullier, & Dartiges, 2015; Thomas, Audvong, Miller, & Gurgel, 2017).

What Happens to Quality of Life When Hearing Loss Goes Untreated?

Untreated hearing loss leads to both social and emotional negative consequences, including less effective social functioning, diminished psychological well-being, poor self-esteem, and reduction in quality of life (e.g., Dalton et al., 2003). An American Academy of Audiology Task Force (Chisolm et al., 2007) conducted a systematic review of published experiments that have considered how the use of a hearing aid affects hearing-loss specific. Such experiments examine the degree to which patients' health status influences their subjective perception of daily functioning and **well-being**. The task force concluded that the use of hearing aids improves HRQoL and leads to a reduction of psychological, social, and emotional effects of sensorineural hearing loss in adults. In a survey of about 2,000 hearing aid users, 75% of respondents reported that at least one area of their lives was improved by using a hearing aid. Improvements included more effective communication in most situations, improved family and social relationships, improved sense of safety and self-confidence, and improved mental and emotional health. Some respondents even reported having a better sense of humor and a better love life (Kochkin, 2012).

Well-being is an intangible concept that encompasses both a physical aspect (e.g., health, protection against pain and disease) and a psychological aspect (e.g., pleasure, absence of stress and worry); state or condition of being well.

Balance Disorders

There is some evidence that older adults who have hearing loss are more likely to experience balance disorders and to fall when ambulating than those who do not have hearing loss. Since the cochlear and vestibular systems have a close proximity within the bony labyrinth of the inner ear, it is quite feasible that damage to one affects the functioning of the other. Moreover, poorer hearing might lead to a decreased awareness of one's spatial environment. Viljanen, Kaprio, Pyykkö, Sorri, Koskenvuo, and Rantanen (2009) studied 434 women between the ages of 63 and 76, of whom 179 had hearing loss. The women with hearing loss had slower maximal walking speeds and lower walking endurance. The women also reported a greater likelihood of falling (see also Lin & Ferrucci, 2012).

The benefits of amplification or use of a listening prosthesis for helping balance is ambiguous. For example, one study found that use of amplification decreased the subjective fear of falling (LaCerda, Silva, Canto, & Cheik, 2012). At least one study has shown that using hearing aids is an effective treatment in older adults who have hearing loss and who experience imbalance (Rumalla, Karim, & Hullar, 2014), whereas another study has shown no benefit of amplification for balance difficulties (McDaniel, Motts, & Neeley, 2018).

AURAL REHABILITATION INTERVENTION

In Chapter 10, the four stages of motivation that adults pass through as they engage in an aural rehabilitation plan were described: contemplation, preparation, action, and maintenance. Older patients may spend an inordinate amount of time in the contemplation and preparation stages, Because hearing loss typically progresses slowly, there is no dramatic "falling off the cliff" or clarion call that signals its presence and a need for action. As a result, many older adults never seek or only belatedly seek aural rehabilitation. In fact, about 70–80% of people with age-related hearing loss do not seek help

(Mahboubi, Lin, & Bhattacharyya, 2018). Only 11% of this group own hearing aids, and of this tiny percentage, only about 75% actually use them (Hartley, Rochtchina, Newall, Golding, & Mitchell, 2010). Less than 25% of people who were recommended for cochlear implantation actually received a cochlear implant (Mahboubi et al., 2018).

Dee Nile is an illustrative patient. Ms. Nile failed a hearing screening test when she was 67 years old. A while later, during her annual medical checkup, she expressed concerns about her hearing and noted that she no longer enjoyed going out to dinner because restaurants are too noisy. Her family doctor calmed her worries, suggesting that "everyone has trouble hearing in noisy dining establishments." As time passed, she began to avoid her favorite restaurant and other social gatherings, and learned to bluff her way through conversations. She did not consult an audiologist until she was 77 years old (Saunders, Chisolm, & Wallhagen, 2012, p. 331).

Patient variables, including readiness for change, self-management skills, and personality influence a patient's decision-making process. Also influencing a decision is the attitudinal environment (e.g., Is the patient's frequent communication partner supportive of a hearing aid evaluation? Does the frequent communication partner believe that the benefits outweigh the barriers?) and overt **cues to action**, such as recommendations from a family doctor (e.g., Convery, Hickson, Meyer, & Keidser, 2018).

Cues to action are strategies, events, or conditions that activate a patient's "readiness."

Hearing Aids

Many of the procedures reviewed for selecting hearing aids for adults apply to the elderly population. When selecting the hearing aid, the audiologist might select one that has easily manipulated battery compartments, especially if manual dexterity is problematic for the patient. Remote controls are the answer to some dexterity problems, as are hearing aids with rechargeable batteries, so that battery insertion is not an issue.

Whether a patient becomes a successful hearing aid user may well hinge on the audiologist's willingness to give a thorough hearing aid orientation. Ample time must be devoted to instructing the patient on how to insert and remove the earmold and how to handle the hearing aid (Figure 11–14). One patient, who stopped using his hearing aid shortly after purchasing it, was asked why he never developed a consistent use pattern. He said he did not know how to work the wax removal device, the battery door was too difficult to operate, and it hurt his ear to remove the aid. This man's audiologist may or

Call Your Mother

"In our work, we have found that adult children are typically very supportive of hearing aid use in their parents. Even if the adult children do not attend the appointment, many feel responsible to support their parents' hearing aid use. One person explained that she called her mother every morning and asked her, 'Have you taken your pills? Are your hearing aids in?' If we can get family members into the appointment, they will see first-hand how a hearing aid improves their loved one's communication. We can then give them tips on how to support their loved one's hearing aid use."

—Jill Priminger, PhD, Division Chief of Communication Disorders at University of Louisville School of Medicine (2018)

FIGURE 11–14 The hearing aid orientation. The older patient may require extra time to learn how to insert the earmold or in-the-ear hearing aid into the ear and to extract it.

may not have provided information about these topics during the hearing aid orientation. However, the audiologist obviously did not take enough time to ensure that the patient had an adequate understanding of how to handle the hearing aid and did not provide enough follow-up support to ensure successful use.

During the hearing aid orientation, family members, caregivers, and others involved in the patient's health care may learn about caring for the hearing aid. They might also develop realistic expectations about what the hearing aid can and cannot do for the patient.

Cochlear Implants

Cochlear implantation remains somewhat controversial for at least very old persons because there has been, at least historically, the question of whether an older patient has the potential to benefit from receiving a device due to reduced neural plasticity (i.e., an older brain may be less likely to learn to interpret the electrical signal than will a younger brain). Other concerns include the following:

- *Surgical risks*, due to increased anesthetic risk, slow wound healing due to a thinning of the skin or reduced blood supply to the skin, or complications from preexisting illness
- *General cognitive considerations*, such as problems with memory, learning new tasks, and ability to manage the device
- *Social considerations*, such as a decreased motivation to use the device and participate in social interactions
- *Cost–utility ratios*, in this day and age of health care rationing, health care providers are increasingly asked to select the best candidates for expensive procedures

Most research supports cochlear implantation for older adults, suggesting that use of cochlear implants lead to improved communication abilities and psychosocial benefits. For example, an investigation conducted by Leung and colleagues (2005) studied 258 patients over the age of 65 years and 491 cochlear implant users under the age of 65 years. The investigators found no significant differences in the two groups' ability to recognize words in an auditory-only condition, suggesting that older adults receive similar benefits as younger adults. Duration of deafness, and not age, appeared to be the best predictor of performance. A meta-analysis of the literature revealed that older cochlear implants have improved confidence and increased participation in social activities, have perceived gains in their communication performance, and have an improved sense of self-worth and health-related quality of life. Moreover, medical complications are comparable between older and younger recipients, suggesting that health-related risks are not problematic (Clark et al., 2012).

Soon to Be a Centenarian Cochlear Implant User

"The ability to hear, just like seeing, tasting, touching, and smelling, has a profound effect on quality of life. Mrs. Christoph [the patient] is just as eager as anyone younger to continue enjoying her life to the fullest. Her spirit and enthusiasm are an inspiration!"

—An otolaryngologist commenting on his 99-year-old patient who has just received cochlear implant surgery

(Mathews, 2010)

Assistive Devices and Over-the-Counter Hearing Technology

The high cost of hearing aids, which average about $3,000 to $6,000 for a pair (Strom, 2013), and the inconvenience of making multiple visits to an audiologist dissuade some older patients from purchasing hearing aids. A viable alternative for some older adults is to purchase an over-the-counter personal sound amplifier. These are significantly less expensive and some incorporate larger ear pieces and easy-to-manipulate batteries.

Besides using hearing aids or a personal sound system, some patients might elect to use other kinds of assistive devices. For example, a patient may be unable to handle a hearing aid because of arthritis and may need a simple FM system instead. Amplified telephones and devices for the television set, such as TV Ears (TV Ears, Inc), are also options.

Not Bad!

"Turn up that speaker phone, and boom! That's not bad. So, you know you hang on to some of the things that sound good."

—An older person, commenting on how a telephone amplifier enhances signal quality

(Southall, Gagné, & Leroux, 2006, p. 256)

When a patient resides in a residential setting, an assistive listening device may be preferable to a hearing aid. Assistive devices can simplify staff training because they are easier to use and troubleshoot, and are less likely to be lost.

Many older persons do not use assistive devices for any of the following reasons (Southall et al., 2006):

- Fear of technology
- Belief that their hearing loss is not problematic enough to warrant use
- Lack of self-confidence or self-esteem
- Fear of stigmatization because of hearing loss
- Vanity
- Secondary health issues, such as reduced fine motor control and visual impairment
- Lack of awareness about assistive devices

Southall et al. (2006) suggest that a series of landmark events occur when an older person goes from not using to using an assistive listening device (Figure 11–15). These landmark events include recognizing that hearing loss limits their participation in valued activities (e.g., talking to a family member), learning about technological solutions, acquiring a device, and adapting to using it.

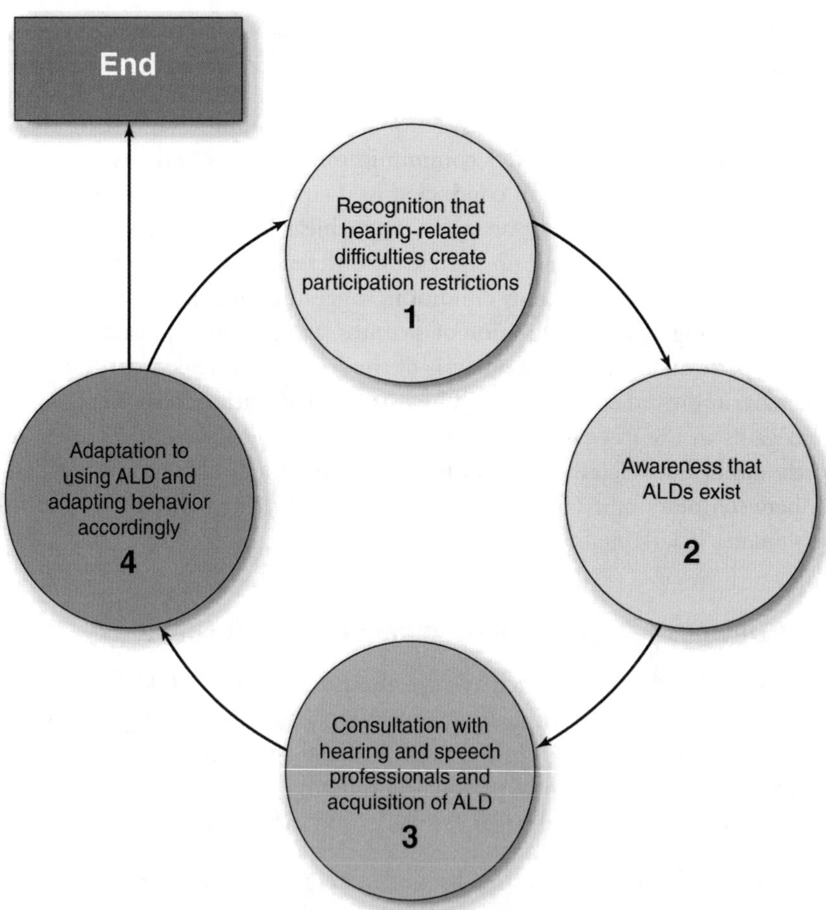

FIGURE 11–15 The four landmark events described by Southall et al. (2006) in acquiring an ALD. Adapted from Southall et al. (2006.)

In recommending assistive technology for a particular patient, an audiologist typically considers the following variables:

- *Affordability*: How expensive is the device? Especially if a patient has recently purchased a hearing aid or cochlear implant, affordability is an important issue to consider when recommending assistive devices. It may be desirable to have the patient prioritize listening needs, and then to select the most useful/versatile assistive device(s) accordingly.
- *Reliability and Durability*: Will the device work as promised, and will it hold up over repeated usage? Many manufacturers are now producing assistive devices, some of which vary in reliability, quality, and durability. When recommending an assistive device, an audiologist will want to balance the features of a particular device against its cost. Reliability may be of paramount consideration when safety is an issue, as in emergency alerting systems like fire detectors.
- *Operability*: How does it work? The patient must be able to manage the device. For example, he or she should be able to replace the batteries, if applicable, and be able to operate the device. Sometimes formal instruction is necessary; therefore, the patient must have the time and the cognitive (and possibly financial) wherewithal to participate in a training session.
- *Portability*: Can the device easily be transported from one locale to another? In some instances, portability is an issue—for example, if a patient is in an assistive living facility and moves from room to room for various activities.
- *Compatibility*: Can the device be used with a hearing aid? In many cases, patients wear their hearing aids at all times and will opt to wear the aid with any assistive device.
- *Cosmetics*: What does it look like when in use? Some people may be self-conscious about using an assistive device. For example, pulling out a wireless FM listening device at a restaurant may be difficult.

In dispensing an assistive listening device, the following steps are usually followed:

- Demonstrate how to use the device(s)
- Review the advantages and disadvantages of the device and its capabilities and limitations
- Describe how the devices work and how to install them
- Demonstrate how to troubleshoot the devices
- Demonstrate the device to family members
- Answer any questions

Other Services

Some patients participate in group aural rehabilitation programs after receiving a listening aid or even without obtaining one. The Key Resources section presents an outline of the first session for a group program for older adults and an outline of how a particular communication difficulty might be addressed during a subsequent group session (Hickson & Worrall, 2003).

Sometimes, family members will participate in the aural rehabilitation program (Figure 11–16). For example, they may learn how to speak with clear speech. They may come

Clear speech is characterized by:

- Accurate pronunciation
- Slightly increased loudness that happens with careful speaking
- Emphasis on important words that convey meaning
- Deliberate pauses at important breaks in the sentence
- Animated and vivacious quality

In the following sentences, please underline the important words that convey meaning and draw a triangle (Δ) to indicate where deliberate pauses might occur in the sentence.

1. The van will pick you up after lunch and bring you to the concert.
2. Cheryl and Darlene bought some chicken broth at the grocery store for their recipe and will be fixing dinner for tonight.
3. Next summer the children and I plan on taking a trip to Bermuda for a golfing vacation.
4. The laundry is in the dryer and should be ready in about fifteen minutes.
5. I brought several magazines so if we have a long wait at the doctor's office we will have something to do.

Please read the sentences aloud. Practice using clear speech—emphasize the words that you underlined and pause at the boundaries denoted by the triangles. Animate and enunciate your words.

FIGURE 11–16 A sample worksheet for providing clear speech training to family members and frequent communication partners.

to understand that conversation can be tiring for older persons who have hearing loss, and they may be encouraged to exercise patience and understanding in their interactions with them.

An Example of Successful Communication Strategies Training for Older Adults

Hickson and her colleagues (Hickson, Worrall, & Scarinci, 2006b) invited 96 people with hearing loss between the ages of 58 and 94 years, and their significant others, when available, to participate in a 5-week interactive group education program called Active Communication Education (ACE; Hickson, Worral, & Scarinci, 2006a), similar to the program formats considered in Chapter 7. The groups met for 2 hours every week. For individual groups, a speech and hearing professional helped participants prioritize their communication needs during the first session so program content for a particular group depended on the particular communication difficulties experienced by the participants. Typical needs included communicating more effectively around the house and listening with greater success to television. Participants completed a modified version of the International Outcome Inventory–Hearing Aids (IOI-HA; Cox & Alexander, 2000), which appears in the Key Resources section in Chapter 10. Frequent communication partners completed a version of the IOI designed for significant others. At the end of the program, more than half of the participants with hearing loss and the significant other participants indicated that participating in the ACE meetings had been "very much worth the trouble." The majority of participants with hearing loss reported using communication strategies on a daily basis, and about half of them reported that they had no remaining difficulties or only slight difficulty in the particular situations that they had identified as being problematic.

Research suggests that older patients benefit from participating in formal aural rehabilitation programs. For example, patients may experience less perceived participation restrictions following a counseling-based aural rehabilitation program (Ventry & Weinstein, 1983), and quality of life may improve when both patients and frequent communication partners participate (Kramer et al., 2005). Older adults may also benefit from receiving auditory training that is game-like (Whitton, Hancock, Shannon, & Polley, 2017).

Older patients who participate in group aural rehabilitation programs receive other, less tangible benefits. First, patients affiliate with peers who are similar to themselves in a variety of ways, and the group experience permits them to expand their network of social contacts. The social contacts not only alleviate age- and hearing-related loneliness, but may also elevate patients' involvement and motivation for seeking hearing health care. Patients can exchange stories and solutions, share frustrations, and talk about their hearing aids. By interacting with an audiologist or other group leader, they may learn more about hearing loss and might receive personalized counseling.

THE FREQUENT COMMUNICATION PARTNER'S JOURNEY

Just like the patient, the frequent communication partner is on a journey, and will pass through a parallel series of phases as the patient. Gregory (2012, p. 14) reviews six phases that are listed below, presented along with a sample of milestones that the frequent communication partner may experience:

1. *What is going on?*—May confuse hearing loss with cognitive impairment; may experience frustration or anger as a result of less social interaction.

When the Frequent Communication Partner Is an Adult Child

When patients are older, their grown children may also suffer third-party disability. Adult children may experience feelings such as frustration and uncertainty and may consider using coping strategies such as yelling. The parent they have known all of their lives has changed, and often so too must they make changes when interacting with that person. Here are some representative comments from adult children about how a parent's hearing loss has affected them (Preminger, Montano, & Tjørnhøj-Thomsen, 2015):

"I have to talk so loud and I'm a really quiet person and I don't want the whole world to hear, because it's usually a private matter. It's hard if there are people around, your conversation is really censored. I have to holler for [Dad] to hear, then I'm sorry about that, but it does keep me from saying some things (p. 723)." —A retired art teacher

"I get angry at times, I lose my patience. I know it's not rational, knowing that it's [Mom's] hearing loss. I remember her being a certain way and now she's different (p. 724)." —A teacher's aide

"I sort of monitor group activity if I'm around to make sure that I can sense if [Mom] is getting it or not, or is engaged or not, or is involved or not (p. 724)." —An audiologist

2. *Awareness*—May recognize changes in family dynamics; may engage in nagging or encouragement.
3. *Persuasion*—May help patient become aware of hearing loss; may consider the implications of moving forward.
4. *Validation*—May consider attending the audiological examination with the patient; may begin to understand the implications of hearing loss and the commitment necessary to facilitate patient's journey.
5. *Rehabilitation*—May realize that hearing aids make the hearing loss public; may wonder whose loss it is and consider own role in the enablement process.
6. *Maintenance*—May experience joy, relief, or disappointment, depending upon the outcome of rehabilitation; may realize that life has changed irrevocably.

AURAL REHABILITATION IN THE INSTITUTIONAL SETTING

Life in the Assisted Living Facility

"Sometimes I don't eat. I just want to get some food that I like. I want to say, 'Are you hearing me?'"

—Louise, resident in an assisted living facility, complaining that the staff does not talk to her because of her hearing loss

(Marrone, Durkin, & Harris, 2012, p. 5)

Since adults are living longer, an increasing number of older adults live in or spend time in nursing homes, residential care communities, adult daycare centers, hospices, and assistive living centers. These adults often have other conditions besides hearing loss, including cognitive impairment and physical limitations, such as chronic pain, incontinence, and the need for feeding tubes. They have a high incidence of depression, hypertension, dementia, arthritis, and diabetes. Residents also tend to be older. About 42% of residents are over the age of 85 years (Department of Health and Human Services, 2015). Many need assistance with activities of daily living such as dressing, walking, personal grooming, bathing, using the restroom, and eating.

For these patients, the aural rehabilitation program may have to be adjusted accordingly. Problems associated with providing hearing health care to patients in a nursing home include:

- *Managing the hearing loss when the patient may also have dementia.* Often patients with dementia also have depression, which can decrease motivation to participate in an aural rehabilitation plan.
- *Preventing hearing aids from being lost.* For example, a patient may place the hearing aid in a bathrobe pocket, and the robe may end up in the laundry before the aid is removed.
- *Maintaining the hearing aids (and cochlear implants and other listening devices).* One study found that 45% of the hearing aids used by patients in four nursing homes and four retirement homes had at least one or more major problems (Ferguson & Nerbonne, 2003), suggesting a need for hearing aid monitoring programs.
- *Involving the staff in the aural rehabilitation plan and providing in-service training.* Personnel should be aware of the communication difficulties associated with hearing loss. They should be familiarized with communication strategies and learn how to optimize the listening environment. Staff need to know how to handle hearing aids; for example, how to change batteries, how to clean earmolds, and how to insert and remove the devices from an older person's ear, as many residents will not be able to manage them alone.
- *Dealing with the high turnover of facility personnel.* An audiologist may provide an in-service in August, only to discover that in December, half of the staff has been replaced.

An **in-service** is continuing education provided to full-time employees.

A nursing home administrator may approach you to perform an **in-service** for the staff, or you might approach the nursing home personnel. An in-service may last anywhere from a couple of hours (more common) to several half-day sessions (less common). Scheduling is often difficult because staff changes occur about three times during a 24-hour shift, so all workers may not be available at any given time. In addition, staff may not receive hourly wages for the time they devote to training. Some attendees may have just finished working an 8-hour shift and be eager to end their workday.

Material should be presented at a level of difficulty that is appropriate for the audience and done in a way that maintains interest and attention, as with the use of visual materials and hands-on teaching aids. In addition, case-study presentation, demonstrations (e.g., "Please try on the ear plugs in the package I gave you at the beginning of the class. Once you have them in place, I'll ask you to try to understand the sentences that I will read"), and group discussion ("Please help me generate a list of conditions that might make speechreading difficult") will engage the staff. The goals of an in-service are to provide basic information about hearing loss and hearing aids, to develop empathy for the patient who has hearing loss and to teach strategies for enhancing communication with patients. For example, a unit about communication may include the objectives:

- Participants will develop an understanding of the limitations of lipreading.
- Participants will identify factors that influence the speechreading task.

Participants will recognize that sometimes communication difficulties that they attribute to a patient's dementia might actually stem from the patient's mild-to-moderate hearing loss.

You may also provide staff with materials citing the effects of noisy environments on the residents' mental, emotional, and physical well-being and consult on the acoustical design of the facility, helping to ensure that background and ambient noise is kept to a minimum (Weinstein, 2018).

CASE STUDY

Staying Active

A case study reported by Aarts (2006) illustrates the steps in planning an aural rehabilitation program for an older adult. The case study begins with an evaluation, then the development of an aural rehabilitation strategy, including prioritizing communication needs, and then the implementation of an intervention plan. Provision is made for follow-up and outcomes assessment.

At the time of his visit to an audiological clinic, "Mr. Whalen" was a 93-year-old widower in good health, other than poorly corrected vision and osteoporosis. He was concerned that poor hearing hindered his ability to participate in local service organizations, community boards, religious services, and out-of-town visits with his children and grandchildren. He came to the audiological clinic wearing two 4-year-old hearing aids. During the case history, he reported that he used only one of the hearing aids' four programs. He did not know if the aids had telecoils (they did). He expressed reluctance to use an FM system that had been recommended to him by another audiologist. Telephone communication was difficult. He reported that he was unable to use the telephone, often unable to hear the telephone or the doorbell ring, and unlikely to hear a smoke alarm when sleeping.

An audiological assessment revealed a sloping moderate-to-profound sensorineural bilateral hearing loss. Speech recognition testing showed that Mr. Whalen received limited benefit in quiet and no benefit in noise by wearing his hearing aids. Real-ear measures revealed that the hearing aids rendered only already loud sounds more audible.

The first step in developing an intervention plan was to prioritize Mr. Whalen's communication needs. His priorities were, in order of importance: (a) to improve functioning in quiet and in group meetings, (b) to improve telephone communication, and (c) to improve ability to hear environmental signals at home.

The next step was to create an intervention strategy that maximized his listening performance while maintaining cost-effectiveness. The audiologist reprogrammed the hearing aids and suggested that if this did not resolve his listening problems, new aids might

(continues)

CASE STUDY

Staying Active (*continued*)

be purchased. The audiologist confirmed that the devices had telecoils and showed him how to work them. The audiologist also recommended a trial period with a mid-priced FM system and a conference microphone. A lapel microphone was recommended, so Mr. Whalen could use the system in meetings as well as one-on-one settings such as in the car or sharing meals. Mr. Whalen also decided to participate in a trial period with a universal transmitter for smoke alarm, phone ringer, and dedicated doorbell, and a hearing aid–compatible device that would work with a cell phone.

In the first follow-up visit, which occurred immediately after the hearing aids were reprogrammed, real-ear measures showed that the hearing aids now somewhat improved the audibility of speech. The FM system's lapel microphone provided appropriate gain for normal conversational speech and the wireless phone devices appeared to provide benefit. Mr. Whalen received instruction about how to use the devices. He then spent the next period using the FM and telephone systems.

About 3 weeks later, Mr. Whalen was seen for a second follow-up appointment. He had used the FM system on several occasions and had used the wireless phone devices, both at home and while traveling. About the FM system he said, "This system is going to be a wonderful gift. I can return to meetings and such, and be an active participant again" (Aarts, 2006, p. 64). During this follow-up visit, he received information about a universal assistive listening device signaler, to be placed near his smoke alarm and landline home telephone.

On a subsequent visit, Mr. Whalen reported continued satisfaction with both the hearing aids and the FM system. He decided to forgo the hearing aid–compatible telephone device so he would not be tempted to talk on the cell phone and drive simultaneously. He also opted against purchasing the alerting devices due to financial concerns. The audiologist encouraged the patient to determine whether he could hear the smoke alarm when not wearing his hearing aids and to place an alerting device for a smoke alarm "at the top of his wish list" (Aarts, 2006, p. 64).

FINAL REMARKS

Working with older people can provide many rewarding professional experiences. For example, one audiologist described how she tested an elderly woman who had terminal cancer. "Mrs. Kramer had a moderate, bilateral hearing loss," the audiologist related. "I knew by talking with her, and reviewing her medical records, that she only had a few months to live. I suggested that she might not be interested in purchasing a hearing aid." Much to the audiologist's surprise, Mrs. Kramer not only wanted to buy a hearing aid, she wanted to buy two. She also wanted to access an internet speechreading training program. Mrs. Kramer's rationale was simple: "There is so much going on in my body that I can't control. It feels good to be able to actually do something positive about my hearing problem."

KEY CHAPTER POINTS

- The elderly represent the fastest growing segment of the U.S. population. By 2030, the number of citizens over the age of 64 years will be 72 million, or about 20% of the American population.
- The first stage of developing an aural rehabilitation plan is to determine a patient's activity limitations and participation restrictions and to establish priorities.
- Degree of hearing loss increases with age. Age-related hearing loss is called presbycusis.
- Some older persons may experience a decline in auditory processing capabilities.
- The impact of hearing loss on older persons may vary as a result of the person's economic status, social circumstances, social contacts, and emotional and physical

health. Two people may be of the same chronological age, yet differ greatly on these variables.

- Three physical conditions that may dramatically influence the design and success of an aural rehabilitation plan include reduced vision, arthritis, and dementia.
- Hearing loss often goes undetected, neglected, or untreated.
- It is important to consider the beliefs and attitudes that motivate an older patient to seek aural rehabilitation.
- Some changes may need to be made in the procedures for assessing hearing status and for providing a hearing aid orientation. In particular, more time usually must be scheduled to provide aural rehabilitation services for an older patient than a younger patient.
- Age should not be a determining factor in deciding whether a patient is a candidate for cochlear implantation.
- Some older patients desire assistive devices in addition to or in lieu of hearing aids.
- Staff at nursing homes and assistive living facilities need to learn about hearing loss, communication strategies, and listening aids.

TERMS AND CONCEPTS TO REMEMBER

Traditional seniors
Baby boomers
Patient priorities
Testing accommodations
Presbycusis
Auditory processing
Self-sufficiency
Self-concept
Vision screening
Arthritis
Dementia screening
Alzheimer's disease
Accommodations for visual impairment
Cochlear implant candidacy
ALD landmark events
Group aural rehabilitation sessions
Untreated hearing loss
In-services

KEY RESOURCES

The Active Communication Education (ACE) program, developed in Australia, is designed for older people who have hearing loss. The program runs for two hours per week for five weeks. In the first session, a "Nominal Group Technique" is used to identify and prioritize the communication needs of the participants. In later sessions, a problem-solving approach is used to address those needs identified. Table 11–3 presents an outline of a typical first session in ACE, whereas Table 11–4 presents a typical problem-solving session.

TABLE 11–3 Outline of the First Session of ACE

Objectives	• To welcome and introduce participants and to explain the aims of the program • To obtain measures of activity limitations, participation restrictions, quality of life, and communicative function • To explore the communication difficulties that participants experience in everyday life • To prioritize communication needs
Materials	• Folders with handouts • Whiteboard • Name tags, Post-it stickers
Introduction and welcome (15 minutes)	• Participants are invited to say who they are, what they have done about their hearing problems, and why they have come to the meeting
Communication needs analysis (20 minutes)	• Participants brainstorm about such questions as (facilitator records answers on whiteboard): • What communication difficulties do you have in everyday life? • What activities do you have difficulty participating in because of your hearing loss? (ensure that every participant is allowed opportunity to speak, without going into too much detail at this stage)
Nominal group technique (15 minutes, followed by 15-minute coffee/tea break)	The group prioritizes communication difficulties: • Participants receive three Post-its, labeled 1, 2, and 3 • Each participant places the three Post-it stickers next to the most important (Label 1) and the least important (Label 3) difficulty listed on the whiteboard
Problem-solving process (40 minutes)	The group takes the top-priority item and considers these issues: • What is involved in the communication activity? Who, what, when, where, why? • What are the sources of difficulty in the activity? • What are some possible solutions? • What information is necessary to apply the solutions? • What practical skills are necessary to apply the solutions? • How can you test the solutions?
Conclusion (15 minutes)	Facilitator and group discuss next classes and facilitator assigns homework activity. Homework may include participants writing in a journal, addressing such issues as: "How do people describe you?"; "How well do you think you have coped with the changes associated with hearing loss?"; and "Describe a hearing-related difficulty when you used a strategy that worked, then describe a hearing-related difficulty where you used a strategy that did not work."

Source: Adapted from Hickson and Worrall (2003, p. 2S88).

TABLE 11–4 Outline of a Problem-Solving Session in the ACE Program: In this session, the topic is conversation in noise.

Objectives	• To work through the problem-solving process as applied to an example situation in noise • To identify the component skills necessary for better communication in noise • To practice the component skills of requesting clarification • To work through the problem-solving process as applied to a situation that is unique to each participant
Materials	• Handouts • Whiteboard • Name tags and paper notebooks
Introduction (15 minutes)	• Discuss homework activity • Write session agenda on whiteboard
Example of a noisy situation (30 minutes)	• Ask each participant to look at the conversation described in a class handout and suggest ways to improve communication in that particular setting • List ideas on the whiteboard • Review a related handout
Identify necessary component skills (15 minutes, followed by a 15-minute coffee/tea break)	After making the modifications to the environment to optimize their chances of successful communication, facilitator suggests that communication breakdowns still occur. • Talk about repair strategies • Talk about the need to practice repair strategies • Review a related handout
Practice clarification skills (20 minutes)	Divide group into two and perform communication exercises. For example, a receptionist in a noisy medical waiting room tells you, "Your appointment will be next Thursday at . . ." You do not hear the time. What do you do?
Discussion of individual noisy situations (15 minutes)	• Have each participant identify a noisy situation that regularly presents communication difficulties • Work through the problem-solving process from Session 1 and ask group members to consider ways to repair likely communication breakdowns
Conclusion (10 minutes)	• Say good-byes and talk about what will happen next

Source: Adapted from Hickson and Worrall (2003, p. 2S89).

PART 3

Aural Rehabilitation for Children

CHAPTER 12

Detection and Confirmation of Hearing Loss in Children

OUTLINE

More than 1.4 million children in the United States have a significant hearing loss, making it the most common birth defect in the United States (Figure 12–1). About three babies born in this country out of every 1,000 have significant hearing loss and more lose their hearing during childhood (White, 2007). Approximately 15% of children between the ages of 12 and 19 years have hearing loss that is measurable in at least one ear (Su & Chan, 2017). In this chapter, we will first consider how prelingual hearing loss is detected and confirmed and then consider the health care follow-up and parent counseling that occurs.

As noted in Chapter 1, children who have prelingual hearing loss had their hearing loss while learning language and speech. They may have been born with hearing loss or they may have lost their hearing early in life, perhaps as a result of meningitis, high fever, or head trauma.

FIGURE 12–1 Incidence of hearing loss. More than 1.4 million children in the United States have significant hearing loss.

OVERVIEW

Figure 12–2 presents an overview of what happens as a baby is identified with hearing loss. The process begins with an evaluation, which entails detection and confirmation of the hearing loss and a consideration of etiology and other health concerns. This is followed by a preparatory process for an early-intervention program, which includes parent counseling and development of an aural rehabilitation strategy. It progresses to the next stage with the implementation of the strategy and the program (Korver et al., 2018).

During the first three years of life, children undergo their most intensive stage of listening and speech/language development. If they are not exposed to language during this time because of hearing loss, they will likely experience delays in acquiring listening, language, and speech skills. During the early years, the brain develops the neural pathways and cognitive skills necessary for acquiring spoken language. If a child with significant hearing loss receives intervention early on, as opposed to later, he or she will have a much better chance of acquiring communication skills that are comparable to a child who has normal hearing.

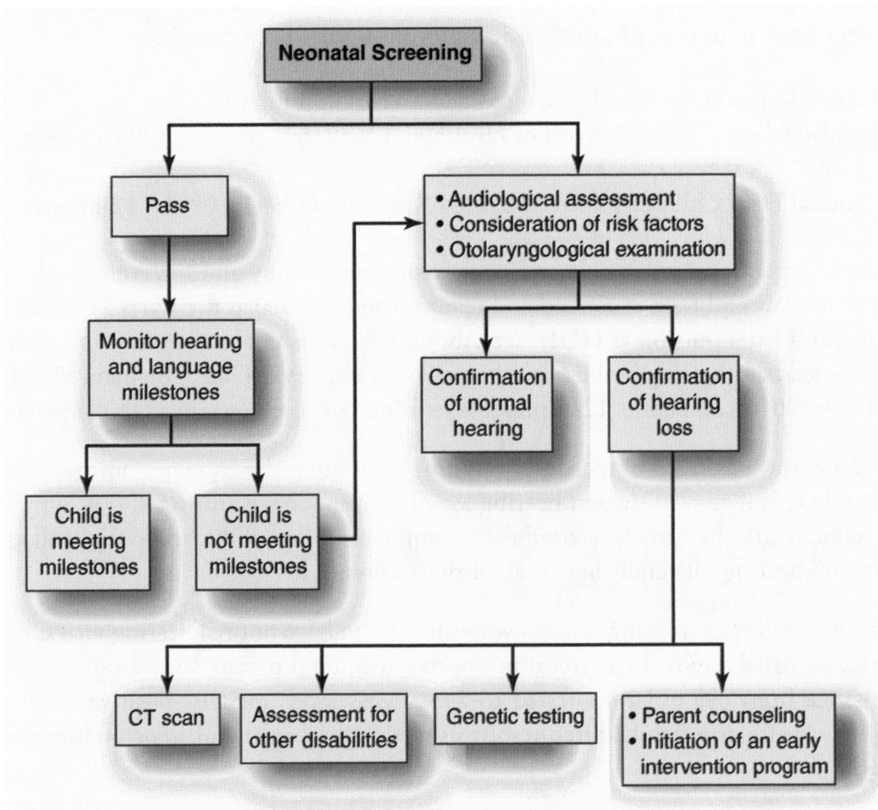

FIGURE 12–2 An overview of what happens when a baby is identified as having hearing loss.

The *patient-centered approach* adopted in Chapter 10 applies to children, but is expanded to be family centered. A **family-centered approach** acknowledges parental expertise, and includes parents and often other family members such as grandparents and siblings in the design and execution of a child's aural rehabilitation plan. Professionals proceed with three assumptions about the family. Families are:

A **family-centered approach** is an intervention approach that places the family as being central to a child's well-being and acknowledges that emotional, social, and developmental support are integral components of the aural rehabilitation plan.

- Unique, with both strengths and weaknesses
- Central to a child's life
- Expert on the child's personality, abilities, and needs

DETECTION OF HEARING LOSS

At least two events may trigger a parent or caregiver to bring a baby or young child for an audiological evaluation. The first is that the child may have failed a screening test and the second is that a parent may have noticed that the child does not respond to sound in the same way as children who have normal hearing.

Universal Newborn Hearing Screening

Universal newborn hearing screening (UNHS) or Early Hearing Detection and Intervention (EHDI), where every baby born is tested for hearing loss in the

Universal newborn hearing screening (UNHS) is the application of rapid and simple audiological tests, typically with automated auditory brainstem response (A-ABR) and otoacoustic emission (OAE) measures, to all newborn babies prior to their leaving the hospital with the goal of identifying those babies who require further diagnostic testing; also called *neonatal hearing screening.*

The **newborn nursery**, also called the well-baby nursery, is a hospital unit designed to provide care for healthy newborn infants.

newborn nursery, has become the standard of care in the United States and in many places throughout the world. Prior to the proliferation of UNHS, children who had hearing loss were often not identified until the age of 2 years or older. This reality was in contrast to goals established by national health organizations. These organizations called for identification to occur in the first few months of life. For example:

- National Institutes of Health, United States (1993): 3 months
- Socialstyrelsen (National Board of Health and Welfare), Sweden (1994): before 1 year
- National Deaf Children's Society, United Kingdom (1994): 80% by 12 months

The **Early Hearing Detection and Intervention (EHDI) Act** provides federal funds for states to develop infant hearing screening and intervention programs, includes provisions to support hearing screening and, when appropriate, full diagnostic evaluation of all newborns, and provides for enrollment into early intervention programs and promotes culturally sensitive family support services.

In 1999, the U.S. federal Newborn Infant Hearing Screening and Intervention Act was signed into law and then expanded and reauthorized in 2010 as the **Early Hearing Detection and Intervention (EHDI) Act**. About 95% of babies born in the United States are screened before going home from the newborn nursery (White, Forsman, Eichwald, & Munoz, 2010). Appendix 12–1 presents terminology often used in a UNHS program.

Screening is a "pass/refer" procedure, meaning either that the baby has normal hearing or that there is reason to suspect hearing loss. If hearing loss is suspected (i.e., a *refer* result is obtained), the baby is referred for a complete audiological workup that will assess the child's hearing bilaterally and at all of the audiometric frequencies.

A **false-positive** occurs when a baby does not have a hearing loss but fails the screening test.

Middle ear effusion is the exudation of fluid from membranous tissue into the middle ear cavity.

Neuromaturational delay occurs when a nervous system function has failed to develop as rapidly as usual.

A **false-negative** occurs when a baby has hearing loss but passes the screening test.

Babies who fail the screening test but who turn out to have normal hearing are examples of **false-positive** results. In a typical newborn screening program, the false-positive rate may range from 2% of babies tested to 7%. Two reasons for false-positive results are **middle ear effusion** (which often resolves shortly after birth) and **neuromaturational delay**.

Babies who pass the screening test but who turn out to have hearing loss are examples of **false-negative** results. Ideally, the false-negative rate of a UNHS program is zero.

Many programs rescreen babies who fail the screening the first time before they leave the newborn nursery. This practice pushes the false-positive rate toward the lower end of 2% (Gorga, Preissler, Simmons, Walker, & Hoover, 2001; Stewart et al., 2000). Rescreening can minimize parents' anxiety. In addition, because many babies who do not pass the hearing screening do not return for follow-up, more accurate screening means that fewer babies are lost to follow-up. Some programs will arrange for the baby to be rescreened in a follow-up appointment, after the baby leaves the hospital, before referring for a comprehensive audiological evaluation.

Other Than a Deaf Cat

"Before leaving the hospital, a nurse told me that Rachel had failed the test and was hearing impaired. *Hearing impaired?* How did this happen? Why did this happen? . . . Other than having a deaf cat when I was a child, I had no experience with hearing loss, hearing aids, or deafness. . . . I was overwrought with grief. My dreams and hopes for my child were shattered."

—Sharon Kane, proud mother of an 11-year-old daughter who testified for a Bill of Rights for children with hearing loss in the state of Connecticut

(Kane & Kane, 2012, p. 47)

Methods used for screening include otoacoustic emissions (OAEs) testing and automated auditory brainstem response (A-ABR) testing, two procedures that will be considered shortly. Screening is designed to pass/fail hearing thresholds of 30 to 40 dB HL in the frequency region of about 500 to 4000 Hz. In some hospitals, parents are invited to view the screening because, as one audiologist noted, "We want the mom to witness the screen because if you screen a baby in the newborn nursery and you give them a piece of paper, it's like a mystery happened and they're not really sure what it meant" (Pallarito, 2012, pp. 20–22).

Support for UNHS stems from research showing that if hearing loss is identified before a child reaches the age of 6 months, and the child receives intervention, then that child will achieve language scores that compare favorably to children who have normal hearing by the age of 3 years. This is not true of children who are not identified early and who do not receive intervention (Nelson, Bougatsos, & Nygren, 2008; Yoshinaga-Itano, Sedey, Coulter, & Mehl, 1998; Figure 12–3).

© Sharomka | Shutterstock.com

FIGURE 12–3 Early identification. Children who are identified as having hearing loss before the age of 6 months and who receive early intervention have a good chance of developing language skills that compare favorably with their peers who have normal hearing.

Willingly Kept in the Dark

"People always seem surprised that I didn't discover my [son's] deafness until he was 19 months old. In fact, the possibility had crossed my mind when he didn't start talking. The pediatrician assured me that since he was babbling, he was also hearing. But I didn't do the one thing that would have told me for sure: I didn't make a loud noise when my baby was asleep to see if it would wake him up. Which is how I know that I had no intention of learning the truth just then."

—Mother of a college student with profound hearing loss

(Lichtman, 2005, p. 120)

Some babies are particularly at risk for hearing loss. Risk factors associated with hearing loss include the following:

- Low birth weight (less than 3.3 pounds)
- Family history of hearing loss
- In utero infections such as cytomegalovirus, rubella, or herpes
- Ototoxic medications
- Low **Apgar scores** (which reflect the normalcy of A = appearance, P = pulse, G = grimace, A = activity, and R = respiration at the time of birth)
- Need for use of a ventilator for five days or longer
- Craniofacial anomalies
- Physical manifestations consistent with a syndrome
- Bacterial meningitis
- Hyperbilirubinemia (severe jaundice) at levels that require an exchange transfusion

An **Apgar score** is a numeric value between 1 and 10 assigned to newborns to describe their physical status at birth.

The **EHDI 1-3-6 guidelines** were developed by the Joint Committee on Infant Hearing and recommend that hearing screening occur by 1 month of age, diagnosis by 3 months, and intervention by 6 months.

The **Joint Committee on Infant Hearing (JCIH)** is a committee comprising professionals from audiology, otolaryngology, pediatrics, education, and speech and language pathology that proffers position papers and establishes practice standards for the early identification of and follow-up care for infants and toddlers who have congenital hearing loss.

Although these risk factors often trigger a suspicion of hearing loss, it is important to recognize that almost 50% of children who have hearing loss do not have risk factors at birth.

The **Joint Committee on Infant Hearing (JCIH)** (2007) developed the EHDI guidelines, which suggest that in addition to screening occurring at 1 month, hearing loss should be diagnosed by 3 months of age, and intervention should be initiated by 6 months of age. These recommendations are referred to as the **EHDI 1-3-6 guidelines**.

Even if a baby passes the newborn screening test, parents should be alerted to watch for the telltale signs of hearing loss, especially if risk factors are present. Childhood hearing loss can occur after birth. Thus, at 6 months of age, babies with a risk factor should be retested, and then retested every six months thereafter until the age of 3 years. A handout, like that presented in the Key Resources section, might be provided to parents when they leave the hospital. Parents might monitor during the first year whether their babies react to loud noises, respond to their names, or localize to sound. At age 2 years, children should imitate simple words and play with their voices. By age 3 years, children usually begin to understand simple phrases, such as *all gone* and *time to go bye-bye.*

The Joint Committee on Infant Hearing (JCIH) 1-3-6 guidelines:

- Screen no later than **1** month of age
- Diagnose no later than **3** months
- Enroll in early intervention programs no later than **6** months

Learning of the Hearing Loss Later On

A Day of Discovery

"My hearing loss was discovered at the age of 2. I was at my babysitter's house playing with toys when the sitter, Nancy, called my name and saw no response from me. Puzzled, she decided to call my parents and explain the odd scenario. My mother was confused. 'What do you mean he is not hearing anything?' she questioned. She agreed to pick me up and take me to the hospital. At the hospital, I received [testing]. . . . The doctors confirmed what Nancy and my mother feared: I had a profound hearing loss. Devastated, my mother broke down crying and called my father to come to the hospital immediately."

—Ryan Lopacinski, a 15-year-old middle school student and cochlear implant recipient

(Lopacinski, 2013, p. 30)

Sometimes parents do not learn of their child's hearing loss until later on, perhaps because the loss occurred after the child left the newborn nursery or occurred later in childhood. Parents may say how they suspected a hearing loss and took the baby to the family physician or pediatrician. The physician may have dismissed the parents' concerns and thereby have delayed diagnosis for several months or even years. As a result, the child did not receive early amplification and intervention services. Some parents may express guilt because they did not follow their instincts and pursue second opinions.

Other parents may express anger because they believe the hearing loss could have been prevented. For example, a child's parents may speak of taking the child to the hospital with a high fever and then being sent home with a diagnosis of a viral infection. Within hours, the child's condition worsened, with increased fever and seizures. Though the child survived a bout of what was ultimately diagnosed as meningitis, the child was left with serious hearing loss that the parents believe could have been prevented.

CONFIRMATION OF HEARING LOSS

A child's hearing may be tested in a variety of ways. The measurement technique depends upon the age of the child and his or her ability to participate in the test procedures. Once a hearing loss has been identified, hearing should be tested twice each year for young children, and four times or more annually if other problems are present or if there is concern about the accuracy of the test results. Older children usually receive testing only once a year.

Objective Tests

Two objective tests are used to determine the presence of hearing loss: auditory brainstem response and otoacoustic emissions.

Auditory Brainstem Response Test

Auditory brainstem response (ABR) is an auditory evoked potential that originates from the eighth cranial nerve and auditory brainstem structures. The electrophysiological record consists of five to seven peaks, which represent the neural functioning of the auditory pathway.

Auditory evoked potential (AEP) is an electrophysiological response to sound, distinguished by latency.

An **automated auditory brainstem response (A-ABR)** is a screening method to measure the auditory brainstem response in which recording parameters are computer controlled and detection of the response is determined by computer-based algorithms.

Auditory brainstem response (ABR) is a type of **auditory evoked potential (AEP)** testing that is often used with babies and older children who are unable to participate in behavioral testing. Surface electrodes are placed on the child's head and neck to record neural activity elicited by the presentation of tone bursts or sound clicks. The ABR is the electrophysiological response to an acoustic stimulus and originates from the eighth cranial nerve and auditory brainstem. Potentials are categorized in terms of their latency, or the time at which they appear following acoustic stimulation. They usually occur between 1 and 15 msec following the presentation of a click. A standard ABR recording contains seven peaks in the recorded waveform. The *wave/peak V detection threshold* correlates well with hearing sensitivity in the 1500 to 4000 Hz region. For a comprehensive ABR test, the child usually must be sedated, or at least asleep, as the child must be very still in order to obtain accurate test results. ABRs can be used to determine the degree of hearing loss at the different audiometric frequencies. For screening purposes, a baby may receive a variation of ABR, called an **automated auditory brainstem response (A-ABR)**. For example, ALGO is an A-ABR screening device, which compares the baby's ABR response to a stored template of expected brain waveforms. Results can either rule out or implicate significant hearing loss.

Otoacoustic Emissions Testing

Otoacoustic emissions (OAEs) are inaudible sounds that are the by-products of the mechanical actions of the outer hair cells in the cochlea. **Outer hair cells** amplify sounds entering the inner ear from the middle ear and potentiate the sensitivity of the inner hair cells. When sound stimulates the cochlea, the outer hair cells vibrate and initiate a signal. Simultaneously, the vibration produces a sound that can be measured with a small probe inserted into the ear canal. Sound is presented, and the OAE is detected and traced. Persons who have normal hearing produce OAEs, whereas those who have hearing loss of 30 to 40 dB HL or greater do not. The procedure is widely used as a screening procedure because it is quick to administer and does not require the cooperation of the patient, other than to remain relatively still (Figure 12–4).

Otoacoustic emissions (OAEs) are low-level sound emitted spontaneously by the cochlea on presentation of an auditory stimulus.

The **outer hair cells** reside in the organ of Corti, amplify vibrations of sound entering from the middle ear, and appear to potentiate the sensitivity of the inner hair cells.

When used for newborn screening, a nurse, technician, or volunteer often collects the OAEs, although a hospital-based audiologist may supervise the overall screening efforts. The screening professional often uses a handheld OAE screener. It flashes a *pass* on the screening unit when an OAE is present, and a *refer* when it is not. Frequencies important for speech recognition are typically tested, such as 2000, 3000, 4000, and 5000 Hz. Children who do not pass are checked for middle ear effusion and then rescreened, if necessary.

Premies

"We typically don't conduct newborn hearing screening before the infant is 34 weeks gestational age because of immaturity within the auditory nervous system. In fact screening is complicated even at this age by continued immaturity or by chronic medical conditions."

—Andrew P. McGrath, AuD, and Betty R. Vohr, MD, Women & Infants Hospital, Providence, RI, talking about infants who are as young as 23–25 weeks gestation and weigh as little as 500 to 750 grams

(McGrath & Vohr, 2017, p. 22)

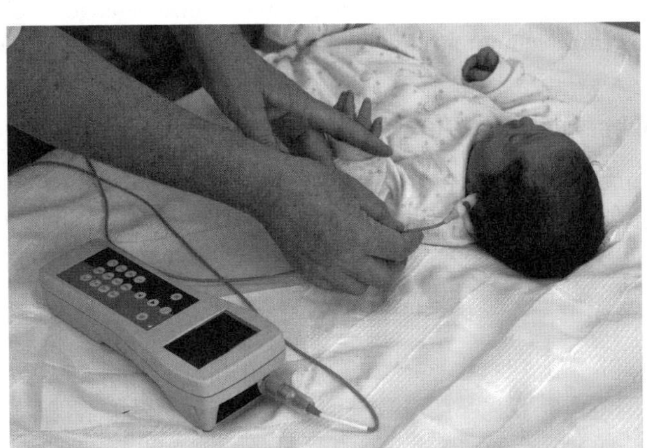

FIGURE 12–4 Testing with otoacoustic emissions.

Guidelines for Breaking the News to Parents

1. The audiologist who administered the tests and will be managing the child's aural rehabilitation should present the diagnosis.
2. Ensure privacy and adequate time, with no interruptions.
3. If feasible, present strengths and positive attributes of the child before communicating the diagnosis.
4. Communicate in clear, simple, and straightforward language.
5. Offer information on prognosis honestly, with a caveat of the difficulty of prediction.

(continues)

Guidelines for Breaking the News to Parents *(continued)*

6. Assess parents' understanding of the situation.
7. Encourage parents to express feelings and attitudes.
8. Respond with warmth and empathy.
9. Give parents a time frame for future decisions and actions, and offer specific advice on next steps.
10. Provide parents with concrete activities to engage in while waiting for a follow-up appointment.
11. Arrange a follow-up appointment.
12. Show respect for the child and family.

(English, 2004; Seligman & Darling, 2007, p. 298)

Behavioral Tests

It may not be possible to obtain an audiogram using traditional behavioral techniques from a very young child. For this reason, to obtain information about the child's ability to detect a range of frequencies, an audiologist may utilize behavioral/observational audiometry, visual reinforcement audiometry, or conditioned play audiometry.

Behavioral/observational audiometry (BOA) is a method of testing a child's hearing in which the tester presents a sound stimulus and observes the child's behavior for change.

Acoustic startle response (Moro reflex) is a baby's response to unexpected loud sound and is typified by a head jerk and outflung arms.

Behavioral/Observational Audiometry

In **behavioral/observational audiometry (BOA)**, sometimes referred to as Auditory Behavior Index (ABI), the audiologist presents a sound stimulus and observes the child's behavior. Response to sound may be manifested by a change in sucking pattern, eye widening, cessation of activity, or a head turn.

The Acoustic Startle Response

Some parents informally test their baby's hearing by eliciting the **acoustic startle response** (also called the **Moro reflex**). They might snap a pan lid against the kitchen counter or clap hands with gusto and simultaneously watch for the startle response. The baby will jerk his or her head and fling out the arms with palms and fingers spread and thumbs bent. The baby's heart rate quickens. The startle response is fully formed at birth, and lasts until about 6 months of age (Figure 12–5).

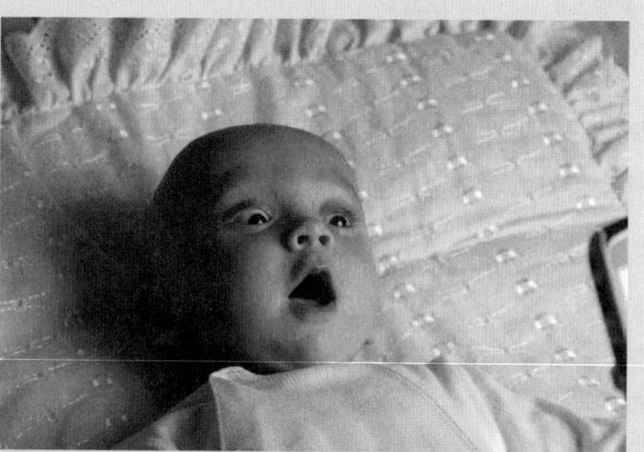

FIGURE 12–5 The acoustic startle response. Babies will jerk their heads and fling their arms in response to unexpected loud noise.

One shortcoming of BOA is that babies vary in their responsiveness. Some 3-month-old babies will react to sound presented at 20 dB HL, whereas others will not react until the sound reaches 80 dB HL. For this reason, the procedure can reliably only eliminate the possibility of profound hearing loss. In addition, babies respond differently to sound, depending on their level of arousal, on how many times they have heard the sound (i.e., habituation occurs), and whether the sound is of interest to them (e.g., speech as opposed to tone pips). Finally, the observer's expectations can color the results: When someone wants to see a response from a baby, the person may see it, whether it really occurred or not.

Visual Reinforcement Audiometry

Visual reinforcement audiometry (VRA) is used with children between the ages of about 6 months and 2½ years. VRA capitalizes on a baby's natural inclination to turn toward sound and utilizes **operant-conditioned responses**. The child is tested in a sound-treated booth. Sound is presented through an audiometer. When sound is presented initially, a box in the booth lights up. Inside of the box, a toy moves or another animated visual image occurs. For example, a box may light up to reveal a toy monkey clashing cymbals or a video clip may play. The child learns to look at the box or video clip when the sound is presented. Testing begins after the child has been conditioned in order to determine the threshold for the frequencies of the audiogram. If the child is willing to tolerate insert earbuds, the audiologist can collect ear-specific information; otherwise,

Visual reinforcement audiometry (VRA) is a method of audiometric testing for young children that entails providing an acoustic signal and reinforcing a head turn with a light stimulus or an activated and illuminated toy reinforcement.

A **conditioned response** is a new or modified response to a previously neutral stimulus.

FIGURE 12–6 Conditioned play audiometry performed in soundfield. A young child listens for a sound before stacking a block in response.

testing occurs in soundfield and the audiogram reflects the performance of the better ear (i.e., unilateral hearing loss cannot be ruled out). One caveat to performing VRA is that not all children who are chronologically 6 months of age are also 6 months of age developmentally, as in the case of prematurity or neurocognitive delay, so some such children may be unable to participate in this procedure.

Conditioned Play Audiometry

Conditioned Play Audiometry (CPA) is a method of testing children 2½ years and older in which the child is trained to perform a task in response to presentation of a sound.

Conditioned play audiometry (CPA) is used to assess children at about the age of 2 or 2½ years to 5 years. Children may insert a peg into a pegboard each time they hear a tone or speech signal or stack blocks (Figure 12–6). An adult encourages a child to wait and listen before performing the response task. The child's parent may sit in the sound-treated room with the child during testing, whereas the audiologist may be in the adjacent room with the audiometer, watching through the window. The parent must be coached to sit quietly and not provide cues about the presence or absence of sound to the child. When a child is capable of participating in CPA, it may also be possible to obtain **speech detection thresholds (SDTs)**. The SDTs will provide a means to cross-check the audiometric thresholds obtained with CPA. As with VRA, if the child is willing to tolerate insert earphones, the audiologist can collect ear-specific information.

Speech detection threshold (SDT) is the level at which speech is just audible.

When the hearing loss is confirmed, an audiologist will convey the diagnosis with sensitivity and launch an intervention plan. Table 12–1 presents guidelines for this process.

TABLE 12–1 Guidelines for Working with Families and Caregivers

AT CONFIRMATION:	PARENTS SHOULD LEAVE WITH:
1. Allow families to "tell their story" 2. Show kindness, empathy 3. Be honest 4. Express hope and confidence	1. Written information (information packet) 2. A plan 3. Phone number (to call whenever clarification is needed) 4. Next appointment scheduled as soon as possible, in writing
WITHIN 4 TO 6 MONTHS OF DIAGNOSIS:	**DURING THIS PERIOD, THE SPEECH AND HEARING PROFESSIONAL WILL:**
1. Recognize/acknowledge the emotional responses 2. Facilitate healthy attachment between child and caregivers 3. Acknowledge imbalance and support work toward reestablishing a healthy family system 4. Actively involve family in intervention choices—avoid "rescuing"—convey hope with all communication modes—convey that there are no failures 5. Support involvement of extended family—siblings/grandparents 6. Connect to other families with children of same age/similar hearing loss and to veteran families	1. Ensure appropriate listening device is being used 2. Model effective communication behaviors 3. Provide parents with information about intervention services 4. Refer to other professionals as necessary

Source: Adapted from Rall and Montoya (2005, p. 1).

HEALTH CARE FOLLOW-UP

Many children who fail a hearing screening and most children who are identified as having hearing loss will be referred to other health care professionals. The purpose is to determine etiology and to determine whether additional conditions exist besides hearing loss, including other disabilities. Referrals may occur shortly after confirmation and several years following, when the child is a toddler or a preschooler.

Causes of Hearing Loss in Children

One of the first priorities of many aural rehabilitation plans for infants or toddlers is to determine etiology. Hearing loss can be sensorineural, conductive, or mixed. Sensorineural hearing loss may be **idiopathic**, meaning that the origin is unknown or uncertain, or may stem from nongenetic or genetic causes. Figure 12–7 presents causes of prelingual hearing loss in children.

An **idiopathic** hearing loss is a hearing loss of unknown origin.

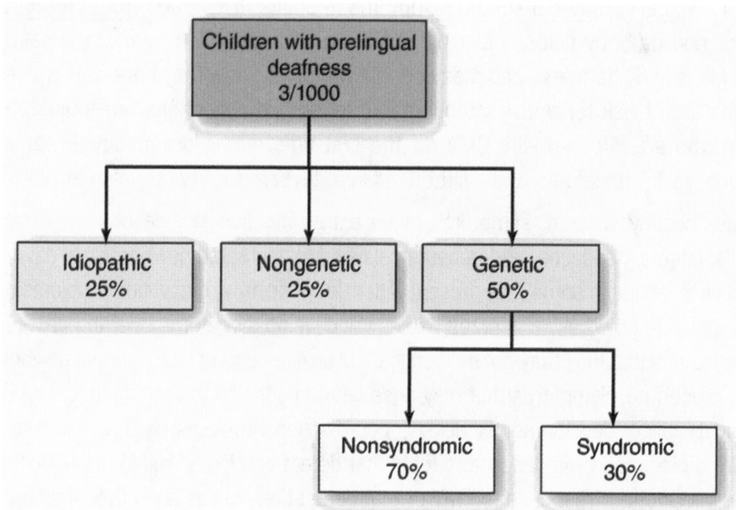

FIGURE 12–7 Causes of prelingual deafness in children (modeled after Smith & Camp, 2007).

Nongenetic Causes of Sensorineural Hearing Loss

Nongenetic causes may be **prenatal** (occurring before birth), **perinatal** (occurring at birth), or **postnatal** (occurring shortly after birth). Prenatal factors that may affect a child's hearing status include the following:

- Intrauterine infections, including rubella, **cytomegalovirus**, and herpes simplex virus
- Complications associated with the Rh factor (wherein maternal antibodies affect the Rh-positive blood cells of the baby)
- Prematurity
- Maternal diabetes
- Parental radiation
- **Toxemia**
- **Anoxia**
- Syphilis

Prenatal means before birth.

Perinatal means during birth.

Postnatal means after birth.

Cytomegalovirus (CMV) is a member of the herpes virus family.

Toxemia is a condition during pregnancy that is characterized by hypertension, or a sharp spike in blood pressure, and edema, or a swelling of the hands and feet as a result of excessive body fluid.

Anoxia refers to a deficiency or absence of oxygen in the body tissues.

Hearing loss may happen during birth, in which case it stems from a perinatal cause. Perinatal causes of hearing loss include anoxia, which may be caused by a prolapse of the umbilical cord and a subsequent blockage of blood to the infant's brain. Although rare, the use of forceps during birth may cause damage to the cochlea, as might severe uterine contractions.

A postnatal loss may occur because of meningitis or other infections or the use of ototoxic drugs. One report suggests that about 25% of bilateral childhood hearing loss is postnatal (Weichbold, Nekahm-Heis, & Weizl-Mueller, 2007), which is good motivation for continued surveillance of children after they leave the newborn nursery, particularly those at risk for hearing loss. A listing of ototoxic drugs appears in Table 12–2. Other postnatal factors include measles, encephalitis, chicken pox, influenza, and mumps.

Cytomegalovirus: A Common Virus with a Potent Kick

Between 20% and 30% of childhood hearing loss may be caused by cytomegalovirus (CMV). CMV is a member of the herpes family that infects 50% to 80% of adults by age 40 years. Members of the herpes family cause chicken pox, infectious mononucleosis, and fever blisters. The herpes viruses can remain alive in the body for a lifetime, even if dormant. Typically, CMV causes no symptoms in adults. It spreads from person to person, carried by body fluids, including blood, urine, breast milk, tears, and saliva. Usually, CMV is fairly harmless and many people will never know they have it. However, babies who are at risk for active infection and serious complications are those born to women who are infected with CMV for the first time during pregnancy. Pregnant women who work with infants and children, as in a daycare facility, are also at risk.

In otherwise healthy children, symptoms of an active infection include prolonged high fever, chills, fatigue, headache, and general malaise. Most infected newborns are asymptomatic at birth, although some may present with **microcephaly**, circulation problems, or abnormal tone. In some cases, infected babies will develop symptoms over the next few years. This means that they may not be identified as having hearing loss during a newborn screening procedure. Symptoms that may arise later, in addition to hearing loss, include intellectual disability, developmental delays, coordination problems, and visual impairment. CMV is diagnosed with laboratory tests that detect antibodies within the body that have been developed in response to CMV or that detect the virus as an active infection.

Microcephaly is an abnormally small head due to a failure of the brain to grow.

TABLE 12–2 Medications That May Be Ototoxic

• Aminoglycoside antibiotics, which are often used against gram-negative bacteria. Hearing loss is often bilateral and sensorineural. Some of the drugs may be more vestibulotoxic than cochleotoxic: **Amikacin** **Dihydrostreptomycin** **Garamycin** **Gentamicin** **Kanamycin** **Neomycin** **Netilmicin** **Streptomycin** **Tobramycin** **Viomycin**
• Salicylates, used in large quantities for the treatment of arthritis and other connective tissue disorders. Their use may result in sensorineural hearing loss and tinnitus: **Acetylsalicylic acid** **Aspirin**
• Loop diuretics, used to promote urine excretion. Their use may result in sensorineural hearing loss: **Ethacrynic acid** **Furosemide** **Lasix**
• Other drugs that may be ototoxic and that are used in chemotherapy regimens: **Cisplatin** **Carboplatin** **Nitrogen mustard**

Genetic Causes of Sensorineural Hearing Loss

Genetic factors cause more than 50% of all incidents of congenital hearing loss in children. More than 400 kinds of genetic-based hearing losses have been described, and with increased activity in genetics research and the Human Genome Project, new types continually are being identified.

Genetic hearing loss is distinguished from acquired (or nongenetic) hearing loss by physical examination, family history, ancillary medical testing such as a **computed tomography (CT) scan** of the skull, and molecular genetic testing. A physician specially trained to recognize genetic conditions may perform the physical examination and may probe for subtle characteristics that relate to specific conditions (e.g., small pits in the front of the ears may implicate branchio-oto-renal syndrome). In considering the family history, a genetic counselor may construct a **family tree**, covering about three generations, giving special attention to family members who have or had hearing losses. Genetic testing may involve **chromosome** tests, where chromosomes are examined under the microscope to see if a part of a chromosome is missing or duplicated. Appendix 12–2 presents a list of terminology and corresponding definitions used to discuss genetic hearing loss.

Hereditary hearing losses are classified according to: (a) the mode of inheritance (**autosomal dominant**, **autosomal recessive**, or **X-linked**), (b) whether they are syndromic or nonsyndromic, (c) the audiological configuration, (d) whether they are bilateral or unilateral, (e) the progression (e.g., sudden or gradual) and the age of onset of the loss, and (f) whether or not the vestibular system is affected. Many people who have a hereditary hearing loss experience a delayed onset that is nonsyndromic. Patients who have a **delayed-onset hereditary hearing loss** may have normal hearing at birth and then begin to lose hearing later, sometimes not until they are in their 20s or 30s. A **nonsyndromic hearing loss** is one that has no other associated findings.

A **computed tomography (CT) scan** creates a series of detailed pictures of areas inside of the body, taken from different angles or planes. The pictures are created by a computer that is linked to an X-ray machine.

A **family tree** is a genealogical diagram of a child's ancestry or kin.

A **chromosome** is a basic unit of genes; structures that carry the genes of a cell.

An **autosomal dominant** condition requires only one parent to have the affected gene in order to pass a trait on to an offspring.

An **autosomal recessive** condition requires both parents to have the affected gene in order to pass a trait on to an offspring; the parents may not exhibit the trait.

An **X-linked** condition involves genes carried on the X chromosome, or the sex chromosome.

A **delayed-onset hereditary hearing loss** occurs when hearing is normal at birth, then declines later in life as a result of a hereditary disorder.

Nonsyndromic hearing loss is a hearing loss that has no other associated findings.

Many hearing losses based in genetics are part of a **syndrome**, which refers to a number of conditions that co-occur and share a common origin. For example, Waardenburg syndrome (WS) is the most common type of autosomal dominant syndromic hearing loss. It is characterized by a varying degree of sensorineural hearing loss, pigmentary discolorations of the skin, a white forelock in the hair, and the two irises of the eyes being of different color.

Usher syndrome is the most common type of autosomal recessive syndromic hearing loss. Affected individuals may be born with normal hearing or a degree of sensorineural hearing loss and experience progressive hearing loss as they age. They often develop **retinitis pigmentosa**, usually sometime after the first decade of life. Retinitis pigmentosa leads to night blindness and loss of peripheral vision and ultimately, possible blindness.

Alport syndrome is an example of X-linked syndromic hearing loss. It is characterized by progressive sensorineural hearing loss, renal disease, and ophthalmologic involvement. In Alport syndrome, the hearing loss usually manifests in the second decade of life. Examples of other syndromes that may affect hearing appear in Table 12–3.

A **syndrome** is a collection of conditions that co-occur as a result of a single cause and constitute a distinct clinical entity.

Retinitis pigmentosa is any number of inherited, progressive conditions that cause abnormal pigmentation on the retina. Retinitis pigmentosa often impairs vision, with first a loss of night vision, then a loss of peripheral vision, and then the development of "tunnel vision." It finally causes blindness.

Questions an audiologist might ask after parents receive genetic counseling in order to ensure they understand the results and to monitor their reactions:

- What did you learn about the cause of the hearing loss?
- What does this mean for your other children or other relatives?
- How are you coping with this diagnosis?

(Arnos, 2012, p. 6)

Mixed and Conductive Hearing Loss

Some children have mixed hearing loss, which is a combination of both conductive and sensorineural components, or a conductive hearing loss alone. The most common cause of a conductive component is otitis media, which is the second most common childhood ailment, second only to the common cold. Other causes of conductive hearing

TABLE 12–3 Examples of Syndromes That May Include Hearing Loss

SYNDROME	CO-OCCURRING CONDITIONS
Alport	Nephritis and sensorineural hearing loss
Alstrom	Pigmentary retinopathy, diabetes mellitus, obesity, malformation of the brain, and progressive sensorineural hearing loss
Bjornstad syndrome	Congenital sensorineural hearing loss and pili torti
Branchio-otorenal	Branchial anomalies, including branchial clefts, fistulas, and cysts; otologic anomalies including malformed pinna or preauricular pits; renal abnormalities; often hearing loss, either conductive, sensorineural, or mixed
Crouzon	Premature closure of sutures, hypertension, downward displacement of eyeballs due to shallow orbits, mild to moderate conductive hearing loss, may entail mixed loss; closure of external auditory canal
Down	Intellectual disability, characteristic facial features, often accompanied by chronic otitis media, and associated conductive, mixed, and sensorineural hearing loss
Edward	Microcephaly, agenesis of bones, congenital heart disease, craniofacial abnormalities, intellectual disability, and outer, middle, and inner ear anomalies
Epstein	Macrothrombocytopathia, nephritis, and sensorineural hearing loss
Fetal alcohol syndrome	Low birth weight, failure to thrive, intellectual disability, wide-set eyes, recurrent otitis media, sensorineural hearing loss
Forney	Joint fusion, mitral insufficiency, and conductive hearing loss
Harboyan	Characterized by progressive sensorineural hearing loss of delayed onset
Hunter	Sensorineural, conductive, or mixed hearing loss, growth deficiency, mental and neurological deterioration, coarse facial features
Jervell and Lange–Nielsen	Electrocardiographic abnormalities, fainting spells, accompanied by congenital bilateral profound sensorineural hearing loss
Latham–Munro	Myoclonus epilepsy, ataxia, and sensorineural hearing loss
Lemieux–Neemeh	Nephritis, motor, and neuropathy with sensorineural hearing loss
Mondini dysplasia	Congenital anomaly of the osseous and membranous labyrinths, severe loss of hearing and vestibular function
Pendred	Goiter and moderate-to-profound congenital sensorineural hearing loss
Pfeiffer	Premature closure of sutures, broad thumbs, broad great toes, short fingers and toes, hypertelorism, high arched palate, downward-sloping eyes, absent external auditory canals, conductive hearing loss
Richards–Rundle	Ataxia, muscle wasting, hypogonadism, intellectual disability, and progressive sensorineural hearing loss
Robinson	Dominant onychodystrophy, coniform teeth, and sensorineural hearing loss
Stickler	Severe myopia, retinal detachment, flat facial profile, cleft palate, ocular anomalies, arthritis, sensorineural, conductive, or mixed hearing loss
Treacher Collins	Pinnae malformations, down-slanting eyes, small chin, depressed cheek bones, large mouth, eyelid coloboma, conductive hearing loss related to atresia and ossicular malformation
Usher	Congenital or progressive sensorineural hearing loss and progressive loss of vision
Waardenburg	Widely spaced eyes, joined eyebrows, a broad nasal root, and a minimal to severe unilateral or bilateral hearing loss (about 30% of patients have a white forelock)

loss include anomalies of the external ear canal (such as atresia), tympanic membrane, or ossicles (such as congenital fixation of the ossicles), and congenital **cholesteatoma**.

A **cholesteatoma** is a tumor-like mass of epithelium cells and cholesterol in the middle ear that may invade the mastoid process and impinge upon the ossicular chain.

As noted in Chapter 1, otitis media is an inflammation of the middle ear, often associated with fluid buildup. The fluid may or may not be contaminated with infection. An estimated 35% of preschool children experience repeated episodes of otitis media (ASHA, 2007). Otitis media can cause a mild or moderate conductive hearing loss, particularly in the low frequencies, and can accentuate the amount of hearing loss in the presence of an existing sensorineural condition. Some children will experience the condition one time and then never again, and only experience slight ear pain and fever. Others will experience repeated bouts, with "glue-like" fluid, excruciating pain, and permanent hearing loss (due to damage to the ossicles or tympanic membrane).

In the absence of pain and fever, the condition may go unnoticed by the child, and hence, untreated. As a result, the child may miss out on being exposed to some speech and language. Although the findings are inconsistent and the results somewhat contradictory, some evidence suggests that academic performance may suffer in the early grades, if children with otherwise normal hearing suffer from chronic otitis media (Golz, Netzer, & Westerman, 2005). Pediatricians report that otitis media between the ages of birth and 2 years can adversely affect speech and language development, although parents and daycare environments can mitigate against this outcome (Sonnenschein & Cascella, 2004). Children with chronic otitis media may have reduced consonant inventories, delayed babbling, and smaller expressive and receptive vocabularies, although these effects may disappear if the otitis media resolves (see Shriberg et al., 2000, for a review). For example, Keogh et al. (2005) reported that on average, children with a history of otitis media recognized connected discourse in noise as well as children without a history by the time they had reached the age of 9 or 10 years. The authors note that their participants who had a history of otitis media exhibited a wider range of performance, suggesting that a subset of children may indeed continue to be at risk for hearing-related difficulties.

Risk Factors for Otitis Media

- Between the ages of 6 and 24 months
- Eustachian tube malfunction or anomaly (e.g., as might occur with Down syndrome)
- Impaired immunologic status (e.g., AIDS)
- Male
- Bottle fed as opposed to breast fed
- Native American
- Placement in a large daycare center
- Poverty status

(Einhorn, 2017)

Some of the symptoms that might alert parents to the presence of otitis media in their young child include the following:

- Inattentiveness
- Reduced ability to discriminate speech
- Wanting the television turned up more loudly than usual
- Hands pulling the ear lobes
- Undue fatigue

Other Disabilities

Nearly 40% of children who have hearing loss have an additional disability (Gallaudet Research Institute, 2003). Co-occurring conditions include intellectual disability, significant visual impairment, learning disabilities, autism, and attention deficit disorder. Emotional or behavioral problems, **cerebral palsy**, and orthopedic problems also may co-occur with hearing loss (Table 12–4). Sometimes, the multiple disabilities stem from similar causes, such as trauma at birth, prematurity, or heredity. A co-occurring condition will affect a child's intervention plan and aural rehabilitation strategy and the composition of the child's multidisciplinary team. The presence of additional disabilities heightens the probability of delays in speech, language, and functional and social outcomes (Ching et al., 2013).

Cerebral palsy is a motor-control disorder caused by insult to the motor cortex of the brain.

Other Hearing-Related Conditions

Children may suffer from other hearing-related conditions besides sensorineural, conductive, and mixed hearing loss. Three such conditions are: (1) central auditory processing disorder (CAPD), (2) auditory neuropathy (sometimes referred to as auditory dyssynchrony), and (3) tinnitus.

TABLE 12–4 Conditions That May Co-occur with Hearing Loss

- Intellectual disability
- Behavior or psychiatric disorders
- Learning disability, related to reading and writing
- Nervous system ailments, such as seizures, vestibular disturbances, or spina bifida
- Eye disease, including optic degeneration, ocular lens abnormalities, and retinitis pigmentosa
- Renal disease
- Musculoskeletal abnormalities in the skull, oral cavity, face, outer or middle ear, limbs, or joints
- Musculoskeletal disease, such as growth retardation or bone disease
- Growth retardation
- Cerebral palsy
- Skin disease, such as pigmentary disorder (e.g., albinism, white forelock, iris bicolor, or heterochromia), keratosis, sun sensitivity, thick, coarse hair, and malformed fingernails and toenails
- Metabolic disease such as diabetes, goiter, liver and spleen enlargement, or impaired metabolism or carbohydrates
- Cardiac and vascular disease
- Autism

Central Auditory Processing Disorders

Some hearing difficulties are due to central causes, which means that sound transmission at and between the brainstem and the cerebrum is disrupted, as a result of either damage or a malformation. Thus, the temporal lobe cortex of the brain may receive incorrect information or the information may not be processed correctly. These deficiencies in auditory processing skills sometimes are referred to as **central auditory processing disorder (CAPD)** and sometimes, *auditory processing disorder*.

Central auditory processing disorder (CAPD) is an inability to differentiate, recognize, and understand sounds. This inability is not due to either hearing loss or cognitive impairment.

CAPD may result from head trauma, neuromaturational delays in the central auditory nervous system, degenerative diseases (e.g., multiple sclerosis), exposure to neurotoxic substances, seizure disorders (e.g., Landau Kleffner syndrome), brain tumors, or autism. Sometimes, a cause cannot be found or it may relate to diffuse central nervous system dysfunction without identifiable lesions.

This is a difficult diagnosis to make. Many times, the problem is not implicit in the audiogram. A parent might comment, "He hears me, but many times I have to repeat myself several times before he gets what I'm saying." A daycare worker might note, "Whenever I talk to Mary, I find myself slowing down how fast I talk and accentuating my articulation. Otherwise, she gets this blank look on her face, as if her mind is somewhere else."

Children who have central hearing problems may experience difficulty in one or more of the following, although their symptoms, behaviors, and degree of impairment may vary widely:

- Sound localization
- Auditory discrimination
- Auditory pattern recognition
- Association of meaning with sound
- Understanding speech in the presence of background noise
- Understanding degraded speech signals, fast speech, or speech with an unfamiliar accent
- Following rhythmic and melodic aspects of music
- Auditory memory
- Following directions

Although screening questionnaires, checklists, and related measures probe the kinds of difficulties included in this list, a universally accepted method of screening does not exist. There are, however, recognized CAPD diagnostic test batteries. The battery may include measures of auditory discrimination, auditory temporal processing and patterning, dichotic listening tests, gap-detection tests, and electrophysiologic tests. These diagnostic test batteries are inappropriate for children 3 years and younger, and diagnosis usually must wait until the child is older, often age 7 or 8 years or older (ASHA, 2005a). Interventions may include tailoring the listening environment (e.g., ensuring good noise reduction), providing an FM system, and providing auditory training.

Auditory Neuropathy

Auditory neuropathy may be related to CAPD, albeit different because it involves the peripheral auditory system. Sound enters the inner ear normally, but transmittal through the nervous system is impaired. Children who receive a diagnosis of *auditory neuropathy* may have audiometrically normal hearing or a hearing loss that ranges from mild to severe, and they will exhibit normal OAEs. They have either absent, negligible, or abnormal ABRs and poor word recognition, poorer than that which would be predicted by their audiological thresholds. Although there are likely many causes, scientists believe that many cases involve impaired inner hair cell functioning, where inner hair cells are either damaged or have faulty connections to the auditory nerve. When hearing is intact, the **inner hair cells** convert vibrations traversing through the cochlea into electrical signals. These signals trigger nerve impulses that travel through the spiral ganglion and auditory nerve and up through the central auditory pathway. Auditory neuropathy has sometimes been associated with jaundice, premature birth, low birth rate, anoxia at birth, and family genetics, such as Charcot-Marie-Tooth syndrome and Friedreich's ataxia.

Auditory neuropathy is a condition where the patient has a pure-tone audiogram that shows any degree of hearing loss, from mild to profound, and shows normal OAEs. ABRs are either absent or degraded, and word discrimination is reduced disproportionately to the pure-tone loss.

Inner hair cells are a single row of auditory receptor cells in the organ of Corti that are in synaptic connect with the fibers of the auditory nerve.

The prognosis varies. Some babies begin to improve and hear normally after a few years, some stay the same, and some worsen. Unfortunately, for many children who have auditory neuropathy, hearing aids are not always helpful. In extreme cases, some experts advocate using sign language with these children to enhance their communication abilities (National Institute of Deafness and Other Communication Disorders, 2013).

PARENT COUNSELING

After their child's hearing loss has been identified, and before or during the time that they learn more about the nature of the hearing loss and related conditions, parents will receive counseling. Between 90% and 95% of children who have a severe or profound sensorineural hearing loss have parents who are normally hearing (Northern & Downs, 1991). This means that, prior to their child's birth, many parents did not know the ramifications of hearing loss. They also are unlikely to belong to the Deaf culture. Thus, they will have much to learn about hearing loss and aural rehabilitation, and they will need to decide whether to try to learn sign language. They may also need to consider issues concerning the Deaf culture. They may or may not want to enculturate their child into a culture that is different from their own.

Families react to the news about hearing loss in many different ways. Some react as if they were experiencing a trauma or crisis, with elevated levels of psychological stress and impaired functioning. Others view hearing loss as a problem to be solved, and even thrive in the face of the challenge. Families' responses will affect the extent to which they seek services, the role they play in the aural rehabilitation plan, and the support they provide toward the child's overall development.

A family-centered approach takes into account the family system by acknowledging "that the well-being and experiences of other family members can impact a child with a developmental disability. In this approach, the 'patient' is no longer simply the child, but his or her family system and its individual members, including parents and siblings, each of whom presents with unique needs and challenges to be assessed, interpreted, and ultimately treated" (Head & Abbeduto, 2007, pp. 293–294).

Sensitive Counseling and Empathetic Listening

"The hallmark of good counseling is careful listening and trusting that the parents will ultimately find the best solution for themselves and their child. Information should be given judiciously and parental confidence enhanced by emphasizing the skills and knowledge the parents already possess."

—David Luterman, D.Ed., Professor Emeritus of Emerson College in Boston and expert in the psychological effects and emotions associated with hearing loss and parenting

(Luterman, 2004, p. 220)

Family systems theory describes how members of a family are interconnected, and how their patterns of communication and interaction affect one another.

Family Systems

FIGURE 12–8 The family system.

Family systems theory recognizes that people do not live in a vacuum. A family consists of interdependent individuals, none of whom can be understood in isolation from the family system. An apt analogy is a mobile: If you move one component of the system, the rest of the system is affected. If homeostasis occurs, all components come to rest (Figure 12–8).

Whereas a family's response to a baby who has hearing loss will be influenced by the family's beliefs and values, the converse also is true. The child with hearing loss will influence the family's beliefs and values. For example, a family may have harbored negative stereotypes about hearing loss prior to the baby's birth, but their beliefs may change with experience.

Psychologists who study family systems take into account how the family interacts. They consider the rules a family follows, rules that govern its level of cohesion, communication style, and adaptability. For example, is emotion freely expressed? Do family members seek social support when they are stressed? Psychologists also consider the family's history, the beliefs that have been passed from one generation to the next, the values, culture, and coping behaviors.

In no small measure, counseling consists of teaching and encouragement, judiciously interwoven. The word "education" is derived from the Latin, meaning to lead out from within, and this is what many times you will do as you interact with parents. In the best case scenario, you will encourage parents to rely upon what they know and have experienced as they make decisions, and provide your knowledge and experience for guidance, realizing that the parent is the expert on the child. The counseling approach and techniques used will hinge upon the decisions to be made at any particular point in time. For example, one approach may meet the situation/information needed when the presence of hearing loss is confirmed, while a different approach may meet the situation/information needed when communication mode options are considered.

The UNHS changed the discovery mechanism of hearing loss. Whereas previously parents often suspected hearing loss through interacting with their baby, now discovery is "institution initiated." Confirmation occurs at a much earlier stage in the relationship formation between parent and baby. Sometimes, from very early on, the hearing loss is an integral part of the child's identity. Within weeks of giving birth, the parents may become involved in an intervention plan. Not surprisingly, many parents feel overwhelmed by the combination of new parenthood and their participation in the plan. Some speech and hearing professionals have suggested that parents may be unable to enjoy their baby before they have to deal with the consequences of the hearing loss. Others have argued that better bonding occurs because parents know from early on that their relationship is with a baby who does not have normal hearing (Figure 12–9). The parent–child relationship does not receive a jolt when the hearing loss is discovered later (McCracken, Young, & Tattersall, 2008; Young & Tattersall, 2007).

Differing Opinions about UNHS

"We just feel so lucky that she has been picked up and we know that she's going to have as much help as she needs and she's going to be able to do as much as she can with it being part of her life."

—Mother of a 6-month-old baby who has a moderate hearing loss

(Young & Tattersall, 2007, p. 213)

"From our point of view it has been a nightmare really. I wish I hadn't been told, I wish I was just finding out now because I would have had nearly eight months to just enjoy him. It has actually been eight horrible months on and off. It hasn't affected me bonding with him or anything but I have not enjoyed him, like I did [my other child]. I wish I had never been told. I wish I was just finding out now."

—Mother of an 8-month-old baby who has a moderate hearing loss

(Young & Tattersall, 2007, p. 215)

FIGURE 12–9 Reactions to early identification. Some speech and hearing professionals suggest that parents who learn of their baby's hearing loss early on are spared the surprise of learning about it later, and learn to accept the hearing loss as part of the baby's identity.

Infancy is a time of great excitement and parent–baby bonding. When parents learn in the newborn nursery that their baby may not be who they had anticipated, the stages of grief that often accompany a child's diagnosis of hearing loss may be amplified, compared with that experienced by parents who learn later of the hearing loss. This occurs because parents of older babies and children have lived with their child and may have gradually grown to suspect a problem. They have observed their child not responding to sound, or have observed the child not developing vocal and listening behaviors that resemble those of his or her peers. Thus, the diagnosis of hearing loss may not surprise them. In contrast, parents who learn that their baby might have a hearing loss while the baby is still in the hospital, and before they have had a chance to get to know and bond with the child, might be handed the news "cold turkey." Add the natural emotions of grief to the emotions associated with postpartum depression, the physical exhaustion of childbirth, and the stress of being a new parent, and the end result may be parents who feel fraught. It is critical that new parents receive counseling and support. They need reason to believe there are mechanisms and support services that will steer them through this initial stage of coping with their baby's hearing loss.

Traditional models of grieving posit that parents and family members pass through discrete stages after learning of their child's hearing loss (e.g., Kubler-Ross, 1969). Certainly these reactions occur, and sometimes in sequential order. More recent models present the grieving process as a circular experience, where stages may be revisited.

Sequential-Stage Model of Grieving

Stage theory suggests that parents pass through stages after learning about their baby's hearing loss, which may include shock and denial, guilt, bargaining, anger, depression or detachment, and finally, acceptance.

Shock, Disbelief, and Anger

"After a diagnosis of hearing loss, some parents may resent the power held by professionals. They may discount the words and guidance offered by professionals because they haven't come to terms with the diagnosis and they don't want the words spoken to be true. Some may even be angry with professionals who delivered the words that will become such a big part of their lives—*hearing loss.* But as we fight through the shock and muck of our child's diagnosis and as the partnership with professionals grows, we will draw strength in the knowledge that you shared with us along the way and in the power that you gave us at a time when we felt completely powerless."

—Statement prepared by a group of parents of children with hearing loss

(Bynum, Hopper, Wolfe, & Smith, 2017, p. 39)

Shock and Disbelief

Shock and disbelief are ways of protecting oneself from a crisis. Initially, parents may feel removed from a diagnosis, as if this were happening to some other family. A parent may deny that the hearing loss exists or may deny the enormity of its consequences. A parent may experience numbness, confusion, and bewilderment, and may harbor the pretense that "nothing has changed."

Guilt

Guilt may occur because parents believe they have done something in the past to have caused the hearing loss. For example, one mother took anti–sea sickness pills while on a cruise in the early weeks of her pregnancy and experienced enormous guilt because she was convinced that the medication had caused her infant's hearing loss.

Bargaining

Bargaining is characterized by magical or fantasy thinking. Parents may believe that their child will improve if they follow certain actions or behave in certain ways. For example, parents may turn to religion for a miracle. They may pledge to seek services and expert opinion until the hearing loss becomes inconsequential.

Guilt Can Be Pernicious

"I need to speak to somebody who is going to tell me as a parent that it is not my fault, it's not something that we brought her to, you know like a concert that was too loud—because you immediately take on that blame, you think: 'Oh my goodness, what did I do to mess up my child for life now!'"

—Parent reflecting about her feelings following her 3-year-old child's diagnosis of hearing loss

(Grandpierre, Fitzpatrick, Na, & Mendonca, 2018, p. 143)

Anger

Anger may occur once parents realize that the hearing loss is permanent, and that denial and bargaining will not change reality. Most parents expected that their child would have normal hearing and would lead a "normal" life. The presence of hearing loss violates this expectation, and unmet expectations often incite anger. Parents' may target their anger on professionals; e.g., *Why can't you heal my child? Why can't you teach my child to speak?* Guilt can also morph into self-directed anger or spouse-directed anger, as parents become angry with themselves or their partner for having inflicted hearing loss on their child. Anger may also be a mask of fear, and may hide feelings of inadequacy to cope with a hearing loss.

Depression or Detachment

Depression or detachment may follow, as parents realize the impotence of their anger and mourn the loss of their *ideal child.* A human tendency is to detach when the emotional strains become overwhelming, like a turtle withdrawing into a protective shell. Detached parents may feel empty, as if life has lost meaning. Some parents will retreat, attempting to avoid the anxiety-ridden implications of hearing loss.

Acceptance

Acceptance occurs when parents accept their child's hearing loss as a reality. In accepting the negative effects of hearing loss, parents recognize that there is work to be done, but the work will lead to favorable consequences. "*Acceptance* is achieved when parents demonstrate some of the following characteristics:

- They are able to discuss their child's [hearing loss] with relative ease.
- They evidence a balance between encouraging independence and showing love.
- They are able to collaborate with professionals to make realistic short- and long-term plans.
- They pursue personal interests unrelated to the child.
- They can discipline appropriately without undue guilt.
- They can abandon overprotective or unduly harsh behavioral patterns toward their child"

(Seligman & Darling, 2007, p. 189).

The Upside of Anger

"Angry people usually get things done and this can be a useful energy if directed appropriately. For parents of children with special needs, the anger often is displaced on to the professional. It behooves the professional to confront the parents' anger and unmask parental fears. This usually results in a fruitful encounter, which benefits the child."

(Luterman, 2004, p. 217)

While these reactions may be very real, they are not stacked like the rungs of a ladder, which parents climb up one step at a time and never climb back down. Rather, parents often experience these stages again and again. For example, when a child enters kindergarten, a child's parents may look at his or her classmates who have normal hearing and realize more fully what a significant hearing loss may mean in terms of their child's academic achievement. This realization may trigger new feelings of depression and sadness, even if they have come to terms with the permanency of the hearing loss.

Circular-Pathways Models of Grieving

Recognizing that grieving may not play out linearly, alternative models depict it as circular or spiraling. For example, Martin and her colleagues present the *Pathways through Grief* model, which includes many of the reactions just described (Martin & Ritter, 2011, p. 15). However, this model portrays grieving as an enduring cyclical process, or a spiraling process where reactions lessen over time. Figure 12–10 depicts two intertwining circular pathways that parents might circumnavigate repeatedly, one positive and one negative. The word *Meanings* is at the center, because parents differ in opinions about the meaning of hearing loss, and they change in their opinions with time and experience.

Dare I Hope?

"In grief nothing stays put. One keeps emerging from a phase, but it always recurs. Round and round. Everything repeats. Am I going in circles, or dare I hope that I am on a spiral?"

—C. S. Lewis, author of *A Grief Observed*

(Lewis, 1976, p. 67)

The Outward-Focused Pathway

Sometimes parents will travel through a hopeful, outward-focused pathway, as depicted in the upper circle, dwelling on what caused the hearing loss, ways to reckon with it, and solutions that will result in a return to "normal." They *explore* by consulting with professionals and reading books, they incorporate *hope* into their lives and look toward the future with optimism, and they *invest,* formulating new plans and cementing commitments.

Providing Perspective

"Our job as professionals is to help parents modify the meanings that determine where they are in the process, which links the circular-pathway model more directly to our diagnostic and treatment process."

—Kathryn Ritter, PhD, listening and spoken language specialist at the University of Alberta

(Personal communication, May 22, 2018)

The Inward-Focused Pathway

Making plans entails risk taking and opens the door for disappointment, which can cause parents to revisit the *meaning* of hearing loss and to enter the pathway depicted in the lower circle. Alternatively, they may begin their journey in this lower circle before moving to the upper one. This phase of the journey includes negative reactions. *Protest,* like the denial we considered above, entails a struggle or an inability to accept the baby's

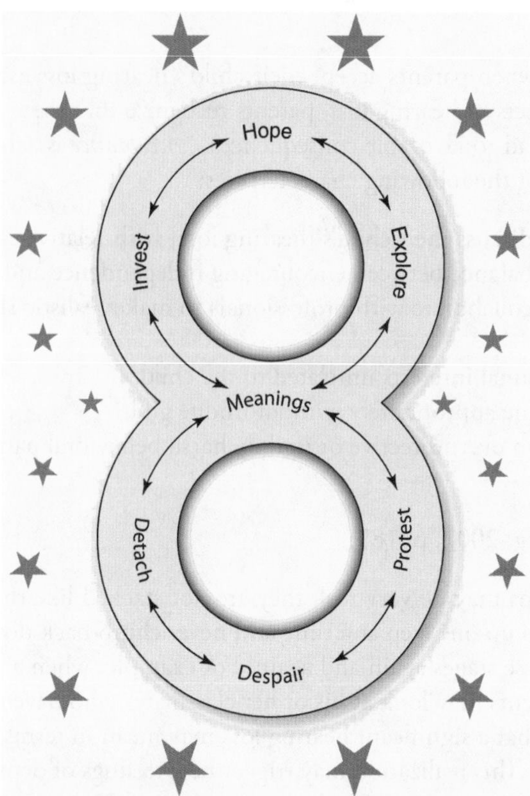

FIGURE 12–10 The Pathways through Grief model. Martin and Elder (1993) constructed this model after analyzing accounts of people who were grieving losses incurred from accidents, illness, divorce, and deaths of loved ones. Unlike stage-based models of grief, it portrays the grieving process as ongoing and as two intertwining circular pathways, one outward focused and one inward focused, with the common link being the meanings associated with hearing loss (modeled after Martin & Ritter, 2011, p. 15).

hearing loss. As reality sets in, *despair,* like the depression considered above, may follow. Parents may perceive the world as chaotic and shrouded in sadness. Parents may also experience anger and feel a loss of control. Parents want to promote their child's best interests. The presence of hearing loss may restrict parents' options, and they may feel anger in response. Protest, anger, and despair can exhaust parents and foster *detachment*, leading parents to resist commitments or participations. Although a parent may get "stuck" at any one of these three-way stations—*protest, despair*, or *detachment*—most of them eventually traverse back to the upper half of the model, with the caveat of perhaps journeying back to the lower half as circumstances change and new meanings materialize.

External Influences

The stars on the model represent people from the parents' past and present milieu, people who exert societal and professional influences about the "right" way to feel and the "right" way to behave. For example, a master teacher can ignite hope, an audiologist can guide exploration, and a speech-language pathologist can oversee investiture. Conversely, having been raised in a remote family can foster detachment.

Clinical Implications of Models of Grief

You might share the Pathway through Grief model with parents as they confront their feelings so they might conceptualize grief as a spiraling process as opposed to a static state or linear path. It may help them to understand that there will be times when one parent resides on the upper circle and the other parent resides on the lower circle, times when they quite literally view the world from two different perspectives. The model may also "normalize" their experience and help them realize that others undergo similar grieving processes.

Models of the grieving process may also help you better understand parents' words and actions. For example, in a discussion about counseling "difficult" or noncompliant parents, Curtin (2006) describes the *bargaining parent* who "was so nice, bringing you gifts of muffins, smiling all the time, and then . . . never following through with your recommendations," and the *angry parent*, who was upset with you "for not providing appropriate recommendations or referrals to their child to get them to talk (pp. 8–9)." She describes the overtly super-dedicated parent who covertly is a *detached parent*, the parent "who had their child with every specialist that exists, the child was enrolled in every activity that money can buy . . . yet, somehow, they [were] never alone with that child (p. 9)." Parents' perceptions and emotions will color how they see the world and how they react to your expertise. By striving to view and understand a situation through the parent's perspective (and stage of grief) as opposed to your own perhaps very different perspective, you may interact with more sensitivity and wisdom, and, in some instances, with immunity from hurt feelings.

Dealing with Feelings and Moving Forward

Kozak and Brooks (2001) suggested ways for parents to deal with their feelings. These practical nuts-and-bolts recommendations are as follows:

- *Accept your feelings*: The situation is difficult and it is understandable and appropriate to be upset. Accept that it hurts and try to find something you can do to help your child. This will allow you to feel something more positive too.
- *Talk to others*: Find a spouse, parent, friend, or parent of another child with a challenge. Tell them what you are feeling and listen to them [talk about] their feelings. Get some support and see if you can give any.
- *Write in a journal*: If thinking and feeling are not enough to help but talking is too much for you right now or if you cannot find the right listener, try writing some notes about your feelings in a journal, notebook or even a letter.
- *Find a group to support you*: You can find good listeners, help, support, and encouragement in a group of parents whose children have any special challenges. . . . Your local children's hospital, clinics, and schools may be resources for finding such a group. . . . Most parents of children with challenges say that other parents of these children provided the most important help they received in the early years. This type of support can help you learn and move forward while you cope with all your feelings.
- *Other ways*: Some parents will look toward their ethical views or their religious values and comrades to help them find the way to feel better. Some people will delve into learning all they can about hearing loss. Some may seek counseling from a professional counselor or physician.
- *Give yourself a break*: Do not demand too much of yourself. Pat yourself on the back for doing what you have already done to help your child. Ask someone who cares about you for some words of encouragement. Get a hug from your child. . . . Cry if it feels better to do so. *Do something good for you*: Take time to watch the quiet beauty of a sunrise or sunset. Be thankful for your child. Do not expect yourself to do every job perfectly. No one is perfect in our imperfect world.

Ask an Expert

"Believe that you and your family will be okay. Take care of yourself and each other. Continue to do what you love. Learn as much as you can about hearing loss as well as about child development so you are aware of what is unique to a particular stage and see your child within the larger world of child development. Meet other parents and children or adults who have hearing losses, and talk to them regularly. Share your joys and concerns with other parents—they are the ones who 'get it.' . . . Be open, flexible and listen to your own voice."

—Dr. Dale Atkins, psychologist, former teacher of children who have hearing loss, popular commentator on NBC's *Today Show*, in response to a question about what advice she would give to parents

(Boswell, 2012, pp. 17–18)

CASE STUDY

A Memorable Journey

Luanna Shibuya relates "one family's journey into the hearing world" (Shibuya, 2006). This journey entails a parent noticing signs of hearing loss in her infant, learning later that the hearing loss is real, the stages of adjustment, and action taken. Along the way, the family encounters helpful speech and hearing professionals, who provide the kinds of education and support we considered in this chapter, and they contact other parents of children who have hearing loss. Shibuya touches on the topic of the family system, as she describes how hearing loss might affect other members of her family.

The journey began with the birth of her son Parker, who was born in November 1998 in Maryland, before the state had implemented newborn screening. During early infancy, Parker did not babble as much as his older sister Sydney had at the same age. His parents wrote this off to gender differences between boys and girls. They suspected a hearing loss only later, when Parker continued not to respond to his name or other auditory stimuli. Shortly before his first birthday, an audiologist confirmed that he had a severe-to-profound hearing loss.

Initially, the parents "mourned the loss of their perfect son" (p. 20). Shibuya writes of unanswerable questions and a sense of unknown fear: What caused the deafness? How should the family change their goals, expectations, and desires for him? How would Parker's life differ from Sydney's? How does a family raise a child who has hearing loss? The parents' one certainty was that they wanted Parker to be a part of the hearing world, and to learn to talk and listen.

Shibuya and her husband received information and advice from an audiologist about cochlear implants and they conducted their own research as well. The parents contacted a cochlear implant center and learned about the different brands of cochlear implants available for children. They talked to as many parents of children who use implants as they could. With the help of their audiologist, they made a "comparison chart" that allowed them to visualize the characteristics of the various cochlear implant models. They selected a particular cochlear implant brand because it had a simple head piece, a body-worn processor, and company commitment to the product. Parker underwent successful surgery, and once having received a cochlear implant, began to progress with his speech and language skills.

In October 2001, the Shibuya family welcomed a third child into the home, Sebastian. The youngest child failed his newborn hearing screening and was later diagnosed as having hearing loss. Although the mother reports of having the same sense of loss at Sebastian's diagnosis, she and her husband were more comfortable navigating the road toward cochlear implantation than they had been three years earlier.

Through the years, the parents have attended numerous audiological appointments and have experienced many challenges. On the whole, however, they are pleased with how well their boys are doing with their cochlear implants. The parents sometimes have to remind teachers and adults that the two boys have hearing loss and that they cannot hear in the swimming pool or at a distance. As of 2006, Parker and Sebastian are "boys who are deaf [but] functioning in the hearing world" (p. 21). A few months before her article was published, Shibuya overheard Parker, then a student in a mainstream kindergarten class, introduce himself to an adult, "Hi, I'm Parker, I'm deaf." He said this in a matter-of-fact way, and it was the first time that his mother had heard him include hearing loss as a part of his identity.

FINAL REMARKS

Dale Atkins has published on the topic of families who have a child with hearing loss and other children who have normal hearing. Importantly, she considers the predicament of the sibling who has normal hearing, and stresses that this child not be overlooked in an intervention plan. Here is what she has to say (Boswell, 2012, p. 18):

> Sometimes the children who have typical hearing are expected to do extra well and assume responsibilities that may be beyond their developmental level. These expectations can be parental or they can come from within the children themselves. Children may see their parents as needing help and

they create ways to be useful, being careful not to "cause" their parents' additional "problems." Other children may feel left out or ignored because their needs are not as "pressing" as [those of] their sister or brother who has a hearing loss. . . . Parents who can continue to share what is happening in an age-appropriate way help brothers and sisters feel that they are part of the family and what the family is facing. All children can stay connected by being reminded, through word and action, that they are equally cherished. It is important to emphasize the ways in which each child is valued because of who they are, not whether they are able to hear well.

KEY CHAPTER POINTS

- A family-centered approach is appropriate for providing aural rehabilitation to children who have hearing loss.
- If children are not exposed to spoken language during the first three years of life, they will likely experience delays in acquiring language, speech, and literacy skills.
- Universal newborn hearing screening (UNHS) requires that every baby born is tested for hearing loss in the newborn nursery, and is increasingly becoming the standard of care in developed countries.
- Methods used for screening include otoacoustic emissions (OAEs) and automated brainstem response testing (A-ABR).
- If hearing loss is identified before a child reaches the age of 6 months, and intervention is begun, the child may develop language skills comparable to those of peers who have normal hearing.
- Behavioral tests for identifying hearing loss in young children include behavioral/observational audiometry (BOA), visual reinforcement audiometry (VRA), and conditioned play audiometry (CPA).
- About 40% of children who have significant hearing loss also have another disability.
- Hearing loss may arise from a variety of causes that may be prenatal, perinatal, or postnatal. The hearing loss may be due to environmental factors or genetic factors.
- Some hereditary hearing losses have a delayed onset, and some are nonsyndromic.
- Otitis media overlaid on a sensorineural hearing loss results in a mixed hearing loss. Some evidence suggests that if untreated, the child may experience related speech and language delays.
- Parents often have difficulty in accepting their children's hearing loss and may pass through a series of psychological stages before acceptance occurs. A primary role of the speech and hearing professional is to empower parents to interact effectively with their child and to make important decisions about their child's aural rehabilitation plan.
- Grieving is a process, and may be depicted as either a series of stages or a circular journey.

TERMS AND CONCEPTS TO REMEMBER

Family-centered approach
Universal newborn hearing screening (UNHS)

Support for UNHS
Risk factors
Objective hearing tests
Behavioral hearing tests
Etiologies
Cytomegalovirus
Syndrome
Ototoxicity
Otitis media
Other disabilities
Auditory neuropathy
Stages of acceptance
Family systems approach
Pathways through Grief

KEY RESOURCES

A Parent's Guide to Hearing and Language Milestones Handout

Your baby will reach a series of milestones as he or she grows. If you suspect that your child is not reaching these milestones, talk to your physician or speech and hearing professional, because your child may have a hearing loss or some other condition that is delaying development.

Newborn

- Cries
- Startles to loud and sudden sound

2 to 3 Months

- Laughs
- Forms sounds in the back of the mouth ("gah")
- Responds to your (parent's) voice
- Distinguishes changes in the tone of voice (happy vs. sad)

4 to 6 Months

- Turns head toward sound
- Begins to put sounds together, typically a consonant and a vowel ("bah")
- Makes nonspeech sounds playfully (squeals, yells, makes "raspberries")

6 to 12 Months

- Babbles strings of syllables ("bah-bah-bah")
- Attempts nonverbal communication through facial expression, eye gaze, vocalization, and gestures such as pointing, reaching, and head shaking
- By 12 months, responds to name; understands the word *no* and simple instructions; gives a toy in response to a request

12 to 18 Months

- Speaks first words
- Understands such phrases as "all gone" and "no-no" and arrival and departure phrases such as "hello" and "bye-bye" and begins to speak these phrases
- Strings sounds together that have an adult-like speech rhythm
- By 18 months, understands about 50 words and speaks about 20 words, usually in isolation and begins repeating words overheard in conversation

18 to 24 Months

- Carries out verbal commands to select and bring a familiar object to the talkee and understands such commands as "sit down" and "stop that"
- Recognizes body parts, such as hair, mouth, and ears
- Enjoys nursery rhymes and songs and can join in
- Understands simple requests and instructions
- Asks simple questions such as "Where Daddy?"
- Asks for names of objects, "What's this?"

24 to 36 Months

- Demonstrates rapid speech development: learns new words rapidly and puts them together in strings of about three
- At about age 24 months, can speak at least 100 recognizable words and recognize several hundred words, and can name familiar objects; by 36 months, can say between 800 and 900 words
- Can say full name
- Understands such concepts as "big" and "little" and "on" and "under"
- Expresses demands verbally
- Enjoys listening to stories and reading from picture books and watching television

36 to 40 Months

- Has an expressive vocabulary of about 1,200 words
- May constantly ask, "Why?"
- Can describe an experience
- Strings together two, three, or more sentences in conversation, with sentence length being about four or five words
- Identifies primary colors, and maybe brown, green, black, and orange
- Can sing songs and often talks to self when playing alone
- Can comprehend compound and complex sentences and answer questions such as "The baby doll is hungry, what should we do?"

Appendix 12–1

A speech and hearing professional might encounter these abbreviations and acronyms when reading the medical or audiological records for an infant or very young child (adapted from Mize & Wigley, 2002):

- BMT: Bilateral myringotomy and tubes
- Chemotx: Chemotherapy
- CHL: Conductive hearing loss
- CNT: Could not test

- DNT: Did not test
- ENT: Ear-nose-throat
- F/u: Follow-up
- H/o: History of
- M/o: Month old
- NBHS: Newborn hearing screening
- PCHI: Permanent childhood hearing impairment
- Pt: Patient
- R/o: Rule-out
- SF: Soundfield
- SLP: Speech-language pathologist
- SNHL: Sensorineural hearing loss
- S/p: Status post
- **TEOAE: Transient evoked otoacoustic emissions**
- TM: Tympanic membrane
- Tymps: Tympanogram
- UNHS: Universal newborn hearing screening
- WNL: Within normal limits
- Y/o: Year old

Transient evoked otoacoustic emission (TEOAE) is a means to access the integrity and function of the outer hair cells by presenting brief clicks. The low-level acoustic response emitted by the cochlea is measured.

Appendix 12–2

Important Terms to Know When Discussing Genetics

Allele: One particular version of a gene.

Chromosome: Structures bearing the genes of a cell and made of a single strand of DNA.

DNA (deoxyribonucleic acid): nucleic acid polymer of which the genes are made.

Dominant allele: The allele whose properties are expressed as the phenotype.

Gene: A unit of genetic information contained within the chromosome that can be inherited.

Genotype: The total genetic makeup of an organism.

Heterozygous: Having two different alleles of the same gene.

Homozygous: Having two identical alleles of the same gene.

Mutation: An alteration in the genetic information carried by a gene.

Phenotype: The visible effect of the genotype.

Recessive allele: The allele for which properties are not observed because they are masked by the dominant allele.

Sex-linked: A gene is sex-linked when it is carried on one of the sex chromosomes.

CHAPTER 13

Infants and Toddlers

OUTLINE

- Legislation Concerning Children Who Have Hearing Loss
- The Individualized Family Service Plan (IFSP)
- Communication Mode
- Listening Device
- Early-Intervention Programs
- Parental Support
- Auditory Training for Infants and Toddlers
- Case Study: A Mother's Karma
- Final Remarks
- Key Chapter Points
- Terms and Concepts to Remember
- Appendix 13–1
- Appendix 13–2

Once a child has been identified as having a hearing loss, an aural rehabilitation strategy will be developed, with the provision of early intervention. Early intervention starts as soon as the hearing loss has been identified. The goals of early intervention are: (a) to enhance the infant's or toddler's development, (b) to minimize the possibility of developmental delay, and (c) to enhance the family's ability to accommodate the child's needs and promote the child's development. Typically, the hospital staff will place the family in contact with personnel from the available early-intervention services in the child's region. A variety of early-intervention services have been established in states, with the help of federal grants, to provide children and their families with appropriate services from birth until the child's third birthday.

In this chapter, we will review legislation about early intervention and related provisions and the decisions that must be made early on, including decisions about communication mode, listening device, and intervention program. We will then consider the importance of and means for providing parental counseling and support and auditory training for infants and toddlers.

LEGISLATION CONCERNING CHILDREN WHO HAVE HEARING LOSS

In the United States, major legislation for children who have disabilities dates back to 1975, when Congress passed the Education for All Handicapped Children Act of 1975, known as PL 94-172, or the EHA law. This law guaranteed a free and appropriate education for all children with disabilities between the ages of 3 and 18 years, in the least restrictive environment possible. The disabilities covered included hearing loss, as well as specific learning disabilities, speech and language impairments, emotional disturbances, cognitive deficiencies, orthopedic impairments, visual impairments, and others. The term **free and appropriate public education (FAPE)** meant that children would receive special education and supporting services at public expense and under public supervision. These services were to comply with the standards of the state educational agency. A **least restrictive environment (LRE)** was deemed one in which a child who had a disability could be placed with the least limitations and still thrive when compared to peers who did not have a disability. The environment had to meet the child's unique needs and allow the child to be educated to the maximum extent appropriate with peers who had typical development.

Free and appropriate public education (FAPE) refers to federal funding provided for the education of children with disabilities, and requires as a condition for receiving federal funds the provision of free and appropriate public education.

A **least restrictive environment (LRE)** is a basic principle of IDEA (Individuals with Disabilities Education Act) that requires public agencies to establish procedures to ensure that to the extent possible, children who have disabilities are educated with children who do not have disabilities, and that special classes, separate schooling, or removal from the regular educational environment occurs only when the severity of the disability is such that education in a regular class environment cannot be achieved satisfactorily.

The Law That Started It All

Public Law 94-142 (November 29, 1975): It is the purpose of this Act to ensure that all handicapped children have available to them, within the time periods specified in section 612(2) (B) a free appropriate public education which emphasizes special education and related services designed to meet their unique needs, to ensure that the rights of handicapped children and their parents or guardians are protected, to assist States and localities to provide for the education of all handicapped children, and to assess and ensure the effectiveness of efforts to educate children.

The **Individuals with Disabilities Education Act (IDEA)** provides for specialized instruction for individuals who have disabilities and who meet eligibility requirements, typically the adverse educational effects that the disability causes.

PL 94-142 was amended in 1997 and reauthorized as PL 105-17, and became known as the **Individuals with Disabilities Education Act (IDEA)**. IDEA encompassed earlier amendments made to the original act, including PL 99-457 and PL 101-476, which mandated services for infants and toddlers and their families. IDEA changed the term *handicapped children* to *children with disabilities*. It expanded the age range of children covered by PL 94-142 to individuals from birth to the age of 21 (up to the 22nd birthday). The key additions afforded by IDEA are the provision of public services for infants and toddlers and their families (**Part C**), assistance to individuals making a transition from secondary school to postsecondary school settings, and the inclusion of assistive technology services in educational planning. The reauthorization underscored parent participation in decision making, made provisions for addressing the general education curriculum in education planning, and promoted high expectations for achievement.

Part C of Public Law PL 108-446 refers to early-intervention services that are available to eligible children from birth through the age of 3 years and to their families.

In 2004, IDEA was revised and issued as Public Law No. 108-446. In particular, the revised law revised performance goals and defined the term *highly qualified teacher*. Provision of services under IDEA for infants might include any or all of the following:

- Family training, counseling, and home visits
- Special instruction
- Speech pathology and audiology
- Occupational therapy
- Psychological services
- Case management
- Medical services for diagnosis or evaluation
- Screening and assessment
- Transportation to and from services

The provisions of IDEA concern both very young children, who are considered in this chapter, and older children, who are considered in Chapter 15, so the list below concerns both groups of children. Key provisions of IDEA include the following:

1. *Identification*—The state and local education agencies must actively seek out and identify children who have special education needs (Child Find).
2. *Evaluation*—A child must be evaluated appropriately prior to placement. All methods used for testing and evaluation must be in the primary language or "mode of communication" of the child. No one test may be the determining factor for placement. The evaluation procedures cannot be racially or ethnically biased. Before a child is placed in an intervention program, a full and individualized evaluation will be conducted to determine the child's educational needs.
3. *Individualized Family Service Plan (IFSP) or an Individualized Education Plan (IEP)*—An IFSP or IEP (an IEP will be considered in Chapter 14) must be prepared for each child based on the child's individual educational needs.
4. *Parents*—Consonant with a family-centered approach, parents are to be considered equal participants in the decision-making process and students may be participants in their IEP development.
5. *Related Services*—Related services shall be provided on an individualized basis to assist the child to benefit from special education.
6. *Least Restrictive Environment (LRE)*—Each child shall be educated to the maximum extent appropriate with children who do not have disabilities, and children should be educated in more restrictive (different) settings only when less restrictive alternatives are not appropriate.
7. *Private School*—When children are placed in private schools by state or local education agencies in order to receive an appropriate education, this must be done at no cost to parents. Private school programs must meet standards set by law.

8. *Early Intervention and Preschools*—IDEA makes early-intervention services available to children ages 0 to 5 years.
9. *Due Process*—Rights of parents and children must be guaranteed by states and localities, including notice, right to hearing, and appeal procedures. If parents have a complaint, they will have an opportunity for a due process hearing that is conducted by the state educational agency, the local educational agency, or intermediate educational unit. Parents have the right to be accompanied by counsel and other individuals with special knowledge with respect to their child's disability.
10. *Advisory Board*—Each state must set up an advisory board, including individuals who have disabilities, teachers, and parents of children who have disabilities.
11. *Funds*—IDEA provides flow-through funds per child per year to supplement state and local program efforts. Funds may be withheld for noncompliance. Payments by the state to local school districts may also be suspended for noncompliance.
12. *Records*—Parents have access to their child's educational records and can request that they be amended.

Similar laws exist in many other countries. For example, the United Kingdom, Ireland, Canada, New Zealand, and Australia call for an Individual Education Plan (also referred to with the acronym IEP), which is a written plan that specifies the special education program or special services required for a child. Like the U.S. equivalent, it stipulates accommodations, annual reviews, assessment, a children's services team, collaborations, interventions, benchmarks of success, and optimal education settings.

THE INDIVIDUALIZED FAMILY SERVICE PLAN (IFSP)

An **Individualized Family Service Plan (IFSP)** is a federally mandated plan for children up to 3 years that ensures appropriate early-intervention services for infants and toddlers and their families. The plan should take into account a child's current level of development, the family's resources and priorities, goals and services necessary for achieving the goals, and a time course.

An **individualized family service plan (IFSP)** is a federally mandated plan for the education of preschool children. In line with the family-centered approach and family systems theory considered in the last chapter, the cornerstone premise of the IFSP is that the family is the child's primary resource, and the child's needs intertwine with the family's needs. The optimum way to support a child's needs is to support and build upon the family's strengths. The IFSP is a plan for the entire family, and the parents play an active role in developing it. IDEA requires that states receiving funding for early intervention provide services to a child who experiences developmental delays, as measured by appropriate test instruments. The IFSP must include a statement of the following:

- The child's present levels of physical, cognitive, communication, social, emotional, and adaptive development, based on objective criteria.
- The family's resources, priorities, and concerns related to enhancing the child's development.
- The major outcomes expected for the child and family, and the criteria, procedures, and timelines to be used in monitoring progress toward achieving the outcomes and whether modifications or revisions of the outcomes or services are necessary.
- Specific early-intervention services necessary to meet the needs of the child and family, including the frequency, intensity, and methods for delivering services.
- The environments in which early-intervention services shall be provided, including a justification of the extent, if any, to which services will not be provided in a natural environment.
- The projected dates for initiation of services and the anticipated duration of the services.
- An identification of a service coordinator.
- Steps to be taken to support the transition of the toddler to preschool or other appropriate services.

The Service Coordinator and the Medical Home

Once a child has been deemed eligible, a service coordinator is assigned to the family and child. The **service coordinator** coordinates the child's evaluations and assessments, facilitates and helps develop the IFSP, assists the family in receiving appropriate services, coordinates and monitors the delivery of services, and then helps develop a transition plan to preschool services if appropriate. Audiologists, family therapists, physical therapists, psychologists, social workers, speech and language pathologists, special educators, pediatricians and other medical specialists, and nutritionists might provide appropriate services.

The **service coordinator** is a designated person who helps the family during the development, implementation, and evaluation of the IFSP.

The pediatrician and any other primary care physician, working in partnership with the child's parents, and other health care professionals such as the audiologist are the infant's **medical home**. The medical home is not a hospital or a building, but rather "an approach to providing health care services where care is accessible, family-centered, continuous comprehensive, coordinated, compassionate, and culturally competent" (Joint Committee on Infant Hearing [JCIH], 2000, p. 801). The professionals act in partnership with the family to develop a global plan of health and rehabilitative care and advocate for the whole child. Often, the pediatrician helps parents to identify both medical and nonmedical services.

The **medical home** is the approach to providing health care services, and involves a partnership of health care personnel and family.

Development of the Individualized Family Service Plan (IFSP)

The IFSP is a written document developed by a team, including the family. Appendix 13–1 presents some of the acronyms that might be encountered during the formulation of an IFSP, and Table 13–1 presents a sample excerpt from an IFSP. The IFSP describes the programs and services for a child, lists goals and objectives and procedures to be undertaken to ensure they are met, and identifies equipment that the public agency will provide the child and the child's family.

Implementation of the IFSP

During and after the IFSP has been developed, the aural rehabilitation plan can be fleshed out and implemented. This will entail selecting a communication mode that will

TABLE 13–1 Example of an Individualized Family Service Plan

This IFSP is for a student named Mary Lombardo, with sample objectives for language, listening, and self-care skills.

Early Intervention Services: Summary

STRATEGY/ ACTIVITY	RESPONSIBLE PERSON/AGENCY	LOCATION	FREQUENCY (PER MONTH)	DURATION OF SESSION	START DATE	END DATE	EVALUATION CRITERIA
Language: Mary will use words to express five different needs across three different people	Speech-language pathologist	The Lombardo home	Once weekly	45 minutes	9/1/19	3/1/20	Preschool Language Scale
Self-care: Mary will brush her teeth herself	Parents and service coordinator	The Lombardo home	Once weekly	Variable	9/1/19	3/1/20	Recorded data of frequency and observation
Listening: Mary will accurately select a crayon from a set of four after hearing the name of the color	Speech-language pathologist	The Lombardo home	Once weekly	45 minutes	9/1/19	3/1/20	8 out of 10 consecutive trials are correct

be used between family and child, providing appropriate amplification, initiating early-intervention services, such as auditory training, and providing parent support, such as giving guidance about communication strategies and encouraging participation in parent support groups.

COMMUNICATION MODE

Use of communication modes by school-aged children in the United States:

- 53.0% use aural/oral
- 12.1% use total communication
- 27.4% use ASL
- 5.0% use Cued Speech
- 2.5% use some other mode

(Gallaudet Research Institute, 2011)

One of the first decisions to make about intervention concerns communication mode. Will the child use primarily speech to communicate? Manually coded English and speech? Sign only? If a sign system is selected, the child as well as the family must learn the system. Research suggests that parents most often receive information about which communication mode to select from their audiologist, speech-language pathologist, and medical professionals, such as the family pediatrician (Decker, Vallotton, & Johnson, 2012). This finding underscores the importance of becoming familiar with the various options and available resources in the community for supporting the family's communication mode of choice.

The majority of persons with significant hearing loss use one of three modes to communicate: (1) a sign system of the indigenous Deaf community, (2) manually coded English, and (3) spoken language. A relatively small minority use a system called (4) Cued Speech.

American Sign Language and Other Sign Systems Used by Deaf Communities

American Sign Language (ASL) is a manual system of communication used by members of the Deaf culture in the United States.

American Sign Language (ASL) is a manual system of communication that is expressed by the hands through configuration, orientation, location in space, and movement. A person does not simultaneously sign ASL and speak English because ASL possesses a different grammar than spoken English and because one ASL sign might represent a concept that requires many English words to express. For example, a student may sign *you* and *name*, asking, "What is your name?" or "You are named what?" Facial expressions and body language can impart a variety of meanings to a sign (Figure 13–1). In both ASL and manually coded English, fingerspelling is used if a sign does not exist for a particular word or concept, where one hand shape corresponds to each letter of the alphabet. For example, a professor might fingerspell the word *photosynthesis* while teaching a botany class. The American manual alphabet appears in Figure 13–2.

FIGURE 13–1 American Sign Language. Hand shape, orientation, movement, and location, in addition to facial expression, determine meaning.

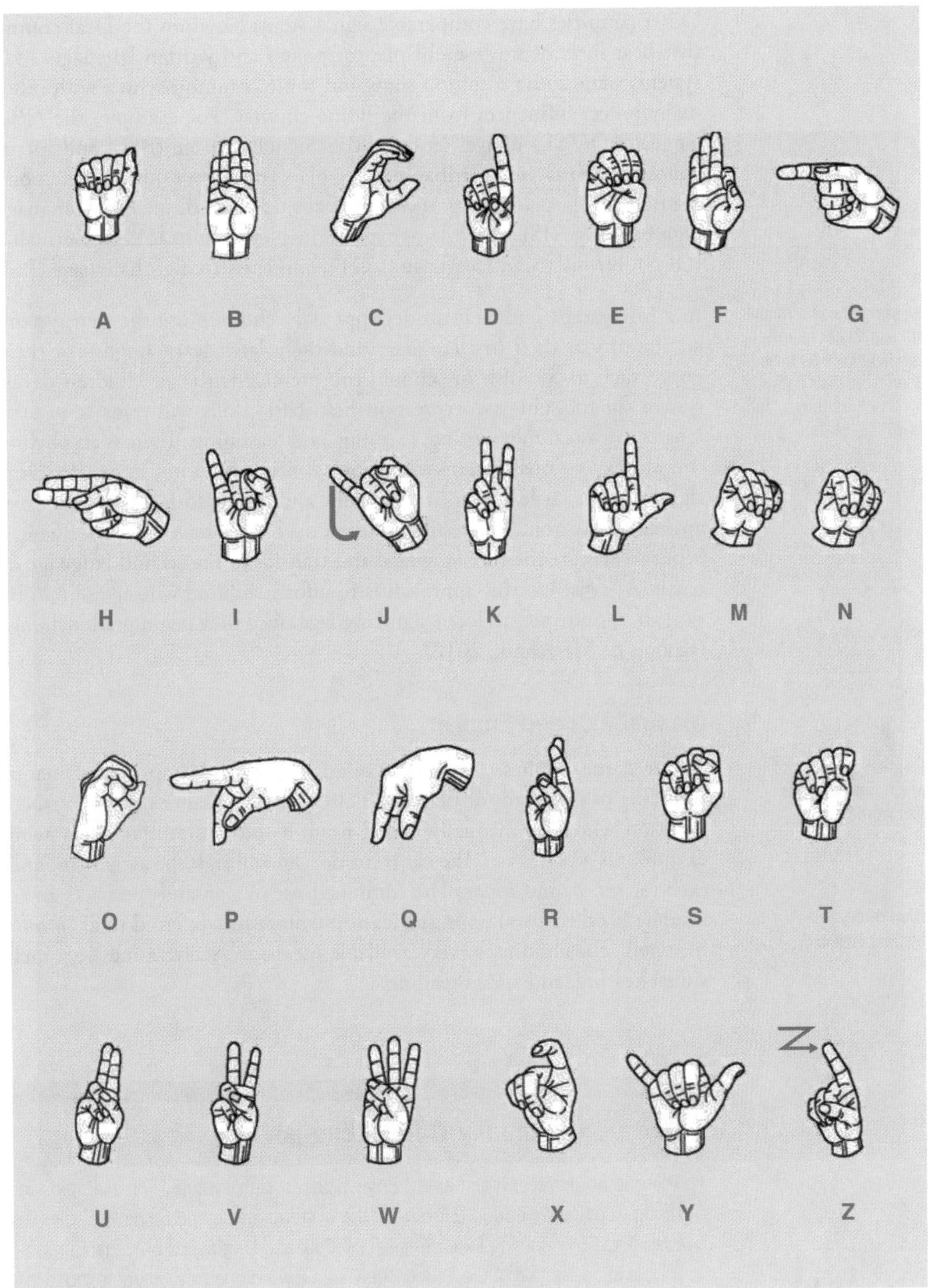

FIGURE 13–2 The American manual alphabet. Words can be spelled out using the alphabet.

Other countries have comparable sign systems based on the Deaf community, systems that bear little or no resemblance to spoken and written language. Many of the sign systems share some common signs and some common syntax with other systems, and many reflect influences from the home country. For example, the New Zealand sign language (NZSL) derives from British Sign Language (BSL) and incorporates Maori concepts such as *marae* (tribal meeting place) and *tangi* (funeral ceremony). The French Sign Language (*Langue des Signes Française*; LSF) is the ancestral language of ASL, Irish Sign Language (ISL), Sign Language of the Netherlands (SLN), German Sign Language (DGS), Flemish Sign Language (VGT), and Russian Sign Language (RSL).

A **bilingual/bicultural model** is a model in which children with significant hearing loss learn a Deaf sign language as their first language and then later their native spoken language in school, as they develop reading and writing skills.

In a **bilingual/bicultural model** approach, children use the sign system of their Deaf community as their first language and then, later, learn English or their national language such as Swedish in school. The premise is that if children develop a language system for thought and expression first, basic skills will transfer to learning a second language for reading, writing, learning, and reasoning. There is an obvious roadblock to this approach: most parents with normal hearing do not know the Deaf community's sign language, at least not immediately, and many do not have the time, resources, or aptitude to learn it. As a result, children may not receive the rich, fluent, and consistent input to acquire the first language and transfer to the second language does not always occur. A "twist" to this approach is to afford children who use aural/oral communication an opportunity to learn sign language once they begin grade school or high school (Knoors & Marschark, 2012).

Manually Coded English

Manually coded English is a form of communication in which manual signs correspond to English words.

Total communication refers to a combined use of sign and speech.

As the name implies, **manually coded English** is comprised of manual signs corresponding to the words of English. It also shares the same syntactic structures. Typically, a person who uses manually coded English speaks simultaneously while signing. For example, as a boy says, "The cat is inside," he will sign the article *the,* and then one sign each for *cat, is,* and *inside.* The combined use of sign and speech as an educational philosophy is called **total communication** (sometimes referred to as *simultaneous communication*). The child uses every available means to receive a message, including sign, residual hearing, and speechreading.

More on Manually Coded English

There is no universally accepted English-based sign system. For example, under the rubric of manually coded English fall the systems of Signed English, Seeing Essential English (SEE I), Signing Exact English (SEE II), and Linguistics of Visual English (LOVE). People in one region of the country may sign a word one way, whereas those in another region sign it in a different way.

Many teachers and children who use manually coded English actually sign a contact form of English, omitting function words such as *the* and morphemes, including those that mark past tense and plurality. For example, in *Conceptually Accurate English (CASE;* also called *Sign Supported English*), a teacher might sign the key words in a sentence in their correct order, but omit function words such as *a* and *the*. Hence, the sentence *We will go to the store to buy groceries* becomes *We go store buy groceries.* Children who receive a contact model of English may be at relatively high risk for developing deficits in language syntax and poor writing skills.

Aural/Oral Language

Aural/oral language (sometimes referred to as an *oral approach*) is the same language used by persons with normal hearing. The child with a hearing loss who uses aural/oral language will speak messages and use speechreading to receive messages. Most children who use aural/oral language are educated with a multisensory approach, but a small number are educated with a unisensory approach.

Aural/oral language is the language used by persons with normal hearing.

Children in a **multisensory approach** utilize both vision and hearing to recognize speech. In learning to talk, children rely on residual hearing, speechreading, and in some instances, touch.

Multisensory approach refers to the use of both vision and hearing, and sometimes touch, to recognize speech.

Children who have a communication mode based on a **unisensory approach** rely only on residual hearing to receive spoken messages. The preschool teacher may sometimes expect a child to recognize the signal auditorily, even if the youngster has minimal residual hearing. Several years ago, this approach was sometimes referred to as an **acoupedic approach**, and was defined by Pollack (1970) as follows: "The term *acoupedics* refers to a comprehensive habilitation program for the hearing impaired infant and his family, which includes an emphasis upon auditory training without formal lipreading instruction" (p. 13). In recent times, a unisensory approach has been often referred to as an **auditory-verbal approach**. The auditory-verbal approach emphasizes the use of audition over vision for the learning of speech and language, and stipulates that a child make habitual and optimal use of amplification or electrical stimulation (i.e., cochlear implant) in order to develop spoken communication. Auditory-verbal is considered to be a way of life. Children are expected ultimately to respond to sound and to use it in the same ways as do children who have normal hearing.

The **unisensory approach** is one that advocates the use of only residual hearing to receive spoken messages.

The **acoupedic approach** is a comprehensive habilitation program for infants and their families that emphasizes auditory training without formal lipreading instruction.

The **auditory-verbal approach** encourages a child to develop listening behaviors and to develop spoken communication by relying on residual hearing rather than vision; the use of appropriate and habitual amplification or electrical stimulation (via cochlear implant) is strongly encouraged.

Cued Speech

Cued Speech is a communication system that uses phonemically based hand gestures to supplement speechreading (Cornett, 1967). Thus, the talker speaks while simultaneously cueing the message. By themselves, the hand signals are uninterpretable. However, when paired with the visual speech signal, the stream of hand signals (i.e., cueing) serves to distinguish the viseme members that compose each of the words in the talker's message. The person with hearing loss thus simultaneously attends to the visual speech signal, the hand cues, and the auditory speech signal. Although a relatively small number of children use Cued Speech, it has become an international phenomenon, having been adapted to more than 60 languages and dialects, including Spanish, Croatian-Serbian, Hindi, Swedish, and Telugu (Beck, 2006).

Cued Speech, a system for enhancing speechreading, uses phonemically based gestures to distinguish between similar visual speech patterns.

In the Cued Speech system, eight different hand shapes distinguish consonants and six locations on the face and neck distinguish vowels. For example, the consonants /p/ and /b/ resemble one another on the mouth. The consonant /p/ is distinguished by a 1 hand shape and the consonant /b/ is distinguished by a 4 hand shape. If a talker said the word *pea*, he or she would hold a 1 hand shape to the corner of the mouth, because a 1 hand shape indicates the phoneme /p/ and a placement at the mouth corner indicates an /i/ vowel. If the talker instead said *bee,* he or she would hold a 4 hand shape at the mouth corner. The word *boo* would be signaled by a 4 hand shape at the throat. Figure 13–3 presents the Cued Speech system. The research about Cued Speech is sparse, although a meta-analysis suggests that it promotes the development of reading abilities (Trezek, 2017).

Selection of a Communication Mode

Some debate and controversy surround the issue of communication mode, and many speech and hearing professionals take firm stands in favor of one mode versus another.

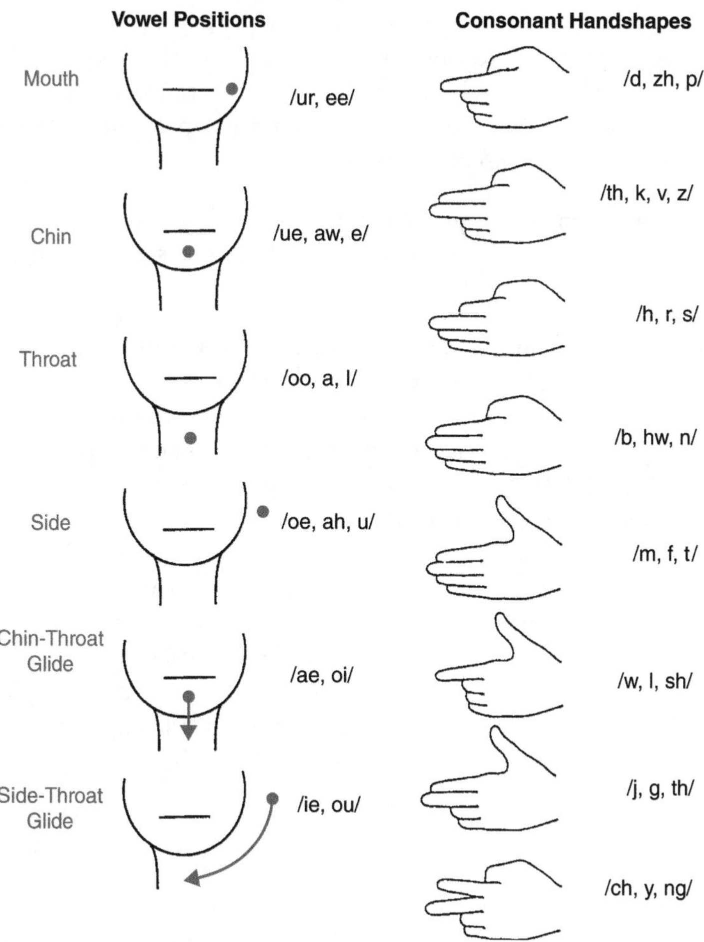

FIGURE 13–3 Cued Speech. Hand configurations and hand placement positions for distinguishing consonant and vowel visemes.

Of all the decisions parents must make about their child's intervention plan, this decision may be the one they revisit most often.

No definitive answers as to the best way to go exist (Fitzpatrick et al., 2016), and it is likely that the best route depends upon the individual child and the kind of benefit he or she receives from a listening device. With this said, some evidence suggests that children who utilize an aural/oral communication mode achieve better speech and language performance and literacy development than do children who rely on sign language. For example, Dornan, Hickson, Murdoch, and Houston (2008) found that a group of 29 children who had severe and profound hearing losses, and who were between the ages of 2 and 6 years at the time of their study, showed the same amount of progress in their speech and language skills over the course of nine months as children who had normal hearing.

Perhaps where the issue of communication mode advantage is best resolved is in the population of cochlear implant users. Numerous studies have shown that children who use a cochlear implant and an aural/oral method of communication develop better speech and language skills than do children who use sign (e.g., Kirk, Miyamoto, Ying, Perdew, & Zuganelis, 2000) and better speech recognition skills (Miyamoto, Kirk, Svirsky, &

Sehgal, 1999). A group of researchers at Central Institute for the Deaf, for example, studied 181 children, 8 and 9 years of age, from across North America. They found that children who were in an aural/oral education program developed better speech (Tobey et al., 2005), language (Geers, Nicholas, & Sedey, 2003), conversational fluency (Tye-Murray, 2003), and reading (Geers, 2003) than did children who were enrolled in a total-communication environment. The aural/oral communication advantage proved robust, even after they factored out child, family, and educational variables. The researchers also found that following cochlear implantation, more children switched from using a total-communication mode to an aural/oral mode than the converse.

Aural/Oral Communication: An Option Now More Than Ever

"Some children need cochlear implants and some don't. Some parents are ready to talk about implants right away and some are not. So we go at their pace. But the most important thing is, the technology we have in 2018 will allow your child to hear, and that will allow your child to listen and learn to speak, and to become anything he or she wants to be."

—Jane Madell, PhD, expert in pediatric audiology

(Beck, 2018, p. 32)

Cochlear implant technology is advancing so rapidly that most young recipients develop the auditory capacity to acquire at least some spoken language. Even if they have begun their language development using sign, children may desist signing with time, as their speech, language, and listening skills emerge. For example, an 8-year-old girl wrote in a personal essay, "When I was 10 months old I got a cochlear implant. My family and I used to sign to communicate. I'm not so good about signing nowadays. I like communication using my voice and hearing" (Iwawaki, 2012, p. 38). New research suggests that children who have never been exposed to sign language before receiving their cochlear implant perform better on tests of auditory-only speech recognition, speech intelligibility, spoken language, and reading than children who were exposed (Geers, Mitchell, Warner-Czyz, Wang, Eisenberg, & CDaCI Investigative Team, 2017). The topic of speech and language development with a cochlear implant will be revisited in Chapter 15.

LISTENING DEVICE

The goal of providing a listening device is to provide the infant or toddler with maximum access to the speech signal at a listening level that is safe and comfortable. For newborns and infants, estimated hearing sensitivity is supported by frequency-specific ABR threshold assessment. Behavioral measures may be available for older babies and toddlers to supplement the electrophysiological measures.

Amplification

Infants and toddlers usually receive hearing aids after a hearing loss is identified, as early as 4 weeks of age. The median delay between identification and hearing aid fitting is about three months (Muñoz, Roberts, Mullings, & Harward, 2012). Even if the child is an excellent candidate for a cochlear implant, he or she must first undergo a trial period with a hearing aid to determine that it is not a viable option. The amplification fitting procedure typically employs prescriptive procedures that include individual real-ear measurements (see Chapter 3). The five steps of the amplification process are: (1) selection, (2) verification, (3) orientation, (4) validation, and (5) follow-up.

Selection

Selecting hearing aids for infants and young children differs in some ways from fitting hearing aids in adults. First, there are physical differences. Children, especially infants, have smaller ears and ear canals, which may limit hearing aid style options. Ear canal size might increase the occurrence of feedback and squeal, and the tiny pinna may not hold a hearing aid behind the ear. Second, because sound is funneled into a small space before the tympanic membrane, the sound pressure delivered to a child's ear might be greater than when the exact acoustic signal is delivered to an adult ear. Thus, it becomes important to ensure that sound is not too loud to cause damage. Finally, babies and young children often cannot participate in the fitting process. They cannot indicate when sound is too loud and they cannot take a word recognition test.

Most young children receive behind-the-ear (BTE) hearing aids (McCreery, Bentler, & Roush, 2013). BTEs typically provide sufficient gain, even for profound hearing losses. Babies' ears are typically too tiny to accommodate an in-the-ear (ITE), completely-in-the-canal (CIC), or in-the-canal (ITC) style of hearing aid. Moreover, these styles are impractical because the baby is growing quickly and would require a new aid more often than with a BTE. Even with a BTE style, parents have to monitor changes in the baby's ear size. New earmolds may have to be fabricated every six to eight weeks.

Verification

As with adults, the goal of verification is to determine whether speech is audible, and entails electroacoustic measures using a probe microphone and insertion gain protocol. Behavioral measures may be included in the verification procedure for older children. Verification provides frequency-specific information about speech audibility and estimates of real-ear aided responses.

Orientation

A **listening check** is an informal check of a hearing aid to ensure that it is functioning.

Once a hearing aid is fitted on a child, the audiologist instructs the parents or caregivers about how to care for the device and how to perform a **listening check**, and provides the equipment to do so. The parent learns about device insertion, removal, overnight storage, and battery insertion and removal. Instruction will also include how to wash an earmold, how to monitor the child's ability to hear with the device, and how to troubleshoot the hearing aid (e.g., what to do if the hearing aid will not turn on, if the sound is weak or distorted, if the hearing aid squeals). Written materials supplement the verbal instruction.

Parents React Differently to Technology

Parent One: I'm not particularly good with equipment. I can just about work the video but you know it was like oh god I don't know what to do with [the hearing aid]. I suppose to start off I was frightened of it.

Parent Two: It just felt overwhelming 'cos [the audiologist] was talking about how to look after them and do the thing, clean them, put them in . . . I was just thinking how am I going to manage this on a little baby . . . it was a nightmare really, it was all very well [to have the] hearing aids, but actually getting him to wear them and use them . . .

Parent Three: It's a normal thing. They're just like putting on his clothes. They are just part of his clothing now and we can both . . . you know at first it was a bit distressing—but really it doesn't take very long to be able to fit them really quickly.

—Three parents of babies identified with hearing loss, talking about becoming "hearing aid managers" while simultaneously trying to establish baby routines

(McCracken, Young, & Tattersall, 2008, p. 59)

Validation

To validate the benefits of amplification, some toddlers of about age 3 years can take speech perception measures, such as the Northwestern University Children's Perception of Speech Test (NU-CHIPS; Elliott & Katz, 1980), a closed-set test of monosyllabic words. Infants and most toddlers will require alternative means, such as parent report or clinician observation. The Early Listening Function (ELF; Anderson, 2002) and the Infant-Toddler Meaningful Auditory Integration (IT-MAIS; Zimmerman-Phillips, 1997) exemplify tests that solicit parent report. These tests assess children's response to sound as well as their emerging speech and language skills, skills which depend upon the child being able to hear the spoken word.

The ELF takes several days to complete and parents typically complete it when their infant reaches 6 months or older. It includes checklists and rating scales. For example, a parent indicates whether the baby can detect the mother saying "sh, sh" or clicking her tongue loudly at distances of six inches, three feet, six feet, ten feet, and then from the next room. The mother must judge whether the baby responds to her voice when the baby is wearing amplification.

The IT-MAIS is a structured interview conducted with the parent by a speech and hearing professional. It assesses a child's vocalization behaviors, alerting behaviors to sound, and ability to derive meaning from sound. One question on the IT-MAIS asks parents to *Describe [the child's] vocalizations when you first put his/her device on each day.* Points are awarded on a graduated scale, ranging from *No difference between when the device is turned on versus off* to *An increase of 100% when the child is wearing the device to when the child is not wearing it.* Parents indicate whether their baby spontaneously responds to his or her name and whether the baby recognizes auditory signals that are a part of the family's everyday routine.

Follow-Up

A typical follow-up schedule for children during the first year of using a hearing aid includes a recheck at one month following the initial fitting and then a visit at every two or three months. After the first year, visits to the audiologist may occur at four- to six-month intervals. At follow-up visits, hearing is assessed and the hearing aids are tested and adjusted as necessary. The follow-up includes a behavioral audiometric evaluation, current assessment of communication needs and abilities, adjustment of amplification system, periodic electroacoustic evaluations, listening checks, earmold fit check, periodic probe-microphone measurements, and long-term follow-up, including a check on ongoing auditory training (American Academy of Audiology, 2004).

Some children reject their devices or want to control when they do and do not use it. Some children react negatively to amplified sound, and some may view the listening device as a means of asserting independence or gaining control over parents. Initially, parents may need to reassure the child and perhaps allow the child to wear the device for only short periods of time. Gradually, use time can increase and eventually, putting the listening device on in the morning becomes part of getting dressed, and removing it becomes part of getting ready for bed in the evening.

The three top challenges experienced by parents in obtaining hearing aids for their infant or young child:

- Paying for the hearing aids and related products (e.g., earmolds, batteries)
- Dealing with their child's other health concerns such as otitis media
- Having confidence in the skill of the audiologist or finding an audiologist who specializes in young children

(Muñoz et al., 2012)

Cochlear Implants

The FDA approved multichannel cochlear implants in 1990 for children who have profound hearing losses and who are between 2 and 17 years of age. Now, the FDA

© Vera Petrunina | Shutterstock.com

FIGURE 13–4 Benefits of early implantation. Research suggests that the younger a child is at the time of implantation, the greater the advantage afforded for speech, language, and auditory development.

guidelines (these are not "laws") endorse cochlear implantation for children as young as 12 months who have profound hearing loss and children 18 months and older who have severe to profound hearing loss. Babies who have had meningitis and are at risk for cochlear ossification might receive a cochlear implant sooner (Figure 13–4) and babies as young as 6 months are receiving implants in the United States (Miyamoto, Colson, & Hening, 2017).

Children who are younger when they receive a cochlear implant perform better on average than children who are older on tests of speech perception, language, and speech production (e.g., Connor, Craig, Raudenbush, Heavner, & Zwolan, 2006; Tye-Murray, Spencer, & Woodworth, 1995). For this reason, some countries and some locales implant children at even younger ages than 12 months. In fact, children as young as 3 months have received a cochlear implant (e.g., Birman, 2009). Results suggest that infants who receive a cochlear implant before their first birthday achieve better growth rates of receptive and expressive language than children who receive a cochlear implant between the ages of 12 and 24 months (Dettman, Pinder, Briggs, Dowell, & Leigh, 2007). Although there are some surgical issues to consider, such as anatomical access being tight and bone marrow ooze occurring in a younger baby, it appears that infants younger than 12 months can safely undergo the surgical procedure (Miyamoto et al., 2017). Thus, in the near future, very early implantation may become routine.

Reasons why parents may opt for cochlear implantation:

- Development and use of child's speech and hearing
- Communication with the family
- Child's safety and environmental awareness
- Concern for the child's self-image

Reasons why parents may opt against cochlear implantation:

- Low priority placed on their child's ability to speak rather than sign
- Financial costs
- Paucity of support services at their community school
- Concern about whether their child will identify with the hearing or Deaf world

(Hyde, Punch, & Komesaroff, 2010)

Candidacy is determined by the degree of hearing loss, demonstration that the child receives minimal or unsatisfactory benefit from using hearing aids (i.e., shows delayed or no gain in vocalization/speech, language, and listening skills after a two- to six-month trial), and the absence of medical contraindications, such as cochlear nerve **aplasia** and complete **agenesis** of the cochlea.

Aplasia is lack or defective development of all or part of a body structure.

Agenesis is an absence of an organ.

The stages involved in a child's receiving a cochlear implant include: (1) initial contact, (2) counseling, (3) formal evaluation, (4) surgery, (5) fitting, (6) follow-up, and (7) aural rehabilitation.

Initial Contact

Parents may first learn about cochlear implants from the child's audiologist, otolaryngologist, pediatrician, or other medical professional. They might then contact the clinical coordinator at a cochlear implant center and ask questions like those listed in Table 13–2. The clinical coordinator will provide initial answers and printed information.

TABLE 13–2 Questions Parents May Ask During the Initial Contact

• Is my child an appropriate candidate?
• How does a cochlear implant work? How does it differ from a hearing aid?
• Will the cochlear implant help my child to talk and hear better?
• Can a cochlear implant electrocute my child? Is it dangerous to use?
• Can my child still play sports if he or she gets one?
• Will the cochlear implant last my child's entire lifetime? What happens if it "wears out"?
• Is the cochlear implant waterproof? Will my child be able to take a bath or shower?
• What happens if my child gets hit in the head?
• How often do the devices break?
• How much do they cost? Will my insurance pay for it?
• What's involved in obtaining a cochlear implant?
• Will my child have to use a particular communication mode?
• Are cochlear implants hard to take care of?

Parents will likely still be grieving as they navigate this new world of infant hearing loss. They may decide very quickly to seek cochlear implantation surgery or they may delay, taking time to gather information and deliberate. Some parents feel rushed or paradoxical. On the one hand, they want to learn as much as possible about risks, alternative choices and options, cultural issues, and possible outcomes, and they want time to see how their baby develops without a cochlear implant. On the other hand, they will have learned from the cochlear implant center personnel that earlier implantation bodes for a better outcome. A survey of 247 parents revealed that almost half found the decision-making process "stressful." As one parent noted, "I was really quite tortured by [making the decision] because we had a fair amount of contact with the Deaf community and had spoken to people who were against cochlear implants . . . . I really didn't know whether when she was an adult, she was going to say, 'I didn't want that.' I felt like I had to make that fairly important decision for her. It was very hard to make" (Hyde et al., 2010, p. 170).

Counseling

One goal of the preimplant counseling session is to establish realistic expectations so that parents are prepared for an array of possible outcomes. A pediatric audiologist might begin by explaining that the child will always have a significant hearing loss and that the cochlear implant is a communication aid and not a bionic ear. The audiologist then may review in layperson's terms how a cochlear implant affects listening and speech and language development, using group data to describe the best and poorest performance of young cochlear implant users, and the average performance.

The audiologist will likely encourage parents to talk with other parents of young cochlear implant users, some of whom receive more and some of who receive less benefit. Parents place high value on the information, personal stories, and emotional support they receive from other families. As one parent said, "I'd spoken to other [parents], and I'd seen other [older] children with the cochlear implant so I made my decision sort of based on, if it worked, it was going to help her" (Hyde et al., 2010, p. 169).

Formal Evaluation

The formal evaluation establishes candidacy. Although the formal evaluation varies amongst cochlear implant centers, children always receive a comprehensive audiological assessment (including ABR), a physical, and a radiological evaluation. Often, a speech-language pathologist who specializes in children who have hearing loss will evaluate speech and language, which may include assessment of vocabulary, language, babbling, and articulation. Depending upon the child and the presence of other disabilities, the formal evaluation may also involve a physical therapist, psychologist, neurologist, ophthalmologist, cardiologist, or family social worker.

Surgery

Regardless of the counseling that has occurred beforehand, families often feel anxious before the surgery. Some worry about the anesthesia, potential surgical complications, the aftermath of surgery, and whether their child will benefit from the device. Some parents may experience guilt for inflicting a surgical procedure on their child. You may play a role reassuring and supporting parents before, during, and after the procedure.

Question: What strategies and activities could help families explain cochlear implant surgery to their toddler or young child?

Answer: Throw a cochlear implant party with hospital props, and make a picture book illustrating the hospital experience.

(Lartz & Meehan, 2009, p. 27)

The Cochlear Implant Fitting

The time necessary to fit and map a cochlear implant varies, depending upon the child's age and cooperativeness. Ideally electrical thresholds (T-levels) can be determined with visual response audiometry (VRA) or conditioned play audiometry (CPA). If necessary, behavioral/observational audiometry (BOA) can be used. Some formulas are available for determining the map when the child cannot participate in behavioral testing and some devices have **neural response telemetry (NRT)** (called neural response imaging [NRI] by some cochlear implant manufacturers), which can help establish thresholds by means of electrical stimulation. NRT records neural responses to electrical stimulation. A pulse is delivered to the electrode. Fibers of the auditory nerve fire in response. The cochlear implant system records the response and delivers it to a computer for analysis. Formulas that utilize behavioral observation (e.g., elicitation of an **auropalpebral reflex**) (e.g., Rance & Dowell, 1997) or NRT/NRI values are sometimes used to establish maximum comfort levels (C-levels).

Neural response telemetry (NRT) records neural responses directly and affords a means to help set threshold values across the cochlear implant electrode array. A pulse is delivered to the electrode. Fibers of the auditory nerve fire in response. The cochlear implant system records the response and delivers it to the programming computer for analysis.

The **auropalpebral reflex** is a wink or twitch of the eye that occurs in response to loud sound.

Initial T-levels may be high and C-levels low. The cochlear implant audiologist may adjust them as the child acclimates to hearing. In addition, due to a child's limited attention span, only a few electrodes may be programmed during the initial fitting session. Although most children use their cochlear implant after one or two fittings, an optimum fitting may require several months to complete.

When the device is activated, a child may show no response to sound or may show happiness, fright, surprise, rejection, distress, or wonderment. Before leaving the cochlear implant center, parents receive instruction about how to handle the device. Topics will include how to turn the device on and off, battery information, troubleshooting, warranty, and general care and maintenance.

Not-to-be-missed YouTube videos that show babies hearing for the first time through a cochlear implant:

Baby suddenly realizes why Mom has been moving her lips all of these months: https://www.youtube.com/watch?v=HTzTt1VnHRM

Baby gives his parents an end-of-the-year holiday present: https://www.youtube.com/watch?v=zb-SU6JUlbc

A baby girl is moved to happy tears: https://www.youtube.com/watch?v=-_Q5kO4YXFs

Follow-Up Visits

After the first year of cochlear implant use, a child returns to the cochlear implant center at regular intervals, often at 6 months or annually. During the follow-up visit, the child typically receives audiological testing, and, when developmentally appropriate, speech recognition testing, speech-language testing (including that of vocabulary, language, and articulation), and in some cases, academic testing. Results provide benchmarks of success and pinpoint areas of concern. Tests of speech recognition are listed in Table 13–3. Chapter 15 presents a review of tests to assess speech, language, and literacy.

TABLE 13–3 Examples of Word Recognition Tests That Use Phoneme, Word, and Sentence Stimuli for Children*

TEST	AUTHOR(S)	STIMULUS TYPE	STIMULUS UNITS	RESPONSE FORMAT	TARGET POPULATION
Speech Pattern Contrast Test (SPAC)	Boothroyd (1984)	Phoneme (also includes test of suprasegmental contrasts, such as word stress)	Words and phrases	Closed set	Children age 10 years and older
Audiovisual Feature Test	Tyler, Fryauf-Bertschy, and Kelsey (1991)	Phoneme	Rhyming words, including *b, c, d, key, me, knee*	Closed set (10-choice)	Children
Nonsense Syllable Test (NST)	Edgerton and Danhauer (1979)	Phoneme	Nonsense bisyllables	Open set	Children and adults
Minimal Pairs Test	Robbins, Renshaw, Miyamoto, Osberger, and Pope (1988)	Phoneme	Monosyllabic word pairs (e.g., *pair* vs. *bear*)	Closed set (2-choice)	Children, about age 4 years and older
Auditory Numbers Test (ANT)	Erber (1980)	Word	Numbers	Closed set (5-choice)	Children
Northwestern University Children's Perception of Speech (NU-CHIPS)	Elliott and Katz (1980)	Word	Monosyllables constructed with the most frequently occurring phonemes in the English language, such as *fork, dog*	Closed set (4-choice)	Children who have the receptive language abilities of age 2.6 years or older
Word Intelligibility by Picture Identification (WIPI)	Ross and Lerman (1971)	Word	Monosyllabic words, such as *bear, pear, stair, chair, ear, hair*	Closed set (6-choice)	Children ages 5–6 years with speech recognition skills associated with moderate hearing loss; ages 7–8 years with severe hearing loss
Phonetically Balanced Kindergarten (PBK)	Haskins (1949)	Word	Monosyllabic words preceded by the carrier phrase *Say the word*	Open set	Children 6 years and older
Early-Speech Perception Test (ESP)	Moog and Geers (1990)	Word	Words varying in number of syllables	Closed set	Children 6 years and older
Early-Speech Perception Test (ESP)–Low Verbal Version	Moog and Geers (1990)	Word	Words varying in number of syllables	Closed set	Children 2 years of age or when vocabulary has been developed
Lexical Neighborhood Test (LNT)	Kirk, Pisoni, and Osberger (1995)	Word	Words, some of which are lexically "easy" and some of which are lexically "hard," with easy words having few other word choices that are phonetically similar (e.g., *thought, live*) and hard words having many words that are similar (e.g., *mole, wed*)	Open set	Children
Children's Realistic Index of Speech Perception (CRISP)	Litovsky (2003)	Word	25 spondees presented in the presence of two competing sentences	Closed set (four-choice)	Children

(continues)

TABLE 13–3 *(continued)*

TEST	AUTHOR(S)	STIMULUS TYPE	STIMULUS UNITS	RESPONSE FORMAT	TARGET POPULATION
Pediatric Speech Intelligibility (PSI)	Jerger, Lewis, Hawkins, and Jerger (1980)	Word; sentences	20 monosyllables known to be familiar to children with normal hearing between the ages of 3 and 7 years	Closed set (five-choice), where words are presented with a carrier phrase or a standard sentence frame	Children
Bamford-Kowal-Bench Sentences (BKB)	Bench, Kowal, and Bamford (1979)	Sentences	Key words in sentences	Open set	Children 6 years old and older
Common Phrases Test	Robbins, Renshaw, and Osberger (1995)	Sentences	List of 10 common phrases	Open set	Children (minimum age not stated)

*These tests typically are administered in an audition-only condition.

Aural Rehabilitation

A concerted, deliberate aural rehabilitation effort is required for children to optimally recognize speech and acquire spoken language. The aural rehabilitation plan must include participation by the parents, speech and hearing professionals, and educators. Ideally, the child will participate in an early-intervention program, one that emphasizes spoken language and includes auditory training.

EARLY-INTERVENTION PROGRAMS

Early intervention ideally begins as soon as the permanent hearing loss is confirmed, and includes receipt of a listening aid. Families may receive a list of all of the available programs in the geographic area or referral to a statewide early-intervention system. Some families will have many options, whereas others will have only a few. The service coordinator assigned to the family typically is responsible for ensuring that the IFSP is developed and that the appropriate services are identified.

The Joint Committee on Infant Hearing (JCIH, 2000, 2007, 2013) presents comprehensive guidelines for early-intervention programs. The goals are designed to support families in developing a child's communication skills, to help the family understand an infant's strengths and needs, and to promote the family's ability to advocate for the child. Early intervention builds upon family support and bolsters the family's confidence in their ability to parent a child who has hearing loss. The best practice goals (JCIH, 2013) are designed to ensure:

- That children with hearing loss and their families have timely access to early intervention programs.
- That they have access to professionals who specialize in working with children who have hearing loss, that their child (and if appropriate, the family) receives sign or spoken language instruction from a qualified teacher.
- That infants and young children have their progress monitored at regular six-month intervals.
- That families be active participants in the development and implementation of the early intervention plan, that families and their children have access to other families of children who have hearing loss and access to individuals who are deaf or have hearing loss and who can provide support, mentorship, and guidance.

- That families from culturally diverse backgrounds or nonnative-speaking homes have access to culturally competent service providers.

Children who have unilateral hearing loss or slight hearing loss also deserve immediate services when appropriate. The newest guidelines include ten appendices, each outlining the knowledge and skill sets necessary for a particular best practice. Examples of these best practices and representative guidelines are listed below:

- Family-centered practices: *Understand family systems and family dynamics*
- Socially, culturally, and linguistic responsive practices: *Promote family's understanding and appreciation of being Deaf or hard of hearing*
- Language acquisition and communication development: *Understand the array of communication approaches such as ASL, bilingual-bicultural, auditory/oral, auditory/verbal, Cued Speech, and simultaneous communication, and resources for observing and demonstrating them*
- Factors influencing infant and toddler development: *Understand auditory, visual, and cross-modal perception and processing in relation to development*
- Planning and implementation of services: *Plan and implement effective parent–child sessions in natural environments*

In concordance with these guidelines, most early-intervention programs provide families with general information about language development and specific information about how hearing loss might affect development. Families are encouraged to engage in home-based activities that facilitate language acquisition. Programs usually ensure access to peer and language models. Peer models include other families who have children with hearing loss, as well as adults who have hearing loss. Language models may include individuals who use an aural/oral mode of communication or a mode that includes the use of sign. Overall, most programs strive to address a child's communicative competence, social skills, emotional well-being, and self-esteem.

Developing an Early-Intervention Program

Parents and professionals will take into account the following when developing an IFSP and choosing directions for early intervention (Cheslock & Kahn, 2011, pp. 10–11; Reed-Martinez, 2013, pp. 24–25):

- *Communication considerations*: The language spoken in the home and the communication options currently used with the child.
- *Family-centered services*: Services that address the family's strengths, needs, priorities, and concerns; families participate actively in the intervention plan.
- *Developmentally supportive services*: "Services that offer children authentic learning experiences to support functional communication development throughout everyday routines specific to the family, as well as interactive participation appropriate to the child's age, developmental level, strengths, needs and family priorities" (Cheslock & Kahn, 2011, p. 11).
- *Assistive technology*: Hearing aids, cochlear implants, FM systems, and any other assistive technology that might promote the child's ability to participate actively in the home, childcare program, school, or community.

(continues)

Developing an Early-Intervention Program *(continued)*

- *Programming options/natural environments*: Description of the available services and the environments where those services might be provided, including the school or aural rehabilitation center or daycare, and the supports the family will need to access these services.
- *Community activities*: The resources and supports (e.g., an FM system) necessary for the child and family to participate in community activities such as playgroups, library story times, and religious services.
- *Proficiency of staff*: A list of qualified service providers on the team who have the requisite expertise, experience, and training to work with children who have hearing loss and who are between the ages of birth and 3 years.

Types of Programs

In a **center-based program**, children attend therapy for a designated number of hours per week.

In a **home-based program**, an early interventionist visits the infant's home and provides instruction for the child and parents.

Parents might consider a center-based program or a home-based program, or a combination of the two. In a **center-based program**, children attend therapy for a designated number of hours each week (Figure 13–5). Their parents may participate too. In **home-based programs**, an early-intervention specialist visits the infant's home and provides instruction to the parents and child (Figure 13–6). Home-based programs occur in the home and emphasize one-on-one rather than group instruction.

Examples of early-intervention programs are the SKI-HI curriculum (www.skihi.org) and the John Tracy Clinic home study programs (www.jtc.org). The SKI-HI curriculum is a family-oriented program for children who are between the ages of infancy and 5 years, and has been implemented throughout the United States and Canada. National and local trainers provide training to service providers in participating states, and some training occurs at the SKI-HI Institute in Logan, Utah. The program includes early

FIGURE 13–5 Center-based programs. The baby or young child receives professional services at a speech and hearing center, often along with other children. Parents may also participate as part of the program.

© BlueOrange Studio | Shutterstock.com

FIGURE 13–6 Home-based programs. A professional provides one-on-one services for the baby in the home environment and works with the baby's family so they can optimize learning during everyday home activities.

amplification, a focus on early communication approaches, language programs, and early literacy. Portions of the curriculum are devoted to natural environments and everyday routines, parent support, and conversation training.

The John Tracy program offers both an on-site early-intervention program for families who reside in Southern California and a correspondence course. Programs are available for infants, toddlers, and preschoolers, and aural/oral communication is promoted. For example, topics included in the infant program are family relationships, deafness, child development, and communication. Videotapes are available to demonstrate techniques, such as those associated with auditory training.

Many early-intervention programs emphasize a coaching model of intervention as opposed to a direct therapy model of intervention (e.g., Rossi, 2003). In a coaching paradigm, the parent implements the program while the professional observes parent–child interactions and provides support and suggestions. In the direct therapy approach, the professional and child interact, and the parent, if present, observes and takes instruction from the professional. In a coaching approach, a speech and hearing professional might say to a parent in the context of modeling language, "You responded to Rachael's signals and you seem to know what they mean. Let's capitalize on this and use something called 'language modeling,' where you can give her words for what she wants, as if she could talk." In a direct therapy approach, in contrast, a speech and hearing professional might instead say, "Let me demonstrate language modeling with Rachael. Try to do what I'm doing throughout her day." The former approach is family-centered and provides the parent with hands-on practice and a sense of self-efficacy; the latter approach is more child-centered and casts the speech and hearing professional as the expert and key to implementation and the parent as an audience member.

Coaching Model of Intervention

In the direct coaching approach, the professional makes home visits and interacts with the family and the child in the home environment. The premise is that one or two hours of therapy performed by the professional each week will have minimal impact on a child's development, whereas the ongoing interactions that occur between family members and the child, day in and day out, will have tremendous effect. The

A Stranger in the Home

Most families appreciate and value the support they receive in the home. However, the reception may not always be welcoming. In a parent survey, one mother wrote, "My husband resents people coming in and out of our home. He says he feels as though he is living in a goldfish bowl. He says getting help means sacrificing our privacy and spontaneity. [Another mother, concerned about appearances, wrote,] You call and tell me you're coming Tuesday morning, so I put the stack of unanswered mail and unpaid bills in the cabinet with the cereal bowls. I race dirty and clean clothes up and down the stairs, shove toys and unmatched shoes in the closet and under the beds, and run the gauntlet with [a cleaning solution] to get fingerprints off everything . . . . (Seligman & Darling, 2007)." Providing services to families in their home requires flexibility, sensitivity, and accommodation.

professional's goal is to help turn everyday activities in the home environment into rich learning experiences for the child. General principles of this approach include the following:

- Parents are the experts when it comes to their child and emphasis is placed on the parent–child relationship. The parents, not the professional, understand the child's personality, preferences, and routines.
- Parents and the professional are members of a team and they have a balanced partnership in decision making.
- Family needs and desires drive the intervention program and the professional adapts to the family's values, culture, ethnicity, socioeconomic status, and background Information.
- The professional does not bring special toys or equipment to the home for providing instruction, but rather, utilizes the child's toys and the family's resources so that learning strategies can be incorporated into everyday activities.

The emphasis is on the function of communication and on embedding learning within ongoing routine interactions. Daily life routines offer families a naturally occurring and supportive framework in which they can use specific strategies to promote their child's language and conversational abilities. By embedding conversational strategies into play and caregiving routines, they become individualized to the family. Parents learn to attend to their child's attentional lead and to stimulate conversation based on the child's focus. They learn to expect participation. Everyday events, such as getting dressed in the morning, playing with toys, or fixing dinner, become opportunities for language development. By embedding conversational strategies into play and caregiving routines, the intervention becomes individualized to the family and becomes part of their unique combination of personal and cultural values, ecological constraints, and resources.

If you are the child's clinician, a home visit during any given week might begin with you asking the parent, "What's new?" or asking a follow-up question about something that happened the week before during your session (e.g., "Is Aubrey still taken with her new coloring book? How's she doing with naming her colors?"). You might also ask about any concerns and priorities. For example, a parent might say, "Aubrey keeps pulling her hearing aid off and I'm at my wit's end about what to do."

Words with Impact

"Your words of affirmation about our children are very powerful. When we get discouraged and overwhelmed . . . getting encouraging words from a professional can be uplifting. Even if there is difficult news, starting the conversation with something positive is a gift. . . . Point out some progress, even when it might be a stretch. Your words of affirmation for parents are also very powerful. We always worry if we are doing what it takes. . . . Your affirmation can be a lifeline that gives us energy to face another week."

—A group statement prepared by parents of children with hearing loss

(Bynum et al., 2017, p. 42)

You might then focus on a particular activity or routine. For example, if you are there at a particular time of day, say lunchtime, you might participate in the meal preparation and as you do, suggest ways that a parent might promote learning and you might reinforce parental behaviors. For example, you might say, "You gave Aubrey a great model of language when you put words to her hand gestures, like when she pointed to the jar of peanut butter and you said, 'We need peanut butter to make the sandwiches.' You gave her the vocabulary for *peanut butter* and put this new vocabulary into the context of a sentence." With this remark, you have not only implicitly reinforced the facilitative language techniques of parallel talk and expansion and modeling (techniques reviewed in Table 13–4), but have also explicitly reinforced the parent's confidence. If during the interaction, the child pulls off her hearing aid, you might observe how the parent responds and comment in a way that reinforces rather than diminishes parental confidence. For example, if the parent says, "See? I just can't get Aubrey to keep the darn thing in her ear," you might observe, "She's been wearing it for the last 30 minutes, so you're doing pretty well today."

In a coaching model of intervention, parents learn to:

- Turn everyday activities such as feeding, diapering, and bathing into learning opportunities.
- Respond to their child's communicative attempts (e.g., through contingent responding, acknowledgements, facial expressions, and turn taking).
- Use the baby's own toys and their household materials as teaching tools.
- Feel confident and empowered to provide learning opportunities to their child throughout the child's waking hours.

During an interaction, you might demonstrate strategies, say, during a play activity, but this should be an inclusive activity wherein the parent is part of the activity and has an immediate opportunity to practice the strategy during the session.

The session ends with a summary of what happened and what was gained, and a discussion about what next steps should occur.

TABLE 13–4 Facilitative Language Techniques and Examples of Each One

COMMUNICATIVE TECHNIQUE	DEFINITION	EXAMPLE
Signaling expectations and time delay	Adult waits for the child's response and signals expectations by tilting the head or raising the eyebrows.	Parent: "Hmmm, you have a block. I wonder what you'll do with it." (Looks expectantly at the child)
Self-talk	Adults speak aloud what they are doing and what they are thinking, thereby illustrating that language can be used to organize, analyze, and direct actions.	Parent: "I'm unpacking the groceries. I'll take out the apples. Maybe we'll make a pie . . ."
Expansion and modeling	Adult copies the meaning of a child's utterance and adds one or more morphemes or words. When new information is included, this technique is sometimes referred to as *expatiation*.	Child: "Baby cry." Parent: "The baby is crying." Child: "Baby sad." Parent: "The baby is sad because she's hungry."
Parallel talk	Adult matches language to an activity a child is performing or an object that the child is looking at.	Parent: "You're holding a teddy. Now you're feeding the teddy. Oh, hug the bear."
Recast	Adult "recasts" a child's utterance into a question.	Child: "Daddy go." Parent: "Did Daddy go into the store?"
Comment	Adult makes a comment to keep the conversation going or to positively reinforce the child.	Parent: "Yes, that's right. Good job!"
Linguistic mapping (labeling)	Adult expresses in words or interprets the child's intended message using context as a clue.	(Child hands parent a toy car and vocalizes) Parent: "That's a car."
Interactive silence	The adult interjects a *self-controlled pause* following the adult's utterance and preceding an utterance by either the child or another by the adult that serves any of the following functions: wait-time (imposing a social obligation to respond), think-time (the child has time to formulate a response), expectancy, and impact.	Parent: "Jack and Jill went up . . ."

Adapted from Spencer (1994), DesJardin and Eisenberg (2007, p. 462), and Rhodes (2013).

Direct Therapy Model of Intervention

In the direct therapy model of intervention, the parent and child might come to an early childhood center or preschool or the professional might come to the home. The professional might work directly with the child or might involve the parent in the learning activity. At the onset, the professional has identified learning objectives and a strategy for pursuing them.

Warren Estabrooks and his colleagues present examples of lesson plans for babies through the age of 3 years. These examples represent the kinds of activities that might be included in direct therapy and how important goals such as mastering the concept of turn taking can be accomplished through simple play routines. Importantly, they involve parents. One lesson plan is reviewed in detail in this section in order to illustrate how a lesson may be implemented.

In this plan, a sample of goals, which was designed for a 6-month-old baby named Arthur who has a bilateral severe to profound hearing loss, included the following (Estabrooks et al., 2006, pp. 91–93):

- *Audition*: To detect environmental and speech sounds, as indicated when Arthur stops the activity, smiles, and widens his eyes; to recognize friendly and angry voices by responding appropriately.
- *Speech*: To experiment and explore his own vocalizations by encouraging cooing and vocal play; to produce varied suprasegmentals.
- *Language*: To listen to the narration of life provided by the caregivers; to encourage vocalization for wants and needs (to develop the vocabulary words of *round, up,* and *down*).
- *Cognition*: To imitate facial expressions; to understand cause and effect.
- *Communication*: To develop joint attention; to develop early turn-taking skills.

In this lesson plan, the clinician first addressed the goals by engaging Arthur and his mother in a game with a jack-in-the-box toy. The clinician began by turning the crank on the box toy (with its lid closed) and singing the child's song "Round and round." When the toy clown popped out of the box, the clinician said, "Oh look! It's a clown. The clown says, *ha ha ha*." Arthur was encouraged to touch the clown and to "push it down—push the clown *dowwwn*." The game was repeated, with the mother turning the crank and engaging in similar repartee. Tips for Arthur's mother, to be pursued later in the home environment, included the following (Estabrooks et al., 2006, p. 93):

- Point out wheels, tops, fans, or mobiles that turn or spin around, and say, "Round and round."
- Think about all the natural ways in which you [the parent] might incorporate the word *round* and its concept throughout the day.
- When you're going down the stairs, or when you are putting Arthur down onto a blanket, use the word *dowwwn*. Contrast "dowwwn" with "up, up, up."

This lesson plan also included activities with a toy airplane, a squeaky toy duck, a ball, a fish, a musical clock, and a toy train. With the musical clock activity, the clinician and mother indicated when the music was playing and when it was not. They provided positive feedback to Arthur when he cooed in response to the music's onset. "Do you want more?" the clinician asked. He waited for a few seconds before answering, "Yes!"

At the end of the lesson, the clinician and parent collaborated in compiling diagnostic information based on their observation of Arthur during the lesson. This information was recorded in Arthur's file and used to tailor his next intervention session. Their observations included the following (Estabrooks et al., 2006, pp. 98–99):

- *Audition*: Alerts to low- and mid-frequency [sounds] by widening eyes and smiling, and searching for toys; does not detect whispered speech.
- *Speech*: Uses a variety of vocalizations (*uh, nn*); quality of vocalizations sounds natural.
- *Language*: Engages in and enjoys vocal play; vocalizes more frequently with intent to make things happen.
- *Cognition*: Demonstrated understanding of "cause and effect" with musical clock; did not demonstrate anticipation in games or routines.
- *Communication*: Laughs, smiles, and coos while socializing; maintains appropriate eye contact.

PARENTAL SUPPORT

Regardless of whether the intervention program is more of a coaching approach or a direct coaching approach, explicit information and instruction should be provided to parents about how they can foster their child's language development and listening abilities. This can be done through both informal and formal means.

Parent instruction often includes training aimed at promoting language development and interactive communication. A professional might encourage parents to use facilitative language techniques. **Facilitative language techniques** are communication acts that facilitate language development in young children. Table 13–4 presents a list of facilitative language techniques and examples of each one. For example, in using **parallel talk**, a mother might comment or relate what a child is doing, thinking, or feeling, as when sharing a picture book: "That's an owl. The owl is snoozing. Okay, you're turning the page . . . Let's see what's on this page." Not only does this technique expand the child's language, but it also establishes joint attention, a basic element for engaging in conversation and for learning language pragmatics (Chapter 15). Studies have shown that facilitative language techniques such as parallel talk and recasting develop a child's conversational turn-taking and joint attention behaviors and increase the child's verbalizations (Cruz, Quittner, Marker, & DesJardin, 2013; Raver et al., 2012), as well as promoting later reading skills (DesJardin, Ambrose, & Eisenberg, 2009).

Facilitative language techniques stimulate language growth in young children through the course of conversational interactions.

Parallel talk is a facilitative language technique wherein the adult provides a commentary to match a child's play, describing what the child is doing and might be thinking and feeling, and does not require the child to answer direct questions.

In addition to learning facilitative language techniques, parents can be encouraged to speak with clear speech. By doing so, they will enhance their child's recognition of their speech, especially in the presence of background noise (e.g., Smiljanic & Sladen, 2013).

Informal Instruction

A clinician might teach facilitative language techniques and shape parent behavior in an informal manner. For example, a clinician might observe parent and child as they engage in a conversation during a play session in the home or clinical setting. Afterward, the clinician might say to the mother, "You seemed very attentive to Terry's focus of attention as you played with the Lego pieces. It was very effective the way you named the colors of each piece he picked up." With this remark, the clinician provides positive reinforcement and instruction about how to increase vocabulary through the use of labeling. As noted above, these kinds of remarks also serve to bolster the mother's self-confidence and sense of satisfaction about the play session.

If you are a child's clinician, when providing informal instruction, you will want to exercise tact and respect for the parent and avoid being critical or negative. The goal is to empower and enable parents to use their own talents, knowledge, and experiences to foster language growth and conversational skills; criticism or an undue display of professional expertise will only diminish well-intentioned efforts.

A parent support group is a group that provides opportunities for parents of children with hearing loss to share their feelings, difficulties, and concerns with others who have experienced them firsthand.

Parents may also learn informally from one another. For example, parents can share their experiences with other families and provide empathetic listening by means of **parent support groups**. Regular interactions with other parents may lessen the stress associated with having a child with a hearing loss. Parent support groups provide a community wherein parents can express and explore their emotions. They can talk about their anxiety, anger, or confusion with others who not only empathize with their situation but have experienced it firsthand. As one parent noted about his experience in a parent group, "just by talking in group sessions, we realized that there are common interests, common concerns, 'I'm not the only one.' In most cases you think, 'I'm the only one that's feeling this way,' and you start discussing and you're going, 'Oh, everybody is in the same boat" (Eriks-Brophy et al., 2007, p. 14). Parent groups are also a means for parents to share suggestions and solutions, say, for encouraging a child to wear a listening device or for teaching vocabulary about a particular topic, such as Halloween.

A Helping Hand to One Another

"By providing structured education in a group setting, parents of children with hearing loss gain easy access to families with similar experiences who can act as personal support. Combining these education sessions with more informal support groups may further ease tension by allowing families to connect with each other and express their emotions openly to an understanding audience."

—Brieana Hester-Keels, a fourth-year extern at UCSF Benioff Children's Hospital, Oakland CA

(Hester-Keels, 2017, p. 30)

Ways for a parent to signal expectation:

- After asking a question, wait for an answer. Cock your head and look expectantly at your child.
- Raise your eyebrows and look inquisitive.
- Shrug your shoulders, holding your palms up.
- Maintain visual contact as you wait for your child to respond.
- Lean forward and look interested.

Formal Instruction

Instruction for parents or primary caregivers might also be more structured and systematic, and might follow a similar model that was considered for communication strategies training in Chapter 8, with the stages of: (1) didactic instruction, (2) guided learning, and (3) real-world practice.

Didactic Instruction

During didactic instruction, you might begin by discussing selected language-stimulation strategies and review related examples. You might jointly "problem solve," brainstorm about intervention strategies, and discuss the pros and cons. The selection of strategies to be taught will depend on the age and language sophistication of the child and the parent's current behaviors. For example, if you observe that a mother routinely uses expansion when interacting with her child, then there is no need to provide further instruction about the technique. If the child never uses language to communicate, then there is no language upon which to expand. You might ask a parent to describe family routines and to identify one or two that happen regularly. Initially, these routines might be selected for practicing the selected strategies. Later, use of the strategies might generalize to other situations.

Instruction may begin with a parent-friendly written handout explaining particular language-stimulation and conversational strategies (e.g., Table 13–4). The strategies can be discussed and parents might be asked to explain the strategies in their own words and to provide examples of when they might use them.

You might also provide audio- or videotaped examples of other parents using the strategies in order to demonstrate how they work (e.g., Lam-Cassettari, Wadnerkar-Kamble, & James, 2015). Two film clips might be shown to a parent (or to a parent group). For example, a first video clip might show an adult who signals low expectations that her child will communicate, as in the following interchange taken from a film transcript (from Spencer, 1994):

Child: (Points toward crayons)
Mother: What are you pointing at?
Child: (Grabs a color)

Mother: You wanted the color. Here's some paper, too.

Mother: What are you drawing? It looks like a cat.

Child: (Continues drawing)

Mother: Here is the black. You can color the tail black. (p. 52)

In this clip, the mother asks questions but does not expect her child to answer them. She does not pause and allow the child to initiate a remark. By providing the paper and crayon to her child, she has eliminated the need for him to ask for them. A second film clip demonstrates how a mother can signal higher expectations for communication, and thereby elicit more language from her child (Spencer, 1994):

Child: (Points toward crayons)

Mother: What? (looks around expectantly)

Child: Ka.

Mother: Color?

Child: Cala.

Mother: Color. Green or black? (waits)

Child: Bak.

Mother: (Gives the child the black crayon . . . waits)

Child: Papa.

Mother: Paper—here's a big piece. (Holds paper up)

Child: Mine.

Mother: Draw me a picture. (pp. 52–53)

After viewing this second clip, the parent and her clinician can talk about how the mother frequently paused and allowed time for her child to talk. She used facial expressions that signal expectation for more information and established a turn-taking pattern. Actually seeing meaningful, concrete examples of strategies in action demonstrates their potency. A clinician can say that a technique works, but observing someone not use a strategy and then comparing the outcome to when someone uses a strategy affords an explicit contrast. In the event that no film clips are available, you can review printed transcripts like the ones presented here.

The clinician might then model the target strategy(ies) with the child, and when possible, do so in a simulation of a family routine or even in the home environment. The parent can observe the clinician and child and then the two of them might discuss the effectiveness of a strategy after the demonstration.

Guided Practice

The parent might then practice the strategy with the child, using the same routine that the clinician engaged in. This is a prime time to use coaching rather than direct therapy. After practicing, the parent and clinician might identify other situations in which the practiced strategy might be implemented or useful. They might complete workbook activities like the one presented in Table 13–5. If groups of parents are involved, parents might share ideas about how they interest their children in using language in the home environment.

Real-World Practice

Parents might tape-record or videotape themselves while playing with their child at home and then review the tapes, checking to see whether they have implemented

Explaining the Language Gap

"I started implanting kiddos and noticed profound outcome differences on children post-implantation that looked like they should have been comparable. Some children would be talking and learning on par with their hearing peers while others would have much more difficulty communicating. . . . I started to educate myself about childhood development and learned that one of the critical factors is early language exposure from birth to age three in his or her environment. A cochlear implant can bring sounds to a child's brain, but there really is more needed for language development. And the role of the parent is really vital to the child and child's brain development."

—Dana Suskind, MD, cochlear implant surgeon and founder-director of Thirty Million Words, speaking on the importance of early intervention

(Carrol, 2018, p. 30)

Navigating the Social Scene

"Some of the daily ways we are able to help Cordelia navigate through life is to aid her in social situations by preparing her ahead of time and checking in with her during the activities to make sure she is able to fill in any gaps in the information. We don't assume she knows what's going on, often because she doesn't overhear, catch some of the social cues, or pay attention. Pre-loading information and language for what she should expect has helped Cordelia get the most out of the moment."

—Nicole Iwawaki, mother of a young cochlear implant user

(Iwawaki & Iwawaki, 2012, p. 37)

TABLE 13–5 Workbook Exercise That a Parent Might Complete to Practice Expansion

On the lines below are some typical utterances a child might say during dinnertime. The meal consists of hamburgers and french fries. Beside each utterance, write ways that you might expand on what the child has said by modeling good grammar or adding a little more information.

CHILD'S UTTERANCE	YOUR EXPANDED MODEL
1. "More."	
2. "Give me."	
3. "Cup fall."	
4. "Down chair."	

Possible expatiations: (a) "I want more french fries, please"; (b) "Give me the ketchup, please"; (c) "The cup fell over"; (d) "You want to get down from your chair."

language-expansion and conversation-stimulating techniques. This practice will help them be more mindful of their efforts as well as provide an opportunity to appreciate the success of their efforts.

Real-world practice might be monitored by asking parents to keep a journal about their communication interactions with their child on a daily basis for a week or two. They might also complete daily checklists, indicating whether they consciously performed any of the techniques that day.

Example

The *Learn to Talk Around the Clock* (Rossi, 2003) program capitalizes on this model. The program was developed for children aged birth to 3 years, and promotes listening and spoken language skills. Activities are designed to be implemented in a child's daily home routine "around the clock," during such regular occurrences as getting dressed, bath time, meal time, and outdoor time.

In a *playtime* activity (Rossi, 2003, the *Playtime, Level 1* handout), a kind of formal or didactic instruction occurs in which the parent and professional meet and talk about strategies and techniques that promote face-to-face, eye-to-eye communication. Together they view examples of face-to-face interaction by watching a video included in the program materials. They review a printed parent handout that includes tactics such as, "If your child is playing on the floor, you need to be playing on the floor, too, or bring your child up to your eye level."

During guided learning, the professional creates an opportunity for the parent and child to play and interact with the child's favorite toys, and provides coaching. For example, the professional might say, "This is a good play area for today [within the home]. Where would you like Johnny to be? On the blanket? Where do you think you should be so you can interact with Johnny? Why don't you lie down on the floor in front of Johnny? Then you can be face-to-face and roll the ball back and forth. Look at that! Johnny looked right at you before you rolled the ball." The professional does not take toys to the child's home but rather uses the toys and other apparatus that the family owns so that the parents can capitalize on the child's natural environment and learn to use their available resources to promote language and listening skills.

After the parent has had an opportunity to gain real-world practice using some of the techniques learned during formal instruction and guided learning, the professional may ask during a next follow-up visit, "How has playtime gone this week? Do you think your interactions with Johnny have gotten better? What have you done that seemed to help the most? I'd love to have you show me." The program includes eight levels for each of the designated daily home routines, so parent and child can graduate from one level to the next. In this example, the second level for *playtime* entails having the parent interpret the child's needs and wants by attending to the child's signals during play activities.

AUDITORY TRAINING FOR INFANTS AND TODDLERS

Young children who have prelingual profound losses may have no memory of how speech sounds, and thus they cannot draw on memories of how speech should sound. During auditory training, these children first must learn to attend to the auditory speech signal. Eventually they must learn to relate the auditory signal to their vocabulary. For children who receive a cochlear implant or a hearing aid early in life, the goal is to accelerate auditory learning and to raise the level at which speech recognition skills plateau.

Children who have more hearing may better deduce meaning from the degraded speech signal, at least initially. The presence of more residual hearing, especially for the mid-frequencies and high frequencies, portends good progress in skill development. These children will probably begin with more difficult tasks than children who have prelingual, profound hearing losses.

Tailoring Auditory Training for the Very Young Child

In Chapter 4, auditory training and the principles underlying many approaches that are taken in providing it were reviewed. When working with very young children who have very little language and only rudimentary listening skills, auditory training tends to be more hierarchical, developing the following set of listening skills that were mentioned in Chapter 4 (Figure 13–7):

- Sound awareness
- Sound discrimination
- Identification
- Comprehension

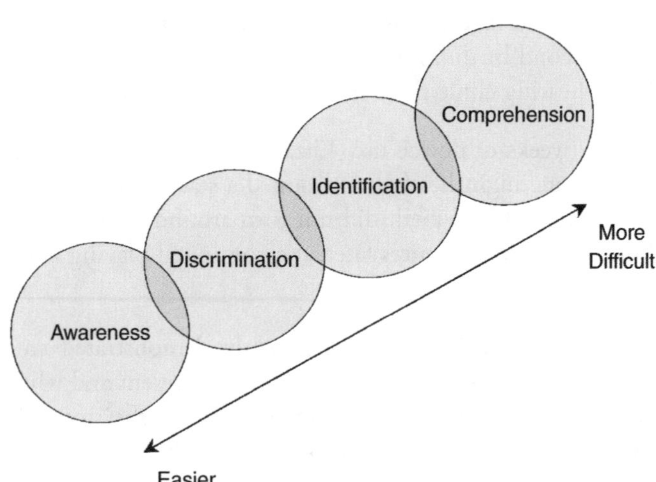

FIGURE 13–7 Four levels of auditory skill development. Auditory skill levels do not represent discrete benchmarks.

As Figure 13–7 indicates, these levels are not discrete benchmarks in auditory development but, rather, represent a continuum of skills. A child might perform some activities associated with a sound discrimination level and some activities associated with identification at about the same time and sometimes will lose ground and have to revisit an earlier stage of skill level. In this section, the four stages are considered by means of a case study. Table 13–6 presents auditory training activities that may be appropriate for each stage.

TABLE 13–6 Auditory Training Activities Appropriate for Each Stage of Auditory Skill Development

AUDITORY SKILL	ACTIVITY
Sound awareness	Play *peek-a-boo*. Play musical chairs. March to the beat of a drum. Push the toy care whenever the clinician says "Vrrrrm."
Sound discrimination	Play a game with toy animals ("The cow says 'moo'; the sheep says 'baaa'"). Respond to commands ("Clap your hands"; "Jump!"). Play a *Same* or *Different* game ("car car"; "car star") using pairs of picture cards where the child has to point to the correct illustration. Repeat what you hear ("Mamma," "Papa").
Identification	Play the game *Candy Land* and listen for the names of the colors. Play with sets of postcards or stickers ("Show me the cat"). Play *Go Fish* with cards ("Give me your sevens"; "Give me your twos").
Comprehension	Listen to a read-aloud story and then answer questions about the plot and characters. Play *I Spy* ("I spy a red sweater"; "I spy some blue jeans"). Play *20 Questions* ("Is it bigger than a chair?"; "Is it alive?").

The four stages of development can be illustrated by way of example: Elizabeth Jenkins was diagnosed with a profound, bilateral hearing loss at the age of 13 months. She received bilateral hearing aids within a month following diagnosis. After five months of using the hearing aids, her audiologist determined that she was not receiving benefit. Shortly before her second birthday, she received a cochlear implant. Her parents took her to a speech and hearing clinic three times a week to receive auditory training.

During the first few weeks of device use, Elizabeth did not respond spontaneously to sound. For example, one night her father dropped a stack of plastic dinner plates near the room where she played. Elizabeth did not turn around to see what had happened. When a telephone rang a few minutes later, she continued playing without an upward glance.

Sound awareness is the most basic auditory skill level, and is an awareness of when a sound is present and when it is not.

Several weeks elapsed before Elizabeth consistently demonstrated **sound awareness** (Figure 13–8), wherein she was aware when sound was present and when it was absent. She searched for sound with eye and head movements or she stopped her activity in response to sound. Sometimes she quieted or startled. She also increased her own vocalizing behaviors. The spontaneous response to sound began to occur once Elizabeth realized that sound has meaning, and that action often produces sound. Her mother promoted sound awareness by playing games of peek-a-boo.

FIGURE 13–8 Sound awareness. Babies must often be explicitly taught that sound has meaning and that action produces sound.

Elizabeth entered the next auditory skill level, **sound discrimination**, during the latter part of her first year of cochlear implant use. Elizabeth now could recognize when two sounds were the same and when two sounds differed, although sometimes she did not associate meaning with the two sounds or name them. For example, she could indicate that an "Eeeeeeeeeeeeee" spoken by her teacher was different from an "Eh." She could distinguish the two-syllable reference to her mother, "Mama," from the single-syllable reference to her father, "Dad." This latter ability is known as **pattern perception**.

Sound discrimination is a basic auditory skill level in which the listener is able to tell whether two sounds are different or the same.

Pattern perception is a kind of discrimination that requires a listener to distinguish between words or phrases that differ in the number of syllables.

After about 10 months of cochlear implant use, Elizabeth entered into the **identification** level of auditory skills development and began to label some auditory stimuli. If her mother asked for a blue crayon, she could pick the blue crayon from a box of four other crayons. This skill relates to awareness that objects have names, and names have auditory representations. She became aware of suprasegmental nuances in speech, such as changes in her mother's speaking rate, intensity, pitch, and stress. For example, she could recognize the difference between her mother saying "Elizabeth?" and "Elizabeth!" She could recognize one or two key words in context.

Identification is a basic auditory skill level in which the listener is able to label some auditory stimuli.

Almost a year and a half elapsed before Elizabeth began to demonstrate some of the listening behaviors associated with the **comprehension** level of auditory skill development, in which she understood the meaning of spoken messages. This stage requires not only advanced auditory skills but some vocabulary and grammar as well. At this time, Elizabeth's mother could ask a question with her face not visible and expect that Elizabeth might answer it appropriately, especially if the question was supported by linguistic and environmental context. Elizabeth could follow simple directions such as, "Clap your hands," and could recognize familiar expressions such as, "It's all gone." Later, her skills would develop to such an extent that she could understand a series of directions and understand connected narratives.

Comprehension is a higher auditory skill level in which the listener is able to understand the meaning of spoken messages.

Children with significant residual hearing or who receive great benefit from an implant or hearing aid may not progress through these four stages of auditory skill development in the same way Elizabeth did. For example, a child who has some residual hearing, or who has incurred a hearing loss gradually over time, will demonstrate more advanced listening skills.

During the awareness phase of auditory learning, a parent might make a point of showing a child the source and meaning of a sound, and reinforce the child when he or she responds to it. For example, a parent might say:

- "I hear a loud noise. [Points upward.] Look, it's a helicopter."
- "I'm turning on the water. [Turns the handle on a water faucet.] Listen. Now you try it."
- "I hear Janie. She must be coming. Listen."

Activities for sound awareness might include asking a child to drop blocks into a container or onto a wooden peg at the onset of a sound stimulus. With each block drop, a clinician might provide animated feedback. A child should be able to recognize when sound is *not* present, or the absence of sound, as this is an essential skill for participating in a hearing test or the programming of a listening device such as a cochlear implant. This means that the child can shake his or her head, knowing that this is an acceptable response.

Once sound awareness has been established, early training activities may involve gross discrimination of loudness, pitch, and rate, as in the following examples performed with a xylophone:

- Loudness: Strike a xylophone softly and ask the child whether the sound is "soft" or "loud."
- Pitch: Play a rising octave and ask whether the sound is going "up" or going "down."
- Rate: Strike a rapid series of notes and ask whether the pattern is "slow" or "fast."

The Suitcase Game

"One of [my son's] favorite activities as a toddler was my suitcase game. I bought a small, old leather suitcase, and filled it with small action figures and wooden animals. . . . Every toy had a sound associated with it. I would line up three or four toys on the table and cover my mouth for him to find the right one to match the sound. It was organized but inherently spontaneous. I followed his lead and made it entertaining. We would swap out the toys each week to make it fun, and the lessons got more challenging as he got better at listening."

—Mother of a child who received a cochlear implant describing an identification task

(Logan, 2013, p. 43)

What's That?

"In the beginning, normal household sounds left [William] feeling very unsettled. The refrigerator running, the back door opening, a car driving by outside, the furnace turning on. These and other sounds would all cause him to ask, 'What's that?' with a worried look on his face. Time and time again we would feel the fridge and talk about why it was running or open the closet that houses the furnace to check it out. Eventually he stopped asking and began to know what these sounds were."

—Amanda Windom, mother of a boy who received a cochlear implant at the age of 2 years and was reluctant to wear it at first

(Windom, 2012, p. 37)

Activities for the discrimination level of auditory skills then gradually can become more advanced. For example, a clinician might ask a child to discriminate between syllables that are short and long (e.g., "The car goes *beep* and the cow says *moooooooo*"), soft and loud (e.g., "The drum beat is *loud* and the drum tap is *soft*"), or continuous and interrupted (e.g., "The whistle goes *eeeeee* and the drum goes *boom-de-boom-de-boom*"). Then the child might discriminate between stimuli that vary in syllable length (e.g., "The dog says *woof* and the cat says *mee-ooow*").

FIGURE 13–9 An example of an activity that promotes identification listening skills. While playing the game *Candy Land*, the child might have to listen for the name of a color and then move a game piece to a game board space that corresponds with that color.

In an identification task, older toddlers might play board games like *Candy Land*, where a clinician might speak which color the child is to move the game piece to on the game board, with your mouth covered by a screen (Figure 13–9). Another activity would be to ask the child to identify a sentence illustration from a set of four dissimilar pictures and then, after practice, from a set of four similar pictures.

In a comprehension task, a clinician might read a story to a child and then ask questions. Coloring books can also provide practice in comprehension; e.g., "Color the cowboy hat next."

Example Programs

In early childhood programs, the instructional materials are often written directly for parents and caretakers because they can play an important role in providing listening practice. They can be encouraged to minimize background noise in the home, to speak on occasion close to the child's listening device with their mouths out of view, to adopt a clear speech speaking style that incorporates **acoustic highlighting** and **auditory spacing**, and sometimes to use language and speech that is repetitive, melodic, expressive, and rhythmic (e.g., "Lilly, Lilly, you're so silly"). They might draw attention to environmental sounds (e.g., "I hear the telephone ringing") and engage the child in singing and light conversation. **Informal training** is meant to be incorporated into everyday routines and conducted simultaneously with language enrichment activities in a fun and playful manner, as in this kitchen sound awareness activity:

Acoustic highlighting occurs when a talker changes duration, intensity, and pitch to highlight a word or to enhance the audibility of a message.

A talker uses **auditory spacing** to chunk information into meaningful phrase units, pausing between each.

Informal training activities occur during the daily routine and are often incorporated into other activities, such as conversation or mealtime.

> Imitate the sounds you hear in the kitchen. Turn on the water. Hear it run. Say, 'I hear that,' and point to your ear. This is something your child will learn as time goes on. He may use it to point out sounds he hears and this gives you the chance to talk about the sound and what it means. Turn off the water and imitate it [make a silent sound with forefinger over pursed lips], 'SHHHHHHH.' For cutting say, 'cut, cut, cut'; for washing vegetables say, 'washh, washhh'; for stirring or wiping sing, 'roundandroundandroundandround.'
>
> (Sindrey, 1997)

The *Learn to Talk Around the Clock* program (Rossi, 2003) is pitched to the clinician who works with parents. It includes materials to help parents achieve eight hierarchical objectives as they help their young children learn to "listen around the clock" through daily activities such as *getting dressed, bath time, little helper time*, and *bed time*. Initially, objectives focus on listening device use, then on sound awareness and the notion that sound conveys meaning, and later on, speech identification and comprehension (Rossi, 2003, compiled from the program's training cards):

1. "Parent will demonstrate a working knowledge of hearing loss and the importance of amplification.
2. Parent will establish hearing aid/cochlear implant use all waking hours, ideally within 6 weeks of fitting.
3. Parent will maintain hearing aid/implant in good working condition and be proactive in hearing aid/[cochlear implant] maintenance.
4. Parent will minimize auditory distractions and provide the best listening environment possible throughout the day.
5. Parent will provide pleasurable and meaningful experiences with sound.
6. Parent will call the child's attention to naturally occurring environmental and voice sounds and talk about them.
7. Parent will know which sounds the child is aware of, and those the child discriminates from other sounds.
8. Parent will associate sounds with meaningful language and concepts."

For example, in achieving the penultimate objective, a parent might say, "Did you hear that noise? I hear the buzzing of the clothes dryer. The clothes must be dry."

This kind of auditory training is informal and is especially appropriate for infants and toddlers. By attending to language spoken in meaningful contexts, they will develop speech and language as well as listening skills. Listening and attending to speech becomes part of their self-identity and modus operandi.

Formal training presents highly structured activities that may involve drill; it usually is scheduled to occur during a designated time of day, either in a one-on-one lesson format or in a small group.

Once the child begins pre-school, more **formal training** may be appropriate. A number of auditory training curricula utilize computerized training (e.g., Fu & Galvin, 2007; Sensimetrics, 2006), and the three major cochlear implant companies (Cochlear Corporation, Med-El, and Advanced Bionics) have web-based programs available.

An example of a more formal training program appears in Table 13–7 and guidelines for providing formal auditory training appear in Table 13–8.

A **reinforcement** is something desirable provided to a child after he or she performs a training activity or performs in a desired manner.

In following a formal lesson plan, a clinician typically will want to provide **reinforcements** to encourage children to participate. After children complete a set number of items or perform so many activities, they receive something desirable, such as a sticker or special privilege. The following are general principles to follow when choosing and providing reinforcements:

- The child should be able to perform a reinforcement activity quickly; he or she should not spend more time with the reinforcement activity than with the training activity.
- Reinforcement activities should not be too challenging or too absorbing; otherwise the child will not attend closely to the training task.
- Activities should be varied; drawing lines on a paper may hold a child's interest for a few minutes, but the activity quickly wears thin.

TABLE 13–7 An Example Lesson Plan for a Formal Auditory Training Session

Title:

Snake and Ice Cream Game

Goal:

Discrimination

Objective:

The student will discriminate a nasal consonant versus non-nasal unvoiced consonant that differs in place of production.

Materials:

1. a picture of a snake to represent the /s/ sound
2. a picture of a boy about to eat an ice cream sundae to represent the /m/ sound
3. a stack of 26 pennies for reinforcements

Procedures:

1. Introduce the picture of the snake by pointing to it and saying "sssssssss . . ." Ask the child to imitate your production. Similarly, introduce the picture of the sundae, and say "mmmmmm . . ." Ask the child to imitate your production.
2. Say each sound with your face visible. After each utterance, ask the child to point to the corresponding picture.
3. Place 13 pennies on each picture. Cover your mouth. Randomly say one sound after another. After each production, the child may pick up a penny from one of the two pictures. If the child removes a penny from the correct picture, he or she can keep it. If incorrect, the penny must be placed back on the picture.
4. Continue until all pennies are spent.

TABLE 13–8 Guidelines for Conducting Formal Auditory Training

1. Training stimuli should become more challenging over time.
2. If feasible, a variety of talkers should speak training items, perhaps by way of computerized training programs or iPads, so that children will learn that the same sounds or words can be acoustically different when repeated or when spoken by different talkers.
3. A great many training items should be presented during a relatively short period of time because concentrated training focuses students' attention on listening and maintains their interest, leading to fast learning.
4. Training typically progresses from closed-set to open-set response modes; for example, early in training a child might be asked to color a shape red and therefore needs to choose between a red or blue crayon (closed set), and then later, the child might be asked to select the red crayon, when crayons from an entire box are available as options (open set).
5. Ten to 15 minutes a day should be devoted to formal auditory training, preferably at the same time every day so it becomes part of the daily routine.
6. Formal training objectives should be pursued informally throughout the day; for example, when opportunity arises during conversation, the child can be presented with listening tasks that reinforce the formal auditory training objectives.
7. Training activities must be engaging and interesting; otherwise, the child may simply pass through the motions of training without receiving benefit or the child may not cooperate.

- Activities should interest the child; for example, if the child enjoys playing with money, he or she might drop coins into a bank.
- Often, it is desirable that the child perform the reinforcement activity immediately after responding to a training item correctly.

Activities should be appropriate for the child's age and gender.

Reinforcements for toddlers and young children include the following:

- Collecting stickers in a sticker book
- Putting features onto a Mr. Potato Head
- Placing puzzle pieces one at a time into a puzzle board
- Blowing soap bubbles
- Stringing beads onto a bead necklace

CASE STUDY

A Mother's Karma

The fates must have known that one day Nicole Iwawaki would give birth to a baby with hearing loss. Iwawaki enrolled in a community ASL class in her early 20s because she was intrigued by the father of a friend who was deaf. He and his daughter communicated via ASL. Iwawaki advanced through several levels of ASL training, gaining enough proficiency to consider becoming a sign language interpreter. However, pregnancy sidetracked her plans, and she gave birth to her first child, Judah. She signed with Judah during his first year, even though he had normal hearing, because she knew that doing so could promote early language learning.

Little Cordelia entered the world about 18 months after her big brother. Cordelia's story illustrates the importance of UNHS, parental reactions to identification, the cochlear implant process, initiation of an early-intervention program, and the strains and stresses stemming from parental involvement. Her story also shows how hurdles and joys crop up along the journey, touches on the issue of Deaf culture, and shows how parents can revisit their decision about communication mode as circumstances change (Iwawaki & Iwawaki, 2012, pp. 36–37).

Cordelia received a hearing screening as a final step before being discharged from the newborn nursery. She failed it. Several weeks later, her parents brought her to the hospital for a second screening. She failed again. At 3 months of age, an audiologist confirmed she had a bilateral profound hearing loss.

"We were devastated," Iwawaki writes, "but not defeated. After weighing the options and researching for hours, we had Cordelia fitted with tiny hearing aids as soon as we could. The aids did not seem to help. We educated ourselves about cochlear implants, becoming experts, so to speak. We attended an AG Bell Convention and went to local seminars and programs about the deaf and hard of hearing."

Iwawaki and her husband opted for a cochlear implant, and Cordelia underwent cochlear implant surgery at the age of 10 months. She heard for the first time at the age of 11 months.

"That is when the real work began. Since we already had a basis of sign language communication, we adopted Signed Exact English [SEE]. In her early years, we simultaneously spoke and signed to her. Cordelia was enrolled in the early education program in our local school district. We had multiple home visits a week with speech-language pathologists and teachers of the deaf as well as audiology appointments. It definitely was tiring running around with two children from appointment to appointment."

Iwawaki and her husband educated extended family members and provided a language-rich environment. They read books to her daily and drew strength from their religious beliefs.

"After she received her implant, Cordelia took to listening and spoken language right away. She enjoyed music, babbling to herself and made great strides in her toddler class. We believe that the fact we used sign language before she could hear meant she was able to use the basic language she already had and put the sign to the word she heard, thus accelerating her speech and language acquisition."

A major hurdle materialized just before Cordelia's third birthday: the internal components of the cochlear implant failed.

"When she could not hear and we signed to her that it was broken, she fell in sadness to the floor. That week she stopped signing with us. She only wanted to hear."

Cordelia underwent surgery for a replacement as soon as possible. She went 21 days without hearing and her mother believes that as a result, she "lost 6–8 months of spoken language ability acquired through therapy."

Following reimplantation, Iwawaki and her husband decided to enroll her in an aural/oral school 60 miles from their home in San Francisco.

"Three times a week I piled the kids in the car and made the trek across the San Francisco Bay (a 1- to 2-hour drive). Cordelia thrived there and Judah joined the school as a language model. That year, in spite of the trek, was a year of great growth in speech, language, and confidence."

And where is Cordelia today?

(continues)

CASE STUDY *(continued)*

A Mother's Karma

"As the years passed, her language grew. What had seemed to be so foreign and unusual—learning about Deaf culture, speech bananas, and [IFSP]—had now become normal. The joy of watching her blossom and become her own person with all her strengths and accomplishments reminded us again that she is just like all the other 8-year-old girls; she just happens to be genetically deaf. It's in her genes and we can't change them."

Iwawaki and her husband want Cordelia to be proud of who she is: "We try to instill in Cordelia that she is her own person. We show her amazing examples of others overcoming difficulties, such as Bethany Hamilton, Temple Grandin, and Helen Keller, among other heroes, artists, and athletes. . . . Our journey into deafness has taught us to be more compassionate, to champion those with struggles and to embrace what has become our 'normal.' . . . Cordelia is our family's perfect gift."

FINAL REMARKS

In this chapter, the focus has primarily been on children who have severe and profound hearing losses. Children with lesser degrees of hearing loss also may experience listening difficulties. For example, a child with a mild, high-frequency hearing loss may appear to have no problem in recognizing speech or responding to environmental sounds. However, the child may not be performing optimally in everyday listening settings, because he or she may have degraded listening performance in the presence of background noise. A child with a mild-to-moderate hearing loss may have decreased speech recognition and may be delayed in both speech and language development if appropriate amplification is not provided.

Children who have a lesser degree of hearing loss represent a fairly significant segment of children in the United States. Ross (1990) suggested that 16 of every 1,000 school-age children have pure-tone averages between 26 and 70 dB HL. These children may need special accommodations in the classroom, as discussed at the end of the next chapter, and may benefit from the use of special assistive listening devices, such as FM trainers. In the next chapter, we will consider these children in more detail.

KEY CHAPTER POINTS

- Public Law 94-142, passed in 1975, was a landmark event in the history of children who have disabilities. It guaranteed a free and appropriate education for all children between the ages of 3 and 18 years, in the least restrictive environment. Many countries have similar legislation.
- The acronym IDEA stands for the Individuals with Disabilities Education Act, which was passed by Congress in 1990. Stemming from Public Law 94-142, it expanded the range of children covered to individuals from birth to the age of 21. It was amended in 1997 and again in 2004.
- Early and appropriate amplification is critical for normal speech and language development. Children often receive behind-the-ear hearing aids. In-the-ear aids usually are not prescribed, for a variety of reasons, including the fact that children's ears may still be growing, so aids must be frequently recast.
- Cochlear implants may be received after an appropriate hearing aid trial.
- Guidelines for early-intervention programs emphasize the importance of family involvement and the need for professionals who have expertise in hearing loss and early childhood development.

- Goals of the early-intervention program are to support families in developing a child's communication skills, to help the family understand the child's strengths and needs, and to promote the family's ability to advocate for the child.
- In a coaching model of intervention, the professional visits the home with the goal of helping the family to capitalize on everyday events in order to promote the child's language and listening abilities.
- In a direct therapy model of intervention, a professional works directly with the child, often involving the parent during a therapy activity.
- During informal instruction, parents and caregivers learn to incorporate language, speech, and listening experiences into their child's everyday routines.
- Regular interactions with other parents may lessen the stress associated with having a child with a hearing loss and provide a community wherein parents can express and explore their emotions.
- During formal instruction, parents and caregivers learn conversational techniques through didactic instruction, guided practice, and real-world practice.
- Many auditory training curricula for very young children are designed to progress a child from one auditory skill level to the next. The four skill levels underlying most auditory training programs are sound awareness, sound discrimination, identification, and comprehension.

TERMS AND CONCEPTS TO REMEMBER

Goals of early intervention
Individuals with Disabilities Education Act (IDEA)
Individualized Family Service Plan (IFSP)
Service coordinator
Medical home
American Sign Language (ASL)
Bilingual/bicultural model
Total communication
Auditory-verbal approach
Validation of hearing aid fitting
Cochlear implant fitting
Family support
Sound awareness

Appendix 13–1

Some of the acronyms used when talking about children and their educational needs include the following:

- FAPE: Free appropriate public education
- IDEA: Individuals with Disabilities Education Act
- IEP: Individualized Education Plan
- IFSP: Individualized Family Service Plan
- IAT: Intervention assistance team, a multidisciplinary group of professionals who work together to provide intervention for a child

- LRE: Least restrictive environment
- SST: Supplemental services teacher, who interacts with a child's regular teacher to help the child

Appendix 13–2

Family Support Services (adapted from the Centers for Disease Control and Prevention [CDC], 2010; Florida Department of Health, 2011)

Agencies:

1. The Alexander Graham Bell Association for the Deaf and Hard of Hearing (www.agbell.org) helps families understand childhood hearing loss and the importance of early diagnosis and intervention. Through advocacy, education, research, and financial aid, the society ensures that children with hearing loss have the opportunity to listen and talk. There are chapters throughout the United States and a network of international affiliates.
2. American Society for Deaf Children (ASDC; www.deafchildren.org) is an organization of parents and families that advocates for children's total quality participation in education, the family, and the community.
3. Babyhearing (www.babyhearing.org), created by Boys Town National Research Hospital, has centers for research and clinical services for hearing loss in children. Parents are invited to ask questions about infant hearing screening and follow-up testing, steps to take following diagnosis, hearing aids, language and speech, and parenting issues.
4. Center for Education Research Partnerships (CERP) (http://www .rit.edu/ntid /cerp/), a part of the National Technical Institute for the Deaf, conducts research and works with schools and organizations on projects that concern children with hearing loss. The organization hosts conferences and workshops, provides information to families, and helps evaluate programs and services for children both nationally and internationally.
5. Family Voices (www.familyvoices.org) is a national organization that is a clearinghouse for information and education concerning the health care of children with special needs.
6. Hands & Voices National (www.handsandvoices.org) is a parent-driven, nonprofit organization supporting families with children who have hearing loss, regardless of communication method or mode. Membership includes families, professionals, and individuals who are deaf or hard of hearing who collaborate to empower families with newly identified babies with hearing loss, to advocate for better educational outcomes, and to provide information and technical support on related subjects without a bias toward one form of communication over another.
7. John Tracy Clinic (www.jtc.org) is a nonprofit organization that provides, worldwide and without charge, parent-centered services to young children with hearing loss. Services include audiological testing, parent/infant programs, parent classes, a preschool, and a correspondence course.
8. Laurent Clerc National Deaf Education Center (http://www.gallaudet.edu/clerc _center.html), part of Gallaudet University, provides information on various topics related to deafness.

9. Marion Downs National Center for Infant Hearing (http://www.mariondowns.com/) provides information on newborn hearing screening, assessment, diagnosis, and early intervention.

10. National Association of the Deaf (NAD; www.nad.org) is the oldest and largest organization representing people with disabilities in the United States. It provides information about grassroots advocacy and empowerment, captioned media, legal assistance, policy development and research, public awareness, and youth leadership.

11. National Cued Speech Association (www.cuedspeech.org) promotes and supports the use of Cued Speech for communication, education, language acquisition, and literacy.

12. National Policy Center for Children With Special Health Care Needs is concerned with the promotion of complete, family-centered systems of health care for children with special needs. The Center is dedicated to producing information that is relevant to benefit managed care organizations, state agencies, families, and program administrators.

13. The SKI-HI Institute (www.skihi.org) is devoted to providing information for assisting infants, toddlers, and young children and their families through research, development, promising practices, training, technical assistance, and information sharing.

Additional Websites

1. Animated American Sign Language Dictionary, www.bconnex.net. Provides animated demonstrations of signs and fingerspelling.
2. Centers for Disease Control and Prevention, http://www.cdc.gov/ncbddd/hearingloss/ehdi-programs.html. Provides information about hearing detection and intervention.
3. Children's Medical Services, www.cms-kids.org. Provides children with special health care needs a family-centered, managed system of care.
4. National Center for Hearing Assessment and Management, www.infanthearing.org. Assists families with managing hearing loss.
5. Oral Deaf Education/Oberkotter Foundation, www.oraldeafed.org. Provides support to parents of children with hearing loss.
6. Sign with Your Baby, www.sign2me.net. Promotes benefits of teaching sign language to babies.
7. ASHA, www.asha.org/slp/clinical/EarlyIntervention. Provides resources for **speech-language pathologists** concerning practice documents, references, brochures, products, and networking opportunities.
8. ASHA, www.asha.org. Provides resources for audiologists concerning practice documents, references, brochures, products, and networking opportunities.

CHAPTER 14

School-Age Children

OUTLINE

- The Transition from Early Intervention Servies to Elementary School
- The Beginnings of Education for Children Who Are Deaf and Hard of Hearing in the New World
- Creation of an Individual(ized) Education Plan (IEP)
- The Multidisciplinary Team
- School and Classroom Placement
- Amplification and Assistive Listening Devices
- Classroom Acoustics
- Other Services
- Children Who Have Mild or Moderate Hearing Loss or Unilateral Hearing Loss
- Case Study: IDEA(s) for All Children
- Final Remarks
- Key Chapter Points
- Terms and Concepts to Remember
- Key Resources
- Appendix 14–1

At about the age of 3 or 4 years, a child who has hearing loss is ready to enroll in preschool. The next decade and a half of formal education will present rewarding and challenging years, as the child continues to develop communication skills, learns to read, studies academics, and socializes with classmates.

In this chapter, we will consider children who are of school age and the aural rehabilitation services that will enhance and promote their educational experiences, and the process of designing an aural rehabilitation plan. The bulk of the chapter concerns children who have bilateral severe and profound hearing losses. At the end of the chapter, we will consider children who have mild and moderate hearing loss and children who have unilateral hearing loss, who are of school age.

THE TRANSITION FROM EARLY INTERVENTION SERVICES TO ELEMENTARY SCHOOL

Factors that facilitate a child's transition from an early intervention program to a classroom:

- Interagency communication; e.g., the professional from the early-intervention program meets with the child's prospective teacher.
- The school personnel observe the child, either at home or in the preschool.
- The child and parent tour the school and meet the school community.
- The school provides printed information and workshops to parents about academic expectations and parent advocacy.

(Curle, Jamieson, Buchanan, Poon, Zaidman-Zait, & Norman, 2016)

Figure 14–1 presents a schematic of a child entering the school system. At the point of entry, the child likely is using a listening device and has begun to use a communication mode, such as spoken language or total communication. The child might have been identified as having other disabilities in addition to hearing loss (e.g., vision difficulties). Changes in either listening device or communication mode may occur once the child enters into a preschool or kindergarten, depending on how well he or she is progressing. The child may have received early intervention services, such as center-based or home-based aural rehabilitation, which will have equipped him or her with school-readiness skills. Examples of school-readiness skills are being able to sit quietly at a table or desk and being able to change in an orderly fashion from one structured activity to the next.

The formation of a multidisciplinary team, the creation of an Individualized Education Plan, and the selection of school and classroom placement are illustrated as sections of a pie chart because these events do not necessarily happen sequentially. Sometimes they happen almost simultaneously and sometimes the determination of one, say selection of a school, will have an impact on the determination of another, say the selection of members for the multidisciplinary team. From this triad, the child enters into a school setting. An aural rehabilitation intervention strategy will ensure that the child's listening device is maintained and that the child receives appropriate assistive devices. Special steps will be taken to promote development of speech, language, and literacy skills and to facilitate social adjustment.

THE BEGINNINGS OF EDUCATION FOR CHILDREN WHO ARE DEAF AND HARD OF HEARING IN THE NEW WORLD

The beginnings of education for children who are deaf and hard of hearing in the New World follow two threads, manual communication and aural/oral communication (or oralism). Although there were sporadic attempts to educate children with significant hearing loss in the United States before Alice Cogswell, many historians date the dawn of deaf education in this country to her birth in 1805. Alice was born into a well-to-do family in New England. At the age of 2 years, she contracted "spotted fever" and lost her hearing. Treatments of salt water poured into her ears, leeches, and special creams could not return what was lost. An ear trumpet bought by her distraught parents allowed her to hear a church bell, but not much more.

Alice's father, Dr. Mason Fitch Cogswell, a physician who performed some of the first cataract surgeries in the United States, commissioned his young neighbor, Thomas Hopkins Gallaudet, to travel to Europe and learn instructional methods for children

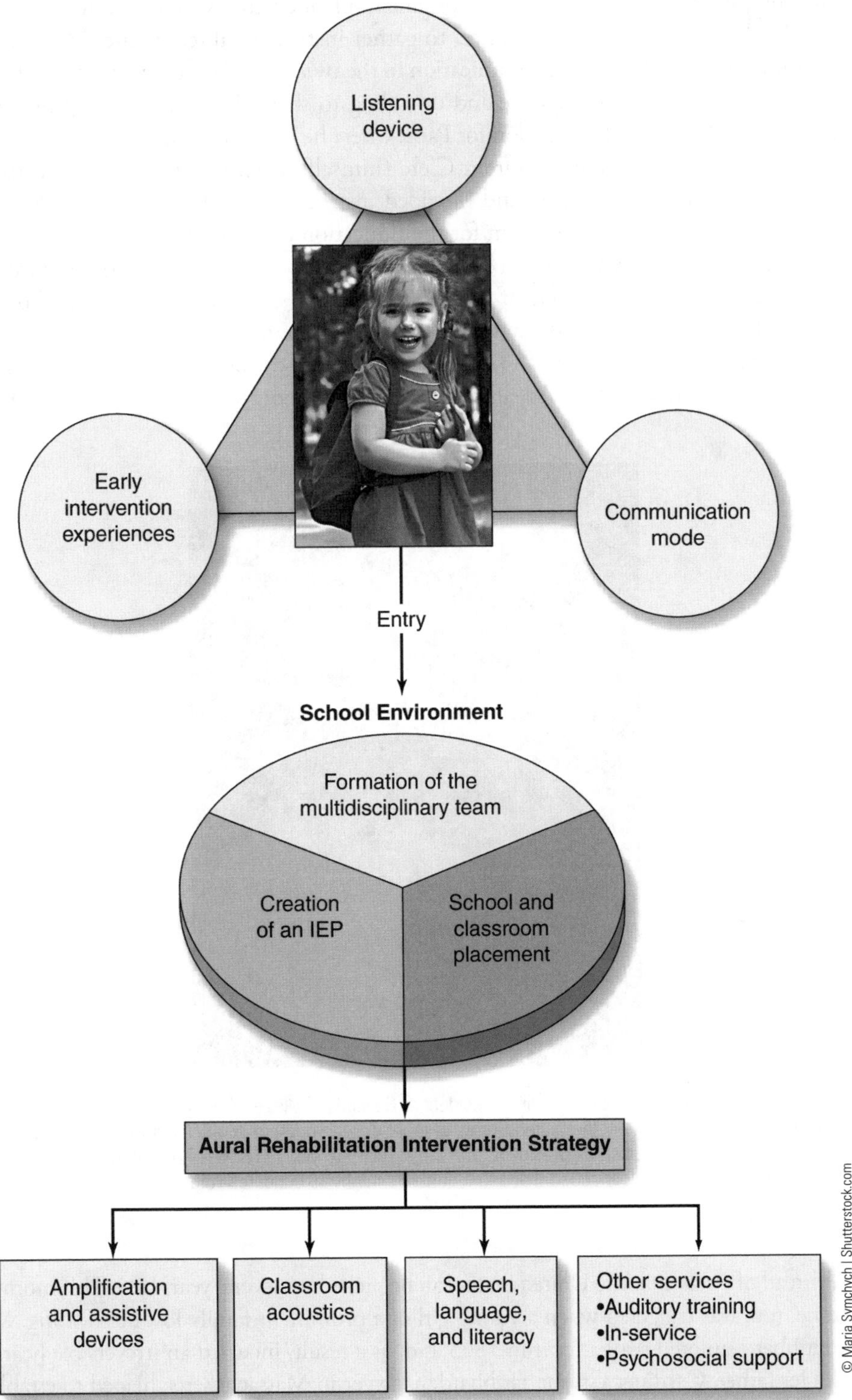

FIGURE 14–1 Entering school. A young child with hearing loss prepares to enter a school setting. She brings with her experience with a listening device, a communication mode, and experiences from an early intervention program.

with profound hearing loss. Gallaudet originally planned to visit the Braidwood family in England and Abbé Sicard in France, to gather instructional techniques in aural/oral communication and manual communication in the two countries, respectively. The Braidwood family proved to be secretive and unwilling to share their oral teaching methods. Thus, in 1816 Gallaudet left London for Paris, where he learned a manual communication system from Abbé Sicard and Laurent Clerc (himself deaf). Gallaudet returned to the United States, along with Clerc, and provided instruction to Alice. The two men went on to establish the American Asylum for the Education of the Deaf and Dumb (now the American School for the Deaf) in 1817, a school with a manual orientation. During the next 40 years, Clerc became one of the most influential educators of children who were deaf and the first (and one of the few) deaf teachers in the nineteenth century. Gallaudet's son, Edward Miner Gallaudet (1837–1917) (Figure 14–2), became the president of the first college for students who are deaf in the New World, now named Gallaudet University.

FIGURE 14–2 Edward Miner Gallaudet, first president of Gallaudet College (now Gallaudet University). Gallaudet was the first college in the United States to grant college degrees to students who were deaf or hearing impaired. Edward served as president for a remarkable 46 years (1864–1910). Although a strong believer in sign language, he conceded that some students might be educated with the "artificial method" of oralism.

The thread of oralism in the United States can be picked up several years later. This moment in time, too, was triggered when a young girl of a prominent family lost her hearing. Mabel Hubbard suffered scarlet fever in 1863 and, as a result, incurred an irreversible hearing loss. Her father, Gardiner Greene Hubbard, a lawyer in Massachusetts, helped to establish the Clarke School in Northampton, Massachusetts, in 1867, with the assistance of Samuel Howe, who also was the principal of the first school for the blind in the United States.

When Mabel Hubbard grew up, she married Alexander Graham Bell. In the latter half of the nineteenth century, Bell became an articulate and passionate advocate for aural/oral education in the United States. In fact, an impetus for developing the telephone was a desire to develop an amplification device for his wife-to-be and for his mother, who also had a hearing loss. His counterpart, who advocated an orientation that incorporated manual communication, was Edward Gallaudet. In the late 1800s, these two men often were engaged in debate as to the merits of one method versus the other.

Throughout the 20th century, debates and controversies flared on and off as to which of the two basic educational approaches, manual or aural/oral, is most appropriate for educating children who are deaf. The debate continues into the twenty-first century.

CREATION OF AN INDIVIDUAL(IZED) EDUCATION PLAN (IEP)

As noted in Chapter 13, an **Individualized Education Plan (IEP)** is a written statement developed for children who have a disability, and many countries now endorse them for children with hearing loss. Not all children with hearing loss receive an IEP, but children performing below grade level or experiencing speech and language difficulties will likely receive one. A schematic of the plan's contents appears in Figure 14–3. The plan includes a description of the following; the child's:

An **Individualized Education Plan (IEP)** is a team-developed, written plan that identifies goals and objectives that address the educational needs of a student aged 3 to 21 years who has a disability. The plan should take into account the family's preferred mode of communication, the child's linguistic needs, academic progress, social and emotional needs, and appropriate accommodations to ensure learning.

- Present level of performance
- Strengths
- Language and communication needs
- Educational needs such as a sign language interpreter
- Opporunity to interact with peers and professionals with his or her preferred communication mode
- Opportunity to learn academic material

The IEP also includes specific goals and objectives and identifies means for assessing their attainment. For example, for the third grader shown in Figure 14–3, the speech-language component of her assessment revealed that she currently has expressive language in the low average range and the writing skills of a first grader. Her strengths include artistic talents, an outgoing personality, good visual memory, and an ability to get along with

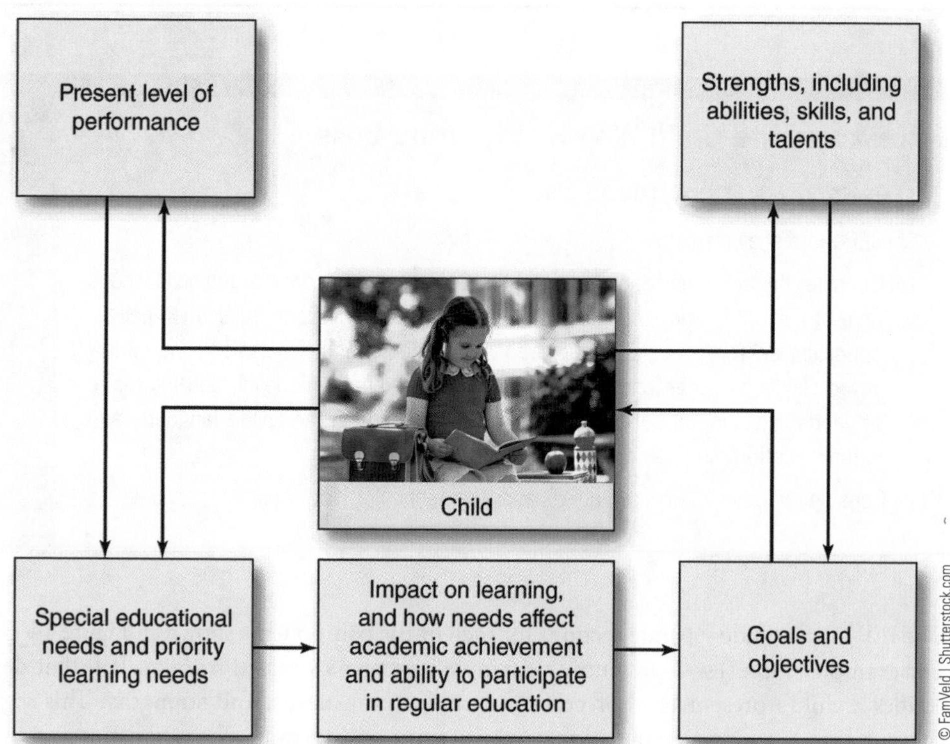

FIGURE 14–3 Components of the Individualized Education Plan (IEP).

her classmates. Her special education needs include an FM trainer in the classroom. Her priority learning needs include acquisition of new vocabulary and language structures and better performance on subtraction and addition problems. The impact on her ability to participate in regular education is that she will have to leave the regular classroom for two hours each week to receive speech-language therapy and two hours each week to receive math tutoring in the resource room. A sample goal may be *Janice will expand her vocabulary and use of prepositional phrases.* The components of the IEP interact. For example, Janice's needs and strengths will influence the development of goals and objectives; achievement of goals and objectives will affect her level of performance. The IEP also includes specific details, such as the location and plan for service delivery, how long services will last, and how and when the child will be promoted within the public school system. Table 14–1 summarizes the components of an IEP in detail.

TABLE 14–1 An Itemized List of Topics Typically Included in a Formal IEP

1. A statement of the present level of performance
2. A statement of annual goals
3. Short-term instructional objectives
4. Special education and related services to be provided
5. Extent of participation in the regular educational program
6. Projected date for services to begin
7. Anticipated duration of services
8. Appropriate criteria to determine if objectives are achieved
9. Evaluation procedures to determine if objectives are achieved
10. Schedules for review
11. Assessment information
12. Placement justification statement
13. A statement of how special education services are tied to the regular education program

IDEA and the Child Who Has Hearing Loss

Section 300.346 of IDEA (1997) states:

The IEP team shall also:

(iv) Consider the communication needs of the child, and in the case of the child who is deaf or hard of hearing, consider the child's language and communication needs, opportunities for direct communications with peers and professional personnel in the child's language and communication mode, academic level, and full range of needs, including opportunities for direct instruction in the child's language and communication mode; and

(v) Consider whether the child requires assistive technology devices and services.

The IEP may include separate sections for each of the components shown in Figure 14–3. For example, Table 14–2 presents an example narrative extracted from an IEP that describes a child's present level of performance, learning needs, and strengths. This segment describes academic/educational achievement and learning characteristics and includes a description of Andrew's present level of performance in the domains of social development, physical development, and needs within a classroom setting.

Table 14–3 presents a segment extracted from an IEP that describes current status, annual goals, and short-term objectives. Although there is no standard form used nationally or internationally, many IEPs include both goals and objectives. A **goal** is the desired aim or outcome and an **objective** is a measurable result expected within a particular time period of class participation, the accomplishment of which represents a milestone toward achieving the corresponding goal.

Children who repeat a grade in school in the United States are:

- 6.1% of children who do not have a hearing problem
- 9.4% of children who have a history of hearing problems
- 19.3% of children who have a current hearing problem

(Gilani, Rodti, & Bhattacharyya, 2016)

TABLE 14–2 An Example Segment from an IEP This IEP describes "Andrew Johnson" and his present level of academic performance. Andrew is an 8-year-old boy with profound hearing loss. Similar descriptions to this one are included in Andrew's IEP that describe his social development, physical development, and classroom needs.

Andrew is a curious boy who enjoys variety. His grades range from Bs to Cs. He responds well to visual aids, hands-on activities, and novelty. Andrew experiences moderate difficulty in working independently, and often requires teacher encouragement to complete an assignment. Andrew recognizes common words during reading class and is performing just below grade level on reading comprehension tests. He enjoys listening to stories and appears to have good auditory comprehension with the use of his cochlear implant. Mathematics may be a strength. He is able to add and subtract three- and four-digit numbers.

TABLE 14–3 Example Segment of an IEP

DOMAIN	STATUS	ANNUAL GOAL	SHORT-TERM OBJECTIVE
Audiologic	Can discriminate two utterances that differ in syllable length and intonation, such as *hello* from *how are you?*	To achieve closed-set identification of monosyllabic everyday words	Will correctly identify a spoken word when presented in the context of four then six alternatives with 80% accuracy
Language	Does not use bound morphemes, such as *-ed* or *-ing*	To establish consistent use of word endings in expressive and written communication	Will demonstrate use of past tense endings in 80% of written samples and in 70% of spontaneous and spoken-language samples
Speech	Neutralizes vowels and omits final word consonants	To improve speech intelligibility	Will distinguish between /i/, /a/, and /u/ in imitated speech tasks with 80% accuracy, and produce final consonants in at least 50% of words spoken during a spontaneous speech task
Psychosocial	Does not follow classroom rules	To demonstrate grade-appropriate classroom behavior	Will receive positive reinforcements for adhering to classroom regulations, and accumulate 100 points during a three-month period
Educational	Reading is delayed by one grade level; can read aloud but has reduced comprehension	To improve reading comprehension	Will demonstrate comprehension on 85% of grade-appropriate reading samples

The IEP might also specify individualized teaching strategies and accommodations. For example, individualized teaching strategies might include the use of supplemental reading material, videotapes, and other audiovisual learning materials that enhance breadth and depth of learning and other enrichment materials. The language used for instructing and assessing the child may be simplified (without sacrificing academic content) and the child might participate in peer partnerships, independent study plans, and mentorship programs. Individualized teaching strategies might include allowing children extra time to complete assignments and tests, allowing them to use alternative methods to complete assignments (e.g., dramatizations, demonstrations), and arranging note-sharing with classmates.

IEP goals must adhere to *DARTS*:

Demonstrable or measurable
Achievable
Realistic
Time-related
Specific

(Department of Education and Children's Services, 2010, p. 21)

The IEP is developed in a meeting attended by representative(s) of the local educational agency, the teacher, the parents or guardians, and sometimes the child or other individuals at the discretion of the parents, such as a friend or an advocate. When the child has a communication disorder, a speech-language pathologist or an audiologist likely attends. These meetings are usually held annually. Appendix 14–1 presents an example of an entire IEP.

If you are the child's speech and hearing professional or teacher, you may want to be especially sensitive to parents' uncertainties during this process and realize that they are new to this process, and will need to be educated. As one parent noted, "In the early years, my full participation in the IEP process was inhibited due to my lack of knowledge of the terminology used for speech-language intervention as well as the IEP process requirements. As I read and studied the paperwork and asked questions, I was able to understand and provide more feedback. The school played a major role in helping me to understand the process" (Boswell & Stern, 2011, p. 27).

THE MULTIDISCIPLINARY TEAM

A **multidisciplinary team** is a group of professionals with different expertise who contribute to the assessment, intervention, and management of a particular individual.

The members of the **multidisciplinary team** implement the IEP. This team may include an audiologist, a speech-language pathologist, an educator, and a psychologist (or a counselor). Depending on the situation, the team also may include an interpreter and an itinerant teacher or a resource teacher. Each professional provides a different perspective of the child's abilities and needs and provides different services.

The Role of the Audiologist

An audiologist may perform any of the following duties:

- Evaluate hearing and speech recognition skills
- Assess central auditory function
- Select, fit, and help maintain appropriate listening devices, including hearing aids and FM systems
- Analyze the classroom environment, which may entail measuring ambient noise levels and **reverberation times (RT60)**, and make recommendations about improving classroom acoustics and reducing classroom noise
- Provide speech perception training
- Provide consultation to parents and other professionals on the multidisciplinary team

Reverberation time (RT60) is the amount of time in seconds it takes for a sound to decay by 60 dB in a room.

Audiologists identify and evaluate children's hearing capabilities and speech recognition skills. Although very young children may not be able to participate in word recognition testing, behavioral assessment of hearing thresholds can be performed with almost all school-age groups. If a child is being identified with hearing loss for the first time, the audiologist may make any necessary referrals, such as to a physician or other health care professional. The audiologist also may initiate the formation of the multidisciplinary team and the case-management process.

Audiologists also select and ensure proper use of listening devices. They may select and fit a new hearing aid or make a recommendation for the child to receive a cochlear implant. They likely will explore the child's home and school environments, either through parent and teacher questionnaires or through site visits to the home and school. For example, the audiologist may see that the child is in a noisy classroom and often misses much of the teacher's speech. The audiologist then may recommend that the child and teacher use an FM system to reduce the effects of background noise. Follow-up maintenance and repair also will be provided.

Sometimes audiologists provide formal speechreading and auditory training rather than, or in addition to, the speech-language pathologist or classroom teacher. In some cases, they may make recommendations to the person who provides training. Finally, audiologists consult with parents and teachers about the child's listening potential and difficulties and ways to encourage the development of listening skills.

The Role of the Speech-Language Pathologist

An ASHA (American Speech-Language-Hearing Association) Omnibus Survey (2003) suggests that about 46% of school-based speech-language pathologists serve children who have hearing loss and on average, they have about three children with hearing loss in their caseloads. A speech-language pathologist may perform any of the following functions (see also ASHA, 2004c):

- Evaluate speech and language performance
- Evaluate preliteracy and literacy skills, including phonological awareness
- Evaluate speechreading skills
- Select assistive listening devices and perform visual inspection and listening check of amplification devices
- Collaborate in the assessment of central auditory processing disorders
- Provide speech and language therapy
- Consult with parents and classroom teachers
- Provide instruction in sign language to the child, classroom teacher, and parents, if appropriate
- Maintain bridges of communication between clinical setting, classroom, and home, and ensure that therapy objectives are reinforced informally throughout a child's day
- Advise audiologists about appropriate language levels for audiological tests
- Provide speech perception training

A speech-language pathologist evaluates speech and language performance and provides speech and language therapy. Test results are used to identify initial therapy objectives and a hierarchy of steps to be followed over time is developed. Often, the objectives coincide with a curriculum that has been developed specifically for children who have hearing loss.

Speech-language pathologists may also provide consultation to parents, teachers, audiologists, and other members of the multidisciplinary team. For example, a speech-language pathologist may familiarize parents and teachers with their child's speech and language skills and how the child's skills compare with those of other children. The speech-language pathologist also might describe how speech and language skills progress in both children with normal hearing and children with hearing loss, and factors that may accelerate or impede progress. Such information helps those who know the child to develop appropriate expectations and provides them with ideas about how best to nurture the child's development.

For families who use total communication or ASL (American Sign Language), speech-language pathologists may help parents and teachers learn sign language. They may recommend printed or video resources that include sign dictionaries, and may even provide direct instruction and practice.

Speech-language pathologists also may suggest ways for helping children generalize what they learned in therapy to more real-world settings by informing parents and teachers about their child's current therapy objectives and by suggesting practice materials. For example, a speech-language pathologist might observe a child in the classroom and then suggest ways the classroom teacher can integrate speech and language practice into the daily routine.

Speech-language pathologists may provide information about the child's language skills to audiologists and help them select appropriate audiological tests. For example, if the speech-language evaluation reveals that a child has an extremely limited vocabulary, the audiologist may opt not to evaluate the child's speech recognition skills with recorded sentence lists.

In some cases, the speech-language pathologist may provide formal speechreading and auditory training and may even perform hearing screenings. Again, the speech-language pathologist interacts with teachers and parents so they can reinforce auditory and speechreading training in everyday communication situations. For example, if an auditory training objective is to identify a word from a closed set of four choices, at home, the child's parent may reinforce the objective by pointedly asking for a specific piece of silverware, say a fork, from a collection of silverware set out on the family dinner table.

The Role of the Educator

The teacher provides academic instruction in the classroom setting. Sometimes the teacher is a regular classroom teacher and will have had little experience in working with children who have hearing loss, and sometimes the teacher has a degree in the education of children who are deaf and who have hearing loss. A regular education teacher knows the general curriculum and knows strategies that might help a child learn appropriate behavior, if behavior is at issue. A teacher of children who are deaf and who have hearing loss has expertise in modifying the curriculum so that a child has optimal opportunity to learn. The teacher of children who are deaf and who have hearing loss has completed a planned curriculum of educational coursework and practicums that include observation, student teaching, planning, implementing, and evaluation of educational outcomes with respect to children who have hearing loss. This teacher can individualize instruction and can advise other adults about modifications in either the physical classroom or classroom procedures that may facilitate learning. The roles of the classroom teacher may include (ASHA, 2004c, p. 3):

- Assessment, diagnosis, and evaluation
- Planning instructional content and practice
- Planning and managing the learning environment
- Managing student behavior and social interactions skills

Ideally the classroom teacher will understand a child's specific needs and will help to ensure that a child receives additional support in relation to his or her listening, speaking, language, and reading comprehension abilities. The teacher may perform a listening check on a child's hearing aid on a daily basis and troubleshoot problems. The teacher may also act as a liaison between the child and the family and the school district.

The Role of the Psychologist

The psychologist often performs a psychoeducational assessment. The psychoeducational assessment may include an evaluation of the following child variables:

- Intelligence, both *verbal* (cognitive abilities demonstrated via language-based performance) and *nonverbal* (cognitive abilities demonstrated by performance that is not language based)
- Verbal function, written language, and reading
- Arithmetic skills
- Visual-motor skills
- Visual and auditory memory and multimodal integration
- Social and emotional function and problem solving
- Attention
- Behavior

The results of this assessment may be used to design a child's intervention plan and to assess whether the child is progressing within his or her current program. The psychologist can also provide support to a student. This professional can talk with a child and provide the youth with the language necessary to express feelings about having a hearing loss, and can help facilitate interactions with fellow classmates.

Sometimes the psychologist is also the school counselor. In this role, the professional can provide structured programs that promote coping skills, psychosocial adjustment, a positive self-concept, and problem-solving abilities. For the older student, the professional may provide information about postsecondary programs that cater to students who have hearing loss.

The Role of the Interpreter

The interpreter presents the ongoing classroom dialogue to the child using the child's preferred mode of communication. Most often, an interpreter is part of the multidisciplinary team when the child uses sign language and the classroom teacher does not sign. The interpreter may provide in-class support as well, especially in elementary schools, where a child stays in the same classroom for most of the day. The interpreter also promotes communication and interactions between the student and classmates by conveying spoken and signed information back and forth.

The Role of the Itinerant Teacher

A general education teacher may receive the assistance of an **itinerant teacher**. The itinerant teacher drives from school to school and works with a student on a one-on-one basis, with the objective of reinforcing classroom instruction. The teacher may review concepts, vocabulary, and literature that have been covered in the regular classroom. The itinerant teacher will receive copies of classroom materials, such as handouts and visual aids, and may go through these with the student. The itinerant teacher may also prepare a student for new material, teaching key concepts, words, and phrases before the student encounters them in the regular classroom. Sometimes the itinerant teacher will provide auditory and speechreading training and sign language instruction, and will sometimes develop individualized programs that promote a student's language, social, and academic skills. The model of service may be a *push-in* model, where the itinerant teacher works with the student in the classroom, or a *pull-out* model, where the itinerant teacher works with the student outside of the classroom. The itinerant teacher also might educate classroom teachers and peers about issues related to hearing loss and might help the teacher learn how to handle listening devices and assistive technology.

Advantages of the push-in model of service provided by an itinerant teacher include:

- Exposure to the general education environment, including high expectations for achievement and exposure to the general curriculum
- An additional teacher in the classroom

Disadvantages of the push-in model of service provided by an itinerant teacher include:

- High noise levels in the classroom
- Language needs of the student may be underserved

(Rabinsky, 2013)

Lifelines

"Itinerant teachers. These people are lifelines or whatever, I mean you can't sing their praises enough."

—Liz, parent of a child with hearing loss who attends a public school, commenting on what makes inclusion possible

(Eriks-Brophy et al., 2006, p. 64)

Itinerant teachers work in several schools, providing support service to children who are deaf and hard of hearing and to their teachers.

SCHOOL AND CLASSROOM PLACEMENT

Because urban and rural areas afford different educational opportunities, decisions about school and classroom placement are to some extent dependent on geographic location. In large cities, parents often have several choices, whereas in rural areas, familial choice may be limited.

School Placement

Options for school placement include public or private institutions and day or residential programs. Public placements are funded by government sources, whereas private placements are funded by tuition and charitable donations.

Challenges if a child lives in a rural community:

- Limited access to special services and to hearing professionals and educators
- High turnover rate of professionals, due to heavy caseloads, restricted career advancement, and lack of support services
- Time spent and costs incurred as a result of having to travel to larger centers for services
- Poor communication and shortage of timely information

(Barr, Duncan, & Dally, 2018)

A residential school provides comprehensive academic, health, and socialization programs. Students live in dormitories with other children who have hearing loss. The staff at the school is expected to communicate with the students fluently, using the students' mode of communication.

A day school employs teachers of children who are deaf and who have hearing loss to teach all academic subjects. These schools have support personnel readily available, such as an audiologist and speech-language pathologist. Children commute to a day school from their homes on a daily basis, and the school is usually located in a central location so it serves children from all over the geographic region. Another version of a day-school placement is enrollment within a general education school, where students receive instruction either in a self-contained classroom or in a regular classroom.

Since the passage of US Public Law (PL) 94-142 (the Education for All Handicapped Children Act) in 1975, there has been a substantial increase in the number of children who remain in their home communities and receive a public education. Concomitantly, there has been a decrease in the number of children who attend residential and day schools for children who are deaf and who have hearing loss. Less than 10% of children between the ages of 6 and 21 years attend a residential facility and less than 10% attend a day school for children who have hearing loss (National Center for Education Statistics, 2011).

Classroom Placement

Self-contained classrooms include only children who are deaf and hard of hearing.

In **mainstream classrooms**, children who are deaf and hard of hearing attend classes with students who have normal hearing.

In **selective mainstreaming**, students typically attend a self-contained classroom for academic subjects such as history and attend nonacademic classes such as art with their students who have normal hearing.

Resource rooms are designated places in a school where instruction in particular areas is provided to children who spend the rest of their day in regular classrooms.

Two distinct classroom placement options, self-contained and mainstream, are available in many public school districts, and a third, resource rooms, may also be available. **Self-contained classrooms** are contained within neighborhood or community schools and include only students with hearing loss (Figure 14–4) or may also include children who have other disabilities, in which case it is classified as a *multicategorical self-contained* classroom. In **mainstream classrooms**, children with hearing loss attend classes together with children who have normal hearing. Some children participate in **selective mainstreaming** and attend a self-contained classroom for part of the school day and a mainstream classroom for some subjects, such as art and physical education. When in a mainstream classroom, children often utilize support services, such as the use of a sign or oral interpreter or an FM system. Some children attend a mainstream classroom as well as receive individualized instruction in a resource room. Children who attend **resource rooms** spend some part of their school day in a regular classroom, and receive instruction from a speech and hearing specialist or a special education teacher for certain topics, such as language.

FIGURE 14–4 Self-contained classroom placement. Class sizes are usually small, and children sit at a table around the teacher.

In some mainstream scenarios, children are treated more like "visitors" to the regular classroom than active members (Antia, Stinson, & Gaustad, 2002). Because of academic or behavioral considerations, the classroom teacher might believe a child is best served in the special classrooms. The upside of this model is that in some ways the child might get the best of both worlds. He or she receives needed support and still has an opportunity to interact with a peer group. The downside of this model is that a student's "visits" to the classroom might be disruptive to the classroom routine, and the child may not be able to slip into the flow of what is happening at the moment (e.g., the child might not have performed an assignment that is under current discussion).

An alternative or a supplement to a resource room is an itinerant teacher. The child attends school in a regular classroom but receives support services from an itinerant teacher, who, as noted earlier, works in several schools and has expertise in issues related to hearing loss.

Three derivatives of mainstreaming are inclusion, coenrollment, and partial mainstreaming. Like mainstreaming, **inclusion** entails placing children who have hearing loss in classrooms with children who have normal hearing. A child in an inclusion classroom is included in most or all aspects of the class life and the school (Figure 14–5) (Antia et al., 2002; Marschark, Young, & Lukomski, 2002). The classroom teacher has the primary job of educating every child in the classroom, but may also have a partnership with a special education teacher in making adjustments to the curriculum and structuring the classroom environment to meet the learning needs of the child with hearing loss. The philosophical difference between mainstreaming and inclusion is that, in the former, the child must adapt to the classroom, whereas in the latter, the classroom must adapt to the child (Stinson & Antia, 1999). Children in an inclusion setting usually communicate with spoken language, total communication, or Cued Speech. Children who use ASL typically are not placed in this setting. Inclusion is not without its challenges. Many classroom teachers feel unprepared to handle the multifaceted needs of both children who have normal hearing and children who have hearing loss (Eriks-Brophy & Whittingham, 2013), and sometimes the child with hearing loss has problems integrating socially with his or her peers who have normal hearing (e.g., Israelite, Ower, & Goldstein, 2002) and feels "different" from classmates. The advantages of inclusion include opportunities for children with hearing loss to participate more readily in extracurricular activities with their neighborhood peers and to learn from speech and language modeling afforded by children with normal hearing. For children with normal hearing, advantages include being exposed from an early age to students with disabilities, which may lead to better acceptance and understanding of differences.

FIGURE 14–5 Inclusion classroom placement. The child with hearing loss is an active member of the classroom, participating in all academic and social interactions.

Who Am I?

"When I attended the school for the deaf, I took deafness for granted, I did not understand then, that if you are deaf, you do not hear. Then you are not like the others. Then you are different. I did not understand it. I took being deaf for granted . . . but when I got my own [hearing] friends and I wanted to talk with them, instead of my family, then I met with obstacles. That was a great barrier. Bang."

—Gro, a high school student living in Norway

(Ohna, 2003, p. 7)

Inclusion integrates all students and activities into the daily routine of the general education classroom.

Transitioning into the Mainstream

"Imagine going to a new school . . . you are 5 years old and deaf and you see other children on the playground. Imagine having butterflies in your stomach. When I first got to Midland Park, I remember I was crying, feeling scared and nervous all at the same time because I missed my old friends from Summit Speech School. I was nervous because I was afraid how people were going to react to me because I am deaf. I was scared because I wanted to meet new friends."

—Anthony Mohan, 14-year-old student at Midland Park School

(Mohan, 2012, p. 34)

A Teacher's Perspective

"[Children with hearing loss] do have deficits in just general knowledge and background knowledge of things that hearing kids understand because they have experience with something similar. . . . [So] you have to be watching all the time for what they don't get because they don't have experience with it before. . . . I think a lot of times regular teachers assume a depth of knowledge that [children with hearing loss] really don't have and they sit a lot of times without having a clue what you're talking about."

—Helen, a regular classroom teacher who taught in a coenrollment class with children with hearing loss

(Jiménez-Sánchez & Antia, 1999, p. 221)

Everybody Wins

The advantages of an inclusion classroom for children who have disabilities include the following:

- Improved academic achievement
- Improved social competence
- Enhanced communication and developmental skills
- Greater opportunity for the generalization of skills and abilities to novel contexts
- Development of positive self-concept
- Access to appropriate models of language and social behavior because of exposure to and interaction with members of a peer group

The advantages of an inclusion classroom for children who have no disabilities include the following:

- Wider social acceptance and understanding of disability
- Increased awareness of and respect for diversity
- Increased tolerance and social cognition
- Enhanced self-concept
- Enhanced socioemotional growth

(Eriks-Brophy & Whittingham, 2013, p. 65)

Coenrollment refers to a model of educating children who have hearing loss that entails a team of teachers, one a regular classroom teacher and the other a trained teacher for children who have hearing loss.

In a **coenrollment model**, the classroom is conducted by two teachers, a regular classroom teacher and a teacher of children who are deaf and who have hearing loss (Antia & Levine, 2001). The class may include students who have normal hearing and students who have hearing loss and who may use sign. The ratio of children who are deaf and who have hearing loss to children with normal hearing is about 1:4 (e.g., Mellon, 2005). When there is a balanced mix of students, the model may be referred to as *reverse mainstream*. All students have access to the school district's adopted grade-level curriculum, and teachers hold the same expectations for students with normal and impaired hearing. This model aspires to place all children on the same playing field. This kind of team-teaching exposes all students to their own culture and to that of others, and helps students establish a self-identity and self-esteem. The students with normal hearing may be expected to learn sign and to learn about the Deaf culture.

Partial mainstreaming usually occurs when a child is about to transition from a self-contained classroom to a mainstream classroom or from a school for children who are deaf and who have hearing loss to a school for children who have normal hearing.

Partial mainstreaming usually occurs when a child is about to transition from a self-contained classroom to a mainstream classroom or from a school for children who are deaf and who have hearing loss to a school for children who have normal hearing. During the final semester in the self-contained classroom, the child may spend one day a week in the general education setting.

Appropriate format accommodations allow children with hearing loss to participate with children who have normal hearing on a "fair playing ground."

The full-time inclusion classroom option may offer various levels of support. Direct services may be provided by an itinerant teacher who works with the child in the regular classroom, either by helping the student to engage in regular classroom learning or by providing direct instruction with a specialized curriculum. Alternatively, an itinerant teacher might provide indirect services by helping the classroom teacher implement **appropriate format accommodations** or by providing training and in-services about how to teach a child with hearing loss. Full-time inclusion with accommodations may mean that the student has access to assistive technology devices, captioning, acoustical improvements to the classroom, and a sign interpreter.

Figure 14–6 illustrates one model for determining classroom placement. The goal is to move the child toward a regular mainstream classroom placement as expediently as appropriate. Only when necessary is a child placed outside of the mainstream classroom or taken out of the classroom to receive special support services.

Introduction to the Mainstream

"At [his school for children who are deaf and hard of hearing] . . . they took him there once a week; he went there in May before he went there in the fall . . . they selected a freshman, a student that was a well-rounded and mature person, to take him around to all his classes every Friday. . . . He felt comfortable going there in the fall because he was familiar with the campus, some of the classrooms, the lunch room, that kind of thing."

—Mother of boy who participated in partial mainstreaming before full mainstreaming

(Rugg & Donne, 2011, p. 335)

Self-contained classroom	Part-time self-contained classroom	Part-time mainstream classroom	Full-time mainstream classroom
	Part-time mainstream classroom	Part-time resource classroom	– Direct services – Indirect services – Accommodations – No services

FIGURE 14–6 One model for determining classroom placement. The goal is to move a child from a placement on the left to one toward the right. Once a child enrolls in a full-time mainstream classroom (far right), the child may receive direct services, as when an itinerant teacher provides ancillary instruction, indirect services, as when the itinerant teacher provides guidance to the classroom teacher, accommodations (e.g., an FM system), or no services.

Not all speech and hearing professionals adhere to such a model. Sometimes a child is placed in a regular classroom at the onset of his or her educational program, so that the youth has normal classroom experiences from the outset and learns to identify with the hearing world. Alternatively, some children are educated in a self-contained classroom throughout their school years, with special emphasis on becoming enculturated into the Deaf community.

An IEP team will deliberate about classroom placement, and in the process, may complete checklists about readiness, such as the Placement and Readiness Checklists for Students Who Are Deaf and Hard of Hearing (PARC; Johnson, 2011). The PARC includes four checklists that assess a student's general readiness to participate in the mainstream and various communication and learning skills, as well as the capacity of the classroom environment to accommodate the child. Sample items for the former include *Knowledge of classroom routines and ability to handle transitions; Following directions; Attention to classroom instruction (compared with classmates);* and *Academic performance (reading, writing, math).* Responses range from 1 to 5 on corresponding scales. Sample items from the latter include yes–no questions such as *Are noise sources in the classroom minimized (e.g., fish tanks, ventilation/heater fans, computers)? And Is there a visual schedule identifying daily routines and student expectations?* Other example instruments sometimes used for this purpose include the Child's Peer Relationship Scale (Anderson & Arnoldi, 2011), Screening Instrument for Targeting Educational Risk (SIFTER; Anderson, 1989), and Listening Inventory for Education (LIFE; Anderson & Smaldino, 1998).

Examples of appropriate format accommodations:

- Abbreviated assignments
- Alternative test format
- Content enhancement
- Content reduction
- Copies of class notes
- Extra credit
- Flexible scheduling
- Interpreter
- Language simplification
- Modified grading
- Paraphrasing
- Study guides

(Burns, 2004, p. 109)

AMPLIFICATION AND ASSISTIVE LISTENING DEVICES

Part B of IDEA states that "each public agency must ensure that hearing aids worn in school by children with hearing impairments, including deafness, are functioning properly" (300.113). Ensuring appropriate amplification requires that good communication

Part B is the section of Public Law PL 105-17 (IDEA) that refers to intervention services for eligible children between the ages of 3 and 21 years in the public school system.

occurs between the school staff, the family, and the members of the child's medical home or audiologic care system. Assistive listening devices may be required to optimize a child's ability to function in the classroom.

Amplification

An audiologic assessment will determine if a child is receiving adequate benefit from a current listening device, or will determine the need for a device if the child is not currently using one, using procedures described in either Chapter 2 or Chapter 12, depending upon the child's age and maturity.

The Ling 6-Sounds Test

Speech-language pathologists or classroom teachers may screen a child's hearing by administering the Ling 6 Sound Test (Ling, 1989). For example, prior to a session, the clinician may administer the test to determine a child's ability to detect, discriminate, and identify each sound. This information can help guide the content of a speech therapy or auditory training session. A classroom teacher may administer the test each morning to see if a child's ability to hear speech sounds has deteriorated, which would suggest that the child's listening device is not working properly.

The sounds span the range of speech frequencies that commonly occurs in running speech and includes the three vowels that make up the vowel formant triangle in English (i.e., the extreme frequency values of the first and second formants). Typically the clinician or teacher covers his or her mouth with an embroidery hoop with an opaque mesh screen and speaks the sounds at a conversational level. The child claps hands after hearing a sound. The six sounds are as follows:

- /m/
- /u/
- /a/
- /i/
- /ʃ/
- /s/

Recommended equipment to have in the classroom:

- **Hearing aid stethoscope** for listening check
- Battery tester
- Air blower to remove moisture and wax from earmold and tubing
- Extra supplies (batteries, and for the FM system, cords, receiver buttons, teacher microphones)

A **hearing aid stethoscope** resembles a clinician's stethoscope and is used to auscultate a hearing aid for the purpose of listening or diagnosing a problem.

Once a student receives an appropriate listening device, then a procedure for ensuring that the device is working properly must be implemented. This may entail periodic checks by an educational audiologist. School staff may learn how to conduct daily visual and listening checks and how to troubleshoot the device for common causes of malfunction. The Key Resources section includes a handout about checking hearing instruments. It is important that school staff, such as the classroom teacher, understand the limitations of amplification. Most students will still experience difficulty in hearing, especially in a noisy classroom.

Assistive Technology

The IDEA defines assistive technology as any equipment or system that will increase, maintain, or improve the functional capabilities of children who have a disability. If the IEP stipulates that assistive technology is needed in order for a child to have access to the regular classroom curriculum, then the school district will provide it at no extra cost to the child's family. The school system may purchase, borrow, or lease the device.

In Chapter 3, FM systems were considered, wherein the speech signal is transmitted via radio signal from a microphone worn by the teacher or speech and hearing professional to an FM receiver worn by the student. The teacher talks into a microphone placed near his or her mouth and the signal passes through to an FM personal receiver, which either stands alone or is incorporated into the child's hearing aid or cochlear implant. Because the signal is conveyed directly to the child's ear, the impact of a noisy classroom environment is minimized. The disadvantage of an FM system is that a child can listen to the speech signal of only one person, the person who is wearing the microphone, although many systems have environmental microphones.

One of the more widely used options is an FM sound field amplification system, which provides an optimal signal-to-noise ratio (SNR) for both children who have hearing loss and children who have normal hearing. As noted in Chapter 3, the FM sound field amplification system is like a public address system, comprising an FM receiver and a microphone for the teacher. Speakers are placed along the periphery of the classroom or on individual students' desks. FM sound field systems have been shown to lead to improvements in academic achievement, speech recognition skills, and students' attending and learning behaviors, for both students with hearing loss and students with normal hearing. Teachers are less likely to suffer laryngitis when using sound field amplification.

The educational audiologist often has the responsibility of ensuring that the classroom teacher is comfortable using the FM system. The audiologist may perform a demonstration and show the teacher how to perform a listening check to make sure that the system is functioning properly and how to troubleshoot it and make minor repairs. The Key Resources presents terminology and definitions likely to be encountered when dealing with an FM system and a troubleshooting guide for a generic FM system.

CLASSROOM ACOUSTICS

Classrooms are noisy environments. Shoes scuffling, children whispering, papers crackling, books slamming, chairs scraping, a student laughing, footsteps falling in the hallway, doors closing, air-handling systems humming—these are just some of the sources blasting sound into the classroom. These background noises can cover up, mask, and even distort speech. Sounds also bounce from wall to wall, and from floor to ceiling, **reverberating** from one hard surface to another. An extensive body of literature documents the deleterious effects of excessive classroom noise and reverberation levels on speech recognition performance and educational/social development (ASHA, 2005b). Classroom noise can also have a negative impact on students' ability to pay attention, their task persistence, and their overall levels of reading achievement (Anderson, 2004).

Reverberation is the persistence of a sound due to the signal being reflected from the surfaces of walls, ceiling, and floor. Long reverberation times (more than 500 msec) cause a speech signal, such as a teacher's words, to merge with other signals and to lose clarity.

Noise may average 50 to 60 dBA SPL in a regular classroom (Crandell & Smaldino, 1995). Children who have hearing loss will be at a double disadvantage in trying to attend to the teacher's speech and to hear other children in a noisy classroom. They experience difficulty even in quiet, and background noise and reverberation exacerbate already degraded word recognition and speech comprehension abilities. For example, if a teacher's voice arrives at a child's desk at a level of 65 dBA SPL (which is about a normal conversational level) and the classroom background noise is 60 dBA SPL, the signal-to-noise ration (SNR) is only +5. Students with normal hearing require an

SNR of about +6 dB for optimal auditory comprehension. Children with even a mild hearing loss perform 13% worse in their speech recognition at the relatively good SNR of +6 and perform 33% worse when the SNR falls to −6. Reverberation magnifies the effects of noise, and many classrooms have reverberation levels long enough to degrade speech recognition for most listeners, even those with normal hearing (Crandell, 1993).

Some simple steps can be taken to minimize the level of noise in a classroom and the amount of reverberation. These include any or all of the following (Johnson, 2000, p. 269):

- Installing carpeting or cork on the floor
- Applying rubber tips on chair and desk legs
- Hanging acoustical panels, cork, felt, or flannel bulletin boards on walls
- Placing bookshelves or wall dividers to create quiet areas within the classroom
- Angling mobile whiteboards to reduce the amount of reverberation
- Applying window treatments such as draperies or shades to reduce the amount of reverberation
- Covering ceiling with suspended acoustic tile
- Using cushions in place of chairs
- Obtaining a solid-core, well-fitted door with a noise lock or doorway treatment
- Arranging desks and tables in a staggered formation, so sound will not travel directly to reflective surfaces
- Arranging the classroom so instruction occurs away from sound sources, such as an air vent

Other strategies include encouraging children to wear soft-sole shoes, such as tennis shoes, and keeping the door and windows closed during academic instruction.

More invasive and global initiatives can be taken to minimize noise and reverberation. The air-handling system can be adjusted to minimize noise generation. Siebein, Gold, Siebein, and Ermann (2000) found that the primary noise source in classrooms came from heating, ventilating, and air conditioning (HVAC) systems. The following air conditioning systems were found to be especially noisy: (a) self-contained, wall-mounted units, (b) decentralized fan coil units, (c) central rooftop units that serve multiple rooms, and (d) central systems with variable air volume systems (p. 380). They suggested possible solutions to HVAC-related noise, including the use of silencers, adequate duct length, and vibration isolators.

Selection of a classroom might be an option. Classrooms that are smaller, with lower ceilings, and classrooms that are not perfect squares or rectangles will minimize reverberation. If the school administration has not selected a classroom for a self-contained or inclusion class, a teacher might encourage them to allocate this kind of room. Moreover, an instructor might select a room away from special-purpose rooms (such as the gym or the band room) and away from environmental noise (e.g., a classroom facing a back alley would be preferable to a classroom facing a busy urban street).

Teachers in noisy classrooms can learn strategies to accommodate students with hearing loss. These strategies include the following:

- Using visual aids for instruction
- Gaining students' attention before speaking so as to optimize their chances for successful speechreading
- Encouraging all students to help minimize the noise level in the classroom
- Facing the students when talking and avoiding covering one's mouth

- Becoming aware that most children with hearing loss cannot simultaneously speechread or read sign and perform another task that requires them to look away (such as using a computer or taking notes)
- Providing handouts to provide context cues for speechreading
- Ensuring that the child with hearing loss has favorable seating, typically at the front of the classroom, where the teacher's face will be most visible

OTHER SERVICES

Other services might include a (1) school in-services, (2) mental health and psychosocial support, (3) assessment and enhancement of social competency, (4) communication strategies training for parents, and (5) communication strategies training for the child in addition to auditory and speechreading training (see Chapters 4, 5, and 13).

School In-Service

A speech and hearing professional might provide school in-service to classroom teachers and other staff about hearing loss and accommodations in the classroom. The contents of the in-service may include the following:

- Hearing loss levels
- Implications for academic achievement
- Social-emotional impact of hearing loss
- Hearing aids (cochlear implants) and assistive technology
- Visual aids and note-taking
- Tips for a successful classroom environment (e.g., ways to minimize noise)
- Importance of speaking with clear speech and expressive facial and body gestures
- Importance of ensuring that the student understands what is being taught and is included in all classroom activities

Classmates might be sensitized to the communication difficulties associated with hearing loss. They may have opportunity to handle a hearing aid, and even listen with a hearing aid stethoscope.

Mental Health and Psychosocial Support

Children with significant hearing loss may have a greater likelihood of experiencing psychosocial problems than those who have normal hearing. For example, a large-scale study that included two groups of children with hearing loss, one tested in 2007 and the other in 2014, showed that both groups had equal levels of mental health problems and that they had levels that were significantly higher than those of children with normal hearing (Niclasen & Dammeyer, 2016). The fact that the two groups of children had comparable levels suggests that the prevalence has not changed, despite early identification programs and improved listening technology. Psychosocial difficulties may emerge as early as the preschool years, and may include emotional issues, hyperactivity, and problems with peers (Laugen, Jacobsen, Rieffe, & Wichstrøm, 2016). Receipt of a cochlear implant does not preclude hearing-realted psychosocial problems (Freeman, Pisoni, Dronenberger, & Castellanos, 2017).

Although children with hearing loss vary from one another as in any group of children, and some children will experience few difficulties in psychosocial adjustment, increasing magnitudes of hearing loss can cause increasing difficulties. Table 14–4 describes how varying degrees of long-term hearing loss may affect psychosocial well-being and associated educational needs.

The Angst of Adolescents Compounded by Hearing Loss

"Sometimes, [classmates] would bug everyone but me more because I have a disability for real. It's a fact that I have a disability. They laugh with one another about others, saying they are stupid or stuff like that; they make fun of everyone's weaknesses. Mostly, they laugh at me because I have a hearing impairment."

—A ninth-grade student with hearing loss

(Zaidman-Zait & Dotan, 2017, p. 262)

Mental health problems that some children with hearing loss might experience:

- Internalizing problems (e.g., somatic complaints, withdrawn behavior)
- Externalizing problems (e.g., rule-breaking behavior, aggression)
- Anxiety/depression
- Attention problems
- Social problems and peer problems
- Hyperactivity

Social problems may include:

- Social isolation
- Naiveté about peer interests and customs
- Difficulty in empathizing
- Limited understanding about internal states such as feelings
- Feelings of frustration or intimidation during social interactions

(Kluwin, 1999; Suárez & Torres, 1996)

TABLE 14–4 Relationship Between the Degree of Hearing Loss and Psychosocial Impact

DEGREE OF HEARING LOSS	POSSIBLE PSYCHOSOCIAL IMPACT	POTENTIAL EDUCATIONAL NEEDS AND PROGRAMS
Minimal or borderline, 16–25 dB HL	May be unaware of subtle conversational cues that could cause child to be viewed as inappropriate or awkward. May miss portions of fast-paced peer interactions that could begin to have an impact on socialization and self-concept. Child may be more fatigued than classmates due to listening effort needed.	May benefit from mild gain hearing aid or personal FM system depending on hearing loss configuration. Would benefit from sound field amplification if classroom is noisy or reverberant and favorable seating. May need attention to vocabulary or speech, especially with recurrent otitis media history. Appropriate medical management necessary for conductive losses. Teacher requires in-service on impact of hearing loss on language development and learning.
Mild, 26–40 dB HL	Barriers beginning to build with negative impact on self-esteem as child is accused of "hearing when he or she wants to," "daydreaming," or "not paying attention." Child begins to lose ability for selective hearing, and has increasing difficulty suppressing background noise, which makes the learning environment stressful. Child is more fatigued than classmates due to listening effort needed.	Will benefit from a hearing aid and use of a personal FM or sound field FM system in the classroom. Needs favorable seating and lighting. Refer to special education for language evaluation and educational follow-up. Needs auditory-skill building. May need attention to vocabulary and language development, articulation or speechreading, or special support in reading. May need help with self-esteem. Teacher in-service required.
Moderate, 41–55 dB HL	Often with this degree of hearing loss, communication is significantly affected, and socialization with peers with normal hearing becomes increasingly difficult. With full-time use of hearing aids/FM systems, child may be judged as a less competent learner. There is an increasing impact on self-esteem.	Refer to special education for language evaluation and for educational follow-up. Amplification is essential (hearing aids and FM system). Special education support may be needed, especially for primary children. Attention to oral language development, reading, and written language. Auditory-skill development and speech therapy usually needed. Teacher in-service required.
Moderate-to-severe, 56–70 dB HL	Full-time use of hearing aids/FM systems may result in child being judged by both peers and adults as a less competent learner, resulting in poorer self-concept and social maturity, and contributing to a sense of rejection. In-service may foster improved self-concept and a sense of cultural identity.	Full-time use of amplification is essential. Will need resource teacher or special class depending on magnitude of language delay. May require special help in all language skills, language-based academic subjects, vocabulary, grammar, pragmatics, as well as reading and writing. Probably needs assistance to expand experiential language base. In-service of mainstream teachers required.
Severe, 71–90 dB HL	Child may prefer other children with hearing impairments as friends and playmates. This may further isolate the child from the mainstream; however, these peer relationships may foster improved self-concept and a sense of cultural identity.	May need full-time special aural/oral program with emphasis on all auditory language skills, speechreading, concept development, and speech. Individual hearing aid/personal FM system essential. May be a candidate for a cochlear implant. Need to monitor effectiveness of communication modality. Participation in regular classes as much as is beneficial to student. In-service of mainstream teachers essential. May be a candidate for a cochlear implant.
Profound, 91 dB HL or more	Depending on auditory/oral competence, peer use of sign language, parental attitude, etc., child may or may not increasingly prefer association with the Deaf culture.	Especially in the early years, may need special program for children who are deaf and hard of hearing with emphasis on all language skills and academic areas. Program needs specialized supervision and comprehensive support services. Early use of amplification likely to help if part of an intensive training program. May be a candidate for a cochlear implant. Requires continual appraisal of needs in regard to communication and learning mode. Time spent in regular classes as much as is beneficial to student.
Unilateral—one normal-hearing ear and one ear with at least a permanent mild hearing loss	Child may be accused of selective hearing due to discrepancies in speech understanding in quiet versus noise. Child will be more fatigued in classroom setting due to greater effort needed to listen. May appear inattentive or frustrated. Behavior problems sometimes evident.	May benefit from personal FM or sound field FM system in classroom. May benefit from CROS hearing aid. Needs favorable seating and lighting. Student is at risk for educational difficulties. Educational monitoring warranted with support services provided as soon as difficulties appear. Teacher in-service is beneficial.

Adapted and updated from Anderson and Matkin, 1991, pp. 17–18.

Assessment and Enhancement of Social Competency

When hearing and speech professionals work with children who have hearing loss, it may be tempting to focus exclusively on listening skills, language development, and, if the child is in an aural/oral or total communication program, speech competency as their benchmarks of success. However, success is also defined by a child's emotional well-being and by how easily he or she can interact socially with other children (Figure 14–7).

© Brocreative | Shutterstock.com

FIGURE 14–7 Social competence. The school years are not just for learning academic materials and developing language and literacy skills. Developing social competency is crucial for a child's emotional and mental health.

Social competence is a multidimensional construct that reflects a child's ability to interact with others effectively, using social skills that include the ability to:

- Engage in conversation
- Take other's perspective
- Maintain appropriate eye contact
- Request help
- Express emotions appropriately
- Exhibit self-control

Social competence is a multidimensional construct that reflects an individual's ability to interact with others effectively and to use social skills in a way that is flexible and adaptable.

Both language age and hearing status predict social competence, with delayed language and poorer hearing being associated with lower competence (Hoffman, Quittner, & Cejas, 2015; Tasker, Nowakowski, & Schmidt, 2010). It is a complex and shifting relationship (Figure 14–8). For example, if children increasingly spend time with their peers, they might experience a burst in language growth, which in turn will enhance social competence; as they gain social competence, they will be more likely to be included in conversations, which in turn will foster language growth.

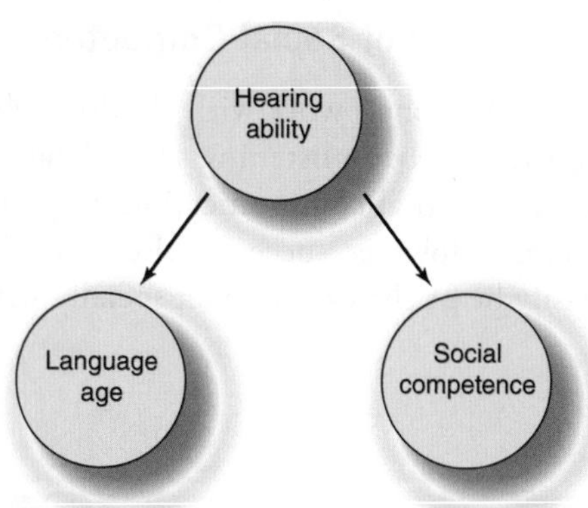

FIGURE 14–8 A model showing the complex relationship between hearing ability, language age, and social competence.

Advice I Would Give to Other Teens

"I would say not to worry that much about what other people think about having a hearing loss. I was quite shy during elementary and middle school, but I eventually grew out of that towards the end of high school when I realized that most people are perfectly willing and happy to speak up a little, speak more clearly, face you directly, whatever accommodations you need in order to hear optimally. Self-advocacy is your best friend and it will get you further than you will by just trying to sneak around your hearing loss."

—Kai Kraus, sophomore at New York University and young man with a severe-to-profound prelingual bilateral hearing loss

(Felzien, 2011, p. 45)

Adolescence may be a particularly difficult time. Adolescents who have hearing loss may have lower levels of self-perceived social acceptance, fewer close friendships, and poorer ego development. They may perceive greater stress from everyday problems than do their peers with normal hearing (Zaidman-Zait & Dotan, 2017).

School Days

High school students who had hearing losses ranging from moderate to profound talked about their school experiences and interactions with their peers. These students live in Toronto, Canada. They attended special classes for hard of hearing students for their elementary schooling and now attend a regular public high school with children who have normal hearing. Here are some of their comments about fitting in to the mainstream (Israelite et al., 2002, pp. 141–142):

About fitting in, a student named Sam said: "My biggest challenge was grade 9. Trying to fit in a school where I had never been, where people from my neighborhood attended too. . . . When I was there, people would put me down because I was different from them. But my challenge was to fit with them, to tell them that I could do the same thing as [they] or possibly better."

About revealing her hearing loss to peers, a student named Kate said: "I realized when I first entered my mainstream English class they don't know I'm hard of hearing so they treat me like everyone else. If I say I'm hard of hearing, then they will treat me differently. . . . So I don't say anything, so they treat me the same as everyone else."

About interactions with the classroom teacher, a student named Jade said: "One thing I hate is when I was in grade 9, one of my English teachers told a teacher I was going into her grade 10 class, and my teacher told her that I was hard of hearing. My teacher was making sure [my grade 10 teacher knew] I was hard of hearing. Every need of mine would be granted. I hated that [grade 10] class so much. The teacher was so nervous around me. I don't need special treatment. I don't like it when I come to a classroom and the teacher knows me because I'm hard of hearing."

An example of an assessment instrument for social adjustment for school-age children who have hearing loss is the Meadow-Kendall Social Emotional Assessment Inventories for Deaf and Hearing-Impaired Students (SEAI; Meadow, 1983). This inventory includes 59 items divided into three subscales: social adjustment, self-image, and emotional adjustment. Norms are established for ages 7 to 21 years and are based on inventories collected from more than 2,400 students. A classroom teacher or other educational professional who is in close contact with the student rates behaviors on a 5-point scale, ranging from *Very true* (description of an observed behavior) to *Does not apply.*

The Minnesota Social Skills Checklist for Students Who Are Deaf/Hard of Hearing: Pre-K to High School (Minnesota Department of Education, 2012) allows teachers to examine a child in terms of social skills and pragmatics or language as it relates to social communication, friendship, and self-esteem. The checklist is designed to follow a child from preschool through the twelfth grade. The checklist designed for grades 3 to 5 include items that assess self-concept and self-esteem (e.g., *Demonstrates pride and confidence in his skills and accomplishments; Identifies self as being deaf/hard of hearing*), friendship (e.g., *Differentiates various levels of friendships, acquaintances, close friends; Respects others' opinions and points of view even if different from his own*), social interaction (e.g., *Accepts constructive criticism; Compromises and accepts a group decision*), and pragmatics (e.g., *Begins to understand the differences between personal and public information; Uses repair strategies during a communication breakdown [talks slower, louder, and repeats]*). The teacher may mark each item as *observed rarely, observed sometimes,* and *mastered.*

Some research suggests that children with severe and profound hearing loss can learn to enhance their social competency. For example, Suárez (2000) developed a program consisting of two parts—(a) an interpersonal problem-solving training program with 15 lessons of a cognitive approach to social competence and (b) six lessons of social skills—and then conducted an experiment to test its efficacy. During the first part, participants developed the interior language for cognitive problem solving (e.g., *What do I have to do? Which way is best? How well did I do?*). Participants learned to identify emotions, with the use of drawings and photographs, and to explore the causes of their emotions. They learned to evaluate solutions to interpersonal problems. In the second part, they learned specific social abilities, including how to apologize, how to negotiate with peers, how to avoid problems with others, how to withstand group influence, and how to cooperate and share in group interactions. Training activities included modeling, role-playing, feedback and reinforcement, and homework. Results showed that the 18 participants improved their social problem-solving skills and increased their assertive behavior, as determined by both teacher- and self-report.

Suggestions for the classroom teacher in a mainstream setting to enhance a child's self-esteem:

- Enable the student to accept how hearing loss makes him or her different, while still enabling him or her to realize that hearing loss is not the student's primary descriptive characteristic.
- Identify attributes that define the student as a valued individual.
- Help the student and classmates to understand the ramifications of hearing loss.
- Develop activities to foster inclusion in classroom activities.

Communication Strategies Training for Parents

Two parents, Mrs. Ansley and Mrs. Kemp, were asked to instruct their children (cochlear implant users) to perform simple tasks, including unwrapping a mint candy (Tye-Murray, 1994b). Each parent and her child sat before a table that held a variety of objects. The goal of the investigation was to determine what would happen in those instances that children misunderstood instructions. Would the parents repeat the message? If so, would these repetitions help their child to recognize the instruction?

In both instances, neither child understood the instruction *Unwrap the mint* after their mothers presented it for the first time. Here is what happened next.

After saying it the first time, Mrs. Ansley repeated the original instruction, "Unwrap the mint." Her daughter, Libby, picked up a red block and threw it gently. "Unwrap the mint," Mrs. Ansley repeated. Libby gave her a puzzled expression. "Unwrap the mint," her mother said again. Libby picked up a cup and set it on a cardboard box. "No, unwrap the mint." Libby shook a sheet of plastic. "Unwrap the mint," her mother said in response. This interchange continued for one minute, until Mrs. Ansley gave up trying to convey the instruction.

In this interaction, the repeat repair strategy was ineffective. No matter how many times Mrs. Ansley repeated the instruction, Libby never understood that she was to unwrap the candy.

The second mother, Mrs. Kemp, adopted a different tack. When her son, Tim, did not understand the instruction, she used different words and said, "Take the paper off the candy." When he still did not comprehend the instruction, Mrs. Kemp said, "Tim, where's the candy?" Tim picked up the mint. "Open it," Mrs. Kemp instructed. Tim looked at his mother and started to open the candy. "Mmmm," she said encouragingly, "Open it." Tim then unwrapped the mint.

Unlike Mrs. Ansley, Mrs. Kemp used repair strategies other than repetition. She rephrased the instruction (i.e., "Take the paper off the candy"), she emphasized an important key word ("Where's the *candy*?"), and provided feedback when her son began to understand the message ("Mmmm"). By using a variety of repair strategies, she was able to convey the message successfully.

This investigation, which also included other parents of cochlear implant users, illustrates two important points. First, the repeat repair strategy is not always the optimal strategy to use in repairing communication breakdowns. Second, parents often do not have an implicit knowledge of communication strategies, even though they live with their child.

Many of the techniques that were considered in Chapter 8 can be used to teach parents optimal ways to repair communication breakdowns. Parents can practice such expressive repair strategies such as rephrasing, simplifying, elaborating, and building from the known.

Very often, communication breakdowns occur because parents do not understand their children, because of either their child's poor speech production skills or limited language abilities. These communication breakdowns should not be considered a "fault" of either the parent (e.g., "I should be able to guess what my child is saying better than I am doing right now") or the child (e.g., "I wish he could speak better"). When conversation breakdowns occur because they cannot understand their children's messages, parents can use the receptive repair strategies listed in Table 14–5. For example, the following is an example of the *Tell me more* strategy:

John: My Legos fell apart.
Mother: When did this happen?
John: In the blue table.
Mother: Tell me more.
John: Chris took my pieces. Whap! He gave big hit.

TABLE 14–5 Receptive Repair Strategies for Parents

- Ask children to repeat the message.
- Encourage them to provide more information (*Tell me more . . .*).
- Restate what they might have said (*I think you said . . .*).
- Ask them to alter the delivery of their messages (*Slow down a little . . .*).
- Go with the flow, in the hopes that you will eventually understand (*How about that ! I see and then what happened . . . ?*).

Other ways to encourage children to provide more information appear in Table 14–6. Parents can also restate what they believe their children may have said (Table 14–7). By using the *Did you say* strategy, a parent demonstrates that at least she or he is trying to understand. Parents might ask their child to change the delivery of a message, or even draw a picture or act out what they mean (Table 14–8).

TABLE 14–6 Ways to Encourage the Child to Provide More Information

- Tell me more about this.
- When did this happen?
- What did you do then?
- Where were you?
- How did this make you feel?
- Who did this?
- (Wait silently for the child to say more.)

TABLE 14–7 Ways to Restate What Children Have Said

- I think you said . . .
- You seem confused. Am I right?
- Let me make sure I understand. You did . . . Your brother did . . .
- (Repeat what you believe your child said, using a questioning intonation) You missed the bus?
- Are you saying . . . ?

TABLE 14–8 Ways to Ask Children to Change Their Delivery of a Message

- Can you slow down a little?
- Can you speak up?
- Please write this down.
- Draw me a picture.
- Show me.
- Act it out.

Communication Strategies Training for Children

Children with hearing loss also may benefit from communication strategies training. This kind of training is usually appropriate for children in the higher grades of elementary school or in junior high school or high school. Some of the concepts underlying communication strategies training may be too abstract for children in lower grades.

The same model that was presented in Chapter 8 may also be followed in providing communication strategies training for children, with the three components of formal instruction, guided learning, and real-world practice. Formal instruction might include a review of effective listening behaviors (e.g., *Pay attention, Watch the talker's face, Try to identify key points*) and how to ask talkers to clarify a message (e.g., *When you don't understand a message, ask the talker to say just one word. This will tell you what he or she is talking about).*

During guided learning, children might watch the clinician or classroom teacher demonstrate the desired behavior and then try to imitate it. Teacher-made or commercially available books might be used to provide vicarious consequences. For example, the drawings in Figure 14–9 present sample pages from a teacher-made story about a young girl who used expressive repair strategies successfully while placing an order at a fast-food restaurant. A teacher and her class might review similar materials before a field trip that includes a lunch outing.

Real-world practice activities help children transfer their use of communication strategies to natural settings. Activities should require them to interact with different talkers, in a variety of contexts. Guidelines for developing real-world activities for children are presented in Table 14–9.

FIGURE 14–9 Sample pages from a teacher-made book about expressive repair strategies. In the story, "Janet," who has hearing loss, is ordering lunch from a fast-food restaurant.

TABLE 14–9 Guidelines for Developing Real-World Practice Activities for Children

A. **Assign a real-world practice activity that the child has performed successfully during guided learning practice.**

If the child is to ask someone to repeat a message following a communication breakdown, the child first should practice asking for clarification in the classroom or clinical setting. Then the child can be asked to attempt the strategy in, for example, art class. Although not necessary, the art teacher can be briefed beforehand that the child will practice repair strategies with her or him.

B. **Select a communication situation in which the child will feel motivated to communicate.**

For example, a young child might be asked to use repair strategies when ordering food at a fast-food restaurant.

C. **Select an interaction that allows the child to experience some success.**

For example, you might ask the child to interact with a familiar teacher before asking the child to try using repair strategies with an unfamiliar store clerk.

D. **Provide instructions for the activity. Present the instructions with simple language and vocabulary.**

The purpose of a homework activity might be to listen for the main points of a one-paragraph narrative. The clinician might provide the following written instructions:

This envelope contains a story. Ask your mother to read it to you. Watch and listen carefully. If you do not understand the story, ask questions. Draw a picture about the story.

E. **Provide a means for the child to record the experience.**

In the activity described in item D above, the record of the experience is the child's drawing.

In addition to learning how to use facilitative and receptive repair strategies, children also can learn to use expressive repair strategies. Expressive repair strategies may be appropriate to use when the child presents a message, usually with speech, and the communication partner does not recognize it. The child then repairs the communication breakdown, perhaps by trying again using his or her best speech or by adding hand gestures.

Table 14–10 summarizes a five-step training plan of action for teaching children to use expressive repair strategies (Elfenbein, 1994). Formal instruction and guided learning occur during the first four steps while real-world practice occurs in the fifth step.

In this plan, children begin by reviewing principles of basic communication processes and consider the sender–message–receiver relationship and the various ways of communicating. Children may create a book about the ways people communicate, tearing pictures from old magazines for illustrations. Step 2 entails talking about communication breakdown: What happens when breakdowns occur? How can you tell that it has happened? Why did it happen? Here, children might generate a list of the ways that people signal a breakdown. In Step 3, the group leader asks the children to consider how best to formulate and transmit their messages. This entails considering the needs of the communication partner, such as how much information the receiver already has. For example, if the child talks about last summer's vacation, will the receiver recognize the locale? The fourth step introduces expressive repair strategies, and children practice revising their own messages using different words and practice modifying their listening environments (e.g., turning off a radio). One of the most important messages conveyed during this step is that children share responsibility in managing their conversational interactions, and they have a variety of options available to them for rectifying their communication breakdowns. The final step provides practice in using repair strategies. At this time, children might talk about their feelings and responses to communication breakdown. Often, it is reassuring to learn that their classmates have experienced similar frustration and embarrassment following a communication breakdown. In practicing

If Only She Could Receive Communication Strategies Training . . .

"I feel that I miss out on many things, particularly with friends. I don't hear what they say and even if I ask 'what?' they repeat it and I don't hear, then I am embarrassed about asking again and give up. That is not a pleasant feeling. I don't feel comfortable in such situations but I try to live with it. Sometimes, I try to continue and be part of the conversation, and sometimes I leave."

—An adolescent with significant hearing loss talking about peer-related stress

(Zaidman-Zait & Dotan, 2017, p. 262)

repair strategies, children progress through increasingly difficult settings: role-playing, then sheltered environments, such as talking to the school administrative assistant, and then real-world situations.

TABLE 14–10 Five-Step Plan of Action for Teaching Children to Use Communication Strategies

Step 1. Understanding Basic Communication Processes
A. Sender–message–receiver relationship
B. Ways to communicate (e.g., speech, sign, writing, mime, gesture)
Step 2. Understanding Communication Breakdowns
A. Definitions and examples
B. Causes of communication breakdown
C. Ways people signal confusion
Step 3. Message Formulation
A. Information to be transmitted
B. Evaluation of the receiver's position (e.g., background knowledge)
C. Evaluation of sender's abilities (e.g., speech proficiency)
D. Environmental constraints (e.g., background noise)
E. Social constraints (e.g., conventions of politeness and etiquette)
Step 4. Introduction of Communication Repair Strategies
A. Receiver's responsibilities
1. Acknowledge confusion
2. Identify causes of breakdown
3. Implement receptive repair strategies
B. Sender's responsibilities
1. Be alert to signals of confusion
2. Identify causes of a communication breakdown
3. Implement expressive repair strategies
Step 5. Practice Using Communication Repair Strategies
A. Move from sheltered environments to the real world
B. Move from transmission of simple to complex to more complex messages
C. Discuss feelings associated with communication breakdown

Source: Adapted from Elfenbein (1994).

CHILDREN WHO HAVE MILD OR MODERATE HEARING LOSS OR UNILATERAL HEARING LOSS

Heretofore, the focus has primarily been on children who have bilateral severe and profound hearing loss. However, there is a huge population of school-age children who have mild and moderate hearing losses who may require services from a speech and hearing professional at some point. Other children in your caseload may have hearing loss in only one ear.

Children Who Have Mild or Moderate Hearing Loss

About 15% of children in the United States (more than 7 million) have a low-frequency or high-frequency hearing loss in at least one ear (Niskar et al., 1998). Etiologies for those who have permanent mild or moderate hearing loss include syndromes, genetics, and ear, nose, and throat anomalies (Fitzpatrick, Whittingham, & Durieux-Smith, 2014).

Mild and moderate hearing loss can affect language development adversely (Carew, Mensah, Rance, Flynn, Poulakis, & Wake, 2017). For example, in a longitudinal study, Tomblin, Harrison, Ambrose, Walker, Oleson, and Moeller (2015) studied children from the ages of 2 to 6 years. The children with hearing loss had poorer language, and by the age of 6, the children with hearing loss still had not lessened the gap in language scores compared with the children with normal hearing. A similar gap was found in a study involving adolescents (Delage & Tuller, 2007). More hearing in the better ear and use of hearing aids are associated with better language development (e.g., Tomblin et al., 2015; but see Carew et al., 2017).

Ensure That a Child Understands What Is Happening in the Classroom

"I got in trouble for cheating on a spelling test because the teacher saw me looking at my neighbor's paper. But I didn't even realize we were being tested because I hadn't heard her say that."

—Carrie Spangler, an audiologist with a prelingual high-frequency hearing loss, reminiscing about an experience in fourth grade

(Rowden-Racette, 2012, p. 36)

Mild and moderate hearing loss can have other adverse effects as well. Some children will produce mild articulation errors, such as errors in the production of fricatives and affricates (Elfenbein, Hardin-Jones, & Davis, 1994). They may experience deficits in speech recognition, academic learning, social skills, and self-image (e.g., Laugen, Jacobsen, Rieffe, & Wichstrøm, 2017). They may experience difficulty in recognizing speech that is spoken quietly or at a distance.

Some children will experience particular difficulty while listening in noisy and reverberant classrooms. For example, one study involving children with mild hearing loss assessed their ability to recognize spoken sentences and to comprehend passages in a simulated classroom. The "classroom" had the reverberation qualities of a typical classroom and was filled with background noise associated with a heating, ventilation, and air conditioning system. The participants with mild hearing loss performed near ceiling on the sentence recognition task, as did the participants with normal hearing, but they performed significantly more poorly on the comprehension task (Lewis, Valente, & Spalding, 2015).

With the advent of newborn screening, children with mild or moderate hearing loss are identified sooner than in previous decades. For example, a **prospective study** of 381 children with mild or unilateral hearing loss revealed that the median age of identification before the implementation of universal newborn hearing screening was 5.0 years compared with 0.8 years post-implementation (Fitzpatrick et al., 2014; Carew et al., 2017). Some children with a mild and moderate hearing loss, however, are diagnosed later in childhood, perhaps during an elementary school screening program when they are 4 or 5 years of age, because they might not demonstrate remarkably delayed speech and language skills and might demonstrate fewer overt listening difficulties than children who have more significant hearing loss.

Prospective studies entail following a group of participants over time and monitoring outcomes, such as language development, during the course of the study and relating those outcomes to other factors, such as degree of hearing loss or socioeconomic status.

Many children with mild or moderate hearing losses receive a hearing aid (or two) and many receive benefit, especially those with moderate hearing loss. Audiologists appear to be routinely fitting children with mild hearing loss, as one study involving 114 children reported that 94% used hearing aids (Walker, Spratford, Ambrose, Holte, & Oleson, 2017). Walker, Holte, McCreery, Spratford, Page, and Moeller (2015) reported that children who had mild hearing loss and used a hearing aid for 8.7 hours or more each day scored significantly better on tests of language than children who wore hearing aids part-time (2 to 8.3 hours per day) or not at all.

Many children with mild or moderate hearing loss will have an IEP developed. The IEP should include recommendation for a speech-language evaluation to determine whether their speech and language acquisition is progressing according to age-level peers with normal hearing. They may or may not need speech-language therapy and they will likely benefit from using a personal or free-field FM assistive listening device system. Often a child's classroom teacher will consult with a speech and hearing professional about how to adjust the classroom environment to accommodate the child with hearing loss. A handout like that presented in the Key Resources might be provided to the classroom teacher.

Why She Did Not Join the Volleyball Team

"You've got the kids all yelling and screaming and shouting at each other, and the echo bouncing off of the walls. She can't hear anything properly down there in that kind of a situation [school gym]."

—Parent of a child who has mild hearing loss

(Grandpierre, Fitzpatrick, Na, & Mendonca, 2018, p. 144)

Unilateral hearing loss is a mild to profound hearing loss in one ear and normal hearing in the other ear.

Retrospective studies entail looking backward and collecting data from past medical or educational records and do not follow the participants going forward in time.

A **restrospective study** conducted with children who have unilateral hearing loss, 87 of whom used a hearing aid in the affected ear and 43 of whom did not, revealed the following findings:

- More than half of the children who used hearing aids felt that it enhanced their directional hearing and their ability to hear in both quiet and noise.
- The children who used hearing aids demonstrated high levels of acceptance, wearing them for at least eight hours per day.
- Both groups had an equally high health-related quality of life.

(Rohlfs, Friedhoff, Bohnert, et al., 2017)

Bringing a Unilateral Hearing Loss to School

"When children with unilateral hearing loss or single-sided deafness start school, that's when we really begin to see the effects of their hearing loss. We start to notice that when they're missing things in the classroom due to background noise, they're not learning to read well. And if a child is not learning to read well, almost everything else falls apart."

—Lisa Christensen, AuD, audiology program manager at Cook Children's Health Care System in Fort Worth, TX

(Abouras, 2018, p. 35)

Children Who Have Unilateral Hearing Loss

One adolescent in the United States in 40 has a **unilateral hearing loss**, with normal hearing in one ear and a loss of 25 dB HL or greater in the other ear (Shargorodsky, Curhan, Curhan, & Eavey, 2010). About 3% to 6% of school-age children have a unilateral loss (Anne, Lieu, & Cohen, 2017). Until fairly recently, a common dictum was "one good ear provides adequate hearing for language learning and cognitive development." As a result, children with unilateral hearing loss historically have received little or no intervention.

Unfortunately, unilateral hearing loss is consequential. These children are at risk for language delay, as they miss out on incidental learning, or opportunities to overhear information from diverse sources. They may miss language spoken at a distance, in noisy places, and when the good ear is turned away. The decrease in incidental learning appears to result in impoverished vocabulary and syntax (Lieu, Tye-Murray, Karzon, & Piccirillo, 2010; Fitzpatrick, Gaboury, Durieux-Smith, Coyle, Whittingham, & Nassrallah, 2018) and may result in impoverished general knowledge about the surrounding environment. Children with unilateral hearing loss may easily fatigue because they exert increased effort to listen in a noisy or reverberant classroom.

Children with unilateral hearing loss are also at risk for decreased educational achievement, and some may exhibit inattentive listening and behavior issues (e.g., they may be accused of "selective listening"). They may seem easily distractible or frustrated. Lieu, Tye-Murray, and Fu (2012) conducted a longitudinal study with 46 children who had unilateral hearing loss, the majority of whom had a severe-profound loss in their poor ear. They found that 39% had received speech-language therapy and 36% had received special education. Teachers had identified behavioral issues in 35% of the children. Parents reported attentional and behavioral problems such as aggressive behavior in 10% of the children.

Children with unilateral hearing loss often receive no aural rehabilitation or special services. They are not automatically entitled to early intervention as part of IDEA nor do they automatically receive an IEP. Lieu et al. (2012) reported that only about half of their participants received an IEP during the three-year course of their study and that only half tried some form of amplification such as a hearing aid or an FM system.

Not all children with unilateral hearing loss develop speech-language delays or educational performance problems. For example, in a systematic review of the literature, Anne et al. (2012) identified seven studies that showed poorer speech and language outcomes for children with unilateral hearing loss compared with children with normal hearing, whereas four studies did not report any differences. However, these children are at increased risk, and it is important to monitor their performance. When you encounter a child with unilateral hearing loss, you might ensure the child has favorable seating in the classroom. You might also arrange for a language and speech assessment, and if appropriate, a hearing aid evaluation, an IEP if the child is demonstrating delays, and any appropriate intervention services such as amplification and auditory training in noise. Other actions may include (Holstrum et al., 2008, p. 40):

- Provide information to parents and classroom teachers about unilateral hearing loss and its possible effects on language development.
- Adapt the environment so that it is acoustically friendly; for example, in the classroom, ensure that the child has a desk that will allow the good ear to be positioned toward the teacher's desk.
- Provide instruction to parents and teachers about how to get the child's attention before speaking to him or her; e.g., make eye contact.

CASE STUDY

IDEA(s) for All Children

Seaver and DesGeorges (2004) present a number of case studies to illustrate the nuances of IDEA. Three of the case studies are summarized in this section.

V.S., Assistive Listening Technology (p. 22)

V.S. has a mild-to-moderate hearing loss and attends a public school. Her classroom faces a busy highway and is heated by a noisy air-handling system. Audiological tests have shown that her speech recognition scores decrease by 50% in the classroom environment compared with a sound-treated booth. An audiologist measured the SNR and the reverberation times of the classroom and found them to be unacceptable. V.S.'s IEP team determines that accommodations are necessary so she can continue to function in her neighborhood school. She is supplied with an FM system, which boosts her speech recognition scores to 84% words correct. The classroom receives carpeting and is treated with acoustic ceiling tiles.

L.R., Least Restrictive Environment (p. 21)

L.R. lives in the suburbs outside of a city. She received a cochlear implant three years ago, at the age of 4 years. She attends a centrally located day school for children who are deaf and hard of hearing, and one that has a total-communication educational philosophy. Until recently, L.R.'s parents used sign with her in the home, but have noticed that her spoken-language skills have progressed to such a level that signing is no longer necessary. Her current teachers are strong advocates of sign language, and they have no prior experience with children who use cochlear implants. The speech-language pathologist at her day school has also never worked with a child who has a cochlear implant, but has opted to treat her like other children who use hearing aids. L.R. has friends at school but has not made friends in her own neighborhood. Her parents decide that she could benefit by being exposed to strong spoken-language models during her school day.

Although L.R.'s original placement in a total-communication program was appropriate, her needs have changed following the receipt of a cochlear implant. Her school district is not large enough to offer an aural/oral option, and there are few children in the mainstream in her district. Her parents would like her to enroll in the neighborhood school and be fully integrated with children who have normal hearing, and receive services from an itinerant teacher. The members of her IEP team agree that L.R. should return to her local school so as to have more spoken-language models, but they also believe that the professionals who work with L.R. should have special expertise with children who have cochlear implants. The special education director from L.R.'s school district performs some field research and learns that a neighboring school district has a cochlear implant staff, assembled to serve a group of four children. The special education director solicits support from this district. Their cochlear implant staff agrees to provide ongoing mentorship to the itinerant teacher who will serve L.R. Their staff also agrees to provide in-services to L.R.'s classroom teacher and help the teacher to understand and implement the accommodations that are appropriate for a cochlear implant user.

J.M., Direct Instruction (p. 19)

J.M. is 4 years old and the daughter of Deaf parents who use ASL. She has a severe-to-profound hearing loss. Currently she is in a center-based preschool for children who have disabilities. Three of her classmates have hearing loss, two have autism, and the other children have other "special needs." The program uses total communication. Her parents want J.M. to have the opportunity to use her native language and to maintain the family's values of culture and community.

The IEP team considers ways to provide direct instruction in J.M.'s primary mode of communication. Because the school uses the SEE sign system, they must accommodate her language through other means. A neighborhood school district has a charter school with teachers who provide instruction using ASL. The IEP team decides that this would be the optimal placement for J.M. This alternative placement will also permit J.M. to interact with other children who use her communication mode. The home school district funds transportation to the ASL charter school. Her parents become a resource for the charter school about Deaf culture and community.

Advocating for Our Child

"We knew our daughter, we knew hearing loss, we knew her goals, we attended every meeting with the school and we knew IDEA as it related to hearing loss."

—Nicole Underwood, who filed for due process so that her daughter would receive the family's preferred school placement and services related to her use of a cochlear implant

(Underwood, 2006, p. 42)

FINAL REMARKS

This chapter presented an overview of school-age children's intervention programs. Federal law mandates that children receive a "free and appropriate public education" in the least restrictive environment, ideally at whatever public school children would have attended on the basis of where they live. However, given the relatively low incidence of hearing loss and deafness, not every school district has the critical mass to justify the expense of either creating a program for children with hearing loss or hiring the appropriate staff. In many cases, creative solutions must be sought, with the overt goal of meeting children's unique communication requirements and related needs. IEP teams have the charge of helping to ensure that children receive the services that they need. Special provisions of the IDEA stipulate accommodations for a child's language and communication needs, for opportunities to interact with peers and teachers, for assistive technology, and for other academic needs. Integral to developing an IEP and ensuring that children receive appropriate services is the child's family. Parents many times must become advocates for their children, participating in the IEP process and ensuring that their children receive the optimal services available.

KEY CHAPTER POINTS

- An Individualized Education Plan (IEP) is a written document that describes the child's current levels of performance, a statement of annual goals, a recommendation for special education support with an indication of how support will be provided, and objective criteria for evaluating progress.
- A multidisciplinary team is assembled to provide support and services to the child and his or her family. The team may include an audiologist, speech-language pathologist, classroom teacher, psychologist, interpreter, itinerant teacher, and resource room teacher.
- School placement may be public or private, residential or day. Classroom placement may be self-contained or mainstream. Variations of a mainstream placement include partial mainstreaming, inclusion, and coenrollment.
- Most children in the United States who have severe and profound hearing loss live at home and attend school in their home community.
- Use of assistive devices and favorable classroom acoustics can enhance a student's academic performance.
- School in-services prepare teachers and classmates for the arrival of students who have hearing loss into the classroom and school.
- Children and teenagers who have hearing loss are at a higher risk for mental and psychosocial problems than those who have normal hearing.
- Assessment instruments are available for evaluating the social skills of children who have hearing loss and some children can benefit from psychosocial social skills training.
- Some communication breakdowns occur because parents cannot understand their children's speech and language, and many parents might benefit from learning to use receptive repair strategies (e.g., "Tell me more. . . .").
- Older school-age children might engage in communication strategies training, following the model we considered in Chapter 8, where the three stages of formal instruction, guided learning, and real-world practice are included.

- Most children with mild and moderate hearing losses can attend classrooms with children who have normal hearing. Usually, they will receive an IEP, although they may or may not require specialized speech and hearing services.
- *Children with unilateral hearing loss are at risk for language delays.

TERMS AND CONCEPTS TO REMEMBER

Individualized Educational Program (IEP)
Multidisciplinary team
Itinerant teacher
Classroom placement
Self-contained classroom
Mainstream classroom
Resource room
Coenrollment
Appropriate format accommodations
Social competence
Unilateral hearing loss

KEY RESOURCES

Checking Hearing Instruments

- Visual inspection: Look for dents, cracks in the hearing aid case, cracks in the tubing, wax in the earmold, moisture in the tubing, corrosion in the battery compartment.
- Listening check: Insert tip of the hearing aid's sound hook tightly into the end of the hearing aid stethoscope, which you wear in the same way that a physician wears a stethoscope. Turn the instrument on and, while speaking into the hearing aid's microphone, rotate its volume control (if the device has one) while listening.
- Battery check: Check and replace the batteries if necessary.

Terminology related to FM trainer use (selected terminology presented by the College of Speech and Hearing Health Professionals of BC, 2011, pp. 4–5)

- **FM channel:** A narrow range of radio frequencies within the band allocated for FM amplification. Each channel is identified by number, letter, or color. The transmitter and the receiver must be set to the same channel.
- **FM level advantage:** The increase in decibel output level when the FM signal is added to, or substituted for, the signal from the aid's own microphone.
- **FM receiver:** The device that detects the transmitted radio wave and recovers the sound signal for delivery to the hearing aid or other hearing device. Connection options include integrated (receiver is built into the personal device), dedicated (the receiver is compatible with one case design), and universal (receiver works with multiple devices depending on the interface between the device and the receiver).

- **FM SNR benefit:** The increase in signal-to-noise ratio when the FM signal is added to, or substituted for, the signal from the aid's or cochlear implant's own microphone.
- **FM trainer:** Classroom assistive listening device in which the teacher wears a microphone and the signal is transmitted to the student(s) by means of frequency modulated radio waves.
- **FM transmitter:** The device that transmits the radio signal that carries the sound signal. Sometimes the microphone and transmitter are incorporated into a single unit.
- **FM transparency:** The condition in which equal inputs to the FM and hearing aid microphones produce equal outputs from the hearing aid (operationally defined for an input of 65 dB HL).
- **Remote microphone hearing assistance technology (RMHAT):** A microphone is placed close to the talker's mouth where the decibel level of the acoustic speech signal is well above that of interfering noise and reverberation. The resulting high quality signal is delivered to the listener via a personal FM receiver or sound ield loudspeaker.
- **Shoe** (also referred to as an ***FM boot***, see Chapter 3): An adapter that is placed on a hearing aid to permit the connection of FM receivers or other accessories.
- A **stetoclip** is a nonelectric device that resembles a stethoscope, which enables someone to perform a listening check on a hearing instrument.

FM Troubleshooting Guide

There are many different personal FM systems available on the market for use with hearing aids and cochlear implants as well as without additional hearing devices. Each device should come with a troubleshooting guide, but here are some general troubleshooting tips for any system.

PROBLEM	SOLUTION(S)
No sound at all	Are the FM or hearing aids/cochlear implant (CI) turned on? Check batteries in FM receiver, microphone, and hearing aids/CI. If the system is rechargeable, make sure FM system microphone or receiver is charged. Check the hearing aids/CI to be sure they are working on their own without the FM system. Make sure the hearing aids/CI are set on the correct program to receive FM input.
No sound from FM (hearing aids/CI are working, but not hearing sound from microphone of FM)	Are the FM receiver or microphone turned on? Check batteries in FM receiver and microphone. If the system is rechargeable, make sure FM system microphone or receiver is charged. If you are using FM boots, be sure they are connected well to the hearing aids/CI and there are no cracks or damage to the boots. If you are using a neckloop, be sure the neckloop is plugged into the receiver and is not cracked or damaged. If you are using a plug from the receiver to the hearing aid/CI, be sure the cord is plugged in correctly to both devices and is not cracked or damaged. Make sure the channels match on the receiver and microphone of the FM system.

Weak or distorted sound (there is sound coming from the FM, but it is not as loud as it usually is or sounds distorted)	Check the hearing aids/CI to be sure they are working on their own without the FM system and are not weak or distorted. Check the earmold of the hearing aids for wax or other blockage. Make sure the volume settings on the hearing aids/CI are correct. Check batteries in FM receiver, microphone, and hearing aids/CI. If the system is rechargeable, make sure FM system microphone or receiver is charged. Be sure the microphone is plugged into the transmitter and the cord is not cracked or damaged. If you are using FM boots, be sure they are connected well to the hearing aids/CI and there are no cracks or damage to the boots. If you are using a neckloop, be sure the neckloop is plugged into the receiver and is not cracked or damaged. If you are using a plug from the receiver to the hearing aid/CI, be sure the cord is plugged in correctly to both devices and is not cracked or damaged.
Static or intermittent sound through the FM (sound cuts in and out or is accompanied by static)	Check the hearing aids/CI to be sure they are working on their own without the FM system and there is no static, intermittent sound, or feedback. Make sure there is no other electronic equipment in the room or nearby that could be interfering (computers, fans, etc.). Make sure there is not someone in a nearby room transmitting on the same channel. Check batteries in FM receiver, microphone, and hearing aids/CI. If the system is rechargeable, make sure FM system microphone or receiver is charged. Check any wires and cords on the FM system and CI for damage or fraying. Make sure the earmold is fitting properly and is not clogged with wax or debris.

Guidelines for the Classroom Teacher

The following suggestions should help ______'s teacher understand that although he/she receives benefits from his/her hearing aid, it does not make speech clearer, only louder. What he hears might be called indistinct speech since there are individual sounds that are distorted or that she may not hear at all. Therefore anything that can be done to improve the listening conditions would be helpful.

1. Let ______ sit as close to the teacher as possible. In this way he/she will be able to benefit from both the auditory and visual cues. This seat should be far away from noisy distractions of hallways, radiators, or windows. Expect ______ to have more trouble listening and paying attention when the room is noisy than when it is quiet.
2. Speak naturally to him/her in a good clear voice. The hearing aid is an amplifier, therefore it is unnecessary to shout.
3. If ______ does not understand something that was said, the teacher can:
   - **a.** repeat—perhaps a little slower.
   - **b.** rephrase.
   - **c.** write the word or sentence on the board.
4. In order to follow a group discussion, it would be helpful if ______ could sit where she could see most of the faces, and if the teacher or children could try to let her know who is talking and let her look before the speaker begins to talk. It is also ideal if the teacher can repeat the most important things said.

5. In order to understand what is said, it is usually helpful for ______ to see the speaker's face and lips. This is called speechreading. For speechreading it is helpful if
   - **a.** ______'s back is to the major light source.
   - **b.** The speaker does not move around too much.
   - **c.** The speaker speaks clearly and distinctly and faces ______ when talking.
6. Sometimes a child with hearing loss may miss the small words and misunderstand a sentence, especially if it is a long sentence and the room is noisy. If ______ seems confused or gives a silly answer, repeat what was said and if he/she said something inappropriate let her in on the joke. ______ may not always tell the teacher if he/she has not understood, but she should be encouraged to do so. Children who are hearing impaired are sometimes embarrassed to keep asking for repetitions.
7. New vocabulary words may be difficult for ______, and he/she may require a little extra help in vocabulary development.
8. In some cases a notetaker can be a help to the student with hearing loss. Sometimes a "buddy" in the class can be assigned to repeat directions to the child with hearing loss without disrupting the classroom routine.

Source: A handout from Central Institute for the Deaf Hearing, Language, and Speech Clinics. Reprinted with permission.

Appendix 14–1

An IEP (adapted from the National Council for Special Education, 2006)

Name: Robert Spencer
Date of Birth: 5-27-06

Address: Deerfield Road, Belleview
Grade: 4th

Classroom teacher: Elizabeth Gump
Itinerant teacher: Cindy Cross

Resource room teacher: Allen Fox
Audiologist: Carla Moses

Speech-language pathologist: Jennifer Lipstein

In attendance: Amy and Charles Spencer, Elizabeth Gump, Cindy Cross, Allen Fox, Carla Moses, Jennifer Lipstein

Nature and degree of special education needs and effects on educational development: Robert has a profound bilateral hearing loss that affects the acquisition and development of language and speech and interferes with his learning of academic material. He received a cochlear implant at the age of 24 months, and wears the device consistently. Learning language in the whole-class setting has proved to be challenging.

Special education and related support services: Robert spends 4 hours in the resource room each week. He receives team teaching with a group of five students who have mixed ability for the subjects of arithmetic and history. He also receives one-on-one speech-language therapy for 30 minutes twice a week. Each session includes 10 minutes of auditory training, speechreading training, or communication strategies training. Twice a week, an itinerant teacher provides support services to Robert for 1 hour. Robert is exempt from Spanish lessons.

Accommodations: Robert's classroom is fitted with an insulated door, and rubber caps have been placed on the leg bottoms of all chairs to reduce echo. A sound field FM system is used during classroom instruction, and he uses a handheld radio microphone for participating in group discussions. He receives preferential seating in both the classroom and the resource room to ensure good view of the teacher and to minimize glare.

Present level of educational performance: [test scores for a psychoeducational assessment, language and speech assessment]

Summary of information from parents, student, class teacher, resource teacher, itinerant teacher, speech-language pathologist

Self-management skills	Approach to schoolwork is organized and thorough.
Motivation	Highly motivated, ambitious, and determined. Has difficulty paying attention during English lessons.
Social and interpersonal skills	Considerate of others. Has many friends, and is a team player. Prefers small groups. Eager to participate in sports but does not pick up the rules through incidental listening. Appears to be embarrassed to ask his friends for help.
Self-esteem	Appears self-conscious about his speech and is loath to ask for clarification following a communication breakdown. Says he sometimes feels different from his classmates.
Language and communication	Good nonverbal skills, including eye contact and animated facial expression. Speech is characterized by sound distortions (especially of the fricatives and glides) and good prosody. Occasionally produces grammatical errors, such as adding "-ing" to irregular verbs. Needs more familiarity with synonyms and idioms.
Literacy skills	Word recognition and spelling skills are near grade level. Reading comprehension needs improvement, especially for the subjects of history and geography. Experiences difficulty in writing creatively.
Mathematical skills	Mathematical skills are at grade level. Can tell time and purchase items in the school supply center. Needs multisensory methods to master new math concepts.
Motor skills	Agile and athletic.
Access to curriculum	Requires pre- and post-tutoring to master academic material, especially history. Important to check for mastery of new vocabulary and concepts.
Computer skills	Learning to touch type. Uses auditory training software.
Learning style	Learns best in small groups or through one-on-one instructions. Visual learner. Needs visual cues and concrete materials to master academic material.
Attendance	Perfect.
Hobbies and interests	Plays soccer. Strong interest in family pets.

ABILITIES	LEARNING NEEDS
• Motivated and cooperative • Team player • Strong computational skills • Strong progress in developing speech and language • Has acquired basic computing skills	• Awareness of own strengths and talents • Skills to express feelings and needs to classmates • Opportunities to participate in playground sports • Access to history and geography lessons (vocabulary and comprehension strategies) • Continued development of vocabulary and syntax • Auditory training and development of listening skills • Speech therapy • Reading comprehension • Creative writing • Understanding Deaf culture

GOALS ROBERT WILL:	PERSONNEL INVOLVED	STRATEGIES AND RESOURCES	BENCHMARKS OF ACHIEVEMENT
Identify and record his strengths, talents, and needs	Resource teacher, itinerant teacher, speech-language pathologist	Make an electronic book called *This Is Me*; read books that have a main character with a disability; create a scrapbook about sports figures and artists who have had hearing loss	Less reluctance in talking about his hearing loss; higher score on the Minnesota Social Skills Checklist for the *Self-concept/self-esteem section*
Use repair strategies following a communication breakdown with classmates	Classroom teacher; speech-language pathologist, audiologist	Disability awareness program for entire class facilitated by audiologist; modeling; role-playing; communication strategies curriculum	Uses repair strategies during circle time; higher score on the Minnesota Social Skills Checklist for the *Pragmatics* section
Participate in playground sports with his classmates	Classroom teacher, resource teacher	Class project, *Games we like to play*; scrapbook of photographs about the rules of baseball, soccer, football, and other playground games; buddy system	Increased involvement with classmates; increased time playing games
Identify place value in whole numbers, up to 1,000	Classroom teacher, itinerant teacher, resource teacher	Use concrete materials such as blocks and number forms to work through operations involved in grouping and exchanging	Competency demonstrated through class tests; math achievement test
Recognize fractions and equivalent forms with denominators 2, 3, 4, 6, 8	Classroom teacher, itinerant teacher, resource teacher	Develop understanding through formal instruction and informal instruction, including cutting simple shapes from paper and paper folding, cutting pizzas into slices, and frequent use of terminology (*quarter; half; third*)	Competency demonstrated through class tests; math achievement test
Verbally define words associated with the history and geography curricula, using clear enunciation	Classroom teacher, itinerant teacher, speech-language pathologist; audiologist	Introduce new vocabulary using photographs and internet searches, record new words in a personal dictionary, coordinate speech-language therapy sessions with classroom instruction, use vocabulary during auditory training lessons	Improvements demonstrated through class tests; standardized vocabulary test
Write a summary of a reading passage, recalling at least three main ideas	Classroom teacher, itinerant teacher, resource teacher, parent volunteer	Before reading—preview and predict and after reading—highlight key words and sentences. Make mind-maps, reread text with a parent volunteer, correct writing sample with itinerant teacher	Improvement demonstrated through class tests and progress on *Reading Rockets* series; standardized reading comprehension test; increased time spent reading for pleasure

CHAPTER 15

Speech, Language, and Literacy

OUTLINE

In the early days of cochlear implant research, the control group used to evaluate the efficacy of cochlear implantation was the hearing aid user who had severe or profound hearing loss. A generic question was *Would the relatively invasive and expensive cochlear implant lead to better performance?* The answer to this question has proved to be a resounding *yes,* so much so that today, most researchers ask the question *To what extent do children with cochlear implants perform like children who have normal hearing?*

We may only be scratching the surface of the potential benefits of cochlear implantation. With implantation ages becoming even younger and technology becoming ever better, results will likely be even more positive in even just a few years from now. Complicating the issue further is that children who use cochlear implants vary greatly in their performance and so generalizations are difficult to make.

In this final chapter, we will consider the speech, language, and literacy difficulties that may co-occur with hearing loss. Because children who use cochlear implants often differ dramatically, under each of these three topics, children who have significant hearing loss and who use hearing aids are considered separately from children who use cochlear implants. The chapter includes an overview, a review of procedures used for evaluating speech, language, and literacy performance, and a review of teaching strategies that foster speech and language skills (Figure 15–1).

Some of the factors that may affect speech, language, and literacy development in young cochlear implant users, and may help account for within-group variability, include the following:

- Age at implantation
- Duration of device use
- Preimplant aided hearing ability
- Consistency of device use
- Cochlear implant model and processing strategy, and appropriateness of map
- Family situation, such as socioeconomic status and mother's level of education
- Family support
- Communication mode
- Educational placement
- Social and world experiences
- Cognitive skills, such as working memory and nonverbal intelligence

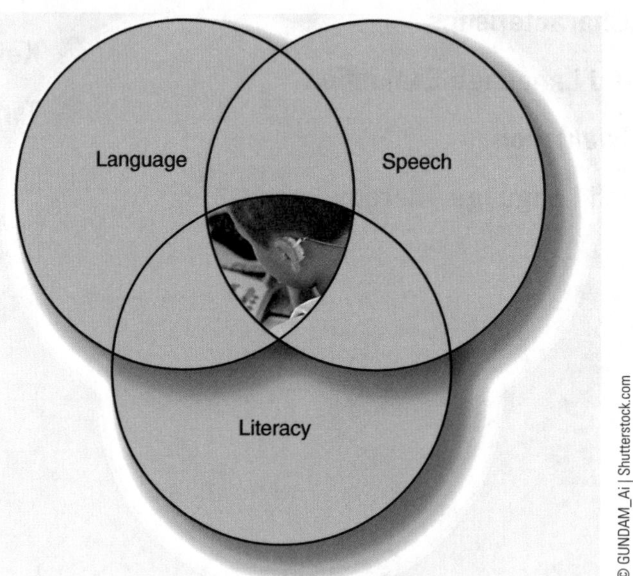

FIGURE 15–1 Language, speech, and literacy skills. The development of skills is often intertwined. For example, a child may become a better reader as he or she acquires more vocabulary and familiarity with syntactic structures and as he or she develops a system of phonology that will allow decoding of the orthographic form.

SPEECH CHARACTERISTICS

The effects of hearing loss are most pronounced with children who have a congenital loss or who lost their hearing in early childhood. In the presence of adventitious hearing loss, even when the loss is profound, speech usually remains intact, although it may have an unusual voice quality.

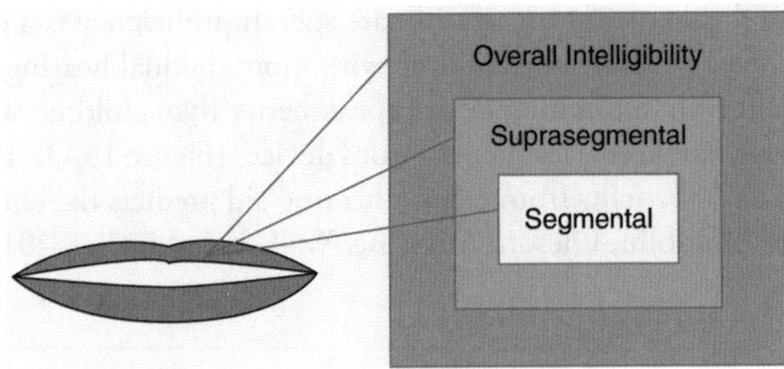

FIGURE 15–2 Assessment of speech production. Speech proficiency is determined with a consideration of overall intelligibility, segmental production, and suprasegmental production.

Overall intelligibility, segmental production, and suprasegmental production are often considered when describing children's speech (Figure 15–2). Numerous factors exert a positive influence on each of these, including the following:

- A child is identified early on as having hearing loss.
- The child begins to use a listening device shortly after identification, and wears the device for most waking hours.
- The child quickly begins to receive intervention services, including speech and language therapy.
- The child is motivated to speak, as when using an aural/oral communication mode.
- The child is raised in a favorable speech environment; for example, the child hears spoken language often, those around the child provide good spoken language models, and the child is reinforced for communicating with speech.
- No other disabilities are present.

Learning to Talk with Little or No Audition

To understand the difficulties children have in developing intelligible speech, it is instructive to think about the ways in which auditory information helps children with normal hearing learn to talk. Auditory information plays at least five important roles; it:

1. Potentiates the development of specific principles of articulatory organization. By listening to the speech of others, children learn how to regulate their speech breathing, learn how to flex and extend their tongue bodies, and learn how to alternate rhythmically between vowels and consonants. Children who cannot hear often do not learn to (a) manage their breath streams for speech, (b) roll their tongue dorsum forward and backward, and concave and convex it to establish vowel postures, and (c) move the articulators smoothly and continuously from one articulatory posture to the next.
2. Differentiates speech events. For example, through listening, children learn to distinguish /p/ with a relatively rapid velocity opening gesture and /w/ with a slow velocity gesture.
3. Leads children to develop a system of phonological performance (i.e., they learn the phonemes of their language community). Often children who cannot hear do not acquire some sounds in their language, especially those associated with high-frequency auditory information, such as /s/ and /ʃ/.
4. Informs children about the consequences of their articulatory gestures and how these consequences compare to sounds produced by other talkers. For example, if a child explodes air through his or her lips, he or she learns that this will produce a stop consonant sound. If the child does it with too much vigor, he or she will hear a sound that may be inappropriately loud. It is not uncommon for children with hearing loss to produce a slight popping sound when producing plosives.
5. Provides a mechanism for monitoring ongoing speech production and for detecting errors. For example, a young girl with normal hearing may hear herself say "See went," and then quickly correct herself and say "She went." Children with hearing loss cannot monitor themselves in this way.

One of the most reliable predictors of ultimate speech proficiency is a child's ability to recognize speech. As a general rule, children with more residual hearing and/or who receive greater benefit from a listening device speak better than children with less residual hearing or children who receive less benefit from devices (Figure 15–3). For example, the extent to which a child benefits from using a hearing aid predicts the child's speech (and language) abilities (Tomblin, Oleson, Ambrose, Walker, & Moeller, 2014).

FIGURE 15–3 The relationship between speech perception and speech production. Children who hear better tend to develop better speech.

What a child can speak relates to what the child can hear, whether at the level of the feature, word, or intonation pattern. For example, children who can hear the place of articulation (e.g., they can distinguish the word *pat* from *cat*), nasality (e.g., they can distinguish the word *nip* from *dip*), and voicing features (e.g., they can distinguish the word *sip* from *zip*) are more likely to speak these features correctly than children who do not hear them very well (Tye-Murray, Spencer, & Gilbert-Bedia, 1995). Children who hear words better also speak them better. Figure 15–4 illustrates the relationship between speech recognition scores on the Word Intelligibility Picture Index (WIPI; Ross & Lerman, 1971) and speech production scores on an imitative sentence test. These data were collected from young cochlear implant users who had at least five years of device experience. A **Pearson correlation**, which tests how well one set of data predicts another, was $r = .88$, denoting a robust relationship. Finally, ability to hear intonation affects ability to speak intonation. Children who can better mimic the intonation patterns of sentences such as *I sit in a chair* that are spoken in an angry, happy, or sad manner can better perceive the emotional content of sentences spoken with one of these three emotional overtones (Nakata, Trehub, & Kanda, 2012) (Figure 15–5).

A **Pearson correlation** is a statistical analysis that indicates the strength and the direction of a linear relationship between two variables.

Overall Intelligibility

Overall intelligibility refers to how well a person with normal hearing can understand a child's speech. A number of speech variables affect overall intelligibility, including how

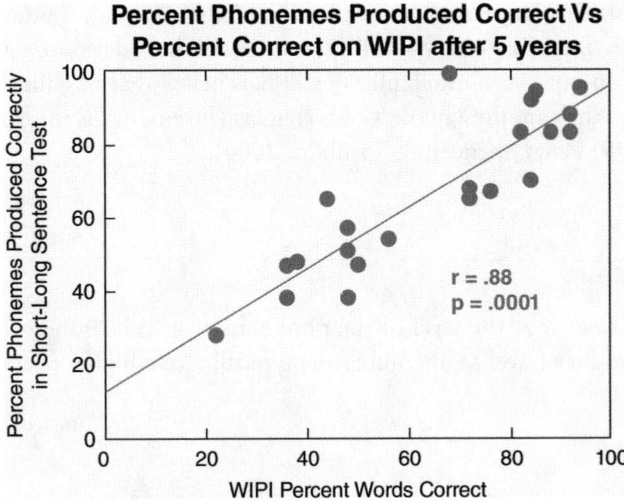

FIGURE 15–4 The relationship between children's speech production and speech recognition skills after 5 years of cochlear implant experience. The Short-Long Sentence Test comprises sentences that have both a short version of a test item (e.g., *How are you?*) and a longer version (e.g., *How are you going to make the sandwich?*) so that the test is easy enough for very young children but difficult enough for older children who have developed relatively good speech skills, and so the effects of sentence length can be assessed (Tye-Murray, Tomblin, & Spencer, 1997). The Word Intelligibility by Picture Identification test (WIPI) is a closed-set six-word recognition where the child responds by pointing to one of six illustrations (Ross & Lerman, 1970).

FIGURE 15–5 Recognizing and producing emotion in sentences. A prompt such as this can be used to direct children to speak with different emotional overtones, and can be used as a response screen in a corresponding test of emotion perception. For example, a child may hear a recorded sentence spoken with a happy emotional intonation and then be asked to point to the corresponding facial expression.

well the child articulates the segmental sounds of the language, how well the child **coarticulates** sounds, and how well the child produces the suprasegmental aspects of speech.

A talker **coarticulates** a speech unit by anticipating the sound during an earlier unit in the string or retains aspects of a unit during production of a subsequent unit; for example, when saying the word *blue*, the lips may round in anticipation of the /u/ as the talker speaks the initial consonant blend.

Children Who Have Significant and Prelingual Hearing Loss and Who Use Hearing Aids

Historically, most children with severe or profound and prelingual hearing loss were difficult to understand. On average, listeners identified less than 20% of their words (Smith, 1975).

Children Who Use Cochlear Implants

Most children who use cochlear implants speak better than children with profound hearing loss who use hearing aids. For example, a group of 40 children with prelingual and profound hearing loss, ranging in age between 2.5 and 15 years, scored 80% words correct when asked to repeat 10 sentences (Habib, Waltzman, Tajudeen, & Svirsky, 2010). However, there is great variability—some children develop very good speech skills and some do not—and intelligibility still falls below that of children with normal hearing, whether they are preschoolers or teenagers (Freeman, Pisoni, Kronenberger, & Castellanos, 2017; Peng, Spencer, & Tomblin, 2004).

A Parent's Insight into the Link Between Perception and Production

"[S]he sort of has trouble sometime saying her 's' clearly or her 'sh' sound or she'll drop some of the consonants sometimes at the ends of words. I think because she doesn't hear them herself, so it's hard for her to remember to make the sounds when she's talking."

—A parent of a child with mild hearing loss

(Grandpierre, Fitzpatrick, Na, & Mendonca, 2018, p. 144)

Segmental Errors

Segmental errors occur at the level of the phoneme or speech sound. Not surprisingly, children who produce fewer segmental errors typically have higher overall intelligibility (Smith, 1975).

Children Who Have Significant and Prelingual Hearing Loss and Who Use Hearing Aids

Children with significant hearing loss often demonstrate different developmental patterns than children with normal hearing and they plateau in their speech development relatively early on. For example, the vocalizations of infants who have significant hearing loss tend to be restricted when compared with their peers with normal hearing. Babies demonstrate delayed onset and fewer instances of **canonical babbling** and a limited range of consonant-like sounds (e.g., Von Hapsburg & Davis, 2006).

Canonical babbling is an advanced form of infant babbling that consists of well-formed consonant–vowel combinations.

As their spoken language emerges, children may produce many segmental errors. For example, one group of hearing aid users who had a mean hearing threshold of 95 dB HL spoke 56% of all of their vowels and diphthongs and 72% of their consonants incorrectly (Markides, 1970).

Children who have significant hearing loss most commonly neutralize vowels so they sound like a schwa (e.g., Verhoeven, Hide, De Maeyer, Gillis, & Gillis. 2016). Results from physiological studies suggest that they may not move their tongue bodies in the anterior–posterior (front–back) dimension as much as talkers with normal hearing and may rely primarily on jaw displacement to distinguish vowel height (e.g., the low vowel /a/ versus the high vowel /I/). This restricted tongue movement contributes to the perceptual phenomenon of neutralized vowels (Tye-Murray, Zimmermann, & Folkins, 1987).

Common vowel error types include the following:

- Neutralizations
- Substitutions
- Diphthongizations
- Prolongations
- Nasalizations

Speaking Sound-by-S-ou-n-d

"The intelligibility of a deaf child's speech is frequently lowered by permitting him to produce each element in a word exactly as it would be produced if it stood by itself."

—S. Sibley Haycock, superintendent of the Langside School for the Deaf, Glasgow, Scotland, 1901–1923

(Haycock, 1933, p. 29)

Many children produce consonants that are visible on the face more accurately than consonants that are not visible on the face. For example, a child more likely will speak the word *pat* correctly than the word *cat.* Affricates, sibilants, fricatives, glides, and laterals pose particular challenge. Characteristic consonant errors include the following:

- Voiced/voiceless confusions
- Substitutions
- Omissions
- Distortions
- Errors in consonant clusters

Children Who Use Cochlear Implants

As they begin to speak, cochlear implant users acquire speech sounds in about the same order (with some exception) as do children who have normal hearing (e.g., Bouchard, Le Normand, & Cohen, 2007; Warner-Czyz, Davis, & MacNeilage, 2010). After prolonged implant experience, they demonstrate greater accuracy in vowel production and a more complete repertoire than children who use hearing aids (e.g., Warner-Czyz, Davis, & Morrison, 2005), although the acoustic characteristics of their vowels remain less distinct than those of children with normal hearing (Verhoeven et al., 2016). They may speak consonants with about a 70% to 90% accuracy rate and their consonantal inventories approach those of children who have normal hearing, even though fricatives and affricates remain problematic, perhaps because they are high-frequency sounds and difficult to hear (Spencer & Guo, 2013). Children who receive their cochlear implants younger than 12 months of age show even better vowel and consonant production than those who are implanted after their first birthday (Dettman, Dowell, Choo, et al., 2016).

Sometimes Progress Occurs in Spurts

"[At the age of 4 years] all of a sudden it clicked with her. Ivy started saying and especially understanding much more. It became fun to do things at home."

—Mother of Ivy, a little girl who received a cochlear implant at the age of 1 year

(Central Institute for the Deaf, 2016)

Suprasegmental Errors and Voice Quality

Suprasegmental effects include intonation, **stress**, tempo, rhythm, and amplitude fluctuations (including silences) that are superimposed across linguistic segments, such as syllables, words, and sentences. Voice quality is sometimes considered as separate from suprasegmental aspects of speech, as it is the vibratory signal that fuels the speech output. Fundamental frequency, **subglottal air pressure**, breath control, **velopharyngeal functioning**, and vocal fold performance affect overall voice quality.

Suprasegmental effects include intonation, stress, tempo, rhythm, and amplitude fluctuations (including silences) that are superimposed across linguistic segments.

Word **stress** is marked by changes in loudness, duration, or pitch, or some combination of the three.

Subglottal air pressure refers to the build-up of pressure below the closed vocal folds in the larynx.

Velopharyngeal functioning refers to the appropriate opening of the velopharyngeal port during nasal consonants (i.e., /m, n, ŋ/) and nasalized vowels and its appropriate closure during "oral" phonemes such as stops and fricatives. The velopharyngeal port connects the oral and nasal cavities.

Children Who Have Significant and Prelingual Hearing Loss and Who Use Hearing Aids

Many children with significant hearing loss speak with faulty stress, rate, and intensity. Their speech may sound staccato or arrhythmic. They may place equal stress on all syllables or stress words inappropriately. For example, children may stress the second syllable in the word *baby* instead of the first, as in "bah-BEE" (e.g., Robb & Pang-Ching, 1992; Tye-Murray & Folkins, 1990). Many children speak very slowly, pausing often both within words and between words. Voelker (1938) found that children with profound hearing loss spoke 70 words per minute as compared with 164 words per minute spoken by children with normal hearing. They also tended to speak too loudly or too softly.

Children with profound hearing loss may have distinctive voice quality. Their speech may sound breathy, strained, hoarse, labored, harsh, strident, nasalized, or denasalized. Their pitch may sound excessively high or variable or may have sounded monotone.

Speech Breathing

For some patients, deviant speech breathing contributes to their frequent pauses and their breathy voice quality. For example, many adults who have significant and prelingual hearing loss demonstrate normal respiratory and aerodynamic behaviors for nonspeech tasks, such as walking, but aberrant behaviors when talking. They produce fewer words per breath cycle than do talkers with normal hearing, and expend more breath saying each word. They may use excessive force while speaking an initial stop consonant, resulting in a plosive popping sound. They may initiate an utterance with less air volume in their lungs and inefficiently valve the air flow at the level of the larynx and velopharynx during expiration. These breathing behaviors contribute to their unique sound quality (Itoh, Horii, Daniloff, & Binnie, 1982; Whitehead, 1982).

Some children produced frequent pitch breaks, where pitch abruptly changed from high to low (Markides, 1970; Smith, 1975).

Children Who Use Cochlear Implants

Cochlear implants do not support pitch perception very well, but can convey timing and loudness cues (see Chapter 3). Thus, there is potential, albeit limited, for receipt of a cochlear implant to influence a child's development of prosody and voice quality. For example, it appears that children struggle to speak a rising intonation, as when asking a question, but do master or approach mastery of other suprasegmental aspects and attain relatively good voice quality. Peng, Tomblin, Spencer, and Hurtig (2007) found that 24 children did not consistently use rising intonation contours when imitating yes–no questions. They also found that acoustic measures of fundamental frequency, intensity, and duration performed on the test sentences differed from those collected from a control group of adults with normal hearing. In a subsequent study, listeners categorized the children's utterances as either statements or questions with 73% accuracy (chance was 50%) as opposed to 97% accuracy for utterances spoken by age-matched peers with normal hearing (Peng, Tomblin, & Turner, 2008). Overall, cochlear implant use leads to better nasalization, speech prosody, and voice quality (e.g., de Souza, Bevilacqua, Braslotto, & Coelho, 2012; Lenden & Flipsen, 2007; Liwo, 2011).

LANGUAGE CHARACTERISTICS

Expressive language refers to the language we speak or sign.

Receptive language refers to the language we either hear or receive via sign.

One way to appreciate how hearing loss affects **expressive language** and **receptive language** development is to compare groups with normal hearing and with hearing loss. Historically, 8-year-old children with normal hearing had better knowledge of grammar than did adults with prelingual profound hearing loss. Moreover, most adults with significant hearing loss never acquired a vocabulary better than that of a fourth grader with normal hearing (Bamford & Saunders, 1985).

As is the case with speech production skills, children who have better speech recognition ability tend to develop better expressive and receptive language skills. For example, Wu et al. (2011) studied 39 Mandarin-speaking children who had received a cochlear implant at age 3 years, on average, and who had 5 to 7 years of cochlear implant experience. The children averaged 78% key words correct on an open-set sentence recognition test administered in an auditory-only condition, with a range of 23% to 100%. The researchers found a strong correlation between these speech recognition test scores and scores from a battery of receptive and expressive language tests (and with a test of reading comprehension too).

The Gap May Be Narrowing

Even though in this chapter a distinction is made between children who use hearing aids and those who use cochlear implants, the gap between their levels of achievement in language and reading appears to be narrowing, thanks to digital hearing aid technology. For example, Harris, Terlektsi, and Kyle (2017) compared two groups of children with severe-profound hearing loss between the ages of 5 and 7 years. The children who use cochlear implants scored similarly to the children who use digital hearing aids on measures of reading comprehension, English vocabulary, and phonological awareness.

Language difficulties are often categorized as problems of: (1) form, (2) content, or (3) pragmatics.

Form

Errors in **form** include errors in syntax and morphology. **Syntax** encompasses the grammatical rules that govern how words combine to form phrases, clauses, and sentences. The sentence *I saw she had a milkshake drank* exemplifies incorrect syntax. **Morphemes** are linguistic units that cannot be subdivided into smaller parts. For example, the word *ties* contains two morphemes, *tie* and *-s,* as does the word *tied* (i.e., *tie* and *-d*). **Morphology** encompasses the rules that govern morphemes and that modify meaning at the word level. A child who says, "He drived the car to the store" presents an example of incorrect morphology.

Form refers to the proper use of the elements of language, such as nouns, verbs, and prepositions.

Syntax is the part of grammar that governs how linguistic units are combined into phrases, clauses, and sentences.

Morphemes are linguistic units that cannot be subdivided into smaller units.

Morphology governs the internal structures of words.

Children Who Have Significant and Prelingual Hearing Loss and Who Use Hearing Aids

The list comprising problems of form is extensive. Children may overuse nouns and verbs and rarely use adverbs, prepositions, or pronouns. They may omit function words. Many of their sentences have a simple subject-verb-object structure, and their sentences have fewer words compared with those produced by children who have normal hearing. Compound or complex sentences are rare, as are morphemes that mark plurality, possession, the third person singular (e.g., *she walks*), or past tense. In telling a story about her cat, one child said, "Socks jump. Cup fall over. Mess big. Mad Mom about Socks." In this narrative, the child omitted function words such as *was,* articles such as *the,* and tense markers such as *-ed.* Her syntactic structures were simple, and one verb form (*fall*) was incorrect. She also reversed the first two words in the final sentence. Although a listener might follow her story, her sentences sound telegraphic.

Not only do they rarely produce compound or complex sentences, many children cannot interpret them when they speechread or listen. For example, someone might say, "The cat was chased by the dog." Children may interpret this sentence in the active tense: *The cat chased the dog.* A talker might speak a nominal sentence, such as, "The ending of the school year saddened the teacher." A child might interpret it in an objective sense: *The school year saddened the teacher* (Russell, Quigley, & Power, 1976).

Children Who Use Cochlear Implants

Children who receive cochlear implants demonstrate accelerated and enhanced development of form compared with hearing aid users but still demonstrate delays when compared with children with normal hearing. For example, Geers, Nicholas, and Sedey (2003) found that about half of their study's 181 children with cochlear implants demonstrated English syntax at a level comparable to their peers who have normal hearing. In a subsequent study of 153 children who attend aural/oral schools across the United States, 47% scored at an age-appropriate level on a receptive language test but only 39% scored at an age-appropriate level on an expressive language test (Geers, Moog, Beidenstein, Brenner, & Hayes, 2009). Performance varies widely, and some children receive more benefit than do others (Inscoe, Odell, Archbold, & Nikolopoulos, 2009; Niparko et al., 2010).

Content refers to the words and meanings.

A **lexicon** is the vocabulary of an individual or a language.

Semantics pertains to both the surface and underlying meanings of words and language, and includes multiple meanings of words.

Content

Content refers to the words and meanings used during communication. The term encompasses a child's **lexicon**, which is the child's vocabulary, and **semantics**, which are word meanings. A child may store a particular vocabulary word in his or her lexicon but may harbor only a restricted meaning. For example, a young child may know that the word *bank* means a depository to store money but not that it also means a river's edge, a series, a way to sink a basketball shot, and a tilting to the left or right (e.g., *The airplane banked left*).

Children with normal hearing acquire new words by interacting with their parents and other communication partners and through incidental learning, such as hearing words spoken on the television and radio and overhearing the conversations of others, as in a physician's waiting room or in a post office. Significant hearing loss, by its very nature, limits children's access to spoken words. Moreover, because the children may have limited language abilities, parents and other communication partners may restrict their vocabulary to simple and frequent words when speaking with them, which in turn may further limit children's vocabulary growth.

Children Who Have Significant and Prelingual Hearing Loss and Who Use Hearing Aids

Whereas an 18-month-old toddler with normal hearing has a vocabulary of about 20 to 50 words, a toddler with significant hearing loss has a vocabulary of less than 10 words (Schafer & Lynch, 1980). A 5-year-old child with normal hearing has a vocabulary of over 2,000 words. His peer with hearing loss has a vocabulary of 250 words (Dale, 1974).

Many children learn only common everyday words. They may have gaps in their vocabularies, wherein they do not know words relating to an entire concept, such as outer space. Hence, words such as *planet, Martian, star, spacemen,* and *rocket* may be unfamiliar. They often use words in limited ways. For example, a child may use a word such as *happy* as a predicate (e.g., *The boy is happy*) but not as a modifier (e.g., *The happy boy is here*). Many children cannot identify synonyms and antonyms or understand idioms such as *She was mad as a hornet.* Similarly, many experience difficulty handling words with multiple meanings. For example, children may understand the word *stand* in the context of *Please stand by the piano,* but not in the context of *Please move the music stand.*

In general, children who have significant hearing loss will learn words that are concrete more readily than they will learn words that are abstract. They may associate meanings with words like *bird, chair, sit, telephone,* and *ball.* Words that do not pair up with a physical object or an overtly observable behavior will be more difficult to learn—for example, words such as *rephrase, sentimental, admirable,* and *wise.*

Children Who Use Cochlear Implants

Cochlear implant use enhances and accelerates vocabulary acquisition, although performance often trails behind that of age-matched children with normal hearing. For example, in the study that included 112 children, 68% of the children scored age-appropriately on a test of receptive vocabulary and 74% scored age appropriately on a test of expressive vocabulary (Geers & Seedy, 2011).

Pragmatics

Pragmatics refers to the use of language in context, along with the societal-dependent aspects of communicative interactions.

Pragmatics is a branch of linguistics that studies the use of language in social interactions, and takes into account the context of the utterance, the goals of the talker, and the implicit rules governing conversation. Pragmatics may play an important role in a child's social functioning, and may contribute to both social competence and behavioral problems.

Many children with significant hearing loss demonstrate pragmatic errors. For example, some may use questions inappropriately. One child's first question to a new acquaintance was to ask how much money the girl's father made. A child may not know how to initiate or maintain a conversation or how to repair breakdowns in communication. In some circumstances, the child may nod and bluff, pretending to understand.

A child also may not know some of the social graces of conversation. He or she may not know how to take turns while conversing, how to acknowledge that the message has been heard, and how to change the topic of conversation. In the following conversation, a child with hearing loss introduced a topic abruptly and did not respond to the adult's request for clarification:

Adult: Do you want to come with me?

Child: Car fell off table, boom!

Adult: What did you say?

Child: Mine.

These inappropriate responses may relate to both the child's hearing loss (the child may not have recognized the adult's utterances) and an unfamiliarity with conversational rules.

In general, there at least three reasons why some children with hearing loss do not learn conversational pragmatics very well. First, they do not receive extensive practice in using language. Their unfamiliarity with many language structures and their reduced vocabulary limit their ability to converse. Moreover, if they do not use an aural/oral communication mode, they have fewer conversational partners to interact with because few persons with normal hearing know manually coded English or a Deaf sign language.

Second, they cannot overhear their parents or other people talking. Thus, as noted earlier, they do not receive the everyday, incidental models of how to use language.

Third, they may not receive the same formal instruction as children who have normal hearing. For example, a parent may carefully explain the rules of politeness to a child with normal hearing (*do not interrupt; say thank you; let someone else say something*). The parent may not explain the rules to his or her child with a hearing loss, either because of the child's limited language or because of the parent's limited skill in using sign.

Children Who Have Significant and Prelingual Hearing Loss and Who Use Hearing Aids

Although relatively few studies have focused on pragmatics, it appears that children who have hearing loss and who use hearing aids sometimes use language in inappropriate ways. For example, teenagers may not conceal their anger or happiness in situations where it might be appropriate to do so (teenagers!) compared with teenagers with normal hearing, as you might do when you want to protect the feelings of another (Hosie et al., 2000).

Toddlers and young children may not maintain the topic of conversation with their mothers as well as their peers with normal hearing. They may ask fewer questions and make fewer comments, refer less often to their feelings and activities, and supply less information (e.g., Lederberg & Everhart, 2000; Nicholas, 2000). They may also repair communication breakdowns less effectively, using nonspecific repair strategies more often and specific repair strategies less often when they are receivers of a message, and using repetition as opposed to rephrasing or expansions when they are senders (Jeanes, Nienhuys, & Rickards, 2000).

Children Who Use Cochlear Implants

Children who use cochlear implants also experience pragmatic difficulties. For example, they experience difficulty in using repair strategies to repair communication breakdowns (Ibertssonn, Hannsson, Maki-Torkko, Willstedt-Svensson, & Sahlen., et al., 2009; Tye-Murray, 2003). In one of the few studies to compare age-matched groups with normal hearing, hearing aids, and cochlear implants, 7-year-old children with hearing aids and cochlear implants were found to have similar pragmatic abilities, and both groups had poorer abilities than the children with normal hearing. In particular, they did not turn-take very well; for example, they did not expand the topic under discussion or they changed the topic abruptly, as in this exchange (Most, Shina-August, & Meilijson, 2010, pp. 432–431):

Adult Tester: It's cold outside today.

Child: Yes.

If the child had been practicing *contingency*, which means continuing the same topic during a turn-take and contributing additional information, he might have instead said, "Yes, I'm glad I have my coat here."

Word decoding is the ability to apply one's knowledge of letter–sound relationships, including a knowledge of letter patterns, to the task of recognizing and interpreting written words.

Results from a study that examined the expressive and receptive language abilities of 302 children with mild to severe hearing loss and 112 children with normal hearing at ages 2 to 6 years:

- On average, the children with hearing loss had delayed language abilities relative to age-matched children with normal hearing.
- The greater the degree of hearing loss, the greater the degree of language delay.
- Children with hearing loss who received greater benefit from using a hearing aid demonstrated better language abilities.
- Receipt of early amplification was associated with better language abilities.
- Children who wore their hearing aids for more hours each day had better language outcomes.

(Tomblin, Harrison, Ambrose, Walker, Oleson, & Moeller, 2015)

LITERACY CHARACTERISTICS

There are at least three reasons for literacy deficits to arise in the face of significant hearing loss. First, reading and writing problems may result from a restricted language system. A child cannot understand text if the child is unfamiliar with the meaning of the constituent words. Vocabulary knowledge is more than just being able to attach words to their meaning; rather, it also entails understanding words' relations to other words and building a semantic network that allows a child to activate possible words in his or her vocabulary as the child progresses through a text. Syntactic knowledge allows the child to understand both simple and complicated sentences, such as passive or causative.

Second, some children do not develop an auditory basis for mapping sound to print (Golding-Meadow & Mayberry, 2001). Typically, when children crack the code of deciphering the written word, they learn **word decoding**, which allows them to associate the orthographic form of a word with its phonological properties and to apply their knowledge of letter-sound relationships and letter patterns to the task of recognizing words. Access to a phonological code allows them to "sound out words" for sound–print mapping. They need to translate graphemes (orthography) into corresponding phonemes and apply their knowledge of letter-sound relationships and of letter patterns to the task of recognizing words. Many children who have never heard sound, or who have had access to degraded speech signals, do not develop the phonological awareness of their counterparts with normal hearing.

Finally, children may have deficits in experience and world knowledge. For example, if a child knows nothing about the United States, the sentence *George took an Amtrak to Washington and visited Mount Vernon* might be misinterpreted. Instead of reading the sentence and coming away with its intended meaning of *a man named George rode a train to the nation's capital and visited the mansion inhabited by its first president,* the child may come away thinking that George took a gift called an *Amtrak* to another man named *Washington* and then visited a mountain called *Vernon.*

Reading

Whether they use a hearing aid or a cochlear implant, many children lack sufficient reading skills to master grade-level academic material.

Children Who Have Significant and Prelingual Hearing Loss and Who Use Hearing Aids

In previous eras, the average reading level of many high school students with profound hearing loss tapered off at about a third- or fourth-grade level (Allen, 1986). This level was barely adequate to allow them to read a newspaper. Rarely did a student with significant hearing loss exceed a 7.5 grade reading level. Even more recently, a study of 106 adults revealed on average a 6.2 grade reading level (Zazone, Meador, Reed, & Gorenflo, 2013). Despite early identification and modern hearing aids, at least one study showed that children still lag their peers with normal hearing by about 2 years (Harris & Terlektsi, 2011). Another showed that only about 35–65% of students in seven states in the United States met their state's definitions of *reading proficiency*, meaning that they could read at grade level or showed mastery of grade-level skills. The participant sample in this latter study included both hearing aid users and cochlear implant users and children with varying degrees of hearing loss (Easterbrooks & Beal-Alvarez, 2012).

Attributes of a successful reader include:

- "Development and maintenance of a motivation to read
- Development of appropriate active strategies to construct meaning from print
- Sufficient background knowledge and vocabulary to foster reading comprehension
- The ability to read fluently
- The ability to decode unfamiliar words
- The skills and knowledge to understand how phonemes or speech sounds are connected to print"

(International Reading Association, 1999)

Children Who Use Cochlear Implants

As a general rule, children with cochlear implants read better than children with hearing aids, but worse than their peers with normal hearing (Marschark, Rhoten, & Fabich, 2007). A meta-analysis of 21 studies that were conducted between 1997 and 2016 and collectively included over 1,000 recipients of cochlear implants concluded that children read in the average to low-average range (Mayer & Trezek, 2018). For example, one study compared high school students who had received a cochlear implant in childhood in the 1990s with high school students who had normal hearing using a test battery that assessed reading vocabulary, comprehension, syntactic and text comprehension, spelling accuracy, and expository writing. Only about half of the cochlear implant users had reading skills commensurate with the participants with normal hearing (Hayes & Geers, 2011).

Writing

Many of the kinds of errors that occur in children's spoken language also occur in their writing samples.

Children with Significant Hearing Loss Who Use Hearing Aids

The writing samples of children with hearing loss often contain syntactic errors, such as omission of articles, inappropriate use of pronouns, and omission of bound morphemes (e.g., *'s* and *-ed*). There is a tendency to overuse subject-verb-object sentences and to rarely construct complex syntactic structures. Use of synonyms, antonyms, metaphors, or cohesive forms of substitution or ellipsis is rare (Yoshinaga-Itano, Snyder, & Mayberry, 1996).

Some children have difficulty writing narratives, in which there is a clear beginning, middle, and end to their story. Sometimes, they have difficulty focusing on the important parameters of a story. For example, a third-grade boy, when asked to write a story about a girl holding a scorched dress and an iron, wrote the following sample: *Girl have red sweater. Hair yellow. Girl work hard!*

High and Low Writing Achievement

"My mom borned me. And my father Don Boone. I really close to my father til I was 5 years old, and Happened My father died in wreak. He was driving w/no seatbelt, and He's drunk. He rolled his Car 4 times. And He jump out He got cut on his face from fence. So sad!!! That hurts me lot! He mades my mom really happy. He takes us to lake w/Many friends. We have wonderful lifes."

—Teenager with profound hearing loss who uses a hearing aid and is considered by the school personnel to have *high* writing achievement

(continued)

(continues)

"Jason enter my house went room then nap for 1 hour. Jason is wake-up and I did see it self open door. Jason won't out my room because I think ghost and me little scared then out room feet same wind. . . . Lacy went to room and Lacy yell I see the ghost and Jason was come to Lora room and Jason saw what want and Lacy say I saw ghost, Jason say that invent."

—Teenager with profound hearing loss who uses a hearing aid and is considered by the school personnel to have *low* writing achievement

(Wolbers, Dostal, & Bowers, 2012, p. 37)

In this example, the child appears to have focused on surface details of the picture rather than the underlying story. The child also used inappropriate verb tense (e.g., *have* instead of *has*) and omitted function words. Most children progress beyond this level of expression and often demonstrate gains in their narrative skills between 7 and 18 years of age, although they rarely achieve the competency of age-matched peers with normal hearing (Yoshinaga-Itano & Downey, 1996).

Children Who Use Cochlear Implants

Relatively few studies have focused on the writing skills of children who receive cochlear implants. Mayer and Trezek (2018) summarized the findings of three studies, concluding that their writing skills are weak but tend to be better than those of children who have not received a cochlear implant. For example, Geers and Hayes (2011) administered a spelling test and an expository writing exercise to 112 students who were enrolled in the ninth through twelfth grades. The teenagers spelled 67% of the test items correctly, compared with 80% by a control group with normal hearing. Fewer than half the cochlear implant users scored within one **standard deviation** of the control group on the accuracy of their writing samples (Figure 15–6).

Standard deviation is a statistic used to describe the dispersion of data, and describes the average distance from the average score.

© Monkey Business Images | Shutterstock.com

FIGURE 15–6 Hearing loss and spelling. Even after receiving a cochlear implant, many children have difficulty learning to spell. In this classroom, the teacher uses letter boards to teach children how to spell simple words.

Why Evaluate

"Few children when first diagnosed as hearing-impaired have skills in spoken language; but for those who have acquired communicative speech, either before or after training, measures of speech production status and growth are essential. One needs such measures both to provide specific guidelines for remedial work and to serve as a base line against which results of training can be compared."

—Daniel Ling, author of one of the most influential books ever written about speech therapy for children with hearing loss

(Ling, 1976, p. 135)

SPEECH AND LANGUAGE EVALUATION

The purposes of conducting a speech and language assessment are at least threefold: (1) determining the need for intervention, (2) developing intervention goals, and (3) evaluating progress and effectiveness of intervention. There are several general principles to remember when testing the speech, language, and literacy abilities of children who have hearing loss. The principles pertain to the following topics:

- *Task type*. Children often use speech and language differently in one setting than in another, and they perform differently on varying tasks. For example, children are more likely to produce a sound correctly when they imitate their speech-language pathologist than when they tell a story to their classmates. By using a variety of speech and language tasks, a clinician can determine how robust certain skills are and whether they have generalized to real-world settings.

- *Mode of communication.* A clinician usually opts to use a child's preferred mode of communication during evaluation, even if it entails using an interpreter. The child must understand the tasks and the test items to provide a true reflection of speech and language skills.
- *Rapport.* Some children with hearing losses are shy about using their voices, especially among strangers. If children do not feel comfortable in a clinician's presence, they will not provide speech or language samples that represent their true skills.
- *Test procedures.* Test procedures should be appropriate for the child's age and language. For example, if an articulation test has picture cards, the child must have the vocabulary necessary to name the pictures.
- *Test norms.* For children who have mild or moderate hearing loss, and for cochlear implant users who have good skills, it is usually standard practice to use assessment instruments that have been developed for use with children who have normal hearing. For children who have significant hearing loss, a clinician usually tries to use at least some tests that have been developed for children with hearing loss, although this may not always be possible, because few tests are available.

Assessing Speech Skills

In assessing speech skills, a clinician may simply administer one test that provides a percent words (and/or phonemes) correct score, or may administer a test battery that provides measures specific to intelligibility, segmental speech production, and suprasegmental speech production.

Assessing Speech Intelligibility

To assess speech intelligibility, a speech sample first must be collected and then evaluated. To obtain a speech sample, a child might be asked to perform any or all of the following tasks:

- *Imitate a series of isolated words or sentences.* The clinician says, "The boy saw the cat," and the child then repeats the sentence. This procedure typically elicits a child's best performance (Figure 15–7).
- *Create a citation speech sample.* The clinician says, "Tell me the name of the picture," or "Tell me what is happening here." The child then speaks the name or describes

FIGURE 15–7 Imitation task. One way to collect a speech sample is to use an imitation task. The clinician speaks an utterance and the child imitates it.

what is occurring in the picture. This task is highly structured like an imitated-sentence task, but the child does not receive a speech or vocabulary model to imitate.

- *Retell a story.* The clinician shows a sequence of pictures (e.g., Figure 15–8) to a child one at a time and tells a corresponding story, picture by picture. The child then retells the story. This procedure constrains the language that children use in the sample, but still allows for the evaluation of spontaneous speech and language production.
- *Speak spontaneously, using continuous speech.* The clinician informally observes a child in therapy, in the classroom, or on the playground while he or she speaks to other children or videotape the child during a play session. For example, a mother and child may play with a set number of toys for 30 minutes.

FIGURE 15–8 Story-retell task. Picture cards such as these can be used to elicit a speech and language sample. A clinician first tells a story, using a prepared text that corresponds to each picture in the picture series (here, organized clockwise, beginning with the top left-hand corner). Then the child tells the story back.

Once a speech sample has been collected, overall intelligibility can be assessed in at least three different ways. First, the recordings can be played to a group of listeners who will assign each sample a value from a rating scale. For example, 1 on a 5-point scale might correspond to *I understood none of the child's message,* and 5 might correspond to *I understood the child's entire message.* Rating scales present some disadvantages. A group of listeners must be assembled, which is not always easy to do in settings such as a public school. Moreover, some have questioned whether rating scales differentiate among children, as judges may cluster scores at one end of the continuum or the other (Samar & Metz, 1988; cf. Wilkinson & Brinton, 2003).

A second way to evaluate intelligibility is to play the speech samples to a group of listeners and ask them to write down what they hear. The number of words correctly identified constitutes a percentage words correct intelligibility score. Alternatively the listeners might estimate how much of the child's speech they understood, such as 10% of the words, 20%, and so forth. Although the transcription procedure also requires a panel of listeners, it has high face validity because it shows how many of their words can be identified by general listeners.

A third way, similar to the second, is for the clinician to transcribe the spoken message and reference the spoken transcription to a printed text (as in the story-retell task), if

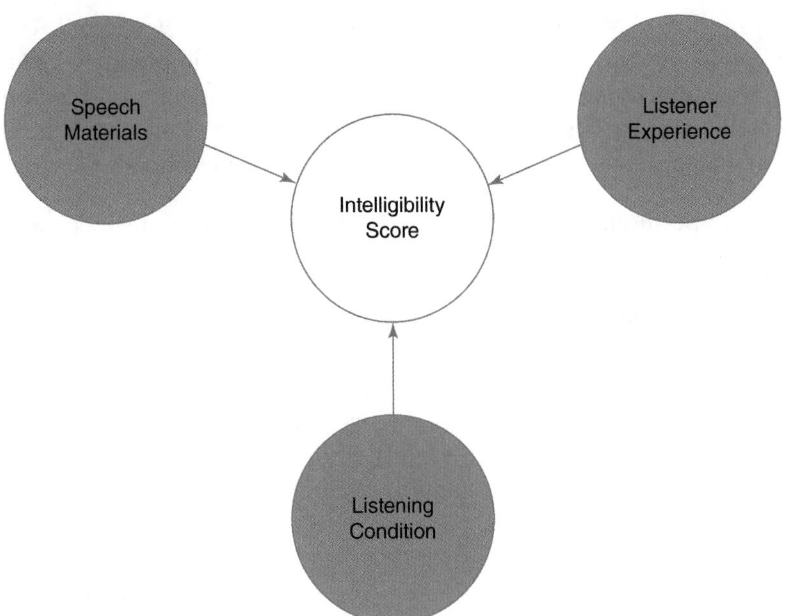

FIGURE 15–9 Factors that may affect speech intelligibility scores. When recording intelligibility scores, it is conventional to comment on these variables.

available. The percentage of words that were spoken correctly can then be computed. This way is probably the most commonly used procedure for assessing intelligibility in clinical and educational settings.

Speech intelligibility scores vary as a function of several different variables (Figure 15–9). For example:

- A child will be more intelligible when reading a paragraph than speaking a list of unrelated sentences.
- Listeners will understand more of a child's speech if they have heard the speech of other children with hearing loss before, than if they are naive listeners.
- Listeners will recognize more speech if they can hear and see children rather than only hear them.

Segmental Speech Testing

Segmental speech testing determines which sounds children can articulate and which sounds they cannot. Variables to consider when selecting test procedures include context and methodology and whether to use conventional tests of articulation.

Segmental speech production can be evaluated with a variety of contexts, including nonsense syllables, isolated words, sentences, and spontaneous speech. It is common to evaluate how well children produce various features of articulation, such as place and manner.

Methodologically, a child may imitate a clinician's speech or might produce the sounds by naming picture cards or reading printed words aloud. The child also may speak spontaneously, and then the clinician determines which sounds were produced correctly in a set number of words (say, the first 200 words spoken by the child).

Often, conventional articulation tests are used to assess segmental speech skills, such as the Goldman–Fristoe Test of Articulation—Second Edition (G-FTA-2; Goldman & Fristoe,

2000) and the Test of Minimal Articulation Competence (T-MAC; Secord, 1981). Representative of many tests, the G-FTA-2 uses colorful pictures to prompt a child to speak sounds in words and sounds in sentences, and includes 39 consonants and consonant clusters. Some clinicians modify tests by eliminating test words that are not in the child's vocabulary. If modifications are made, they should be described alongside the child's scores.

Tests designed specifically for children with significant hearing loss include the following:

- The *Phonetic Level and the Phonologic Level Speech Evaluation* (Ling, 1976): In the phonetic level segment, children's imitative vocal characteristics are judged on the basis of pitch, duration, and intensity. Children are asked to produce vowels and diphthongs as single syllables, repeated syllables (e.g., *ba ba ba*), alternated syllables (e.g., *ba bee ba bee*), and syllables with varying pitch and loudness. The phonologic level segment of the test focuses on the quality and complexity of the child's speech at a discourse level. The clinician completes a checklist that concerns the child's vocal control, linguistic structure, phonemic inventory, and intelligibility.
- The *CID Phonetic Inventory* (Moog, 1988): Very similar to Ling's (1976) phonetic level test in structure, this inventory also bases the evaluation of a child's speech production primarily on the syllable unit. Children are shown printed cards and then asked to imitate the clinician's spoken model. Vowels, diphthongs, and consonants in a variety of syllable configurations are tested.
- The *Speech Intelligibility Evaluation* (SPINE; Monsen, 1981): The SPINE documents overall intelligibility at the single-word level. It consists of 40 cards with a single word printed on each (the cards must be constructed by the clinician, as they are not commercially available). The cards are sorted into contrastive sets of four, each set designed to contrast vowel characteristics and voicing. The child sees a set of four cards at a time and speaks the name of one of the depicted images. The clinician records what he or she hears. The percentage of words correctly recognized constitutes the child's intelligibility score.
- The *Beginners' Intelligibility Test* (BIT; Osberger, Robbins, Todd, & Riley, 1994): The BIT contains four lists of 10 sentences and was developed for children with cochlear implants. The sentences include vocabulary that is familiar to young children, and range in length from two to six words. Pictures are presented along with the sentences to provide meaningful context. Typically, the examiner speaks a sentence while showing the picture and then the child imitates the production.

Suprasegmental Speech Testing

Methods to assess suprasegmental speech production include checklists, rating scales, acoustical analysis (e.g., Peng et al., 2007), and imitation tasks. For example, Smith (1975) used a checklist to note whether segmental errors were *present* or *not present* in children's speech, and McGarr and Osberger (1978) used a 1–5 rating scale to assess voice quality. Levitt (1987) implemented an imitation task where he asked children to sustain the vowel /a/ for 5 seconds (to assess breath management) and speak two-syllable phrases with correct stress and pitch variation (to assess his or her ability to imitate stress patterns). Chin et al. (2012) have also created an imitation measure, called the Prosodic Utterance Production (PUP) task, where children imitate recorded sentences that convey one of four grammatical or emotional moods: statement, question, happy, or sad.

Assessing Language Skills

When assessing language skills, a clinician might administer a formal test. Alternatively, the clinician might collect a spontaneous or structured language sample, in much the way one might when collecting a speech sample, using a story-retell task or a spontaneous play session, and then perform a language sample analysis. One problem with using formal tests is that children may not hear the language. For example, the Reynell Developmental Language Scales (Reynell & Gruber, 1990) includes the item *What does* sleeping *mean?* A child who cannot hear an /s/ will hear *leaping*, and likely respond incorrectly. The advantage of using a formal test is that it can systematically assess skills and competencies that might not surface during a language sample. For example, a young girl may never have reason to speak a past-tense verb during a play session with her mother.

Formal Tests of Language

Table 15–1 presents examples of tests that are sometimes used to assess the expressive and receptive language of children who have hearing loss. They are organized according to whether they primarily assess form, content, or pragmatics. Many tests evaluate multiple aspects of language, and include subtests, so the categorization in Table 15–1 is somewhat arbitrary. For example, the MacArthur-Bates Communicative Development Inventory (Bates et al., 2007) appraises the expressive vocabulary of children as well as their grammatical skills, such as use of irregular word forms and syntactic complexity of sentences.

A typical item on a test of form would ask a child to follow directions using toys (e.g., *Put the car under the chair; Put the car on the chair*). A typical item on a test of content would ask the child to identify the word *dog* from a closed set of four pictures (Figure 15–10). A typical test of pragmatics would ask a parent or teacher to complete a rating scale about a child's conversational skills (e.g., *On a scale of 0–4, where 0 = never and 4 = always, how often does your child participate in or initiate a conversation in a quiet situation?*).

The five most often-used instruments to assess the language of children who use cochlear implants are as follows:

- Peabody Picture Vocabulary Test (PPVT)
- Reynell Developmental Language Scales (RDLS)
- MacArthur-Bates Communicative Developmental Inventories (MCDI)
- Meaningful Use of Speech Scale (MUSS)
- Clinical Evaluation of Language Fundamentals (CELF)

(Silva, Comerlatto, Bevilacqua, & Lopes-Herrera, 2011)

TABLE 15–1 Language Tests That Are Sometimes Used to Test Children Who Have Hearing Loss

Form
Clinical Evaluation of Language Fundamentals (CELF) (Semel, Wiig, & Secord, 2013)
Comprehension Assessment of Spoken Language (CASL) (Carrow-Woolfolk, 2017)
Cottage Acquisition Scales for Listening, Language & Speech (CASLLS) (Wilkes, 2001)
Index of Productive Syntax (IPSyn) (Scarborough, 1990)
Oral and Written Language Skills (OWLS) (Carrow-Woolfolk, 2011)
Preschool Language Scales–5 (PLS-5) (Zimmerman, Steiner, & Pond, 2011)
Test for Auditory Comprehension of Language (TACL) (Carrow-Woolfolk, 2014)
Test of Adolescent and Adult Language—4th Edition (TOAL-4) (Hammill, Brown, Larsen, & Wiederholt, 2007)
Test of Language Development–Primary and Intermediate—4th Edition (TOLD-4-PI) (Newcomer & Hammill, 2008)
Content
Expressive One-Word Picture Vocabulary Test (EOWPVT) (Martin & Brownell, 2001)
Expressive Vocabulary Test (EVT) (Williams, 2007)
MacArthur-Bates Communicative Development Inventory (CDI) (Bates et al., 2019)
Peabody Picture Vocabulary Test (PPVT) (Dunn & Dunn, 2019)
Receptive One-Word Picture Vocabulary Test (ROWPVT) (Martin & Brownell, 2001)
Reynell Developmental Language Scales (Reynell & Gruber, 1990)
Test of Narrative Language (TNL) (Gillam & Pearson, 2017)
Pragmatics
Children's Communication Checklist–2 (CCC-2) (Bishop, 2006)
Meaningful Use of Speech Scale (MUSS) (Robbins & Osberger, 1994)
Parents' Evaluation of Aural/Oral Performance of Children (PEACH) (Ching & Hill, 2007)
Pragmatic Language Skills Inventory (PLSI) (Gilliam & Miller, 2006)

Courtesy of the author.

FIGURE 15–10 A language test that assesses content. The clinician speaks a vocabulary word and the child selects a response from a closed set.

Children who use a Deaf sign system such as American Sign Language (ASL) should be monitored for their language development, and a variety of tests are available not only for ASL but for other sign systems as well, including British Sign Language, Sign Language of the Netherlands, Deutsch Gebärdensprache, and Langue de Signes Française.

Language Sample Analyses

An analysis of children's spontaneous language might include a description of the semantic classes that they use and recognize, their syntactic structures, and their pragmatic skills. For example, the following language sample was elicited during a play session between a mother and her 29-month-old son who uses a cochlear implant (Nicholas & Geers, 2006, p. 297) (Figure 15–11):

Son: I want train.
Mother: You want the train?
Son: (nods)
Mother: Oh, okay. I'll give you some pieces.
Son: I hold.
Mother: You're going to help?
Son: (nods)
Mom: Okay.
Son: This go there? This working?
Mom: Does that work, you think?
Son: Yeah.

Type-token ratio (TTR) is the ratio between the number of different words that occurred in a language sample and the total number of words within the sample.

Quantitative measures for a sample like this might include **type-token ratio (TTR)**, which is the ratio of the number of different words compared with the total number

FIGURE 15–11 Obtaining a spontaneous speech sample. A mother and child may engage in a play session. The session is recorded, and the language elicited during the session is analyzed.

of words used, **mean sentence length** (MSL), which is the mean number of words per sentence, total number of words, and the number of different words. In the sample above, the boy's TTR is 11:9 and the MSL is 2.75. A total of 11 words occurred in his sample, and 9 different words. An in-depth analysis might also include a tally of bound morphemes (e.g., zero in the sample above) and of different bound morphemes (e.g., zero), and a description of the syntactic sentence structures (in the sample above, *subject-verb-object* and *subject-verb*). A pragmatic analysis might tally such functions as *response, statement, question, imitation/repetition,* and *directive* (e.g., Nicholas, 2000). In the sample above, the child both speaks questions (and waits for an answer) and responds to his mother's questions, and exhibits appropriate turn-taking behaviors.

Mean sentence length (MSL) is the mean number of words per sentence, and is computed when analyzing a language sample.

LITERACY EVALUATION

Assessing literacy skills is important for at least two reasons. First, test results can inform decisions about classroom placement and the need for support services. For example, does a child have the reading skills necessary to understand the content of a fifth-grade history book? Can the child write a book report independently? Might the child benefit from ancillary instruction in the resource room or from an itinerant teacher? Second, test results can inform the teacher about a child's strengths and weaknesses, and help the teacher target teaching efforts.

Reading

Although a few assessment tools have been designed specifically for children who have hearing loss (e.g., the Test of Early Reading Ability–Deaf or Hard of Hearing [Reid, Hresko, Hammill, & Wiltshire, 1991]), instruments developed for children with normal hearing are often used to evaluate a child's reading readiness and reading skills. The disadvantages of using assessment instruments designed for children with normal hearing are, first, test items may be too difficult and, second, a child's performance cannot be compared with a peer group of children who have hearing loss. On the other hand, if a child is in a mainstream or an inclusion classroom, test scores may indicate how well he or she may be expected to perform in that setting and how well the child performs with respect to classmates who have normal hearing.

Table 15–2 presents a sample of instruments used for assessing reading, as well as the grades (for children who have normal hearing) appropriate for testing and the areas of skill evaluated. These areas of skill include reading and language comprehension, phonology, syntax and semantics, decoding, phoneme awareness, alphabetic principles, letter knowledge, and concepts about print.

TABLE 15–2 A Sample of Instruments Used to Assess Reading Performance

ASSESSMENT	GRADE	AREAS ASSESSED
Analytical Reading Inventory (Woods & Moe, 2014)	K, 1, 2, 3, and higher	Reading comprehension, language comprehension, decoding
Bader Reading and Language Inventory (Bader & Pearce, 2012)	Pre-K, K, 1, 2, 3, and higher	Reading comprehension, language comprehension, phonology, syntax, semantics, decoding, phoneme awareness, letter knowledge, concepts about print
Brigance Comprehensive Inventory of Basic Skills–Revised (CIBS-R) (Brigance, 2010)	Pre-K, K, 1, 2, 3, and higher	Reading comprehension, phonology, semantics, decoding, letter knowledge
Gray Oral Reading Test–Diagnostic (GORT) (Wiederholt & Bryan, 2012)	K, 1, 2, 3, and higher	Reading comprehension, syntax, decoding
Kaufman Assessment Battery for Children II (K-ABC-II) (Kaufman & Kaufman, 2004)	Pre-K, K, 1, 2, 3, and higher	Reading comprehension, semantics, decoding
Reading and Oral Language Assessment (ROLA) (LitConn Inc., 2000)	K, 1, 2, 3, and higher	Reading comprehension, language comprehension, decoding, lexical knowledge, phoneme awareness, letter knowledge, concepts about print
Signposts Early Literacy Battery and Pre-DRP Test (Touchstone Applied Science Associates, Inc., 2001)	K, 1, 2, and 3	Reading comprehension, language comprehension, syntax, semantics, decoding, phoneme awareness, letter knowledge
Test of Early Reading Ability–Deaf or Hard of Hearing (TERA-D/HH) (Reid et al., 2018)	Pre-K, K, 1, and 2	Letter knowledge, concepts about reading
Woodcock Diagnostic Reading Battery (WDRB) (III Woodcock, 2004)	K, 1, 2, 3, and higher	Reading comprehension, semantics, decoding, letter knowledge
Woodcock-Johnson Psycho-Educational Battery (WJ-R) (Woodcock & Johnson, 2010)	K, 1, 2, 3, and higher	Reading comprehension, lexical knowledge

For children who are on the cusp of reading readiness, a clinician might complete a simple checklist to assess preliteracy performance. For example, the clinician might indicate whether a child *never, sometimes,* or *always* demonstrates some of the following developmental benchmarks (adapted from Bodrova, Leong, Paynter, & Semenov, 2000):

- Holds a book upright and turns the pages of the book from front to back
- Pretends to read familiar books; joins in with predictable phrases (e.g., "I will huff and puff and blow your house down")
- Reads environmental print (such as a McDonald's sign or a stop sign)
- Identifies letters in his or her name
- Tells a story when stimulated with a sequence of pictures
- Pretends using or creates language
- Listens responsively to narratives and books
- Tells stories

Writing

An assessment of writing ability can provide important information about how the child is developing, and often the classroom teacher maintains a folder of writing samples collected over time.

One assessment means is to ask children to write a paragraph or short narrative about a topic, such as a vacation, and then apply a scoring rubric to the resultant sample. Schley and Albertini (2005) developed a scoring rubric for assessing the writing abilities of postsecondary Deaf students, which has been modified and applied to younger children (Geers & Hayes, 2011). The four scoring categories are *organization* (e.g., clear statement of the topic), *content* (e.g., persistent and noteworthy ideas), *language use* (e.g., correct use of grammatical structure), and *vocabulary use* (e.g., appropriate semantic use of vocabulary).

Other means that researchers have used to assess written language samples include the following (Wolbers et al., 2012):

- Documenting the number of sentences and length of composition
- Evaluating the complexity of syntactic forms used
- Counting, analyzing, and categorizing the errors
- Performing a quantitative analysis of the various parts of speech and types of transformational grammatical structures included
- Assessing sentence awareness by computing the percentage of sentences that were fragments or run-on
- Counting the number of function words that are correct, incorrect, or omitted

SPEECH AND LANGUAGE THERAPY

Most children with significant hearing loss benefit from receiving speech and language therapy. Speech and language skills often do not emerge spontaneously. Concerted attention over many years must be placed on developing skills if a child is to develop functional speech and language.

Approaches

There are two general educational approaches for developing spoken language skills that differ in their emphasis on visual information.

Unisensory Approach

In a unisensory approach, children receive instructions and correction about their speech and language via the auditory modality primarily, although in some applications, no attempt is made to limit children's use of nonauditory cues, such as natural facial cues.

In a very strict incantation of an auditory approach, children are not allowed to watch the talker's face or may do so for only a limited amount of time (Pollack, 1970). For example, a teacher may use a speech hoop or cover his or her mouth with the flat, slanted hand during instruction (Estabrooks, 2001; Rhodes, Estabrooks, Lim, & Maclver-Lux, 2016). One rationale for this approach is that if you do not allow the child to capitalize on visual speech information, then regions of the brain that are dedicated to processing auditory information will not be repurposed for processing visual information via neuroplasticity but will remain dedicated to auditory speech perception (e.g., Sharma,

Campbell, & Cardon, 2015). By limiting speechreading cues, children learn to process the auditory signal and develop auditory representations of words.

A Strong Opinion

"There can be no compromise, because once emphasis is placed upon 'looking' there will be divided attention, and the unimpaired modality, vision, will be victorious."

—Doreen Pollack, who was the developer of a language program called *Acoupedics* and was one of the most vocal advocates of an auditory approach, writing about why clinicians should obscure their mouths during speech and language therapy

(Pollack, 1970, p. 18)

Multisensory Approach

In a multisensory approach, speech and language instruction is presented through more than one sensory modality, usually audition and vision. The assumption is that by allowing children to speechread, they will have better access to spoken words as they greatly benefit when facial speech cues are added to the degraded auditory speech signal. Moreover, **auditory enhancement**, which is the amount of improvement in word recognition when going from an auditory-only condition to an audiovisual condition, has been shown to be positively correlated with receptive and expressive language and speech intelligibility in children with hearing loss (e.g., Bergeson, Pisoni, & Davis, 2003; Kirk, Pisoni, & Lachs, 2002). Given that most communication occurs face-to-face, allowing children to both see and hear the talker during language instruction seems an ecologically valid way to maximize speech and language outcomes.

Auditory enhancement is the amount of improvement in word recognition when being tested first in an auditory-only condition and then being tested in an audiovisual condition.

Comparison of Approaches

Although some clinicians favor a unisensory approach (e.g., Rhoades, Estabrooks, Lim, & MacIver-Lux, 2016) and others favor a multisensory approach (e.g., White & Voss, 2015), few have directly compared their effectiveness. One that did include a direct comparison found them to be equally effective (McDaniel, Camarata, & Yoder, 2018).

Speech Therapy

Goals for a comprehensive speech development program may include the following (Carney & Moeller, 1998, p. S62):

- Increase vocalizations that have appropriate timing characteristics and that require numerous vocal tract movements
- Expand phonetic and phonemic repertoires
- Establish link between audition and speech production
- Improve suprasegmental aspects of speech
- Increase speech intelligibility

Results from the speech evaluation can guide therapy goals. The phonetic transcriptions of elicited and spontaneous speech may be used for phoneme and phonological error pattern analysis. Phonetic error analysis yields an inventory of sounds a child can produce, as well as a catalog of the child's deletions, substitutions, and distortions. Phonological error analysis reveals phonological process errors. These may include final-consonant deletions, cluster reductions, and frontings. Therapy goals may focus on increasing a child's phonetic repertoire and on reducing phonological process errors. Auditory modeling is used extensively, sometimes in conjunction with a visual and tactile supplement.

Misperceptions

"I've always wanted to write a book relating my experiences growing up as a deaf child in Chicago. Contrary to what people might think, it wasn't all about hearing aids and speech classes or frustrations."

—Marlee Matlin, Academy Award–winning actress and television star

(Brainy Quote, 2013)

Therapy curricula often differ according to the way speech is presented to the child and how feedback is provided and may relay more on an auditory approach or a visual approach. For example, Daniel Ling (1976) developed a speech therapy program based on an auditory approach. This program rests on the premise that there exists a hierarchy of speech skills. The most effective and efficient way to learn how to talk is to learn skills in an appropriate sequence and to build on an existing skill to develop a new one. For example, before a child can learn specific speech sounds, he or she must first learn to regulate voice level and pitch. A child should be able to speak homophenous syllable strings, such as *bee-bee-bee,* before being asked to speak heterogeneous strings, such as *bee-boo-bee-boo.*

In a more visual approach, visual stimuli are presented purposefully to supplement the auditory signal. A visual program may entail the use of mirrors, and graphic symbols may be paired with specific speech sounds or prosodic features. Figure 15–12 presents an example of a visual approach, where a speech-language pathologist is using cue cards of alphabet letters to elicit an /s/ sound from the child.

© Katarzyna Bialasiewicz | Dreamstime.com

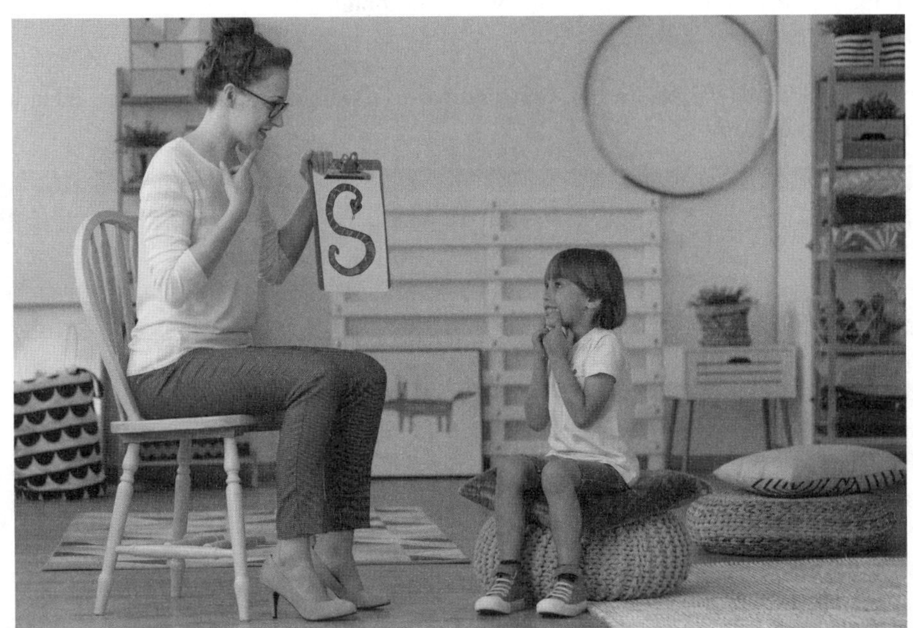

FIGURE 15–12 Visually oriented speech therapy. Sounds may be paired with their orthographic representation.

Tips for Fostering Preliteracy Skills

Teachers and speech and hearing professionals can use the following techniques to foster good preliteracy skills while reading aloud to the child (adapted from DesJardin et al., 2014; Wauters & Dirks, 2017, p. 248):

Engagement. Provide positive feedback, read and comment with emotional language and intonation, expend effort to engage the child, maintain close proximity, and monitor the child's comprehension (Figure 15–13).

Literacy strategies. Point to and label pictures, ask questions about the book, and point to words, letters, and sentences.

Teaching techniques. Relate content to the child's previous experiences, elaborate on the child's remarks about the book, define new vocabulary, and ask the question, "What do you think will happen next?"

Interactive reading. Let the child hold the book and turn the pages, respond to the child's remarks and questions, let the child take the lead, and allow time for the child to process the content.

© Robert Kneschke | Shutterstock.com

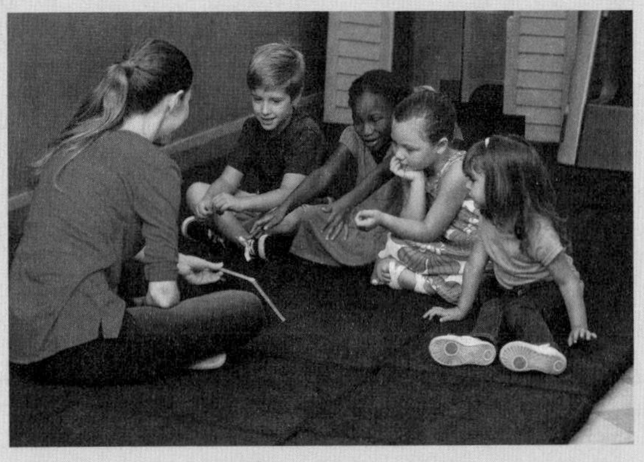

FIGURE 15–13 Promoting preliteracy skills.

Language Therapy

Therapy goals in language development may include the following (Carney & Moeller, 1998):

- Increase communication between parent and child
- Promote an understanding of complex concepts and discourse units
- Enhance vocabulary growth
- Increase world knowledge
- Enhance self-expression
- Enhance growth in use of language syntax and pragmatics
- Develop narrative skills

Language curricula vary from highly structured to naturalistic and very often include a combination of both.

The Difficulty in Acquiring Bound Morphemes and a Structured Language Activity That Might Help

Children with significant hearing loss often have difficulty acquiring bound morphemes, such as the plural *-s* and the past tense *–ed* (e.g., Spencer, Tye-Murray, & Tomblin, 1998). Drawing from the literature on second language learning, it may well be because bound morphemes carry less meaning than the content words to which they attach and sometimes are redundant with other sentence content. For example, in the grammatically incorrect sentence "The boy walk yesterday," the listener will know that the action happened in the past, despite the missing past-tense bound morpheme. This phenomenon is known as *the primacy of meaning principle* (VanPatton, 1996) and includes the following subprinciples:

- P1a. *The primacy of content words principle.* Listeners process content words in the input before anything else.
- P1b. *The lexical preference principle.* Listeners tend to rely on lexical items as opposed to grammatical form to get meaning when both encode the same semantic meaning.

In other words, the less communicative value a form has, the more likely listeners are to "skip" it in the input. Structured language therapy can be tailored explicitly to teach bound morphemes. For example, Figure 15–14 shows two pictures, one of a single cookie and the other of three cookies. A teacher says, "The cookies smelled good," and asks the child to select the appropriate illustration, thereby forcing the child to attend specifically to the bound morpheme. Other examples of training stimuli that might be included in this kind of structured language exercise include the following:

- *The bird's cage; The bird cage*
- *The boy can swim; The boy can't swim*
- *The girls walked; The girls walk*

The exercise would have corresponding picture pairs, like that shown in Figure 15–14.

FIGURE 15–14 Teaching bound morphemes.

Structured Language Therapy

Structured models usually exploit teacher modeling, student imitations, and sometimes metalinguistic symbols (such as a symbol that distinguishes a noun from a verb), and are most often used with school-aged children. By focusing on structured stimuli, children may learn to perceive language patterns, practice them, and eventually produce them spontaneously.

An example of a structured language curriculum is *A Patterned Program for Linguistic Expansion Through Reinforced Experiences and Evaluation* (APPLE TREE; Anderson, Boren, Kilgore, Howard, & Krohn, 1999). Designed for children in the primary and intermediate grades, the program consists of a sequence of procedures for developing children's ability to construct and comprehend 10 basic sentence patterns. Structures taught early in the curriculum include NOUN + VERB (BE) + ADJECTIVE (e.g., *The ball is red*) and NOUN + VERB (e.g., *The boy walks*). A structure taught later is NOUN1 + VERB + NOUN2 + VERB (e.g., *The boy sees the bird sit in the tree*). Sentence patterns build upon a previous pattern, and students advance to increasingly difficult levels of syntactic and semantic complexity. The curriculum also includes vocabulary building, spontaneous sentence production prompted with visual aids such as a picture story, and construction of transformations, such as asking a child to convert one of the sentence patterns into a question format. A sample activity is illustrated in Figure 15–15. Here, a child has been asked to arrange a set of word cards into patterns corresponding to the NOUN + VERB (BE) + ADJECTIVE sentence structure.

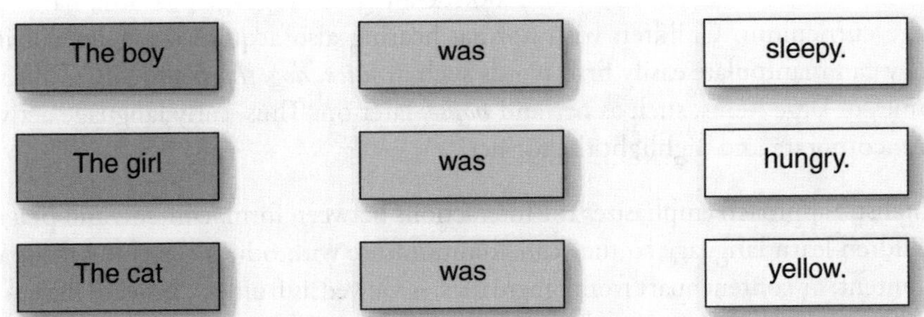

FIGURE 15–15 Structured language activities. During a structured language activity, a student might be asked to arrange word cards into a NOUN + VERB (BE) + ADJECTIVE pattern.

Other activities that might be included in a structured language curriculum are worksheets or sentence strips that require students to do any of the following:

- Complete phrases, such as *The bird ___ through the sky*
- Unscramble sentences, such as *Boy the school walked to*
- Indicate whether a sentence is right or wrong, as in *The boy walked to school tomorrow*

Naturalistic Language Therapy

Many modern curricula advocate naturalistic methods, where language is learned in the context of everyday meaningful communication, particularly for students who are infants and small children. Teachers and clinicians exploit conversations and experiences to expand vocabulary and model syntax and pragmatics (Figure 15–16). The underlying premise is that children learn language when they are surrounded by a language that describes what is relevant, meaningful, and of interest to them at the moment.

FIGURE 15–16 Naturalistic methods of language instruction. Naturalistic methods include optimizing everyday events (and structuring the environment so that events occur) to promote the growth of form, content, and pragmatics. In this encounter, the teacher is using snack time to develop children's concept of the prepositions *on* and *off*. The children place a puzzle piece on and off their juice containers and body parts. In this scene, the teacher turns to the little girl on her right side and asks, "Where is John's puzzle piece?" The little girl responds, "On." The teacher repeats the child's production of the word *on* and expands on it by saying, "John's puzzle piece is *on* the bottle."

In a naturalistic approach, therapy goals often are based on information about the language development of children with normal hearing. For example, children with normal hearing use phrases that indicate plurality relatively late in language development (e.g., *two cats*), so mastery of plurality would not be an early language goal in a naturalistic language curriculum. Children with normal hearing also acquire the names of items that they can manipulate easily first, words such as *juice, dog, shoes,* and *ball.* They learn the names of large items, such as *tree* and *house,* later on. Thus, early language activities would incorporate and highlight the former.

A naturalistic approach emphasizes the interactions between form, content, and pragmatics. Children learn language so they can communicate with others. Teaching form apart from content, or content apart from pragmatics, is viewed as fruitless. Instead, the emphasis falls on creating experiences and contexts that foster semantic intentions and meanings and that encourage children to use content and form in pragmatically appropriate ways and in a variety of settings and situations. One implication of this approach is that vocabulary words are never taught in isolation, as when learning a "vocabulary list." In addition, a teacher who adheres to a naturalistic approach would never require a child to perform word-for-word imitation, as in this example (Rose, McAnally, & Quigley, 2004, p. 98):

Child: Mother store.

Teacher: Say, Mother went to the store.

Child: (no response)

Teacher: No, let's say a whole sentence. Mother . . .

Child: Mother

Teacher: went

Child: went

Teacher: to

Child: to

Teacher: the

Child: the

Teacher: store.
Child: store.
Teacher: Good. Now say, Mother went to the store.
Child: Mother store.

Even though some schools might use this kind of teaching, imitation like this may not only NOT promote language acquisition, but may hinder it because the child loses the meaning and perhaps loses the motivation to converse in the process.

An example of a naturalistic language activity entails a teacher and a child making a peanut butter sandwich. The goal of the activity is to develop the child's use of negative forms. The teacher makes atypical ingredients available, such as noodles, hot dogs, dog food, and even marbles. After making the sandwich, the teacher models negative forms, as in this interchange (Fey, Long, & Finestack, 2003, p. 8):

Teacher: We use/ate/needed cheese.
Child: No, we not use cheese.
Teacher: Right, we didn't use cheese. What about dog food?

Fey et al. (2003) call this technique *Manipulate the social, physical, and linguistic context to create more frequent opportunities for grammatical targets.* The teacher might also manipulate the conversation to emphasize negatives and to contrast them with a positive statement by saying, "We did NOT eat the marbles" and "We put the peanut butter on the bread, but we did NOT put it on the hot dog." This latter technique is called *Manipulate the discourse so that targeted features are rendered more salient in pragmatically felicitous contexts.*

Combined Formal and Naturalistic Instruction

Learning opportunities for language cannot always be created in a classroom setting or within a completely naturalistic approach and some vocabulary and concepts simply are not suited for an entirely formal or entirely naturalistic approach. Therefore, some schools use a combination of structured and naturalistic instruction in a way that closely resembles the framework that was considered in Chapter 8 for conceptualizing the stages of communication strategies training (Figure 8–2) and again in Chapters 13 and 14.

Classroom practices that follow a naturalistic approach to language learning include the following:

- Language goals are sequenced to mirror the stages and sequences of normal language development.
- The teacher accepts "child language" that is appropriate for a particular language stage and does not expect or require a child's utterances to have adult syntax.
- The teacher frequently uses the language facilitation technique of expansion (Chapter 13) to maintain a conversation and to model and present new language information at a time when the child is attending.
- The teacher responds to the child's semantic and communicative intent rather than interrupting and requiring the child to use adult syntax.
- The teacher provides both common and novel experiences to increase the child's experiential background and to gain opportunity for language input and communication

(Paraphrased from Rose et al., 2004, p. 101)

FIGURE 15–17 Example of how structured and naturalistic language instruction may be combined. This figure represents a science unit about the plant life cycle and how it can be structured to promote language development.

This combined method includes the three stages of formal instruction, guided learning, and real-world practice. For example, Figure 15–17 shows these three stages as they are implemented in an introductory science/language unit about the plant life cycle.

During formal instruction, children learn basic plant vocabulary and play a flashcard game and a computer-based game about the principles of plant growth. The teacher emphasizes other related vocabulary and concepts, such as the words *measure* and *underground* and the concepts of energy and sunlight.

During guided learning, children plant seeds in two beacons or paper cups. They place one of the plantings by a sunny window and the other in a closet, the pedagogical goal being to demonstrate the importance of sunlight in the growing process. The class keeps a journal about how the seeds germinate and grow, and the students regularly measure the height of their plants with individual rulers. Throughout, the target vocabulary is integrated into the activity and reference is made back to the photographs and drawings that were used during formal instruction.

Finally, in real-world practice, the children plant an outdoor garden and monitor the progress of the plants, eventually harvesting a crop of vegetables. They become

Tips for Fostering Writing Skills

Teachers and speech and hearing professionals can use the following techniques to foster good writing skills (adapted from Fernandes, 1998):

- *Language experience/writing*. The teacher and students write a story, essay, or poem together or create a cartoon strip, either on a poster board or on manila paper and big books. They may write about a shared experience, such as a field trip, or sporting event.
- *Dialogue journals*. Create a written conversation between the teacher and the student. The teacher does not correct the child's grammar or spelling but rather, models appropriate language and punctuation. Both teacher and student make an entry daily.
- *Journals and daily logs*. Members of the class maintain a log about a science project or other school event. Each day, they write about observations, predictions, and outcomes. They might include visual information such as graphs, maps, and charts.
- *Shared writing*. The teacher writes a passage on a whiteboard with the students, thinking aloud about his or her process of deciding about grammar, spelling, and punctuation (e.g., *Since this is a question I'm writing, I need to end it with a question mark*). The teacher solicits ideas from the class about what to include and how to write it.
- *Guided writing*. In comparison to shared writing, students are more independent. Students might work in small groups, making a first draft and then jointly refining this draft into a final draft.
- *Writer's workshop*. The teacher first gives a brief lesson about a topic pertaining to grammar, spelling, or punctuation. Afterward, one or two students sit in the "writer's chair" and share a writing sample with the class. The teacher and classmates provide feedback.
- *Weekly newspaper*. Children receive assignments, such as interviewing the school principal, and then write a news article to be included in a weekly class newspaper.

comfortable with the vocabulary, using it spontaneously in this naturalistic setting. The activity culminates with a luncheon of salads and raw vegetables, which could then segue into a next science/language unit about the five food groups.

CASE STUDY

Writing Samples from 10- and 11-Year-Old Children

Three children—Michelle, Jelyyn, and Allison—who attend a private aural/oral school for children who have hearing loss wrote the stories that follow. The children have severe-to-profound hearing loss and have been using hearing aids since early childhood. The samples are characteristic of the writing skills demonstrated by a group of children of this age and with severe-to-profound hearing loss, both in terms of variability in their length and in their types of errors. The class assignment was to describe the scene depicted in Figure 15–18. The children were shown this picture after their teacher read them a story about a girl and her purchase of a magic sled.

Michelle wrote only two sentences:

FIGURE 15–18 The picture that was used to elicit the written language samples presented in the case study. The picture illustrates a story about a magic sled that can glide uphill. The teacher first told the story and then showed the picture. Students wrote a paragraph describing the picture.

> *The gril [sic] going up the hill.*
>
> *The boys look the gril [sic] going up the hill.*

Michelle described the key element of the picture: The girl was sledding upward and the boys were impressed enough by the action that they stopped and watched. Some of the errors include omission of the function word *is* in the first sentence, and the word *at* in the second sentence. She also misspelled the word *girl*. She used the commonplace word *going* in lieu of the more descriptive word *sledding*.

Although Jelyyn's writing sample also included many errors characteristic of children who have significant hearing loss (including spelling errors, tense disagreement, omission of morphemes, omission of function words, run-on sentences, verb disagreement, and inappropriate change in verb tense), her narration of the story and of the accompanying picture was more complex and more informative than that of her classmate, Michelle. She also used more appropriate punctuation. However, notice how she missed writing about the key element of the story: The sled was magic and hence able to glide uphill.

(continues)

CASE STUDY *(continued)*

Writing Samples from 10- and 11-Year-Old Children

> *A girl name Tiffany. She walking by the stroe and she saw a macigi sleding and she went into the store and buy the macigi sleding and she can't wait to go sled down the hill. When she finish buy the sled. She was in a hurry. When she got home she put her snowpant on, hat, boots, mittens, scarft. And ran up the hill and she try to sleding down.*

The final sample presents the most narratively sound and grammatically correct paragraph of the three. In writing it, Allison described the key elements of the story. Also, in the final sentence, she inserted dialogue, which is an advanced component in narrative writing. Grammatically, even though Allison did not use quotation marks and did not use a question mark where appropriate, she preceded the dialogue with a comma and capitalized the first word. Other grammatical errors included the omission of function words and inappropriate changes in verb tense. Allison wrote:

> It was winter time and it was snowy in the picture. Dave, Kathy and Dan went sleding on big hill. They are tired to walk up on big hill but Kathy and her sled went up! Fanilly they get on top of hill. They ask her, How your sled went up.

FINAL REMARKS

Technology has exerted an enormous effect on how children with hearing loss acquire speech, language, and literacy skills. For example, teachers can now video record events that occur in the classroom and then send the recordings home via the internet that same night, perhaps with comments about how parents might reinforce learning objectives in the home. Children can watch television with closed-captioning and thereby develop both their language and reading skills. Handheld phones can be used to access printed information and photographs that were once accessible only through encyclopedias and dictionaries.

Telepractice is the delivery of services by means of telecommunications and electronic communications.

One of the most exciting uses of technology is in telepractice. **Telepractice** allows clinicians and teachers to reach children and parents who live at a long distance from a clinic or from a school with special services. For example, children in rural areas and in lower-income countries can receive speech and language therapy or auditory training from a professional who may reside in a distant, urban area. Someday, you might interact with a parent via telecommunication so as to help implement a child's Individual Family Service Plan (IFSP) and suggest ways to accomplish goals in the child's home environment, using daily routines and activities.

KEY CHAPTER POINTS

- Hearing ability and ability to recognize spoken language strongly relate to a child's eventual abilities in speech production, language, and reading.
- Children with significant hearing loss may make characteristic speech errors, such as neutralizing vowels and omitting final consonants. These errors underlie generally low intelligibility levels.
- Children's production of suprasegmental aspects of speech may be aberrant, and their voice quality may sound strained and harsh.
- Children who receive cochlear implants, especially those who receive one at an early age, typically acquire better intelligibility and segmental and suprasegmental

speaking abilities than children who have significant hearing loss and who use hearing aids.

- Children with significant hearing loss often have problems in content, form, and pragmatics of language. For example, many have reduced vocabulary and have mastered fewer syntactic structures than children with normal hearing. Use of a cochlear implant can ameliorate these problems.
- Children with significant hearing loss often experience difficulty in learning to read. Many adults never attain better than a fourth-grade reading level. They also typically have poor writing skills. Use of a cochlear implant can ameliorate these difficulties.
- Speech and language can be assessed with formal tests or by collecting a language sample and performing an analysis on the content.
- Results from a literacy assessment battery test can inform a teacher about a child's strengths and weaknesses, and guide teaching efforts.
- Speech and language therapy may follow an auditory, visual, or multisensory approach.
- Language therapy may follow a structured or naturalistic approach.

TERMS AND CONCEPTS TO REMEMBER

Segmental speech errors
Suprasegmental speech errors
Roles of auditory feedback
Form
Content
Pragmatics
Literacy
Impact of cochlear implants
Transcription procedures
Language sample analysis
Preliteracy skills
Structured language curriculum
Bound morphemes
Naturalistic language instruction
Telepractice

GLOSSARY

Terms and acronyms used in this text and other terms related to aural rehabilitation.

AAA: American Academy of Audiology.

A-ABR: Automated auditory brainstem response.

AARP: American Association of Retired Persons.

ABR: Auditory brainstem response.

Academy of Doctors of Audiology (ADA): A national organization that fosters and supports qualified audiologists in their efforts to dispense hearing aids and to provide related aural rehabilitation services; formerly known as the Academy of Dispensing Audiologists.

Acknowledgment gesture: May consist of a head nod or a head shake; often made in response to a remark from a frequent communication partner who is familiar with the signaling system.

Acknowledgment tactic: Used by people with hearing loss to disclose their hearing loss when talking to an unfamiliar communication partner for the first time.

Acoupedic approach: A comprehensive habilitation program for infants and their families that emphasizes auditory training and listening without formal lipreading instruction and without reliance on the visual speech signal for communication.

Acoustic feedback: Occurs when the output from a hearing aid receiver reenters the microphone, sending the system into oscillation and creating a "squeal."

Acoustic feedback cancellation: Occurs so that hearing aids will not "whistle" or produce acoustic feedback when sound escapes from the receiver.

Acoustic highlighting: Occurs when a talker changes duration, intensity, and pitch to highlight a word or to enhance the audibility of a message.

Acoustic lexical neighborhood: Comprised of a set of words that are acoustically similar and have approximately the same frequency of occurrence within a language.

Acoustic neuroma: A tumor of the auditory or eighth nerve, usually benign, which may cause gradual hearing loss, tinnitus, and dizziness.

Acoustic startle reflex: An infant's response to unexpected loud sound that is typified by a head jerk and out flung arms; also called a *Moro reflex.*

Acquired hearing loss: Hearing loss that is acquired after birth.

Activity: The execution of a task or action by an individual; with respect to aural rehabilitation, an endeavor that a patient wants or needs to do with hearing; e.g., alerting to sound; recognizing speech.

Activity limitation: A change at the level of the person brought about by an impairment at the levels of body structure (e.g., loss of hair cells in the cochlea) and function (e.g., loss of an ability to discriminate pitch); for example, a patient may no longer be able to engage easily in casual conversation.

Acute otitis media: Inflammation of the middle ear that lasts for 3 weeks or less.

AD: Alzheimer's disease; assistive device.

ADA: Academy of Doctors of Audiology; Americans with Disabilities Act.

Adaptive strategies: Methods of counteracting maladaptive behaviors that stem from hearing loss.

ADD: Attention deficit disorder.

Adjacency pairs: Linked speaking turns; e.g., *How are you?: Fine.*

ADM: Automatic directional microphone.

Adventitious hearing loss: Hearing loss occurring after birth.

AEP: Auditory evoked potential.

Affective filter hypothesis: A hypothesis that acknowledges that affective factors can impede perceptual and linguistic learning.

Affricate: Consonants that, when spoken, entail a vocal tract obstruction (or a stop consonant) and a prolonged frication; e.g., /tʃ/.

AGC: Automatic gain control.

Agenesis: An absence of an organ.

Aggressive conversational style: Conversational style in which the person may blame others for misunderstandings and may not take ownership of communication difficulties; e.g., *Quit muttering!*

Aided thresholds: Hearing thresholds obtained from a patient using hearing aids, indicated by an *A* on the audiogram.

Air–bone gap: The difference between air- and bone-conduction thresholds; a difference may indicate a conductive component in the hearing loss.

Air conduction: Refers to when sound travels through the air into the external auditory canal and stimulation progresses through the middle ear, inner ear, and then to the brain.

ALD: Assistive listening device.

ALGO: An automated ABR screening device used for screening newborn infants.

Algorithm: A mathematical formula that provides step-by-step rules for performing a specific function or task, such as processing and amplifying an acoustic signal.

Allele: One of two or more alternative forms of a gene, occupying the same position on paired chromosomes, which are responsible for alternative traits or for controlling the same inherited characteristic.

Altered speech: Human speech that is recorded and then altered in some way.

Alzheimer's disease (AD): A form of dementia that causes irreversible loss of brain cells.

Ambient noise: Noise that is present in a room when it is unoccupied.

American Academy of Audiology (AAA): A professional organization for audiologists that advances the profession of audiology through leadership activities, advocacy, educational programs, public awareness, and research support.

American Association of Retired Persons (AARP): Consumer group for persons over the age of 50 years.

American National Standards Institute (ANSI): A group that determines standards for measuring instruments, including audiometers.

American Sign Language (ASL): A manual system of communication used by members of the Deaf culture in the United States.

American Speech-Language-Hearing Association (ASHA): A professional, scientific, and credentialing organization for audiologists, speech-language pathologists, and speech, language, and hearing scientists in the United States and internationally.

American Tinnitus Association (ATA): An organization that supports self-help groups for tinnitus sufferers and funds research about tinnitus.

Americans with Disabilities Act (ADA): A civil rights law that prohibits discrimination on the basis of disability in employment and in services and activities of federal, state, and local government agencies, as well as in goods, services, facilities, advantages, privileges, and accommodations of public places.

Amplification: Provision of increased intensity of sound.

Amplifier: Increases the intensity of sound.

Analytic training: In auditory and speechreading training, emphasizes the recognition of individual speech sounds or syllables.

Anoxia: Deficiency or absence of oxygen in the body tissues.

ANSI: American National Standards Institute.

Anticipatory strategies: Methods of preparing for a communication interaction.

Aperiodic: Not occurring at regular intervals; not periodic.

Apgar score: A numeric value between 1 and 10 assigned to newborn infants to describe physical status at birth.

Aplasia: A lack of development of all or part of a body structure, or defective development.

Appropriate format accommodations: Accommodations that allow children with hearing loss to participate with children who have normal hearing on a "fair playing ground."

Arthritis: Inflammation of a joint, often accompanied by pain, swelling, stiffness, and redness of the skin.

Articulation: Movement and positioning of the oral-cavity structures, including tongue tip, tongue body, jaw, and lips, during speech production.

ASHA: American Speech-Language-Hearing Association.

ASL: American Sign Language.

ASSEP: Auditory steady state evoked potential.

Assertive conversational style: Conversational style in which a person takes responsibility for managing communication difficulties in a way that is considerate of communication partners; e.g., *I'm going to turn down the car radio so that I can hear you better and so you won't have to repeat so much.*

Assertiveness training: Training or behavioral therapy that teaches patients to express themselves in a confident way, and in a way that does not offend or alienate others, and teaches them to state both requests and feelings directly and courteously with an appropriate balance of passivity and aggression.

Assistive device (AD): A device designed to overcome limitations imposed by hearing loss, inclusive of assistive listening devices.

Assistive listening device (ALD): Instrument designed to provide awareness or identification of environmental signals and speech and to improve signal-to-noise ratios.

Assistive living facility: A living arrangement where patients with special needs, especially older patients, reside and receive help with everyday tasks such as bathing, dressing, and taking medication.

Asymmetrical hearing loss: Hearing loss in which the degree or configuration of loss in one ear differs from that in the other ear.

ATA: American Tinnitus Association.

Atresia: A congenital closure of the external auditory canal.

Attack time: The time between when a signal begins and the onset of its steady-state amplified value.

Attention: A selective narrowing of mental focus and receptivity.

Attention deficit disorder (ADD): Cognitive deficit that limits an individual's ability to pay attention and stay focused on a task; may involve restlessness, distractibility, and hyperactivity.

Audible: Loud enough to be heard.

Audio boot: A device that is used with a behind-the-ear hearing aid for coupling to a direct audio input cord or wireless system; also called a *shoe.*

Audiogram: A graphic representation of hearing thresholds as a function of stimulus frequency.

Audiologic rehabilitation: Term often used synonymously with aural rehabilitation or aural habilitation; sometimes may entail greater emphasis on the provision and follow-up of listening devices and less emphasis on nontechnology-based solutions and interventions.

Audiologist: Allied health care professional who has academic accreditation in the practice of audiology; professional who provides an array of services related to hearing evaluation and rehabilitation.

Audiometer: An instrument for measuring hearing sensitivity for a range of frequencies.

Audiometric zero: Lowest sound pressure level that can just be detected by an average adult ear at any particular frequency; designated as 0 dB Hearing Level (HL) on an audiogram.

Audiovisual: Situation in which speech is presented with both the auditory and visual signals.

Audiovisual integration: Occurs when information from the auditory and the visual signals combine to form a unified percept.

Audition-only: Presentation of only the auditory signal during a testing or training session.

Audition-plus-vision: Presentation of both the auditory and visual signals simultaneously during a testing or training session.

Auditory brain training: Speech perception training that has a heavy emphasis on exercising those cognitive skills that are necessary to recognize speech (e.g., auditory attention, auditory working memory, auditory processing speed) as well as a classic emphasis on analytic and synthetic speech recognition.

Auditory brainstem implant: Implant that has an electrode that implants to the juncture of the eighth cranial nerve and the cochlear nucleus in the brain stem.

Auditory brainstem response (ABR): Auditory evoked potential that originates from the eighth cranial nerve and auditory brainstem structures; the electrophysiological record consists of five to seven peaks, which reflect the neural functioning of the auditory pathway.

Auditory canal: External auditory meatus.

Auditory cortex: The region of the brain that is responsible for processing auditory information and is located in the temporal lobe of the cerebral hemisphere.

Auditory enhancement: The amount of improvement in word recognition when being tested first in an auditory-only condition and then tested in an audiovisual condition.

Auditory evoked potential (AEP): An electrophysiological response to sound, distinguished by latency.

Auditory feedback: One's own speech signal that is heard while speaking.

Auditory memory: Acquisition, storage, and retrieval of previously experienced auditory sound patterns.

Auditory neuropathy: Condition in which the patient has a pure-tone audiogram that shows any degree of hearing loss, from mild to profound, and shows normal otoacoustic emissions and either absent or degraded auditory brainstem responses; also called *auditory dyssynchrony*.

Auditory spacing: A talker uses auditory spacing to chunk information into meaningful phrase units, pausing between each phrase unit.

Auditory training: Instruction designed to maximize a patient's use of residual hearing or electrical hearing by means of both formal and informal listening practice.

Auditory-verbal approach: Encourages a child to develop listening behaviors and to develop spoken communication by relying on residual hearing rather than vision; the use of appropriate and habitual amplification or electrical stimulation (via cochlear implant) is strongly encouraged.

Auditory-verbal therapy: An intervention in which technology, techniques, and strategies are used to enable children to listen and understand spoken language, with a primary emphasis on the auditory modality for learning.

Aural habilitation: Intervention for persons who have not developed or who are currently acquiring listening, speech, and language skills; e.g., infants and toddlers.

Aural/oral communication: The communication mode used by persons with normal hearing, which entails listening and speaking; also called *oralism*.

Aural/oral language: The language used by persons with normal hearing.

Aural/oral method: An instructional method used to teach children with significant hearing loss and one that encourages to use hearing, speechreading, and spoken language for learning; a teaching method that does not incorporate manual sign language.

Aural rehabilitation: Intervention aimed at minimizing and alleviating the communication difficulties associated with hearing loss with a primary goal of enhancing conversational fluency.

Auricle: Pinna; external or outer ear.

Auropalpebral reflex: A wink or twitch of the eye that occurs in response to loud sound.

Automated auditory brainstem response (A-ABR): A screening method to measure the auditory brainstem response in which recording parameters are computer-controlled and detection of the response is determined by computer-based algorithms.

Automatic directional microphone (ADM): Automatically switches between an omnidirectional and directional mode according to environmental conditions.

Automatic gain control (AGC): Nonlinear hearing aid compression circuitry that changes gain as signal level changes or limits the output of the hearing aid when the level reaches a specified value.

Autosomal dominant: One parent passes a dominant allele to the child and the probability of the trait being expressed in the child is 50%.

Autosomal recessive: Transmission of genetic characteristics in which both parents must pass on matching alleles to the child in order for the characteristic to be expressed.

Autosome: Any of the 22 pairs of 23 chromosome pairs not related to determination of gender.

Baby boomers: The generation born between the years 1946 and 1965.

Background noise: Undesirable noise that masks the auditory signal of interest.

BAHA: Bone-anchored hearing aid.

Band-pass filter: An electronic filter that allows a band of frequencies to pass, while blocking the passage of frequencies below or above the band of specified limits.

Barotrauma: Damage to body tissue, typically in the ears or lungs, caused by increased air or water pressure.

Basic knowledge: Allows the recall of specifics, universals, methods, and processes, or the recall of a pattern, structure, or setting.

Battery: A cell that provides electrical power.

Behavioral audiometry: Pure-tone and speech audiometry that requires a behavioral response from the patient.

Behavioral/observational audiometry (BOA): A method of testing a child's hearing in which the tester presents a sound stimulus and then observes the child's behavior for change.

Behind-the-ear hearing aid (BTE): A hearing aid worn over the pinna and coupled to the ear canal by means of an earmold.

Bilateral: On both sides; involving both ears.

Bilateral contralateral routing of signals (BICROS): A hearing aid fitting designed for asymmetrical hearing loss and one that entails a microphone at each ear, with both microphones routing the auditory signal to a single amplifier and receiver in the better ear.

Bilingual: A term that describes a person who speaks two languages.

Bilingual/bicultural model: An instructional model in which children with significant hearing loss learn a Deaf sign language as their first language and then later learn their native spoken language in school, as they develop reading and writing skills.

Bimodal stimulation: The use of a cochlear implant in one ear and a hearing aid in the other.

Binaural: For both ears.

Binaural advantage: The advantage of using both ears instead of one, such as better hearing thresholds and enhanced listening in the presence of background noise.

Binaural squelch: Improvement in listening in noise when hearing with two ears instead of one, as a result of interaural phase and intensity differences.

Binaural summation: The advantage of binaural versus monaural hearing, expressed in dB, when listening in a noisy soundfield, with binaural thresholds being approximately 3 dB than monaural thresholds.

Biomedical orientation: Reduces hearing loss to the biological dimension of disease and illness and focuses more on the organs and mechanisms of hearing rather than on the person as an individual.

Biopsychosocial: Implies that biological, psychological (e.g., thoughts, emotions, behaviors), and social factors (e.g., friends) influence how a health condition may affect human functioning.

Biphasic pulses: A square wave that has equal amplitude for the positive and negative phases.

Blindness: Described by the World Health Organization as vision of 20/500 or worse in the better eye.

Bluffing: Pretending to understand an utterance and behaving in a way that suggests that understanding occurred, even if little or none of the message was recognized.

BOA: Behavioral/observational audiometry.

Body functions: Physiological functions of body systems, including psychological functions.

Body hearing aid: A hearing aid that includes a box worn on the torso and a cord connecting it to an ear-level receiver.

Body structures: Defined by the World Health Organization as an anatomical part of the body, such as organs (e.g., the cochlea) and limbs.

Bone-anchored hearing aid (BAHA): A bone-conduction hearing aid anchored to the mastoid via a titanium screw and attached percutaneously to an external processor; primarily used for conductive hearing loss and when there is an intractable middle ear disorder or significant atresia.

Bone conduction: Sound is delivered by means of vibrating the skull.

Bone-conduction hearing aid: A hearing aid that delivers the amplified signal via a bone vibrator placed over the mastoid process and provides stimulation director to the inner ear, bypassing the outer and middle ear.

Bone conductor: A small device, about a square inch in diameter, that is used to transmit sound to the bones of the skull by means of vibration; also called a *bone oscillator*.

Bottom-up processing: The processing of sound that is influenced primarily from input from the auditory periphery, with minimal cognitive processing in terms of expectations or prior knowledge.

BTE hearing aid: Behind-the-ear hearing aid.

Calibration: Electric or psychoacoustic checking of a measuring instrument, such as an audiometer, against an accurate standard to determine whether deviations or errors exist, and if they do exist, usually entails the correction of the instrument.

Canonical babbling: An advanced form of infant babbling that consists of well-formed consonant–vowel combinations.

CAPD: Central auditory processing disorder.

Carrier phrase: In speech audiometry, a phrase that precedes the target word, such as, *Say the word* ___., and which prepares the patient for the target word.

Case study: A research study that involves an in-depth examination of a patient, either because the patient is considered to be unusual or representative of a larger group.

Cataract: Progressive retinal disorder that entails a clouding of the lens, causes blurred vision, and impairs contrast sensitivity. Lens-replacement surgery is available as a treatment.

CAT scan: Computerized axial tomography scan.

CC decoder: Closed-caption decoder.

Center-based program: Program in which children attend therapy at a center, clinic, or school for a designated number of hours per week.

Central auditory processing disorder (CAPD): Difficulty in differentiating, recognizing, and understanding sounds that is not due to either hearing loss or intellectual impairment.

Cerebral palsy: A motor-control disorder caused by insult to the motor cortex of the brain, characterized by a lack of muscle control, especially in the limbs.

Cerumen: Earwax.

Cholesteatoma: A tumor-like mass of epithelium cells and cholesterol in the middle ear that may invade the mastoid process and impinge upon the ossicular chain.

Chromosome pair: The basic unit of genes; structures carrying the genes of a cell and made up of a single strand of DNA.

Chronological age: Age of an individual referenced to birth.

CIC: Completely-in-the-canal hearing aid.

CICI: Completely implantable cochlear implant.

Clarification: A counseling technique in which clinicians abstract the essence of a patient's remarks and then summarize them back to their patient.

Classroom acoustics: The background noise and reverberation properties of a classroom, determined by the size and surfaces of the room, the sound sources inside and outside, furnishings, people, and other factors.

Clear speech: A way of speaking to enhance one's intelligibility; it entails speaking with a slowed rate and good but not overly exaggerated enunciation.

C-level: With reference to cochlear implants, the amount of electrical current level needed to hear a comfortably loud sound; the loudest comfortable stimulation level on a channel.

Clinical significance: Whether an experimental or test result has practical meaning to either the patient or the clinician.

Clock-time orientation: An orientation driven by the clock and characterized by an adherence to time as a factor in determining the length of an interaction or the time course of an intervention.

Closed-caption (CC) decoder: In a television set or electronic appliance, extracts previously encoded closed-caption data from a received video signal and displays it on a screen.

Closed captioning: Printed text or printed dialogue that corresponds to the auditory speech signal from a television program or movie.

Closed-ended questions: Questions used to gather quantitative or categorical information and which typically elicit a response from a close-set of possible responses; e.g., *yes, no.*

Closed set: A stimulus or response set that contains a fixed number of items that are known to the patient; e.g., four pictures of four different types of fruit.

Cluster analysis: A statistical approach to information in a database that aims to determine which data points fall into groups or clusters; for example, it is not uncommon for the phonemes /b,d,g/ to cluster together because they often sound similar to people who have significant hearing loss.

CMV: Cytomegalovirus.

CNT: Could not test.

Coaching model of intervention: An approach to early intervention in which the professional usually comes to the child's home one or two hours per week and helps caretakers learn to optimize everyday activities such as feeding and bathing so that they promote the child's hearing, language, and speech (or sign) abilities.

Coarticulate: In speech production, anticipating the sound during an earlier unit in the string or retaining aspects of a unit during production of a subsequent unit; for example, when saying the word *blue,* the lips may round in anticipation of the /u/ as the talker speaks the initial consonant blend /bl/.

Coarticulation: In speech production, the influence of one phoneme on either a preceding or succeeding phoneme.

Cochlear implant: Device implanted in the skull that permits persons with significant hearing loss to receive stimulation of the auditory mechanism and is typically comprised of a microphone, a speech processor, a transmitter, and an electrode array inserted into the cochlea that directly stimulates the auditory nerve by means of electrical current.

Cochlear implant mapping: Process of programming the cochlear implant's speech processor.

Cochlear implant team: The group of professionals who are part of the cochlear implant process and which often includes an otolaryngologist, audiologist, and clinical coordinator, and which may include an educator, aural rehabilitation specialist, speech-language pathologist, psychologist, and/or social worker.

Cochlear nucleus: Cluster of cell bodies in the brain stem where the fibers of the auditory nerve (8th cranial nerve) leading from the cochlea enter and synapse.

Coenrollment: A model of educating children who have hearing loss that entails a team of teachers, one a regular classroom teacher and the other, a trained teacher for children who have hearing loss.

Cognition: Those mental processes involved in obtaining knowledge, in comprehending, and in thinking, including such mental acts as remembering, judging, and problem solving.

Color sensitivity: The ability to detect colors of different wavelengths.

Comfortable loudness level: Intensity level at which it is comfortable to listen to sound; also referred to as the *most comfortable listening level.*

Communication: The act of exchanging messages, and may entail the use of speech, sign, writing, facial expressions, and/or hand gestures.

Communication breakdown: Occurs when one communication partner does not recognize another's message.

Communication disorder: An impairment in one's ability to communicate.

Communication mode: The means used by a sender to share information with a receiver and may include speech, sign, writing, hand gestures, or any other system of shared symbols.

Communication partner: Person with whom one engages in conversation.

Communication strategies training: Instruction provided to persons with hearing loss or to their communication partners which helps them to maximize their communication potential and conversational fluency and to minimize the occurrence of communication breakdowns.

Communication strategy: A course of action taken to enhance communication.

Completely implantable cochlear implant (CICI): A cochlear implant comprised of only internal components.

Completely-in-the-canal (CIC): A hearing aid that fits entirely within the external ear canal.

Comprehension: An auditory skill level in which the listener is able to understand the meaning of spoken messages.

Compressed speech: Speech that has been modified to have segments removed and then has been compressed in such a way that the signal is still intelligible, but the duration is shorter than the original version.

Compression: A nonlinear form of amplifier gain used to determine and limit output gain as a function of input gain.

Compression ratio: The decibel ratio of acoustic input to amplifier output.

Computerized axial tomography scan (CAT scan): A computer-generated picture of a section of the brain compiled from sectional radiographs obtained from the same plane; also known as a *CT scan.*

Concha: The bowl-like depression of the outer ear that forms the mouth of the external ear canal.

Conditioned play audiometry (CPA): A method of testing children 2½ years and older in which the child is trained to perform a task in response to presentation of a sound.

Conditioned response: A new or modified response to a previously neutral stimulus.

Conductive hearing loss: Hearing loss that results from an obstruction within the outer or middle ear.

Configuration: Refers to the extent of the hearing loss at each frequency and gives an overall description of the hearing loss.

Congenital: Present at birth.

Congruence with self: The first tenet of person-centered counseling in which clinicians act as themselves in interactions with patients and do not assume a facade of professionalism.

Consonant-vowel-consonant (CVC): A monosyllabic word structure; CVCs often are used as stimuli in isolated-word speech recognition tests.

Construct: An abstract or general idea that is inferred or derived from a constellation of measures or from a group of specific instances.

Construct validity: Statistical term meaning the extent to which a test measures what it is supposed to measure, usually a trait or skill; e.g., speech perception.

Constructive strategy: Tactic designed to optimize the listening environment for communication.

Content: In terms of language acquisition, refers to vocabulary words and their meanings.

Content validity: Statistical term meaning the extent to which a test adequately samples what it is supposed to measure.

Contextual information: Linguistic support available for identifying a target word, phrase, or sentence.

Contralateral routing of signals hearing aid (CROS): A hearing aid fitting designed for unilateral hearing loss that entails placing the microphone on the poorer ear and the amplifier and receiver on the good ear so that sound can be routed to the good ear.

Contrast sensitivity: The ability to detect differences in luminance.

Control group: Comprised of a group of research participants who closely resemble members of the experimental group but who do not receive the experimental treatment, and thereby serves as a standard against which to detect and measure changes in the experimental group due to the treatment.

Conversational fluency: Relates to how smoothly conversation unfolds.

Conversational rules: Implicit rules that guide the conduct of participants in a conversation.

Conversational turn: The period during which a participant delivers a contribution to the conversation.

Coping: Refers to a patient's mental and behavioral efforts to manage difficult or demanding situations, even when a situation is perceived as taxing or beyond their resources.

Corner audiogram: An audiogram that displays a profound hearing loss with thresholds measurable only in the low frequencies.

Cost-effectiveness: The relationship between the money spent and the benefits accrued.

Counseling: With respect to aural rehabilitation, a professional service designed to help patients better understand and solve their hearing-related problems.

CPA: Conditioned play audiometry.

Critical period: The early years of a child's life in which the language and vocal patterns of the child's language community are acquired most easily.

CROS hearing aid: Contralateral routing of signals hearing aid.

Crossmodal enhancement: Occurs when the response to a stimulus presented through one modality (e.g., hearing) is augmented or modulated by another stimulus presented through a different modality (e.g., sight).

Cued Speech: A system for enhancing speech reading that uses phonemically-based hand gestures, placed at different locations around the face and neck, to distinguish between similar visual speech patterns.

Cues to action: Strategies, events, or conditions that activate a patient's "readiness."

Cultural and linguistic competence: A set of congruent behaviors, attitudes, and policies that come together in a system, in an agency, or among professionals that enables effective work in cross-cultural situations.

Culture: A conglomeration of the thoughts, communications, actions, customs, beliefs, values, learned behaviors, and institutions of racial, ethnic, religious, or social groups.

CVC: Consonant-vowel-consonant.

Cytomegalovirus (CMV): A member of the herpes virus.

DAI: Direct audio input.

Daily log: Self-report of behavior used by respondents for self-monitoring.

dB: Decibel.

dB nHL: Decibels normalized hearing level.

Dead-air spaces: Unventilated air spaces.

Deaf: Having minimal or no hearing.

Deaf culture: A subculture in society that shares a common language (e.g., American Sign Language; British Sign Language), beliefs, customs, arts, history, and folklore and that is primarily comprised of individuals who have prelingual hearing loss.

decibel (dB): The decibel is a logarithmic unit of sound pressure that is one-tenth of a Bel and is a unit for expressing sound intensity.

Delayed-onset hereditary hearing loss: Hearing is normal at birth and then declines later in life as a result of a hereditary disorder.

Dementia: A term that refers to a number of diseases that affect reasoning and intellectual faculties, with symptoms that may include memory loss, deterioration of thought processes, and orientation disorders.

Dependent variable: The factor or item measured in an experiment.

Describing: In aural rehabilitation, a language-stimulation technique in which an adult describes an ongoing event for the purpose of helping a child develop vocabulary and language structures that pertain to the event.

Desensitization: A way to reduce a patient's negative reactions in specific situations by means of repeatedly exposing the person to a situation in mild form, either in reality, role-playing, or imagination.

Detection: The ability to recognize when a sound is present and when it is absent.

Developmental delay: A condition in which a child lags behind in development relative to age-matched peers.

Diabetic retinopathy: A condition resulting from long-standing diabetes, causing blurred and distorted vision in the central visual field or patchy vision, and sometimes a detached retina; management of the diabetic condition and laser surgery can limit damage to the eye.

Dichotic-syllable identification task: A task in which two consonant-vowel syllables are presented to a patient, one to each ear, and the patient must identify the two syllables, sometimes from a closed set of alternatives.

Digital hearing aid: Hearing aid that utilizes digital technology to process the signal.

Digital noise reduction (DNR): Processing designed to reduce gain in the low frequencies or specific frequency bands when noise is detected.

Digital signal processing (DSP): When performed by a hearing aid, a procedure that converts the signal from analog to digital form, processes the signal to achieve a target, and then converts the signal back to analog form.

Digit-span tasks: Measure a person's working memory capacity to store a string of digits, and the longest string stored is that person's digit span; e.g., a string of 6 digits; a string of 7 digits.

Direct audio input (DAI): A hardwired connection that leads directly from the sound source to the hearing aid or other listening device.

Direct therapy model of intervention: An approach to early intervention in which the professional provides direct therapy to an infant or toddler and teaches parents how to promote their child's hearing, language, and speech (or sign) abilities.

Directional microphone: A microphone that is more sensitive to sound originating from in front of the hearing aid user than to sound coming from behind the user.

Disability: A physical or mental impairment that substantially limits one or more life activities in the individual.

Discourse: Communication of thoughts by use of language.

Discrimination: In speechreading or auditory training, the ability to distinguish whether stimuli are the same or different.

Disorder: An abnormality in functioning.

Distortion: Undesirable change in the audio signal.

DNA: Deoxyribonucleic acid.

DNR: Digital noise reduction.

DNT: Did not test.

Dominant hereditary hearing loss: Hearing loss that stems from a genetic characteristic on at least one gene of a pair.

Dominating conversational behaviors: Behaviors that are characteristic of an aggressive conversational style, which may include interrupting, taking long speaking turns, and dominating the topic of conversation; e.g., *Speaking of summer vacations, let me tell you about the time my son and I went to Sweden and we went on a three week extravaganza. . . and then. . . . . . and then. . . . . . and then. . . .*

DPOAE: Distortion product otoacoustic emission.

Dri-aid kit: A small package used to keep moisture out of the internal components of listening devices.

Drill activity: Repeated exercises and rote activities.

DSP: Digital signal processing.

Dyalog: A computer-based technique that analyzes conversations and may include measuring the length of speaking turns and silences by means of pressing a keyboard key.

Dynamic range: The difference in decibels between a person's threshold for just being able to detect speech and the person's threshold for uncomfortable listening.

EAA: Educational Audiology Association.

Early Hearing Detection and Intervention (EHDI) Act: Legislation that mandates federal funds for states to develop infant hearing screening and intervention programs and includes provisions to support hearing screening and when appropriate, to support full diagnostic evaluation of all newborn infants. It also provides for enrollment into early-intervention programs and promotes culturally sensitive family support services.

Early Hearing Detection and Intervention (EHDI) 1-3-6 Guidelines: These guidelines were developed by the Joint Commission on Infant Hearing and recommend that hearing screening occurs by 1 month of age, diagnosis occurs by 3 months, and intervention begins by 6 months.

Ear protection: A term used to refer to hearing protectors such as ear plugs and ear muffs.

Earmold: A coupler customized to fit into the auricle that channels sound from the earhook of a hearing aid into the auditory canal.

EBP: Evidence-based practice.

Educational Audiology Association (EAA): An international organization for audiologists and related professionals who deliver hearing-related services to children, particularly those in educational settings.

Effusion: In the middle ear, exudation of body fluid from the middle ear membranous walls as a result of inflammation.

EHDI Act: Early Hearing Detection and Intervention Act.

Eighth cranial nerve: The cranial nerve consisting of an auditory and vestibular branch.

Electrical auditory stimulation (EAS): Presents combined electrical and acoustic stimulation to the same ear; developed for patients who have profound hearing loss in the high frequencies and significant residual hearing in the low frequencies.

Electrical threshold (T-level): With reference to cochlear implants, the amount of current that must be passed through a channel so that the cochlear implant user is just aware of sound sensation.

Electrode: Metal ball or plate through which electrical stimulation is applied to the body or electrical energy is measured.

Electrode array: A component of a cochlear implant that is composed of electrodes separated by insulation and that is inserted into the cochlea and placed in close approximation to the ganglion cells that are responsible for transmitting electrical impulses to those brain regions responsible for processing sound.

Elicitation technique: Techniques that a clinician might use to ensure that a desired event or behavior occurs.

Empathetic understanding: In aural rehabilitation, a tenet of person-centered counseling in which clinicians assume that patients know best and assume that patients have the inner resources to overcome their conversational difficulties.

Empathizing: Occurs when clinicians place themselves in their patient's situation while still remaining objective.

Encephalitis: An inflammation of the brain, often caused by a viral infection.

Environmental factors: Factors that are external to a patient and that are comprised of the physical, social, and attitudinal environment in which the patient lives and conducts his or her life.

Equivalent lists: Typically in the context of speech recognition tests, lists in which the collection of items comprising each list are presumed to be equally difficult to recognize in the aggregate.

Event-time orientation: An orientation that is process-driven in which issues are pursued to their natural conclusions, no matter how long that might take.

Evidence-based practice (EBP): Clinical decision-making that is based on (a) a review of the scientific evidence regarding benefits and costs of alternative forms of diagnosis or treatment, (b) on clinical experience, and (c) on patient values.

Evoked potential: Electrical activity generated in the brain in response to a sensory stimulus.

Expanded speech: Recorded speech that is altered by duplicating small segments of the signal so that the speech sounds like it has a slowed speaking rate.

Expansion: A language-stimulation technique in which an adult copies the meaning of a child's utterance but modifies or expands the grammar or vocabulary of the message.

Experimental group: A group comprised of research participants who receive the treatment under study.

Explicit categorization: An informational counseling technique used to ensure retention in which the clinician enumerates the topics that will be covered and then announces each one before talking about it.

Expressive language: The language we speak or sign.

Expressive repair strategy: Repair strategy used by the sender (talker) when the sender produces an unintelligible utterance or otherwise incomprehensible message and the communication partner cannot decipher it; for example, the talker might point to the object that is the subject of the misunderstood utterance.

Extended repair: Occurs when many repair strategies are needed to mend a communication breakdown.

External auditory meatus: External ear canal.

External components: In cochlear implants, the external components are worn on the outside of the body.

External ear canal: The canal of the outer ear leading from the concha to the tympanic membrane.

Facilitative language techniques: Techniques used to stimulate language growth in young children through the course of conversational interactions.

Facilitative strategies: A class of communication strategies typically used by the person with hearing loss that include instructing the talker and structuring the listening environment so to enhance listening and speechreading performance.

False-negative: Occurs when a baby has hearing loss but passes a hearing screening test.

False-positive: Occurs when a baby does not have a hearing loss but fails a hearing screening test.

Familial deafness: Deafness reoccurring in members of the same family.

Family-centered approach: An intervention approach that places the family as being central to a patient's well-being and acknowledges that emotional, social, and (in the case of children) developmental support are integral components of the aural rehabilitation plan.

Family lifecycle: Represents the milestones and emotional and intellectual stages a person passes through as a member of a family and is often described in terms of age, marital (partner) status, and ages and the presence or absence of children.

Family systems theory: Describes how the members of a family are interconnected and how their patterns of communication and interaction affect one another.

Family tree: A genealogical diagram of a child's ancestry or kin.

FAPE: Free and appropriate public education.

Favorable seating: For speechreading, includes being close enough to see the talker's lip movements and being able to see the talker full-face rather than in profile.

FDA: Food and Drug Administration.

Filtered speech: Speech that has been passed through filter banks for the purpose of removing or amplifying frequency bands in the signal.

Fingerspelling: A kind of manual communication in which words are spelled letter-by-letter using standard hand configurations.

Flat audiogram: An audiogram configuration in which the thresholds across frequencies are similar.

Fluctuating hearing loss: A hearing loss that varies in magnitude over time.

FM: Frequency modulation.

FM boot: A small boot-like device worn on the bottom of a user's hearing aid that attaches to or contains an FM receiver.

FM level advantage: The increase in decibel output level when the FM signal is added to, or substituted for, the signal from the aid's own microphone.

FM receiver: The device that detects the transmitted radio wave and recovers the sound signal for delivery to the hearing aid or other hearing device. The connection options include integrated (receiver is built into the personal device), dedicated (the receiver is compatible with one case design), and universal (receiver works with multiple devices depending on the interface between the device and the receiver).

fMRI: Functional magnetic resonance imaging.

FM trainer: A classroom assistive listening device in which the teacher wears a microphone and the signal is transmitted to the student(s) by means of frequency modulated radio waves.

FM transmitter: The device that transmits the radio signal that carries the sound signal.

Food and Drug Administration (FDA): The U.S. government agency that oversees the regulation of a large range of products, including medical devices such as hearing aids and cochlear implants.

Form: In terms of language acquisition, refers to the proper use of the elements of language, such as nouns, verbs, and prepositions.

Formal instruction: The first stage of a three-stage learning model (i.e., *formal instruction, guided learning, real-world practice*) where children or adults receive explicit instruction, often in a classroom or therapy setting, and may be used during the teaching of communication strategies, language stimulation techniques, and language structures and vocabulary.

Formal training: A type of training that presents highly structured activities and that is usually scheduled during designated times of the day, either in a one-on-one lesson format or in a small group; e.g., drill activities.

Formant: A resonance in the vocal tract that results in some frequencies in the speech signal having more energy than other frequencies.

Free and appropriate public education (FAPE): Refers to federal funding provided for the education of children with disabilities and requires as a condition for receiving federal funds the provision of free and appropriate public education.

Frequency: The number of regularly repeated events in a given unit of time, usually measured in cycles per second and expressed in hertz (Hz).

Frequency modulation (FM): The process of creating a complex signal by means of sinusoidally varying a carrier wave frequency.

Frequency of occurrence: The frequency in which a word is likely to occur in everyday speech or common usage, also called *frequency of usage*.

Frequency response: The output characteristics of a listening device that is usually denoted by gain as a function of frequency.

Frequency selectivity: The auditory system's ability to respond differentially to different frequencies and bands of frequencies.

Frequent communication partner: A particular person with whom another often converses, a person who is often a family member or close friend.

Fricative: A speech sound generated by creating turbulent airflow through a constriction in the oral cavity; e.g., /f, s/).

Full-on gain: Hearing aid setting that results in the maximum acoustic output.

Functional gain: Difference in decibels between unaided and aided thresholds.

Functional magnetic resonance imaging (fMRI): An imaging technology used to study the activity of the brain; the computerized images show which brain structures are active during a particular mental activity.

Gain: In hearing aids, the difference in decibels between the input level of an acoustic signal and the output level.

Gain/frequency response: The difference between the amplitude of the input signal and the amplitude of the output signal across frequencies.

Gallaudet University: Founded in 1864, Gallaudet University is the world's first university that has programs and services designed specifically for students who are deaf and hard of hearing.

Gaze behavior: In reference to lipreading or speechreading, refers to how the eyes shift their focus around the talker's face as the talker speaks.

Generous listening: Listening in a way that lets patients know that they are being heard without being judged and listening in a way that provides positive attention, regard, and acknowledgment.

Genetic counseling: Provision of information to prospective parents about the likelihood of an inherited condition or disorder in their children or future offspring.

Genotype: The genetic makeup of an individual.

Glaucoma: A health condition caused by high fluid pressure within the eye that may damage the optic nerve and result in reduced vision, especially in the peripheral visual field.

Glide consonant: A consonant that, when spoken, is characterized by a gradual change in the acoustic signal; e.g., /w, l, r/.

Goal: The desired result of training or instruction.

Grounding: A conversational occurrence in which communication partners establish a body of information as shared common ground for an ongoing conversational interchange. It usually entails the presentation of information by one communication partner and the confirmation of mutual understanding by another.

Group discussion: Provides a forum for class members to discuss communication issues.

Guided learning: The second stage of a three-stage learning model (i.e., *formal instruction, guided learning, and real-world practice*) where children or adults receive practice and informal instruction in a structured setting, and may be used during the teaching of communication strategies, language stimulation techniques, and language structures and vocabulary.

Habilitation: A program or an intervention aimed at the initial development of skills and abilities.

HAE: Hearing aid evaluation.

Hair cells: Sensory cells in the cochlea that attach to the nerve endings of the eighth cranial nerve.

HAO: Hearing aid orientation.

Handicap: A term that today is rarely used to refer to the the psychosocial disadvantages that result from a functional impairment.

Hard of hearing (HOH): A term that is used to denote hearing loss, typically one that is not a profound loss.

Hardwired: Directly connected by wires.

Hardwired assistive listening devices: Devices that are directly connected by wires.

HATS: Hearing assistive technology system.

Head shadow: The attenuation of sound to one ear because of the presence of the head between the ear and the sound source.

Health maintenance organization (HMO): An HMO is a type of insurance plan that stipulates which doctors and medical facilities can be used by a patient and which medical tests and procedures will be covered.

Health-related quality of life (HRQoL): HRQoL refers to the impact of a health condition on the well-being experienced by an individual or a group of people and includes such dimensions as physiology, function, social activity, cognition, emotions, energy, vitality, health perception, and general life satisfaction.

Hearing aid: An electronic listening device designed to amplify and deliver sound from the environment to the listener; includes a microphone, amplifier, and receiver.

Hearing aid evaluation (HAE): A procedure in which an appropriate hearing aid is selected for a patient.

Hearing aid orientation (HAO): The process of instructing a patient (and a family member) to handle, use, and maintain a new hearing aid.

Hearing aid stethoscope: Resembles a physician's stethoscope and is used to auscultate a hearing aid for the purpose of listening or diagnosing a problem; also called a *stetoclip.*

Hearing aid test box: A chamber that provides an electroacoustic analysis of hearing aids and probe-microphone measurements.

Hearing aid use pattern: The times, situations, and locations in which a hearing aid user wears the hearing aid(s).

Hearing assistive technology system (HATS): Listening, alerting, and signaling devices that facilitate patients' communication with the environment or enhance their personal safety through the use of auditory, visual, or tactile modalities.

Hearing conservation: Prevention or reduction of hearing loss through a program of identifying and minimizing risk, monitoring hearing sensitivity, education, and providing protection from noise exposure.

Hearing culture: The mainstream culture in the United States that includes persons whose primary mode of communication is spoken language.

Hearing level (HL): Decibel level referenced to audiometric zero.

Hearing loss: Abnormal or reduced hearing sensitivity.

Hearing Loss Association of America (HLAA): A self-help organization for people with hearing loss that provides information, education, support, and advocacy.

Hearing loss-specific quality of life (HLQoL): The activity limitations and participation restrictions imposed by hearing loss, and its impact on psychosocial functioning.

Hearing meetup: A support network of patients who meet regularly to discuss hearing loss and audiology related topics and to provide psychosocial support to one another.

Hearing protection: Means to prevent or minimize the deleterious effects of loud sound on the auditory system.

Hearing-related disability: A loss of function imposed by hearing loss. The term denotes a multidimensional phenomenon, and may include pain, discomfort, physical dysfunction, emotional distress, and the inability to carry out typical activities.

Hearing-related stress: Includes the stress of adjusting to a new self-concept, the stress of living with an impaired sensory system, and the stress of living with the reactions of society to people who have a disability and who experience communication difficulties.

Hearing screening: Presents a rapid and truncated audiological assessment to a large group of individuals with the goal of identifying those who require additional diagnostic procedures.

Hearing threshold: Level of intensity at which a sound is just audible to an individual.

Hearing wellness advocate (HWA): A patient with hearing loss or a community member or professional who has a "can-do" attitude and who is willing to share his or her patient healthcare journey or expertise with other people who have hearing loss; e.g., a physician.

Hertz (Hz): A unit of frequency that is equal to one cycle per second.

High frequency of usage: Words that occur frequently in everyday conversation.

High-pass filtered speech: Speech that has been passed through filter banks that removed the lower, but not the higher, frequencies.

HL: Hearing level.

HLQoL: Hearing loss-specific quality of life.

HMO: Health maintenance organization.

Home-based program: An early education program in which an early interventionist visits the infant's home and provides instruction for the child and parents.

Homophenes: Words that look identical on the mouth.

HRQoL: Health-related quality of life.

Hybrid: Listening aids that combine a cochlear implant system with hearing aid technology.

Hz: Hertz.

ICF: International Classification of Functioning, Disability and Health.

IDA Institute: A non-profit organization that sponsors a website (https://idainstitute.com) that provides free tools and resources designed to promote person-centered hearing health care worldwide.

IDEA: Individuals with Disabilities Education Act.

Identification: In auditory training, a basic auditory skill level in which the listener is able to label some auditory stimuli.

Idiopathic: In reference to hearing loss, a loss with unknown origin.

IEP: Individualized educational plan.

IFSP: Individualized Family Service Plan.

Immittance: The energy flow through the middle ear, and includes admittance, compliance, conductance, impedance, reactance, resistance, and susceptance.

Impairment: Reduced or abnormal function.

Impedance audiometry: Battery of measures designed to assess middle ear functioning, including tympanometry and acoustic reflex threshold determination; immittance audiometry.

Incidence: Frequency of occurrence.

Inclusion: Integrates all students and activities into the daily routine of the general education classroom.

Independent variable: The experimental factor that is manipulated or influential.

Individual(ized) Education Plan (IEP): A team-developed written plan that identifies goals and objectives that address the educational needs of a student aged 3–21 years who has a disability. The plan takes into account the family's preferred mode of communication, the child's linguistic needs, academic progress, social and emotional needs, and appropriate accommodations to ensure learning.

Individualized Family Service Plan (IFSP): Federally mandated plan for children age birth to 3 years that ensures appropriate early-intervention services for infants and toddlers and their families. The plan takes into account a child's current level of development, the family's resources and priorities, goals and services necessary for achieving the goals, and a time course.

Individuals with Disabilities Education Act (IDEA): A piece of United States legislation that ensures that public schools serve the needs of children with disabilities.

Induction loop system: A system that works by running a wire around the circumference of a room or table that conducts electrical energy from an amplifier and thus creates a magnetic field, which induces the telecoil in a hearing aid to provide amplified sound to the user.

Informal training: Occurs during the daily routine and is often incorporated into other activities, such as conversation or academic learning.

Information transmission analysis: A statistical procedure that analyzes the transmission of speech features by scoring confusions between test stimuli that are grouped based on the presence or absence of those features; for example, the phonemes /p/ and /t/ share the feature of being "unvoiced."

Informational counseling: In aural rehabilitation, a counseling method that includes imparting information about the hearing loss and hearing disability and the recommended steps for management.

Infrared system: Assistive listening device that broadcasts from the sound source to a receiver/amplifier by means of infrared light waves.

Inner ear: Part of the hearing mechanism that houses the structures for hearing and balance and includes the cochlea, vestibules, and semicircular canals.

Inner hair cells: A single row of auditory receptor cells in the organ of Corti that are in synaptic connect with the fibers of the auditory nerve, to which the primary afferent nerve endings of the 8th cranial nerve attach.

Insert earphone: An earphone whose receiver is attached to a tube that leads to an expandable cuff and that can be inserted into the ear canal.

In-service: Continuing education provided to employees of an organization.

Instructional strategy: A communication strategy in which the listener asks the talker to change the delivery of the message.

Intelligibility: The degree to which speech can be recognized.

Interactive behavior: The use of cooperative conversational tactics, consistent with an assertive conversational style; e.g., *How interesting! Tell me more. . . .*

Interdisciplinary team: A group of professionals with different expertise working together for the purpose of providing assessment and intervention in a coordinated and cooperative fashion.

Interleaved pulsatile stimulation: A cochlear implant processing strategy in which trains of pulses are delivered across electrodes in the electrode array in a non-simultaneous fashion.

Internal components: Components of a cochlear implant that are implanted within the skull.

International Classification of Functioning, Disability and Health (ICF): An internationally recognized classification system for describing consequences of health conditions and for considering the dimensions of health and functioning.

Interpreter: A person specially trained to translate oral or signed communications from one language to another.

Interview: In aural rehabilitation, a basic assessment procedure used to elicit specific information about an individual's hearing-related communication difficulties.

In-the-canal hearing aid (ITC): Hearing aid that fits in the external ear canal, with only a partial filling of the concha.

In-the-ear hearing aid (ITE): Hearing aid that fits into the concha of the ear.

Ipsilateral: Pertaining to the same side.

ITC hearing aid: In-the-canal hearing aid.

ITE hearing aid: In-the-ear hearing aid.

Itinerant teachers: Teachers who work in several schools, providing support services to children who are deaf and hard of hearing and to their teachers.

JND: Just noticeable difference.

JNIH: Joint Committee on Infant Hearing.

Joint Committee on Infant Hearing (JNIH): A committee comprised of professionals from audiology, otolaryngology, pediatrics, education, and speech and language pathology that proffers position papers and establishes practice standards for the early identification of and follow-up care for infants and toddlers who have congenital hearing loss.

Joint goal setting: The patient and clinician creating a partnership to identify meaningful goals and desired outcomes for the aural rehabilitation plan.

Just noticeable difference (JND): The smallest increment of stimulus change in which the stimulus can be perceived as different; difference limen.

Keying: Occurs when a talker's tone of voice, cadence, lexical emphasis, prosody, and other speaking characteristics imbue an emotional stance to an utterance.

Kneepoint: Point on an input–output function where compression is activated.

Labeling: A language-stimulation technique in which an adult provides names for objects, actions, and events.

LD: Learning disability.

LDL: Loudness discomfort level.

Learning disability (LD): A lack of ability in an area of learning that is inconsistent with an individual's cognitive capacity and is not a result of a deficit in sensory, motor, or emotional functioning.

Learning effect: Occurs when performance on a test improves as a function of familiarity with the test procedures or test items and not because of a change in ability.

Least restrictive environment (LRE): A basic principle of IDEA (*Individuals with Disabilities Education Act*) that requires public agencies to establish procedures to ensure that to the extent possible, children who have disabilities are educated with children who do not have disabilities, and that special classes, separate schooling, or removal from the regular educational environment occurs only when the severity of the disability is such that education in a regular class environment cannot be achieved satisfactorily.

LEP: Limited English proficiency.

Lexicon: The vocabulary of an individual or a language.

Life factors: Conditions that help define one's life, such as relationships, family, and vocation.

Life stages: Age ranges in which a hearing loss may have a different impact.

Limited English proficiency (LEP): Used in reference to persons who are limited in their English proficiency.

Linear amplification: Hearing aid amplification system in which there is a one-to-one correspondence between the input and output until the maximum output level is reached.

Linked adjacency pairs: Two remarks that often are linked in conversation, as when one communication partner asks, "How are you?" and another responds, "Fine, thank you."

Lipreading: The process of recognizing speech using only the visual speech signal and other visual cues, such as facial expression.

Listening check: Informal check of a hearing aid to ensure that it is functioning properly.

Live-voice testing: Testing in which the stimuli in a test of speech recognition are spoken by a talker in real time as opposed to being recorded and played back.

Localization: The ability to locate the source of a sound in space due to the normal ears' sensitivity to interaural differences in phase and intensity.

Long-term memory: The cognitive mechanism used to maintain information for extended periods of time, even a lifetime.

Loudness balancing: Programming the speech processor so that stimulation follows the loudness contour of the incoming speech signal.

Loudness comfort level: Level at which sound is perceived to be comfortably loud.

Loudness discomfort level (LDL): Level at which sound is perceived to be uncomfortably loud.

Loudspeaker: A device that converts electrical energy into sound.

Loudspeaker azimuth: The position of the loudspeaker relative to the listener, measured in angular degrees in the horizontal plane.

Low frequency of usage: Words that occur infrequently in everyday conversation.

Low-pass filtered speech: Speech that has been passed through filter banks that removed the higher, but not the lower, frequencies.

LRE: Least restrictive environment.

Luminance: The intensity of light per unit area of the source.

Macula: A small area at the back of the eye where vision on the retina is keenest.

Macular degeneration: Deterioration of sensory cells in the central region of the retina that may result in a progressive loss of both close vision and distance vision.

Mainstream classrooms: Classrooms in which children who are deaf and hard of hearing attend classes with students who have normal hearing.

Mainstreaming: Reassignment of children with disabilities from a special education classroom to a classroom in the regular school environment.

Maladaptive strategies: Inappropriate behavioral mechanisms for coping with the difficulties caused in conversation by hearing loss. These behaviors sometimes yield short-term benefits but incur long-term costs.

Managed care: A health care reimbursement plan in which an organization intercedes between patient and provider and determines the kind and extent of services that will be provided.

Manual alphabet: A series of hand configurations that correspond to each letter in the alphabet and are used to fingerspell words in manual communication.

Manual communication: Communication modes that entail the use of fingerspelling, hand signs, and gestures.

Manually coded English: A form of communication in which manual signs correspond to English words, typically in a one-to-one fashion.

Map: With respect to cochlear implants, specifications of threshold, comfort levels, loudness levels, and frequency by which the speech processor of a cochlear implant processes the speech signal and delivers it in electrical form to the electrodes in the electrode array.

Mapping: The process of programming the speech processor of a cochlear implant.

Masker: For tinnitus, an electronic listening device that delivers low-level noise to the ear for the purpose of masking the presence of tinnitus.

Masking: Noise that interferes with the perception of another sound.

Maximum comfort level (C-level or M-level or MCL): The maximum intensity level that can be listened to comfortably for a prolonged duration of time.

Maximum power output (MPO): The maximum intensity level that a hearing aid can produce, sometimes called *saturation sound pressure level.*

MCL: Most comfortable loudness; also maximum comfort level.

Mean length of speaking turn (MLT): Computed by determining the average number of words spoken during a set number of conversational turns, or the average duration of conversational turns in seconds.

Mean length turn ratio (MLT ratio): The ratio of the mean length of speaking turns spoken by two communication partners during the course of a conversation.

Mean sentence length (MSL): The mean number of words per sentence.

Meaning-based orientation: Refers to using tasks in auditory training that require a student to engage in meaning-related processing and to activate the semantic regions of the brain.

Medicaid: A program in the United States authorized by Title XIX of the Social Security Act that is jointly funded by the federal government and state governments, which reimburses hospitals and physicians for providing health care to qualified people who cannot otherwise afford services.

Medical home: An approach to providing health care services that involves a partnership of health care personnel and family.

Medicare: A program under the U.S. Social Security Administration that reimburses hospitals and physicians for medical care they provide to qualified people who are 65 years or older and to some younger people who have disabilities.

Melody: A sequence of musical tones that is perceived as a single entity.

Ménière's disease: An inner ear disorder that is related to idiopathic endolymphatic hydrops and may cause vertigo, hearing loss, tinnitus, and the sensation of fullness in the ear.

Meninges: The membranes that cover the brain and spinal cord.

Meningitis: A common cause of childhood sensorineural hearing loss caused by bacterial or viral inflammation of the meninges.

Mental health problem: A psychological or physiological pattern that is not expected as a part of normal functioning, behavior, or culture.

Message-tailoring strategy: A communication strategy that is a way of phrasing one's remarks so to constrain the response of a communication partner.

Meta-analysis: A study that combines the results of a set of studies on the same topic to reach a general conclusion.

Metacommentary: A comment about the talk or conversation.

Metacommunication: Communication about communication, and that indicates how verbal communication should be interpreted.

Microcephaly: An abnormally small head associated with a failure of the brain to grow.

Microphone: Transducer that converts an audio signal into an electronic signal.

Microtia: A congenitally small external ear.

Middle ear: Portion of the hearing mechanism extending from the tympanic membrane to the oval window of the cochlea and that includes the ossicles and middle ear cavity.

Middle ear effusion: The exudation of fluid from membranous tissue into the middle ear cavity.

Mimetic: Imitating or copying movements.

Mismatched Negativity (MMN): A component of the event-related potential which arises from electrical activity in the brain and occurs after a change in a repetitive sequence of syllables, such as *dah dah dah dah dah tah.*

Mixed hearing loss: A hearing loss that has a conductive and sensorineural component.

MLT: Mean length of speaking turn.

MLT ratio: Mean length turn ratio.

MMN: Mismatched negativity.

Mobile unit: A mobile van that is equipped to screen hearing; often used for educational and on-site industrial hearing screening programs.

Modeling: The act of representing or demonstrating a behavior.

Monaural: Concerning one ear.

Monolingual: Term that describes a person who speaks only one language.

Monosyllabic word: A word comprised of one syllable.

Morphemes: Linguist units that cannot be subdivided into smaller units.

Morphology: Governs the internal structures of words.

Most comfortable loudness level (MCL): The intensity level at which sound is most comfortable for a listener, usually expressed in dB HL.

MSL: Mean sentence length.

MTO: An acronym that refers to the three settings of a hearing aid on–off switch: **M**icrophone, **T**elephone, and **O**ff.

Multiband compression: A method of shaping the loudness growth of a signal to maximize speech for the listener using different degrees of compression and output limiting for different frequencies.

Multichannel: With respect to cochlear implants, a term used to describe cochlear implants that present different channels of information to different regions of the cochlea.

Multidimensional scaling: A statistical procedure whereby data points are represented in a geometric space; for example, two phonemes that sound similar to a patient will be plotted near to each other; two phonemes that sound dissimilar will be plotted far from each other.

Multidisciplinary team: A group of professionals with different expertise contributing to the assessment, intervention, and management of a particular individual.

Multiple channels: A listening aid that filters the signal into frequency bands so that some bands (usually the high-frequency bands) can receive more gain than others.

Multiple-memory hearing aid: A hearing aid that provides access to different amplification characteristics.

Multisensory approach: Refers to the use of both vision and hearing, and sometimes touch, to recognize speech.

Myringitis: Inflammation of the tympanic membrane.

NAD: National Association of the Deaf.

Narrative therapy: An interview/counseling technique that focuses on the narrative during clinician–patient encounters, and holds that our identities are shaped by the stories we derive from our life experiences.

Nasal consonant: A consonant, that when spoken, entails creating resonance in the nasal cavities and a lowered velum; e.g., /m, n/.

National Association of the Deaf (NAD): An organization of more than 22,000 members that advocates for the use of sign language and the rights of Deaf people.

National Institute on Deafness and Other Communication Disorders (NIDCD): A United States federal agency that supports research activity concerning the normal and disordered processes of hearing, speech, language, balance, taste, and smell and about problems that people with communication impairments might experience.

National Institutes of Health (NIH): The medical research agency of the United States whose mission is to acquire knowledge to help prevent, detect, and treat disease and disability.

Neckloop: A transducer worn around the neck, often as part of an FM assistive device system, which transmits signals via magnetic induction to the telecoil of the user's hearing aid.

Neonatal: Concerning the first 4 weeks of life.

Neuromaturational delay: Occurs when a nervous system function has failed to develop as rapidly as usual.

Newborn nursery: A hospital unit designed to provide care for healthy newborn infants; also called a *well-baby nursery.*

NIHL: Noise-induced hearing loss.

NIPTS: Noise-induced permanent threshold shift.

NITTS: Noise-induced temporary threshold shift.

Noise: Unwanted sound.

Noise exposure: Level of noise and duration of exposure to which a person is subjected.

Noise-induced hearing loss (NIHL): A permanent sensorineural hearing loss caused by exposure to excessive sound levels.

Noise notch: Refers to the characteristic dip in hearing sensitivity at around 4000 Hz that is associated with an audiogram for a patient who has noise-induced hearing loss.

Noninteractive behavior: Characteristic of a passive behavioral style and is one in which the individual does little to advance the course of the conversation.

Nonsense syllable: Syllable of speech that has no meaning; e.g., *kah.*

Nonspecific repair strategy: A communication strategy that simply indicates a lack of understanding without providing instruction or other feedback to the communication partner about how to repair the communication breakdown.

Nonsyndromic hearing loss: A hearing loss that has no other associated findings.

Norm: Standards derived from a sample of the population of interest, thought to represent typical values of the characteristic under study or test.

Normalizing: A counseling technique that helps patients realize that their feelings are *normal* and helps to decrease any negative emotions, such as shame or embarrassment, that they may have about their hearing loss.

NR: No response.

Nursing home: A residential, institutionalized facility that has three or more beds and provides nursing care. Patients usually require constant nursing care and may require physical, occupational, and other rehabilitative therapies.

Nystagmus: A pattern of eye movement characterized by a slow lateral drift in one direction followed by a saccade or fast movement in the opposite direction.

OAEs: Otoacoustic emissions.

Objective: A result, ideally one that is measurable, which is expected within a particular time period or after a lesson or training program.

Objective tinnitus: Tinnitus which can be heard by placing a stethoscope over the patient's ear.

Occlusion effect: The enhancement of low-frequency sounds that occurs via bone conduction and is caused by the occlusion of the ear canal.

Omnidirectional microphone: Microphone that is sensitive to sound coming from all directions.

On–off control: A small switch that moves back and forth to turn the hearing aid off when not in use and on when needed, which may be incorporated into the volume wheel.

Open-canal fitting: A hearing aid fitting that has an open earmold or a tubing-only to the ear canal, with no earmold.

Open-ended questions: Questions that do not confine responses to a closed set of options as might a yes–no question; e.g., *What's for dinner tonight?*

Open-set: A testing or training task that does not provide a closed set of response options.

Oral interpreter: A professional who silently repeats a talker's message as it is spoken so that a person with hearing loss may lipread the message.

Oralism: Method of instruction for children who have significant hearing loss that emphasizes spoken-language skills to the exclusion of manual communication; also called *aural/oral*.

Oral transliteration: The act of lagging a talker by a few words, mouthing or speaking the words with a normal speaking rate and good enunciation, and which usually does not entail the use of sign language, but natural body language, expressions, and gestures are typically presented that support the content of the words.

Organized messages: Communications that are not too wordy, do not use complex verbiage, and use precise terminology; e.g., *Tom bought the bread*, as opposed to, *Tom just arrived home with a couple loaves of bread.*

OSPL: Output sound pressure level.

OSPL90: An electroacoustic assessment of a hearing aid's maximum level of output signal, expressed as a frequency response curve to a 90-dB SPL signal, with the hearing aid volume control set to full on; also called *SSPL90*.

Ossicular chain: Located within the middle ear and comprised of the three small bones, the malleus, incus, and stapes, and extending from the tympanic membrane through the tympanic cavity to the oval window.

Ossification: A conversion of tissue into bone.

Otitis media: Inflammation of the middle ear often accompanied by the accumulation of fluid in the middle ear cavity.

Otoacoustic emissions (OAEs): Low-level sound emitted spontaneously by the cochlea on presentation of an auditory stimulus.

Otolaryngologist: A physician who specializes in the diagnosis and treatment of medical conditions of the ear, nose, and throat, including diseases of the related structures of the head and neck; also called an *ear, nose, and throat doctor.*

Otologist: A physician who specializes in the diagnosis and treatment of diseases and conditions of the ear.

Otoscope: An instrument used for visual examination of the external ear and tympanic membrane.

Ototoxic drugs: Drugs that are harmful to the structures of the inner ear and the auditory nerve.

Outcome measure: A measure that indicates the amount or type of benefit experienced by either an individual or a group of individuals to a treatment or series of treatments, and indicates a response.

Outer ear: The peripheral part of the auditory mechanism that includes the pinna, the concha, the external auditory canal, and the lateral wall of the tympanic membrane.

Outer hair cells: Sensory cells within the organ of Corti that are aligned in three rows, and which have rich efferent innervation.

Output sound pressure level (OSPL): Maximum output generated by a hearing aid receiver, determined when the hearing aid has its gain turned full on and is receiving a 90-dB SPL signal.

Oval window: The opening in the cochlea that leads to the scala vestibuli, into which the footplate of the stapes fits.

OTC: Over the counter hearing aid.

Over-the-counter hearing aids (OTC): Hearing aids meant for adults who have mild-to-moderate hearing loss and are available without involvement of an audiologist or licensed hearing healthcare professional.

Parallel talk: A facilitative language technique in which the adult provides a commentary to match a child's play, describing what the child is doing and might be thinking and feeling, and one which does not require the child to answer direct questions.

Parent support group: A group that provides opportunities for parents of children with hearing loss to share their feelings, difficulties, and concerns with others who have experienced them first-hand and allows for exchange of information, resources, and ideas.

Part B: The section of the United States Public Law PL 105-17 (IDEA) that refers to intervention services for eligible children between the ages of 3 and 21 years in the public school system.

Part C: The section of the United States Public Law PL 108-446 that refers to early-intervention services that are available to eligible children from birth through the age of 3 years and to their families.

Partial mainstreaming: A child with a hearing loss has some classes with children who have normal hearing and some in a self-contained classroom or resource room with a teacher for children who are deaf and hard of hearing.

Participation: Refers to a patient's involvement in a life situation and represents the societal perspective of functioning; e.g., participating in a dinner table conversation.

Participation restriction: An effect of an activity limitation that results in a change in the broader scope of a patient's life; e.g., a patient may avoid social gatherings.

Passive-aggressive conversational style: A conversational style in which aggression is expressed in indirect ways; e.g., *Don't worry about me, you two have fun at the party and I'll stay home, all alone, and read a cookbook or maybe see if there is something on TV that's worth watching, I'd just be a bother if I tagged along with you. . . .*

Passive conversational style: Conversational style in which a person plays a lesser role than the communication partner in advancing a conversation, and is characterized by not taking conversational turns and by bluffing and pretending to understand; e.g., *Yes, hmmm, for sure, I see. . . . . . oh, right. . . yeah, yeah. . . .*

Patient-centered model: Focuses on providing care that is respectful of and responsive to individual patient preferences, needs, and values, and ensuring that patient values guide all clinical decisions.

Patient-centered orientation: An orientation centered on the patient's background, current status, needs, and wants, on which the design and delivery of aural rehabilitative services are based.

Patient journey: The sequence of experiences and phases a patient passes through during a treatment regimen.

Pattern perception: A kind of discrimination that requires a listener to distinguish between words or phrases that differ in the number of syllables.

PB: Phonetically balanced.

Peak-clipping: A method of limiting hearing aid output in which a constant or linear amount of gain is provided across a range of input levels until it reaches a saturation level at which the amplifier begins to "clip" off the peaks of the signal.

Pearson correlation: A statistical analysis that indicates the strength and the direction of a linear relationship between two variables.

Perceived barriers: A patient's belief in the tangible and psychological costs to taking advised actions.

Perceived benefits: A patient's belief in the benefits of the advised action to reduce the seriousness of the impact of the health condition.

Perceived quality of life: Reflects how people assess their current life experiences, and encompasses such constructs as enjoyment, meaning, purpose, usefulness, value, freedom of choice, and independence.

Perceived severity: A patient's belief of how serious a condition is or how serious are the possible consequences.

Perceived susceptibility: A patient's belief about the chances of contracting a condition or of an existing condition worsening.

Perceptual effort: The effort that a person expends to recognize speech, sometimes at the cost of using cognitive processing resources that might otherwise be allocated towards encoding speech into memory.

Perilingual: Hearing loss acquired during the stage of spoken-language acquisition.

Perinatal: During birth.

Personal adjustment counseling: Counseling that focuses on the permanency of the hearing loss and on psychological, social, and emotional acceptance.

Personal factors: Factors that pertain to the patient, and encompass the patient's age, lifestyle, race, coping styles, attitudes, self-efficacy, lifestyle, habits, preferences, socioeconomic background, and other health conditions.

Personal FM system (trainer): A listening device in which the talker wears a wireless microphone and the speech is frequency modulated on radio waves transmitted through the room to the listener, who wears a receiver.

Personal sound amplification products (PSAPs): Listening aids that are worn in the ear and that amplify sounds, but they do not address other aspects of hearing loss, such as the configuration of the loss or distortion caused by hearing loss.

Phonetically balanced (PB): A word list that presents a set of words that contain speech sounds with the same frequency in which they occur in everyday conversation.

Pinna: Auricle; the cartilaginous structure of the outer ear.

Pitch ranking: In cochlear implants, determines the patient's ability to discriminate pitch from stimulation of the basal to apical electrodes.

Place of articulation: Classification of a speech sound according to where in the vocal tract it is produced; e.g., bilabial.

Plasticity: A term used to refer to the physiological changes in the central nervous system that occur as a result of sensory and perceptual experiences.

Play audiometry: A behavioral method for testing the hearing thresholds of young children, in which correct identification of a stimulus presentation is rewarded by allowing the child to perform a play-oriented activity.

Postlingual: Hearing loss incurred after the acquisition of spoken language.

Postnatal: After birth.

Pragmatics: In terms of language acquisition, the use of language in context, along with the societal-dependent aspects of communicative interactions.

Preamplifier stage: In hearing aids, the stage where the signal from the microphone is amplified.

Predicament: The relevant aspects of a patient's state and situation, including disabilities, participation limitations, environments, demands, resources, attitudes, and behaviors.

Prelingual: Hearing loss incurred before the acquisition of spoken language.

Prenatal: Before birth.

Presbycusis: Generic term for age-related hearing loss.

Prescribed gain: The gain and frequency response of a hearing aid that are determined by use of a prescriptive formula.

Prescription procedures: Strategies for fitting hearing aids by using a formula to calculate the desired gain and frequency response.

Prevalence: The percentage of a population that experiences a particular health problem at a particular point in time.

Probe microphone: A microphone transducer that is inserted into the external ear canal for the purpose of measuring sound near the tympanic membrane.

Processing speed: In cognition, the rate at which information is conducted and manipulated throughout the nervous system.

Processing strategy: A strategy used by cochlear implants to determine how the input signal is processed, including the degree of amplification of different frequency bands and the manner in which the signal is delivered by different electrodes in the electrode array.

Program: The setting of a speech processor or hearing aid according to the user's measured thresholds, comfort levels, and other subjective responses to stimulation.

Programmability: Refers to a feature of some hearing aids, wherein several parameters, such as gain, may be adjusted and controlled by a computer.

Progressive hearing loss: A hearing loss that increases over time.

Prompting: A language-stimulation technique in which remarks serve to inspire a behavior or an utterance and a technique that is also designed to assist an individual in formulating or remembering a remark.

Prosodic cues: Cues about the meaning of an utterance that are provided by variations in intonation, rate, and duration of speech sounds and words.

Prosody: Suprasegmental aspects of the speech signal, including fluctuations in voice pitch, rhythm, rate, intensity, and stress patterns; also called *intonation*.

Prospective study: A study that follows a group of research participants over time and monitors outcomes, such as language development, during the course of the study and relates those outcomes to other factors, such as degree of hearing loss or socioeconomic status.

PSAPs: Personal sound amplification products.

Psychological costs: The nonmonetary costs that relate to a person's psychological well-being.

Psychological factors: The factors that pertain to an individual's attitudes, self-image, motivation, and assertiveness.

Psychosocial support: The means by which speech and hearing professionals help patients achieve long-term self-sufficiency in managing the psychological and social challenges that result from hearing loss.

Psychosocial therapy: A therapy approach that challenges a patient's erroneous assumptions and helps the patient to develop a positive self-image.

Psychosocial well-being: The extent to which the patient has a positive self-image and feels like an integral and important part of social relationships.

Psychotherapy: A treatment for an emotional or behavioral problem in which a mental health expert (e.g., psychiatrist, psychologist, counselor) discusses feelings and potential solutions with a patient, with the goals of providing relief of symptoms, changes in behavior leading to improved social, emotional, and vocational functioning, and personality growth.

PTA: Pure-tone average.

Pure tone: A pure tone has only one frequency of vibration.

Pure-tone average (PTA): Average of hearing thresholds at 500 Hz, 1000 Hz, and 2000 Hz.

Quest?AR: A structured communication procedure used to assess communication difficulties.

Random assignment: A method of placing research participants into the conditions or treatments of an experiment in such a way that every participant has an equal chance of being assigned to any of the conditions or to any level of the independent variable.

Randomized controlled trial: Investigators randomly assign eligible research participants into treatment and control groups and then compare outcomes. The chance assignment reduces the likelihood that differences stem from preexisting differences between the two groups.

Rational emotive behavior therapy (REBT): A solution-oriented counseling (or therapy) approach that focuses on resolving specific problems using cognitive, behavioral, and affective elements. Its central premise is that emotions result from beliefs rather than events or circumstances.

Reactive: Acting in response to a stimulus or an experience rather than initiating or controlling it.

Real-ear gain: The gain of a hearing aid at the tympanic membrane, measured with a probe microphone, and is the difference between the dB SPL in the external ear canal and the dB SPL at the field reference point for a specified sound field.

Real-ear measures: The use of a probe microphone to measure hearing aid gain and frequency response delivered by a hearing aid at the tympanic membrane.

Real-time captioning: Captioning of a person's speech in real time using computer technology.

Real-world practice: The third stage of a three-stage learning model (i.e., *formal instruction, guided learning, real-world practice*) where children or adults practice a new skill or behavior in an everyday environment.

Reassurance: Instilling or restoring confidence.

REBT: Rational emotive behavior therapy.

Receiver: An instrument that converts electrical energy into acoustic energy, as in a hearing aid. The term also refers to a component of an FM system worn by the listener to receive signals from an FM transmitter.

Receptive language: The language that we either hear or that we receive via sign.

Receptive repair strategy: Repair strategy used by the receiver (listener) when he or she has not understood a message spoken by a communication partner; for example, the individual might ask the communication partner to repeat the last part of a sentence.

Recorded stimuli: Test items that have been previously recorded and that are presented via an audiometer, computer, tape recorder, compact disc (CD) player, iPod, or a DVD player.

Reflection: A counseling technique in which clinicians paraphrase or summarize what their patient has just said, and thus demonstrate that they are listening carefully and accurately, and which also provides their patients with an opportunity to examine their own views or feelings by hearing them expressed by another person.

Reframing: A counseling technique that provides the patient with an alternative frame of reference from which to view a problem.

Rehabilitation: An intervention designed for the re-teaching or recovery of particular skills.

Reinforcement: Something desirable provided to a student after he or she performs a training activity or performs in a desired manner.

Relay system: System used by persons with significant hearing loss for telephone access; an individual contacts a relay operator who serves to transmit messages between the caller and the person called by means of teletype, captioning, or voice.

Release time: The time it takes for an amplifier to return to its steady state after a loud sound ends.

Remote control: A handheld device that permits adjustments in the volume or changes in the program of a programmable hearing aid.

Repair strategies: A class of communication strategies that include tactics implemented by a participant in a conversation to rectify a breakdown in communication.

Residual hearing: The hearing remaining in a person who has hearing loss.

Resource rooms: A designated place in a school where instruction in particular areas is provided to children who spend the rest of their day in regular classrooms.

Retinitis pigmentosa: Any number of inherited, progressive conditions that cause abnormal pigmentation on the retina. The condition often impairs vision, with first a loss of night vision, then a loss of peripheral vision, and then the development of "tunnel vision," and the finally, may cause blindness.

Retrospective study: A study in which the investigator looks backwards and collects data from past records and does not follow the research participants going forward in time.

Reverberation: The persistence of a sound due to the signal being reflected from the surfaces of walls, ceiling, and floor. Long reverberation times (more than 500 msec) cause a speech signal, such as a teacher's words, to merge with other signals and to lose clarity.

Reverberation time (RT60): The amount of time in seconds it takes for a sound to decay by 60 dB in a room.

Rhythm: A pattern of sounds and silences that is repeated.

Role-playing: Individuals participate in hypothetical real-world situations and interactions.

Round window: Membrane-covered opening between the middle ear space and the scala tympani section of the cochlea in the inner ear.

Saccade: A rapid and intermittent eye movement such that the eyes fixate on one point and then on another point in the visual field.

Sales orientation: An orientation to providing aural rehabilitation services in which emphasis is placed on persuading the patient to pursue and procure services, interventions, and listening devices.

Saturation level: The point at which an amplifier no longer provides an increase in output compared to input.

Saturation sound pressure level (SSPL): The maximum sound pressure level that can be delivered by a hearing aid with its volume at full on.

Screening: The use of tests that are quick and easy to administer to a large group for the purpose of identifying individuals who require further diagnostic testing.

SDT: Speech detection threshold.

SEE: Seeing Essential English.

Seeing Essential English (SEE): A manual communication system that incorporates some signs of American Sign Language and some English syntax.

Segmental errors: Errors in articulation pertaining to the sounds of speech.

Selective attention: A selective narrowing of mental focus and receptivity.

Selective mainstreaming: Students who have hearing loss typically attend a self-contained classroom for academic subjects such as history and attend nonacademic classes such as art with students who have normal hearing.

Self-concept: How persons view themselves.

Self-contained classrooms: Classrooms that contain only children who have hearing loss.

Self-efficacy: The confidence a person has for performing a particular task and the person's belief in his or her ability to do something.

Self-image: An individual's awareness of his or her biological or physical self and personality in addition to the individual's sense of identity and self-worth.

Self-stigma: Occurs when a patient is aware of stereotypes (e.g., *Persons with hearing loss are old and decrepit*), agrees with the stereotypes (e.g., *That's right, persons with hearing loss are old and decrepit*), and applies the stereotypes to him or herself (e.g., *I have hearing loss therefore I'm old and decrepit*).

Self-sufficiency: The extent to which a person can conduct day-to-day activities without undue reliance on others.

Self-talk: A language-stimulation technique in which an adult describes what he or she is doing or thinking for the purpose of promoting language development in a child.

Semantics: Pertains to both the surface and underlying meanings of words and language, and includes multiple meanings of words.

Sensation level (SL): The level of a sound in dB above a person's threshold.

Sensorineural hearing loss (SNHL): Hearing loss with a cochlear or retrocochlear origin.

Service coordinator: A designated person who helps the family during the development, implementation, and the evaluation of the Individualized Family Service Plan (IFSP).

Shaping: Serves to reinforce those conversational turns that increasingly approximate sought-after behaviors.

Shared decision making: Entails the patient and clinician (and family member) jointly considering the options to achieve a goal and then making a selection after reviewing related information and taking time for discussion and deliberation.

Shoe: An adapter that is placed on a hearing aid to permit the connection of FM receivers or other accessories; also called a *boot*.

Sign interpreter: A professional who translates the spoken signal into a form of sign language or vice versa.

Sign language: A system of manual communication in which hand configurations, positions, and movements are used to express concepts and linguistic information.

Signal processing: Manipulation of various parameters of the acoustic signal.

Signal-to-noise ratio (SNR): The level of an auditory signal relative to a background of noise.

Signed English: A manual communication system that utilizes English word order and syntax.

Simple amplification systems: Systems that amplify the audio signal so that it is more audible to a person with hearing loss.

Simultaneous communication: An educational approach used with individuals with severe and profound hearing loss that integrates spoken language and manual communication; also called *total communication*.

SL: Sensational level.

SLP: Speech-language pathologist.

SNHL: Sensorineural hearing loss.

SNR: Signal-to-noise ratio.

Social competence: A multidimensional construct that reflects an individual's ability to interact with others effectively and to use social skills in a way that is flexible and adaptive.

Social factors: The prevailing viewpoints of one's society.

Social identity: One's sense of belonging to a particular social group, and comprises a part of person's self-concept.

Social stigma: A condition that is devalued because it deviates from a societal norm and results in a negative status being placed on a person or group of persons.

Socioeconomic status: A person's position within a hierarchical social structure that is determined by such variables as occupation, wealth, education, income, and place of residence.

Sociolinguist: A scientist who belong to a branch of linguistics that studies the effects of social and cultural differences within a community on its use of language and conversational patterns.

Somatization: A process in which a mental or emotional experience or event is converted into bodily symptoms.

Sound awareness: The most basic auditory skill level; awareness of when a sound is present and when it is not.

Sound discrimination: A basic auditory skill level in which the listener is able to tell whether two sounds are the same or different; e.g., *pah-pah* versus *pah-bah*.

Sound field: A free-field environment where sound is propagated.

Sound-field FM system: A listening system, similar to an FM trainer, in which sound from a microphone is transmitted to loudspeakers that are positioned throughout the room.

Sound field testing: Determines a patient's hearing sensitivity or speech recognition ability by presenting signals in a sound field through a loudspeaker.

Sound level: The intensity of a sound expressed in decibels.

Sound level meter: An instrument designed to measure the intensity of sound in dB according to an accepted standard.

Sparse lexical neighborhood: Has few lexical members.

Spatial working memory: Responsible for temporarily storing visual information and permits active utilization and updating of visual information from the environment and about one's spatial position.

Special knowledge: Allows application, analysis, synthesis, and evaluation, allowing a person to apply and elaborate upon that knowledge.

Specific repair strategy: A communication strategy that provides explicit instructions to the communication partner about how to repair a communication breakdown.

Spectrogram: A three-dimensional graph of speech that displays frequency on the ordinate (y-axis), time on the abscissa (x-axis), and amplitude by the density of the tracing.

Speech audiometry: The measurement of speech-listening skills, including speech awareness and speech recognition.

Speech detection threshold (SDT): The level at which speech is just audible.

Speech discrimination score: The percentage of monosyllabic words presented at a comfortable listening level that can be correctly repeated (a term not often used).

Speech features: Categorical properties of phonemes.

Speech-language pathologist (SLP): Professionals who provide diagnosis and treatment of speech and language disorders.

Speech-language pathology: Professional discipline related to the study, diagnosis, and treatment of speech and language disorders.

Speech noise: Broadband noise that has been filtered so that it resembles the speech spectrum.

Speech processor: The component of a cochlear implant where the input signal is modified for presentation to the electrodes in the electrode array.

Speech reception threshold (SRT): The lowest presentation level for spondee words at which 50% can be identified correctly.

Speech recognition: The ability to perceive a spoken message and make decisions about its lexical composition using auditory and sometimes visual information.

Speech recognition testing: Testing performed in order to determine how well a patient can recognize speech units; e.g., phonemes, words, sentences.

Speechreading: Speech recognition using auditory and visual cues.

Speechreading enhancement: Computed by comparing a patient's speech recognition score in a vision-only condition to the score obtained in an audition-plus-vision condition.

Spiral ganglion: Comprised of the nuclei of the auditory nerve fibers that connect to the hair cells and meet in the central core (which is called the modiolus) of the cochlea.

Spondee: A two-syllable word that has equal stress on each syllable; e.g., *baseball, sidewalk.*

SRT: Speech reception threshold.

SSPL: Saturation sound pressure level.

SSPL90: Saturation sound pressure level 90.

Stage of life: The phases in the life cycle, including childhood, young adulthood, middle age, and old age.

Standard deviation: A statistic used to describe the dispersion of a data set, and describes the average distance from the average score.

Stetoclip: A nonelectric device that resembles a stethoscope, which enables someone to perform a listening check on a hearing instrument; also called a *hearing aid stethoscope.*

Stigmatization: A process whereby one's self-identity is spoiled by the reactions of others, usually because the person deviates in some way from the prevailing social and cultural norms, and is usually described in terms of stereotypes, prejudices, and discriminations.

Stop consonant: Speech sounds that are produced by building up air pressure behind a closure in the oral cavity and then releasing it; e.g., /p, t, k/.

Stress: Of words, is marked by changes in loudness, duration, or pitch, or some combination of the three.

Structured communication interaction: Simulated conversations that are used to assess or elicit a patient's communication difficulties.

Subglottal air pressure: Refers to the build-up of pressure below the closed vocal folds in the larynx.

Sudden hearing loss: Hearing loss that has an acute and rapid onset.

Suprasegmentals: Variations in pitch, rate, intensity, and duration, which are superimposed on phonemes and words.

Suprasegmental effects: Include intonation, stress, tempo, rhythm, and amplitude fluctuations (including silences) that are superimposed across linguistic segments.

Suprasegmental errors: Prosodic errors; e.g., inappropriate syllable stress.

Syndrome: Collection of conditions that co-occur as a result of a single cause and constitute a distinct clinical entity.

Syntax: The part of grammar that governs how linguistic units are combined into phrases, clauses, and sentences.

Synthesized speech: Speech that is created with a computer and not the human vocal tract.

Synthetic sentences: Syntactically correct but meaningless sentences that usually include a noun, verb, and object.

Synthetic training: In auditory and speechreading training, emphasizes the understanding of meaning and not necessarily the identification and comprehension of every word spoken in an utterance.

T-switch: Telecoil switch.

Tactile aid: A listening aid that converts sound into mechanical vibration to provide tactual stimulation, often to the wrist of the user, to provide sound awareness and gross sound discrimination.

Target gain: The gain prescribed for each frequency against which the actual hearing aid output is compared.

Telecoil: An induction coil that receives electromagnetic signals from a telephone or loop amplification system.

Telecoil switch (T-switch): A switch on a hearing aid that activates the telecoil.

Telecommunication device for the deaf (TDD): Telephone device for persons with deafness or significant hearing loss in which messages are typed on a keyboard, transmitted over telephone wires, and displayed on a small monitor screen; also called a *text telephone (TT)* or *teletypewriter (TTY).*

Telegraphic speech: Spoken-language patterns that are characterized by the omission of function words and, sometimes, incorrect word order; e.g., *Car go fast, boom, over into ditch fall.*

Telephone amplifiers: Device or mechanism that amplifies sound from a telephone receiver.

Telepractice: The delivery of services by means of telecommunications and electronic communications.

Temperament: Stable personality traits.

Temporal-order discrimination: Requires a patient to attend to the order in which auditory stimuli are presented.

Temporal resolution: The auditory system's ability to perceive or discriminate sound segments occurring closely in time as separate events.

Test battery approach: A testing approach that employs more than one type of assessment procedure.

Test–retest reliability: The degree to which a group of test takers will achieve the same scores with repeated administrations of a test.

Test–retest variability: A measure of the consistency of a test-taker's or group of test-takers' performance on a test from one presentation to the next.

Third-party disability: The changes in life functioning that accrue as a result of a family member's health condition.

Threshold: The level at which sound can be detected only 50% of the time.

Threshold shift: The change in hearing sensitivity expressed in dB.

Timbre: The quality of a musical note that distinguishes different sound sources, such as wind instruments (e.g., a flute) and string instruments (e.g., violin).

Time-talk: A language-stimulation technique in which an adult purposely incorporates time-related language into conversation.

Tinnitus: The perception of sound in the head without an external cause.

Tinnitus masker: An electronic hearing aid that generates and outputs noise at low levels for the purpose of masking an individual's tinnitus.

T-level: An electrical threshold and is the amount of current that must be passed through an electrode so that the patient is just aware of a sound sensation.

Tone-decay test: A test of auditory adaptation during which a continuous tone is presented at about threshold and any change in perception is monitored over a set time interval. An abnormal adaptation may indicate a retrocochlear site of lesion.

Tonotopic organization: Structures within the peripheral and central auditory nervous system are arranged topographically according to tonal frequency.

Top-down processing: The processing of a speech signal that is influenced by expectations and prior knowledge and a way that advanced cognition affects perception of sensory inputs.

TOPICON: An example of a structured communication interaction activity. The clinician and patient are independently provided with conversational topics. One of them selects a topic and initiates a conversation about it. The two then conduct a brief conversation on the chosen topic, during which the clinician monitors and evaluates the events. The clinician might evaluate "naturalness" and "topic maintenance" and might maintain a count of communication breakdowns.

Topic shading: Occurs when a new emphasis is derived from an ongoing topic of conversation such that the topic remains the same but the relevant details shift.

Total communication: Refers to a combined use of sign and speech; also called *simultaneous communication.*

Toxemia: A condition during pregnancy that is characterized by hypertension, or a sharp spike in blood pressure, and edema, or a swelling of the hands and feet as a result of excessive body fluid.

Transcription analysis: A recorded conversation is transcribed word for word, and then analyzed.

Transfer-Appropriate Processing (TAP) theory: Implies that the benefits of auditory training will be tied to what is transfer appropriate: the greater the overlap between what is trained and what is the desired outcomes, the greater will be the training benefits.

Translator: A person specially trained to translate written text from one language to another.

Troubleshoot: A series of steps to follow when a listening device will not turn on, if the sound is faint or distorted, or feedback occurs, the objective being to locate and correct the source of malfunction.

TTR: Type-token ratio.

Tune-up: Mapping, establishing a map for a cochlear implant speech processor.

Tx: Therapy or treatment.

Tympanogram: Graph of middle ear immittance as a function of air pressure in the external auditory canal.

Type-token ratio (TTR): The ratio between the number of different words that occurred in a language sample and the total number of words within the sample.

UCL: Uncomfortable loudness level.

UL: Uncomfortable level.

ULL: Uncomfortable loudness level.

Uncomfortable level (UL): The level at which sound is judged to be so loud as to be uncomfortable to the listener.

Uncomfortable loudness level (ULL or UCL): The intensity level at which a listener judges a sound to be uncomfortably loud; also called *loudness discomfort level (LDL)* and *uncomfortable level (UL).*

Unconditional positive regard: The second tenet of person-centered counseling in which clinicians assume that patients know best and assume that they have the inner resources to overcome their conversation difficulties.

Underserved: A group of patients receiving less than ideal services.

UNHS: Universal newborn hearing screening.

Unilateral: Pertaining to one side.

Unilateral hearing loss: A mild to profound hearing loss in one ear and normal hearing in the other ear.

Unisensory approach: Advocates the use of only residual hearing to receive spoken messages.

Universal newborn hearing screening (UNHS): The application of rapid and simple audiological tests, typically with automated auditory brainstem response (A-ABR) and otoacoustic emission (OAE) measures, to all newborn infants prior to their leaving the hospital with the goal of identifying those babies who require further diagnostic testing; also called *neonatal hearing screening.*

Unserved: Refers to a group of patients in need of but not receiving services.

Use gain: Amount of gain provided by a hearing aid when the volume control is set where it is commonly used.

Validation: With respect to hearing aid fitting, determines the extent to which hearing-related disability has been reduced by an intervention, such as receipt of a hearing aid. With respect to counseling, it lets patients know that a clinician understands their feelings and hears what they are expressing, and that their feelings make sense.

Validity: With respect to testing, the extent to which a test measures what it is assumed to measure.

Variable: Something that can vary and that a researcher can measure.

Velopharyngeal functioning: Refers to the appropriate opening of the velopharyngeal port during the production of nasal consonants (i.e., /m, n, ng/) and nasalized vowels and its appropriate closure during "oral" phonemes such as stops and fricatives.

Velopharyngeal port: Connects the oral and nasal cavities.

Ventriloquism illusion: Occurs when a ventriloquist induces the perception of speech as coming from a puppet's mouth by moving the puppet in synchrony with the sound.

Verification: The determination of whether a hearing aid meets a set of standards, including standards of basic electroacoustics, real-ear electroacoustic performance, and comfortable fit.

Vertigo: Dizziness, including a sensation of spinning or whirling.

Vestibular system: The biological system that includes the semicircular canals, the vestibule (otolith and saccule), and the vestibular nerve, and functions to maintain equilibrium and balance, in conjunction with the ocular and proprioceptive systems.

Vibrotactile: Pertaining to the detection of vibrations through the sense of touch.

Vibrotactile aid: A listening device that converts acoustic energy into vibratory patterns that are delivered to the skin; also called a *tactile aid.*

Vicarious consequences: Students observe the consequences of a model's behaviors.

Videotaped scenarios: With respect to communication strategies training and assertiveness training, recorded vignettes that provide examples of communication interactions that can be used to stimulate discussion about communication strategies and assertive behaviors.

Viseme: A group of speech sounds that appear identical on the lips; e.g., /p, m, b/.

Vision-only: Presentation of only a visual stimulus in testing or training.

Visual alerting systems: Assistive devices that include alarm clocks, doorbells, and smoke detectors in which the alerting mechanism is a flashing light.

Visual field: The entire expanse of space visible to the immobile eye at any point in time.

Visual fixation: Occurs when the eyes fixate gaze on a single location.

Visual impairment: A vision loss that cannot be compensated through corrective lenses.

Visual lexical neighborhoods: Groups of words that look alike on the face and have approximately the same frequency of occurrence.

Visual reinforcement audiometry (VRA): A method of audiometric testing for young children that entails providing an acoustic signal and reinforcing a head turn with a light stimulus or an activated and illuminated toy reinforcement.

Voicing: Classification of a speech sound according to whether it is produced with or without voice; e.g., /b/ vs. /p/.

Volume control: On a hearing aid, a control that is used to adjust its output, and which may be manual or automatic.

VRA: Visual reinforcement audiometry.

WATCH: An acronym for an example of a short-tutorial program of communication strategies training.

Well-being: An intangible concept that encompasses both a physical aspect (e.g., health, protection against pain and disease) and a psychological aspect (e.g., stress, worry, pleasure).

White noise: A broadband noise that has equal energy at all frequencies.

WHO: World Health Organization.

Wireless system: An assistive listening device in which wires are not necessary to connect the sound source to the listener, and includes FM and infrared systems.

Word decoding: The ability to apply one's knowledge of letter–sound relationships, including knowledge of letter patterns, to the task of recognizing and interpreting written words.

Word recognition: Ability to perceive and identify a word.

Word recognition score (WRS): Percentage of words presented at a comfortable listening level that can be correctly repeated.

Working memory: The cognitive system used to temporarily store information that is required to perform complex cognitive tasks such as reasoning, comprehension, and learning, and is thought to have limited capacity.

World Health Organization (WHO): An agency within the United Nations system that is responsible for providing leadership on global health issues, for setting health research agendas and health standards and norms, for dispersing evidence-based policy options, and for monitoring and assessing international health standards.

WRS: Word recognition score.

X-linked: Refers to a trait related to the X chromosome; transmitted by mothers to 50% of their sons who will be affected and to 50% of their daughters who will be carriers and transmitted by fathers to 100% of their daughters.

Years lived with a disability (YLD): A term used by the WHO and refers to years of life lived with a disability, taking into account severity.

YLD: Years lived with a disability.

REFERENCES

Aarts, N. L. (2006). Go for the gold. *Advance for Audiologists, 8*, 59–64.

Abouras, T. (2018). Managing single-sided deafness and unilateral hearing loss. *The Hearing Journal, 71*, 32–34.

Abrahamson, J. A. (1991). Teaching coping strategies: A client education approach to aural rehabilitation. *Journal of the Academy of Rehabilitative Audiology, 24*, 43–54.

Abrams, H., Chisolm, T., & McArdle, R. (2005). Health-related quality of life and hearing aids: A tutorial. *Trends in Amplification, 9*, 99–109.

Affiliate Representatives (2003). A primer on evidence-based clinical practice. *Canadian Cochrane Network/Centre*. Retrieved March 28, 2013 from http://www.cochrane.uottawa.ca/pdf/presentations/EBCPPrimer_July_2003.pdf

Alcantara, J. I., Cowan, R. S., Blamey, P. J., & Clark, G. M. (1990). A comparison of two training strategies for speech recognition with an electrotactile speech processor. *Journal of Speech and Hearing Research, 33*, 195–204.

Alexander Graham Bell Association for the Deaf and Hard of Hearing (1988). *Speechreading for better communication*. Washington, DC: Alexander Graham Bell Association for the Deaf and Hard of Hearing.

Allen, J. (2012, December). It's a noisy, wonderful world. *Good Housekeeping*, 59–65.

Allen, T. E. (1986). Patterns of academic achievement among hearing impaired students: 1974 and 1983. In A. N. Schildroth & M. A. Karchmer (Eds.), *Deaf children in America* (pp. 161–206). San Diego, CA: College-Hill Press.

Alzheimer's Association (2007). *Every 72 seconds someone in America develops Alzheimer's*. Chicago, IL: Alzheimer's Association.

American Academy of Audiology (2004). Pediatric amplification guidelines. *Audiology Today, 16*, 46–53.

American Academy of Audiology (2006). Guidelines for audiologic management of adult hearing impairment: Summary guidelines. *Audiology Today, 18*, 32–36.

American Speech-Language-Hearing Association (1998). Guidelines for hearing aid fitting for adults [Guidelines]. *ASHA*. Retrieved March 28, 2013 from http://www.asha.org/policy/GL1998-00012.htm

American Speech-Language-Hearing Association (2002). Knowledge and skills required for the practice of audiologic/aural rehabilitation [Knowledge and Skills]. *ASHA*. Retrieved March 28, 2013 from http://www.asha.org/policy/KS2001-00216.htm

American Speech-Language-Hearing Association. (2003). *2003 Omnibus survey caseload report: SLP*. Rockville, MD: Speech-Language-Hearing Association.

American Speech-Language-Hearing Association (2004a). Evidence-based practice in communication disorders: An introduction [Technical Report]. *ASHA*. Retrieved March 28, 2013 from http://www.asha.org/policy/TR2004-00001.htm

American Speech-Language-Hearing Association (2004b). Knowledge and skills needed by speech-language pathologists and audiologists to provide culturally and linguistically appropriate services [Knowledge and Skills]. *ASHA*. Retrieved March 28, 2013 from http://www.asha.org/policy/KS2004-00215.htm

American Speech-Language-Hearing Association (2004c). Roles of speech-language pathologists and teachers of children who are deaf and hard of hearing in the development of communicative and linguistic competence [Guidelines]. *ASHA*. Retrieved March 28, 2013 from http://www.asha.org/policy/GL2004-00202.htm

American Speech-Language-Hearing Association (2005a). (Central) auditory processing disorders—the role of the audiologist [Position Statement]. *ASHA*. Retrieved March 28, 2013 from http://www.asha.org/policy/PS2005-00114.htm

American Speech-Language-Hearing Association (2005b). Acoustics in educational settings: Technical report [Technical Report]. *ASHA*. Retrieved March 28, 2013 from http://www.asha.org/policy/TR2005-00042.htm

American Speech-Language-Hearing Association (2007). Causes of hearing loss in children. *ASHA*. Retrieved March 28, 2013 from http:// www.asha.org/public/hearing/Causes-of-Hearing-Loss-in-Children/

American Speech-Language-Hearing Association (2009). Audiology information series: Ask your audiologist about hearing assistive technology and audiologic rehabilitation. *ASHA*. Retrieved March 16, 2013 from http://www.asha.org/uploadedFiles/aud/InfoSeriesAssistTech.pdf

American Speech-Language-Hearing Association (2011). Cultural competence in professional service delivery. *ASHA*. Retrieved October 23, 2012 from http://www.asha.org/policy/PI2011-00326.htm

American Speech-Language Hearing Association (2013). Top tasks and earnings for audiologists. *The ASHA Leader, 18*, 22.

American Speech-Language Hearing Association (2015). 2014 Audiology survey report: Private practice. ASHA. Retrieved July 10, 2018 from hhttp://www.asha.org

Americans with Disabilities Act of 1990, Pub. L. No. 101–336, 104 Stat. 328 (1990).

Amieva, H., Ouvrard, C., Giulioli, C., Meillon, C., Rullier, L., & Dartigues, J. F. (2015). Self-reported hearing loss, hearing aids, and cognitive decline in elderly adults: A 25-year study. *Journal of the American Geriatrics Society, 63*, 2099–2104.

Anderson, K. L. (1989). S.I.F.T.E.R.—Screening Instrument for Targeting Educational Risk. *Success for Kids with Hearing Loss*. Retrieved February 11, 2013 from https://successforkidswithhearingloss.com/uploads/SIFTER.pdf

Anderson, K. L. (2002). *ELF—Early listening function. Phonak Pro*. Retrieved March 27, 2013 from http://www.phonakpro.com/content/dam/phonak/b2b/Pediatrics/Junior_Reports/Fitters /com_elf_questionnaire_gb.pdf

Anderson, K. L. (2004). The problem of classroom acoustics: The typical classroom soundscape is a barrier to learning. *Seminars in Hearing, 25*, 117–129.

Anderson, K. L., & Arnoldi, K. (2011). Children's peer relationship scale. Retrieved February 11, 2013 from https://successforkidswithhearingloss.com/wp-content/uploads/2011/08/Childrens-Peer-Relationship-Scale.pdf

Anderson, K. L., & Matkin, N. D. (1991). Relationship of degree of long-term hearing loss to psychosocial impact and educational needs. *Educational Audiology Association Newsletter, 8*, 17–18.

Anderson, K. L., & Smaldino, J. (1998). *Listening inventory for education (L.I.F.E.)*. Tampa, FL: Educational Audiology Association.

Anderson, M., Boren, N. J., Kilgore, J., Howard, W., & Krohn, E. (1999). *The apple tree curriculum for developing written language (2nd ed.)*. Austin, TX: Pro-Ed.

Andersson, U., & Lidestam, B. (2005). Bottom-up driven speechreading in a speechreading expert: The case of AA. *Ear and Hearing, 26*, 214–224.

Andersson, G., Melin, L., Lindberg, P., & Scott, B. (1995). Development of a short scale for self-assessment of experiences of hearing loss: The hearing coping assessment. *Scandinavian Audiology, 24*, 147–154.

Anne, S., Lieu, J. E., & Cohen, M. S. (2017). Speech and language consequences of unilateral hearing loss: A systematic review. *Otolaryngology–Head and Neck Surgery, 157*, 572–579.

Antia, S. D., & Levine, L. M. (2001). Educating deaf and hearing children together: Confronting the challenges of inclusion. In M. J. Guralnick (Ed.), *Early childhood inclusion: Focus on change* (pp. 365–398). Baltimore, MD: Paul H. Brookes.

Antia, S. D., Stinson, M. S., & Gaustad, M. G. (2002). Developing membership in the education of deaf and hard-of-hearing students in inclusive settings. *Journal of Deaf Studies and Deaf Education, 7*, 214–229.

Armero, O., & Thomas, G. (2018). Patient-centered counseling for older adults. *The Hearing Journal, 71*, 18–19.

Arnold, P., & Hill, F. (2001). Bisensory augmentation: A speechreading advantage when speech is clearly audible and intact. *British Journal of Psychology, 92*, 339–355.

Arnos, K. (2012). Talking to parents about genetics: With new technologies, families seek information on causes of hearing loss. *The ASHA Leader, 17*, 5–7.

Auer, E. T., & Bernstein, L. E. (1997). Speechreading and the structure of the lexicon: Computationally modeling the effects of reduced phonetic distinctiveness on lexical uniqueness. *Journal of the Acoustical Society of America, 102*, 3704–3710.

Auer, E. T., & Bernstein, L. E. (2007). Enhanced visual speech perception in individuals with early-onset hearing impairment. *Journal of Speech, Language, and Hearing Research, 50*, 1157–1165.

Backenroth, G. A. M., & Ahlner, B. H. (2000). Quality of life of hearing-impaired persons who have participated in audiological rehabilitation counseling. *International Journal for the Advancement of Counseling, 22*, 225–240.

Baddeley, A. (1992). Working memory. *Science, 255*, 556–559.

Bader, L. A., & Pearce, D. L. (2012). *Bader reading and language inventory* (7th ed.). Bloomington, MN: Pearson Education.

Baker, C. (1993). *Foundations of bilingual education and bilingualism*. Clevedon, Avon, UK: Multicultural Matters.

Balik, B., Conway, L., Zipperer, J., & Watson, J. (2011). *Achieving an exceptional patient and family experience in inpatient hospital care*. Cambridge, MA: Institute for Health Care Improvement.

Bamford, J., & Saunders, E. (1985). *Hearing impairment, auditory perception, and language disability*. London, UK: Edward Arnold.

Bandura, A. (1994). Self-efficacy. In V. S. Ramachaudren (Ed.), *Encyclopedia of human behaviour* (Vol. 4, pp. 71–81). New York, NY: Academic Press.

Bandura, A. (2001). Guide for constructing self-efficacy scales. In F. Pajares & T. Urdan (Eds.), *Self-efficacy beliefs of adolescents* (pp. 307–337). Greenwich, CT: Information Age Publishing.

Banks, W. A., & Morley, J. E. (2003). Memories are made of this: Recent advances in understanding, cognitive impairment, and dementia. *Journal of Gerontology: Medical Sciences, 58A*, 314–321.

Barcroft, J. (2007). Effects of opportunities for word retrieval during second language vocabulary learning. *Language Learning, 57*, 35–56.

Barcroft, J. (2015). *Lexical input processing and vocabulary learning* (Vol. 43). Amsterdam, Netherlands: John Benjamins Publishing Company.

Barcroft, J., Sommers, M., Tye-Murray, N., Mauzé, E., Schroy, C., & Spehar, B. (2011). Tailoring auditory training to patient needs with single and multiple talkers: Transfer-appropriate gains on a four-choice discrimination test. *International Journal of Audiology, 50*, 1802–1808.

Barcroft, J., Spehar, B., Tye-Murray, N., & Sommers, M. (2016). Task- and talker-specific gains in auditory training. *Journal of Speech, Language, and Hearing Research, 59*, 862–870.

Barr, M., Duncan, J., & Dally, K. (2018). A systematic review of services to DHH children in rural and remote regions. *Journal of Deaf Studies and Deaf Education, 23*, 118–130.

Bates, E., Dale, P., Fenson, L., Marchman, V., Thal, D., Reznick, J., & Jackson-Maldonado, D. (2007). *MacArthur-Bates CDI words and gestures: Second edtion*. Baltimore, MD: Paul H. Brookes Publishing Company.

Bauman, S. L., & Hambrecht, G. (1995). Analysis of view angle used in speechreading training of sentences. *American Journal of Audiology, 4*, 67–70.

Beattie, G. (1983). *Talk: Analysis of speech and non-verbal behavior in conversation*. Milton Keynes, UK: Open University Press.

Beck, A. T., & Emery, G. (1985). *Anxiety disorders and phobias*. New York, NY: Basic Books.

Beck, P. H. (2006). Cued Speech across cultures. *Volta Voices*, September/October, 26–28.

Beethoven, L. v. (2013). Beethoven's heiligenstadt testament. *Awesome Stories*. Retrieved March 28, 2013 from www.awesomestories.com/assets/heiligenstadt-testament

Benitez, L., & Speaks, C. (1968). A test of speech intelligibility in the Spanish language. *International Audiology, 7*, 16–22.

Bentler, R. A. (2009). Developments in hearing aid technology and verification techniques. In J. J. Montano & J. B. Spitzer (Eds.), *Adult audiologic rehabilitation: Advance practice* (pp. 145–167). San Diego, CA: Plural Publishing.

Bentler, R. A., & Kramer, S. E. (2000). Guidelines for choosing a self-report outcome measure. *Ear and Hearing, 21*, 37S–49S.

Benyon, G., Thornton, F., & Pool, C. (1997). A randomized, controlled trial of the efficacy of a communication course for first time hearing aid users. *British Journal of Audiology, 31*, 345–351.

Berg, A. I., & Johansson, B. (2014). Personality change in the oldest-old: Is it a matter of compromised health and functioning? *Journal of Personality, 82*, 25–31.

Berger, K. W. (1972). *Speechreading: Principles and methods.* Baltimore, MD: National Education Press.

Bergeson, T. R., Pisoni, D. B., & Davis, R. A. (2003). A longitudinal study of audiovisual speech perception by children with hearing loss who have cochlear implants. *Volta Review, 103,* 347.

Bergman, B., & Rosenhall, U. (2001). Vision and hearing in old age. *Scandanavian Audiology, 30,* 255–263.

Beyer, C. M., & Northern, J. L. (2000). Audiologic rehabilitation support programs: A network model. *Seminars in Hearing, 21,* 257–265.

Bilger, R. C., Nuetzel, J. M., Rabinowitz, W. M., & Rzeczkowski, C. (1984). Standardization of a test of speech perception in noise. *Journal of Speech and Hearing Research, 27,* 32–48.

Binnie, C. A. (1977). Attitude changes following speechreading training. *Scandinavian Audiology, 6,* 13–19.

Bishop. D. V.M. (2006). *Children's Communication Checklist–2.* Bloomington, MN: Pearson Education.

Blackwood, M. J. (2006). Rediscover sounds of life. *Ladue News, 5,* 25.

Blood, I. M., & Blood, G. W. (1999). Effects of acknowledging a hearing loss in social interactions. *Journal of Communication Disorders, 32,* 109–120.

Bloom, B. S., Hastings, J. T., & Madaus, G. F. (1971). *Handbook on formative and summative evaluation of student learning.* New York, NY: McGraw-Hill, Inc.

Bochner, J., Garrison, W., Palmer, L., MacKenzie, D., & Braveman, A. (1997). A computerized adaptive testing system for speech discrimination measurement: The speech sound pattern discrimination test. *Journal of the Acoustical Society of America, 101,* 2289–2298.

Bode, D., & Oyer, H. (1970). Auditory training and speech discrimination. *Journal of Speech and Hearing Research, 13,* 839–855.

Bodrova, E., Leong, D. J., Paynter, D. E., & Semenov, D. (2000). *A framework for early literacy instruction: Aligning standards to developmental accomplishments and student behaviors.* Aurora, CO: Mid-continent Research for Education and Learning.

Boothroyd, A. (1984). Auditory perception of speech contrasts by subjects with sensorineural hearing loss. *Journal of Speech and Hearing Research, 27,* 134–144.

Boothroyd, A. (2007). Adult aural rehabilitation: What is it and does it work? *Trends in Amplification, 11,* 63–71.

Boothroyd, A. (2008). Caspersent: A program for computer-assisted speech perception testing and training at the sentence level. *Journal of the Academy of Rehabilitative Audiology, 41,* 31–52.

Boothroyd, A., Hanin, L., & Hnath-Chisholm, T. (1985). *The CUNY sentence test.* New York, NY: City University of New York.

Boswell, S. (2012). Inspire: Learn how with Dr. Dale Atkins. *Volta Voices,* January/February, 16–19.

Bouchard, M., Le Normand, M., & Cohen, H. (2007). Production of consonants by prelinguistically deaf children with cochlear implants. *Clinical Linguistics and Phonetics, 21,* 875–884.

Boylan, J. F. (2017, October 31). Glasses are cool. Why aren't hearing aids? *New York Times,* A25.

Brainy Quote (2013). Marlee Matlin quotes. *Brainy Quote.* Retrieved March 29, 2013 from http://www.brainyquote.com/quotes/authors/m/marlee_matlin.html

Brewer, D. (2001). Considerations in measuring effectiveness of group audiologic rehabilitation classes. *Journal of the Academy of Rehabilitative Audiology, 34,* 53–60.

Bridges, J. F. P., Lataille, A. T., Buttorff, C., White, S., & Niparko, J. K. (2012). Consumer preferences for hearing aid attributes: A comparison of rating and conjoint analysis methods. *Trends in Amplification, 16,* 40–48.

Brigance, A. H. (2010). *Brigance comprehensive inventory of basic skills-revised (CIBS-R).* North Billerica, MA: Curriculum Associates.

Briggs, R. J., Eder, H. C., Seligman, P. M., Cowan, R. S., Plant, K. L., Dalton, J., Money, D. K., & Patrick, J. F. (2008). Initial clinical experience with a totally implantable cochlear implant research device. *Otology and Neurotology, 29,* 114–119.

Bronus, K., El Refaie, A., & Pryce, H. (2011). Auditory training and adult rehabilitation: A critical review of the evidence. *Global Journal of Health Science, 3,* 49.

Brooks, D. N. (1979). Counseling and its effect on hearing aid use. *Scandinavian Audiology, 8,* 101–107.

Brooks, D. N., & Hallam, R. S. (1998). Attitudes to hearing difficulty and hearing aids and the outcome of audiological rehabilitation. *British Journal of Audiology, 24,* 229–233.

Brooks, D. N., Hallam, R. S., & Mellor, P. A. (2001). The effects on significant others of providing a hearing aid to the hearing-impaired partner. *British Journal of Audiology, 35*, 165–171.

Brown, G. R. (2004). Tinnitus: The ever-present tormentor. *The Hearing Journal, 57*, 52–54.

Brown, P. M., & Cornes, A. (2015). Mental health of deaf and hard-of-hearing adolescents: What the students say. *Journal of Deaf Studies and Deaf Education, 20*, 75–81.

Brownell, R. (2000). *Receptive one-word picture vocabulary test.* Novato, CA: Academic Therapy.

Bruce, R. V. (1973). *Bell: Alexander Graham Bell and the conquest of solitude.* Ithaca, NY: Cornell University Press.

Bruhn, M. E. (1947). *The Mueller-Walle method of lip reading for the hard of hearing.* Boston, MA: M. H. Leavis.

Bunger, A. M. (1944). *Speech reading—Jena method: A textbook with lesson plans in full development for hard-of-hearing adults and discussion of adaptations for hard-of-hearing children.* Danville, IL: The Interstate.

Burk, M. H., & Humes, L. E. (2007). Effects of training on speech recognition performance in noise using lexically hard words. *Journal of Speech, Language, and Hearing Research, 50*, 25–40.

Burk, M. H., Humes, L. E., Amos, N., & Strauser, L. (2006). Effect of training on word-recognition performance in noise for young normal-hearing and older hearing-impaired listeners. *Ear and Hearing, 27*, 263–278.

Burns, E. (2004). *The special education consultant teacher: Enabling children with disabilities to be educated with nondisabled children to the maximum extent appropriate.* Springfield, IL: Thomas.

Busacco, D. (2011). Rehabilitation strategies for older adults with dual sensory loss. *Hearing Review, 18*, 40–42.

Bynum, W., Hopper, K., Wolfe, J., & Smith, J. (2017). What parents want from hearing professionals. *The Hearing Journal, 70*, 39–40.

Caissie, R. (2001). Conversational topic shifting and its effect on communication breakdowns. *Volta Review, 102*, 45–56.

Caissie, R., Campbell, M. M., Grenette, W., Scott, L., Howell, I., & Roy, A. (2005). Clear speech for adults with a hearing loss: Does intervention with communication partners make a difference? *Journal of the American Academy of Audiology, 16*, 157–171.

Caissie, R., & Gibson, C. L. (1997). The effectiveness of repair strategies used by people with hearing losses and their conversational partners. *Volta Review, 99*, 203–218.

Caldrone, J. (2017, February 2). Can PSAPs help your hearing? *Consumer Reports.* Retrieved October 28, 2018 from https://www.consumerreports.org/hearing-ear-care/can-psaps-help-your-hearing/

Caplan, D., & Waters, G. (1999). Verbal working memory and sentence comprehension. *Behavioral and Brain Sciences, 22*, 77–126.

Carew, P., Mensah, F. K., Rance, G., Flynn, T., Poulakis, Z., & Wake, M. (2017). Mild–moderate congenital hearing loss: Secular trends in outcomes across four systems of detection. *Child: Care, Health and Development.* Retrieved July 13, 2018 from https://doi.org/10.1111/cch.12477

Carhart, R. (1947). Conservation of speech. In H. Davis (Ed.), *Hearing and deafness, a guide for the laymen* (pp. 300–317). New York, NY: Murray Hill Books.

Carhart, R. (1963). Conservation of speech. In H. Davis & S. R. Silverman (Eds.), *Hearing and deafness* (pp. 387–402). New York, NY: Holt, Rinehart & Winston.

Carney, A. E., & Moeller, M. P. (1998). Treatment efficacy: Hearing loss in children. *Journal of Speech, Language, and Hearing Research, 41*, S61–S84.

Carroll, B. (2018). Parents to prime children for academic and long-term success. *Audiology Today, 30*, 29–34.

Carrow-Woolfolk, E. (1996). *Oral and written language scales (OWLS).* Circle Pines, MN: American Guidance Services.

Carrow-Woolfolk, E. (1999a). *Comprehensive assessment of spoken language (CASL).* Bloomington, MN: Pearson Education.

Carrow-Woolfolk, E. (1999b). *Test for auditory comprehension of language–III.* Austin, TX: Pro-Ed.

Cassell, J. (2001). Nudge nudge wink wink: Elements of face-to-face conversation for embodied conversational agents. In J. Cassell (Ed.), *Embodied conversational agents* (pp. 1–27). Cambridge, MA: MIT Press.

Casserly, E. D., & Barney, E. C. (2017). Auditory training with multiple talkers and passage-based semantic cohesion. *Journal of Speech, Language, and Hearing Research, 60*, 159–171.

Centers for Disease Control and Prevention (CDC). (2010). Intervention and family support services. *CDC.* Retrieved

March 22, 2013 from http://www.cdc.gov/ncbddd/hearing loss/links.html

Center for Hearing and Communication (2018). Statistics and facts about hearing loss. Retrieved July 10, 2018 from http://www.chhearing.org/facts-about-hearing-loss

Central Institute for the Deaf (2016). One family's journey to conversation. *Sound Effects, Winter,* 1.

Chandrasekaran, C., Trubanova, A., Stillittano, S., Caplier, A., & Ghazanfar, A. (2009). The natural statistics of audiovisual speech. *PLoS Computational Biology, 5,* 1–18.

Cheesman, M. G. (1997). Speech perception by elderly listeners: Basic knowledge and implications for audiology. *Journal of Speech Language Pathology and Audiology, 21,* 104–110.

Cherry, R., & Rubinstein, A. (1988). Speechreading instruction for adults: Issues and practices. *Volta Review, 90,* 289–306.

Cheslock, M. A., & Kahn, S. J. (2011). Supporting families and caregivers in everyday routines. *The ASHA Leader, 16,* 10–13.

Ching, T. Y. C., Dillon, H., Marnane, V., Hou, S., Day, J. et al. (2013). Outcomes of early- and late-identified children at 3 years of age: Findings from a prospective population-based study. *Ear and Hearing, 34,* 535–552.

Ching, T., & Hill, M. (2007). The parents' evaluation of aural/oral performance of children (PEACH) scale: Normative data. *Journal of American Academy of Audiology, 18,* 221–237.

Ching, T., & Incerti, P. (2012). Bimodal fitting or bilateral cochlear implantation? In L. Wong & L. Hickson (Eds.), *Evidence-based practice in audiology* (pp. 213–233). San Diego, CA: Plural Publishing.

Ching, T., Incerti, P., & Hill, M. (2004). Binaural benefits for adults who use hearing aids and cochlear implants in opposite ears. *Ear and Hearing, 25,* 9–21.

Chisolm, T. H., Abrams, H., & McArdle, R. (2004). Short and long-term outcomes of adult audiologic rehabilitation. *Ear and Hearing, 25,* 464–477.

Chisolm, T. H., Johnson, C. E., Danhauer, J., Portz, L., Abrams, H., Lesner, S., McCarthy, P. A., & Newman, C. W. (2007). A systematic review of health-related quality of life and hearing aids: Final report of the American Academy of Audiology task force on the health-related quality of life benefits of amplification in adults. *Journal of the American Academy of Audiology, 18,* 151–183.

Christopherson, L. A., & Humes, L. E. (1992). Some psychometric properties of the test of basic auditory capabilities (TBAC). *Journal of Speech and Hearing Research, 35,* 929–935.

Cienkowski, K. M., & Carney, A. E. (2002). Auditory-visual speech perception and aging. *Ear and Hearing, 23,* 439–449.

Clark, D. P., & Russell, L. D. (1997). *Molecular biology made simple and fun.* Vienna, IL: Cache River Press.

Clark, J. G., & English, K. M. (2004). *Counseling in audiologic practice: Helping patients and families adjust to hearing loss.* Boston, MA: Pearson.

Clark, J. G., Maatman, M. A., & Gailey, L. (2012). Moving patients forward: Motivational engagement. *Seminars in Hearing, 33,* 35–45.

Clark, J. G., Yeagle, J., Arbaje, A., Lin, F., Niparko, J., & Francis, H. (2012). Cochlear implant rehabilitation in older adults: Literature review and proposal of a conceptual framework. *Journal of the American Geriatric Society, 60,* 1936–1945.

College of Speech and Hearing Health Professionals of BC (2011). Guidelines: Best practices: Fitting of remote microphone hearing assistance technology for children in an educational setting. Vancouver, British Columbia. Retrieved March 23, 2013 from http://cshhpbc.org/docs/fm_micro_guideline.pdf

Compton, D. O. (1995). A note on new product development. *Generations*, Spring, 30–31.

Connor, C. M., Craig, H. K., Raudenbush, S. W., Heavner, K., & Zwolan, T. A. (2006). The age at which young deaf children receive cochlear implants and their vocabulary and speech-production growth: Is there an added value for early implantation? *Ear and Hearing, 27,* 628–644.

Contrera, K.J., Betz, J., Deal, J., Choi, J.S., Ayonayon, H.N., Harris, T. et al. (2017). Association of hearing impairment and anxiety in older adults. *Journal of Aging and Health, 29,* 172–184.

Convery, E., Hickson, L., Meyer, C., & Keidser, G. (2018). Predictors of hearing loss self-management in older adults. *Disability and Rehabilitation,* 1–10.

Convery, E., Meyer, C., Keidser, G., & Hickson, L. (2018). Assessing hearing loss self-management in older adults. *International Journal of Audiology, 57,* 313–320.

Cornett, R. O. (1967). Cued Speech. *American Annals of the Deaf, 112,* 313.

Cowie, R., & Douglas-Cowie, E. (1992). *Postlingually acquired deafness: Speech deterioration and the wider consequences.* New York, NY: Mouton de Gruyter.

Cox, R. M. (2003). Assessment of subjective outcome of hearing aid fitting: Getting the client's point of view. *International Journal of Audiology, 42*, S90–S96.

Cox, R. M. (2005). Evidence-based practice in provision of amplification. *Journal of the American Academy of Audiology, 16*, 419–438.

Cox, R. M., & Alexander, G. C. (1999). Measuring satisfaction with amplification in daily life: The SADL scale. *Ear and Hearing, 20*, 306–320.

Cox, R. M., & Alexander, G. C. (2000). Expectations about hearing aids and their relationship to fitting outcome. *Journal of the American Academy of Audiology, 11*, 368–382.

Cox, R. M., & Alexander, G. C. (2002). The international outcome inventory for hearing aids (IOI-HA): Psychometric properties of the English version. *International Journal of Audiology, 41*, 30–35.

Cox, R. M., Alexander, G. C., & Gilmore, C. (1987). Development of the connected speech test (CST). *Ear and Hearing, 9*, 198–207.

Cox, R. M., & Gilmore, C. (1990). Development of the profile of hearing aid performance (PHAP). *Journal of Speech and Hearing Research, 33*, 343–357.

Cox, R. M., Gilmore, C. G., & Alexander, G. C. (1991). Comparison of two questionnaires for patient-assessed hearing aid benefit. *Journal of the American Academy of Audiology, 2*, 134–145.

Cox, R. M., Hyde, M., Gatehouse, S., Noble, W., Dillon, H., Bentler, R., Stephans, D. et al. (2000). Optimal outcome measures, research priorities, and international cooperation. *Ear and Hearing, 21*, 106S–115S.

Cox, R. M., & Rivera, I. M. (1992). Predictability and reliability of hearing aid benefit measured using the PHAP. *Journal of the American Academy of Audiology, 3*, 242–254.

Crandell, C. C. (1993). Noise effects on the speech recognition of children with minimal hearing loss. *Ear and Hearing, 14*, 210–216.

Crandell, C. C., & Smaldino, J. J. (1995). An update of classroom acoustics for children with hearing impairment. *Volta Review, 97*, 4–12.

Cruz, I., Quittner, A. L., Marker, C., & DesJardin, J. L. (2013). Identification of effective strategies to promote language in deaf children with cochlear implants. *Child Development, 84*, 543–559.

Curle, D., Jamieson, J., Buchanan, M., Poon, B. T., Zaidman-Zait, A., & Norman, N. (2016). The transition from early intervention to school for children who are deaf or hard of hearing: Administrator perspectives. *Journal of Deaf Studies and Deaf Education,* 1–10.

Curtin, J. (2006). Counseling the "difficult" or non-compliant parent. *Hearing and Hearing Disorders in Childhood*, April, 7–12.

da Silva, M. P. D., Comerlatto, A. A., Bevilacqua, M. C., & Lopes-Herrera, S. A. (2011). Instruments to assess the oral language of children fitted with a cochlear implant: A systematic review. *Journal of Applied Oral Science, 19*, 549–553.

Dale, D. (1974). *Language development in deaf and partially hearing children.* Springfield, IL: Charles C. Thomas.

Dalton, D., Cruickshanks, K., Klein, B., Klein, R., Wiley, T., & Nondahl, D. (2003). The impact of hearing loss on quality of life in older adults. *Gerontologist, 43*, 661–668.

Dancer, J. (2006). Celebrate diversity. *Advance for Audiologists*, July/August, 24–26.

Dancer, J., & Gener, J. (1999). Survey on the use of adult hearing assessment scales. *Hearing Review, 6*, 26–35.

Davis, K. (2018). Organizing hearing meetups: The new support group in audiology. *The Hearing Journal, 71*, 22–23.

Davis, H., & Silverman, R. (1978). *Hearing and deafness* (4th ed.). New York, NY: Holt Rinehart & Winston.

Deal, J. A., Sharrett, A. R., Albert, M. S., Coresh, J., Mosley, T. H., Knopman, D., Wruck, L. M. & Lin, F. R. (2015). Hearing impairment and cognitive decline: A pilot study conducted within the atherosclerosis risk in communities neurocognitive study. *American Journal of Epidemiology, 181*, 680–690.

Decker, K. B., Vallotton, C. D., & Johnson, H. A. (2012). Parents' communication decision for children with hearing loss: Sources of information and influence. *American Annals of the Deaf, 157*, 326–339.

Delage, H., & Tuller, L. (2007). Language development and mild-to-moderate hearing loss: Does language normalize with age? *Journal of Speech, Language, and Hearing Research, 50*, 1300–1313.

Department of Education and Children's Services (2010). Individual education plans for children and young people under the guardianship of the minister. *Government of South Australia.* Retrieved February 11, 2013 from http://www.decd.sa.gov.au/docs/documents/1/IepPart1StakeholdersManua.pdf

Desai, M., Pratt, L., Lentzner, H., & Robinson, K. (2001). Trends in vision and hearing among older Americans. *Aging Trends, 2*, 1–8.

DesJardin, J. L., Ambrose, S. E., & Eisenberg, L. S. (2009). Literacy skills in children with cochlear implants: The importance of early oral language and joint storybook reading. *Journal of Deaf Studies and Deaf Education, 14*, 22–43.

DesJardin, J. L., Doll, E. R., Stika, C. J., Eisenberg, L. S., Johnson, K. J., Ganguly, D. H. et al. (2014). Parental support for language development during joint book reading for young children with hearing loss. *Communication Disorders Quarterly, 35*, 167–181.

DesJardin, J. L., & Eisenberg, L. S. (2007). Maternal contributions: Supporting language development in young children with cochlear implants. *Ear and Hearing, 28*, 456–469.

de Souza, L., Bevilacqua, M. C., Brasolotto, A. G., & Coelho, A. C. (2012). Cochlear implanted children present vocal parameters within normal standards. *International Journal of Pediatric Otorhinolaryngology, 76*, 1180–1183.

Dettman, S. J., Dowell, R. C., Choo, D., Arnott, W., Abrahams, Y., Davis et al. (2016). Long-term communication outcomes for children receiving cochlear implants younger than 12 months: A multicenter study. *Otology & Neurotology, 37*, e82–e95.

Dettman, S., Pinder, D., Briggs, R., Dowell, R., & Leigh, J. (2007). Communication development in children who receive the cochlear implant younger than 12 months: Risks versus benefits. *Ear and Hearing, 28*, 11S–18S.

Dietrich, V., Nieschalk, M., Stoll, W., Rajan, R., & Pantev, C. (2001). Cortical reorganization in patients with high frequency cochlear hearing loss. *Hearing Research, 158*, 95–101.

Dillon, H., Birtles, G., & Lovegrove, R. (1999). Measuring the outcomes of a national rehabilitation program: Normative data for the client oriented scale of improvement (COSI) and the hearing aid user's questionnaire (HAUQ). *Journal of the American Academy of Audiology, 10*, 67–79.

Dillon, H., James, A., & Ginis, J. (1997). Client oriented scale of improvement (COSI) and its relationship to several other measurements of benefit and satisfaction provided by hearing aids. *Journal of the American Academy of Audiology, 8*, 27–43.

DiLollo, L., DiLollo, A., Mendel, L., English, K., & McCarthy, P. (2006). Facilitating ownership of acquired hearing loss: A narrative approach. *Journal of the Academy of Rehabilitative Audiology, 39*, 49–67.

Donaldson, N., Worrall, L., & Hickson, L. (2004). Older people with hearing impairment: A literature review of the spouse's perspective. *Australian and New Zealand Journal of Audiology, 26*, 30–39.

Dornan, D., Hickson, L., Murdoch, B., & Houston, T. (2008). Outcomes of an auditory-verbal program for children with hearing loss: A comparative study with a matched group of children with normal hearing. *Volta Review, 107*, 37–54.

Dowell, R. (2005). Evaluating cochlear implant candidacy: Recent developments. *The Hearing Journal, 58*, 9–23.

Dowell, R. (2012). Evidence about the effectiveness of cochlear implants for adults. In L. Wong & L. Hickson (Eds.), *Evidence-based practice in audiology* (pp. 141–165). San Diego, CA: Plural Publishing.

Driscoll, V. (2012). The effects of training on recognition of musical instruments by adults with cochlear implants. *Seminars in Hearing, 33*, 410–418.

Driscoll, V., Oleson, J., Jiang, D., & Gfeller, K. (2009). Effects of training on recognition of musical instruments presented through cochlear implant simulations. *Journal of the American Academy of Audiology, 20*, 71–82.

Dryden, W., & Branch, R. (2008). *The fundamentals of rational emotive behavior therapy*. Chichester, UK: John Wiley and Sons Ltd.

Dunn, D. M. (2019). *Peabody picture vocabulary test—* (4th ed.). Circle Pines, MN: American Guidance Service.

Early Hearing Detection and Intervention Act of 2010 (2010). H.R. 1246/S. 3199.

Easterbrooks, S. R., & Beal-Alvarez, J. S. (2012). States' reading outcomes of students who are Deaf and hard of hearing. *American Annals of the Deaf, 157*, 27–40.

Edgerton, B. J., & Danhauer, J. L. (1979). *Clinical implications of speech discrimination testing using nonsense stimuli*. Baltimore, MD: University Park Press.

Education for All Handicapped Children Act, Pub. L. No. 94-172 (1975).

Education for All Handicapped Children Act Amendment, Pub. L. No. 99-457 (1986).

Einhorn, K. (2017). Ear infections over the ages. *Hearing Review, 24*, 18.

Eisenberg, A. (2012, May 5). For hard of hearing, clarity out of the din. *New York Times*, p. BU3.

Ellersten, P., Lai, T., O'Donnell, J., & Saunders, C. (2012). *Patient stories and the role of the audiologist as listener in hearing loss treatment.* Paper presented at the the Academy of Rehabilitative Audiology Institute, Providence, RI.

Elfenbein, J. (1994). Communication breakdowns in conversations: Child-initiated repair strategies. In N. Tye-Murray (Ed.), *Let's converse: A how-to guide to develop and expand the conversational skills of children and teenagers who are hearing impaired* (pp. 123–146). Washington, DC: Alexander Graham Bell Association for the Deaf.

Elfenbein, J. L., Hardin-Jones, M. A., & Davis, J. M. (1994). Oral communication skills of children who are hard of hearing. *Journal of Speech and Hearing Research, 37,* 216–226.

Elkayam, J., & English, K. (2003). Counseling adolescents with hearing loss with the use of self-assessment/significant other questionnaires. *Journal of the American Academy of Audiology, 14,* 485–499.

Elliott, L., & Katz, D. (1980). *Development of a new children's test of speech recognition.* St. Louis, MO: Audiotec.

Ellis, A. (2001). *Overcoming destructive beliefs, feelings, and behaviors.* Amherst, NY: Prometheus Books.

Ellis, A., & Grieger, R. (1977). *Handbook of rational-emotive therapy.* New York, NY: Springer.

Ellis, A., & MacLaren, C. (1998). *Rational emotive behavior therapy: A therapist's guide.* Atascadero, CA: Impact.

English, K. (2004). Informing parents of their child's hearing loss: Breaking bad news guidelines for audiologists. *Audiology Today,* March/April, 10–12.

English, K., Mendel, L. L., Rojeski, T., & Hornak, J. (1999). Counseling in audiology, or learning to listen: Pre- and post-measures from an audiology counseling course. *American Journal of Audiology, 8,* 34–39.

Erber, N. P. (1974). Visual perception of speech by deaf children: Recent developments and continuing needs. *Journal of Speech and Hearing Disorders, 39,* 178–185.

Erber, N. P. (1988). *Communication therapy for hearing impaired adults.* Abbotsford, Victoria, Australia: Clavis.

Erber, N. P. (1996). *Communication therapy for adults with sensory loss* (2nd ed.). Melbourne, Australia: Clavis.

Erber, N. P. (1998). Dyalog: A computer-based measure of conversational performance. *Journal of the Academy of Rehabilitative Audiology, 31,* 69–76.

Erber, N. P., & Lind, C. (1994). Communication therapy: Theory and practice. *Journal of the Academy of Rehabilitative Audiology, 27,* 267–287.

Erdman, S. A. (1994). Self-assessment: From research focus to research tool. *Journal of the Academy of Rehabilitative Audiology, 27,* S67–S92.

Erdman, S. A. (2011). *The art and science of counseling and rehabilitative audiology.* Paper presented at the ASHA Online Conference.

Eriks-Brophy, A., Durieux-Smith, A., Olds, J., Fitzpatrick, E., Duquette, C., & Whittingham, J. (2006). Facilitators and barriers to the inclusion of orally educated children and youth with hearing loss in schools: Promoting partnerships to support inclusion. *Volta Review, 106,* 53–88.

Eriks-Brophy, A., Durieux-Smith, A., Olds, J., Fitzpatrick, E., Duquette, C., & Whittingham, J. (2007). Facilitators and barriers to the integration of orally educated children and youth with hearing loss into their families and communities. *Volta Review, 107,* 5–36.

Eriks-Brophy, A., & Whittingham, J. (2013). Teacher's perceptions of the inclusion of children with hearing loss in general education settings. *American Annals of the Deaf, 158,* 63–97.

Estabrooks, W., De Melo, M., Katz, L., Maclver-Lux, K., Tannenbaum, S., & Walker, B. (2006). Auditory-verbal therapy in action: Babies through age 3. In W. Estabrooks (Ed.), *Auditory-verbal therapy and practice* (pp. 89–132). Washington, DC: Alexander Graham Bell Association for the Deaf and Hard of Hearing.

Etchison, M., & Kleist, D. (2000). Review of narrative therapy: Research and unity. *The Family Journal: Counseling and Therapy for Couples and Families, 8,* 61–66.

Etymotic Research (2001). *Quick speech in noise test (quick-SIN).* Elk Grove Village, IL: Etymotic Research.

Executive Order No. 13166, 65 Federal Registry 159 (August 16, 2000).

Fagan, J. J., & Jacobs, M. (2009, March). Survey of ENT services in Africa: Need for a comprehensive intervention. *Global Health Action, 2. doi:* 10.3402/gha.v2i0.1932

Feld, J., & Sommers, M. (2009). Lipreading, processing speed, and working memory in younger and older adults. *Journal of Speech, Language, and Hearing Research, 52,* 1555–1565.

Feld, J., & Sommers, M. (2011). There goes the neighborhood: Lipreading and the structure of the mental lexicon. *Speech Communication, 53*, 220–228.

Felzien, M. (2011). Meet Kai Kraus. *Volta Voices*, November/December, 44–45.

Ferguson, N. M., & Nerbonne, M. A. (2003). Status of hearing aids in nursing homes and retirement centers in 2002. *Journal of the Academy of Rehabilitative Audiology, 36*, 37–44.

Fernandes, J. K. (1998). *Literacy—it all connects: Nine important pieces*. Laurent Clerc National Deaf Education Center. Washington, DC: Gallaudet University.

Fey, M. E., Long, S. H., & Finestack, L. H. (2003). Ten principles of grammar facilitation for children with specific language impairments. *American Journal of Speech-Language Pathology, 12*, 3–15.

Firszt, J., Holden, L., Reeder, R., Cowdrey, L., & King, S. (2012). Cochlear implantation in adults with asymmetric hearing loss. *Ear and Hearing, 33*, 521–533.

Fitch, J. L., & Holbrook, A. (1970). Modal vocal frequency of young adults. *Archives of Otolaryngology, 92*, 379–382.

Fitzpatrick, E. M., Gaboury, I., Durieux-Smith, A., Coyle, D., Whittingham, J., & Nassrallah, F. (2018). Auditory and language outcomes in children with unilateral hearing loss. *Hearing Research*, https://doi.org/10.1016/j.heares.2018.03.015

Fitzpatrick, E. M., Hamel, C., Stevens, A., Pratt, M., Moher, D., Doucet, S. P., . . . Na, E. (2016). Sign language and spoken language for children with hearing loss: A systematic review. *Pediatrics, 137*, e20151974.

Fitzpatrick, E. M., Whittingham, J., & Durieux-Smith, A. (2014). Mild bilateral and unilateral hearing loss in childhood: A 20-year view of hearing characteristics, and audiologic practices before and after newborn hearing screening. *Ear and Hearing, 35*, 10–18.

Flexer, C. (1999). *Facilitating hearing and listening in young children* (2nd ed.). Clifton Park, NY: Delmar Learning.

Florida Department of Health (2011, May). *Florida resource guide for families of young children with hearing loss*. Tallahassee, FL: Children Medical Services.

Folstein, M. F., Folstein, S. E., & McHugh, P. R. (1975). Mini-Mental State: A practical method for grading the cognitive state of patients for the clinician. *Journal of Psychiatric Research, 12*, 189–198.

Freeman B. A. (2017). The changing landscape of hearing aid batteries. *Hearing Review, 24*, 34–36.

Fu, Q. J., & Galvin, J. J. (2007). Computer-assisted speech training for cochlear implant patients: Feasibility, outcomes, and future directions. *Seminars in Hearing, 28*, 142–150.

Gagné, J. P., & Boutin, L. (1997). *The effects of speaking rate on visual speech intelligibility*. Paper presented at the ESCA Workshop on Audiovisual Speech Processing, Rhodes, Greece.

Gagné, J. P., Charest, M., Monday, K. L., & Desbiens, C. (2006). Evaluation of an audiovisual-FM system: Speechreading performance as a function of distance. *International Journal of Audiology, 45*, 295–300.

Gagné, J. P., Dinon, D., & Parsons, J. (1991). An evaluation of CAST: A computer-aided speechreading training program. *Journal of Speech and Hearing Research, 34*, 213–221.

Gagné, J. P., & Jennings, M. B. (2000). Audiological rehabilitation intervention services for adults with acquired hearing impairment. In M. Valente, H. Hosford-Dunn, & R. J. Roeser (Eds.), *Audiology treatment* (pp. 547–579). New York, NY: Thieme.

Gagné, J. P., Stelmacovich, P., & Yovetich, W. (1991). Reactions to requests for clarification used by hearing-impaired individuals. *Volta Review, 93*, 129–143.

Gagné, J. P., Tugby, K. G., & Michaud, J. (1991). Development of a speechreading test on the utilization of contextual cues (STUCC): Preliminary findings with normal-hearing subjects. *Journal of the Academy of Rehabilitative Audiology, 24*, 157–170.

Gagné, J. P., & Wyllie, K. M. (1989). Relative effectiveness of three repair strategies on the visual-identification of misperceived words. *Ear and Hearing, 10*, 368–374.

Gallaudet Research Institute (2003). *Regional and national summary report of data from the 2001–2002 annual survey of deaf and hard of hearing children and youth*. Washington, DC: Gallaudet University Press.

Gallaudet Research Institute (2011, April). *Regional and national summary report of data from the 2009–2010 annual survey of deaf and hard of hearing children and youth*. Washington, DC: Gallaudet University Press.

Galvin, J., Fu, Q., & Nogaki, G. (2007). Melodic contour identification by cochlear implant listeners. *Ear and Hearing, 28*, 302–319.

Gans, J. J. (2010). Mindfulness-based tinnitus therapy is an approach with ancient roots. *The Hearing Journal, 63*, 52–56.

Garstecki, D. C., & Erler, S. F. (1998). Hearing loss, control, and demographic factors influencing hearing aid use among older adults. *Journal of Speech, Language, and Hearing Research, 41*, 527–537.

Gatehouse, S. (1999). Glasgow hearing aid benefit profile: Derivation and validation of a client-centered outcome measure for hearing aid services. *Journal of American Academy of Audiology, 10*, 80–103.

Geers, A. E. (2003). Predictors of reading skill development in children with early cochlear implantation. *Ear and Hearing, 24*, 59S–68S.

Geers, A. E., & Hayes, H. (2011). Reading, writing, and phonological processing skills of adolescents with 10 or more years of cochlear implant experience. *Ear and Hearing, 32*, 49S–59S.

Geers, A. E., Mitchell, C. M., Warner-Czyz, A., Wang, N. Y., Eisenberg, L. S., & CDaCI Investigative Team. (2017). Early sign language exposure and cochlear implantation benefits. *Pediatrics, 140*, e20163489.

Geers, A. E., Moog, J. S., Biedenstein, J., Brenner, C., & Hayes, H. (2009). Spoken language scores of children using cochlear implants compared to hearing age-mates at school entry. *Journal of Deaf Studies, 14*, 371–385.

Geers, A. E., Nicholas, J., & Sedey, A. L. (2003). Language skills of children with early cochlear implantation. *Ear and Hearing, 24*, 46S–58S.

Geers, A. E., & Sedey, A. L. (2011). Language and verbal reasoning skills in adolescents with 10 or more years of cochlear implant experience. *Ear and Hearing, 32*, 39S–48S.

Gellis, Z. D., & McCracken, S. G. (2009). Depressive disorders among older adults. In *Mental health resource review*. Alexandria, VA: National Center for Gerontological Social Work Education. Retrieved March 27, 2013 from http://www.cswe.org/CentersInitiatives/GeroEdCenter/Programs/MAC/Reviews/MentalHealth.aspx

Getty, L., & Hétu, R. (1991). Development of a rehabilitation program for people affected with occupational hearing loss. *Audiology, 30*, 317–329.

Gfeller, K. (2009). *What the experts say*. Centennial, CO: Cochlear Americas. Retrieved March 27, 2013 from http://www.cochlear.com/files/assets/music_tips_enjoy_exp.pdf

Gfeller, K., Jiang, D., Oleson, J., Driscoll, V., Olszewski, C., Knutson, J. et al. (2012). The effects of musical and linguistic components in recognition of real-world musical excerpts by cochlear implant recipients and normal-hearing adults. *Journal of Music Therapy, 49*, 68–101.

Gfeller, K., Mehr, M. A., & Witt, S. (2001). Aural rehabilitation of music perception and enjoyment of adult cochlear implant users. *Journal of the Academy of Aural Rehabilitation, 34*, 17–27.

Gfeller, K., Oleson, J., Knutson, J., Breheny, P., Driscoll, V., & Olszewski, C. (2008). Multivariate predictors of music perception and appraisal by adult cochlear implant users. *Journal of the American Academy of Audiology, 19*, 120–134.

Gfeller, K., Turner, C., Mehr, M., Woodworth, G., Fearn, R., & Knutson, J. (2002). Recognition of familiar melodies by adult cochlear implant recipients and normal-hearing adults. *Cochlear Implants International, 3*, 29–53.

Gfeller, K., Witt, S., Stordahl, J., Mehr, M., & Woodworth, G. (2000). The effects of training on melody recognition and appraisal by adult cochlear implant recipients. *Journal of the Academy of Rehabilitative Audiology, 33*, 115–138.

Gil, D., & Lorio, M. (2010). Formal auditory training in adult hearing aid users. *Clinics (Sao Paulo), 65*, 165–174.

Gilani, S., Roditi, R., & Bhattacharyya, N. (2016). Grade repetition and parents' perception of hearing loss: An analysis of data from children in the United States. *The Laryngoscope*, https://doi.org/10.1002/lary.26131

Gillam, R. B., & Pearson, N. A. (2017). *Test of narrative language (TNL)*. Austin, TX: Pro-Ed.

Gilliam, J. A., & Miller, L. (2006). *Pragmatic language skills inventory (PLSI)*. Austin, TX: Pro-Ed.

Gitles, T. (1999). Re-inventing the profession: The relationship model of hearing care. *The Hearing Journal, 52*, 53–56.

Golding-Meadow, S., & Mayberry, R. I. (2001). How do profoundly deaf children learn to read? *Learning Disabilities Research and Practice, 16*, 222–229.

Goldman, R., & Fristoe, M. (2000). *Goldman-Fristoe test of articulation* (2nd ed.). Circle Pines, MN: American Guidance Service.

Golz, A., Netzer, A., & Westerman, S. T. (2005). Reading performance in children with otitis media. *Otolaryngology Head & Neck Surgery, 132*, 495–499.

Gorga, M. P., Preissler, K., Simmons, J., Walker, L., & Hoover, B. (2001). Some issues relevant to establishing a universal newborn hearing screening program. *Journal of the American Academy of Audiology, 12,* 101–112.

Grandpierre, V., Fitzpatrick, E.M., Na, E., & Mendonca, O. (2018). School-aged children with mild bilateral and unilateral hearing loss: Parents' reflections on services, experiences and outcomes. *Journal of Deaf Studies and Deaf Education, 23,* 140–147.

Grant, K. W., Bernstein, J. G. W., & Summers, V. (2013). Predicting speech intelligibility by individual hearing-impaired listeners: The path forward. *Journal of the American Academy of Audiology, 24,* 329–336.

Grant, K. W., & Seitz, P. F. (2000). The recognition of isolated words and words in sentences: Individual variability in the use of sentence context. *Journal of the Acoustical Society of America, 107,* 1000–1011.

Grant, K. W., Walden, B. E., & Seitz, P. F. (1998). Auditory-visual speech recognition by hearing-impaired subjects: Consonant recognition, sentence recognition, and auditory-visual integration. *Journal of the Acoustical Society of America, 103,* 2677–2690.

Greenburg, J. H., & Jenkins, J. J. (1964). Studies in the psychological correlates of the sound system of American English. *Word, 20,* 157–177.

Gregory, M. (2011). Self-efficacy and successful hearing rehabilitation. *Hearing Review, 18,* 28–32.

Gregory, M. (2012). A possible patient journey: A tool to facilitate patient-centered care. *Seminars in Hearing, 33,* 9–15.

Grice, H. P. (1975). Logic and conversation. In P. Cole & J. Morgan (Eds.), *Syntax and semantics 3: Speech acts* (pp. 41–58). New York, NY: Academic Press.

Gussenhoven, A. H. M., Jansma, E. P., Goverts, T., Festen, J. M., Anema, J. R., & Kramer, S. E. (2013). Vocational rehabilitation services for people with hearing difficulties: A systematic review of the literature. *Work, 46,* 151–164.

Habib, M. G., Waltzman, S. B., Tajudeen, B., & Svirsky, M. A. (2010). Speech production intelligibility of early implanted pediatric cochlear implant users. *International Journal of Pediatric Otorhinolaryngology, 74,* 855–859.

Hager, R. M. (2007). Obtaining hearing aids for children. *Volta Voices, July/August,* 20–24.

Hale, S., & Myerson, J. (1996). Experimental evidence for differential slowing in the lexical and nonlexical domains. *Aging, Neuropsychology, and Cognition, 3,* 154–165.

Hall, J. W. (2018). Educating AuD students for the practice of evidence-based audiology. *Audiology Today, 30,* 85–87.

Hallam, R. S., & Corney, R. (2014). Conversation tactics in persons with normal hearing and hearing-impairment. *International Journal of Audiology, 53,* 174–181.

Hallberg, L. R. M. (1999). Hearing impairment, coping, and consequences on family life. *Journal of the Academy of Rehabilitative Audiology, 32,* 45–59.

Hammill, D. D., Brown, V. L., Larsen, S. C., & Wiederholt, J. L. (2007). *Test of adolescent and adult language* (4th ed.). Austin, TX: Pro-Ed.

Hampton, D. (2005). Desertion or retention? *Advance for Audiologists,* September/October, 59–79.

Hanin, L. (1988). *The effects of experience and linguistic context on speechreading.* Unpublished doctoral dissertation, City University Graduate School, New York, NY.

Harris, M., Terlektsi, E., & Kyle, F. E. (2017). Literacy outcomes for primary school children who are deaf and hard of hearing: A cohort comparison study. *Journal of Speech, Language, and Hearing Research, 60,* 701–711.

Hartley, D., Rochtchina, E., Newall, P., Golding, M., & Mitchell, P. (2010). Use of hearing aids and assistive listening devices in an older Australian population. *Journal of the American Academy of Audiology, 21,* 642–653.

Harvey, M. A. (2012). A narrative psychological framework for audiologic care. *Audiology Today,* November/December, 50–57.

Harvey, M. A. (2018). Paving the clinical road: Managing, utilizing patients' traumatic transference. *The Hearing Journal, 71,* 12–13.

Haskins, H. (1949). *A phonetically balanced test of speech discrimination for children.* Unpublished master's thesis, Northwestern University, Evanston, IL.

Hawkins, D. B. (2005). Effectiveness of a counseling-based adult group aural rehabilitation programs: A systematic review of the evidence. *Journal of the American Academy of Audiology, 16,* 485–493.

Haycock, G. S. (1933). *The teaching of speech.* Washington, DC: Alexander Graham Bell Association for the Deaf.

He, W., Sengupta, M., Velkoff, V. A., & DeBarros, K. A. (2005). *65+ in the United States: 2005.* Washington, DC: US Department of Health and Human Services.

Head, L. S., & Abbeduto, L. (2007). Recognizing the role of parents in developmental outcomes: A systems approach to evaluating the child with developmental disabilities. *Mental Retardation and Developmental Disabilities Research Reviews, 13,* 293–301.

Hear-It Organization (2012). *More and more hearing-impaired people. Hear-it.* Retrieved August 29, 2012 from http://www.hear-it.org/More-and-more-hearing-impaired-people

Helfer, K. S. (1997). Auditory and auditory-visual perception of clear and conversational speech. *Journal of Speech, Language, and Hearing Research, 40,* 432–443.

Henry, J. A., Dennis, K. C., & Schechter, M. A. (2005). General review of tinnitus: Prevalence, mechanisms, effects, and management. *Journal of Speech, Language, and Hearing Research, 48,* 1204–1235.

Henry, J. A., Zaugg, T. L., & Schechter, M. A. (2005). Clinical guide for audiologic tinnitus management I: Assessment. *American Journal of Audiology, 14,* 21–48.

Henshaw, H., & Ferguson, M. A. (2013). Efficacy of individual computer-based auditory training for people with hearing loss: A systematic review of the evidence. *PLos One 8*(5), e62836. doi:10.1371/journal.pone.0062836

Hernandez, D., & Amlani, A. M. (2004). Patient, client or consumer? *Audiology Today, 16,* 34–35.

Hester-Keels, B. (2017). Audiologists can assist families through their journey by giving them informational and emotional guidance necessary to feel confident in managing their child's condition. *Audiology Today, 29,* 27–33.

Hétu, R., & Getty, L. (1991). Development of a rehabilitation program for people affected with occupational hearing loss. 1. A new paradigm. *Audiology, 30,* 305–316.

Hétu, R., Reverin, L., Getty, L., Lalande, N. M., & St-Cyr, C. (1990). The reluctance to acknowledge hearing difficulties among hearing-impaired workers. *British Journal of Audiology, 24,* 265–276.

Heydebrand, G., Mauzé, E., Tye-Murray, N., Binzer, S., & Skinner, M. (2005). The efficacy of a structured group therapy intervention for adult cochlear implant recipients. *International Journal of Audiology, 44,* 272–280.

Hickson, L. (2012). *How can the uptake and outcomes of hearing rehabilitation be improved?* Paper presented at the Academy of Rehabilitative Audiology Conference, Providence, RI.

Hickson, L., & Scarinci, N. (2007). Older adults with acquired hearing impairment: Applying the ICF in rehabilitation. *Seminars in Speech and Language, 28,* 283–290.

Hickson, L. & Singh, G. (2018). Mythbusters' myth #3: Many patients do not want their family in the room. *Hearing Review, 25, 26.*

Hickson, L., & Worrall, L. (2003). Beyond hearing aid fitting: Improving communication for older adults. *International Journal of Audiology, 42*(Suppl. 2), 2S84–2S91.

Hickson, L., Worrall, L., & Scarinci, N. (2006a). *Active communication education (ACE): A program for older persons with hearing impairment.* Brackley, UK: Speechmark.

Hickson, L., Worrall, L., & Scarinci, N. (2006b). Measuring outcomes of a communication program for older people with hearing impairment using the International Outcome Inventory. *International Journal of Audiology, 45,* 238–246.

Hickson, L., Worrall, L., & Scarinci, N. (2007). A randomized controlled trial evaluating the active communication education program for older people with hearing impairment. *Ear and Hearing, 28,* 212–230.

Hines, J. (2000). Communication problems of hearing-impaired patients. *Nursing Standard, 14,* 33–37.

Hirsh, I. J., Davis, H., Silverman, S. R., Reynolds, E. G., Eldert, E., & Benson, R. W. (1952). Development of materials for speech audiometry. *Journal of Speech and Hearing Disorders, 17,* 321–337.

Hjaldahl, J., Widén, S., & Carlsson, P. I. (2017). Severe to profound hearing impairment: Factors associated with the use of hearing aids and cochlear implants and participation in extended audiological rehabilitation. *Hearing, Balance and Communication, 15,* 6–15.

Hoffman, M. F., Quittner, A. L., & Cejas, I. (2015). Comparisons of social competence in young children with and without hearing loss: A dynamic systems framework. *Journal of Deaf Studies and Deaf Education, 20,* 115–124.

Hogan, A. (2001). *Hearing rehabilitation for deafened adults: A psychosocial approach.* Philadelphia, PA: Whurr.

Horowitz, A., Teresi, J. A., & Cassels, L. A. (1991). Development of a vision screening questionnaire for older people. *Journal of Gerontological Social Work, 17,* 37–56.

Hosie, J. A., Russell, C. D., Gray, C., Scott, C., Hunter, N., Banks, J. S. et al. (2000). Knowledge of display rules in prelingually deaf and hearing children. *Journal of Child Psychology and Psychiatry, 41,* 389–398.

Hull, R. H. (2018). Aural rehabilitation: What's in a name? *The Hearing Journal, 71*, 40–43.

Humes, L. E. (1996). Speech understanding in the elderly. *Journal of the American Academy of Audiology, 7*, 161–167.

Humes, L. E. (2005). The contributions of audibility and cognitive factors to the benefit provided by amplified speech to older adults. *Journal of the American Academy of Audiology, 18*, 590–603.

Humes, L. E., Burk, M., Stauser, L., & Kinney, D. (2009). Development and efficacy of a frequent-word auditory training protocol for older adults with impaired hearing. *Ear and Hearing, 30*, 613–627.

Humes, L. E., Coughlin, M., & Talley, L. (1996). Evaluation of the use of a new compact disc for auditory perceptual assessment in the elderly. *Journal of the American Academy of Audiology, 7*, 419–427.

Humes, L. E., Kinney, D. L., Brown, S. E., Kiener, A. L., & Quigley, T. M. (2014). The effects of dosage and duration of auditory training for older adults with hearing impairment. *Journal of the Acoustical Society of America, 136*, EL224–EL230.

Hutchby, I., & Wooffitt, R. (2008). *Conversational analysis*. Cambridge, UK: Polity Press.

Hutton, C. L. (1980). Responses to a hearing problem inventory. *Journal of the Academy of Rehabilitative Audiology, 13*, 133–154.

Hyde, M. L., Punch, R., & Komesaroff, L. (2010). Coming to a decision about cochlear implantation: Parents making choices for their deaf children. *Journal of Deaf Studies and Deaf Education, 15*, 162–178.

Hyde, M. L., & Riko, K. (1994). A decision-analytic approach to audiological rehabilitation. *Journal of the Academy of Rehabilitative Audiology, 27*, 337–374.

Hygge, S., Rönnberg, J., Larsby, B., & Arlinger, S. (1992). Normal and hearing-impaired subjects' ability to just follow conversation in competing speech, reversed speech, and noise backgrounds. *Journal of Speech and Hearing Research, 35*, 208–215.

Ibertsson, T., Hansson, K., Mäki-Torkko, E., Willstedt-Svensson, U., & Sahlén, B. (2009). Deaf teenagers with cochlear implants in conversation with hearing peers. *International Journal of Language and Communication Disorders, 44*, 319–337.

Immersion Active (2017). 24 stats marketers need to know about baby boomers in 2017. Retrieved May 9, 2018 from https://www.immersionactive.com/resources/24-stats-marketers-need-to-know-about-baby-boomers-In-2017/

Individuals with Disabilities Education Act, Pub. L. No. 101-476 (1990).

Individuals with Disabilities Education Act Amendments, Pub. L. No. 105-17 (1997).

Individuals with Disabilities Education Act Amendments, Pub. L. No. 108-446 (2004).

Inscoe, J., Odell, A., Archbold, S., & Nikolopoulos, T. (2009). Expressive spoken language development in deaf children with cochlear implants who are beginning formal education. *Deafness and Education International, 11*, 39–55.

International Reading Association (1999). *Using multiple methods of beginning reading instruction: A position statement of the International Reading Association*. Newark, DE: International Reading Association.

Israelite, N., Ower, J., & Goldstein, G. (2002). Hard-of-hearing adolescents and identity construction: Influences of school experiences, peers, and teachers. *Journal of Deaf Studies and Deaf Education, 7*, 134–148.

Itoh, M., Horii, Y., Daniloff, R., & Binnie, C. (1982). Selected aerodynamic characteristics of deaf individuals' various speech and nonspeech tasks. *Folia Phoniatrica, 34*, 191–209.

Iwawaki, C. (2012). Nothing stops me. *Volta Voices*, March/April, 38–39.

Iwawaki, N., & Iwawaki, J. (2012). Our journey into deafness. *Volta Voices*, March/April, 36–37.

Jeanes, R. C., Nienhuys, T. G., & Rickards, F. W. (2000). The pragmatic skills of profoundly deaf children. *Journal of Deaf Studies and Deaf Education, 5*, 237–247.

Jeffers, J., & Barley, M. (1971). *Speechreading (lipreading)*. Springfield, IL: Thomas.

Jennings, M. B. (2005). *Factors that influence outcomes from aural rehabilitation of older adults: The role of perceived self-efficacy*. Unpublished dissertation, University of Ontario, Ontario, Canada.

Jennings, M. B., Cheesman, M. F., & Laplante-Lévesque, A. (2014). Psychometric properties of the self-efficacy for situational communication management questionnaire (SESMQ). *Ear and Hearing, 35*, 221–229.

Jennings, M. B., Southall, K., & Gagné, J. P. (2013). Social identity management strategies used by workers with acquired hearing loss. *Work, 46*, 169–180.

Jerger, J., Speaks, C., & Trammell, J. L. (1968). A new approach to speech audiometry. *Journal of Speech and Hearing Disorders, 33*, 318–329.

Jerger, S., Lewis, S., Hawkins, J., & Jerger, J. (1980). Pediatric speech intelligibility test. I. Generation of test materials. *International Journal of Pediatric Otorhinolaryngology, 2*, 217–230.

Jessen, D. (2018). Make auditory rehabilitation work in any practice. *The Hearing Journal, 71*, 12–14.

John Tracy Clinic (2012). *Parent distance education*. Retrieved March 23, 2013 from http://www.jtc.org/services/parent-distance-education

Johnson, C. D. (2011). PARC: Placement and readiness checklists for students who are deaf and hard of hearing. *Hands and Voices*. Retrieved February 11, 2013 from http://www.handsandvoices.org/pdf/PARC_2011.pdf

Johnson, C. E. (2000). Children's phoneme identification in reverberation and noise. *Journal of Speech, Language, and Hearing Research, 43*, 144–157.

Johnson, C. E., Jilla, A. M., & Danhauer, J. L. (2018). Developing foundational counseling skills for addressing adherence issues in auditory rehabilitation. *Seminars in Hearing 39*, 013–031.

Johnson, S. M., & Wilhite, G. (1971). Self-observation as an agent of behavioural change. *Behavior Therapy, 2*, 488–497.

Joint Committee on Infant Hearing (2007). Year 2007 position statement: Principles and guidelines for early hearing detection and intervention programs. *Pediatrics, 120*, 898–921.

Joint Committee on Infant Hearing (2013). Supplement to the JCIH 2007 position statement: Principles and guidelines for early intervention after confirmation that a child is deaf or hard of hearing. *Pediatrics, 131*, e1324–e1349.

Joosse, L. L. (2011). Sound levels in nursing homes. *Journal of Gerontological Nursing, 37*, 30–35.

Jordan, T. R., & Bevan, K. (1997). Seeing and hearing rotated faces: Influences of facial orientation on visual and audiovisual speech recognition. *Journal of Experimental Psychology: Human Perception and Performance, 23*, 288–403.

Kaiser, A. R., Kirk, K. I., Lachs, L., & Pisoni, D. B. (2003). Talker and lexical effects on audiovisual word recognition by adults with cochlear implants. *Journal of Speech, Language, and Hearing Research, 46*, 390–404.

Kane, S., & Kane, R. (2012). Hearing-impaired girl advocates law for deaf students. *The Hearing Journal*, November, 47–48.

Kantrowitz, B., & Springen, K. (2007, June 18). Confronting Alzheimer's. *Newsweek*, pp. 55–64.

Kaplan, H., Bally, S. J., & Garretson, C. (1985). *Speechreading: A way to improve understanding*. Washington, DC: Gallaudet University Press.

Kaufman, A., & Kaufman, N. (2004). *Kaufman assessment battery for children–II (K-ABC-II)*. Circle Pines, MN: American Guidance Service.

Keate, B. (2006). Diet and tinnitus. *Advance for Audiologists*, September/October, 55–58.

Keidser, G. (2012). Evidence-based practice and emerging new technologies. In L. Wong & L. Hickson (Eds.), *Evidence-based practice in audiology* (pp. 119–137). San Diego, CA: Plural Publishing.

Keogh, T., Kei, J., Driscoll, C., Cahill, L., Hoffmann, A., Wilce, E. et al. (2005). Measuring the ability of school children with a history of otitis media to understand everyday speech. *Journal of the American Academy of Audiology, 16*, 301–311.

Kessels, R. P. C. (2003). Patients' memory for medical information. *Journal of the Royal Society of Medicine, 96*, 219–222.

Killion, M. C., Niquette, P. A., Gudmundsen, G. I., Revit, L. J., & Banerjee, S. (2004). Development of a quick speech-in-noise test for measuring signal-to-noise ratio loss in normal-hearing and hearing-impaired listeners. *Journal of the Acoustical Society of America, 116*, 2395–2405.

Killion, M. C., & Villchur, E. (1993). Kessler was right—partly: But SIN test shows some aids improve hearing in noise. *The Hearing Journal, 46*, 31–35.

Kirk, K. I. (1998). Assessing speech perception in listeners with cochlear implants: The development of the lexical neighborhood tests. *Volta Review, 100*, 63–86.

Kirk, K. I., Miyamoto, R. T., Ying, E. A., Perdew, A. E., & Zuganelis, H. (2000). Cochlear implantation in young children: Effects of age at implantation and communication mode. *Volta Review, 102*, 127–144.

Kirk, K. I., Pisoni, D. B., & Lachs, L. (2002). Audiovisual integration of speech by children and adults with cochlear implants. In *Proceedings: ICSLP. International Conference on Spoken Language Processing* (Vol. 2002, p. 1689). NIH Public Access.

Kluwin, T. N. (1999). Co-teaching deaf and hearing students: Research on social integration. *American Annals of the Deaf, 144*, 339–344.

Knoors, H., & Marschark, M. (2012). Language planning for the 21st century: Revisiting bilingual language policy for deaf children. *Journal of Deaf Studies and Deaf Education, 17*, 291–305.

Kochkin, S. (2005). Customer satisfaction with hearing instruments in digital age. *The Hearing Journal, 58*, 30–43.

Kochkin, S. (2007). MarkeTrak VII: Obstacles to adult non-user adoption of hearing aids. *The Hearing Journal, 60*, 24–51.

Kochkin, S. (2012). MarkeTrak VIII: The key influencing factors in hearing aid purchase intent. *Hearing Review, 19*, 12–25.

Kochkin, S., & Tyler, R. (2008). Tinnitus treatment and the effectiveness of hearing aids-hearing care professional perceptions. *Hearing Review, 15*, 14–18.

Korver, A. M., Smith, R. J., Van Camp, G., Schleiss, M. R., Bitner-Glindzicz, M. A., Lustig, L. R. et al. (2017). Congenital hearing loss. *Nature Reviews Disease Primers, 3*, 16094.

Kozak, V. J., & Brooks, B. M. (2001). *Baby talk: Helping your hearing-impaired baby listen and talk*. St. Louis, MO: Central Institute for the Deaf.

Kramer, S. E. (2008). Hearing impairment, work, and vocational enablement. *International Journal of Audiology, 47*, S124–S130.

Kramer, S. E., Allessie, H. M., Dondorp, A. W., Zekveld, A. A., & Kapteyn, T. S. (2005). A home education program for older adults with hearing impairment and their significant others: A randomized clinical trial evaluating short- and long-term effects. *International Journal of Audiology, 44*, 255–264.

Krashen, S. D. (1985). *Inquiries & insights: second language teaching: Immersion & bilingual education, literacy*. Hayward, CA: Alemany Press.

Kraus, N., & White-Schwoch, T. (2017). Neurobiology of everyday communication: What we have learned from music? *The Nueroscientist, 23*, 287–298.

Kricos, P. B. (2006). Audiologic management of older adults with hearing loss and compromised cognitive/psychoacoustic auditory processing capabilities. *Trends in Amplification, 10*, 1–28.

K's Blog (2011). Deaf technology—Real time texting for deaf people and new phone apps. *My Space*. Retrieved November 5, 2012 from http://us.myspace.com/557931525/blog/542466290

Kubler-Ross, E. (1969). *On death and dying*. New York, NY: Macmillan.

Kuhl, P. K., & Meltzoff, A. N. (1982). The bimodal perception of speech in infancy. *Science, 218*, 1138–1141.

Lacerda, C. F., Silva, L. O., Canto, R. S. D. T., & Cheik, N. C. (2012). Effects of hearing aids in the balance, quality of life and fear to fall in elderly people with sensorineural hearing loss. *International Archives of Otorhinolaryngology, 16*, 156–162.

Lam-Cassettari, C., Wadnerkar-Kamble, M. B., & James, D. M. (2015). Enhancing parent–child communication and parental self-esteem with a video-feedback intervention: Outcomes with prelingual deaf and hard-of-hearing children. *Journal of Deaf Studies and Deaf Education, 20*, 266–274.

Lansing, C. R., & McConkie, G. W. (1999). Attention to facial regions in segmental and prosodic visual speech perception tasks. *Journal of Speech, Language, and Hearing Research, 42*, 526–539.

Laplante- Lévesque, A., Hickson, L., & Worrall, L. (2010a). A qualitative study of shared decision making in rehabilitative audiology. *Journal of the Academy of Rehabilitative Audiology, 43*, 27–43.

Laplante- Lévesque, A., Hickson, L., & Worrall, L. (2010b). Factors influencing rehabilitation decisions of adults with acquired hearing impairment. *International Journal of Audiology, 49*, 497–507.

Laplante-Lévesque, A., Hickson, L., & Worrall, L. (2012). Stages of change in adults with acquired hearing impairment seeking help for first time: Application of the transtheoretical model in audiologic rehabilitation. *Ear and Hearing, 34*, 447–457.

Lartz, M., & Meehan, T. (2009). Preparing professionals to foster social-emotional development within the family context. *Volta Voices*, July/August, 26–29.

Laugen, N. J., Jacobsen, K. H., Rieffe, C., & Wichstrøm, L. (2016). Predictors of psychosocial outcomes in hard-of-hearing preschool children. *Journal of Deaf Studies and Deaf Education, 21*, 259–267.

Laugen, N. J., Jacobsen, K. H., Rieffe, C., & Wichstrøm, L. (2017). Social skills in preschool children with unilateral and mild bilateral hearing loss. *Deafness & Education International, 19*, 54–62.

Lawson, J. (2009). Federal laws governing education for exceptional students. *Livestrong Foundation*. Retrieved March 22, 2013 from http://www.livestrong.com/article/14755-federal-laws-governing-education-for-exceptional-students/

Lederberg, A. R., & Everhart, V. S. (2000). Conversation between deaf children and their hearing mothers: Pragmatic and dialogic characteristics. *Journal of Deaf Studies and Deaf Education, 5*, 303–322.

Lee, C. Y., Harrison, M., & Wiener, S. (2017). The role of familiarity in audiovisual speech perception. *Journal of the Acoustical Society of America, 142*, 2705.

Lenden, J. M., & Flipsen, P. (2007). Prosody and voice characteristics of children with cochlear implants. *Journal of Communication Disorders, 40*, 66–81.

Lesner, S., Sandridge, S., & Kricos, P. (1987). Training influences on visual consonant and sentence recognition. *Ear and Hearing, 8*, 283–287.

Leung, J., Wang, N., Yeagle, J., Chinnici, J., Bowditch, S., Francis, H. et al. (2005). Predictive models for cochlear implantation in elderly candidates. *Archives of Otolaryngology—Head & Neck Surgery, 131*, 1049–1054.

Levitt, H. (1987). *Fundamental speech skills test*. New York, NY: City University of New York.

Lewis, C. S. (1976). *A grief observed*. New York, NY: Harper Collins.

Lewis, D. E., Valente, D. L., & Spalding, J. L. (2015). Effect of minimal/mild hearing loss on children's speech understanding in a simulated classroom. *Ear and Hearing, 36, 136.*

Lichtman, W. (2005, May). Seeing kids clearly. *Good Housekeeping*, 120.

Lieu, J. E., Tye-Murray, N., Karzon, R. K., & Piccirillo, J. (2010). Unilateral hearing loss is associated with worse speech-language scores in children. *Pediatrics, 125*, e1348–e1355.

Lin, F. R., & Ferrucci, L. (2012). Hearing loss and falls among older adults in the United States. *Archives of Internal Medicine, 172*, 369–371.

Lin, F. R., Metter, E. J., O'Brien, R., Resnick, S., Zonderman, A., & Ferrucci, L. (2011). Hearing loss and incident dementia. *Archives of Neurology, 68*, 214–220.

Lin, F. R., Yaffe, K., Xia, J., Xue, Q. L., Harris, T. B., Purchase-Helzner, E. et al. (2013). Hearing loss and cognitive decline in older adults. *JAMA Internal Medicine, 173*, 293–299.

Lind, C. (2009a). Conversation repair strategies in audiologic rehabilitation. In J. J. Montano & J. B. Spitzer (Eds.), *Adult audiologic rehabilitation: Advance practice* (pp. 217–239). San Diego, CA: Plural Publishing.

Lind, C. (2009b). Conversation therapy: Interaction as intervention. *Phonak Pro*. Retrieved December 10, 2012 from http://www.phonakpro.com/content/dam/phonak/b2b/Events/conference_proceedings/chicago_2009/proceedings/18_P69344_Pho_Kapitel_9_S103_110.pdf

Lind, C., Campbell, K., Davey, A., Rodgers, L., Seipolt, C., & Akins, C. (2010). Some prosodic characteristics of repeated talk following conversation repair requests by adults with hearing impairment. *Seminars in Hearing, 31*, 127–139.

Lind, C., Hickson, L., & Erber, N. P. (2006). Conversation repair and adult cochlear implantation: A qualitative case study. *Cochlear Implants International, 7*, 33–48.

Ling, D. (1976). *Speech and the hearing-impaired child: Theory and practice*. Washington, DC: Alexander Graham Bell Association for the Deaf.

Ling, D. (1989). *Foundations of spoken language for hearing impaired children*. Washington, DC: Alexander Graham Bell Association for the Deaf.

Liquid Lock Media (2017). Outstanding statistics on baby boomers and social media. Retrieved May 9, 2018 from https://medium.com/@LiquidLockMedia/12-outstanding-statistics-on-baby-boomers-and-social-media-2be6c49b5b91

LitConn, Inc. (2000). *Reading and oral language assessment (ROLA)*. Fresno, CA: LitConn, Inc.

Litovsky, R. (2003). *Method and system for rapid and reliable testing of speech intelligibility in children*. US patent allowed in March 2003.

Liwo, H. (2011). Cochlear implant as an important factor of the development of prosodic features in prelingually deaf children under 2 years of age. *Journal of Hearing Science, 1*, 73–75.

Lockey, K., Jennings, M. B., & Shaw, L. (2010). Exploring hearing aid use in older women through narratives. *International Journal of Audiology, 49*, 542–549.

Logan, L. (2013). Using creativity and arts for language development. *Volta Voices*, November/December, 42–43.

Looi, V., King, J., & Kelly-Campbell, R. (2012). A music appreciation training program developed for clinical application with cochlear implant recipients and hearing aid users. *Seminars in Hearing, 33*, 361–380.

Lopacinski, R. (2013). Discovering new sounds. *Volta Voices*, January/February, 30–31.

Luce, P. A. (1986). A computational analysis of uniqueness points in auditory word recognition. *Perception and Psychophysics, 39*, 155–159.

Luce, P. A., & Pisoni, D. B. (1998). Recognizing spoken words: The neighborhood activation model. *Ear and Hearing, 19*, 1–36.

Luterman, D. (2004). Counseling families of children with hearing loss and special needs. *Volta Review, 104*, 215–220.

Luxford, W. M., & Brackmann, D. E. (1985). The history of cochlear implants. In R. F. Gray (Ed.), *Cochlear implants* (pp. 1–26). San Diego, CA: College-Hill Press.

Lyman, R. (2006, March 10). Census report foresees no crisis over aging generation's health. *New York Times, 1*, 17.

Lyxell, B. (1994). Skilled speechreading: A single-case study. *Scandinavian Journal of Audiology, 35*, 212–219.

Lyxell, B., & Rönnberg, J. (1987). Guessing and speechreading. *British Journal of Audiology, 21*, 13–20.

Macherey, O., & Delpierre, A. (2013). Perception of musical timbre by cochlear implant listeners: A multidimensional scaling study. *Ear and Hearing, 34*, 426–436.

MacLeod, A., & Summerfield, Q. (1987). Quantifying the contribution of vision to speech perception in noise. *British Journal of Audiology, 21*, 131–141.

Mahboubi, H., Lin, H. W., & Bhattacharyya, N. (2018). Prevalence, characteristics, and treatment patterns of hearing difficulty in the United States. *JAMA Otolaryngology–Head & Neck Surgery, 144*, 65–70.

Mak, M., Grayden, D., Dowell, R. C., & Lawrence, D. (2006). Speech perception for adults who use hearing aids in conjunction with cochlear implants in opposite ears. *Journal of Speech, Language, and Hearing Research, 49*, 338–351.

Margolis, R. H. (2004a). Audiology information counseling: What do patients remember? *Audiology Today*, March/April, 14–15.

Margolis, R. H. (2004b). Boosting memory with informational counseling: Helping patients understand the nature of disorders and how to manage them. *The ASHA Leader, 9*, 10–28.

Margolis, R. H., & Morgan, D. E. (2008). Automated puretone audiometry: An analysis of capacity, need, and benefit. *American Journal of Audiology, 17*, 109–113.

Markides, A. (1970). The speech of deaf and partially hearing children with special reference to factors affecting intelligibility. *British Journal of Disordered Communication, 5*, 126–140.

Marrone, N., & Harris, F. (2012). A multifaceted living well approach to the management of hearing loss with adults and their frequent communication partners. *Perspectives on Aural Rehabilitation and Its Instrumentation, 19*, 5–14.

Marschark, M., Rhoten, C., & Fabich, M. (2007). Effects of cochlear implants on children's reading and academic achievement. *Journal of Deaf Studies and Deaf Education, 12*, 269–282.

Marschark, M., Young, A., & Lukomski, J. (2002). Perspectives in inclusion. *Journal of Deaf Studies and Deaf Education, 7*, 187–188.

Martin, F. N., & Clark, J. G. (2006). *Introduction to audiology* (9th ed.). Boston, MA: Allyn & Bacon.

Martin, K., & Elder, S. (1993). Pathways through grief: A model of the process. In J. Morgan (Ed.), *Personal care in an impersonal world* (pp. 73–86). Amityville, NY: Baywood Publishing Company.

Martin, K., & Ritter, K. (2011). Navigating the emotional impact of diagnosis. *Volta Voices*, May/June, 14–16.

Martin, M. (2007). Software-based auditory training program found to reduce hearing aid return. *The Hearing Journal, 60*, 32–35.

Martin, N., & Brownell, R. (2011). *Receptive one-word picture vocabulary test*. Austin, TX: Pro-Ed.

Massaro, D. (1998). *Perceiving talking faces: From speech perception to a behavioral principle*. Cambridge, MA: MIT Press.

Mathews, J. (2010). 99-year-old SMG patient receives cochlear implant. *Summit Medical Group*. Retrieved January 10, 2013 from http://www.summitmedicalgroup.com/article/99-year-old-SMG-Patient-Receives-Cochlear-Implant/

Mayer, C., & Trezek, B. J. (2018). Literacy outcomes in deaf students with cochlear implants: Current state of the knowledge. *Journal of Deaf Studies and Deaf Education, 23*, 1–16.

McCormack, A., & Fortnum, H. (2013). Why do people fitted with hearing aids not wear them? *International Journal of Audiology, 52*, 360–368.

McCoy, S., Tun, P., Cox, L., Colangelo, M., Stewart, R., & Wingfield, A. (2005). Hearing loss and perceptual effort: Downstream effects on older adults' memory for speech. *Quarterly Journal of Experimental Psychology, 58A*, 22–33.

McCracken, W., Young, A., & Tattersall, H. (2008). Universal newborn hearing screening: Parental reflections on very early audiological management. *Ear and Hearing, 29*, 54–64.

McCreery, R. W., Bentler, R. A., & Roush, P. A. (2013). Characteristics of hearing aid fittings in infants and young children. *Ear and Hearing, 34*, 701–701.

McCullough, J. A., & Wilson, R. H. (2001). Performance on a Spanish picture-identification task using a multimedia format. *Journal of the American Academy of Audiology, 12*, 254–260.

McCullough, J. A., Wilson, R. H., Birck, J. D., & Anderson, L. G. (1995). A multimedia approach for estimating speech recognition of multilingual clients. *American Journal of Audiology, 3*, 19–22.

McDaniel, J., Camarata, S., & Yoder, P. (2018). Comparing auditory-only and audiovisual word learning for children with hearing loss. *Journal of Deaf Studies and Deaf Education,* Retrieved May 29, 2018 from https://doi.org/10.1093/deafed/eny016

McDaniel, D. M., Motts, S. D., & Neeley, R. A. (2018). Hearing aids and balance improvement. *The Hearing Journal, 71*, 6.

McFall, R. M. (1970). Effects of self-monitoring on normal smoking behavior. *Journal of Consulting and Clinical Psychology, 35*, 135–142.

McGarr, N., & Osberger, M. J. (1978). Pitch deviancy and intelligibility of deaf speech. *Journal of Communication Disorders, 11*, 237–247.

McGrath, A. P., & Vohr, B. R. (2017). Ear care for the most vulnerable infants: Hearing screening and intervention prove particularly challenging with NICU babies. Extra vigilance and parent support are required. *The ASHA Leader, 22*, 20–22.

McGurk, H., & MacDonald, J. (1976). Hearing lips and seeing voices. *Nature, 264*, 746–748.

McKenna, L., Marks, E. M., & Vogt, F. (2018). Mindfulness-based cognitive therapy for chronic tinnitus: Evaluation of benefits in a large sample of patients attending a tinnitus clinic. *Ear and Hearing, 39*, 359–366.

Meadow, K. P. (1983). An instrument for assessment of social-emotional adjustment in hearing-impaired preschoolers. *American Annals of the Deaf, 128*, 826–834.

Mellon, N. (2005). The River School: Educating children with hearing loss in an inclusion model. *The ASHA Leader, 10*, 6–24.

Mendel, L. (2011). *Subjective and objective evaluation of hearing aid outcomes.* Paper presented at the ASHA Audiology 2011 Online Conference.

Mendel, L., & Danhauer, J. (1997). *Audiologic evaluation and management and speech perception assessment.* San Diego, CA: Singular Publishing Group.

Miller, D. A., & Fredrickson, J. M. (2000). Implantable hearing aids. In M. Valente, H. Hosford-Dunn, & R. J. Roeser (Eds.), *Audiology treatment* (pp. 489–510). New York, NY: Thieme.

Miller, G. A., & Nicely, P. E. (1955). An analysis of perceptual confusions among some English consonants. *Journal of the Acoustical Society of America, 27*, 338–352.

Miller, J. L., Grosjean, F., & Lomanto, C. (1984). Articulation rate and its variability in spontaneous speech: A reanalysis and some implications. *Phonetica, 41*, 215–225.

Mills, J. H., Schmiedt, R. A., & Dubno, J. R. (2006). Older and wiser, but losing hearing nonetheless. *Hearing Health,* Summer, 12–19.

Minnesota Department of Education (2012). Minnesota social skills checklist for students who are deaf/hard of hearing. *Success for Kids with Hearing Loss.* Retrieved February 6, 2013 from https://successforkidswithhearingloss.com/wp-content/uploads/2011/08/Minnesota-Social-Skills-Checklist-for-Students-who-are-Deaf-Hard-of-Hearing-Chap-3.pdf

Miyamoto, R. T., Colson, B., Henning, S., & Pisoni, D. (2017). Cochlear implantation in infants below 12 months of age. *World Journal of Otorhinolaryngology–Head and Neck Surgery, 3*, 214–218.

Miyamoto, R., Kirk, K. I., Svirsky, M. A., & Sehgal, S. T. (1999). Communication skills of pediatric cochlear implant recipients. *Acta Otolaryngologica, 119*, 219–224.

Mize, J., & Wigley, H. (2002). *Hearing the truth about pediatric audiology.* Paper presented at the American Speech-Language-Hearing Association Convention, Atlanta, GA.

Mohan, A. (2012). Being deaf in the mainstream. *Volta Voices*, September/October, 34–35.

Monsen, R. (1981). A usable test for the speech intelligibility of deaf talkers. *American Annals of the Deaf, 126*, 845–852.

Montgomery, A. A. (1994). WATCH: A practical approach to brief auditory rehabilitation. *The Hearing Journal, 10*, 10–55.

Monzani, D., Galeazzi, G., Genovese, E., Marrara, A., & Martini, A. (2008). Psychological profile and social behavior of working adults with mild or moderate hearing loss. *Acta Otriholaryngoloy Italica, 28*, 61–66.

Moog, J. (1988). *The CID phonetic inventory*. St. Louis, MO: Central Institute for the Deaf.

Moog, J., & Geers, A. E. (1990). *Early speech perception test (standard version; Low verbal version)*. St. Louis, MO: Central Institute for the Deaf.

Moore, D. R., Rosenberg, J. F., & Coleman, J. S. (2005). Discrimination training of phonemic contrasts enhances phonological processing in mainstream school children. *Brain and Language, 94*, 72–85.

Most, T., Shina-August, E., & Meilijson, S. (2010). Pragmatic abilities of children with hearing loss using cochlear implants or hearing aids compared to hearing children. *Journal of Deaf Studies and Deaf Education, 15*, 422–437.

Mueller, H. G. (2010). Brain plasticity: There's more to hearing than you think. *Hearing Journal, 63*, 10–16.

Mueller, H. G., & Palmer, C. V. (1998). The profile of aided loudness: A new "PAL" for 98. *The Hearing Journal, 51*, 10–19.

Muller, J., Brill, S., Hagen, R., Moeltner, A., Brockmeier, S., Stark, T. et al. (2012). Clinical trial results with the MED-EL fine structure processing coding strategy in experienced cochlear implant users. *Journal of Oto-Rhino-Larngology, Head and Neck Surgery, 74*, 185–198.

Muñoz, K., Roberts, M., Mullings, D., & Howard, R. (2012). Parent hearing aid experiences. *Volta Review, 112*, 63–76.

Myerson, J., Spehar, B., Tye-Murray, N., Van Engen, K., Hale, S., & Sommers, M. S. (2016). Cross-modal informational masking of lipreading by babble. *Attention, Perception, & Psychophysics, 78*, 346–354.

Nachtegaal, J., Smit, J., Smits, C., Bezemer, P., van Beek, J., Festen, J. et al. (2009). The association between hearing status and psychosocial health before the age of 70 years: Results from an internet-based national survey on hearing. *Ear and Hearing, 30*, 302–312.

Nakata, T., Trehub, S. E., & Kanda, Y. (2012). Effect of cochlear implants on children's perception and production of speech prosody. *Journal of the Acoustical Society of America, 131*, 1307–1314.

Nash, S. D., Cruickshanks, K. J., Klein, R., Klein, B. E., Nieto, F. J., Huang, G. H., . . . Tweed, T. S. (2011). The prevalence of hearing impairment and associated risk factors: The Beaver Dam Offspring Study. *Archives of Otolaryngology–Head & Neck Surgery, 137*, 432–439.

National Center for Education Statistics (2011). *Digest of education statistics, 2010*. NCES Report No. 2011–2015.

National Center for Health Statistics (2002). *Chartbook on trends in the health of Americans from health United States, 2002* (Centers for Disease Control and Prevention/National Center for Health Statistics, Vital Health Statistics, Series 10, No. 209). Washington, DC: U.S. Government Printing Office.

National Council for Special Education (2006). *Guidelines on the individual education plan process*. Dublin, Ireland: Stationery Office.

National Council on Aging (1999). *The consequences of untreated hearing loss in older persons*. Washington, DC: National Council on Aging.

National Deaf Children's Society (NDCS) (1994). *Quality standards in paediatric audiology.: Guidelines for the early identification of hearing impairment* (Vol. I). London, UK: National Deaf Children's Society.

National Eye Institute (2000). Visual functioning questionnaire-25 (VFQ-25). *National Eye Institute*. Retrieved July 6, 2007 from http://www.nei.nih.gov/resources/vision function/vfq_ia.pdf

National Institute on Deafness and Other Communication Disorders (2013). Auditory Neuropathy. Retrieved June 1, 2013 from http://www.nidcd.nih.gov/health/hearing/Pages /neuropathy.aspx

National Institutes of Health (1993). *NIH consensus statement: Early identification of hearing impairment in infants and young children*. Washington, DC: NIH.

Nelson, H., Bougatsos, B., & Nygren, P. (2008). Universal newborn hearing screening: Systematic review to update the 2001 US Preventive Services Task Force recommendation. *Pediatrics, 122*, 266–276.

Newby, H. A., & Popelka, G. R. (1992). *Audiology* (6th ed.). Englewood Cliffs, NJ: Prentice Hall.

Newcomer, P. L., & Hammill, D. D. (2008). *Test of language development—primary and intermediate* (4th ed.). Austin, TX: Pro-Ed.

Nicholas, J. G. (2000). Age differences in the use of informative/heuristic communicative functions in young children with and without hearing loss who are learning spoken language. *Journal of Speech, Language, and Hearing Research, 43*, 380–394.

Nicholas, J. G., & Geers, A. E. (2006). Effects of early auditory experience on the spoken language of deaf children at 3 years of age. *Ear and Hearing, 27*, 286–298.

Niclasen, J., & Dammeyer, J. (2016). Psychometric properties of the strengths and difficulties questionnaire and mental health problems among children with hearing loss. *Journal of Deaf Studies and Deaf Education, 21*, 129–140.

NIDCD (National Institute on Deafness and Other Communication Disorders) (2017). *Quick statistics about hearing.* Retrieved July 10, 2018 from https://www.nidcd.nih.gov/health/statistics/quick-statistics-hearing

Nilsson, M., Soli, S. D., & Sullivan, J. A. (1994). Development of the hearing in noise test for the measurement of speech reception thresholds in quiet and in noise. *Journal of the Acoustical Society of America, 95*, 1085–1099.

Niparko, J. K., Tobey, E., Thal, D. J., Eisenberg, L., Wang, N., Quittner, A. et al. (2010). Spoken language development in children following cochlear implantation. *The Journal of the American Medical Association, 303*, 1498–1506.

Niskar, A. S., Kieszak, S. M., Holmes, A., Esteban, E., Rubin, C., & Brody, D. J. (1998). Prevalence of hearing loss among children 6 to 19 years of age. *Journal of the American Medical Association, 279*, 1071–1075.

Nitchie, E. (1912). *Lip-reading principles and practice.* New York, NY: Frederick A. Stokes Publisher.

Nitchie, E. (1930). *Lip-reading principles and practices (New Edition).* New York, NY: Frederick A. Stokes Publisher.

Noble, W. (2000). Self-reports about tinnitus and about cochlear implants. *Ear and Hearing, 21*, 50S–59S.

Noble, W. (2002). Extending the IOI to significant others and to non-hearing-aid-based interventions. *International Journal of Audiology, 41*, 27–29.

Noffsinger, D., Wilson, R. H., & Musiek, F. E. (1994). Department of Veterans Affairs Compact Disc (VA-CD) recording for auditory perceptual assessment: Background and introduction. *Journal of the American Academy of Audiology, 5*, 231–235.

Nondahl, D. M., Cruickshanks, K. J., Dalton, D. S., Klein, B., Klein, R., Schubert, C. R. et al. (2007). The impact of tinnitus on quality of life in older adults. *Journal of the American Academy of Audiology, 18*, 257–266.

Northern, J., & Beyer, C. M. (1999). Reducing hearing aid returns through patient education. *Audiology Today, 11*, 10–11.

O'Brien, E., Wu, K. B., & Baer, D. (2010). *Older Americans in poverty: A snapshot.* Washington, DC: AARP Public Policy Institute.

Ohna, S. E. (2003). Education of deaf children and the politics of recognition. *Journal of Deaf Studies and Deaf Education, 8*, 5–10.

Olson, A. (2010). *Auditory training at home for adult hearing aid users.* University of Kentucky Doctoral Dissertations, Paper 11.

Olson, A., Preminger, J. E., & Shinn, J. B. (2013). The effect of LACE DVD training in new and experienced hearing aid users. *Journal of the Academy of American Audiology, 24*, 214–230.

Osberger, M. J., Robbins, A. M., Todd, S. L., & Riley, A. I. (1994). Speech intelligibility in children with cochlear implants. *Volta Review, 96*, 169–180.

Ouni, S., Cohen, M., Ishak, H., & Massaro, D. (2007). Visual contribution to speech perception: Measuring the intelligibility of animated talking heads. *EURASIP Journal on Audiology, Speech, and Music Processing.* Article ID 47891.

Pallarito, K. (2012). Quality improvement efforts target gaps in newborn hearing screening programs. *The Hearing Journal, 65*, 18–22.

Palmer, C., Bentler, R., & Mueller, H. G. (2006). Evaluation of a second-order directional microphone hearing aid: II. Self-report outcomes. *Journal of the American Academy of Audiology, 27*, 190–201.

Palmer, C. V., & Mormer, E. (1999). Goals and expectations of the hearing aid fitting. *Trends in Amplification, 4*, 61–71.

Palmer, C. V., Mueller, H. G., & Moriarty, M. (1999). Profile of aided loudness: A validation procedure. *The Hearing Journal, 52*, 34–42.

Pelli, D., Robson, J., & Wilkins, A. (1998). The design of a new letter chart for measuring contrast sensitivity. *Clinical Vision Science, 2*, 187–199.

Peng, S., Tomblin, J. B., Spencer, L. J., & Hurtig, R. (2007). Imitative production of rising speech intonation in pediatric cochlear implant recipients. *Journal of Speech, Language, and Hearing Research, 50*, 1210–1227.

Peng, S., Tomblin, J. B., & Turner, C. W. (2008). Production and perception of speech intonation in pediatric cochlear implant recipients and individuals with normal hearing. *Ear and Hearing, 29*, 336–351.

Peterson, G. E., & Lehiste, I. (1962). Revised CNC lists for auditory tests. *Journal of Speech and Hearing Disorders, 27*, 62–70.

Picheny, M. A., Durlach, N., & Braida, L. D. (1985). Speaking clearly for the hard of hearing I: Intelligibility differences between clear and conversational speech. *Journal of Speech and Hearing Research, 28*, 96–103.

Picheny, M. A., Durlach, N., & Braida, L. D. (1986). Speaking clearly for the hard of hearing II: Acoustic characteristics of clear and conversational speech. *Journal of Speech and Hearing Research, 29*, 434–446.

Picheny, M. A., Durlach, N. I., & Braida, L. D. (1989). Speaking clearly for the hard of hearing III: An attempt to determine the contribution of speaking rate to differences in intelligibility between clear and conversational speech. *Journal of Speech, Language, and Hearing Research, 32*, 600–603.

Pichora-Fuller, M. K. (2016). How social psychological factors may modulate auditory cognitive functioning during listening. *Ear and Hearing,* 37, 92S-100S.

Pichora-Fuller, M. K., & Cicchelli, M. (1986). *Computer-aided speechreading training: Owner's manual (CAST).* Mississauga, Ontario: Department of Psychology, University of Toronto.

Pichora-Fuller, M. K., & Levitt, H. (2012). Speech comprehension training and auditory and cognitive processing in older adults. *American Journal of Audiology, 21*, 1–7.

Pichora-Fuller, M. K., & Souza, P. E. (2003). Effects of aging in auditory processing of speech. *International Journal of Audiology, 42*, 2S11–2S16.

Picou, E. M., & Ricketts, T. A. (2013). Efficacy of hearing-aid based telephone strategies for listeners with moderate-to-severe hearing loss. *Journal of the American Academy of Audiology, 24*, 59–70.

Pimperton, H., Ralph-Lewis, A., & MacSweeney, M. (2017). Speechreading in deaf adults with cochlear implants: Evidence for perceptual compensation. *Frontiers in Psychology, 8*, 106.

Piquado, T., Benichov, J., Brownell, H., & Wingfield, A. (2012). The hidden effect of hearing acuity on speech recall, and compensatory effects of self-paced listening. *International Journal of Audiology, 51*, 576–583.

Plant, G. (2009). Music and cochlear implants in audiologic rehabilitation. In J. J. Montano & J. B. Spitzer (Eds.), *Adult audiologic rehabilitation: Advance practice* (pp. 354–365). San Diego, CA: Plural Publishing.

Pollack, D. (1970). *Educational audiology for the limited hearing infant.* Springfield, IL: Thomas.

Preminger, J. E. (2003). Should significant others be encouraged to join adult group audiologic rehabilitation classes? *Journal of the American Academy of Audiology, 14*, 545–555.

Preminger, J. E. (2007). Issues associated with the measurement of psychosocial benefits of group audiologic rehabilitation programs. *Trends in Amplification, 11*, 113–123.

Preminger, J. E. (2011). Group audiologic rehabilitation for adults and their communication partners. *The ASHA Leader, 16*, 14–17.

Preminger, J.E. (2018). Building trust and improving outcomes with family-centered hearing care: What are strategies for better partnering with patients and their families in audiologic care? Jill Preminger shared some in a recent online chat. *The ASHA Leader, 23*, 28–28.

Preminger, J. E., & Meeks, S. (2012). The hearing impairment impact-significant other profile (HII-SOP): A tool to measure hearing loss-related quality of life in spouses of people with hearing loss. *Journal of the American Academy of Audiology, 23*, 807–823.

Preminger, J. E., Montano, J. J., & Tjørnhøj-Thomsen, T. (2015). Adult-children's perspectives on a parent's hearing impairment and its impact on their relationship and communication. *International Journal of Audiology, 54*, 720–726.

Preminger, J. E., & Yoo, J. (2010). Do group audiologic rehabilitation activities influence psychosocial outcomes? *American Journal of Audiology, 19*, 109–125.

Preminger, J. E., & Ziegler, C. (2008). Can auditory and visual speech perception be trained within a group setting? *American Journal of Audiology, 17*, 80–97.

Primeau, R. L. (1997). Hearing aid benefit in adults and older adults. *Seminars in Hearing, 18*, 29–36.

Rabinsky, R. (2013). Itinerant deaf education and general educator perceptions of the D/HH push-in model. *American Annals of the Deaf, 158*, 50–62.

Rall, E., & Montoya, L. A. (2005). *Pediatric audiology counseling guidelines: Birth-adolescence [Handout]*. Philadelphia, PA: Children's Hospital of Philadelphia.

Rance, G., & Dowell, R. (1997). Speech processor programming. In G. M. Clark, R. S. C. Cowan, & R. Dowell (Eds.), *Cochlear implantation for infants and children: Advances* (pp. 147–170). San Diego, CA: Singular Publishing Group.

Ratner, N. B. (2006). Evidence-based practice: An examination of its ramifications for the practice of speech-language pathology. *Language, Speech, and Hearing Services in Schools, 37*, 257–267.

Raver, S. A., Bobzien, J., Richels, C., Hester, P., Michalek, A., & Anthony, N. (2012). Effect of parallel talk on the language and interactional skills of preschoolers with cochlear implants and hearing aids. *Literacy Information and Computer Education Journal, 3*, 530–538.

Reed-Martinez, E. (2013). Helping you navigate IDEA Part C. *Volta Voices*, January/February, 24–25.

Reese, J. L., & Hnath-Chisolm, T. (2005). Recognition of hearing aid orientation content by first-time users. *American Journal of Audiology, 14*, 94–104.

Reid, K., Hresko, W., Hammill, D., & Wiltshire, S. (2018). *Test of early reading ability—Deaf and hard of hearing (TERA-D/HH)*. Austin, TX: Pro-Ed.

Reisberg, D., McLean, J., & Goldfield, A. (1987). Easy to hear but hard to understand: A speechreading advantage with intact stimuli. In R. Campbell & B. Dodd (Eds.), *Hearing by eye: The psychology of lip-reading* (pp. 97–113). London, UK: Erlbaum.

Reynell, J. K., & Gruber, C. P. (1990). *Reynell development language scale*. Los Angeles, CA: Western Psychological Services.

Rhoades, E. A. (2013). Interactive silences: Evidence for strategies to facilitate spoken language in children with hearing loss. *Volta Review, 113*, 57–73.

Rhoades, E. A., Estabrooks, W., Lim, S. R., MacIver-Lux, K., & MacIver, K. (2016). Strategies for listening, talking, and thinking in auditory-verbal therapy. *Auditory-verbal Therapy*, 285–326.

Ridgway, J., Hickson, L., & Lind, C. (2017). What factors are associated with autonomous and controlled motivation for hearing help-seekers? *Journal of the American Academy of Audiology, 28*, 644–654.

Rishiq, D., Rao, A., Koerner, T., & Abrams, H. (2016). Can a commercially available auditory training program improve audiovisual speech performance? *American Journal of Audiology, 25*, 308–312.

Robb, M., & Pang-Ching, G. (1992). Relative timing characteristics of hearing-impaired speakers. *Journal of the Acoustical Society of America, 91*, 2954–2960.

Robbins, A. M., & Osberger, M. J. (1994). *Meaningful use of speech scale (MUSS)*. Valencia, CA: Advanced Bionics.

Robbins, A. M., Renshaw, J. J., Miyamoto, R. T., Osberger, M. J., & Pope, M. L. (1988). *Minimal pairs test*. Indianapolis: Indiana University School of Medicine.

Rogers, C. R. (1980). *A way of being*. Boston, MA: Houghton Mifflin.

Rohlfs, A. K., Friedhoff, J., Bohnert, A., Breitfuss, A., Hess, M., Müller, F. et al. (2017). Unilateral hearing loss in children: A retrospective study and a review of the current literature. *European Journal of Pediatrics, 176*, 475–486.

Roman, A. M. (2018). It takes a village: Lessons in group aural rehabilitation therapy. *Audiology Today, 30*, 12–14.

Rönnberg, J. (1995). What makes a skilled speechreader? In G. Plant & K. Spens (Eds.), *Profound deafness and speech communication* (pp. 393–416). London, UK: Whurr.

Rönnberg, J. (1996). Speech gestures and facial expression in speechreading. *Scandinavian Journal of Psychology, 37*, 132–139.

Rönnberg, J., Andersson, J., Samuelsson, S., Söderfeldt, B., Lyxell, B., & Risberg, J. (1999). A speechreading expert: The case of MM. *Journal of Speech, Language, and Hearing Research, 42*, 5–20.

Rose, S., McAnally, P., & Quigley, S. (2004). *Language learning practices with deaf children (3rd ed.)*. Austin, TX: Pro-Ed.

Rosen, S. M., Fourcin, A. J., & Moore, B. C. J. (1981). Voice pitch as an aid to lipreading. *Nature, 291*, 150–152.

Ross, M., & Lerman, J. A. Y. (1970). A picture identification test for hearing-impaired children. *Journal of Speech, Language, and Hearing Research, 13*, 44–53.

Ross, M. (1990). Definitions and descriptions. In J. M. Davis (Ed.), *Our forgotten children: Hard of hearing pupils in the schools (pp. 2–10)*. Washington, DC: Self Help for Hard of Hearing People.

Ross, M., & Lerman, J. (1971). *Word intelligibility by picture identification*. Pittsburgh, PA: Stanwix House.

Rossi, K. (2003). *Learn to talk around the clock*. Washington, DC: Alexander Graham Bell Association for the Deaf and Hard of Hearing.

Rowden-Racette, K. (2012). Hitting her stride. *The ASHA Leader, 17*, 36.

Rubinstein, A., Cherry, R., Hecht, P., & Idler, C. (2000). Anticipatory strategy training: Implications for the postlingually hearing-impaired adult. *Journal of the American Academy of Audiology, 11*, 52–55.

Rugg, N., & Donne, V. (2011). Parent and teacher perceptions of transitioning students from an auditory-oral school to general education. *Volta Review, 111*, 325–351.

Rumalla, K., Karim, A. M., & Hullar, T. E. (2015). The effect of hearing aids on postural stability. *The Laryngoscope, 125*, 720–723.

Russell, K., Quigley, S., & Power, D. (1976). *Linguistics and deaf children: Transformational syntax and its applications*. Washington, DC: Alexander Graham Bell Association for the Deaf.

Samar, V. J., & Sims, D. G. (1983). Visual evoked response correlates of speechreading performance in normal-hearing adults: A replication and factor analytic extension. *Journal of Speech and Hearing Research, 26*, 2–9.

Sardone, R., Battisa, P., Tortelli, R., Piccininni, M., Coppola, F., Guerra, V. et al. (2018). The great age study. Retrieved July 12, 2018 from https://www.aan.com/PressRoom/Home/PressRelease/1625

Saunders, G., Chisolm, T., & Wallhagen, M. (2012). Older adults and hearing help-seeking behaviors. *American Journal of Audiology, 21*, 331–337.

Saunders, G. H., Frederick, M. T., Arnold, M. L., Silverman, S. C., Chisolm, T. H., & Myers, P. J. (2018). A randomized controlled trial to evaluate approaches to auditory rehabilitation for blast-exposed veterans with normal or near-normal hearing who report hearing problems in difficult listening situations. *Journal of the American Academy of Audiology, 29*, 44–62.

Saunders, G. H., Frederick, M. T., Silverman, S., & Papesh, M. (2013). Application of the health belief model: Development of the hearing beliefs questionnaire (HBQ) and its associations with hearing health behaviors. *International Journal of Audiology, 52*, 558–567.

Saunders, G. H., Smith, S. L., Chisolm, T. H., Frederick, M. T., McArdle, R. A., & Wilson, R. H. (2016). A randomized control trial: Supplementing hearing aid use with listening and communication enhancement (LACE) auditory training. *Ear and Hearing, 37*, 381–396.

Scarborough, H. (1990). Index of productive syntax. *Applied Psycholinguistics, 11*, 122.

Scarinci, N., & Hickson, L. (2018). Implementing family-centered care in adult audiological rehabilitation: The hows and whys of family-centered care in private practice. Workshop presented at the American Academy of Audiology Conference, Nashville, TN.

Scarinci, N., Worrall, L., & Hickson, L. (2009a). The effect of hearing impairment in older people on the spouse: Development and psychometric testing of the Significant Other Scale for Hearing Disability (SOS-HEAR). *International Journal of Audiology, 48*, 671–683.

Scarinci, N., Worrall, L., & Hickson, L. (2009b). The ICF and third-party disability: Its application to spouses of older people with hearing impairment. *Disability and Rehabilitation, 31*, 2088–2100.

Scarinci, N., Worrall, L., & Hickson, L. (2012). Factors associated with third-party disability in spouses of older people with hearing impairment. *Ear and Hearing, 33*, 698–708.

Schafer, D., & Lynch, J. (1980). Emergent language of six prelingually deaf children. *Teachers of the Deaf, 5*, 94–111.

Schley, S., & Albertini, J. (2005). Assessing the writing of deaf college students: Re-evaluating a direct assessment of writing. *Journal of Deaf Studies and Deaf Education, 10*, 96–105.

Schooling, T., & Solomon, M. (2017). Mapping your way to evidence-based practice: Want a fast, easy way to find the most up-to-date, evidence-based approaches to treating students? Read on. *The ASHA Leader, 22*, 34–35.

Schow, R. L. (2001). A standardized AR battery for dispensers is proposed. *The Hearing Journal, 54*, 10–20.

Schreitmüller, S., Frenken, M., Bentz, L., Ortmann, M., Walger, M., & Meister, H. (2017). Validating a method to assess lipreading, audiovisual gain, and integration during speech reception with cochlear-implanted and normal-hearing subjects using a talking head. *Ear and Hearing, 39*, 503–516.

Schulz, K. A., Modeste, N., Lee, J. W., Roberts, R., Saunders, G. H., & Witsell, D. L. (2017). Burden of hearing loss on communication partners and its influence on pursuit of hearing evaluation. *Ear and Hearing, 38*, e285–e291.

Schum, D. J. (1999). Perceived hearing aid benefit in relation to perceived needs. *Journal of the American Academy of Audiology, 10*, 40–45.

Schum, R. L. (1991). Communication and social growth: A developmental model of social behavior in deaf children. *Ear and Hearing, 12*, 320–327.

Scott, A. O. (2007, March 4). Kiss, kiss, talk, talk. *NY Times Book Review, 11*.

Seaver, L., & DesGeorges, J. (2004). Special education law: A new IDEA for students who are deaf and hard of hearing. In R. J. Roeser & M. P. Downs (Eds.), *Auditory disorders in school children* (4th ed., pp. 2–24). New York, NY: Thieme.

Secord, W. (1981). *T-MAC: Test of minimal articulation competence*. Columbus, OH: Merrill.

Seitz, P. R. (2002). French origins of the cochlear implant. *Cochlear Implants International, 3*, 77–86.

Seligman, M., & Darling, R. B. (2007). *Ordinary families, special children: A systems approach to childhood disability*. New York, NY: The Guilford Press.

Semel, E., Wiig, E., & Secord, W. (2013). *Clinical evaluation of language fundamentals* (5th ed.). San Antonio, TX: Psychological Corporation.

Seniorcare.com (2018). The growth of the U.S. aging population. Retrieved May 9, 2018 from https://www.seniorcare.com/featured/aging-american

Sensimetrics (2006). Seeing and hearing speech. *Sensimetrics*. Retrieved April 24, 2007 from http://www.seeingspeech.com

Shatner, W. (1997). Sound of silence. *People, 47*, 153–155.

Shargorodsky, J., Curhan, S. G., Curhan, G. C., & Eavey, R. (2010). Change in prevalence of hearing loss in US adolescents. *Journal of the American Medical Association, 304*, 772–778.

Sharma, A., Campbell, J., & Cardon, G. (2015). Developmental and cross-modal plasticity in deafness: Evidence from the P1 and N1 event related potentials in cochlear implanted children. *International Journal of Psychophysiology, 9*, 135–144.

Shaw, L., Tetlaff, B., Jennings, M. B., & Southall, K. E. (2013). The standpoint of persons with hearing loss on work disparities and workplace accommodations. *Work, 46*, 193–204.

Sheikh, J. I., & Yesavage, J. A. (1986). Geriatric depression scale (GDS): Recent evidence and development of a shorter version. In T. L. Brink (Ed.), *Clinical gerentology: A guide to assessment and intervention* (pp. 165–173). New York, NY: The Haworth Press, Inc.

Shelton, C., & Faucette, R. (1999). Preparing the patient for amplification. In R. Sweetow (Ed.), *Counseling for hearing aid fittings* (pp. 23–52). San Diego, CA: Singular Publishing Group.

Shibuya, L. (2006). One family's journey into the hearing world. *Volta Voices*, January/February, 20–21.

Shinn-Cunningham, B. G., & Best, V. (2008). Selective attention in normal and impaired hearing. *Trends in Amplification, 12*, 283–299.

Shiovitz-Ezra, S., & Ayalon, L. (2010). Situational versus chronic loneliness as risk factors for all-cause mortality. *International Psychogeriatrics, 22*, 455–462.

Shriberg, L., Flipsen, P., Thielke, H., Kwiatkowski, J., Kertoy, M., Katcher, M. et al. (2000). Risk for speech disorder associated with early recurrent otitis media with effusion: Two retrospective studies. *Journal of Speech, Language, and Hearing Research, 43*, 79–99.

Shultz, D., & Mowry, R. B. (1995). Older adults in long-term care facilities. In P. B. Kricos & S. A. Lesner (Eds.), *Hearing care for the older adults: Audiologic rehabilitation* (pp. 167–179). Newton, MA: Butterworth-Heinemann.

Siebein, G. W., Gold, M. A., Siebein, G. W., & Ermann, M. G. (2000). Ten ways to provide a high-quality acoustical environment in schools. *Language, Speech, and Hearing Services in Schools, 31*, 376–384.

Silverman, R. S., & Hirsh, I. (1955). Problems related to the use of speech in clinical audiometry. *Annals of Otology, Rhinology, and Laryngology, 64*, 1234–1244.

Sims, D., Dorn, C., Clark, C., Bryant, L., & Mumford, B. (2002). *New developments in computer assisted speechreading and auditory training*. Paper presented at the American Speech-Language-Hearing Association convention, Atlanta, GA.

Sininger, Y. S. (2002). Otoacoustic emissions in the diagnosis of hearing disorder in infants. *The Hearing Journal, 55*, 22–26.

Skinner, B. F. (1953). *Science and human behavior*. New York, NY: Macmillan.

Skinner, B. F. (1971). *Beyond freedom and dignity*. New York, NY: Knopf.

Smiljanic, R., & Sladen, D. (2013). Acoustic and semantic enhancements for children with cochlear implants. *Journal of Speech, Language, and Hearing Research, 56*, 1085–1096.

Smith, C. (1975). Residual hearing and speech production in the deaf. *Journal of Speech and Hearing Research, 19*, 795–811.

Smith, L., Bartel, L., Joglekar, S., & Chen, J. (2017). Musical rehabilitation in adult cochlear implant recipients with a self-administered software. *Otology and Neurotology, 38*, e262–e267.

Smith, S. L., & Fagelson, M. A. (2011). The tinnitus self-efficacy questionnaire. *Journal of the American Academy of Audiology, 22*, 424–440.

Smith, S. L., Pichora-Fuller, K., Watts, K., & La More, C. (2011). Development of the Listening self-efficacy questionnaire (LSEQ). *International Journal of Audiology, 50*, 417–425.

Smith, S. L., & West, R. L. (2006). The application of self-efficacy principles to audiologic rehabilitation: A tutorial. *American Journal of Audiology, 15*, 46–56.

Socialstyrelsen (National Board of Health and Welfare, Sweden) (1994). Kvalitetssakring av barnhalsovhrd. Att skydda skyddsnatet [Quality Management in Well-Baby Care. To Secure the Safeguard]. *SoS-rapport, 19*.

Sommers, M., Hale, S., Myerson, J., Rose, N., Tye-Murray, N., & Spehar, B. (2011). Listening comprehension across the adult life span. *Ear and Hearing, 32*, 775–781.

Sommers, M. S., Tye-Murray, N., Barcroft, J., & Spehar, B. (2015). The effects of meaning-based auditory training on behavioral measures of perceptual effort in individuals with impaired hearing. *Seminars in Hearing, 36*, 263–272.

Sommers, M., Tye-Murray, N., & Spehar, B. (2005). Audiovisual integration and aging. *Ear and Hearing, 26*, 263–275.

Sonnenschein, E., & Cascella, P. W. (2004). Pediatricians' opinions about otitis media and speech-language-hearing development. *Journal of Communication Disorders, 37*, 313–323.

Southall, K., Gagné, J. P., & Jennings, M. B. (2010). Stigma: A negative and a positive influence on help-seeking for adults with acquired hearing loss. *International Journal of Audiology, 49*, 804–814.

Southall, K., Gagné, J. P., & Leroux, T. (2006). Factors that influence the use of assistance technologies by older adults who have a hearing loss. *International Journal of Audiology, 45*, 252–259.

Southall, K., Jennings, M. B., & Gagné, J. P. (2011). Factors that influence disclosure of hearing loss in the workplace. *International Journal of Audiology, 50*, 699–707.

Spahr, A., Dorman, M. F., Litvak, L. M., Van Wie, S., Gifford, R. H., Loizou, P. C. et al. (2012). Development and validation of the AzBio sentence lists. *Ear and Hearing, 33*, 112–117.

Speaks, C. S., & Jerger, J. (1965). Performance-intensity characteristics of synthetic sentences. *Journal of Speech and Hearing Research, 9*, 305–312.

Special Report (2017). NASEM committee looks into OTC hearing device regulations. *Hearing Review*. Retrieved July 10, 2018 from http://www.hearingreview.com/2017/06/nasem-committee-looks-regulations-otc-hearing-devices/?ref=cl-title

Special Report: Part 1 (2018). Audiologists get real on impact of OTC devices. *The Hearing Journal, 71*, 20–23.

Spehar, B., Goebel, S., & Tye-Murray, N. (2015). Effects of context type on lipreading and listening performance and implications for sentence processing. *Journal of Speech, Language, and Hearing Research, 58*, 1093–1102.

Spehar, B., Tye-Murray, N., & Sommers, M. (2008). Intra- versus intermodal integration in young and older adults. *Journal of the Acoustical Society of America, 123*, 2858–2866.

Spence, C., Senkowski, D., & Röder, B. (2009). Crossmodal processing. *Experimental Brain Research, 198*, 107–111.

Spencer, L. (1994). Some ways to nurture children's conversational and language skills. In N. Tye-Murray (Ed.), *Let's converse: A how-to guide to develop and expand the conversational skills of children and teenagers who are hearing impaired* (pp. 51–84). Washington, DC: Alexander Graham Bell Association for the Deaf.

Spencer, L., & Guo, L. (2013). Consonant development in pediatric cochlear implant users who were implanted before 30 months of age. *Journal of Deaf Studies and Deaf Education, 18*, 93–109.

Spencer, L. J., Tye-Murray, N., & Tomblin, J. B. (1998). The production of English inflectional morphology, speech production and listening performance in children with cochlear implants. *Ear and Hearing, 19*, 310.

Srinivasan, R. J., & Massaro, D. W. (2003). Perceiving prosody from the face and voice: Distinguishing statements from echoic questions in English. *Language and Speech, 46*, 1–22.

Stacy, P., Raine, C., O'Donoghue, G., Tapper, L., Twomey, T., & Summerfield, A. Q. (2010). Effectiveness of computer-based auditory training for adult users of cochlear implants. *International Journal of Audiology, 49*, 347–356.

Staehelin, K., Bertoli, S., Probst, R., Schindler, C., Dratva, J., & Stutz, E. Z. (2011). Gender and hearing aids: Patterns of use and determinants of nonregular use. *Ear and Hearing, 32*, e26–e37.

Stanton, J. F. (2005). Captioning in theaters: What will it take? *Volta Voices*, May/June, 28–30.

Stecker, G. C., Bowman, G., Yund, W., Herron, T., Roup, C., & Woods, D. (2006). Perceptual training improves syllable identification in new and experienced hearing aid users. *Journal of Rehabilitation Research and Development, 43*, 537–552.

Stephens, D., France, L., & Lormore, K. (1995). Effects of hearing impairment on the patient's family and friends. *Acta Otolaryngologica, 115*, 165–167.

Stephens, S. D., Jaworski, A., Lewis, P., & Aslan, S. (1999). An analysis of the communication tactics used by hearing-impaired adults. *British Journal of Audiology, 33*, 17–27.

Stevens, M. N., Dubno, J. R., Wallhagen, M. I., & Tucci, D. L. (2018). Communication and healthcare: Self-reports of people with hearing loss in primary care settings. *Clinical Gerontologist,* 1–10.

Stevenson, R. A., Nelms, C. E., Baum, S. H., Zurkovsky, L., Barense, M. D., Newhouse, P. A., & Wallace M. T. (2015). Deficits in audiovisual speech perception in normal aging emerge at the level of whole-word recognition. *Neurobiology of Aging, 36*, 283–291.

Stewart, D. L., Mehl, A., Hall, J. W., Thomson, V., Carroll, M., & Hamlett, J. (2000). Universal newborn hearing screening with automated auditory brainstem response: A multisite investigation. *Journal of Perinatology, 20*, S128–S131.

Stinson, M. S., & Antia, S. D. (1999). Considerations in educating deaf and hard-of-hearing students in inclusive settings. *Journal of Deaf Studies and Deaf Education, 4*, 163–175.

Stone, B. (2002, June 24). How to recharge the second sense. *Newsweek*. Retrieved April 2, 2013 from http://www.thedailybeast.com/newsweek/2002/06/23/how-to-recharge-the-second-sense.html

Stouffer, J. L., & Tyler, R. S. (1990). Characterization of tinnitus by tinnitus patients. *Journal of Speech and Hearing Disorders, 55*, 439–453.

Strawbridge, W. J., Cohen, R. D., Shema, S. J., & Kaplan, G. A. (1996). Successful aging: Predictors and associated activities. *American Journal of Epidemiology, 144*, 135–141.

Strom, K. (2007). Hearing aids are not only for old people. *Hearing Review, 14*, 8.

Strom, K. (2014). Hearing Review 2013 dispenser survey: Dispensing in the age of internet and big box retailers. *Hearing Review, 21*, 22–28.

Su, B. M., & Chan, D. K. (2017). Prevalence of hearing loss in US children and adolescents: Findings from NHANES 1988–2010. *JAMA Otolaryngology–Head & Neck Surgery, 143*, 920–927.

Suárez, M. (2000). Promoting social competence in deaf students: The effect of an intervention program. *Journal of Deaf Studies and Deaf Education, 5*, 323–336.

Suárez, M., & Torres, E. (1996). Dyadic interactions between deaf children and their communication partners. *American Annals of the Deaf, 141*, 245–251.

Sumby, W. H., & Pollack, I. (1954). Visual contribution to speech intelligibility in noise. *Journal of the Acoustical Society of America, 26*, 212–215.

Swanepoel, D., Clark, J. L., Koekemoer, D., Hall, J. W., Krumm, M., Ferrari, D. V. et al. (2010). Telehealth in audiology: The need and potential to reach underserved communities. *International Journal of Audiology, 49*, 195–202.

Sweetow, R. (2006). *Tinnitus patient management.* Paper presented at the meeting of the American Academy of Audiology, Denver, CO.

Sweetow, R., & Jeppesen, A. M. (2012). A new integrated program for tinnitus patient management: Widex zen therapy. *Hearing Review, 19*, 20–30.

Sweetow, R., & Palmer, C. (2005). Efficacy of individual auditory training in adults: A systematic review of the evidence. *Journal of the American Academy of Audiology, 16*, 494–504.

Sweetow, R., & Sabes, J. H. (2006). The need for and development of an adaptive Listening and Communication Enhancement (LACE) program. *Journal of the American Academy of Audiology, 17*, 538–558.

Sweetow, R., & Sabes, J. H. (2007). Listening and communication enhancement (LACE). *Seminars in Hearing, 28*, 133–141.

Sweetow, R., & Sabes, J. H. (2010). Auditory training and challenges associated with participation and compliance. *Journal of the American Academy of Audiology, 21*, 586–593.

Sydlowski, S. A. (2018). Preparing your practice pre-otc. *Audiology Today, 30*, 18–29.

Taitelbaum-Swead, R., & Fostick, L. (2016). Auditory and visual information in speech perception: A developmental perspective. *Clinical Linguistics and Phonetics, 30*, 531–545.

Takeoka, A., & Shimojima, A. (2002). Grounding styles of aged dyads: An exploratory study. *In Proceedings of the Third SIGdial Workshop on Discourse and Dialogue*, 188–195.

Tannen, D. (2000). "Don't just sit there—Interrupt!" Pacing and pausing in conversational style. *American Speech, 75*, 393–395.

Tasker, S. L., Nowakowski, M. E., & Schmidt, L. A. (2010). Joint attention and social competence in deaf children with cochlear implants. *Journal of Developmental and Physical Disabilities, 22*, 509–532.

Taylor, K. S., & Jurma, W. E. (1999). Study suggests that group rehabilitation increases benefit of hearing aid fittings. *The Hearing Journal, 52*, 48–54.

Tecca, J. E. (2018). Are post-fitting follow-up visits not hearing aid best practices? *Hearing Review, 25*, 12–22.

Thomson, R. S., Auduong, P., Miller, A. T., & Gurgel, R. K. (2017). Hearing loss as a risk factor for dementia: A systematic review. *Laryngoscope Investigative Otolaryngology, 2*, 69–79.

Tillman, T. W., & Carhart, R. (1966). *An expanded test for speech discrimination utilizing CNC monosyllabic words: Northwestern University auditory test no. 6* [Tech. Rep. No. SAM-TR-6655. USAF School of Aerospace Medicine]. San Antonio, TX: Brooks Air Force Base.

Tobey, E., Devous, M., Buckley, K., Overson, G., Harris, T., Ringe, W. et al. (2005). Pharmacological enhancement of aural habilitation in adult cochlear implant users. *Ear and Hearing, 26*, 45S–56S.

Tomblin, J. B., Harrison, M., Ambrose, S. E., Walker, E. A., Oleson, J. J., & Moeller, M. P. (2015). Language outcomes in young children with mild to severe hearing loss. *Ear and Hearing, 36*, 76S.

Tomblin, J. B., Oleson, J. J., Ambrose, S. E., Walker, E., & Moeller, M. P. (2014). The influence of hearing aids on the speech and language development of children with hearing loss. *JAMA Otolaryngology–Head & Neck Surgery, 140*, 403–409.

Touchstone Applied Science Associates (2001). *Signposts early literacy battery and pre-DRP test.* Brewster, NY: Touchstone Applied Science Associates.

Townshend, P. (2013). *Hearing loss quotes.* Retrieved March 28, 2013 from http://www.hearinglossweb.com/hearing-loss-quotes/

Treille, A., Vilain, C., Kandel, S., & Sato, M. (2017). Electrophysiological evidence for a self-processing advantage during audiovisual speech integration. *Experimental Brain Research, 235*, 2867–2876.

Tremblay, K. L., Kraus, N., Carell, T., & McGee, T. (1997). Central auditory system plasticity: Generalization to novel stimuli following listening training. *Journal of the Acoustical Society of America, 102*, 3762–3773.

Trezek, B. J. (2017). Cued Speech and the development of reading in English: Examining the evidence. *Journal of Deaf Studies and Deaf Education, 22*, 349–364.

Trychin, S. (2003). *Did I do that?* Erie, PA: Samuel Trychin.

Trychin, S. (2012a). Factors to consider when providing audiological services to people who have hearing loss and their communication partners. *Seminars in Hearing, 33*, 87–96.

Trychin, S. (2012b). *Living with hearing loss presentations, workshops, and training programs.* Retrieved December 5, 2012 from www.trychin.com/workshops.html#work

Tucci, D. L., Merson, M. H., & Wilson, B. S. (2009). A summary of the literature on global hearing impairment: Current status and priorities for action. *Otology and Neurology, 31*, 31–41.

Tuokko, H., Hadjistavropoulos, T., Miller, J. A., & Beattie, B. L. (1992). The clock test: A sensitive measure to differentiate normal elderly from those with Alzheimer disease. *Journal of the American Geriatrics Society, 40*, 579–584.

Tye-Murray, N. (1991). Repair strategy usage by hearing-impaired adults and changes following communication therapy. *Journal of Speech and Hearing Research, 34*, 921–928.

Tye-Murray, N. (1994). Some conversation strategies for adults who interact with hard-of-hearing children. In N.

Tye-Murray (Ed.), *Let's converse! A how-to guide to develop and expand the conversational skills of children and teenagers who are hearing impaired* (pp. 11–50). Washington, DC: Alexander Graham Bell Association for the Deaf.

Tye-Murray, N. (2003). Conversational fluency of children who use cochlear implants. *Ear and Hearing, 24*, 82S–89S.

Tye-Murray, N. (2012). Counseling for adults and children who have hearing loss. In L. V. Flasher & P. T. Fogle (Eds.), *Counseling skills for speech-language pathologists and audiologists* (2nd ed., pp. 313–340). Clifton Park, NY: Delmar Cengage Learning.

Tye-Murray, N. (2016a). Gaming technology for customized aural rehabilitation and hearing healthcare. *Hearing Review, 23*, 20.

Tye-Murray, N. (2016b). Better Hearing? Game On!: An auditory training game program can help you customize care for your patients. *The ASHA Leader, 21*, 18–19.

Tye-Murray, N. (2018). A perfect storm: Integrating auditory brain training into hearing care. *The Hearing Journal, 71*, 12–14.

Tye-Murray, N., Barcroft, J., & Sommers, M. (2011). I hear what you mean: The state of the science in auditory training. *ENT & Audiology News, 20*, 84–86.

Tye-Murray, N., & Folkins, J. (1990). Jaw and lip movements of deaf talkers producing utterances with known stress patterns. *Journal of the Acoustical Society of America, 87*, 2675–2683.

Tye-Murray, N., Knutson, J. F., & Lemke, J. (1993). Assessment of communication strategies use: Questionnaires and daily diaries. *Seminars in Hearing, 14*, 338–353.

Tye-Murray, N., Mauzé, E., & Schroy, C. (2010). Receive readily, recognize genuinely: Casual conversation and cooperative behaviors. *Seminars in Hearing, 31*, 154–164.

Tye-Murray, N., Purdy, S. C., Woodworth, G., & Tyler, R. S. (1990). Effects of repair strategies on visual identification of sentences. *Journal of Speech and Hearing Disorders, 55*, 621–627.

Tye-Murray, N., Sommers, M., Mauzé, E., Schroy, C., Barcroft, J., & Spehar, B. (2012). Using patient perceptions of relative benefit ad enjoyment to assess auditory training. *Journal of the American Academy of Audiology, 23*, 623–634.

Tye-Murray, N., Sommers, M., & Spehar, B. (2006). *The build-a-sentence test*. St. Louis, MO: Washington University School of Medicine.

Tye-Murray, N., Sommers, M., & Spehar, B. (2007a). Audiovisual integration and lipreading abilities of older adults with normal and impaired hearing. *Ear and Hearing, 28*, 656–668.

Tye-Murray, N., Sommers, M., & Spehar, B. (2007b). Lipreading and aging: Does gender make a difference? *Journal of the American Academy of Audiology, 18*, 883–892.

Tye-Murray, N., Sommers, M., & Spehar, B. (2008). Auditory and visual lexical neighborhoods in audiovisual speech perception. *Trends in Amplification, 11*, 233–241.

Tye-Murray, N., Sommers, M., Spehar, B., Myerson, J., & Hale, S. (2010). Aging, audiovisual integration, and the principle of inverse effectiveness. *Ear and Hearing, 31*, 636–644.

Tye-Murray, N., Sommers, M., Spehar, B., Myerson, J., Hale, S., & Rose, N. (2008). Auditory-visual discourse comprehension by older and young adults in favorable and unfavorable conditions. *International Journal of Audiology, 47*, S31–S37.

Tye-Murray, N., Spehar, B., Barcroft, J., & Sommers, M. (2017). Auditory training for adults who have hearing loss: A comparison of spaced versus massed practice schedules. *Journal of Speech, Language, and Hearing Research, 60*, 2337–2345.

Tye-Murray, N., Spehar, B., Myerson, J., Hale, S., & Sommers, M. (2013). Reading your own lips: Common-coding theory and visual speech perception. *Psychonomic Bulletin and Review, 20*, 115–119.

Tye-Murray, N., Spehar, B., Myerson, J., Hale, S., & Sommers, M. (2015). The self-advantage in visual speech processing enhances audiovisual speech recognition in noise. *Psychonomic Bulletin and Review, 22*, 1048–1053.

Tye-Murray, N., Spehar, B., Myerson, J., Hale, S., & Sommers, M. (2016). Lipreading and audiovisual speech recognition across the adult lifespan: Implications for audiovisual integration. *Psychology and Aging, 31*, 380.

Tye-Murray, N., Spehar, B., Sommers, M., & Barcroft, J. (2016). Auditory training with frequent communication partners. *Journal of Speech, Language, and Hearing Research, 59(4)*, 871–875.

Tye-Murray, N., Spencer, L., & Gilbert-Bedia, E. (1995). Relationships between speech production and speech perception skills in young cochlear-implant users. *Journal of the Acoustical Society of America, 98*, 2454–2460.

Tye-Murray, N., Spry, J., & Mauzé, E. (2009). Professionals with hearing loss: Maintaining that competitive edge. *Ear and Hearing, 30*, 475–484.

Tye-Murray, N., Tomblin, B. J., & Spencer, L. (1997). *Speech and language acquisition over time in children with cochlear implants.* Paper presented at the American Speech-Language-Hearing Convention, Boston, MA.

Tye-Murray, N., Tyler, R. S., Woodworth, G., & Gantz, B. (1992). Performance over time with a Nucleus or Ineraid cochlear implant. *Ear and Hearing, 13,* 200–209.

Tye-Murray, N., & Witt, S. (1996). Conversational moves and conversational styles of adult cochlear-implant users. *Journal of the Academy of Rehabilitative Audiology, 29,* 11–25.

Tye-Murray, N., Witt, S., & Schum, L. (1995). Effects of talker familiarity on communication breakdown in conversation with adult cochlear-implant users. *Ear and Hearing, 16,* 459–469.

Tye-Murray, N., Witt, S., Schum, L., & Sobaski, C. (1995). Communication breakdowns: Partner contingencies and partner reactions. *Journal of the Academy of Rehabilitative Audiology, 25,* 1–27.

Tye-Murray, N., Zimmermann, G., & Folkins, J. (1987). Movement timing in deaf and hearing speakers: Comparison of phonetically heterogeneous syllable strings. *Journal of Speech and Hearing Research, 30,* 411–417.

Tyler, R. S., & Baker, L. J. (1983). Difficulties experienced by tinnitus sufferers. *Journal of Speech and Hearing Disorders, 48,* 150–154.

Tyler, R. S., Preece, J., & Tye-Murray, N. (1986). *The Iowa phoneme and sentence tests.* Iowa City: University of Iowa Hospitals and Clinics.

Uchanski, R., Choi, S. S., Sunkyung, S., Braida, L. D., Reed, C. M., & Durlach, N. I. (1996). Speaking clearly for the hard of hearing IV: Further studies of the role of speaking rate. *Journal of Speech and Hearing Research, 39,* 494–509.

Underwood, N. (2006). A family's journey through due process. *Volta Voices,* May/June, 40–44.

UK Cochlear Implant Study Group (2004). Criteria of candidacy for unilateral cochlear implantation in postlingually deafened adults I: Theory and measures of effectiveness. *Ear and Hearing, 25,* 310–335.

US Bureau of the Census (2004). International programs center, international database. *US Department of Commerce.* Retrieved May 23, 2007 from http://www.census.gov/ipc/www/idbnew.html

US Bureau of the Census (2017). The nation's older population is still growing, census bureau reports. Retrieved from https://census.gov/newsroom/press-releases/2017/cb17-100.html

US Department of Health and Human Services, & Centers for Medicare and Medicaid Services (2015). Nursing home data compendium. Retrieved May 9, 2018 from https://www.healthdata.gov/dataset/nursing-home-data-compendium

US Department of Health and Human Services (2017). Administration on Aging (AOA). Administration for Community Living. Profile of older Americans.

US Department of Justice (2002). *Guidance to federal financial assistance recipients regarding title VI prohibition against national origin discrimination affecting limited English proficient persons.* Federal Register.

Utah State University (n.d.). Ski-Hi institute. *Utah State University.* Retrieved March 23, 2013 from http://www.skihi.org/

Utley, J. (1946). A test of lipreading ability. *Journal of Speech Disorders, 11,* 109–116.

VanPatten, B. (1996). *Input processing and grammar instruction in second language acquisition.* Norwood, NJ: Alex Publishing Corp.

Venezia, J. H., Vaden Jr, K. I., Rong, F., Maddox, D., Saberi, K., & Hickok, G. (2017). Auditory, visual and audiovisual speech processing streams in superior temporal sulcus. *Frontiers in Human Neuroscience, 11,* 174.

Ventry, I. M., & Weinstein, B. E. (1982). The hearing handicap inventory for the elderly: A new tool. *Ear and Hearing, 3,* 128–134.

Ventry, I., & Weinstein, B. (1983). Identification of elderly people with hearing problems. *ASHA, 25,* 37–47.

Verhoeven, J., Hide, O., De Maeyer, S., Gillis, S., & Gillis, S. (2016). Hearing impairment and vowel production. A comparison between normally hearing, hearing-aided and cochlear implanted Dutch children. *Journal of Communication Disorders, 59,* 24–39.

Viljanen, A., Kaprio, J., Pyykkö, I., Sorri, M., Koskenvuo, M., & Rantanen, T. (2009). Hearing acuity as a predictor of walking difficulties in older women. *Journal of the American Geriatrics Society, 57,* 2282–2286.

Voeks, S., Gallagher, C., Langer, E., & Drinka, P. (1990). Hearing loss in the nursing home: An institutional issue. *Journal of the American Geriatrics Society, 38,* 141–145.

Voelker, C. (1938). An experimental study of the comparative rate of utterances of deaf and normal-hearing speakers. *American Annals of the Deaf, 83,* 274–284.

Von Hapsburg, D., & Davis, B. L. (2006). Auditory sensitivity and the prelinguistic vocalizations of early-amplified infants. *Journal of Speech, Language, and Hearing Research, 49*, 809–822.

Von Hapsburg, D., Champlin, C. A., & Shetty, S. R. (2004). Reception thresholds for sentences in bilingual (Spanish/English) and monolinugual (English) listeners. *Journal of the American Academy of Audiology, 16*, 88–98.

Von Hapsburg, D., & Peña, E. D. (2002). Understanding bilingualism and its impact on speech audiometry. *Journal of Speech, Language, and Hearing Research, 45*, 202–213.

Walden, B. E., Demorest, M. E., & Helper, E. L. (1984). Test-retest reliability of the hearing handicap inventory for the elderly. *Ear and Hearing, 7*, 295–299.

Walden, B. E., Prosek, R. A., Montgomery, A. A., Scherr, C. K., & Jones, C. J. (1977). Effects of training on the visual recognition of consonants. *Journal of Speech and Hearing Research, 20*, 130–145.

Walker, E. A., Holte, L., McCreery, R. W., Spratford, M., Page, T., & Moeller, M. P. (2015). The influence of hearing aid use on outcomes of children with mild hearing loss. *Journal of Speech, Language, and Hearing Research, 58*, 1611–1625.

Walker, E. A., Spratford, M., Ambrose, S. E., Holte, L., & Oleson, J. (2017). Service delivery to children with mild hearing loss: Current practice patterns and parent perceptions. *American Journal of Audiology, 26*, 38–52.

Warner-Czyz, A. D., Davis, B. L., & MacNeilage, P. F. (2010). Accuracy of consonant-vowel syllables in young cochlear implant recipients and hearing children in the single-word period. *Journal of Speech, Language, and Hearing Research, 53*, 2–17.

Warner-Czyz, A. D., Davis, B. L., & Morrison, H. M. (2005). Production accuracy in a young cochlear implant recipient. *Volta Review, 105*, 151–173.

Wauters, L., & Dirks, E. (2017). Interactive reading with young deaf and hard-of-hearing children in eBooks versus print books. *The Journal of Deaf Studies and Deaf Education, 22*, 243–252.

Wayner, D. S., & Abrahamson, J. A. (1996). *Learning to hear again: An audiologic rehabilitation curriculum guide*. Austin, TX: Hear Again.

Weatherhead, D., & White, K. S. (2017). Read my lips: Visual speech influences word processing in infants. *Cognition, 160*, 103–109.

Wedenberg, E. (1951). Review of the literature. *Acta Oto-Laryngologica, 39*, 14–30.

West, J. S., Low, J. C., & Stankovic, K. M. (2016). Revealing hearing loss: A survey of how people verbally disclose their hearing loss. *Ear and Hearing, 37*, 194–205.

Weichbold, V., Nekahm-Heis, D., & Wilzl-Mueller, K. (2007). Universal newborn hearing screening and postnatal hearing loss. *Pediatrics, 117*, e631–e636.

Wiederhold, J. L., & Bryant, B. (2001). *Gray oral reading test–diagnostic (GORT-4)*. Austin, TX: Pro-Ed.

Weinstein, B. E. (2018). Hearing loss in nursing homes. *The Hearing Journal, 71*, 10–12.

Weikum, W. M., Vouloumanos, A., Navarra, J., Soto-Faraco, S., Sebastian-Galles, N., & Werker, J. (2007). Visual language discrimination in infancy. *Science, 316*, 1159.

Weisleder, P., & Hodgson, W. R. (1989). Evaluation of four Spanish word-recognition-ability lists. *Ear and Hearing, 10*, 387–393.

Welsh, K., Breitner, J., & Magruder-Habib, K. (1993). Detection of dementia in the elderly using telephone screening of cognitive status. *Neuropsychiatry, Neuropsychology and Behavioral Neurology, 6*, 103–110.

West, R. L., & Smith, S. L. (2007). Development of a hearing aid self-efficacy questionnaire. *International Journal of Audiology, 46*, 759–771.

White, K. (2007). Early intervention for children with permanent hearing loss: Finishing the EHDI revolution. *Volta Review, 106*, 237–258.

White, K., Forsman, I., Eichwald, J., & Munoz, K. (2010). The evolution of early hearing detection and intervention programs in the United States. *Seminars in Perinatology, 34*, 170–179.

White, M., & Epston, D. (1990). *Narrative means to therapeutic ends*. New York, NY: W. W. Norton & Company.

White, E., & Voss, J. (2015). *Small talk: Bringing listening and spoken language to your young child with hearing loss*. St. Louis, MO: Central Institute for the Deaf.

Whitehead, R. L. (1982). Some respiratory and aerodynamic patterns in the speech of the hearing impaired. In I. Hochberg, & M. J. Osberger (Eds.), *Speech of the hearing impaired: Research, training, and personnel preparation*. Baltimore, MD: University Park Press.

Whitestone, H. (2007). *Frequently asked questions. Heather Whitestone*. Retrieved August 1, 2007 from http://www.heatherwhitestone.com/site/content/faqs.html

Wilkinson, A. S., & Brinton, J. C. (2003). Speech intelligibility rating of cochlear implanted children: Inter-rater reliability. *Cochlear Implants International, 4*, 22–30.

Williams, K. T. (2019). *Expressive vocabulary test-Third edition*. Bloomington, MN: Pearson Education.

Williams, K. C., Falkum, E., & Martinsen, E. W. (2015). Fear of negative evaluation, avoidance and mental distress among hearing-impaired employees. *Rehabilitation Psychology, 60*, 51.

Willott, J. F. (1996). Physiological plasticity in the auditory system and its possible relevance to hearing aid use, deprivation effects, and acclimatization. *Ear and Hearing, 17*, S66–S77.

Wilson, A. H., Alsius, A., Paré, M., & Munhall, K. G. (2016). Spatial frequency requirements and gaze strategy in visual-only and audiovisual speech perception. *Journal of Speech, Language, and Hearing Research, 59*, 601–615.

Wilson, R. H., Carnell, C. S., & Cleghorn, A. (2007). Words In Noise (WIN) test with multi-talker babble and speech-spectrum noise maskers. *Journal of the American Academy of Audiology, 18*, 522–529.

Windom, A. (2012). The geese can eat it. *Volta Voices*, November/December, 36–37.

Wolbers, K. A., Dostal, H. M., & Bowers, L. M. (2012). "I was born Deaf." Written language outcomes after 1 year of strategic and interactive instruction. *Journal of Deaf Studies and Deaf Education, 17*, 19–38.

Woodcock, R. (2004). *Woodcock diagnostic reading battery (WDRB)*. Boston, MA: Houghton Mifflin Harcourt.

Woodcock, R., & Johnson, M. B. (2014). *Woodcock-Johnson psycho-educational battery (WJ-R)*. Boston, MA: Houghton Mifflin Harcourt.

Woods, D. L., & Yund, E. W. (2007). Perceptual training of phoneme identification for hearing loss. *Seminars in Hearing, 28*, 110–119.

Woods, M. L., & Moe, A. (2014). *Analytical reading inventory* (10th ed.). Columbus, OH: Merrill Education (Prentice Hall).

Woodward, M. F., & Barber, C. G. (1960). Phoneme perception in lipreading. *Journal of Speech and Hearing Research, 17*, 212–222.

Worcester, A. E. (1915). Pronunciation at sight. *Volta Review, 17*, 85–93.

World Health Organization (WHO) (2001). *International classification of functioning, disability, and health*. Geneva, CH: WHO.

World Health Organization (WHO) (2006). *Primary ear and hearing care: Training resource—advanced level*. Geneva, CH: WHO.

World Health Organization (WHO) (2008). *The global burden of disease: 2004 update*. Geneva, CH: WHO.

World Health Organization (WHO) (2018). Deafness and hearing loss. Retrieved July 10, 2018 from http://www.who.Int/news-room/fact-sheets/detail/deafness-and-hearing-loss

Wu, C., Chen, Y., Chan, K., Lee, L., Hsu, K., Lin, B. et al. (2011). Long-term language levels and reading skills in Mandarin-speaking prelingually deaf children with cochlear implants. *Audiology and Neurotology, 16*, 359–380.

Yi, A., Wong, W., & Eizenman, M. (2013). Gaze patterns and audiovisual speech enhancement. *Journal of Speech, Language, and Hearing Research, 56*, 471–480.

Yoshinaga-Itano, C., & Downey, D. M. (1996). Development of school-aged deaf, hard-of-hearing and normally hearing students' written language. *Volta Review, 98*, 3–7.

Yoshinaga-Itano, C., Sedey, A., Coulter, D. K., & Mehl, A. L. (1998). Language of early and later identified children with hearing loss. *Pediatrics, 102*, 1161–1171.

Yoshinaga-Itano, C., Snyder, L. S., & Mayberry, R. (1996). How deaf and normally hearing students convey meaning within and between written sentences. *Volta Review, 98*, 9–38.

Young, A., & Tattersall, H. (2007). Universal newborn hearing screening and early identification of deafness: Parents' responses to knowing early and their expectations of child communication development. *Journal of Deaf Studies and Deaf Education, 12*, 209–220.

Zaidman-Zait, A., & Dotan, A. (2017). Everyday stressors in deaf and hard of hearing adolescents: The role of coping and pragmatics. *Journal of Deaf Studies and Deaf Education, 22*, 257–268.

Zazove, P., Meador, H. E., Reed, B. D., & Gorenflo, D. W. (2013). Deaf persons' English reading levels and associations with epidemiological, educational, and cultural factors. *Journal of Health Communication, 18*, 760–772.

Zeng, F. (2012). William F. House, MD, audiology pioneer. *The Hearing Journal, 65*, 32–36.

Zeng, F., & Turner, C. (1990). Recognition of voiceless fricatives by normal and hearing-impaired subjects. *Journal of Speech and Hearing Research, 33*, 440–449.

Zimmerman, L., Steiner, V. G., & Pond, R. E. (2011). *Preschool language scale-5 (PLS-5)*. Boston, MA: Pearson.

Zimmerman-Phillips, S. (1997). The infant-toddler meaningful auditory integration scale (IT-MAIS). *Advanced Bionics.* Retrieved March 23, 2013 from http://www.advancedbionics.com/content/dam/ab/Global/en_ce/documents/libraries/AssessmentTools/3-01015_ITMAIS%20brochure%20Dec12%20FINAL.pdf

Zipoli, R. P., & Kennedy, M. (2012). Evidence-based practice among speech-language pathologists: Attitudes, utilization, and barriers. *American Journal of Speech-Language-Pathology, 14*, 208–220.

INDEX

I

J

K

L

M

N

O

T

U

V

W

X

Y